P9-BJL-999

Also by Alexis Lichine ❧

WINES OF FRANCE *(4th edition, revised 1951, 1955, 1960, and 1963)*

This is a BORZOI BOOK *published in New York by* ALFRED A. KNOPF

Alexis Lichine's Encyclopædia of

WINES AND SPIRITS

Alexis Lichine's Encyclopædia of

WINES & SPIRITS

in collaboration with WILLIAM FIFIELD

and with the assistance of

Jonathan Bartlett** and **Jane Stockwood

NEW YORK *ALFRED · A · KNOPF* 1967

THIS IS A BORZOI BOOK / PUBLISHED BY ALFRED A. KNOPF, INC.

First Edition • *© Copyright 1967 by Alexis Lichine*

Distributed by Random House, Inc., and in Canada by Random House of Canada Limited, Toronto. Published in Great Britain by Cassell and Company Ltd.

Library of Congress Catalog Card Number: 66–19385

Manufactured in the United States of America

To Sacha and Sandra,
who were raised in the Médoc—
in the hope that this will give them taste

Contents

Preface

This book is written for the consumer and those in the trade whose function is to relate the taste, traditions and knowledge of wine, the subtle changes between one vineyard and another, and the inescapable limitations of fine wines produced from limited acreage. Such knowledge adds immeasurably to the real enjoyment of a good bottle. Also, it helps to blow away the cobwebs from a subject which, for too long, has been shrouded in mystery. Some of the people who approach it with awe are not even sure that wine is made from grapes: that is why so much importance has been given in this book to the sciences of viticulture and wine-making. Detailed information on these matters—as well as on the history, value and serving of wine—will be found in the chapters which precede the alphabetical encyclopædic section.

It has been impossible, because of restrictions of space, to give every topic its own entry, and some subjects will be found included under an entry of greater importance. No hard and fast rules have been laid down, however. Wine is a subject of infinite flexibility and every aspect is treated according to its individual merits, and placed where it seems to fit best. It should therefore be stressed that full use must be made of the index, which in cases of doubt will quickly pinpoint all references to a particular aspect of any subject. The Appendixes supply complete documentation of such matters as cooperage and bottle sizes, useful conversion tables, and lists of worthy but non-classified châteaux of the Bordeaux region. Any production figure quoted in the text is a mean average unless a specific figure is given as representing a typical year. These figures are naturally subject to the fluctuations of season from year to year. Any regulations quoted in the Encyclopædia are in force at the time of going to press but some are liable to annual amendment.

In order to make quite clear when reference is being made to the genuine wine and when to an imitation of it, wines such as Sherry, Port, Burgundy, etc., are given an initial capital letter in the text only when they are the legally restricted wines coming from Spain, Portugal, or France.

My first book, *Wines of France*, was so well received and widely bought that I decided to embark, in somewhat the same manner, on the wines and spirits of the world. This volume would not, however, have been possible without the particular collaboration of the following persons:

Herr Karl Ress, not only a great taster, but one whose sincere dedication to his beloved Rheingau has been an invaluable source of information for this and other important German wine regions.

Dr. Maynard Amerine, the leading œnologist of the United States, whose technical assistance has been sought by governments throughout the world. His books, reflecting his knowledge of the science of modern wine-making, are respected by such experts as Dr. Peynaud and Dr. Ribéreau-Gayon of France; and he is a wine-lover who realizes that wine is not only a science, but is also one of the civilizing graces.

Monsieur Pierre Gauthier, the wine-buyer of Alexis Lichine & Co., who spent long hours and many late nights checking the small vineyards of France and their production, with the result that no other book published, even in France, can approach this one in the wide range of statistics surveyed.

Monsieur Claude Taittinger, who has given of his time and knowledge to ensure that the Champagne entry is as complete and authoritative as it can possibly be.

Monsieur François Hine, Cognac-shipper of Jarnac, whose jovial nature is as internationally esteemed as is his product.

Monsieur Pierre Bréjoux, President of the I.N.A.O., who personally checked the entries on his native Anjou.

Dr. Philippe Dufaye, who abandoned medicine to become a wine grower in Châteauneuf-du-Pape, feeling that he could find a fuller and happier life dealing with the nature of the soil than with human nature.

Monsieur Georges Dubœuf, an up-and-coming young man who started off as a grower and broker, and who today, with his qualifications for selecting wines and working towards the unity of the Beaujolais growers, is well on the way to becoming the outstanding personality of his famous wine region.

Miss Jane Stockwood, who has worked diligently with me over the past eight years, who shared my frustration when 20 per cent of the manuscript was inadvertently destroyed by a typist, and gave me a helping hand in getting the missing sections into order again. If it had not been for her, this book would never have reached the publishers.

My publisher's Chief Editor, Miss Annette Carter of Cassell, who has given freely of her time, as well as her professional expertise and meticulous attention to detail, in co-ordinating corrections and seeing the proofs through the final stages.

All those who have been close to me in the eleven years, starting in 1956, when I optimistically believed this book would be finished at the end of three years.

Many other people, too many to name here, have given me considerable help and these are listed on pages 649–53. I also wish to acknowledge my indebtedness to Yves Renouil's and Paul de Traversay's *Dictionnaire du Vin* (Féret et Fils, Bordeaux, 1962), from which the tables on pages 48–9 and 375–6 were taken.

ALEXIS LICHINE

Introduction

I can truthfully say that since I reached the age of discretion I have consistently drunk more than most people would say was good for me. Nor do I regret it. Wine has been to me a firm friend and a wise counsellor. Often wine has shown me matters in their true perspective, and has, as though by the touch of a magic wand, reduced great disasters to small inconveniences.

Wine has lit up for me the pages of literature, and revealed in life romance lurking in the commonplace.

Wine has made me bold but not foolish; has induced me to say silly things but not to do them.

Under its influence words have often come too easily which had better not have been spoken, and letters have been written which had better not have been sent.

But if such small indiscretions standing in the debit column of wine's account were added up, they would amount to nothing in comparison with the vast accumulation on the credit side.

Duff Cooper: OLD MEN FORGET

Wine as a business is of international importance, an affair of vast ramifications. It provides a livelihood for some 35 million people throughout the world. More than 27,181,000 acres of the earth's surface are planted in vines. The world's harvest in 1964 was 6,115,444,000 imp. gallons (7,344,148,400 U.S.), one-quarter of which came from the Common Market countries. If all the vineyards were to be laid low by a sudden plague, millions of people would be thrown out of work, or ruined; many others would be hard hit; and an unmanageable economic crisis would follow.

As the world becomes increasingly industrialized and standards more materialistic, as automation brings more leisure, people everywhere expect a share in the good things of life—the pleasures of civilized eating and drinking among them. It is harder now to find young men prepared to devote the necessary time and devotion to the cultivation of the vine. Yet, in the cities, interest in wine, far from declining, is growing and spreading all the time.

Thus wine, one of the first interests of civilized man, is at once a major industry and a major pleasure of life. The widely differing figures in yearly consumption per head in different countries make interesting reading. France is well ahead, with 27·28 imp. gallons (32·76 U.S.). Italy comes second, with 23·10 imp. gallons (27·74 U.S.); Argentina, with 19·14 imp. gallons (22·98 U.S.), is third. Spaniards enjoy a modest 14·74 imp. gallons (17·70 U.S.) *per capita* of their own production. In the course of a year, an average American will drink 0·84 imp. gallons (1·00 U.S.); an Englishman, 0·62 imp. gallons (0·74 U.S.); a German, four times as much. A Russian, who used to consume very little wine, has lately seen his country's vineyards expand by 75%, and drinks rather more of it than does the American; but the wine itself will probably be inferior in quality to that which the American will put in his glass.

Countries whose inhabitants drink the greatest quantity are not always those which take the best. England and the United States buy some of France's finest bottles and, in spite of comparatively low *per capita* consumption in these countries, each will dispose of more great French wines in a year than will the French themselves.

As more and more people travel and acquire a taste for good wine, the civilized custom of having a bottle on the table is gaining ground. 'Will demand outrun supply?' one is asked sometimes. Yes, if Chambertins are sold which are not Chambertins and Montrachets which do not come from that patch of soil famous throughout the world for making one of the greatest dry white wines, and if that label is stuck indiscriminately on to wines that have never seen Burgundy, which regrettably is sometimes the case. Some regions can still increase their vineyard acreage. Burgundy has reached its maximum—and some fine and famous areas are extraordinarily small: 4,700 acres for the whole Chablis district. Compare this figure with the thousands of bottles labelled Chablis to be found on restaurant tables all over the world, and draw your own conclusions.

The present cry is for more of everything, turned out faster and more cheaply. If there is one thing which does not respond to this call, it is great wine. It can be made expensively, but will not, still, increase in quantity. It can be made in bulk, but will not then be a fine wine. The best wines have always been those from comparatively non-productive grapevines—which are pruned short in order to reduce output and channel the plant's energy into the production of superior fruit. Because the grower cannot at the same time obtain both quantity and quality, enlightened laws have been set up to limit production. That is why the statistics of this book represent the amount the soil can produce—*not* the amount to which an unscrupulous merchant may, accordion-like, stretch his merchandise, while his labels claim for it the geographical limitations of a vineyard, a district, or even a region to which it has no right. In these malpractices, many countries have been at fault. Italy, for instance. Too often the famous growths of the north have been cut with cheaper wines coming from the south; and it will take a few years yet for the recently enacted laws to put a stop to such 'sophistications'.

In this book, I have set out to represent wine in terms of today. By stressing the small production of the great vineyards, I hope to be able to guide the consumer through the mazes of nomenclature and of impermissible—as against permissible and honest—blending. For the contemporary trend towards a standard product (much favoured in England) is one which creates difficulty for the wine-maker. His harvest will be different in different years. He may honestly blend them towards uniformity—but no blending vat in the world is capable of turning out a standard wine of the highest quality. Fine wines will survive if the consumer insists on higher and more regular standards. That is what this book is dedicated to.

Clearly, the average wine-drinker cannot expect to enjoy the greatest wines every day. Even if he could afford to, there would soon not be enough to go round. But the supply of sound, honest wines is fortunately not short. Bordeaux is one region which has been able to increase the size of some of its classified vineyards by as much as 30%; and the American customer, who once believed he must always aim as high as Château Lafite, has learned to extend his knowledge not only to Fourth and Fifth Growths, but also to sound regional wines. He will be quite content if he—and the shippers—will get used to honest labelling, and does not expect a true Pommard for the price of an ordinary red Burgundy. Conversely, experience will teach him that for the price of a commercial Liebfraumilch (a meaningless name if ever there was one) he may find a wine from a good vineyard and double his enjoyment.

As Ernest Hemingway wrote, in *Death in the Afternoon*, 'A person with increasing knowledge and sensory education may derive infinite enjoyment from wine.'

In this book I have tried to help the reader to distinguish the small wine from the great, and by comparing one with the other, to educate his palate and develop his taste and his pleasure. To quote again from Hemingway: 'Wine is one of the most civilized things in the world, and one of the material things of the world that has been brought to the greatest perfection and which offers a greater range of enjoyment and appreciation than, possibly, any other purely sensory thing which may be purchased.'

CANADA
U.S.A.
MEXICO
COLOMBIA
PERU
BRAZIL
BOLIVIA
CHILE
URUGUAY
ARGENTINA
AUSTRALIA
NEW ZEALAND

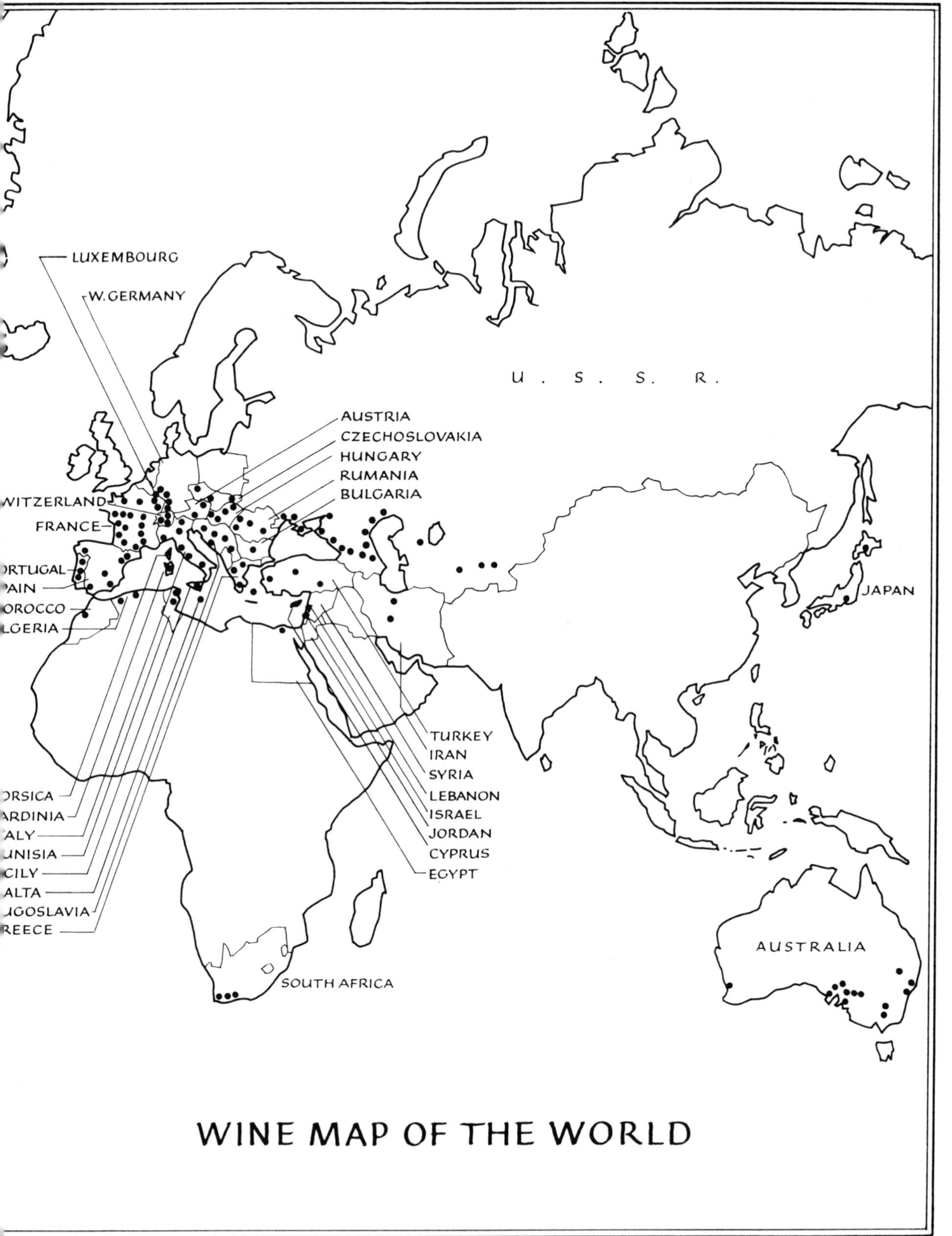

LUXEMBOURG
W. GERMANY
U. S. S. R.
AUSTRIA
CZECHOSLOVAKIA
HUNGARY
RUMANIA
BULGARIA
WITZERLAND
FRANCE
RTUGAL
AIN
OROCCO
LGERIA
JAPAN
TURKEY
IRAN
SYRIA
LEBANON
ISRAEL
JORDAN
CYPRUS
EGYPT
RSICA
RDINIA
ALY
UNISIA
CILY
ALTA
GOSLAVIA
REECE
SOUTH AFRICA
AUSTRALIA

WINE MAP OF THE WORLD

Alexis Lichine's Encyclopædia of

WINES AND SPIRITS

Chapter One

History of Wine

The history of wine is inextricably interwoven with the history of man. It has been said that civilization grew out of agriculture: when the first nomads planted seeds and waited for the crop to grow, their wandering ceased. It might be even truer to say that it was with wine that civilization began, for the vine takes longer to mature than any other crop, and does not produce grapes for the *vendange* until its fourth year—after four years in one place, the nomad tribe would be well settled and already practised in domestic arts.

We do not know when men first had wine, but it was accepted as a gift from the gods: the Egyptians attributed it to Osiris, the Greeks to Dionysos; the Armenians maintained that Noah planted the first vineyard near Erwan. Since grape-seeds have been found in prehistoric caves, it is conceivable that wine is older than history—although it is unlikely that the cavemen knew how to ferment their grapes. The discovery, when it came, was probably accidental. According to one legend, a Persian king who was very fond of grapes stored some away in a great jar marked *Poison*. Some time afterwards, one of the neglected beauties of his harem, tired of life, drank from the jar—and the poison was now so delicious that, much revived, she took a cup to the king, who drank from it, took the lady back into favour, and ordained that thereafter the grapes should be allowed to ferment. However they discovered it, the Persians evidently loved wine: according to Herodotus, all important matters were discussed twice in the councils of state—once when they were drinking, and again when they were sober.

Mesopotamia and the Caucasian slopes were no doubt early sources of wine: the Libation Scene in the 'Standard' panel from Ur (now in the British Museum) dates from the first half of the third millennium before Christ. In Egypt vineyards were being planted for funerary wines soon after 3000 B.C.; and legendary tales of wine-drinking in China (*q.v.*) date from much the same period. In any case, it is believed that Greece, the first European country to make wine, received the art from the East, and also, no doubt, from Egypt.

The earliest records of wine in Egypt are the sealing inscriptions on the stoppers of amphoræ found in pre-Dynastic tombs. In early days, the king had his own vineyard, from which the funeral wines came and (according to H. F. Lutz) a domestic vine-plot to provide his table-wine. Vineyards belonging to important persons were given names: Rameses III (1198–1166 B.C.) made the famous Ka-n-komet, as well as new plantations in oases. Another, more long-winded name was King Zoser's 'Praised be Horus, who is in the front of Heaven'—the wine from there was sometimes more succinctly described as 'Beverage of Horus'. Wine labels, on the other hand, could be models of clarity: 'In the year xxx Good wine of the large irrigated terrain of the Temple of Rameses II in Per-Amon. The chief of the wine-dressers, Tutmes.' Would that all labels were as honest, explicit, and simply expressed.

In the unchanging climate of Africa, vintage years were not very important. But soil matters vitally to the vine, wherever it grows, so that the Egyptians were concerned about the sites of their vineyards. The vines grew best near the Delta, where they were irrigated by the annual flooding of the Nile—but since marsh is not the land for them, the walled vineyards would be planted on artificially raised plots.

The reliefs and wall-paintings in the tombs in which so clear a picture of Egyptian life is preserved show workers harvesting the vine with curved knives like the hand-sickles still occasionally in use, the grapes being picked by women and dropped into wicker baskets to be carried on the men's backs —or balanced on shoulder yokes—to the press. The Egyptians used fermenting vats of acacia wood, in which they trod the grapes to a compulsive rhythm, sung and clapped out by hand—this is a sight familiar to everyone who has watched the vintage on the Douro or in Spain. Nor does the parallel with modern times end there: a certain Bilgai, 'Overseer of the Fortress of the sea', shamelessly recorded, on a stele, that he had assessed the people 23,568 measures of wines in excess of his tax-collector's due. Moreover, the Code of Hammurabi (Babylon, 2000 B.C.) stipulates the conditions under which wine may be bought; and a seller who gave short measure was to be thrown into the water—then, as now, there was fraud in the business.

We know little about the wine of the common people, because they lacked the means to have themselves buried in great tombs or to have their thoughts and histories carved out in stone—probably they drank the wines made from palms and dates, and the barley beer. The wine of the royal and the rich was mainly white. The most celebrated kinds were as follows. *Mareotic*: grown near what was to be the city of Alexandria—a white wine, sweet and light, long-lasting, and with a fragrant bouquet. Centuries later, it was known in Rome: Horace wrote that this was the wine which fired Cleopatra. *Tæniotic*: Athenæus (*c.* A.D. 200) declared that this was even better than the Mareotic—an unctuous, greenish-white wine, sweet and aromatic, and of a slightly astringent character. (He went on to say that the wine-loving Egyptians often ate boiled cabbage before a feast, and took cabbage-water to cure a hangover.) *Sebennyticum*: described by Pliny as being the product of three different grapes, the Thasian, the soot grape, and the pitch-pine. Egyptian wines were sealed up in amphoræ of the Greek pattern—and since they were not sufficient for the people of the country, many more came in from Greece, from Phoenicia, and from Syria.

It has been reckoned that wine is mentioned 155 times in the Old Testament and ten times in the New. In the Book of Numbers it says that, at the time of the Exodus, the Hebrews regretted leaving behind the wines of Egypt: but they need not have feared, for the land of the Philistines and the plain of Sharon were green with the vine, and Palestine came to be rich in vineyards. Indeed, vines flourished prolifically in the eastern Mediterranean countries and around the Caspian and the Black Seas. In Ezekiel, Chapter xxvii, we read about Damascus, that great centre of the wine trade: 'thy merchant . . . in the wine of Helbon'. The wine of Byblos was celebrated, too. The Syrians and the Phœnicians sent their wine by the old caravan routes to Arabia and Egypt, to India and as far as China; and their famous Chalybon went to the Persian kings. Vines were planted in Arabia, too, and large quantities of wine—mostly red—were made there.

There are many references to wine in the Babylonian Talmud also; in their inscriptions and their art. The southern parts of the country were not very suitable to the vine, and here, as in the Nile Delta, plots had to be raised by human labour. But in the north, soil and climate were favourable, and at one time Babylonian wines were much esteemed, and travelled as far as Arabia. Wine was blessed and offered to Abraham by King Melchizedek (Genesis, xiv): libations were made with the daily burnt offerings at the Feast of the Tabernacles, and so a link is made with King Nebuchadnezzar, dedicating wines with strange names to the pagan god, Marduk; and with Assurbanipal in Nineveh, making libations freely—pouring wine on corner-stones, on sacred objects, on lions killed in the hunt or on beheaded enemies. In the voodoo ceremonies of Haiti, libations are still offered to the gods; nor is there anything surprising about this custom, since primitive gods are largely anthropomorphic— and what more natural than to offer wine to an honoured guest?

The ancient Greeks also poured libations to their gods, and from Homeric times and earlier they were a wine-drinking people. Vines decorated the shield of Achilles; the gold cup of Nestor is still famous; and Odysseus and his men washed down 'abundant flesh with sweet wine'. The Greeks liked their wines old and watered down. These sweet wines, trodden in stone vats and matured in earthenware crocks, may have borne some resemblance to Malmsey. Hesiod, the Bœotian farmer-poet, who was writing his *Works and Days* in about 700 B.C., pruned and planted his vines in the ways that were to be followed by countless generations (*see* CLASSICAL WINES). The Pramnian and pure Maronean first described in Homer are still discussed, and regretted —some writers are of the opinion that the well-matured vintages of ancient Greece were the quintessence of fine wine. Nobody alive is in a position to dispute this view. Yet the pitched vessels in which much of the Greek wine was stored, the mixture, with some of it, of sea-water, the addition of perfumes, must have combined to produce flavours not much to our taste.

Some of the grapes which yielded the Greek wines were almost certainly transplanted to the Greek colonies in Sicily and southern Italy, and the wine would surely have been made there in the same way. Up on the mainland, the Etruscans (migrants, it has been said, from Asia Minor) were already a wine-drinking people, loving luxury and splendid banquets in which their women took a prominent part. The Etruscans' wine god was called Fufluns. In the same province of Tuscany some of the best Italian wines are made today.

Viniculture, therefore, would have been a natural heritage of the Romans. Like the Greeks, they made red, white, and amber wines; and they, too, could drink them 'pitched and pickled', sometimes mixed with sea-water or exposed in smoky rooms. In old age some of them would be, as Tovey said, 'reduced to a syrup and rendered so muddy and thick they had to be strained through cloths and dissolved in hot water'. But the *fumarium* was intended to mellow the wine by heat rather than by smoke—the principle was not unlike that of maturing Madeira near ovens—and the jars were protected by a thick coat of plaster or pitch. The Romans themselves complained of 'smoky wines' when they came in from

Marseilles—settled about 600 B.C. by Greeks from Phocæa, and surely the first place in Gaul to have made real wine. The wines most prized in Rome were luscious, less in need of acrid preservatives—they probably resembled the *lagrima* of today (*see* CLASSICAL WINES).

Where the Romans went, conquering and colonizing, the culture of the vine went with them. In A.D. 92 the Emperor Domitian, in an attempt to boost agriculture and to control the surplus production of wine, ordered that half the vines throughout the Empire should be uprooted. It is not to be supposed that all of them were; the French character being what it is, orders are not much regarded; but however half-heartedly the growers carried out the order, their descendants must have been relieved when, in 280, the Emperor Probus repealed it.

When the vines were openly planted again, they spread beyond the old vineyard regions of Marseilles, Bordeaux, the Rhône Valley and the Iberian Peninsula, to the more northerly regions of France and Germany, and to Britain also. In Germany, as in France, viticulture was encouraged by Charlemagne. Soon, in an age when most wine was only fit to drink when young, the Germans, storing theirs in huge casks, promoted a taste for 'old Rhenish'. Christianity spread, too, monasteries sprang up, and all through the early Middle Ages the Church was the principal producer—because of their learning and their industry, the monks took the lead in viticulture: the pure wine of the grape was needed both for sacrament and for sustenance. Cluny, in Burgundy, was the great monastic centre. When life there became too luxurious, the ascetic Cistercians broke away, disseminating the Gospel and the culture of the vine wherever they went, inside France and across her frontiers.

In early mediæval times, vines were grown, largely by monks, in the southern counties of England. But wine was imported, also, from the Rhine and the north of France. In spite of the marriage of Henry II and Eleanor of Aquitaine (*see* BORDEAUX), it was not until the beginning of the thirteenth century that Bordeaux (Gascon) wines began to come in any quantity to England, Flanders, and the Hanseatic ports.

The Gascon wine was soon much loved in England, where it was known as clairet; and by the early fourteenth century, the people were able to enjoy table wines from Spain.and Portugal, as well as the sweet wines of Crete and Cyprus. Malvasia, or Malmsey, came originally from Greece; but when the Turks occupied the mainland, the wine was shipped from Candia (Crete) and other islands, often in the vessels of the powerful Venetians who, in the reign of Richard III, were bringing the legendary Helbon of Damascus to western Europe. To England, they were obliged to bring with each cask ten Levantine yews to be made into bows. Inside the country also, there were strict controls. Officials boarded the merchant ships to supervise the cargoes and test the quality of the wine, and the king took his *prise* from every load. Although the wine was cheap, the common people did not drink very freely. Each town was allowed only a specified number of taverns; and no man except a peer or one with a considerable income and household was permitted to keep more than ten gallons of wine at home. Yet an Archbishop of York bought and dispensed one hundred tuns at his enthronement—wine was not, however, as strong then as it is now.

In the meantime, the wine which had come so early to the Middle East had been forbidden to the followers of Mohammed—yet the prohibition must not be taken too seriously since certain Turks are known to have been devoted to drink. But as the power of the Moslems spread, so did the rule of abstinence; and when the practical monks of Carbonnieux wanted to sell their wine to the Turks, they labelled it 'Mineral Water of Carbonnieux'. The Crusaders, however, are said to have found new vines in the lands of the Saracen, and to have brought back with them sweet muscat grapes which they planted at the foot of the Pyrenees, to produce Muscat de Frontignan, Lunel, and Rivesaltes. It was from the abstemious Saracens that Europe learned the art of distilling spirits.

Since in the Middle Ages all wine was drunk young, some of it must have been very acid and crude; and this, especially at banquets, was made palatable by admixtures of honey and spices known as *piments*, which combined 'the strength of wine, the sweetness of honey, and the perfume of aromatics'. Of these liqueur-like drinks, the most celebrated were hippocras, about which poets rhapsodized, and clarry—the basis, clearly, was claret.

By Elizabeth I's time, although the gentry still drank a lot of wine, the price of French wines had risen, the common people drank less of it—and more beer—and sack and Sherry were already well established (the name sack was applied to wines from the Canaries, and other places besides Jerez). James I loved his claret; Oliver Cromwell, who hated fun and destroyed beauty, was yet human enough to approve of good wine; Charles II brought back from France a new taste for Champagne. But under William of Orange and his German successors, crippling duties were put on French wine;

and the Methuen Treaty of 1703 gave overwhelming preference to Port—not then the fortified drink we know, but simply Portuguese table wine which was, as Englishmen complained, much inferior to Bordeaux. Many of them refused it, and turned to 'Florence' wine instead. The poorer people turned, regrettably and excessively, to gin. Rhenish, also, was to be had, and some Spanish table-wine, as well as Sherry—by the early eighteenth century, sack was seldom heard of. Claret, of course, was smuggled in; but gradually people took to Port—perhaps the first 'brandying' (which started, probably, about 1715) had something to do with it. In time, the shippers of Oporto learned to fortify and mature the wine as they do now, and by the end of the century it was first in popularity, although Hermitage, Champagne, and Madeira were doing well. During these years, wine-bottles, which had formerly been nothing more than squat jugs for holding wine taken fresh from the barrel, had developed more or less the form they have now, and so, in 1781, the first Claret to be stored in a well-rounded bottle was laid down in the cellars of Château Lafite.

When the French Revolution broke out, the vineyards were taken from the nobles and the Church and given to the people. A few years later, Napoleon secularized the vineyards of Germany—almost as great a revolution, from the point of view of the German growers. In France, ever since, the Burgundian holdings have mostly been divided into small parcels, although in Bordeaux the big estates were soon re-established. Talleyrand became the owner of Château Haut-Brion, and some sharp wits attributed his diplomatic successes at the Congress of Vienna to the talents of his cook. At delicious dinners, he would ply his guests with fine wines, and then play them off against each other. The chief opponent of Talleyrand was Metternich, later proud possessor of the great German vineyard, Schloss Johannisberger.

By the middle of the nineteenth century, new vineyards were established in new countries: in South Africa and Australia and, most importantly, in America. When Leif Ericson crossed the Atlantic, he found a country green with wild vines and called it 'Vineland'. Later settlers made many experiments with European vines transplanted; finally, they discovered that, while the *Vitis vinifera* would grow in California, it was better to stick to the native species in the Eastern States (*see* AMERICA).

It was never guessed that the American vine, living independently, was developing an immunity to certain vine pests and diseases, themselves strengthened continually in the competition. But when American vines were brought to Europe, a hundred years ago, the pests struck, and in the second half of the century nearly all the vineyards of Europe were decimated by the burrowing plant louse, phylloxera. Indeed, the plagues swept over the world, and wine, as we know it, might have vanished. Luckily, the growth which brought disaster also contained the cure. American roots became immune to phylloxera, and it was found that the European varieties would grow on American root-stocks. What will be the final result, in terms of quality, of grafting on to American stocks cannot yet be determined. Some people say that the wines are better than 'before phylloxera'; others deny this. The long adjustments of the vine to soil and weather, changes very gradual in all wine history, must be given their own time.

Besides this effect of American vines on Europe is the story of wine in America itself. At first, in the Colonies, European wines were drunk. How discriminating were the drinkers, and of what kinds the wines, can be judged from records of the time. The writer Washington Irving was a famous lover of wine and we have many of his letters and receipts for orders of hogsheads from France and Spain. There were a great number of others but we will cite excerpts from two letters of Thomas Jefferson, a true expert, the first written in 1792 to Henry Sheaff, a Philadelphia merchant, and the second in 1817 to President James Monroe at the White House . . .

Burgundy. the best wines of Burgundy are Montrachet, a white wine. it is made but by two persons, to wit, Mons[r] *de Clermont, & Monsieur de Sassnet. the latter rents to Mons*[r] *de la Tour. this costs 48 sous the bottle, new, and 3 livres when fit for drinking.*

Meursault, a white wine. the best quality of it is called Goutte d'Or. it costs 6 sous the bottle new. I do not believe this will bear transportation. but the Montrachet will in a proper season.

Chambertin, Vougeau, Beaune, are red wines, of the first quality, and are the only red wines of Burgundy which will bear transportation and even these require to be moved in the best season, & not to be exposed to great heat or great cold. These cost 48 sous the bottle, new & 3 livres old. I think it next to impossible to have any of the Burgundy wines brought here in a sound state.

Champagne. the Mousseux or sparkling Champagne is never brought to a good table in France. the still, or non-mousseux is alone drunk by connoisseurs.

Bordeaux red wines. There are four crops of them more famous than all the rest. These are Chateau-Margau, Tour de Segur, Hautbrion, & De La Fite. they cost 3 livres a bottle, old: but are so engaged beforehand that it is impossible to get them. the merchants, if you desire it, will send you a wine by any of those names, & make you pay 3 livres a bottle: but I will venture to affirm that there never was a bottle of those wines sent to America by a merchant, *nor is it worthwhile to seek for them; for I will defy any person to distinguish them from the wines of the next quality, to wit.*

Rohan-Margau, which is made by Madame de Rohan. this is what I import for myself & consider as equal to any of the four crops.

There are also the wines of Dabbadie, la Rose, Quirouen & Durfort which are reckoned as good as Madame de Rohan's. yet I have preferred hers. these wines cost 40 sous the bottle, when of the proper age for drinking.

Bordeaux white wines.

Grave. the best is called Pontac, & is made by Mons[r] *de Lamont. it costs 18 sous a bottle.*

Sauterne. this is the best white wine of France (except Champagne and Hermitage) the best of it is made by Mons[r] *de Lur-Salur and costs at 4 years old (when fit to drink) from 20 to 24 sous the bottle. there are two other white wines made in the same neighborhood called Prignac & Barsac, esteemed by some. but the Sauterne is that preferred at Paris, & much the best in my judgment. they cost the same. a great advantage of the Sauterne is that it becomes higher flavored the day the bottle has been opened, than it is at first.*

Mr. Fenwick, Consul of the U.S. at Bordeaux, is well informed on the subject of these wines, and has supplied the President and myself with them genuine & good. he would be a proper person to endeavor to get from the South of France some of the wines made there which are most excellent & very cheap, say 10 or 12 sous the bottle. those of Rousillon are the best . . .

I promised you, when I should have received and tried the wines I had ordered from France and Italy, to give you a note of the kinds which I should think worthy of your procurement. They are the following:

Vin blanc liquoreux d'Hermitage de M. Jourdan à Tains. This costs about .82 a bottle put on shipboard. . . .

There is still another wine to be named to you, which is the wine of Florence called Montepulciano, with which Appleton can best furnish you. There is a particular very best crop of it known to him, and which he has usually sent to me. He knows too from experience how to have it so bottled and packed as to ensure its bearing the passage, which in the ordinary way it does not. I have imported it through him annually 10 *or* 12 *years and do not think I have lost* 1 *bottle in* 100.

By the middle of the nineteenth century, tariffs between England and France had been so much lowered that the English bourgeoisie became Claret-drinking people again—although Cyrus Redding, a few years earlier, wrote that the English palate, coarsened by a long diet of brandied wines, could not appreciate a great growth of Bordeaux in its pure, natural state, and so, especially for the English market, fine Clarets were 'sophisticated' with Cahors, Hermitage, Benicarlos, and even brandy. But Burgundy, Redding believed, could not be successfully adulterated—because its exquisite delicacy and bouquet were inimitable. (That he should have supposed blended and over-chaptalized imitations to be unacceptable seems odd today.) Burgundy was also held by the eighteenth-century writer, Barry, to be too delicate a wine to travel, and it was not, in fact, widely known in England in his time.

It must be added that, even if Mr. Redding's strictures on the Clarets prepared for England were deserved, a race of keen connoisseurs was to spring up in the second half of the century, whose rhapsodies over the great pre-phylloxera vintages of the eighteen-sixties and seventies are still quoted today. By their day, Englishmen must have earned the right to buy their Claret pure. About mid-century, also, came the first of two disastrous vine diseases—the oïdium mildew, considered the greatest of plagues until it was followed by phylloxera.

The other momentous event was the Official Bordeaux Classification (based on earlier, unofficial ratings) of the great growths of the Médoc. The age of jurisprudence in the organization of the wine-trade was beginning. It was clearly necessary that place-names should be controlled in a way which would make it difficult if not impossible for an inferior wine to masquerade as a great one. The campaign, which began on the Douro to protect the good name of Port, was carried on in France through the early years of this century until, in 1936, the laws of Appellation Contrôlée were passed—models of their kind, which the other vine-growing countries of the world would do well to imitate (*see* APPELLATION D'ORIGINE).

Wine is getting more expensive, but the demand for it is greater than ever, and, in spite of bad summers in Europe, production flourishes. The Office International du Vin, a working group of wine growers and legislators, has assessed the production of forty-four member countries; in 1964 it amounted to 6,121,335,373 imp. gallons (7,351,384,958 U.S.). In this age of mechanization, man is returning to the wine of the soil, the drink of civilization.

NOTE: *See* CLASSICAL WINES, page 203, for additional history. Also regional entries: America, Bordeaux, Burgundy, etc. for local history.

Chapter Two

History of Spirits and Distillation

In the Middle Ages spirit was known as *aqua vitæ*, a term which survives today in Swedish and Norwegian aquavit and Danish akvavit. This was symptomatic, because the name means 'water of life'.

In ancient Greece, Aristotle wrote: 'Sea water can be rendered potable by distillation. After it has been converted into humid vapours it returns to liquid.' A Greek is said to have discovered this simply by noticing how steam condensed on the inner lid of a dish.

The principal remedies of the ancients were, as we know, wine and herbs. From the time of the Egyptians onward, great use was made of flowers, plants, and spices, cooked, macerated, or infused for pharmaceutical or culinary purposes. With wine or water, the healing, perfumed liquid was preserved in airtight jars. The science of distillation, if not continuously practised, crops up again and again in history. The distillates, as far as we know, were water and scents. The discovery of the distillation of alcohol was made by the Arabs in the early Middle Ages. The philosopher Avicena in the tenth century produced a complete description of the alembic, but did not mention alcohol—although it must have been discovered about that time. Like alchemy, the word 'alcohol' derives from the Arabic. A certain black powder was liquefied, converted to vapour, allowed to solidify again, and then used as eye-paint by the harem beauties. This was *kohl*, which is in use throughout the Arab world today. And when the spirit of wine began to be distilled, the Arabic name for this distilled powder —*Al Koh'l*—was adopted, because of the similarity of the process.

In fact, we inherited the Arabian science of distillation by way of alchemy, which played a larger part in the mediæval world. The two earliest names of genuine importance in distillation are those of Arnáu of Vilanova (d. 1313), Catalan professor at the University of Montpellier—and probably the first to write of alcohol—and his pupil, Raimundo Lulio (or Raymond Lully), the philosopher and chemist who carried on with Arnáu's experiments. Lulio was born in 1235 at Mallorca. Arnáu's treatise on wine and spirits was a handbook of the time.

Eau-de-vie, Lulio wrote, is 'an emanation of the divinity, an element newly revealed to men but hid from antiquity, because the human race was then too young to need this beverage destined to revive the energies of modern decrepitude'. Arnáu of Vilanova was more ecstatic. To him, the liquor was the long-sought panacea, the elixir of life itself, the dream of the alchemists. Although they never found what they were looking for—the secret of transmuting base metal into gold, or the elixir of everlasting life—the alchemists discovered a great many other things by the way. They developed the science of chemistry; and while they did not discover *aqua vitæ*, they used it extensively and bequeathed its uses to us.

To the general public *aqua vitæ* was a medicine and tasted like one. Another name for it was *aqua ardens*—fire-water. The fruit and herbs with which the spirit was doctored helped to hide the taste as well as to heal the patients. When, later on, people began to think of brandies and liqueurs primarily as drinks, there was much experimenting with different plants, to improve the flavour; and, except in such favoured regions as Cognac, Frenchmen were still tackling the same problem at the end of the eighteenth century. Then, in 1800, Adam invented the process of rectification or rectifying—that is, a redistillation which removed the *mauvais goût*. Unfortunately, it removed all taste, good as well as bad, and the French, who had been adding herbs and fruit concoctions to hide the nasty taste, had to restore them again to give flavour to their neutral spirit.

Aqua vitæ was on sale in Italy in the Middle Ages; at about the same time, or a little earlier, it appeared in Ireland, gælicized into *uisge beatha* and distilled from a barley beer. Variants of this name for 'the water of life' persisted throughout the centuries, but in the end it was unquestionably whisky.

Scotch whisky originated in the Highlands. By the fifteenth century, it was a familiar drink there—this was purely malt whisky. Gradually it seeped through to the Lowlands and the Scottish Court.

The English at first preferred the fine French Cognac brandies miraculously distilled from the thin, sharp wines of Charente. In early days, ships from the north used to put in at La Rochelle, principally to pick up salt. Then the inhabitants began to sell their wine as well; and afterwards, to save space in the ships—and perhaps to avoid taxes, too—they began to boil down the wine, which travelled much better when it was thus metamorphosed. At first the idea was to restore the wine by adding water when it reached land again; but it was soon discovered to taste better as it was. A gentleman called Croix-Maron, who is supposed to have had a lot to do with the boiling down of the wine, is said to have remarked: 'In cooking my wines, I have discovered their soul.'

A report from 1688 says that very little wine of the Charente region could be sold abroad, but '. . . when the white wines are converted to *eau-de-vie*, which is the customary thing, then the English and Danish fleets come to the ports of the Charente in search of it'. So, by that date, the brandy of Cognac was established. The name 'brandy' may well have come from the Germanic *Branntwein*—burnt wine. There are mentions of 'brand wine' in English in 1622 and 1650.

It is interesting that much of the early distilling was done in the house, and the politest ladies were proficient in this domestic art, as common as cooking. Scotch whisky was at first almost entirely made at home: the best was for the Highland chiefs; the crofters mashed their surplus grain into whisky. When, in that mountainous and inaccessible country, the domestic stills were banned by the Hanoverian Kings, and heavy taxes and duties began to be placed on the spirit, the distillers quite naturally took to the hills.

It is estimated that of the roughly half a million gallons of Scotch whisky being made annually in 1800, the amount made legally was approximately nil. Some 300,000 illegal gallons are said to have eluded the Excise men and now flowed down over the border into England year after year. At one time there were 200 illicit stills in the famous glen of Glenlivet, where perhaps the finest unblended whisky in the world is made today.

The Scottish distillers were defiant men, who brewed their illegal potions quite openly. All that was necessary was to choose a defendable glen, and then go about armed to the teeth. In 1823, the English Government lowered the duty on whisky in order to encourage the open and legal distillation of good spirit. Yet the illicit stills were so well established that when a dare-devil named George Smith came to Glenlivet itself and set up a legal distillery, he was considered to have shown great effrontery. His memoirs tell nothing of how he made his whisky, but they do tell the secret of his success. He hired the toughest men he could find, and by standing watch in turn with them around the clock he saved his still from being burnt out, the fate that befell the few others as bold as himself. Smith's foothold in Glenlivet was the beginning of the end. The sad decline in illegal distilling can be read in the statistics of illicit stills detected in Scotland: in 1834, 692; in 1835, 177; in 1854, 73; in 1864, 19; in 1874, 6. Whisky-runners were a dying race, like the romantic highwaymen of the previous century.

American whiskey (the word is spelt whisky in Canada, England, and Scotland, whiskey in the United States and Ireland) began to be made in the eighteenth century. Distilling of rye and barley grains had become so strong a habit by the year 1794 that such interferences as taxation and control were resented to the point of armed revolt—this was the year of the Whiskey Rebellion in Pennsylvania. The distillers, losing the fight, moved west in large numbers, preferring Red Indians to revenue men. A few years before, in Bourbon County, Kentucky, they had started making corn whiskey: with the arrival of the refugees from the east, the trade prospered. At first corn whiskey was made to reduce the carrier's load: the pack-horses winding down the narrow mountain trails of Kentucky could carry only four bushels of corn each; when the corn was distilled down to whiskey, they could carry the equivalent of twenty-four bushels. This corn whiskey took its name Bourbon from Bourbon County.

There was another incentive for home distilling, and that was the whiskey price in Kentucky. In 1782, about the time when the first Bourbon stills were set up, the price fixed by the Court in Jefferson County, Kentucky, was fifteen dollars a half-pint and 240 dollars a gallon. The Indian had already set the example, making a corn spirit he called Nohelick (the Apaches, further west in undiscovered territory, were brewing their Teeswin from boiled corn), and the settlers pitched in. The first may have been Elijah Craig. At any rate, that intrepid Baptist preacher 'considered it as honourable a business as any. Even preachers did not deem it derogatory to their high calling to lend their countenance to its manufacture and engage in it themselves, or drink a little for the stomach's sake.'

That process of rectification or redistilling, invented in 1800 by Adam and mentioned earlier, eventually set off a complete revolution in the manufacture of spirits. Even Cognac (which even now is never rectified, but is pot-distilled by the ancient method derived from the alembic) changed its manner of exportation some three-quarters of a century ago as a consequence of the growing competition from rectified spirits. Traditionally shipped in barrel, it began to be exported in bottle, so that the distillers and shippers could be sure of having full control over the liquid they were selling—sent abroad in cask, it was increasingly likely that it would be stretched and adulterated at the end of its journey. One important consequence was that the brandy began to be called after the little river-town from which it was shipped, and for the first time it was known as Cognac.

Rum—the sugar-cane spirit of the West Indies—had a riotous history in those islands. It was the traditional drink of the fighting men along the sea-lanes of the Empire-builders—and if the sailors did not get their issue of rum, there was danger of mutiny. The blazing cane-juice brew was the drink, also, of the western American colonies and, in one sense, fired them to revolt and form an independent United States—for England's taxing of rum was resented at least as bitterly as her taxing of tea. Even more romantic was the connexion of rum with the pirates of the Spanish Main. In the coves of Barbados, Jamaica, and the other islands, the privateers hove to for concealment—and a fresh load of rum.

We drink—by and large—rather tamed rum to-day. Once again it is rectification that has brought about the revolution. By repeated redistilling, all by-products can be eliminated from any base liquid—in many a light modern rectified rum little of the lustiness of the pungent cane is left. These light rums are the Puerto Rican and Cuban—different from the heavier, pungent, sweeter liquors of Demarara and Jamaica, and more to the modern taste.

It is in the vast popularity of gin and vodka that the true effects of rectification appear. Both are, fundamentally, spirits made neutral by rectification, then—in the case of gin—reflavoured. The persisting predilection for gin may be called the vogue of the Martini. During Prohibition, complex mixtures of alcohol appeared all over North America, and spread their influence over the world. These mixtures were known as cocktails. Evolving perhaps from cold punches or mint juleps, they certainly developed and multiplied as they did because illicit synthetic 'bath-tub' gins needed to be well disguised by other, less disgusting flavours. Nowadays, the cocktail—once so complex—grows simpler and simpler. The overwhelming preference is for the Martini—simply gin with a touch of vermouth, a concoction which is only possible when the basic ingredients are good.

Vodka is the latest craze. Originally a Russian, Polish, Balkan, Lithuanian, and Estonian spirit, it is now made from grain, in the United States and in England, France, and elsewhere in Europe. The Smirnoff vodka formula bought by an American firm in 1939 from a White Russian refugee started this post-war fashion.

Chapter Three

Wine and Food

Match-making, always a diverting occupation, becomes a positive pleasure when its object is a marriage between food and wine: once complementary flavours are brought together, the two combine in a gastronomic treat infinitely more delicious then either could provide alone. A fine meal, well cooked, and served so that it is as seductive to the eye as to the appetite, is a delight in itself; add a glass of wine—gleaming red or a translucent greenish-gold—and delectation will be doubled. The flavour and aroma of wine enhance enormously the taste of the food; moreover, it induces a sense of well-being—euphoria—and stimulates the imagination. That is why, since the days of Socrates, a dinner-table is the traditional setting for good talk.

The tradition was, indeed, broken by the contemporary habit of sitting over cocktails before dinner, and hurrying out of the dining-room afterwards to look at television; but fortunately there is, all over the world, a reviving interest in wine, and people who plan their dinner-parties with care and round out the meal with several good bottles, usually see to it that the aperitifs are Sherry, dry Champagne, or dry vermouth well iced—one of the best of these is a dry Chambéry. It is a waste of time to achieve felicitous matches between the wine and the food unless the drinks also complement each other: wine should be preceded (and followed) by the products of the grape, not of the grain—wine and spirits, excellent apart, do not go well together.

That wine and food *do* go well together was discovered by our remotest ancestors. In the old days, vast meals would be washed down by jugs of new wine, fresh from the wood. In the eighteenth century, the wine began to be matured in glass bottles, and by 1800 it was no longer a refreshing drink to be gulped down: the country gentleman still ate hugely and sometimes downed his three bottles a day; but in the renaissance of the fine French cuisine, in the time of Carême and the other great cooks, dinners began to be planned with finesse and the carefully selected wines were appreciatively sniffed and sipped. Even then, and until late in the nineteenth century, meals were, by our standards, enormous and endless, with a formidable array of glasses beside each plate.

In comparison with the vigorous Victorians, we eat and even entertain very sparingly; yet at a special dinner where three or more wines are served (each course planned so that the accompanying bottle may be greater than the one before) it is still possible to play the classic music of the wines: instead of draining your glass, leave a little in it to taste against the wine which comes with the next course, and so on, until the best bottle arrives with the cheese.

The meal may start with a dry white wine, go on to a red one, and then an older or finer red—for instance, a Chablis, a Claret, and an older or greater Claret; or, depending on the dishes served, there may be three red wines, beginning with the youngest and ascending to the finest. In France, the cheese always comes before the pudding, and the red wine is finished with this course. Then, if the host has a luscious dessert-wine to offer, it will make its own counterpoint of sweetness with the sweet. Champagne (semi-sweet) and Vouvray are perfect with fruit; Sauternes or Barsac with desserts, tarts, and sweet fruits.

To offer wine is the most charming gesture of hospitality, and a host brings out for his guests the finest he has. Whether there are four wines or one, the gesture is the same. A single wine, chosen for the main dish, will be more of a success if it goes with the first course, too; if, for instance, it is a Bordeaux, the meal might start with a cheese soufflé. It is worth considering, however, that a bottle of white wine and a bottle of red may be just as easy to produce as two of red. In France, where almost everybody drinks wine every day, most households content themselves on ordinary occasions with a single, modest wine. A Frenchman's dinner table always shows if it is Sunday, a holiday, a christening . . . because then a special bottle of good wine appears. And there will be chicken, fish, or meat for dinner according to which will best show off the qualities of that wine.

Combinations of Food and Wine

Traditionally, certain wines accompany certain dishes—Chablis and oysters go together like bread and butter—and wine-bores (of whom, unfortunately, there are plenty, since on no other subject is a little learning such a tedious thing) tend to be extremely didactic about it. Most of the rules are sound, however, since they are the result of experiment over the centuries: dry white wines taste best before red ones, the great ones taste better when they follow lesser ones of a similar type; sweet wines are not at all good with meat—and all this was discovered long ago. Moreover, many wine and food partners are near relations: with the famous sausages of Lyons, no wine is so good as a fruity young Beaujolais grown in the region; and in the Loire Valley they wash down the Rillettes de Tours with local Sancerre, Vouvray, or Pouilly-Fumé.

The man who likes to make up his own mind would be wise, then, not to reject the rules—even if they are laid down for him by wine-snobs—but to prove them for himself and to test them against his own experiments. In choosing the wine for his meal, the important consideration is, after all, that it should please *him*. He should remember, though, when he makes his experiments, that time and place must be taken into account: the light rosé, which goes so well with a midday sandwich, will be out of place with a fine dish at dinner-time. The author remembers drinking, on a torrid night in the Caribbean, a fine Bordeaux, followed by a great red Burgundy; and although the food suited them, the temperature did not. (Rules are only useful to those who know how to break them; and in the tropics, chilled pink or white wines are most agreeable, whatever the menu.) Conversely, the cool rosé one enjoyed on a warm day in the South of France would not do with a big steak on a cold winter's night.

Some foods clash resoundingly with some wines: a hot curry will kill a Claret; but a white wine with a distinctive flavour (a Gewürztraminer, for example), can hold its own against the spicy taste. As for such things as anchovies, kippers, and vinegary salad-dressings—they are deadly to all wines and should not be served with them.

Types of Wine

Some wines are good to drink alone or with a biscuit—these are usually the very sweet Sauternes, Barsacs, and the German Beerenauslesen, Trockenbeerenauslesen, and Auslesen, or the fortified wines —Sherry, Port, Madeira. Natural still wines cannot be truly appreciated without the harmonious taste of food. A great dish needs wine to set it off; and a fine bottle is wasted when it is accompanied by a discordant series of food flavours.

Table Wines

These are the still beverage wines we drink with meals. They are light—from 7% to 15% in alcohol —and may be red, pink, or white; dry or sweet; light or heavy.

Dry White Wines are traditionally associated with sea-food. Chablis, as we have said before, is perfect with oysters—but so are Champagne, Muscadet, Riesling, and other dry wines; and white Burgundy is excellent also with shrimp or lobster, with ham, veal, or chicken cooked in a white wine sauce. With poached sole, a Montrachet is magnificent; and a dry white Hermitage is so distinctive in taste that it can balance curry and other highly spiced dishes. As a general rule, it should be remembered that dry white wines are light, and delicate in flavour, and so they should be accompanied by food in the same category. Rich, heavy dishes will usually overpower them.

Sweet White Wines, we know, are delicious with sweet fruits and puddings. At the start of a meal, the sugary content kills the taste buds and spoils the appetite; whereas at the end these same characteristics are precisely what is needed to induce a feeling of satisfaction and content. Yet in the early years of the century, Sauternes was constantly served with the fish; and even today some Frenchmen in the Bordeaux country consider that this is the wine which goes best with a rich fish such as salmon.

Red Wines are almost exclusively dry. (Some sweet red wines do exist, but they fall into much the same category as red sparkling wines—pleasant if you like that sort of thing, but not generally distinguished; and their sweetness renders them incompatible with food.) Everywhere in the world, more red wine than white is consumed; on the continent of Western Europe, *vin ordinaire* is the workman's staple beverage.

The outstanding characteristic of red wines is their variety: white wines are either dry or sweet, still or sparkling; dry red wines range from lightness to full-bodied robustness, each with its own distinctive taste derived from differences in soil and grape variety. Clearly, the heavier the food, the heavier the wine you will want to drink with it. Fowl, veal, and other light meats are excellent with light red wines—as with white; but full-blooded meats need heartier company, and *pasta* with meat sauce, and game, usually demand the sturdiest of wines. The best accompaniment for red wine is cheese; but it must not be too strong, especially if the wine is old and delicate. On account of this affinity, the finest wine always comes on with the cheese—which is always mild.

Sparkling Wines

Most fully sparkling wines are white, but a very few are red, and they range from dry to sweet— sometimes too sweet. Sweet red sparkling wines are generally shunned by experienced wine drinkers, because many of them are quite mediocre, and even the best lack the distinction of their fine white counterparts. Moreover, they do not go well with food. On the other hand, the Italians, among others, have been making them for centuries and seem to enjoy them.

Champagne, of course, is far and away the best sparkling white wine. Many others have borrowed this famous place-name; but only the French wine, made by the true Champagne process, in the region of Champagne, is entitled to bear it. And it is easy enough to distinguish the original from the imitations at the first sip. Yet many white sparkling wines are very agreeable and, like Champagne itself, these may be dry, semi-sweet, or sweet. There are people who consider Champagne to be the only drink; and certainly it is delicious late in the evening: before meals, if it is dry; with fruit or dessert at the end of a meal, if it is fairly sweet. By its devotees, it is sometimes drunk all through dinner; this is not to be recommended, yet there is no valid reason why you should not do so, as long as you don't go on with a Champagne *brut* into the sweet course, and once you have tried other wines and decided that you really enjoy the Champagne most. The general opinion is, however, that when it comes to balancing the wine against the food, Champagne has too little body and too many bubbles. But there is no doubt that for launching ships, for toasting the New Year and the new bride, this bubbly wine is superlative.

Fortified Wines

These may be white or red, dry or sweet. Dry Sherry (Fino or Manzanilla) is generally considered to be the perfect aperitif, particularly before a meal at which fine wines are to be served. After dinner, Port is held by many to be incomparable; yet some people prefer sweet Sherries or Madeiras. There is also a variety of lesser fortified wines, esteemed, as a rule, in their own country—the Italian Moscato, for instance, and the *vin de liqueur* of Banyuls. It is as well to know, however, that in certain parts of the world, outside Europe, fortified wines of a kind are made, cloyingly sweet and excessively alcoholic—really nothing but a substitute for cheap spirits. Naturally, nobody would think of drinking fortified wines with meals—except, perhaps, for a dry Sherry with the soup.

A Few Simple Rules

It is possible to make endless permutations and combinations of food and wines—and everyone can discover new ones for himself. He will not, however, waste good wine on unnecessary mistakes if he observes these simple rules.

Dry white wines taste best before red; and red wines are better when they are served after others of the same type but lesser quality. In the second instance, it is an elegant—and most enjoyable—practice to serve more than one red wine with a fine meal. In this case, it is a good idea to stick to the wine of one region, offering, for example, Bordeaux after Bordeaux, and Burgundy after Burgundy, rather than mixing the two. And it is advisable to serve the wines in reverse order of age—the youngest first. With wines of the same age, the lesser should come first.

Certain foods and flavours simply do not harmonize with wine. Vinegar has been mentioned; and such pungent things as onions, garlic, and fishy *hors d'œuvres* spoil the palate for wine. Spices, curry, and mustard also have a regrettable effect, unless the wine itself has a taste so definite that it can prevail over the others.

Once these obvious pitfalls have been avoided, it is as well not to worry too much (unless you are planning a dinner-party) about what to drink with what. Wine and food have a natural affinity, and in more cases than anyone would think possible, they unite with felicitous results.

Chapter Four

Serving Wine

White wines are served chilled, red ones at room temperature—but a good deal of care must be expended on them before ever they reach the table.

In the Cellar. To begin with, if you have bought an old red wine which will probably have formed a sediment, let the bottle stand upright for a day or two before laying it down in the bin; in this way, the deposit stirred up on the journey will not come up into the neck. Afterwards, lay the bottle flat in the rack, label upwards, to be read at a glance (this applies, of course, to all table wines, red or white). Again, before bringing an old red wine out of the cellar to the table, it should be stood upright for some hours, so that the sediment may sink.

Halves and Magnums. Half-bottles are good buys when you want to try out a wine, or if you are in the habit of using a small quantity at a time; but only young or average wines should be bought in this way, since great wines age prematurely in small bottles, and are, indeed, happier in magnums. In extra big bottles, wine matures more slowly and this, in a great wine, is a guarantee that it will eventually achieve real quality—a quickly matured wine will never attain great heights.

Age and Temperature. White wines should mostly be drunk young: the chances are that after five years many of them will lose their freshness and start oxidizing. Yet a good white Burgundy may live some years longer. (What is a young wine? In Bordeaux of good vintage, less than four years old. In red Burgundy, less than two-and-a-half years.)

White wines need to be chilled—the sweeter, the colder; but it is a mistake to freeze wines too much, since this kills the taste and destroys the character. Rather drink a fine white Burgundy under- than over-chilled. Most people now put their wine in the refrigerator. One or two hours is sufficient, as 40° to 50°F. (5° to 10°C.) is the ideal temperature for dry white wines, although an ice bucket is said to be a better cooler, because less time is required, twenty minutes being sufficient. Naturally, the time for chilling a wine largely depends on the temperature the bottle was at before chilling. If you have no ice bucket, lay the bottle in a big salad bowl full of crushed ice or ice cubes with some water. Just before you are ready to serve it, take the bottle from the freezer and pull the cork.

Pink wines, as well as white, are served chilled.

Red wines which are young and full-bodied (great young Médocs, for instance) should be uncorked several hours before dinner; a very young one may even benefit from being opened the day before—this extra time for breathing will help it to achieve some maturity and softness. In Beaujolais, extreme youth is an advantage: nine months to under three years is its age cycle; treat it like white wine, and uncork it immediately before serving. Although it need not be chilled in a cold climate, Beaujolais is better chilled in a very hot one. A Claret between five and fifteen years old should be opened about two hours before drinking; but a very old wine needs less breathing space—if it is really old and delicate (earlier than 1928), decant it at dinner: even then, it may have faded and died a little by the time you pour the second glass—whereas a younger red wine will expand and develop in the glass.

Decanting. Wine which contains sediment a quarter of an inch or more thick should be taken up very gently, held steady in the position in which you first grasped it, and poured in one continuous movement into a clean crystal decanter, until the deposit begins to rise to the neck of the bottle—then stop at once. So that you may keep an eye on the sediment, hold the bottle in front of the light. As the process of decanting enables the wine to breathe, there is no need to leave the stopper out. Here again, the age of the wine will determine how much it should be exposed to air before drinking. However, all red wines should be brought into the dining-room a couple of hours before the meal, so that they may come up to room temperature (or become *chambrés*): to warm them suddenly before a fire or in hot water is injurious. The purpose of a wine-basket is to hold steady a bottle which may contain sediment; since in restaurants many waiters pour the wine in jerks, and wave these baskets about, they are usually superfluous adjuncts to the often meaningless ritual which has grown up about wine.

Opening

When you open a bottle of wine, cut the capsule and tinfoil below the tip with a knife; use a clean cloth to remove the mould which usually forms under the capsule; draw the cork and then carefully clean the lip of the bottle inside.

Corkscrews. Don't choose a fancy one, with all

kinds of levering gadgets. These are all right for young wines but not for old ones, where the cork is apt to break or crumble into powder. The best is the old-fashioned T-screw: look for one with a long stem (great wines have long corks) which is rounded—not sharp enough to cut the cork. If the cork *should* break or turn out to be old and powdery, it can be got out by leverage: insert the screw delicately, slightly sideways; set the bottle on its side, so that the pressure of the wine is against the inside face of the cork, then turn the screw gently, using some leverage to lift the bottom of the cork towards the upper side of the bottle. One occasionally finds a defect in even the finest of corks—sometimes an invisible vein which, with age, is liable to deteriorate and turn mouldy (this is not the fault of the wine-maker and may happen to the best wines). The wine will then have an unpleasant, corky taste and smell—and the cork will smell of itself and not of the wine. In a restaurant, the waiter should smell the cork, and then bring it to you; and the reason why a little wine is poured first into the glass of the host is that he may make sure the wine is not corked, before it is offered to his guests. Sometimes the infection is so slight that only the first glassful is spoiled; therefore, when you open the wine at home, it is worth putting the bottle aside to see if it will afterwards be fit for you yourself to drink. In a restaurant, it must, of course, be sent back at once.

Serving

At a small dinner for four or five people, given in a private house, the bottle of wine is set on the table in front of the host, who will pour it; if the party is larger, a second bottle should be given to the hostess to pass round at her end of the table. When the wine is brought round by a servant, he serves the ladies first, starting on the right side of the host and moving, clockwise, to the lady on his left; then the men, beginning with the one sitting on the right of the hostess. Never make the mistake of leaving the wine until after the food has been served. At his own table, a host does not taste the wine first, because, having opened it himself, he knows that it is not corked.

For the order in which wines should be brought on, see Chapter Three, p. 11.

Glasses. Choose plain crystal to display the sparkle of the wine itself. Great wines can be ruined in small glasses; there should be room for the wine to be swirled around and for it to breathe and reveal its bouquet. The best glass is large and tulip-shaped, clear and thin, without markings, the bowl the size of an apple or orange. Different shapes exist for different wines; but this tulip glass serves equally well for all, including Champagne—in the shallow 'Champagne glass' the carefully manufactured bubbles will be dissipated and the flavour lost. (Incidentally, the swizzle-stick is a negative instrument, designed as it is deliberately to destroy the sparkle which is the distinctive characteristic of Champagne, and the result of years of labour. People who do not care for bubbles would do better to order a still Champagne to begin with.)

The *Brandy* served with the coffee should be poured, not into a small liqueur glass but into one big enough to be warmed in the palm of the hand and to allow the brandy (serve good Cognac, Armagnac, or marc) to be rolled around in it. For *eau-de-vie* or white spirits (such as Framboise, Mirabelle, Quetsch, or Kirsch) chill the glass first by swirling a piece of ice in it: this chilling of the glass mellows the taste of the very alcoholic drink.

Port. It is the custom, particularly in England, to serve Port wine at the end of dinner and before the coffee. Very often, the ladies leave the dining-room and the men remain to enjoy their wine alone. The decanter is passed clockwise.

Smoking. In England, it is bad form to smoke with good wine. The French are less strict in some ways, and many growers smoke when they are drinking wine—between meals. The French have never adopted the American custom of smoking between courses.

Chapter Five

Value and Wine

Wine is good value when you find the right bottle for the right purpose, and at the right price. A bogus Burgundy at thirteen shillings (two dollars) is expensive; a genuine Richebourg is reasonable at two pounds (six dollars). A regional wine, or a shipper's Monopole (wine with a brand name, blended for consistent year-after-year quality and character by a shipper whose own name is its guarantee) may be the same price as a classified Bordeaux growth; but even though the shipper's blend be a reliable one, the first is a bad buy—whereas if it were to be sold for a few shillings less it would be a good one. In every case, the important factor of personal choice must be considered: no wine, however honest, can be good value unless it pleases you and goes well with the food you are going to eat.

The obvious way for an amateur in wine to find out what he likes best, and to learn which wines traditionally accompany which dishes, is to cultivate a wine merchant who knows his business, and who is a man of integrity and taste as well. In England more than anywhere else, and recently in America, in a number of old-established houses, such sound traditions of wine-selling flourish—and one of their lists alone is a store of information and advice. In France, they hardly exist; people buy direct from the grower—or from the grocer; and it is not always easy, in one part of the country, to find wine from elsewhere. A village shop in Burgundy will stock the local wine, but is unlikely to supply you with Bordeaux. In France, however, wine-drinking, chauvinistic as it may be, is part of a way of life; in America, it is not, and wines are sold, too often, by shop-assistants (or clerks) who don't know one from another. Yet well-informed wine merchants do exist in the United States, and the increasing number of tourists who return from Europe with a new appreciation of wine is encouraging them to expand their business. The good customer is now getting the service he deserves, serious wine merchants are spreading all over the U.S.A. Often, the local wine merchant has developed because the state and federal laws make it difficult, or impossible, for a buyer in one part of the country to have wine shipped to him from another state. In spite of great improvements, then, the standard of wine-selling in American stores and restaurants still leaves a good deal to be desired. In the restaurant, the customer has matters very much in his own hands: he has only to refuse to pay an absurd price for poor wine and bad service.

Wine for the House

Wine is bought either to be drunk within the next month or two, or to be laid down for future use. In the old days, when life was stable and people lived in houses with large cellars, it was customary to buy wines of a fine vintage, as soon as possible and at a good price, and lay them away to mature. By the time they had reached their peak, the retail price would have risen considerably and the early purchaser—or the son who succeeded him—would congratulate himself on his foresight. Nowadays, when the tendency is to live in the present rather than plan for the future—and to live also in apartments where storage space is limited—there is less laying down of wine. The small quantity that can be fitted into a modern cupboard should be chosen with extra care: for suggestions on cellarage conditions and the contents of a model cellar, see Chapter Six.

Inexpensive Wines

Many of the wines bought for immediate consumption will probably be unpretentious regional types: but there is every reason why these should still be sound and palatable, living honestly up to the statements on the bottle label—and some labels offer a better guarantee of validity than do others. On French wines, look for the words Appellation Contrôlée; on Spanish, Denominación de Origen; on Italian, the seal of a *Consorzio*. The better bottles from the vineyards of South Africa, Australia, and California will, at a moderate price, be good value; but they will be better value if you avoid those bearing such meaningless generic names as 'South African Claret' and 'Californian Burgundy' (for neither Claret nor Burgundy could come from anywhere outside the Bordeaux and Burgundy regions of France) and look instead for 'varietal wines'—that is, wines named for the dominant grape variety, such as Riesling, Cabernet, Pinot Noir. If the specific place of origin is also named, the wine will probably be above average in quality.

Some South American wines—notably, those from Chile—are good bargains and very agreeable to drink—as are many from Italy, Spain, and Portugal.

Pleasant wines can be found, also, from Yugoslavia and Hungary: the best are those bearing a State seal. Look for vintages on the labels, for the date will give an indication of the amount of ageing the wine has undergone; and, if possible, choose any of these wines when they are from three to five years old.

In France and Germany, the choice becomes infinitely expanded and the price-range wider: and the first question to ask yourself about such wines is simply: 'Is this what it pretends to be—is it authentic?'

French Wines

Most of the French wine sold abroad will bear the words Appellation Contrôlée, signifying that it has been made in accordance with the strict laws of place-name (*see* APPELLATION D'ORIGINE) and that it conforms to certain minimum standards. Since France produces more than 210 million imp. gallons (253 million U.S.) of wine of Appellation Contrôlée in an average year, even bottles carrying this legend will vary considerably. In buying fine wines, the rule is: the more specific the place, the better the wine will be (i.e. Médoc should be better than simply Bordeaux; Margaux will be better than Médoc). The exception is the wine of Alsace, where grape variety takes precedence over place, the better bottles selling as Alsatian Riesling, Alsatian Gewürztraminer and so on—and in rare cases bearing the vineyard as well as the grape name. Clearly, then, some detailed knowledge of the geography of France will be invaluable in selecting French wines: it is impossible to choose the bottle from the more specific place unless you know whether Saint-Julien, say, is in the Haut-Médoc (as it is) or the Haut-Médoc in Saint-Julien (which it isn't).

Fine French Wines

Apart from Champagne, the great wines of France are those from Bordeaux or Burgundy, and the finest examples carry the name of one vineyard where the grapes were grown. If you are prepared to spend the not unreasonable sum demanded for some of these great wines, the surest indication that you are getting your money's worth is the guarantee on the label that the wine (if it is a Bordeaux) was bottled at the château where it was made: the French words are *Mis en bouteilles au Château*. Burgundies bottled by the growers are rarer, since the Burgundian estates are so small (*see* BURGUNDY); but domaine-bottled Burgundies—than which nothing could be finer—are labelled *Mis au Domaine*, or something similar. Failing one of these, look for the label of a reliable shipper: among the good ones are Bouchard Père et Fils, Louis Jadot, and Louis Latour.

The system for labelling wines from other districts is much the same—except that individual vineyard names do not occur so frequently. Champagne is usually a blend of wines from that region, made by one of the big firms whose names are famous. The best carry vintage years. (Other sparkling wines are poor value compared with Champagne, since none of them can compare with it, and yet taxes on sparkle put them in the same high price-range.) Wines from other regions are often blended, although some come from specific vineyards; and one such from Châteauneuf-du-Pape, Hermitage, Côtes du Rhône, or Tavel in the Rhône Valley; or from Anjou, Vouvray, or Pouilly-sur-Loire in the Loire Valley, can be not only pleasant but admirable.

German Wines

Because of their northerly climate, it is almost impossible for the Germans to make great wines inexpensively, and the finest are admittedly very dear. But, fortunately, many sound, agreeable wines do exist at prices which are not extreme. Since, however, in Germany, as elsewhere, unscrupulous wine merchants are to be found, it is wise to look for a bottle named for the place of origin, the grape variety, and the date of vintage (e.g. Hattenheimer Riesling 1964er—i.e. town, grape variety, and date.) The better wines will bear the name of the vineyard as well (e.g. Hattenheimer Nussbrunnen Riesling 1964er); or may omit the grape and simply read, for instance, Hattenheimer Nussbrunnen 1964er, since in many of the fine German vineyards only Riesling is grown. The next thing to look at is the name of the bottler: if one of the owners of this particular vineyard has bottled the wine, there will be a complete degree of authenticity. Certain aristocrats among the wines, such as Schloss Johannisberger, Schloss Vollrads, and Steinberger state only the name and year, and these three are always estate-bottled and almost always expensive. Buyers of the sweet Trockenbeerenauslesen Steinberger 1959 paid as much as £15 ($45) for a single bottle: this acknowledged king of the Rheingau is made in minute quantities and sold for whatever price customers are willing to bid. Schloss Johannisberger has invented a system of coloured seals to distinguish the various types of estate-bottled, personally selected, and late-picked wines (*see* RHEINGAU) and some other vineyards have followed this example. The Spätlese and Auslese wines of the great vineyards are those which have been late-harvested and selected after the noble rot or *Edelfäule* has set in, and these, as well as the Edelbeerenauslese and especially the Trockenbeerenauslese, like the Sauternes which is harvested in the same way, will be luscious dessert wines. Yielded by grapes grown so far north, this sweetness is a *tour de force*: indeed, in some of the great years these wines, although extraordinary, may even be too sweet; whereas in lesser years they may have less than the expected sweetness.

Again, because of the harsh climate in which they are grown, vintage years in authentic German estate-bottled wines are unusually important. (The further north you carry the cultivation of the vine, the greater the variation in the seasons—and a summer without sunshine means grapes lacking in sugar. Yet a northern wine which does succeed will have more finesse than one grown in the south.)

As a rule, German wine labels carry a wealth of information—if you can understand them. It was always said that only an expert could find his way around one of these; and although in recent years the tendency has been to standardize and simplify, the labels are still confusing. (*See* the explanatory paragraph on *Wine Labels* under GERMANY in the encyclopædic section.)

Finally, there are several German wines which can usually be depended on to be of no value at all. One of these is the celebrated Liebfraumilch: the name applies to no place, but is given to any unspecified Rheinhessen—or indeed to wines of even more indefinite origin. Moselblümchen and Zeller Schwarze Katz are in the same category, as they never exhibit the potential greatness of a Moselle.

The Greatest Wines

Sooner or later, every amateur of wine will be tempted to taste one of the world's great growths. First, let him educate his own palate, starting with lesser wines, learning to recognize a good bottle when one comes his way, before he sits down to savour the best. A great wine must be sufficiently aged if its true excellence is to be appreciated—and it is axiomatic that it will not be cheap, especially if (as now is so often the case) it must be bought fully aged from a wine merchant. Whether you buy it young, for laying down, or later, for immediate use, it is wise to take no risks in planning such a treat, but to decide on one of the illustrious names among the acknowledged élite (Château Margaux, Chambertin, Château d'Yquem, Montrachet) and from a great year. Vintage charts, as we have said elsewhere, are not as infallible as they seem: a great vineyard is unlikely to produce a poor wine, however bad the summer may have been, and a Chambertin or a Château Lascombes of an off-beat year may be very good and less expensive than usual: but the fully matured fine wine of a great year will be an incomparable experience. Look for these supreme names in the First, Second, or Third Growths (*Premiers, Seconds, Troisièmes Crus*) of Bordeaux (*see* MÉDOC *and* BORDEAUX: CLASSIFICATION), among the Burgundian *grands vins* (*see* BURGUNDY) or the fine German wines (*see* GERMANY).

Wine in the Restaurant

Getting value for your money in a restaurant is rather different from doing the same thing in a shop. In many restaurants in France, diners-out discard the list of mediocre wines at inflated prices and order the carafe Beaujolais or rosé instead—and these, incidentally, are often quite good value. This is the easier way out but it is not the answer; constructive criticism would be much more effective. Complain, complain, complain—but make allowances for the fact that the management must make a fair percentage on the bottle. A number of restaurants keep good cellars and present excellent wine-lists: it is easy to find out which these are, since their reputations will be generally known; at other places, the manager may really know very little about wine, and, tactfully handled, might be willing to learn and to change his source of supply to one of the more reliable shippers or merchants. It cannot be repeated too insistently that in a restaurant the regular customer gets the wine he deserves.

Vintage Charts

As for the great years, read the vintage charts but do not let yourself be hypnotized by them: in the small space of one of these printed lists, only the broadest generalities can be included. The vintage notes in the catalogue of the first-class wine merchant will be fuller and therefore more reliable—but even those cannot possibly cite the many exceptions to every rule.

The men who devote their lives to making wine are agreed on one point: wine is a living, constantly changing complex. In any given year, it will start out 'green', generally fruity, often harsh, and will mature, first in barrel and then in bottle, until it is soft and mellow. Then (it may be years after bottling) the wine is at its peak—a state of excellence which endures for varying lengths of time. Those wines which, in the opinion of the experts, will slowly mature to greatness and hold it are given high marks on vintage charts; if a wine is marked low, it may be not unpleasant but one which should be drunk when it is young. What the marking system cannot take into account is the fact that individual wines are full of surprises. Wines from adjoining vineyards, each made by experienced and devoted men, may yet vary enormously. In Burgundy, 1947 was a fabulous year, yet many growers made poor wine, because their grapes were too high in sugar; 1945 was a good vintage—but not in Chablis, where the vineyards were spoiled by hail.

Once its limitations are realized, however, a chart is useful and some notes on recent vintages follow.

Recent Vintages

The factors determining quality are the soil, the climate, and the man who makes the wines, taking for granted that the grape varieties will be suited to the vineyards in which they are planted. When all these elements are perfectly married, the buyer will be justified in expecting value in a bottle of wine. Vintage years are important; yet over-emphasis on vintage charts will not solve all the buyer's problems.

Provided the possibilities of fraud have been set aside, the expert can select in any given year the best wines from the château-bottlings of Bordeaux and the estate-bottlings of Burgundy, eliminating the failures of both nature and man. Some great vintage years will produce some disappointing wines through premature picking or faulty winemaking. Nature does not bless a large area with a uniform balance of sunshine and rain when needed.

Vintage charts, at best, can only generalize. In lesser years, often condemned categorically as 'poor', the wine buyer can find well-selected, good, enjoyable values, and occasionally he will find an absolute delight. This especially applies to red wines. A minimum amount of sunshine is required for white wines; otherwise, excessive acidity will throw the wines out of balance. In a perfect vintage, a red wine will have a higher degree of alcohol, plus an abundance of tannin. This will make for a slow-maturing wine, one which often disappoints the early drinker and requires ageing to carry it to a high level of quality where well-matured velvet will replace the harsh bitterness of tannin.

A great vintage in a red Bordeaux is one which, thanks to the abundance of sunshine, will have a high sugar content that is transformed into a high degree of alcohol. To some great years, like 1928, 1945, and 1961, vintage chart makers will, perhaps sincerely, give the highest possible rating, but they will be rating in terms of the 'high' the wine will reach once it is fully matured. Sometimes, such memorable vintages have an over-abundance of tannin. This tannin acts like a corset, to hold the wine together over a period of years, until it reaches its apex. This may only be attained at the end of some fifteen or twenty years. To drink the 1945 in 1949 might have been a disappointing experience. If you had waited until 1960, that wine—from a great vineyard—would have been one of the most memorable experiences available to living man in the enjoyment of wines.

If one must generalize, one can say that vintage charts are much more important in white wines than in reds, since in the poor years the high acidity caused by lack of maturity is expressed in a certain greenness, and the defects of the wine are more apparent. In red wines, one must consider the district, as to whether its wines are generally fast or slow in maturing. Another generalization is that the greater the wine, the more slowly it matures. Bearing these facts in mind, here are the generalities, always remembering that they may be upset by the storage and the climate in which the wines will be drunk, for hot storage ages the wines prematurely and perfect cool storage will allow the wines to reach their potentials naturally.

Bordeaux

1952—A great year for red wines. The top wines, slightly on the hard side, were slower to mature than the 1953s. In the Saint-Émilion and Pomerol, the '52s were much greater than the '53s, but the same is not true in the Médoc. As a whole, the '52s will last longer than the '53s.

1953—This was a very great year for red wines, well adapted to the United States, where lack of cellerage generally means that a wine is consumed quickly. The '53s have great softness, roundness, and perfect balance. They may not last as long as the '52s, but are certainly sheer perfection now. Don't push your luck beyond 1970.

1954—Pessimistic forecasters have had to eat their words. When inexpensive, red wines were excellent value and their short-lived pleasantness was apt to confound vintage chart makers. Bordeaux merchants bought heavily in 1952, borrowed to buy the '53s, were delighted by bad prospects during the summer of 1954 and took a strongly condemnatory position on the '54s. Late September sun notwithstanding, the chartists rated the wines as 'poor'. Although on the thin side, and very light, they were pleasant drinking throughout 1959.

1955—This very great year for red wines is definitely better than 1952. In some vineyards, greater than 1953. In others, the contrary is true. Magnificently balanced.

In white wines this was a perfect year for those who find Sauternes over-sweet. Many of the Graves had a tendency to hardness and dryness. They are now oxidized.

1956—Red wines ranged from fair to good, with a tendency to hardness. The expected amount of the softening Merlot was lacking because of the February freeze and pre-harvest over-maturing. The prices, nevertheless, warranted an interest in these wines which were bottled between the autumn of 1958 and the early spring of 1959. Here again is a year when you could pick and choose your values.

The white Bordeaux were rather small wines. The top-notch vineyards proved to be disappointing.

1957—Small, very good vintage for red wines. This and inflation caused high prices. Vineyards that harvested late benefited from a uniquely warm October. Quantities in the Médoc were half of normal—only 30% in Saint-Émilion. A tendency to hardness makes the wines relatively slow-maturing. They suffered from harshness and lack of roundness when young. Beautiful bottles may now be had, for these are wines that require ten years' maturing if they are to be drunk with pleasure.

White Bordeaux was tiny in quantity; some wines are very fine—some even great.

1958—A small yield of red wines. The vineyards still suffered from the 1956 freeze. Very light, fast-maturing, lacking the character to warrant keeping for any length of time, they should be drunk when five to ten years old.

Of the white wines the dry Graves are clean and pleasant. The sweet wines lacked sunshine to give them the sweet, full richness that has made Barsacs and Sauternes universally known as the greatest sweet white wines made by man. Yet many light wines with a slight, sweet after-taste can be found among the '58s.

1959—Has been optimistically heralded as the year of the century. This great vintage, however, was not greater than 1929. Whereas the '29s were unnoticed at birth, due to world depression and Prohibition, the '59s made banner headlines throughout the civilized world. The quantity in the Médoc was smaller than '53 and '55 because the vines were still recovering from the 1956 freeze. In Saint-Émilion and Pomerol the quantity was, tragically, 40% below normal. The red wines are full, harmonious, and rich in natural glycerine. They are big and are beginning to soften.

For those who like Barsacs and Sauternes for what they are—the richest, most luscious sweet white wines with breed in the world—1959 is the year. Perfectly balanced, the '59s should help to re-establish a dying custom, the serving of Sauternes with desserts.

1960—A large quantity of red wine. Much rain during the summer created a great deal of mildew. In the Médoc the harvest took place in good conditions. A wine that began with a bad classification but gave to those who waited a pleasant surprise: in attaining maturity, it is fulfilling itself remarkably well. The Médoc growths Château Latour, Château Montrose, Château Grand-Puy-Lacoste and Château Prieuré-Lichine, for example, have given good-quality, distinguished wines which will be quickly consumed in the years to come. They will last and will show that the great vintages are not always the best to be drunk quickly.

The white Graves had a certain success but the Sauternes lacked sugar for the reason that the 'noble rot' was replaced by grey mildew.

1961—One of the smallest years remembered in the Médoc. Fertilization during the cold and rainy month of May resulted in a diminution in production of 50–60% in comparison with the previous year. Then a hot summer, followed by a superb September, gave us (in quality if not in quantity) the greatest red wine vintage since 1945, taking into consideration the change in vinification methods. The wines are softer than those of 1945 but they will not be at their best until 1970. This was a very great vintage, and a great success, also, in Saint-Émilion and Pomerol.

The white vintage was a success also. Dry white wines had a high degree of alcohol; some were sturdy and slightly hard. This was a good vintage for the sweet wines of Sauternes and Barsac. The Sauternes produced great bottles which will last ten, fifteen, or twenty years. Some of the sweet wines were less successful because of the lack of maturity and bad weather during the harvest which had to be late (in the Sáuternes district this means the end of October).

1962—A plentiful year. Very soft red wines of such a quality that certain old growers have compared it with 1953. These wines will be ready before those of 1961. Although one can find some good bottles in Saint-Émilion and Pomerol, success there was not as great as it was in the Médoc.

The great white wines were rather on the light side, but fruity and pleasant. The dry whites are too soft and lack body.

1963—Some light and drinkable wines in the Médoc, a disaster in Saint-Émilion and Pomerol. After a rainy summer, the harvest took place in bad conditions—with a few exceptions, depending upon the time of harvest.

1964—A very plentiful year for red wines. A magnificent summer was followed by an excellent September, and the grapes achieved maturity in good conditions. Certain châteaux in the Médoc waited to harvest late, but unfortunately it rained incessantly from 8 October onwards. This year which started so well is now going to prove a disappointment in wines harvested late. However, 1964 was generally an excellent vintage in the Médoc. Very successful in Saint-Émilion and Pomerol where the harvest finished before the rain started.

A good year for the dry, white wines which had been harvested at the end of September or in the first few days of October, at the latest. For the Sauternes growers who waited until the end of October, it was a disaster.

1965—The summer was rainy. A few vineyards harvested late under fair conditions. If well selected, there will be some good-quality wines which will not last long, but to those who appreciated the 1960s, some of the '65s will prove even better.

1966—Uniformly a great vintage. A very dark deep colour with perfect balance made these round wines outstanding. The best since 1961, but different in character as they closely resemble the 1953s. Fast maturing. White Graves—very good. Barsac and Sauternes—one-third very good. The remainder disappointing.

Burgundies

1957—Very great in Beaujolais, where a third of the normal quantity was harvested, to be drunk as soon as possible. A normal quantity was produced in the Côte d'Or. The wines are big, strong, and hardy. The prices for the authentic estate-bottlings were high, as a result of inflation in France and a general shortage of great wines throughout France in this particular year.

Burgundy whites were great. Quantity was half of normal. In Chablis, a premature May frost destroyed 90% of the potential harvest; the remaining 10% proved to be undrinkable, hard and high in acid.

1958—As a whole, the red wines of the Côte d'Or were very disappointing, lacking in taste and character. In the Beaujolais, 20% of the wines from the good communes, Fleurie, Brouilly, Moulin-à-Vent, produced typical Beaujolais wines: fresh, light, fruity, flowery. These fast-maturing wines were delightful. The white wines of both the Côte d'Or and southern Burgundy—namely, those of Beaujolais Blanc, Mâcon, and Pouilly-Fuissé—were good.

1959—Very abundant. Quantities are so large that the maximum production permitted by law was increased by more than 25%. For Burgundy, this was sensational, because quality was undoubtedly great. The red wines have depth, and enough sustaining backbone to make them into *vins de grande garde*, wines that will repay patience with the glorious maturity they can achieve. Yet the natural glycerine, suppleness, and elegance will give them the roundness that has made Burgundy renowned. And this, without the abusive addition of sugar during fermentation. In Burgundy, as in other districts, faulty fermentation and poor production methods will warrant selectivity. We do not believe that 1959 will have the big fullness of the '29s. In white wines, the high peaks of quality were great. In retrospect, the white wines did not have enough fixed acidity to give them lasting freshness and they oxidized prematurely.

1960—Light and disappointing in both Côte d'Or and in the Beaujolais. Some white wines were made which were delightful when young, but did not last.

1961—A very great year for red Burgundies. Rich, tannic, and well-balanced wines with a beautiful colour. A high degree of alcohol counterbalanced by acidity gave the white Burgundies an excellent, well-deserved reputation. This was also a great year for Beaujolais, both red and white.

1962—Very fine, light, and well-balanced red Burgundies with a tendency towards early maturity. Will be ready before the 1961s. The white Burgundies are very pleasant to drink. They are lighter in alcohol than the '61s and have less character, but a good acidity gives a freshness to this wine. A good year for red and white Beaujolais.

1963—Red Burgundies were disastrous. The white Burgundies were quite drinkable but no more.

1964—In some instances the red Burgundies were better than the red Bordeaux. These well-rounded wines can be drunk fairly early, as was the case with the 1962s. They have plenty of bouquet—although the white Burgundies are well balanced there is a tendency towards lack of acidity. They will mature quickly. A very great year for Beaujolais.

1965—The floods which spoiled many vineyards, and the lack of maturity, together made the red wines a disaster. Some light and fruity red Beaujolais were drunk with great pleasure in France.

1966—The red Beaujolais resembled the 1962s. The wines from the village of Brouilly were exceptional. The Burgundies from the Côte d'Or had many of the 1964 characteristics, being full, round, and fast maturing. The white wines were really exceptional, with that perfect balance that is found in the 1962s.

Rhônes

1959—The sun-drenched valley of the Rhône got an over-abundance of heat, which scorched the vines. The grapes matured so rapidly that they rotted before they could be picked; hence, selectivity should be shown in buying Châteauneuf-du-Pape. The grapes from the other Rhône districts enjoyed the same healthy ripeness as the other districts of France.

1960—A very great vintage. The only region in France that produced great-quality wines that year. Favoured by remarkably good weather, both during the development of the grape and the harvest. One of the best vintages for the past fifteen years.

1961—Unlike any other region in France, the Rhône Valley produced a good vintage, but nothing more.

1962—A small vintage which gave flat wines lacking in character. There were, however, some isolated successes.

1963—A very small vintage. Wine completely lacking in colour. Very clearly inferior to the 1962s.

1964—An average vintage. Slightly similar to the 1961s.

1965—A good vintage. The Côtes du Rhône region, unlike other parts of France, did not lack sunshine. The harvest weather was ideal.

1966—A top vintage. The best since the great 1960 which was exceptional in the Rhône. Some growers claim that the great 1966s have even surpassed it.

Loire

1959—Great, from one end of France's longest river to the other. Starting with the very inexpensive Muscadets, through the rich and perhaps over-sweet Vouvrays, to Pouilly-Fumé.

1960—A small vintage. Green and acid wines, lacking body.

1961—A good vintage, but a small harvest. The wine had a high degree of alcohol, but lacked balance because the degree of alcohol, fruit, and body were out of proportion.

1962—A very great success. Better balanced than 1961s, and in some cases of better quality.

1963—A small vintage. Ordinary wine. Well balanced but not showing any particular quality.

1964—A good vintage. Rather like the 1962s, but a bit lighter and more hollow.

1965—An ordinary vintage. Too light. The best wines of this vintage should be drunk early.

1966—A very good quality. A little more sprightly than the 1964s, with the exception of Muscadet, much of which was disappointing.

Alsace

1962—A very good vintage. Remarkably well balanced. A wine which will last.

1963—A small vintage.

1964—A good vintage. Some wines lacked roundness and fruitiness.

1965—A very small vintage.

1966—Excellent wines. Well balanced.

Champagne

1955—Magnificent wines. Fruity, with great finesse and excellent body. The best vintage of the fifties. 235,000 barrels were produced.

1956—Small yield, small quantity. 94,000 barrels were produced.

1957—Disastrously small quantity. Unlike most other regions, quality was not up to expectations. Lack of balance, lack of body, and excess of acidity. 84,000 barrels produced. Because of the catastrophic spring freeze, and the rains during the harvest, 1957 cannot claim to be a vintage year.

1958—Small production. Better quality than 1957; nevertheless, still undeserving of being labelled a vintage year.

1959—The very great 1893 alone can claim to be a peer of 1959. Fortunately, the excellent weather towards the end of May and the beginning of June permitted bountiful flowering of the vine; hence, the quantity of approximately 65 million bottles is more than three times that produced in 1957, and 10% more than 1955.

1960—Not a vintage year. Of little interest.

1961—A very good vintage.

1962—Some firms will produce a vintage, others will not.

1963—A lack of sunshine produced wines on the acid side, which will be useful in the blending of non-vintage wines.

1964—A very good vintage, plentiful in quantity. The wines are round and full. 93 million bottles were produced.

1965—A non-vintage year.

1966—Magnificent wines. Excellent bouquet with great finesse. Well balanced. Some 80 million bottles were produced.

Rhine and Moselle

1952—Above average and well balanced; pleasant for those liking a little less softness. Some very good noble wines to be found. Too old now.

1953—Must be put on par with 1949 as a very great year. Quite outstanding in the noble wines.

1955—Rhine front: medium to good. Others: lower quality. Quantity small.

1957—A good year. The wines were fruity and elegant, with a natural fragrance. Not a great vintage, but an average one; with some excellent Spätlese and Auslese in the Moselle.

1958—Clean, dry wines appreciated mainly by connoisseurs in Germany.

1959—A very great year comparable to 1949 and 1953. High in alcohol, rich in sugar. The rare sweeter wines made history.

1960—A very large crop but below average in quality. Light but pleasant.

1961—The Moselle was good. Along the Rhine there were some disappointments.

1962—The Rheingau was favoured, the Moselle was not.

1963—Large quantity in all wine regions. Small in quality.

1964—Good vintage with many very high peaks. A vintage which will not soon be forgotten.

1965—Uninteresting.

1966—Good, especially in the big estates, where they started picking on 28 October.

Chapter Six

Starting a Cellar

Until I was nearly forty such liquids as I possessed had to endure very inferior accommodations.

Notes on a Cellar-Book,
George Saintsbury

A wine cellar conjures up a picture of a more spacious age when men laid down their crusted Port and pre-phylloxera Claret—or when their fathers were drinking their three bottles a day and suffering from gout. A country house with ample cellars is an undeniable asset; but even the owner of a modern '2½ room' apartment may emulate Professor Saintsbury's 'very inferior accommodations', if he exercises some ingenuity.

The ideal wine cellar should be roomy, airy, and dry, away from light, free from vibration, and maintaining a constant temperature of about 55°F. (13°C.). Obviously this ideal is not very often attainable, and even in France only a few cellars approach it. The next best thing is to contrive a store-place which satisfies as many of these conditions as possible. An understanding of why they are ideal, and how they affect the wine, is a great help.

'A roomy, airy, consistently cool, dry place.' Lack of room, of course, means simply that you will be cramped for storage space, and so you lay down less wine. Proper ventilation will ensure that the air doesn't get stale and musty, creating an atmosphere which will eventually permeate through the corks, slowly imparting a mouldy taste to the wine. Dryness is not essential. A certain amount of humidity is to be sought for. This prevents the corks from drying up prematurely. A good 'flooring' is to cover the ground with an inch of small gravel, sprinkling a little water over it periodically. The gravel will contain the humidity. Excessive humidity is injurious to the labels but rarely to the wine. For the fortunate one owning a large cellar, it would be wise to have the bottles recorked every twenty-five to thirty years. This is the maximum expected life-span of a good cork.

'Away from light and free from vibration.' Some of the diseases that afflict wine—such as proteic casse, a precipitate formed by the presence of excess protein—react only in the presence of light. Strong light may also 'bake' your wine, maderizing or oxidizing it—i.e. turning it prematurely flat, musty, and brown like Madeira in colour. Then vibration agitates wines and also ages them prematurely: a house near a railway is therefore a bad place for a wine cellar, although if the disturbance is not too great, and the wine placed close to the ground, there may be no ill effects.

'A constant temperature of about 55°F.' This is almost certainly the biggest bugbear of the would-be wine keeper. Yet wines will not be ruined by temperatures rising as high as 75°F. (24°C.) provided that the rise has been gradual, although they will age faster; old wines in particular are fragile and will not keep very long above 60°F. (16°C.). Between 50° and 57°F. (10° and 14°C.) wines age normally, and although they can generally adapt themselves to an almost imperceptibly rising temperature, sudden changes will soon kill them. To keep them near hot pipes is particularly injurious; and any house where the temperature rises during the day and drops suddenly during the night is a bad wine-store. In general, red wines are less susceptible to heat than are white ones; and white wines are best kept closest to the floor in the coolest part of the cellar.

It will be perfectly obvious that a 'wine-cellar' need not necessarily be in the cellar. With a little ingenuity, it is often possible to convert some corner into a store for wines that are to be consumed reasonably soon. It will not then be possible to buy great wines very young—when prices are most advantageous—and keep them until they are old and mature; yet a variety of good wines can be kept on hand at all times. A hall cupboard, for instance, would do—or the space under the stairs. Once you have found the place for your miniature cellar, you can start planning what you will put into it.

To begin with, all natural wines—that is, wines not fortified with brandy—should be stored lying on their sides, so that the wine wets the cork, keeping it from shrinking and letting air into the bottle, and so ruining the wine. Sherry, Port, spirits, and liqueurs can be stored standing up since the higher alcoholic content will preserve them; but since—with the exception of Vintage Port and Madeira—these do not improve in bottle, there is little point in keeping a great store on hand. As you will probably want to keep both wines and spirits in your cellar you will need shelves on which to stand the spirits, and bins and racks in which to lay the wines.

Many wine shops have metal and wooden racks at fairly reasonable prices, and they make excellent containers for wines. As a substitute, a whisky carton, laid on its side, is a simple and effective arrangement; or special bins may be made. These should be of stout wood, preferably in the shape of a honeycomb or lozenge to keep the bottles from rolling when one of them is removed. Clay pipes, fifteen inches round, may also be used; these provide a protective cover for the bottles and insulate them from sudden changes in temperature. The bins need not be large—one a foot and a half square will hold almost a case of wine—but unless you plan to keep large quantities of the same wine on hand, they should not be too deep either. Wines keep best when they are not disturbed, and scrambling through them to find a bottle at the bottom of the pile is restful neither for the wine nor for the searcher.

Once you have your racks or bins installed, the cellar needs very little extra equipment: the main things are a thermometer, some tags, and a cellar-book.

Of these, the thermometer is the most important, since it shows at once if the temperature of your store-place is proper for the normal ageing of wines. Tags come in handy for identifying bottles which are laid on their sides, and helping you to find the one you want without upsetting all the others. Finally, the cellar-book. While it may seem pretentious to keep a book if you only have half a dozen bottles or at most a case of wines on hand, the book will nevertheless be useful—and a pleasure to look back on, later. For the cellar-book is the history of the wines you drank and what you thought of them; a record of the comparative prices and qualities of wines from your various sources of supply; and it supplies an invaluable running commentary on your own tastes and preferences. The book itself may be of any kind. Special cellar-books exist, bound in leather, with ruled columns properly marked for each page, and may even have your name engraved on the front; others are simple note-books. The famous pages from which Professor Saintsbury wrote his *Notes on a Cellar-Book* were those of 'an ordinary exercise book, cloth-backed, with mottled paper sideboards outside, and unruled leaves within, undecked with the pompous printed page headings for different bins and vintages, and the dispositions for entering consumption and keeping an eye on the butler. . . .' Whatever book you choose, your entries in it will run true to form: the wine, its name and year; the amount purchased, from whom, and on what date; the name of the shipper, and the price paid. On the other side of the page you will want space to enter the date of drinking and your comments. It is a good idea to devote one full page to a wine, particularly if you have bought a number of bottles.

Once the bins are in place, the cellar equipped and the book opened, only one thing is lacking to make it complete—the wine. Cellars provide the most enjoyment if the selection is a balanced one with a variety from which to choose. This variety may include wines of different types, qualities, and prices. Some ideas for a 'model' cellar are given below, each one being balanced in its selection. In establishing a large and elaborate cellar, it is best to call in an expert wine merchant who will be familiar with the market and can secure the best values.

36-bottle Cellar

4 bottles of rosé, the all-purpose pink wine, to be served chilled. Choose a Tavel, Provence, or Bordeaux wine—such as Rosé de Lascombes; or a Californian Almadén Grenache Rosé—not more than three years old.

4 bottles of red Burgundy, inexpensive: Mâcon, Beaujolais, Moulin-à-Vent, Fleurie—less than two or three years old.

4 bottles of red Burgundy: Pommard, Nuits-Saint-Georges, Vosne-Romanée, Clos de Vougeot, Chambolle-Musigny, Beaune, Volnay, Chambertin, less than ten years old.

4 bottles white Burgundy: Chablis, Chassagne-Montrachet, Meursault, Pouilly-Fuissé, or Puligny-Montrachet, each preferably bearing a vineyard name in addition to that of the parish, such as Les Preuses, Blanchots, Vaudésir, Les Clos, Vaillon, Fourchaume, or Montée de Tonnerre, for the wines of Chablis; Les Perrières, Blagny, or La Goutte d'Or for Meursault; Les Pucelles, Les Combettes, or Les Chalumeaux for Puligny-Montrachet. Vintages: less than five years old.

4 bottles red Bordeaux: a shipper's bottling of Saint-Émilion, Saint-Estèphe, Saint-Julien, or Margaux, or preferably an inexpensive château-bottled Claret from one of the Bourgeois Growths (*Crus Bourgeois*).

4 bottles of château-bottled red Bordeaux (for great occasions): Beychevelle, Cheval-Blanc, Calon-Ségur, Cos d'Estournel, Haut-Brion, Lafite, Lascombes, Latour, one of the three Léovilles, Margaux, Mouton-Rothschild, Palmer, Pichon-Longueville, Prieuré-Lichine, or Talbot. Vintages: a good vintage in the last twenty years: see chart, pp. 643–4, and pp. 17–19.

1 bottle of sweet wine—Barsac or Sauternes, either from a shipper or, preferably, a château-bottled wine such as Climens, Coutet, Filhot, Guiraud, La Tour-Blanche, Rabaud, or the very expensive Château d'Yquem. Vintages: less than ten years old.

2 bottles of young Rhine wines (less than five years old): Hattenheimer, Hochheimer, Niersteiner, Rüdesheimer, Schloss Johannisberger, Schloss Vollrads. Wines bottled by the grower at the estate are indicated in Germany on the label with the word: *Originalabfüllung*. These are preferable. A vineyard name in addition to that of the district is likewise desirable. Labels often have the word Auslese (selected) or Spätlese (late-picking) after the name of the wine. These are usually sweeter. Avoid Liebfraumilch—a name which gives no guarantee of quality or origin.

2 bottles of young Moselle wine less than five years old, such as: Bernkasteler, Wehlener, or Zeltinger. (*See* remarks on Rhine and Moselle wines.)

1 bottle of Loire Valley wine, such as Pouilly-Fumé, Sancerre, Saumur, or Vouvray, not more than seven years old.

2 bottles of dry white Bordeaux from the Graves district, either from a good shipper (in which case the price should not be high) or a château-bottled Graves such as Domaine de Chevalier, Couhins, Haut-Brion Blanc, Carbonnieux, La Tour-Martillac, Olivier, or Laville-Haut-Brion.

4 bottles of Alsatian wine, such as Riesling or Gewürztraminer, less than four years old.

In America, you might cut down the bottles of rosé to two, cut out altogether the Loire Valley and Alsatian wines, and the Graves, and substitute:

2 bottles of California Cabernet, preferably from the northern districts surrounding San Francisco Bay. Among the best of these wines are Almadén, Beaulieu, Inglenook, Krug, and L.M. Martini.

2 bottles of California Pinot Noir.

5 bottles of American white wines (dry) from Livermore in California or from New York State. The grape variety names to look for are: Sémillon, Riesling, Sauvignon, Traminer, or Delaware. Among the good firms are: Almadén, Beaulieu, Inglenook, Krug, Martini, Wente, for California; High Tor in New York State and Boordy Vineyard in Maryland (the best wines made east of the Rockies).

Chapter Seven

Wine and Health

Wine can be considered with good reason as the most healthful and the most hygienic of all beverages.

Louis Pasteur

Wine is one of the noblest cordials in nature.

John Wesley, founder of Methodism

Wine is a food.

Oliver Wendell Holmes

The magic of wine is intrinsic and complete. It induces confidence, a sense of well-being, euphoria, thus conditioning a moderate, wine-drinking man to be happy and healthy—for good wine is a tonic in convalescence. It disposes him to relax, and encourages his appetite; a process well understood in this age of psychological study, but one which can only partially be demonstrated scientifically. A laboratory rat cannot show how wine will influence a tired or debilitated man: nor would the man feel the same after a hypodermic injection of wine as he does when he holds a sparkling glassful up to the light, sniffs the bouquet, and rolls the first sip around on his tongue. The secret is not in the alcoholic content alone, for wine has virtues which other alcoholic beverages do not share. In the chemical compound wine, which awaits final analysis, there are infinitesimal esters, contributing largely to the smell, taste, and character of the whole, but too subtle to have been trapped by the chemist so far. Its main ingredients have nevertheless been long established. The astonishing thing about modern scientific research is the way it proves that wine-making traditions dating from the earliest times are, according to our lights, perfectly logical and sane. Practices which might, at first glance, seem to be dictated by superstition have taken on a new authority in the cold light of science.

The study of wine is necessarily the study both of the particular and of the general effect—of the component and the composite. In France it is held that men who drink wine are gay, men who drink beer are heavy and often slower-witted; men who drink spirits may be hectic and are often ugly-tempered. Professor Arnozan said:

'Wine taken every day in moderation gently excites the intellectual faculties of him who absorbs it. It ends by giving him certain special characteristics: sharpens his wits, animates, renders more amiable, confers a great facility of assimilation, producing a sort of self-confidence—such are the traits of the man who every day makes use of wine.'

It is worth remembering that not only were the Greeks and Romans wine-drinking people, not only are the French, Spanish and Italians today, but the English, during their most vivid and adventurous period, the Elizabethan age, were wine-drinkers too.

Wine as Food

Depending on its richness in sugar and alcohol, a litre of wine is equal to 600–1,000 calories. More than one hundred chemical ingredients have been isolated in wine. It contains vitamins A, B, and C; and all thirteen of the minerals established by E. J. Underwood in 1940 as necessary to human life are also present. These are: calcium, phosphorus, magnesium, sodium, potassium, chlorine, sulphur, iron, copper, manganese, zinc, iodine, and cobalt.

Vitamin B is significantly present in wine. Red wine is richer than white in many food elements, because it is obtained by maceration or steeping with the skins during fermentation; this is not the case with white wine, yet studies at the College of Agriculture, in the University of California, have established that in vitamin B content there is no difference between red and white wine, nor between dry and fortified wine. In riboflavin, white wines tend to lead, some of them having two-thirds the value of fresh milk. The vitamin B complex in wines remains stable and does not deteriorate as they age; but the freezing or pasteurizing necessary to preserve unfermented grape juice destroys vitamin B, including riboflavin, the content of which may reach 120 microgrammes in 100 grammes, with 50 microgrammes of thiamin and other elements.

Besides these vitamins and minerals, which help to maintain the body and its metabolism, are the nutritive components in the grape sugars (dextrose is valuable here), polyphenols, proteins, and alcohol. ('It has been demonstrated that natural grape sugars in wine are readily absorbed by the human system and are desirable in the diet, that the alcohol in wine is a quick source of caloric energy, that wine has a definite blood-building iron content.' . . . *Encyclopædia Britannica.*) 95% of the energy in alcohol is converted for immediate use—so Neumann said in Germany at the beginning of the century, and it has been confirmed by Atwater and Benedict. 'Ethylic alcohol is absorbed directly and progressively unless the stomach is empty.' (Starling.) 'Carried by the blood to every part of the system, it is burned up in the tissues.' (Duroy, Perrin and Lallemand.) The nutritive value of wine has been recognized in Spain, where it is placed under the same price controls as bread. Because of the nourishing quality of the other ingredients in wine the alcoholic content is taken into the body more slowly and utilized more efficiently than when it is absorbed in a higher percentage from more potent drinks. Research by Professor Georges Portmann of Bordeaux, President of the International Committee for the Scientific Study of Wine, and by Max Eylaud has revealed that while a small amount of alcohol can increase the vigour of the human machine by 15%, a double and triple dose does not have a proportionately greater effect, and it has been found, independently, that in larger quantities of alcohol there is an inhibition which actually decreases its utility. The approximate 11% of alcohol in natural wine is believed to be the most effective proportion. Even more surprising is the claim that alcohol as an internal disinfectant seems to be most powerful in solution in wine and even in wine-and-water. The increase of prophylactic effect with the *decrease* of proportion of alcohol remained totally baffling until very recently, when it was discovered that certain elements of wine, other than alcohol, prevent or impede the growth of the germs of certain diseases in the human body.

Wine in Weight Reduction

Various investigations and experiments have established in graphable figures the predictable effects of wine on the human system. Taken in dilution of about 10% to 11%—the saturation of natural wine—the body oxidizes approximately half a gramme of alcohol per pound of body-weight in twenty-four hours, provided that the drinks are taken at well-spaced intervals. This quantity completely disappears in the vital processes, leaving no residue in the blood, urine, or other analysable media. It is excess alcohol, not this assimilable amount, which causes inebriation. The ideal intake, therefore, totally used by the system in restoration and in generating energy, with nothing left over, is the number of pounds of body-weight multiplied by half a gramme of alcohol.

In a man of average size this comes to a rough 500 calories per day, a gramme of alcohol providing seven calories. (150 pounds of body-weight multiplied by half a gramme of alcohol = 75 grammes; 75 × 7 calories = 525 calories.) The average daily caloric expenditure under normal conditions is 3,000 calories; wine therefore can supply 17% of the calories needed in daily life. In fact, in a great part of the world, it does—here is a laboratory experiment verified on a gigantic scale in many lands and over thousands of years, where wine has always been a chief element of diet. This vast human experiment was confirmed under closely controlled conditions by W. O. Atwater and others of the American Academy of Science. Three healthy men between the ages of twenty-five and thirty-three and conditioned by different environments, a Swede, an American, and a Canadian, one an individual accustomed to drink wine and two tee-totallers, were observed in a calorimetric chamber. They were given a diet which included seventy-two grammes of alcohol a day. The heat production and by-products of their bodies were studied. The alcohol provided 20% of total calories during rest and 14% during work, and was found to be capable of replacing proteins, carbohydrates, and fats, and of protecting proteins and other tissue-substances ingested from other sources. The weight of all three men remained constant throughout the experiment.

The significance of wine in diet has been summarized as follows by Georges Portmann, professor of medicine, who is one of Europe's outstanding authorities on wine and health: 'Wine can be used to replace 500 calories of fat or sugar intake in the daily diet. These calories will be completely consumed and will not add an ounce of body-weight. So employed, wine is very useful in reducing—it being understood that the food intake will be reduced by the 500 calories replaced by the wine.'

Experiments in the United States and Italy have shown that wine not only replaces carbohydrate calories but in doing so reduces carbohydrate hunger, making it easier to do without the weight-producing sugar foods. Although there may be disagreement on the subject, it was shown that in lessening the type of intake and thus the food mass, alcohol has been demonstrated to lighten proportionately the work of the digestive glands.

The standard bottle of wine (three-quarters of a litre), if it is at 10% of alcohol, provides 525 alcoholic calories. Considered as food alone, a bottle of natural wine a day is the desirable average for a person of normal size, although for one not engaged in manual labour, a little less wine (say half a litre) may be sufficient. While providing about one-sixth of required nourishment, it cannot add weight.

Wine in Anorexia (Lack of Appetite)

While it has been found to reduce carbohydrate hunger, wine—dry white wine and especially red wine—excites the olfactory nerves and the taste-buds, and so sharpens sluggish appetite.

Taken in the heavy-artillery concentration of the before-dinner cocktail or highball, alcohol *inhibits* appetite.

Alcohol in the dilution in which it is found in natural wine (in combination with sugars, with acidity and vitamin B_2) prompts the flow of saliva, hydrochloric acid and gastric secretions—as, to some extent, does fruit juice. In other words, wine starts hunger and appetite into action. S. P. Lucia, Professor of Medicine in the University of California School of Medicine, describes what happens when too brutal a dose is taken. 'If, however, the concentration of alcohol surpasses the optimum, then the albumin-coagulating action of the alcohol, the changes in osmotic pressure, and other physico-chemical alterations will induce a suppression of secretion.'*

Tartaric and acetic acids and the tannins in dry wine, white or red, stimulate appetite quite apart from the influence of the alcohol. In order to investigate this, the acids alone in non-alcoholic solutions were fed to twenty-one men and women between twenty-two and fifty-three years of age in an experiment conducted in 1953 by the Institute of Medical Research in Oakland, California. The individuals were engaged in their regular clerical work, and on certain test days took the wine-derived acids with their meals, or even, in a few cases, in place of their meals.

After the normality of the subject's nasal passages had been established by making him breathe on a polished metal surface (which should show cloudy patches of equal size and consistency), a nosepiece was fitted on, attached by pure gum rubber tubes to a bottle from which air could be injected into his nostrils under completely controlled conditions. By this method, the exact amount of any given odour projected to the subject could be known. The odour selected for the entire experiment was a standard brand of coffee.

It was found that after a normal meal olfactory sensitivity always decreased. This was graphed. When the acids accompanied the meal olfactory sensitivity remained constant, the graph line cutting straight through the sharp zag which indicated the individual's usual loss of capacity to respond to the smell of an appetite-provoking substance. This corresponded more or less exactly with the capacity of the acids to remove the sensation of satiety usual after a large meal.

Independently, in 1955, an appetite-stimulating ingredient, apart from the acids and still incompletely understood, was isolated in red wine.

Wine as Medicine

Wine serves as medicine, either as a general tonic, or as a specific in the cure of a large number of diseases. Its greatest value is probably in the way it can stimulate energy and give moral support, preparing the ground for recovery. It is an alkaline agent.

From very early times, the therapeutic and antiseptic properties of wine were known and valued. Medical papyri of ancient Egypt have preserved prescriptions in which wine played an essential part. Xenophon, in his *Anabasis*, recorded Cyrus's orders to his troops to take wine with them and, while it lasted, mix it with the unaccustomed water of foreign lands; and in the nineteenth century wine was still recommended to be mixed with the impure water that caused cholera. From Homeric days until a few centuries ago, wine was used for the cleansing and poulticing of wounds: Hippocrates advised it also as a diuretic, and for cooling fevers; Galen made a list of wines and their different healing virtues. During the Middle Ages and after, the various theriacs and pharmaceutical compounds of herbs, spices, and magic animal ingredients, were mixed in wine; and right up to the last century wines were employed in great quantity in hospitals and in private practice: white wines as diuretics, red Burgundy for dyspepsia, red Bordeaux for stomach trouble and diarrhœa, German wines for nerves, Champagne for nausea and catarrh, Port and Sherry in convalescence. Even now, a base of wine is not unknown in medical prescriptions. Its falling out of favour in many of these instances was due in the first place to American agitation against intoxicants and, secondly, to the discovery of new drugs.

Some specific curative effects of pure, unadulterated wine in cardiology, neurology, geriatrics, etc., are as follows:

1. In France the general opinion is that by their richness in tartrates, certain wines add to the intestinal secretion, although red wines with high tannin content decrease it. Such red wines have long been well known for relieving diarrhœa,

* *Wine as Food and Medicine* (Blakiston Co. Ltd., New York and Toronto, 1954).

particularly through the influence of the tannin in red wine on the large intestine. (But this is only true of good wine, especially Bordeaux; it is not suggested that a wine which has been adulterated with coarser blends will have the same beneficial effect.) Wine is beneficial also in cases of colitis and hæmorrhoids.

2. It is indispensable in low-sodium diets: a glass of wine contains from 1·3 to 9·9 milligrammes of sodium, whereas an egg contains 40 milligrammes; a glass of milk, 120 milligrammes; an ounce of Cheddar cheese, 210 milligrammes; a slice of white bread, 215 milligrammes.

3. Regular wine-drinkers are less apt than others to develop gall-stones.

4. 'It is the safest of all sedatives' (according to Haggard and Jellinek).

5. Wine that is rich in iron counteracts iron deficiency in anæmia.

A Germ Killer

Wine and alcohol have always been known as germ-killers both inside and outside the body. Curiosity about the effectiveness of wine prophylactics dating back to the time of the Romans caused a student at the University of California College of Pharmacy, John Gardner, to track down an ingredient in red wine—not the alcohol—capable of killing *staphylococcus aureus* and other bacteria. Numbers of germs, including that of typhus, had long been known to succumb to alcohols and certain of the acids in wine. Ordinary wine is equally capable of killing the dysentery bacillus, and even in great dilution red wine has been effectively utilized in purifying polluted water. The universal use of red wine in drinking water in the past, and throughout much of the world today, has contributed immeasurably to the preservation of human life. Even in countries where the water supply is pure, this bactericidal action is useful. Wine taken with the meal functions in the system against such germs as may have been eaten on leafy vegetables or fruit, or derived from infectious organisms present in uncooked shellfish and other foods.

A wine of 9% or more alcohol has been shown to delay or prevent digestive liberation of trichinosis (J. B. McNaught and G. N. Pierce, Jr.: *The Protective Action of Alcohol in Experimental Trichinosis*, American Journal of Clinical Pathology, 1939). 'I should be sorry to give up the use of wine in severe forms of enteric and pneumonic fever,'—so said Sir William Osler, the distinguished Canadian physician. And wine is well known in the treatment of bronchitis and influenza.

Wine is not all Alcohol, and Alcohol does not necessarily lead to Alcoholism

It is now certain that small quantities of wine stimulate and large amounts of alcohol stun. Cocktails are depressants, only appearing to be otherwise because they release the inhibitions. But natural wine is generally only one-tenth alcohol, whereas a cocktail will be 40% or over. Another difference is the presence in wine of the many elements, other than alcohol, which have their effect. A big dose of alcohol will inhibit the flow of bile; a 10% dose in natural wine will cause the flow to increase. Professor Georges Portmann once said: 'Wine is a total complex—balanced, living, and in existence nowhere else. Do you know anything about food and life and think that balance and vitality count for nothing? It is the only thing man consumes that comes to him direct from the earth and alive.'

Excess, not habit, in wine as in spirits, may lead to harm. In wine, where the amount of alcohol is less, the danger is less. Old theories regarding the diseases caused by alcohol are now mostly exploded; these were often caused by vitamin and food deficiencies. Bright's disease, or inflammation of the kidneys, supposed in 1827 by Bright to have been sometimes caused by alcohol, has been established as having no connexion with alcohol, which actually helps the kidneys to function. If the drinker eats properly, it is only with some difficulty that heavy consumption of alcohol can cause cirrhosis of the liver; and taken in moderation alcohol has a stimulating effect on the liver. There is at present no known ailment caused by natural wine, provided it is not consumed in very great excess.

Chapter Eight

The Vine

Grape-vines belong to the botanical family Ampelidaceæ, a family which includes such other assorted plants as the Virginia creeper (*Ampelidaceæ*, *Parthenocissus quinquefolia*) and other climbing, berry-bearing growths, but not common ivy (*Hedera helix*). Of the ten genera of the family, only one—the genus *Vitis*—is important to the wine-maker, although others are capable of producing grapes. (Wine has been attempted from grapes of the genus *Ampelocissus* but the result was light and sour and the experiment should not be repeated.) The genus *Vitis* suffices, however, for its vines are found virtually everywhere in the temperate world, growing wild generally between 35° south latitude and 50° north latitude and cultivated between 38° south and 53° north. The genus embraces two sub-genera (*Euvites* and *Muscadiniæ*) and numerous species. The varieties within the species proliferate enormously.

Genus *Vitis* (sub-genus *Euvites*) species *vinifera* is responsible for all the world's great wines. Thought to have originated in Transcaucasia, *Vitis vinifera* found its most successful home in the warm Mediterranean basin where early civilization domesticated it; and from there it has been transplanted to California, Australia, North and South Africa, and South America. It has rivals as far as wine-making is concerned—but none serious—in species native to eastern Asia and America. None of the eastern species is of particular note for the viticultor, although a few are planted in Japan and some wines of *Vitis coignetiæ* were imported into France at the height of the phylloxera influx. (Even with *Vitis vinifera* stock grafted on to them they bore an attractive, distinctive fruit, which fermented into something nearer to a sweet liqueur than a wine.) Nor are the American species of vines of much importance in the development of wine, although they are used extensively in the eastern United States and Canada. Otherwise, they are useful in France, and other places, as root-stocks, resistant to phylloxera, on to which *Vitis vinifera* species are grafted.

The classification of the species of genus *Vitis* is open to considerable debate; botanical classifications are arbitrary things at best and scientists often disagree about them. Perhaps the most widely accepted—especially in Europe and academic American circles—is that used by Professor Branas (perhaps the world's foremost ampelographer) in his classes at the École Nationale d'Agriculture at Montpellier, in southern France. This classification divides the species as follows:

I—sub-genus *EUVITES*

A American species
- (1) Temperate regions
  - (eastern zone)
    - *Vitis labrusca* — *Vitis æstivalis*
    - *Vitis lincecunici* — *Vitis bicolor*
  - (central zone)
    - *Vitis riparia* — *Vitis rupestris*
    - *Vitis rubra* — *Vitis monticola*
    - *Vitis berlandieri* — *Vitis cordifolia*
    - *Vitis candicans* — *Vitis cinerea*
  - (western zone)
    - *Vitis Californica* — *Vitis Arizonica*
- (2) Torrid regions
  - (Florida and the Bahamas)
    - *Vitis coriacea* — *Vitis gigas*
  - (tropical and equatorial zones)
    - *Vitis Bourgœana* — *Vitis Caribœa*

B Eastern Asian species (incomplete)
- (1) Temperate regions
  - *Vitis amurensis* (Japan, Mongolia, Sakhalin Is.)
  - *Vitis coignetiæ* (Japan, Sakhalin Is., Korea)
  - *Vitis Thunbergii* (Japan, Korea, Formosa, South-West China)
  - *Vitis flexuosa* (Korea, Japan, India, Nepal, Cochin-China)
  - *Vitis Romaneti* (China)
  - *Vitis Piasezkii* (China)
  - *Vitis armata* (China)
  - *Vitis Wilsonœ* (China)
  - *Vitis rutilans* (China)
  - *Vitis Pagnucii* (China)
  - *Vitis pentagona* (China)
  - *Vitis Romanetia* (China)
  - *Vitis Davidii* (China)
- (2) Sub-tropical regions
  - *Vitis Retordi* (Tonkin)
  - *Vitis Balansœana* (Tonkin)
  - *Vitis lanata* (India, Nepal, Dekkan, Southern China, Burma)
  - *Vitis pedicellata* (Himalayan Mountains)

C European and East and Central Asian species
- *Vitis vinifera*

II—sub-genus *MUSCADINIÆ*

A North American species
- *Vitis rotundifolia*
- *Vitis Munsoniana*
- *Vitis Popenœi*

On the American side of the Atlantic, most practising viticulturists have adopted the classification of the American scientist, Bailey. Considered by Europeans to be scholastically less accurate—but extremely effective from a practical standpoint—the Bailey classification includes several variations in nomenclature and some slightly different divisions. The notable changes are in nomenclature: *Vitis riparia* becomes *Vitis vulpina*, *Vitis bicolor* is *Vitis argentifolia*. Bailey also divides *Vitis Caribœa*, recognizing two distinct species (*Vitis tiliœfolia* and *Vitis sola*) where Europeans see mutations of the same one.

Hybridization

A distinct difficulty in the classification of vines is that they can be interbred, and the result may be a new vine with some characteristics from both parents, but all the characteristics of neither; and such a hybrid may seem to be a new species altogether. In the United States, artificial hybridization has been practised to a large degree and many of the better wines of the eastern part of the country—where for various reasons *Vitis vinifera* simply will not grow—result from efforts made over the past century and a half.

Americans are not the only people interested in hybrids. Practically every wine-growing country in the world has its viticultural stations, and the French in particular have experimented widely. The French hybrids—crosses between *Vitis vinifera* and American species or *Vitis vinifera* and hybrids—are named after the men who developed them, and some of the achievements of Baco, Seibel, and Couderc are known to vineyard owners the world over. Hybrids of varying sorts occupy large areas of vineyards in the eastern United States and Canada, in southern France, in Italy and Spain; and while they produce more than do *Vitis vinifera*, and are more resistant to disease, they give wine which is sound and reasonably priced, but nothing more. Yet the search for a better hybrid continues. Throughout the world, researchers strive to perfect the cross which will combine vigour, resistance to disease, and productivity with fruit of the quality of *Vitis vinifera*. The world's great wines continue, however, to come exclusively from *Vitis vinifera*. What is perhaps more, they continue to come, as they have for the past several centuries, from the same handful of vineyards.

Soil

Œnologists, or wine scientists, maintain that four factors determine the quality of any wine: soil, climate, vine type, and man. Other minor factors such as the prevailing yeasts, may enter the equation as sub-headings, but these are the essentials. In order to arrive at a great wine, they must all be linked together, each one supporting and complementing the others, each adding its indispensable qualities. In this combination the vine is of paramount importance; and after it comes the soil it grows in.

The elements that make soil 'noble' for wine are many and difficult to analyse. The outstanding attribute of the soil of fine wine vineyards is its obvious poverty, for vines often do their best in land where nothing else will grow. The oolitic debris of Burgundy prompted the Burgundian paradox: 'If our soil weren't the richest in the world it would be the poorest'; and the scarcely fertile chalk of Champagne, the sandy gravel of Bordeaux, and the slate sections of the German Moselle Valley nourish plants whose grapes yield some of the world's greatest wines. By the same token, such rich and fertile soils as those of France's Mediterranean coastline and Italy's Po Valley produce little more than a good *vin ordinaire*.

Together with the poverty of the soil must go certain types of richness: a richness in trace elements. One of wine's greatest glories resides in the nuances of taste and aroma and these come—at least in part—from the action and interaction of the elements that nourished the vine.

These elements, broadly speaking, are present in rock or soil in relatively small quantities. Among them may be such minerals as boron, cobalt, copper, iodine, manganese, molybdenum, nickel, selenium, vanadium, and zinc. These, if they are too concentrated, can be harmful to plant life; but they are often essential in small quantities. While tests have not been extensively performed on vines, the effects of trace elements on plant life have been dramatically demonstrated in orchards and vineyards in the United States, where even a small increase in the boron content of the soil has eliminated a defect in the flesh of apples. Similar results with other elements have been obtained in other parts of the world, such as Germany and Australia.

It is thought that trace elements affect wines by controlling the rate of growth and the processes of the vine and by modifying the enzyme complex of the growth. The soil elements that nourish the vine affect taste and aroma. The type and number of fermentation-causing yeasts can have considerable effect upon wine (*see also* Chapter Nine).

Very small transformations in soil may affect wine made from grapes grown in it, but obviously the basic essentials must be present before these trace elements can assume any importance. Vines produce their finest fruit generally in quartz, calcareous, or slate soil, and where soil composition is large grained and consequently well drained. This leads to riper grapes. Nitrogenous and humus materials prompt the vine to produce luxuriant foliage, but the quality of the fruit suffers. Small amounts of iron are to be found in most fine vineyards, but if there is too much the wine may be difficult to clarify and stabilize (although some experts maintain that it is the iron in the wine-making equipment rather than in the soil which causes this trouble). A plenitude of elements will be present in one degree or another, and the components and the interplay between them dictate the quality of the fruit. The result is that a prospective vineyard owner can tell with little difficulty where the vine will grow well; to tell where it will produce with grandeur is a matter of time, trial, and a large measure of luck.

Climate

Heat and rainfall are the direct climatic influences on vines. Moderately cold, rainy winters and fairly long hot summers with some—but not much—rain are the most desirable. The first cold of the late autumn or early winter encourages the vine to become dormant, and allows the wood to toughen and mature; but severe cold during the winter will kill it. Sufficient summer heat is necessary to mature the fruit: and later summer sunshine, in particular, will soon mature the grape internally, and therefore growers in cool, temperate regions must harvest as late as possible, taking advantage of any late summer sun they may get. The quality of a marginal harvest may not be decided until the final week or so of the summer when a sudden burst of sunshine may produce a very pleasant wine, whereas the result of rain will be a mediocre wine, at best. Most of the rain a vine gets should come during the winter and early spring, for the diseases that afflict vines are most active in hot, humid weather, and in very wet years the fruit is apt to rot on the vine. Moreover, the lack of sunshine will mean that grapes do not mature so well as they would in a sunny year.

Among the indirect climatic influences are the frequency and severity of frosts, hail, and wind. A late frost, occurring in May, just before or during the flowering of the vine, may destroy the entire year's crop; and late summer hail or a very strong wind can easily remove the grapes before the harvest. Other important factors are the proximity of water—for lakes and rivers have a tempering effect upon heat and cold—and the situation of the vineyard on the slope. For proper drainage and exposure to the sun most great vineyards are on slopes, ranging from the gently rolling near-plains of Bordeaux to the swift-plunging cliffs of the German Rhine and Moselle valleys.

For any specific conditions of soil and climate the right vine-type—of the thousands that exist—must be found. An example of the importance of grape variety is Burgundy, where the noble red vine is the Pinot Noir along the Côte d'Or, and the Gamay some thirty miles to the south in the Beaujolais. Even in so small a distance as this, the difference is markedly great: Gamay, on the Côte d'Or, gives ordinary wine; Pinot Noir, in the Beaujolais, produces flat and insipid wines; yet put the two where they belong, and the results may be superlative.

The last major factor is man. Human error is always to be considered in human endeavour and only when man is most skilful and nature most bountiful will great wine be made. Much of the skill will be needed after the harvest; but unless the grapes are brought to proper maturity, the harvest will hardly be worth the effort. Tending these grapes is arduous and exacting work, and the conscientious grower finds little time for other pursuits.

Vineyard Preparation

The preparation of a new vineyard requires the greatest care and backbreaking labour. In some sections of the world—such as the steep Rhine Valley in Germany or Portugal's River Douro—the grower may have to blast rock, build terraces, and even carry earth to his high site simply to get enough soil to nourish his vine. In parts of Europe, 'trenching' is a necessity. This may be a very deep plough, but it can be more—depending upon the needs of the specific soil. The ground may be ploughed so that topsoil and subsoil both benefit without the two being mixed; or both may be mixed together; or topsoil may be turned under and subsoil over, each taking the place of the other; or subsoil may be ploughed without too much disturbing the topsoil. This process is often desperately complicated, because so many European vineyards are planted on slopes which cannot always be worked by tractor, and sometimes not even by horses, so that man has to plod away alone. After this ploughing, a cover crop is usually planted, and in one or two years the vineyard is ready for its vines. These, when they are set out, are sometimes one, more often two years old.

In California and other newer grape areas where

land in most cases can be levelled, or the lower slope levels (workable by tractor) are available, it is customary to clear, plough, and plant the vines within a few days. Most soils are virgin and quite fertile, so that cover crops to enrich the soil are not necessary. Mechanization of the work allows many acres to be planted in a day by very few men.

Propagation of the Vine

There are various ways in which vines can be made to reproduce, not all of them useful to the viticulturist. The original purpose of the grape was to carry seeds, and vines will reproduce by seedlings, but this is perhaps the most impracticable method for the vineyard owner. In order that they may reproduce, vines must be pollinated; and they may or may not be pollinated by plants of the same variety. If not, the seedlings will not be of the same variety as the parent, they will be hybrids. Since the vineyard owner is looking for an exact replica of his bearing vine, and since seedlings require such expensive extras as greenhouses and potting sheds, he leaves this to the nurseryman and hybridist and this to the grower is the most efficient means.

Layering or *marcottage* was the traditional way of propagating vines, but is rarer since the phylloxera outbreak of the last century. It allows vine-shoots to establish roots of their own before being cut from the parent vine—which permits the shoot to draw nourishment from the old vine until its own roots are strong enough to support it. The usual practice was to lead one shoot—still attached to the vine—down, into the ground, then out again. The nodes along the buried section of the shoot sent forth roots while the exposed end developed foliage. When the new roots were considered fully developed, the shoot was cut from the parent. *Provignage* is a variation by which an old vine was buried with one single shoot coming forth from the ground. This shoot developed roots but also drew nourishment from the old ones as long as they lived, and the fruit had characteristics of the old vines. Neither of these methods is widespread today, because of phylloxera. In most cases, modern vines are made up of *Vitis vinifera* tops grafted on to American or hybrid roots. If either *marcottage* or *provignage* were used, it would mean establishing a vine with *Vitis vinifera* roots and these would probably be open to attack by phylloxera; although *marcottage* has been extensively used in a part of Château Prieuré-Lichine vineyard since 1958, with no visible ill-effects. In California, however, where soil and climate are not conducive to the growth of phylloxera, 65% of the vines are planted on their own roots. Similar conditions prevail in Turkey, in Asia Minor generally, and in some parts of Germany.

The only practical means of allowing vines to reproduce today is by cuttings. Vine canes—cut in the autumn or winter from the dormant vine and kept until the spring in sawdust or sand—are placed in fertile ground until the roots develop. At the end of a year or so, these roots are strong enough to support transplantation. The rooted portions, of course, are normally of American or hybrid stock, and the *Vitis vinifera* bearing wood is grafted on to them.

Bench grafting and field-budding or grafting are the two methods usually found in vineyards. In bench grafting, the two sections—scion (top of the vine—*Vitis vinifera*) and stock (root)—are joined at a nursery and only after the graft has healed is the new vine placed in soil to develop roots. In field-budding, the stock forms the roots, is placed in its proper spot in the vineyard, the top is cut off when the bud has become established, and the scion is grafted or budded on in its place.

Whichever method is chosen, the result is the same—a new vine is in existence. Four years after the vine has been planted it will start producing fruit worthy of being made into wine, although many varieties produce grapes of sorts after three years.

Care of the Vine

Although this is an over-simplification, it might be said that during the first year of the vine's life the major preoccupation of the grower is to make sure that his vine develops good roots; during the second year, strong and well-placed branches; in the third year (and thereafter) that the fruit be of the best possible quality. All of these considerations will be concurrent throughout the life-span of the vine, but in the early years they take on extra significance. The above-ground portions of the vine can be divided into the following parts:

The TRUNK—the body of the vine. From it come:
- ARMS—or branches. These in turn, support:
  1. SHOOTS—the current season's growth, including
     - (a) new foliage
     - (b) tendrils (slender, winding shoots that twine around trellises and other supports)
     - (c) watersprouts (shoots growing on wood more than one year old)
     - (d) suckers (shoots which appear below the ground)

2. CANES—one-year-old matured shoots. The most important are
   (a) fruit canes (or canes that will bear the current year's crop)
3. SPURS—short canes, divided into
   (a) fruit spurs (intended to bear fruit)
   (b) renewal spurs (intended to bear the next season's canes)
   (c) replacement spurs (used to replace existing branches)

Pruning and training—two technically separate but interrelated practices—are the methods the vine grower uses to keep the vegetative parts of his vine in order and to ensure a fairly—and consistently—large quantity of good fruit. Pruning is the removal of excess portions of the vine's growth; training, the directing of the vine into conformations that will make it easy to handle and convenient to work.

Pruning

There are two kinds of pruning: long and short. The type chosen will depend upon the fertility of the soil, the vigour of the vine, and the warmth of the climate. When the weather is hot, the soil fertile, and the vine vigorous, long pruning—leaving four or more 'eyes' on each cane—will be used, for the vine has the energy to support large crops and plenty of foliage. In California, where the weather is often hot, long spur pruning is rarely used. Vigour is controlled by leaving more spurs of normal length. The form of a long-pruned head or cordon-trained vine is very difficult to maintain, and at the present time the cost of trellising required for the espalier system is prohibitive for wine grapes. In regions where the weather is reasonably cold—such as Germany and northern France— the vine will be feebler and short pruning—leaving up to four 'eyes'—is generally adopted. In some cases the buds close to the base of the cane are infertile, and long pruning is mandatory, other influences notwithstanding. The Cabernet is an example of a vine where canes are often retained to give the vine more crop. The type of pruning may also depend upon the particular vine; a plant which overproduced one year may have to be more severely pruned the next, and vice versa.

Training

The method of pruning chosen, and the conditions which dictated the pruning, will also have an effect upon the way the vine is trained. The three major methods of training are: (1) *cordon*, (2) *gobelet* or head, and (3) *espalier*.

(1) A *cordon*-trained vine has the trunk extended in a single direction, be it vertical, horizontal, or oblique.

There are numerous variations of cordon training but the most frequently encountered consists of a trunk coming out of the ground, bent sideways to run parallel with the ground, usually supported by a wire or style. The quantity of spurs that grow up and down from this trunk may be regulated as well as the number of buds or 'eyes' on each spur, and the method—although requiring some skill to establish—rewards the skilful with large harvests. It is not applicable to all vine varieties and cannot normally be used for the finer—and less fruitful—types. Perhaps the most important of the *cordon* styles is the Guyot—one of the most widespread in the world of fine wines—which consists usually of a trunk and one arm. Canes coming forth from that arm are trained along wires. It is particularly effective for vines with infertile basal nodes and those that form small and compact bunches of grapes.

(2) *Gobelet* (or head) training leaves a single vertical trunk terminating in several arms rising in approximately the shape of a vase or goblet (French *gobelet*). It has the particular virtue that no support is needed for the vine and it is simple to establish and maintain. However, if the basal buds of the vine are infertile it cannot be used, and in some cases very vigorous vines tend to set their fruit badly.

(3) *Espalier* training leaves a trunk terminating in one or two arms and several canes, most often all trained in the same plane. Like the *cordon*-trained vine, it must have a trellis or wire for support. There are a number of variations on this system, including the decorative trellis-trained vine—so often found in formal gardens.

Cycle of the Vine

The growth-cycle of the vine starts in the spring when the dormant winter stage has passed and sap begins to flow. Five to six weeks after the rising of the sap, the vine begins to produce foliage and the buds along the canes swell, bursting out of the brown scaly wood which has covered and protected them during the winter, and revealing a small, woolly bud. Tiny, delicate leaves form, and from this point until the vine flowers—for unlike many fruits the vine does not put forth fruit and leaves at the same time—it is budding out, a time of growth before floral parts develop (French *débourrement*). The time this occurs depends mainly upon the warmth of the soil, but also to a certain extent upon the time chosen for pruning.

If a vine is pruned during the winter season—as most are—budding will occur naturally; but if it is pruned after the sap has begun to flow, budding will be delayed by as much as two weeks. Late pruning involves loss of a considerable amount of sap and although this sap has practically no nutrient value, growers usually feel that such a loss could only be detrimental to the vine, and so they tend to avoid late pruning. In areas where late frosts prevail, however, it can be valuable, retarding budding until the danger of frost has abated. 'Green' or 'summer pruning' implies the removal of succulent growth.

A variation of this used in California is called 'double pruning'; the vines are pruned in the normal manner in the fall or mid-winter except that long spurs are left, 4–8 buds instead of 2–4 buds. The apical buds are allowed to push, and the spurs are immediately cut to normal length before excessive starch reserves are used up. Using this method initial pruning may be done at leisure with no worry that growth will commence before pruning is complete, and yet the bud-push is delayed 5–14 days.

The young shoots of the vine put forth leaves and later flower clusters. On each cluster is a group of tiny blossoms, in the form the grape bunch will eventually take. At first, each flower in the cluster is covered by a cap—which slips away, revealing the flowering parts of the vine.

In most vines, the flower consists of a cone-like female pistil and five male stamens, equally vigorous. The pistil has an ovary, style, and stigma, and the stamens are composed of filaments carrying anthers, tiny sacs of pollen. When the sacs open, pollen is discharged, the grains are trapped by the stigma, where the pollen germinates. The pollen tube grows down the style and into the ovary where fertilization takes place.

Most *Vitis vinifera* vines are hermaphroditic and both male and female organs of the same vine are equally developed. In some other vines one set of organs may be stunted and the vineyard owner will need both female (to bear fruit) and male (to fertilize the female) vines. Hermaphroditic vines usually fertilize themselves—the pollen falling from the male to the female portions—but unisexual vines *must* be cross-pollinated. It is a curious fact that cross-pollination has little or no effect whatsoever upon fruit. The grape will always run true to the bearing vine and changes take place only in the seeds, which are of no interest to the viniculteur.

The vine flowers for a period of about two weeks. During this time the weather is of the utmost importance, for on it depends the fruit the vine will yield. Failure to flower properly or completely is the condition known as *coulure* (*see* VINE PATHOLOGY below) and, if serious, this may mean that the plant will develop no grapes at all. At the end of a normal flowering a tiny green berry will form, growing and maturing into the grape.

The flowering (*floraison*) is followed by the slow preliminary maturing of the fruit. The grapes, green with chlorophyll, assimilate carbon in exactly the same manner as the leaves; they grow in bulk, and chemically they show very little change beyond a slight rise in acidity. The next stage, usually starting in August, is the *véraison* when the grape changes colour, turning from the early green to its final red-purplish hue, or translucent greenish-white, after which the final maturing will occur. The approximate duration of these various operations is:

Putting forth leaves	72–75 days
Flowering	10–20 days
Developing grape	40–45 days
Maturing grape	48–50 days
Total	170–190 days

This chart is only valid for grapes of 'First Epoch', because different varieties of grape mature their fruit at different intervals. The most widely accepted classification of *time* of maturing is that of the Frenchman Pulliat, devised toward the end of the last century. Pulliat took the Chasselas doré grape as a 'standard' and from its cycle built up the following table.

Designation		*Time of Maturing* Before or after Chasselas doré
'Precocious'	Very early	10 days before
First epoch	Early	about same time
Second epoch	Early mid-season	12 days after
Third epoch	Mid-season	24 days after
Fourth epoch	Late	36 days after

The system of Pulliat is not the best guide to predict the days to maturity, as it does not account for environmental influences. It does allow comparison of the relative *rate* of maturation of different varieties. A more precise determination of the time to mature is the method of Winkler and Amerine, based on the total heat summation required to mature a given variety. With knowledge of the required heat summation, and weather records, the number of days to mature a given variety in a given area may be predicted.

After the *véraison* the grape starts its significant

change. It has already achieved its acid, and from this point on acidity will decrease and sugar content will increase. The bulk also increases and the reaction speeds its pace as the grape approaches maturity. Full maturity is attained when no more sugar is generated, and the grapes are then ready for picking, or for the second stage of going into the noble rot. In some cases there will be an increase in *apparent* sugar content after final maturation, but this is due to evaporation of water rather than to increase in sugar. (In certain parts of the world, as in the Barsac–Sauternes districts of Bordeaux and, to a much smaller extent, the Moselle and Rhine districts of Germany, the mould *Botrytis cinerea*, the noble rot, forms on the grapes, hastening the process and resulting in an extremely sweet wine.) During the ripening period of the fruit a waxy 'bloom' forms on the outside, protecting the grape from sunburn, and trapping the yeasts that will cause the fermentation (*see* BOTRYTIS CINEREA).

While the vine is preparing itself and producing its fruit, there are a number of maladies to which it may succumb. The most crippling of these thrive in wet weather, since they multiply faster under humid conditions and since rain washes off the chemical sprays used by the grower in an attempt to counteract or control them. Some of the more important diseases—and their antidotes—are outlined below.

Vine Pathology

The ills to which the vine is prone fall into two major categories: (1) accidents and non-parasitic maladies and (2) maladies of parasitic origin. The first group embraces afflictions caused by climate, soil, vine, and man, and the second is caused by viruses, bacteria, cryptogams, and animal parasites.

1. ACCIDENTS AND NON-PARASITIC MALADIES

(a) *Climate*

Frost is the most important climatic danger. Although most vineyards are so situated that frosts will have a minimal effect, those that do occur can be devastating. The severe winter of 1956 in Bordeaux caused a decrease in production of as much as 90% in some districts; but it is partly because such winters are so rare (1956 was the second worst winter in the region since 1709) that growers are unprepared to cope with them. In general, winter temperatures below 5°F. (−15°C.) are dangerous for vines and spring temperatures even a few degrees below freezing (25°F. or −4°C.) are equally critical. Many American vine types are more resistant to cold than are *Vitis vinifera*, and the Beta grape—a crossing of *Vitis labrusca* and *Vitis riparia* found in the northern United States and Canada—can withstand temperatures as low as −4°F. (−20°C.) while *Vitis amurensis* can live at fantastically low temperatures. (At the present time, unfortunately, *Vitis amurensis* has not given useful grapes.) In exceptionally cold vineyard areas, vines may be protected from winter cold by covering them completely with soil, a practice occasionally followed in Russia, Hungary, Bulgaria, Asia Minor, and Canada. Late spring frosts are also a great hazard, but late pruning will sometimes retard flowering until the danger has passed.

Heat, if excessive, may damage vines although temperatures must rise above about 110°F. (43°C.) before the critical limit is reached. This kind of heat is unusual in vineyards elsewhere than in North Africa, where the hot, dry, dehydrating, sustained winds of the sirocco sometimes wreak enormous damage.

Hail scars leaves and branches or may remove vegetation, weakening the vine. Late summer hailstorms are called 'harvesters' by vine growers, and may destroy or remove the entire crop. Rockets fired into hail clouds sometimes cause them to burst before they come over the vineyards, but it is not easy to do this successfully because of the height of the clouds and the speed with which they form.

Wind breaks off or cracks shoots, fruit, and vegetation, and salt winds blowing in from the sea as sometimes in the Médoc—even as far as fifty miles inland—can wither the leaves.

(b) *Soil*

Drought causes vine leaves to turn yellow, and unless some manner of irrigation is installed the plant eventually degenerates or dies.

Excess moisture may drown the plant, but only after some time. If the vine is flooded for less than ten weeks, it is able to survive. This has led to flooding as a counter-measure to phylloxera; the water drowns the pest, and is then drained off before the vines are affected

Chlorosis is a yellowing of the leaves caused by a lack of chlorophyll. In Europe it is often due to an excess of calcium in the soil which results in iron deficiency. Vines differ in degrees of resistance to it, and most *Vitis vinifera* varieties are practically unaffected. Treatment is with ferrous sulphate, on the theory that a comparative excess of calcium impedes the vine from assimilating iron, thus causing the disease. *Vitis berlandieri* is somewhat resistant and is thus used as root-stock.

Soil deficiencies are principally caused by lack of boron, potassium, or zinc. Zinc deficiency is fairly common in California and Australia and the vine is treated with zinc, while the more widespread boron deficiency is treated in various ways, either by increasing the soil's boron content or by injecting boron into the vine.

Soil toxicity comes mainly from an excess of salt. Selection of root-stock may overcome it (hybrids and particularly those from *Vitis candicans*, whose native habitat is the swamps of Mississippi, are highly resistant); or the land may be 'washed' by flooding for a short period with clear water. Micronutrients, especially boron, are occasionally present in toxic amounts.

(c) *Vine*

Coulure is the dropping of flowers, flower clusters, or of the tiny berries during the period of their initial development; or is their failure to develop. Its most important cause is bad weather, for proper flowering can only take place under rainless, warm, sunny skies. Too rapid growth can also cause *coulure*, in which case the vines would be better grafted on to root-stock more appropriate to their vigour.

Shot berries (*millerandage*) is the name given to grape clusters with grapes of varying sizes. If the flowering has not been complete, some or all of the grapes may remain small, green, and hard, resembling buckshot. It is an aftermath of *coulure*.

Leaf reddening (*rougeau*), if not caused by a virus, is due to a wound which interrupts the flow of sap to the roots. The wound may be on the aboveground portion of the vine—in which case the afflicted part will be removed, if possible. If it is due to wounds on the roots, potassium fertilizers sometimes have a restorative effect by translocating more potassium, especially when the root growth is restricted.

(d) *Man*

Browning (*brunissure*) is a result of overproduction, of not pruning the vine sufficiently. Brown stains appear on the leaf, which drops off; the quality of the fruit suffers, and eventually the vine may lose some of its reserves of strength, and die. Decreasing the number of grape bunches may combat the malady in its early stages; but if the disease exhausts the vine too much, there is no cure.

Burning of leaves by insecticides, chemical fertilizers, or even, in some instances, by smoke from nearby factories may do damage to the vine, whether caused by the carelessness of man, or by unfavourable vineyard sites.

2. MALADIES OF PARASITIC ORIGIN

(a) *Viruses*

Infectious degeneration or *fanleaf* (*court noué*) is a virus disease that apparently appeared only in the wake of phylloxera. Fan leaf is spread in the soil by the vector *Xiphema index*. The leaf turns yellow along its veins and in patches between them; leaves grow misshapen, shoots bifurcate and multiply laterally, and flowers form double clusters. The malady forms in 'stains' or patches throughout the vineyard and spreads slowly. Its insidious character is threefold: it progressively shortens the life of the vine; it lives in the soil; there is no known treatment. It is spread and intensified by ploughing and the only present solution is to pull up affected vines and plough lightly, if at all. The progressive action means that, while a pre-phylloxera vine might have lived a hundred years, the first generation thereafter may survive only for forty years, and the second for fifteen. When this life-span gets down to four years there will be no more wine from that vineyard. The infected soil may be cleaned up by removing vines from infected areas, allowing the land to lie fallow until all the old roots rot, and fumigating with D.D. (dichloropropane dichloropropylene).

Pierce's disease is found in California. The leaves yellow along the veins, the edges burn, the vine puts out dwarf shoots, fruit wilts and colours prematurely, and the vine dies in from one to five years. The disease is caused by the same virus which causes alfalfa dwarf, and it is spread by insects, i.e. sharpshooters. Treatment: pulling up the affected vines is useless; the insect-carriers of the disease must be attacked with powerful insecticides. Other widespread virus diseases which cause considerable damage are *corky bark*, *yellow vein*, *leaf roll*, and the *mosaic complex*.

(b) *Bacteria*

Oleron's disease or *bacterial blight of vines* causes stains on leaves and flower clusters and destroys intercellular walls. European in origin, it is of little importance today outside the vineyards of South Africa. It is thought that widespread use of copper sprays and sterilization of pruning instruments have led to its disappearance in Europe.

(c) *Cryptogams* or *fungus diseases*

Downy (or *false*) *mildew* (in Europe known as mildew) is the most crippling fungus disease of the vine. American in origin, it is caused by *Plasmospora vitacola* and attacks the green portions of the vine, but only before the *véraison*—the changing of colour in the grape. On leaves, an oily stain later turning to white forms on the undersides and spreads. It also appears on shoots just below the buds, and it can attack flowers and fruit. Downy mildew needs high humidity and heat to generate, and since it is partly spread by wind, it can be devastating once it gets started. (Most American vine types are resistant to downy mildew and American vineyards are not treated for it. The fungus is thus allowed to run rampant and this has been one of the major factors in keeping *vinifera* vines out of eastern America although the primary problem with *vinifera* in the eastern United States is winter cold, and black rot, if not controlled, is a menace.) Treatment is by copper sulphate ($CuSO_4$), eighty thousand tons of which are used annually in France to combat mildew. It is usually applied in the Bordeaux mixture, made up of varying amounts of copper sulphate, chalk, and water.

Powdery (or *true*) *mildew* (in Europe known as oïdium) also attacks only green organs. Introduced into Europe from America, it caused widespread damage in 1854, reducing the crop in France by 20%. Powdery mildew limits growth, attacks leaves, and splits berries, and if untreated will kill the vine—especially the susceptible *vinifera*—in a few years. Wines made from grapes affected by this disease will have a disagreeable taste and smell, a poor colour, and a low degree of alcohol. Even when the leaves of a plant alone have been attacked, the ensuing wine will be tainted. Finely ground sulphur—seventy-five thousand tons of which are used annually in France—combats it.

Black rot is also of American origin. It forms stains speckled with black on green organs, and the fruit shrivels and turns brown. It is most virulent when the temperature is about 70° F. (21° C.) and when humidity is high. The treatment, which is copper sulphate, is the same as for downy mildew, and since this has little or no effect in the eastern United States, black rot is most vicious there.

Anthracnose is the only important vine disease of European origin. It forms small polygonal stains on leaves, fruit, and shoots. It develops under the same conditions as does black rot, and treatment is the same as for downy mildew.

Excoriose is exceedingly rare and attacks mainly branches. Treatment is to spray with a concentrated Bordeaux mixture.

Grey rot (*pourriture grise*) is caused by the same fungus which is the 'noble rot' responsible for the sweet white wines of Sauternes, Germany, and Hungary—*Botrytis cinerea*. At an optimum temperature of about 77° F. (25° C.), in moist weather, and often after other diseases have weakened the vine, grey rot forms, causing stains on the leaves and alterations within the fruit. Only under certain conditions—i.e. high humidity followed by hot weather—can it become *pourriture noble* (noble rot) and in most areas and under most conditions it is simply a hazard (*see* BOTRYTIS CINEREA).

White rot (*rot blanc*) forms on ripening berries, splitting them. Prompt treatment with copper or sodium bisulphite counters it.

Brenner is a browning between the veins on basal leaves, caused by a fungus. Early sulphate treatment will counter it, and it only occurs where winters are cold and dry—the conditions of life for the fungus. It is most prevalent in Germany.

'*Apoplexy*' (*Esca*) gets its name from the spectacular way the vine dies in the hottest part of the summer. It is a disease found in all plants in all parts of the world and is caused by a cryptogamic growth entering the wood and liberating an enzyme that kills the wood ahead of it. Sodium arsenite seems to combat it, although the reasons are as yet unknown.

Armillaria root rot (*pourridié*) develops on shoots, trunk, and roots, with the result that the upper roots develop at the expense of the lower and more useful ones, which remain weak. It is especially virulent in sandy soils and is often found near streams. There is no effective treatment short of pulling up the vine, disinfecting the soil, and letting it rest until all traces of the causative fungi—*Armillaria mellea* and *Rosellinia necatrix* or *Dematophora necatrix*—have been killed.

(d) *Animal parasites*

Animal parasites differ widely from one place to another, and those found in France will not necessarily be the same as those in South Africa or California, or even in Spain. However, some of the most important are:

Phylloxera, found the world over (with the exception of the vineyards of Chile and a few isolated sections elsewhere). A burrowing vine louse native to America, phylloxera caused the greatest single viticultural disaster since the Flood, necessitated significant changes in viticulture, and started off the Great Debate among connoisseurs: is post-phylloxera wine equal to that of pre-phylloxera days? Phylloxera and the questions and problems it raised are all discussed in the encyclopædic section of this book (*see* PHYLLOXERA).

Grape berry moths (*Eudemis, Cochylis,* and *Polychrosis viteana*) produce larvæ which feed on grape bunches, leaving those not completely ruined open to attack from other quarters. Treatment is by arsenic or D.D.T.

Meal-moth (*Pyralis*) feeds on foliage and fruit. Arsenic and D.D.T. are the most effective insecticides.

Altise, a type of beetle, feeds on leaves, reducing them to the aspect of very fine lace. Killed with insecticides.

Cochineal (*cochnilles*) bugs, of varying sorts, attack vines—and other plants—feeding on sap and weakening the vine until it dies. Various emulsions of oil, applied both during winter and summer, are used to combat them.

Acariose, a species of mite, feeds on fruit and foliage. Destroyed by copper sprays.

Erinose (*Phytoptus vitis* or *Eriophyes vitis*) is a microscopically small mite which causes blisters on leaves, grapes and flower clusters. Most vines are resistant to it; and those that are not are treated with the same solution as is normally used against powdery mildew.

Eelworms (*anguillules*) are nematodes, or threadlike parasitic worms, which puncture roots and form nodosities resembling those of phylloxera. *Vitis vinifera* vines are particularly susceptible, but proper choice of root-stock on which the *Vitis vinifera* will be grafted obviates much of the danger. Sterilization of the soil by D.D. is necessary if the nematodes become too numerous. Next to phylloxera this is by far the most important animal parasite.

Japanese beetles are a considerable menace in the eastern United States but have not as yet appeared in California or in Europe. D.D.T. and arsenic compounds are used to fight them.

In addition to the combating of diseases, there is a considerable amount of work to be done in a vineyard. The details of the labour and the time chosen for each chore will vary according to the situation of the vineyard and the traditional practice of the area. The following chart represents a part of the seasonal division of labour at the author's Château Lascombes in the town of Margaux in the Bordeaux region of France. Usual practice elsewhere will be very similar to that represented here, although there are slight variations even among the other vineyards in Margaux.

A Vineyard Calendar

Autumn. In late September or October the harvest, which lasts for more than two weeks, is followed by a general cleaning up of ditches and the turn-around spaces in the vineyard. Autumn ploughing aerates the soil and covers and protects the sensitive graft zone of the plants against the cold.

Winter. Pruning continues throughout the winter. Pickets and support wires are replaced and repaired as needed and the trunks and branches attached to them.

Spring. A second ploughing, for the same reasons as before; and women follow with special rakes to draw out the soil from between the plants where it cannot be reached by the plough. During budding, excess buds are removed from the vines and 'suckers' growing below the graft are removed. A third ploughing is done and any necessary planting of vines (April–May).

Summer. Weeds are removed and in June shoots are attached with reeds to the supporting wires. The ends of the shoots are trimmed—to curb excessive growth—and the spraying treatments against vine maladies started (there may be anything from three to eight during the course of the summer). A fourth ploughing does away with summer weeds and the grapes are left to ripen.

Autumn. When the grapes reach maturity, the harvest starts. After this the cycle recommences with the cleaning up.

Chapter Nine

Wine: What it is, How it is Made

Wine comes from the fermentation of grape sugar. Dandelions, parsnips, and elderberries can be made to yield a kind of 'homemade wine', but properly wine comes from grapes and nothing else—and it is the natural product of grapes which have been gathered, carted to the wine-shed, pressed, and left in large vats until the grape sugar has fermented into alcohol. The chemical reactions of wine fermentation are due to yeast. These microscopic plants grow in the rich natural medium of the fresh juice and produce enzymes which convert the sugar, through an intricate series of biochemical reactions, to alcohol, carbon dioxide, and other fermentation products.

The result of such a haphazard process as natural fermentation would, indeed, be a wine of doubtful quality—although the first wine known to man must have been just that, the historic consequence of a felicitous accident. But fine wine comes from good management rather than good luck, and over the centuries men have been learning, first by trial and error and later by scientific experiment, how to improve the technique of making it. The discoveries of Louis Pasteur (1822–95) shed a new light on the scientific theories of earlier wine-makers and provided a logical explanation for many time-honoured practices, some of them dating from ancient Greece and Rome. The scientists did not, in fact, add very much that was new to the practical art of wine-making, but they did show contemporary vintners *why* certain things should be done, and encouraged them to use the wisest methods. And they cut out the 'lows' of the poor vintage years by teaching growers how to salvage a harvest that might have been a disaster fifty years before.

The Grape

The basic ingredient of wine is clearly the grape. At perfect maturity it will have certain specific characteristics, although fruit from different vine varieties will differ considerably. Skins, pulp, and —with some exceptions—seeds each donate certain qualities to the wine.

Grape skins give mainly tannins and colouring matter. The colour and tannin are generally conceded to be bound in the internal portions of the skin cells. Until these cells are killed it is very difficult to remove the pigments. Several methods are available to cause cell death and cell wall collapse—heat, alcohol, or physical disintegration. The second method is usually used and this is accomplished by allowing the juice and skins to ferment together until sufficient alcohol is produced to cause the cell walls to become permeable and the colour to be released. The extraction of colour rises to its peak after a few days, then diminishes; but duration of vatting time is the most important factor in colouring wines. Rosés, which are separated quickly from the skins, are vatted for a shorter time than reds, whilst white wines are made from grapes that have been separated from the skins at the outset. Some minor grape varieties keep the pigment in the inner layers of the skin and yield tinted juice, while a very few have coloured flesh and give deep red juice. The tannins also pass from skin and pulp to juice during vatting—the essential difference between red and white wines lies more in tannin content than in colour.

In some cases the skin contributes another element—an odorant which may be either agreeable or disagreeable. In many *Vitis vinifera* varieties this odorant imparts a fresh, light perfume—a whiff of the grape. This is most apparent when the wine is young but tends to disappear as it ages and bouquet develops. In some eastern American vines—notably *Vitis labrusca*—the odorant gives a 'foxy' scent and taste, strange and sometimes disagreeable to those brought up on European wines, and the variety is not allowed in France. Many eastern American and Canadian wine-makers keep the vatting period of their wines as short as possible to prevent this characteristic developing.

The bulk of the grape is pulp, comprising from 80% to 90% of its weight. While composition of a ripe grape varies, an approximate breakdown has been given by the French scientist Jules Ventre in his *Traité de Vinification Pratique et Rationelle* (*see* table on p. 40).

The skin and pulp of the grape are the important elements for the wine-maker. Seeds contain tannin and an oily, resinous material that would render the wine unpalatable if released, and so care must be taken not to break the seeds in the pressing.

Another element that may figure in the constitution of wine is the stalk or stem of the grape bunches. Rich in tannin, it will be included in the materials vatted in areas giving soft wines. In most cases, however, stems are taken out before grapes

COMPOSITION OF A RIPE GRAPE

Constituent	*Range (per cent)*	*Remarks*
Water	70–80	
Extract	15–30	
Carbohydrates		
Sugars	12–27	Dextrose and levulose
Pectins	0·1–1·0	Includes gums, etc.
Pentosans	0·1–0·5	Also small amounts of pentoses
Inositol	traces	
Acids, total		
Malic	0·1–0·5	Varies with region, variety, and season
Tartaric	0·2–0·8	Mainly potassium bitartrate
Citric	traces	
Tannin	0·0–0·2	
Nitrogen	0·01–0·20	Mostly proteins, amino acids, ammonia
Ash	0·2–0·6	

and juice go to the fermenting vats, removed either by hand in the very small European wineries or by a device called a stemmer or *égrappoir*. In white wines seeds are definitely obnoxious, because of an enzyme (œnoxidase) which may impart to the unfermented grape juice, or must—and later to the wine—a brown stain, like an apple that has been bitten into and exposed to air. This stain may take as little as an hour or so to develop.

HARVEST

The time chosen for the harvest (or *vendange*) may have an important effect upon the quality of the wine. In the fine wine districts, the grapes are tested for maturity with great care and are picked only at the latest possible moment in the cooler regions where it is extremely difficult to obtain maturity. In the warmer areas the grapes are harvested when the sugar and acid have the proper balance to make the desired wine. Once picked, they are de-stemmed immediately and run off into the fermenting vats. A delay, even of little more than twelve hours, could result in serious difficulties: (1) the elements that naturally form the bouquet might oxidize in the presence of too much air, giving the wine an unpleasant aroma; (2) undesirable or unwanted bacteria or tiny sugar-flies might begin to attack the sugar, spoiling the wine.

FERMENTATION

Alcoholic fermentation is defined by Yves Renouil and Paul de Traversay as the biochemical phenomenon which causes sugar to be transformed into ethyl alcohol and carbon dioxide.

Before the experiments of Pasteur (*c.* 1857) fermentation was largely a mystery, and only in comparatively recent times have the processes of fermentation been studied at all. The following list shows the elements present in must and wine:

Must	*Wine*
Water	Water
Sugars:	Sugars:
glucose	glucose
fructose	fructose
pentoses	pentoses
sucrose	
	Alcohols:
	ethanol
	glycerol
	2, 3-butanediol
	acetoin
	isoamyl
	active amyl
	isobutyl
	n-propyl
Esters:	Esters:
	ethyl acetate
	ethyl succinate
	ethyl lactate
	other esters
Acids:	Acids:
tartaric	tartaric
malic	malic
citric	citric
ascorbic	succinic
	lactic
	acetic
Minerals:	Minerals:
sodium	sodium
potassium	potassium
calcium	calcium
iron	iron
phosphate	phosphate
	copper
	sulphate

Must	*Wine*
Nitrogenous substances:	Nitrogenous substances:
ammonia	ammonia
amino acids	amino acids
proteins	proteins
	Acetaldehyde
Phenolic substances	Phenolic substances
Colour pigments	Colour pigments
Vitamins	Vitamins

For an up-to-date summary of the approximate amounts of these materials present in wine see Ribéreau-Gayon and Peynaud's *Traité d'Œnologie.*

Most of the constituents found in the must remain to some degree in the wine. The sugars are greatly depleted and usually are found only in small amounts in dry wines. However, many new products appear during the fermentation and it is these that make wine different from solutions of water, acid, and alcohol.

In plain language, the process is essentially the changing of hexose sugars—dextrose and levulose—into alcohol and carbon dioxide gas through the action of yeasts. The classic chemical expression is that of Gay-Lussac:

$$\underset{\text{(hexose sugar)}}{C_6H_{12}O_6} \longrightarrow \underset{\text{(ethyl alcohol)}}{2C_2H_6O} + \underset{\text{(carbon dioxide)}}{2CO_2}$$

While this formula remains the basic statement of the beginning and end of fermentation, it is only 90% valid—10% of the sugar is fermented into by-products such as glycerin, butylene glycol, aldehydes, etc.—and is actually a simplified statement of a complicated series of chemical reactions. According to Amerine and Joslyn (*Table Wines*, University of California Press, 1951), the dextrose molecule alone passes through twelve stable intermediary stages before forming alcohol. Actually decarboxylation takes place all along the way and CO_2 is given off at several places. In addition there are thirty-odd organic and inorganic substances which must be present if the process is to succeed. The Amerine-Joslyn definition of fermentation is: 'Essentially a process of a series of reversible inter- and intra-molecular oxidation reductions, phosphorylations, and an irreversible decarboxylation.'

Yeasts

The yeasts themselves do not directly cause fermentation; they excrete certain enzymes that make the reaction possible. A number of micro-organisms are capable of accomplishing fermentation, but not all are useful to the wine-maker. Yeasts differ according to genus, species, and variety, and the combination of varieties found in one place will never be exactly the same as that found in any other.

The yeast strain *Saccharomyces cerevisiæ* var. *ellipsoideus* is the work-horse of the wine-maker. (It should be noted that yeasts are classified according to morphological and physiological traits. Nomenclature is made possible by the fact that the twenty-odd genera of yeasts that exist recur identically throughout the world.) Occurring in numerous mutations and variants, this strain is valued for its ability to ferment sugar more completely than can any of the others. But it is not the only yeast to contribute to fermentation; others help to develop bouquet and flavour, and it is thought that the number and type of yeasts active in fermentation have a considerable effect upon the wine. Not even the finest yeasts will make a good wine of mediocre grapes, but in providing the last nuance of quality, subsidiary yeasts may play an important part. In the traditional fine wine regions, the yeasts used are those trapped by the waxy 'bloom' on the outside of ripe grapes and are thus completely natural to the region. One reason perhaps why such newly developed countries as California and Australia do not produce strikingly original wines is that single-strain yeasts obtained from laboratories are used, generally selected for their efficient conversion of sugar into alcohol. Yeast variations contribute minor amounts of 'nuances' of flavours but the climate and the choice of varieties have greatly overriding effects. The final touch of glory on a superlative wine might be the slight increase in esters caused by an ester-forming wild yeast. However, the same wine could be ruined by the same yeast if it produced too much ester. Common sense and scientific knowledge demand that in order to obtain the greatest degree of continued success yeast cultures of pure yeast of known quality should be used. The study of these organisms is not so far advanced that laboratory-procured mixed cultures may always be used with complete assurance. Actually, because of certain problems arising from the uncertainty of the natural yeast more new wine areas are culturing the yeast and using a pure strain for fermentations. This strain may come from the wild yeast material of the area.

To the uninitiated the rapid wine fermentation appears to be a seething cauldron and may sound like a hive of angry bees. However, this type of fermentation is rapidly disappearing. As the technical skills and mechanical equipment become available, musts are being fermented at lower temperatures, sometimes in closed tanks, and the wines may take weeks instead of days to complete their fermentations.

The yeasts multiply very rapidly in fresh must

and the usual number of live yeast cells in one millilitre of must after initial yeast growth will be above one hundred million. This will vary with temperature and the nutrient qualities of the must.

If no yeast culture is added, then usually no sulphur dioxide, or only minor amounts, can be added as wild yeast is easily inhibited by the sulphur dioxide. But, if pure yeast cultures are employed then a little sulphur dioxide may be used to inhibit the growth of wild yeast. The pure culture can be acclimatized to the sulphur dioxide and will grow vigorously in its presence without delay.

Wine yeasts ferment effectively over a wide temperature range of 50° to 90° F. (10° to 32° C.). However, white wines are usually of the best quality if fermented at the lower temperatures. Red wines are improved in quality by fermenting on the skins at slightly warmer temperatures, i.e. 65° to 85° F. (18° to 29° C.).

The danger of 'sticking' a fermentation or causing the yeast to be inhibited by excess production of toxic material by heat-resistant bacteria through letting the fermentation exceed 100° F. (38° C.) is obvious to all competent wine-makers and every effort is made to avoid this situation.

Wines with incomplete fermentations are a big problem in some areas. The reasons for this are not always apparent but can be due to the use of yeast with low tolerance for alcohol, low nutritional value of grapes or too high or low a fermentation temperature.

Red Wines

For red wines, grapes are fermented with their skins, for varying lengths of time, depending upon the type of wine, upon the specific characteristics of the vintage, and upon the traditions of the region. In Bordeaux, the old style—followed decreasingly by a very few vineyards—was to leave the wines in the fermenting vats for from three to four weeks. The modern method is to vat for from nine to fourteen days, with the result that the wines are lighter, more supple, and ready to drink sooner, since they do not pick up so much tannin from the skins. (But some of the younger growers in Bordeaux are returning to the longer vatting time of three weeks.) In Burgundy the practice is totally different. Since the end of the First World War, wines have been vatted for the shortest possible time, and five to seven days is considered optimum, eight to nine days, extreme.

During fermentation, the pulp and mass of colour- and tannin-imparting skins float on top of the juice, forming the *chapeau* or 'hat'; in a large vat, this may attain a thickness of two or three feet. Various methods exist for diffusing the elements contained in the *chapeau* throughout the wine: (1) the *chapeau* may be punched down two or three times a day, (2) a sort of chimney may be inserted into the vat, through which the wine rises and spills over to water the 'hat'; (3) a false top may be put on, forcing the *chapeau* down into the seething grape juice. Pumping the wine through a thick hose affixed to the lower spigot in the vat and up over the *chapeau* on top of the vat is the method most commonly used in France.

When fermentation is over, the wine is drained off and the *chapeau* falls to the bottom of the vat. This residue is then pressed for whatever wine it still contains. The first lots of the 'press wine' may be kept separate or added to the free-run juice, and the later ones will be vinified separately into ordinary wine for the workers. When drained off after vatting, the wine is put into oak barrels to age.

Wine is aged in the wood to allow it to clarify and throw off its 'gross lees', and to permit it to complete any remaining chemical changes—continuation of fermentation, precipitation of various compounds, etc.—before bottling. Many of the reactions that must take place need the presence of oxygen—which comes through the pores of the wood and through the bung—of which the wine will be deprived in bottle.

In his *Études sur le Vin*, Pasteur observed that, without oxygen, wine could not mature or outlive its early sharpness. The wine, on ageing in a wooden cask or barrel, will usually change in alcohol concentration. If the humidity is low the water will evaporate at a greater rate than the alcohol, but if the humidity is high then the alcohol will evaporate more quickly than the water. The evaporation will slightly increase the concentration of the non-volatile constituents but not enough to be noticeable in most dry wines. But oxidation of the sulphurous salt ($SO_2 + O_2 \rightarrow SO_4$) will increase the wine's acidity, as will concentration of the liquid (10%–15%) and the action of bacteria.

Initial ageing and racking

For the first year of ageing of a red wine, it is kept in a lightly bunged barrel—one that can always be kept filled. In most *chais* (wine sheds or cellars) twice weekly in winter and three times in summer, a worker will 'top' the barrel to compensate for evaporation. (This is called *ouillage*, ullage.) If the level were allowed to go down there would be an air space in which undesirable bacteria could set to work creating volatile acidity. As the months go by, the wine, losing some of the astringency of its tannin, becomes gradually less harsh to the taste—malolactic fermentation (see below, under Secondary Fermentation) mitigates the bitterness. The colour, growing less vivid, will by the end of the year have achieved its deepest red, although the hue may be affected by variations in the wine's sulphurous acid content.

During the early phase, the wine is in repose and any particles left over from fermentation slowly settle to the bottom; after this the wine is 'racked'—racking is the draining or pumping of wine from one barrel into a clean, sterile one, leaving the lees or sediment behind.

The ideal time for racking wine is when the moon is full, the wind in the north, and the weather clear—science supports these superstitions. Such conditions imply high atmospheric pressure, conditions in which the wine will be at its least active. (When atmospheric pressure is low, the dissolved gases coming out of solution are apt to stir up the lighter lees which will then be less liable to stay behind in the old barrel.) However, few vineyards of any size can afford the luxury of waiting on Nature to this extent. The changes due to atmospheric variations are extremely small and can be neglected with little penalty. Since most of the harmful bacteria collect in the lees, racking helps to free the wine from infection. These lees are then gathered together and, by further settling, give a small amount of wine, one of inferior quality, usually for the staff. Racking is generally done about four times during the first year—and if the wine is a small one, it is bottled at the end of this year or is sold to be served straight from the barrel. A fine wine requires more care.

Quality wines, to be barrel-aged further, are kept in the barrels usually for another year and rarely longer. During this second year of ageing the barrels are tightly bunged and put on their sides so that the bung will stay wet and seal well. Oxidation still proceeds, as the barrels allow a certain amount of air-transfer through the wood. The wine may be racked twice or three times during this period. When it is removed from the barrel it is usually fined and filtered and may be stabilized by certain treatments, depending on the standard practices of the area. Oxidation is replaced by reduction, and the bouquet begins to develop. During the second year, changes in the wine are not so noticeable. It goes on deepening in colour and flavour, deriving character and mellowness from contact with the wood. There will still be some precipitation.

The wine rests in this way for another year—longer in some cases—during which time the rackings will continue; just before being bottled or shipped the wine undergoes a 'fining'.

Fining

Fining, or *collage*, ensures that a wine will be perfectly clear and free from any suspended particles and also helps stabilize the wine against precipitation of certain protein, colour, or polyphenolic material, depending on the type of fining material used. Colloidal matter is added to the cask; it coagulates, attracting to itself any minute particles which may be floating in the wine, and the whole mass settles to the bottom. The recommended colloidals for red wines are gelatine, white of egg, blood, etc. These organic agents perform a chemical action—or one which is at once chemical and physical. Inorganic clarifiers, such as Spanish clay, with its active ingredient kaolin and the special clay of Wyoming, 'bentonite', are also used, especially in California. When the sediment has settled, the wine is racked once more and bottled or shipped in barrel.

For satisfactory results, clarification should be effected six months at least after vintage, when both fermentation and malolactic fermentation (*see* below under Secondary Fermentation) are complete. At the same time, the wine must be inert, so that there shall be no agitation of the sediment; it follows that the wine must have been adequately racked. The task will be more easily accomplished on a day when the temperature is stable.

Where wines need sulphite treatment, this should be given the day before the fining. The added sulphurous acid temporarily inhibits the active micro-organisms in the wine.

In some modern French plants outside the fine wine regions fining is an almost obsolete practice, and filtration has taken its place. Filters differ in type and design, but the object is to clear the wine with the least possible exposure to the air. In other large wineries centrifuges are used to clarify rapidly the wine which is to be sold as quickly as possible (within several months of fermentation) and the procedure in these plants is to rack and centrifuge the new wine several times, put it into a cold tank (39° F.; 4° C.) for a week or two, centrifuge, filter, and bottle.

Filtration in itself does no harm to a wine if the necessary competent help and the proper filters are available. Filtering is used in most modern wineries after each racking or fining and certainly before bottling. As long as the filter is made of suitable materials and the pumps used are of a non-aerating type the wines profit by this treatment.

Fining is not replaced by filtration. Fining does more than clarify a wine; it also makes a wine of improved flavour and balance and one which will remain clear in the bottle for a longer period.

White Wines

It should be made clear at the outset that the methods of making dry and sweet white wines are not the same. And special cases such as Sherry, which is a fortified wine, are discussed separately in this book and are not considered here (*see* SHERRY).

White wines are sweet, semi-sweet, or dry, depending upon how complete is the conversion of sugar into alcohol. Sweet wines result from the fact that sugar will not normally ferment after 15% to 16% of alcohol has been generated. In practice dry wines are allowed to proceed until all the sugar is fully fermented.

Sweet white wines

Sweet wines are made by four methods: (1) by using grapes so rich in sugar that all will not be converted, (2) by stopping the fermentation artificially, usually by chemical means, (3) by racking several times during fermentation, and (4) by fortifying the wine either before or during fermentation with brandy or wine alcohol. (An alternative to (4) is the addition of sugar to wine, but the results are poor and the practice is generally frowned upon.)

1. Grapes rich enough in sugar to stop fermentation are rare. They are found mainly in the Sauternes district of France, in the German Rhine and Moselle valleys, and in a part of Hungary. In all these cases, the grapes are left on the vine until the special mould *Botrytis cinerea*—known to the French as *pourriture noble* and to the Germans as *Edelfäule*, both meaning 'noble rot'—has formed, to cause certain chemical changes. These grapes, in fact, contain not an abnormal amount of sugar—merely less water. Another way of getting the same result is to dry grapes—as is done in sections of France, Italy, and Spain; but drying can never, as does *Botrytis*, proportionately decrease acidity as well as water.

2. The commonest way of stopping fermentation artificially is by the addition of sulphur dioxide. This invaluable chemical has the ability to stun or kill yeasts and micro-organisms, but has a lesser and later effect upon the desirable ones than on the undesirable. If it is added in large quantities, the good as well as the bad microbes will be killed and fermentation will cease altogether, leaving any remaining sugar unresolved. The danger is that too much SO_2 might stay in the wine, and impart to it the unpleasant flavour and aroma of sulphur—a fault of many mediocre sweet and semi-sweet white wines. Alternative methods are pasteurization, severe and sterilizing filtration, or the use of diethylpyrocarbonate (a highly effective fungicide); in all cases the ferments will be killed or removed before all the sugar has been resolved.

3. Whatever the method used, the wines must be chilled to a temperature close to 32° F. (0° C.) or lower for the treatments to be effective.

4. Alcohol added before or during fermentation prevents or stops it, and guards all or part of the sugar unresolved. Many of the world's sweet fortified wines are made on this principle. An alternative method is also used by wine-makers, both for red and white wines. Starting with a base of grape juice, the maker adds sugar and alcohol, a concoction which some people feel should not be allowed the name of wine.

Pressing the grapes

The significant practice in the making of all white wines is the removal of the grape juice from the skins at the earliest possible moment: grapes are crushed and pressed immediately upon arrival at the vatting-shed and the juice collected in tanks or barrels to ferment. Fine white wines are made only from the 'free-run' juice and that of the earliest pressings, for as pressure increases, quality decreases.

Fermentation and racking

White wines are fermented either in large vats (bulk method) or small barrels of about 50 imp. gallons (60 U.S.) maximum (quality French method). The exception is Germany, where great wines are fermented in large barrels. The secret of a fine white wine is in a slow, cool, controlled fermentation. Oxygen plays a less important role in the maturing in wood of white wines than it does with a red, nor is oxygen necessary for the improvement of white wine.

Vats are only partially filled, for the must expands and quantities of foam and grape particles rise to the top; if the containers were filled, the must would overflow and be wasted.

However, white wine fermentation that takes place in barrels is probably of a lesser quality than that in a 1,000-gallon tank if starting with the same juice. The *only* reason for the French using barrels in their vineyards is because formerly it was all they had. It has become a tradition and it allows some, but not much, temperature control. White wines to be at their best must be protected from oxygen and a half-full 60-gallon barrel is poor protection.

When the first tumultuous fermentation has ended, the lees begin to settle, and afterwards a light racking is done—a more thorough racking would remove active as well as spent yeasts, and any further fermentation that might remain might become 'stuck'. In many wine regions, this first racking is extremely light, for removal of all the particles would hinder the secondary or malolactic fermentation (*see* below) which diminishes acidity. In hot areas (California, for example) the contrary is true, for in making their low-acid wines great care is taken to ensure that malolactic fermentation does not start.

In addition to the periodic light rackings, fermentation is controlled by temperature. Most growers consider that a fermentation temperature of 60° to 70°F. (16° to 21°C.) is optimum, but some prefer an even lower one. A slow, cool fermentation extracts the fruity quality of the grape and results in a wine with greater finesse than is possible if fermentation is fast.

In the warmer countries where the addition of acid is permitted, malolactic fermentation is sometimes encouraged and the wine acidity is adjusted with tartaric or citric acid to an optimum amount after the malolactic fermentation is completed. It is desirable that it should be controlled as it can occur many times during the initial fermentation or within a month afterwards. There is no sure way to control it but judicious use of sulphur dioxide and the lowering of the acidity, as well as thorough rackings and early clarifications, do help. The fermentation at lower temperatures will also reduce the likelihood of a malolactic fermentation.

The fermentation temperature is usually kept as low as the vineyard can manage with its facilities. Some well-equipped Californian wineries ferment all their white wines at less than 60° F. (16° C.) and at an average temperature of slightly above 50° F. (10° C.). Racking can be used to reduce fermentation rates but the danger of 'sticking' the wine is always present.

Initial ageing of white wines

White wines are conserved at lower temperatures than are reds. Tartrates and other dissolved substances—more noticeable in white wine than in red —precipitate best at low temperatures, and nowadays most people like their wines perfectly clear. In spite of every precaution, suspended particles of potassium bitartrate sometimes show, forming white flecks like snow and, though generally tasteless, detract from the appearance of the wine. If the wine is kept at the proper low temperature, and is not bottled too early—before the particles have had a chance to precipitate—these flecks do not appear as a general rule.

Fining and bottling

Dry white wines are bottled young—younger than sweet white wines. A year or eighteen months in the barrel often suffices for clarification and the wines are fined, racked, and either bottled or sold in barrel. Fining white wines is a process similar to the fining of red, except for the choice of the fining agent which is slightly different: isinglass is the preferred substance, followed by blood and casein. Actually most dry white wines are best if only fined with bentonite. Unless they are kept in very new wood and have picked up a lot of wood tannin the use of organic fining agents is questionable. There are also some new agents in use—nylon powder and P.V.P. (polyvinylpyrrolidone). These substances help stabilize the wines against changes to brown colour. Sweet white wines are often, nowadays, fined with bentonite, which removes protein matter from them, helping to establish proper stabilization. Bottle ageing is similar in principle for white and red wine: less time for dry, longer for sweet wines. In general it is the fresh, early scent of the grape that is appreciated in dry white wines while the sweet varieties develop bouquet after several years in glass and keep far longer; some of the great ones have been known to hold their excellence for a half-century or even longer.

Secondary Fermentation in Red or White Wines

Many wines undergo a secondary fermentation sometimes concurrent with, often after, the first. Not a sugar-alcohol process, it is called malolactic fermentation and is caused by bacteria attacking the malic acid and turning it into much weaker lactic acid and carbon dioxide gas. It is *not* responsible for Champagne and other sparkling wines. These are produced by a second sugar–alcohol fermentation, generally induced artificially, either in the bottle—Champagne process—or in enclosed tanks or vats—Charmat process (*see* CHAMPAGNE, CHARMAT).

If secondary fermentation occurs before bottling, the gas will escape and the result will simply be a wine with reduced acid strength. An extra racking will often be a good thing. In the normally high acid wines of Switzerland, malolactic fermentation is considered of enormous importance; and the Bordeaux œnologists hold it responsible for much of the excellence of the wines of the region, both red and white. In the cases of red wines, it is a good thing to have the secondary fermentation completed soon after the first. If this does not occur, it may take place six or nine months—or even a year or more—later. There is no known process for bringing about this biological de-acidification at a given time. Once begun, however, it can be helped by the use of big butts: the reason, that a large volume of liquid will retain the heat generated by the alcoholic fermentation longer than will a small quantity. If secondary fermentation starts or continues in the bottle, the gas is confined and the wine becomes turgid and gassy, frequently unpleasant. If the bubble is a slight one, it can sometimes be eliminated by airing the wine—either by swirling it around in the glass or by pouring it from one glass to another; but if such a wine is served in a restaurant, it is best to send it back.

Recently, scientific knowledge has increased to the point where specific malolactic bacteria can be cultured in the laboratory and added to must prior to fermentation, thus inducing the malolactic fermentation to proceed along with the primary fermentation. Occasionally a bad strain of malolactic bacteria, which produced off-aromas and flavour, could occur in the wine, spoiling it. This can now be avoided by the controlled use of a known strain. This also allows the wines to be brought to maturity sooner and avoids the occurrence of secondary fermentation in the bottles.

Ageing of Wines

Not all wines improve with age. Some—notably the dry whites—are at their best when young. Most fine wines improve, both in barrel and in bottle, but eventually pass their prime, decline and finally fall apart altogether. What happens to wine while it is ageing? Decrease in acidity, transformation in alcohol, acids, and other components to form innumerable complex compounds—esters, aldehydes, acetals, and the like—and the precipitation of salts all play a part. Professor E. Peynaud of the Bordeaux Œnological Station recognizes two sharp divisions in wines: (1) those such as Port, Sherry, and the sweet fortified wines in general, whose excellence comes from a process of oxidation and the forming of aldehydes, notably acetaldehyde (other oxidative changes occurring at the same time give this wine an aged character as well as the components picked up from the barrels); and (2) those wines which can only develop their best characteristics in the absence of air. In the case of wines of the second category, the characteristics come from the grape used; for example, Bordeaux mainly comes from the Cabernet grape, and Burgundy from the Pinot Noir. Bouquet is an important product of ageing, and this can only come about, in wines of the second category, when there is an odorant supplied by the grape, when the wine is effectively sealed from air, and when good reducing conditions are provided.

Barrel-ageing is important in hastening the clarification and stability of wines, and in imparting certain characteristics donated by wood—for, once bottled, the wines can no longer be treated and cared for—but the amount of oxygen that enters the wine, and its importance, is disputed and perhaps over-estimated. Bottle-ageing of fine wines is very incompletely understood, but the scientists differ from the wine-maker, maintaining that the amount of air which enters a bottle through the cork plays a very small role, if any. Professor J. Ribéreau-Gayon, of the University of Bordeaux, states in his impressive *Traité d'Œnologie*: 'The quantity of oxygen that normally penetrates into bottles is infinitesimal if not nil; it is improbable that an important role could be attributed to it.' He supports his statement with the observation that wines age as well in hermetically sealed tubes as in corked bottles. With these matters so incompletely understood, it seems unlikely that artificial ageing, a process which has received a good deal of attention, will very soon become practical.

What is generally overlooked by the non-scientist is that there is some air in the wine when it is bottled and this can play a role in the changes which occur. Actually 8 to 10 millilitres of air are present in the average bottle of wine. If the cork is kept wet little or no air transfer would be expected to occur but the air already there would cause certain variations to take place. Extreme care should be taken to reduce the amount of air at the time of bottling so that bottle oxidative changes are at a minimum and reductive changes can proceed. Bottle age bouquets can be developed by artificial treatments and do show some promise for certain common wines.

Exceptional Practices

The wine-maker must always reckon with the possibility of unfavourable weather during the growing season of the vine and thus with the prospect of immature or badly matured grapes. In earlier times this spelled disaster, but today there are ways of bringing the wine up to standard. Some of these methods are:

Chaptalisation. Named after its French inventor, Dr. Chaptal, who proposed the idea about the turn of the nineteenth century, it is also called in Germany Gallization (after Dr. Gall) and *Verbesserung* (meaning 'improvement'). *Chaptalisation* is the addition of sugar to sugar-deficient musts—but never wines—to make certain that the wine will have an alcoholic content commensurate with its other qualities. Regular sugar (sucrose) hydrolyses into hexose sugars (dextrose and levulose) when added to the must, and ferments normally. Used discreetly, *chaptalisation* may bring the alcohol into better balance with the other constituents of the wine, but abused—as it unfortunately is in some areas—it results in 'wine' being made from grape skins, sugar and acids. *Chaptalisation* is widespread in Germany and Burgundy, and may sometimes be found as far to the south as Bordeaux—but only when specifically authorized by the Government. In Burgundy, where it is a yearly practice unfortunately, some of the great wines are now allowed to be over-abundantly sugared. In regions where the sun is hot enough to generate the requisite amount of sugar in the grapes, it is not necessary. In their *Dictionnaire du Vin*, Messieurs Renouil and de Traversay say that *chaptalisation* could with advantage increase the alcoholic content, since the fermentation of sugar gives rise not only to alcohol but also to side-products (such as glycerol, succinic acid, etc.) which exert a considerable influence on the flavour of wine. The operation also decreases the excessive tartness of certain wines by precipitating the cream of tartar.

De-acidification. When the weather is really bad, the grapes may be too high in acid as well as deficient in sugar. The common way of handling this is to blend the wine with low-acid wines, a perfectly proper procedure providing the wine is not then sold under an *appellation*, or place-name, to which it has no right. A rarer method is to add calcium carbonate. This reacts with the acids and mainly precipitates out, but calls for very careful handling and usually gives poor results.

Acidification. After an exceptionally hot summer, grapes may have too little acid, resulting in a flat and tasteless wine. This may be corrected quite legally by adding to the must either a small amount of tartaric acid (which does not improve the quality of fine wines) or the less mature—and therefore more acid—grapes from a late flowering of the vine; or by blending with high-acid wines.

De-coloration. If a white wine is tinged with red —or a pink wine too deeply coloured—fining with charcoal will remove as much of the colour as desired. Unfortunately it also removes any character the wine might otherwise have had.

Concentration. Sugar deficiency may be corrected by adding concentrated must, from which some of the water has been boiled off. Alcohol-deficient wines may similarly be treated by adding wine from which some of the water has been removed by freezing. In either case, the sugar or alcohol of the must or wine will be proportionately raised. The drawbacks are that in some countries these practices are illegal, and while they increase sugar or alcohol, they also increase acidity, sometimes to the detriment of the wine.

Pasteurization. The applicability of the method of sterilization by heat is still disputed. Many experts feel that heat kills wine, although the Bordeaux œnologist, Professor Ribéreau-Gayon, says that this is true only under certain conditions. Pasteurization, or heating wine quickly up to a temperature of 130°F. (54°C.), effectively sterilizes wines in barrel, destroying all bacteria—but it is impracticable, if not impossible, for wines already bottled. It is also a cumbersome procedure, partly because the mechanics of it have never been satisfactorily worked out. In certain circumstances it can be very useful; but in the fine wine districts it is best avoided, since wines so treated tend to become inert. However, in sweet or semi-sweet table wines of many countries it is routine to pasteurize before bottling or during bottling. The common wines are heated to 180° F. (82° C.) for one minute or may be bottled at 130° to 140° F. (54° to 60° C.) and then cooled slowly. Some large wineries selling competitive wines have the systems so perfected that not one bottle would spoil from yeast or bacteria out of the thousands of bottles bottled every hour unless a defective closure or something unforeseen occurred. The mechanical conditions for wine pasteurization are well understood.

Basic Rules of Wine-Making

Recommendations to follow	*Faults to be avoided*
1. Cleanliness is essential. See that all equipment coming into contact with the wine is kept clean. Avoid iron utensils or copper-containing metals—certain plastics, glass and stainless steel or wood are recommended for tools, tanks, pipes, etc., where the wine is contacted.	Unpleasant taste or smell. Metallic casse (or breakdown) of the wine; deterioration, and microbial cloudiness.
2. Gather the grapes in as sound a condition as the year permits, and in a suitable state of ripeness. Bring them whole to the presses, and free of soil.	Unpleasant taste of mould. Turning sour (for mildewed wines). Excessive, or insufficient, acidity. Depreciation and microbial cloud, breakdown due to metal content.
3. Pressing must be done rapidly for white musts, nor should the grapes be over-pressed. Avoid oxidation of the musts by maceration in the open air of the crushed grapes.	Lack of freshness and fruitiness. Excessive tannin. Colloidal cloud. Excess of proteids. Oxidasic breakdown, moulding.
4. Cleanse the must—and so the wine—by the addition of a small but adequate dose of sulphurous acid.	Deterioration and microbial cloud, oxidasic casse.
5. Control fermentations at suitable temperatures, as low as possible but not too low, otherwise the fermentation may be arrested. With red wines, time the fermentation periods very carefully. Beware of deterioration which may be caused by the exposure to air of the top crusts.	Excess of reducing sugars, mouldiness. Scouring or excessive volatile acidity and ropiness (if the temperature is too high).
6. As soon as fermentation is complete, the wines should be ullaged (i.e. the barrels topped up). Never leave a broached wine in contact with air.	Fungoid growth, deteriorations, and microbial cloud.
7. Red, rosés, and dry white wines must not retain the slightest trace of reducing sugars. (Yet in many places small amounts of residual sugars in dry white and rosé wine are tolerated or even encouraged (without excessive alcohol). It is quite possible to preserve such wines successfully by use of sorbic acid and sulphur dioxide. Many German wines have residual sugar and this is thought of as a necessity for quality in some instances.)	Lactic acid mouldiness. Mannitic fermentation.
The high alcoholic content of the great sweet and mellow white wines helps to preserve them without much sulphur dioxide. Conversely, the lesser white wines, sweet and mellow, are difficult to keep.	Secondary fermentation.
To avoid giving the wines large doses of sulphur dioxide they may be sterilized before bottling.	Development and depositing of yeast.
8. Carry out rackings at the right time, and sufficiently often, either with æration or away from air as the case may be. Do not forget that malolactic fermentation to a certain extent may either be achieved or avoided according to the amount of acidity which the wine should retain. This operation calls, however, for constant care, particularly as regards white wines. Other factors besides acidity determine whether or not there will be malolactic fermentation. Fornachon points out that it depends on	Excess or deficiency of acidity. Ropiness.

Recommendations to follow	*Faults to be avoided*
nutrients, aeration, pH, and sulphur dioxide. It is a very complex system and interactions exist, making it impossible to predict with assurance if a wine will naturally undergo a malolactic fermentation. Filtering will assist the maturing of all wines.	
9. The wine will attain physical maturity during the first winter by means of precipitation of the various tartars. The ordinary wines, drunk a few months after the harvest, may be treated with metatartaric acid or, preferably, they may be refrigerated. Filtering will assist the maturing of all wines.	Crystalline precipitations. Colloidal cloudiness.
Clarification, without excessive use of fining agents, will help the maturation of wines.	Over-fining, making a thin wine lacking in character. Coagulation of the proteids.
10. The blending of wines can only be recommended when it is possible to marry qualities which complement each other. It is better to lower the classification of an inferior wine if these inferior qualities can only be diluted rather than improve it by blending in a better wine and give it the somewhat misleading classification of the superior component.	No character.
11. In order that the maker may guarantee his product, it is essential for the wine to be delivered in bottle to the consumer, and bearing a label with the bottler's guarantee, as is the case with mineral waters, soda-waters, beers, etc.	Deterioration and microbial cloud. Poor keeping qualities. A loss of authenticity.
12. Put the bottles up for sale in such a way as not to mislead the consumer.	Reprehensible labelling. (Regulatory action by the enforcing agency of the country.)

The Composition of Wine

Wine is an extraordinarily intricate and inconstant complex of different ingredients. It is because of its ability to change in many ways from the time the grape is picked until the wine is poured, that wine is said to 'live'—as indeed it does.

Alcohol

The most obvious, but not the most important element of wine, alcohol, derived from the fermentation of the non-alcoholic grape-juice, comprises from 7% to 24% of the contents by volume; most is ethyl alcohol, but some—less than 0·15%—is methyl alcohol, present in wine in quantities varying between 36 and 350 milligrammes. In addition there are varying amounts of such higher alcohols as amyl, isoamyl, *n*-propyl, isopropyl, *n*-butyl, *sec*-butyl, isobutyl, *a*-terpineol, and perhaps *n*-hexyl, *n*-heptyl, and *sec*-nonyl.

Ethyl alcohol (*ethanol*). The degree of this essential component is decided by the amount of sugar in the must. It varies, according to the maturity of the grape, between 7% and 16% of the volume (higher when extra alcohol has been added). In fine wines, the amount, which influences both quality and longevity, is of vital importance. As the acids in the wine gradually combine with the alcohol to produce esters, so the elements that compose the bouquet develop. The antiseptic properties of the ethyl alcohol help to inhibit the growth of the various bacteria and yeast disorders to which wine is prone.

Acids

Acids give freshness and tartness to the taste. An acid-deficient wine is flat; a too-acid wine undrinkable. The organic acids (malic, tartaric, etc.) are those which impart the characteristic flavour, sharp on the tip of the tongue—a sensation caused by the presence of hydrogen ions. A wine vinified from unripe grapes will have a high total acidity and a low pH. In brandy, a high degree of acid is a fault, although a moderate content gives it body.

Acidity, by preventing, or slowing down, the development of such harmful bacteria as the mannitic (which turns wine sour), helps to preserve the wine. It affects also stability and colour—the higher the acid content, the more brilliant the hue. The total acidity of a young, healthy wine averages 4 to 5 grammes a litre, expressed in sulphuric acid. This will be less, by about 25%, than the acidity of the original must.

Three of the major acids in wine are naturally present in the grape (tartaric, malic, and citric; it is interesting that the grape is the only temperate fruit in which there is tartaric acid) and the rest are the result of fermentation. Most of the acid content is tartaric, and about 10% to 40% is malic, so called because it is present in apples and supposedly responsible for the 'fruitiness' of many wines. Citric acid is found in very small amounts, as are succinic, lactic, and acetic acids; there are minute traces of butyric, capric, caproic, caprylic, formic, lauric, propionic, and, in sparkling wines, carbonic. Acetic, butyric, carbonic, formic, and propionic acids are the 'volatile' acids and chemists consider volatile acidity in wines to be of the same order as temperature in man: it is always present, but when it deviates from normal there is something wrong. The others are the 'fixed' organic acids. The sum of the fixed and volatile acidity makes up the 'total acidity' of the wine; that is, the titratable acidity expressed usually as grammes of tartaric acid.

Tartaric acid. This is the most important of the fixed acids in wine and the one particularly associated with the grape; it is rarely found elsewhere in nature. The quantity of the acid present in the grape is decreased by respiratory combustion, during the periods of high temperature. The addition of tartaric acid to the must is allowed in cases of low acidity. At too high a concentration, however, it will impart to the wine a certain astringency, even harshness, and the great wines, both red and white, are usually low in this acid.

Malic acid. The principal acid in many fruits and vegetables. The quantity present in grapes at the *vendange* is of considerable importance in wine-making. While the fruit is ripening, cellular respiration causes the malic acid concentration to be lowered. Under the influence of bacteria, it undergoes lactic fermentation. The tartness of wines made after a cold summer, and the sharpness of young wines, is due to the malic acid which determines, almost by itself, the state of ripeness of the grape.

Citric acid. This occurs in all varieties of grapes, both ripe and unripe—and to a greater extent where *Botrytis cinerea* has developed. Wines made from grapes in a state of 'noble rot' may contain as much as 1 gramme of citric acid. Normal quantities (usually increasing somewhat during fermentation) vary between 1 and 10 grammes, and tend to be much lower in red wines than in white. The bacteria which cause malolactic fermentation may ferment the citric acid and produce volatile acidity. Wines vary in the amount of citric acid naturally present and this may affect a casse formation. Amounts which may be added to wine vary from country to country.

Carbonic acid. Carbon dioxide (CO_2) and carbonic anhydride are often called incorrectly by this name. Carbonic acid is, in fact, the acid with formula H_2CO_3 corresponding to the anhydride. Carbon dioxide is formed in sound wine primarily by the decomposition of sugar during fermentation. Relative equilibrium of pressure between it and the outside air is arrived at after a long time, sometimes as much as six months. Another cause of the gas is the secondary fermentation of certain wines in bottles or closed vats after sugar has been added—the method which produces Champagne and other sparkling wines. Or malolactic deterioration may break up malic acid into carbon dioxide and lactic acid. Finally, the purely physiological transformation—breathing of the ferments, of the yeast—may induce carbon dioxide which, colourless and one-and-a-half times as heavy as air, is unbreathable and poisonous to living creatures. Because of its noxious action, wine-making premises should be spacious and sufficiently well ventilated.

Sulphurous acid (or *Sulphurous anhydride* or *Sulphur dioxide*). Sulphur dioxide (SO_2) is frequently (and incorrectly) referred to as sulphurous acid. Sulphurous acid has the formula H_2SO_3, corresponding to the anhydride—a gas with a choking smell which is produced by burning sulphur in air: $S+O_2=SO_2$. The resulting sulphur dioxide is used for preserving casks of wood and, being antiseptic, is carefully added to wine which it protects against deterioration. Sulphurous acid and sorbic acid are at present the only two antiseptics allowed under French law. Sulphur dioxide is soluble in water and in wine to produce a molecule of sulphurous acid: $SO_2+H_2O=H_2SO_3$. Sulphurous acid, an anti-oxidant, is a reducing agent.

Among the useful properties of this acid are its antiseptic qualities, effective against such microbial diseases caused by harmful yeasts and bacteria. Sulphite treatment is used to subdue too violent fermentation. Sulphurous acid has its drawbacks, however. Because it is solvent in contact with various metals and minerals, it is apt to cause ferric casse, both blue and white, and, in white wines, cuprous casse. It is likewise well known that wines which have been over-dosed with it retain a disagreeable smell and taste of sulphur.

In the French vineyards, when a wine is to receive sulphite treatment, it (or the must) is poured into a cask in which a stick of sulphur has been burned. This old-fashioned method is not accurate, since unburned sulphur is liable to remain at the bottom of the barrel, and sulphur dioxide may escape through the bung. The theory that 10 grammes of sulphur will produce, when burned, 20 grammes of sulphur dioxide is incorrect—under favourable conditions the sulphur may make 15 grammes, which will only be completely effective if put in through the bung of the cask. Barely half a stick (about 20 grammes) can be burned in a cask of 225 litres: it can be estimated therefore that the sulphur burned introduces into the wine the equivalent of its own weight in sulphur dioxide.

An ordinary water solution of sulphur dioxide is saturated at about 5% to 6% sulphur dioxide and cannot be further concentrated. Of course, a solution of sodium sulphite or sodium bisulphite or metabisulphite can be made more concentrated. The 5% to 6% solution is extremely corrosive to metal.

Bisulphites or metabisulphites should be used in the form of pellets or crystals. In all wine-making countries, sulphite treatment is restricted in terms of free and total sulphurous acid content. Total sulphur dioxide is the aggregate of free sulphur dioxide and compound sulphur dioxide. The amount of free sulphur dioxide decreases steadily to an equilibrium level because part is combined with aldehydes, colour pigments, sugars, etc. Some sulphur dioxide is oxidized to the sulphate by the oxygen in solution. The amount of free sulphur is proportionate to the amount of the total once an equilibrium is reached with the combining materials (generally about two weeks). After this there is a slow loss by chemical change but the relative amounts of the total and free sulphur dioxide stay the same.

Usually sulphur dioxide is added at the time of bottling as a protection against oxidation and to combine an inactivated acetaldehyde. Over a period of years the total sulphur dioxide will become greatly reduced. However, if the wine is well made and in the bottle, little will happen because of this loss.

Table of Wine Acids

(according to J. Ribéreau-Gayon and E. Peynaud)

Name of Wine Acid	*Remarks*
Fixed organic	
Tartaric Malic Citric	These acids come from the grape
Succinic Lactic	Produced by fermentation
Gluconic Glycuronic	Eudemized grapes
Dioxymalic Dioxytartaric	Oxidation of the tartaric acid
Glycolic Glyoxylic Glyceric Saccharic High fatty	Not as yet studied thoroughly in wines
Volatile organic Formic Acetic	Acetic alone is always present in wine
Mineral	
Hydrochloric Sulphuric Sulphurous Orthophosphoric	Authorized antiseptics
Carbonic	Produced by fermentation

Acidification Procedures Permitted in Various Wine-producing Countries

Algeria: Musts: tartaric acid, without restriction (during fermentation); citric acid: 50 grammes per hectolitre maximum (after fermentation). Wines: tartaric acid forbidden; citric acid: maximum 50 grammes per hectolitre, providing the original must has not been acidified at this dose.

Germany: During blending.

Austria: Forbidden in principle to increase the acid content.

Bulgaria: Tartaric and citric acid only for the sparkling wines.

Spain: Pure citric acid, maximum 1 gramme per litre; tartaric acid only in musts or wines of low acidity, but not for other usages.

U.S.A.: Tartaric, malic, and citric acids—within specified limits.

France: Musts: tartaric acid; Wines: citric acid, maximum 0·50 gramme per litre.

Volatile acidity. The primary source of volatile acidity in most wines is acetic acid. However, other acids—such as formic or sulphurous acid, or any other steam-distillable acid—do contribute. The actual smell of 'acetic' wine can be attributed to ethyl acetate in many instances. The presence of these chemicals is normal and only when they are in excess do they become objectionable. In France, wine volatile acidity is expressed in sulphuric acid, averaging between 0·3 and 0·7 grammes per litre. When this figure is exceeded, the wine is affected.

In France there have from time to time been strict regulations about the degree permissible in wine to be sold: the current law lays down that a wine is spoiled at 0·9 gramme per litre at the wholesale, and 1·2 grammes at the retail stages.

Sugar and glycerin

In a sugar–alcohol fermentation, the most important by-product is glycerin (or glycerol). This donates some of the sweetness and smoothness to a wine and was once erroneously thought to be responsible for the 'legs'—the streaks that run down the side of a glass in which wine has been swirled. (Legs are now known to be a result of ethyl alcohol.) Compounds related to glycerin, and found in very small quantities, are 2,3-butylene glycol, acetylmethylcarbinol, and diacetyl. Sugar will also be present—even in a completely 'dry' wine. (Less than 0·2% sugar is about standard for dry wines; this amount can neither be tasted nor will it ferment further.) Some of this is hexose sugar—dextrose and levulose, of which levulose is the sweeter—and some are pentose sugars, mostly arabinose and some xylose. There are also related compounds such as rhamnose, pentosans, methyl pentosans, dihydroxymaleic acid, and pectins.

Aldehydes and esters

Aldehydes are a half-way step between alcohols and acids and are formed by the oxidation of alcohols; esters are the result of a combination of acid and alcohol. Both play an important part in wines, particularly in bouquet.

The most important wine aldehyde is acetaldehyde. In addition there are traces of formaldehyde, propionaldehyde, cinnamaldehyde, cenanthaldehyde, vanillin, methyl ethylketone, acetal, capraaldehyde, and benzaldehyde—and probably furfural and acrolein, although these two have not been sufficiently established for the chemists to be quite sure. In certain sweet wines—those that have been heated, such as Madeira and some imitation 'sherries'—there is also a trace of hydroxymethylfurfural.

Esters fall into two groups: (1) volatile, odoriferous esters usually formed from acetic acid, and (2) the neutral and acid esters of the fixed acids, mostly tartaric and malic. Ethyl acetate is by far the most prevalent ester, but others, formed from all the acids mentioned above plus those of valeric, caproic, and pelargonic acids, will be present to a greater or lesser degree.

Dry extract and ash

When wine is placed in a test tube and carefully heated, the liquid boils away leaving salts, and these, when heated to high temperatures, form the ash, useful to the wine chemist in determining what is there, and in what quantity. The salts include chlorides, phosphates, silicates, and sulphates; and the minerals include potassium, calcium, magnesium, sodium, iron, copper, and small amounts of boron, iodine, manganese, molybdenum, titanium, vanadium, and zinc, among others. The type and amount of minerals present will largely depend upon the soil in which the grapes were grown and what minerals nourished the vine, and the elements which came into contact with the wine.

Nitrogen, and vitamins

The most important nitrogen by-products are the amino acids, some of which disappear during fermentation or are used by yeasts to form the higher alcohols. Other amino acids are formed by the yeast. Common amino acids are alanine, arginine, aspartic acid, cystine, glutamic acid, glycine, histidine, isoleucine, leucine, lysine, methionine, proline, serine, threonine, tryptophan, tyrosine, valine, and phenylalanine. Vitamins include vitamin A, ascorbic acid, thiamin, riboflavin, pyridoxin, nicotinic acid, pantothenic acid, *p*-aminobenzoic acid, biotin, and inositol.

Tannin

This is contributed by the skins, pips, and stalks of grapes and is dissolved in the liquid during fermentation. It adds flavour, body, and lasting properties to the wine. It also has certain antiseptic qualities, obstructive to noxious bacteria. Its astringency, which may amount to harshness in some young red wines (such as the Bordeaux), decreases with age and is the result of precipitation, combining as it does with aldehydes to form a deposit. Addition of proteins may also help to clear the wine, and it is sometimes made use of in fining. The quantity of tannin present in a wine varies with vine varieties and harvesting conditions. White wines are low in tannin; red ones may contain up to 3 grammes or more per litre.

The tannins found in wine are made up of polyphenols: leuco-anthocyanin, leuco-cyanidol, catechins, pyrogallics, and œnological tannins.

Wine Disorders

Young wine is a living thing in the sense that biochemical processes are taking place continuously.

It is subject to diseases and disorders of various sorts. These may be divided into maladies caused by biological disorders and those caused by the physical environment.

1. *Biological disorders*

Bacterial or yeast spoilage can take place under either ærobic or anærobic conditions. In many cases it is extremely difficult to pinpoint the organism causing the trouble; the same bacteria may cause apparently different diseases under different conditions. Over the years the nomenclature of the various diseases also changes. The most common bacteria are the lactobacilli, which will ferment malic acid and also citric acid under certain conditions. These are only dangerous if the strain metabolizes other than desired substances or gives off odour or flavours, or the wine is so low in acid as to become flat and unbalanced after the secondary fermentation. Some widely recognized diseases are:

Flowers of wine (*Flor*). Flowers of wine is the name given to a particular film-forming yeast which will grow on the surface of young wines if they are exposed to air. This is not a disorder when used to produce the distinctive character of Spanish Sherry or the *vin jaune* of the French Jura. This yeast growth generally has to be encouraged and can easily be prevented by keeping the wine container full.

Microderma (*Fleur*). This is a fairly harmless microbe which grows rapidly on the surface of young wine, forming a film. It is often mistaken for 'Flor' but under microscopic observation the difference is easily determined. This disease can also be prevented by limiting the exposure of the wine surface to the air.

Acescence (*Piqûre*) or *Acetification*. Like 'Fleur', acescence is marked by the formation of a film on the surface of the wine—but of a translucent grey rather than white in many instances. *Acetobacter* causes a rapid decrease in alcohol and sugar and produces varying amounts of acetic acid and ethyl acetate which give the wine the disagreeable vinegary taste, thus ruining it. Again, this disease can be easily prevented if the wine is not subject to excess aeration by exposure of the partly full container to air and by good cellar practice.

Tourne. The wine becomes gassy—with a thoroughly disagreeable aroma and taste resembling that of acescence—hazes, and loses its colour. Tourne is caused by bacteria attacking tartaric acid and chemically shows a loss of tartrates, an increase of volatile acidity, and a decrease of fixed acidity and acid strength (as shown by a rise in pH value).

Graisse (*Fatty degeneration*). The wine becomes turgid and viscous and flows like oil. There is a decrease in sugar, an increase both in total and volatile acidity, and a gummy deposit. The disease is often found in Champagne where it affects the *rebêche* (the low-quality, last-run-of-the-wine press) which is vinified and given to the workers.

Amertume (*bitterness*). The wine throws a deposit and becomes bitter and very acid. It is caused by bacteria attacking glycerin and chemically shows a decrease in glycerin and an increase in total and volatile acidity.

These last three diseases are generally considered to be caused by either lactobacilli, leuconostoc, or bacilli.

Mannitic fermentation occurs when the temperature of the fermenting vat becomes excessive, the useful yeasts die and other bacteria take over, attacking the sugar. The resultant wine is cloudy and has a curious bitter-sweet, sometimes 'mousy' taste. Instead of converting grape sugar to ethyl alcohol and carbon dioxide, these bacteria convert it to acetic acid, lactic acid, carbon dioxide, and mannite, a non-fermentable sugary substance. It is a particular menace in hot countries.

2. *Chemical disorders* (*casses*)

There are four types of *casse*: oxidasic, protein, ferric, and cuprous.

Oxidasic casse. Caused by an enzyme (polyphenol-oxidase), it makes wine cloud upon exposure to air and change colour—red wines turning brown and white wines yellow, and, after a time, forming a deposit. It is often present in wines made from slightly overripe or mouldy grapes. Wines containing a fairly high proportion of alcohol, or acid, and especially of tannin, are best qualified to resist this breakdown. Preventive treatments for the condition are: judicious use of sulphur dioxide; the addition of ascorbic acid in its natural state, at 100–200 milligrammes per litre; heating of the musts (to 158°–167°F., 70°–75°C.) in a pasteurizer, by the addition of bentonite and yeast.

Protein casse. There is always a certain amount of protein matter in white wines and, if it is present in too great a degree, this reacts with the tannins to coagulate, first turning the wine hazy, later forming a precipitate. Once troublesome to makers of sweet white wines, the importance of protein casse has been reduced by the practice of fining with bentonite, which removes protein matter, so that wines must no longer be aged until enough tannin has been absorbed to cause the reaction.

Ferric casse. In primitive times, nothing but bare feet and wood touched grapes. In installing labour-saving devices, wine-makers found that iron and copper often contaminated wines, imparting off-tastes and cloudiness. Ferric (iron) casse is caused by a high iron content, reacting with phosphates in the presence of air and causing blue or black clouding and precipitation, in a wine which may also be rich in tannin but of low acidity. Sometimes the casse is allowed to run its course, and then the wine is clarified. Many red wines, young and older, will become cloudy as a result of oxygen dissolving or exposure to the air. White wines also are subject to a form of phosphato-ferric casse when they are rich in iron or phosphoric acid and are exposed to the air in the course of racking, bottling, or, especially, filtering. The deposit, which forms slowly, is greyish in colour; the cloudiness will sometimes disappear when the wine is kept airtight and away from the light. One remedy is to add to the wine a solution of sodium bisulphite—not more than 1 gramme per litre. In this case too, the best preventive measure is to keep the wine away from metal utensils. Ferric, like cuprous casse, can be prevented by 'blue fining'—precipitating the metal with minute amounts of potassium ferrocyanide. Officially forbidden in many countries, including France, 'blue fining' is, in some places such as Germany, allowed under rigid governmental control; while not expressly forbidden in the United States, it is not encouraged.

Two forms of iron compounds can form precipitate in wine. One, called 'white casse', is due to ferric phosphate and the other, called 'blue casse', is due to ferric tannate. The first forms if the pH of the wine is below 3·60 and sufficient iron (above 5 mg/l) is present. If conditions are favourable then the compound will usually form as there are sufficient phosphates present normally. The iron must be oxidized to the ferric state. The most obvious preventive measure is to have no iron in contact with the wines. However, this is not always a practical solution. Therefore wines are either aerated and the casses allowed to form or, better, the metals are removed by the proper fining. This is accomplished by treating the wines with ferrocyanide in countries where this is allowed and with safer compounds (such as 'Cufex' in the United States) if the use of ferrocyanide is forbidden. As a help against formation of these casses citric acid can be added and it will chelate the iron and prevent casse formation.

Cuprous (or copper) casse. Copper casse is usually considered as cupric sulphide. It will not form in the absence of protein but will quickly flocculate in its presence. Sulphur dioxide, or hydrogen sulphide, must be present and if they are not then a copper-protein precipitate will form slowly. Aeration will hinder formation of these compounds, as will organic acids to a small extent. Cold treatments, metal removal and filtration and the usual methods of control will save the wine.

Cuprous casse may occur in white wines containing even a few tenths of a milligramme per litre of protein, and copper, when these wines have been kept for some time away from air and in a warm, light place. The condition can be remedied by aerating the wine, by adding a few drops of hydrogen peroxide, or by clarification with bentonite to remove the protein matter. Since cuprous casse requires light to develop, vulnerable wines are often put into dark green bottles. Like ferric casse, this form of breakdown responds to 'blue fining' with potassium ferrocyanide in the few countries where its use is not forbidden.

Copper, exposed simultaneously to light and air, becomes oxidized—and so does the wine. Preventive measures can therefore be taken before introducing the wine into copper pipes or containers, by washing them out with a solution of tartaric acid at a concentration of 5 grammes per litre, and then rinsing with clear water. Better still, do not allow the wine or the must to come in contact with copper at all.

3. *Accidents*

Most accidental off-tastes in wines are caused by carelessness on the part of the maker. Extraneous odours affect wines to a far greater extent than is generally realized, and wines may be spoiled by being stored in places where they come into contact with such strong-smelling things as petrol, insecticides, tobacco, or even scent.

The odour caused by mouldy barrels and unclean hoses or tools is dangerous because it may help to impart an off-taste to wine. The so-called 'romantic' cellars shown with pride by their European owners all contribute to the creation of this problem.

Off-odours and flavours can also be caused by the addition of excessive chemicals such as sorbic acid, sulphur dioxide, diethylpyrocarbonate, etc.

Steps to be taken against Wine Disorders

Sterilizing of utensils. Cobwebs clustering on the walls of the wine-sheds harbour harmful bacteria. They must be cleared away, and the dirty walls sprayed with whitewash solution mixed with 1% of copper sulphate. Mouldy walls should be rubbed over with carbonate of soda—about 2 lb. to 10 litres (2·2 imp., 2·6 U.S. gallons) of boiling water. After rinsing with clear water, the walls may be brushed over with a tepid solution of 1% potassium permanganate. The floor, when it has been scrubbed, can be treated with calcium chloride (1% solution) and then rinsed with water.

Fermenting vats must, from time to time, be descaled; and wine presses and wooden vats (which should always be well scrubbed and rinsed) ought, when they accumulate a layer of grey mould, to be washed first in a 10% solution of carbonate of soda, then with clear water.

Wine: the Sum Total

If in wine, as in geometry, the whole is the sum of its parts, it is at least theoretically possible to duplicate wine in the laboratory. The overwhelming complexity of such a job can be seen from the foregoing list of some of the ingredients and components of wine. At present, according to Professors Ribéreau-Gayon and Peynaud of Bordeaux, the scientist has successfully isolated and measured some seventy different compounds, comprising about 97% to 98% of wine's composition. Of the nature of its all-important remaining 2% to 3%, we have little or no idea, nor how many separate compounds they represent. More important still, if we take the known ingredients and mix them together in their proper proportions, we obtain nothing resembling wine. With this in mind, there can be no wonder that leading wine chemists admit that the final judgement of a wine must not be in the test-tube but in the wine-glass.

Chapter Ten

Spirit Making

Potable spirits are beverages of high alcoholic content obtained by distillation—that is, the separation, by heating, of ethyl alcohol from wine or other spirituous liquids. Alcohol vaporizes at a lower temperature than does water, and the process of distillation makes use of the differences in their volatility. Under normal atmospheric pressure, water boils at 212°F. (100°C.) and alcohol at 173·5°F. (78·4°C.). When heat is applied to a diluted mixture of water and alcohol between these temperatures, the alcohol will be converted to vapour; and if it is then drawn off through a tube and condensed by cooling, it will become separated from the original liquid—which may be wine, or the fermented product (or *mash*) of grain, from which whisky and many vodkas are made; of molasses, the basis of rum; of potatoes, for some vodka; of apples, for applejack. These various liquids will evaporate at different temperatures, depending on the percentage of alcohol each contains—the smaller the amount of alcohol in the mixture, the greater proportionately will be the quantity of alcohol in the distillate.

Apparatus

The apparatus in which the liquid is distilled is called a still, and the simplest form, known as a 'pot still', consists of a pot where the mixture can be heated, a head, or alembic, through which the vapours pass, and a condenser in which the vapour is cooled and transformed into liquid again. The pot is heated either by direct firing, or by steam, the heat being introduced by means of a heating jacket, or a coil. To obtain a purer distillate, the mixture may undergo this process a second or third time, until spirit of the desired purity and strength is obtained (this is the disadvantage of the pot still; the advantage is that a finer flavour is preserved by this method). In the first distillation, the wine or mash is brought to the boil and yields a spirit of some 25% alcohol by volume or about 45° British proof or 50° U.S. proof. When it is distilled again, the first and last of the steam—the head and tail—are discarded and only the middle distillate, called the heart, is kept. This finishes at between 60% and 70% alcohol by volume, 105° to 122° British proof.

The ancient pot-still is still used in the distillation of Cognac and native Scotch and Irish malt whiskies; but most spirits are now made by a continuous process in patent stills derived from the one invented by Coffey, about 1830. Basically, this consists of two columns, long and rectilinear, and known as the rectifier and the analyser. Each of these contains several compartments divided horizontally by perforated copper plates and communicating with each other by means of a drop-pipe—while the columns themselves are connected by two pipes, one of which carries vapour from the top of the analyser to the bottom of the rectifier while the other, in reverse, takes the wash from the bottom of the rectifier to the top of the analyser. Steam enters the still at the bottom of the analyser (the left-hand column), and the cold wash comes in near the top of the rectifier (on the right), passes through a zigzag tube to the bottom of the column and up the connecting pipe to the top of the analyser. As it enters this left-hand column, the now-heated wash meets the ascending vapours; and while it drips down step by step, on to the successive plates, the steam heats it, and carries off its content of alcohol, so that in the final stage the spent wash falls as waste to the bottom of the analyser and is drawn off—while the alcohol is carried up with the steam which passes out of the column and is conducted by the vapour pipe to the bottom of the rectifier. Here again, the alcoholic vapour rises to the top, warming, as it goes, the zigzag pipe which is introducing the new wash, and itself, in consequence, growing cooler as it rises. Near the upper part of the rectifier, the vapours reach the 'spirit plate' and here they condense. This plate is fitted with a pipe which leads the alcohol to a cooler. Finally, it is collected in a spirits receiver. By means of strategically placed condensing coils, the alcohol is separated from certain aldehydes and volatile substances, particularly fusel oil.

Where a pot still can distil only one lot of wash at a time, the continuous still, which does not need to be emptied and recharged, is more economical in use and also enables the operator to exercise greater control over the product.

Raw Materials

Wine is the foremost of the alcoholic liquids used to produce spirits, in the sense that it is itself already an alcoholic liquid; but sugary substances are fermented into alcohol and then distilled; or the starch of cereals is converted into fermentable sugar, which in its turn is fermented to obtain alcohol. (For a fuller description of the processes by which ingredients for different spirits are fermented and distilled *see* GIN; RUM; COGNAC; WHISKY—SCOTCH; etc.)

By-products

The principal component of all spirits is ethyl alcohol diluted with water and various secondary and tertiary ingredients to give the spirit its essential characteristics. The raw material incorporates a quantity of substances which are carried throughout the fermentation and the distillation and enter into the ageing process. The various processes influence the conditions and the proportion of the secondary ingredients which will be present in the final alcoholic spirit. Brandies, such as Cognac and Armagnac, after fermentation contain substances coming from wine—mineral salts, fixed acids, tannic, and organic substances which are not desirable in the distillation procedures. The distiller of brandies is concerned with the volatiles—alcohols (butyl, amyl, propyl, caproic, etc.), aldehydes, esters (for the bouquet of the finished product), and acids. These volatiles pass from fermentation into the distillation and distribute their value. Aldehydes, extremely volatile, pass into the distillate and a proportion of them may combine with alcohol to form certain acetals. Acetification and esterification action, which develop in the latter stages, contribute to the flavour and aroma of the brandy; but the complexity of the aldehydes, if it is not properly managed, may impart a certain bitterness to the brandy—and so an excess of aldehydes is undesirable.

The secondary substances of spirits can be classified as follows:

1. *Higher alcohols*—fatty alcohols higher than ethanol. The make-up of the higher alcohols depends on the raw material of the spirit. Pot-still whiskies produce a higher alcohol mixture composed of iso-amyl and iso-butyl ingredients as well as propyl alcohol. Patent-still whiskies, of higher proof and rectified, while containing a smaller amount of total higher alcohols than pot-still whisky, have a greater proportion of propyl and iso-butyl and a low proportion of iso-amyl ingredients. Neutral grain spirit for gin contains no appreciable amount of higher alcohols. Potato spirits produce iso-butyl.

2. *Esters.* These are formed during the fermentation period and are a result of the intermixture of alcohol and acids. Some of the esters arise from the fatty acids combining with a small amount of ethyl or amyl alcohols; e.g. ethyl acetate, the principal ester, known as acetic ester, ethyl valerate, butyrate, etc.

3. *Acids.* Acetic acid forms the greater percentage, although acidity will vary according to the spirit. Butyric, tartaric, and succinic acids are among the best known.

4. Aldehydes result from the oxidation of the ethyl alcohol. Furfural or pyromucic aldehyde is formed at the beginning of distillation and diminishes as the spirit develops in the casks.

5. Other substances such as essential oils, terpenes, and minor volatile ingredients are called tertiary constituents and add to the character of the spirits.

Ageing

The time the spirit spends in the wood, the maturation stage, depends on its character. Brandy is all the better for fifteen or twenty years' ageing; gin, a highly refined spirit, need not be very much aged, and would not benefit from maturation of more than one year. Generally, all the secondary ingredients—total acids, aldehydes, esters, etc.—tend to increase with age. Furfural increases in whiskies, but in some spirits it diminishes with ageing. The type of cask and the condition of storage are of major importance in this process. Limousin oak is the special wood used to heighten the quality of Cognac during the long time of maturation; charred white oak imparts flavouring and tannin substances to whiskies—especially American whiskies. Water usually evaporates through the wood as time goes on, and the percentage of alcohol increases in proportion to the loss of liquid: after one year in barrel, an American whiskey will have an average proof of 116·5; after six years this will increase to 122·7, and at eight years, the whiskey will be 124·9 proof. The evaporation of liquid through the barrels will be greater in a dry cellar than a damp one: and the temperature of a cellar in which spirits are stored is generally constant.

See separate entries for BRANDY; COGNAC; GIN; RUM; VODKA; WHISKY.

A

Abboccato

Term for semi-dry or semi-sweet wine in Italy.

Abocado

Spanish term for wine which is of delicate bouquet and medium sweet.

Abricotine

French apricot liqueur made by steeping apricots in brandy. It is tawny in colour and tastes of apricots, with a slight hint of almonds from the apricot stones.

Abruzzi

Red and white wines. District: East-Central Italy.

An east-central portion of Italy which makes a few pleasant but unimportant wines. Montepulciano d' Abruzzo and Cerasuolo d' Abruzzo are red, light, and pleasant enough, particularly at lunchtime; Trebbiano d' Abruzzo is straw-coloured and equally agreeable. None of these is found outside its native region.

See ITALY.

Absinthe

A light green, extremely potent liquor of spirits infused with herbs, chiefly anise and wormwood (*Artemisia absinthium*). Because of its potency and the harmful effect it is considered to have on the nerves, its sale has been banned in most western countries. This is not so in Spain, where the dangers of absinthe will be hotly denounced over full glasses of the cloudy liquid.

Absinthe was invented in Couvet, Switzerland, by Dr. Ordinaire, a Frenchman, who sold the recipe to a M. Pernod in 1797. It enjoyed great popularity throughout Europe until it was banned, and many substitutes have taken its place, similar in taste but without the dubious wormwood. Of these, anis and pastis (*qq.v.*) are the favourites, particularly in the south of France, and two of the best-known proprietary brands are Pernod and Ricard. The firm of Pernod still manufactures absinthe in its Spanish distillery.

Acariose

A species of mite which feeds on the fruit and foliage of vines.

See CHAPTER EIGHT, p. 38.

Acescence

The formation in wine of an excessive quantity of acetic acid, often caused by too prolonged exposure to air, and apparent in the formation of a translucent grey film caused by the *Acetobacter* microbe. The result is a wine which is vinegary or *piqué* (pricked).

See CHAPTER NINE, p. 53.

Acetic Acid

An acid (CH_3COOH) always present in wine in very small quantities. This is one of the volatile acids. If it is allowed to form freely, it will 'acetify' the wine, turning it vinegary or *piqué*.

See CHAPTER NINE.

Acetification

See ACESCENCE.

Acid

The generic term applies to substances which may exchange one or more hydrogen atoms for a metal or its basic radical. Acids, which give freshness and tang, are essential constituents of wine. An acid is known as mono-acid, bi-acid, or tri-acid, according to whether it contains one, two, or three exchangeable hydrogen atoms.

Hydracids are combinations of hydrogen and certain metalloids. The term 'hydro' or 'hydric' appears in their names (e.g. hydrochloric acid, sulphydric acid). Oxyacids derive from the action of an anhydride on water: generally speaking their names end in -ic (e.g. nitric, sulphuric), but certain simple substances form different oxyacids according to valencies. They can be distinguished in order of decreasing valency as follows:

per——ic	persulphuric acid	$H_2S_2O_8$
———— ic	sulphuric acid	H_2SO_4
———— ous	sulphurous acid	H_2SO_3
hypo —— ous	hyposulphurous acid	$H_2S_2O_4$

(Yves Renouil and Paul de Traversay: *Dictionnaire du Vin*)

Acidity

Acids, which give freshness and tang, are essential constituents of wine. Without acidity, it would be insipid; with too much, sharp or vinegary. But when the proper balance is reached, the wine is flavoursome and fresh. Some acids are natural in grapes, some the result of fermentation; but the type and quantity in any wine will depend upon the grape variety, the soil of the vineyards, the climate during the growing season, the yeasts and other micro-organisms and the additions made to the wine during vinification.

Among the acids desirable in wine are tartaric and malic. The most undesirable is acetic. Citric acid is one of several found in very small quantities; and in sparkling wines some carbonic acid is present.

The expert recognizes three types of acidity: volatile, fixed, and total. Acetic is the predominant volatile acid, although the insignificant amounts of butyric, formic, and propionic acids which may be present are also in this category. Volatile acid is indispensable to the stability and bouquet of wine, yet can be most unpleasant if it is present in excess, giving the wine a vinegary character. Of the fixed, or stable acids, the most important are tartaric, malic, and citric. Together, the two types make up total acidity.

See CHAPTER NINE.

Aconcagua Valley

Red wines. District: Central Chile.

One of the best vine regions of Chile, specializing in Cabernet and Malbec wines, and producing wines which are strong in finesse, well balanced and long-lasting.

See CHILE.

Acquavite

Italian spelling of *aqua vitæ*, or brandy (*qq.v.*).

Acquit

More exactly *acquit-à-caution*; an official French document that accompanies all shipments of wines and spirits on which internal taxes have not been paid. (For tax-paid shipments, the *congé* is used.) The *acquit* is employed for exports—exempt from taxation—and for shipments made in bond. The colour of the paper changes with the type of wine or spirit to facilitate identification. Green signifies table wines of controlled place of origin, yellow-gold is for Cognac and Armagnac, orange for sweet, fortified wines of controlled place of origin, etc. If importing countries were to demand that these papers, which usually stop at the French border, accompany each shipment and be subject to strict controls, the amount of fraudulent wine now going out of France would be considerably curtailed.

In 1959 the United States Customs authorities declared this document legally necessary in the commercial importation of French wines.

Adega

The Portuguese name for a *bodega* (*q.v.*).

Adom Atic

Leading red wine of Israel.

See ISRAEL.

Advocaat

A beverage resembling 'egg-nog', usually made of brandy and egg yolks, and bottled. In the Netherlands it has a rather low alcoholic content of 15% to 18% and is so thick that it is often taken with a spoon.

Agave

This, known also as the century plant, is the source of tequila, pulque, and mescal.

See TEQUILA.

Aglianico del Vulture

A deep red, sturdy, warm wine from Aglianico grapes in the vineyards of Monte Vulture in Southern Italy.

See BASILICATA.

Agrafe, Agraffe

A clamp used to hold on the first Champagne cork, prior to *dégorgement* and final corking.

Aguardiente

The name for spirits in Spanish-speaking countries. Specifically, a spirit distilled from grapes in grape-growing countries and from molasses or sugar cane in cane-growing countries.

Ahr

Red and white wines. District: North-West Germany.

The proportion of red Ahr wines to white is about three to one. The vineyards have some claim to be the oldest in Germany, and certainly they are among the oldest; definite records date from the third and seventh centuries A.D. Cultivation of red wine grapes began at the end of the seventeenth century, when the Pinot Noir plant was brought from Burgundy, and for nearly two-and-a-half centuries the Ahr wines were almost exclusively red. The descendant of the French plant is called Spätburgunder, and comprises 60% of all the vines in the Ahr Valley today. Ahr wines do not reach the outside world except in tiny amounts and as curiosities because they can in no sense be compared with better French red wines; in Germany, however, they are well known. Lately, more white wine varieties are being planted and the red wine seems to have fallen off.

The most remarkable thing about Ahr wine is that it exists at all. The Ahr is north of the Moselle, and so the smaller vineland (about one-twentieth of the acreage) challenges the Moselle's claim to be the northernmost in the world. Cold snaps, especially a deadly May frost, threaten the crop nearly every year, and the vine could not ripen if it were not for the steep, narrow valleys which trap the sun's heat. Ahrweiler and Walporzheimer reds are the best-known growths; and a small quantity of quite good red wine is made at Bad Neuenahr.

Aiguebelle

French liqueur produced near Valence, France. It is said to be made according to an ancient formula discovered in a Trappist monastery and its taste derives from a blend of some fifty herbs. There are two varieties—green and yellow—of which the green is the stronger.

Aiven

Tartar spirit made from fermented milk.

Aix-en-Provence

Red, white, and rosé wines. District: South of France.

In and around Aix, the ancient capital of Provence, in vineyards that stretch from the rocky inland slopes down to the Riviera itself, some pleasant wines are made. They are usually heady and sturdy and are perfect to drink in their own district, slightly chilled, in the summer. Red, white, and rosé are made, but the rosés are generally the best.

See PROVENCE; COTEAUX D'AIX; COTEAUX DES BAUX.

Akevit

See AQUAVIT.

Akvavit

Danish spelling for aquavit (*q.v.*).

Alasch

A variant spelling of Allasch (*q.v.*).

Alavesa

One of the best types of Spanish Rioja wine, frequently so identified on the label. It is somewhat like a Rhône wine.

See RIOJA.

Alba Flora

A white wine of Majorca, Spain.

Albana di Romagna

The principal white wine of the Emilia-Romagna region of Italy. It may be dry or sweet, and in the good years it has a noticeably velvety quality.

See ITALY.

Alcohol

In wine, one of the principal components. During fermentation, the enzymes created by yeast cells convert the sugar in the grape juice into alcohol as well as into carbon dioxide gas. In fermented grape-juice, alcohols combine with acids to produce esters. In general, alcohol is defined by Yves Renouil and Paul de Traversay as 'the derivative resulting from the substitution of a hydroxyl radical for an atom of hydrogen in a hydrocarbon'. Pure alcohol is colourless, and will ignite at temperatures ranging between 10·4° F. (−12° C.) (absolute alcohol) and 51·8° F. (11° C.) (95% alcohol). It is antiseptic—admirably so in wine. A rectified alcohol is one which has been distilled.

See CHAPTERS NINE AND TEN; RECTIFICATION.

Alcoholic Content (by volume)

The proportion of alcohol contained in a wine, or the alcohometric strength of that wine, is always expressed in France in terms of its volumetric alcohol content at 59°F. (15°C.), determined in accordance with the Gay-Lussac principle: pure alcohol has a strength equal to 100 degrees, and the alcohol content is equal to the number of litres of ethyl alcohol contained in 100 litres of wine, both these volumes being measured at a temperature of 59°F. (15°C.). One degree of alcohol then corresponds to 1 c.c. of pure alcohol contained in 100 c.c. of wine. The amount of alcohol can be expressed in grammes per litre at 68° F. (20° C.). (Renouil and de Traversay: *Dictionnaire du Vin.*)

As far as the British evaluation is concerned, this is based on the 'proof gallon' and on 'proof spirit'.

The proof gallon is a unit of volume and alcoholic content corresponding to 4·5459631 litres of standard 'proof spirit'.

Proof spirit is a standard alcohol which weighs exactly, at a temperature of 51°F. (11°C.), twelve-thirteenths of an equal quantity by volume of distilled water. It is in point of fact a mixture of water and alcohol containing 49·28% by weight and 57·1% by volume of alcohol at 60°F. (15.6°C.).

For the calculation of alcoholic content, the graduation by Sikes degrees is used. Since 'proof' corresponds to 57·1 degrees by Gay-Lussac, a higher alcoholic content is expressed in degrees Sikes O.P. (over proof) and 100 degrees Gay-Lussac is represented by 75·09 degrees Sikes O.P. Conversely, a lower alcoholic content is expressed in degrees Sikes U.P. (under proof) and in this case 100 degrees Sikes U.P. corresponds to 0 degrees Gay-Lussac.

See APPENDIX C.

Aldehyde

A volatile fluid obtained by the oxidation of alcohol; a large class of compounds intermediate between alcohol and acids. These play an important part in wines, particularly in bouquet.

See CHAPTER NINE, p. 52.

Ale

A malt beverage.

See BEER.

Aleatico

A grape of the Muscat family which produces a sweet, aromatic wine. Used in various parts of Italy for red wine.

Aleatico di Portoferraio

Sweet red dessert wine from Elba.

See TUSCANY.

Aleatico di Puglia

Deep-coloured, sweet, strong Italian dessert wine.

See APULIA.

Alella

Principally dry white wine produced north of Barcelona in the Catalonian village of that name. Some red is made.

See SPAIN.

Aleyor

A red wine of Majorca, Spain.

See SPAIN.

Algeria

With an annual output of nearly 344 million imp. gallons (413 million U.S.) in 1961, falling to some 240 million imp. gallons (288 million U.S.) in 1962, Algeria was the sixth largest wine-producing country in the world, following France, Italy, Spain, Argentina, and Portugal. In 1964 it took seventh place, having been overtaken by Russia, and produced 230 million imp. gallons (277 million U.S.). The indigenous population of the country did little towards the consumption of all this wine, since, although 35–40% of the working population is employed in wine-making, most Algerians are Moslems for whom the drinking of wines or any sort of alcoholic beverage is forbidden by their faith. The dark, heady wine of Algeria had to find other outlets. In 1964 201 million imp. gallons (242 million U.S.) were exported.

A great deal of it went anonymously abroad to be blended with the wines of France (particularly those of the Midi); and of the rest, millions of gallons went to France and other places abroad under its own labels, as useful, ordinary wine for washing down everyday meals. But with the declaration of Algerian independence, in the summer of 1962, quality began to fall off: the Moslem workers missed the guidance of their French supervisors. There was a slight drop in imports into France; but the growers of the Midi and other bulk-producing areas started to protest and to put pressure on the Government to reduce the quantity. This had been laid down, however, in the Evian Treaty, and the Algerian Government, insisting on its rights, has so far dictated the policy of the French. The matter remains a political issue.

Not all Algerian wine is *vin ordinaire*: other wines are made of a very pleasant quality, most of them sold as V.D.Q.S. (*Vin Délimité de Qualité Supérieure*—'Delimited Wine of Superior Quality') the French secondary classification following their Appellation d'Origine Contrôlée. The greater quantity produced is bulk wine, however, and the growing is done (as it is in California) strictly on an industrial basis. Throughout the vast domains modern machinery is found, and the grapes are brought to the enormous wine-sheds where they are processed on a production-line basis into the huge cement vats where they ferment. So that the vats will be ready for the next batch of grapes coming in from the vineyards, selected yeasts are added to the grape must, to ensure a quick and sound fermentation. When the fermentation is over, the wines are stored in other enormous vats, and are later sold by the barrel, truckload, or tank car, the price depending on alcoholic content. The vines used are the lesser varieties—Carignan, Cinsault (or Cinsaut), Alicante-Bouschet, Aramon, Morrastel, and Mourvèdre for red wines, and Clairette, Listan, Ugni Blanc, Faranan, Maccabéo, and Merseguéra for whites.

Algerian wines are generally heavy, coarse, dark

in colour, and running in alcohol from 11% up. It is not unusual to find some which are naturally of 15% with very low acidity—an alcoholic content that would be extremely rare in cooler countries, where the summer sun is not sufficiently hot to generate so much sugar in the grapes. Since the wines of the French Midi may be light in acid and low in alcohol (sometimes no more than 9%), these Algerian wines are often used to 'correct' them, adding colour, body, and alcoholic content. Unfortunately, they may be used as well to 'correct' better wines where the deficiency is not so much in the colour or body as in the quantity produced. The wines of Mascara are notoriously the base for many a shipper's 'Burgundy'.

Not only are the methods used in Algeria like those of southern and central California, the climate is often very similar too. The outlook is different, however, since Californians claim that, in their sunny country, every year is a vintage year, while the Algerian growers simply maintain that the vineyards are far enough to the south for vintage years to be unimportant. Both places also grow grapes of the same general type—the quantity-producing varieties, and those which flourish in a hot climate. Most of these grapes reach maturity at the end of August or the beginning of September, whereas the temperate European varieties would mature too quickly and produce a wine so lacking in acidity that it would be flat and unpalatable. But the vines found in this North African country today are not those which have always been planted there.

Wine History

Grape-growing in Algeria started in ancient times and the wines—or some of them—were known to have been transported to Rome for the delight of the rulers of the Mediterranean world. The arrival of the Moslem faith did not spell the end of all the vineyards, despite the interdiction of alcohol in any form, for table grapes and raisins have always been appreciated there. It is probable, as has been suggested, that the Muscat types exist solely because of the Moslem prohibition of alcohol and the resulting search for table grapes of quality. But table grapes could not keep many of the vineyards alive, and these declined in size and in numbers.

In about 1830 the French colonized Algeria, eventually making it a part of metropolitan France rather than a colony (until its independence in 1962) and under French rule viticulture revived. The first vineyards appeared in 1865. Later in the century, as the phylloxera, the devastating plant louse, took its toll of the French vineyards, various growers gave up their ruined fields and moved to Algeria; and in many cases the vines they planted were those they were accustomed to use at home. Colonists from Lyons imported the Gamay and Pinot vines; Burgundians leaned towards the same plants; Bordelais colonists put in Cabernets; ex-inhabitants of the Midi planted Aramon; and refugees from Alsace and Lorraine (some of them fleeing German occupation of their homeland as well as the phylloxera) nurtured Chasselas and Pinot Gris. Throughout, also, were found Mourvèdre, Morrastel, and Grenache. When the phylloxera finally hit Algeria, too, many of these vines were abandoned and the vineyards were replanted mostly in Carignan, with some Cinsault and Alicante-Bouschet, all of them grafted on to American roots. Some Aramon remains in Algeria, but although the production of this vine is huge, it is losing ground with the growers because of its low alcoholic content and lack of colour. In the case of white wines, the vines used are mostly Clairette, Merseguéra, Maccabéo, and Ugni Blanc.

Vine-growing Regions

Algeria has some 890,000 acres of vines spread throughout the three departments of Oran, Constantine, and Alger. Most of these are planted along the plains and they yield the great bulk wines. But the departments of Oran and Alger have between them some 175,000 acres of vines planted along the slopes and these give wines classified as V.D.Q.S. The better Algerian wines, seldom found in France, are often of extremely pleasant quality, suppler than the wines of the Midi, and with more fatness, and most of them are sold in the former French overseas possessions and in Germany, Switzerland, Belgium, Great Britain, and other wine-drinking countries.

The V.D.Q.S. wines of Algeria are mostly made from the Cinsault, Carignan, Grenache, and Morrastel vines, although some other varieties are allowed in certain cases. The whites come generally from grapes of the Clairette and Muscat varieties. On the slopes, some vines of the Cabernet, Grenache, Mourvèdre, Pinot, and Syrah varieties are cultivated also. All of these wines must have an alcoholic content of at least 12%, and in many cases the minimum is 13%. Under the hot Algerian sun the grapes usually ripen well enough to produce from 12% to 15% of alcohol in the wines. Red wine predominates, and is customary throughout Algeria, but there is also a good deal of rosé (some of it very good when young) and some white—quite a large quantity is produced in Oran. In each case, the wines that are to benefit from the designation

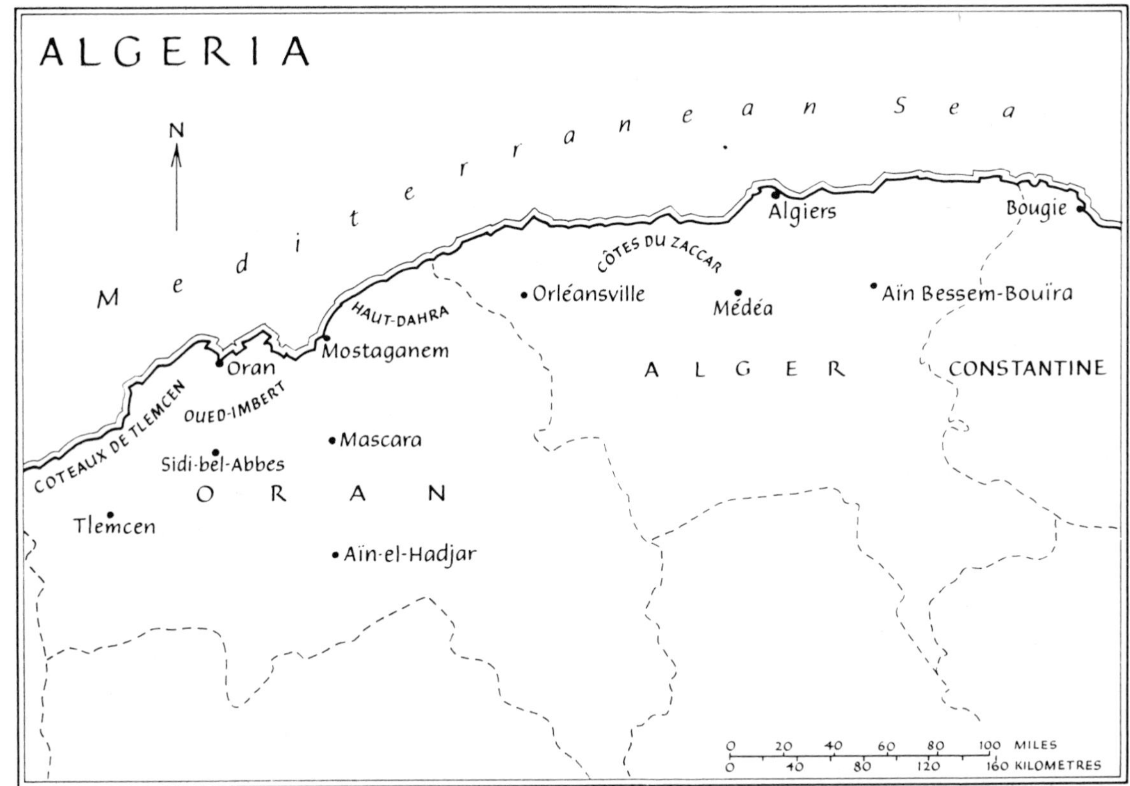

V.D.Q.S. must be tasted by a local committee of experts and tested in the laboratory before the right is conferred. The following wines are those which were recognized by the French authorities, when they were in control.

Department of Alger

Aïn-Bessem-Bouïra: red and white wines—minimum 12% of alcohol.

Côtes du Zaccar: red and white wines—minimum 12% of alcohol.

Haut-Dahra: red wines only—12% of alcohol.

Médéa: red and white wines—minimum 12% of alcohol.

Department of Oran

Aïn-el-Hadjar: red, white, and rosé wines—minimum 12·5% of alcohol.

Coteaux de Mascara: perhaps the best of the Algerian wines, from the slopes around Mascara. (The word Mascara without the 'coteaux' refers to wines grown lower down and without quite the same degree of quality.) These wines are red, white, and rosé and must have at least 12·5% of alcohol.

Coteaux de Tlemcen: red and white—minimum 12·5% of alcohol.

Mascara: red, white, and rosé—minimum 12·5% of alcohol.

Monts du Tessalah: Red, white, and rosé—minimum 12·5% of alcohol.

Mostaganem: red wines (minimum 12·5% of alcohol) and some white and rosé wines (minimum 12% of alcohol).

Mostaganem-Kenenda: red wines—minimum 12·5% of alcohol.

Oued-Imbert: red, white, and rosé wines—minimum 12·5% of alcohol.

Alicante

Red Spanish wine, known in Shakespeare's time as 'Tent'.

See SPAIN.

Alicante-Bouschet

Extremely productive red-wine grape developed in the nineteenth century by the French hybridizers, L. and M. Bouschet. It is grown throughout the French Midi, Algeria, and California, but everywhere gives the same inferior, characterless wine with low acidity and intense but quickly fading colour.

Aligoté

Burgundian white grape which gives pleasant but unexceptional wines; these are at their best when young, as they tend to oxidize within three years.

Alkermes

A red cordial once made from the kermes insect of the Cochineal genus, long supposed (because invariably found on the tree) to be the berry of the Mediterranean kermes oak.

Allasch, Alasch

A type of kümmel favoured in England, Poland, and Russia. The liqueur draws its name from Allasch near Riga (U.S.S.R.), a place famous for its caraway seeds, which are the essential flavouring agents of kümmel.

Almadén Vineyards

Los Gatos, California, U.S.A.

These vineyards produce some of the finest wines made in California. About eight miles south of San José and between Los Gatos and the former quicksilver mining town of Almadén stands the California State Historical Landmark No. 505. 'In 1852 Charles Le Franc made the first commercial planting of fine European wine grapes in Santa Clara County and founded Almadén Vineyards.' Whether Le Franc or Étienne Thée, his French compatriot from Bordeaux, was the original founder, is open to debate, but it was undeniably Charles Le Franc who planted choice European grape varieties at the foot of the Santa Cruz Mountains, where the heat of the constant Californian sun is tempered by cool evening breezes from the Pacific. The rocky soil is not fertile enough for large yields, but the hillsides of Almadén offer grapes of special quality.

Almadén wines are almost all varietal wines, bearing the grape name on the label. Only a few acres of the United States are planted with the Pinot Chardonnay, but some of these are in Almadén, and its Chardonnay is generally acknowledged to be one of America's best white wines; the local Cabernet Sauvignon also is a red wine of distinction. The pride of this winery is probably its particularly fine rosé—the Almadén Grenache Rosé, a really delightful pink wine.

Louis Benoist, a San Francisco businessman, bought the vineyards in 1941 and increased the acreage in varietals by securing, under the recommendation of soil experts, two vineyard tracts totalling 300 acres. One of these, in the Santa Cruz Mountains near Eagle Rock, is planted entirely with Johannisberg Riesling; the other, the Foothill Vineyard, lies two miles south of the main ranch and its principal growths are Cabernet Sauvignon and Pinot Chardonnay.

In 1959 the 3,500-acre Rancho Paicines, one hundred and fifty miles south of San Francisco in San Benito County, was purchased by Almadén Vineyards, and grapes are being planted in hillside land—among them Pinot Noir, Cabernet Sauvignon, Johannisberg Riesling, Gewürztraminer, Sémillon, Pinot Chardonnay, etc. The property, classified as a mountain vineyard with elevation ranging from 700 to 1,000 feet, includes several soil types and climate exposures, particularly adapted to the cultivation of fine varietal wine grapes. This transaction followed within six months the leasing of the 500 acres of Valliant Vineyards and winery from the W. A. Taylor Co., which is four-and-a-half miles south of the Rancho Paicines property. These vineyards were eventually purchased and are now known as Almadén Vineyards, Cienega.

See also AMERICA: CALIFORNIA.

Aloxe-Corton

Burgundy red and white wine. District: Côte de Beaune, France.

The commune is at the northern end of the Côte de Beaune but its finest white wines rank with those from the unofficial 'Côte de Meursault'—the great white wine-giving southern end of this famous slope—and its reds are the finest of the Côte de Beaune, among the finest of all Burgundy. But in order to get what you want, you must know what to ask for.

Some of the wines are sold as Aloxe-Corton. These are communal wines—pleasant and enjoyable, sometimes distinguished, seldom great. Others have, as well, the full communal name such as Aloxe-Corton Les Maréchaudes, signifying that they come from one, selected, excellent vineyard and that the wine has attained higher than minimum standards. The most magnificent wines do *not* bear the name Aloxe; they are either Corton alone, or Corton followed by some other, more specific designation. The three greatest names are:

Corton: more red wines than white, sometimes further defined to determine the exact portion of the vineyard from which they come (e.g. Corton-Bressandes, Corton-Renardes, etc.).

Corton-Charlemagne: the superb full-bodied white wine of Aloxe.

Charlemagne: applicable to certain outstanding white wines but rarely used since these wines have equal right to the preferred Corton-Charlemagne.

See each under separate heading.

The vines grow on a prominent hill known as La Montagne, which stands back from the main road, its gentle slopes crowned with the Bois de Corton, a quiet, peaceful woodland. The vineyard strip fronting these woods is Corton, but farther down are the even more outstanding sections of the same vineyard: Bressandes, Renardes, and the Clos du Roi. On a level with Corton is Charlemagne, and both Charlemagne and the upper portion of Corton are planted in Chardonnay. Local growers say that the upper sections are best for white wines, the middle and lower parts for red. The soil itself is the clue. At the top it is light and dry, with a whitish tinge from the chalky subsoil; farther down, it becomes ferruginous and reddish.

Aloxe is one of the oldest of the wine-growing communes along the ancient Slope of Beaune. Charlemagne, Henry II, and Charles the Bold (the Burgundian duke who lost both his life and his lands to Louis XI) have been growers, and Voltaire was one of the most celebrated admirers of the wines. In the famous letter to Monsieur Le Bault—who built the commune's Château Corton-Grancey—he said: 'Your wine has become a necessity for me. I give a very good Beaujolais to my friends from Geneva but in secret I drink your Corton.' Le Bault's reply was a note scribbled in the margin: 'This man is a *villain,*' implying Voltaire was at the very least a miser and a scoundrel. The château has been renovated a number of times since its construction in 1749, and today—thoroughly modernized—it is in the hands of the good shipping firm of Louis Latour.

Whether red wine or white comes first in Aloxe is a matter of choice, but most wine lovers are willing to settle for both. The reds are powerful, full, and big, tending towards harshness when young but maturing beautifully and taking on a great balance. They have a magnificent aroma with sometimes a hint of violets. Corton, of all Côte de Beaune wines, is the one to lay down, for it develops slowly and holds its majesty for years. The best Corton whites are sometimes in the same class as Montrachet—the wine from the south of the Côte de Beaune which many experts consider the greatest dry white wine in the world. These wines have a firmness that borders on a touch of steel and an almost overwhelming perfume of the grape, especially when young. Some connoisseurs maintain that they can also detect a scent of cinnamon in the bouquet; and the wines have exceptional breed and a lingering aftertaste with an enormous range of sensations.

The area on which the vines are grown is not large. The total for Aloxe-Corton is about 600 acres, and the best vineyards cover considerably less ground (some of these, entitled to the Appellation Contrôlée of Aloxe-Corton, are partly in the neighbouring Pernand-Vergelesses and Ladoix-Serrigny). Production in an average year for quantity may amount to 57,000 imp. gallons (68,000 U.S.) of red wine, and less than 420 (500 U.S.) of white. These statistics do not include the production of the vineyards Corton and Corton-Charlemagne (*qq.v.*). Those vineyards which may produce wines that will carry both commune and vineyard name—the First Growths (*Premiers Crus*)—have only tentatively been established and the list is provisional—the acreage has not, at the time of writing, been fixed.

GREAT GROWTHS (*Grand Crus*)

Vineyard		*Acres*
Le Corton	(*Red wine and some white*)	192·8
Corton-Charlemagne	(*White wine*)	61·5
Charlemagne	(*White wine*)	88

The minimum degree of alcohol allowed for these wines is: red, 11½%; white, 12%. Maximum production must not exceed 312 imp. gallons (374 U.S.) to the acre. The *appellation* Charlemagne is seldom used as most of the land is entitled also to the name Corton or Corton-Charlemagne.

FIRST GROWTHS (*Premiers Crus*)

Le Clos du Roi	Les Chaillots
Les Bressandes	Les Guérets
Les Renardes	Les Brunettes
Les Chaumes	Les Sallières
Les Fiètres	Les Genevrières
Les Meix	Les Maréchaudes
La Vigne au Saint	Les Combes
Les Languettes	La Boulotte
Les Petits Vercots	Les Fournières
Boulmeau	Les Planchets
Les Grèves	Les Vercots
Les Perrières	Les Paulands
Les Pougets	Suchot
Clos Boulmeau	Les Valozières

The following vineyards in Ladoix-Serrigny, bordering on Aloxe-Corton, are allowed the place-names of Corton and Corton-Charlemagne:

Les Vergennes-Corton	Le Rognet-Corton
Clos de Corton	

The following top vineyards in Ladoix-Serrigny may take the *appellation* Aloxe-Corton:

La Maréchaude	La Toppe-au-Vert
La Coutière	Les Grandes-Lolières
Les Petites-Lolières	Basses-Mourettes

Alsace

Rhine wines of France. District: North-East France.

The route of the wine runs from Thann by the Swiss border, northward to Marlenheim, near Strasbourg, skirting the eastern side of the Vosges, a black-pine barrier between France and Germany which has not always kept the Germans out of Alsace. The sixty miles of vineyard, cut up into small holdings (35,000 growers hold the approximately 40,000 acres), lie in among orchards from which the fruit is gathered for the famous Alsatian *eaux-de-vie*: kirsch, quetsch, mirabelle, and framboise.

Wine History

From pre-Roman times, Alsace has made wine. The Rhine is its waterway, and in the Middle Ages Alsatian wine flowed downriver to Cologne, to be shipped to Scandinavia and England. Alsace was then called Aussay—spelled in various ways—and the wines of Osoy are mentioned by Shakespeare. The Thirty Years War put a stop to all this; it was the first of many crushing blows to the wine industry of the contested Rhineland. At this time (1635–48) France participated with Sweden in the final stages of the war—their common enemy being the troops of the Emperor and of southern Germany. Under the Peace Treaty of Westphalia (1648) France received sovereignty over the Landgravate of Upper and Lower Alsace, and the government of ten imperial cities in Alsace.

In the eighteenth century, Alsatian wines were popular in Austria and Switzerland. Quality controls very much like the French wine laws of today, although in primitive form, had already been put into force, and shipments were rigorously inspected by the *magistrats de la vigne*, forerunners of I.N.A.O. inspectors and of our modern wine brokers, still known here as *gourmets*. Place of origin of the wine, conditions of production, and so on, were all carefully inscribed on the invoices. Vine control laws also prohibited the planting of a larger proportion of quantity-producing vines than of quality producers.

The French Revolution brought drastic changes, breaking up all the large holdings and establishing the pattern of small ownership still in effect today. Yet, by 1870, the vineyards were flourishing again and the wines, known as Vins d'Alsace du Rhin Français, were good. But in that year war broke out between France and Germany and, in 1871, Alsace became German. To protect their own Rhine wines, the Germans forbade the Alsatians to call theirs Vins du Rhin; and so the name was cut down to Vins d'Alsace. The economics of German wine production also put Alsace into a position where every incentive was given to the producer of cheap stuff. This attempt to lower the quality of Alsatian wine remained in force until 1918, when France liberated Alsace.

With the return to France in 1918, there was a disheartening collapse of the market. It looked as if liberation carried a fatal sting in its tail for the Alsatian wine growers. In Germany, where the wines produced along the Rhine and Moselle are fine but not plentiful, there had been an enormous demand for cheap table wines. But in France, the largest producer in the world of every kind of wine, from superb down to ordinary, this need did not exist. Cheap Alsatian wines, produced on a mass scale, had nowhere to go.

The decision now taken was courageous—and it proved to be right. Alsace returned to making the best possible wines, and is still doing so today. Success came from the fact that, many as her wines were, France had lacked native wines of the Rhine type. The light, pleasant wines of Alsace, designed for drinking rather than sipping, filled a necessary place with the French. Now they have won themselves a world market, and 625,000 imp. gallons (750,000 U.S.) are being exported yearly.

Alsace experienced another tragedy in 1944–45, when the battle for the liberation of the province caused wide devastation. Yet travellers driving up, now, from Lorraine into the peaceful mountains would never guess how many of the towns were levelled and the vineyards destroyed; and Obey, which lies waiting in the valley, is placid-looking and rich with good living—*foie gras* and trout, sausages and succulent ham, and piles of whipped cream. Progressing through the pass into the foothills, they would get some idea of what Alsace suffered; but the people have been quick to rebuild their towns, to reconstruct their cellars, and to replant their vines. The wine business is brisk again, although sales dropped temporarily as a result of the

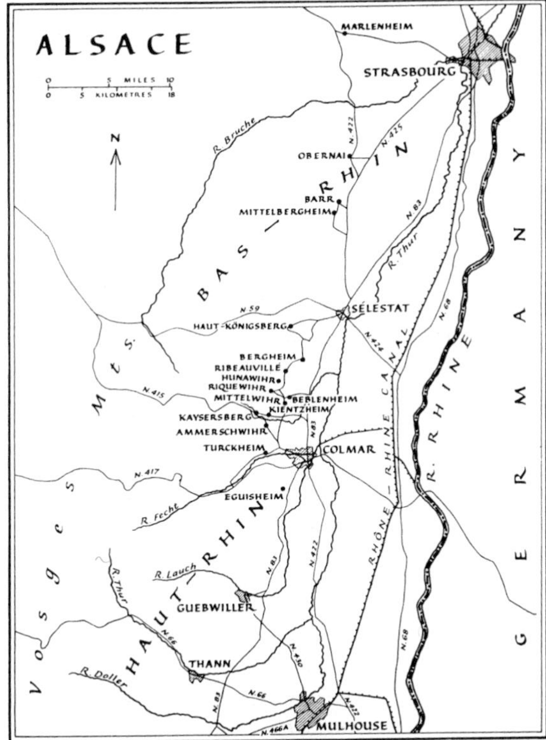

1956 frosts which destroyed large areas of vineyard, hence pushing up these formerly inexpensive wines into a higher price bracket.

Wines named by Vine Type

In all fine French wines except Alsatian, the place of origin is the thing to look for on the label. If the soil is worthy, it pays the grower to produce the best wines he can. The laws of Appellation Contrôlée, based on soil and location of vineyards, guarantee that the quality he achieves will be recognized, because the higher his wine's qualifications, the higher and more choice an *appellation* it will merit; and the higher the prices he can legitimately ask.

Alsace was the only important still-wine zone in France which had no Appellation Contrôlée. If you asked until very lately the reason, you were told that control in this one French province was by grape-variety; and that the statute of 2 November 1945 served as a wine control.

(Statute of 2 November 1945 governing the wines of Alsace: *The designations 'Grand Vin' and 'Grand Cru', indicating superior quality, may be used only for wines from noble grape varieties having at least 11% of alcohol. Such wines, if sold in bottle, may be sold only in the type of bottle designated 'Alsatian Wine Bottle'* . . .)

Alsatian wine-makers considered the regulation concerning the type of bottle unfair, since it obliged them to use this bottle but did not protect them from the competition of other growers in other regions copying the shape; so they began a fight in the French wine jurisdiction which ended in the winning of the decree of 21 May 1955. By this decree, the typical tall, slender, tapering bottle was limited almost entirely to Alsatian wines.

In 1962 the tighter Appellation Contrôlée laws superseded those denoting origin. This form of control specifies that only wines from certain kinds of vines may call themselves Alsatian Vins d'Origine. These are wines from the Chasselas, Sylvaner, Riesling, Muscat, Pinot Blanc, Pinot Gris (which, in this region, has for centuries been called the Tokay d'Alsace) and Gewürztraminer varieties.

Only in Alsace is the right to the Appellation d'Origine given according to the vine type instead of geographical location of the vineyard. It is in accordance with the *usage local, loyal et constant,* the phrase that forms the cornerstone of all the French wine laws, and it is the reason why Alsatian wines alone are known primarily by the name of the grape variety—and only secondly by the name of the place they come from. So take care *not* to buy Alsatian wines which carry only the name of the place of origin. Nearly always these will be of the poorer grape varieties or will be blends. Do not, however, exclude the few fine bottles which carry first the grape-variety name, and then that of shipper, commune, or vineyard. These hold some of the best wines.

Alsace cannot at present qualify for an Appellation Contrôlée because there are no limitations as to the permissible amount of wine made per acre, a fundamental restriction in the French Appellation Contrôlée areas, since large quantities are never obtained by the methods which produce high quality. In Alsace, your protection is the name of the grape used. The better varieties produce the best wine, and less of it.

Place-names

Officially, Alsace is divided into the two departments of Bas-Rhin and Haut-Rhin. The band of vineyard is one continuous strip stretching north–south along the eastern fringe of the Vosges Mountains, where the range touches the Rhine plain. The most important areas are the section between Riquewihr and Ribeauvillé and also the clusters around the villages of Barr to the north and Guebwiller to the south. First-class wines are produced all along the strip beginning somewhat south of

Ammerschwihr and extending to Bergheim, a little beyond Ribeauvillé. The famous names of the Alsace wine villages which lie back from the Rhine, surrounded by their vineyards, are Ammerschwihr, Bergheim, Eguisheim, Guebwiller, Hunawihr, Kaysersberg, Kientzheim, Mittelbergheim, Mittelwihr, Obernai, Riquewihr, Ribeauvillé, and Turckheim.

There are exceptions to the rule of the general unimportance of vineyard names, e.g. Kaefferkopf in Ammerschwihr, Kanzlerberg at Bergheim, Wannen at Guebwiller, Sporen at Riquewihr, Rangen at Thann, Sonnenglanz at Beblenheim, and Brand at Turckheim. All of these are officially approved vineyard names which may be added after the designation Vin d'Alsace. According to the decrees covering these place-names, the wines must come from noble plants—Pinot, Traminer-Gewürztraminer, Muscat, and Riesling—and must attain the 11% of alcohol that is demanded for the Alsatian denomination Grand Vin. The wines from these vineyards may be Edelzwicker (blends of the noble grape varieties) and still be entitled to the name. Other names, such as the Clos Sainte-Odile, Clos des Sorcières, etc., apply not to specified vineyards but to the trade-marks of shippers.

The Famous Wine Towns

Sparingly dotted along the curve of the plain, with the steep forests clothing the mountain palisade behind them, the wine villages of Alsace are surrounded by their vineyards.

Colmar

The commercial centre of the wines; site of the August Wine Fair, which attracts a great number of visitors every year. There is a special link between Colmar and the United States, for it was Bartholdi, a native of Colmar, who sculpted the Statue of Liberty. The museum of Colmar contains the extraordinary altar-piece of Grünewald.

Ammerschwihr

The ancient vineyards surrounding the town on the mountainward side are in some places scored by the ridges and moats and battlements of vanished castles and fortresses. The town itself is utterly clean, modern, and completely new—for ancient Ammerschwihr disappeared almost to the last stick and stone in the bombardments of December and January 1944–5. The population huddled in the wine cellars under the houses: even some of these were blasted, and most of the wine stocks, much of the vineyard, and a number of lives, were sacrificed to the liberation. Rebuilt Ammerschwihr is as functional as a fine machine. The Gaertner is one of the best regional restaurants in France, proudly serving, with *foie gras* or *choucroute*, the wines from Ammerschwihr's reborn vineyards. A mark of the change of the times is the alteration of the ancient wine brotherhood from the Herrenstubengesellschaft (German) to the Confrérie Saint-Étienne (French). To become a member, a man must be able to distinguish by blind tasting between a common Alsatian wine and an Alsatian Grand Vin —not very difficult; but to rise to the rank of Master, he must distinguish and name every varietal wine of Alsace and give the vintage.

Kaysersberg

Testing the wines in a *cave* such as that of Salzmann in Kaysersberg is as romantic an experience as the vinous life offers. The courtyard is Gothic and unspoiled, a relic of the Middle Ages, overshadowed by the ruin of the old castle on its crag across the river. Coincidentally this charming village was the birth place of Dr. Schweitzer. The wines of Kaysersberg are tapped from great oval vats taller than a man and carved with harvest scenes and garlands.

Riquewihr

Circled by its city walls and untouched by war, Riquewihr is lovelier than any wine town in France, except Saint-Émilion and perhaps Sancerre. The cobbled streets, lined with houses of the sixteenth and seventeenth centuries, bright with painted shop signs and flowering window-boxes, are cooled by splashing fountains. A vine-trellised courtyard of one of the old inns is the best place in the world to taste the fresh Alsatian wines, green-gold in a green-stemmed glass.

Ribeauvillé

Ribeauvillé is slightly less important. Three castles look down from the mountains on this village, which preserves the charming tradition of being the town where the pipers of France are protected. Each year the old, winding streets of Ribeauvillé resound with the Festival of the Pipers (who themselves have long disappeared) and there is much wetting of whistles with Alsatian wines.

Bergheim

Bergheim has a high reputation for its wines, especially the Traminers, and more especially those from the Kanzlerberg site. It is a charming walled village, approached through an archway on which the date 1300 is carved. In some of the old streets, the splashing gutters are so wide that they have to be bridged, and women still wash clothes in the clear water. The centre of the town is a shady square with a handsome town hall on one side, and a parish church which has a tower called *la tour des sorciers* because here the alleged witches of the sixteenth century were tried and condemned.

Guebwiller

Very good wines, mainly Rieslings, are produced with painstaking care from the terraced vineyards to the north and south of the building.

Barr

Barr is a lesser-quality producing area, specializing mainly in Sylvaner grapes. The small amount of Riesling that is produced is excellent. The small city lies near the mouth of a valley descending from 3,000-foot crests, the highest in that part of the Vosges, and opening into the broad Rhine Valley. Although Alsatian wine labels do not usually indicate the place of origin, there is always a perceptible difference between wines from the Barr–Strasbourg region, the Ammerschwihr–Riquewihr–Ribeauvillé region, and Guebwiller.

The Grape Varieties

Riesling and Gewürztraminer (or Traminer-Gewürztraminer) are the finest wines, the crown perhaps going to the Rieslings. There is much argument among non-Alsatian lovers of Alsatian wine as to which of these ought to stand first, but no knowledgeable drinker would claim first place for any other than the Riesling. Alsatians themselves say firmly that the Riesling is the king of wines. The bulk of the common wines of the better type are Chasselas and Knipperlé.

Traminer-Gewürztraminer

There is still some confusion as to whether or not there is any actual difference between the Gewürztraminer (spicy Traminer) and the Traminer. In fact, the Gewürztraminer is a variety of the Traminer vine—very like it, but a little more cherished. This wine can be slightly sweetish in the biggest years, but is generally fairly dry. It has a high alcoholic content for an Alsatian wine, reaching nearly 14% in the supreme year of 1959, with unresolved sugar remaining in the wine; and it differs from the Riesling in that the latter, when very ripe, may have a slight suggestion of Muscat while the Traminer-Gewürztraminer, equally ripe, has a trace of perhaps violet or rose in the nose; it just lacks the breed, distinction, and steeliness of a really fine Riesling, and its pronounced taste and bouquet may be too unsubtle for some tastes. Traminer-Gewürztraminer is the most individual-tasting white wine in France; a delicious, fruity wine when good and an excellent accompaniment to such strong-tasting, highly spiced dishes as curry.

Riesling

The grape which produces the great German Rhines and Moselles. Alsatian Riesling can be a splendid wine with oysters, fish, and all sea food, and with cheese. It has less body than the Alsatian Tokay, and it is less individual than a Traminer, but unquestionably it has more class than either. Riesling is dry, fruity, and fresh, and can achieve great elegance.

Tokay d'Alsace or *Pinot Gris*

Many people consider this next in quality after the Rieslings and Traminers. A very full-bodied wine, either dry or slightly sweet, it improves in bottle. There is a theory that it is called 'Tokay' because the grape variety may have been imported, 300 years ago, from the Tokaj district of Hungary. The wine has no other connexion with the Hungarian Tokay, which comes from the Furmint, and there is some opposition to this misleading name; the *Dictionnaire du Vin* states simply the name Tokay is generally used for wines made from the Pinot Gris.

Muscat d'Alsace

A very dry, fruity Muscatel, often with a fine bouquet.

Sylvaner

Intermediate in quality between the more common wines such as the Chasselas and the finer wines. A pleasant, light luncheon wine, sometimes refreshingly prickling—or with a *pointe de fraîcheur*—comparable with Sylvaners of the same class from across the Rhine in the German Palatinate. It ought to be drunk young. Under certain conditions it may qualify as a *Grand Vin*.

Pinot Blanc

This has more body generally than the Sylvaner, which it resembles slightly, but is not among the distinguished wines. It may sometimes be slightly prickling.

Chasselas

The largest producer of carafe wines, light and agreeable, with the alcoholic content of average Alsatian wines (about 9%–10%). It is seldom bottled, and so is rarely, if ever, exported.

Müller-Thurgau

This crossing of Riesling and Sylvaner, which is gaining much headway in Germany, is quite rare. In Alsace it produces a wine somewhat like, but not as good as, the Chasselas.

Knipperlé

Another of the common wines of Alsace, not quite as good as the Chasselas.

Zwicker

Not a grape variety but, on a bottle label, it indicates that the wine is a blend of both noble and common varieties. Most Alsatian wines bearing the invented name given by a shipper or grower are Zwickers.

Edelzwicker

A blend exclusively of noble grape varieties. *Edel* is the German word for noble.

Vins Gris

Famous—except in Alsace—as the Alsatian vin rosé or pink wine, but more apt to be a blend of red and white wines than a true rosé (which is lightly fermented wine exclusively from red grapes). Important Alsatian wine authorities, such as René Kuehn of Ammerschwihr—a leading grower, ex-member of the French Chamber of Deputies, and former delegate to the United Nations—state that the best pink wine of Alsace is Rosé d'Alsace, which must come from the Pinot Noir grape, and be made at the only two or three vineyards in each of the three or four communes throughout Alsace which produce true rosé. Vins gris are made on a considerable scale in nearby Lorraine.

Vintages

Alsatian wines are bottled young. They are aged in huge oak casks, not barrels as is usual with French wines; but they are not aged long. In anything from seven to twelve months after their harvesting, having been racked off the lees once in the January after the *vendange*, they are bottled. In Alsace, they say the wine should be drunk young: owing to special efforts to protect it from oxidation, it retains an extraordinary fruitiness and freshness. Therefore, although they are ready very young, the wines do not fade quickly, but hold their level for some years—the time depending on the quality. But after the first year or two, they do not gain much with bottle age. For this reason, some shippers say they do not put the vintage on the label, except in important years—thus following the custom of Champagne and Port shippers.

Spirits

The *eaux-de-vie* of Alsace are many and famous: these fruit brandies are called *alcools blancs* because they are aged not in wood but in crockery. Vineyards alternate with orchards along the east slope of the Vosges Mountains skirting the Rhine plain. The blue-plum trees producing quetsch fan out on to the plain; in the forest crown of the range are the wild strawberries, raspberries, and holly.

Kirsch

This is the most important of all the *eaux-de-vie*. It is distilled from cherries, including their stones, as the German name indicates. Some sixty pounds of fruit render about eleven bottles at 50% of alcohol. The best section for the wild-cherry tree which produces kirsch is along the middle height of the Vosges slope half-way between valley and summit, especially around Trois-Épis, directly above Ammerschwihr, Haut-Koenigsbourg, and Sainte-Odile.

Fraise

The spirit is distilled from both wild and cultivated strawberries. The genuine *eau-de-vie* is very good and very expensive.

Framboise

Since it takes sixty pounds of raspberries to make a single bottle of framboise, the cost is fabulous and completely authentic bottles are almost non-existent. When found, framboise is unquestionably the most splendid achievement of Alsace.

Mirabelle

Made from yellow plums of a size that can be enclosed in the hand. The finest mirabelle comes from neighbouring Lorraine.

See MIRABELLE DE LORRAINE.

Quetsch

This brandy comes from blue plums. This more common and hardy tree produces successfully on the broad plain.

Houx or Holly Spirit

This extraordinary beverage distilled in the mountains above Ammerschwihr is one of the rarest, and at over £7 (20 dollars) a bottle probably one of the most expensive, in the world. Less than five hundred bottles of it are produced a year, by fermenting together holly berries and sugar, then distilling.

Enzian

This spirit is distilled from the astonishingly long roots of the yellow gentian.

Reine-Claude

This variety of plum (the greengage), named, in French, after the daughter of Louis XII, is infrequently distilled, but it gives a spirit with an almost overwhelming bouquet.

Other spirits are made from apricots, peaches, rowan or sorb-apples (*alises*), bilberries (*myrtilles*), and blackberries (*mûres*).

Altar Wine

Wine used for sacramental purposes. It must be pure, unadulterated natural wine.

Altise

A beetle that feeds on vine leaves.

See CHAPTER EIGHT, p. 38.

Amber Dry

Name under which Clairette de Languedoc (*q.v.*) is often sold in Great Britain.

Ambonnay

Village of the Mountain of Reims district, producing a first-growth Champagne (*q.v.*).

Amelioration

Any treatment of, or addition (such as sulphur or sugar) to grape juice or new wine for the purpose of improving the quality.

Amer Picon

A proprietary French bitters used as an aperitif, made with a wine and brandy base to which has been added quinine (to impart a bitter taste), orange peel, and innumerable herbs. It is drunk with ice, diluted with water, and usually sweetened with grenadine or cassis.

America: Eastern States

There is a wide disparity between Californian wines and those produced elsewhere in the United States. California's product is made almost exclusively from European grape varieties; all other wines made in the United States come either from native American grapes or from hybrids—because the unsuitability of weather and climate outside California virtually precludes the growing of European *Vitis vinifera* grape vines. There is, however, some *vinifera* grown in Oregon, Washington, and Arizona. It is thus obviously impossible to discuss the two regions—California and the rest of the United States—together. Hereafter, 'American wines' will therefore be understood to refer to wines grown in any part of the United States except California (*see also* AMERICA: CALIFORNIA).

Eastern American wines have little in common with those made in Europe. This difference, however, should not be taken as an immediate sign of inferiority. The native wines of any country in the world have their own merits and their own occasions, and when the grower realizes his function and produces wines that fulfil their proper part, such wines cannot be replaced by the product of other lands. Some growers, of course, understand their role better than do others. This explains the rivalry between those who are realistically trying to adapt their vineyards to the existing conditions of soil and climate and those who still vainly try to reproduce wines that can only be the output of Europe or are suitable solely to the conditions of California. To confound the confusion, there is a further rivalry amongst America's more realistic growers—a struggle between those who advocate the use of native American vines and others who are tending more and more towards the use of hybrid vines. At present native American vines have the larger following, but hybrids may well be the vines of the future.

Wine History

The Vikings are said to have made the first trip from Europe to the New World. What they saw, apparently, were vines, for they named the new country 'Vineland'. History neglects North America for several centuries thereafter, but conditions on the continent remained so far unchanged that early settlers almost to a man were fired by the prospect of making wine in their new territory. The first wines were produced from wild grapes—and were found to be thoroughly unsatisfactory. European vines were imported—and speedily died. The first grape that has come down to us as being even remotely suitable for making palatable wine is the Alexander, an accidental cross between an American (perhaps *Vitis labrusca*) and a European vine. It is named for its discoverer, John Alexander, the gardener of William Penn.

With the example of the Alexander in front of them, the workers in the vineyards made various attempts to develop a grape vine more suitable to the wine-maker. Numerous grapes were brought forward, most of which flourished briefly, if at all, then fell into a well-deserved oblivion. Some have continued. Catawba, Concord, Delaware, Elvira, and smaller amounts of Diana, Dutchess, Noah, and a few other early crossings may still be found here and there, but with the exception of Concord, the amount of land devoted to them is small and getting smaller. Concord is enjoying new life, thanks to its adaptability for making sweet 'Strictly Kosher' wine, and for reasons not connected with the making of wine. Its potential for use in table wines is nil.

All of these grapes were technically hybrids, the result of crossing different vines. But in all cases they were crossings of two or more native American vines and had no European blood. Later hybridizers have been crossing European with American vines, aiming at some combination of European grape quality and American vine hardiness. The search for the better vine continues, but a significant number of these 'French hybrids' have been tested and set out in American vineyards. In many cases the results have been remarkably good.

At present it is impossible to pinpoint specific regions for vineyards planted in native vines as against those planted in hybrids. Both types of vine may be found throughout the eastern United States, sometimes side by side in the same vineyard. It is equally difficult to tell whether any specific bottle found on a wine merchant's shelf holds wine of hybrid or native grapes. Labels rarely reveal this sort of information. And many wines are a judicious mixture of juice from hybrid grapes and native varieties.

With certain exceptions, the blending of wine from native grapes with that from hybrids infuriates the hybrid advocates. Even a small addition of native juice gives the characteristic 'foxiness' of American vines, and this foxiness is the crux of the problem. The expression has nothing to do with foxes. Probably it came from the pronounced taste and pungent aroma of the wild or 'fox' grape. Wine drinkers who do not like this characteristic—and many do not—insist that it must be eliminated before Eastern America can produce any wines it can put forward with pride. Those drinkers who are not disturbed by foxiness—and again many are not—feel that it is the traditional mark of Eastern American vines and that to do away with it would be to rob them of their most distinctive heritage. History alone will judge between them.

Vine-growing Regions

The vineyards of America—exclusive of California—are widely distributed. The most important commercially are in New York State, with Ohio a distant second. Wine-making is also fairly important in Maryland, Michigan, New Jersey, and Washington. There are wineries, and some vineyards too, in Arkansas, Georgia, and Illinois.

New York

This state is a large producer of sparkling wines and, often wrongly, these wines are considered to be better than those made in California. New York also produces more than 11,500,000 U.S. gallons (9,600,000 imp. gallons) of still wine annually. Its regions are: Hudson River Valley, Finger Lakes, Chautauqua, and Niagara.

1. *Hudson River Valley*. The region extends from Newburgh (seventy-one miles from New York City) northward for roughly fifteen miles. It is actually more of a centre for table than wine grapes, although many growers sell their Concord grapes to be made into Kosher wine.

The district's best vineyard is unquestionably High Tor, situated on the famous hill from which it derives its name—the hill immortalized by Maxwell Anderson. The owner-operator, and ex-radio writer, Everett Crosby, experiments both with native American grapes and hybrids. His white table wine, for example, is produced mostly from Delaware grapes, while his red and rosé come from hybrids.

The Valley's other wine of note is made slightly up-river, near Highland, on a bluff overlooking the river. The Hudson Valley Wine Company, owned by the Bolognesi family, takes a more traditional stand than does Crosby. The company has been making wines from native American vines since 1907 and still does. Delaware and Catawba are among the grapes used.

2. *Finger Lakes*. The important vineyards border Lakes Keuka and Canandaigua, and to a lesser extent, Seneca and Cayuga. The Finger Lakes form a series of slits gouged out by some ancient glacier and extending like outstretched fingers into the gently rolling countryside. Upper New York's normally

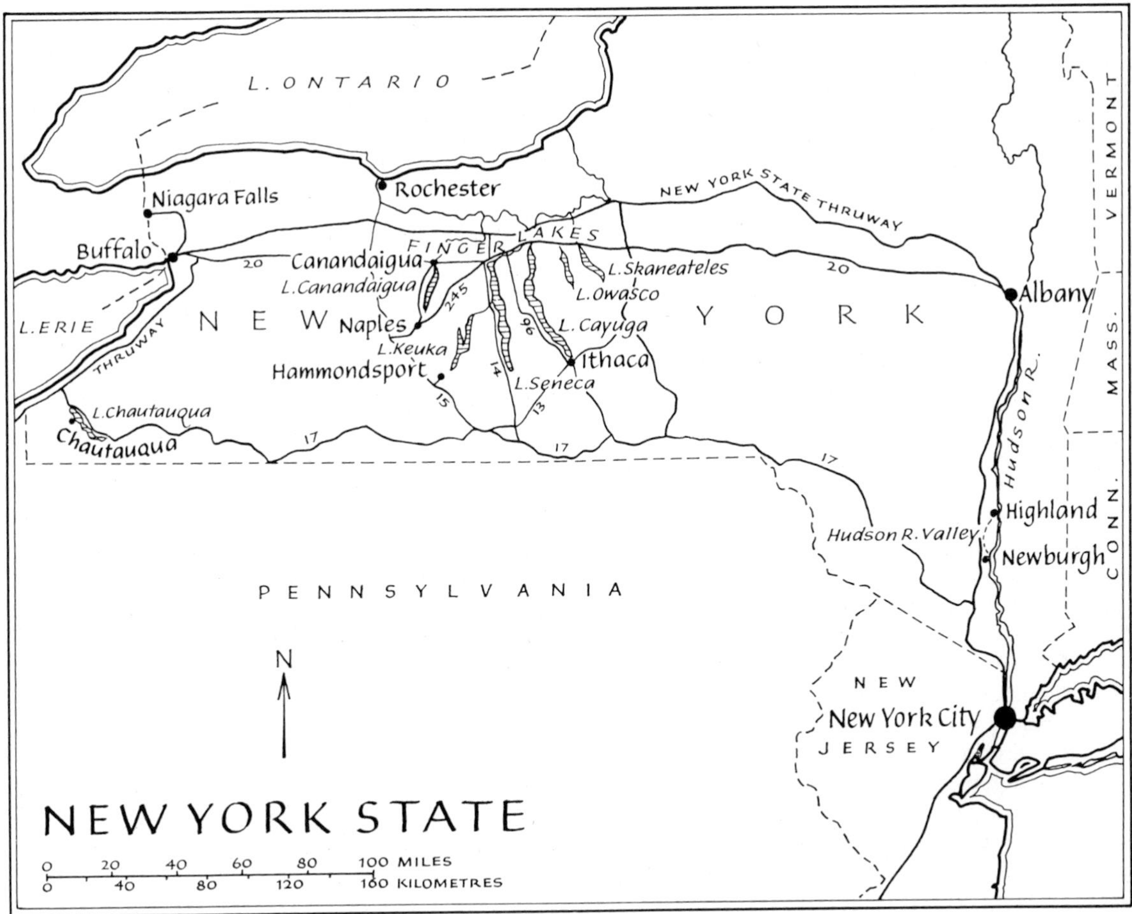

harsh climate is tempered by the waters into something nearly ideal for grapevines. Sparkling wines are dominant, but still wines are by no means overlooked.

The firms in the Hammondsport-Pleasant Valley section, at the southern end of Lake Keuka, include the Pleasant Valley Wine Company, Taylor Wine Company, Urbana Wine Company, and several smaller concerns. The first-mentioned firm produces the Great Western New York State champagne-type, using both hybrid and native American grapes; Taylor makes still and sparkling wines of all types, from both hybrid and native grapes; Urbana, the Gold Seal and Charles Fournier brands of sparkling wine. In the Urbana vineyards, a certain number of European *vinifera* vines have been planted as an experiment, to see if modern methods of vine-tending can overcome the *vinifera*'s refusal to thrive in eastern America. At the same time, however, Urbana is also experimenting with hybrids on a far larger scale. Yet most of the Hammondsport-Pleasant Valley sparkling wines are still made from Catawba, Delaware, Elvira, and some Isabella grapes, with, in most cases, neutral or flat-tasting wines from California. This blending with Californian wines is necessary to reduce the overbearing taste of foxiness of the eastern varieties. Most of these sparkling wines are fermented in the bottle. Table wines are made—mostly by Taylor and Gold Seal (Urbana)—and some dessert wine.

Naples, on Lake Canandaigua, is the headquarters of Widmer's Wine Cellars, run by Widmer Brothers. Will Widmer, a skilful technician in wine-making, stubbornly maintains the traditional native vines, and consequently most of his wines have a greater or lesser amount of the traditional 'foxy' taste and aroma. Catawba, Delaware, Diamond, Diana, Dutchess, and Elvira grapes predominate in the vineyards. Most Widmer wines are light table wines and certainly represent the best that can be produced from the native grapes of Eastern America.

3. *Chautauqua*. The Chautauqua 'belt' starts west of Buffalo, skirts along to the south of Lake Erie, cuts

a path through a piece of Pennsylvania, and ends up at last in Ohio. Its vineyards abound in Concord grapes, most of which are for use as table grapes. Chautauqua's wine is 'Kosher'.

4. *Niagara.* The vineyards stand on both sides of the Niagara River between Lake Erie and Lake Ontario, partly in New York State and partly in Canada. On the American side, considerable quantities of table wine are made, partly from hybrids and partly from the native grapes which are grown generally east of Buffalo. (*See also* CANADA.)

Ohio

Ohio's largest wine district borders Lake Erie, running roughly from Vermillion westward to Port Clinton, with Sandusky as its geographical and vinicultural centre. The most important vineyards are on Middle Bass Island—although of almost the same importance are those at Kelley—and on North Bass and South Bass (or Put-in-Bay) islands. The Catawba grape is the traditional favourite although recently other native varieties and some hybrids have replaced it in a number of instances.

The wines may be either red or white and mostly still, although there are some good sparkling wines. For the most part, the still wines are treated with sugar, a practice that raises alcoholic content but generally does little for quality. They are also often blended with neutral Californian wines, with the result that quantity is increased and some of the wine's wild foxiness is toned down. It might be thought that these practices would destroy any intrinsic Ohio characteristics the wines might have, and such is certainly the case with many of them. But at their best, they have a forthright individuality of character, and are sound and presentable table wines. The best still wines are white, but the sparkling wines outshine them.

Meier Wine Cellars is Ohio's leading firm, with wineries near Cincinnati and others at Sandusky. Other notable companies include Engels & Krudwig and George Lonz.

Maryland

Maryland's climate is eminently suited to the culture of the grapevine, but with one notable exception little advantage is taken of it. The exception is the admirably run Boordy Vineyard in Ryderwood, near Baltimore, where J. & J. Wagner (Mr. and Mrs. Philip M. Wagner) not only make wines but experiment widely with different types of grapes. Their sizeable nursery contains a variety of hybrid vines—it was the Wagners who introduced the French hybrids commercially to the United States—and the nursery end of the business is the part that interests them most. However, they also make wines, if only to demonstrate how good eastern American wines from hybrid grapes can be, if properly handled. The result, so far as quality goes, is laudable, and their contribution to American wine-making is enormous.

Michigan

The grapes are grown in the southern part of the state at Benton Harbor and Paw Paw, near Lake Michigan. Concord grapevines take up most of the vineyard space, together with some Catawba and Delaware, but the dry, sweet, and sparkling wines—all three types are made—are inferior to those produced elsewhere in the United States. Michigan's growers enjoy a considerable tax advantage in their home state with the result that wines grown elsewhere are penalized, competition is sluggish, and interest in the poor local wine remains at a low ebb.

New Jersey

New Jersey wines are slowly disappearing. A major one closed in 1967. Consumers prefer to buy Eastern Finger Lake wines or those from California.

Virginia

The vineyards in this state are few in number but the wine is good. They are situated principally in Albemarle and Clack counties.

NATIVE AMERICAN WINE GRAPES

A large number of grapevines have been developed in the United States, but most have, for one reason or another, proved themselves unsuitable for the production of wine grapes. A few have been satisfactory and are still under cultivation. Some of the more important are:

Concord. The most widely-planted, blue-black grape of the eastern United States. It is adaptable to a wide variety of soils and climates, has several uses, and is hardy and productive. However, it is useless for the purposes of the wine-maker, on account of its strong foxy attributes. In recent years it has enjoyed a considerable vogue, thanks to its suitability for making very sweet Kosher wines.

Fredonia. A close relative of the Concord. Fredonia is planted in New Jersey, but is rare elsewhere. It is of little interest to the informed wine-drinker.

Isabella. A dark red, almost black grape now found in the New York Finger Lakes region. It is often used with Catawba and Delaware for the New York State sparkling wines.

Norton. A poor producer, and easily killed in a bad winter. Its grapes are red and extremely high in acidity.

Catawba. The most ubiquitous white-grape-producing vine. It is used both for still white wines and for sparkling wines, notably in New York State and Ohio.

Delaware. Beyond any doubt the best of the native American white wine grapes. Although not a heavy producer, it is widely planted wherever American white wines are made.

Diana. A delicate vine producing white grape. Its culture is almost entirely confined to the vineyards of Widmer's Wine Cellars in New York State.

Diamond. Not an outstanding wine grape, but one still to be found in the New York Finger Lakes region.

Dutchess. An 'average' grape found today, as is Diana, almost entirely in New York.

Elvira. Produces grapes for white wine, but has almost disappeared from the American scene because of its low sugar content and the consequent low alcoholic content of the wine that comes from it.

Noah. Another white grape which is slowly dying out. A few plantations may still be found in New Jersey.

Hybrid Wine Grapes

Every country has experimented with hybrids. American hybrids are given names whereas the French (these two being of the most importance in American viticulture) carry only the name of the hybridizer and a number. Some outstanding grapes are:

Alpha. An American hybrid for red-wine grapes. It is praised for its ability to withstand ferociously cold winters, but its wine is extraordinarily high in acid.

Baco 1. A French hybrid for red wines. It is far more satisfactory in the northern United States than it is in its native France.

Foch. An early-ripening, red-wine grape, originally from Alsace. It is vigorous and easy to handle.

Seibel 5455. A good, steady, red-wine variety, making a sound, well-balanced wine.

Seibel 7053. A heavily-producing vine giving grapes that make a sound, ordinary red wine.

Seibel 13053. A vigorous vine for grapes which make either a light attractive red wine or a good rosé.

Seibel 5279. A French hybrid giving a pale, light wine bearing some resemblance to the wines of Alsace.

Seibel 9110. Gives a white grape that is particularly suitable as a table grape but can be used to make a perfumed white wine.

Seyve-Villard 5276. A productive vine. Gives a white wine that is clean and fresh and is generally excellent. One of the most promising of the French hybrids.

Seyve-Villard 12375. Gives a white grape that can be used either as a table grape or to make a sound white wine.

America: California and the West

Climate, soil, and other conditions conducive to the production of good wine are in California equal to those in most of the great vine-growing regions of the world. The great handicap in the production of fine wines comes from the enormous acreage of poor and mediocre grape varieties in the many districts.

Plantings of the finer vines are rather limited, while such red-wine grapes as Zinfandel, Carignane, Alicante-Bouschet, and white-wine grapes like Burger, French Colombard, Thompson Seedless, and Sauvignon Vert, all of which usually produce only ordinary wines, abound. Zinfandel may be the exception for when grown in the proper area it makes a distinctive red wine of better than average quality for a Californian wine and when properly aged can make a superior wine as such. For the most part, the cooler regions in north California—Napa, Sonoma, Livermore Valley, Santa Cruz, and Santa Clara—yield table wines, some of excellent distinction and flavour, and the warmer regions give dessert wines. It is perhaps unfortunate that approximately 60% of Californian wines are of the sweet, fortified variety (such as the miscalled sherries and ports) and sacramental wines, rather than table wines. The real nobilities of the Californian vineyards are found in the northern counties.

In the United States, there are two types of vines, the indigenous American, found wild in the east, and the *Vitis vinifera*, or the European variety, imported into California. It is the *Vitis vinifera* which forms the basis of the wine industry, both of Europe and California.

Wine History

The history of California goes back to Cortez, the

Spanish conqueror of Mexico who, in 1524, ordained that wine-making should become one of the industries of the New World. The vines were probably of Spanish origin, although it is not certain that cuttings or seeds were brought from Spain. In time, the new wines were competing with the wines of Spain, and the Spanish, like the Emperor Domitian before them, ordered that the colonial vineyards be uprooted. Wine growing continued, however, and for many years the wine industry in Mexico and Lower California was carefully concealed from Spanish officials. A Jesuit priest, Father Juan Ugarte, planted what were probably the first wine grapes to be grown on the west coast in about 1697 at Mission San Francisco Xavier in Lower California. This was a European variety, the only one to be planted by the Fathers, and it was named, appropriately enough, 'Mission'—and still has that name today. While the Spanish missions were being established and spreading slowly northward, the Mission grapes made their appearance in the vineyards of Alta California. The Franciscans, led by Padre Junipero Serra, brought them into what is now California, planting them at Mission San Diego de Alcala soon after its establishment in 1769. The vines prospered and the harvest was said to have been better than any known before in the New World. Padre Serra's Franciscan missionaries constructed twenty-one missions, most of them with vineyards, from San Diego to Sonoma, the northernmost point of the Camino Real, or 'King's Highway'—a great thoroughfare today—but the missions were largely confined to southern California. Descendants of the vines they cultivated are still living. San Gabriel Arcangel Mission near Los Angeles was chosen as the site for their largest winery and the mission still preserves the little adobe building where the Indians trampled the juice from the grapes. Today visitors come from far and wide to see the Trinity vine which was planted, probably, before 1780.

Between 1770 and 1830, when the missions were flourishing, wine was produced according to the needs of the Fathers. In the 1830s the Mexican Government secularized the missions and these vineyards were mostly abandoned; but it had now been established that wine and brandy could be produced in the State.

New Vineyard Owners

The downfall of the missions and the resulting ruin of the vineyards and wine presses roughly marks the beginning of the modern industry. Before 1830, private holdings of vineyards were rare. As early as 1824, however, Joseph Chapman, one of the first Americans to settle in Los Angeles, planted 4,000 vines. He was followed by Jean-Louis Vignes, a Frenchman from Bordeaux, who started his commercial venture in wine-making approximately where the new Los Angeles Union Station now stands, and by 1833 his successful wine and brandy were acclaimed throughout the State. As others followed him, viniculture expanded and within a generation became the principal industry of the Los Angeles district. Vignes was one of the first to advocate the planting of noble grape varieties. In the early 1830s, he imported cuttings of choice European vines which were delicately packed and shipped from France to Boston and then around Cape Horn to California. The long journey did not damage the vines; they were planted and some bore fruit and were used in Californian wines. Another of the newcomers to Los Angeles who built up, also in the 1830s, an extensive business in grapes and wines, was William Wolfskill, a Kentucky trapper. By 1858, two years before his death, Wolfskill had increased his holding to 145 acres with 55,000 vines, and he had a wine cellar with a capacity of 60,000–100,000 U.S. gallons (50,000–83,000 imp.).

Along with Vignes and Wolfskill, the names of Charles Kohler and John Frohling are important in this pioneering record. These two partners of German descent purchased a vineyard of 3,000 vines near Los Angeles, and at the same time they opened a wine shop in a San Francisco basement, the first of its kind, starting with 500 U.S. gallons (416 imp.) in the cellars; by 1862, they had 500,000 U.S. gallons (416,340 imp.) of wine and 20,000 U.S. gallons (16,650 imp.) of brandy in storage vaults.

The Mission grape was introduced into the earliest commercial vineyards by Chapman, Vignes, and other pioneers who planted it first in southern, then in northern California. The vine was a rough, prolific producer, lacking character and ill suited to the production of table wines; yet for more than eighty years it dominated Californian viticulture.

During the 1850s, each wine district was known by the kinds of wines it manufactured. Port-type came from Los Angeles, hock, 'sauterne', and claret from Sonoma and Napa; 'sherry' came from Sonoma and El Dorado Counties. One contemporary writer on wine said: 'But we shall not probably make our best wines till we cease to strive for foreign imitations and strike out boldly for the manufacture of new kinds of wine, which will bring out the excellence with which nature has no doubt enriched the grape in this peculiar climate.' This is a

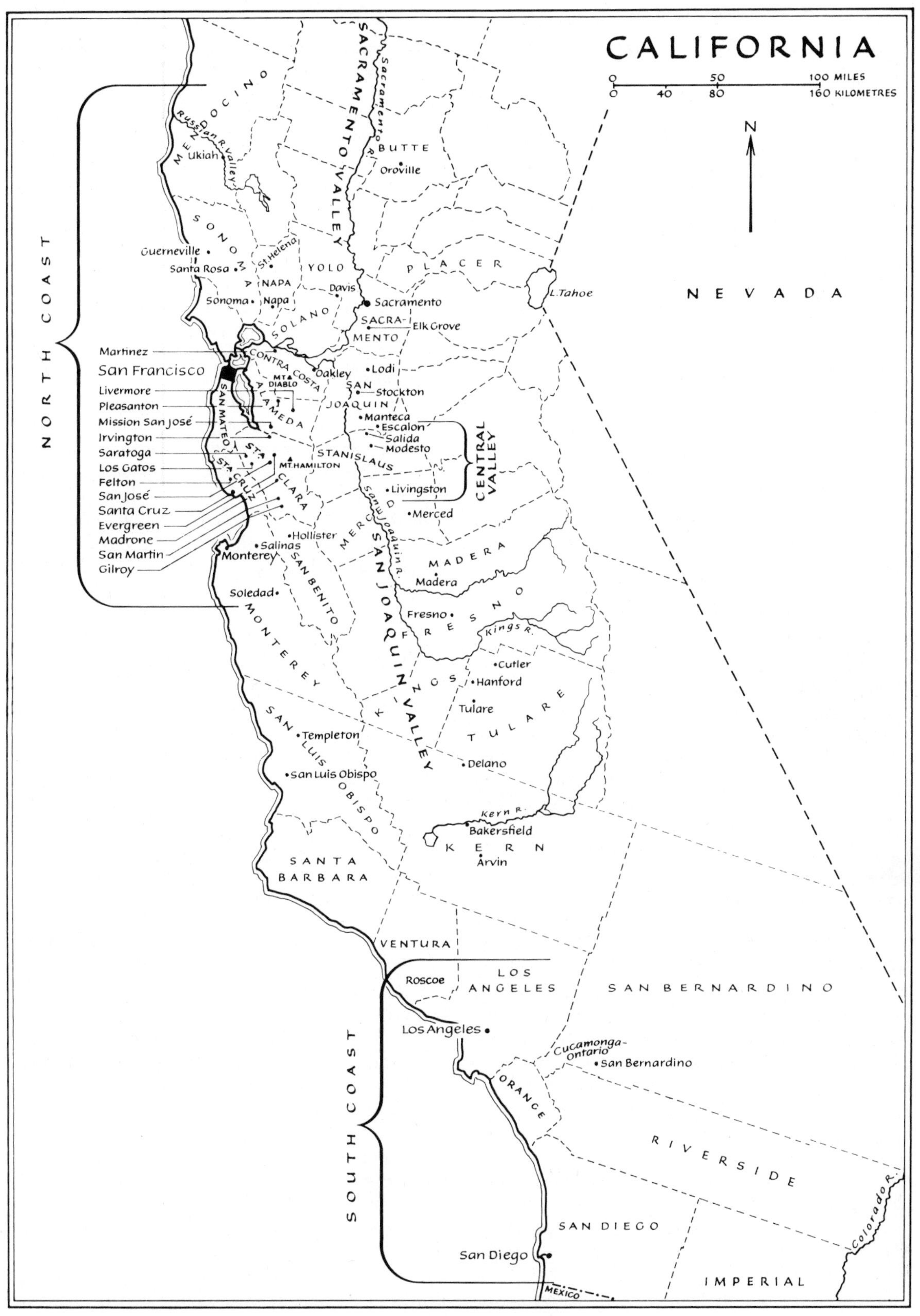
CALIFORNIA
0 50 100 MILES
0 40 80 160 KILOMETRES
N
NEVADA
NORTH COAST
SOUTH COAST
CENTRAL VALLEY
SACRAMENTO VALLEY
SAN JOAQUIN VALLEY
MENDOCINO
Russian R. Valley
Ukiah
SONOMA
Guerneville
Santa Rosa
Sonoma
St. Helena
NAPA
Napa
YOLO
Davis
SOLANO
BUTTE
Oroville
Sacramento R.
PLACER
L. Tahoe
Sacramento
SACRA-MENTO
Elk Grove
Martinez
San Francisco
CONTRA COSTA
Oakley
Lodi
MT. DIABLO
SAN JOAQUIN
Stockton
Livermore
Pleasanton
ALAMEDA
Mission San José
Irvington
Saratoga
Los Gatos
Felton
San José
Santa Cruz
Evergreen
Madrone
San Martin
Gilroy
SAN MATEO
STA. CLARA
STA. CRUZ
MT. HAMILTON
Manteca
Escalon
Salida
Modesto
STANISLAUS
Livingston
Merced
MERCED
San Joaquin R.
Hollister
Salinas
Monterey
SAN BENITO
Soledad
MONTEREY
MADERA
Madera
FRESNO
Fresno
Kings R.
Cutler
Hanford
KINGS
Tulare
TULARE
Delano
SAN LUIS OBISPO
Templeton
San Luis Obispo
Kern R.
Bakersfield
KERN
Arvin
SANTA BARBARA
VENTURA
Roscoe
LOS ANGELES
Los Angeles
SAN BERNARDINO
Cucamonga-Ontario
San Bernardino
ORANGE
RIVERSIDE
SAN DIEGO
San Diego
IMPERIAL
Colorado R.
MEXICO

point on which Californian vintners are still being attacked.

European plantings increased by Colonel Haraszthy

The great transition from the use of the Mission grape to fine European varieties was brought about by a new settler in California, twelve years or so after Jean-Louis Vigne's success with foreign cuttings from France. The extraordinary newcomer on the scene was Agoston Haraszthy, a Hungarian nobleman, who has since been recognized as the father of Californian viticulture. The first considerable importation of foreign vines began early in 1851, when Colonel Haraszthy introduced 100 cuttings and six choice rooted vines which he planted in San Diego. Among these was the famous Zinfandel which was later to be used in the making of a very popular dry red wine. At first, growers clung to the Mission grape and were slow to buy the new variety, believing that the colonel was only speculating on the cuttings, but by 1878 extensive acreages were planted with Zinfandel. Colonel Haraszthy, convinced that the finest foreign grapes could grow in California, experimented with his cuttings to determine the regions of the state best suited to the different kinds. He also believed that, to get the best and quickest results, many types should be introduced.

In 1861, he was assigned by Governor John G. Downey to a viticultural expedition, to gather all varieties that might prove satisfactory. He selected some 100,000 cuttings from 300 varieties and all were shipped to California in the course of one year. Some of these were planted in his Buena Vista vineyard at Sonoma, but the majority were sold to growers from all parts of the state. In 1863, Haraszthy organized the Buena Vista Vinicultural Society, to which he conveyed his 6,000-acre farm in Sonoma Valley with its 400 acres in vines; it was his gift of a wide assortment of grapes and his continual research that stimulated the great modern expansion of the industry. Most of the superior varieties of imported vines during this period were planted around San Francisco Bay, which was one of the areas to benefit enormously from Haraszthy's practical demonstration that superior wine can come from non-irrigated grapes.

The great plunge into the wine industry attracted the inexperienced farmers and seekers after immediate profits, indifferent as to the choice of vine varieties, soil, or location. The realization of Haraszthy's ideal was postponed and even today it has not been fully achieved. In the 1860s, Los Angeles, Anaheim, and Sonoma stood out as the three major wine and grape districts, possessing more vineyards than any others.

It was the discovery of gold which originally brought the prosperity of the liquid gold—the wine—to California. The wine market prospered in proportion to the gold discovered, and wine from Los Angeles was a luxury even to the Forty-Niners. When the gold rush was over, wine prices dropped drastically and the State Legislature was forced to keep viticulture alive by exempting new vineyards from taxes. In 1870, the future looked brighter: the new European grape varieties, Haraszthy's success, and the beneficial legislation of the state and national government led to expansion and national recognition. But this did not last. In the slump caused by national economic crises, between 1875 and 1877, the wine industry slumped too.

After 1878, however, things began to improve again. The depression had frightened away the amateurs and the speculators, and those who continued in the industry were producing better wines from finer grape varieties. They survived not only the depression but the phylloxera pest as well.

The Coming of Phylloxera

The phylloxera, a burrowing plant louse fatal to the vine, had appeared in California before 1870; but in 1876 it became a real plague, which went on for at least three years, ravaging vineyards in Sonoma, Napa, Yolo, El Dorado, and Placer Counties, as it had been devastating most of the vineyards of Europe. The French were the first to succeed in combating the disease, by grafting their *vinifera* vines on to phylloxera-resistant Eastern American vines; and soon the Californian growers were adopting the same measures.

The Beginning of Legislation

Valuable aid in stamping out phylloxera came from the California State Board of Viticultural Commissioners. This organization was formed in 1880 and did much to stabilize the industry. The Commission helped growers to find the best climates and soils for each grape variety and gave vital assistance in the control of vine maladies. An elaborate experimental grape-growing station under the College of Agriculture of the University of California also contributed to the progress of the industry. The college has continued the research and teaching of viticulture and œnology to this day; and it has been under the capable guidance of Professor A. J. Winkler and Dr. Maynard Amerine, who have earned the respect of œnologists and viticulturists throughout the world. The Commission sponsored state control laws which established California's earliest standards of quality in wine.

Between 1880 and 1895, viticultural ideas, conditions, and policies within the state were transformed. Tariff, taxation, and the fight for control wine laws were important matters to every grower and vintner in California. Before the turn of the century, the wines were taking prizes in international exhibitions, and California was competing with Europe for world markets.

Between 1900 and 1915 there was a further increase both in cultivation and in sales—but movements towards total abstinence were growing, and when the Prohibition Law was passed, viticulture in California suffered a severe blow, and many of the new wineries stopped functioning. Production dropped from about 50 million U.S. gallons (42 million imp.) of wine in 1912 to approximately 27 million U.S. gallons (22 million imp.) in 1919. But Prohibition was not altogether disastrous: the law still allowed wine to be used for medicinal and sacramental purposes, thus enabling a part of the commercial wine industry to remain. When Prohibition was finally acknowledged to be a failure, and the Volstead Act was repealed in December 1933, those growers who had not given up were able to resume full-scale production almost immediately. For a time, the demand for wine far exceeded the supply, prices were exaggerated, and inferior wines were sold. Not until 1938 could the market be said to have settled down.

In 1934, standards of quality were laid down for Californian wines by the Californian Department of Public Health and the Federal Government. Federal regulations were amended to safeguard the controls which ruled that all the wine, wherever it should be sold, must meet Californian requirements.

Perhaps the most important step in the whole history of Californian wines has been the effort of the vintners to improve varietal plantings and to produce good varietal wines—named after the grape variety (Cabernet Sauvignon, Pinot Chardonnay, etc.) from which they are produced. Unfortunately, the attempt to eliminate the Mission grape in the cooler regions, and cut down the percentage of Alicante-Bouschet, has not been entirely successful. The industry has never completely recovered from Prohibition. At that time the demand was for tough-skinned, very productive grapes, which could be shipped to eastern markets. A vine of such high quality as the Cabernet Sauvignon, producing scarcely more than 3 short tons (2·7 long tons) to the acre, was overlooked in favour of Carignane and Alicante-Bouschet, which would yield as much as 15 short tons (14·3 long tons) to the acre. These impaired the quality of post-Repeal wines and are still largely the cause of much criticism. Even today, some 60% of all the grapes used for wine in California are not wine-grapes but raisins or table grapes.

In general, however, the story since Repeal has been one of improvement, as there have been numerous plantings of fine varietals which can produce the best white and red table wines. Producers such as Martin Ray, who owned the Paul Masson Winery before the war, Louis M. Martini, the late Georges de Latour of the Beaulieu Vineyards, H. Wente of Wente Bros., John Daniel of Inglenook, Chaffee E. Hall of Hallcrest, the Mondavi Brothers of Krug Winery, and the Almadén Vineyards, who have applied large-scale business methods, have likewise done much to maintain the quality of American wines, in spite of the pressure of 'mass production'. And Frank Schoonmaker, a New York wine merchant who, with the help of the author, introduced fine American wines east of the Rockies, is another of the people who have fought for quality over quantity in the United States.

There are some 350 bonded wineries in California, but only a few of those producing directly to the public consistently make fine wines. The scene changes as the years advance. There are newcomers such as Weibel Champagne Vineyards and there are those who are forced to leave the wine trade for one reason or another—the Fountaingrove Vineyard is an example. Some vineyards have become too commercialized, sacrificing quality for quantity. Paul Masson and Cresta Blanca, which formerly produced excellent wines, are examples of this, although they are now making a notable effort to achieve a higher standard. Only a few select wineries insist that Californian wines should be called by original Californian names: for this reason, the late Paul Rossigneux, President of Napa and Sonoma Wine Company, John Daniel of Inglenook, and Carl Wente, have always been respected for their uncompromisingly high standards.

Today Californian growers are faced with the task of getting the industry to the point at which it can compete on equal terms with the European market—and this can only be done with varietal wines, not with imitations. Sherry comes from Spain, Port from Portugal, Burgundy, Chablis, and Sauternes from France, and to name a Californian wine for one of these is to admit its inferiority. Good grapes, aided by suitable soil and climate, will produce good wines. The planting of fine varietals in Californian soil certainly should result in wine worthy of being judged on its own merit.

Vine-growing Regions

There are five natural vine-growing regions in California—the North Coast, the Sacramento, the Central, the San Joaquin valley, and the South Coast. Each has its well-known districts, and almost every grape and type of wine is produced in one or more of these.

North Coast

The North Coast region is to the north and south of San Francisco Bay in the many valleys which lie parallel to the coastal ranges, and is generally characterized by warm summers and moderate annual rainfalls. The best dry table wines, both red and white, are grown here. The four principal districts are Sonoma-Mendocino, Napa-Solano, Livermore-Contra Costa, and Santa Clara–San Benito–Santa Cruz.

1. *Sonoma-Mendocino.* This district, which lies directly north of San Francisco, yields some excellent table wines and sparkling wines which rank with the very best in the state. Sonoma is one of the three top wine-producing counties in California with an average total of 11,850 acres planted in vines, and it leads all the other counties in the number of its bonded wineries. Unfortunately, however, although in this district conditions seem perfect for the production of fine wines, quantities of rather ordinary table wines are in fact made here. The wines of Sonoma County come from the Sonoma Valley, Santa Rosa, and the Russian River Valley.

The Sonoma Valley runs parallel to the Napa Valley, separated from it by the high peaks of the Mayacamas Mountains; this is the original 'Valley of the Moon' of Jack London, who wrote and died in this beautiful country. The Buena Vista Wineries (*q.v.*) are the most important quality vineyards.

Santa Rosa derives its name from the Santa Rosa Creek which empties its waters into the Russian River. The Fountaingrove Vineyard, founded in 1873, has been uprooted and is now a cattle ranch. Wine is no longer produced on this romantically named estate.

In the Russian River Valley are forty of the area's fifty-six wineries, many of them centred around Guerneville. The most important of them is the Korbel Vineyard (*q.v.*). The wines, which account for about 90% of the Sonoma output, are for the most part undistinguished red table wines, many of which are marketed in the eastern part of the United States.

Mendocino County produces mainly dry red table wines of average quality, but recently has begun to cultivate finer varietals. The most prominent wineries of this county are found in Ukiah.

2. *Napa-Solano.* This is undoubtedly the most famous red wine district in California, with thirty-eight bonded wineries and some of the finest vineyards in the country. Napa is the Indian word for 'plenty', and the valley abounds in rich, fertile land, while the hillsides are planted in fine grapes. There are approximately 12,000 acres of vineyard, and in 1955, 35,000 short tons (31,250 long tons) of grapes were crushed; two-thirds of the production is in red wine. The Cabernet Sauvignon is the royal grape of Napa, producing better than the Pinot Noir. The Cabernet, the same variety as is used in the great red Bordeaux, is very slow to mature in the Napa region and the wine is sometimes left in casks to age for as long as four years.

Napa is divided into the Upper Valley and the Lower Valley. The centre of the Upper Napa Valley is the dignified town of St. Helena, but the district stretches seven miles north towards Calistoga, and in the south it goes as far as Rutherford and Oakville. The Lower Valley covers the area around the city of Napa, an hour's drive from San Francisco, and takes in the north-western part of a wide valley bottom running up to the Sonoma County border. The soil in the southernmost part of Napa County is heavy and this region is the coolest, owing to its proximity to the Bay. The Upper Valley has a gravelly soil and the mountains influence both the climate and the exposure.

It is a general opinion in Napa that if more grapes were planted on the slopes, better wine would be made—three-quarters of the vines are planted on the flats; and this is one of the few districts where the growers admit that they have good and bad years, so that some will be regarded as vintage years and others not. Another sign of progress in the valley has been the establishment of many group co-operatives; and since 1942 there has been a Vintners' Association to deal with recurrent problems.

The most important vineyards are those of Beaulieu, Beringer, The Christian Brothers, Inglenook, Charles Krug, and Louis Martini Company (*qq.v.*).

The Lower Napa Valley and Solano County are relatively small producers but the area has recently expanded into neighbouring Chiles Valley.

3. *Livermore–Contra Costa.* This is a district noted for its production of many fine wines. Alameda County's Livermore Valley is known throughout the country for its good Sauternes-type, as well as for other outstanding white wines. The valley was named after the pioneer Robert Livermore who, as early as 1848, had a vineyard near the town that bears his name.

The Livermore Valley (more of a basin than a valley) comprises two important wine-growing areas—the vineyards surrounding the town of Livermore, and the neighbouring sector of Pleasanton. In 1887, Charles A. Wetmore said of the valley: 'Here every condition known to be essential for the production of the highest grades of wines and brandies, approximating the noblest French types, exists.' With cuttings he brought directly from the vineyards of Margaux and Château d'Yquem in Bordeaux, Wetmore founded in 1882 the concern which won renown as Cresta Blanca, but which is unfortunately not maintaining its former standards. Today, the two outstanding wineries of Livermore Valley are Concannon Vineyard and Wente Bros. (*qq.v.*).

The soil of most of the vineyards in this section is made up largely of coarse, arid-looking gravel like that of the Châteauneuf-du-Pape vineyards of the Rhône Valley and some of those in Graves and the Médoc. This soil is, in California, particularly adapted to the production of full-bodied white wines ranging from very dry to sweet. Recent attempts to make the wines lighter have been successful, and early bottling has done much to improve these wines which only ten years ago were considered by many to be very heavy. Because of the climate and the nature of the soil, it is doubtful if the Pinot Noir will ever be successfully cultivated in Livermore.

South-west of Livermore and very close to the tip of San Francisco Bay are the wine-growing centres of Mission San José and Irvington, extending almost to Santa Clara County. In this southern Alameda district the red wines are almost as successful as the white; and sparkling wines, aperitifs, and dessert wines are all produced here too. The most important winery is Weibel Champagne Vineyards (*q.v.*).

Contra Costa County, directly north of Alameda County, is best known for its table wines. The vineyard area lies around the town of Martinez, between Mount Diablo and Suisun Bay. Here, on the slopes of Mount Diablo, the Gamay grape of Burgundy plays an important role.

4. *Santa Clara–San Benito–Santa Cruz.* The district centralizes most of its wine-growing in Santa Clara County where there are thirty-nine bonded wineries. This county consists of three vineyard areas. West of the Santa Clara Valley and at the foothills of the Santa Cruz Mountains lies Los Gatos, and, a little to the north-west and higher up the mountain slopes, Saratoga. This Los Gatos–Saratoga area produces some of the finest table wines and sparkling 'champagnes' of California. The principal vineyards are those of Almadén, Martin Ray, Chaffee Hall's Hallcrest, and San Martin (*qq.v.*).

The second area of Santa Clara lies to the east of San José and the vineyards of the Evergreen area stretch on to the slopes of Mount Hamilton. Although this district does not produce heavily, the wines are generally superior.

The third area is in the southern part of Santa Clara County near the towns of Madrone, San Martin, and Gilroy. This has many small wineries making good average wine and catering to the local trade. Santa Clara County is one of the world's greatest fruit-growing districts, and its viticultural past goes back to the days of the Spanish padres who planted the valley's first domestic grapes.

Santa Cruz County is separated from Santa Clara only by the bordering Santa Cruz Mountains. Although there are only three bonded wineries, the vineyards produce good sound grapes. The most important winery is the Hallcrest Vineyard (*q.v.*).

The counties of San Benito, Monterey, and San Luis Obispo lie south of Santa Clara and Santa Cruz, and their output of table wines is comparatively small. The San Benito wine area is planted around the town of Hollister; in Monterey the principal vineyards are north of Soledad in the Salinas Valley foothills; and at San Luis Obispo they are concentrated around the quiet town of Templeton. Many of the vineyards are planted in Zinfandel grapes.

Sacramento Valley

The region extends from the northern part of San Joaquin County up as far as Oroville in Butte County and comprises Sacramento, Placer, Yolo, Amador, Butte, and northern San Joaquin counties. The Sacramento Valley is merely an extension of one great inland valley region marking the heart of Californian agriculture, but with its variations in soil, contour, and climate it is one of three important subdivisions. This region is somewhat affected by the moderating influence of San Francisco Bay and consequently the summers become slowly hotter and the winters cooler. Some parts of the valley, particularly where the winter frosts are negligible and the summers mild, may eventually prove to be the home of better wines. Much of the land to the north is broken and irregular and entirely unsuitable to the planting of wine grapes.

Most of the region's vineyards are found in the northern section of San Joaquin County and in Sacramento County. The majority go in for mass production, and ordinary table wines and dessert wines abound.

The major district of the Sacramento Valley region is the Lodi–Sacramento, which dominates the better part of the region's wine-growing area. From the state capital of Sacramento southwards to the town of Elk Grove, table and dessert wines are bulk-produced and types of 'burgundies' and 'ports' are made from inferior as well as from good grape varieties. At Elk Grove in Sacramento County many fruit and berry wines are produced and dessert wines and aperitifs are preferred to table wines.

In northern San Joaquin County, Lodi, a lively little city, is noted for its many wineries almost exclusively given over to dessert wines. However, the Lodi area, which branches out in all directions from the city, is now starting to convert to some table-wine production.

Central Valley

The major district in the Central Valley, known as the Escalon-Modesto, contains some of the largest distributing Californian wineries. Escalon and Manteca are south of Stockton in the southern part of San Joaquin County and the vineyards mostly lie in an east–west direction between these two small cities. The Central Valley region covers the southern San Joaquin and Stanislaus Counties and takes in northern Merced County in the vicinity of Livingston. It is a large producer of table grapes —Flame Tokay and Thompson Seedless or Sultanina —and unfortunately too many of them are used in the making of wines. The important wineries in Stanislaus County are in Modesto and Salida.

The Central Valley produces enormous quantities of mediocre wines—mostly dessert wines and a few ordinary table and sparkling wines made from grape varieties that are considered heavy producers and even from table grape varieties producing a sub-standard quality. Approximately 375,000 short tons (334,800 long tons) of grapes are crushed yearly in this region. The area has a marked resemblance to the southern part of France and to a lesser degree Algeria, not only in climate but in the wines produced.

San Joaquin Valley

The region forms the southern branch of the great inland valley. It is the warmest area, a typical valley climate with its lack of moderating sea breezes. The annual rainfall is negligible and irrigation is necessary; daytime temperatures in July and August average over 80°F. (27°C.). The San Joaquin is a great raisin area, and it produces sweet fortified wines of better than average quality. Dry table wines are also made, but they lack quality, mainly on account of the poor balance between sugar and acid in the grape varieties grown.

The principal district of the region is the Fresno–San Joaquin Valley, comprising five counties. From north to south they are: Madera (lying south of Merced County), Fresno, Kings, Tulare, and Kern Counties.

Madera County vineyards surround the city of that name, the most important in quantity being Ficklin (*q.v.*).

Fresno County, with the city of Fresno as its centre, has thirty-three bonded wineries, many of them producing wines misnamed port, sherry, sauternes, etc.—handicaps to a promising industry. The wines of the inland valley regions may be improved by the planting of better varieties. Around Fresno there are many towns with large wineries—Fowler, Selma, Reedley, Parlier, and Sanger.

Kings County's vineyards are near Hanford, while Tulare has its centres in Tulare and Cutler.

Kern County's large acreage of vineyards stretches from Delano to Arvin, outside the city of Bakersfield. There are few wineries in Kern, but although they do not produce directly to the public, they play a considerable role in supplying wine to major firms in other areas. Approximately 680,000 short tons (607,500 long tons) of grapes are crushed annually in the San Joaquin Valley.

South Coast

This region is a combination of three districts—Los Angeles County, San Diego, and Cucamonga-Ontario districts. Los Angeles and San Diego counties, lying in the southern coastal valley region, are cooled by sea breezes, while the inland district of Cucamonga-Ontario—synonymous with San Bernardino County—is an extension of the desert area and its summers are comparable with those of the San Joaquin Valley. This warmer area is less suitable for the production of dry table wines, although quite good sweet wines are made.

The Los Angeles district takes in the San Fernando Valley, around the cities of San Fernando and Roscoe, and the eastern part of Los Angeles, from San Gabriel and Rosemead, south to Whittier.

The small Escondido district in San Diego County devotes most of its wine-growing to muscatels made from the Muscat of Alexandria grape.

The most famous district in southern California is around Cucamonga. Light wines which are produced in large quantities here should be consumed early because the warm climate is not conducive to the production of full-bodied, lasting growths. Red table wine made from grape varieties which go into so-called chiantis, clarets, and burgundies is a speciality. There are a few vineyards in this area which make a fair Grignolino Rosé. Wines of all natures are produced in the Cucamonga-Ontario district ranging from red table wines and sparkling 'champagne'-types to aperitifs and dessert wines. Quality in this sun-parched region depends on the grower's integrity and his willingness to substitute quality for quantity. Grapes grown in the warmer parts of the hot desert region—such as the Coachella and Imperial valleys—are not suitable for wine and not used for such, although this area does well with its early-maturing table grapes.

Aperitifs

Aperitifs or appetizer wines are technically classed as dessert wines because of their alcoholic content, but are classified separately because they are drunk before instead of after meals. The two main aperitifs in California, as elsewhere, are sherry and vermouth. Californian sherry should, of course, not be confused with the real Sherry, which can come only from the region of Jerez de la Frontera in Spain.

Californian 'sherry'

The 'sherry'-type wine has the characteristic nutty flavour obtained through processes of ageing and warm temperatures. In California many different regions are used to make these wines. The best quality grape for the purpose is the Palomino or Napa Golden Chasselas (not a real Chasselas). Authentic Spanish Sherry is made almost entirely from the Palomino. This grape has become a varietal in California and is used for the best sherries, although most growers continue with such varieties as the Flame Tokay, Mission, Thompson Seedless, and Feher Szagos, which produce lesser wines of the type.

Three styles of sherry-type wines are produced in California: a dry aperitif with a sugar content of from 0% to 2½%; Californian 'sherry', with 2½%–4% of sugar; and a sweet Creme 'sherry' with over 4%. All these wines have about 20% of alcohol.

Most of the Californian 'sherry' is made by heating the fortified wine in concrete or steel tanks for from two to six months, at temperatures varying from 120° to 140°F. (49° to 60°C.). It is then stored in small oak barrels, to be aged for six months—or longer, in the case of better-quality wines.

Scarcely any 'sherry' is made by the Spanish 'flor' method, although some is produced for blending purposes by a newly developed method known as the 'submerged flor' technique. The finest 'sherries' of the region are allowed to mature for a considerable time in their oak casks.

Californian vermouth

There are two kinds of vermouth—the dry French type (pale amber) and the sweet Italian type (dark amber). The first step in the making of Californian vermouth is to select and age neutral white wines. These are then flavoured with herbs and other aromatic substances (usually imported), which are introduced into the wine—or an infusion of aromatic herbs is added to the basic fortified wine and the mixture is aged in barrel. Vermouth producers all have their secret formulæ containing sometimes as many as fifty different herbs, roots, seeds, barks, flowers, dried fruit, wormwood, etc. Vermouth ranges from 15% to 20% in alcoholic content—a very light type has recently become popular in California and elsewhere in the United States.

Dessert Wines

Dessert wines generally have an alcoholic content of about 20% and range from medium-sweet to sweet. There are four distinct Californian dessert wines—'port', 'white port', muscatel, and 'tokay'. Unfortunately, place-name controls are particularly negligent where Californian dessert wines are concerned; but there are a few bearing such varietal names as Palomino, Muscat de Frontignan, and Tinta port varieties which are usually of better quality. The hot interior valleys produce the best grapes for dessert wines.

Californian 'port'

This is made from many grapes—but rarely from those which go into genuine Port. Carignane, Petite-Syrah, Trousseau, Grenache, Valdepeñas, and Zinfandel are most commonly used in Californian ports; while Alicante-Bouschet, Alicante Ganzin, and Salvador are added, for the dark colour they contribute in blending. Californian port is usually deep red in colour, fruity, and heavy-bodied. It ranges from 8% to 14% natural grape sugar content and is usually sweeter and darker in colour than the Ports from Portugal. There is also a lighter-coloured, lighter-bodied wine known as tawny port. Ficklin is by far the outstanding producer of port in California.

Californian ports, like other dessert wines, thrive best in the warmer regions. The better quality wines are made with Tinta Madeira, Tinta Cão, and Touriga (choice Portuguese grape varieties). A great deal of credit must go to the Ficklin Vineyard (*q.v.*) of Madera in Madera County, which is producing the best 'port-type' wines in California, using the methods employed in Portugal (*see* PORT).

White 'port'

The California style is made from the Thompson Seedless, actually a white table grape, and from Grenache and Mission red grapes which are fermented without the skins, so that the colour may be pale. It is a sweet wine (10% to 15% natural grape sugar content), straw-coloured, and made, unfortunately, from any number or quality of grape varieties.

Californian Muscatel

This is a dessert wine made from Muscat grapes (which are used also for a light Muscat white table wine). Muscatels, which have an unmistakable aroma and flavour, are, on the whole, a drug on the market, and are only rarely agreeable wines. They range in colour from golden and dark amber to red, and in sweetness from 10% to 15% natural grape sugar content. These muscatels are sometimes sold as cheap substitutes for whiskey, especially in monopoly state stores.

The better varieties of grapes are used in the making of Muscats as table wines, which can be considered as finer wines. The white grapes used are the Muscat de Frontignan (sometimes called Muscat Canelli in California) and Malvasia Bianca, while the red grapes are Malvasia and Aleatico.

Most Muscatels are made from the Muscat of Alexandria (also a table grape) and have a golden colour, but there are at least seven other Muscat grape varieties used in California. In the Santa Clara Valley, the Black Muscat or Muscat Hamburg is grown. Californian Muscat varieties find their proper home in the warm climate of the San Joaquin Valley region where the grapes attain a high sugar content.

California 'tokay'

This is made by blending other dessert wines, such as port, angelica, and sherry, and bears no relationship to Hungarian Tokay wines, nor is it necessarily made from the Flame Tokay, a table grape planted extensively in the Lodi area. This tokay ranges from 7% to 10% natural grape sugar content, and has a slightly nutty flavour reminiscent of Sherry. The colour of Californian tokay is amber-pink; it is a wine of less than average quality and is the lowest in production of the better-known dessert wines.

Angelica is an original Californian wine and is not one for Californians to be proud of. This white dessert wine, very sweet and straw-coloured, and blended with brandy, is more of a cordial than a wine. The Mission grape and the cheaper Grenache—the Spanish variety—go into the making of the highly fruity Angelica. 'Winos' (those who get drunk on cheap dessert wines) usually buy Angelica in small bottles.

Aleatico wine has the spicy, fruity flavour of the Aleatico grape, and resembles the red muscatels. There is also an Aleatico table wine, inferior and rarely to be found.

'*Malaga*' in California is just a name referring to a cordial wine of no particular distinction, and quite unconnected with the Málaga of Spain.

Berry wines in California have the distinct taste of the berries used in such sweet, fruity wines as blackberry, raspberry, etc. The Sacramento Valley area near Elk Grove is a noted berry-wine producing region.

Other dessert wines include Californian grenache, (made from the Grenache grape in the San Joaquin Valley); Californian marsala, rarely found on the market, and having nothing in common with the Marsala from Sicily; and Californian madeira, which is usually a poor imitation of genuine Madeira.

One of the better Californian appetizer wines is the Palomino, a varietal containing 17% alcohol per volume. It is very much like a Californian sherry, but owing to its lower alcoholic content, the State Law does not allow it to take the name. 19·5% alcoholic content must go into the making of 'sherry'-type wines. Californian legislators would be well advised to taste the best dry Sherries of Spain which when sold in their homeland rarely exceed 17·5% alcoholic content.

SPARKLING WINES

These may be red, pink, or white, and their alcoholic content ranges from 10% to 14% by volume. The most popular sparkling types in California are 'champagne' and 'sparkling burgundy'. Although no wines outside France have any right to the title of 'champagne', some of the Californian sparkling wines are made by the true Champagne method in which secondary fermentation takes place in the bottle. When this happens, the wine is allowed to bear the label of bottle-fermented champagne, provided the words 'Californian' or 'American' are added, and a statement that it is a sparkling wine made by the Champagne method in California, the state of New York, etc. The alternative method is the Charmat process, in which secondary fermentation takes place in bulk in huge glass-lined vats.

In France, however, only bottle-fermented sparkling wine is allowed to be authentic Champagne (*q.v.*) and only if it has been made in the Champagne region.

Californian 'champagnes' are produced throughout the state, but the finest come from the cooler regions —the counties of Sonoma, Santa Clara, Napa, and Alameda. Sweeter types come from the Cucamonga district in southern California; bulk-process types are made in both these regions, as well as in the inland valley. Bottle-fermented types are mostly found in the areas which produce fine table wines: the Almadén Vineyards of Los Gatos (Santa Clara Valley), F. Korbel & Bros. of Guerneville (Sonoma County), Weibel Champagne Vineyards of Mission San José (southern Alameda County), Hans Kornell, and Beaulieu Vineyards are probably the best champagne producers in California.

Pinot Noir and Pinot Chardonnay, the grapes that go into the making of French Champagnes, yield the best quality; other good grapes for Californian champagnes are the Pinot Blanc, Sémillon, Sauvignon Blanc, White Riesling, and Folle Blanche. Some of the inferior grape varieties are the Sauvignon Vert, Burger, French Colombard, and Green Hungarian. Californian champagnes range from dry to sweet and are dosed with sugar in the usual way; but a real *brut* champagne is rare in California (*see* CHAMPAGNE).

Pink champagnes from California may be either bottle-fermented or bulk-processed (the Government requires labels to designate bulk-process champagnes as well as the bottle-fermented types).

Of the sparkling wines, Sparkling California 'burgundy', after champagne the most popular in the country, is red wine made sparkling by either of the two methods used for champagnes. It is usually semi-sweet or sweet, and produced from Pinot Noir, Carignane, Mondeuse, and Petite-Syrah. Of the sparkling wines, moselle- and sauternes-types are treated by the Champagne method and are made from the table wines bearing the same names. Sparkling muscats are made from light Muscat wines, usually Muscat Canelli (Muscat de Frontignan): they tend to be very sweet and are sometimes sold under the Italian name 'Moscato Spumante'. Another wine is made from the Malvasia Bianca which produces a sweet Muscat-flavoured sparkling wine.

Californian carbonated wines are made to sparkle by artificial carbonation and under Californian law must be designated as such. Sometimes known as effervescent wines, they are mass-produced and much cheaper than the relatively better quality and naturally fermented sparkling wines. A limited quantity of red and white, dry and sweet wines is marketed as carbonated burgundy, carbonated moselle, carbonated sauterne, etc.

Grape Varieties

A few of the red-wine grape varieties successfully planted in California are the Cabernet Sauvignon (sometimes referred to simply as Cabernet but not to be confused with the Cabernet Franc), Pinot Noir, Gamay Beaujolais, Grenache, Barbera, and Zinfandel. Some of the recommended white grape varieties are the Pinot Chardonnay or Chardonnay, Sauvignon Blanc, Sémillon, Pinot Blanc, White Pinot, White or Johannisberger Riesling (sometimes referred to as Riesling), Sylvaner or Franken Riesling, and Traminer (also called the Red Traminer).

Leading Red Wine Grapes

Cabernet Sauvignon. Of the large number of red-wine grape varieties, very few have been recommended for planting in California. Of those that have passed rigorous tests, the Cabernet Sauvignon is still the most valuable: it is the best adapted to the cooler parts of the coastal valleys and usually ripens about mid-season; it matures more slowly than the same variety in the Bordeaux region, and produces a fuller, heavier wine. In California, the Cabernet lacks bouquet, but is known to have produced, in tiny quantities, some remarkably great wines which can compare with some of the better red wines anywhere in the world. The Cabernet Sauvignon from northern California has out-produced in terms of quality some of the best red wines of Italy, Spain, and Portugal and attains an even fuller wine than those made from the same variety in Chile. In the suitable northern coastal regions it gives a wine of pronounced varietal flavour, high acidity, and good colour, holding its own with some of the better Bordeaux. Cabernet Sauvignon attains its highest quality after ageing; but only recently have most Californian growers come to realize that their table wines improve with bottle age—and so more matured red Cabernet Sauvignons are appearing on the market. As the price goes up, the value goes down.

Varietal wines, according to Californian wine laws, can bear on the label the name of the grape variety provided the wine is made out of a minimum of 51% of that particular grape variety.

Pinot Noir. This grape is recommended for planting in the cooler northern regions. It is the outstanding variety of Burgundy and in California it is sometimes confused with Pinot Meunier, Pinot Pernand, and Pinot St. Georges (which is not a real Pinot). It ripens early and is not always easy in fermentation and ageing. The Pinot Noir, although an excellent variety from which some very good wines have been made, does not produce as successfully in California as does the Cabernet Sauvignon.

Gamay Beaujolais. Although this grape, which is, generally speaking, a variety of the Pinot Noir family, is a little easier to handle than the Pinot Noir, it needs a great deal of attention. Like the Pinot Noir, it ripens early and improper handling will spoil the wine. The true Gamay, the variety which is associated with the red Beaujolais of France, is found here mainly in Napa, where it has produced delightful light wines which have in some instances possessed the much-needed bouquet lacking in many Californian wines. In the parts of the Napa Valley where the late-ripening variety of the Gamay (the Napa Gamay) is produced, it differs from the Gamay Beaujolais in flavour and aroma.

Grenache. The Grenache is a good producer, strong and resistant to disease—a much sought-after variety. The grape, which is successful in the making of Tavel rosé in the Rhône Valley, is often used for rosés in California also, because of its pinkish colour. The Grenache Rosé from the Almadén Vineyards in the Santa Clara Valley is the most popular of its kind.

Barbera. In Italy, Barbera at its best is sometimes likened to the Nebbiolo and ages almost as well; in California, it is a high-acid variety of only average vigour and production. Blending is not recommended, but with ageing and special care Barbera may yet yield a wine comparable with some of those in Piedmont. It does best in the coastal valleys and the intermediate Central Valley region, where it produces a full-bodied, honest wine.

Zinfandel. This is the most widely-planted red-grape variety in California; its exact origin is unknown and it is not grown extensively in any other country. It is subject to mildew and any excessive humidity or irrigation may lead to rotting; generally it is harvested early and finds a growing place in practically all of the regions of California, although the best dry wines of this variety are made in the cooler areas. Zinfandel, a very productive variety, produces some pleasant, straightforward wines, and its multiple appeal of bouquet, good colour, and wholesome aroma and flavour account for its popularity. A red and a rosé wine can be made from the Zinfandel.

Three more red wine grape varieties of some distinction are Ruby Cabernet, Tannat, and Grignolino. These are lesser-known varietals and their full potential has not yet been realized in the Californian vineyards.

Ruby Cabernet. This is a new hybrid developed by the California Agricultural Experimental Station. It has shown itself to be a good producer with a high acid content.

Tannat. This variety, rare in California, is grown in the French Pyrenees where for hundreds of years, in the vineyards of Madiran, it has produced a deep-coloured, full-bodied wine. It is a vigorous grape of moderate productivity, not as rich in quality as Cabernet Sauvignon or Pinot Noir but, planted in the cooler regions, it is quite capable of producing a pleasant wine. When properly aged it improves in quality, giving a better-balanced, full-flavoured wine with a distinctive aroma. Tannat is very little grown in California where it easily might find a future home.

Grignolino. This grape is one of the several Californian varieties which are native to Piedmont in Italy. It produces a highly characteristic wine ranging from orange-pink to orange-red in colour, and it is sometimes bottled as a natural rosé. Grignolino has a unique aroma and an exceptionally high tannin content and, to be at its best, should be aged for at least three years. It flourishes in the warmer regions.

Less Important Red Wine Grapes

Some of the other red wine varieties that produce heavily but are not fine grapes are Alicante-Bouschet, Carignane, Petite-Syrah, and Refosco. The Alicante-Bouschet is a large producer of common wine; unfortunately, too much is still grown in California and finds it way into the so-called burgundies, clarets, and chiantis of the middle and southern regions. Carignane, which is not bad in a good soil, is heavily produced in the warmer regions and often used in blending. Petite-Syrah, a superior variety, is favoured in Napa.

Leading White Wine Grapes

Fine dry white wine varieties are found mainly in the northern coastal and cooler regions of California.

Pinot Chardonnay or Chardonnay. This is not a good producer generally; but it is the grape of French Chablis and the true white Burgundies, Meursault, and Montrachet. The Chardonnay has all the virtues needed to produce good wine. It ripens well, particularly in the cooler regions, and attains an excellent balance of sugar and acid. Because it adapts itself so well in the cooler parts of Alameda, Napa, and Santa Clara counties, it makes the finest white wines of California. The cultivation of the Chardonnay is not an easy task, but the results seem to be worth the trouble. It produces a blander wine in California by not attaining the richness it has in France, and it has a different bouquet here.

Sauvignon Blanc. This is the principal grape variety used in the production of the white Graves of France, and, with the Sémillon, it is the base of all the great Sauternes. It is used extensively in France for Pouilly-Fumé, Sancerre, and for Chavignol in the Cher. In California, this variety thrives particularly well in the North Coast regions. It is an early-ripening vine which produces better with age, becoming more vigorous as the years roll on. As in the French Sauternes, the Sauvignon Blanc is blended with Sémillon—plus Muscadelle of Bordelais—to produce a California-type sauterne. This is an exceptional wine, rich and aromatic. The blend with Sémillon is usually preferred to the wine of either variety used alone.

The Sauvignon Blanc should not be confused with the Sauvignon Vert (Colombard), an inferior grape variety.

Sémillon. This is another variety best suited to the North Coast regions. The dryness of the Californian climate does not permit the noble rot—the *pourriture noble* found in the French plantings for Sauternes—to set in while the grapes are ripening, nor does the mature wine have the aroma and flavour of French Sauternes. (This is an excellent reason why wines made with Sémillon from California should not be called sauternes. Sémillon is one of the world's finest grapes and is quite capable of making an original dry or sweet wine in California.) When grown in the warmer regions it produces a natural sweet wine low in acid.

Pinot Blanc. This is the grape variety used in the making of many white French Burgundies and a few Alsatian wines. In California, it seems to preserve its ancestral virtues, although until now it has not been widely planted. It has a good quality, and is a strong, disease-resistant grape with a distinction of its own. Its productivity is rather higher than that of the Pinot Chardonnay, but it rarely exceeds 3 short tons (2·68 long tons) per acre. The Pinot Blanc has often been confused with the Chardonnay, but many experts consider the Chardonnay an entirely different variety and not a true Pinot at all. Tests have shown that the Pinot Blanc is beginning to do well in the slightly warmer regions as well as in the cooler districts.

White Pinot. This variety is also known as the Chenin Blanc and should not be confused with Pinot Blanc. The White Pinot produces and adapts well to regions varying from slightly cool to warm. In France this variety, known as Pineau de la Loire as well as Chenin Blanc, produces delightful white wines of which Vouvray and Saumur are the most familiar. It is above average in quality but lacks the distinction of Pinot Blanc. White Pinot is versatile, since it sometimes produces a fresh, light, fruity wine, slightly sparkling, and at other times it is apt to make a much sweeter wine, according to the whim of the vintner.

Riesling. The Riesling, or White Riesling, or Johannisberger Riesling, is responsible for the outstanding reputation of all the famous wines of the Rhine and Moselle Valleys as well as most of the fine Alsatian wines. It performs at its best under relatively cool conditions, which California's somewhat Mediterranean climate cannot quite give. The Riesling is one of the finest grape varieties in the world and produces throughout Europe (except in the Mediterranean region) a wine of excellent quality. The cooler parts of California produce a wine above average, but lacking the balance and delicacy of the Riesling wines of Europe. In the North Coast region of California, it produces a little better than the Chardonnay and ripens much later.

Sylvaner. In California this variety is also known as the Franken Riesling. In the valleys of the Rhine and the Moselle, and in Alsace, it is grown only where the Riesling does not produce well. Its wine is generally of good character and balance, and above average in California where it does relatively better than the Riesling (Johannisberger Riesling) when planted in a slightly cool to warm district. Sylvaner is a delicate, early-maturing grape with a certain distinction of character and a good balance of sugar and acid. Light and dry, the wine is usually drunk when it is quite young.

Traminer. The 'Red' Traminer is often favourably compared to the very best Rieslings when grown in the better parts of Alsace and the Jura Mountains in France. In the cooler parts of California it produces a wine with a distinctive, delicate aroma and proper balance. It is also called the Red Traminer because of the red flush of the ripening grape. The Krug Winery of St. Helena in Napa Valley produces a small quantity of superior Traminer wine. Selected strains of the Traminer are called Gewürz-Traminer or Gewürztraminer in Alsace and Germany. It has an unmistakable bouquet and spiciness.

Less Important White Wine Grapes

Some of the other dry white wine grape varieties, widely produced but lacking in distinction, are the French Colombard, Folle Blanche, Burger, and Sauvignon Vert.

The Burger is extensively planted in California, chiefly for its high production and a supposedly neutral character which allows it to 'stretch' other wines of superior quality. The Sauvignon Vert, another coarse heavy grape, is frequently substituted in blending for the Sauvignon Blanc. The Sauvignon Vert is sometimes called Colombard, which should not be confused with the French Colombard. The latter, formerly called West's Prolific or Winkler (after Dr. A. J. Winkler, Professor of Viticulture of the University of California) is a vigorous, highly-productive grape of high acid content used for blending in the chablis-type and Rhine-type of Californian wines. Sauvignon Vert, French Colombard, Burger, and Folle Blanche are favourably grown in the warmer inland valley regions.

It is safe to say that the growers in California are still experimenting and searching for land which may potentially be better than any that has yet been found in the country. A good grape grown in suitable soil and with favourable climate will produce a fine wine. Excellent varieties are available, better soils will probably be found, and with proper care choice wines will result.

There are times when the wine-maker has little choice in the varieties of grapes he can use, but must take those which are available. In such cases, it is advisable to avoid low-acid grapes such as the Palomino (Napa Golden Chasselas), Sauvignon Vert, Burger, etc. When there is little choice, it is better to choose grapes from a cooler region and from mature vines rather than young vines. But at all times, the consumer should be informed as to what he is getting by a varietal label; in this way wines will gain a better reputation and the wine-maker a better market.

WASHINGTON AND OREGON

Washington has two different vineyard regions, each presenting entirely different characteristics. The inland Yakima Valley region, in north-central Washington, offers one of the few places outside California where European grapevines can flourish. Much of the land is irrigated and much of the 'wine' is made from berries of various sorts, but grapes are also grown. Sylvaner, Pinot Blanc, Pinot Noir, Zinfandel, Carignane, Gutedel, and Muscat of Alexandria are among the more widely planted varieties. Washington's other region, the 'bay' area fronting Puget Sound, is planted with native vines. Catawba, Delaware, Niagara, and Norton are fairly numerous. The Island Belle or Campbell's Early is also to be found, despite the blatant mediocrity of the wine from its grapes. There are some indications that Washington growers are becoming interested in hybrid vines too, and this development may promise a bright future.

The State of Oregon is potentially a fine wine producing region of the United States, as it is one of the few where *Vitis vinifera* will grow successfully.

Amertume

Bitterness in wine, when it throws a deposit and turns acid.

See CHAPTER NINE, p. 53.

Aminæan Wine

One of the most lasting and famous of the Augustan era, to which 'even the royal Phanæan' paid homage. (Virgil *Georgics II.*)

See CLASSICAL WINES.

Ammerschwihr

Wine town in Alsace (*q.v.*).

Amontillado

A kind of Spanish Sherry, not so pale in colour as the Finos and with more bouquet. It is naturally dry; but for the Anglo-Saxon trade sweeter wine, made from the Pedro Ximénez grape, is often added to it.

See SHERRY.

Amoroso

Sweetened Oloroso Sherry prepared for the British market. Unknown in Spain.

See SHERRY.

Ampelidaceæ

Botanical family to which the grapevine belongs. Of the ten genera of the family only one, the genus

Vitis, is important in wine-making, although others are capable of producing grapes. *Vitis* embraces two sub-genera, *Euvites* and *Muscadinia*, and numerous species. Of these, *vinifera* is the most important, for it yields the great wines of the world. Native to Europe, it has been transplanted to other continents.

See CHAPTER EIGHT, p. 29.

Amphora

A two-handled vessel—pitcher or jar—used in ancient times for holding wine or oil.

See CLASSICAL WINES.

Angelica

1. A sweet yellow liqueur, somewhat similar to Chartreuse, made in the Basque country.

2. A very sweet Californian mixture of partially fermented grape-juice and brandy.

Château Angludet

Bordeaux red wine. District: Haut-Médoc, France. Commune: Cantenac-Margaux.

Rated an Exceptional Growth (*Cru Exceptionnel*), just below Fifth Growth (*Cinquième Cru*), in 1855. The vineyard was going through a bad period then, for it had in earlier times always been considered at least equal to a Fourth Growth (*Quatrième Cru*). Recently, owned and run by the son-in-law of the owners of Château Coutet, it is now the property of the Sichel family, which has restored part of the vineyard. Angludet deserves a higher classification. Ever since the turn of the century this wine has been very popular in England, and it is so still.

Characteristics. Because of recent re-planting, this vineyard is not quite in the class of some of those which surround it. The wine will be hard because of the large quantity of young vines; but eventually, thanks to its excellent soil, it will regain the quality that made it famous.

Vineyard area: 50 acres.

Average production: 5,000 cases.

Angola Wine

Palm sap fermented in West Africa.

Angostura

Rum-based bitters made in Trinidad, from a formula still the secret of the Siegert family, heirs of the inventor. Dr. Siegert was a Frenchman who became Surgeon-General to Simón Bolivar during the liberation of South America. He developed his bitters, from various herbs and plants, to counteract the enervating effect of the tropical climate. The product proved so popular that in the early nineteenth century he founded the firm which still manufactures it.

Anis

Popular French and Spanish liqueur and aperitif. The dominant taste derives from the seeds of the star anise plant (an important ingredient of Absinthe) whose pods resemble starfish. Anis was developed as a substitute for absinthe (*q.v.*) and, like absinthe, can be drunk diluted with water, turning cloudy with a pale greenish tinge when the water is added. A similar drink is pastis (*q.v.*). The difference between the two is that liquorice replaces aniseed as the principal flavouring ingredient of pastis. One of the best-known brands of anis is that of the firm of Pernod, known as Pernod 45, although Ricard has now become the best-selling French aperitif of this type. The anis liqueur is the most popular of all the cordials in Spain.

Anisette

Liqueur of aniseed flavour. A well-known formula is said to have been confided by a West Indian traveller to Marie Brizard of Bordeaux.

Anjou

White, rosé, and red wines. District: Loire Valley, France.

There are over 14,000 wine producers in the historic province of Anjou (now the department of Maine-et-Loire) which embraces a large vineyard area on the slopes west of Touraine and rising from the left bank of the Loire. Anjou and Touraine are alike in many ways: the hills around Saumur are made of the same chalky limestone deposit as those at Vouvray, and in both districts the wine is aged in caves dug deep into the hillside. In Anjou, west and south of Angers, however, the shallow soil covering a bed of hard rock resembles that of Brittany. The château country proper is within Touraine, but in Anjou also the wide River Loire flows through a peaceful green countryside, past old manors and castles, relics of the days when the Plantagenet Kings of England were also Counts of Anjou. In the thirteenth century the wines were very popular in England. Later on, when the English were importing mainly Bordeaux, the people of the Netherlands were the biggest buyers, sailing up the river as far as Rochefort and Saumur to collect the barrels. In those days, the best wines were saved for the foreign trade and the lesser ones sent to Paris.

The Anjou wines, like those from other parts of the Loire Valley, are fresh and sprightly; even the lesser growths are often charming, but these are seldom seen outside their native region. Best known abroad are now the Muscadet and the Anjou rosés.

Three-fifths of the 4 to $5\frac{1}{2}$ million imp. gallons ($4\frac{3}{4}$–$6\frac{1}{2}$ million U.S.) of wine produced annually in Anjou is white, and rosé makes up most of the remaining quantity, although a small amount of relatively minor red wines is produced also. The best Angevin white wines are sweet, as were the vast majority at one time; but changes in taste have converted many growers to vinifying their wines at least comparatively dry, and this trend is healthy for Anjou. Those vineyards capable of producing natural sweet wines continue to do so; others—where doses of sugar once had to be added to impart the requisite sweetness—have turned to drier and better wines. A percentage of the annual output is made into sparkling wine, especially in and around Saumur, but the finest Angevin remains non-sparkling.

Soil and Vines

It has already been stated that the region divides into two basic types of soil: chalky clay around Saumur and along the slopes of the little Loir River; and a hard schist covered with a thin layer of flinty clay elsewhere. This is so thin that growers are often forced to use dynamite to loosen the earth in which to plant their vines—or, if not dynamite, then many weary hours with a pickaxe.

The only grape allowed for fine white wine is Chenin Blanc, a standard in Anjou since the ninth century. Red wines—made principally in Saumur in the communes of Souzay, Champigny, Chacé, Dampierre, and Varrains, as well as in Saint-Cyr-en-Bourg, Brézé, and Brain-sur-Allonnes—come from Cabernet Franc grapes with some Cabernet Sauvignon, and ever-decreasing amounts of Pineau d'Aunis, which is giving way to the Cabernets. Two kinds of rosé are produced: Rosé d'Anjou from Groslot, Gamay, Cot, Noble, and Pineau d'Aunis grapes; and Rosé de Cabernet, entirely from Cabernet grapes. The latter is the better—fruitier, fresher, cleaner-tasting and with a more appealing colour. It tends, also, to be higher in alcohol, the legal minimum being 10%. Some of the Anjou rosés are dry, others are sweet. There is a growing tendency for the ordinary consumer in the region itself to ask for a sweeter pink wine.

Only about a third of the wine is labelled Anjou. The rest (including the best) bears the name of one of the sub-districts with the Appellation Contrôlée, and these names are more likely to be found on bottles sent abroad.

Angevin Sub-districts

Coteaux de la Loire

This area, on both banks of the river, is one of the best and most well-known in Anjou. In soils of varying consistency and quality, it grows Chenin Blanc grapes which give way, west of Montjean, to the Muscadet. The wines, therefore, also vary; sweet yet in general drier than those of the Layon district, they are lively and well made. A few, rather sharp when young, take some time to come round. Others will be mature after years in bottle.

Savennières, an attractive village and the best wine-town on these slopes, has its own Appellation Contrôlée. The wines incline to dryness, are high in alcohol and slow to mature. The leading vineyards are La Coulée-de-Serrant, La Roche-aux-Moines, both of which make fine, very elegant wines; Château de Savennières, Château d'Epiré, Château de la Bizolière, Clos du Papillon.

Other communes worth noting are Bouchemaine, La Possonnière, Saint-Georges-sur-Loire, Champtocé and Ingrandes, Montjean, La Pommeraye, and part of Chalonnes.

Coteaux du Layon

This is the other leading district of the region. Thirty miles of vineyard are scattered along the banks of the little stream, the Layon, which descends from the hills near Les Verchers to meander through a string of wine-growing villages until, just above Chalonnes, it enters the Loire. The wines are high in alcohol, and some of the best vineyards are picked only after the *pourriture noble* has set in. These sweet wines are probably the finest of all the sweet wines of Anjou, but dry white wines, also, are made in the area. The sweet whites are fuller in body and longer lasting than any from the Coteaux de la Loire.

Bonnezeaux. This great growth of the region has its own Appellation Contrôlée and ranks almost as a sub-district on its own. The vineyards, in the commune of Thouarcé, sprawl down the slopes towards the river bank, and a solitary windmill stands guard above—once there were three. They produce a limited quantity of sweet white wine, soft and fruity.

Quarts de Chaume. Almost equally distinguished (indeed, some say it is really the best of the Layon slopes) is the sweet wine from this vineyard, near the village of Chaume in the commune of Rochefort. It resembles a sweet Vouvray, and is more flowery than a Sauternes. In lightness and bouquet, it is unique, and yet in most years its alcoholic content is between 13% and 16%. At one time, the

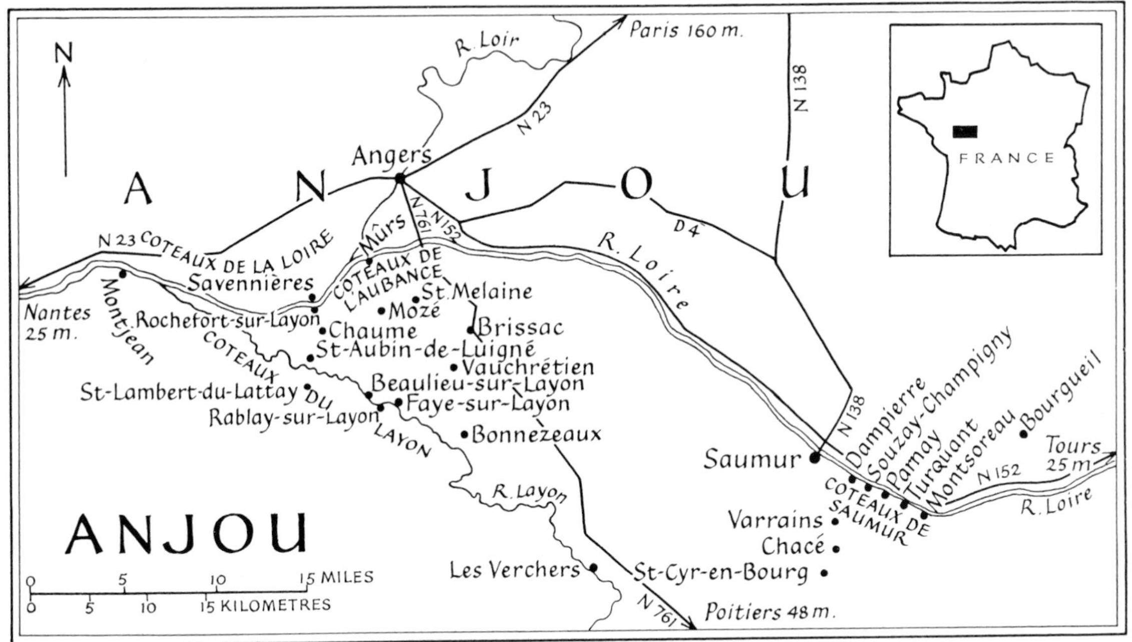

vineyards belonged to a single proprietor, who rented it out in return for a quarter share of each vintage. He reserved the right to choose which section of the vineyard his quarter should come from, and so it came to be called Quart de Chaume.

Six more communes in this area add their names to the Appellation Contrôlée of Coteaux du Layon. These are Beaulieu-sur-Layon, Faye d'Anjou, Rablay-sur-Layon, Rochefort-sur-Layon, Saint-Aubin-de Luigné, and Saint-Lambert-du-Lattay.

From the middle reaches of the Layon comes a quite considerable quantity of white wine permitted the more general Appellation Anjou, although this is predominantly a district for vin rosé.

Coteaux de l'Aubance

The wines of this small district north of the Coteaux du Layon are better known in their own part of the country than elsewhere. Yet they are pleasant, typical Anjou wines. Most of them are white, but rosé is produced as well. The whites have not all the rich mellowness of a wine from the slopes of the Loire or the Layon, but are often outstanding—especially the medium dry, which have character and an agreeable bouquet. The leading communes are Brissac (making mainly good pink wines from Cabernet and Groslot grapes); Vauchrétien, producer of good white wines; Saint-Jean-des-Mauvrets, Juigné-sur-Loire, Saint-Melaine, Soulaines, Mozé, Mûrs, and Denée, which is near Rochefort and makes very similar wines.

Coteaux du Loir

A district on a small tributary of the River Loire. The wines are white and pleasant, red and indifferent, rosé and charming.

Saumur and Coteaux de Saumur

The old town of Saumur is dominated by a rambling castle which has been turned into an equestrian museum—this is where the cavalry school of the French army is stationed. The riverside bluffs are tunnelled with vast caves, perfect for ageing, and the sweeter white growths make a sparkling wine. A good deal of the wine, however, is dry or semi-dry, with 10% to 13% of alcohol, and sometimes it is slightly *crémeux*.

The sparkling Loire wines preserve their own flavour; they are different from Champagne, and Saumur is overpriced if it costs the same—the producers suffer from the fact that it is usually taxed as much. Made of two-thirds Chenin Blanc and one-third Cabernet, it is fuller and heavier than sparkling Vouvray.

Thirty-seven communes share the Appellation Saumur in the department of Vienne. They include Pouançay, Berrie, Saint-Leger-de-Montbrillais, Ternay, and Ranton.

On the Coteaux de Saumur, with its châteaux, its chalky hills, and cave dwellings, Dampierre is the leading commune, with a good production of two-thirds white wine, one-third red and rosé. Souzay-

Champigny, Parnay, and Turquant make fresh, fruity wines; the white wine of Montsoreau has a definite character. Varrains and Chacé are better known for their rosé and red wines than for their smaller harvest of white; Saint-Cyr-en-Bourg makes more white; Brézé, Epieds, and Saix do quite well with their red wines, but the white have the greater reputation.

Muscadet

Far down the Loire, near Nantes, these vineyards, the only ones in Brittany to be classified, are planted in muscadet grapes—the same as the Melon of Burgundy. Those vineyards which grow on the slopes of the Loire are small, planted on the river shores. The pale, light, dry wines—very agreeable with oysters and sea-food—are at their driest and most robust in this section.

See under individual headings.

Anthracnose

A vine disease of European origin.

See CHAPTER EIGHT, p. 37.

Apoplexy

A spectacular vine malady.

See CHAPTER EIGHT, p. 37.

Appellation d'Origine

Guaranteed place-name for a French wine. Champagne, for example, is a name which can properly be applied only to the products of certain approved vineyards and wine-making processes inside that region. No other sparkling wine (even when made by the authentic Champagne process) has a right to the name; and in France this rule is enforced by the laws of Appellation d'Origine. For an account of the events and legislation which led to the formulation of these laws, and of further controls over the viticultural and vinicultural standards essential for the production of fine wines, see Appellation d'Origine Contrôlée, *below*.

Appellation d'Origine Contrôlée (Control Laws)

Literally 'controlled place of origin'; on a bottle of French wine the guarantee not only of place of origin but of the quality standards traditionally associated with wines from that place. These control laws represent the most flexible, most enlightened, and most effective body of legislation existing at present for the protection of fine wines.

How the Laws work

Fine wines always bear the stamp of the place where the grapes were grown and—given the conditions necessary for producing fine wines—the more restricted the place, the better the wine. Recognizing this fact, the Frenchman drew his control laws as a series of concentric circles, selecting more *élite* terrain and stiffening the wine's minimum requirements as he narrowed the circles. The result: the more specific the name or *appellation*, the higher the guarantee of quality.

A typical example is the large Bordeaux wine region in south-west France. Imagine a great circle drawn around the city of Bordeaux and the land surrounding it. Everything within this circle (excepting land obviously unfit for the purpose) has the right to grow grapes for Bordeaux. Just north-west of the city—but within the circle—is the district of the Haut-Médoc; to the south-east are Graves, Barsac, and Sauternes; to the north-east, Saint-Émilion and Pomerol. These are all districts represented by smaller circles within Bordeaux, and although their wines have the right to bear the more general name, they will always take the more specific if they can qualify for it. Within these smaller circles, the terrain is finer, the requirements higher, and the wines better. The contraction of the circles does not end there. Within, for example, the Haut-Médoc, yet smaller circles represent specific towns or communes, the best of which are Margaux, Saint-Julien, Pauillac, and Saint-Estèphe. Again, growers always choose the most specific name for which their wines qualify, and again the quality of the wines is raised and the characteristics more specifically determined. The system reaches its logical conclusion in Burgundy where certain superb vineyards (one—La Romanée—a mere 2·1 acres) have special, separate *appellations* and highly stringent requirements for their magnificent wines.

The system has the confidence of both grower and consumer and thus prices for wines with specific names are higher than for those with general names, and the more specific, the higher. It is to the credit of the French law-makers that such wines are almost invariably worth the increased price.

What is controlled

These laws control every factor that contributes to the wine, every process that may affect it—in fact, every detail literally from the ground up is regulated until the bottle of wine is sold to the consumer or leaves the boundaries of France. An easy and harmonious working relationship between the technical and administrative experts of the Institut National des Appellations d'Origine in Paris and technical experts in each wine region make this complex and seemingly cumbersome system workable. The Institut National des Appellations d'Origine (it is usually referred to as the I.N.A.O.) sets down the broad outline of the controls, the local people contribute the specific points, the Minister of Agriculture makes it law, and the Fraud Inspectors see that the law is carried out. While each control law will be adapted to its specific area, all will contain the following broad general points:

1. *Area of Production.* The geological composition of the soil deemed fit for the production of the wine in question is outlined. The land is then studied and marked out by experts in the region, and only vineyards within the delimited area are permitted to use the name.

2. *Permissible Grapevine(s).* In different soils and under different skies, the same vine will produce grapes of different characteristics. Selection of varieties follows the best traditional practices of each area.

3. *Minimum Alcoholic Content.* Alcohol helps to give wine its staying power—its ability to live long enough to develop into greatness. If vines are allowed to over-produce, the grapes may develop so little sugar that the wine will end up unbalanced, with too little alcohol to match its other characteristics. Stipulation of alcoholic content before enrichment of the wine is thus an assurance of quality.

4. *Viticultural Practices.* Pruning, fertilizing, and the handling in general of the vine show in the quality of the wine. Viticultural practices are closely regulated, hence the type of pruning is specified for each area, with special emphasis on the outlawing of methods which produce huge crops but mediocre fruit.

5. *Permissible Harvest.* Since quality is inversely proportional to quantity, the amount of permissible harvest is specified. This is expressed in hectolitres/hectare (which may be converted into gallons/acre) and usually drops sharply as names get more specific.

6. *Vinicultural Practices.* The traditional wine-making procedures of any region are largely responsible for the reputation of each of the great wines, instilling much of the wine's distinctive character. These have thus been codified into law. Tasting contests have become more frequent, especially in the Bordeaux region.

7. *Distilling.* The I.N.A.O. also controls the fine spirits of France. The procedures that made the fame of these spirits are also formalized into law.

The Evolution of the Laws

The outlook for French wines at the turn of the twentieth century was bleak and unpromising. Phylloxera had invaded France in the middle of the last century, reducing vast areas of vineyard to rows of bare, wooden stumps—resembling huge graveyards. Once-flourishing vineyards were replanted in different crops or in bulk-producing hybrid vines which, more often than not, yielded wine which was common and harsh and of inferior quality. A not uncommon practice, despite strict laws forbidding it, was the addition of sugar and water to grape pomace, or pulp, letting the concoction ferment, and then selling it as wine. Fine wines had been hit as badly as ordinary ones, and in many cases there was no connection between bottle contents and label. Into this chaos the French legislature stepped, in 1905, passing *Lois Administratives* against misrepresentation of the place of origin of any product, and establishing the Fraud Brigade to back them up. In helping to bring the ordinary wines back to standard, the laws were excellent—the pattern for all agricultural controls of place-names, they were often imitated abroad but never equalled; but where fine wines were concerned, they did no more than sketch a plan which, in fact, turned out badly. Nor were matters helped by the more explicit legislation of 1908.

The trouble was that the legislators, whose knowledge of viniculture was mainly theoretical, did not understand that fine wines are produced not only by the place and the soil where they are grown, but also by the grapes planted and the manner in which they are cultivated. In controlling the geographical place of origin without either exacting certain traditional practices of cultivation, or imposing tests of tasting or analysis, they opened the way to two abuses: 1. That wines of great name would be made without the care to which they owed their superlative characteristics. 2. That some proprietors would take advantage of the geographical guarantee to plant grafted hybrid vines in the finest soil, and so produce quantities of inferior wine which, under the letter of the law, were entitled to bear the label of a greater growth.

The legislation of 1908 codified for wines that of 1905. As a result, certain sections of France—including Champagne and Bordeaux—were staked out and only wines from within the delimited areas were allowed the place-names. The delimitations were arbitrary and administrative, again made by the overworked bureaucracy of France, few of whose members were qualified to make such tricky and technical decisions. The results were alarming.

The plain of Champagne extends over several French departments, and by 1908 growers in the Marne and those in the Aube had long been locked in a bitter feud over who had the right to the great wine name. The administration's delimitation was a compromise, intended to please both factions. Like so many decisions of the sort it pleased neither. There was little outcry, however, before 1910. In that year severe frosts ushered in one of the most disastrous harvests in Champagne history and the growers erupted. They said that, had the limits of the region been more tightly drawn, and had the shippers respected the limits, the normal price of grapes would have been higher and the growers would have been able to save enough to tide them over a poor year. As it was, riots broke out in January 1911, and troops had to be sent to restore order. In June, the limits of the region were amended—and again there were riots. The situation was similar—if less violent—in Bordeaux, where growers were equally disgusted with the arbitrary manner of delimiting vineyards. Thus, later in the year, the legislature declared the law unworkable and set it aside, without offering anything to replace it.

Yet the Government was beginning to listen to men like the Baron Le Roy du Boiseaumarié, and Deputy Capus who, ever since 1906, had been fighting for improvements in the Appellation d'Origine. In 1911, a sensible modification of the previous laws was prepared and discussed in the Chamber. The opponents' argument, however, was: 'Can you contest the right of a cultivator to make what use he pleases of the name of his property and the fruits of his soil?' The result was that no reforms were made. Trying again in 1914, Deputy Jenouvrier pointed out the collective character of the Appellation d'Origine: 'The reputation attached to these products is the result of the sustained effort of successive generations; the fruit of their combined labour became famous, and the proprietorial right was thus established for the whole commune or region.'

When, after the war, a new law was passed in 1919, Monsieur Jenouvrier's modification was incorporated; but there was still no clause controlling varieties of grapevine, methods of cultivation, and other guarantees of quality. The results of this law, therefore, were disastrous—the more so since the first Article affirmed that any man who claimed that an Appellation d'Origine was contrary to his interests and right or to customs *locaux, loyaux, et constants* (local, loyal, and constant) could go to law to demand an interdiction. The consequence of this clause was, of course, a great deal of senseless litigation.

The law of 1919 was again interpreted by the courts as applying only to geographical control; and this precipitated a movement to create new and inferior vineyards in delimited areas. Deputy Capus, in his account of the long struggle to obtain the control law as we now know it, recalls the effect of the 1919 Act on his native Barsac, a district of Bordeaux. The sweet, rich, justly famous white wines of Barsac traditionally stem from Sauvignon and Sémillon grapes grown on the hilly sections of the commune. In the valleys and along the *palus*—the moist low land near the River Garonne—the traditional vines had been for red wine, none of it Barsac, all of it ordinary. In the litigation following the law, the courts suddenly discovered that the *palus* is in Barsac and gave it the right to grow the famous white wine, overlooking the fact that legal right could not endow the land with the proper geological conditions. A few growers balked, since the law of 1919 said nothing about vines, but most accepted the ruling and did the legal but improper thing. As Capus said: 'Bad laws make bad citizens.' The vines in the *palus* were rooted out, those for bulk production of white wine were planted or grafted with hybrids, and for the first time Barsac was grown in the *palus*. A further result was that the small-bearing noble vines of the slope could not match the productivity of the newcomers and in some vineyards they were replaced by bulk varieties, often hybrids. So, great seas of wines ranging from mediocre to frightful went to market emblazoned with the famous name. Prices, of course, dropped. So did the reputation of Barsac, and the situation was duplicated in other regions of France. Whenever a local court ruled in favour of the traditionally acceptable land only, the ruling was overthrown by a higher court, farther removed from the mysteries of wines. Fraud had suddenly become respectable.

This state of things was bad for the cultivator as well as for the consumer; the honest man who spent money on his vineyard and worked hard to produce a small quantity of great wine was hit by less scrupulous competitors, turning out far more and far worse wine which would bear the same label of authenticity. Soon the buyers from abroad began to complain that their customers were refusing to pay the prices asked for such inferior stuff; and when the agitators for a stronger law increased their activity, it became clear that public opinion was changing. Monsieur Cheron, the Minister of Agriculture, had been shocked, when he paid a visit to the

Gironde, by the number of vines in the Great Growths (*Grands Crus*) which were being uprooted to make room for the more prolific hybrids; and a Commission was set up to enquire into the affair.

In all these years, the troubles in Champagne had never been settled, and now the two parties appealed to Monsieur Édouard Barthe, President of the Groupe Viticole, to mediate for them. He drew up a plan which fixed satisfactorily both the question of delimitation and also every necessary condition for the production of fine Champagne. This plan, since it had the approval of all the associations of viticulture concerned, was able to be incorporated intact into the new Law of 1927, which added to the regulations of 1919 amendments (1) restricting the place of origin to 'the surface areas comprising communes or parts of communes for the production of wine of the *appellation*'; and (2) forbidding the right of *appellation* to wines produced from hybrids or from any vines other than those traditionally bearing the great wines. This was known as the Appellation Simple. The consequence was that the *palus* and other unsuitable lands dropped back to inferior status and the noble vines returned—in those regions which observed the Law. For one of the Law's weaknesses was that it was optional. Some districts did observe it—in the region of Châteauneuf-du-Pape the Baron Le Roy, a proprietor himself, went further and persuaded the other growers to endorse a plan similar to that accepted in Champagne—but some districts ignored the amendments and went on in the bad old ways.

The Law of 1927, although a great improvement on its predecessors, was still imperfect—because, except in the separate clause dealing with Champagne, it ignored all guarantees of quality except those of soil and place-name: that is, it overlooked the extent of permissible harvest and the minimum alcoholic content of the wine, as well as the necessary standard of vine-tending and wine-making practices.

In spite of the imperfections of the Appellation Simple, it was significant that for the first time the French legislature admitted that the name of a wine embraced something other than geography. The way to the present stricter controls was not to be smooth; but from that point it had been marked out and paved. In 1935 these stricter controls began going into operation, and the fine French wines became the province of a committee, now the Institut National des Appellations d'Origine des Vins et Eaux-de-Vie (the National Institute of Place-names of Wines and Spirits), whose capable hands guide the fortunes of French wines both in France and in some instances abroad.

The Effect of the Laws

In the case of every Appellation Contrôlée that has gone into effect, the result has been an immediate and marked increase in quality. Passage of a control law would cut out the lesser wines, and the grower—conscious that his efforts would be reimbursed—strove for high quality. The existence of an Appellation Contrôlée is of itself immediate evidence that the wine is fine, and the gain is twofold: the grower gets more money for his wine, and the consumer gets better wine for his money. It is only unfortunate that other wine-producing countries have not followed the example more closely. It is as well to understand that it is the place-name which is controlled and not always the wine, i.e. Pommard Appellation Contrôlée means that geographical boundaries and minimum standards have been set up for Pommard. But the controlling of the wine in the bottle is much more difficult, with a limited 'police-force'. Therefore there are still loopholes in the enforcement of authenticity of the wine.

Appellation Simple

'Simple name of origin'; a predecessor of the system of Appellation Contrôlée which at present protects the quality and origin of fine French wines. The earlier law was passed by the French legislature in 1927 and provided a measure of control by regulating the precise area where the grapes could be grown and the type of grape that was permissible. Since this system overlooked the amount of permissible harvest, vine-tending and wine-making practices, and minimum alcoholic content of the wine, it proved generally insufficient, although it is still the rule, with minor modifications, in Alsace.

See APPELLATION D'ORIGINE CONTRÔLÉE.

Apple Brandy

Brandy made from apples; distilled cider. The best French apple brandy is Calvados; the American variety is applejack.

See CALVADOS; APPLEJACK.

Apple Jack

Applejack, strictly speaking, is the American name for apple brandy. Americans do not always speak strictly about applejack, however, since the name applies both to apple brandy, which is a spirit made by the distillation of fermented apple juice, and to a rougher spirit made by a more primitive process. The second method, nowadays confined to a few back-country areas, is to let cider ferment completely, and then to freeze it. Since water freezes at a higher temperature than alcohol, the ice which forms and is skimmed off is almost pure water and the unfrozen liquid left behind is almost pure alcohol. This potent and slightly oily spirit is applejack.

In the early days, both methods were used in making applejack, which was for a long time one of the most popular spirits in America. This was partly, perhaps, because at that time the common drink was cider. This was comparatively low in alcohol (about 6% by volume) and, if contemporary reports are to be believed, the early American liked his liquor as potent as it was plentiful.

Actually, neither cider nor applejack was popular, nor even available, when the first settlers came to America, for the simple reason that there were no apple trees. The English and the Dutch brought beer with them; and the English set about planting hops and barley in New England—where they did not thrive. Then they planted fruit-trees, which flourished exceedingly and began to bear fruit (so it was said) much sooner than they would have done in England, where cider was already being drunk in the sixteenth century, and probably earlier. The word, spelled 'sider' in earlier times, comes from the Hebrew *shekar*; at first it may have meant any strong drink, although by the sixteenth century it was specifically the strong drink made from apple juice.

Since New England had proved to be a poor place for the growing of hops, the taste for beer changed to a liking for cider, for rum—imported from the West Indies and later made in New England from West Indian molasses—and for applejack, which was soon being carried inland by travellers and Indians. As time went on, the Dutch and German settlers in the State of Pennsylvania began brewing beer with great success; and the Scots and the Irish, who arrived early in the eighteenth century, started the whiskey industry; but for a long time after this, the common drink in rural areas was still applejack.

The economic factors which encouraged the Pennsylvania grain-growers to start making whiskey in quantity worked in the same way upon the New England apple growers. Since roads were universally poor, it was risky to try to transport heavy or bulky cargoes, and so both grain and fruit were fermented or distilled. The lighter loads of liquor, much easier to carry, commanded better markets, too. In the cider industry, New England, with Connecticut outstanding, led other producers. The ingenious Connecticut Yankee, in addition to making himself famous by selling wooden nutmegs, proved his adaptability in the field of spirituous beverages. By taking cider, colouring it with Indian corn, and letting it age for three months, he got fairly strong liquor quite like Madeira in colour, and sold it as such to gullible Europeans. How much of this went on is not known, but the practice could not have been extensive, for cider was too much in demand at home to be wasted on others.

One of the strongest beliefs held by the American of revolutionary times was that the drinking of strong spirits was necessary to the health—and, with great gusto, he set about taking care of his health, not infrequently starting with cider or applejack for breakfast and then carrying the jug out to the fields with him. Social events of all kinds, from weddings to funerals, and from church suppers to political rallies, were well supplied with rum, cider (or applejack), or some kind of strong punch, and sometimes with all three at once. At one church function in New England, thirty bowls of punch were drunk before the morning meeting by eighty Christians—and a great deal more of a formidable mixture of drinks that same evening. As stills became easier to buy, many farms set up their own, thus raising applejack to the level of a distilled spirit, although much of the primitive, frozen type was made, too. That the product was powerful is proved by the way it was referred to in the local taverns, where customers would ask for a 'a slug of blue fish-hooks', 'essence of lockjaw', or, after the centre of the trade had moved to New Jersey, for 'Jersey lightning'.

For the making of applejack only the cider from sound, firm, well-matured apples would be chosen. For commercial applejack the product is distilled. The kind of still used in the old days (and often, but not always, found today) was the pot still. In modern applejack-making, the fluid is distilled twice, the first time coming through at about 60° of proof, and the second time at anywhere from 110° to 130° of proof. (In America, a spirit that contains 50% alcohol by volume is said to be at 100° of proof.) Today, after distillation, the applejack is cut with water and grain neutral spirits to bring it down to 85° or 100° proof as the distiller desires—since apples are more expensive than grain, a pure applejack would cost the customer too much. In the more robust frontier days, applejack was often put on sale raw and fiery, straight from the still. It is placed in oak casks today and kept in bonded warehouses to age—anything from one to five years.

In other times, a rougher and inferior spirit was

sometimes obtained by the slapdash method of distilling the pomace without pressing it first. Alternatively, the pomace from which all the juice had been pressed out was sometimes taken and soaked in water. The water was then fermented, and became a weak spirit known as ciderkin which, in colonial days, was considered fit for children.

Among the terms for applejack are: apple brandy, cider brandy, cider spirits, cider whiskey, and sometimes just plain 'apple'. Although the name applejack is strictly an American one, apple brandy is made in various parts of the world, the most famous being that from the Calvados area in the province of Normandy in France.

See CALVADOS.

Apricot Brandy

A dry, unsweetened brandy made from the distilled juice of apricots. The original, and most famous, apricot brandy was Barack Pálinka, made in Hungary (*q.v.*).

Apricot Liqueur

A beverage, not to be confused with apricot brandy, made of mashed apricots and sweetened brandy.

Apry

Tawny-coloured liqueur made from apricots soaked in sweetened brandy. It is produced by the firm of Marie Brizard et Roger in Bordeaux, France.

Apulia (Puglia)

Red and white wines. District: South-east Italy.

Apulia comprises Italy's south-east corner, jutting down into the Mediterranean to form the 'heel' of the Italian 'boot'. The sun-drenched, shadeless, wheat-bearing plain changes as you go farther south into a huge rolling sea of vines and gnarled olive trees, the two often rubbing branches in the same field. The soil is as poor as the sun is hot, but the vine adapts itself so prolifically that Apulian grapes are crushed into 166,500,000 imp. gallons (200 million U.S.) of wine annually, mostly red, mostly run from fermenting vat to tank or barrel to be sold throughout the country as the indispensable ordinary table wine. Some of it is used for blending—sought after for its rough body and high alcoholic content—and much floods into the vermouth plants or is concocted into the various wine-based aperitifs Latin countries consume in such abundance. As in the French Midi (Mediterranean) regions, the emphasis is on output, not quality: no one pretends that these bulk wines are fine. There are, nevertheless, some delightful exceptions.

Sansevero is a pale, light, dry and eminently drinkable straw-coloured wine from the northern end of Apulia's *tavoliere*, the 'chessboard' or plateau extending around Foggia. The wine is of medium strength (perhaps 13%) and from Bombino grapes, and some experts consider it among Italy's finest white wines. Torre Giulia (white) and Santo Stefano (red) are other offerings from the chessboard and both are agreeable though not in the class of Sansevero. Barbera, Pinot, and Montepulciano grapes are responsible for the bright red Santo Stefano, Bombino for Torre Giulia.

Among other wines of note are Aleatico di Puglia and Moscato del Salento—but not for people who do not care for sweet wines. The former is a warm orange-red, sweet, strong (15%) dessert wine with a special pungency that betrays its origins, the sun-dried Aleatico grape, which is something like a Black Muscat and leaves an unmistakable trace in the perfume of the wine it makes. Most Apulian Aleatico is grown around Bari, Brindisi, and Taranto. Muscat grapes grown along the Salento peninsula are both red and white and the wine also may be either. Both types are strong and sweet, but neither has quite the virtue of the Aleatico.

The lesser wines include Martina Franca, Locorotondo, Barletta, and Squinzano. They mostly derive their names from the towns near which they are made and all are produced in enormous quantity. As a rule they are distinctly minor wines.

Aqua Vitæ

The early name for brandy, from the Latin, meaning water of life. The Italians claim, however, that the original name was not *Aqua Vitæ* but *Aqua Vite*, or *Acqua di Vite*, the Italian for water of the vine, and referring to the colourless fluid which has been distilled from wine. Later, they say, either because of the power of liquor to stimulate and revive, or through a simple mistake in spelling, the more familiar term came into use.

Aquavit, Akvavit, Akevit

A spirit, found generally in the Scandinavian countries, distilled from grain or rectified potato spirit and flavoured with certain aromatic seeds and spices—caraway seeds in particular. Aquavit is drunk chilled and traditionally accompanies Scandinavian smörgåsbord. The name, a contraction of the Latin *aqua vitæ*, meaning water of life, was coined during the thirteenth century in Italy to designate the first distilled liquor produced from wine.

Today, Sweden is generally considered the world's foremost producer of aquavit, or 'snaps', as it is often called in that country. The first licence to sell aquavit in Stockholm was granted in 1498. During the next century, the liquor was produced merely by distilling wine, and as the requisite grapes are not grown in Sweden, the wine had to be imported from abroad, which made aquavit so expensive that it was used mainly for medicinal purposes. Not until Swedish soldiers learned to produce the spirit from grain did it become more common. During bad harvest years, however, the authorities had to prohibit all distilling of aquavit, and so the search for substitutes continued. Experiments were made with roots and berries; but in the eighteenth century the potato was found to be so suitable for the purpose that it has been the main source of aquavit ever since.

Most of the potato distilleries in Sweden today are situated in the southern province of Skåne. The clean potatoes are first boiled in steam under pressure, and the resultant starch mass is then mixed with crushed malt (made from barley or mixed grains) to convert the starch into sugar. Yeast culture is added to the mash, and in the ensuing fermentation the sugar is converted into alcohol. The spirit is rectified again before it is used as an ingredient in the finished product, to remove the taste of potato.

A high-quality aquavit cannot be obtained merely by diluting such alcohol with water, for it would have no flavour. It is for this reason that the diluted spirit is allowed to come into contact with birch charcoal made active through the effect of steam at high temperature. This not only increases the aldehyde content of the alcohol, but also forms small quantities of taste elements called esters. A few selected spices are generally accepted as especially suited to flavouring aquavit, the most popular of which are caraway seed, aniseed, fennel seed, and bitter orange.

There is a general misconception that aquavit must be strictly an unsweetened spirit. In fact, the term aquavit has been adopted as a general term both for the spiced and sweetened liquor—specifically known in Sweden as aquavit—and for Brännvin, which is usually (but not always) unspiced and unsweetened.

At present there are some twenty aquavit brands in Sweden. The O. P. Anderson Aquavit is a leading export mark made with caraway seed, aniseed, and fennel seed. Another well-known brand is Ödakra Taffel Aquavit, which was brought into the market in 1899: it is lightly spiced and comparatively dry. Överste Brännvin has a stronger spice aroma than O. P. Anderson and contains somewhat more sugar; while Skåne Aquavit very much resembles the O. P. Anderson, although it is less spicy.

Second to Sweden in the production of aquavit is Denmark, where this beverage, usually known as 'schnapps', is looked on as the national drink—it accounts for 70% of Danish spirit consumption. Schnapps is generally a non-sweetened, colourless beverage.

The Danish Distilleries were founded in 1881, and up to 1914 aquavit could be purchased for about the equivalent of sevenpence (fifteen cents) a bottle. Today there is one distillery only, owned by Danish Distilleries, which since 1923 has enjoyed the sole right of producing alcohol and yeast in Denmark. The Danes sometimes use potatoes and grain. The latter is invariably used for export.

Aalborg Taffel Akvavit, which was first produced in 1846 and which is the best-known brand in Denmark and abroad, is seasoned with caraway seeds and contains 43% alcohol by volume. Other brands worthy of mention are Brøndūm Kummenaquavit, a caraway seed aquavit with cinnamon; Aalborg Export Akvavit, which has a slight taste of Madeira; Harald Jensen Taffel Akvavit; and Perikum-Snaps.

Norway produces less of the spirit than does either Sweden or Denmark, and its best-known brands are: Lysholm Aquavit, a light, elegant, and rather delicate type matured in newly-empty Sherry casks; Løiten Aquavit, a full-bodied, more robust type; and Linie Aquavit, a rather interesting type, the name of which refers to a 'crossing of the Line' (i.e. the Equator). This is in keeping with the old tradition that the liquor improves with a sea voyage—and today it is sent to Australia and back on the Wilhelmsen cargo liners.

Aramon

An enormously productive grape variety, giving ordinary wines, and cultivated principally in southern France and in California.

Arbois

White, red, and rosé wines. District: South-East France.

The best-known wine district of the Jura in France. White and red wines are made here, and rosés which are among the best in France.

See JURA.

AREOMETER (*see* p. 100)

Equivalence Table for Baumé Degrees, Potential Alcohol Degrees and Specific Gravity (at a Temperature of 59°F. (15°C.))

Baumé Degrees	*Alcohol Content Potential Coeff.* 17	*Corresponding Specific Gravity*
6	5	1043
7	6·2	1051
8	7·4	1058
9	8·6	1066
10	9·9	1074
11	11·1	1082
12	12·4	1090
13	13·7	1099
14	15	1107
15	16·4	1116
16	17·7	1124
17	19·1	1133
18	20·5	1142
19	22	1151
20	23·4	1160
21	24·9	1170
22	26·4	1179
23	27·9	1189
24	29·5	1199
25	31	1209
26	32·6	1219
27	34·3	1230
28	35·9	1240
29	37·6	1251
30	39·3	1262
31	41·1	1273
32	42·9	1284
33	44·7	1296
34	46·5	1308
35	48·4	1320
36	50·3	1332
37	52·3	1344
38	54·2	1357
39	56·3	1370
40	58·5	1383

Equivalence Table for Baumé Degrees, Œchslé Degrees and Specific Gravities (at Temperature of 59°F. (15°C.))

Baumé Degrees	*Œchslé Degrees*	*Corresponding Specific Gravity*
0	0	1000·0
0·1	0·7	1000·7
0·2	1·4	1001·4
0·3	2·1	1002·1
0·4	2·8	1002·8
0·5	3·5	1003·5
0·6	4·2	1004·2
0·7	4·9	1004·9
0·8	5·6	1005·6
0·9	6·3	1006·3
1·0	7·0	1007·0
1·1	7·7	1007·7
1·2	8·4	1008·4
1·3	9·1	1009·1
1·4	9·8	1009·8
1·5	10·5	1010·5
1·6	11·2	1011·2
1·7	11·9	1011·9
1·8	12·6	1012·6
1·9	13·3	1013·3
2·0	14·0	1014·0
2·1	14·7	1014·7
2·2	15·4	1015·4
2·3	16·1	1016·1
2·4	16·8	1016·8
2·5	17·5	1017·5
3·0	21·2	1021·2
4·0	28·5	1028·5
5	35·9	1035·9
6	43·4	1043·5
7	51·0	1051·0
8	58·7	1058·7
9	66·5	1066·5
10	74·5	1074·5
11	82·5	1082·5
12	90·7	1090·7
13	99·0	1099·0
14	107·4	1107·4
15	116·0	1116·0
16	124·7	1124·7
17	133·5	1133·5
18	142·5	1142·5

Ardine

Apricot brandy made by the French firm of Bardinet.

Areometer

Device for measuring specific gravity—a form of densimeter (*q.v.*) with arbitrary graduations. There are different versions of the instrument: the Œchslé, for one, and, of particular interest here, the Baumé.

This areometer (French: *mustimètre*) has always been used since the time of Chaptal (*see* Chapter Nine, p. 47) to check the density of the grape must, since luck would have it that the graduation so obtained represents approximately the proportion of alcohol which wine will contain after fermenting—so that 1 degree Baumé corresponds nearly enough to the density of 17·18 grammes of sugar in a litre of water.

The instrument shows 0° in distilled water, 15° in a solution of 15 parts (by weight) sea salt in 85 parts water.

See TABLE, p. 99.

EQUIVALENCE TABLE OF THE DENSITY OF A WINE AND THE WEIGHT OF SUGAR IT CONTAINS

Specific Gravity of Dry Wine at Equal Strength	*Sugar to be Added to Achieve Specific Gravity of* 1,000 (*in grammes per litre*)	*Specific Gravity of the Same Wine after Adding Sugar per litre*					
		9g	18g	27g	36g	45g	54g
990	25	994	998	0°1	0°6	1°1	1°6
991	22	995	998	0°3	0°8	1°3	1°8
992	20	996	1,000	0°4	0°9	1°4	1°9
993	17	997	0°2	0°6	1°1	1°6	2°1
994	15	998	0°2	0°7	1°2	1°7	2°2
995	12	999	0°4	0°9	1°4	1°9	2°4
996	10	1,000	0°5	1°0	1°5	2°0	2°5
997	7	0°1	0°6	1°1	1°6	2°1	2°6
998	5	0°2	0°8	1°3	1°8	2°3	2°8
999	2	0°4	0°9	1°4	1°9	2°4	2°9

Argentina

Argentina, with some 638,000 acres of wine-producing vines, is the largest wine-producing country in South America and ranks fourth among the world's wine makers, with an annual average of over 430 million imp. gallons (516 million U.S.). Of this huge quantity, only a small amount reaches the world market. The highest figure—reached at the end of the last war—was approximately 2,500,000 imp. gallons (3 million U.S.), the major share of which went to England. Since 1947–8, exports have diminished steadily, dropping in 1962 to 9,900 imp. gallons (11,880 U.S.). The estimated figure for 1964 charts a rise to 87,990 imp. gallons (106,000 U.S.). Among South American wines, the Chilean are better known abroad; but the main reason is that the Argentinian is a wine-drinking man. Total domestic consumption in 1964 was 423,798,500 imp. gallons (508,958,500 U.S.)—that is 19·1 imp. gallons (22·9 U.S.) a head, a very high average. Even so, certain sparkling wines and vermouths from Argentina are occasionally to be found in the United States and in Europe. A tremendous quantity of vermouth is made, and sparkling wines are produced by all three methods: secondary fermentation in bottle (the Champagne method), bulk fermentation, and carbonation. About 80% of the country's production is in *vin ordinaire*; but some *bodegas* specialize in the production of quality wines.

WINE HISTORY

The Jesuits brought wine to the land of the Pampas; in 1566 a Jesuit priest named Father Cedron planted the first vineyard in the region of Cuyo. The very early Jesuit plantings survive in the form of the Criollas grape variety, a descendant of the vines brought to Argentina 400 years ago and today still the leading producer of white and rosé wine.

The modern story of Argentine wine is an Italian and not a Spanish missionary story, however. A century ago, Argentinians of Italian origin began to sluice the snow waters out over what was then the unpromising desert of Mendoza, the province that lies against the mile-high boundary with Chile, towering up in the sky along the Andes. The snow water from the Andes worked the same miracle that has been worked by irrigation in Algeria and California. A new vineland was born.

VINE-GROWING REGIONS

Today Mendoza Province produces nearly 70%

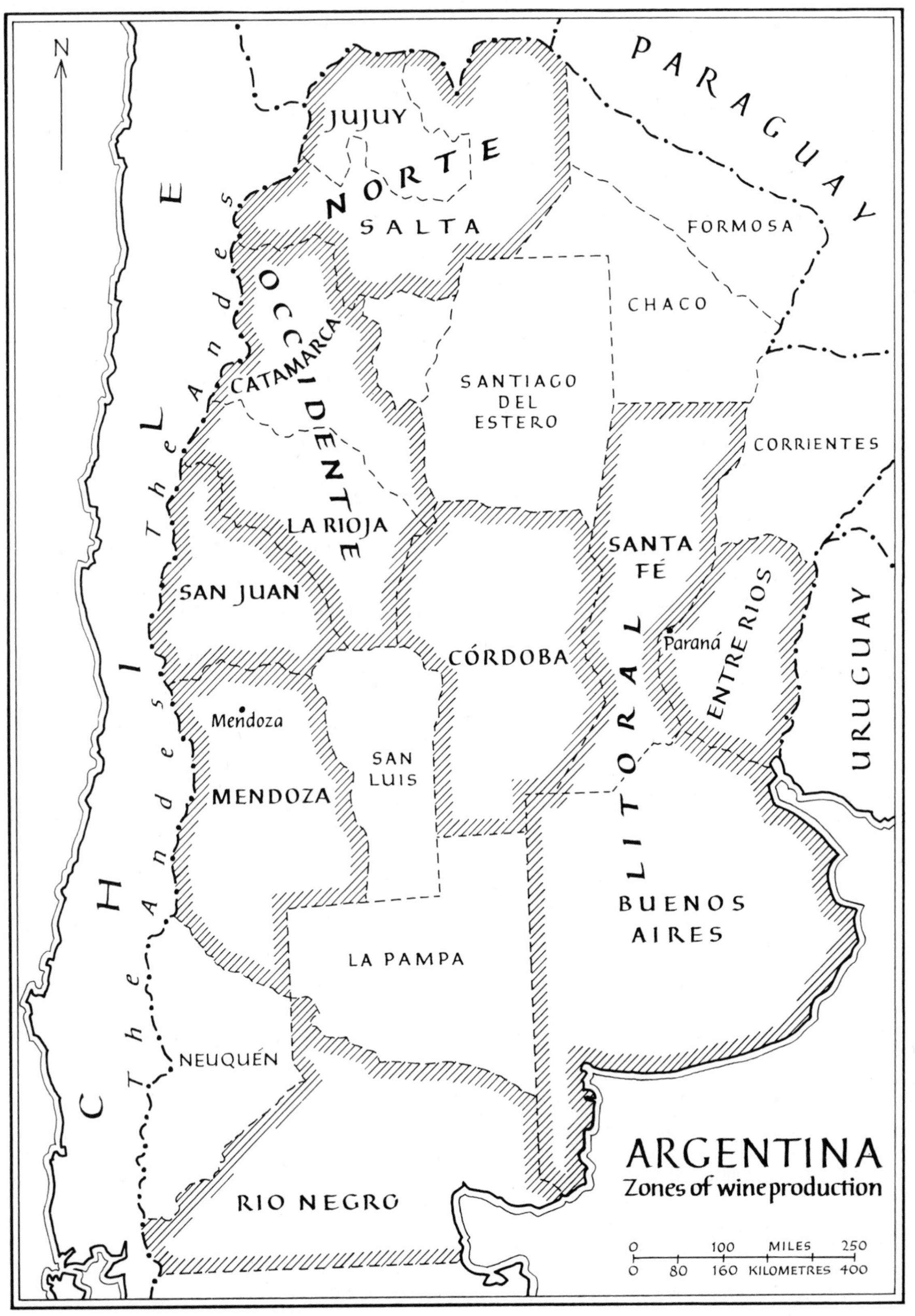
N
PARAGUAY
JUJUY
NORTE
SALTA
FORMOSA
CHACO
OCCIDENTE
CATAMARCA
SANTIAGO DEL ESTERO
CORRIENTES
LA RIOJA
SANTA FÉ
SAN JUAN
ENTRE RIOS
Paraná
CÓRDOBA
URUGUAY
Mendoza
SAN LUIS
MENDOZA
LITORAL
BUENOS AIRES
LA PAMPA
NEUQUÉN
RIO NEGRO
The Andes
CHILE
ARGENTINA
Zones of wine production
0 100 MILES 250
0 80 160 KILOMETRES 400

of the wine of Argentina, and 40% of its entire cultivated acreage is devoted to the vine. In this province, wine-making is the only important industry. The total number of vine-growers is about 40,000, but as much as 16% of the output is produced by nine large firms, each of which maintains its own vineyards, bottling plants, and sales organizations throughout Argentina. Red wines outnumber the white and pink wines by a little more than two to one. As might be expected in a new wine area and under Italian influence, the methods are chiefly the modern ones of mass-production. It is the French and not the Italian wine-maker who has traditionally troubled to refine his art. Mendoza, and the neighbouring province of San Juan, are gigantic flat platters of green vines stretching like an ocean, with island wineries that utilize some of the highest fermentation vats on earth. The positive and unsubtle qualities of the wines stem from these mass vinification methods, where, in lots sometimes exceeding 200,000 imp. gallons (250,000 U.S.), the wines are fermented and matured. In such conditions, individual care is impossible. One winery in the town of Mendoza processes the staggering total of about 20 million imp. gallons (24 million U.S.) a year. There are over two hundred *bodegas* (wineries) in the town of Mendoza, a true honeycomb. Altogether, 250,000 acres are in vineyard in Mendoza Province.

Directly north of Mendoza in the Province of San Juan, also lying against the continental spine of the Andes, a heavier, richer wine is produced. This is, of course, nearer the Equator and the climate is hotter, producing, consequently, a heavier wine. 26% of Argentine wine is made in San Juan. Since irrigation is essential in both San Juan and Mendoza, the familiar slope wines of European vineyards are unknown. The water coursing through the veins of the table-flat vineyards has brought death as well as life to the vines. While in most other countries the lethal vine louse phylloxera has travelled in the air or been transported on infected vine stalks, in Argentina the parasites may also have been flushed from one region to the next in the ducts of the irrigation system. Conversely, Argentinians utilize irrigation in fighting phylloxera. Attacked areas are flooded and kept under water for a short period; the pest is drowned and the vineyards are then phylloxera-free.

South of Mendoza in Río Negro about 3% of Argentina's total output is grown. Here, following the European pattern in reverse in the southern hemisphere, the lighter wines are found to the south, and excellent dry white wines and sparkling white wines are produced in the colder, more rigorous climate. These are often considered the best wines in Argentina. The remaining quantity, about 1% in each case, is grown in the Provinces of La Rioja and Salta in the north of the country, and in nearly all parts small amounts of wine are made.

The Malbec grape produces two-thirds of the total amount of red wine, followed by other familiar European varieties, principally French and Italian. The largest part of the white wine is made from the Criollas variety, which may now be considered native after four centuries in the country, next in order being the Pedro Ximénez from Spain, followed by such European plants as Sémillon, Sauvignon, Malvasia, Pinot Blanc, Riesling, and others.

The following are zones of production in the Republic of Argentina: Mendoza, San Juan, Río Negro, Litoral (the adjoining provinces of Buenos Aires and Sante Fé), Córdoba, Occidente (La Rioja and Catamarca), Norte (Salta and Jujuy), and Entre Ríos.

The tremendous expansion of Argentina's wine industry over the past years is certainly in part due to the fine set of laws that regulates the labelling and bottling of its wine. No country outside France has done so much to eliminate fraud. In Argentina, the laws governing place-name denomination are exemplary. No cheese may be named except as of the district where the cow gave the milk and the curd was made, the particular grass, climate, and technique having created the taste. And no wine may carry the place-name of a locality unless the bottle is of that locality and has its typical characteristics. Foreign wines may not be blended with national wines, and (as is unfortunately not the case in too many countries) in Argentina no wine may call itself 'chablis', 'bordeaux', or any other famous and specific foreign place-name unless it really is an imported wine from the place indicated. There have been inconsistencies, such as referring to the champagne-type sparkling wine of 1953 as Champaña, yet using likewise the labels 'Fine Champagne'; but in general Argentina must be highly praised for laying this sound foundation for its growing industry.

Arjan

Another name for koumiss or fermented sour mare's milk made by the Tartars.

Arkansas

Small wine-producing region of the United States. The vineyards are centred around the northern sector, in the Ozark Mountains.

Armagnac

Brandy. District: South-West France.

Armagnac comes from the land of d'Artagnan, a land of vines, geese, horses, of the bland, cream-coloured cattle of the Pyrenees and swarthy, hot-blooded people, some of them descended from the Goths and Vizigoths who came from Spain to settle in the wide spaces of Gascony. They say that witches are still to be found in Armagnac, to bring luck to their friends and put curses on their enemies; but here, in the birthplace of Henry IV, there are many good Protestants, their farms marked by cypress trees as a sign of their faith. The landscape is blackened with short, knotty oak and pine; in winter, a cold wind howls down from the Pyrenees, and in summer the rolling plain, veined with streams, is burned brown by a searing sun. Armagnac brandy, matching the extreme climate in which it is nurtured and the determined character of the people who make it, is full-bodied, pungent, and strong. Much of it goes to market in a flat, fat, long-necked flagon, known as a *basquaise* and labelled, usually, Armagnac or Bas-Armagnac. Ténarèze and Haut-Armagnac also are permitted place-names but are seldom seen, since they are the lesser designations of the region. (This is the supreme example of the foolishness of assuming that *bas*—lower—must necessarily mean of lower quality than *haut*—higher; these words are used in France simply in the geographical sense.)

Delimitation

In 1909, in order to establish the name and capture a market after the example of Cognac, the region of Armagnac brandy was marked out. It is mostly in the department of Gers, although a little of the best corner juts into Les Landes, south of Bordeaux. The chief centres are Condom, for Ténarèze; Auch, for Haut-Armagnac; and Eauze, in Bas-Armagnac, scene of the Thursday market in Armagnacs, when the narrow streets bulge with men buying and selling the brandy, testing the quality by rubbing a drop between their hands and sniffing it.

Bas-Armagnac, to the west, flattening into the pine-forest which extends to the dunes along the Atlantic, gives brandy of the greatest finesse, from a mainly sandy soil. This brandy, if it is to carry the choice name of Bas-Armagnac, must not only be 100% Bas-Armagnac, but must also have been blended in a separate warehouse, apart from any other types which might be handled by the same shipper. The brandies from the south part of Ténarèze, where the soil is clay, are lighter and develop more quickly. Haut-Armagnac, to the east, is predominantly chalky—and although it is chalk content which determines the finest Cognacs, here the brandy is of a ruder type, and seldom appears on the market, except as a basis for liqueurs, an important part of the Armagnac business.

Vintage

The question of vintage is disputed in Armagnac, as it is in Cognac. Commercially, vintage brandy is an insignificant business in either region, although Armagnac, being more individualistic and less commercially developed, tends to make a little more. There are no such great firms here as are seen along the river banks in Jarnac and Cognac, although some quite large houses do exist in Condom.

Some shippers claim that blending is on a lesser scale. Here, also, opinions differ as to whether vintage brandy is superior to that obtained by blending over the years.

In Armagnac, as in Cognac, Three Star, V.S.O.P., Extra, and other 'type' brandies are sold. They will conform to a style—Three-Star being a five-year-old 'type', V.S.O.P. twenty-year-old; Extra, forty-year-old (always with considerable latitude from firm to firm), and usually the blend will contain brandy both older and younger than the type age. Generally, Armagnac will be a little older than Cognac of a similar style, because there is not the same market pressure demanding a very quick turn-over.

Since certain growers consider that vintage brandy is better than a blend (although, as in Port or Champagne, only in certain years), some firms produce an occasional vintage Armagnac, putting the other years into blends. Exceptionally, a producer will deal exclusively in vintage Armagnac. In the *chai* of one such grower, connected with his house beneath one long-sloped Basque roof in Bas-Armagnac, barrels of Armagnac are ranged on their scantlings into two tiers, each dated in chalk with the vintage. The proprietor, in sabots, Basque beret peaked forward over his eyes, will tell how the greater number of his customers come in person, from various parts of France and even from abroad, to taste the brandies of the different years, and make their choice. A larger shipper-grower a few miles away has the only glass-lined storage tanks in Armagnac. This might be thought a sad departure

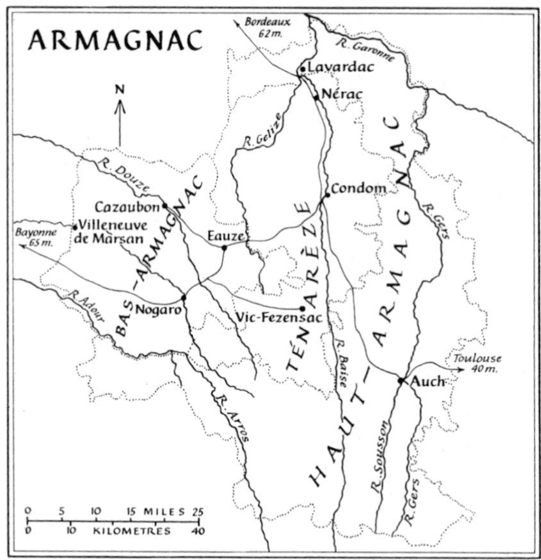

from tradition, an infiltration from the French Midi or Algeria—until the magic 1904, 1891, 1888, and other old vintage Armagnacs are drawn one by one with the little silver spigots and nosed and tasted. After about fifty years, Armagnac will no longer improve in the wood but will begin to go down; when in glass, like every other spirit, it does not change. That is why the Bas-Armagnac shipper-grower has captured his old brandies at their height and put them into glass.

Nearly black from age in oak, smouldering with a fresh fire that seems to burn inside velvet, and with such an aroma that the perfume sometimes lingers for over a week in the emptied glass, these vintage Armagnacs are indeed supreme.

To bear a date on the label, an Armagnac need not be from a single year; the brandy blended across the years will sometimes be dated, but in this case the date is required by law to be the year of the youngest brandy included.

Authorized Vines

For the white wines of the Gers from which Armagnac is made, Folle Blanche, Picpoule, Saint-Émilion, Colombard, and Jurançon are the chief vines. Blanquette, Mauzac, Clairette, Meslier, and Plant de Grèce are also authorized, but are very little seen. Folle Blanche, which used to be the leading variety, is steadily giving way to the Saint-Émilion and other sturdier plants.

In recent years, the hybrid vine Baco 22A, a cross of the Folle Blanche and the American Noah, has been included among the authorized vines, but only in the sandy terrains of Bas-Armagnac. Its merits are hotly debated in Armagnac. A basic rule of French viticulture is that hybrid vines produce grapes inferior in quality, and in every vineyard with a controlled place-name, for wine, they must be rooted out. In the sandy vineyards of Bas-Armagnac, the Baco seems, so far, to produce a wine which can be distilled into a brandy as fine as that from the Picpoule or Folle Blanche. It is early, however, to judge the ingredients of a product which must mature for forty years to reach its best.

Comparison with Cognac

Armagnac differs basically from Cognac in several ways. The best of it comes from a sandy soil, while the fine Cognac is from the area richest in chalk. The climate is different, for in Cognac it is maritime, mellow, and misty; in a more primitive region, Armagnac is closer to its origins than Cognac, not so smoothed-out by blending, a natural product to which no sugar need be added.

Many Frenchmen besides the Gascons prefer Armagnac, at its best, to Cognac—but unfortunately, it is not always at its best. Cheap Armagnacs are too prevalent, and some of the people who are in the habit of buying these are unacquainted with the finer types. In the United States no good was done to the name by false claims to great age; ninety-nine years was a frequent boast until the 1951 law stamped out this practice. Now, an Armagnac label may state (if true) that the brandy is 'at least ten years old', but no greater claim can be made.

Different also in Armagnac and Cognac are the methods of ageing and distilling—a difference deliberately emphasized.

In the brandy co-operative at Réans, on the edge of Eauze, new distillations of Bas-Armagnac wine, all from the same still and all 1952, were put into a row of barrels, half of which were of the native oak of Armagnac, and half of the Limousin oak in which Cognac is aged. The bung of every barrel was wax-sealed and officially taped. Tasted in 1956, the brandy in the Armagnac oak barrels was good, but the Limoges oak barrels contained something which was neither Armagnac nor Cognac. There was a practical reason for the experiment: Armagnac oak is slowly running out and is consequently soaring in price; yet again it had been proved that Armagnac must be made in Armagnac oak and nothing else.

Distillation of Armagnac in Cognac stills has often been tried. The result is indicated by the fact that since 1936 a law has decreed that Armagnac must be made in the native continuous still. Cognac is double-distilled, the final issue being around 70% of alcohol. Armagnac cannot exceed 63% and is usually 10% less. This means more non-alcoholic grape products in the brandy and more native taste. Originally, the Armagnac still resembled the one used in Cognac—but by the nineteenth century the present continuous still was becoming common. Fundamentally, it is a pot still in which the vapours are refined by the wine itself (*see* CHAPTER TEN, p. 56), and it is designed to distil wine of 9% to 10% of alcohol—a more highly alcoholic wine is not desirable, as the aim is to pass over as much as possible of the non-alcoholic taste and aroma-giving quality. The result is that Armagnac, retaining many of the original elements of flavour and scent, has an astonishing perfume, even when it is less than a year old, and is too fiery to drink. This young brandy is often taken in coffee, to which it gives a heady burst of fragrance.

Many of the smaller growers share a perambulating still, and this alembic is one of the sights of the countryside: like an ancient black locomotive drawn backwards, it moves slowly across the Armagnac landscape, pulled by blond yoked oxen; or else it halts somewhere in the night, its mouth gushing fire as the sticks of oak are thrust in, while everywhere else is silence and darkness. From peasant to peasant it goes—and thus the product of those without an alembic of their own is distilled. Now, however, the leading firms are studying a new type of alembic which will produce an equally pure *eau-de-vie* while eliminating certain ethers. This will cut short the period of ageing.

The reason why some Armagnac was bad was lack of tradition among the shippers; and the reason why Armagnac is still exported in smaller quantities than Cognac is that the growers did not know how to advertise their brandy. These matters have now been taken in hand by some of the better shippers and the more important growers. At the head of these is the Marquis de Montesquiou, Duc de Fézensac, a parliamentary Deputy who works his estate, the Château de Marsan, as a model farm and experimental station, and who has made strenuous efforts to maintain the highest standards of Armagnac and to protect the small peasant grower from the sharp practice of certain shippers, who would try to buy their brandy for the lowest price and then sell it at the highest. A visitor to the Château de Marsan may dine off the traditional Gascon dish, Henry IV's favourite *poule au pot,* followed, at the end of dinner, by a fine old Armagnac. And in his bedroom, he will find more Armagnac, in a small decanter—another tradition in which the host believes.

Because this is the country of the famous companion of The Three Musketeers, most firms have their Réserve d'Artagnan: the one who is entitled to this splendid name is the Marquis de Montesquiou. He is a descendant of the hero, who really lived at the Château de Castelmore, near Lupiac, although his name was not d'Artagnan. The plaque over the gate of the neglected seventeenth-century building bears these words: *Ici naquit vers 1615 d'Artagnan, de son vrai nom Charles de Batz* (Here d'Artagnan was born, about 1615, under his real name, Charles de Batz).

Since 1951, Armagnac has had a brandy fraternity comparable with the wine orders of the Chevaliers du Tastevin in Burgundy and the Commanderie du Bontemps in the Médoc. These fraternities provide a good deal of dressing-up, oath-swearing, and other amusement for the members, and excellent means, also, of attracting attention to the brandy of the region. In Gascony, the Company of the Musketeers dress up in high boots, plumed hats, and magnificent moustaches; Cardinal Richelieu and the King of France appear, too. The hill-top city of Auch is crowned by a cathedral begun in the fourteenth century and finished by Louis XIV. It contains a choir-seat decorated with hundreds of wooden figures marvellously carved by a pupil of Michelangelo, and approached by a fine flight of steps. Up these steps sweep the modern Musketeers; and at the top stands d'Artagnan, in stone—a surprisingly young and girlish figure, looking out over the land whose character he personifies.

Armillaria Root Rot

A fungus disease of the vine.
See CHAPTER EIGHT, p. 37.

Arrack, Arraki, Arack, Arak, Raki, etc.

The name derives from the Arabic for 'juice' or 'sweat' and generally designates 'native spirits', so there are probably as many types of arrack as there are of native spirits in the Orient and in Eastern Europe. Arrack has been distilled in the East Indies from fermented palm-sap and from rice; from grain spirits in Greece; from dates in the Middle East and Egypt; and Batavia arrack is a highly aromatic rum distilled in Java. The number and type of herbs and spices which have been used as flavourings are probably as wide as the human imagination. In any case arrack is a coarse drink made for tough palates. A French proverb states that: 'He who has once tasted arrack never forgets the taste.'

Arroba

Spanish wine measure of 11·5 kilogrammes (25·36 lb.), approximately equal to one basket of grapes. Sixty arrobas theoretically give one butt of 516 litres (113·5 imp. gallons; 136·3 U.S.) of wine. The liquid arroba equals 16·0–16·5 litres (3·52–3·63 imp. gallons; 4·23–4·36 U.S.).

Artichoke Brandy

Spirit distilled in France from the Jerusalem artichoke.

In Italy there is an aperitif called Cynar which is made from artichokes.

Asali

An East African beverage fermented from honey.

Asciutto

Italian term for dry wine.

Assmannshausen

One of the two best red wines of the German Rhine. The German red wines are never important, nor to be compared with the great white wines; a considerable amount is seen in Germany, but it is of no significance in the export market.

See RHEINGAU.

Asti

Italian town celebrated for its sparkling white wine, Asti Spumante—which is sweet and bubbly—and, to a lesser extent, for its Moscato d'Asti.

See PIEDMONT.

Astringency

With reference to wine, this means sharpness from acid content and tannin and sometimes indicates that the wine will be long-lived.

Asztalibor

Hungarian term for common wine. *Bor* means wine.

Athol Brose

Scottish drink based on whisky, mixed with honey and/or oatmeal.

Attemperators

Spiral-shaped, metal coils which are immersed in fermenting vats, and through which hot or cold water is run to regulate the temperature of the fermenting must or grape juice.

Aubance

See COTEAUX DE L'AUBANCE; ANJOU.

Aude

Red and some white wines. District: Southern France.

One of the three most important wine-producing departments of France, quantitatively speaking. The other two are Hérault and Gard. All three make up the bulk wine area known as the Midi. The Aude vineyards in the Roussillon region, near the Franco-Spanish border, produce very large quantities of undistinguished wines, mostly red; also a very limited quantity of fair white and rosé wines, more particularly those of Limoux, Corbières, and Minervois.

Aurum

A proprietary Italian liqueur, pale gold in colour, and with an orange flavour.

Auslese

A German term meaning wine made from selected bunches of grapes. Beerenauslese is the selection of individual grapes from the bunches, Trockenbeerenauslese the selection of overripe individual grapes.

See GERMANY.

Château Ausone

Bordeaux red wine. District and Commune: Saint-Émilion, France.

Traditionally first among the wines of Saint-Émilion, Ausone is now sometimes held to have fallen behind Cheval-Blanc—and is considered by some to be below Gaffelières-Naudes. A portion of the harvest is aged in old barrels rather than new ones, and this failure to obtain the tannin which fresh oak would give is believed to be partly responsible for a decline in the wine. When Saint-Émilion wines were officially classified in 1955, however, Ausone and Cheval-Blanc were placed in their traditional position at the head of the First Great Growths (*Premiers Grands Crus*), the others following alphabetically, although they were not ranked in a class apart.

Ausone is believed, by some, to stand on the site of the villa of the fourth-century Roman poet Ausonius—and, if what Ausonius wrote is true, the wine was a favourite of Julius Cæsar. In any case, the vineyard is magnificently placed on the western edge of the eleventh-century hill-top village of Saint-Émilion; the château looks over its terraced and sloped vines, all facing south. Because of its high situation, Ausone escaped the terrible frost of February 1956, in which so many other vineyards, including Cheval-Blanc, were frozen—they not only lost their 1956, 1957, and some later vintages, but the effect on the wines is still felt in the sixties. The Ausone cellar is a deep, rocky cave hewn centuries ago out of the soft stone upon which Saint-Émilion stands. Château Belair wine—the vineyards adjoin—is also aged in the Ausone *cave*. Both châteaux are owned by Monsieur Dubois-Challon, who is the leading figure in the Saint-Émilion wine society—the Jurade.

Characteristics. Less robust than many of the Saint-Émilions; nevertheless a full wine of considerable distinction.

Vineyard area: 17 acres.

Average production: 2,800 cases.

Australia

Australia is a land endowed by nature to produce abundantly all the fruits of the earth. This is especially true of 'God's greatest gift to man'—the vine and wine. Not only does the vine flourish where it grows, but it is capable of limitless expansion in large tracts of land equally suitable to bear it. It is regrettable, however, that the vintners still parade their wines under European place-names instead of building up their own.

In 1801, Napoleon Bonaparte sent a delegation to spy out the land so recently discovered, and it was then reported to him that because of Britain's great consumption of wine, Australia was destined to become the vineyard of Britain. Years later, Hubert de Castella (original planter of the famous Lilydale vineyard of St. Hubert's) wrote a small book which he entitled *John Bull's Vineyard.*

In Australia, as also in California, conditions are so congenial for vine growing that almost every year is a vintage year and there is no necessity for that ceaseless control that is essential on the European continent. This evenness in climate does away with certain 'lows' but does not necessarily increase the 'highs'.

The versatility of Australian soil has been amply demonstrated over the years by its ability to produce from, for example, Cabernet Sauvignon either a classical claret-style wine or a good Vintage port-type, and from Tokay either a dry white or a luscious dessert wine. Many other varieties are capable, in this country, of such a dual function. It is this adaptability that marks the difference between Australian and European wine practice. Years of experience have shown the old world's vine-growers that their soil and climate are particularly adapted to certain varieties of grapes, and they concentrate on these to the exclusion of all others.

Wine History

The vine in Australia is as old as the settlement itself. When Captain Arthur Phillip set sail from the Thames with his fleet of eleven ships, he included in the cargo 'plants for the settlement', among which were the first vines to enter Australia. He landed in Sydney on 26 January 1788, and planted the vines on the site where the Botanical Gardens now stand. It was soon found that this location was far from ideal for the propagation of the vine, since the humid conditions on the waterfront encouraged the development of a fungoid disease later identified as anthracnose—more familiarly known as 'black spot'. It was decided to replant in a more congenial area, and in 1791, three acres were planted by Governor Phillip twelve miles away from Sydney, on the Parramatta. At the same time, a settler named Schaffer planted an acre, and thus can be given credit for being the first private *vigneron* in Australia. Unfortunately, however, his further activities appear to have been very obscure.

The first man to make any serious attempt to produce wine on a commercial scale was Captain John McArthur, who was given a grant of land some thirty miles from Sydney. This he named Camden Park. Rootlings of all procurable varieties were obtained from the official collection and afterwards a certain number of seedlings were planted with a fair measure of success. Later, Captain McArthur was joined by his two sons—James, born in 1798, and William, born 1800. The feud between McArthur and Governor Bligh is common knowledge, and it was even carried into the ordinary procedure of wine-making: when, in 1807, McArthur imported two stills for making brandy from some of his wine, Bligh had these confiscated, re-packed, and returned to England. At the same time, he had McArthur tried in the Criminal Court, holding that the stills were illegally imported to produce rum—the currency of the N.S.W. Corps. The McArthur family, nevertheless, continued to thrive and to play an important part, not only in Australian viticulture, but in the public affairs of the state.

Another important individual in the early history of Australian wine was Gregory Blaxland, who was the first grower in Australia to export his wine to London. Certainly the quantity involved was not great, being only a quarter-pipe of red wine, but it can be cited as the forerunner of the subsequent very considerable trade in export 'burgundy'. Five years later, Blaxland exported from the same Parramatta vineyard three half-pipes of wine. He achieved further fame when, with Wentworth and

Lawson, he crossed the formidable barrier of the Blue Mountains and explored the fertile plains beyond—a venture which was to mean much to the development of agriculture in New South Wales.

In 1824 a remarkable young man arrived in Sydney. His name was James Busby and he was then twenty-four years old. While still in Scotland, with only the viticultural background of a few months spent in the best wine districts of France, he was imbued with the belief that there was a great future for the vine in Australia. Shortly after his arrival he wrote his first book, *A Treatise on the Cultivation of the Vine and the Art of Making Wine.* On 8 May 1824, a grant of 2,000 acres of land in the Hunter River district was made to him. He named it Kirkton, afterwards well known for its wine. After five years' experience in Australia, Busby wrote a second book, *A Manual of Plain Directions for Planting and Cultivating Vineyards and for Making Wine in New South Wales.*

At this time Busby arranged with McArthur, Blaxland, and others who had established vineyards, for their surplus cuttings to be distributed among intending planters. Busby's crowning work, however, was his voyage of viticultural research into southern European wine regions and the introduction to Australia of his great vine collection which included nearly all the best varieties grown in France and southern Spain at that time. The vines reached Sydney in good condition, and Busby offered them to the Government for the formation of an experimental garden there, 'to prove their different qualities and propagate, for general distribution, those which may appear most suitable to the climate'. The vines were planted in the Botanical Gardens, and of 678 varieties, 362 were successfully struck. This collection has been the basis of the vine population of Australian vineyards since 1833.

Right up until 1925, nearly all the wine exported from Australia was of the export burgundy-type. In 1854, consignments were only of a token nature, and it was not until 1872, when the firm of P. B. Burgoyne & Company started operations, that the wine trade showed any important development. It grew, and was maintained at around 750,000 imp. gallons (900,000 U.S.), and distributed throughout the United Kingdom by such firms as Burgoyne's, with Harvest and Tintara; as Gilbey's, with Rubicon; as Stephen Smith, with Keystone, and Pownall's, with Emu. Then, at the end of the First World War, it became the responsibility of the Bruce-Page Government to absorb the returning soldiers into sound occupations. At that time, as established growers on the Murray were gathering crops of Gordo Blanco grapes at the rate of about 10 tons (11 short tons) to the acre, at £A12 per ton, grape-growing appeared to be the ideal occupation for the repatriated men. Despite warnings from the industry itself that only limited settlement was possible, the Government went ahead with the greatest vigour, so that when the vines bore their fruit, there was an inevitable glut of grapes, accompanied by an economic crisis of the worst kind. The Government was impotent to solve this problem, which was flung back upon the industry itself. The Federal Viticultural Council advised that the only possible remedy was to establish new markets by the granting of an export bounty, which would have the effect of creating a demand for fortifying spirit for this new market, and thus absorb the glut of Doradillo grapes—which were the distilling variety. Having no better plan, the Government announced a bounty of 2*s.* 9*d.* a gallon, and gave a drawback of excise on the fortifying spirit used, which was considered equivalent to 1*s.* 3*d.* a gallon, making a total remission of 4*s.* a gallon on all the sweet wine exported. Within a few years these measures had proved successful. The export of fortified wine sustained a great impetus, and in 1927 the total export of wines rose to 3,773,000 imp. gallons (4,553,000 U.S.).

At the present time, the export trade in Australian wine has considerably receded and is round about the 1,538,000 imp. gallon (1,847,000 U.S.) mark per annum.

New South Wales

The Hunter River Valley was important in the early viticultural experiments of the Australian continent. Later growers of note there included the Lindeman family; in 1842, Dr. H. J. Lindeman planted Cawarra, famous for many years for its high-quality, claret-type wines. In 1914 he acquired the vineyard of Kirton from Catherine Busby: her daughter later married Dr. Lindeman's son. This vineyard was to become one of the best-known of the many vineyards subsequently owned by the Lindemans. The Ben Ean Vineyard, planted by J. McDonald in 1870, was purchased by the Lindemans in 1912 and is still flourishing and producing first-quality wine for the table.

Other vineyards still actively producing in this area are Penfold's Dalwood; the late Hector Tulloch's Glen Elgin, now under the management of his brother Keith; McWilliam's Mount Pleasant and several more. It is unfortunate that the vineyards on

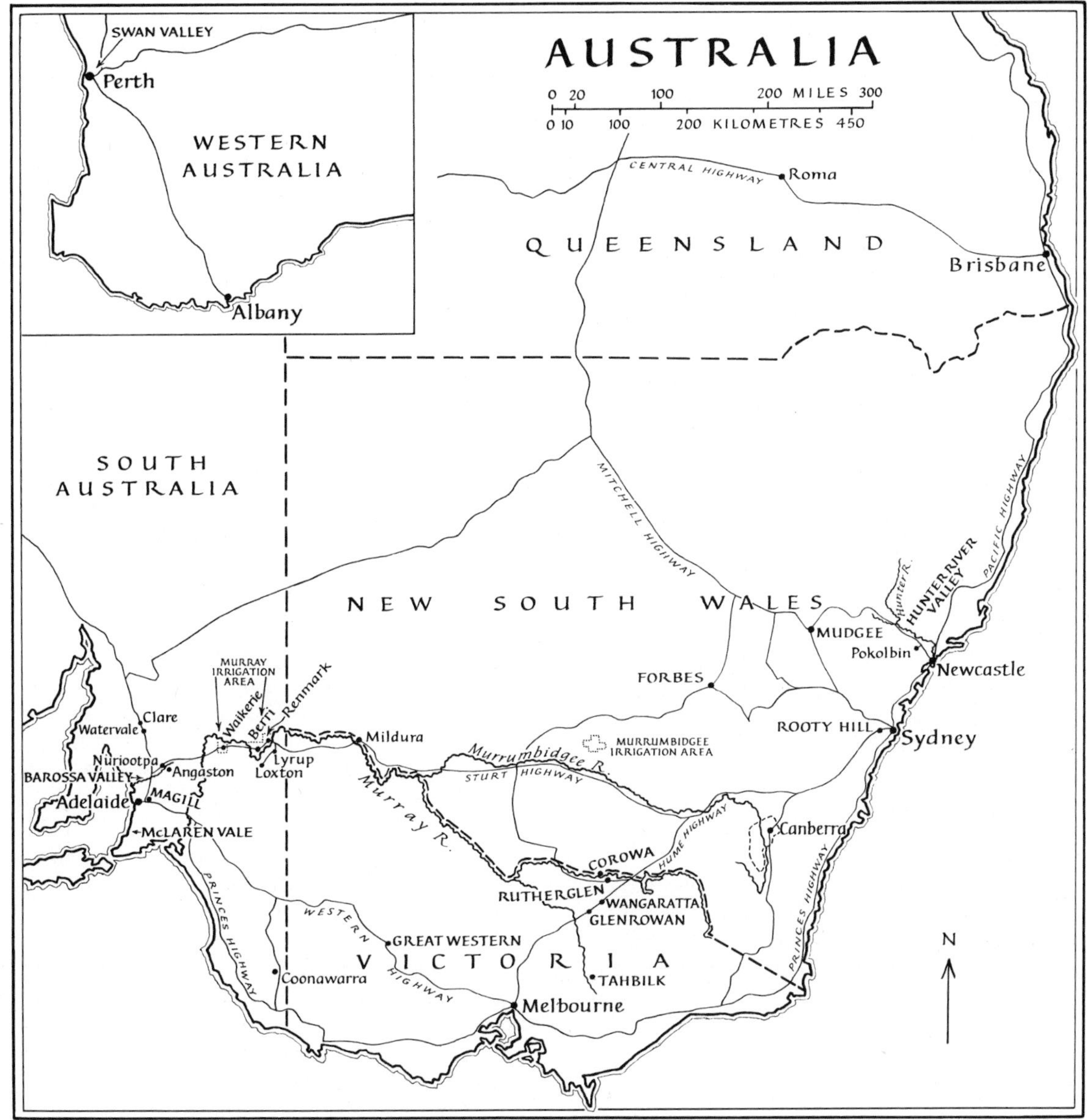

the Hunter River do not share the otherwise uniformly good vintages, with the result that there are now fewer growers in this area.

Another important district in New South Wales is the Murrumbidgee Irrigation Area, the principal centres of which are Griffith, Leeton, Beelbangeira, and Mirroul. Large quantities of wine (more of the commercial sweet style) are produced, and help to make New South Wales the second largest wine-making state in Australia. Most of the vineyards here are planted with true wine varieties, in contrast to the irrigation areas of the Murray River in South Australia where the main varieties used are Doradillo, Sultana, and Gordo Blanco. A third important vineyard area is Corowa which, though small, produces the best quality dessert wines of Australia. In the 1951–2 season the total yield of wine for New South Wales was 5,280,000 imp. gallons (6,341,000 U.S.), made up of:

	gallons	
	imp.	*U.S.*
Hunter River	80,000	96,000
Corowa	333,000	399,000
Murrumbidgee Irrigation Area	4,833,000	5,804,000

The balance was made up from small yields from

Mudgee, Forbes, and Rooty Hill. Mention can be made here of Penfold's Minchinbury sparkling and table wines, which enjoy a uniformly good reputation.

Victoria

The first record of a vineyard in Victoria was that planted at Yering in Lilydale in 1838 by William Ryrie, from vine cuttings obtained from Camden Park. In 1839 Charles LaTrobe was appointed first Superintendent of Port Phillip—he afterwards became first Governor of the Colony of Victoria. La Trobe married, in 1835, a Swiss lady (Mademoiselle de Montmollin) and there is no doubt that this union prompted the departure of a number of Swiss *vignerons* for Australia, and more particularly Victoria. Eleven of these settled in Geelong, and very soon after their arrival they all possessed their own small vineyards. In 1848 Paul de Castella arrived in Victoria and took up land at Yering. George de Pury settled in Yeringberg, and in 1854 Hubert de Castella arrived and planted St. Hubert's. By 1886 Yering had 100 acres of vines; Yeringberg, 70 acres; and St. Hubert's, 260 acres. The vines were mostly White Hermitage and Tokay, Red Hermitage and Cabernet Sauvignon.

Although vine culture in Victoria started later than in New South Wales and South Australia, the congenial conditions in Victoria attracted a number of settlers to the cultivation of the vine, so that by 1900 there were over 1,200 separate vineyards, distributed throughout almost every part of the state, and Victoria was by far the biggest wine producer at that time. In 1889–90 production was as follows:

	gallons	
	imp.	*U.S.*
South Australia	510,674	613,294
New South Wales	688,685	827,076
Victoria	1,578,590	1,895,808

Unfortunately for Victoria, however, the dread scourge of phylloxera began to make its appearance, first in Geelong, then in Bendigo, and later in the vineyards of the north-east, with the ultimate result that the main areas devoted to viticulture were devastated. In many cases, the costly process of reconstitution with phylloxera-resistant vines from America proved too frightening and the land concerned was turned to other, more stable forms of agriculture. Another factor which reduced the number of growers, particularly of the lighter types of wine, was the lack of appreciation, inside Australia, of the quality of Australian wines, so that it often happened that a wine-maker was faced with the problem of storing the forthcoming vintage whilst his cellars were already filled to overflowing. The uncertainty, the comparatively poor prices, and the low yields per acre were also contributing factors to the loss in production.

The irrigated area of Mildura plays a dominant part today in the state's wine production, and this area is coming into prominence by reason of the increasingly high quality of the wines made there. The districts still producing, but in much smaller quantities, are: Rutherglen, Glenrowan, Wangaratta, Tahbilk, and Great Western. This last area is noted as the largest producer of Australian sparkling wine, its cellars being somewhat similar to those in the Champagne area of France.

South Australia

Inferior, in earlier years, to Victoria, this state has shown steady progress because it escaped the vicissitudes of Victoria. From the earliest plantings in 1834, vine areas suffered no setbacks and there are at least a dozen firms which have already celebrated their centenaries. Wine-making in South Australia ranks very high in popular esteem; it is classed with grazing as the most important rural industry. The principal 'dry' area is the Barossa Valley, probably the most successful of all from the point of view of production and the quality of its product. In this region are Penfold's, Seppelt's, Smith's of Yalumba, Gramp's of Orlando, Saltram of Angaston, Tolley of Nuriootpa, Thomas Hardy & Sons—to mention just a few. The area is planted with all the best grape varieties for the production of high quality wines: Rhine Riesling, Hermitage and Cabernet, Pedro and Palomino, Grenache, Dolcetto, and many others.

It was in this district that the Barossa Wine Festival originated, to celebrate the harvest on the lines of the old festivals in Germany. Nothing could more adequately symbolize the spirit of the vine than the sight on a glorious day in early June of the red-gold sea of the vines in their autumn colours spreading as far as the eye can reach.

Quite close to Adelaide lies the district of Magill and here fine wines of diverse types were successfully grown from the characteristic grape varieties common to the best areas of Europe. As Adelaide has expanded almost all the vineyards have been given over to housing. Another fruitful area is McLaren Vale, in which the principal firms are Hardy's of Tintara, Emu, Ingoldby, and A. C. Johnston. This area has been the principal source of supply to the export burgundy-style trade.

Various small vine-growing districts in South

PRODUCTION FIGURES FOR A TYPICAL YEAR

	Total gallonage		*Gallonage exported*	
	imp.	*U.S.*	*imp.*	*U.S.*
South Australia	25,060,800	30,096,768	1,812,105	2,176,247
New South Wales	5,343,700	6,417,516	49,560	59,519
Victoria	3,613,900	4,340,113	33,165	39,829
West Australia	985,800	1,183,896	282	339
Queensland	21,193	25,452	152	182
Total	35,025,393	42,063,745	1,895,264	2,276,116

Australia are Coonawarra, Clare, Watervale, Modbury, Hope Valley, and Highercombe, of which the first two are by far the most important.

Another important district is the Murray Irrigation Area, which includes Renmark, Lyrup, Berri, Waïkerie, and Loxton. Up till 1921 vines were made in these areas simply to be distilled into fortifying spirits; otherwise the main preoccupation of the growers was with drying varieties, such as sultanas, currants, and lexias. Since then, more attention has been paid to table wine and today a high percentage of the fortified wine produced in South Australia comes from the Co-operative Wineries in these localities. Evidence of its importance is the recent purchase of virgin river land at Cadell by several large firms in non-irrigated areas. Some of these are already planted.

In 1921, however, Leo Buring—then an advisory expert—introduced the idea of producing commercial sweet wine of the same nature as that obtained from the dry, non-irrigated districts. In the beginning, such wine-making was not an unqualified success, but today, forty years later, wines of quite exemplary quality are coming from this area. This is fortunate, because of the augmentation it provides when lack of rain seriously depletes yields in the older 'dry' districts. Most of the growers in this region are on a co-operative basis, the chief firms being Berri, Loxton, Renmark Growers, and Waikerie. The exceptions are Angove's Ltd. and the Lyrup Wine Company, which are proprietary.

Taking as an example 1952—when the total production in the state amounted to 25,800,000 imp. gallons (30,840,000 U.S.)—9,300,000 imp. gallons (11,169,000 U.S.) came from the River Murray Irrigation Area. (Although classed as a small vine-growing district it is, in fact, the largest vineyard area of South Australia.)

WESTERN AUSTRALIA

In 1952, 700,000 imp. gallons (841,000 U.S.) of wine were made in this state, the principal *vignerons* being Valencia and Houghton's, both acquired in recent years by the Emu Wine Company. The other principal winery is Sandalford.

Western Australia is noted for the number of Yugoslavs who have settled there, some of whom carry on what may be called 'back-yard' operations, because of the primitive nature of their wine-making and the unofficial methods of distribution. Houghton Vineyard is probably the most versatile in Australia, owing to the remarkable diversity of the types produced there, from the lightest white burgundy-type to the luscious liqueur Muscat.

QUEENSLAND

This is the least significant of all the Australian wine-producing states. The total production rarely exceeds 100,000 imp. gallons (120,000 U.S.).

PRODUCTION FIGURES

(*see* table above)

Austria

Austrian wines are predominantly white and light, some crisp and tempting to gulp down, some fresh and fruity, with a few red. This small country, the heart of Europe (and, in the great days of the Habsburgs, the heart of the Holy Roman Empire), touches at its borders six others: Switzerland, Italy, Yugoslavia, Hungary, Czechoslovakia, and Western Germany—and its grapes are as variegated as the landscape. Vine growing is older than the name Österreich, going back nearly a thousand years.

The word Austria conjures up pictures of Viennese cafés, zithers, and cream cakes, of Baroque architecture, Strauss waltzes, and horses dancing—or else of a pastoral land of mountain lakes and wild flowers, of winter sports, and haymaking farmers, jolly in *Lederhosen*. Austria is all these things and more—although it is not true that the Danube is blue. The vast ranges of the Alps tower over the land. In Carinthia, on the higher slopes of the Gross Glockner, one of the highest mountains in Europe, is a remote glacial world where the snow never melts. But eastwards, the steep massif declines towards the slopes outside Vienna, and the great plains of Burgenland and Lower Austria.

The spectacular western provinces of Tyrol and Vorarlberg produce little wine, all of it consumed locally. The approximately 99,000 acres planted in vine lie mainly in Lower Austria, Burgenland, Styria, and in the neighbourhood of Vienna—in order of size. The vineyards, where some eighty thousand workers are employed, are mostly cut up into parcels of less than twenty-five acres, and the annual production of wine averages 28,600,000 imp. gallons (34,300,000 U.S.)—85% white, and 15% red. Most of the harvest is stored by the growers in their own vaults, but in big harvests part of it is taken over by the wine trade and the growers' associations. They combine voluntarily in these co-operatives, surrendering their crops for storage and for sale on a trust basis. In the whole country, there are forty such associations, with a storage capacity of 10,559,000 imp. gallons (12,689,000 U.S.)—or a quarter of the country's harvest. The societies have a reputation for good quality wines. The number of people employed, directly or indirectly, in the wine industry is estimated as some two hundred thousand. Consumption of wine per head is 4·84 imp. gallons (5·81 U.S.).

Wine labels state whether the wine is a natural one (*naturbelassen*) and, most important, if it is hand-picked (*gerebelt*). The labels carry either the name of the village or district of origin, or, less often, of the individual vineyard; or they may state the name of the grape variety, as in Alsace. Occasionally, both will be found. (For example, Wachauer 1959, i.e. wine of the 1959 vintage from the important Wachau region of Lower Austria; Grüner Veltliner 1959, i.e. wine of the 1959 vintage of the Grüner Veltliner grape; Steiner Veltliner 1959, i.e. wine of the 1959 vintage from Stein in the Wachau region and from the Grüner Veltliner grape.) Schluck is the light, dry wine that asks to be swallowed. Among the better bottles, Riesling and Traminer will be found, and also some Spätlese wine from late-picked grapes; and ice-wines, such as the Nicholas wine from Krems. Among important place-names to look for on labels are Krems, Klosterneuburg, Gumpoldskirchen, Retz, Vöslau, Nussdorf, Grinzing, Oggau, and Rust—they will usually appear with the possessive 'er', e.g. Ruster Gumpoldskirchner.

Austria imports a good deal of wine, especially from the South Tyrol, once Austrian, now in Italy. Until a few years ago, most of the native harvest was consumed at home. The situation has now changed and Austrian wines are seen abroad—from Schluck, made perhaps from Sylvaner grapes, to luscious Spätlese, and estate-bottled Auslese. In 1964, the export figure had risen to 410,000 imp. gallons (493,000 U.S.).

Wine History

In A.D. 955 Otto I ordained the replanting of the Austrian vineyards, for the first time since the departure of the Romans. Here, as elsewhere, the vines were to be tended principally by monks, in the monasteries of Bavaria and Salzburg. Those wines which were shipped up the Danube to Bavaria were known as *Osterweine*. The Austrian vineyards were most extensive in the sixteenth century, when Hungary came under Turkish rule and wine-making virtually ceased. Austria was free of her chief competitor, and soon her vineyards were ten times the size they are today. Upper Austria, which now makes no wine, was then a leading producer.

About 1580, Johannes Rasch wrote the most important book on Austrian viticulture. In 1673, the *Landkompass* printed by imperial patent the classification of the vineyards, which had actually been graded in 1646: good, fair, ordinary. Over the years changes have occurred. The Wachau, now one of the best regions, was then in the third class, its wine, proverbially sour (*Sauer wie der Wachauer*) —nothing could be sourer than Wachau wine. In 1780, the Empress Maria Theresa, setting out to simplify the administration of her dominions, revised the wine taxes (*Tranksteuer*). Under the new law, the aristocracy and the higher clergy were absolved from paying them, but as many as eight different taxes were levied on the rest of the population. Maria Theresa also approved some complicated regulations for the stocking and shipment of wines that were not unlike those in use in the United States today.

All producers were now allowed to sell their own wine (*Eigenbauwein*) free of tax. This law was extended to certain items of food—and still causes trouble at the *Heurigen*, based even now upon the laws of Maria Theresa, although many foods are served that were not included in the fêtes of the eighteenth century.

When a grower wished to announce that stocks of his new wine were on sale, he hung up branches outside his house. The German verb 'to hang out' is *aushängen*; hence, the name of these wines became

AUSTRIA
CZECHOSLOVAKIA
HUNGARY
YUGOSLAVIA
STYRIA
BURGENLAND
VIENNA
N
0 MILES 25
0 KILOMETRES 40
Retz
Pulkau
Haugsdorf
Falkenstein
Poysdorf
Mailberg
Eggenburg
R. Kamp
Kamp Valley
Schönberg
Ravelsbach
Hollabrunn
Mistelbach
Weinviertel
BRÜNNERSTRASSE
Zistersdorf
Zöbing
Langenlois
Strass
Dürnstein
Weissenkirchen
Spitz
Wachau
Krems
Stein
Loiben
Arnsdorf
Traismauer
Am Wagram
Tullnerfeld
Klosterneuburg
Wolkersdorf
Bisamberg
Matzen
R. Danube
Hainburg
Brünn am Gebirge
Gumpoldskirchen
Baden
Traiskirchen
Vöslau
Bruck
Neusiedlersee
Leitha Mountains
St. Margarethen
Steinfeld
Gr. Höflein
Kl. Höflein
Eisenstadt
St. Georgen
Gols
Podersdorf
Oggau
Rust
Illmitz
Apetlon
Mörbisch
Pottelsdorf
Rosalien Mts.
Neckenmarkt
Deutsch-Kreutz
Lutzmannsburg
Rechnitz
Eisenberg
Graz
Hitzendorf
Ligist
Stainz
Deutschlandsberg
R. Mur
Fürstenfeld
Feldbach
Sausal
Leibnitz
Ehrenhausen
R. Sulm
Eibiswald
Mureck
Klöch
Radkersburg
Leutschach

Hengelweine—and the most prominent wine-selling family in Grinzing today bears the name Hengl. According to the dispensation of Maria Theresa, a man could sell only his own wine free of tax; therefore a true *Heuriger,* when his barrels were dry, must close his doors until next season.

Wine Regions

Lower Austria

This eastern province, with over 55,000 acres of vineyard, watered by the Danube, is the granary of Austria—a country of cornfields, market-gardens, and vines; a country, also, of churches, baroque monasteries, and romantic castles. It is the only district in Europe which produces oil actually in a vineyard region. The vineyards fall into the Danube area on both banks of the river—the hilly Weinviertel, and the Wienerwald-Steinfeld district.

Prevailing grape varieties: Rheinriesling, Grüner Veltliner, Neuberger, Riesling-Sylvaner, Welsch-Riesling, Müller-Thurgau, Zierfandler ('Spätrot'), Muscat-Ottonel, Traminer, for white wines; Rotgipfler, Blauer Portugieser, Blauburgunder, Blaufränkisch, Sankt Laurent for red.

The Danube section begins west of Willendorf with the Wachau, a lovely stretch of country between there and Krems-Stein, where the vines climb up steep terraces of gneiss and mica-schist. At Stein, the district of Krems begins. This belongs to the Wachau with its loess terraces, but the centre is Krems itself, a historic wine town with big vaults for bulk storage, a school of viniculture, and a fascinating wine museum. In 1964, the last harvesting in Strass bei Krems was completed on 10 December. In addition to those places already mentioned, Spitz, Dürnstein (lying picturesquely at the foot of a ruined castle), Weissenkirchen, and Loiben are worth noting. In both the Krems and the Wachau districts, the Riesling produces wines with a fine bouquet, and is becoming increasingly popular.

On the right bank of the Danube, the vineyards follow the river from Ober-Armsdorf to Traismauer. The Kamp Valley, on the left bank of the Danube, is an important wine-growing area in which the most important place is Langenlois. East of the Kamp Valley is the district known as Am Wagram, its vines planted along a terraced ridge of hills very like those at Krems. Downstream, on the right bank of the river, the valley widens into the fertile Tullnerfeld until, at Greifenstein, the mountains close in again, and the vines climb their slopes. Here the Klosterneuburg region begins. Klosterneuburg itself is a town celebrated for fine wines. It contains an experimental school of viticulture, a wine museum, and the enormous vault of the Chorherrenstift, three stories deep.

The principal place-names besides those cited above are Zöbing (distinguished for its excellent Riesling), Strass, and Schönberg; in the Klosterneuburg area: Kahlenberg and Buchberg.

Northward, on the left bank of the Danube, good wines grow on the slopes of the Bisamberg. Below Vienna, on the right bank, is the Hainburg and Bruck district.

The *Weinviertel* lies north of the Danube and consists of the countryside around Retz and south to the Eggenburg, Hollabrunn, and Ravelsbach districts. It includes also the 'Brünnerstrasse' district, on both sides of the old main road between Vienna and Brünn, which is one of the most productive areas in the country. Light, palatable wines come from this fertile country, although in the south-west the Veltliner produces spiced and fruity growths, and Matzen has some good red wines.

The principal place-names in the Weinviertel are Retz, Pulkau, Haugsdorf, and Mailberg; Eggenburg, Hollabrunn, and Ravelsbach; Poysdorf, Zistersdorf ('Steinberg'), Matzen, Wolkersdorf, and Falkenstein.

The Wienerwald-Steinfeld district. Some excellent vineyards are planted on the hill-slopes of the Vienna Woods. Gumpoldskirchen, at the foot of the Anningen Mountain, where in good years luscious grapes are gathered late in the season is the best-known wine town. From Baden and Traiskirchen come fiery, spicy wines; and in Vöslau a red wine (Vöslauer Rotwein) is made from the Blauer Portugieser.

Burgenland

Until 1919, this south-eastern province was part of Hungary, and even now some of the villages are entirely Magyar or Croat. The landscape here is different, too; its dominant feature, set in the midst of *Puszta*, a kind of steppe, is the Neusiedlersee, a great lake rimmed with reeds—and exotic birds nesting on its marshy shores. The country, rich in orchards and vegetable gardens, also bears vines—24,700 acres of them, shared among four different areas, the Lake District, Eisenstadt and Mattersburg districts, and South Burgenland.

Prevailing grape varieties: Welsch-Riesling, Muscat-Ottonel, Furmint (Mosel), Traminer, Weissburgunder (Klevner or Pinot Blanc), Ruländer, Müller-Thurgau, Neuburger, and Bouviertraube for white wines; Blaufränkisch, Blauburgunder, Portugieser, and Sankt Laurent for red.

The Lake district is the most important for wine,

with vineyards bordering the Neusiedlersee on three sides. The vines are protected by the Leitha Mountains, and the glassy surface of the vast lake retains and reflects the warmth of the sun's rays. Excellent white wines are made here from Welsch-Riesling and Muscat-Ottonel, and some pleasant red ones from Blaufränkisch. At the end of a good summer there will be some fine Ruster Ausbruch from late-picked grapes, notably the Furmint. On the sandy soil of the Seewinkel the original vines escaped the phylloxera plague; this is one of the very few places in Europe where wine is still made from ungrafted vines. The principal place-names are Oggau, Mörbisch, St. Margarethen, and Rust.

The Eisenstadt district. The great centre is Gols with 2,000 acres of vineyard. Close to the lake, vines planted in sandy soil, immune from phylloxera, produce Sandweine. The principal place-names are Gross-Höflein, Klein-Höflein, St. Georgen, Podersdorf, Illmitz, and Apetlon.

The Mattersburg district. South of Eisenstadt, in the foothills of the Rosalien Mountains, the vineyards produce mainly red wines—one of them the fiery Kadarka. The principal place-names are Pöttelsdorf, Trauersdorf, Neckenmarkt, Deutsch-Kreutz, and Lutzmannsburg.

South Burgenland. The wine-growing districts here centre around Eisenberg and Rechnitz.

Styria

Lying between the lovely lakes of the Salzkammergut (where St. Wolfgang and the White Horse Inn are to be found) and Yugoslavia, Styria is the green province, a country of meadows and woodlands, of fat cattle and plodding cart-horses, of rolling hills and rivers well stocked with fish. Its capital, Graz, is the second largest town in Austria. Once it was the peaceful resort of retired officers; now it is a busy industrial city. The *Steirergewand*—the grey loden suit with green facings—worn all over Austria, originated in Styria, where it is the national dress. The province has almost 5,000 acres of vineyard, scattered over five districts, the Schilcher, the Sausal-Leibnitz, the Leutschach-Ehrenhaus, the Klöch, and East Styria.

Prevailing grape varieties: Furmint, Riesling, Sylvaner, Traminer, Weissburgunder, Ruländer, Morillon, Müller-Thurgau, Muscat-Ottonel, and Sauvignon for white wines; Blauer Portugieser, Blaufränkisch, and Sankt Laurent for red. The blue Wildbacher also is of local importance, since it is the basic grape for a wine of special character and subtlety—the Styrian Schilcherwein.

Schilcher district. This extends from Graz to Eibiswald on the southern frontier. In Stainz, a light red wine is made, and in Deutschlandsberg, a dark red one—fresh, spicy, digestible: this is the Schilcherwein. Other names to remember are Hitzendorf and Ligist.

Sausal-Leibnitz district. A stretch of country lying east of the Schilcher district, between two streams, the Lassnitz and the Sulm, the latter the home of the world's finest capons. It highest point is Demmerkogel, where the vineyards are planted at 1,920 feet.

Leutschach-Ehrenhausen district. Extending to the northern slopes of the Windische Bühel, this is similar in soil and grape varieties (Welsch-Riesling, Sylvaner, Weissburgunder, and Traminer) to the Sausal-Leibnitz vineyards, but the wines are stronger and fuller.

The *Klöch district* produced wines of quality, some of them sparkling, with a charming bouquet. They are particularly agreeable when young. The principal place-names are Radkersburg and Mureck.

East Styria. Viticulture is not taken over-seriously in this district. Wines are made, however, and the vineyards struggle up the slopes of the hills as high as 2,000 feet. The best-known places are Hartberg, Fürstenfeld, and Feldbach.

Vienna

The beautiful city is almost encircled by trees and meadows—the Vienna Woods, on the slopes of which the vines grow—nearly 1,500 acres of them. From two of the hills, Kahlenberg and Leopoldsberg, the Turks were driven back from western Europe—but their oriental languor is said to persist in the leisurely café life. The wine villages of Grinzing, Sievering, and Nussdorf are now within the suburbs, and the stinging new *heurige* wine served in their wine-garden is, for the tourists who flock there, the essence of Viennese gaiety. Outside the little vine-covered houses, green boughs are hung out when the wine of the year is ready. Some may actually come from the proprietor's vine plot, but he will need more than he is likely to make to satisfy all the customers who come to the long wooden tables in his garden and sing to the music of zithers and guitars. A new law has been passed which permits them only to sell wine which has been produced in their own vineyards. If they wish to sell wine from other vineyards they have to get a special permit to do so.

Prevailing grape varieties: Grüner Veltliner, Riesling, and Weissburgunder.

Auxerrois

Grape grown in the Lorraine district for the light pink *vin gris.*

Auxey-Duresses and Auxey-Duresses-Côte de Beaune

Burgundy red and white wine. District: Côte de Beaune, France.

Auxey is one of the poor relations of the Côte de Beaune. Its wines are about 80% red and, while they are considered pleasantly sound enough in body, fragrance and colour, they are rarely, if ever, distinguished otherwise. Yet, on account of the difference in price between these and others from the famous slope, they are often good value.

The vineyards are set back in the hills, slightly too high to be first-rate. They cover about 370 acres, and wines from grapes grown in about 250 acres within this area may add the term Côte de Beaune to the commune name. Such wines may occasionally be slightly superior to the communal ones. In 1962 Auxey produced 38,000 imp. gallons (45,600 U.S.) of red wine and 18,000 imp. gallons (21,600 U.S.) of white. Wines from the best vineyards may add vineyard name to commune name and although the final list of these First Growths (*Premiers Crus*) has not yet been drawn up, the following vineyards are considered the best.

FIRST GROWTHS (*Premiers Crus*)

Vineyard	*Acres*
Les Duresses	19·5
Les Bas-des-Duresses	5·9
Reugne	7·8
Les Grands-Champs	12·0
Climat-du-Val (or Clos du Val)	23·0
Les Écusseaux	15·9
Les Bretterins	5·0

N.B. Wines sold as La Chapelle come from grapes grown in a once separate vineyard now split between Reugne and Bretterins.

Ava-Ava

Another name for Kava (*q.v.*).

Avelsbach

German commune in the triangle between the Moselle and Ruwer. The wines are classed sometimes with one group, sometimes with another. The best known vineyards are: Altenberg, Dom Avelsbach, and Dom Herrenberg.

See RUWER; MOSELLE.

Avize

Village in Champagne which produces one of the finest wines of the Côte des Blancs.

See CHAMPAGNE.

Ay

Town in the Marne Valley near Épernay, whose cellars lie underneath the fine Champagne red-wine vineyards of that region.

See CHAMPAGNE.

B

Bacardi

A well-known brand of Cuban, Puerto Rican, Brazilian, Mexican, and Bahamanian rum. Also a cocktail based on the rum.

See RUM: PUERTO RICO.

Bacchus

1. From the Greek Bacchos—an alternative name for their wine god, better known as Dionysos. The Romans adopted him as Bacchus, identifying him with their own wine deity Liber.

2. An American hybrid grape, small and black, which at best produces wines with body and of fair quality.

See DIONYSOS; CLASSICAL WINES.

Baco

French hybridizer Maurice Baco, whose grapes are grown in France and America. Baco 1 is widespread but produces better wine in New York State than in France; Baco 22A is legally allowed in the sandy soils of France's Bas-Armagnac to be used in making the region's fine brandy, but its merits are still disputed.

Bacterium (*pl.* Bacteria)

'Genus of schizomycetæ, microscopic rod-shaped unicellular organisms, in decomposing liquids' (*Oxford English Dictionary*).

Certain wine maladies are caused by the presence of bacteria—notably acescence, bitterness, fatty degeneration, tourne.

Bad Dürkheim (Dürkheim)

See DÜRKHEIM; PALATINATE.

Bad Kreuznach

Wine town and region in the Nahe (*q.v.*).

Badacsonyi Kéknyelü

The best-known of the Badacsonyi wines—a dry, greenish-white dessert wine. Both red and white wines are grown in this region.

For this and other Badacsonyi fine wines *see* HUNGARY.

Baden

White and red wines. District: South-West Germany.

The Baden vineyard, like an edging worked in vine and grape motif, borders the extreme south-west corner of Germany. It begins along the south shore of Lake Constance (or Bodensee, as it is called in German), skirts the thickly wooded slopes of the Black Forest on the fringes of Switzerland and France, and then marches parallel with Alsace on the other side of the Rhine, past Strasbourg on the Alsace side and Baden-Baden on the German side, until it reaches the Heidelberg region.

The wines are not among the most important in Germany and they are practically unknown abroad. In the 1860s, Baden was the largest German vineyard, but shortly afterwards the phylloxera plague struck, reducing the plantation by almost half. A second catastrophe for local production—although good was expected to come out of it—was the law of 1938–40 which required the uprooting of hybrid vines. The Baden vine area then shrank another 20%; but the replanting with Ruländer, Sylvaner, Traminer, some Riesling, and Müller-Thurgau gives promise of generally improved wines as the vineyards age. The Müller-Thurgau crossing of Riesling and Sylvaner is gaining rapidly in this district, as it is elsewhere.

Much of the common wine comes from the Elbling grape; and better quality red wines are made from Spätburgunder, the variety brought originally from Burgundy, where it is called Pinot Noir—this is the standard grape for such good red wines as are found in Germany. In Baden, the Burgundy-import variety is known as the Blauer Spätburgunder; a wine called *Weissherbst* (White Autumn, or White Vintage) is made from the grapes, sometimes with the addition of a little Traminer or Riesling. It is really a rosé, very light in colour and surprisingly heavy and full-bodied for a pink wine.

Gutedel, a grape variety brought from Vevey on Lake Geneva in 1780, produces the Markgräfler wines grown below Freiburg in the south-west corner of Germany. It is also found in considerable quantities over the Swiss border to the south, and the French border to the west. In the German corner, Gutedel wine is often called Moster.

The Ruländer grape variety is actually the French Pinot Gris. Its German name derives from the fact that the grape was brought from France to Germany in 1711 by one Ruländ, a merchant of the town of Speyer. It gives a golden wine which can be very rich and fruity, and in the big years quite full-bodied.

Riesling is not very common in Baden. There is some on the south face of the Kaiserstuhl and some in the Ortenau, the areas producing the best Baden wines.

Vine-growing Regions

The long hook-shape of Baden, following the Rhine from Lake Constance to Heidelberg, includes several distinct vineyard areas with their own characteristics of soil and climate, and therefore of wines. The main ones are Bodensee and the pleasant Seeweine (Lake Constance); and then, following the Rhine rather than any order of importance, Markgräfler, Kaiserstuhl, Ortenau, Kraichgau, and Bergstrasse. The Bergstrasse, above and slightly below Heidelberg, is in both Baden and Hessen and is considered separately.

See BERGSTRASSE.

Bodensee

The wines are known as the *Seeweine,* or Lake Wines. The name refers to the influence on them of the large lozenge-shaped lake along which they lie. Even more influential than the mild climate of the lake is the *Föhn*, a warm wind peculiar to the surrounding alpine area in Germany, Austria, and Switzerland. The hot breath (which has such a disturbing effect on plants, men, and animals that it commonly causes insects to swarm and milk to turn sour, and the penal laws of Austria to take it into account in crimes of violence) brings the grapes quickly to ripeness. The better types are Burgunder, Ruländer, and Traminer. Each little lake port has its vineyard, but nearly all the wine of consequence grows around Meersburg, where sixty acres are cultivated by the Baden State, and called Domäne Meersburg. None of the Bodensee wine escapes the tourists and you must go there if you want to taste it. You could hardly do better. The little lake steamer glides along from port to port, first in Switzerland and then in Germany; speed-boats and sailboats cross from the Swiss shore where snowy peaks tower in the distance. Meersburg itself is a mediæval jewel set in vines; it has a castle which is thirteen hundred years old and still carefully preserved. In the lantern-hung outdoor restaurants on the shore of the lake, accompanying the characteristic Bodensee blue trout, the wines taste better than they really are.

Markgräflerland

The name comes from Markgraf, a German title approximately equivalent to Count. Markgraf Karl Friedrich planted vines in this extreme south-west tip of Germany in the late eighteenth century. It was during this period that the Gutedel, the dominant variety, was brought from Vevey in Switzerland; but the best wines are the Sylvaners, Ruländers, and Traminers.

Kaiserstuhl

Crossing the little bridge over the Rhine in the vicinity of Riquewihr in Alsace and going towards Freiburg, you see on your left hand a low, cone-shaped hill ringed around with vine. The Kaiserstuhl is of volcanic origin; and the mingled clay and volcanic soil gives rich red wines, and darkish white wines with an amber tinge, all of which are likely to have the fieriness of their origin and to be definitely full-bodied, yet rather soft. Common vines, mostly Elbling, grow on the north and the east faces. From the south and south-west slopes come the best Baden wines from the grape varieties Riesling, Sylvaner, Traminer, and Ruländer for white wines; and for red wines, the Blauer Spätburgunder. Among the best *Gemarkungen* or townships are Achkarren, Ihringen, and Bickensohl. Wines are named both by the usual German method of village name followed by vineyard parcel name, and by the Alsatian method of naming the wine after the grape variety. Thus two excellent white Kaiserstuhl wines are Ihringen Sylvaner and Achkarrer Schlossberg.

Ortenau

After the very circumscribed area of the Kaiserstuhl, the best Baden wines come from the region called the Ortenau. Also known as the Ortenau and Bühler Gegend (Bühl is a village and valley in the area, and *Gegend* means region), it stretches along the thin plantable zone from the Rhine to the forested mountains, from the town of Offenburg up to Baden-Baden. The soil is mainly crumbled granite. The best white wines are the Rieslings, the Traminers, the Ruländers; and in reds, the Blauer Spätburgunders. Red and white vineyards are intermingled, but among the best *Gemarkungen* for white wines are Durbach, Fessenbach, Ortenberg, and Neuweier; and for red wines, Affental, Zell-Weierbach, and Durbach. Here, near Offenburg, the Riesling is called Klingelberger, a name taken from a property of Markgraf Staufenberg. A further peculiarity is that the white wines around Neuweier are bottled in the Franconian flask, or Bocksbeutel (*q.v.*).

Kraichgau

This is the region lying between the Ortenau and the section just below Heidelberg where the Bergstrasse begins. Kraichgau is a zone where much of the vineyard had to be torn up when hybrids were outlawed in 1938–40. Where there has been post-war replanting, much of it has been in Ruländer and Blauer Spätburgunder.

Bagaceira

Portuguese spirit made from grape skins.

Balaton, Lake

Centre of one of the principal wine regions of Hungary.

See HUNGARY.

Balthazar, Balthasar

A bottle—notably in Champagne—more suitable for display purposes than for holding wine or spirits. It has a capacity of sixteen normal bottles.

Banadry

French banana liqueur made by Bardinet of Bordeaux.

Bandol

Controlled place-name for certain wines of Provence, France.

See PROVENCE.

Banyuls

Sweet wines. District: South of France.

Area on the Mediterranean border between France and Spain. Banyuls produces a sweet fortified wine known as *vin de liqueur*, of little interest in countries where Sherry and Port can be had. Banyuls is a sweet, natural wine, often drunk before meals by those French who like sweet aperitifs; and it is taken also as a dessert wine.

See SWEET FORTIFIED WINES OF FRANCE.

Barbados Rum

See RUM, BRITISH WEST INDIES.

Barbados Water

One of the earliest names for rum. From Barbados, a British island in the West Indies where rum originated.

Barbaresco

A red wine from Piedmont. One of the better red wines of Italy—big, strong, slow-maturing, with considerable depth and pungency.

See PIEDMONT.

Barbera

Italian red-wine grape, used especially in Piedmont (*q.v.*).

Barbera Amabile

Sweet, slightly sparkling, red Italian wine from the Barbera grape, grown widely in north Italy.

Bardolino

Red wine grown in the vineyards between Verona and Lake Garda, Italy.

See VENETO.

Bärentrank

A beverage from East Prussia, distilled from potatoes and flavoured with honey. The name in German means 'bear's drink'.

Barolo

A red wine from Piedmont. One of the best red wines of Italy—robust, heavy, and slow-maturing, with a pungent aftertaste.

See PIEDMONT.

Barossa Valley

Vine-growing district near Adelaide, South Australia.

Barr

Wine town in Alsace, France.

See ALSACE.

Barrel

Standard container. In England, a barrel contains 36 imperial gallons; in America, 31·5 U.S. gallons. For table of capacities of barrels, casks, and containers of various nations, see APPENDIX B.

Barricas

Spanish for the Bordeaux *barrique*, or barrel, found in Spain.

See BARRIQUE.

Barriquant

Old French for small barrel or keg.

Barrique

French barrel or hogshead, especially the *barrique bordelaise*, or Bordeaux hogshead, containing 225 litres (49·5 imperial gallons; 59·4 U.S.). A *barrique* contains the equivalent of 288 bottles, or twenty-four cases of twelve bottles each. In Bordeaux, 4 *barriques* make up a *tonneau* (*q.v.*).

See APPENDIX B, p. 628.

Barsac

Sweet white wines. District: Bordeaux, France.

Even in the minds of people who are knowledgeable about wine, there is apt to be some confusion between Barsac and Sauternes—is Barsac a Sauternes or is it a place-name on its own? In fact, it is both.

The natural sweet white wine district of Barsac surrounds the town of that name in the northern stretch of the official Sauternes region, about twenty-five miles south-east of Bordeaux. Sauternes is composed of five communes, of which Barsac and Sauternes itself are two. (*See* map on p. 485.) All were once separate and known in their own right; but the production of the commune of Sauternes was small, and some considerable time ago it was decided to include in the *appellation* the similar wines grown in neighbouring villages, in order to have a large enough production to make the wine known in the world market. But Barsac, although it was brought into the Sauternes communes, was considered too famous to give up its own name. Consequently, the French wine law authorities decided that Barsac wines (grown in the vineyard region of Sauternes as now constituted and having all the characteristics of the wines of Sauternes, yet remaining in the traditional district of Barsac) were entitled to both the place-names Barsac and Sauternes. In practice, some are called Sauternes, some Barsac. Either is correct; the greatest are likely to keep the *appellation* Barsac.

Of the thirteen Second Growths (*Seconds Crus*) classified in Sauternes, eight are in Barsac which, however, possesses only two of the eleven First Growths (*Premier Crus*). Château d'Yquem, the single First Great Growth (*Premier Grand Cru*), classed above all the others, is in the south of Sauternes. Yet Barsac can boast of Château Coutet and Château Climens, the two First Growths which deserve to be placed immediately after Château d'Yquem. The most aristocratic of the five Sauternes communes is Bommes, with one-third of its vineyards classified First Growths. In general, quality is spread quite evenly over the region of Sauternes, Barsac, and Preignac, where the soil is intermediate between that of the other two areas. The wines from the stonier, hillier southern section are slightly more unctuous and richer in sugar; the Barsacs tend to be lighter and more fruity and to develop more quickly. Differences, however, are very subtle, and grape varieties, methods of production, and general characteristics are identical.

The Barsac section is flat—in contrast to the rest of Sauternes which is hilly—and its boundary runs roughly parallel with a brook called the Ciron, which runs diagonally across the region and empties into the Garonne. It was tragic, in the summer of 1956, to drive along the Circuit du Sauternais, a winding lane which follows golden arrows in among the greatest vineyards and to pass one blighted vineyard of Barsac after another, the leafless stumps of vine like scorched arms. The February frost in that year was most devastating in the low-lying areas. On the slope vineyards of Sauternes, losses were not nearly as heavy as they were in Barsac, which lost most of its wine for the 1956 and 1957 vintages, and was able to produce little during the recuperative replantation period which followed. The soil of Barsac is less stony, more chalky, than that across the Ciron—hence the difference, slight though it is, between Sauternes and Barsac wine.

Classified Growths (1855 Classification) of Sauternes Situated in Barsac

FIRST GROWTHS (*Premiers Crus*)

Château Coutet	Château Climens

SECOND GROWTHS (*Seconds Crus*)

Château Myrat	Château Broustet
Château Doisy-Dubroca	Château Nairac
Château Doisy-Daëne	Château Caillou
Château Doisy-Védrines	Château Suau

See Château CLIMENS, Château COUTET, SAUTERNES.

Bartzch

A spirit made from fermented hogweed in North Asia. Hogweed is a general name covering various coarse plants such as ragweed, sow thistle, and the like.

Basi

A Philippine Islands spirit of fermented sugar cane.

Basilicata

Red and white wines. District: Southern Italy.

In this region, once known as Lucania, Aglianico del Vulture is the wine of note; a garnet red, sturdy, warm wine from the vineyards of Monte Vulture, and one which is often very agreeable. Southern Italian wines tend to pick up a tang from the volcanic soil, strange and rather unpleasant at first tasting; but the soil of Monte Vulture does not impart too strong a flavour and consequently its Aglianico is more appreciated by outsiders.

Muscat and Malvasia vines abound here, as they do throughout Italy. Both are most at home in hot climates, and both lend themselves well to *passito* treatment—that is, letting the grapes dry before vinifying them, in order to obtain a stronger, sweeter wine. Both normal and *passito* styles are made in Basilicata and may be either red or white. Normal wines run to about 12% of alcohol, *passito* up to 15%, but neither is in the class of Aglianico.

Basler Kirschwasser

A Swiss kirsch.

See KIRSCH.

Bastardo

Important grape in the making of Port (*q.v.*).

Château Batailley

Bordeaux red wine. District: Haut-Médoc, France. Commune: Pauillac.

Situated a mile back from the River Gironde on the high land just south of Pauillac, the vineyard overlooks the two châteaux Pichon-Longueville and Latour. Owned since 1942 by Monsieur Marcel Borie—also proprietor of Château Trottevieille, one of the finest Saint-Émilion vineyards—the estate is a Fifth Growth (*Cinquième Cru*) of Médoc according to the 1855 classification. Château Grand-Saint Julien is a secondary vineyard of the same property. The wine enjoys a limited reputation.

Characteristics. Fairly robust wines but not one of the leaders.

Vineyard area: 47 acres.

Average production: 5,400 cases.

Bâtard-Montrachet

Burgundy white wines. District: Côte de Beaune, France. Commune: Puligny-Montrachet (and in part Chassagne-Montrachet). Official Classification: Great Growth (Grand Cru).

This is one of the magnificent Montrachets which are the greatest of all white Burgundies and consequently among the most superb white wines in the world. Bâtard ranks next to Chevalier-Montrachet, which is second only to the great Montrachet itself. The vineyard, some twenty-nine acres in size, is walled in from the road behind the village of Puligny. It is on the left, with Bienvenue-Bâtard-Montrachet beside it, and across the road, approached through stone archways, is Le Montrachet, backed by Chevalier and the vineyard once known as Les Demoiselles, now discreetly renamed Le Cailleret. Nearby is the remaining vineyard of the Bâtard trio—Criots-Bâtard-Montrachet, a small property of three to four acres, which falls entirely in the commune of Chassagne-Montrachet. Bienvenue-Bâtard, not a great deal larger, with nine acres, is, like Montrachet itself, partly in Puligny, partly in Chassagne. The average yield for Bâtard-Montrachet is about 7,145 imp. gallons (8,581 U.S.), not a great deal for a delicious wine which is in demand all over the world, and it is not surprising that much spurious Montrachet is sold. This is why it is so important to get to know the names of shippers, and of those growers who bottle their own good wines at the domaine. In its characteristics, Bâtard resembles the greater Le Montrachet: it is dry yet rounded, with great elegance and breed and a seductive bouquet. Often this wine is better made than Montrachet itself.

See MONTRACHET; PULIGNY-MONTRACHET.

Batavia Arrack

See ARRACK.

Batzi

A Swiss apple brandy. The French equivalent is known as Calvados, and the American as applejack.

Beaujolais

Red wine. District: Southern Burgundy, France.

Beaujolais is now one of the most widely drunk red wines in the world. Like a blooming country girl, whose freshness is her charm, it has been captivating the capitals of the world, and it remains to be seen whether the quality of the wine will survive the inordinate demand.

Above all, Beaujolais is a wine to be taken young and to be drunk, not sipped. As it is made nowadays, it is fermented very quickly, depending on the maturity achieved on the vine in the particular summer, and this is why it is light, fruity, and flowery. Such a quintessential Beaujolais as Fleurie will be more characteristic than the bigger wines—the Morgon and Moulin-à-Vent. Tasters sometimes say that they detect the taste or scent of peach, of apricot, or of rose in the wine: but whatever the individual may find, it will always be the flower and fruit and freshness that will give the distinction and beauty. This is the reason for drinking Beaujolais young—although to some degree, exception may be made for the Morgon and Moulin-à-Vent. Obviously such a wine is in danger of being ruined by success, and both the *vin bourru* which fills the carafes in Paris cafés, and the more consequential Beaujolais which goes abroad, are increasingly apt to be stretched with the lesser wines of more prolific regions.

Beaujolais, lying in the Saône–Rhône Valley which cuts France in two, has always been on a highway travelled by man. Plentiful relics remain from the Stone Age. Julius Cæsar conquered the tribes of Beaujolais, and his name, and vestiges of Roman occupation, remain in ruined walls and chapels, especially in the north, on the border of the Mâconnais, and in the names of such regions and villages as Juliénas and Romanèche-Thorins. At the time of the Crusades, the River Saône was the eastern frontier of France, and even in very recent times it was still the habit of the river pilots on that broad stream to call out 'Turn to the Kingdom!' if they wanted the helmsman to steer towards the Beaujolais side, or 'Turn to the Empire!' if they meant the other.

Yet the wine of Beaujolais is comparatively modern, and its wide success is quite new. In the eighteenth century, a certain amount of Beaujolais began to be carried over to the nearby Loire—the land route through Burgundy was then all but impassable—and ferried in boatloads down to Paris. Until lately, the young Beaujolais was strictly a child of Lyons, which lies just to the south. The saying is: 'Three rivers flow into Lyons—the Rhône, the Saône, and the Beaujolais.' Even today, a Lyonnais calls for his Beaujolais by the *pot*, not the bottle. A *pot* is now actually larger than a half-bottle, containing 50 centilitres or 17 fl. oz., but not long ago it was a grey mug with blue trimming. These mugs sat in rows in the cafés of Lyons, and down the throats of the men of Lyons was poured practically all the Beaujolais that existed.

Beaujolais stands on the parallel which divides the north of France from the Mediterranean south. Above this region, roofs are pointed; below, they tend to be flat. The accent changes, and the game of bowls, *boules*, becomes the rage. All Beaujolais takes the pitching and knocking together of the balls with deadly seriousness: there are clubs, leagues, and whole newspapers devoted solely to the sport. Every village café has its court of *boules*, its row of *pots*, and usually the 'Fanny', an impudent figure of a young girl to be kissed by the losers.

Out of this country backwater existence, Beaujolais wine has come suddenly into the world. The people themselves show the change. Beaujolais was at least as peasant and country-mannered as any other wine area of France; but now the peasants begin to be arrogant and difficult, because they are sought-after and successful. The wine shows the change: it is not called Burgundy any longer—which it may be, if it conforms to certain conditions, as, for instance, that the wine must come from the Pinot grape instead of the now all but universal Gamay. But '*Beaujolais suis*...' they say—'Beaujolais I am.'

A wine which is drunk very young, and is sometimes very light in alcohol, does not travel well. Ideally, a Chiroubles, for example, should not even be bottled, but should be drunk fresh from the barrel. Yet such wines may be exported to the far corners of the globe. Moreover, high alcoholic content is taken by too many people to indicate value. This has its effect in Beaujolais, where they shudder to hear their wine spoken of condescendingly as a 'nice little wine'. Many growers are trying, in fact, to make it 'bigger'—that is, more alcoholic—and this means longer vatting, which is likely to ruin its freshness. Others begin to talk of the *goût parisien*; they are afraid that too much Beaujolais is going to conform to the Parisian taste, which seems to be for higher alcohol content at the expense of freshness.

Restrictions, Production and Geographical Limits

Most Beaujolais is red wine, but not all the wine made in the Beaujolais region is red. Some Pinot Chardonnay white wine growing on the boundary line of Beaujolais and Mâconnais is known as Mâcon—except for a small quantity known as Beaujolais Blanc. This, superior to the Mâcon, is of a quality equal to that of Pouilly-Fuissé but does not come from communes entitled to that name.

The red wines from the important place-name districts may be labelled Burgundy. They are Burgundies; but nowadays the tendency is to use the popular name of Beaujolais. The production is in Gamay grape, which makes a delightful wine here, although it produces a common wine further north on the Côte d'Or.

The region is divided into two sections from the viticultural standpoint: Haut-Beaujolais and Bas- (or sometimes Bâtard) Beaujolais. The geographical division is the little stream of the Nizerand which cuts across the region at Villefranche-sur-Saône; Haut-Beaujolais extends north to the border of Mâconnais, and Bas-Beaujolais stretches south. But the reason for the division is a distinct difference of soils. With the Gamay grape, the climate balanced

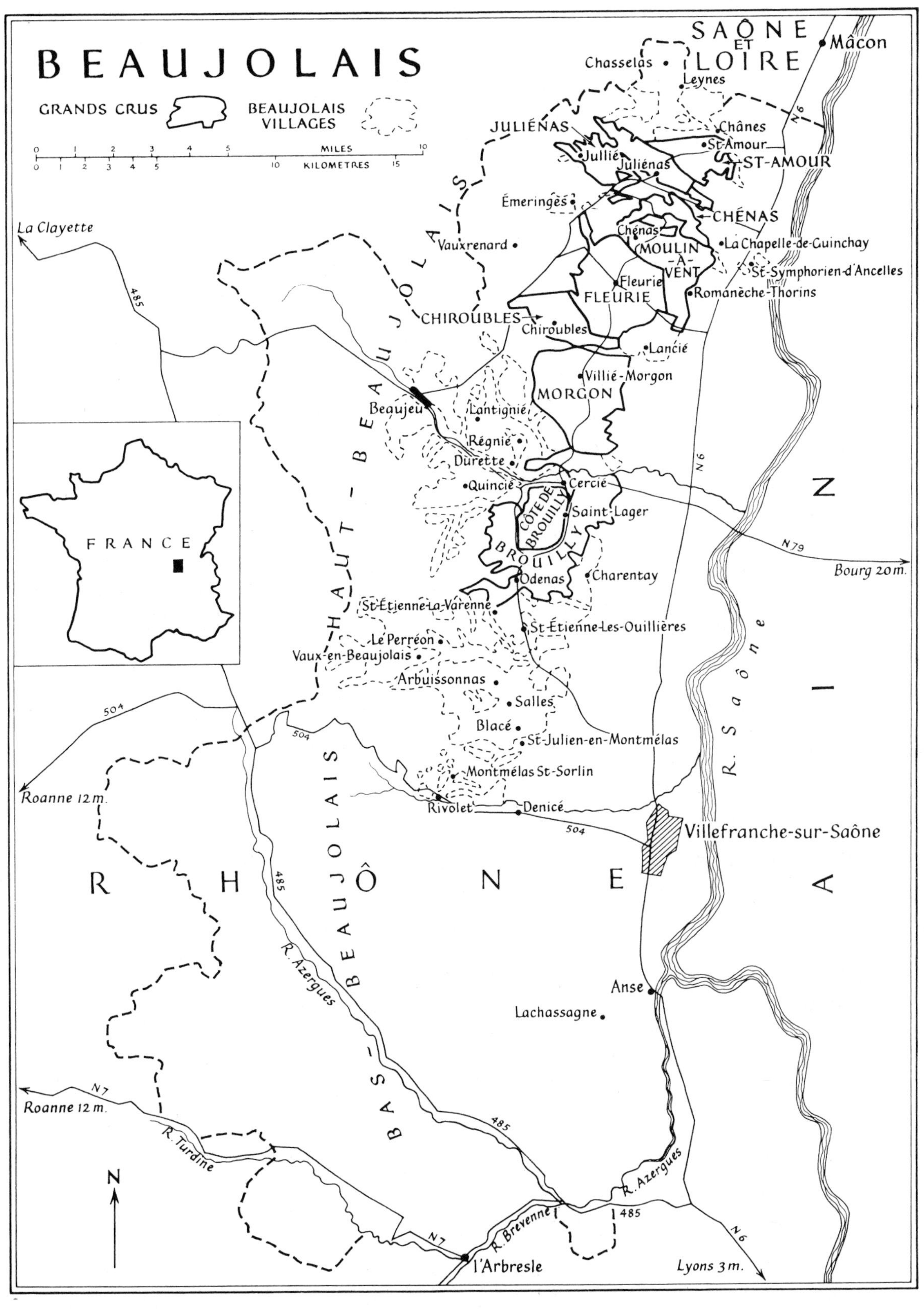
BEAUJOLAIS
GRANDS CRUS
BEAUJOLAIS VILLAGES
MILES
KILOMETRES
SAÔNE ET LOIRE
Mâcon
Chasselas
Leynes
JULIÉNAS
Chânes
St-Amour
ST-AMOUR
Jullié
Juliénas
Émeringes
CHÉNAS
Chénas
La Chapelle-de-Guinchay
MOULIN-A-VENT
St-Symphorien-d'Ancelles
Vauxrenard
Fleurie
FLEURIE
Romanèche-Thorins
La Clayette
CHIROUBLES
Chiroubles
Lancié
Villié-Morgon
MORGON
Beaujeu
Lantignié
Régnié
Durette
Quincié
Cercié
CÔTE DE BROUILLY
Saint-Lager
BROUILLY
Charentay
Odenas
FRANCE
St-Étienne-la-Varenne
St-Étienne-Les-Ouillières
Le Perréon
Vaux-en-Beaujolais
Arbuissonnas
Salles
Blacé
St-Julien-en-Montmélas
Montmélas St-Sorlin
Rivolet
Denicé
Villefranche-sur-Saône
HAUT-BEAUJOLAIS
BAS-BEAUJOLAIS
RHÔNE
AIN
R. Saône
N79
Bourg 20 m.
Roanne 12 m.
Roanne 12 m.
R. Azergues
Anse
Lachassagne
R. Turdine
R. Brevenne
l'Arbresle
Lyons 3 m.
N
485
504
N6
N7

between the sharp north and soft south, and the short fermentation period, the soil characteristic accounts for the nature of the wines. The best come from Haut-Beaujolais, where the soil is characteristically granitic, with a good deal of manganese in the sub-soil—near Moulin-à-Vent and Fleurie there is the site of a manganese mine which was worked from the time of the French Revolution until the First World War. The soil of the lesser Beaujolais is more chalky.

The Beaujolais vineyard begins about five miles south of the city of Mâcon and extends with a width of never more than nine or ten miles for a distance of about forty-five miles to the outskirts of Lyons. The zone is very carefully marked out by the French wine authorities, and technically is delimited by the Turdine on the south, by the natural termination of vineyards at an altitude of about 1,500 feet on the slopes of the Monts du Lyonnais to the west, by the national Paris–Riviera route and the Saône on the east, and by a boundary-line with the Mâconnais to the north just above a stream called the Arlais. Except for a little bulge at Saint-Symphorien-d'Ancelles in front of Moulin-à-Vent, the vineyard never crosses the highway, for the good reason that the rest of the distance to the river is a flat plain which could never produce wine worthy of the name Beaujolais.

Within this expanse are four grades of wine: Beaujolais, Beaujolais Supérieur, Beaujolais-Villages, and the nine Growths (*Crus*)—Saint-Amour, Juliénas, Chénas, Moulin-à-Vent, Fleurie, Chiroubles, Morgon, Brouilly, and Côte de Brouilly.

Beaujolais, with less than 10% of alcohol, is the wine of fifty-nine communes not entitled to a higher classification. Except for narrow strips on both the mountain and river sides of the greater areas in Haut-Beaujolais, it is almost entirely made in Bas-Beaujolais, and nearly all is bought in barrels by shippers for their blends. Beaujolais Supérieur is wine from the same communes which surpasses 10% of alcohol. The yield of Beaujolais may not exceed 445 imp. gallons (535 U.S.) per acre, that of Beaujolais Supérieur 400 imp. gallons (481 U.S.). If it does, the wine must be called simply Vin Rouge.

There are two ways of pruning the vine in Beaujolais. The one called Guyot is the method for the more ordinary wines, and the plant is trained on wires. The Gobelet method calls for pruning very close, and the vines, not trained on wires, are usually hardly a foot high. It is the system for obtaining quality and is obligatory for wines entitled to be called either Beaujolais-Villages or listed among the nine Growths.

Haut-Beaujolais

The wines of the nine Growths must not exceed 356 imp. gallons (428 U.S.) per acre or they drop to the simple class of Beaujolais, although in certain great years the French wine authorities may allow the classification to wines surpassing the maximum if they are satisfactory in quality.

The nine select areas of the Growths lie islanded within the section of Beaujolais-Villages and Beaujolais Supérieur, which is all in Haut-Beaujolais above Villefranche and is the heart and nearly the whole bulk of the zone. The wines not in the Growth area but entitled to the classification Beaujolais-Villages, an official place-name, may be called by their commune name, if 'Beaujolais' is attached.

The some 36,000 acres of vineyard making up all Beaujolais produce 12–15 million imp. gallons (14½–18 million U.S.) yearly, a little more than half of which is Beaujolais. The nine Growths account for about two-thirds of the rest with approximately 3,500,000 imp. gallons (4 million U.S.) a year; and there are also about 850,000 imp. gallons (1,020,000 U.S.) of Beaujolais-Villages and Beaujolais Supérieur.

Bas-Beaujolais

The wines, not having the advantage of the granite soil, lack distinction and are generally less complete, and lighter, than Haut-Beaujolais wines. Although lighter, they are a little like the wines in the Mâconnais, as if the same general characteristics established themselves on both sides of the true Beaujolais area.

Topographically, the region is a vast bowl dotted with small farmhouses, and at certain points nearly a hundred village steeples may be seen. The slopes are rolling rather than sheer, but the peasants consider their domain wild and rough. It must once have been so, in manners if not in landscape, if we are to believe the stories told in the town of Anse. There, if a girl tosses her head at men and looks hard to handle they say: 'She's walked in front of the oven at Anse.' Apparently, in Napoleon's day, the women of Anse ran the men like horses and if they balked they tortured them in front of the oven. When a village priest tried to stop them, they popped him into the oven.

Beaujolais-Villages

The following communes are entitled to the official place-name or Appellation Contrôlée Beaujolais-Villages; or may couple their names with Beaujolais:

Leynes, Pruzilly, Chânes, Saint-Vérand (which have also white wine called Mâconnais Blanc), and

Arbuissonnas	Odenas
Beaujeu	Le Perréon
Blacé	Quincié
Cercié	Régnié
La Chapelle-de-Guinchay	Rivolet
	Romanèche-Thorins
Charentay	Saint-Étienne-des-Ouillières
Durette	Saint-Étienne-la-Varenne
Emeringes	Saint-Julien-en-Montmélas
Jullié	Saint-Lager
Lancié	Saint-Symphorien-d'Ancelles
Lantigné	Salles
Montmélas-Saint-Sorlin	Vaux-en-Beaujolais
	Villié-Morgon

Growths (*Crus*)

(Ranged from the heaviest to the lightest)

Moulin-à-Vent

Known as the king of Beaujolais wines, it is generally considered first among the noble growths —with the possible exception of Fleurie.

It is the bigness and fatness of a Moulin-à-Vent that gives it its character, but even this monarch of Beaujolais usually loses some of its fruitiness and freshness when it is bottled for more than two years.

The windmill itself, which has given its name to the wine and terrain, is a stone cone standing up like a lighthouse, three hundred years old, in a rolling sea of vines. Far newer-looking is the stretch of the Paris–Riviera road passing a mile or so towards the Saône; neon signs flash on and off, several saying 'Moulin-à-Vent'; yet it is the best place to taste the real Moulin-à-Vent.

Chénas is a place-name itself. Nevertheless, the best part of the commune of Chénas, about 1,200 acres, is within the zone of the place-name Moulin-à-Vent, and the wines are sold under this, the more famous name of the two. Three-quarters of the commune of Romanèche-Thorins, 1,500 acres, is in Moulin-à-Vent. Thorins and Moulin-à-Vent wines, always famous in the past, frequently compared for their very similar qualities and now joined as Moulin-à-Vent, grow on a very shallow soil of decomposed granite. The vine roots drive right down into the rock, so that it crumbles even more. The manganese, strong in the subsoil here, undoubtedly contributes to the breed of the wines.

Juliénas

The wines sometimes preserve the pleasant fruitiness of their youth into a lusty age—for these wines and the Morgons are the longest-lasting of the Beaujolais.

An average 400,000 imp. gallons (480,000 U.S.) is made from some 1,100 acres. Château Juliénas is one of the best vineyards. Bessay and Château Les Capitans are well-known names.

Morgon

This, the hardest of Beaujolais wines and very full-bodied, is unlike the others in that it is not so delightful when young, but improves with some ageing; a 'true Morgon' is not bottled until seven or nine months after the harvest and needs a year in the bottle. The heaviest of the Morgons stands on the dividing line of characteristics between a more typical Beaujolais and a Burgundy; and in fact a considerable amount of it is used by shippers for its strength in blending, and never reaches the consumer in its true state. The area entitled to the name Morgon, with its 1,765 acres, is one of the largest of the Growths, but there really is no typical Morgon wine because the soil varies greatly. The part in Morgon is called 'true Morgon', and that in Villié-Morgon produces a generally lighter wine. Not all Villié-Morgon can call itself Morgon, the remainder being Beaujolais-Villages. The best parcels of all lie on a ridge called the Côte de Py, where the brownish decomposed slate soil may be seen on the surface—the 'rotted soil' as the peasants inelegantly put it, that gives the special *goût de terroir* often present in a Morgon. Robust, usually fat, these wines are the only Beaujolais which generally repay laying down. As the local peasants put it: '*Ils morgonnent*'—they morgonize. An unfortunate tendency now is to leave the wine too long on the lees, making it even harder than is typical. The largest top-quality estate of the Beaujolais is at Villié-Morgon and is known as the Château Pizay.

Chénas

Most of Chénas lies within Moulin-à-Vent. A small slice of the commune, however, caps Moulin-à-Vent on the north and its wine is sold as Chénas. The production is not large and the wines are not quite as good as Moulin-à-Vent, yet often they closely approach it in character and they are likely to be excellent value.

Fleurie

If Moulin-à-Vent is the king of Beaujolais wines, Fleurie is the queen, best of all the fine growths if the standard is the most typically Beaujolais. Before the strict place-name laws were drawn up—between the world wars—most of the wine was sold as Moulin-à-Vent, which adjoins Fleurie on the south side. The result is that the name is not nearly as well known as Moulin-à-Vent today. Fleurie is the only one of the best Growths entirely within one commune, that of Fleurie, but not quite all the wine is entitled to the place-name. A little produced to the west and south must be sold as Beaujolais.

The characteristic of the wine is its exceeding fruitiness and while it is among the heavier Beaujolais, it does not seem as heavy as a Moulin-à-Vent, or, in their different ways, a Morgon or a Chénas.

Roughly 520,000 imp. gallons (624,000 U.S.) are made each year on 1,700 acres, about a quarter of this coming from the Cave Coopérative. The best vineyards are Clos de la Roilette; Grand Cour; La Madone; Les Moriers; Augarant. There are approximately 400 vineyard owners.

Saint-Amour

This is the furthest north of the Growths, nearly touching the domain of Pouilly-Fuissé in the Mâconnais. About 12,500 imp. gallons (15,000 U.S.) of white wine are made, and 115,000 imp. gallons (138,000 U.S.) of red. The white wine, sold as Mâcon Blanc or Beaujolais Blanc, bears a considerable likeness to the Pouilly-Fuissés and is definitely fruity and to be drunk young. This is equally true of the red, which carried the *cru* designation Saint-Amour and is one of the lightest of all fine-growth Beaujolais.

The wine grows on a granite and slate soil pebbled with stones sometimes as large as eggs. Most of the slopes face east and south-east on the mountain of Bessay, bordering Juliénas, and a smaller hill called l'Église.

Côte de Brouilly

The centre of Brouilly. The wines from these 462 acres have more character, longer life, and are fuller-bodied than those labelled simply Brouilly.

In the exact middle, and in vine only half-way to the summit, is the Mont de Brouilly. At the top of the hill, on the bush-covered crown, is Notre-Dame du Raisin (Our Lady of the Grape). Built a hundred years ago by penitents seeking to exorcize the vine plague of *oïdium*, it is the goal of a pilgrimage on 8 September each year, preceding the harvest. The friends of the wine wind up the long climb, acquiring a proper thirst. At the top there is a religious ceremony and protection is asked for the coming crop. And then thirsts are whetted under the September sun, welcoming the Côte-de-Brouilly Beaujolais.

Château de la Chaize, built by a nephew of the confessor of Louis XIV, makes Côte de Brouilly in its vast cellars. With its dignified, rather frigid rooms, preserved exactly in the style and spirit of the period, it is the tourist haven of the area. Even more at the heart of things is the pretty Château Thiven.

Brouilly

This, the southernmost of the Growths, gives the lightest wine. The 2,162 acres are in the communes of Saint-Lager, Cercié, Odenas, Charentay, and a small segment of a little over 100 acres in Quincié. The centre and best part of Brouilly has the separate *appellation* Côte de Brouilly.

Chiroubles

The wine is usually as elegant as a Fleurie and less hard than a Morgon. The vineyards adjoin both districts on the west.

This is a wine to be taken very young, and ideally it should never be drunk in bottle but only from the barrel. Although until recently it was the least known, it is now becoming the Growth best liked in France as a fast-maturing light Beaujolais.

The alcoholic content is actually fairly high, but this does not show in the wine, which is soft, light, exceedingly fruity, and, when very young, a fresh and typical Beaujolais. It can be drunk as early as two months after the harvest, and generally ought to be. Production averages 190,000 imp. gallons (228,000 U.S.).

In the square of the village of Chiroubles itself, facing the church, is what must be one of the most appropriate statues in any wine town of France. Not Napoleon, nor Joan of Arc, is commemorated here, but one Pulliat, the man who planted the first grafted vine in Beaujolais during the crisis of the phylloxera vine louse. The best grower is Jean Desvigne.

Beaujolais-Villages

Name applied to the wines of thirty-five communes or townships in the French Beaujolais. After the fine-growth Beaujolais such as Fleurie, Moulin-à-Vent, Morgon and others, the Beaujolais-Villages are the best of these pleasant, fresh red wines now the rage in France and growing popular everywhere.

See BEAUJOLAIS.

Beaulieu-sur-Layon

Commune with the right to an Appellation Contrôlée in the Coteaux du Layon district of Anjou, France.

See ANJOU: COTEAUX DU LAYON.

Beaulieu Vineyards

Rutherford, Napa Valley, California.

George de Latour founded this beautiful estate and the vineyards in 1900. He imported many cuttings from his native France and found the ideal site for them near Rutherford, where the gravelly soil holds the annual rains without need of irrigation. Beaulieu has maintained a continuous operation right from its beginning: the winery made sacramental wines during Prohibition, and when Repeal followed, Beaulieu enjoyed a success it had never had before with a wide distribution of wines throughout the United States.

There are now four vineyards with about 600 acres in active production, all of them in the centre of Napa Valley. The principal varieties grown are Pinot Chardonnay, Johannisberger Riesling, Sauvignon Blanc, Pinot Noir, and Franken Riesling. The Muscat de Frontignan is not too often seen in California, but at Beaulieu this variety thrives abundantly and makes a fine varietal wine. The soil varies quite markedly and the vines are planted accordingly.

See AMERICA: CALIFORNIA AND THE WEST.

Beaumes-de-Venise

Vin Doux naturel and *vin de liqueur* are made in this area of Vaucluse, from the Muscat grape.

See SWEET FORTIFIED WINES OF FRANCE.

Beaune

Burgundy red and white wine. District: Côte de Beaune, France.

The ancient city of the same name is the largest and most important of the Côte de Beaune and is called—not without reason—the 'Capital of Burgundian Wines'. It dates from the fifth century or earlier—there are grounds for believing that Beaune may have been the Bibracte mentioned by Cæsar in his chronicles. Beaune's long history has been one of storm and terror, for many ambitious nobles converged there as they struggled for supremacy among themselves. Walls have been built and razed, castles constructed and toppled, and the city archives hold more stories of intrigue and violence than do those of many a Hollywood producer. Lying between the once-powerful strongholds of Autun and Besançon, Beaune was strategically placed, and its wines added to its desirability. Characteristic of the change that has come over the city is that the one remaining mediæval fort is now the residence of the manager of the wine-shipping firm of Calvet et Cie., and the pillars—all that remain of the stout walls which once girdled Beaune—are used today to house wine instead of broadswords.

The great change in the life of the place occurred in the seventeenth century, when the citizens beat their swords into pruning knives and turned their attention to wine. Beaune's undisputed place as the centre of the Burgundian wine trade, and its aura of bustling commerce and prosperity, date from that era. As a result of its energy and enterprise, the economy not only of the Côte de Beaune but of the entire Côte d'Or is based on the cellars of Beaune and the city lives for its wines. Cellars tunnel and wind beneath the twisting streets, wine slogans adorn walls of buildings and restaurants, and billboards lure passing tourists and wine-buyers from all over the world into the storerooms of the great firms. Finding these firms is no trouble, but discovering the difference between them sometimes is. The Beaune telephone directory carries a couple of dozen under a single number; names of established and reliable firms are imitated by fly-by-nights to within an inch of a lawsuit, and merchants abound who will agree to sell any wine in any quantity, sometimes in excess of its production. Yet behind it all lies a genuine love of Burgundian wines, a conviction that there are no others in the world to rival them, and an enthusiasm unequalled in any region of the world.

There is more to Beaune than the winding streets, the clatter of great tank-trucks carrying wine, and the hum and buzz of conversations about vintages, comparative tastings, and prices. Outside the city, but still within the limits of the commune of Beaune, are more vineyards planted in fine vines than in any other commune of the Côte d'Or, although both Pommard and Meursault generally make more wine each year. The wines from these vineyards—both red and white—are sold as Beaune or may have the vineyard name following that of the commune. Sometimes they are sold as Côte de Beaune, which means simply that they come from any vineyard allowed to use the name Beaune, and from several others as well. (When blended with wines from specified other communes of the slope they may also be sold as Côte de Beaune-Villages.)

The outstanding vineyards of Beaune today are substantially the same as those which received top rating when the vineyards of the Côte d'Or were classified in 1860. At that time, there were eight Outstanding Vineyards (*Têtes de Cuvées*) and all but one of them are still considered outstanding. The French authorities included all eight in their list of the thirty-four First Growths (*Premiers Crus*) —superior vineyards whose wines have the legal right to carry both commune and vineyard name on the label—established in 1936. The best growth is generally considered that from the vineyard of Grèves and particularly from the section called L'Enfant Jésus. The name is said to have been bestowed by early monks and comes from the expression: 'It goes down the throat as easily as the little Jesus in velvet trousers.' Since the monks did not consider this irreverent, no one in Burgundy does either. Grèves is one of the fullest wines of Beaune and one of the suavest. Les Clos des Mouches is another wine noted for its body (considerable for a Beaune) and for its elegance. Slightly behind these is Fèves, a smaller vineyard and thus one with far less output, its wines noted for their fineness and delicate yet pronounced aroma. Beaune Bressandes —not to be confused with Corton-Bressandes in nearby Aloxe-Corton—and Marconnets, Champimonts, and Cras are also highly reputed and the wines are light but firm with a distinctive bouquet. Finesse, delicacy, and an expressive and often remarkable bouquet are the characteristics which excel in all Beaune wines.

In the past, Beaunes were considered at their best immediately after harvest. During the seventeenth century, wines were generally drawn straight from the barrel instead of being bottled, and were vinified to be very light, very fast maturing, and for immediate drinking. Beaunes are still reasonably light and reasonably fast maturing, but the drinking is nowhere near so immediate as it once was and a couple of years in the bottle will aid them considerably. Some of the better wines will hold for a number of years but they are the exception to the rule; five years in glass will usually suffice. After this the wines tend to fade.

The great event in Beaune each year is the annual auction sale at the impressive Hospices de Beaune, the charity hospital which has been in continuous operation since the fifteenth century and which gains some of its revenue from the sale at auction of wines coming from vineyards donated by philanthropic Burgundians. The sale, usually held in mid-November, gathers swarms of buyers, mostly from France and Belgium, and the prices determine the value of the harvest throughout the Côte d'Or. The Hospices has holdings all over the Côte de Beaune; it vinifies its own wines, and also distils a Marc de Bourgogne which is sold at the same time as the wine (*see also* HOSPICES DE BEAUNE).

Within the limits of the commune there are 1,329 acres of vineyard allowed for grapes going into Beaune, and this and twenty-two more for wines labelled Côte de Beaune. In an average-quantity year Beaune produces 191,500 imp. gallons (230,000 U.S.) of red wine and about 4,400 (5,300 U.S.) of white. The white is rarely in the class of the red, but some may be delicate and perfumed, and it is often excellent wine. Beaune is sold mostly in France but large quantities go to the Low Countries —partly on account of geographical proximity, and partly because of the historical links forged when the Burgundian Ducal family held court in the Netherlands, and strengthened by the Huguenot refugees from Beaune, in the sixteenth century, many of whom settled in Belgium and Holland and retained, as do their descendants today, their traditional drinking preferences. England, Switzerland, the United States, and Austria are also big buyers.

FIRST GROWTHS (*Premiers Crus*)

Vineyard	*Acres*
Les Marconnets	25·2
Les Fèves	10·6
Les Bressandes	45·8
Les Grèves	78·5
Les Clos des Mouches	61·4
Clos du Roi	34·3
Sur-les-Grèves	11·3
Aux or Les Cras	12·5
Le Clos de la Mousse	8·4
Les Teurons	38·4
Champimonts (or Champ Pimont)	41·0
Aux Coucherias	55·9
En l'Orme	5·1
En Genêt	12·5
Les Perrières	8·0
À l'Écu	7·7
Les Cent Vignes	57·6
Les Toussaints	16·1
Les Chouacheux	12·7
Les Boucherottes	21·4
Les Vignes Franches	24·6
Les Aigrots	35·7
Pertuisots	13·7
Tiélandry	4·4

Vineyard	*Acres*
Les Sizies	20·4
Les Avaux	33·1
Les Reversées	12·9
Le Bas des Teurons	17·9
Les Seurey	3·1
La Mignotte	5·9
Montée Rouge	41·0
Les Montrevenots	22·4
Les Blanches Fleurs	22·9
Les Epenottes	33·7
Les Chilènes	42·5
Chaume-Gaufriot	48·0

See CÔTE DE BEAUNE.

Château Beauséjour-Duffau-Lagarrosse

Bordeaux red wine. District and commune: Saint-Émilion, France.

Placed on a little hill outside the walls of Saint-Émilion, with a view over the lazy curve of the Dordogne, the two Beauséjour vineyards were a single property until 1869, when they were divided between two branches of the Ducarpe family. Mademoiselle Ducarpe had become Madame Duffau-Lagarrosse by marriage and it is in her line that the original château and the immediately surrounding part of the vineyard descend. Both Beauséjour-Duffau-Lagarrosse and Beauséjour-Fagouet, which adjoins it, were ranked First Great Growths (*Premiers Grands Crus*) of Saint-Émilion in the official classification of 1955. Care must be taken not to confuse them, since in both cases the words Château Beauséjour will generally be found on the labels printed in large letters, with the proprietor's name in smaller print.

Characteristics. The vineyards are well placed between Canon and Fourtet, and they yield an agreeable wine, rather on the light side in poor years, perfectly successful in the good years.

Vineyard area: 17 acres.

Average production: 2,000 cases.

Château Beauséjour-Fagouet

Bordeaux red wine. District and commune: Saint-Émilion, France.

Owned by Dr. Jean Fagouet. Impressive underground cellars hewn in rock.

Characteristics. Fine wine, with a fine bouquet in a good vintage year.

Vineyard area: 23 acres.

Average production: 2,500 cases.

See château BEAUSÉJOUR-DUFFAU-LAGARROSSE.

Beer

The origins of beer go almost as far back as those of wines; it has been made by virtually all people in all stages of civilization. African tribes produce it from millet, the Japanese from rice; Europeans, Americans of both continents, Australians, and countless others make their beer mainly from barley. It is consumed the world over—most of all in Belgium whose citizens manage to down an impressive 29·5 imp. gallons (35·5 U.S.) per head of the population a year.

Beer is the general term for all classes of beers, both draught, bottled and canned, pale ales, lagers, and stouts. It is brewed from malt, sugar, hops, and water and fermented with yeast. Beer quality is largely dependent on the suitability of these main raw materials for the type of beer being produced.

Malt begins its life as barley. Special types are grown and carefully ripened. In the malting, barley is dampened with water and allowed to germinate under controlled conditions in order to convert the insoluble starch to soluble sugar: it is then dried and cured to a pale colour for pale beers and to a richer colour for dark beers.

Sugars used in brewing are manufactured from cane sugar which is treated in different ways to give various flavours and sweetness.

Hops are specially grown for brewing, only the flower, which is a cone of golden petals carrying resin and oils, being used. They give beer its bitter flavour.

The water used in brewing is usually specially treated with mineral salts for the particular type of beer being processed. Before the days of water analysis, famous brewing centres emerged because the local water was particularly suitable for the brewing of certain types of beer. For example, the famous beer of Pilsen in Czechoslovakia is brewed with natural water and Pilsener is recognized as one of the finest beers in the world.

Yeast, a living organism, is the agent which ferments the beer.

The brewing process is not a very complicated operation. The malt passes through a mill and is crushed, after which it is mixed with water at a carefully controlled temperature. The sugar solution from the mixture is drawn off from the vessel. Rotating water sprinklers spray the grain to ensure that all the malt extract is used, leaving only husks which are usually sold as cattle food.

The solution, called wort, is pumped to the boiling coppers where hops and sugar are added. The resultant mixture is boiled for an hour or two and, in the process, the aroma and distinct bitterness of hops combine with the sweetness and flavour derived from the wort and sugar. After boiling, the hops are removed by straining, and the wort is cooled and collected in a vessel where yeast is added. It splits the sugars into alcohol and carbon dioxide gas: the gas is usually collected for later use in carbonating bottled and canned beers.

Fermentation takes several days, at the end of which the bulk of the yeast, in the case of lager, settles on the bottom of the fermenting vessel. In the case of ale it rises to the top of the beer. In both cases it is collected. The yeast produced during fermentation is several times the original quantity and is used for subsequent fermentations, the surplus forming a very valuable by-product as it is a source of vitamins for humans or animals.

In most beer-consuming countries the beer is stored in large cold tanks at near freezing point to improve its stability and ensure long and satisfactory quality, after which it is filtered, carbonated, and filled into a cask, bottle, or can for dispatch to the consumer. Most beers are now pasteurized (heated to 140° F.; 60° C.) to ensure that any minute quantities of yeast which may be left in the beer after filtration do not ferment and multiply and in so doing turn the beer cloudy.

Draught beer, which is drawn from a cask, now usually metal, is still very popular in most beer-drinking countries. All containers are washed and sterilized before being filled with beer. Bottles and cans are filled, labelled, and packaged on high-speed machines which can work at the rate of up to 600 bottles a minute.

The quality of beers varies widely, depending upon the skill, plant, and management of the manufacturer. One of the most famous is the Tuborg plant in Copenhagen which produces a product known throughout the beer-drinking world. Other countries and cities have become famous for their beers; Pilsen of Czechoslovakia, Carlsberg of Denmark, Heineken of Holland, the Munchener beer of Munich. England and Eire are renowned for their heavier ales and stouts. The beers of Mexico, U.S.A., Australia, Cuba, and Canada are also very good.

The major types of beer are:

Lager

Light highly carbonated beer. The name comes from the German *lagern* 'to store', and lager beer is one that is allowed to rest until all the sediment of the fermentation has cleared, is then carbonated and bottled. Most American beers—unless the labels bear a statement to the contrary—are lager beers, although the term itself is seldom used.

Ale

A kind of beer, formerly made without hops and drunk fresh. Nowadays, there is little difference in Great Britain between this and other beers. In the U.S.A., ale is usually fermented at a higher temperature than beer and different yeast strains are used.

Stout

A dark, heavy ale, often slightly sweet, with a pronounced taste of malt, usually heavily flavoured with hops. Great Britain and Eire are most famous for their stouts, which include the famous name of Guinness and Oyster Stout.

Porter

Similar to stout but not so strong, usually with a heavy creamy foam. The name is said to derive from the fact that it was the favourite drink of the London porters.

Bock

Special, heavy beer made in the United States in the spring, purportedly from sediment taken out of the fermenting vats in their annual cleaning. The Bock Beer season usually lasts for about six weeks. In France, however, bock is the term for a mugful of light beer.

Beerenauslese

German wine term for the selection of individual grapes from bunches.

See GERMANY.

Beeswing

A light, thin crust—resembling the transparent wing of a bee—which forms on some old bottled Ports.

Château Belair

Bordeaux red wine. District and commune: Saint-Émilion, France.

Owned by the same grower (Dubois-Challon) as Château Ausone, matured in the Ausone cellars and divided from the latter vineyard only by an arbitrary space between ranks of vines on the same slope, many people feel that the distinction between Belair wine and the much more famous Ausone is not very real. Others maintain that Belair closely resembles Ausone but in most years is less generous and less fine. While Roman origins are often claimed for the vineyard, it is certain that in the fourteenth century it was the property of the Englishman Robert Knolles, when he was Governor of Guyenne. Until recent times the estate belonged to the French family Cannolle—French descendants of Knolles. Belair was named a First Great Growth (*Premier Grand Cru*) in the Saint-Émilion Classification of 1955.

Characteristics. A subtle, very agreeable wine.

Vineyard area: 32 acres.

Average production: 7,500 cases.

Château Belgrave

Bordeaux red wine. District: Haut-Médoc, France. Commune: Saint-Laurent.

(*Saint-Laurent is not a place-name and the wine has the place-name of Haut-Médoc.*)

Classified a Fifth Growth (*Cinquième Cru*) in 1855 and on the boundary line of Saint-Julien, the estate was known by varying names in the past. The name Belgrave, which it shares with a few other Bordeaux vineyards, is claimed to be the inspiration for the naming of Belgrave Square in London. This wine should not be confused with a lesser wine called 'Château Bellegrave'.

Characteristics. Frequent changes in proprietors have made for a certain amount of variation in this wine which is usually fairly full.

Vineyard area: 72 acres.

Average production: 7,200 cases.

Bellegarde

A commune on the great Languedoc plain of southern France in the confines of which Clairette grapes are planted for making a small white wine.

See CLAIRETTE DE BELLEGARDE.

Bellet

Controlled place-name near Nice in the south of France. This is one of the best vineyard districts planted along the Riviera.

See PROVENCE.

Ben Ean

Important vineyard in New South Wales.

See AUSTRALIA.

Bench Grafting

For description of this method of grafting vines, *see* CHAPTER EIGHT, p. 32.

Benedictine D.O.M.

A famous, very popular liqueur supposed to have been first compounded about 1510 at the Benedictine monastery in Fécamp, France, by Dom Bernardo Vincelli, to fortify and restore the weary monks. The liqueur is said to have found royal favour in 1534, when Francis I passed through the region and tasted it, but at the time of the French Revolution the monastery was destroyed, the Order dispersed, and manufacture of Benedictine halted. Some seventy years or so later, the formula came into the hands of Monsieur Alexandre Le Grand, who established the present secular concern which produces the liqueur—it no longer has any connexion with Benedictines or any other religious order. Every true bottle of Benedictine (numerous unsuccessful attempts have been made to counterfeit it) still carries the ecclesiastical inscription D.O.M. which means not 'Dominican Order of Monks', as it has sometimes been construed, but *Deo Optimo Maximo*—'To God, most good, most great.'

The liqueur is greenish-yellow and flavoured with a variety of herbs, plants, and peels on a base of brandy; and it is claimed that no more than three people, at any given time, know its exact formula. In recent years the firm realized that great numbers of people were ordering their Benedictine mixed half-and-half with brandy in order to reduce sweetness slightly, and an official 'B & B' (Benedictine and Brandy) has also been put on the market.

Benicarlo

Muscular red wine from the region of Castellón de la Plana in Valencia, Spain.

Benin Wine

Nigerian palm 'wine', or fermented palm sap.

Bentonite

Bentonite (a kind of clay) is an excellent clarifying agent for white wines, one which resists proteid precipitation and discoloration from copper. Its use is allowed by law.

The bentonite (hydrated silicate of aluminium composed mainly of montmorillonite) swells in water to form a gelatinous paste. After dilution, it should be stirred briskly into the wine to be treated. The most satisfactory dose is usually about 100 grammes per hectolitre, diluted in at least two litres of water.

See CHAPTER NINE, p. 43; FINING.

Bergerac

Red and white wines. District: South-West France.

Bergerac's proximity (eighty miles) to Bordeaux and the similarity in wines, vines, and viticultural practices leads to widespread and—for Bergerac—unfortunate comparisons. With one exception—sweet, white Monbazillac—the wines of Bergerac are simply not in the same class.

The city itself is dull and quiet—hardly worth visiting were it not for the castles and strongholds which guard the beautiful wide valley of the Dordogne above it. Many battles in the Hundred Years War were fought along these hills and it is easy to imagine the mounted knights emerging from the ancient structures in full battle array.

The vines are planted along the hills girdling the city in soil ranging from sandy gravel to flinty clay and ending in a chalky clay with traces of iron. The grapes planted are Bordeaux varieties: Cabernet Sauvignon and some Cabernet Franc for red wines; and Sémillon, Sauvignon, Muscadelle, Ondenc, and Chenin Blanc for whites. For red wines benefiting from the most general place-name—Bergerac—the Fer and Périgord vines are permitted. The place-names of the Bergerac region are:

Monbazillac. The most important. Sometimes known as the 'poor man's Sauternes', it will, in good years, have much of the full, sweet richness of Sauternes but generally fails in its full finesse, tending to be too obvious. It is grown in the parishes of Monbazillac, Pomport, Rouffignac, Columbier, and a part of Saint-Laurent-des-Vignes, and its vineyards extend on the south side of the Dordogne and face north. This is an exception to the general rule that southerly facings are best for vines. The soil is a chalky clay with occasional veins of gritty sandstone, and the grapes stay on the vines until late in the autumn, as in Sauternes, when the 'noble rot' of the mould *Botrytis cinerea* attacks them, drying up much of the water. The vineyards cover some 6,000 acres and production averages slightly more than 1,250,000 imp. gallons (1,500,000 U.S.) annually.

Pécharmant. The best of the red Bergeracs. Light and sometimes bearing a resemblance to wines made in the lesser areas around Saint-Émilion—the closest of the Bordeaux districts—it is made in four communes to the north and east of Bergerac. The slopes closest to the city are thought to be the best. It is seldom that more than 8,500 imp. gallons (10,000 U.S.) are produced annually.

Rosette. Only applicable to white wines. Semi-sweet and rarely distinguished, the wine comes from six communes, three of which have the title to the name Pécharmant for red wines. About 83,000 imp. gallons (100,000 U.S.) are made annually.

Montravel. Includes Haut-Montravel and the Côtes de Montravel. Grown in fifteen communes downstream—almost due west at this point—from Bergerac, the vines are all on the north side of the river. Like Rosette, the wine is semi-sweet. Montravel and Haut-Montravel each produce about 416,000 imp. gallons (500,000 U.S.) annually, and the Côtes de Montravel about 666,000 (800,000 U.S.).

Bergerac and the Côtes de Bergerac. These two produce about 1,700,000 imp. gallons (2 million U.S.) of wine annually, two-thirds of which is white. They make up the most general place-names of the region, and thus the wine will be less good than those carrying more specific names.

Bergheim

Beautiful old wine village in Alsace (q.v.).

Bergstrasse

White, and some red, wines. Districts: Hesse and Baden, Germany.

The line of tumbled hills to the north and a little to the south of Heidelberg is known as the Bergstrasse. It divides into two sections: Hessen Bergstrasse in the province of Hesse in the north, and Baden Bergstrasse in Baden near Heidelberg. The wines are seldom, if ever, seen abroad, because they are all consumed on the spot by the hordes of tourists who flock to the timbered inns and the open-air restaurants where once students fought their duels with sabres. It is said that those bottles of Bergstrasse wine which do not reach the tourists are snatched by the Heidelberg students. Most of the wines are bottled in the spring following the harvest, and few are left to see the summer. Moreover, some of these cheap wines may be blended with such better-known Rhine wines as Liebfraumilch.

The wines vary surprisingly, considering the small size of the district. This is because, in an area where there has been much geological upheaval, the soil characteristics change almost from hill to hill. Certain Bergstrasse Rieslings grown on a shale soil will taste like lesser Moselles, while Sylvaner wines will have the fullness and body of some of the Rheinhessens. None of them is particularly distinguished, and too often they are likely to be over-sulphured. Both red and white wine is made, but the majority is white, especially in the Rheinhessen section.

Bensheim and Heppenheim are the two leading Hessen Bergstrasse wine towns. The Kirchberg vineyard, comprising most of Bensheim, is the most important on the Bergstrasse.

The State Domain owns fifty or so acres of vineyard in this district.

Other vineyards. Streichling and Pfaffenberg in Bensheim. In Heppenheim: Krück, Steinkopf, Schlossberg. The vineyards of Auerbach just above

Bensheim, once well known, are dying, perhaps on account of a strangling quantity of sand in the soil.

Beringer Brothers

St. Helena, Napa Valley, California.

Two German brothers, Fredrick and Jacob Beringer, assured the success of this well-known winery founded in 1876 at St. Helena in the Napa Valley on the north coast of California. The vineyard known as Los Hermanos has been active from the very beginning and even flourished during Prohibition by selling sacramental wines to the clergy throughout the country. The most celebrated brand is Beringer Private Stock, and their Los Hermanos is a close second. The more expensive wines bear the Beringer Family bottling label.

See AMERICA: CALIFORNIA AND THE WEST.

Bernkasteler Doctor (or Doktor)

The most famous great Moselle wine. If it is not absolutely first or always first among Moselles, it is nevertheless a great wine. The market pressure of its fame causes it to be somewhat over-priced.

See MOSELLE.

Bernkasteler Graben

There is little to differentiate this magnificent wine from Bernkasteler Doctor, its near neighbour and the most famous wine of the Moselle. In fact, many men of the region say Graben is frequently the better of the two wines. Of late years, the Graben have been sold with the neighbouring Doctors. The labels read Bernkasteler Doctor und Graben.

See MOSELLE.

Château Beychevelle

Bordeaux red wine. District: Médoc, France. Commune: Saint-Julien.

Owned today by Monsieur Armand Achille-Fould, former Minister of Agriculture, Beychevelle is one of the largest Médoc vineyards, and commands a reputation, fame, and prices considerably higher than its official position as Fourth Growth (*Quatrième Cru*), Classification of 1855.

The château, long and low, with a great wing, is perhaps the most imposing and beautiful in the Médoc. It stands on the site of earlier feudal fortresses and was reconstructed in its present style in 1757. An enormous belvedere, at least fifty yards long, commands a vista of lawns running down for more than three-quarters of a mile to the River Gironde, a prospect reminiscent of Versailles on a small scale.

Monsieur Achille-Fould tells an amusing story of how Beychevelle came into the family. His father went to the United States and married an American wife. While on a tour of France, he was pleased to hear her say at Beychevelle, 'This is where I would like best to live,' whereupon he bought the estate.

The name Beychevelle comes from *baissez les voiles* (strike sail), the salute given to the Duke of Épernon, Grand Admiral of France, by ships passing on the river when he was lord of the domain in feudal times. A further remembrance of the Grand Admiral is the secondary wine, Clos de l'Amiral.

Beychevelle is very well known in England, where Monsieur Achille-Fould, an Oxford graduate, has kept up his connexions; and also in the United States, whither it has been shipped for a century.

Characteristics. Great finesse. This vineyard has a fantastic following: some of its vintages are definitely remarkable; others may be rather disappointing.

Vineyard area: 150 acres.

Average production: 19,000 cases.

Bhang, Bang

A 'wine' made in India from hemp leaves and twigs infused in water.

Bianco

White. Italian term for white wine.

Bienvenue-Bâtard-Montrachet

Burgundy white wine. District: Côte de Beaune, France. Commune: Puligny-Montrachet (and in part Chassagne-Montrachet). Official Classification: Great Growth (Grand Cru).

One of the memorable Montrachets which are the greatest of the great white Burgundies. The vine yard, covering only about nine acres, is beside that of Bâtard-Montrachet. In character and quality the wines are similar. It is only in the past ten years that a distinction has been made between Bienvenue, Criots, and Bâtard. Before that, all three wines were sold under the last name. The average production of this wine is about 1,550 imp. gallons (1,860 U.S.).

See BÂTARD-MONTRACHET; PULIGNY-MONTRACHET.

Bin

English term for the place in which bottles of wine are stored in a cellar; or, in a flat, in a cupboard. When a merchant sells wine 'in bin' (or 'ex-bin'), it means that the customer must pay the cost of packing and delivery.

Binger Rochusberg

An outstanding wine of Bingen on the German Rhine. It has great character, from slate-quartz soil.

See RHEINHESSEN.

Bishop

Mulled Port. The Port wine is heated up with sugar, orange, and cloves, and set alight before it is poured. Some authors give Claret as the wine in a Bishop, but others say that Claret is used in an Archbishop.

Bitters

Spirits of varying alcoholic content flavoured with roots, barks, and herbs, having in common only their bitterness and their claims to medicinal powers. Originally they were elixirs and some are still so called. Bitters are used either as flavouring for mixed drinks, or may be taken as aperitifs, or liqueurs, or digestives. Some of the better known ones are: Amer Picon (France) (*q.v.*), Angostura (Trinidad, British West Indies) (*q.v.*), Boonekamp's (Holland), Campari (Italy) (*q.v.*), Abbot's Aged Bitters (U.S.A.), Fernet Branca (Italy) (*q.v.*), Law's Peach Bitters (England), Orange Bitters (England), Pommeranzen (Holland and Germany), Secrestat (France), Toni Kola (France), Unicum (Hungary), and Welling's (Holland).

Black Death

Popular name for the aquavit—and the national drink—of Iceland. This spirit is flavoured with caraway seeds.

See AQUAVIT.

Black Rot

A vine disease of American origin.

See CHAPTER EIGHT, p. 37.

Black Velvet

A mixture of stout and Champagne, popular in England in Edwardian days and still in existence. Usually associated with oysters.

Blackberry Liqueur

A cordial made by steeping blackberries in sweetened brandy.

Blagny

The only Burgundian communal place-name that has no accompanying commune. Blagny is a hamlet, divided between Meursault and Puligny-Montrachet on the Côte de Beaune. Its wines are similar in almost all respects to those of Meursault. Meursault-Blagny denotes the wines from the best part of Blagny, adjoining Meursault.

See MEURSAULT.

Blanc

White. French term for white wine.

Blanc de Blancs

Champagne made from the Pinot Blanc grape only. It is easily distinguishable by its light colour from the golden wines made from red grapes. Blanc de Blancs is also becoming a widespread term for the white wines made from white grapes in many of France's lesser-known wine districts.

See CHAMPAGNE.

Blanc Fumé de Pouilly

Dry white Loire Valley wine usually called Pouilly-Fumé.

See POUILLY-SUR-LOIRE.

Blanc de Noirs

White wine from red grapes.

See CHAMPAGNE.

Blanco

Spanish term for white wine.

Blanquette de Limoux and **Vin de Blanquette**

Sparkling, and some still, wines. District: South-West France.

Limoux, a small town near Carcassonne, makes two types of wine, both from the same grape. That called Blanquette de Limoux is a sparkling wine and the Vin de Blanquette is the still variety. Made from grapes of the Mauzac (at least 90%) and Clairette Blanche (no more than 10%), the wines come from a delimited area of thirty-five communes of which Limoux is the centre.

The sparkling Blanquette de Limoux has won some small renown. The wines contain at least 10% of alcohol and have been made sparkling by the Champagne process, that of secondary fermentation in the bottle. Despite its renown, the wine is a sweetish, small, rather peculiar one—and is a good point in the argument for drinking only real Champagne.

The Vin de Blanquette is that amount of the wine that is not rendered sparkling—always a small proportion. It too must have at least 10% alcohol, and it usually has a slight sparkle to it. Together the wines are produced on some 500 acres with an average yearly output of 41,600 imp. gallons (50,000 U.S.).

Blauer Portugieser

A grapevine producing red wines and grown in the Vöslau region of Austria.

Blaufrankische

A red-wine grape cultivated in Austria, Hungary, and elsewhere.

Blaye, Premières Côtes de Blaye, Côtes de Blaye

Red and white wines. District: Bordeaux, France.

White and red wines lacking in distinction and produced in a large and ancient vineland on the Gironde in south-west France. The three distinct place-names or Appellations Contrôlées apply to the same area, circling the historic river-town of Blaye, and indicate gradations of quality. Blaye (or Blayais) is the most common, chiefly white; Côtes de Blaye is entirely white wine, to which slightly more exacting quality restrictions apply; Premières Côtes de Blaye, 15% white and the remainder red, alone merits consideration for certain bottles, and alone is restricted to noble grape varieties (except that, in red wine, Prolongeau, Cahors, and Béquignol are permitted up to 10%).

The white wines are dry, or, if they are labelled 'sweet', will be found to be semi-sweet. The red wines are lighter than those from the adjoining region of Bourg, and if tasted together with red Bourgs in the Blaye-Bourg House of Wine opened in Blaye in 1955 they will be found to be less distinguished, if smoother and suppler.

Separated from the Médoc by the considerable width of the River Gironde, Blaye is a romantic-looking region of rolling hills, its chief landmark a huge fortress, starfish-shaped, originally built in the eleventh and twelfth centuries, rebuilt by General Vauban, strategist of Louis XIV, and now largely in ruins. From thimble-topped watchtowers in the corners of its walls, the view over the Gironde includes Pauillac, in the distance on the opposite shore, and in the wide river a trio of large islands given over to vineyard. From the river in the vicinity of Blaye comes the only true caviar produced outside Russia or Rumania.

Bleichert

German term for rosé wine.

Blending

The practice of mixing together or 'marrying' wines or spirits to obtain uniform quality from year to year, or to obtain a product better than any one of the components taken individually. In some cases, blending is a practical way of increasing quantity—but not quality; for if the original wine or spirit has been a fine one, quality is lowered and all individuality or distinction lost.

All Sherry is blended, as is most Champagne, Cognac, and Whisky. In these instances the practice often enhances the product.

Blue Fining

Fining or clearing wines with crystals of potassium ferrocyanide. This is effective in stabilizing white wines, but the results of an overdose are so dangerous that those countries which permit it only do so under very strict regulations. Blue fining is allowed in Germany but forbidden in France; whereas in the United States it is permissible but not encouraged.

See FINING; CHAPTER NINE, p. 54.

Bõa Vista

One of the best known Quintas of the Alto Douro in Portugal, for many years the property of the Forrester family.

Boal, Bual

A type of Madeira: full, sweet, rich in colour, and with an extraordinary bouquet.

See MADEIRA.

Bock

See BEER.

Bocksbeutel, Boxbeutel

The flat, flask-shaped wine bottle of Franconia (Germany) and Styria (Austria), rarely used except for these wines—although Undurraga, in Chile, has a somewhat similar bottle for Riesling, and some Australian wines and some Portuguese rosés are now being marketed in flasks of this type. While a variety of Franconian wines appear in the Bocksbeutel inside Germany, it is principally the green-gold Steinwein which is found abroad.

The origin of the flask is accounted for in several ways. Obviously, it resembles the once common leather wine skin. A Bocksbeutel carry-all favoured by old-fashioned German women is also cited as a possible pattern—and so is an organ of the goat, which takes much the same shape. In any case, the Bocksbeutel has been in use for some time: in 1728, the Burgerspital wines of Würzburg began to be bottled in these flasks.

See FRANCONIA.

Bocoy

Chestnut barrel used for shipping Spanish wines, holding usually 650 to 700 litres (143–154 imp. gallons; 172–185 U.S.). There is also a Media Bocoy, or half-bocoy, containing generally 350 litres (77 imp. gallons; 92 U.S.). The two measures are the same in content as the German Halbstück (half 'piece') and Viertelstück (quarter 'piece').

Bodega

In Spain a place for storing wine, not a cellar usually, but above ground; and, colloquially, a wine shop. The term is often used in England for a wine-bar.

Body

A wine with substance or body fills the mouth. Alcohol and tannin give the characteristic. Many great white wines, such as Moselles, can be light, lacking body, but all great red wines will have it. When young, a great wine often has excessive body. With age, if the wine succeeds, this modifies and becomes part of the full roundness. The French term is *corsé*.

Bois Ordinaires

See COGNAC.

Bolivia

Not one of the more important of the South American wine-producing countries, Bolivia has about five thousand acres planted in wine-producing vines. In addition there are about four thousand acres more, producing table grapes. The wine made amounts to a negligible 132,000 imp. gallons (158,500 U.S.) or so a year; and in addition there is an almost equal amount of brandy. Bolivian brandy is usually Pisco brandy, as in Peru and Chile.

See PISCO BRANDY.

Bombom Crema

A honey-flavoured Cuban liqueur.

Bonarda

Grape used for dark red wine made principally around Asti in Italy. The wine is sometimes sparkling.

See PIEDMONT.

Bonde

French term for a barrel stopper, or bung (*q.v.*).

Bonded Spirits, or Wines

Spirits or wines held in store by Customs and Excise until duty is paid by the purchaser. In the United States, a bonded whiskey must remain a minimum of four years in bond before it can be called Bonded Rye or Bourbon. Until 1958, these whiskies could be aged for eight years only. After that, Internal Revenue taxes had to be paid.

Bonnes Mares

Burgundy red wine. District: Côte de Nuits, France. Communes: Chambolle-Musigny and Morey-Saint-Denis. Official classification: Great Growth (Grand Cru).

The origin of the name is obscure, but no one has seriously put forth the theory that it has anything to do with stagnant pools (the French word *mare*), good or otherwise.

A large vineyard by Burgundian standards, 37·8 acres, Bonnes Mares is split with 4·6 acres in Morey-Saint-Denis and the rest in Chambolle. It borders Morey's Clos de Tart and the twisting vineyard road (on the uphill side). Although it lies in two communes, the name of neither will normally appear on bottle labels. Bonnes Mares is a Great Growth (*Grand Cru*), one of only thirty-one so designated among the hundreds of Burgundian vineyards, and is put on sale with no further indication of source than the vineyard name. The information on labels should include vineyard, year, grower, and/or shipper and his address—anything else is superfluous.

Like most Burgundian vineyards, Bonnes Mares is divided among a number of growers (one of whom is the author of this book) who all tend their own sections; but for some reason the very great wine they make is not very well known abroad. The peer of most red wines of the Côte de Nuits, and finer than most on the Côte de Beaune—with the exception of Corton—it is overshadowed nonetheless by many lesser but more widely recognized growths. Perhaps it has been eclipsed by the fabulous Musigny—on the opposite side of Chambolle—or by-passed by wine lovers speeding north towards the fine wines of Gevrey-Chambertin.

As is true of all the great Côte d'Or reds, the grape used is the Pinot Noir. In the soil of Bonnes Mares, it produces wines which are generally softer than most of the great Moreys, with much of the elegance and delicacy of Musigny. Richer in tannins than most Burgundies, they have a firm strength which permits them to age and to round out beautifully, and they keep longer than many other red Burgundies.

No great quantity is made. In an average quantity year production amounted to 6,093 imp. gallons (7,317 U.S.) or the equivalent of only 3,050 cases.

Bonnezeaux

A small choice section of the Coteaux du Layon district of Anjou, France, with the right to an Appellation Contrôlée.

See ANJOU.

Bons Bois

See COGNAC.

Boordy Vineyard

Riderwood, Maryland, U.S.A.

This small, prosperous U.S. vineyard specializing in French hybrids is at Riderwood, Maryland—which is not otherwise much of a wine-growing state. Boordy is owned by Philip Wagner, author of books on grape-growing in the United States, and former editor of the *Baltimore Evening Sun*, who has made a very great contribution to improving all Eastern wines through his intelligent, extensive experiments with French hybrids.

See AMERICA: EASTERN STATES.

Bor

Hungarian term for wine.

Bordeaux

Red, white and rosé wines. District: South-West France.

Bordeaux is the most important wine region of France. More than half of the fine wines of the world come from France, and about half of these from Bordeaux, which has a long and troubled history.

When the Romans arrived in 56 B.C. to occupy what was then Burdigala, it was already a port (although not yet the most important of the Gironde) doing some trade with Britain and other northern ports; and it was connected by road and river with the earlier colony of Narbonne in the south. According to the Bordeaux writer, Gaston Marchou, Roman rule was lenient in Burdigala and the native Bituriges were easily and happily Latinized. The city flourished and so did the surrounding vineyards—Pliny mentions the wines that were being made here in the first century A.D.; and in the fourth century, Ausonius was writing from his agreeable villa on an estate outside the town. This good life lasted his time. Afterwards, the Visigoths came and a dark age set in for the vineyards as well as for the city. Luckily Christianity had arrived first, and here, as elsewhere, it was the Church that preserved a vestige of the old learning and saved the culture of the vine—but with many setbacks, over several hundred years.

In 1152, Eleanor of Aquitaine married Henry Plantagenet, Count of Anjou and King of England, bringing Guyenne (Gascony) and Bordeaux as her dowry. At first the Bordelais resented their new rulers. Richard Cœur de Lion spent some time in the city and seems to have charmed them. Yet, in an edict of his successor, King John, on the French wines selling in England in about 1200, no mention was made of any from Bordeaux. Soon, however, and in spite of heavy tolls and taxes at each end of the voyage, the wines began to be shipped. By the end of the reign of Henry III (1216–1272), the Bordeaux merchants had gained many privileges: easing of taxes, the right to sell in English markets, freedom to set up a council (or Jurade) in their own city, and to elect their Mayor. Although ships still sailed from Soulac and other harbours, the crescent-shaped port of Bordeaux (*le port de la lune*) was now first in importance, bristling with the masts of merchant ships. The wines of Graves became the fashion in England (as late as the sixteenth century, the Médoc was described as a savage district, and its wines were to be little known for another hundred years); the *bourgeoisie* began to build new houses. By the fourteenth century, the Jurade was very powerful. No one was allowed to sell his wines until the big burghers had made all the sales they wanted—even aristocratic families with estates outside the city were asking to be accepted as *bourgeois*. As for the wines of other towns (Libourne, Poitiers, Cahors), these could not be brought in for sale to foreign buyers until the very end of the autumn wine fair—in those days, wines were drunk from the wood in their first year, and the English ships had to be home before Christmas with the new vintage. The under-privileged barrels were kept apart on the Quai des Chartrons, which was afterwards to become the preserve of the great Bordeaux merchants themselves. When the Hundred Years War (1337–1453) began, the Bordelais, now quite happy under a rule so beneficial to them commercially, took the English side. In 1356, after the battle of Poitiers, the Black Prince held the French King prisoner and brought him into Bordeaux. 'It cannot be recorded', said the chronicler

Froissart, 'the great feast and cheer that they of the city, with the clergy, made to the Prince.' King Jean also seems to have had a fair share of the good time before he was taken off to England. Next year came the Black Death, but as soon as the plague had died down the war revived. In his last years the Black Prince, spent out, ill and sadly changed from the magnificent conqueror of Poitiers, carried out senseless destructive raids in the country beyond Bordeaux, and what he did not destroy was ravaged afterwards by the French armies in the struggle to recapture the whole of Gascony. For a long time, the Bordeaux vineyards remained untouched and overseas trade went on. Even when the helpless Henry VI became king of England, Bordeaux and the famous Archbishop Pey Berland believed the English could defend them still. They asked for help. Little came. A small force under the eighty-year-old John Talbot, Earl of Shrewsbury, brave but outnumbered, was defeated at Castillon. Talbot was killed (his name survives at Château Talbot in the Médoc) and Bordeaux was French again. This was in 1453. At first the burghers were not pleased. The city lost its privileges and the foreign trade on which, in those days of bad roads to Paris, they depended, was almost at a stop. But Louis XI, when he succeeded Charles VII of France, realized the value of a flourishing wine trade and restored many of the privileges, even at the expense of some of the up-river towns which had been loyal to the French kings. He allowed the Bordelais to elect their own parliament and the English to return for their wine.

In the next century, the troubles were religious. Calvinism spread in the district. There were religious persecutions, uprisings, and in 1572 Bordeaux had its own version of the Massacre of Saint Bartholomew. Henry IV, with his Edict of Nantes, recognized the Protestants (or Huguenots) and things began to look up again. By the seventeenth century, Bordeaux wine was known in Paris and at court. When Cardinal Richelieu planted a new vineyard in the Loire region, he sent for vines from Bordeaux. Madame de Sévigné said Bordeaux would soon go out of fashion 'like coffee and Racine' but time has proved her wrong on every count. Louis XIV is said to have washed down big helpings of meat with Saint-Émilion and Chambertin. But his rule was oppressive to the *grands bourgeois* of Bordeaux, who found all their power transferred to the King's Intendant, while the King's wars were bad for trade. His unfriendly relations with England (and the change there to Dutch and German kings) led to the Methuen Treaty, which announced new customs duties, favourable to Peninsular wines, taxing French ones almost out of the market. Yet the English upper classes wanted their Claret, and smugglers brought it in.

The middle of the eighteenth century was the *belle époque* in Bordeaux—in spite of the fact that at one time the Intendant ordered growers to root up their vines and grow corn instead. Orders like that have never been universally obeyed, and one who defied this one was the writer and grower, Montesquieu. The wine trade was always first, but other industries (distilling, ship-building, glass-blowing, sugar refinery) were started. Now Bordeaux had an important new customer in North America. The town grew rich, and elegant houses and public buildings appeared: the Place de la Bourse, the Allées de Tourny, and the splendid theatre of Victor Louis—all these are still to be seen. When, in 1758, the Duke de Richelieu followed Tourny as Intendant, he brought down troupes to act in the theatre and invited actresses to supper. He was frivolous, to say the least, and quite unlike the rich *bourgeoisie* of Bordeaux, some of them Protestants, who lived well but rather austerely. It was in this period that many of the foreigners whose names have become local in Bordeaux first settled in—Barton, Lawton, Johnston—their descendants are there today.

The first Claret to be put down for ageing, in one of the first bottles sufficiently well rounded to be laid on its side, was the Château Lafite 1797. A dusty old bottle of that vintage is even now on show in the cellars of the château.

The Revolution and the Napoleonic Wars brought particularly bad times for Bordeaux. Cut off from English, American, and Colonial trade, some of the merchants were reduced to selling prunes instead of wine. By 1808, there was no life in the port. Napoleon paid a visit and promised a subsidy, but nothing came of it—except the warm support of Bordeaux for the Restoration. When the wars were over, trade naturally picked up. England lowered taxes in the eighteen-twenties and 'thirties. In the 'fifties came the terrible mildew epidemic, but in spite of it the Classification of 1855, based on earlier classifications and on current prices for the different wines, was drawn up so that the best wines of Bordeaux could be recognized when they were shown at the Paris Exhibition of that year. In 1860, Gladstone's Government lowered the duties on wines coming into England and allowed grocers to sell them. The result was lower prices, bigger trade, and a boom in the import of Claret. The twenty pre-phylloxera years, from 1858 to 1878, produced some memorable vintages—ten good years, of which the greatest were 1858, 1864, 1865, 1870, and

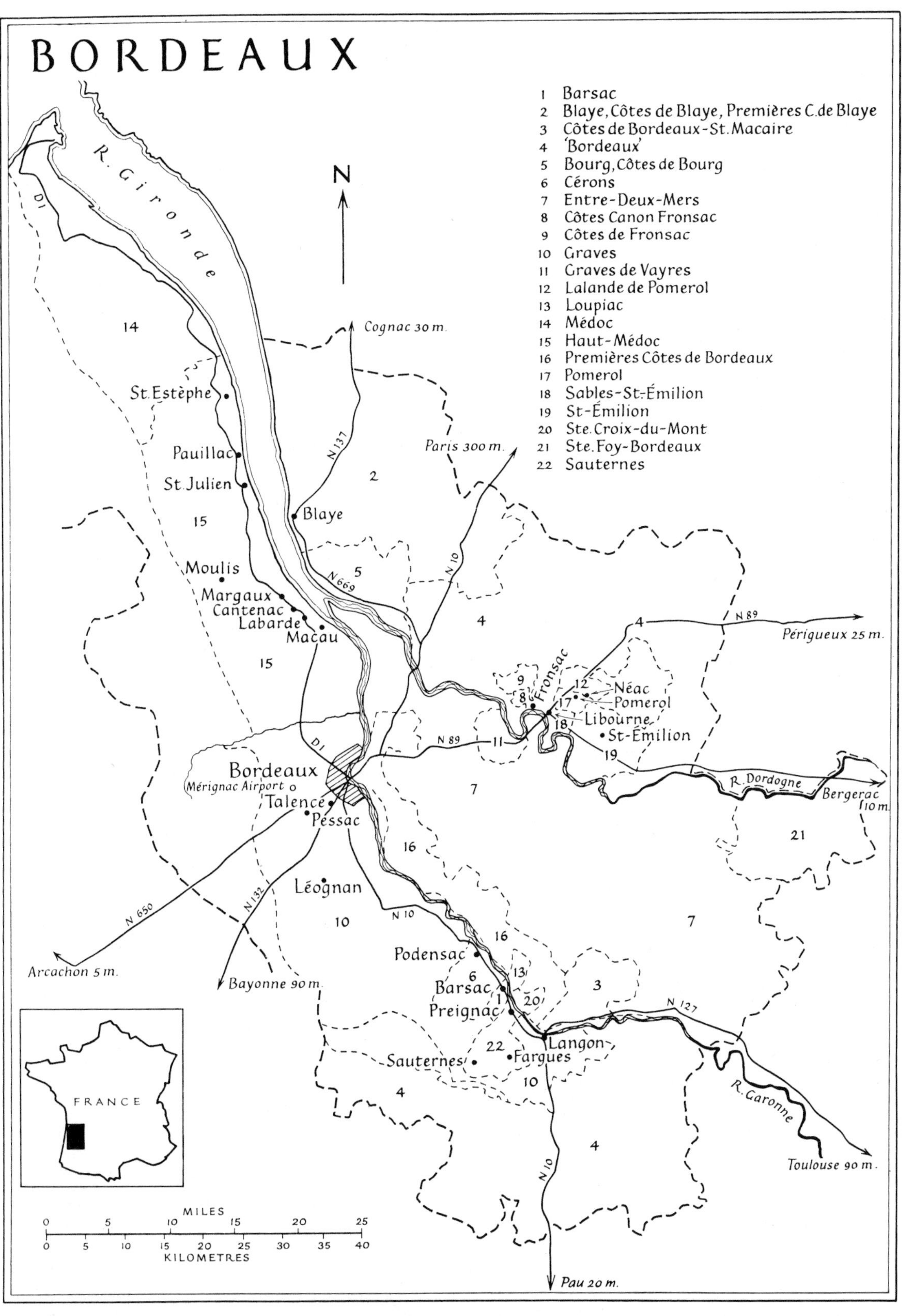
BORDEAUX
1 Barsac
2 Blaye, Côtes de Blaye, Premières C. de Blaye
3 Côtes de Bordeaux-St. Macaire
4 'Bordeaux'
5 Bourg, Côtes de Bourg
6 Cérons
7 Entre-Deux-Mers
8 Côtes Canon Fronsac
9 Côtes de Fronsac
10 Graves
11 Graves de Vayres
12 Lalande de Pomerol
13 Loupiac
14 Médoc
15 Haut-Médoc
16 Premières Côtes de Bordeaux
17 Pomerol
18 Sables-St-Émilion
19 St-Émilion
20 Ste. Croix-du-Mont
21 Ste. Foy-Bordeaux
22 Sauternes
R. Gironde
N
Cognac 30 m.
Paris 300 m.
Périgueux 25 m.
Bergerac 10 m.
Toulouse 90 m.
Pau 20 m.
Bayonne 90 m.
Arcachon 5 m.
St. Estèphe
Pauillac
St. Julien
Blaye
Moulis
Margaux
Cantenac
Labarde
Macau
Fronsac
Néac
Pomerol
Libourne
St-Émilion
R. Dordogne
Bordeaux
Mérignac Airport
Talence
Pessac
Léognan
Podensac
Barsac
Preignac
Langon
Sauternes
Fargues
R. Garonne
N 137
N 10
N 669
N 89
N 650
N 132
N 127
D1
FRANCE
MILES
0 5 10 15 20 25
0 5 10 15 20 25 30 35 40
KILOMETRES

1875. Connoisseurs still alive who tasted these wines maintain that nothing like them will ever be seen again. Even if we do not agree that the great days are over, it must be allowed that today's fine wines are to some extent different, because they are the product of vines grafted on to American rootstocks, whereas the earlier wines were purely from *Vitis vinifera*. Nevertheless, 1893, 1899, and 1900 are agreed to have been excellent years in Bordeaux, as were 1904, 1906, and 1914. The post-First World War vintages of 1924, '28, '29, '34, and '37 are everywhere remembered—indeed, the '34s are not yet past their prime, and the '37s, exceptionally stubborn, are only now reaching it. People who bought these wines to lay down before the last war were lucky: claret was unprecedentedly cheap in the nineteen-thirties. We know from Professor Saintsbury's *Notes on a Cellar-Book* that château-bottled wines were being sold for much the same figure in the eighteen-sixties, when money was worth much more.

Bordeaux Place-names

In 1911, after long litigation and dispute, the boundaries of the zone of Bordeaux were fixed as those of the department of the Gironde—except for the strip of dune soil along the Atlantic coast, which is not accepted.

The Gironde, largest of the French departments, produces 55 million imp. gallons (66 million U.S.) of wine each year on the 550,000 acres of vineyard which comprise one-eighth of its entire land surface. The name is derived from the French *hirondelle* (a swallow). The two rivers Dordogne and Garonne meet a little below Bordeaux and flow into the broad tidal Gironde which descends another fifty miles into the Atlantic. The graceful confluence of the two tributaries sketches a swallow's tail; and around the *hirondelle* and the wider estuary, with Bordeaux at its centre, the departmental boundaries of the Gironde are flung. The wines are mostly river wines—all the great ones, except the Saint-Émilions and the Pomerols, grow within sight of flowing water.

Within the region, at least three dozen place-names, or Appellations Contrôlées, designate different wines. All these are Bordeaux, although the wines carrying the looser designation Bordeaux are less distinguished than those with a more specific place-name. Yet, not all wine grown in the district is labelled Bordeaux, because, to be entitled to the *appellation*, minimum standards of viticulture and viniculture must be met (*see* APPELLATION D'ORIGINE CONTRÔLÉE). The more restricted regional *appellations*—Haut-Médoc, Saint-Julien, etc., will nearly always have been bought from different vineyards within the given region by a Bordeaux shipper, and blended by him. His reputation will be the additional—and usually soundest—indication of the value of the wine. The Monopole Bordeaux of the various shipping houses are wines of this class, on which the shipper means to stake his name. Nearly all these regional wines are blends. If the vintage year appears on the bottle, it is a blend within the stated year; when the vintage date does not appear, the blend may be from different vineyards and different years. The best shippers blend with the intention of producing a consistently good wine, a 'type' which can be reproduced year after year and which can therefore 'follow itself'—a basic principle in the making of all the better blended wines and spirits. This means, nevertheless, that year-to-year conformity brings the standard down to a common denominator which can never be very high.

Bordeaux Rouge, Bordeaux Blanc, regional bottlings, and château bottlings are the types to be found on the market. The latter are wines from individual vineyards or blends from several lesser vineyards or even from small châteaux, as Bordeaux vineyards are nearly always called, even when they do not possess a 'castle' or big house—for, compared with the châteaux of the Loire, many of these are modest country houses, some of them merely villas. Château wine is never blended with wines from outside the limits of the château itself, and is always marked with the vintage year—thus, it is the wine of one vineyard and one harvest. With weather and other viticultural conditions fluctuating as they do, these wines will never have the year-to-year consistency of regional bottlings; but they will touch the highest peaks in the finest years. They are bottled at the château itself and carry on the label the words *mis en bouteilles au château*—or some slight variant of this phrase, which is the owner's guarantee that the wine is authentic, a guarantee that he could not make with assurance if it had left his premises unbottled.

Approximately 200 of the more than 2,000 châteaux of Bordeaux have been officially classified at various times, beginning in the sixteenth century. Three of these lists—the Médoc and Sauternes Classification of 1855, the Graves Classification of 1953, and the Saint-Émilion Classification of 1955—are extant today (*see* MÉDOC, SAUTERNES, GRAVES, SAINT-ÉMILION). All châteaux classified as outstanding are treated individually (*see Château* LAFITE, *Château* LATOUR, *Château* D'YQUEM, *Château* CHEVAL

APPELLATIONS CONTRÔLÉES OF THE BORDEAUX REGION

Place-name	*Date established*	*Maximum gallons permitted per acre* imp.	U.S.	*YIELD IN 1962 in imperial gallons (U.S. gallonages in parentheses)* white		red	
Barsac	11 Sept. 1936	223	267	404,052	(485,244)		
Blaye or Blayais	11 Sept. 1936	400	481	8,051,562	(9,669,480)		
Bordeaux	14 Nov. 1936	445	535	27,918,122	(33,528,119)	7,110,746	(8,539,613
Bordeaux Clairet or Rosé	14 Nov. 1936	445	535	—		97,383	(116,952)
Bordeaux supérieur	14 Oct. 1943	356	428	2,138,519	(2,568,243)	5,596,387	(6,720,952)
Bordeaux Mousseux (sparkling Bordeaux)	16 Mar. 1943	445	535	—		—	
Cérons	11 Sept. 1936	356	428	573,983	(689,322)		
Côtes de Blaye	11 Sept. 1936	374	449	104,643	(125,670)		
Côtes de Bordeaux Saint-Macaire	31 July 1937	374	449	731,420	(878,395)		
Côtes de Bourg, Bourg or Bourgeais	14 May 1941 (white)	356	428	1,013,627	(1,217,310)		
	11 Sept. 1936 (red)	445	535			2,115,201	(2,540,240)
Côtes Canon Fronsac	1 July 1939	374	449			271,538	(326,104)
Côtes de Fronsac	14 March 1938	374	449			726,867	(872,927)
Entre-Deux-Mers	31 July 1937	445	535	1,991,289	(2,391,428)		
Graves	4 March 1937	356	428	81,963	(98,433)	390,743	(469,261)
Graves supérieures	4 March 1937	356	428	1,542,692	(1,852,687)		
Graves de Vayres	31 July 1937	374	449	772,798	(928,087)	5,015	(6,023)
Haut-Médoc	14 Nov. 1936	320	385			873,987	(1,049,610)
Lalande de Pomerol and Néac	8 Dec. 1936	356	428			502,029	(602,909)
Listrac	8 June 1957	320	385			239,906	(288,115)
Loupiac	11 Sept. 1936	356	428	329,920	(396,217)		
Lussac-Saint-Émilion	14 Nov. 1936	374	449			777,923	(934,243)
Margaux	10 Aug. 1954	303	363			345,626	(415,078)
Médoc	14 Nov. 1936	338	406			882,544	(1,059,886)
Montagne-Saint-Émilion	14 Nov. 1936	374	449			984,393	(1,182,201)
Moulis	14 May 1938	320	385			120,591	(144,823)
Parsac-Saint-Émilion	14 Nov. 1936	374	449			161,440	(193,882)
Pauillac	14 Nov. 1936	303	363			524,599	(630,014)
Pomerol	8 Dec. 1936	356	428			655,704	(787,463)
Premières Côtes de Blaye	11 Sept. 1936	374	449	25,143	(30,196)	717,694	(861,910)
Premières Côtes de Bordeaux	31 July 1937	356	428	2,717,210	(3,263,218)	666,637	(800,594)
Puisseguin-Saint-Émilion	14 Nov. 1936	374	449			612,963	(736,135)
Sables-Saint-Émilion	4 March 1937	374	449			154,093	(185,058)
Sainte-Croix-du-Mont	11 Sept. 1936	356	428	412,411	(495,283)		
Saint-Émilion	14 Nov. 1936	374	449			4,883,357	(5,864,642)
Saint-Estèphe	14 Nov. 1936	320	385			768,376	(922,777)
Sainte-Foy-Bordeaux	31 July 1937	400	481	1,012,923	(1,216,465)	25,957	(31,173)
Saint-Georges-Saint Émilion	14 Nov. 1936	374	449			243,711	(292,685)
Saint-Julien	14 Nov. 1936	303	363			351,632	(422,290)
Sauternes	30 Sept. 1936	223	267	765,890	(919,792)		

BLANC, *etc.*). The sub-regional and communal names or Appellations Contrôlées in Bordeaux wines are as follows:

APPELLATIONS CONTRÔLÉES OF BORDEAUX

(*see all place-names as entered individually*)

Most Important Regions

Sauternes (including Barsac)	white sweet wines	5,000 acres
Médoc	red wines	15,500 acres
Pomerol	red wines	1,500 acres
Saint-Émilion	red wines	10,750 acres
Graves	red wines and white dry wines	8,750 acres

Characteristics

It is evident, from the multiplicity of names, that the range of Bordeaux wines is the greatest anywhere. Roughly, it may be said that red wines are made north of the city and white wines to the south, with the Graves district, in which the actual town is set, forming an intermediate zone where both white and red wines are grown, frequently in a single vineyard. The white wines tend—though again there are exceptions—to change gradually from dry to sweet through the vineyards in Graves on the edge of Bordeaux to Sauternes at the southern extreme of the region.

Red Bordeaux is, in its own delicate, feminine style, the finest of its kind in the world. Yet its characteristic softness and subtlety comes only with age. The tannin content—which, with alcohol, decides the 'heaviness' or 'lightness' of any wine—in a Bordeaux is actually higher than in an authentic and natural Burgundy. This might be said to disprove the theory that the wines of Bordeaux are light and those of Burgundy are heavy. This is not the case, but there are, in fact, a number of exceptions to the rule. The delicate characteristics of 'light' Bordeaux are exemplified in the wines of Margaux, in the middle of the Médoc, which are definite in taste but mild in texture. Generally speaking, however, natural Bordeaux are sturdy when young, but mature beautifully and attain softness with age; the greater the Bordeaux, the greater will be the recompense of patience, especially in the case of the wines grown around the village of Pauillac, and of the very sturdy wines of Saint-Estèphe, where the softening qualities of age are most necessary. Red Graves, also, is earthy and full when young and attains a magnificent splendour later on. In Burgundy, on the other hand, young wines tend to mature much faster; and some of those from the Beaujolais region of Burgundy are among the lightest red wines of France, if not of the world. A Côte de Nuits may well be more delicate than a Saint-Émilion, which usually has great fullness and is sometimes referred to as the 'Burgundy' of Bordeaux.

Certain generic characteristics the great gamut of Bordeaux wine does share. Uniquely, for such volume, it is perfectly natural. White or red, dry or sweet, the châteaux wines never have anything added to them; and for this reason, and also because of their iron content, they are wonderfully health giving. (Occasionally—1958 and 1960 are modern instances—the process of *chaptalisation*, or adding sugar before fermentation, a common practice elsewhere, is authorized in Bordeaux.) When necessary Bordeaux are characterized, too, by their longevity, tremendous for purely natural wines. Some of the greatest Médocs will live for a century in the bottle (the stubborn 1870 vintage did not fulfil its early promise until it was between fifty and seventy years old); and among the sweet white wines, Château d'Yquem also has been known to last a hundred years. In spite of the huge multiplicity and range, there is something peculiar to the scent of Bordeaux, especially the aged reds; a woodland freshness or an earthy smell of low-growing violets which is found in no other wine.

Soil and Climate

Such a diversity of wines indicates an equal variety of vineyard soils. The most characteristic soil element, very widespread, is the presence on the surface, and in the subsoil, of pebbles, forming either the gravel or *graves* which give the name to several of the finest vineyard areas, or the egg-sized and even fist-sized *cailloux* (pebbles) figuring proudly in the names of such vineyards as Château Beaucaillou in Saint-Julien, and contributing largely to the character of, for example, Château Latour, Château Margaux, or Château Lascombes. With only a few exceptions, the finest wines come from the vineyards planted on soil deposited in the Quaternary era. The extreme of this principle is that the most recent river soils are excluded as vineyards for wines accorded any of the Bordeaux Appellations Contrôlées. The late alluvial strips and marshy areas are called *palus*; an interesting sidelight on the changing tastes in wine is that a few hundred years ago these were the most sought-after areas in the four categories of land then established.

All Bordeaux wines—though not all to the same degree—are influenced by the mildness and humidity of the climate created by the rivers and the nearness of the sea and by the pine forests which blanket the land towards the ocean. Summer heat rarely fails to generate a sudden thunder-shower, and long parched stretches are uncommon. Winters are very short and are seldom cold. The chief menace to the vines is hail, which in recent years has struck most often in the regions of Barsac–Sauternes, more than once destroying the crops of Château d'Yquem, Château de Rayne-Vigneau, and adjacent vineyards. Frosts are a danger, but are less frequent than in most fine vine-land. For this very reason, the unprecedented freeze of February 1956 killed hundreds of acres of vineyard; vines unprepared to resist frost failed to withstand the coldest Bordeaux winter since 1709, and the crop was reduced by some 50% with a loss of about 58 million imp. gallons (70 million U.S.) of unmade wine.

Grape Varieties

Bordeaux red wine must be made from varieties of the Cabernet vine (Cabernet Sauvignon and Cabernet Franc), the Carménère, Merlot, Malbec, and Petit-Verdot. White wines are limited to the grapes of the Sémillon, Sauvignon, Muscadelle, and Merlot Blanc. Only very rare instances exist of a wine made from a single variety, and practically all are blends of the permitted grapes, varying somewhat in proportion according to the theories of the different growers, but tending to follow the rough formula which time has proved to be best suited to that particular section. Until 1953 a number of other, less noble vines were tolerated, up to a maximum of 10% of the wine; but in the decade beginning in March 1943 these had all to be systematically uprooted. The writings of Montesquieu indicate a very different situation in his time. In 1785, according to him, no less than twenty-seven varieties of red and twenty-two varieties of white vine contributed to the wines.

Vintages

Vintage is very much over-emphasized in Bordeaux wines. From 1795 to 1870, 40% of the years were poor or mediocre, and 60% were good or better. Since 1870, the proportion has been 80% good or excellent, and 20% mediocre: thus the number of poor years before 1870 was proportionately double the number today. Modern science has eliminated the conditions which gave rise to emphasis on vintage by helping to cut out the 'lows'.

This does not mean that vintages do not differ—they only fail to differ in commonplace wine zones—but it does mean that the terms used to describe vintages, and especially in the highly abbreviated and therefore misleading and sometimes biased vintage charts, no longer conform to the real case. On these lists, the opposite of a 'great' year is always a 'poor', or perhaps a 'small' one. In fact, small years occur in quantity, but never in terms of wine character or quality, and it is a distinct misnomer to refer to a light wine as 'small'. A 'great' red Bordeaux is simply a Bordeaux which has been produced in a 'big' year—when continuous sunshine has made a wine destined to develop slowly and to last a long time. A 'small' year is merely one when there was less sun; and the wines of this year will mature relatively quickly. Deluded by vintage charts, too many people suppose that they must buy the wines only of the big years, usually indicated by outsize ciphers on the vintage chart; but when they do this they are buying essentially what ought properly to be called long-lasting wine; and, too often, they drink it before it has come to its proper bottle-age. Had they chosen instead the wine of a lighter year, they would have paid less and had a better bottle *at the time when they drank it.*

Yet it would not be correct to say that the big vintages are overvalued, for, properly laid down and waited for, they will finally achieve the highest peaks. It is true, however, that the lighter years are undervalued, for the wines of those years, ready to be drunk much earlier, are not always inferior but are merely going to develop more quickly and fade sooner.

Harvesting

Bordeaux is usually harvested at the end of September, sometimes in early October, and very rarely in August or November. As a general rule, the hotter the summer the earlier the harvest. In a little more than a century and a half, the following were the number of vintages starting in the effective months: August (1822 and 1893), 2; September 122; October, 51; November (1816), 1. Red wines and most white wines are picked straight over the vineyard, but the extra-sweet Barsacs and Sauternes are selectively picked, bunch by bunch and almost grape by grape as the individual berries reach super-ripeness. Therefore, Barsac and Sauternes harvests take about twice as long as they do elsewhere, often ending in November. The following chart depicts the cycle of the vine over more than a century in certain significant years.

Ripening of the Vine at Château Mouton-Rothschild (great vintages only)

Year	*Flowering*		*Beginning of reddening of the grape*	*Start of harvest*
	Beginning	*End*		
1966	25 May	15 June	25 July	26 Sept.
1952	19 May	5 June	8 July	18 Sept.
1947	26 May	15 June	15 July	17 Sept.
1945	11 May	1 June	2 July	7 Sept.
1929	24 May	25 June	22 July	21 Sept
1921	19 May	13 June	18 July	10 Sept.
1900	29 May	14 June	26 July	25 Sept.
1893	28 April	20 May	23 June	22 Aug.
1870	18 May	5 June	12 July	10 Sept.
1822	13 May	31 May	3 July	24 Aug.

Maturing

Wines of Bordeaux previously stored in jars, or amphoræ, began to be kept in cask at the suggestion of Charlemagne. Centuries later—not long before the French Revolution—a greater integrity was established by the enforced use of the *barrique bordelaise,* the barrel which survives today and which was at that time forbidden to all other wines. It is an ideal size—225 litres—for maturing red Bordeaux, although in white Bordeaux some experiments are being made to see if a larger barrel, slowing the development of the wine and keeping it fresher and fruitier, will not better accord with the taste for ever younger white wines. The cost of the barrel itself, in Bordeaux as elsewhere, has risen sensationally and become a factor in the price of the wine. The raw oak alone, at the time of writing, costs well over 100 francs (£7 or 20 dollars) per barrel with an additional approximate 40 francs to be added for labour and the iron of the hoops. Oak used to be imported from Poland, Sweden, and the United States; but since the war a great deal of it has come from Yugoslavia and the Limoges forest (where the wood is shared with makers of Cognac); and a certain amount of poorer quality wood from Alsace is used to make up the deficit.

White wines are both fermented and matured in cask; red wines are matured in cask, but are fermented in large vats, generally oak, although at some vineyards they are now made of cement or stainless steel. Controversy rages between traditionalists and modernists in Bordeaux over the use of concrete vats, but no one has been able to prove that the modern method of fermenting in concrete is less efficient or entails loss of quality; and it is fast gaining adherents. There are a few vineyards which have begun cautiously to experiment with maturing red Bordeaux in the oak vats in which it is fermented, an innovation which, if it is successful, will both reduce cost, by eliminating expensive casks, and produce a lighter wine which can be drunk sooner. The great red Bordeaux will never be made by this method, because part of the tannin which gives it longevity is absorbed from the new oak of the barrels, renewed for each vintage; but perhaps there will be room also for the lighter, younger wine. It is, however, understandable that since the war there has been a widespread tendency in Bordeaux to hurry on the bottling by additional rackings, which hasten the development of the wine. Thirty-five years ago, red Bordeaux was always kept for a minimum of three years in the wood. Nowadays, all the châteaux are bottling at anything from eighteen to thirty months; while most châteaux bottle their wines at the end of about two years.

Bordeaux Bottles

The characteristic Bordeaux bottle has shoulders to retain the sediment and a neck very suited by its straight length to the long corks which distinguish and preserve the finest wines. Half-bottles, called in Bordeaux *fillettes* (little girls), are becoming common, especially for dry white wines which ought to be drunk very young. A wine will mature more quickly in a half-bottle than in a bottle because its ripening is partly caused by oxygen coming through the cork, relatively greater in proportion to the lesser quantity of wine in the small bottle. For this reason, a young wine may be good from the half-bottle, but old wines from the half-bottle will be 'gone'. The ideal bottle for great old Bordeaux is the magnum, with double the content of the standard bottle, in which the wine matures more slowly. The double magnum and the six-bottle *jéroboam* are rare; and the *impériale*, with the content of eight normal bottles, has not often been seen since the war. Some experts contend that the old red Bordeaux are better in the sizes greater than the magnum, on the same law of ever lesser cork dimensions in relation to wine mass; while others believe the magnum is the optimum size. This is an argument limited almost entirely to the Bordelais, and almost impossible to settle, since it concerns wines half a century old, bottled long ago and subject to dozens of subtly influential conditions.

Export

Export of Bordeaux wine in casks in 1965 amounted to 8,755,000 imp. gallons (10,514,000

U.S.). Some of the bottled red and white Bordeaux wines, both regional and château types, bear an identifying seal on the throat of the bottle. In this form 875,000 imp. gallons (1,051,000 U.S.) of wine were exported to the United States in 1965. This figure represents an increase of 148% on the amount exported in 1957; in value the increase was 322%. The shield-shaped gold and black seal with the device of the French fleur-de-lis and the leopard of Bordeaux certifies that the wine has been taste-tested in Bordeaux by a changing committee of shippers and brokers, and has met with approval as representative of its region and vintage. At present this seal is kept exclusively for the American market.

Bordeaux Growths: Classification

In 1855 there was a great Exhibition in Paris; the organizers sent to Bordeaux for samples of its best wines, and this set off the local notables on a classification of their finest growths. Only two districts were dealt with—the Médoc and Sauternes. At that time Graves, which had once been the leading district, had fallen behind, and these two regions produced the recognized quality wines of Bordeaux, whose wine merchants discriminated (partly out of snobbery) against the merchants of Libourne and its adjoining vineyards in Saint-Émilion and Pomerol. Hence Château Pétrus of Pomerol, Château Cheval-Blanc and Château Ausone (celebrated as the oldest fine vineyard of the region) in Saint-Émilion were omitted from the 1855 Classification of the Wines of the Gironde and had to wait until 1955 to be officially rated. The grading was done by the Bordeaux brokers (or *courtiers*) who sell the product of the various vineyards to the shippers and are therefore considered to know the wines better than anybody else. The brokers based their judgements on soil, prestige, and prices.

That this was a sensible decision has been proved by the long life of the 1855 Classification. Climate, soil, and surface-exposure of vineyards do not change, and these elements have exercised the same beneficial influence since 1855 as they did before; but owners change, some tend their vines and make their wine better than others do—and there is no doubt that this century-old assessment is now, in some parts, obsolescent. There are few important châteaux which have not changed their holdings. Patches of vineyard are continually being bought and sold. The classification is still, however, completely valid for the First Growths (*Premiers Crus*)—the three great Médoc châteaux, Lafite, Margaux, and Latour; and Haut-Brion, which has always been on the list. Although it is actually in Graves, Haut-Brion wine was too good to be left out and so, defying geography, was classed in with the Médocs. As for Château Mouton-Rothschild, listed first of the Second Growths (*Seconds Crus*) in 1855—the high prices it has commanded for the past thirty years entitle it to be included among the First Growths.

In considering the 1855 Classification, it should be emphasized that a Second, Third (*Troisième*), Fourth (*Quatrième*), or Fifth Growth (*Cinquième Cru*) is not a second-, third-, fourth-, or fifth-rate wine. Actually, only sixty-two amongst approximately two thousand vineyards were considered worthy of being listed Great Growths (*Grands Crus*) —whether First or Fifth—and they are the absolute cream of the vineyards which, as a group, are probably the world's finest in red wine. To be second after only Lafite, Latour, Margaux, and Haut-Brion is very far from being second-rate. Moreover, it is only on an average that the first are the best; in certain years, others equal and even surpass them. Anyone can be sure of a superb bottle when he buys the best years of the famous vineyards (at a price); but there is adventure—and economy—in seeking out other years and other vineyards from the splendid list of Bordeaux wines.

Exceptional Growths (*Crus Exceptionnels*) are *not* classed higher than the Great Growths, but are those classified, in 1855, after the sixty-two great vineyards—and were themselves followed by the Bourgeois and Artisan classes (*Crus Bourgeois* and *Crus Artisans*). Among these are some fine wines which now deserve to be elevated to greater recognition.

In fact, the old classification no longer tells the whole truth; and opinions expressed in the press and elsewhere have proved that even in Bordeaux uneasiness has, in certain quarters, been steadily increasing—although the general view was that, while the ruling of 1855 had its faults, it was impossible to improve upon it. And this in spite of the fact that some of the vineyards then listed are no longer in existence.

In 1959, a committee was formed to decide what was to be done about reclassifying the work of 1855. Two alternatives were discussed: should the 1855 Classification be amended to reflect the changes of today; or should the Classification of 1855 remain untouched and a new one be drawn up? The author, feeling that many alterations are needed, was a member of one of the original committees, which consisted of leading Bordeaux growers, shippers, and brokers; and he published, in 1959, a private classification of all the red wines of Bordeaux, on the lines of the recent official ratings for Saint-Émilion and Graves—Pomerol has not even yet been classified. While this was in preparation, each expert was interviewed privately and 'off the record', and no one person's views, therefore, are quoted: but it was soon evident that on certain points there was no difference of opinion. Investigation of land records in the various communes revealed that some of the châteaux no longer occupied the same terrain as they did in 1855; in many cases changes were insignificant, but in others important transfers of parcels of land had been made—and therefore even the essential qualification of first-rate soil cannot, in these instances, go unchallenged. Other classified châteaux, including some Second and Third Growths, no longer make any wine; the names stand for Great Growths of 1855 as a Roman ruin may persist as a reminder of a vanished monument of classical times. This absurdity does harm to the Bordeaux wine trade; and the reverse case, of a vineyard classed as a Fifth or even a Bourgeois Growth, when it deserves to be sold as a Second or Third Growth, deprives both grower and customer (who is misled by the wine's rating) of a satisfactory transaction.

It was generally agreed that if the 1855 standards were applied today, they would have to rate as a First Growth Château Pétrus—still unclassified in the as yet unclassified district of Pomerol; would have to advance Château Mouton-Rothschild from Second to First Growth, and elevate Cheval-Blanc from a First of Saint-Émilion to a Bordeaux Great Growth. Indeed, so many vineyards of Saint-Émilion, Graves, and Pomerol clamoured for their rightful place that it became obvious that any workable classification should include all Bordeaux wines. In fact, the system of 1855 should not now be used, for if a guide is no longer completely reliable, the public loses confidence. This is now happening.

As to the form a new classification should take, opinions were almost unanimous that the error of grading vineyards First, Second, and so on, must not be repeated. In an age of publicity and competitive salesmanship, any wine listed as a Second, Third, or Fourth would be unfairly handicapped; and the newer classifications for Saint-Émilion and Graves have not followed this pattern, but have graded their wines 'First Growths', 'Great Growths', and 'Other Principal Growths' (*see* Appendix A, III and VII). In his suggested revision of the Classification, the author has adapted and expanded these as follows: Outstanding Growths (*Crus Hors Classe*), Exceptional Growths (*Crus Exceptionnels*), Great Growths (*Grands Crus*), Superior Growths (*Crus Supérieurs*), and Good Growths (*Bons Crus*).

Finally, most of the experts consulted were of the opinion that, in assessing the position of the vineyards, price would still be (as it was in 1855) the most reliable indicator; and it was on this basis, of the prices the individual wines command in today's market, that the following classification was prepared. The fact that a great soil, given proper management, will produce great wines, was taken into account: certain vineyards have not been downgraded as much as their present management warrants, because the soil is intact and, under new management, these vineyards may rise again.

A classification should not be planned for a shorter span than twenty-five years or a half-century. The present condition of the 1855 list proves that no such ruling can remain valid indefinitely; but, conversely, too frequent change would cause confusion and loss of confidence among buyers.

In 1960, after the committee had made a formal request for a revision of the 1855 Classification, the Institut National des Appellations d'Origine was called in to arbitrate. Two years later, however, it was decided in Bordeaux that the jurisdiction of this body was too limited for it to resolve a matter so complex and so controversial. The Bordeaux Chamber of Commerce and the Académie des Vins de Bordeaux then took up the question of the proposed reforms. At the time of writing, it is still being debated and may not be settled for some time.

CLASSIFICATION DES GRANDS CRUS ROUGES DE BORDEAUX

Revised as from July 1966 and based on the standing of the Bordeaux vineyards in 1959. Wines other than those in the *Crus Hors Classe* category are listed alphabetically.

Crus Hors Classe (*Outstanding Growths*)

MÉDOC	Château Lafite-Rothschild (*Pauillac*)
	Château Margaux (*Margaux*)
	Château Latour (*Pauillac*)
	Château Haut-Brion (*Pessac, Graves*)
	Château Mouton-Rothschild (*Pauillac*)

Crus Hors Classe (Outstanding Growths)—Contd.

SAINT-ÉMILION
Château Cheval-Blanc
Château Ausone

POMEROL
Château Pétrus

Crus Exceptionnels (Exceptional Growths)

MÉDOC
Château Beychevelle (*Saint-Julien*)
Château Brane-Cantenac (*Cantenac-Margaux*)
Château Calon-Ségur (*Saint-Estèphe*)
Château Cantemerle (*Macau*)
Château Cos d'Estournel (*Saint-Estèphe*)
Château Ducru-Beaucaillou (*Saint-Julien*)
Château Gruaud-Larose (*Saint-Julien*)
Château Lascombes (*Margaux*)
Château Léoville-Barton (*Saint-Julien*)
Château Léoville-Las-Cases (*Saint-Julien*)
Château Léoville-Poyferré (*Saint-Julien*)
Château Lynch-Bages (*Pauillac*)
Château Montrose (*Saint-Estèphe*)
Château Palmer (*Cantenac-Margaux*)
Château Pichon-Longueville (Baron) (*Pauillac*)
Château Pichon (Longueville, Comtesse de) Lalande (*Pauillac*)
Château Rausan-Ségla (*Margaux*)

SAINT-ÉMILION
Château Belair
Château Canon
Château Figeac
Château la Gaffelière

POMEROL
Château La Conseillante
Château l'Évangile
Château Vieux-Château-Certan

GRAVES
Domaine de Chevalier (*Léognan*)
Château La Mission-Haut-Brion (*Pessac*)

Grands Crus (Great Growths)

MÉDOC
Château Branaire-Ducru (*Saint-Julien*)
Château Cantenac-Brown (*Cantenac-Margaux*)
Château Duhart-Milon (*Pauillac*)
Château Durfort (*Margaux*)
Château Giscours (*Margaux*)
Château Grand-Puy-Lacoste (*Pauillac*)
Château d'Issan (*Cantenac-Margaux*)
Château La Lagune (*Ludon*)
Château Malescot-Saint-Exupéry (*Margaux*)
Château Mouton-Baron Philippe (*Pauillac*)
Château Pontet-Canet (*Pauillac*)
Château Prieuré-Lichine (*Cantenac-Margaux*)
Château Rauzan-Gassies (*Margaux*)
Château Talbot (*Saint-Julien*)

SAINT-ÉMILION
Château Fourtet
Château Magdelaine
Château Pavie

POMEROL
Château Certan-de-May
Château Gazin
Château Lafleur
Château Lafleur-Pétrus
Château Petit-Village
Château Trotanoy

GRAVES
Château Haut-Bailly (*Léognan*)
Château Pape-Clément (*Pessac*)

Crus Supérieurs (Superior Growths)

MÉDOC
Château Batailley (*Pauillac*)
Château Chasse-Spleen (*Moulis*)
Château Ferrière (*Margaux*)
Château Gloria (*Saint-Julien-Beychevelle*)
Château Grand-Puy-Ducasse (*Pauillac*)
Château Haut-Batailley (*Pauillac*)
Château Kirwan (*Cantenac-Margaux*)
Château Langoa-Barton (*Saint-Julien*)
Château La Tour-de-Mons (*Soussans-Margaux*)
Château Marquis-d'Alesme-Becker (*Margaux*)
Château Marquis-de-Terme (*Margaux*)

Crus Supérieurs (*Superior Growths*)—Cont.

Saint-Émilion
- Château l'Angélus
- Château Beauséjour-Duffau-Lagarrosse
- Château Beauséjour-Fagouet
- Château Canon-la-Gaffelière
- Château Croque-Michotte
- Château Curé-Bon-la-Madeleine
- Château Larcis-Ducasse
- Château Ripeau
- Château Trottevieille
- Château Villemaurine

Pomerol
- Château Beauregard
- Château Certan-Giraud
- Clos de l'Église-Clinet
- Clos l'Église
- Château Lagrange
- Château Latour-Pomerol
- Château Nenin
- Château La Pointe

Graves
- Château Carbonnieux (*Léognan*)
- Château Malartic-Lagravière (*Léognan*)
- Château Smith-Haut-Lafitte (*Martillac*)
- Château La Tour-Haut-Brion (*Talence*)
- Château La Tour-Martillac or La Tour-Kressmann (*Martillac*)

Bons Crus (*Good Growths*)

Médoc
- Château Angludet (*Margaux*)
- Château Bel-Air-Marquis-d'Aligre (*Soussans-Margaux*)
- Château Belgrave (*Saint-Laurent*)
- Château Boyd-Cantenac (*Cantenac-Margaux*)
- Château Capbern (*Saint-Estèphe*)
- Château Clerc-Milon-Mondon (*Pauillac*)
- Château Cos-Labory (*Saint-Estèphe*)
- Château Croizet-Bages (*Pauillac*)
- Château Dutruch-Lambert (*Moulis*)
- Château Fourcas-Dupré (*Listrac*)
- Château Fourcas-Hostein (*Listrac*)
- Cru Gressier-Grand-Poujeaux (*Moulis*)
- Château Haut-Bages-Libéral (*Pauillac*)
- Château Lagrange (*Saint-Julien*)
- Château Lanessan (*Cussac*)
- Château Lynch-Moussas (*Pauillac*)
- Château Les Ormes-de-Pez (*Saint-Estèphe*)
- Château Paveil (*Soussans-Margaux*)
- Château de Pez (*Saint-Estèphe*)
- Château Phélan-Ségur (*Saint-Estèphe*)
- Château Poujeaux-Theil (*Moulis*)
- Château St. Pierre (*Saint-Julien*)
- Château Siran (*Labarde-Margaux*)
- Château La Tour-Carnet (*Saint-Laurent*)

Saint-Émilion
- Château Baleau
- Château Balestard-la-Tonnelle
- Château Cap-de-Mourlin
- Château Le Chatelet
- Château La Clotte
- Château Corbin (*Giraud*)
- Château Corbin-Michotte
- Château Coutet
- Château La Dominique
- Château Fonroque
- Château Grand-Barrail-Lamarzelle-Figeac
- Château Grand-Corbin
- Château Grand-Corbin-Despagne
- Château Les Grandes-Murailles
- Clos des Jacobins
- Château Saint-Georges-Côte-Pavie
- Château Soutard
- Château La Tour-du-Pin-Figeac
- Château Troplong-Mondot

Pomerol
- Château La Croix
- Château La Croix-de-Gay
- Château Feytit-Clinet
- Château Gombaude-Guillot
- Château la Fleur-Pourret
- Château Mazeyres
- Château Rouget
- Château de Sales

Graves
- Château Bouscaut (*Cadaujac*)
- Château Fieuzal (*Léognan*)

Note: All Saint-Émilion and Pomerol châteaux classified above bear the strict commune designations of Saint-Émilion and Pomerol respectively.

Bordeaux: Mousseux, Supérieur

Mildly sparkling wines with Appellations Contrôlées in the Bordeaux region.

See BORDEAUX.

Borderies

Lesser region of Cognac, producing brandies with considerable body, and usually lacking in finesse.

See COGNAC.

Bosa

Malvasia di Bosa is a richly-coloured red wine of Sardinia (*q.v.*).

Bota

1. Wine bag; the modern conventional Spanish wine bag is of untanned goatskin, holding about a litre. It has a bone or wooden nozzle out of which the wine may be squirted by squeezing the bag. It is thus possible for several different persons in turn to drink from the bota without touching the nozzle with their lips.

2. Spanish wine barrel of 500 litres (110 imp. gallons; 132 U.S.) widely used for storing and ageing wines. A Sherry butt. There is also a media bota, or half-bota, with a capacity of 250 litres (55 imp. gallons; 66 U.S.).

Botrytis cinerea

A parasitic fungus or mould that attacks grapes with the result that in certain climates the grapes develop grey rot and spoil, while in others the *Botrytis cinerea* produces some of the greatest sweet white wines of the world. Called *pourriture noble* by the French (literally, noble rot), it is carefully cultivated in Sauternes, Monbazillac, Anjou, and Touraine—as well as in Germany, where it is known as *Edelfäule* and is responsible for the Auslese, Beerenauslese, and Trockenbeerenauslese wines of the Rhine and Moselle. It also produces Tokay in Hungary. In no other area has it so far proved possible to make those late-gathered sweet wines from overripe grapes, since the climate must be exactly right for them. (The proper weather conditions have reportedly been found in the New York State Finger Lakes district and in California, but there have been no further developments.)

The fungus penetrates, without breaking, the skin of the fruit, and thus without exposing the pulp to the air. If all is in order, the grape begins to wither and become desiccated, and there is a corresponding concentration of the juice. In the shrinking of the fruit, loss of acidity is greater than loss of sugar. Consequently the percentage of soluble solids becomes greater, sugar and glycerin mounting faster than acidity. When vinified, the wines become smooth and almost oily in texture, very sweet and high in alcohol. The climatic conditions must be such that as the grapes mature, there must be moisture in the air to allow the fungus to grow, alternating with periods of dry weather to cause the water in the grapes to evaporate and so keep the mould from growing too fast—yet if the temperature rises too high, the fungus will be killed. At the end of this uncertain and difficult culture, the juice that remains in the grape makes only a small amount of wine, which is thus extremely expensive.

See CHAPTER NINE, p. 44.

Bottle Sickness

A temporary indisposition to which wine is sometimes subject when it is first bottled.

Bouché

French term for a wine-bottle stoppered with a cork; not to be confused with *bouchonné*, spoiled by the cork.

Bouchet

One of the grape varieties of the Saint-Émilion and Pomerol districts of Bordeaux; synonymous with Cabernet Franc and Cabernet Sauvignon.

Bouchon

French term for cork.

Bouchonné

A bottle of wine spoiled by a bad cork. Corky.

Bouquet

Volatile acidity is responsible for the bouquet of a wine. It should be clean, with no trace of mouldiness. The scent is produced by the vaporization of esters and ethers, those elusive chemical components which the wine contains. When a wine is cold or when a bottle is first opened, the bouquet is faint and hard to identify. (The first perfume is the bouquet; the later, more lingering odour, the aroma.)

Bourbon

A type of American whiskey.

See WHISKEY, BOURBON.

Bourg, Bourgeais, Côtes de Bourg

Red and white wines. District: Bordeaux, France.

Official French wine place-names, all applying to the red and white wines made in nearly equal quantity on the hills of Bourg fringing the River Gironde and the River Dordogne as they enter the Gironde, and all but enclosed within the larger Blaye wine region. The two ancient fortified towns of Bourg and Blaye are less than half a dozen miles apart, and the wines can be considered together. Red Bourg is fuller-bodied than red Blaye, and, all in all, is superior. Some of the white Premières Côtes de Blaye are the best white wines of the linked regions. The red Blayes have not been granted the Appellation Contrôlée.

Bourgogne: Aligoté, Mousseux, Passe-tout-Grains

Wines with Appellations Contrôlées in Burgundy (*q.v.*).

Bourgueil and Saint-Nicolas-de-Bourgueil

Loire Valley red and rosé wine. District: Touraine, France.

The growing areas are separate and distinct but are adjacent; and the wines are so alike that they are invariably classed together. They have also in common the fact that they are the only Loire vineyards where the place-name is restricted to red and rosé wines; white can be called only Touraine.

The wines are light, soft, and delicate, with a pronounced fruitiness and a strong bouquet which calls to mind raspberries, or perhaps violets. Wine labelled Saint-Nicolas-de-Bourgueil comes from grapes grown only there and is generally better than Bourgueil, for which the grapes may be grown in seven parishes. Soil throughout is a gravelly sand enriched with limestone and clay and the only permissible grape is Cabernet Franc. Wines must have a minimum alcoholic content of 9·5%. About 935,000 imp. gallons (1,125,000 U.S.) are made annually.

Château Bouscaut

Bordeaux red and white wine. District: Graves, France. Commune: Cadaujac.

Classed in 1953 among the five top Graves vineyards making white wine and the eleven top Graves vineyards making red wine, Château Bouscaut is the first important estate on the Graves–Sauternes road leading to Toulouse. The house is a handsome mixture of mediæval and modern, with its tapestries, swimming pool, and huge walled park. The *chais* divide in two for the making of red wines—which are fermented in huge oak vats—and white wines, which are crushed in electric presses, contained in a reservoir the first day but then tapped off directly into barrels in the *chai*, where they both ferment and age. Once in barrel, red and white wines age side by side.

Bouscaut continues the ageing and selling of its wine in bottle—a practice instituted by the father of Robert Place, the present owner. Few large vineyards could start today the expensive process of having to wait over a number of years, without income, before selling bottle-aged wines; but behind the barrel-stores at Bouscaut are a dozen room-sized lockers containing thousands of bottles of wine. This is a usual sight at a shipper's cellar—rare at a château.

Adjoining the Bouscaut vineyard is a secondary growth, Château Valoux, under the same ownership.

Characteristics. Strong and full; rather lacking in breed.

Vineyard area: 87 acres.

Average production: 3,000 cases white, 6,000 cases red.

Bouzy

Village of the Mountain of Reims district, producing red grapes for a First Growth Champagne, and a red still wine.

See CHAMPAGNE.

Boxbeutel

See BOCKSBEUTEL.

Château Boyd-Cantenac

Bordeaux red wine. District: Haut-Médoc, France. Commune: Cantenac-Margaux.

There is no château; but the vineyard itself, owned by Monsieur P. Guillermet, is a Third Growth (*Troisième Cru*) of Médoc according to the Classification of 1855. The wine is made at Monsieur Guillermet's Château Pouget. Until recently, the vineyard did not deserve its high classification, and it was the opinion of many local brokers that it should be reclassified.

Characteristics. Light and generally on the thin side. Disappointing.

Vineyard area: 15 acres.

Average production: 1,800 cases.

Brachetto

Red wine grape of Italy, which produces a wine of strong colour and agreeable flavour.

See PIEDMONT.

Château Branaire-Ducru

Bordeaux red wine. District: Haut-Médoc, France. Commune: Saint-Julien.

Facing Château Beychevelle across the Médoc vineyard road as it winds north into Saint-Julien, Château Branaire, Fourth Growth (*Quatrième Cru*) by the 1855 Classification, is now owned by Monsieur Jean Tapie, an enterprising Algerian wine grower who in the early fifties acquired interests in France. The previous owner, Monsieur Ducru, figures in the vineyard name, but Monsieur Tapie is simplifying the nomenclature and probably in the future the Growth will be simply Château Branaire. The vineyard is well placed on the flattish top of rising ground and there is an excellent large *chai* for old wines sunk underground to two-thirds its height to achieve a beneficial dampness.

Characteristics. Sturdy, big wines, sometimes quite hard at the outset; but among the best of Saint-Julien.

Vineyard area: 92 acres.

Average production: 10,000 cases.

Brandy

The word alone means distilled wine. It has been appropriated to refer to distillates from other fruits —apples, pears, cherries, etc.—but in such cases will always be qualified by the source. Brandy, when it stands alone, is a product of the grape, and is distilled throughout the world.

The best brandies are the French Cognac and Armagnac. A fact too often overlooked is that Cognac is not brandy, but *a* brandy. It is perhaps, at its best, the world's most exquisite example of spirits of this type; Armagnac can be almost as perfect. Brandies are made in most wine-growing countries, sometimes of extraordinarily good quality, sometimes not. The secret of a fine brandy is partly in the wine distilled, partly in the distilling process (the best is made in pot stills), but also in the age and the wood in which it is aged. Cognac, for instance, matures best in Limousin oak. It should be remembered that once brandy is bottled, it ceases to improve, and may even deteriorate after a certain time. Such labels as 'Napoleon Brandy' thus become meaningless or worse, as any brandy kept in barrel since the days of Napoleon would have evaporated, and any kept in bottle would be the same, or perhaps not so good as when it was placed in glass. In any case, there is none left.

Fruit brandy is made from all kinds of fruit.

Other leading brandies of the world are:

Calvados: the apple brandy of France.

Marc: distilled from grape pomace.

Grappa: another name for marc.

Applejack: American apple brandy.

See under separate headings.

Château Brane-Cantenac

Bordeaux red wine. District: Haut-Médoc, France. Commune: Cantenac-Margaux.

Once famous as Château Gorce, the vineyard was acquired by the 'Napoleon of the Vines', Baron de Brane. In 1820 he gave it his name, a bold gesture for the day. 'Gorce is widely known', he wrote to the press, 'but I have faith in the name of Brane.' Acquiring a vineyard in Pauillac named Château Pouyallet, he named it Brane-Mouton; this is now Mouton-Rothschild. In those days, Brane-Cantenac was considered the superior vineyard, and the Baron disposed of the present Mouton-Rothschild in order to devote all his attention to it. Lucien Lurton, a young and energetic wine-grower, is owner of this fine Second Growth (*Second Cru*) today.

Brane has long lingered in a twilight zone of quality. Some rather mediocre wines were made in this very great vineyard which disappointed many Médoc admirers. Some recent vintages, however, have definitely re-established its waning reputation.

Characteristics. The wine has the delicacy and suppleness of a typical Margaux, and a particularly delightful perfume.

Vineyard area: 136 acres.

Average production: 20,000 cases.

Brännvin

An alternate name for aquavit (*q.v.*).

Brauneberger Falkenberg

One of the two best of the elegant wines of Brauneberg on the German Moselle.

See MOSELLE.

Brauneberger Juffer

The more famous of the two best wines in the Brauneberg vineyard section, one of the top quality regions of the German Moselle. Flowery, elegant wines.

See MOSELLE.

Brazil

Brazil, three million square miles in extent, is the largest of the South American countries. Roughly

170,000 acres of the country are cultivated in vines. Of late years there has been considerable development in wine production, and a greater demand for wine inside the country. Growers have introduced modern fertilizers and more efficient methods of processing and purifying, and so quality has been improving. About 30 million imp. gallons of wine (36 millions U.S.) are now being made each year. In 1964, production figures fell to 27·8 million imp. gallons (33·3 millions U.S.). Some 19,000 imp. gallons (23,000 U.S.) of wine were exported to the United States in 1959. Wine was exported also to Argentina and to Germany.

Brazil was colonized by wine-drinking Portuguese, yet vine-tending was not one of their early occupations. Few vines were brought into the country until the turn of this century, and most of them were planted after the First World War by settlers from Italy.

The principal wine region is the southern state of Rio Grande do Sul. Flanked by the Atlantic, by Argentina, and by Uruguay, it lies in the southern temperate zone and is the part of the country where the climate is most favourable to the wine. Other centres are São Paulo, and the states of Rio de Janeiro, and Minas Gerais, at an altitude of between 2,300 and 6,000 feet. Santa Catarina, also, is expanding its vineyards, and shipping the harvest to São Paulo to be fermented into wine.

The vine planted most abundantly in Brazil is Isabella, an American hybrid which gives a good, sound wine, but a rather ordinary one. This variety supports the hot, damp climate better than does *Vitis vinifera*. Other grapes are: Duchesse (also known as Riesling de Caldas); Niagara, Folha de Figo (Fig Leaf); Black July, Seibel, Two 10096, 6905, several of the Couderc types, Delaware, Jacques Gaillard, and different kinds of Bertille-Seyve. In Santa Catarina, Concord, Cintiana, Herbemont, Gothe, Trebbiano, Poverella, and several of the Moscatelle type are planted too. For quality wines, some distinguished European stocks are cultivated.

The leading types of Brazilian wine are:

Cheaper Table Wines. Reds of the 'burgundy' and 'claret' types, rosés, and white wines—dry, semi-dry, sweet and sparkling.

Good Table Wines. Reds from the Barbera, Bonarda, Cabernet, Merlot, and other fine vines. White wines from Trebbiano, Poverella, Malvasia, Riesling, and others.

Expensive Wines. Espumante (fermented in bottle and in vat) Moscatels, Malvasias.

Brazil's best wine is made by the firm which is also the largest producer, turning out some 6 million imp. gallons (7 million U.S.) a year. This firm—with the somewhat staggering name of Indústria, Comércio e Navegação, Sociedade Vinícola Rio Grandense, Ltda.—distributes its wines under the label *Granja União*. These are both red and white. Some of the reds come from Merlot and Cabernet (or Caberat) grapes; the white are Trebbiano (Trebiano) and Riesling. Trebbiano is the Italian name for the Ugni Blanc—this shows the Italian influence at work.

Special Wines. Vermouths, medicinal wines and others.

Distilled Liqueurs. Conhaques, and liqueurs of various types.

Most Brazilian wines are sold inside Brazil. São Paulo and Rio de Janeiro are the heaviest consumers, but the rest of the country absorbs most of what is left over. Wines are imported, also: from Europe, and from South American neighbours, particularly Chile. Among the sixty-odd wine firms in Brazil, the most important, after the one already cited, are: Luiz Antunes & Cia., Luiz Michielon S.A., Sociedade Vinhos Unico, Ltda., Carlos Dreher Neto, E. Mosele S.A., and Sociedade Brasileira de Vinhos, Ltda.

Breathing

A wine breathes or oxidizes when it comes in contact with air. In general, red wines need more airing than whites, and young red, with high tannin content, require most of all. To enjoy the bouquet of a wine at its best, uncork the bottle and let the wine breathe for an hour or two—the best way of letting it show to its best advantage.

See CHAPTER FOUR, p. 12.

Château de la Brède

Bordeaux white wine. District: Graves, France. Commune: La Brède.

La Brède, the home of Montesquieu at the end of the seventeenth and the beginning of the eighteenth centuries, was the estate not only of a great writer, but also of a great wine-grower. Montesquieu's vineyard was much larger than the La Brède of today, spreading over miles of Graves and including many of the vineyards now famous under other names. The great author plied his vines as actively as his pen, and pushed the sale of his wines with energy both in France and England. Today La Brède is only of historical interest, although the château remains Bordeaux's most beautiful castle. The small quantity of wine made is undistinguished;

it is bottled in Bordeaux by the firm of Sichel et Fils Frères and sold entirely in England and the United States.

Vineyard area: 15 acres.
Average production: 900 cases.

Breed

Delicacy and discretion are the attributes of breed in wine. This undisputed superiority comes from the soil (or *terroir*). The French words for it are *race* and *finesse*.

Brenner

A fungus disease of vines found notably in Germany.

See CHAPTER EIGHT, p. 37.

Breton

The Cabernet Franc grape is so called in the Touraine region of France.

See CABERNET.

Bristol Cream

Sweetened old Oloroso Sherry bottled in Bristol, England.

Bristol Milk

Sweetened Oloroso Sherry, less rich than the 'Cream', bottled in Bristol, England.

British Compounds

British excise term for redistilled, rectified, or flavoured spirits.

British Isles

Vines are grown and wine made in England on a very limited scale but despite the antiquity of the endeavour (Bede mentions flourishing vineyards as early as A.D. 631), the term 'British wines' does not usually refer to this natural wine from British grapes, but is more generally applied to wines made from raisins or concentrated, unfermented grape juice which have been imported into the British Isles and vinified. The result is recognizably wine but is not inspiring. Wine from British grapes was made possibly in Roman times; certainly on a fairly considerable scale in the early Middle Ages, before the trade with Bordeaux began to boom; and that it is still possible to produce it in modern times has been proved by the Viticultural Research Station at Oxted, Surrey, where they experiment with various types of grapes, and give advice mostly to amateurs interested in producing their own wines at home. Serious private growers in England are Sir Guy Salisbury-Jones and Mr. Edward Hyams.

Brizard

Firm of Marie Brizard & Roger, liqueur-makers in Bordeaux, France.

Brolio

An excellent classical chianti; the best is sold, not in the popular *fiasco*, but in bottle.

See TUSCANY.

Brouilly

See BEAUJOLAIS; CÔTE DE BROUILLY.

Brown Sherry

Sweet, dark Oloroso Sherry.

See SHERRY.

Brunissure (Browning)

Vine disease. Brown skins appear on the leaf, which drops off—the result of over-production and insufficient pruning of the vine.

See CHAPTER EIGHT, p. 36.

Brut

This word on the label of a bottle of Champagne indicates that the wine is very dry, and is, in fact, drier than that labelled Extra Sec—or Extra Dry.

See CHAMPAGNE.

Bual, Boal

A full, sweet Madeira wine.

Bucelas

A golden Portuguese wine, once world-famous but now little seen.

See PORTUGAL.

Buchu

A South African liqueur virtually unknown elsewhere. The reason for this may be inferred from C. de Boscari's account of Buchu in his *Wines of the Cape*, where he describes it as: 'The herb with which savage Africa cured all its ills, from stomach-ache to snake-bite, from housemaid's knee to witch-doctor's spell, for centuries before the White Man appeared. Grafted on to the European pharmacopœia, buchu is today cultivated as a farm crop round Paarl: its extract is used externally as an embrocation and internally, mixed with brandy, for disorders of the digestive tract. It is credited with miraculous powers of healing, and it certainly tastes noxious enough to possess them.'

Buena Vista Vineyards

Sonoma, California, U.S.A.

These are the historic vineyards originally planted by the great Californian viticulturist, Colonel Agoston Haraszthy, who wrote his classic *Report on Grapes and Wines of California* on the terrace of his Buena Vista house and advised growers from many parts of California on the cultivation of their vines. After his death in 1869, his winery was carried on by his sons Attila and Arpad. The phylloxera plague destroyed many of the European vines at Buena Vista, and the final catastrophe came with the earthquake of 1906, when the winery and storage caves collapsed in ruins. Thereafter viniculture at this famous vineyard remained at a standstill until 1943, when the two wineries were restored and more acreage was bought. At present, the vineyards are planted with such grapes as the Pinot Noir, Cabernet Sauvignon, Riesling, Traminer, and Sylvaner. The present owner, Frank Bartholomew, is a journalist and world traveller.

See AMERICA: CALIFORNIA AND THE WEST.

Bulgaria

Fundamental political changes at the end of the Second World War have produced changes also in Bulgarian viticulture. Thus it is necessary to consider the wines as of before and after that time.

Bulgaria has always been a wine-growing country. From the time of the First World War, a steady and gradual increase in vineyard acreage and in wine production had caused, by 1945, a tripling of the area planted and a quadrupling of production. At that time Bulgaria stood fifteenth among wine-producing countries.

In the disturbed times immediately after the last war, production fell off very steeply. In 1947 Bulgaria made only about 8,300,000 imp. gallons (10 million U.S.) of wine, a mere fifth of war-time production.

Exports dropped just as sharply. Having reached 7 million imp. gallons (8·4 million U.S.) in 1940, they fell to 789,000 imp. gallons (947,500 U.S.) in 1946.

In 1947, the Vinprom State Enterprise was established and put in charge of all wine production and trade was united under the one head. Modern technical methods were introduced, large cellars were built in the principal growing regions and stocked with up-to-date equipment, and a wine institute was installed. One special technique was the development of large experimental vineyards where grape varieties were tried out on a big scale. This was possible under the centralized control of the industry.

What success has been achieved by these changes cannot be determined precisely since the minimum of information is obtainable from the authorities. On the negative side, *Zemedelsko Zname,* a Bulgarian agricultural journal, complained a few years ago that in spite of the advanced viticultural advice circulated by the government wine stations, the peasant was going on stubbornly in the old ways. The journal also mentioned a shortage of materials. It would be expected that in the modernization of an industry a country like Bulgaria would encounter these obstructions, and from occasional and more recent reports progress does appear to have been made. That there was considerable progress in quantities of wine produced and exported is evident from the 1961–2 figures published in the Bulletin of the Office International du Vin. Production has almost doubled since Vinprom took over, rising to the figure of some 86½ million imp. gallons (103,900,000 U.S.); and export figures to more than 18 million imp. gallons (21,600,000 U.S.). The principal customers are of course countries behind the Iron Curtain but in 1958 France, with 11·5%, took more than Poland or East Germany; Switzerland bought 6·9% and Great Britain a mere 0·1%. In 1964 production dropped to 63,800,000 imp. gallons (76,700,000 U.S.) but 21,200,000 imp. gallons (25,400,000 U.S.) of wine were exported.

White Wines

White wines are very much appreciated in Bulgaria, and are produced mainly from grape varieties native to the different regions.

South Bulgaria is divided into two important districts south of the Balkan mountains: Karlovo, around Levskigrad, and Songoularé. The dominant variety in this part of the country is the Cherven Misket (red Muscatel), from which the best of the white wines come.

Karlovo White Muscatel is one of the Bulgarian wines best known abroad. It is produced in the same rose valley as the attar of roses, and there is a faint trace of roses in the bouquet of the straw-coloured wine—a bouquet which develops with age. This wine, which has between 11% and 13% of alcohol, is exported principally to Poland, Czechoslovakia, Hungary, the Soviet Union, and East Germany.

Songoularé Misket is produced in the Songoularé Valley, nearer to the Black Sea. Again, the Cherven Misket is the dominant grape. It gives a wine of a greenish colour with a slight perfume of muscat. The alcoholic content is 11% to 12·5%.

Slavianka, a dessert wine from the white muscatel, is full flavoured and golden, with the characteristic flavour and savour of the grape.

White Dimyat. The grape that yields this wine flourishes along the coast of the Black Sea and in south-west Bulgaria. The important wine centres are Varna, Pomoriye, Preslav, and Bourgas—and the wine will be labelled Varna Dimyat, Pomoriye Dimyat, Preslav Dimyat, etc. These wines, grown in sunny vineyards near the sea, have a pleasing freshness and distinctive aromas. In colour, they vary from greenish to pale gold, and develop in bouquet and flavour as they age. The degree of alcohol is 11% to 13·5%. Both the Dimyat and the Songoularé Misket may be blended with other growths to produce sparkling wine of the Champagne type. The Dimyat grape also makes wines with residual sugar and a distillate from which brandy is obtained.

Evxinograd is made from Riesling, Cherven Misket, and Dimyat grapes at Varna, 'the pearl of the Black Sea'. The wine is delicate and of a greenish colour.

Other white wines produced in Bulgaria are Vinenka and Keratsouda. And there have, latterly, been plantings of grape varieties from other countries—Furmint, Traminer, Riesling, and Ugni Blanc, all of which are doing well.

RED WINES

Red wines, also, are being made, from Gamza, Mavroud, Melnik, and Pamid grapes.

Mavroud. The Mavroud grape produces a wine with approximately 11% to 13% of alcohol and high acidity. A special feature is its dark ruby colour, on account of which it is often used to improve the tint of lighter red wines.

Melnik is a wine of superior quality, dark and rather heavy, and the high sugar content is not always fermented. The Melnik grape has grown in the country since very early times, and is believed to have come from France. It flourishes in the long, dry autumns and in the soil around the town of Melnik, a little north of the Thracian border.

Pamid is the commonest wine of its kind in Bulgaria, sweet and low in acidity, light in colour, and suitable for drinking soon after fermentation. It is therefore a popular wine for general domestic consumption.

Gamza has, when young, a pleasant, fruity aroma, and after it is aged it develops considerable bouquet. In degree of alcohol and acidity it is much the same as the Mavroud. Some white Gamza is also made.

SPIRITS

Considerable quantities of various rakis are produced from fruits, wine, and grape residues. The usual production process consists of a single distillation of the fermented materials. The resulting raki usually contains about 50% alcohol.

The most popular rakis are those distilled from sloes and apples, as well as from grape residues after their fermentation. Plum raki, obtained from the fermentation of blue Balkan plums and containing 38% to 40% of alcohol, is the favourite type both in Bulgaria and abroad.

Bulk Gallon

A gallon (160 imp. or 128 U.S. fluid oz.) of wine or spirits irrespective of proof or alcoholic strength; a wine gallon.

See PROOF GALLON.

Bumper

A cup or glass filled to the brim. To 'drink a bumper' is an old English expression specially used for a toast.

Bung

The cork for a wine cask. It may be made of wood, earthenware, or glass. The last two types are generally used as light stoppers for barrels of new wine, in which secondary fermentation may occur. Some contain a device to facilitate the escape of carbonic gas. In the second year of ageing, the racked wine is sealed into its barrel with a wooden cork, often bound in linen; or with a patent unbroachable stopper, such as the *Bonde Bordelaise de Sûreté*. The barrel is then set on its side, or *couché*.

See CHAPTER NINE.

Burdin

A French hybridizer who has developed a red-wine grape, Burdin 4503, out of a white-wine grape, comparable with the Sylvaner, and known as Burdin 5201.

Burgenland

White and red wines. District: South-east Austria.

Wine region of Austria. The principal vineyard towns are Rust, Oggau, Saint-Margarethen, and Mörbisch. Burgenland touches the Hungarian border, and one of the principal grape varieties is the Furmint, which also goes into Tokay.

See AUSTRIA.

Burgunder

The Pinot grape of Burgundy transplanted to German-speaking countries, where vines of this variety are known as Spätburgunder, Frühburgunder, Weissburgunder (white), or Grauerburgunder (grey). The more usual name for the Pinot Gris, however, is Ruländer.

Burgundy

Red and white wines. District: Eastern France.

The ancient realm of the Dukes of Burgundy is neither the largest nor the financially most important wine region in the world, but it is one of the very greatest. Nowhere else is wine so much a part of daily life and conversation, and nowhere is there such honest love of wine and such pride in its perfection, except in Bordeaux.

For more than two thousand years Burgundians have been planting the vine continuously in the same soil, devoting themselves to its care, making and drinking magnificent wines and shipping them to all the corners of the world. From father to son the tradition has been passed, from noblemen to priest to peasant. Over the centuries, the finest vineyard sites have been discovered; the best vines for the soil have been found and planted there and cherished with loving care. The result is Burgundy as we know it today.

It is true, unfortunately, that one man's Burgundy is another man's *ordinaire*, for no other name is so persistently misapplied. In large areas of the world 'Burgundy' has become almost synonymous with a heavy, dark red wine, sometimes too rough, sometimes oversweetened; and the buyer (if not the seller) is often unaware that many Burgundies are light, subtle wines—and that some of the greatest Burgundies are white.

The red wines of the Burgundian district of the Beaujolais, for example, are at their best light and fresh and fruity; and the red wines of the Côte d'Or vineyards of the communes of Volnay, Pommard, or Beaune can be exquisitely fine and delicate. The misconception is encouraged by sellers the world over who do not hesitate to put the name 'Burgundy' on red wines, no matter where they originated. In fact, the only wines with any historical, geographical, moral, or (in France at least) any legal right to the name, are those from certain clearly defined sections of the French departments of the Côte d'Or, Yonne, Saône-et-Loire, and the *arrondissement* of Villefranche-sur-Saône in the department of the Rhône. As is the case with all French wines of Appellation Contrôlée, the permissible vines are legally controlled, the amount of harvest is legally controlled, and the methods of pruning, growing, and fertilizing, as well as of vinifying and ageing, are all legally controlled—and if the resultant wine does not meet the minimum standards it is not Burgundy. (These controls are applied not in Burgundy alone, but to all French wines of Appellation Contrôlée.) This means that bottles labelled California burgundy, South African burgundy, or Chilean burgundy may all have their merits but will *not* be Burgundy (*see* APPELLATION D'ORIGINE CONTRÔLÉE).

History

It is not known who first introduced the vine into Burgundy. It has been established that the Romans found vines when they made their conquest: that under their influence the vineyards certainly increased and prospered; and it is probable that the barbarians who followed destroyed the plantations, and the Burgondes began to reconstitute them at the end of the fourth century.

In the year 581, Gontran, King of Burgundy, gave the vineyards of Dijon to the Abbey of Saint Bénigne, a move that was to have far-reaching consequences. The monks were happy to receive the gift, which assured a steady source of pure wine for their services. In the centuries that followed, Burgundy changed from a kingdom to a duchy and various nobles, following Gontran's example, gave to different religious orders such vineyards as those of Aloxe, Fixey, Fixin, Santenay, Auxey, Comblanchien, Chassagne, Savigny, Pommard, and Meursault.

To the mediæval world wine was wealth, and overwhelmed by the sudden influx some of the clergy began to forget the strict monastic rules and live too well. By the twelfth century the great reformer, Saint Bernard of Clairvaux, was denouncing this luxuriousness and greed. He came, in 1112, to the Cistercian monastery at Cîteaux, and transformed it. With the Benedictine monastery of Cluny, Saint Bernard was at complete odds. Cluny had been the most powerful arm of the Church in France and its vineyard holdings were substantial. Adopting the motto *Cruce et Aratro* (By Cross and Plough) the Cistercians began cultivating sections of the desolate countryside. In Burgundy, nothing else thrives so well as the vine, and viticulture became one of the main occupations of the order. Their greatest accomplishment was the founding of the Clos de

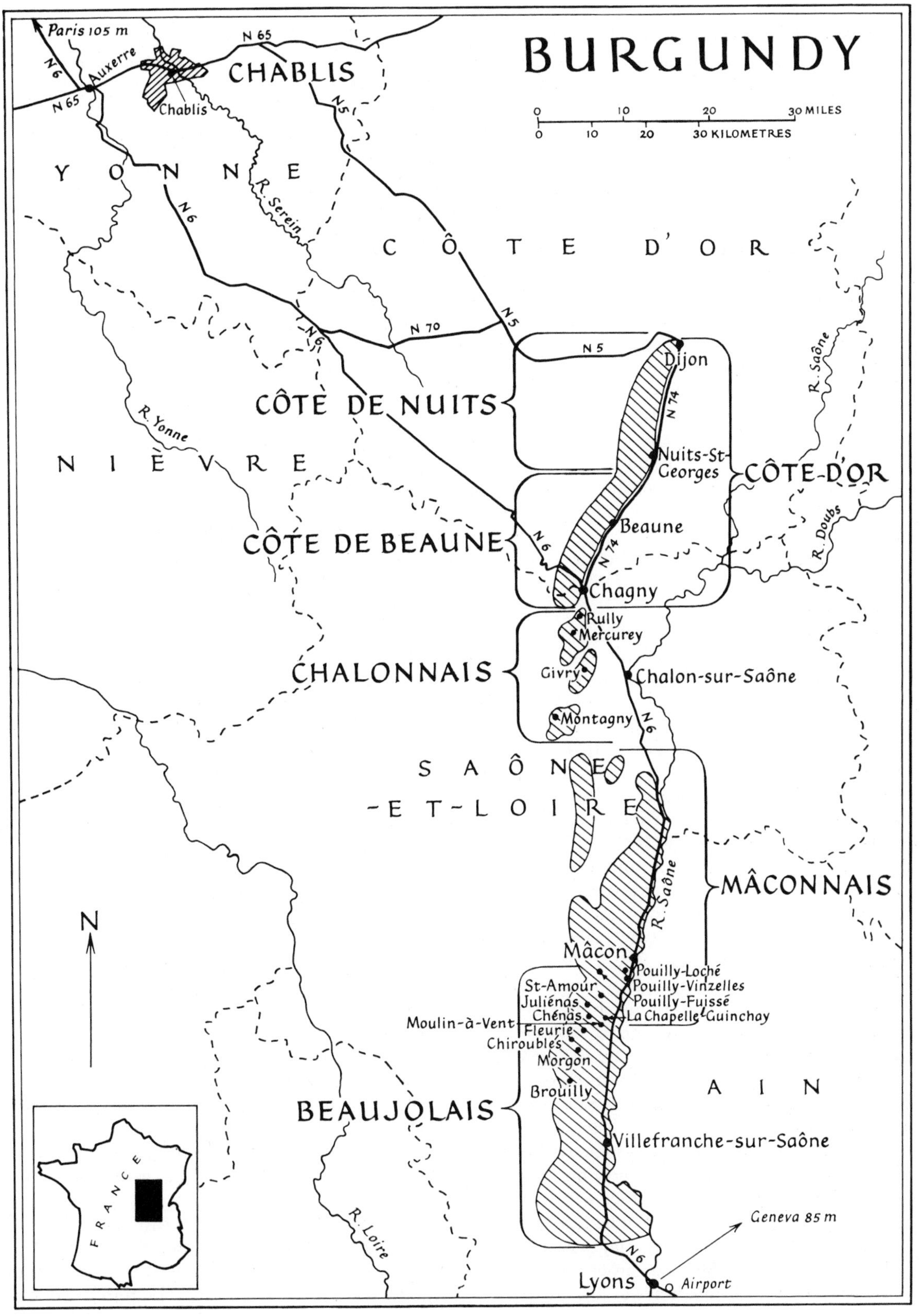
BURGUNDY
0 10 20 30 MILES
0 10 20 30 KILOMETRES
Paris 105 m
N 6
N 65
Auxerre
Chablis
CHABLIS
N 5
Y O N N E
R. Serein
C Ô T E D'O R
N 70
CÔTE DE NUITS
N 5
Dijon
N 74
Nuits-St-Georges
CÔTE-D'OR
R. Saône
R. Yonne
N I È V R E
CÔTE DE BEAUNE
Beaune
R. Doubs
Chagny
Rully
Mercurey
CHALONNAIS
Givry
Chalon-sur-Saône
Montagny
S A Ô N E
-E T-L O I R E
MÂCONNAIS
N
Mâcon
Pouilly-Loché
St-Amour
Pouilly-Vinzelles
Juliénas
Pouilly-Fuissé
Chénas
La Chapelle Guinchay
Moulin-à-Vent
Fleurie
Chiroubles
Morgon
A I N
Brouilly
BEAUJOLAIS
Villefranche-sur-Saône
FRANCE
R. Loire
Geneva 85 m
Lyons
Airport

Vougeot, built up slowly from grants given by landowners who were impressed by the sanctity and industry of the monks. Their sister order founded the Clos des Dames de Tart, later shortened to the Clos de Tart.

As the Middle Ages wore on, the vines flourished and increased—too much in variety if not in quantity. In 1395, Philip the Bold, Duke of Burgundy, banned from Burgundian vineyards the grape he refers to as the 'disloyal Gaamez', that gives wine in abundance but full of 'very great and horrible harshness'. The introduction into fine wine regions of inferior grapes which produce quantity rather than quality is a recurrent evil. The Gamay vine mentioned by the Duke is not unknown in Burgundy today; one of its varieties is responsible for the excellent wines of Beaujolais, but on the Côte d'Or it gives a wine similar to that described by Duke Philip more than five centuries ago. Another ducal edict of the Middle Ages attempted to ban the storage of wines coming from any other district.

The wines of Burgundy, of Beaune especially, appealed to the kings of France. Philip Augustus, faced by the Imperial Army, is said to have called for a barrel of Beaune; during the coronation of Philip VI, at Reims, the wine flowed from the nostrils of a bronze stag set up outside the cathedral. Louis XI was extremely fond of Volnay and he had the happiness, in his reign, of adding the rebellious Dukedom of Burgundy to the French crown.

At peace at last from ducal wars, Burgundy was to be trampled in the wars of religion—and again in the Thirty Years War (1618–1648). Here, as in Bordeaux, there were sporadic orders to root up vines and plant more corn, but this does not seem seriously to have prevented the sale of wine. As late as the seventeenth and early eighteenth centuries, Burgundy (in great favour with Louis XIV) came back into favour. It was not yet the wine we know: it was very much lighter, and sometimes white grapes were mixed with the red to produce the pinkish, partridge-eye colour which was then preferred. Foreign customers—particularly Germans and Dutch—are said to have wanted a heavier drink and for them, before the days of *chaptalisation*, sugar was sometimes introduced when the vintage was not big enough. Stories about Napoleon and various wines of Burgundy have been too often told to be repeated here —it seems certain that a heavy luggage of casks followed some of his Marshals around the battlefields of Europe. Chambertin was the growth of which Talleyrand is quoted as saying: 'Sir, when one is served such a wine, one takes the glass respectfully, looks at it, inhales it, then, having put it down, one discusses it.' And of the same wine Dumas said: 'Nothing inspires such a rosy view of the future.'

When the French Revolution erupted, a great part of the Burgundy vineyard was in the hands of the Church. So the established pattern of Burgundian viticulture was completely disrupted by the wave of anti-clericalism that swept France in the 1790s and through the First Empire. The vineyards were seized by the State, and afterwards sold to the people. The most important consequence was the setting up of the pattern of small ownership that still prevails in this region: the system has been maintained as a primitive kind of insurance. A grower who has all his grapes in one vineyard might be ruined if hail should hit that vineyard; whereas, if he owns only part of that one and part of another some miles away, he is likely to salvage something from the storm. The result was—and is —that the great vineyards continue to exist as entities, but each one is divided between a number of owners, each with his own parcel of land. Thus, two bottles of wine coming from the same vineyard, in the same year, may be quite different from each other, their characteristics depending to some extent upon the wine-maker's industry and talent. The Bordeaux system of large estates—unified under one ownership—is today practically unknown in Burgundy; with a very few exceptions, there are no Burgundian châteaux in the Bordeaux sense of the word, and a domain may include bits and pieces of a number of widely scattered vineyards unified only in the ownership of one man. In Burgundy, there are more than a hundred separate place-names; at first glance the system appears complicated and confusing. Actually it is neither.

Burgundian Place-names

There is a large number of different controlled place-names in Burgundy simply because there is an equivalent number of separate and distinct wines. The names run from the general to the particular, and—as is true with all French wines of Appellation Contrôlée—the more specific the name, the better the wine. As an example of how the system works there is the vineyard of Chambertin.

Chambertin is one of the greatest of Burgundian vineyards and its wines, when well made and from a good year, are unsurpassed. The thirty-two-acre vineyard is legally rated a Great Growth (*Grand Cru*)—one of only thirty-one of the hundreds of Burgundian vineyards to receive this distinction. Its wine can take the name Chambertin, the commune name of Gevrey-Chambertin, the district name of Côte de Nuits, or the general name of Burgundy (Bourgogne); yet it will always be labelled with the famous name of Chambertin if the wine meets the high minimum standards demanded. The name is more specific, the minimum standards are higher, the wine is finer, and the system is strong enough to guarantee the grower a higher price for the better wine as reflected by the name. Vineyard name—commune name—district name—regional name. Chambertin—Gevrey-Chambertin—Côte de Nuits—Burgundy. The formula is repeated over and over again in each commune along the famous Côte d'Or or Slope of Gold, and through the other sections of Burgundy (although here and there may be minor exceptions to the rule).

The fact that there will be a number of growers in even so small a vineyard as Chambertin—32·5 acres—has given rise to a special way of handling the wines and putting them on sale—a method that was worked out to decrease the inherent confusion. Under this system, the shipper (*négociant*) buys wines from various growers in, for example, Chambertin, blends them together and sells them labelled as Chambertin from his own particular firm. The wines will be so blended that they will be reasonably the same year after year. The system has this advantage, that a number of growers will not each be putting out different wines under the same name and the customer can learn the name of the wine and the firm he prefers and feel comfortably sure that he can buy the wine year after year and it will always be very similar. The disadvantages are that, in spite of the shipper's care, the wine will not be identical, and that when wine from a talented winemaker is blended with that from an inept one, the quality of the finer wine is inevitably dragged down.

Burgundy is not large and the 23 million imp. gallons (28 million U.S.) of wine made each year does not, for example, compare with the annual 54 million imp. gallons (65 million U.S.) that comes out of Bordeaux. Furthermore, authentic Burgundy is not cheap, nor can it be. The weather is too often unfavourable for growers to count on a good harvest every year, and the proceeds from good years must tide them over the others. When quantity is lowest the revenue to the grower is correspondingly small—although he must still eat, and the vines must receive the usual expensive care, to keep them healthy. This does nothing to reduce prices. Since these prices are rather high, and variations in the wines considerable, it is more important to know what you are buying from Burgundy than from any other fine wine region, for get-rich-quick shippers have for centuries found it expedient to buy wines other (and cheaper) than the great Burgundies and use them to stretch the supply when it runs low, so that they can sell more wine at lower prices and make a higher profit on each sale. The great epoch of fraud occurred shortly after the First World War and was flourishing in the 1930s when some enlightened Frenchmen banded together to amend and perfect the laws of Appellation d'Origine which gave wide powers to the Inspectors of Fraud. The laws have not completely done away with deceit, but they have made it much more difficult. And some of the growers themselves are adopting a system (modelled on the château-bottling of Bordeaux) which makes fraud practically impossible. This is known as estate or domain bottling. An estate-bottled wine is simply a wine that has been grown, made, and bottled by the same man, usually a small peasant grower with anything from two to ten acres of vines. In such a case, the label will tell the name of the wine, the year, the name of the grower, and the fact that the wine is *Mis au domaine* (bottled at the domain). Alternative phrases are *Mise du Domaine* or *Mis en bouteilles par le propriétaire*, or else *Mis en bouteilles à la propriété*.

The greatest wines come from the golden slopes of the Côte d'Or, a low range of hills, topped by brush and scrub, and rolling along the western edge of the Burgundian plain. Geographically, it begins at Dijon (in days gone by, there was a Côte de Dijon, too, and an effort has been made to bring it back into currency, particularly with the rosés of Marsannay), and ends just south of Santenay. It is divided into two sections: the Côte de Nuits, to the north, making the regal reds, Chambertin, Musigny, Romanée—the first great vineyard the motorist sees is Clos de Vougeot; and, to the south, the Côte de Beaune with its more delicate red wines (Beaune, Pommard, Volnay) and the magnificent whites of Meursault and Montrachet.

Of the great number of Burgundian place-names there are several that will seldom or never appear on bottles outside Burgundy. These most general names are applied to wines which often make very pleasant drinking if caught young and near the place where they were made, but which neither age nor travel well. Among them may be such names as:

Place-name	*Date established*	*Permissible yield (gallons per acre)* imp.	U.S.	*YIELD IN 1962 in imperial gallons (U.S. gallonages in parentheses)* red		white	
Bourgogne	31 July 1937	400	481	869,708	(1,044,476)	216,679	(260,221)
Vins Fins des Hautes Côtes							
(The most general name of all. It is allowed to any wine coming from the specified area of Burgundy—red wines to be made from the Pinot Noir grape (with allowances for the Pinot Liebault and Pinot Beurot, for the César and Tressot in the Yonne, for Gamay in certain parts of southern Burgundy); white wines from the Chardonnay. The wines must have a minimum alcoholic content of 10% if red, 10·5% if white.)							
Bourgogne-Passe-Tout-Grains	31 July 1937	400	481	499,208	(599,524)	—	
(Once made in enormous quantity, this is a mixing or vatting together of grapes of Pinot Noir and Gamay—at least one-third Pinot. The wine must have an alcoholic content of 9·5% and can often be pleasant on the spot but does not travel or keep well.)							
Bourgogne Aligoté	31 July 1937	400	481	—		1,412,406	(1,696,229)
(White wines exclusively, from the Aligoté grape. Chardonnay may also be used, but in practice it is not. Alcoholic content of 9·5%.)							
Bourgogne Ordinaire	31 July 1937	400	481	(no figures available)		276,961	(332,616)
Bourgogne Grand Ordinaire	31 July 1937	400	481	542,940	(652,044)	—	
(Only in France could a wine be 'great' and 'ordinary' at the same time. These two place-names cover red, white, and rosé made from Pinot and Gamay grapes (and Tressot in the Yonne) and white from Pinot Blanc, Chardonnay, Aligoté, Melon de Bourgogne, and, in the Yonne, Sacy. At least 9% of alcohol for red and rosé, 9·5% for white.)							
Bourgogne Mousseux or **Sparkling Burgundy**	16 March 1943	400	481	(no figures available)			
(Sparkling Burgundy may often be pleasant enough, but too often is mediocre or worse. It is vinified from any red or white wine that has the right to a general Burgundy *appellation* but rarely from those with any merit or distinction. Since taxes are as high in Great Britain and the United States on this as on Champagne, the latter is almost inevitably much better value.)							

Listed below are the districts of Burgundy, followed by the place-names of the Appellations Contrôlées, making wines more distinguished than the foregoing:

Côte d'Or	red and white wines	Mâconnais	red and white wines
Chablis	white wines	Chalonnais	red and white wines
Beaujolais	red (and very few white) wines		

See under individual headings.

APPELLATIONS CONTRÔLÉES OF THE BURGUNDY REGION

Vineyards benefiting from special, controlled place-names are indented under pertinent commune.

Place-name	*Date established*	*Maximum gallons permitted per acre* imp.	U.S.	*YIELD IN 1962 in imperial gallons (U.S. gallonages in parentheses)* red		white	
I—Côte d'Or—best communes marked with an asterisk (*).							
*Aloxe-Corton	11 March 1938	312	374	88,826	(106,676)	572	(687)
Corton	31 July 1937	267	321	51,364	(61,686)	572	(687)
Corton-Charlemagne	31 July 1937	267	321			14,400	(17,200)
Charlemagne		a small quantity of red wine sometimes produced					

Place-name	*Date established*	*Maximum gallons permitted per acre* *imp.*	*U.S.*	*YIELD IN 1962 in imperial gallons (U.S. gallonages in parentheses)* *red*		*white*	
Auxey-Duresses	31 July 1937	312	374	37,550	(45,096)	18,148	(21,795)
*Beaune	11 Sept. 1936	312	374	211,661	(254,194)		
Blagny	31 July 1937	312	374	3,718	(4,465)	66	(79)
*Chambolle-Musigny	11 Sept. 1936	312	374	108,272	(130,029)		
Bonnes Mares	8 Dec. 1936	267	321	9,283	(11,148)		
Musigny	11 Sept. 1936	267	321	6,555	(7,873)		
*Chassagne-Montrachet	31 July 1937	312	374	125,122	(150,266)	62,187	(74,684)
Bâtard-Montrachet	31 July 1937	267	321			7,259	(8,718)
Chevalier-Montrachet	31 July 1937	267	321			2,333	(2,800)
Criots-Bâtard-Montrachet	13 June 1939	267	321			1,100	(1,321)
Montrachet	31 July 1937	267	321			3,455	(4,148)
Cheilly-les-Maranges	31 July 1937	312	374	14,782	(17,753)	396	(476)
Chorey-les-Beaune	31 July 1937	312	374	51,870	(62,294)	22	(26)
Côte de Beaune	31 July 1937	312	374	3,301	(3,963)	418	(502)
Côte de Beaune-Villages	31 July 1937	312	374	96,020	(115,315)		
Dezize-les-Maranges	31 July 1937	312	374	10,031	(12,047)		
*Fixin	8 Dec. 1936	312	374	9,415	(11,307)		
*Gevrey-Chambertin	11 Sept. 1936	312	374	237,574	(285,314)		
Chambertin	31 July 1937	267	321	11,879	(14,266)		
Chambertin-Clos de Bèze	31 July 1937	267	321	8,271	(9,933)		
Chapelle-Chambertin	31 July 1937	285	342	3,103	(3,725)		
Charmes-Chambertin	31 July 1937	285	342	21,327	(25,599)		
Griotte-Chambertin	31 July 1937	285	342	1,255	(1,506)		
Latricières-Chambertin	31 July 1937	285	342	5,367	(6,446)		
Mazis-Chambertin	31 July 1937	285	342	5,653	(6,789)		
Mazoyères-Chambertin		(same as Charmes-Chambertin)					
Ruchottes-Chambertin	31 July 1937	285	342	1,827	(2,193)		
Ladoix	31 July 1937	312	374	29,983	(36,008)	770	(925)
*Meursault	31 July 1937	312	374	12,759	(15,322)	227,895	(273,690)
Monthélie	31 July 1937	312	374	43,379	(52,096)	704	(845)
*Morey-Saint-Denis	8 Dec. 1936	312	374	46,855	(56,270)	462	(555)
Bonnes Mares		(see under Chambolle-Musigny)					
Clos de la Roche	3 July 1944	267	321	9,481	(11,386)		
Clos Saint-Denis	3 July 1944	267	321	4,224	(5,072)		
Clos de Tart	4 Jan. 1939	267	321	2,729	(3,276)		
*Nuits-Saint-Georges	11 Sept. 1936	312	374	200,706	(241,038)	418	(502)
Pernand-Vergelesses	8 Dec. 1936	312	374	21,888	(26,286)	3,587	(4,306)
*Pommard	11 Sept. 1936	312	374	228,973	(274,985)		
*Puligny-Montrachet	31 July 1937	312	374	8,733	(10,488)	88,628	(106,438)
Bâtard-Montrachet		(see Chassagne-Montrachet)					
Bienvenue-Bâtard-Montrachet	13 June 1939	267	321			2,619	(3,144)
Montrachet		(see Chassagne-Montrachet)					
Saint-Aubin	31 July 1937	312	374	25,341	(30,434)	15,354	(18,440)
Saint-Romain	14 Oct. 1947	312	374	4,070	(4,887)	13,265	(15,930)
Sampigny-les-Maranges	31 July 1937	312	374				
Santenay	8 Dec. 1936	312	374	160,714	(193,010)	3,674	(4,412)
Savigny	8 Dec. 1936	312	374	159,769	(191,874)	1,409	(1,691)
Vins Fins de la Côte de Nuits	31 July 1937	312	374	109,416	(131,403)		
*Volnay	9 Sept. 1937	312	374	157,393	(189,021)		
*Vosne-Romanée	11 Sept. 1936	312	374	119,315	(143,291)		
Échezeaux	31 July 1937	267	321	18,434	(22,138)		
Grands-Échezeaux	31 July 1937	267	321	6,929	(8,322)		

Place-name	*Date established*	*Maximum gallons permitted per acre* *imp.*	*U.S.*	*YIELD IN 1962 in imperial gallons (U.S. gallonages in parentheses)* *red*		*white*	
La Tâche	11 Sept. 1936	267	321	4,422	(5,310)		
Richebourg	11 Sept. 1936	267	321	5,917	(7,106)		
Romanée-Saint-Vivant	11 Sept. 1936	267	321	6,005	(7,212)		
Romanée-Conti	11 Sept. 1936	267	321	1,409	(1,691)		
La Romanée	11 Sept. 1936	267	321	660	(793)		
*Vougeot	8 Dec. 1936	312	374	14,650	(17,594)	1,365	(1,638)
Clos de Vougeot	31 July 1937	267	321	32,182	(38,650)		
II—Chablis							
Chablis	13 Jan. 1938	356	428			206,909	(248,488)
Chablis Grand Cru	13 Jan. 1938	312	374			24,461	(29,377)
Petit Chablis	5 Jan. 1944	356	428			92,434	(111,008)
Chablis Premier Cru	13 Jan. 1938	356	428			217,402	(261,089)
III—Beaujolais							
Beaujolais	12 Sept. 1937	445	535	4,930,652	(5,921,440)	33,744	(40,525)
Beaujolais Supérieur	12 Sept. 1937	400	481	719,563	(864,156)		
Beaujolais-Villages	12 Sept. 1937	400	481	2,952,694	(3,546,022)		
Brouilly	19 Oct. 1938	356	428	631,221	(758,062)		
Chénas	11 Sept. 1936	356	428	118,699	(142,552)		
Chiroubles	11 Sept. 1936	356	428	152,685	(183,367)		
Côte de Brouilly	19 Oct. 1938	356	428	128,796	(154,677)		
Fleurie	11 Sept. 1936	356	428	414,347	(497,609)		
Juliénas	11 March 1938	356	428	312,982	(375,875)		
Morgon	11 Sept. 1936	356	428	622,796	(747,944)		
Moulin-à-Vent	11 Sept. 1936	356	428	420,902	(505,480)		
Saint-Amour	8 Feb. 1946	356	428	151,761	(182,258)		
IV—Mâconnais							
Mâcon	31 July 1937	445	535	84,361	(101,313)	162,606	(195,282)
Mâcon: Pinot-Chardonnay-Mâcon	31 July 1937	445	535	——	——	——	——
Mâcon Supérieur	31 July 1937	400	481	1,273,661	(1,529,596)	901,528	(1,082,685)
Mâcon-Villages	31 July 1937	445	535			1,663,459	(1,997,722)
Pouilly-Fuissé	11 Sept. 1936	400	481			473,630	(568,804)
Pouilly-Loché	27 April 1940	400	481			20,040	(24,067)
Pouilly-Vinzelles	27 April 1940	400	481			31,655	(38,016)
V—Chalonnais							
Givry	8 Feb. 1946	356	428	34,206	(41,080)	5,785	(6,948)
Mercurey	11 Sept. 1936	312	374	269,603	(323,779)	15,376	(18,466)
Montagny	11 Sept. 1936	356	428			57,920	(69,559)
Rully	13 June 1939	356	428	5,521	(6,631)	23,207	(27,871)

Burgundian Vines

Vines for red wines

Pinot Noir. The noblest vine of them all. Head of a distinguished family (although the other members do not generally come up to the excellence of the 'Noiren', as it is sometimes called), it adapts itself in the varying soils of the Côte d'Or to produce grapes giving some of the world's most magnificent wines. Oddly enough, in the granite of the Beaujolais it can give no better than flat and undistinguished wine and is replaced by the Gamay.

Gamay. Except in the Beaujolais—where it gives a fruity, light, and eminently delightful wine—Burgundian Gamay wine tends to be common, acid, and harsh. Much was once planted on the Côte d'Or, but this practice is passing and most of the Gamay today is maintained by the workers for their own consumption. However, a very small amount of

Passe-Tout-Grains (a vatting together of Gamay and Pinot Noir) is still put on the market.

Pinot Liebault. Indistinguishable, to all intents and purposes, from the Pinot Noir, except to a specialist.

Pinot Gris. No wine is made exclusively from the Pinot Gris in Burgundy as it is, for example, in Alsace. Some plants may be found, however, and growers claim that the addition of some of this to Pinot Noir results in a wine with more elegance, finesse, and delicacy.

César. Only allowed in the Yonne for wines taking the most general of place-names.

Tressot. Only allowed in the Yonne for wines taking the most general of place-names.

Vines for White Wines

Chardonnay (also called Aubaine, Beaunois). Once erroneously thought to be a member of the Pinot family (and called Pinot Chardonnay), this vine is responsible for all the great white wines of Burgundy. In chalky soil—as on the Côte d'Or, Chablis, and the Mâconnais—it gives wines that vary with local conditions, but tend at their best to be rather full yet delicate, imbued with the scent of the grape, beautifully balanced and with enormous finesse.

Pinot Blanc. The white grape of the Pinot family. It is added to the Chardonnay in the making of the better white wines.

Aligoté. The grape that makes the common secondary white wine of Burgundy. The wine rarely has much breed and does not travel well, but when young and drunk on the spot, it can be extremely pleasant; it is sometimes made to be slightly sparkling or *pétillant.*

Sacy. Only allowed in the Yonne for wines taking the most general of place-names.

Melon de Bourgogne. Allowed throughout Burgundy, but only for wines taking the most general of place-names.

Burgundian Viniculture

Burgundian red wines are not long-vatted. Here, as elsewhere, red wines are fermented in their skins, white are pressed from their skins and fermented apart; but in Burgundy, red wines only stay in contact with the skins for from five to eight days—the optimum is about six. This contrasts markedly with Bordeaux—where wines are vatted for ten to fifteen days—and the results are apparent.

Long-vatted Bordeaux reds pick up more tannin —from the skins, seeds, and stems—than do Burgundies. This makes them harder at the outset and allows them to reach a greater 'high' with longevity; only with age do the great reds of Bordeaux achieve their full glory. Red Burgundies, not having so much tannin, will be ready to drink far sooner, often from two to five years after harvest. Furthermore, the Cabernet Sauvignon grape of Bordeaux produces wines that are bigger and fuller than those produced by the Pinot Noir of Burgundy. Thus a natural Burgundy may, by its lightness, confound the traditional notion that all Burgundies are full-bodied and all Bordeaux light.

Apart from the duration of vatting time, wine-making in Burgundy does not differ significantly from standard practice as outlined in Chapter Nine (*q.v.*). The only major modification is the widespread use of *chaptalisation*—adding sugar to sugar-deficient musts—for in most years the Burgundian summer sun does not generate enough sugar in the grapes to make a perfectly balanced wine. The additional sugar—added under strict control by the Government—ferments with the natural grape sugar and results in a wine with a higher alcoholic content than it would otherwise have had, and sometimes with more force and body as well. Yet the present regrettable tendency is to overchaptalize fine wines.

Burgundian wines are aged, from eighteen to twenty-four months, in containers of varying sizes. Wines for current consumption are kept in large vats, but finer wines need smaller cooperage. The standard barrel size is the *pièce*, holding 228 litres (about 50 imp. gallons; 60 U.S.). Very occasionally, reference is made to the old measure *queue* which is simply two *pièces*; there is no actual barrel of this size. Half-barrels are called *feuillettes* and quarter-barrels *quartauts*, and they each hold exactly what one would expect. In Chablis, however, there is another *feuillette* holding 132 litres (about 29 imp. gallons; 34·9 U.S.); the traditional *pièce* of the Mâconnais holds 215 litres (about 47·3 imp. gallons; 56·8 U.S.), and that of the Beaujolais 216 litres 47·5 imp. gallons; 57·1 U.S.). Fortunately these odd sizes are rapidly being replaced by the more standard Burgundian *pièce*.

White wines in Burgundy are given less ageing than was once customary: twelve to twenty months is now standard practice. This results in a cleaner, fresher, fruitier wine than heretofore, and experts feel that the change is thoroughly justified. When bottled, Burgundian wines are always put in the typical, squat, slope-shouldered Burgundian bottle.

Although many a Burgundy will be ready to drink any time from a few months to a few years after being put into bottle, others will sometimes hold their excellence as long as a half-century or perhaps more. Unfortunately these old bottles are becoming exceedingly rare. Burgundies are not made in the same way as they used to be. Before the First World War the wine was long-vatted and the extra tannin it picked up naturally from the contact with the skins and the wood gave it longevity. Tannin occasionally added to young wine by some shippers does not have the same effect, but serves instead to deform the taste of the wine. Another deformation suffered by a great deal of the Burgundy in shippers' (or *négociants*') cellars, is caused by the practice of giving the wine a so-called 'Burgundy' character by blending it with heavy wines from other regions. The past hundred years have seen the supply of honest Burgundy running so far short of the demand that cheap, heavy wine from the Rhône valley or Algeria has been brought in to stretch the precious supply. As the contents of Burgundian bottles grew further and further away from the characteristics of real Burgundy wine, a market was built up among inexperienced wine-drinkers who were taught to believe that if a wine did *not* have the thick or oversugared consistency they had come to associate with Burgundy, it lacked the true characteristics. This puts them in the paradoxical position, when they manage to obtain a bottle of estate-bottled wine or one put out by an honest shipper, of finding fault with it, because it is utterly different from any 'Burgundy' they have ever drunk. To those who judge wine by taste rather than by labels, it is often a revelation.

See CÔTE DE BEAUNE: CÔTE DE NUITS; CÔTE D'OR.

Butt

Standard British cask. A butt of ale contains 108 imp. gallons (129·6 U.S.); of Sherry and Malaga, 108 imp. gallons (129·6 U.S.); of wine other than Sherry or Malaga, 126 imp. gallons (151·3 U.S.). In general use, a synonym for a cask or barrel to hold wine, beer, or rainwater. More specifically, a cask with a capacity of 108–140 imp. gallons (129–168 U.S.).

Buza

Alcoholic beverage of Egypt distilled from fermented dates.

See EGYPT.

Buzz

British university term for a glass of Port from the bottom of the decanter.

Bybline

A sweet Phœnician wine mentioned in classical writings. Native to Byblos, it was probably grown afterwards in Thrace also.

See CHAPTER ONE, p. 2; CLASSICAL WINES.

Byrrh

Very popular French proprietary aperitif based on wine, flavoured with quinine and fortified with brandy. It is made at Thuir on the Mediterranean coast near the Spanish border.

C

Cabernet

The outstanding grape variety used for the finest Clarets of the Médoc district of Bordeaux, for superior wines in California, in Chile, in Australia, and elsewhere. The finest and most widespread is Cabernet Sauvignon; Cabernet Franc is grown in the Médoc, in Graves, and the Loire Valley but is spreading slowly; Ruby Cabernet is an American hybrid that combines Cabernet Sauvignon and Carignane. Only the first two are really important for the wine-maker.

Cabinet Wine, Kabinettwein

A term applying chiefly to German Rhine wines, which originally meant the special reserve of the vineyard owner. It may have originated at Kloster Eberbach on the Rhine where the finest Steinbergers were kept in a special small cellar called Das Kabinett, which may be seen today. The importance of Cabinet wines was and is based on the fact that fine German wines are not only harvested and barrelled individually from the different parts of the vineyard, but also on different days of the harvest. The barrels therefore vary greatly in quality. In most vineyards today the designation Cabinet may be applied to a wine and put on the label if the barrel has surpassed a certain price when sold. This price level varies at different vineyards, but always marks off the small, very superior upper portion of the vintage.

Cachiri

Guiana liqueur from the cassava plant from which tapioca is also obtained.

Cahors

1. Red grape, not a noble variety, permitted in limited quantities in, for example, the district of Bordeaux. Known also as Malbec and Cot.

2. The wines from the vineyards around the town of Cahors in the Lot department of France. These are the darkest of French wines, often used to mix in with weaker qualities and commonly known as 'the black wines of Cahors'.

Château Caillou

Bordeaux white wine. District: Sauternes, France. Commune: Barsac.

Château Caillou, classified a Second Growth (*Second Cru*) in 1855, adjoins the two Barsac First Growths (*Premiers Crus*), Château Climens and Château Coutet. *Caillou* is French for 'pebble'; and pebbles are thick in the vineyard soil which gives so much to the quality of the Bordeaux wines. Monsieur Bravo, the proprietor, also owns the Barsac vineyards, Château Baulac and Château Petit-Mayne.

Characteristics. Small and pleasant yet high in alcohol.

Vineyard area: 41 acres.

Average production: 4,000 cases.

Cairanne

One of the best communes of the Côtes-du-Rhône, producing red, white, and rosé wines.

See RHÔNE.

Cajuada

A West African beverage made from fermented cashew nuts.

Calabria

White and red wines. District: South Italy.

Calabria, in the 'toe' of the Italian 'boot', is hot, mountainous, and poverty-stricken, although along the coast, cooled by the sea, the more fertile land is fruitful with orange and lemon trees. The soil is largely volcanic, and vines do as well as anything here, yet most Calabrian wines are not of the first order.

An exception might be made for Greco di Gerace, a sweet, yellow wine moderately high in alcohol from 14% up to 18% and famous for its flowery bouquet. It comes from Gerace in the Calabrian Apennines, and only about 2,500 imp. gallons (3,000 U.S.) are made annually. The wine was held in high esteem in classical Rome.

Ciró di Calabria and Savuto are two of the more frequently encountered red wines. In spite of the dissimilarity in the grapes used, the wines share certain characteristics, notably a harsh, pungent strength and headiness. The former comes from Gaglioppo and some Greco vines and the latter from Arvino, Pecorello, Greco, and some Malvasia. Lacrima di Castrovillari and Moscato di Cosenza (sometimes Moscato di Calabria) complete the list of the better-known wines. The first is a red table wine from the Pollino Mountains near the Ionian Sea, the second the inevitable Muscat, sometimes from dried grapes. It is not one of Italy's more distinguished Muscats.

Caledon

Wine-growing district of the Cape Province, South Africa.

See SOUTH AFRICA.

Calisaya

A Spanish liqueur with the bitter taste of quinine.

Château Calon-Ségur

Bordeaux red wine. District: Haut-Médoc, France. Commune: Saint-Estèphe.

The vineyard is a classified Great Growth. Here, as at Château Latour, the wines are allowed to achieve their maximum age and are not uprooted by sections; individually removed and replaced, some live for ninety years and more. Quality at the expense of quantity is the consequence of this method: the vine produces better and better wine all its life, but there is less and less of it after the twelfth or fifteenth year. Yet, since the vineyards are large, there is no shortage of Calon-Ségur.

In early times, Calon-Ségur was one of only three vineyards in Saint-Estèphe. It is ironical to consider that while in 1855 Calon-Ségur was classed a Third Growth (*Troisième Cru*) and Château Montrose was classed a Second Growth (*Second Cru*), in 1825 Montrose was a forest-land parcel of the Calon-Ségur estate. Today Calon-Ségur could be classed as a Second Growth. It is the best of all the Thirds and better than many Seconds.

The word 'Calon' comes from a little river skiff used in the Middle Ages to ferry timber across the Gironde; eventually the name spread to the whole district of Saint-Estèphe, which was known as the Calones or Saint-Estèphe-de-Calon, until the eighteenth century. At this time the property had passed, by marriage, into the hands of the Président de Ségur—Marquis de Ségur-Calon. He was the proprietor, at the same time, of the great Châteaux Lafite and Latour, but Calon was his favourite, apparently, for he said: 'I make wine at Lafite and Latour, but my heart is at Calon'—and this motto is still inscribed on an archway in the courtyard. Hence the heart on the label.

The soil is of three types: sandy gravel, giving finesse and nose to the wines; fatty gravel, or a limy and heavy soil, which, if it were not blended with the other, would give common but full-bodied wines; thinnish gravel, which alone could produce wines with breed but with considerable harshness. It is the scale of these soils that the late proprietor, Édouard Gasqueton, played to produce his outstanding wine. Since his death, in 1962, the vineyard is owned by his widow and his heirs.

Characteristics. Body is the foremost characteristic, although this robustness is held in the traces of a certain suppleness. The wines of Saint-Estèphe are the heaviest and most masculine of the Médocs and generally Calon-Ségur produces the most powerful wine of the Saint-Estèphes, and the longest lived. The 1955, unlike most Médocs, will take a long time to mature; and Calon-Ségur 1906 is still at its peak.

Vineyard area: 168 acres.

Average production: 20,000 cases.

Calvados

Apple brandy, the finest in the world. It is distilled from cider, in Normandy: the name is taken from the department of Calvados, and the best comes from the Vallée d'Auge, its greatest cider-making district. When old, Calvados can be a magnificent brandy, but fine ones can rarely be found outside the cellars of Normandy. When cider is being produced, a distillation is made from the residue of apple pressings, and this is usually called Eau-de-vie de Marc de Cidre.

Château Camensac

Bordeaux red wine; some experimentation has been made with white in recent years. District: Haut-Médoc, France. Commune: Saint-Laurent.

(*Saint-Laurent is not a place-name and the wine has the* appellation *Haut-Médoc.*)

A little-known and almost-forgotten Fifth Growth (*Cinquième Cru*) as classified in 1855. In recent years the vines have been dwindling, as a result both of frosts and of the relatively weak growth of the young vines in the poor soil of the vineyard.

Characteristics. Not distinguished.

Vineyard area: 26 acres.

Average production: 2,100 cases.

Campania

Red and white wines. District: South-West Italy.

Campanian wines are the very essences of the sunny province which produces them. Nowhere else is life so exuberant and carefree as it is in Naples, Campania's capital, but without its wines even Naples might lose some of its gaiety. The city is surrounded by beaches and islands—Sorrento, Capri, Ischia—of such legendary beauty that ever since classical times they have been resorts of pleasure.

The entire coast of the Bay of Naples might be Paradise on earth—and this, according to Neapolitan mythology, is precisely the case.

Lacrima (or Lacryma) Christi, the 'tear of Christ', is a dryish pale golden wine, made from grapes grown along the southern slope of Mount Vesuvius. The story they tell about it may well have been established to rival that of Latium's Est! Est!! Est!!!, but the Neapolitans swear that it is true. They say that when Lucifer fell from grace, he and his retinue landed with such a crash that the land beneath them collapsed, to form the Bay of Naples. Lucifer soon realized that he was in the place nearest to his lost Paradise, and so he populated Naples and its surrounding areas with his demons—with the result that Naples soon became a citadel of wickedness. The Saviour, looking down one day, grieved to see the terrestrial paradise so steeped in sin and He wept, His tear falling on Mount Vesuvius. From the tear a vine sprang up, and it multiplied into a vineyard, and every year the tear is reproduced in the wine vat as a reminder of the glory which awaits the honest wine-maker. This all happened, of course, a very long time ago, and Greco and Fiano have been planted to replace the original vines, but the story still lives on, retold with each glass. The wine, incidentally, has nothing in common with Spanish Lagrima Christi (*see* MÁLAGA) except that Italian and Spaniard each claim the original inspiration for the name.

Falerno is another wine with a long history. In Roman times it was known as Falernum and seems to have been considered almost as one of the wonders of the ancient world, but unfortunately we do not know from what grapes it was made, and have only an imperfect idea of how it tasted. Modern Falerno is made in Campi Flegrei, Capua, Sessa Aurunca, and Mondragone and the wine today, from Falanghino grapes, is generally golden-yellow, semi-dry, and of medium strength. Much of it is exported. Red Falerno is made also, mainly from Aglianico grapes, and this is pleasant enough provided that the price is reasonable.

Capri and Ischia. These white wines are more typical of Campania than the more famous Lacrima Christi and Falerno. The better of the two is Capri, from Greco and Fiano grapes grown on the island and vinified into a heady, sprightly, dry (or sometimes semi-sweet) white wine which is perfect with sea-food fresh from the Bay, with a sandwich or a meal, or as an aperitif sipped on a vine-shaded terrace. This is a delightful wine and one almost never found outside Capri, for it is made in such small quantities that it could never satisfy the thirst even of Capri itself—and so rather similar wines are imported to masquerade under Capri labels. The same is true of the comparable wine of the neighbouring island of Ischia—some of which is sold as Arturi. Some red and rosé Capris are also made, but there is even less of them than there is of the white.

Gragnano. The last of the Campanian red wines, made inland from Amalfi on the peninsula which juts out between Naples and Sorrento. It has a rich, deep hue but a light texture, and its outstanding charm is its freshness and a bouquet recalling violets or fresh strawberries. These, of course, are characteristics of young wines, and it follows that Gragnano should be taken fairly young. Jaculillo, Piede di Palumbo, and Aglianico grapes are the traditional components and the wine is now and again brought out *frizzante*, or slightly sparkling, but whether by accident or design it is difficult to say.

Lesser Wines of Campania

Conca. Made from Sangiovese, Canaiolo, Malvasia, and Aglianico grapes grown on slopes overlooking the Bay of Sorrento.

The wine is red, sometimes slightly coarse, generally high in alcohol. It is typically Italian and like so many Italian wines is excellent with pasta and other Italian dishes, but usually disappointing with more subtle fare.

Fiano di Avellino. Light, white, slightly flowery wine grown from Fiano grapes about thirty miles east of Naples.

Greco di Tufo. White wine made near the vineyards of Fiano di Avellino which it resembles—from Greco and Coda di Volpe grapes. It may be either dry or semi-sweet.

Ravello. Red, white, and rosé wines are made in (and named for) this flower-filled resort; the rosé, or Rosato, is the most appealing. Greco and Fiano grapes produce the white, the others are from Aglianico.

Solopaca. Red and white wines from the small city in northern Campania from which they take their name. They are made from Mangiaguerra, Oliveto, and Aleatico grapes.

Taurasi. Strong, vigorous red wine from Aglianico grapes, often too sturdy or even harsh when young. Proper vinification and suitable ageing might improve it considerably.

Vesuvio. Red wine from Aglianico and also white from other grapes grown along the slopes of Mount Vesuvius. Not very distinguished, but it can be agreeable if the price is reasonable. It is said that

Vesuvio is used to augment the production of red Capri, at a distinct mark-up in price.

Campari Bitters

Reddish-brown Italian bitters flavoured with herbs and orange peel, made by Fratelli Campari of Milan. It is used in the Americano and Negroni cocktails or drunk straight with a twist of lemon peel and a dash of soda.

Campbeltown

One of the two chief centres for West Highland malt whisky: the other is the nearby island of Islay. Campbeltown is on the sea-girt peninsula of Kintyre, extending southward down the Firth of Clyde. Until two centuries ago Kintyre was always considered a detached island of the Inner Hebrides.

See WHISKY, SCOTCH.

Canada

The vineyards of Canada are mainly in the Niagara peninsula of southern Ontario and in the Okanagan Valley of British Columbia, but the first of these regions is by far the more important.

About 95% of the grapes grown in Canada come from the fertile alluvial soils of the peninsula, bordered by Lake Erie, the River Niagara, and Lake Ontario. Although the climate of the country is generally supposed to be cold and harsh, the Niagara region has an average growing season of 173 days. Because it is near these large bodies of water, the district actually has more frost-free days than do many areas 200 to 300 miles south. The winters are mild, and the average temperature during the dormant season is about 25°–30°F. (−4° to −1° C.). Rainfall is adequate, and the hot summer and the long autumn season provide the right conditions for growth and harvesting.

Wine History

It is told in the Norse Sagas that Leif the Lucky first discovered North America and, because of the profusion of wild vines there, named the country Vineland. The first wines were probably made by French missionaries for sacramental purposes, for in LeJeune's *Relation of the Jesuits for 1636* it is stated that: 'In some places there are many wild vines loaded with grapes. Some have made wine of them through curiosity. I tasted it, and it seemed to me very good.' While this is the first record of wine-making in Canada it was not until much later that viticulture assumed commercial importance, and then it was due to German, not to French, influence. In 1811, John Schiller, an ex-corporal of the German Army, settled in Cooksville near Toronto, Ontario, and established a vineyard and a small winery. Canadians accept this date as the beginning of their wine industry. By the year 1890, grape growing had become established principally in the Niagara peninsula with about 5,000 acres planted. These have increased through the years to approximately 22,000 acres in 1961. There is an average annual yield of 40,000 tons (45,000 short tons) and in 1964 wine production in Canada was 8,711,000 imp. gallons (10,461,000 U.S.).

Modern Developments

A major portion of the vineyard is still planted with North American varieties, but these are gradually being changed over to European hybrids and *Vitis vinifera*. At first, it was thought that *Vitis vinifera* could not be grown in Canada but research and experimentation indicate that it is possible. Vineyards of this variety are not yet extensive, but they are being expanded. The focal point of Canadian viticultural research is the Ontario Department of Agriculture Experimental Station at Vineland, Ontario, where more than 300 varieties of vines have been under test for wine-making qualities. While most of the wine produced is still of the sweet dessert class, the demand for table wines has been growing, production of these wines is now about 20% of the total, and demand is increasing. With the exception of table varieties, most of the wines are blends of different years and different vineyards. They are aged in wood, and must be produced from grapes grown within the Province. Contrary to European practice, the wines must be marketed by the winery producing them. In all provinces, except Ontario, wineries may sell only to the Liquor Control Boards or Commissions which sell retail through their stores to consumers and to hotel and restaurant establishments. In Ontario, wineries sell to the Liquor Control Board, which operates 360 retail stores and to consumers through a limited number (51) of winery-operated retail stores.

The industry is relatively young, but it has developed considerably in the last twenty-five years, and there is no doubt that it will make even greater progress in the years to come.

See also WHISKY, CANADIAN.

Canadian Whisky

See WHISKY, CANADIAN.

Canaiolo

One of the red grapes used in making Chianti.

See TUSCANY.

Canary

See SPAIN.

Candia

Crete. This name is sometimes to be found on the labels of Cretan wines.

See GREECE.

Cannelle

Cinnamon-flavoured liqueur.

Château Canon

Bordeaux red wine. District: Haut-Médoc, France, Commune: Macau.

Classed a First Great Growth (*Premier Grand Cru*) in 1955, the vineyard is planted right over some of the ancient quarries out of which the building stone of the mediæval town of Saint-Émilion was dredged. The 'château' is an unprepossessing farmhouse. The 1929 is outstanding even among the great bottles of that year. Canon has always been one of the top Saint-Émilions, its recognition antedating by generations the recent official classification.

Characteristics. A supple, generous wine with considerable finesse.

Vineyard area: 50 acres.

Average production: 7,200 cases.

Canteiro

A rather rare type of Madeira: the designation means that the wine was matured in the heat of the sun.

Château Cantemerle

Bordeaux red wine. District: Haut-Médoc, France. Commune: Macau.

(*Macau is not a place-name and the wine has the* appellation *Haut-Médoc.*)

Classified a Fifth Growth (*Cinquième Cru*) in 1855, Cantemerle is now universally considered to be very much superior to its official classification. Actually it deserves to be reclassed as a Second Growth (*Second Cru*). The second great Médoc vineyard north of Bordeaux (the first is Grand La Lagune), Cantemerle lies about two miles south of the first cluster of famous growths within the grouped communes entitled to the place-name Margaux. The château is surrounded by one of the largest and most beautiful parks in Médoc, and the vines planted at either side of the woodland produce an excellent wine.

Cantemerle existed long before many of today's famous vineyards were established. In the Middle Ages it was the site of a fortress called Sauves, and it played its part in the turbulent history of that time as a portion of the Barony of Cantemerle. Acquired in 1759 by the family of Jehan de Villeneuve, it remained in their hands until 1892, when it was bought by the father of the late Monsieur Pierre J. Dubos, who died recently; the vineyard is now run by his son-in-law.

The present high reputation of the wines was achieved largely through the efforts of old Monsieur Dubos, a twinkling little man with his sturdy legs wrapped in field puttees, still remembering the English he learned to speak in England decades ago, and revered as one of the most dedicated wine men of Médoc. His Vintage Book is a legend in Bordeaux, recording unfailingly every morning, afternoon, and evening, for more than sixty-five years, wind direction, temperature, and barometer readings, with, alongside, the behaviour of the vine, its flowering, ripening, etc. His dictum: 'You must harvest ninety-five days to 105 days after the flowering regardless of the weather through the summer,' is an opinion considered unorthodox in the Médoc. When the vintage arrived, each day was graphed by Monsieur Dubos—section harvested, yielding how many tubs, put to ferment in which vat, day's weather, condition of the grapes at picking. All other processes throughout the life of the wine were charted just as carefully. This tremendous care has borne splendid fruit in the fine wines of Cantemerle.

Château La Tour de Mons in Soussans-Margaux, in his wife's family for three centuries, came to Monsieur Dubos by marriage, and is one of the highest-rated of the non-classified vineyards. A dependent vineyard of Château Cantemerle is Château Royal.

Characteristics. Beautiful, light, supple, fast maturing wines with remarkable finesse. Another example of how obsolete is the 1855 Classification, since Cantemerle, a Fifth Growth, has come up with many a superb bottle. Very popular in Holland.

Vineyard area: 49 acres.

Average production: 6,200 cases.

Cantenac

Sometimes Cantenac-Margaux. A village of the Haut-Médoc district of the Bordeaux wine region in south-west France. The wines are sold under the controlled place-name of the adjoining commune, Margaux. There is no appreciable difference in quality or style between the wines of the two communes. Six vineyards of Cantenac were classified in 1855: Château Brane-Cantenac, a Second Growth (*Second Cru*), Châteaux Kirwan, d'Issan, Palmer, Boyd-Cantenac, and Cantenac-Brown, Third Growths (*Troisièmes Crus*); and Châteaux Prieuré-Lichine and Pouget, Fourth Growths (*Quatrièmes Crus*).

See under individual headings.

Château Cantenac-Brown

Bordeaux red wine. District: Haut-Médoc, France. Commune: Cantenac-Margaux.

Accorded the right in 1954 to the place-name Margaux with the other vineyards of Cantenac, Brown faces the village of Margaux from a distance of half a mile. The huge red-brick château with its many chimneys, looking like an English prep. school, is now privately owned and not connected with the vineyard.

The vineyard, a Third Growth (*Troisième Cru*) as classified in 1855, was established by Armand Lalande and is still in the same family. Vine types going into the wine are the same as in the other vineyards of the Médoc—Cabernet Sauvignon, Cabernet Franc, Merlot, and Petit-Verdot. Château Lamartine, whose wines grown in river soil are entitled to the rating Bordeaux Supérieur, is a secondary vineyard.

Characteristics. Big full wines, rather heavier than those of the neighbouring châteaux.

Vineyard area: 55 acres.

Average production: 7,200 cases.

Cap Corse

French wine-based aperitif made with the heady wines of the Cap Corse (northernmost) peninsula of Corsica and flavoured with quinine and herbs.

Château Capbern

Bordeaux red wine. District: Haut-Médoc, France. Commune: Saint-Estèphe.

The property of 150 acres, approximately half of it in vine, is set on high gravelly land at the edge of the village of Saint-Estèphe and overlooking the River Gironde. Directly across the town is Château Calon-Ségur, which nowadays produces one of the finest red Bordeaux; both châteaux are owned and worked by the Gasqueton family. Capbern wines are as well cared-for by these expert vinicultors as the famous Calon-Ségur, and deserve elevation to classification among the Great Growths (*Grands Crus*). Various parts of the production are sold as Château Capbern, Château Grand-Village-Capbern, Château La-Rose-Capbern, and Château Latour-Lichine.

Characteristics. A full-bodied, round wine combining a certain amount of hardness and finesse. Better made than many classified growths.

Vineyard area: 80 acres.

Average production: 8,000 cases.

Cape Smoke

South Africa's cheapest and worst brandy. A wise policy of favourable taxes on high quality brandy and high taxes on the poorer examples is causing it to disappear.

Cape Wines

See SOUTH AFRICA.

Caperitif

South African aperitif, deep gold in colour, based on wine, blended with spirit, and flavoured with herbs. It is bitter but reminiscent of vermouth.

Capri

Mainly a dry white wine from the island of Capri. Some of this is made in Capri itself, some in Ischia and other neighbouring places. A small quantity of red and rosé wine is also made.

See CAMPANIA.

Carafe

In French, a decanter or glass bottle for serving wines. In French restaurants the ordinary wine is usually drawn straight from a cask and brought to the table either in a carafe or a *carafon*, a small carafe.

Caramel

Burnt sugar added to spirits as colouring matter. All spirits emerge pale and colourless from the still, and unless colour is absorbed from the wooden barrels during ageing, caramel—tasteless and practically odourless—must be used.

Carbon Dioxide

CO_2, produced in approximately equal weight with alcohol when sugar is fermented by the action of yeast. Normally it escapes, but it is trapped in the fluid in the production of sparkling wine, beer, and cider. In French, *gaz carbonique*.

Carbonated Wines

Wines in which an unnatural sparkle has been induced by gasifying with carbon dioxide.

See SPARKLING WINES.

Château Carbonnieux

Bordeaux red and white wine. District: Graves, France. Commune: Léognan.

With the charming wine goes a charming story. To sell their wines in Turkey (which meant getting round the Islamic interdiction on wine) the fathers of the Abbey of Sainte-Croix of Bordeaux, then owners of the vineyard, sent off bottles of Carbonnieux labelled as mineral water. The Sultan tasted it and said: 'If the French mineral water is so good, why do they take the trouble to make wine?'

Set in the ancient vineyard, where only the crest and slopes of the hill are devoted to wine, the château dates from the fourteenth century. In 1953 both red and white Carbonnieux wines were classified as among the leading Graves growths. Excellent and consistent though the red wine is, it is the dry, brilliant white wine that has made the great fame of the vineyard.

Characteristics. A wine with both vigour and finesse. The preponderance of Sauvignon grapes gives it a particularly agreeable flavour.

Vineyard area: 100 acres.

Average production: White—7,000 cases.
Red—3,700 cases.

Carboy

A large bottle of glass, or occasionally earthenware, with a wicker or wooden frame. The name is derived from the Persian *garabana*, 'large flagon', a demijohn.

Carignan

Grape grown mostly in southern France and similar hot climates for robust, heady table wines and dessert wine. It has also been transplanted to America, where it is spelt Carignane.

Cariñena

Best-known wines of Aragón, both red and white.

See SPAIN.

Carmel

Some of the wines of Israel bear this name, followed by a grape variety or wine type, e.g. Carmel muscat, Carmel port.

See ISRAEL.

Carta Blanca (White Label)

A light-bodied Puerto Rican or Cuban rum, a little lighter, paler, and less sweet than Carta Oro.

See RUM: CUBA, PUERTO RICO.

Carta Oro (Gold Label)

A light-bodied Puerto Rican or Cuban Rum which, owing to the addition of caramel colouring, is slightly darker than Carta Blanca. It is usually a little heavier and sweeter, too.

See RUM: CUBA, PUERTO RICO.

Case

A case of wine contains twelve bottles of 24 to 26 oz.; twenty-four half-bottles; forty-eight splits of Champagne; six magnums, or three jeroboams. The cases used to be made only of wood but today, when so many wines are being shipped in cardboard cartons, these cartons are also called cases.

Casein

This useful protein is employed in the ageing of white wines, both as a clarifier and as a remedy against maderization. The substance, which contains phosphorus, is generally extracted from milk, where it is present as a calcic salt. When it has been washed, dried, ground, and sieved, it can be used, in doses of from 5 to 20 grammes per hectolitre, for clearing wines; or from 25 to 30 grammes per hectolitre as a preventive and curative treatment for oxidation, or maderization.

Cask

A wine barrel, usually of wood bound with hoops. Sizes and capacity vary widely following traditional customs of particular localities (for standard casks and containers, *see* APPENDIX B). Casks are used for maturing, storing, and transporting wines, spirits, and beers. In Europe ordinary wine is always sold in cask, the wine being drawn off as needed.

Casse

Clouding and precipitation, with an off-taste, caused in wine by the presence of too much air, protein, iron, or copper.

See CHAPTER NINE, p. 53.

Cassis

1. Controlled place-name in the wines of Provence, France. The vineyards are planted on the hillsides behind the picturesque fishing village of Cassis, some 200 odd kms. east of Marseilles, along the Riviera.

See PROVENCE.

2. Sweet, dark red liqueur made from blackcurrants. The most notable Cassis is that of Dijon, in north-east France, although it is also made elsewhere. Around Dijon it is used as a popular

aperitif, a little Cassis being put in a glass that is then filled with a fairly neutral, dry white wine. The local and somewhat inelegant name for this is *rince cochon*—pig rinse. Also called kir.

Castelli di Jesi

See VERDICCHIO DEI CASTELLI DI JESI.

Castelli Romani

Inexpensive wines very popular in the restaurants of Rome.

See LATIUM.

Catawba

Pink American grape of uncertain origin, said to draw its name from the River Catawba in western North Carolina. Its juice is white, dry, and heavy-flavoured, and was widely used in the nineteenth century, particularly for sparkling wine. 'Sparkling Catawba', the most famous of which was made by the Longworth Vineyards of Cincinnati, Ohio, was extremely popular.

Caudle

Spiced and sweetened hot wine or ale, with an egg yolk beaten in.

Cave

French term for cellar.

Cavistes

French term for cellarmen.

Cellar

Place for storing wine.

See CHAPTER SIX, p. 22.

Centerbe

Italian liqueur said to be made from a hundred different herbs, with mint outstanding. It is also called Silvestro from the reputed originator, Fra San Silvestro, an Italian monk.

Central Valley

Californian wine region. The major district is Escalon-Modesto, in San Joaquin County. The area comprises also part of Stanislaus and Merced counties.

See AMERICA: CALIFORNIA AND THE WEST.

Cépage

French term for grape variety, e.g. Pinot or Riesling.

Cerasella

Dark, red, sweet Italian liqueur made from and flavoured with cherries, although the taste is enriched by the addition of a number of herbs.

Cerasuolo d' Abruzzo

Italian light red wine.

See ABRUZZI.

Ceres

Wine-growing district of Cape Province, South Africa.

See SOUTH AFRICA.

Cerise d'Alsace

White *eau-de-vie* made with cherries.

See ALSACE.

Cérons

White wines. District: Bordeaux, France.

The vineyard road which goes down the left bank of the River Garonne, past the great châteaux of Graves and eventually in among the hills of Sauternes, winds through a flat country of neatly kept vines as solid as a carpet and beaded along the highway with gaudy stands, some in the shape of wine bottles or clapboard castles, into which the public is urged to step, and taste the wines. The district is Cérons and its wines are neither as dry as the white Graves nor as sweet as Sauternes. They are produced by impeccable wine-making methods from the same grapes as Sauternes—Sémillon, Sauvignon, and some Muscadelle—and according to the Sauternes system of letting the grapes achieve a sugar-rich overripeness, in which condition they are selectively picked. Finally, as indicated by the many stands along the road, Cérons white wine is far more popular in France than might be imagined from its small fame abroad.

(In Bordeaux it is assumed that as Cérons is an in-between style, neither sweet nor dry, it has failed to make a definite impression in the world market, where there are so many names to choose from.)

A considerable amount of dry Cérons is being made now, however, in response to present market conditions. But the typical Cérons is a little less sweet than a Barsac, which region it touches and of which it once was a part, just as a Barsac will be a little less sweet than a Sauternes. Cérons makes about 500,000 imp. gallons (600,000 U.S.) of white wine a year, as compared to about 333,000 imp. gallons (400,000 U.S.) from adjoining Barsac and 666,000 imp. gallons (800,000 U.S.) of Sauternes.

Certosa

Red Italian liqueur resembling Chartreuse.

Cesanese

Grape variety found in Italy.

Cesanese di Piglio

The outstanding red wine of Latium, made from Cesanese grapes.

See LATIUM.

Chablis

White wine. District: Burgundy, near Auxerre, Central France.

Chablis is one of the most famous wine names in the world but, used correctly, it refers to one of the world's rarest great wines—to the steadily decreasing quantity of magnificent, flinty-dry white wines which are made from grapes grown on hilly acres in and around the Burgundian town of Chablis, about 110 miles south-east of Paris.

The village lies in a small valley in the department of the Yonne, surrounded by gently rolling hills on which the vines are grown—but not in any great numbers. The bare hills overlooking the town are astonishingly empty and it is sometimes said that if present trends continue the wines of Chablis may cease to exist within a few generations.

The soil is hard, and hard to work. Easily exhausted, the vineyards must rest as much as twenty years at a time, and at present about half of the land is resting. The topsoil is thin and in many spots the white, marly, calcium-rich subsoil (a formation known as Kimmeridge Clay) shows through. The thin top layer is easily washed down the slopes by the rains, and must be carried up again on the backs of the workers, for only at mid-slope can the greatest wines have their source.

A further hazard is the inclemency of the climate, for Chablis is more to the north than any other fine-wine district of France except Champagne and Alsace. When the vine is planted so far north it must expend a great part of its vigour simply struggling to survive the hard winters, the uncertain summers and the often disastrous frosts—the month of May is by far the most critical, for a May frost can ruin the prospects for the entire year.

The Burgundian *vigneron* is passionately attached not only to his land but to his wine. For the older growers, no sacrifice is too great if the result may, in very favourable years, be great wine. The younger men, however, are not inspired with this ideal of perfection, and many are leaving to find occupation elsewhere. In regions as unrewarding as Chablis, the exodus is greater than in more favoured spots. Thus the amount of land in cultivation and the quantity of wine being made is slowly but steadily dropping. In the past century the vineyards have dwindled by more than half and the Yonne, once the most productive department of Burgundy, now makes a negligible amount of wine.

The greatest Chablis vineyards are on one hill visible from the main square of the town; they cover a mere 247 acres of which only a half is usually in production, and are generally sold with the name of the vineyard or the words *Grand Cru* (*see Grand Cru* below in this entry). Another 1,112 acres, half of which are in production, are divided into vineyards designated First Growth (*Premier Cru*) and these form the second-rank vineyards, producing excellent wines which only occasionally reach the high level of the Great Growths (*Grands Crus*). Chablis and Petit Chablis end the list and these are the minor wines—but minor only in comparison to their splendid cellar-mates.

All the vineyards fit into an area about ten miles long by six miles wide encompassing some 4,700 acres. They fall in the communes of Chablis, Chichée, Chemilly-sur-Serein, Poilly-sur-Serein, Préhy, Fyé, Fleys, Rameau, Courgis, Beines, Poinchy, Maligny, Milly, Béru, La Chapelle-Vaupelteigne, Villy, Lignorelles, Ligny-le-Châtel, Fontenay, and Viviers, but the name of the town will rarely be found on the labels. The single permissible grape is Chardonnay, Burgundy's only noble white-wine vine, known in the district as Beaunois. At one time, Sacy, Melon, and Aligoté vines were fairly prevalent, but these have been rooted out and their grapes forbidden. The present vines are grown low to the ground—to allow the brown and white, chalky soil to deflect the sun's rays on to them, and so hasten the maturing of the fruit—and they are severely pruned, with the result that the amount of fruit they give is small, even in the finest years.

Chablis growers normally have a number of small and often widely separated vineyard plots, their total acreage amounting to anything between two and twenty acres. The famous vineyards, small though they are, may be divided into half a dozen sections, each one owned and worked by a different man and, for this reason, the wine shippers adopted the general Burgundian practice of blending wine from different growers in any given vineyard and selling it under the firm's label. Many growers, however, have started estate-bottling their wines—harvesting the grapes, making the wine, caring for it themselves and bottling it under their own labels.

The low-lying vines are planted in rows running up and down the slopes—in contrast to the planting of earlier days, when they followed the ridge lines. Both cultivation and drainage are enhanced by this method.

Harvest time in Chablis generally falls in the first two weeks of October and the weather is often chilly. As soon as the grapes are ripe they are picked and taken, the same day, to be pressed. If they were left overnight, fermentation might start by itself, bringing trouble for the vintner.

The great heaps of grapes are brought and taken off the stems, to prevent the bitter tannin in the stems from imparting harshness to the eventual wine. The grapes are then crushed lightly in presses and the juice run off into barrels: the Chablis barrel is traditionally the *feuillette*, containing 132 litres or about 29 imp. gallons (35 U.S.). Many growers are abandoning this slightly odd-sized container and adopting the more widespread Burgundian *pièce* of 228 litres or about 50 imp. gallons (60 U.S.) or the larger *fûts* of 400 litres or 88 imp. gallons (105·7 U.S.). Once the juice is in the barrel, fermentation begins.

In all the cellars and *chais* of Chablis, in the autumn just after harvest time, there is a pungent sweetness mixed with the unpleasant smell of gases rising from the fermenting grapes. During the first tumultuous days of fermentation, wine-makers are careful not to remain too long in the cellars, for the gas is powerful and could overcome them. Cellars are small and dark, usually with rows of barrels stacked two or three high down both sides and sometimes with another row down the centre. In one corner will be a small stove, for the weather gets cold quickly and unheated cellars might become too cold for the yeast to work and the wine to ferment.

In most years the summer sun does not instil enough sugar into the grapes to produce the amount of alcohol essential for great wine and so the vintner has to resort to the addition of sugar or *chaptalisation*. In many years this is necessary; in some years it is advised; occasionally it is unnecessary. *Chaptalisation* has the full sanction of the French law and is carried out under Government control.

When the grape must has fermented, the wine is ready for its first clearing or racking—normally done in the February after the harvest. The slow, careful pumping from one barrel to another—leaving behind the deposit and a small amount of wine, which together form the lees—both airs the wine and clarifies it. Some of the very minor wines (such as Petit Chablis) are bottled in the summer following the harvest, but the great ones are left to sleep longer in wood. Bottling for them will not usually occur until fourteen to twenty months after the harvest. The smallest wines are never bottled at all, but are sold to restaurants and served directly from the barrel.

Wine History

The fame of Chablis goes back to very ancient times. It is one wine which has kept its reputation and renown while others once equally well known have been forgotten. The department of the Yonne once produced two-thirds of all Burgundies but now Chablis is the only significant area remaining. (Minor red wines are still grown in the villages of Irancy, Saint-Bris-le-Vineux, Chitry, and Joigny, but production is small and the wines command neither great acclaim nor high prices.)

No one knows when the first vines were planted in Chablis. It is certain that, whether or not Julius Cæsar found vines in the region when he arrived in Gaul, they were there when the Romans departed. The decline of the Roman Empire was accompanied by a decline of the vineyards, but in the twelfth century they revived under the care of the monks. The Cistercian Abbey at Pontigny, ten miles from Chablis, had extensive holdings throughout the vineyards and it is thought that the Chardonnay vine was introduced then. Most of the monks came from the Côte d'Or, where the Chardonnay rules the slope for white wines, and the Chablis word *beaunois* (plant of Beaune), for the Chardonnay, supports the theory. Other orders had portions of the Chablis vineyards too: the Church of Saint Martin at Tours, for example, whose vineyards were donated to one of the abbots by his brother, Charles the Bald, in the ninth century. The association between Tours and Chablis lasted until 1790, when the Revolutionary State confiscated all church property.

One factor in the decline of Chablis is the lack of adequate compensation for the amount of labour required, another was the onset of phylloxera.

This lethal vine louse came to Chablis about 1893. Previously discovered in other French vineyard regions, it had caused little trouble in Chablis until an extremely hot summer gave it the conditions in which it thrived. By this time, the French growers had discovered that grafting French *vinifera* vines on to hybrids or American root-stock was an

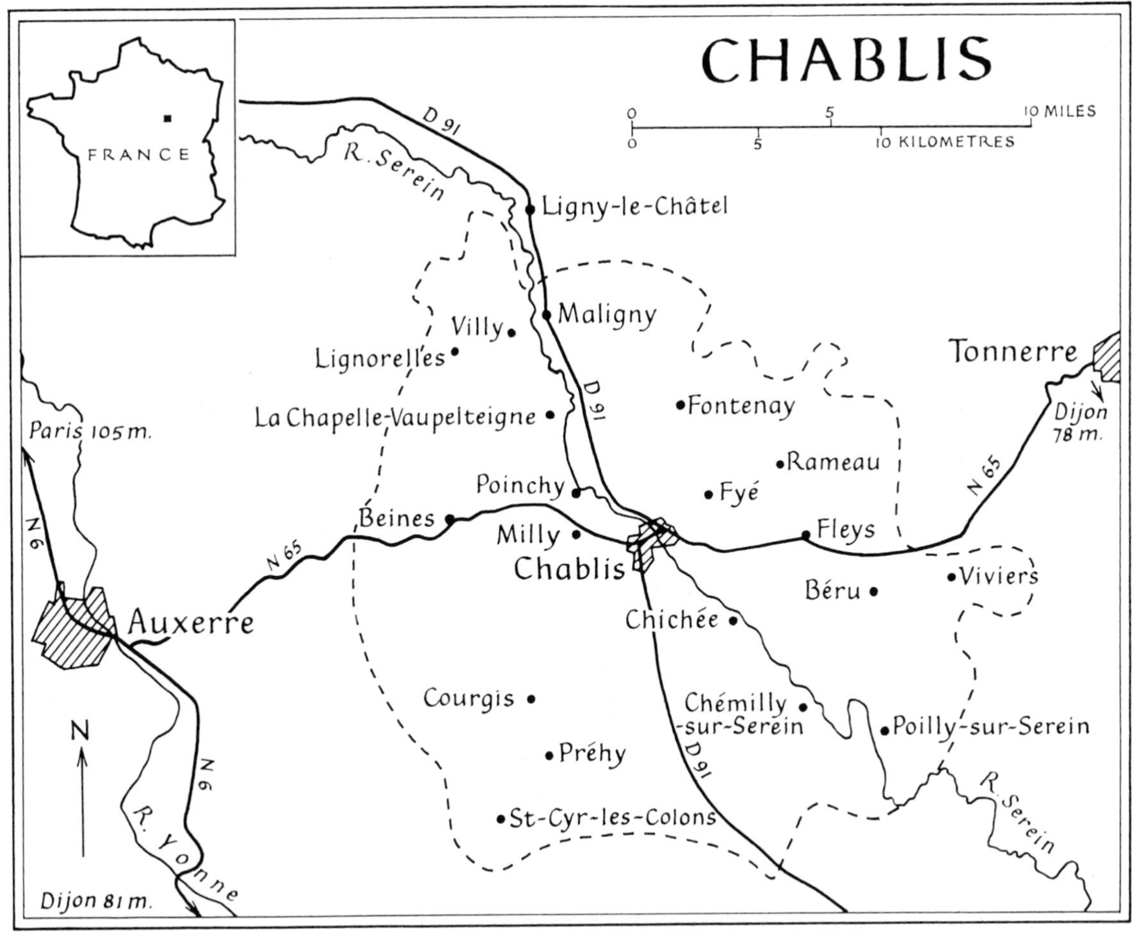

effective way of combating the scourge and many Chablis vineyards were quickly reconstituted in vines grafted on to roots with such numerical tags as 161–49, 3·309, 41–B and B.31. But, because of the expense of reconstitution, some growers took this opportunity to find different employment.

In the 1930s, Chablis was again in production, but again in trouble. Fame had brought the wines into great demand and much wine was supplied which was white and dry but otherwise had nothing in common with Chablis. The French control laws, beginning in 1936, have taken the matter in hand, and today the amount of fraudulent Chablis found on the market is nothing compared to what it was.

Great Growths (Grands Crus)

Seven vineyards, totalling ninety acres, comprise the Great Growths of Chablis. They are adjoining vineyards half-way up the south-westerly slope, and with one exception are all within the limits of the town of Chablis (the exception is Blanchots, in neighbouring Fyé). The wines are almost always sold with vineyard names on the labels, the vineyards being Blanchots, Les Clos, Valmur, Grenouilles, Vaudésir, Les Preuses, and Bougros. Another one which might have been included is La Moutonne: but it has never received official recognition although such action was considered.

The somewhat hazy status of La Moutonne began with the French Revolution when the vineyard was taken over by the State and sold to a local grower. The document accompanying the sale seems to have been extremely vague and the location of the vineyard not well established, although people in Chablis can point it out with no trouble. (It takes in about five acres between Vaudésir and Les Preuses.) In 1951, the French wine authorities recommended to the Minister of Agriculture that the vineyard be recognized as a Great Growth of Chablis but, as the quality was disappointing, the request was never followed up and the edict died a quiet, bureaucratic death.

Just what makes these vineyards clearly superior to the others—and even to those close by—is impossible to define. The interplay of soil, sunlight, and whatever other mysterious elements combine to produce just exactly the right grapes for making a specific wine are too complex for analysis. The differences between them will, however, be abundantly clear in the wines themselves.

Wines from these Great Growth vineyards are Chablis: but they are Chablis with a difference. All Chablis has a certain green-tinged, yellow-gold colour, an impeccable dryness, and a delicate, light perfume. The greater the wine, the more varied and richer it will be, and the more it will have that indescribable quality known as elegance or breed. Since the wines from these specific vineyards are consistently superior, they alone are rated Great Growths. In addition to their source in a Great Growth vineyard, these wines must have a minimum of 11% alcohol. Wines of a good year may be expected to hold their greatness as long as ten years—a considerable life-span for a dry white wine. In most cases, however, the rewards for keeping them more than five are not great enough since only about 12,500 imp. gallons (15,000 U.S.) are made annually—the equivalent of six thousand cases—and the greater part is exported to the United States.

FIRST GROWTHS (PREMIERS CRUS)

Twenty-two vineyards in various towns around Chablis on both sides of the River Serein have the right to the name. The wines stand just below the Great Growths, but are often so similar that even the most accomplished wine-taster finds it difficult to differentiate between them. They are usually sold with the name Chablis and that of the vineyard (e.g. Chablis-Montée de Tonnerre).

Wine must have an alcoholic content of 10·5% or forfeit the right to the designation. An average 119,000 imp. gallons (143,000 U.S.) (the equivalent of about 59,000 cases) are made each year.

The vineyards, and the towns from which they come, are as follows:

Right bank of the Serein

Vineyard	*Commune*
Chapelot	Fyé
Côte de Fontenay	Fontenay
Vaupulent	Fontenay (part), La Chapelle-Vaupelteigne (part)
Fourchaume	La Chapelle-Vaupelteigne
Mont de Milieu	Fyé and Fleys
Montée de Tonnerre	Fyé
Pied d'Aloup	Fyé
Vaucoupin	Chichée
Vaulorent	Poinchy

Left bank of the Serein

Vineyard	*Commune*
Beauroy	Poinchy
Beugnon	Chablis
Butteaux	Chablis
Châtain	Chablis
Côte de Léchet	Milly
Les Forêts or Forests	Chablis
Les Lys	Chablis
Mélinots	Chablis
Montmain	Chablis
Séchet	Chablis
Troesme	Beines
Vaillon and Côte de Vaillon	Chablis
Vosgros or Vogiras	Chichée

CHABLIS

On a wine label, Chablis, without any further qualification, means a wine from one of the slopes in the district, but not one of the outstanding ones. About 200,000 imp. gallons (240,000 U.S.) of this wine, which must contain at least 9·5% of alcohol, are made annually, much of it being sold in barrel. Some is also bottled.

PETIT CHABLIS

The least of the wines made mostly from grapes grown in the Chablisian hinterlands. The towns in which the vineyards lie are Lignorelles, Ligny-le-Châtel and any allowed the place-name Chablis. The wines are mainly sold in barrel, mostly in France or the Low Countries. However, much of the better wines are shipped in bottle to the U.S.A. Annual output averages about 80,000 imp. gallons (96,000 U.S.).

Chai

A wine shed, or place above ground where wine is stored in cask. In Bordeaux, where virtually all wine is kept in such sheds, there is one *chai* for *vin nouveau* or wine of the year and another for *vin vieux* or wine of the previous year not yet bottled.

Chalonnais

Red and white wines. District: South Burgundy, France.

The slope is almost an extension of the Côte de Beaune and there is a distinct resemblance between the wines of the two districts. The Chalonnais are lesser wines, indeed, only rarely attaining the same level of excellence, but they are well known, produced in considerable quantity, relatively inexpensive, and often very good.

The name derives from Chalon-sur-Saône, a small quiet town about five miles to the west of the vineyards. Vines are grown between these vineyards and the city, but the output is not, oddly enough, Chalonnais. To benefit from the name, the grapes must be grown along specified hillsides in the four communes of Givry, Mercurey, Montagny, and Rully. Anything else in the vicinity cannot hope for a place-name more specific than Burgundy.

The favoured slopes generally face east, although some look south-east and a very few face directly south. The soil is virtually the same as that of the Côte de Beaune but more fertile.

The standards ordained for these wines do not differ markedly from those in other sections of Burgundy. Red wines must be from Pinot Noir (with allowance for the almost identical Pinot Liebault and Pinot Beurot) grapes, and the white are restricted to Pinot Blanc and Chardonnay; the permissible amount of harvest amounts to 312 imp. gallons (374 U.S.) of wine per acre of vine for Mercurey, 356 imp. gallons (428 U.S.) for the other three (all subject to modification in abnormal years); red wines must have a minimum alcoholic content of 10·5%, white of 11%. No rosé is made.

Chalonnais red wines are usually lighter than Côte d'Or Burgundies, often have considerable perfume, and do not hold for any length of time. A bottle which is more than five to eight years old could conceivably be excellent, but the odds are against it. White wines are pleasant enough as a rule, but seldom worth exporting. As for sparkling Burgundy—vast quantities of which are made in the Chalonnais—this is a drink which has its followers, but it is not to be taken seriously.

Place-names

Rully

Most of the output is sparkling. Rully, northernmost of the Chalonnais wine communes, has been a centre for sparkling Burgundy since 1830 and for a considerable period it supported itself almost entirely on the sales of these wines, which are not made from top Burgundies.

At the end of the First World War, once-prosperous wine-growers of France found themselves in serious difficulty. No provision had been made to protect the names of fine wines, and in the chaotic aftermath of the war, many members of the trade found more incentive in fast profits, so the market was flooded with cheap, bulk wine sold under famous names. Simultaneously, agitation for workable controls was gaining strength. The growers of Rully found themselves in trouble. The wines were—and are—above the average; but Rully had been selling them under the name of neighbouring Mercurey, whose growers were not entirely pleased with this practice. When they drew up their controls, they excluded the wines of Rully from the place-name Mercurey.

Three courses were open to the vintners of Rully: to press Mercurey to readmit their wines; to establish a control of their own; or to sell their wines simply as Burgundy, at a considerable reduction in price. Rather than try to establish Rully as a name in its own right—which might have taken a considerable time—the growers chose the first course; but, fortunately for them, the town had its sparkling Burgundy trade to support it, for the French wine authorities proved as stubborn as the Mercurey growers. In 1939 the fight was given up and Rully, benefiting from its own controls, has become a producer of still as well as sparkling wines.

Both red and white wines are made, but the white shows more quality—and in fact, is considered one of the better offerings of southern Burgundy, just below the whites of the Mâconnais. Rully's still white is marked by a pronounced bouquet and a winy flavour described as 'vinosity', but, like most dry white wines, it should be consumed young. Wine stemming from one of the better vineyards is elevated to the rank of First Growth (*Premier Cru*)—assuming that it attains a half-degree of alcohol more than the normal minimum. These vineyards, some of which produce red as well as white wines, are:

Vauvry	Raboursay
Mont-Palais	Ecloseaux
Meix-Caillet	Marisson
Les Pierres	La Fosse
La Bressande	Chapître
Champ-Clou	Préau
La Renarde	Moulesne
Pillot	Margoty
Cloux	Grésigny
Raclot	

Mercurey

The best-known and the best wines of the Chalonnais. The grapes are grown in the communes of Mercurey, Saint-Martin-sous-Montaigus and Bourgneuf-Val d'Or and, although the law permits growing grapes for both red and white wines, those of Mercurey are about 95% red.

The wines are often very like those of the Côte de Beaune, light but sometimes surprisingly rich, not generally as fine, yet they come astonishingly close in good years. These are definitely wines to be consumed when young—from two to five years old. They are sound and pleasant but rarely stamped with greatness. One of the best organizations of the commune is the Cave Coopérative, run in a more than usually enlightened manner, respectful of the wines of each one of its members, and used as a source of supply rather than as a blending mill. Each member has his own wines, his own tools, and his own equipment, and the great advantage is that he can procure his supplies more cheaply since the organization buys in bulk and at wholesale prices.

The fame of Mercurey is so widespread that it is one of the few communes which did not go through the periods of recession after the two world wars. The renown of the wines, coupled with the fact that they are generally less expensive than comparable wines from the Côte de Beaune, was the dominant contributing factor to Mercurey's continued prosperity. The grapes are mostly Pinot Noir and the amount of wine grown is about 125,000 imp. gallons (150,000 U.S.) per year.

Here, as elsewhere, certain vineyards have the right (if their wines attain half a degree of alcohol higher than the standard minimum limit) to add the words First Growth to the label, or to be sold as Mercurey, followed by the name of the vineyard. These vineyards are:

Clos-du-Roi	Clos-des-Fourneaux
Les Voyens	Clos-des-Montaigus
Clos Marcilly	

Givry

The wines are predominantly red, although some white is grown. Tradition claims that Givry was one of the favourites of Henry IV of France, a monarch who seems to have had a colossal thirst and a penchant for almost every wine in France. The red wines of Givry are slightly lighter and generally coarser than those of Mercurey, although very often wines of the finer vineyards (Clos-Saint-Pierre, Clos-Saint-Paul, Cellier-aux-Moines, and Clos-Salomon) stand on a pretty equal footing with them. One of the more important owners is Baron Tenard, who has holdings in numerous vineyards, including Givry's Cellier-aux-Moines and the famous Montrachet on the Côte de Beaune. His cellars in Givry house wines from all his holdings. They consist of caves dug deep below the town; huge ornate chambers which look like the set for a Hollywood costume-piece.

About 11,000 imp. gallons (13,000 U.S.) of wine are made each year, most of which is sold as Givry. Provision has been left in the decree of 1954 for certain vineyards to be designated First Growths, but the French authorities have not as yet drawn up a definite list of those that may add vineyard name to that of the commune.

Montagny

The only name of the Côte Chalonnaise which applies to white wines exclusively. The vineyards are in the towns of Montagny, Buxy, Saint-Vallerin, and Jully-les-Buxy, but only in those portions selected by the experts as fit and proper for growing Montagny wines. All told, the permitted area measures just over 760 acres.

After Mercurey, Montagny is the largest producer of the district but little of the wine is of first quality. 'Pleasant' is the word most frequently used to describe it, and it is particularly apt if the wines are caught young. The dominant grape is the Chardonnay, and about 33,000 imp. gallons (40,000 U.S.) of wine are made annually.

A surprising number of vineyards have been selected as superior, their wines allowed to be sold with the designation First Growth, the vineyard name following that of the commune. Although bottles carrying these indications are rare, the vineyards are:

Sous-les-Roches	Les Bouchots
Les Combes	Les Vignes-sur-le-Clou
Les Saint-Catages	Les Vignes-Couland
Les Vignes-Saint-Pierre	Les Trouffières
Les Charmelottes	Les Vignes-du-Soleil
Les Champs-Toizeau (or Chantoiseau)	Les Marais
	Les Perrières
Les Garchères	Le Pallye
Les Chacolets	Le Varignus
Les Clouseaux	Les Thilles
Les Carlins	La Vigne-Devant
Le Breuil	La Corvée
Les Champs-de-Coignée	Les Vignes-Dessous
	Les Marcques
Les Burnins	La Thi
Les Montcuchots	Les Mâles
Les Crets	La Condemine
Les Beaux-Champs	Les Vignes-Longues
Les Pandars	Les Vignes-Blanches
Les Jardins	Cornevent

Les Saint-Morille	Le Mont-Laurent
Le Clou	Les Bonnevaux
Les Vignes-Derrière	Les Bassets
Les Resses	La Mouillère
Le Perthuis	Les Pasquiers
Les Gouresses	Les Coères
Les Bordes	Les Thillonnés
Les Las	Les Chandits
Clos-Chaudron	Les Chazelles
La Grande Pièce	Le Vieux-Château
Les Pidans	Les Vignes-du-Puits

Chambertin

Burgundy red wine. District: Côte de Nuits, France. Commune: Gevrey-Chambertin. Official classification: Great Growth (Grand Cru).

Chambertin is the *Grand Seigneur* of Burgundy, partly on account of the unquestionable magnificence and nobility of the wine, and partly in deference to Napoleon, who preferred it to all others. It is not surprising that the commune of Gevrey chose to add this name to its own, becoming Gevrey-Chambertin—although this does tend to confuse inexperienced buyers.

When buying Chambertin, make sure the label says simply Chambertin. If it says Gevrey-Chambertin, the wine is regional, could come from any vineyard in the commune, and will be a lesser wine (albeit lesser only in respect of its great neighbour). It hardly needs to be pointed out that a bottle of Chambertin should always carry the vintage year.

The vineyard lies on the gently sloping mid-section of the hill to the south of the village, next to the Route des Grands Crus (Route of the Great Growths), which leads to Morey-Saint-Denis. It directly adjoins the vineyard Clos de Bèze—the only other which has the right to produce wines to be called Chambertin. Since the Clos de Bèze is less well known—but no less outstanding—than its neighbour, this clause was inserted in the law. In practice, some of its wine is sold as Chambertin-Clos de Bèze and the rest simply as Chambertin. But Chambertin has no right to the name Clos de Bèze.

Together, the two vineyards comprise some 70 acres—32·5 as Chambertin and 37·5 as Clos de Bèze. Within this area are more than two dozen growers. Each one of these tends his own vines, harvests his own grapes, makes his own wines, and sells to whom he pleases and, for this reason, there is always a certain amount of variation between bottles. The scrupulous care of one grower contrasted with the more casual methods of another creates shades of difference even in wines from the same small vineyard and the same year. Yet there will also be a strong family resemblance between Chambertins from different growers in the same year, and between wines from Chambertin and from the Clos de Bèze. Some local experts maintain that the wines from the two vineyards are so similar that it is impossible to tell them apart.

At its finest, Chambertin is big and sturdy with a deep, strong colour—the colour or *robe* is one of the wine's most distinctive characteristics—and a pronounced, lingering, and glorious aftertaste. It is a wine with a tremendous 'nose' (for the wine-taster often transfers the perceptive organ to the wine itself). The nose is so outspoken that bouquet—the usual term—fades into insignificance beside it. In a well-made and distinctive Chambertin of a good year, all the characteristics are welded together into a balanced unity, and the wine improves with age, developing the wonderful austere masculinity which causes experts to exclaim 'Chambertin', and novices, 'Great wine!'

The quantity made is not great; yet it is perhaps greater than might be expected from the size of the vineyard, because of the amount of Clos de Bèze which assumes the name; but in 1958—an average year for quantity—only 6,361 imp. gallons (7,639 U.S.) were made. This is the equivalent of about 3,200 cases and obviously not enough to satisfy the clamorous demand for Chambertin all over the world.

Chambertin-Clos de Bèze

Burgundy red wine. District: Côte de Nuits, France. Commune: Gevrey-Chambertin. Official classification: Great Growth (Grand Cru).

In A.D. 630, Almagaire, Duke of Lower Burgundy, founded the Abbey of Bèze near Dijon, endowing it with near-by lands and fields from which to draw support. One such holding was a wooded lot of thirty-seven acres in what is today the commune of Gevrey-Chambertin, and the monks cleared the land, planted vines, and established the vineyard of Clos de Bèze. They tended it until the thirteenth century when it passed into the hands of another order: but the vineyard did not really become exceptional until the eighteenth century when a man named Jobert—secretary to the king's legal representative and reputedly a very clever business-man—took over both Chambertin and the Clos de Bèze and proceeded to make them famous. The vineyard was so good that its reputation lasted, and when the French wine authorities classified Burgundian vineyards in 1937, it was recognized as a

Great Growth (*Grand Cru*)—one of only thirty-one outstandingly great vineyards of Burgundy.

The Clos de Bèze stands just to the south of Gevrey-Chambertin, on the twisting, winding vineyard road. On the side away from the village, and adjoining it, is Chambertin, and the two vineyards are the commune's finest although there are others near them. Wines from both may legally be sold as Chambertin; and although the Clos de Bèze is considered slightly the superior of the two, many growers take advantage of this rule, feeling that the shorter and simpler name is the better known and the easier to sell.

The official name—that which will be found on bottle labels—is Chambertin-Clos de Bèze, and not very much is made in any year. The figure in an average year for quantity amounted to a little more than 8,870 gallons (10,650 U.S.) or the equivalent of about 4,400 cases, not including the amount sold as Chambertin. The characteristics of the two wines are virtually the same and are discussed under Chambertin (*q.v.*).

Chambéry

An old city of Savoy in France, famous for the extra dry vermouths produced there.

Chambolle-Musigny

Burgundy red and some white wine. District: Côte de Nuits, France. Commune: Chambolle.

The red wines are delicate, elegant, entrancingly perfumed, and have the fragile yet resolute charm of 'feminine' wines. The whites—made in very small quantities—share this same charm, but tend to lack some of the finesse of their great counterparts.

The wines have been famous for centuries and they succeeded for a long time in overshadowing those of neighbouring Morey-Saint-Denis, with which in fact they have little in common. Morey's wines tend to be big, hard, assertive—the reverse in every way of the Chambolles. Yet much of the production of Morey once went to market under Chambolle place-names until the laws of Appellation d'Origine outlawed the practice and established Morey as a place-name in its own right. One outstanding vineyard—Bonnes Mares—is shared by the two communes; but the wines tend to affiliate themselves with the Chambolle characteristics rather than with those of Morey.

Bonnes Mares and Musigny (*see* under individual headings), lying on opposite sides of the town, are Chambolle's greatest vineyards. Both are legally rated Great Growths (*Grands Crus*) and the wines are labelled only with the name of the vineyard, signifying outstanding excellence. Other superb wines are included among the First Growths (*Premiers Crus*)—wines that have stature and breeding but generally fall just below the topmost two, and this status is signified by labels bearing both communal and vineyard name. The best is Les Amoureuses, directly below the vineyard of Musigny and lying on the imaginary dividing line which separates Chambolle-Musigny and Vougeot. 'Women in Love' is the meaning of the name, and Burgundians consider it highly appropriate. The wines are slightly—but only slightly—less distinctive than those of Musigny, and in a good year and from an able wine-maker are delicate and feminine, with beguiling grace and a captivating, warming bouquet.

Nineteen other vineyards are considered in the same category as Les Amoureuses, and while their output seldom attains the same extraordinary quality, they too may often be perfectly made and beautiful wines. The wines which do not stem from one of these, or from other vineyards classified but not tested here (and do not otherwise meet the elevated minimum standards demanded for these ratings), are sold as Chambolle-Musigny and will have many of the same characteristics but not to the same sublime degree.

Chambolle-Musigny has 427 acres planted in fine vines and production in 1960—an average quantity year—was just over 117,000 gallons (140,500 U.S.), entirely red wine.

GREAT GROWTHS (*Grands Crus*)

Vineyard	*Acres*
Les Musigny	24·8
Les Bonnes Mares (*in part*)	33·9

(*see under individual headings*)

FIRST GROWTHS (*Premiers Crus*)

Vineyard	*Acres*
Les Amoureuses	13
Les Charmes	14·4
Les Cras	10·4
Les Borniques	3·6
Les Baudes	8·8
Les Plantes	6·3
Les Hauts-Doix	4·3
La Combe d'Orveau	12·5
Les Chatelots	6·3
Les Gruenchers	7·3

Vineyard	*Acres*
Les Groseilles	3·7
Les Fuées	15·3
Les Lavrottes	2·5
Derrière-la-Grange	1·8
Les Noirots	7·1
Les Sentiers	12·2
Les Fousselottes	10
Aux Beaux-Bruns	6
Les Combettes	1·6
Aux Combottes	5·6

Chambrer

French term for bringing a red wine slowly to the temperature of a room (*chambre*), the best temperature for most red wines. Warming the wine by plunging the bottle in hot water or putting it before a fire is not to be recommended: such sudden shocks are apt to change the chemical equilibrium of a wine with the result that its excellence is impaired or destroyed. A too-cold wine can be warmed by the heat of the hands on the glass, but one that has been heated too quickly is ruined.

Champagne

Principally white sparkling wines; some still white wine and a small quantity of red and rosé. District: North-East France.

The deliciously sparkling wines of Champagne are the most famous in the world. There are indeed some people who feel that Champagne should be reserved for launching ships and debutantes, and others who would like to drink it with meals, before meals, after meals, in the middle of the morning, or in the middle of the night. But most of them experience a thrill of pleasure as the cork slowly pops out of the bottle, the whiff of smoke curls up into the air, and the pale-gold wine foams into the tall glasses. Champagne is unique—a fact which, outside France, is too often ignored.

The only wine with any right to the name Champagne is that made from certain legally specified grapes grown in limited and well-defined sections of the province of France called Champagne, vines tended and vinified according to a body of strict local rules. It is partly soil, partly climate, partly vines, and partly labour and tradition which make Champagne what it is. Sparkling wines produced in other parts of the world may be good, but none will ever be Champagne—although some of them masquerade under the name. What is not universally known is that several wines of Champagne are not sparkling. Still wines are also made in the province, but they do not travel well and are little known abroad. The French Government forbids the export of the still wines, selling at a cheaper price than the sparkling, thus achieving greater foreign exchange revenue.

The fertile region of Champagne, some ninety miles to the east and slightly to the north of Paris, is a vast chalky plain, carefully cultivated, broken only now and again by an occasional river and dominated by the Mountain of Reims. Between the city of Épernay, on the Marne, and Reims on the Vesle, a deformed hunch rises from the sturdy back of Champagne; an outcropping of chalk which, when viewed from above, resembles a huge question-mark superimposed on the plain. This Mountain of Reims could only be a mountain in a flat country since its average height is 600 feet, with a maximum of about 900 feet in a few places. The stem of the question-mark extends beyond Reims, moving north to the section known as the Petite Montagne—the 'little Mountain'—and the arc curls round towards Épernay to the south, terminating in the section known as the Côte de Bouzy, after the principal town. At Épernay, the region of the great growths splits, one part following the Marne towards Château-Thierry, and the other heading due south, to form the famous Côte des Blancs where the Pinot Noir gives way to the white-grape Chardonnay vines. These sections are not all of Champagne, but they are the best. All are in the department of the Marne, but the limits of Champagne extend slightly beyond these borders. Four-fifths of Champagne comes from the Marne, the rest from the adjoining departments of Aube, Aisne, and Seine-et-Marne.

From these three lesser departments flow many of the cheap Champagnes which are sold throughout the world.

History

The vines in Champagne are among the oldest in Europe; there is adequate fossil evidence that vines were there during the Tertiary era, which geologists set at from 1 to 60 million years ago. The use of the vine for the making of wine may have been established before the Romans, although there are no records, but the Romans increased the planting of the vine throughout Champagne, as they did throughout France. The wines were originally still, however, and provided strong competition for Burgundy. A bitter rivalry broke out between these two districts, eventually coming to a head over the question: which is better for the health? The point was finally decided when the court physicians of Louis XIV cast their votes in favour of Burgundy.

Sparkling wines did not make any headway in

Champagne until the seventeenth century, when, it is said, the discoveries of a Benedictine monk, Dom Pérignon, drastically changed the methods of wine-making. Sparkling wines have certainly been known over the centuries. All the growers of the world must have noticed that certain wines refermented in the spring and, if enclosed, became sparkling, usually breaking the container in which they were kept. Such wines were often referred to as *saute bouchon* (cork popper) or as *vin diable* (devil wine). Dom Pérignon (or some of his contemporaries) realized that the pressure built up was due to carbon dioxide, and recommended that stronger bottles be used. Until this time, stoppers had been made not usually of cork, but of cotton wadding soaked in oil. Now, they began to make thicker ones and tied them down with a string. Dom Pérignon is also credited with being one of the pioneers in blending the wines of Champagne—most of which need the additional qualities which only blending can give. He was cellar-master at the Benedictine Abbey of Hautvillers for forty-seven years until his death in 1715, and his name is still honoured in Champagne. Once each year there is a wine festival in Hautvillers celebrating the achievements attributed to him.

Classification and Rating

The small towns of Champagne, and the vineyards lying within them, are classified according to a complicated percentage scale, and the rating given the town will determine the price for the grapes in any given year. Each autumn, the growers meet with the shippers who will be buying their harvests and haggle over the prices to be paid. Seldom do the growers in Champagne vinify their own grapes, and price must be decided in advance: once the harvest is started, there can be no delay if the grapes are not to suffer. The price decided upon is for the very best growths, officially rated at 100%; that for the produce of other places will be proportionate to the town's percentage rating. In lesser districts, premiums may also be paid for certain types of grapes, to encourage the growers, to plant the vines which give better fruit but less of it. In 1966, for the first time a premium of 0·20 francs was paid for each kilo of white Chardonnay grapes whether or not they came from the Côte des Blancs, which shows the increasing demand for lighter Champagne.

The Mountain of Reims boasts five growths rated at 100%: Beaumont-sur-Vesle, Mailly, Sillery (at one time the most renowned wine-name in England), Puisieulx, and Verzenay. Moving south towards the Marne Valley, off the Mountain and into the Côte de Bouzy, the best growths are Ambonnay, Ay-Champagne, Bouzy, Louvois, and Tours-sur-Marne, and on the Côte des Blancs are Avize and Cramant. In towns where there are both red and white grapes grown, the percentage will be different for each, and except in the Côte des Blancs, the higher rating nearly always goes to the red, plants giving white grapes being more or less curiosities in other sections.

Growths (Crus)

ARRONDISSEMENT DE REIMS

Canton d'Ay		%
Ambonnay		100
Avenay		93
Ay-Champagne		100
Bisseuil		90
Bouzy		100
Champillon		93
Cormoyeux		83
Cumières		90
Dizy		95
Hautvillers		90
Louvois		100
Mareuil-sur-Ay		98
Mutigny		93
Romery		83
Tauxières		99
Tours-sur-Marne red		100
Tours-sur-Marne white		90
Canton de Beine		
Nogent-l'Abbesse		85
Cernay-les-Reims		85
Canton de Bourgogne		
Cauroy		81
Cormicy		81
Merfy		82
Pouillon		82
Saint-Thierry—basses vignes		87
Thil		82
Villers-Franqueux		82
Canton de Reims		
Reims (lot Brisset)		88
Trois-Puits		94
Canton de Verzy		
Beaumont-sur-Vesle		100
Chamery		88
Chigny-les-Roses	red	94
	white	86
Ludes	red	94
	white	86
Mailly	red	100
	white	86
Montbré		94

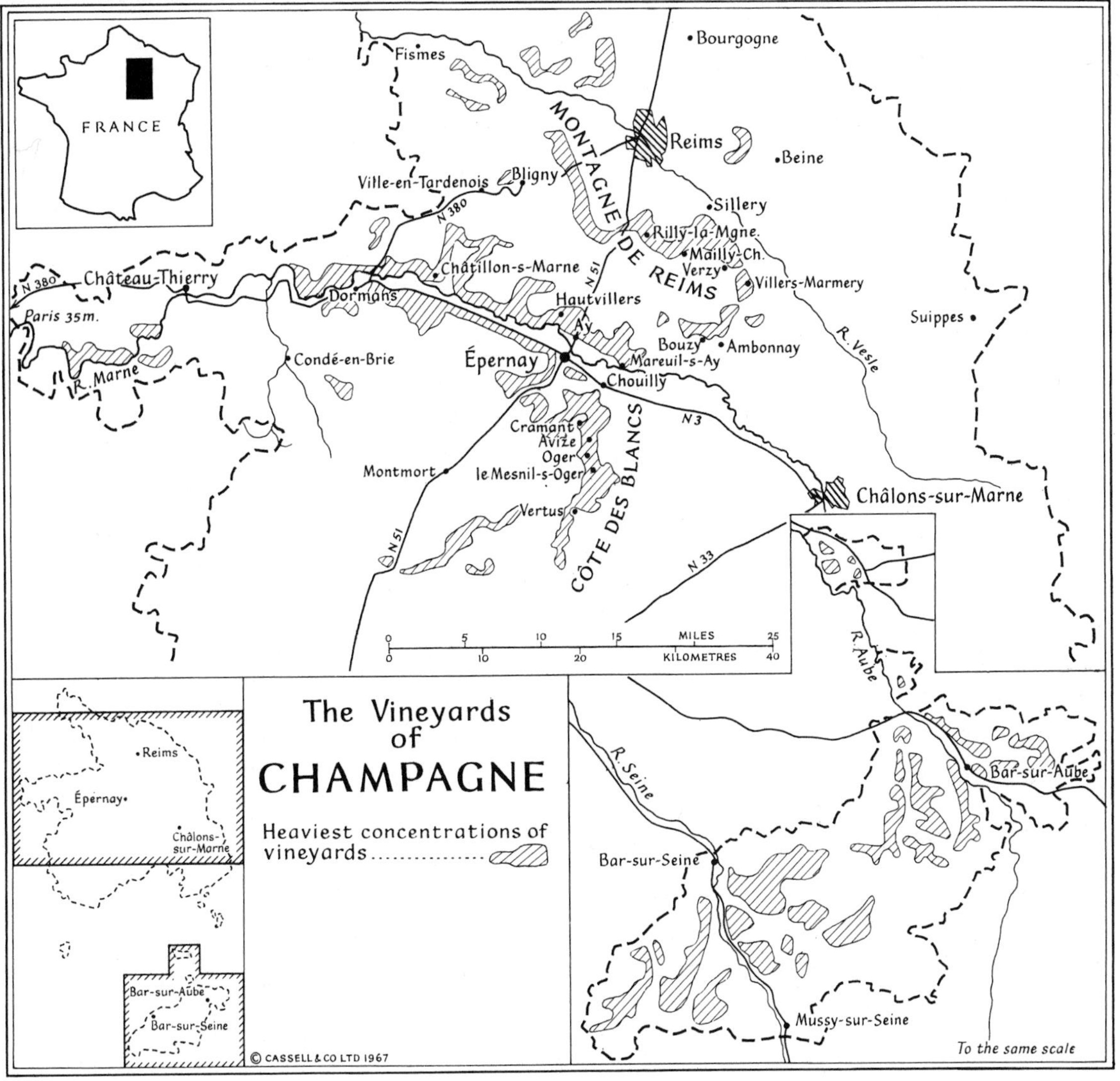

Growths (Crus)		
Puisieulx		100
Rilly-la-Montagne		94
Sermiers		88
Sillery		100
Trépail		90
Verzenay	red	100
	white	86
Verzy	red	99
	white	86
Villers-Allerand		90
Villers-Marmery		90

Canton de Châtillon-sur-Marne

Baslieux	81
Belval-sous-Châtillon	81
Binson-Orquigny	83
Champlat-Boujacourt	81

Growths (Crus)	
Châtillon-sur-Marne	82
Cuchery	81
Cuisles	82
Jonquery	82
Montigny-sous-Châtillon	83
La Neuville-aux-Larris	81
Olizy-Violaine	82
Passy-Grigny	82
Pourcy	82
Reuil	83
Sainte-Gemme	82
Vandières	82
Villers-sous-Châtillon	83

Canton de Fismes

Chenay	82
Crugny	86

Growths (Crus)		
Hermonville		82
Hourges		86
Pévy		81
Prouilly		82
Trigny		82
Unchair		86
Vandeuil		86
Canton de Ville-en-Tardenois		
Bligny		81
Bouilly		86
Branscourt		86
Brouillet		86
Chaumuzy		81
Coulommes-la-Montagne		89
Courmas		87
Écueil		90
Faverolles		86
Germigny		85
Gueux		85
Janvry		85
Jouy		89
Lagery		86
Les Mesneux		90
Marfaux		82
Pargny		89
Poilly		81
Rosnay		81
Sacy		90
Sainte-Euphraise		86
Sarcy		81
Savigny-sur-Ardres		86
Serzy-et-Prin		86
Tramery	red	86
	white	86
Treslon		86
Villedommange		90
Ville-en-Tardenois		79
Vrigny		89

ARRONDISSEMENT D'ÉPERNAY

Canton d'Avize		
Avize		100
Brugny-Vaudancourt		86
Chavot-Courcourt	red	87
	white	88
Cramant		100
Cuis	red	90
	white	93
Grauves	red	90
	white	93
Le Mesnil-sur-Oger		99
Mancy	red	86
	white	88
Monthelon		88
Morangis		84
Oger		99
Oiry		99

Growths (Crus)		
Canton de Dormans		
Boursault		80
Champvoisy		82
Comblizy		81
Courthiézy		81
Dormans (Try, Vassy, Vassieux, Chavenay)		81
Festigny		81
Le Breuil		81
Leuvrigny		82
Mareuil-le-Port		82
Le Mesnil-le-Hutier		82
Nesle-le-Repons		81
Œuilly		81
Soilly		81
Troissy-Bouquigny		81
Verneuil		82
Vincelles		83
Canton d'Épernay		
Chouilly	red	90
	white	93
Damery	red	85
	white	86
Épernay		88
Fleury-la-Rivière	red	83
	white	83
Mardeuil		82
Moussy		88
Pierry		90
Saint-Martin-d'Ablois		86
Vauciennes		81
Venteuil		85
Vinay		86
Canton de Montmort		
Baye		85
Beaunay		85
Broyes		85
Cogny		85
Coizard-Joches		85
Courjeonnet		85
Étoges		85
Fèrebrianges		85
Oyes		85
Talus-Saint-Prix		85
Villevenard		85

ARRONDISSEMENT DE CHÂLONS

Canton de Vertus		
Bergères-les-Vertus	red	90
	white	93
Vertus		93
Givry-les-Loisy		85
Loisy-en-Brie		85
Vert-la-Gravelle		85
Coligny		85
Soulières		85

Growths (Crus)	
Toulon-la-Montagne	85
Villeneuve-Renneville	93
Canton de Suippes	
Billy-le-Grand	90
Vaudemanges	90
Marne (crus non côtés)	75

ARRONDISSEMENT DE CHÂTEAU THIERRY

Canton de Condé-en-Brie	
Barzy-sur-Marne	82
Passy-sur-Marne	82
Treloup-Chassins	82
Baulne-en-Brie	81
Aisne (less the communes of the Canton de Condé-en-Brie listed above)	75
Canton de l'Aube	
Les Riceys	73
Neuville-sur-Seine	73
Buxeuil	73
Gye-sur-Seine	73
Courteron	73
Balnot-sur-Laignes	73
Polisy	73
Montgueux	73
Other Growths of Aube	70

Most of the sparkling wines of Champagne are made from a blend of red and white grapes. Some are Blancs de Noirs, or white wines made from black grapes; and a few are Blancs de Blancs, or white wines made from white grapes—the latter are almost entirely confined to the Côte des Blancs south of Épernay. (Most Champagnes do not carry any designations, although it is fairly common practice to use them on labels for still Vin Nature de la Champagne.) Some Champagne makers say that white grapes tend to improve the final blend. The present vogue is towards the Blancs de Blancs. Thus whether for blending with red grapes or not, the increased demand for Chardonnay has made them more expensive than the Pinot Noirs. A certain small amount of pink, or rosé, Champagne is also made, as well as various still wines known correctly as Vin Nature de la Champagne, or commonly as Champagne Nature, Bouzy Rouge, and Rosé de Riceys. But the name Champagne, with no other qualification, always refers to the sparkling variety.

The total area of Champagne planted in fine vines amounts to about 36,750 acres. Of this 22,180 are in the Marne, 3,470 in the department of Aube, 1,160 in Aisne, and only seventeen in Seine-et-Marne. Rather more than half a century ago, the area planted came to about 40,000 acres, but the rapacity of the vine-louse phylloxera, which arrived in Champagne about 1890, and the ravages of the First World War (throughout the war, from 1914 until 1918, the countryside was cut up with trenches) combined to decrease the vineyard area. However, each year over 8 million imp. gallons (10 million U.S.) of wine are taken to the cellars to be made sparkling. The amount of still wine varies considerably. No matter how abundant the crop, the grapes for sparkling wine cannot be harvested in excess of about $1\frac{3}{4}$ tons (2 short tons) per acre, and everything else must be vinified into Vin Nature de la Champagne. In some years there may be as little as 83,000 imp. gallons (100,000 U.S.) and in others as much as 1,665,000 imp. gallons (2 million U.S.). The still Bouzy Rouge (red Bouzy) hardly ever exceeds 20,000 imp. gallons (24,000 U.S.); and Rosé de Riceys is made virtually every year but in negligible amounts.

Almost all Champagne is made sparkling in the cellars of the big shipping firms, most of which are in Reims and Épernay. Deep below the cities, the chalk subsoil has been cut out into vast caves and cellars. One firm has eleven miles of underground cellars so deep that the visitor must descend 116 steps to reach them. Most of these cellars are laid out in broad alleyways, named after the principal cities of the world where Champagne is sold. Statues carved into the chalk walls give them a certain resemblance to art galleries. These cellars were used during the war as underground shelters, but they provide a better home for wine than for refugees. Holding their temperature of about 40°F. (4°C.) the year round, they are fresh and clean and require no attention to keep them fit for the storage of wine.

Épernay and Reims, in whose splendid cathedral the kings of France were once crowned, are the two main headquarters for the shipping firms, many of which maintain offices in both. Some of the more important firms with their main headquarters in Reims are: Veuve Clicquot-Ponsardin, Heidsieck Monopole, Charles Heidsieck, Mumm, Piper-Heidsieck, Pommery and Greno, Louis Rœderer, and Taittinger. Those which have their main offices in Épernay include Mercier, Moët et Chandon, Perrier-Jouet, Castellane, and Pol Roger. In addition to these, there are a few firms in the small city of Ay overlooking the Marne, among them Ayala, Besserat de Bellefon, and Bollinger.

Climate, Soil, and Vines

The vineyards of Champagne are the farthest north of any producing French wines of Appellation Contrôlée. When a vineyard is so critically close to the northern limit, every care must be taken to protect the vine from the unfavourable climatic conditions not only because of the natural hazards which afflict it, but also because a plant's vitality is lowered in its struggle for existence and it is less fitted than vines grown in more favourable climates to combat the dangers of frost and disease. Yet it is this northerly climate which is responsible for the exquisite delicacy of Champagnes. The situation and exposure of the vineyards is important, and most of the vines look to the south and south-east. The exceptions are those of the Côte des Blancs, which look east, and of the town of Verzenay (rated 100%) which actually faces to the north. Southern exposure means that the hills will provide a shield against harsh winter winds and the vines will get the full benefit of the summer sun. The frosts and cold waves of the winter have a tendency to settle in the valleys and depressions and therefore the vines are mostly planted along the mid-section of the hills where they are relatively unaffected, although disastrous frosts are not unknown. Humidity is not excessive, and this factor is important since most fungus diseases which attack vines thrive on moisture. The important Chardonnay vine is also very subject to the *pourriture grise*, a type of rot which is at its worst in humid climates.

Climate is only one factor which contributes to making Champagne what it is. Another is the exceptional soil from which the vines draw their nourishment and whose qualities are reflected in the grapes and in the wines. Chalk is the major element, but there are others. Silicon and clay give the soil a workable consistency and various trace elements add to the mixture. Most of the chalk in Champagne is Kimmeridge clay and is the same formation found in the soil of Chablis (*q.v.*) and in the village of Kimmeridge in southern England where it was first studied and identified. The coarse-grained composition of this soil throws off excess moisture, but holds at the same time enough to nourish the vine. The white pebbles absorb the heat of the sunshine, reflecting and radiating it evenly on to the ripening fruit and holding it well after the sun has disappeared below the horizon. Without this extra source of heat, the grapes, in some years, would never ripen at all.

The vines which may be planted in Champagne are closely controlled, and the Pinot Noir predominates, a vine which gives red grapes for the making of the wines of purest gold. Pinot Noir is far and away the major vine, but Pinot Meunier and Chardonnay (sometimes called Pinot Chardonnay, although modern research has established that it is not a member of the Pinot family) are important; and a very little of Meslier and Arbanne is also planted. In the department of Aube there were still some plantations of Gamay after the war and the result was not particularly happy. Originally, all the Gamay vines were to have been rooted out by 1942, but because of the war the date was postponed until 1962. The firms which buy the grapes generally pay a slight premium over the fixed price to any grower who brings in grapes from the permissible vines, but not for Gamay, which, latterly, has gone only into the cheapest Champagnes.

The vines are generally planted in rows some three feet apart, the plants about thirty inches from each other and trained along wires which run the length of the rows. There are generally two or three rows of wires along which the vine tendrils grow, bending their bunches of fruit towards the ground. Pruning is controlled by law and the only permissible methods are Chablis, Royat Cordon, Guyot, and Gobelet—all measures to ensure that the vines will give a moderate production of high quality grapes year after year.

The grapes are usually small and quite acid. The comparatively cold climate of Champagne matures them slowly and in some years incompletely. Acidity drops as the summer wears on and the sugar content rises, but never gets so high as it does in warmer regions. Yet in some years these acid-high grapes are capable of producing 12% of alcohol; in exceptionally hot years the wine-maker may even be forced to add acid; and in most years the grapes are vinified into a delicate sparkling wine with the sublest combinations of colour, aroma, and taste.

Champagnes, like all great wines, are dependent upon the weather, and like all great wines they will, in some years, be superb. Some of the better years for Champagne have been: *1928*, 1929, 1934, 1937, 1945, *1947*, 1949, *1952*, *1953*, 1955, *1959*, 1961, 1962, *1964* and *1966* (greatest years in italics).

Wine-making in Champagne

As is the case with any wine, the making of Champagne begins in the vineyards at the harvest. In ancient times, the date of the harvest was set by law and anyone who started too early was brought before the regional officials for punishment. The Ban de Vendange, the official proclamation, still exists, although now as a formality rather than a legal requirement. The deciding factor today is the grape, which must be ripe but not overripe. Harvests are fairly late in the autumn, usually beginning during the second and third weeks in October; the minimum amount of sugar in the grapes and the minimum alcoholic content to be formed by this sugar in fermentation are decided each year by the Comité Interprofessionel du Vin de Champagne (Interprofessional Committee for the Wine of Champagne)—the semi-official body in Épernay which governs all Champagne activity, including promotion.

When the harvest starts, the women and children go out into the vineyards, their heads protected by characteristic faded blue sun-bonnets, and cut the heavy, ripe bunches of grapes. The younger men patrol the rows with cone-shaped baskets on their backs and carry the grapes to the ends of the rows where they are inspected, the overripe or defective ones discarded and the others placed in *caques* or *mannequins*, deep wide baskets holding about 150 to 175 pounds of grapes. The baskets are loaded on to carts and are then taken to the *vendangeoir*, or press-house.

Only in a few isolated cases does the grower in Champagne vinify his own grapes—they are nearly always sold to one of the shipping firms, sometimes before the harvest has started, and the firm makes the wine and carries it through the extensive series of operations which will result in Champagne. Most of these shipping firms have their own holdings in the vineyards to ensure at least a part of each year's harvest, and an estimated 5,000 to 6,000 of the 36,750 acres are owned by them. They maintain *vendangeoirs* in all the important towns and the grapes are pressed on the spot. Here and there, however, co-operative cellars can be found where the growers themselves make the wine. Such is the case in the 100%-rated town of Mailly. During the depression, the big wine firms refused to buy grapes from the Mailly growers, who banded together and built a co-operative, in their spare time, starting with no capital, and doing all the work themselves after they had finished in the fields. Today, the co-operative has some seventy members; it makes both pink and white vintage Champagnes and ships them all over the world.

Throughout the harvest, the roads are packed with the laden carts on their way to the press-houses, and pressing starts as soon as they arrive. Most of the grapes in Champagne are red, and if the juice is left in contact with the colour-imparting skins, an undesirable tinge may discolour the wines. This can be removed by passing the juice through charcoal, but the wine-makers prefer to press their grapes immediately, before the colour has had time to form. Pink (or rosé) Champagne is sometimes made by adding some red wine to the white, a practice held in the lowest esteem except in Champagne alone where the results seem to justify the practice. However, the usual way is by short-vatting red grapes, ensuring only a small amount of coloration. Either way, Champagne makers consider the pink variety something of an oddity and not in the same class as the rest.

The oak presses are round and wide and built close to the ground with a trough around them to collect the juice as it runs out. The size and shape of the presses are such that they take exactly four tons of grapes, evenly distributed in a thin layer. The first pressings, called first, second, and third *serre*, give the high quality wine and the last, or *rebêche*, produces common wine to be given to the workers. The first *serre* gives the top quality wine, the *vin de cuvée* amounting to 2,000 litres or 440 imp. gallons (528 U.S.) or the equivalent of ten *pièces*, or barrels. The second gives from one and a half to two barrels of wine, called *première taille*, and the third, another one and a half of *deuxième taille*, both of which go into the secondary wine of the makers. Between each *serre* the mass of grapes is spaded over with wooden spades (in none of the fine-wine districts does metal ever touch the grapes) to ensure that the pressure, which is greatest in the middle of the press, is equally applied to all the grapes. Before the marc, or pomace, is pressed for the *rebêche*, it is moistened slightly and again spaded over.

The wine which flows from the presses usually goes into huge vats and then into barrels, to be sent to the cellars of the firms in Ay, Épernay, and Reims. The pressing takes place in the vineyards, but everything else is done by the firms, and the newly extracted juice is usually given a light dose of sulphur to stop fermentation from starting before the wine-maker is prepared for it. Once in the cellars, it is tested to determine its consistency. In many years, in Champagne, sugar must be added, a practice known as *chaptalisation*, which is widespread in Burgundy and is even found in a very few vintage years as far south as Bordeaux. The aim in Champagne is to make a wine which will have from 10% to 12% of alcohol and a moderate acidity. Depending upon the year, the wine-maker may add sugar, or he may de-acidify his must, or unfermented grape juice. Sometimes citric or tartaric acid has to be added. Apart from sugar, which is added fairly frequently, these measures are exceptional and undesirable except in difficult years.

After the additions are made, the wine begins to ferment. For eight to ten days, it boils ferociously in the barrels, sounding like a hive of angry bees. After this preliminary action, it calms down considerably and for another ten to twenty days bubbles serenely and quietly. During this fermentation, the sugar is converted by the action of yeasts into alcohol and carbon dioxide gas, and the gas is allowed to pass off into the air through the bung-hole of the barrel. When the fermentation is finished, the wine is allowed to rest and clarify.

In the December after the harvest, the wine will have settled and all the grape particles left from the pressing as well as the spent yeasts will have fallen to the bottom of the barrel. The wine is ready for its first racking, in which it is carefully drawn off from the barrels and the lees, or impurities, are left behind. After the first racking, the *assemblage* of wines from different vineyards, which have fermented separately in the same cellar, takes place. This is the blending of wines from a single town, and when it is done, all those from Ay or from Sillery or Verzenay will be uniform and consistent throughout. After a second racking at the end of January and a third just before the wine is bottled, the wines are ready for the second fermentation which will make them full-blown Champagnes. Those which are to remain non-sparkling undergo the racking, but their development stops there and they are sold as Vin Nature de la Champagne.

The Champagne Process

The Champagne process is the name for the traditional method of making a wine sparkle by allowing it to ferment a second time in the bottle. The preparations for it usually start after the second or January racking when the *coupage* or blending is done. Some firms specialize in *vins de cru*, or wines which come from one town only, but most Champagnes are blends. The wines from a single town are almost certain to be from one of the Côte des Blancs, usually Cramant or Avize. Most of the rest are blended, and the top quality wine of any firm is referred to as the *vin de cuvée*. Sometimes only wines from 100%-rated towns are used and may be sold as Champagne Grand Cru.

The delicate blending process starts with samples being taken from the various barrels of wine in the firm's cellars. These samples are taken up to special tasting rooms—spotlessly clean, airy, and hygienic, free from any extraneous odours or anything which might divert the taster's attention from the wine. These measures are of great importance, since the man is working with raw wines and he must be able to detect any flaws or possible impurities before they develop. The desired result is a Champagne which will resemble the product the firm has put out in the past. When the proportions have been decided, the chosen wines are blended together and the lesser ones kept aside to be bottled under another label as the second quality of the firm.

After the wine has been made and racked and blended, it is ready to be bottled and to undergo the secondary fermentation which will impart the sparkle. Bottling usually starts about April and lasts until July. The first step is the addition of the *liqueur de tirage*, usually a solution of cane sugar dissolved in wine, very occasionally with a little citric acid added. (The acid speeds up the splitting of cane sugar into the fermentable grape sugars.) The amount of sugar added is usually calculated at twenty to twenty-six grammes per litre of wine to be treated (equivalent to about one and a half pounds for each ten gallons). Sometimes less liqueur is added, and the result is a Champagne which is *crémant*, or only lightly sparkling. The word *crémant* (literally 'creaming') should not be confused with the town of Cramant, one of the leading or 100%-rated towns of the Côte des Blancs.

The sugar added as *liqueur de tirage* ferments to make the wines sparkling. It ferments under the action of yeasts which may already be present in the wine or which may be added from special strains. The fermentation is the exact replica of the first, forming alcohol (the alcoholic content of the wine will be raised by about 1%) and carbon dioxide gas. This time, however, the wine is not lying free in an open barrel, but is confined in a stout bottle and capped with an extra heavy cork wired in place.

As the sap begins to rise in the vines in the spring, the wine mysteriously starts its second fermentation, as though there were some mystic bond between the two. The cellars are cool and prevent temperature from speeding the action of the yeasts, since experience has shown that a better wine will result if the fermentation is allowed to proceed slowly. The bottled wine is laid in great stacks in the cellars, and every six months or so the stacks are moved and the bottles are given a hearty shake to free any sediment which may have formed. Marks painted on the bottoms of the bottles indicate which way they were lying, and they are always put back in the same position. As they are restacked, those which were in the middle of the pile are placed on the outside and vice versa, since the warmth generated in the middle will be greater than at the sides.

As fermentation continues, the carbon dioxide generated builds up pressure. Eventually, this pressure will amount to some five to six times that of the atmosphere and it is for this reason that the bottles and corks are of such heavy construction. Occasionally during this process a bottle will break, because the mounting pressure exceeds it in strength, and each time the bottles are moved from place to place these broken ones must be abstracted. The fermentation itself will only take about three months, but the wines are left in these cellars for a period of years to 'ripen', during which time the bottles are shaken occasionally to keep the sediment from forming permanently. At the end of this ripening period, the wines are ready for the *remuage* and *dégorgement*, the long series of operations which will remove the sediment from the bottle.

Remuage means 'shaking', and bottles of Champagne must be shaken in a particular manner. The first step is the gradual *mise sur pointe*, turning them upside down. This is done in special racks or *pupitres*—hinged, sloping boards, much like an artist's easel. Holes are cut on both sides of the *pupitre* in such a way that they will hold a bottle firmly when it is inserted neck first in any position between the horizontal and the vertical. The bottles are put in at a very slight angle—usually about thirty degrees—and over a period of time are slowly changed until they are literally upside down. Each day a trained man, a *remueur*, goes through and carefully shakes each bottle, putting it back at a slightly more elevated angle, and turning it about a quarter turn each time. This slightly shakes the sediment, and slowly, as the bottle is raised, it slides down to the neck, where it rests against the cork. The *remueur* is a highly expert man, one who works at top speed, using both hands; and he is capable of turning 32,000 bottles a day. To ensure that the bottles are absolutely sound, he is given a bonus for any defective ones he finds. When he has finished, the bottles are standing on their heads in the racks, the sediment is next to the cork and the wine is ready for the next step—the *dégorgement* which will shoot out the sediment.

Dégorgement is another ticklish procedure, particularly if it is done in the old, traditional manner. The bottles are taken, the cork slowly prised off, and the sediment is allowed to shoot out, propelled by the pressure in the bottle. The trick is to lose as little wine as possible but not to leave any sediment. The high degree of skill and practice necessary for this job has been modified by the more modern method of freezing the necks of the bottles. The sediment and a small amount of the wine become frozen, and again the pressure that has been built up shoots it out in a solid lump. The wine is then brought back to its original level with a little of the same wine from another bottle and is ready for *dosage* and the final cork.

The *dosage* of a Champagne depends on the potential clientèle. Sophisticated customers usually prefer their Champagne *brut*—that is, as dry as possible, except when it is to be served with sweets or fruit when a Champagne of one of the varying degrees of sweetness should be chosen. The wine is sweetened by the addition of sugar. Generally only the best quality wines are used for *brut* Champagne since any defects, which in the others will be masked by the added sugar, will here be apparent.

The sweetening is referred to as *liqueur d'expédition* and consists of a small amount of sugar mixed up with a little of the same Champagne to be dosed, and a little brandy. The amounts generally added are:

French Name	*Percentage*	*English Name*
Brut	0 to 1½	Brut
Extra-sec	1 to 2	Extra Dry
Sec	2 to 4	Dry
Demi-Sec	4 to 6	Semi-dry
Doux	8 to 10	Sweet

After the *liqueur d'expédition*, the bottles are ready for their final corking. Although the cork changes, the wine remains in the same bottle throughout its development, except where it is to be transferred into larger bottles. Champagne is always re-fermented in the regular Champagne bottle of twenty-six ounces, in magnums of fifty-two ounces, or in half-bottles of thirteen ounces. As 2% to 3% of the bottles break each year, it is too risky to use the larger sizes, into which the wine is poured only at the time of *dégorgement*. The corks, however, change. The best come from Spain or Portugal, from special cork trees from twelve to fifteen years old. However, many firms are now using plastic corks until the final bottling and some Champagnes are retailed with plastic stoppers.

All corks used finally, according to French law, must have the word 'Champagne' printed on them. If the word does not appear, the wine is not Champagne. These corks are soaked in water to soften them and are driven into bottles which are then returned to the cellars for another period of checking and ageing. Watched fairly closely, to ensure that the *liqueur d'expédition* has mixed well into the wine, and to see that no unwanted third fermentation will start, they remain there sometimes for as much as two years. In total, the finer Champagnes may be six to seven years developing before they are ready for the consumer, and a bottle may be handled from 150 to 200 times before it leaves the cellar.

Champagne Bottle Sizes

Champagne is sold in bottles of varying sizes; the traditional ones are:

Name	*Size*
Split	Half-pint
Pint	$\frac{1}{10}$ gallon
Quart	$\frac{1}{5}$ gallon
Magnum	2 quarts
Jeroboam	4 quarts
Rehoboam	6 quarts
Methuselah (Methusalem)	8 quarts
Salmanasar	12 quarts
Balthazar	16 quarts
Nebuchadnezzar	20 quarts

See APPENDIX B.

Serving Champagne

It is usually considered that Champagne is at its best served chilled—not iced. The makers generally take a slightly more tolerant view about opening the bottle than do some drinkers, suggesting that the cork should come out in your hand rather than being encouraged to career across the room to the accompaniment of popping noises and spilled Champagne. Letting the cork come out too fast, they say, allows too much pressure to escape, and with it some of the bubbles which have been so carefully developed over the years. Swirling Champagne with swizzle sticks has the same effect. That and dropping ice cubes into the wine are looked upon with horror by connoisseurs.

Some Champagne growers also suggest that tall flute-shaped glasses be used rather than the wide shallow ones; an eight-ounce tulip-shaped glass is even better. The bubbles disappear too quickly in the open-bowled glasses; and it is the bubbles which make Champagne. As the columnist, Art Buchwald, put it: 'I like Champagne, because it always tastes as though my foot's asleep.'

Chantepleure

In Anjou, a *pipette* or tube for removing wine from cask or other bulk container.

Chapeau

A 'hat' or thick layer of solids consisting of pulp and skins, which forms on the must in the vats during fermentation.

See CHAPTER NINE, p. 42.

Chapelle-Chambertin

Burgundy red wine. District: Côte de Nuits, France. Commune: Gevrey-Chambertin. Official Classification: Great Growth (Grand Cru).

Chapelle is one of the more delicate of the wines of this northerly commune of the Côte de Nuits. Generally, the wines of Gevrey are full-bodied and robust, assertive and strictly masculine; and while those from Chapelle share these qualities, they have a lightness, a fruitiness sometimes, and a certain finesse which tends to set them apart.

All of the nine vineyards which make up the family of Chambertin are clustered around the nucleus of Le Chambertin and Chambertin-Clos de Bèze, and either adjoin or are visible from the little road which runs through the vineyard joining Gevrey and Morey-Saint-Denis. Leaving Gevrey by this road, Chapelle is the first of the important vineyards on the left, though there is little chance that the newcomer will notice it unless a local inhabitant points it out. Throughout these renowned wine communes there is little to distinguish one great vineyard from another, the significant differences becoming apparent only in the wines themselves.

The vineyard of Chapelle has been rated as Great Growth (*Grand Cru*) and covers some 13·3 acres. The amount of wine made by the several growers who own sections of it came to 2,900 imp. gallons (3,500 U.S.) in 1958, an average year for quantity. This is the equivalent of about 1,400 cases.

Chaptalisation

The addition of sugar to the fermenting wine must, in order to build up the alcoholic content.

See CHAPTER NINE, p. 47.

Chardonnay

Excellent white grape grown, notably, in Burgundy. It resembles the Pinot Noir but is not a true Pinot, although in the past it was supposed to be a white variant of that grape and therefore is sometimes called Pinot Chardonnay. Other local names include Arnoison, Aubaine, Beaunois, Melon blanc. It yields rich, well-balanced wine with a distinctive aroma and a superb, lingering aftertaste.

Charente Wines

Principally, the light, thin, tart white wines which are distilled into Cognac brandy, although this district does also produce some red wine (from which Cognac is never made) and some white wine which is not made into Cognac.

See COGNAC.

Charlemagne

Burgundy white wine. District: Côte de Beaune. Commune: Aloxe-Corton. Official Classification: Great Growth (Grand Cru).

The vineyard area is about eighty-eight acres, and the white wines are excellent, but the name Charlemagne is rarely used alone, since growers are entitled to the preferred Corton-Charlemagne. The Emperor Charlemagne once owned the vineyards that bear his name and which he afterwards gave to the Church, in the person of the Abbot of Saulieu. In the sixteenth century the lands were leased to an innkeeper of Beaune, appropriately named Charles; by the seventeenth century the holdings had been carved up, and some of them became the property of the Hospices de Beaune.

Charmat

In 1910 the French wine-scientist, Eugene Charmat, developed a process for making sparkling wines in bulk which is still, with modifications, used today.

The original Charmat process required four tanks—three for wine and the other for yeasts. Still wine is run into the first tank and artificially aged by being heated for twelve to sixteen hours, then cooled. Pumped into the next tank, it has yeast and sugar added and ferments for ten to fifteen days; then it is pumped into the third tank, where it is clarified by refrigeration; and finally it is filtered and sent to the bottling machine. The entire process is interconnected and the wine never loses the pressure built up during fermentation.

Although no replacement for the Champagne process of second fermentation in the bottle, the Charmat system allows the wine-maker to produce a continuous flow of sparkling wine of sound but uninspiring quality.

Charmes-Chambertin

Burgundy red wine. District: Côte de Nuits, France. Commune: Gevrey-Chambertin. Official Classification: Great Growth (Grand Cru).

Charmes-Chambertin and Mazoyères-Chambertin form a partnership with Mazoyères—the silent senior partner. The ruling is that wine from either Charmes or Mazoyères may be sold as Charmes but that Charmes may not be sold as Mazoyères. In practice it is all Charmes.

The two vineyards form an unbroken expanse to the left of the vineyard road as you move south towards Morey-Saint-Denis, with the smaller Charmes coming up first, directly opposite Le Chambertin, and Mazoyères following, opposite Latricières-Chambertin. Together they compose some 65·29 acres. The wines are considered by local growers to be almost identical; Charmes has slightly more body and Mazoyères more finesse. Mazoyères, they say, would be the superior growth except that it is sold as Charmes, with the result that there is no way of telling between them.

Whichever vineyard it comes from, wine sold as Charmes is remarkably light and delicate for this commune where the emphasis generally is on austere masculinity. Classified in 1937 as a Great Growth (*Grand Cru*), the highest rating given to Burgundian wines by the Institut National des Appellations d'Origine des Vins et Eaux-de-Vie (National Institute of Place-Names of Wines and Spirits), the wines must live up to the rigid standards demanded by both law and tradition (for standards, *see* CÔTE DE NUITS). The vineyard is reasonably divided up among several growers. The average amount of wine grown in the two vineyards comes to about 22,000 imp. gallons (26,400 U.S.), a fairly representative figure. It is roughly the equivalent of 11,500 cases.

Charnu

French term for full in body; that is, literally, fleshy.

Chartreuse

The famous liqueur made in Tarragona, Spain, and Voiron, France, by monks of the Carthusian (Charterhouse) Order. The Spanish distillery was established in 1903 when the Order was expelled from France for the second time (the first: from the Revolution until 1815) and they have continued to operate it since their return in 1932. In the early part of the present century there was considerable confusion because the goods of the Order were seized and sold at the time of their expulsion; the trade-mark went, but not the formula. The 'Chartreuse' thus sold in France was no more than a pallid imitation of the real liqueur, and the monks were forbidden to use the name and resorted to the inscription: Liqueur fabriquée à Tarragone par les Pères Chartreux. This has, of course, been changed since the return and the name now belongs exclusively to the rightful owners.

Chartreuse is made on a base of brandy, with extracts of a considerable number of herbs and plants, to provide the flavouring. The still-secret formula is said to have been given to the order in 1605 and perfected some time thereafter by Father Jérôme Maubec; but it was not sent outside the monastic walls until 1848, when a group of French Army officers tasted it and were so impressed that they undertook to make it known everywhere. The original liqueur was the Elixir, white and stronger than it is now, but its manufacture has been discontinued. Chartreuse is either green or yellow, the green the stronger and the yellow less alcoholic and sweeter.

Chassagne-Montrachet and Chassagne-Montrachet-Côte de Beaune

Burgundy red and white wine. District: Côte de Beaune, France. Commune: Chassagne.

At the southern end of the Côte de Beaune is the Côte des Blancs where the finest white wines of the Côte d'Or are produced. The greatest by far is wine from the vineyard of Montrachet—shared in almost equal parts by Chassagne-Montrachet and Puligny-Montrachet—but those just a shade below it are still magnificent. Chassagne also makes some very good red wines which, because they are little known and are slightly eclipsed by the celebrated whites, are often comparatively inexpensive and sometimes exceptional value. This has not always been the case.

During the eighteenth century Chassagne was famous for red wines. It is reported that red wine from the vineyard of Morgeot was so highly thought of that the rate of exchange was two bottles of Montrachet for one of Morgeot. The tables are so far turned today that Morgeot no longer makes red but, although they do not merit the ancient exchange rate, its whites are among the finest in the commune.

Chassagne is the last of the important communes of the Côte de Beaune. To the south is Santenay, where the wines are often good, seldom extraordinary; and after Santenay the slope tails off eventually to merge with the Côte Chalonnaise. But the wines of Chassagne are often exceptional.

The leading vineyard is, of course, the incomparable Montrachet, but Bâtard-Montrachet and Criots-Bâtard-Montrachet are others of top-most rank (*see each under individual heading*). These are all Great Growths (*Grands Crus*) as rated by the French Government and are thus on a level with the handful of the finest wines of Burgundy. Slightly behind them in the legal hierarchy—but often their equal in quality—are such vineyards as Morgeot, Ruchottes, and Caillerets. Chassagne's whites share many of the characteristics of Puligny—the dry, firm, but never hard, full, flowery richness and lingering aftertaste. Montrachet itself has astonishing stamina for a dry white wine, but the others tend to maderize reasonably quickly. Ten years will usually kill them, and they are generally at their best when from two to five years old.

The reds of Chassagne are generally finer than those of Puligny and often finer than the better-known Santenays. They are hardish, well-rounded wines, with a *goût de terroir* which is characteristic, and they form a transition between the other reds of the Côte d'Or and those of the southern Burgundian wine districts. Boudriottes is the most masculine at the outset, but it matures into a mellow and not over-assertive richness; while Clos Saint-Jean reaches its peak rather faster, has more finesse and develops its bouquet considerably earlier. In general, the red wines of Chassagne are at their peak after about five years but can be drunk when younger with considerable enjoyment.

Chassagne has about 860 acres planted in vines. The wine—when it meets the legal minimum standards—is allowed to use the commune name and if it comes from an 820-acre section of this greater whole, may add the designation Côte de Beaune to the common name.

The better vineyards are the First Growths (*Premier Crus*), which are entitled to be labelled with vineyard name and commune name, and the finest are the Great Growths, which carry the vineyard name only. Average production in Chassagne is about 70,750 imp. gallons (85,000 U.S.) of red wine, 37,500 imp. gallons (45,000 U.S.) of white.

GREAT GROWTHS (*Grands Crus*)

WHITE WINES

Vineyard	*Acres*
Montrachet (*in part*)	8·8
Bâtard-Montrachet (*in part*)	14·4
Criots-Bâtard-Montrachet	3·5

See PULIGNY-MONTRACHET.

FIRST GROWTHS (*Premiers Crus*)

WHITE WINES AND RED

Vineyard		*Acres*
Les Grandes Ruchottes	(*White wines only*)	1·59
Les Ruchottes	(*White wines only*)	4·26
Morgeot		9·75
Les Caillerets		13·6

FIRST GROWTHS (*Premiers Crus*)

WHITE WINES AND RED

Vineyard	*Acres*
Clos Saint-Jean	35·5
Clos de la Boudriotte	5
Les Boudriottes	44·3
La Maltroie	22·8
Champgain	70·7
La Romanée	3·2
Les Brussanes	43·8
Les Chaumées	2·5
Les Vergers	23·6
Les Macherelles	19·8

Chasselas

This is one of the best European table grapes, but it is used only for small light wines: although these have a delicate bouquet, they are low in acid and do not keep well. Varieties of this family are the Gutedel (Germany), the Fendant (Switzerland), and the Chasselas Doré (California).

Château Chasse-Spleen

Bordeaux red wine. District: Haut-Médoc, France. Commune: Moulis.

Moulis is an official place-name in its own right, and the commune lies a little to the north and to the west of Margaux. Its best wine is Chasse-Spleen, classified Exceptional Growth (*Cru Exceptionnel*) in 1855. A re-classification of Médoc wines today would find this vineyard rated higher, among the great classified growths. Served frequently in recent years at banquets of the Médoc wine fraternity, the Commanderie du Bontemps, it has held its own among Médocs of high classification and world-wide reputation.

Characteristics. One of the best of its class, round and full. Very good breed.

Vineyard area: 57 acres.

Average production: 5,700 cases.

Château

In the wine world this means not a great castle, like a château of the Loire, but a wine estate (especially in the region of Bordeaux) where vineyards and wine-sheds are controlled as a rule from the country house which is the centre of the estate. This may look like a small castle; it may just as well be an average villa. The wine made and bottled on the estate is the fine château-bottled wine always more prized than regional wines, which may be blends.

For the names of the wine châteaux of Bordeaux (e.g. Château Haut-Brion, Château Lascombes) *see* under individual names.

Château Bottled

Wine bottled at the château where it was grown and made: a guarantee that it is untampered with and authentic. At most leading vineyards the legend *mis en bouteilles au château* is also a guarantee of quality. If the vintage of any year does not come up to standard it will be disposed of to shippers to be sold as regional wine.

Château-Chalon

A *vin jaune* wine of the French Jura. Yellow-coloured, this wine is akin to Sherry and can last up to sixty or seventy years.

See JURA.

Château-Grillet

Rhône Valley white wine. District: Rhône Valley, France.

The estate, perched above the River Rhône, covers about three and a half acres of the communes of Verin and Saint-Michel-sous-Condrieu, and produces some 250–420 imp. gallons (300–500 U.S.) or roughly 200 cases of wine annually. The wine is dry, white, heady, well balanced, and full, and sometimes has a slight aroma of Muscat grapes although it is made entirely from Viognier. In good years it can be wonderful, among the best of the Rhône Valley's white wines, surpassing or ranking with white Hermitage, but its production is so small that it is rarely seen outside the district. Much of it is sold at the Restaurant de la Pyramide, in near-by Vienne, where wines must meet rigorous standards before they are admitted to the cellars. Nevertheless, the wine is renowned more for its scarcity than for its quality.

Châteauneuf-du-Pape

Rhône Valley red, and some white wines. District: Rhône Valley, France.

Midway between Avignon and Orange, on the left bank of the Rhône, Châteauneuf has about 6,000 acres of vines, producing one of the Côtes du Rhône's finest red wines, and boasts the most stringent wine controls in the world. Were it not for Châteauneuf and its most distinguished grower —the Baron Le Roy de Boiseaumarié—there would probably be fewer controls in France today, for, in 1936, the authorities followed the rules which had already been established by the Baron and others in Châteauneuf since 1923, and applied them to other fine French wines. Today, Philippe Dufaye, who abandoned medicine for viticulture, is a moving spirit in the commune.

Legislation, in Châteauneuf, came about through force of necessity, for after the First World War a bottle was apt to contain something quite other than its label claimed, and anything but good wine. Since 1923, however, the picture has changed drastically, and fraud, while not completely rooted out, has been given an almost mortal blow.

Most Côtes du Rhône wines are the produce of one grape, but in Châteauneuf there are thirteen varieties. On this account, there will be differences between wines coming from different growers, all of whom maintain that each type of grape adds certain characteristics and that only by playing the scale of the varieties can a Châteauneuf-du-Pape be achieved.

Grenache gives mellowness and alcohol; Mourvèdre, Syrah, Muscardin, and Vaccarese add body, colour, and firmness; Counoise, Picpoule and Cinsault vinosity, bouquet, and freshness; Clairette and Bourboulenc, finesse and warmth. Terret Noir, Picardan, and Roussanne are also allowed. The vines grow far apart, with often as much as five feet between rows, in soil covered with flattish stones, the size of small coconuts. The bunches of grapes mature, caught between the scorching heat of the sun and the reflected heat from the stones. As a result of this roasting and of new, shorter vatting methods, the wines usually surpass the required 12·5% of alcohol (a legal minimum matched by few French wines and exceeded by none) and often reach 13% or even 14%. The wine is characteristically deep in colour and full-bodied, but softer than either a Hermitage or a Côte Rôtie, and is much quicker to mature than are most Côtes du Rhônes. It is often ready after three or four years. The wine has a good bouquet (though not so intense as in the Côte Rôtie) and a special winy taste termed 'vinosity'.

Some very pleasant white wines are made and, while conserving the same distinctive taste, they are less well known—almost curiosities compared with the reds.

The name Châteauneuf-du-Pape comes from the crumbling ruins of an old castle built in the time known as the Babylonian Captivity (1305–1377), when successive Popes were French and Avignon, not Rome, was the seat of the Papacy. The 'New Castle' was to be their summer headquarters and was started by Clément V, a lover of wine and former Bishop of Bordeaux—in which region Château Pape-Clément still stands in tribute to him. The building of the castle was finished by Pope Clément VI, although the vines were probably established by an intervening pontiff, John XXII. The holdings were attacked during the religious wars and the castle burned in 1502.

It is probable that wine from the district was not called Châteauneuf-du-Pape much before the nineteenth century; in earlier times it was 'Wine of Avignon'. Today a varying amount is made each year, for in areas as dry as this the grapes sometimes remain small from lack of water; but in a good year there will be about 13,000 imp. gallons (15,600 U.S.) of white wine and 1 million imp. gallons (1,200,000 U.S.) of red.

The word Châteauneuf, with its associations with châteaux and Bordeaux, is attractive to the public. In the last year or two, some of these wines have been bottled within twelve months of the harvest, and are thus lighter than the traditional Châteauneuf-du-Pape, and comparable with the best growths of Beaujolais.

Some important Châteauneuf-du-Pape vineyards are:

Vineyards	*Acres*
Domaine des Fines Roches	117
Domaine de la Nerthe	115
Clos Saint-Jean	109·9
Domaine de Nalys	115
Château de Vaudieu	73·04
(about 40% of this is actually in production, although the whole rates an Appellation Contrôlée)	
La Gardine	60·5
Château Fortia	63·9
Domaine des Sénéchaux	58·3
Clos-des-Papes	33·4
Domaine de Saint-Préfert	35

Chauché Gris

This grape is grown in the Livermore and Santa Cruz regions of California. The wine it makes is sold as 'Grey Riesling' or 'Rhine Wine' (although the grape is not a Riesling) or even as a 'Chablis'.

Chaume

See QUARTS DE CHAUME.

Chautauqua

Wine-growing district in New York State.

See AMERICA: EASTERN STATES.

Cheilly-les-Maranges and Cheilly-les-Maranges-Côte de Beaune

Burgundy red and white wines. District: Côte de Beaune, France.

Cheilly and its neighbours (Sampigny and Dezize)—all of which have added the name of the vineyard they jointly share to their own—make up the southernmost communes of the Côte de Beaune. Cheilly's wines are usually blended with those from other communes along this famous slope and sold as Côte de Beaune-Villages, but may occasionally be found over some 310 acres, and grapes grown on 106 acres—enclosed within the larger area—may be made into wine that has the right to add Côte de Beaune to the communal name. The vineyards Les Maranges, Plantes-de-Maranges, and La Boutière are the commune's best, and wines from these three may—although they almost never do—carry both commune name and vineyard name on the bottle label.

Chénas

Wines of Beaujolais, France, grown in small quantity, generally inside the famous district of Moulin-à-Vent; not quite of Moulin-à-Vent excellence, they are nevertheless first-rate and, being much cheaper, are outstanding value.

See BEAUJOLAIS.

Chenin Blanc

The dominant white grape of the lower Loire Valley, going into Vouvray and other wines of the Touraine, and into most of the white wines of Anjou. Sometimes known as Pineau de la Loire, Blanc d'Anjou, etc.

See ANJOU; TOURAINE.

Cherry Brandy

Technically a brandy distilled from fermented cherry juice, but in practice it is a liqueur derived from it, containing a proportion of crushed cherry stones to impart a bitter-almond taste.

Cherry Heering

This cherry liqueur made by the firm of Peter Heering of Copenhagen in Denmark has made its name throughout the world. Having a true cherry flavour and made according to Heering's special formula, it is not over-sweet, on account of the proportion of cherry stones used in the distillation. This is one of the most popular cordials sold in the United States.

Cherry Liqueur

Cherry cordial made by steeping cherries in sweetened brandy. Cherry Rocher is famous in France. An English variety is produced by Thomas Grant & Sons.

See CHERRY HEERING; MARASCHINO.

Château Cheval-Blanc

Bordeaux red wine. District and Commune: Saint-Émilion, France.

Generally considered the best Saint-Émilion wine today, Cheval-Blanc is one of the twelve vineyards officially classified First Great Growth (*Premier Grand Cru*) of Saint-Émilion in 1955, and privileged to stand with Château Ausone at the head of the list, the others following alphabetically. The vineyard, predominantly gravelly although it covers various soils, lies on flat land on the north-east borders of Saint-Émilion, on the edge of Pomerol. As a building the château is not distinguished.

The geographical position, otherwise excellent, proved disastrous in the freeze of February 1956. The Pomerol area was the hardest hit; and as the frost lay on the lower flatter land and spared the hills, Cheval-Blanc suffered most of all the great Saint-Émilion vineyards. The owner, Monsieur Fourcaud-Laussac, in whose family the property has been for a little more than a hundred years, afterwards predicted an average of about eight barrels of wine in each of the vintages of 1956, 1957, and perhaps 1958 (his usual yield is 360 barrels), because the cold killed the productive shoots and branches, which cannot be renewed under three or four years. Approximately a quarter of the plantation was actually destroyed so that the vineyard was unable to return to normal production until the early 1960s.

Characteristics. Undoubtedly one of the greatest red vineyards of Bordeaux, on a par with the First Growths of the Médoc. Its reputation has grown tremendously in recent years and three qualities may be said to have contributed to its success. It is one-third Pomerol, for the vineyard touches the Pomerol boundary, it is one-third Graves, since the soil is gravelly, and the remaining one-third is a typical Saint-Émilion. The result is a strong, supple, excellent wine.

Vineyard area: 87 acres.

Average production: 9,100 cases.

Chevalier-Montrachet

Burgundy white wines. District: Côte de Beaune, France. Commune: Puligny-Montrachet. Official Classification: Great Growth (Grand Cru).

These wines are the closest to the great Montrachet itself. They have the same enveloping richness with no trace of sweetness, and the same overwhelming perfume and magnificence. This is not really surprising, since the vineyards are contiguous. Chevalier is lighter and not as powerful a wine as Montrachet, but, depending upon the skill of the grower, it can sometimes be as great or even greater. Superb finesse is the attractive characteristic of this beautiful white wine.

The Chevalier is directly above Montrachet in the commune of Puligny-Montrachet. On one side of it is Cailleret—good, but not in the same class as the other two—and on the other two sides no vineyards at all.

Chevalier, not much more than a dozen acres in size, is split among several owners. Madame Boillereault de Chauvigné is one; and much of the rest is in the hands of Bouchard Père et Fils, Jadot and Latour (joint ownership), and Chartron. The average production of the vineyard is 2,000 imp. gallons (2,400 U.S.).

Chian Wine

A Greek wine famous in antiquity.

See CLASSICAL WINES.

Chianti

Chianti is one of the most abused names in the world of wines. Almost every wine-growing country has taken the name and applied it to almost any red wine as long as it is sold in straw-covered flasks. Real Chianti is made in a small district in the region of Tuscany in central Italy, and it may come in a flask (*fiasco*) or in a bottle. In either case, 'classical' Chianti will have on the neck of the bottle or flask a seal depicting a black cockerel on a gold background; and other permissible Chianti from a wider area in Tuscany will show a white cherub on the seal. Anything else, in spite of what the label may say, is *not* Chianti.

See TUSCANY: ITALY.

Chiaretto

An Italian rosé from Lake Garda.

See ITALY.

Chica

South American drink, brewed from maize by the Indians.

Chicken

General name covering various types of native American grapes, some of which can be used by the wine-maker.

Chile

Chile makes the best wines in South America, and in quantity produced is counted thirteenth among the wine-producing countries of the world. Soil and climate helped by irrigation are favourable to viticulture; the French *vignerons* who planted the better vineyards have left behind them a high tradition of wine-making—although the Spaniards have been growing vines in Chile ever since they conquered it; and finally, the Chilean Government takes a progressive and enlightened interest in wine and the vine.

On its roughly 276,000 acres of vineyard, Chile makes almost 106,400,000 imp. gallons (127,800,000 U.S.) of wine a year. About 1½ million imp. gallons (1,860,000 U.S.) are exported, mainly to the other South American countries, to the United States, to Belgium, and to Switzerland and other European countries. It is everywhere appreciated, for although not great wine, it is good—and usually an extraordinarily good buy at the price. The amount of wine consumed annually inside Chile is limited to 60 litres (13·2 imp. gallons; 15·9 U.S.) per inhabitant, and average consumption is just about that. This limit was imposed by the Government in an attempt to check the growth of alcoholism in the country. More than 7% of the cultivated land, and 2% of all the land in Chile, is planted in vines and about 50,000 workers are constantly employed—as compared with 11,000 men in the big copper mines.

Three types are produced: fortified wines in the north, good table wines in central Chile, and ordinary table wines in the south. Those of the central section often bear a close resemblance to the lesser Bordeaux wines. This is not really surprising for the soil and climate in the two regions are very similar and the vines and viticultural practices are direct imports. Chilean wines might not, of course, match a château-bottled Claret of a good year; but they often equal or surpass some of the regional bottlings—and they have the advantage of being much cheaper. In addition to the wines of the Bordeaux type from Cabernet grapes, there are some Burgundy types from Pinot Noir, but the former is by far the more successful.

One of the best Chilean white wines is the Riesling, but its production is reduced, not because of the quality of the wines but because the growers find the results too expensive. Chilean white wines are

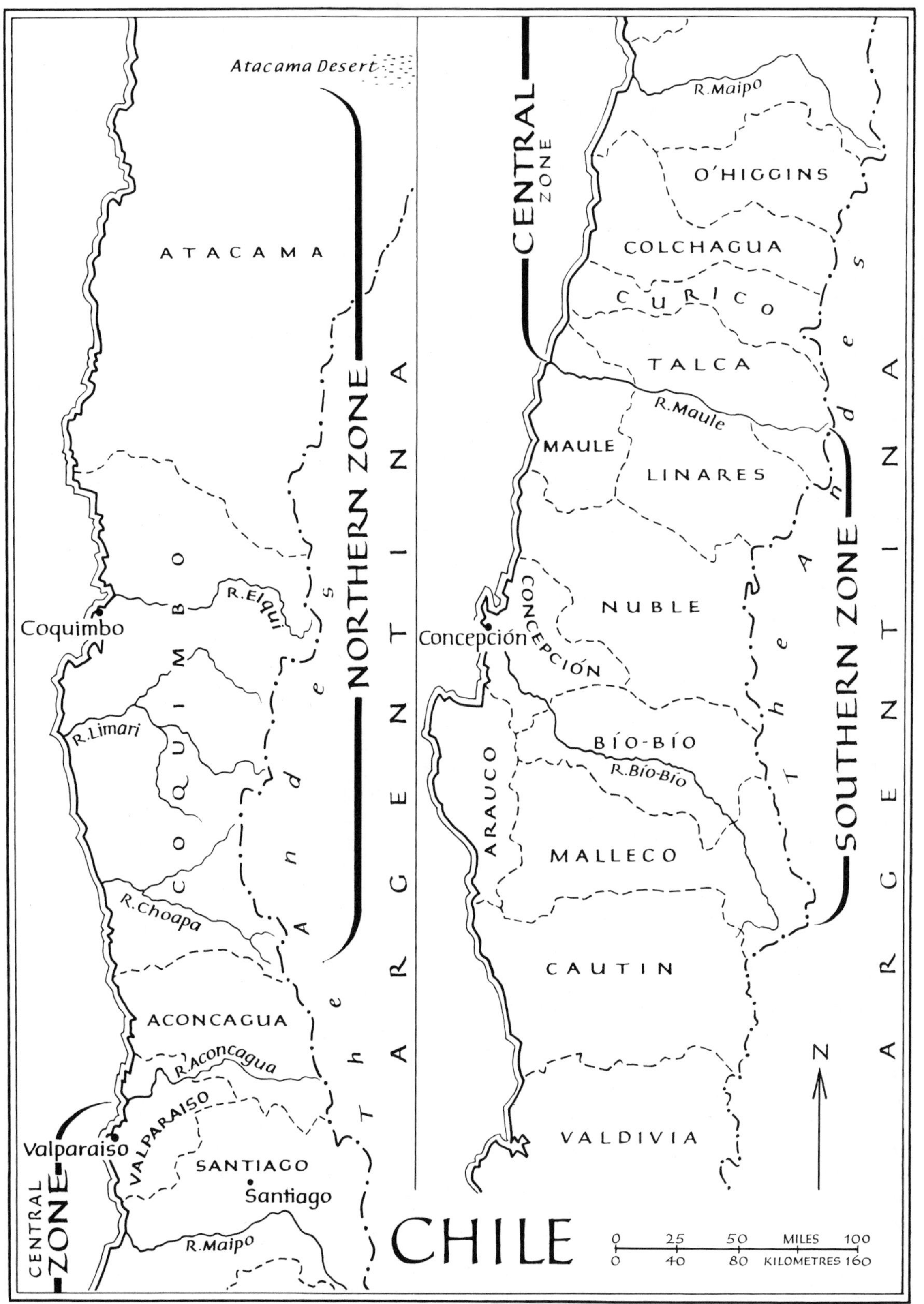
Atacama Desert
ATACAMA
NORTHERN ZONE
ARGENTINA
The Andes
COQUIMBO
R. Elqui
Coquimbo
R. Limari
R. Choapa
ACONCAGUA
R. Aconcagua
VALPARAISO
Valparaiso
SANTIAGO
Santiago
R. Maipo
CENTRAL ZONE
CHILE
CENTRAL ZONE
R. Maipo
O'HIGGINS
COLCHAGUA
CURICO
TALCA
R. Maule
MAULE
LINARES
NUBLE
CONCEPCIÓN
Concepción
BÍO-BÍO
R. Bío-Bío
ARAUCO
MALLECO
CAUTIN
VALDIVIA
SOUTHERN ZONE
N
0 25 50 MILES 100
0 40 80 KILOMETRES 160

now made from the Pinot Blanc, Sauvignon, and Sémillon vines, for the most part. The red *vin ordinaire* grown in the southern section of the country comes both from grapes of French stock and from the Païs, a vine of Spanish origin which has been in Chile long enough to be considered a native.

Terrain and Climate

Chile is so fortunately situated that the country has so far escaped the devastation of mildew—the most crippling fungus disease of the vine—and of phylloxera, although this vine louse has taken its toll in the vineyards of Argentina to the east and Peru to the north. Chileans say that the Andes, which lie between Chile and Argentina, have prevented the influx of the pest from that side; that the desolate Atacama Desert has obstructed its entry from Peru; and that the prevailing winds blowing in from the sea guarantee that it will not make its entrance by air. The result is that in Chile even the most tender of European vine-types need not be grafted on to American roots; yet experiments have been made, and this could be done with a minimum of confusion should phylloxera ever get into the country—precautions taken at Chilean border stations make this improbable.

As there are three types of wine, so there are three zones of grape-production. The northern zone, from the Atacama Desert to the River Choapa, consists of vineyards planted mostly in Muscat and produces the country's best table grapes. Irrigation is a vital necessity since as a rule the rainfall is negligible; what there is, however, is closely connected with the cold Humboldt Current off the coast and when—as sometimes happens—this current is displaced by warmer water, catastrophic rains result, ruining the vineyards and everything else in the region. The vines are mostly cultivated in the transversal valleys, and irrigation is based on the occasional rivers which flow down from the mountains. The wines are strong and high in alcohol, and some are fortified to resemble Sherry, Port, or Madeira.

From a quality standpoint, the most important vine-growing region is the central portion which runs from the Aconcagua River to the River Maule. Here the influence is almost entirely Bordelais both in viticultural practices and in vine planting. The most important vines are Cabernet Franc, Cabernet Sauvignon, Merlot, Malbec (here spelt Malbeck), and Petit Verdot for red wines, and Sémillon and Sauvignon for whites. All these come from the Bordeaux area. Other important vines are Pinot Noir, Pinot Blanc; and, of lesser importance, Riesling and Païs. The vines are tended and cared for according to traditional Bordeaux methods, with the single important exception that they are virtually all irrigated, and therefore give more output than those which are watered naturally. This factor is not prejudicial to the quality of the wine. Since all the best vineyards of Chile are irrigated, it cannot at this point be decided whether or not the wine would improve under different conditions.

The two best sections of the central region (and thus the best of Chile) are the Aconcagua valley and the valley of the River Maipo. Both specialize to a large extent in Cabernet vines, and the wines are strong in finesse, are well balanced, and tend to hold their excellence longer than most other Chilean growths. The Maipo Valley, in the section south-east of the Chilean capital city of Santiago, is the top vineyard district. The soil has more limestone than elsewhere (there is generally a higher percentage of sand and slate) and the Cabernet Franc and Cabernet Sauvignon produce wines which are strong and stable, deep in colour and rich in perfume. There is a good yield per acre in this district, although this claim can be attributed partly to irrigation.

The southern section of Chile is the area between the Rivers Maule and Bio-Bio. With a few exceptions in the extreme north, the vineyards are not irrigated. The subsoil is hard and the topsoil is made up of slate and mud, sometimes rich in iron, with occasional outcroppings of lime. These wines are distinctly less interesting than those farther to the north, and while there are some vines of French origin (Cabernet, Malbec, Sémillon) and a little Riesling, much of the area is in the bulk-giving País. A certain amount of blending is done with these wines and the rest make up the everyday wine of the Chilean.

Wine History

Despite the fact that they were conquered and settled by wine-drinking Latin people, most of the countries of South America had to await the influx of Italians after the First World War before they had substantial vineyards of their own. But both Chile and Peru have had vines for just about as long as they have had Spaniards.

Vines were brought into these countries by the missionaries who followed the Conquistadores, and were established as a source for altar wine. It is thought that the first vines were carried into Chile by either Francisco de Carabantes or Bartoloméo de Terrazas—two missionaries who were instrumental in planting vines in neighbouring Peru. One of these two—it is not known definitely which—took part in the expedition into Chile of Diego de Almagro, somewhere between 1535 and 1537. The vine they brought with them is recorded as giving grapes which were small and red and extremely tasty.

Culture of the vine received its first impetus about 1556, in the neighbourhood of Santiago, whence it spread to what is today Argentina. The important vines of this era were Muscats, in particular the Muscat of Alexandria. Another useful variety was one that Chileans, for lack of a better name, call the País; it is known to have come from Spain, but otherwise its origins are shrouded in mystery. The wines were mostly altar wines, or were modelled on Spanish types; and the real upsurge in the industry had to wait until the middle of the nineteenth century.

In 1851, the 'Father of Chilean viticulture', Silvestre Ochagavia, realized that the country had the potential of becoming one of the best vineyard regions of the American continent. Acting on his conviction, he imported from France a number of viticultural experts. In addition, he imported a variety of cuttings from the better French vines, which were mostly planted in the central valley of Chile, where the better vineyards are still to be found. As his experiment turned out to be an almost unqualified success, the Chilean Government stepped in and had more French vines imported and the new industry was well launched.

Today, the typical vineyard of Chile is a small one indeed. Of the 32,000-odd vineyards, more than 18,000 are two and a half acres or less; another 9,000 range from two and a half to ten and a quarter acres; and less than 180 vineyards contain more than 250 acres. This raises various problems of cultivation; problems which have a direct bearing on the quality of the wine. A small Chilean grower who has neither the capital nor the proper equipment cannot hope to produce a really fine wine and stay in business. But the Chilean Government has established a fund to provide loans for the building of co-operative cellars. This eliminates the necessity for each grower to buy all the expensive machinery he would otherwise need, and provides a central place for a technical expert to advise growers on the latest and best methods.

Government Controls

The Chilean wine industry is one of the best regulated in the world. Perhaps the main reason for this is the effort to control alcoholism; but the outcome is that the wine which is encouraged is of high quality.

Chilean growers have a production figure they may not exceed—and if by any chance they do exceed it, they must get rid of their surplus, the two most popular methods being the attempt to export and distillation to industrial alcohol. In any year, each grower must declare to the Government how much wine he has made. If the total comes to more than the legal maximum for the country, he must dispose of a certain amount, depending on the national total and the percentage of the wine he has made in proportion to his acreage. He must also declare to the Government how much wine he eventually disposes of, and the way in which he has done it. The dumping of poor wine on the export market is prevented by restrictions imposed by the National Council of External Commerce. These rules decree that, for export, white wines must have at least 12% of alcohol, red wines 11·5%; and that the wines must be clear, healthy, and at least one year old.

The final control placed on Chilean wines by the Government refers to age. There are four classes of export wines: *Courant* refers to wines one year old; *Special* to two-year-olds; *Reserve* to four-year-olds; and *Gran Vino* applies to wines six years old or more. In many cases the *Reserve* wines may be Chile's best.

Spirits

Much of the production of fine muscat wine made in the northern zone is used for the distillation of fine brandy native to Chile and to some other South American countries.

See PISCO BRANDY.

China

From very early times, wines have been made sporadically—but seldom in any significant quantity—in China. During the past decade or so, returning travellers have told of wild vines still growing in the south; of experimental stations for viticulture; and of a small number of co-operative vineyards, part of the agricultural plan of the State. Some European grapes (such as Pinot and Riesling) appear to have been introduced; and visitors have seen American-type vines, descended from *Vitis labrusca*, as well as native Asian stock. Some of the vines are cultivated in irrigated land, on a curious system by which the plants are supported on a fan-shaped trellis work of wires; in other, non-irrigated vineyards, the pergola method of training was seen.

According to these reports, the Chinese generally drink lemonade at meals, or beer; wine is for special occasions. One visitor was offered red wine—sweet, and low in alcohol—poured from a bottle of the Bordeaux type; and a white wine, served warm in a cup, which bore some resemblance to *vin jaune* and turned out to be rice wine. There was also a drier wine, of an aromatic kind, with a slightly bitter aftertaste.

Officials of the Chinese Government confirm that grape, fruit, and rice wines are now being made, and that between 1952–1964, total output of wine increased 2·6 times.

Wine History

Chinese history has it that wine-making started as early as 2140 B.C., when the wine was called Li or Chang instead of Chieu, its present name. Wine was brought into China as well, coming from the Mediterranean and Persia on the long, slow relays of caravans which had brought silk westwards. Sometimes barbarian wars interrupted this trade for years at a time; but about 130 B.C. vines are said to have been taken in from Persia and planted near the Emperor's palace. Yet it was not until the seventh century A.D., when the Chinese dominated all Central Asia, that the art of wine-making spread more widely. By the time of the Chou Dynasty (1066) it had made considerable progress. It was not a drink for the masses, but poets and mandarins loved it. In the resplendent period of the T'ang Dynasty art and poetry flourished and the drink of the courtiers and the artists was wine. The famous poet, Li-Po, a sort of innocent Villon, who wandered from tavern to tavern writing and reciting his poems, and always praising wine, was most poetically drowned: being drunk, and wanting to clasp the reflection of the moon in his arms, he plunged into the river.

In 1322, the Emperor ordered the vines in his territory to be uprooted to make way for cereals: in the town of Chang-Si, wine was offered to Hong-Wu 'for the last time'. But such edicts occurred everywhere. Marco Polo was to find wine plentiful in Tai-Yuan. In the late seventeenth century, the Emperor K'an-hi was introducing new vines from Turkestan.

Today, red and white wines, dry, sweet and sparkling, are being made from grapes, as well as some rosé. Vermouth and Cassis are produced, too. And fruit wines are made from apples, oranges, lychees, peaches, etc; while medicinal wines, with herbs steeped in them, are based on ancient recipes.

Rice Wine

This traditional Chinese drink is made by sweetening and fermenting glutinous rice or millet. The wines have an individual bouquet, and an alcoholic content ranging from 11°–18° proof. The best-known brands are Chai Fan and Hsiang Shueh of Shao-Hsing in Chekiang province, Tsen Gon in Foochien province, Mai Lao in Shantung Province.

Spirits

The principal spirits of China come from grain which has undergone various processes known as yeasting, sweetening, and fermenting. Alcoholic content is usually about 50°–60° proof. Different methods produce spirits with a flavour and smell that varies from rich to mellow to sharp. Leading types are Mou-Tai, Feng Chu, Lu-Chou-Dai-Ch'u, Wu Liang Yea and Shi Fung.

Chinchon

Spanish anis-flavoured spirit diluted with water and drunk in a tall glass.

Chinon

Loire Valley red, white, and rosé wine; still, semi-sparkling, and sparkling. District: Touraine, France.

The ruined mediæval fortress of Chinon rising above the quiet River Vienne stands on the top of a steep hill, to the slopes of which cling the picturesque buildings of the old town. Chinon, a wine centre for a considerable period, claims as its most exuberant admirer the writer Rabelais, who once tended a vineyard—La Devinière—near by and made there what he described as 'taffeta wines', soft and velvety. The description has lived on in Chinon and is still apt.

Red, rosé and white wine is made, the red being the most interesting. White Chinon is almost invariably overshadowed by Vouvray or Montlouis and the rosé by Anjou, but the reds are apt to be soft, flowery, and have a bouquet often compared with raspberries. To be good, Chinon requires great vintage years; and such vintages only fall about twice in a decade. Red and rosé—a fresh and clean-tasting if unexceptional wine—are made from Cabernet Franc grapes grown in flinty clay soil; white from Chenin Blanc grapes grown in chalky soil. All wines must have at least 9·5% of alcohol. About 333,000 imp. gallons (400,000 U.S.) are made annually.

Chiroubles

A village in the Beaujolais producing an excellent light red wine, now becoming most popular of all red Beaujolais wines in Paris and throughout France.

See BEAUJOLAIS.

Chlorosis

A vine disease caused by an excess of calcium in the soil. This prevents the vine from assimilating iron. It is treated by adding iron to the soil, by injecting iron into the vine or replanting with vines grafted on to calcium-resistant root-stock.

See CHAPTER EIGHT, p. 35.

Chopine

French pint.

Chorey-les-Beaune

Burgundy red and white wines. District: Côte de Beaune, France.

A Burgundian wine village where there is more village than wine. Like so many of her sister communes, Chorey has the option of selling her wines either as Chorey or, after blending with those from other specified communes, as Côte de Beaune-Villages (*q.v.*). The result is that one year may see 16,500 imp. gallons (20,000 U.S.) declared as communal wine and the next a scant 2,500 imp. gallons (3,000 U.S.).

Chorey is on the right side of the railway but the wrong side of the road. Throughout the Côte d'Or the hills descend gently to a plain, the start of which is marked by *Route Nationale* (National Highway) No. 74. As you drive south, you will see vines on both sides of the road; but only on the hilly right are the vineyards really good. To the left, on the plain which extends to the railway, they are distinctly minor—and most of Chorey is on the left. A small pocket, amounting to 412 acres, crosses the road but does not climb far enough up the hill to make a great deal of difference; and none of the vineyards is classified First Growth (*Premier Cru*). Both red and white wines could be made, but in practice all are red.

Christian Brothers Vineyard

Napa Valley, California, U.S.A.

Known in the United States as 'The Brothers of the Christian Schools', these are members of a monastic order founded in the early eighteenth century, in France, by St Jean-Baptiste de La Salle, primarily for teaching. The winery of the Brothers is now one of the most important producers in the North Coast region of California. The large vineyards are at Mont La Salle on the edge of the Napa Valley; the big cellars, at St Helena. Table wines are made, and labelled with the varietal names of the grapes; fortified wines also are produced, as well as 'California champagne'. The total production amounts to nearly a million cases a year. The Christian Brothers make a good deal of Californian brandy, too.

See AMERICA: CALIFORNIA AND THE WEST.

Chromatography

This process of analysis by selective absorption of a mixture of substances on a porous material is employed in wine-making, where paper is generally used. Chromatography has been found to be effective in assessment of certain organic acids, as well as in the differentiation between *Vitis vinifera* and hybrids.

Chusclan

One of the best communes of the Côtes du Rhône, producing rosé wines.

See RHÔNE.

Cider

Fermented juice of sweet apples, commonly made in England, France and other parts of Europe. English settlers introduced it into North America.

The apples were first reduced to a pulp known as 'pomace'. At first this was done by beating the apples in a stone or wooden trough with wooden paddles; but the earlier practice was supplanted by the cider 'mill', consisting of a large wheel that revolved on its side in a circular trough filled with apples, and reduced the fruit to a jelly. (The modern method is to place the apples between two cylinders equipped with sharp knives which, when revolved at high speed, perform the same operation much more quickly.) The pomace was then made into a 'cheese' to be pressed. This 'cheese' was produced by putting on a bed of straw enough of the pomace to make a pile several inches high, followed by another layer of straw at a different angle from the first, and then more pomace. Care was taken that the straw was not only on the top and bottom of the 'cheese' but could fold over the sides as well to keep it in shape and act as a filter during pressing. When the 'cheese' was about three feet high, it was taken to a press and then squeezed until all the juice had been taken out of it. Today, the substitution of collapsible forms which mould the 'cheese' and are removed before pressing, using cloths instead of straw, brings the procedure up to date without changing any of the essentials. Now, however, the dry pomace is no longer fed to the pigs as it often was in earlier times. Once the juice of the pomace had been expressed, it was put into vats or barrels to ferment until it was quite dry.

On some of the Somerset and Normandy farms, it will then be aged for a year or more and will be unexpectedly strong. Commercially manufactured cider will sometimes have cultivated yeasts added to the natural fermentation. Sweet cider is filtered before all the sugar has fermented out; the champagne type continues to ferment in the bottle; the cheaper sparkling ciders are carbonated.

Cinque Terre

White Italian wine made from Vernaccia grapes. *See* LIGURIA.

Cinsault (or Cinsaut)

Grape used in the wines of south-west France, the Midi, the Rhône Valley, and Algeria. It is known also as Picardan Noir, Espagne, Malaga and by other local names. In combination with Grenache, this produces warmth and fullness in the wine.

Cirò di Calabria

One of the best-known red wines of Calabria (*q.v.*), Italy.

Clairet

In French, formerly a light blend of red and white wine or sometimes simply a very light red one. From the word was derived the English 'Claret', applied to the red wines of Bordeaux.

Nowadays, a clairet is not a rosé but a light red wine, supple and fruity but lacking in tannin—one that can be drunk cool and young. A good clairet is the product of grape varieties which tend to give a delicate wine of this nature, and which, because of its low acidity, has been allowed to achieve full maturity. The skins of the fruit are not left in the fermenting vat for more than a day or two. In order that malolactic fermentation may not be hindered, the wine is lightly treated with sulphur. Once alcohol and malolactic fermentation have been fully achieved, the wine is stabilized by fining or with sulphur treatment.

Clairette de Bellegarde

White wine. District: Southern France.

The commune of Bellegarde, about ten miles from Nîmes, southern France, makes a small, light yellow wine, from the Clairette grape variety. Grown on a mass of pebbles washed down by an arm of the River Rhône, it is one of the few white wines of the so-called Languedoc area enjoying an Appellation Contrôlée, or legal place-name. Subject to the usual restrictions of geographical area and pruning, and required to attain 11·5% of alcohol, the wine must also—and this is not universal under French wine law—submit to a committee of tasters and receive their seal of approval, which will go on the bottle. Otherwise, it cannot be called Clairette de Bellegarde. The commune produces an average of 125,000 imp. gallons (150,000 U.S.) of Clairette each year.

Clairette de Die

White wine. District: Southern France.

A semi-sparkling, yellowish-gold wine made in twenty-five parishes around the village of Die on the River Drôme—a tributary of the Rhône—in south-east France. Produced from grapes of the Clairette and Muscat de Frontignan, Clairette de Die dates back to Roman times, when it was the wine of Dea Augusta.

In making the wine, the growers must use a minimum of 50% Clairette and may vinify by either one of two methods. The modern way is the Champagne process of secondary fermentation in the bottle. The other is the more traditional 'rural' way. Following this method, the maker allows his wine to ferment slowly, filtering frequently and adding sulphur in small quantities, to slow down the yeasts. The sulphur has a cleansing effect, killing all the harmful bacteria. When the wine has finished its first fermentation, the vintner closes it up tightly in the barrel and allows any unresolved sugar to re-ferment. He puts it through a pressure filter and effectively stops all action, purifying his wine but allowing the carbon dioxide gas which has been generated to remain in it. This is the more usual process at present.

The result is a more or less sparkling wine with a pronounced flavour of Muscat, and an alcoholic content of at least 10·5%. The average yearly output is 50,000 imp. gallons (60,000 U.S.). Appreciation of this wine is generally considered to be an acquired taste.

Clairette du Languedoc

White wines. District: Southern France.

The great plain of Languedoc in southern France stretches from Arles, near the River Rhône, towards the Spanish border and produces almost half of the wines of France. Very few of these, however, are more than the most ordinary of *vins ordinaires*. Scattered here and there are small holdings of vineyards whose product has been considered good enough to be controlled by French law as wines of Appellation d'Origine Contrôlée. Clairette du Languedoc is one example.

The wine is grown principally in the seven communes of Adissan, Aspiran, Paulhan, Fontès, Cabrières, Péret, and Ceyras, somewhat to the west of Montpellier in the department of Hérault. Two types of wine are made along the sun-scorched slopes, both coming only from grapes of the Clairette vine, with some Picpoule and Terret. The first is that wine carrying on its label simply Clairette de Languedoc, with or without the name of the commune of origin. This is a dry, heavy, white wine of at least 13% of alcohol, sometimes sold in Great Britain as Amber Dry. The other has the qualification 'rancio' added to it. To earn the name of rancio, this unpleasant wine must come from grapes which have been left on the vine until well after they are ripe. The wine must have an alcoholic content of at least 14%, must be allowed to maderize and age for at least three years before it is put on sale, and must have the taste characteristics associated with a rancio (*q.v.*).

The vineyards growing the Clairette du Languedoc comprise about 2,800 acres and average production is less than 25,000 imp. gallons (30,000 U.S.), well under the permitted 312 imp. gallons (374 U.S.) per acre.

Claret

In Great Britain, and frequently in the United States, red Bordeaux is known as Claret.

From the first days of the wine trade with the Bordelais (which began to flourish early in the thirteenth century), the pinkish, light wine became a favourite in England, and has remained so ever since. The French called it clairet; the blunter English tongue clubbed it into Claret—but the wine was not Claret as we know it now. At the time of the Roman occupation, wines were aged; but not again, until almost modern times, was Bordeaux anything but 'wine of the year', drunk sometimes as early as two weeks after its harvesting—or the time it took the fleet of wine ships to return to England. It was a wine very briefly fermented. The practice was for a listener to stand posted with ear to the vat, and soon after the boiling of fermentation was heard, the wine was run off.

Today, too, some wine is made after a short fermentation of less than four days. With the new taste for young, light wine, clairet is again being produced in Bordeaux, and it is so called to distinguish it from Claret, now the term for the old red wine of Bordeaux. It is also called rosé; and recently this rosé from Bordeaux has become very popular and many excellent examples are made.

Bordeaux clairet—or rosé—is not red and white wine blended together. In the past, the light Claret sometimes was—*vinum claratum*, or clarified wine, being confused with *vinum clarum*, or wine light and clear by its nature. Clarified wine was common, white wine being added traditionally to red wines which were too murky; but the mingling of red and white wine to make clairet or rosé is forbidden by law throughout France today.

See BORDEAUX.

Classical Wines

A great deal is known about wine and the vine in ancient Greece and Rome. In viticulture, in particular, methods have not changed radically since, in about 700 B.C., Hesiod wrote of the planting and pruning of the vines on his Bœotian farm. What we cannot learn from books is exactly how the wines tasted, and so modern specialists in the subject pursue their own fancies. One says that the liquors would have been disgusting to us, boiled down to a muddy sediment, smoked, cloyed with honey, ruined with resin or salt water. Another will maintain that those Greek wines which were kept to a ripe age actually were what the primitive heroes believed them to be—the most divine drink ever enjoyed by man. A few shipwrecked amphoræ dredged up from the bottom of the Mediterranean are still in existence and still sealed. The date and the name of shipper or grower are decipherable; but if the jars were opened, the tantalizing liquid inside—brackish and half-evaporated—would not taste like wine. It was the opinion of the nineteenth-century wine historian, Cyrus Redding, that the better growths probably tasted like Malvasia, or the sweet wines of Cyprus which (in his day as, sometimes, in ours) were made by the traditional methods.

Greece

Vines grew from earliest times in Greece and the Greek islands, and the inhabitants were naturally wine-drinking people. In the adventures of Odysseus wine played an important part. Nausicaa, when she found Odysseus by the stream, revived him with food and the wine she had brought in a goatskin bottle. Later on, in the King's palace, he ate and drank with Alcinous and the chieftains; and afterwards the King said: '"Mix the bowl and serve out the wine to all in the hall, that we may pour forth before Zeus" . . . and Pontonius mixed the honey-hearted wine and served it out to all when he had poured for libation into each cup in turn.' (A custom that might be compared with the loyal toast.)

Sweet Wines. Generally, the wine seems to have been sweet. That with which Odysseus made the Cyclops drunk was given to him by Maron—'sweet wine, unmingled, a draught for the Gods'. When Maron broached this best vintage (he kept it hidden from his servants), 'that red wine, honey sweet', he would mix it in the silver bowl with twenty parts to one of water, 'and a marvellous sweet smell went up from the mixing-bowl'. Hesiod's wine would have been sweet, too—he spread the grapes in the sun for ten days after they were picked. Just so, Mago of Carthage, about 550 B.C., and Columella repeating, six hundred years later, his instructions for making *passum optimum* (the best luscious wine), said that the sun-dried grapes should be laid out on a raised frame and covered with reeds, until they were sufficiently shrivelled—after which they would be kept in a jar of good must for six days, before pressing. The practice is near enough to that followed in the making of straw wines today. Sweet wines have never lost their appeal for the people of southern Italy, of Cyprus and the Aegean. It is not surprising that the ancient Greeks liked them, and that they preferred old wine to new—even now, the rich Commandaria of Cyprus may live to a great age. The best wines are said to have been made from a blend of red and white grapes; and the famous Pramnian must have been an essence like Tokay.

Mixing of Wines. Not all Greek wines, however, were pure and unmingled. Sometimes honey was put in the wine-jars. Pliny was later to describe the Greek habit of invigorating wine with potter's earth, powdered marble, and salt water. And, although the use of resin in ancient Greece is not unanimously accepted, it is improbable that the pitch-pine so common in early Roman viniculture, and surviving in the peasant wine-making of modern Greece, was really avoided in classical Greece. The mixing of sea-water in the must was not quite as crude as it sounds. The water (taken from the sea when it was calm) was boiled down to one-third of its original volume, with spices for flavouring, strained, and kept for several years before use. One wine would be improved by blending with another—great growths which had been kept until they were sticky and thick as honey were often fit for nothing else, and many of the well-matured sweet vintages had to be strained before drinking. These would be mixed with water—indeed, the Greeks usually drank their wine well diluted. Sometimes, as a finishing touch, they would add perfumes.

Wine-jars and pots. At an Athenian dinner-party, while the guests (all men as a rule) reclined on sofas, slaves would mix wine and water in bowls, take the mixture round in jugs, and pour it into each cup. First a libation would be offered; then the host or leader of the feast would decide how much wine was to be taken, and how strong. In summer, the wine would be cooled with snow brought down from the mountains. Many of the pots and jars for the keeping and serving of wine have been preserved. *Pithoi* (Latin: *dolia*) were the fermenting jars. For the better conservation of lighter wines, these would be smeared with pitch and sunk in the ground. Amphoræ were the tall, two-handled jars in which the wine was aged and brought from the store-room; the squatter *hydria* was the covered water-pot, which was taken out to be filled at the fountain; the *krater* was a wide bowl for mixing wine and water; the *kantharos*, a ladling cup with two handles; the *kylix*, a shallow goblet, somewhat like a Champagne glass—when the wine was drained, a surprising picture would sometimes be discovered at the bottom. In classical Greece, where there was no paper and little papyrus, talented artists and topical illustrators used wine-jars as their canvases. On these we can see the Greeks at their banquets, and expensive flute-players and dancing-girls who sometimes came to entertain them, or the young men aiming their heel-taps into a raised saucer in the game of kottabos, said to have been invented in Sicily. As he flung the dregs, the youth would often invoke a girl's name.

Women and Wine. Women, apart from *hetairæ* and flute-girls, seldom came to these parties, but some of the courtesans had strong heads, and from Nausicaa onwards, Greek women generally drank wine—which is only to be expected in a country where it is the normal drink. A lot has been written by old writers about almost legendary times in Greece, and the austere early days in Rome, when women drank nothing but innocuous *sapa* (unfermented wine); but the women of a more sophisticated Rome drank with the men and sometimes got very drunk. As for the rites of Dionysos, in Greece, a fever which broke out originally in Thrace, women were the more numerous of the worshippers, and the more violent—and even when the worship of the wine god had sobered down to a ritual without Mænad dances and destruction, women, as Mr. Charles Seltman has pointed out, still made Bacchic pilgrimages to Delphi.

Rome

Wild vines flourished in the temperate zones that border the Mediterranean, and no doubt the primitive people who lived there made a weak kind of wine. But the Greeks, the Phœnicians—wine-makers also—and ultimately the Romans, taught the natives to prune their vines and make a wine that would keep. The Greeks were early and adventurous navigators, and their first Italian settlement is believed to have been made by Eubœans at Cumæ, on the coast of Campania, probably in the eighth century B.C. By the end of the seventh century B.C. there were Greek cities along the east coast of Sicily and round the Tarantine Gulf, as well as on the mainland. Whether or not it is true that the Greeks found the Etruscans already making good wine from cultivated vines, it is accepted as fact that these people were fond of luxury and feasts, in which the women took part and drank their share. In general, it is assumed, the Romans learned viticulture and viniculture from the Greeks and passed on the knowledge to most of the people they conquered. The first true wine was precious and used sparingly: a victorious general vowed only a single cup to Jupiter. At a time when small cultivators were being persuaded to take vine-tending seriously, Numa Pompilious (715–673 B.C.) is said to have forbidden the people to make libations with wine from unpruned vines.

Roman Viticulture. The earliest first-hand account, in Latin, of Roman vines and wines comes down to us from Cato the Censor (234–149 B.C.). From *De Agri Cultura*, his book on farming (referred to with admiration by Pliny two hundred years later), from Pliny the Elder himself, and from Columella (roughly contemporary with him), we get the most connected account of vine-growing—how to plant and graft, when to prune—and of wine-making in the first century A.D. and earlier. Pliny relates that, even in his day, some of the vines, particularly in Campania, were allowed to grow as tall as houses, and to twine round tree-tops, so that a man hired to prune them had to ask for danger money. But 'here our vines are kept short by pruning', he wrote, 'in order that their strength may be concentrated in the shoots.' Grape varieties in Greece he believed to be uncountable, and in Italy he knew of eighty sound wines, the best of which were from the Aminean grape (dividing into five varieties), the Nomentane vines with red-tinged stalks, and the Muscatel, which flourished greatly in Tuscany. All these were indigenous. Among others, transplanted from Greece and the islands, he picked out the Græcula (rivalling the Aminean), and the Eugenia, successfully imported from Taormina to the Alban district. The Rhætian and the pine-flavoured Allobrogian from Gaul would not produce quality wines on Italian soil, but they made up for it in quantity.

How the Wine was Made. The natural flavour of pitch (or resin) in the Allobrogian grape was considered desirable, since the Romans smeared not only the outsides of their wine-jars, but the insides also, with this piny gum. In the twelfth book of his *Res Rustica*, in which he outlines the innumerable duties of a steward's wife, Columella gives clear instructions for doing this. Then he describes various ways of preserving the must: with liquid resin mixed with vine-ash; with salt water, and sweet herbs and spices. So that they might age more quickly, the wine-jars would be kept in a loft above the *fumarium*, or smoke-room, where wood was seasoned. In the city, those not in need of smoking would be kept in public cellars (or in private ones) and treated much as wines are today. Even the apparently superstitious rule that wine should never be racked except in a north wind becomes reasonable when one realizes that the opposing wind in parts of Italy is apt to be the sirocco, maddening men and turning milk sour. Pliny considered that, within reason, smoking improved the flavour of wine; but he had hard things to say of the forced ageing by smoke of wines imported from Narbonne, some of which might also be adulterated with obnoxious herbs and drugs. The only Gallic wine he seems to have found passable was that from Marseilles. The Spanish he liked better, rating the growths of Tarragona, Lauron, and the Balearics as high as the best Italian.

The Prized Wines. Imported Greek wines, of course, were held in high esteem, although no longer so rich and rare in Pliny's lifetime as they had been two generations earlier, when guests at a dinner-party would not be offered more than one glass. In the first century A.D., the Greek was rivalled by the Falernian. The Greek islands (Lesbos, Chios, Thasos) which shipped the favourite wines knew the value of publicity: they had their coinage stamped with clusters of grapes or with the head of Dionysos. All these expensive growths, Greek and Italian, must have gone untasted by the common people, who no doubt washed down their meals with draughts as new and as ordinary as our *vin ordinaire*.

The Romans made black (very dark red) wines, clear red, amber, and white ones; those they laid down for ageing would be as concentrated as the old vintages of Greece. In the *Satyricon* of Petronius, the newly rich tycoon, Trimalchio, produces at his supper-party (overloaded, pretentious, but not well conducted) a little glass amphora labelled 'Opimian Muscadine, a Century old'. 'Alas', he said, 'that wine should live longer than man. We'll try if it has held good ever since the consulship of Lucius Opimius.' This wine of a vintage year (121 B.C.), as celebrated as the Comet Year of 1811, was one of the longest lived in history. When Pliny tasted it, it was so dried and thick that it had to be scraped off the sides of the amphora and mixed with a younger wine. Trimalchio offered his guests, as well, a *vino cotto* 'boiled off a third part and kept underground to preserve its strength'. Before the meal, there had been *antepasti*—a honey-sweet aperitif, and the olives and hot sausages that would appear at a cocktail party today; also dormice covered with honey and poppy-seed, which would not.

Some Literary Sources of Classical Wine Lore

Greek

Homer. From references throughout the *Iliad* and the *Odyssey*, a few of which have been quoted above, we know that the heroes of epic times—and their women—habitually drank wine. We know they liked it sweet and diluted with water; and how they served it and poured libations, in princely gatherings, between the eleventh and the eighth centuries B.C.

Hesiod. The first plain, if limited, account of viticulture in Europe is to be found in Hesiod's *Works and Days*. The Bœotian farmer-poet, writing in about 700 B.C., reckoned his calendar by the stars, but he pruned and planted his vines much as small-holders do to this day. It is clear that he had to work hard on his land, and he complained of the oppressions of the local princes.

Alcaeus. The lyric poet of Mytilene, who flourished a hundred years after Hesiod, was himself one of the nobles of Lesbos. Island tyrants rose and fell, and his love-songs and verses in praise of wine ('Hurry, my boy, and pour me out a cup of luscious Lesbian wine') were interspersed with patriotic odes. His 'Let us drink and dance, since Myrsilus is dead' is the model for Horace's ode on the death of Cleopatra, which begins *Nunc est bibendum*. Alcaeus was banished for his political behaviour, and Sappho may have been exiled at the same time.

Anacreon. A generation or so later, Anacreon of Teos came to Athens. He was another lyric poet and boon companion, singing of wine and garlands. He referred to the game of kottabos—'heel-taps flying from the Teian cup'.

Plato, Xenophon, Aristophanes. In the great classical age of Athens, they described the drinking customs of their time: Aristophanes, by topical references in his comedies; Plato and Xenophon each wrote a *Symposium* in which Socrates took part, and each gives a valuable account of a Greek supper-party.

Dioscorides. For 1,600 years from the time when it was written (in the first century A.D.), his *Materia Medica* remained the authority on every vegetable substance used in medicine, and on natural, medicinal, and doctored wines, both Greek and Roman.

Galen. This great physician, born in Asia Minor, court doctor to Marcus Aurelius, was also a connoisseur of wines. Searching in the Palatine cellars for the best Falernian for his master, he would only consider that which had reached twenty years of age. Athenæus referred to his surpassing output in philosophical and medical writings, and to his *Treatise on Wines*—but these were lost.

Athenæus. The author of the long-winded *Deipnosophists* (learned, indeed pedantic, banqueters) is an unrivalled source of gossip and information, accurate or not. In long dialogues and discussions on fish, riddles, wine-making, cheesecakes, the use of words, wine again—he inserts quotations from almost every author of his day (*c*. A.D. 230) and earlier. His accounts of different kinds of wine are valuable; his preserving fragments of lost writers, even more so. Athenæus himself was born at Naucratis in Egypt. As his work proves, he was a great reader and amasser of encyclopædic knowledge. *The Deipnosophists* is a description of a banquet at the house of Laurentinus, a Roman noble. Galen was one of the guests.

Latin

Cato. The first practical account, written in Latin, of Roman wine-growing appeared in *De Agri Cultura* by Cato the Censor, a hard-headed old Roman born on a farm in 234 B.C. Pliny, writing two hundred years later, quoted some of his precepts with approval.

Marcus Varro. This 'learned historian', who lived in the time of Julius Cæsar and Augustus Cæsar, wrote a handbook on farming, *De Re Rustica*, always considered one of the best of its kind, and not begun until his eightieth year. He gives lucid instructions on vine tending and wine-making, and cites in his work the maxims of earlier Greek writers—and of Mago of Carthage.

Virgil. Because of his supremacy as a poet, Virgil's *Second Georgic* is one of the (if not *the*) best-known works on the vine. Yet he was not an experienced cultivator (although his father was a farmer), and Varro was said to be his authority. Pliny remarked that, gracious poet though he was, Virgil only mentioned fifteen varieties of grape.

Pliny. This is Pliny the Elder (A.D. 23–79). Book XIV of his *Naturalis Historia* is devoted to vines and different kinds of wine with recipes for making them. He referred in his work to most of the important wine writing then extant. Always keen in pursuit of scientific knowledge, he died investigating an eruption of Vesuvius.

Horace. He knew wine (and grew it) and famous vintages are mentioned in the *Odes* and *Satires*—Chian, Lesbian, Cæcuban, and Falernian. The Lesbian, he said, was harmless, leaving no headache. Calenian, produced near the Falernian vineyards, was one of the wines he liked, and he offered it to his patron Mæcenas in place of the Falernian he could not afford.

Juvenal and Martial. Both were writers of satire, flourishing about A.D. 100. Each writes of wines, and of customs, fashionable at the time. Martial, especially, has a lot to tell—of old wives' tales about wine, about faked wines from Marseilles, etc.

Petronius. Very little is known about him. He may have been the same Titus Petronius who was known for a lazy, dissipated fellow, yet managed to be a Consul. His account of Trimalchio's feast in the *Satyricon* has already been mentioned.

Columella. Of this writer, also, little is known. From internal evidence he seems to have been born about the beginning of the first century at Cadiz. He had an uncle, also Columella, a farmer in Spain, whom he sometimes quoted. He wrote a book about trees, and twelve books of *Res Rustica*, a remarkably clear and complete treatise on Roman farming and viniculture. In Books III and IV are detailed directions for planting and dressing a vineyard; in Book XII (the responsibilities of the steward's wife) instructions on preparing the vintage, making wine, correcting the must, and so on.

Ausonius. The Bordeaux professor who became tutor to the future Emperor Gratian (son of Valentinian), and afterwards Governor of the Province of Gaul and a Consul, retired in old age to his villa and his vineyards—he had one at Pauillac, another small property on the Dordogne, and later, a property in the Charente district. It is by no means certain that he ever lived on the site of Château Ausone. During his travels with the Emperor he visited the Moselle Valley, which delighted him, because it reminded him of the Bordeaux vineyards. In his writings, however, he had more to say about food than about wine.

Some Ancient Wines

Descriptions of the following wines whose names have not been forgotten are collected from the writers listed above. Sometimes they contradicted each other. Some of them would grow lyrical about rose and violet in the bouquet of a wine, as writers on wine do now.

Greek

Maronean. This, already referred to as the wine that Odysseus gave to Polyphemus, was described by Pliny as the most ancient of all—grown near the Thracian shore, dark in colour, and generally mixed with eight parts of water to one of wine. According to Pliny, the Maronean retained in his day all its strength and vigour.

Pramnian. This most glorious wine of antiquity was said by Homer to be Nestor's favourite, and the wine, 'very strong and nutritious', which he gave to the wounded Machaon, with relishes of goat cheese and raw onions. It was the base of Circe's magic potion, and still known in Athens when Aristophanes was writing—he did not care for it. It was the opinion of Dioscorides that the grapes pressed out the must by their own weight (thus producing a rich essence); but Athenæus reported that it was neither a sweet nor a thick wine, but dry and hard, and extraordinarily strong.

Chian. According to more than one writer, this was the best of Greek wines, 'faultless, never causing a headache', and the island's first growths appear to have been Phanean and the wine of Arisium. Horace got in a cask of Chian for a party, and gave orders that half of it should be mixed for the temperate guests, nine cups of water to three of wine; the rest for the hard drinkers, nine cups of wine to three of water. The Chians, who were great gourmets, had a legend that the son of Dionysos first taught them to make the dark red wine. Evidently it was sweet and rather thick.

Lesbian. This was a sweet wine. 'How sweet the Pramnian Lesbian wine', said one of the characters quoted by Athenæus (thus, Pramnian must have been a type, not a place-name). Some declared it the nicest of all but, in the opinion of Athenæus, it was less astringent, more diuretic than the Chian, and not so pleasant. No sea-water was mixed with it, he said.

Thasian. A 'rich and rosy' wine, said to have been a noble growth when mellowed by age. Theophrastus told that it was 'wonderfully delicious and well flavoured; they knead dough with honey and put that in the jars, so that the wine receives sweetness from the honey and fragrance from itself'. It was a wine that had to be strained.

Coan. The wine of the island of Cos, where Hippocrates wrote his famous treatise on medicine, was heavily mixed with sea-water, and white in colour. Cato gives a recipe for faking it with Italian wine and salt. It has been described as headachy.

Bybline. Originally the famous wine of ancient Byblos in northern Syria. Vines were probably transplanted to Thrace afterwards. It must have been sweet and fragrant. Hesiod wrote: 'In weary summer, when the goats are fattest and the wine is at its best, then let me have the shadow of a rock and some Bybline wine.'

Helbon, or Chalybon. A celebrated sweet wine of Syria, made near Damascus and mentioned in the Bible. It was a favourite of the Persian kings.

Roman

Falernian. The most famous of all the Roman wines was often praised by Horace, although Pliny classified it among the second growths, while admitting that it ranked high at that time. He added that it was the only wine which would take fire when lighted, and that it came in three styles: light and dry, yellow, sweet and dark. Trimalchio's Opimian wine was a Falernian. Galen's view was that the wine (of other years than the Opimian, presumably) was not fit to drink until it was ten years old, at its best between fifteen and twenty, and liable to give one a headache after that. Redding, describing the Falernian that grew in volcanic Campania near Naples, where Massic was also produced—rough, dark, and strong until it grew mellow—guessed that it would have resembled Lacrima Christi.

Setine. The favourite of Augustus Cæsar, diplomatically placed in the first class by Pliny. Athanæus also recorded that it was first-class, 'like Falernian', but lighter and not so apt to make one drunk. It was produced at Setia on the Appian Way.

Cæcuban. Another of Pliny's Firsts. Athanænus said it was a wine of breed, generous and heady, not reaching its peak for many years. Horace knew it; but the vineyards disappeared when Nero started to make a canal from Lake Baiæ to Ostia.

Alban. The wine of Alba, referred to by various writers, seems to have been of two kinds, sweet and dry. Pliny classified it a Third, and it was said to be good for the stomach.

Sorrentine. Opinions differed about this. Galen considered it was no good until it was twenty-five years old. Doctors recommended it for the health, but Tiberius called it 'generous vinegar'. Pliny said it was made from Aminean grapes, grown low on props.

Mamertine. The wine was produced near Messina, in Sicily. Galen found it light, well balanced, and pleasing. Julius Cæsar brought it into fashion when, to celebrate his third Consulship in 46 B.C., he dispensed not two wines but four: Falernian, Chian, Lesbian, and Mamertine. A wine of that name, pale in colour, high in alcohol, is still made in the same district.

Château Clerc-Milon-Mondon

Bordeaux red wine. District: Haut-Médoc, France. Commune: Pauillac.

Adjoining Châteaux Lafite and Mouton-Rothschild, the vineyard is a Fifth Growth (*Cinquième Cru*) of Médoc as classified in 1855. The wine is a monopoly of the Dourthe wine shipping firm in Moulis, Médoc.

Characteristics. Well-made wines with typically Pauillac characteristics: hard at the outset, full-bodied, and quite rich.

Vineyard area: 25 acres.

Average production: 2,100 cases.

Climat

Burgundian term for a vineyard, equivalent of Growth (*Cru*) in Bordeaux.

Château Climens

Bordeaux white wine. District: Sauternes, France. Commune: Barsac.

One of the two best vineyards in Barsac—the other is Château Coutet, an eighth of a mile away—Climens stands in a winding country lane running between old stone walls and marked at turnings with golden arrows to direct visitors along the Route de Sauternes. Entitled to either of the place-names, Barsac or Sauternes, the wine often uses Barsac-Sauternes. (In the past Barsac was a celebrated district; but since 1936 the wines of the commune have been allowed to take the name of Sauternes, which had become more famous. Barsac wines are legitimate Sauternes, although they are inclined to be slightly lighter and drier.)

In 1855, the year Climens was classified a First Growth (*Premier Cru*) of Sauternes, Monsieur Henri

Gounouilhou acquired the property, and it is in his family today. The unpretentious, low wooden château is not lived in by the proprietors; but the *chais* across the gravel courtyard from it are large and impressive. The vineyard is four-fifths in Sémillon vine and one-fifth in Sauvignon and Muscadelle, and in the summer after the February 1956 freeze it presented a tragic picture. Most of the vines were blackened stubs, with hardly a sprout of green, and Climens vintages of 1956 and 1957 were non-existent. Afterwards, the vines began to bear again, except in patches so badly struck that they had to be replanted. All the flat-lying Sauternes vineyards were in the same plight.

Characteristics. A wine which is much better when young. It reaches the height of finesse in great years. For sheer delicacy in sweetness, the beautiful 1929s, 1947s, and 1949s were classics. In such years, Climens excels Château d'Yquem—it is lighter, with less vinosity and body, yet miraculously subtle.

Vineyard area: 70 acres.

Average production: 4,500 cases.

Clinton

Productive American vine giving small, black, spicy grapes yielding wines suitable for blending but little else. The vine is mostly cultivated for root-stock, for other vines rather than for its fruit.

Clos

A walled vineyard—or a vineyard which was once enclosed by a wall. These occur mainly in Burgundy. Some of their wines are sufficiently important to be entered under individual headings. Other well-known vineyards are as follows: Le Clos (Pouilly-Fuissé); Les Clos (Chablis); Les Clos (Côte Rôtie); Clos des Arlots (Nuits-Saint-Georges-Prémeaux); Clos Blanc (Pommard); Clos de la Boudriotte (Chassagne); Clos du Chapitre (Fixin); Clos de la Commaraine (Pommard); Clos des Corvées (Nuits-Saint-Georges-Prémeaux); Clos des Ducs (Volnay); Clos des Forêts-Saint-Georges (Nuits-Saint-Georges-Prémeaux); Clos des Lambrays (Morey); Clos de la Maréchale (Nuits-Saint-Georges-Prémeaux); Clos des Mouches (Beaune); Clos du Papillon (Savennières-Loire); Clos des Perrières (Meursault); Clos des Porrets-Saint-Georges (Nuits); Clos des Réas (Vosne); Clos du Roi (Aloxe-Corton); Clos du Roi (Beaune); Clos Saint-Jacques (Gevrey); Clos Saint-Jean (Chassagne); Clos Saint-Paul (Givry); Clos Saint-Pierre (Givry).

Clos de Bèze

See CHAMBERTIN-CLOS DE BÈZE.

Clos Fourtet

See FOURTET, CLOS.

Clos Haut-Peyraguey

See HAUT-PEYRAGUEY.

Clos de la Roche

Burgundy red wine. District: Côte de Nuits, France. Commune: Morey-Saint-Denis. Official Classification: Great Growth (Grand Cru).

Clos de la Roche is one of the least-known wines of this section of the Côte de Nuits and is thus often good, and sometimes exceptional, value. Throughout the centuries of its existence, it has been overshadowed by Bonnes Mares, by the Clos de Tart and Clos des Lambrays, and by the unfortunate circumstance that wines of Morey were more often than not sold under the name of one of the two famous adjoining communes—Gevrey-Chambertin and Chambolle-Musigny—probably more to the advantage of the two neighbours than to their loss.

The vineyard is the largest of the important Growths of Morey, covering some thirty-seven acres. It stands up the hill, above the road that goes through the vineyards, along the boundary between Gevrey and Morey. Its nobility is such that it is one of the rare Great Growths (*Grands Crus*) of Burgundy, and bottles are not labelled with both vineyard name and commune name—vineyard name alone is sufficient. To earn the name, of course, the wine must meet the rigorous Great Growth standards. Like most of the wines of Morey, it is sturdy and rich yet curiously delicate, much like a Clos de Tart. Draw a graph from the sturdy nobility of the great Chambertin to the elegance of Musigny, and Clos de la Roche stands perhaps just below Chambertin, lacking some of its austere majesty but adding a beguiling grace.

As is the case with most Burgundian vineyards, this one is divided among a number of growers. All together, in 1954—an average year for quantity—they produced 9,000 imp. gallons (10,800 U.S.) of wine or the equivalent of about 4,500 cases.

Clos Saint-Denis

Burgundy red wine. District: Côte de Nuits, France. Commune: Morey-Saint-Denis. Official Classification: Great Growth (Grand Cru).

The vineyards of the Clos Saint-Denis stand alongside the Route des Grands Crus, the road that threads through the middle of the Côte d'Or vineyards, slightly before you reach the village of Morey heading south. In 1927, the village chose to add the vineyard name to its own although the Clos was not at that time classed among the topmost of the commune. This was remedied in 1937 when Clos Saint-Denis was ranked among the Great Growths (*Grands Crus*)—the thirty-one outstanding vineyards of the Côte d'Or.

The wine which starts its career in the vineyard of Clos Saint-Denis is among the lightest of the top-rated wines of the Côte de Nuits. In fine years, delicacy and finesse are the characteristics to look for, rather than the full, robust strength of its peers, Clos de Tart, Clos de la Roche, and Clos des Lambrays. (This last is an outstanding wine despite its classification among the First Growths (*Premiers Crus*) instead of among the Great Growths.)

Within the 16·2 acres of the vineyards there are a number of growers who together declare to the French Government 4,000 imp. gallons (4,800 U.S.) of wine in an average year for quantity. This works out at about 2,000 cases.

Clos de Tart

Burgundy red wine. District: Côte de Nuits, France. Commune: Morey-Saint-Denis. Official Classification: Great Growth (Grand Cru).

The Clos de Tart received its present name in 1141 when the vineyard called *Climat de la Forge* was sold to the Bernardines de l'Abbaye de Notre-Dame de Tart, a feminine offshoot of the Cistercian order. A Bull of Pope Lucius III confirmed the sale in 1184 and the vineyard has been the Clos de Tart ever since. The sisters cultivated the vineyard—expanding it slightly in 1240—until the French Revolution, when it was seized and sold by the State. Unlike most Burgundian vineyards, the Clos de Tart has been kept intact through the changes it has undergone since the Revolution, and today it is entirely in the hands of the shipping firm of J. Mommessin, whose headquarters are in Mâcon.

Clos de Tart lies just north of the village of Morey, to the right of the vineyard road as you go south, and between Bonnes Mares and the Clos des Lambrays. Its 17·8 acres are entirely enclosed within an ancient wall which borders the road along the mid-section of the hill. The wine is often known as a 'ladies' wine', but this is in deference to the distaff side of the Cistercians, for it is sturdy and big. To its Morey characteristic of robustness is added a special delicacy and subtlety, and it ages exceedingly gracefully. The vineyard has been rated a Great Growth (*Grand Cru*) by the French wine authorities, the highest rank a Burgundian vineyard can receive; and while it may not have all the fiery strength of neighbouring Clos des Lambrays—ranked only as *Premier Cru* (First Growth)—it sometimes merits the considerable renown it has received.

Production in an average-quantity year is 4,200 imp. gallons (5,095 U.S.) or the equivalent of about 2,000 cases.

Clos de Vougeot

Burgundy red wine. District: Côte de Nuits, France. Commune: Vougeot. Official Classification: Great Growth (Grand Cru).

The 124 acres of the Clos de Vougeot (or Clos Vougeot) are so famous that the vineyard is practically a national asset of France; and it was a tradition for passing regiments of the French Army to salute the vines. Started in the twelfth century by Cistercian monks, on the slopes above their monastery, it remained in the hands of the clergy until the French Revolution, when the State confiscated church property. The monks did not plant the entire vineyard; some of it they accepted as a gift from early Burgundians with names such as Hugues le Blanc, Eudes-le-Vert, and Wallo Gile, but they consolidated the holding and built a wall around it.

In the sixteenth century the vineyard was so big that it was felt that a château and a house for the wine-press should now be added to the buildings inside the wall. The drawing-up of the plans for this building was entrusted to a young and zealous monk and he went to work with fervour, but made the mistake of signing the completed blueprint with his own name. The Abbot informed him that he had committed the deadly sin of pride, and ordered that the plans should be given to other monks to complete. These new hands botched them hopelessly. Legend has it that the original architect, following the strict code of the Middle Ages, repented his sin and died of chagrin, and the Clos was built complete with all its structural faults as a monument to his sinful pride and fall from grace.

Since its foundation, the building has undergone repeated additions and renovations. The last—although this is almost a continuous process—was at the hands of the Confrérie des Chevaliers du Tastevin de Bourgogne, the society which makes sure that the rest of the world does not forget the wines of Burgundy. The members of the order, who are mostly shippers, growers, and visiting dignitaries interested in wines, meet every month or so in the great dining-room of the château, and the halls which once resounded with the plainsong of the Church now reverberate with the noise and tumult of the Chevaliers singing the songs—and the praises—of Burgundy. The great dining-hall can seat 500 people, and the towering stone pillars are decorated with coats of arms, with baskets which once were used to carry in the grapes, and with the dates of the most famous vintage years, dating back to 1108.

Since the vineyard was confiscated, after the Revolution, it has seldom been under one ownership—the last proprietor lived in the nineteenth century, and his grave lies beside the terraced drive leading up to the forbidding gates of the château. Since his death the ownership has become more and more diverse and today there are about 100 people with holdings within the walls.

Each one of the owners has his own plot. His vines will be of varying ages, and age has a direct effect on quality. The vines will be tended as each owner desires, the grapes will be picked when he feels that it is time, and wine-making procedures will vary according to his talent, conscience, and ability. Once made, the wines will be sold to different people, some in barrel to shippers and some bottled by the growers. Apart from all else, the vineyard itself is divided into three different sections and the wines will vary accordingly. As a result, drawing a common set of taste characteristics which are distinctly Clos de Vougeot is difficult in the extreme. If the job had to be done, it would be fair to say that in a good year a characteristic Clos de Vougeot will be relatively full-bodied and with a big nose, which will not have all the austere majesty of a Chambertin nor the delicate grace of a Musigny or a Romanée-Saint-Vivant but will incline towards the latter. In any case, it will be a mouth-filling wine, and the aftertaste will be glorious and lingering.

Average yearly production for the whole 124 acres is about 25,000 imp. gallons (30,000 U.S.).

Of the three sections of the Clos as set up by the early monks, that just behind the château, leading up to the wall, is traditionally the best part, with the middle section just behind it; and the bottom, close to the *Route Nationale* (national highway), distinctly inferior. The difference is partly in the pitch of the slope—very flat at the bottom, becoming steeper towards the château—and partly in the soil. Chalky clay, reddish-brown in colour and rich in pebbles, makes up the top parts; and the bottom, more brown than red, has more humus and fewer pebbles. The land at the bottom is prone to hold moisture and only in dry years do the vines produce in a way comparable with those planted higher up.

At one time the vineyard was divided into plots, and despite the divided ownership many of these still retain their traditional identity. In the uppermost part are Musigny de Clos de Vougeot (closest to Chambolle-Musigny), Garenne, Plante Chamel, Plante Abbé, Montiottes Hautes, Chioures, Quartier de Marci Haut, Grand Maupertuis, and Petit Maupertuis. The middle is made up of Dix Journaux, Baudes Bas, and Baudes Saint-Martin; and the bottom, where the wine is generally inferior but commands nevertheless the same high price, has Montiottes Bas, Quatorze Journaux, and the bottom portions of Baudes Bas and Baudes Saint-Martin.

Some white wine is made in the little commune of Vougeot. This is not entitled to the name Clos de Vougeot but is sold as Clos Blanc de Vougeot.

Cloudy

Cloudiness in wine is caused by tiny particles in suspension and often clears spontaneously. This condition is sometimes brought on by a rapid and excessive change in temperature.

Cobblers

In America, long iced drinks concocted with fruit juice, wine, or spirits and decorated with pieces of fruit or berries.

Cochineal

Grubs of various sorts which attack the vines (*see* CHAPTER EIGHT, p. 38).

Cochylis Moth

The Cochylis pest, attacking by laying eggs on the grapes and eventually smothering them in cocoons, was formerly one of the most dangerous enemies of the vine. It was fought ineffectively by nicotine and arsenic. Now, however, the Swiss chemicals Nirosan and Gesarol, sprayed individually or used in combination with Bordeaux mixture (copper-sulphate and chalk solution), are successful in eradicating the pest.

See CHAPTER EIGHT, p. 37.

Cocktail

A mixed aperitif, containing spirits and served iced in small glasses. The best-known examples are the Manhattan (two parts rye whiskey to one of Italian vermouth, and a dash of bitters) and the Dry Martini (four parts gin, one part French vermouth; but in the United States, the latter is sometimes sprinkled in with an atomizer).

Cocuy

Venezuelan liquor from the desert plant sabila.

Coffey Still

The Coffey (or patent) still, developed by the Irish Inspector-General of Excise whose name it bears, made possible the rapid and therefore large-scale production of grain whisky. Other patent stills, such as the Barbet and Ilye, are now also in use.

Cognac

Brandy. District: Western France.

In 1860 a French geologist named Coquand made a trip to the Charente district of France on the Bay of Biscay, an often misty seaboard region irradiated with a strange quality of ultra-violet light. With him he took an odd companion for a scientific excursion —a professional taster of brandies and wines. From farm to farm the pair went, from one brandy warehouse to another, each pursuing his own science. Coquand, the geologist, went into the vineyard and analysed the soil; the taster merely stayed inside and sniffed and sipped the brandy. At the end of the trip the two compared notes on the qualities and characteristics of each of the Cognac brandies—one as he had deduced them from the soil, the other as he discovered them in the grape. And their notes tallied in every single case.

Coquand had proved his theory on the relationship of the soil and the Cognac, and this changing relationship accounts completely for the division of the region into six zones—Grande Champagne, Petite Champagne, Borderies, Fins Bois, Bons Bois, and Bois Ordinaires—but it does not quite account for Cognac.

It is interesting to speculate upon the unique excellence of Cognac, and its causes. To begin with, there is the chalk in the soil—the exact degree decreasing from Grande Champagne down the range of officially marked-out areas to Bois Ordinaires, the value and the quality of the brandy decreasing with it. But chalk does not create a fine wine beverage in Cognac only—it produces Champagne and Sherry too. Chalk-lime is a mother-bed for exceptional vines.

Cognac wine (or, correctly, Charente wine—the name of the town had not then overspread the district) was always sourish, it seems; but in early days it was not distilled, and the acidity had not become a virtue. English and Norse seamen used to come to the Charente not for the wine but for the salt in the region; but once they were there they bought wine as well. In the centuries that followed the vineyards were encouraged to over-produce. The next development was that, to save space in the ships which carried them away, to strengthen them before the North Sea voyage, and finally to avoid taxation which was then on bulk—the wines were boiled down. The idea was to reduce them and later on to restore them with water. Nobody could have imagined what a miraculous essence would be distilled from the hard Charente wines.

When Cognac was first distilled, sometime after 1600, other brandies were already being made in France: but where Charente wine gave a drinkable natural brandy, all other spirits—until the invention of multiple distillation a century later—had to be doctored by herb and fruit flavours to hide the bad taste. The final contributing factor to the unique perfection of Cognac was the barrel in which it was aged.

Immediately to the east above Charente, in the first rises of the Massif Central where the River Charente has its source, is a forested district around Limoges, the land of Limousin oak.

When the distillation of Cognac was an art almost two hundred years old, the makers began to age the brandy in barrels of the Limousin oak which happened to be at hand. The result was Cognac as we know it now. Prices these days are high, and the oak forests of the world have been combed for another wood that would do for the brandy what the Limousin oak does. But there is no substitute. 'It's hard to say which is more important, the wood or the wine,' they tell you in Cognac. In 22 imp. gallons (26·4 U.S.) of the brandy aged twenty-five years in the oak there will be one pound of wood extract, an immense factor in the bouquet and taste of old Cognac. The oak from the forest of Tronçais in the Allier was used extensively on account of its fine grain. It gave excellent results though slightly more slowly than the Limousin oak. It is used less and less as its prices are extremely high.

Until 1860 Charente brandy was not shipped in bottle, and it probably was not called Cognac. Old-timers in the industry opposed shipping in bottle, saying that as brandy ages only in wood, it would be better for it to travel in the barrel. True though this was, bottling the brandy for the first time gave the makers control over what would be in the bottle when it reached the consumer. This is an example of a fundamental law in wine; the surest bottle is the one that passes through the hands of middlemen with the cork in. Moreover, the name on the label of the place the brandy came from became famous, until finally the brandy was known as Cognac.

Today there may be Coñacs and Koniaks (a Greek imitation now suppressed)—but there is only one Cognac by law in France, and in many other countries. It is specifically a brandy distilled from the wine of certain varieties of grapes, grown in delimited areas of the Charente and Charente-Maritime departments of France (and to a very small extent in two others), and which has been twice distilled in a pot still—never in the more common continuous still—and has then been aged.

Roughly eighty-eight years ago the whole vineyard was wiped out by the vine pest phylloxera, and the industry had to be restarted. The makers, while they were doing this, realized that the many neutral spirits then being developed by multiple distillation were competing in their own market, and since, therefore, with the growing tendency to vend in bottle the spirit could no longer be aged abroad, the Cognac firms themselves undertook the ageing of the brandies. The financial load may be assessed when it is considered that the sale of Cognac now touches 300 million new francs (around £22 million or 60 million dollars) a year and that a man selling five-year-old Cognac must, of course, have the full supplies for five different years in stock. If his sales were exclusively of forty-year Cognac he ought theoretically to have forty years' worth in stock—which would demand an astronomical capital sum, and warehouses of a size to cover half the Charente. With proportionately small stocks of old brandy, two firms today hold supplies worth, in each case, approximately £18 million (50 million dollars)—about 52,000 barrels each.

Types of Cognac

Nowadays most firms concentrate on three types of Cognac. The youngest, still rather raw, is best drunk with soda. Then there is Three-Star, which amounts to about 90% of the Cognac sold. Various legends account for the star device; it began to be used three-quarters of a century ago, when the blending of Cognacs to type was coming into fashion—it is said in Cognac that the first Three-Star was made and shipped for the Australian market. It is important to know that this sign does not mean that the brandy is three years old. It does, however, indicate a Cognac usually older than those designed for mixing with soda, and one always younger than a V.S.O.P. Generally, with many important firms, the Three-Star has about five years of barrel-age (spirits do not age in glass as wine does, so that an 1860 Cognac bottled in 1900, and a 1900 Cognac bottled in 1940, are exactly the same age).

The third type is V.S.O.P.: the letters stand for Very Superior Old Pale—somewhat contradictorily, because the longer a Cognac is left in the barrel to age, the more of the darkening tannin it absorbs from the oak. It begins as a colourless liquid; tannin tans it. Very Superior Old Dark would be a more logical name.

As with Three-Star, V.S.O.P. is really a style of brandy, not a brandy of any specified age. It is the oldest of the three types described here; but many firms put out a Reserve, Extra, X.O., Cordon Bleu, or in rare cases even a straight vintage brandy, all in relatively small quantities.

In fact, a V.S.O.P. put out by one of the better houses may approach twenty years of barrel-age. It is essential to understand, however, that 'twenty years old' refers to a type; for Cognac, except in the 'straight Cognacs' seldom made commercially now, is always a blend of brandies from different areas and different years. Each firm establishes its V.S.O.P.—the process is exactly the same for its Three-Star—and continues by skilful blending, to copy the original model and so to repeat the same bottle over and over again. Master samples are kept, and with great care and art—by 'sniffers', because they smell the Cognacs rather than taste them—diverse brandies are mixed to reproduce the sample, always from year to year in differing proportions to equalize the differences of the years. A 'twenty-year-old' brandy is likely to contain Cognacs both older and younger than twenty years.

V.S.O.P. describes what the brandy is: i.e., such-and-such a firm's interpretation of V.S.O.P. style. V.S.E.P. (E for Extra) is also seen sometimes on the U.S. market.

It is worth mentioning that the buyer gets greater value for his V.S.O.P., or the other older Cognacs, than for Three-Star. Duty, casing, bottling, etc., are the same, and the extra cost for a much finer Cognac is often comparatively little, whereas enjoyment will be doubled.

Vintage and Age

Age is considered the great virtue in Cognac, and at present there are four age-indications for the British–American market that are based on checkable fact. They are:

1. In England, Cognac must be at least three years old by British law.
2. In the United States, Cognac must be at least two years old by American law.
3. V.S.O.P., by French law, must be at least four years old to be exported from France.
4. 'British Bonded'—Cognac shipped in cask to England and matured in the warehouses of London docks—is aged in bond and a record of the years is kept. This record is generally authentic, and at the present time a British Bonded may be seen not only

in England but also in the United States, because it bears the only age indication beyond the American legal minimum, and the Cognac can be sold at a premium which makes transhipment worth the trouble. In the trade, British Bonded is also known as 'Old Landed' because it is landed before it is bottled. The style, matured in the London climate, very different from that of Cognac, has a somewhat clean, melted taste (which some people like and some do not); and it may be expected to have lost strength, as brandies do when they age in damp places. Yet some of the greatest Cognacs available today are London bottlings which have never been blended but are straight vintage brandies. These can be superb. Delicate with age, they often become the prototypes of great Cognac. Since the war, shipment in cask to England has dwindled greatly.

In Cognac itself, the age of brandy is not controlled beyond five years. Five official categories exist after the new brandy: (1) one year old; (2) two years old; (3) three years old; (4) four years old; but (5) five years old and any number of years beyond. Like every other regulation in Cognac, these controls are rigid and reliable.

There is sound sense in limiting age control at a five-year maximum. Cognac is aged by shippers, by farmers and by co-operatives. There are 322 Cognac firms, numerous Co-operative distillers, and, of the approximately 70,000 peasants and others who grow wine to make Cognac, a little over 7,000 distil and age some or all of their own product. In addition to this multiplicity of individuals, the great Cognac stores of the principal firms are spread in series of warehouses over the towns of Cognac and Jarnac and into the countryside. This is done to prevent a fire from destroying the stock; although indemnified by insurance, a firm wiped out by fire would be years building up old brandies in order to re-establish its brands, and by that time would have lost its customers. Faced with so many owners and so many small collections of casks, Cognac authorities know that a realistic control of very old brandies is impossible. 'Most of all we value public confidence and we prefer not to certify anything we can't be absolutely sure of,' they rightly say.

Except for an occasional British Bonded, no Cognac can be positively known to be more than five years of age. (The V.S.O.P. and older brands of all reputable houses of course *are* older, and the rare straight vintage Cognac from a fine firm will be exactly what it claims to be and perhaps very old—the point is that it can't be proved.) Less and less, Cognac makers themselves like to talk about age. 'We go to the impractical, enormous cost of producing a twenty-year-old Cognac,' they say, 'and our reward is that the public thinks it is too young because it did not travel to and from Russia with Napoleon.' The brandies would be no older than the day they were bottled if they *had* been on that march to Russia; and in fact, no brandy from that time is on the commercial market. Undoubtedly, the worst deception in Cognac brandies is the fraud and fakery connected with alleged 'Napoleon' brandy—but a distinction must be made between brandies pretending to derive from Napoleon's time, and the Napoleon style. The latter is an indication akin to V.S.O.P., and the Cognac will be at least five years old.

Beyond an optimum of about forty years—it depends both on the Cognac and how it is housed—barrel-ageing itself ceases to be a good thing. 1815 to 1850 Cognacs, which may still be tasted in the *paradises*—inner sanctums of the oldest casks—of firms in Jarnac and Cognac, are only echoes, although they are still useful in blends of very old Cognacs, because they keep their bouquet after they have lost everything else.

The consensus of opinion in Cognac seems to be that within a dozen years V.S.O.P. brandies will not be more than ten years old and that Three-Star will dominate the output. Interest rates, duties, and taxes multiplying the price of Cognac by about two or three in most countries have made the price of a bottle so high that the makers cannot add on the real cost of ageing old brandy; to do so would be to price it out of the market. V.S.O.P. of twenty years old is already considered by many firms to be a losing proposition. (A bottle of Cognac costing 2 dollars when it leaves France costs 7 dollars when it is sold in the U.S.; leaving France at 10 Norwegian krøne, it rises to 83·32 krøne in Norway. These figures illustrate the effect of duties.) The debatable question is whether small firms selling very old Cognacs to a select clientèle are going to be able to survive. It is regrettable that Three-Star Cognacs of the smaller houses are being driven out of business as the advertising campaigns of the biggest brands gather cumulative force, and some makers believe that in a generation there will be only a half-dozen or so mammoth firms; others, while admitting that the monopolies are likely to corner Three-Star and perhaps V.S.O.P., contend that there will always be sufficient demand for brandies too old ever to be produced on a big scale to keep small, de luxe houses alive.

Vintage in Cognac brandy is a debatable point. A 'straight' Cognac is the brandy of one area and one

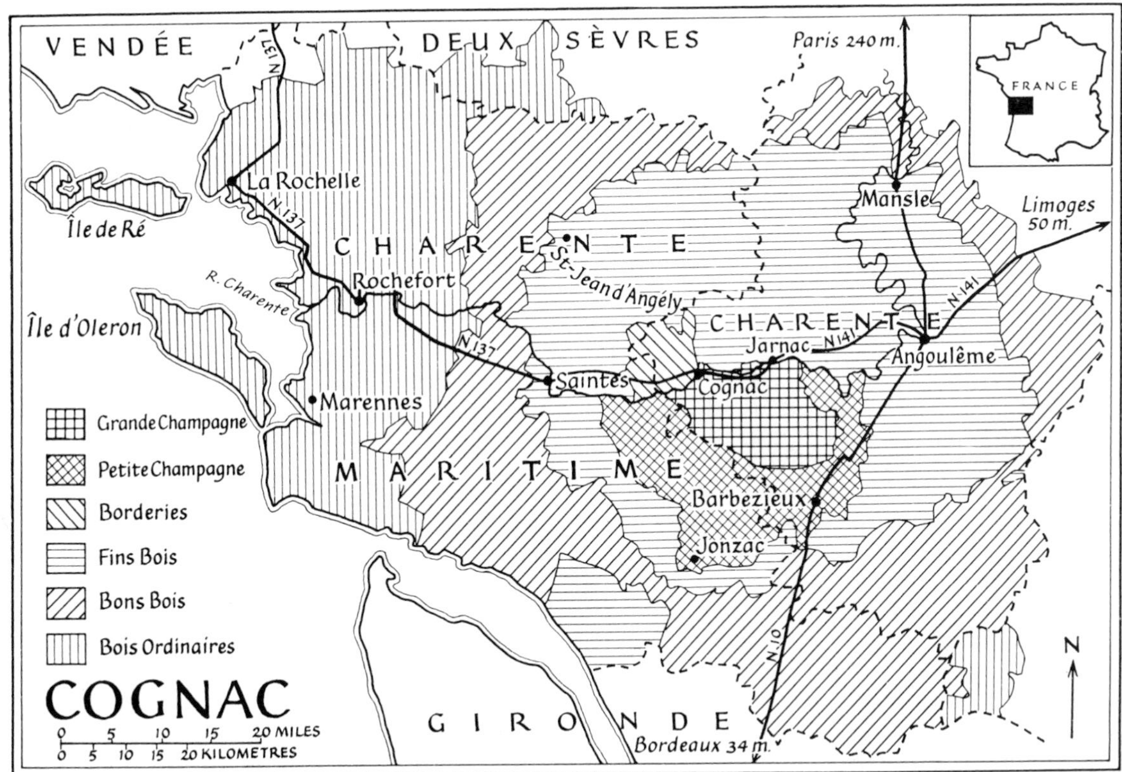

year. Blending—the nearly universal practice in Cognac—clips off the peaks to fill up the valleys. If this were always true, all blend Cognac would be a mere compromise, a concession to marketing conditions and the demand for a stable product. But most houses in Cognac contend that it is not all. No region, they say, and seldom any year, produces by itself a fully balanced, complete, and harmonious Cognac. Granting that Grande Champagne is the best region, finest in bouquet, finesse, elegance, and charm, they point out that the Borderies sector produces Cognacs with more body—a touch of heartiness often needed in a too-princely Grande Champagne.

Grande Champagne, Petite Champagne, Fine Champagne, Fine Maison, Borderies, and Bois

Vineyards as such play no role in Cognac and do not appear on labels, but the following districts are important to know and are often indicated on labels of bottles in the higher categories. The vineland of Cognac—within the boundaries of which all wine which is to become Cognac must grow—is geographically proportioned as follows:

	%
Grande Champagne	10·8
Petite Champagne	10·3
Borderies	3·9
Fins Bois	33
Bons Bois	29
Bois Ordinaires	13

The order of quality, downwards from Grande Champagne to Bois Ordinaires, is also a rough indication of the geographical order, Grande Champagne being the heart and the other zones circling it. All the districts produce some red wine (from which Cognac is never made) and some white wine which is not made into Cognac; the poorer the district, the greater the proportion of these non-Cognac wines. Altogether, Cognac accounts for about half of the crude wine.

Grande Champagne

The best and the most expensive. But the difference in price is nothing like that between the wines of great vineyards and lesser ones in other famous areas. Grand Champagne has great finesse, bouquet, and elegance; but it is hard to the taste when young, and must age fifteen years or longer; it has less body than Borderies, but more body than Petite Champagne. It is also called Grande Fine Champagne.

Petite Champagne

Similar to Grande Champagne except that the characteristics appear in slightly lesser degree, and it matures rather more quickly. The difference is due to a somewhat smaller proportion of chalk in the soil. 'Champagne' in French indicates a region of chalky soil.

Fine Champagne and *Fine Maison*

The old blend of brandies exclusively from the Grande and Petite Champagne district. The so-called house speciality of a restaurant in France is called Fine Maison and will vary in quality, from fair to excellent, depending on the desire and ability of the restaurant to give something special.

Borderies

The district does not, as is frequently supposed, 'border' the regions of Petite and Grande Champagne. It faces them—and the town of Cognac—from across the River Charente on the north. It gives the Cognacs with the greatest body.

Fins Bois, Bons Bois, Bois Ordinaires

The lesser zones, much larger in area but less thickly planted in vine. All but a patch of the Bois Ordinaires lies along the shore, and the sea air has a tangible effect on the brandy.

Official Regions of Cognac: Communes Entitled to the Most Important Names

The zone within which Cognac may be produced is divided into six regions, of which Grande Champagne, Petite Champagne, and Borderies are the most important.

Grande Champagne (or Grande Fine Champagne)

Communes: Ambleville, Angeac-Champagne, Bonneuil, Bourg-Charente (right bank of River Charente), Bouteville, Château-Bernard, Cognac (left bank of Charente), Critéuil-la-Magdeleine, Éraville, Gensac-la-Pallue, Genté, Gimeux, Gondeville, Juillac-le-Coq, Lignières-Sonneville, Mainxe, Malaville, Merpins, Salles-d'Angles, Saint-Brice (left bank of Charente), Saint-Fort-sur-le-Né, Saint-Même, Saint-Preuil, Segonzac, Touzac, Verrières, Viville.

Petite Champagne

Communes in the department of Charente: Angeac-Charente, Ars, Barbezieux, Barret, Birac, Bourg-Charente, Châteauneuf, Graves, Guimps, Jurignac, Lachaise, Ladiville, Lagarde-sur-le-Né, Montchaude, Mosnac, Nonaville, Saint-Amant-de-Graves, Saint-Bonnet, Saint-Hilaire-de-Barbezieux, Saint-Médard-de-Barbezieux, Saint-Palais-du-Né, Salles-de-Barbezieux; Vignolles.

Communes in the department of Charente-Maritime: Allas-Champagne, Archiac, Arthenac, Biron, Bougneau, Brie-sous-Archiac, Brives-sur-Charente, Celles, Chadenac, Champagnac, Cierzac, Coulonges, Clam, Échebrune, Germignac, Jarnac-Champagne, Jonzac, Lonzac, Meux, Moings, Montils, Neuillac, Neulles, Pérignac-de-Pons, Peaux, Rouffiac, Saint-Ciers-Champagne, Saint-Eugène, Saint-Germain-de-Lusignan, Saint-Germain-de-Vibrac, Saint-Martial-de-Coculet, Saint-Martial-de-Vitaterne, Saint-Maurice-de-Tavernolles, Saint-Lheurine, Saint-Seurin-de-Palenne, Saint-Sever, Salignac-de-Pons.

Borderies

Communes: Burie, Chérac, Cherves, Cognac (right bank of River Charente), Javrezac, Louzac, Saint-André, Saint-Laurent-de-Cognac, Saint-Sulpice, Richemont.

The Vine and the Wine

The vine used to be largely Folle Blanche. By law, sub-regional Cognac—that is, entitled to one of the district names of Grande Champagne, etc.—may be distilled from wine of only the Folle Blanche, Colombard, and Saint-Émilion vines—and five others, under certain conditions, but never to a total of more than 10%. The law is very exact, and since 1955 any grower planting any part of his vineyards in unauthorized vine has his total crop refused.

Colombard and Folle Blanche together now account for less than 6% of the total yield, nearly all of which is Saint-Émilion, a variety of Ugni Blanc. In Cognac perhaps alone, the quantity of yield does not affect quality—and enormous quantity is achieved from the Saint-Émilion; whereas in all fine wine areas yield is strictly limited by law to protect quality.

This is one indication of the peculiar relationship between the wine and the brandy. It is a local axiom that the best Cognac comes from the worst wine. Rightly understood, this is true. The wine is tart, fit only to be drunk with shellfish—or not at all, if anything better is handy. On the other hand, it must be *sound.* Distillation removes neither perfections nor imperfections—it emphasizes them; if there is a taint in the wine, the Cognac distilled from it will be undrinkable. But the virtues in wine for drinking and in wine for making Cognac are not the same. Technically the Saint-Émilion is a third-epoch vine. It is the grape called the Trebbiano in Italy and the Ugni Blanc in Algeria and the extreme south of France and in California. In those hotter regions—in what viticulturalists, marking off growing zones for the vine, call the Third Epoch—it is quite at home. But in Cognac, much farther north, it is not: it seldom ripens properly and gives a sourish, highly acid wine low in alcohol—which happens to be the perfect basis for the world's best brandy.

Life-cycle of a Cognac

The countryside, rolling and misty, infused with that special clarity of actinic sunlight said to account in part for the taste of Cognac, possesses a few great stone châteaux, but the feeling of the landscape is much more primitive and simple than it is in the Loire Valley. The living unit in Cognac is not the castle but the close, a Saracen heritage. A wall encloses house, courtyard, sheds, and hen-coops: it is broken only by two arched portals, which may be closed by great wooden doors.

Inside one of these domestic forts that dot the vineland, it may well seem that time has stood still since the Saracens—and in a way it has. No peasant is more individual and independent than the Cognac grower. After all, he makes it his business to keep a supply of something far stabler than the fluctuating post-war franc in his sheds.

The grapes are brought in from the vines, and the wine-making is much the same as in other regions. With distillation, the difference—and the Cognac—begins.

The wine is heated in a massive fixed copper kettle sitting in its bed—a square brick furnace—and after a time the furious brandy elements pass up as steam, into the gracefully curved 'swan-throat'. Condensed by cooling, the steam becomes the *brouillis*—a milky liquid with an alcoholic strength of from 20% to 30%. The process is repeated: this second time, the 'head' which comes over first—and the 'tail' which comes last—are eliminated—and only the 'heart' of the distillate used. This is the infant Cognac, raw, and unsophisticated, a white brandy of 70% alcohol.

In spite of the seeming timelessness of the walled houses and the way of life, there have been changes here as everywhere else. All through the winter, patient men and women must sit beside the pot stills—and the older generation was more willing to do this than the young people are. More and more shippers are finding that they must do their own distilling because the farmers' sons and daughters won't stay beside the stills.

Once distilled, Cognac goes into a Limousin oak barrel—not too full, so that the liquid may be in contact with oxygen, and in a spot which is to some extent affected by outside temperatures. In theory, the Cognac goes into a new barrel for a year and is transferred to one that has still some tannin left. This move leads to a certain additional amount of evaporation. In practice, to overcome this loss, about half of the Cognac is put into new barrels and the other half straight into used barrels. In this way the brandy absorbs enough tannin from the new oak, but does not stay in contact with it too long. Ideally, the cask should be made from a tree eighty to a hundred years old, for its tannin imparts a mellow flavour to the brandy, whereas young wood may produce harshness. Here again is an influence driving Cognac away from the growers to the dealers. Only Limousin oak and that from the Tronçais forest in the Allier department may be used—and it must be weathered four or five years out-of-doors beforehand. The price for a single stave has now climbed so high that peasant-growers tend to put their brandies into old barrels, to save buying new ones, and a paler Cognac is the result.

During the ageing period, various changes occur: a decrease in the volume of the brandy, a change of degree, dissolution of tannins. At the same time there are less evident chemical changes: oxidation, hydrolysis, acetylization, and the development of the rancid taste.

Blending is always done in the establishments of the shippers—some as large and grim as prisons; others, converted mediæval castles. Barrels of different Cognacs are opened over gutters in the floor above the blending vats. The liquid streams into the vat below, where great paddles moved by machinery slowly turn and agitate it. Blending is done a stage at a time, with long halts in between to let the brandies rest. Slowly they 'marry'.

In about half a century, evaporation will reduce a new Cognac of 70% to the proper drinking and shipping strength of 40%. As it is not economically possible to wait for this natural process, Cognac must be 'reduced' before bottling. This is done by adding distilled water either directly or indirectly. As the draught of water tends to shock the brandy, a few of the better firms reduce indirectly by means of *faible*, or weak brandy. This is Cognac which has been brought down by distilled water to about 27%, and then been given a long rest. Fit again, it is used to reduce other Cognacs—even then reduction is only 8% or 9% at a time. (The brandy is filtered and allowed to rest after each operation.) The addition of the *faible,* and the more elaborate process, increases loss by evaporation. This is the costly element in Cognac-making: the special porousness of the Limousin oak which allows the brandy to ripen, also lets in air—and so it lets out the brandy. The loss by evaporation into the sky above Charente is almost precisely the yearly figure of consumption in France, and one-fifth of that throughout the world.

The Cognacs age in low, above-ground storehouses called *chais,* easily distinguishable by the blackening on the walls, which looks like soot but is a wine fungus. The casks or *tierçons* hold from 75 to 100 imp. gallons (90 to 120 U.S.). Some makers contend that ageing in the bigger barrel is better, others dispute it. At the end of each row of barrels is the *chanteau*—usually marked CH—the partly empty barrel used to replenish the others. Evaporation is encouraged, expensive as it is, for without it there would be no ageing, and the sheds are airy.

When it is ready, the brandy is put into a bottle which has been rinsed with Cognac, and a cork which has been dipped in Cognac is flogged home. It is ready to go out to the world.

Export

Roughly 80% of Cognac is exported. England remains the largest customer, with the United States second. Cognac brings in the largest revenue of any French agricultural product exported.

Sales are going up in both Britain and the U.S.A.—annual import has passed 400,000 cases in the U.S.A. and is approaching 1,000,000 cases in England.

All wines and spirits in France must have a tax certificate, or *acquit,* even if they are moving only from one warehouse to another. By this means, every movement can be traced. An adaptation of the domestic French *congé* is the *Acquit Jaune d'Or* which now accompanies every Cognac shipment exported. Though originally devised to expedite processes of export, the yellow-gold certificate in effect guarantees the important specifications of the brandy.

Cointreau

A famous proprietary liqueur of the Curaçao type made in Angers, France, and in the United States by the Cointreau family. Although the bottle and label are always identical, the alcoholic content varies from country to country. The original name for it was Triple Sec White Curaçao, but so many makers started using the name Triple Sec that it was changed to Cointreau.

See CURAÇAO.

Colares, Collares

Port wine apart, this is the most distinctive wine of Portugal. Grown on sandy vineyards overlooking the Atlantic, a forty-minute drive from Lisbon, the wine achieved prominence during the invasion of the vine pest phylloxera which devastated world viticulture about twenty years before the end of the last century. Sand-grown wines were immune and thus sold at an enormous premium during the phylloxera wine drought. A liking for the wine itself (which is often matured in Angola mahogany or American redwood for as long as a decade and a half), is an acquired habit, for it has an individual—some would say a shocking—taste.

See PORTUGAL.

Collage

The fining process to which wine must be subjected before it is ready to be bottled.

See CHAPTER NINE, p. 45; FINING.

Collar

Label on bottle neck. The French term is *collerette.*

Colmar

Wine town in Alsace.

See ALSACE.

Colombard

White wine grape grown in the Dauphiné region, where it is also known as Bon Blanc; in Charente as Pied-Tendre; in Tarn-et-Garonne as Blanquette.

Colombia

There are an estimated 500 acres of vineyard in Colombia, producing some 2,000 imp. gallons (2,600 U.S.) of wine, almost entirely sweet and fortified with brandy. These are generally called vermouth and Muscatel or mis-called 'manzanilla' and 'port'. Some light table wines are made, too; but these also are distinctly sweet.

Native fruits, such as bananas, oranges, and blackberries, provide the source for most of the alcoholic beverages, and the making of spirits is a monopoly of the provincial governments. Aguardiente, rum, types of whisky and gin are produced in various parts of the country, but the more popular drinks are whisky among the more influential classes, Guarapo and Anisado among the others. Anisado is a species of brandy flavoured with aniseed, while Guarapo is made from fermented sugar and water. Guarapo is not commercially sold and it generally constitutes a home-made beverage for the peasants in certain regions of the country. When fresh, this has some resemblance to new apple cider.

Colour in Spirits

Spirits and liqueurs are by nature colourless, and the colour is added after they leave the still. They may darken somewhat in the barrel, but most tawny spirits take their colour from a dose of caramel; and the green colour of crème-de-menthe is likewise added.

Comète, Vin de la (Comet Wine)

It sometimes happens that a good vintage year is glorified by the appearance of a comet. 1630 was such a year, but 1811, more famous (and not so long ago), is the vintage usually referred to as the 'comet year'.

Commandaria

The great wine of Cyprus and one of the longest-lasting wines in the world.

See CYPRUS.

Commanderie du Bontemps de Médoc

The local wine society and promotional organization of the Médoc, composed of growers, shippers, and various dignitaries interested in wine. Dressed up in mediæval caps and long robes, the members hold meetings, inauguration ceremonies, and luncheons. The society now includes Graves also.

Common Clean

The light style of Jamaican rum.

See RUM, JAMAICA.

Commonwealth Wines

Wines from British Commonwealth countries, notably Australia, Canada, and New Zealand (*q.v.*). Not of the same quality as European fine wines, they are not in the same price class either and may prove extremely enjoyable—if unexceptional—and inexpensive drinking.

Commune

In France, parish or township. In the fine wine areas, the wines of a district clustered around one or more parishes are likely to take the name of the commune, as an official place-name or Appellation Contrôlée—meaning they are legally recognized to have a certain alikeness and certain standards of quality. For example, Margaux, Saint-Julien, Saint-Émilion are important commune names in Bordeaux red wine.

Coñac

Designation improperly used for Spanish brandy.

See SPAIN.

Concannon Vineyard

Livermore Valley, California, U.S.A.

This winery produces red and white table wines, and also a vintage Muscat de Frontignan dessert wine. It was founded by James Concannon in 1883 when forty-seven acres of land of gravelly composition were purchased in the heart of the Livermore Valley. Then, in 1889, he convinced President Porfirio Díaz of Mexico that viticulture should be established in that country on a commercial basis. Díaz approved of this idea, and the Irishman from Livermore was able to ship cuttings from his vineyards to be planted in suitable areas in Mexico. Today, the Livermore vineyards are managed by Captain Joseph S. Concannon who has been at the head of the company since the death of James Concannon in 1911. The 350 acres are planted in Zinfandel, Cabernet Sauvignon, Sémillon, Sauvignon Blanc, Petite-Syrah, and so on.

Concord

The most important blue-black grape of the American East Coast, hardy and productive, adaptable to an astonishing variety of soils and climates, but yielding incredibly mediocre wine—which is, however, widely sold throughout the United States, either blended with others or as Kosher wine—sweet, strong, and utterly undistinguished. Concord wine is known for its pronounced foxy taste and aroma.

Condrieu

Rhône Valley white wine. District: Rhône Valley, France.

The wines are heavily perfumed, with a distinctive taste—or *goût de terroir*—picked up from the granitic soil of the vineyards, and are practically unknown outside the district. They are, however, gaining in popularity and also in quality. Modern methods of vinification and early bottling are doubtless responsible for the latter development; and the rising reputation of the wines is due to the patronage of the widow Point, owner of the great Michelin three star restaurant, the Pyramide, at Vienne, south of Lyons.

Confrérie

French term for Wine Society (*q.v.*).

Congé

Official French document which accompanies shipments of wines and spirits and indicates that internal taxes have been paid. It is used when wine or spirits are sent to a wholesaler, retailer, or to the consumer, inside the country—but not for export. There are about six different types of *congé*, distinguished by different initials and colours for various types of wine, e.g. the green ARB for wines of Appellation d'Origine; the gold 4B for Cognac and Armagnac. For shipments on which taxes have not been paid, the *acquit* (*q.v.*) is used.

Congenerics, Congeners

Distilling term for the characteristics of taste and aroma retained by distilled spirits coming from the material distilled. When distillation is done at a very high proof the spirit will carry over less congenerics and will be more 'neutral' than if distilled at a low proof.

Connétablie de Guyenne

Society devoted to the promotion of white, sweet wines in the Bordeaux region. The members are descendants of the *connétables* (constables) of Bordeaux who, in the Middle Ages, judged the wines passing on the river and decreed whether or not they could go to market.

See PREMIÈRES CÔTES DE BORDEAUX.

Consorzio

Italian term for a group of wine growers and shippers who have banded together to introduce some control on the use of place-name in Italian wines. They are voluntary organizations in which members are bound to respect the geographical limits imposed on the wine in question, and to observe certain minimum standards of quality. For this they get a seal—which differs with each *consorzio*—to put on the neck of every bottle. The seals have a distinctive design and are consecutively numbered. A brief discussion of *consorzi* can be found in the section on Italian wines, and a discussion of the workings of a typical *consorzio* appears under Tuscany.

See ITALY; TUSCANY.

Constantia

Celebrated Cape wines which were already being exported from South Africa by the beginning of the nineteenth century.

See SOUTH AFRICA.

Consumo

Portuguese term for ordinary wine.

Cooper

1. A craftsman who makes casks.
2. A merchant occupied with the sampling and bottling of wine.
3. An English drink made from a mixture of stout and porter.

To Cooper

1. To make or repair casks.
2. To stow away in casks.

Cooperage

General term for casks or the manufacture and repair of casks or barrels; the fee charged for the work done by a cooper.

Corbières

The sturdy wines grown on beautiful rolling hills near the Mediterranean are separated into three districts which have been accorded the V.D.Q.S. stamp of recognition; Corbières, Corbières Supérieur, and Corbières du Roussillon.

Although these wines come from the Midi, a mass producer of *vin ordinaire*, Corbières can be of exceedingly good value.

Corbières Supérieur is of a superior grade and Corbières du Roussillon, which is equally good wine, comes from vineyards in the department of Pyrénées Orientales.

Cordial

A beverage compounded from spirits with fruit or aromatic substances added by a variety of methods such as maceration, steeping, or simply by mixing. They are always sweetened. The word has come to be almost synonymous with liqueur.

Cordon

Method of training vines. Usually, the trunk of the plant is bent sideways to run parallel with the ground, and is supported by a wire or style. The number of canes that grow up and down from this trunk, as well as the number of buds on each cane, may be regulated.

See CHAPTER EIGHT, p. 33.

Corkage

A fee charged for opening and serving a customer's own bottle in a restaurant or hotel, or sometimes an additional charge made on any bottle that is opened and consumed on the premises.

Corky or Corked Wine

Spoiled by a bad cork. The defect originates in the cork; it can happen to any wine if a faulty cork is used. The French term for corky is *bouchonné*.

Cornas

Rhône Valley red wine. District: Rhône Valley, France.

The wine is never great, often good, and seldom expensive. It is red, comes from Syrah grapes, and contains the characteristics generally expected of the Rhône Valley (*see* RHÔNE) although not to the same exalted degree as some of its neighbours. It is usually good value, however.

As is the case throughout the Côtes du Rhône, the vines grow on terraced plots carefully built into the slopes so steep that they must be cultivated by hand. There are some hundred acres of vineyard, and annual production averages 28,300 imp. gallons (34,000 U.S.).

Coronata

Thin, light, white Italian wine.
See LIGURIA.

Corowa

Vineyard region in New South Wales.
See AUSTRALIA.

Corsé

French term used of a robust, full-bodied wine.

Corsica

The island of Corsica lies to the south of France and to the west of Italy in the Mediterranean Sea, and the climate is almost ideal for growing vines. Climate is not the only vital factor in agriculture, however; and of the island's 2,125,000 acres, only 27,500 are fit for any cultivation. Of these, some 20,000 acres are in vines.

The wines produced are not of any high degree of quality, with the exception of a very few grown around the principal city of Ajaccio, and a few more around Sartène. Most Corsican wines are rough and common, haphazardly vinified, and improperly cared for. The 12,000 growers on the island live a generally poor and wretched existence and have neither the money nor the time to improve their product, and perhaps for this reason the wines are rarely, if ever, found outside the island. Corsica does not generally make enough for its own consumption; and in many years wines must be imported, the major sources being Algeria, the mainland of France, and Tunisia. Much of this wine is drunk by the tourists who flood the island for about two-and-a-half months each year, most of them more interested in the island's savage beauty than in the wines it can offer.

Among the better wines of Corsica are those grown on the Cap Corse, the peninsula which points like a finger at the French Côte d'Azur. The best are the whites and rosés, and these, the Corsicans say, were the preferred wines of the island's most spectacular son, Napoleon Bonaparte. The peninsula is also noted for the only considerable wine-export of Corsica—the fortified, wine-based aperitif, Cap Corse, about 75,000 imp. gallons (90,000 U.S.) of which are sent to the mainland of France each year. Other wines (mostly white) are grown around Bastia, around Corte in the centre of the island (red and white), Ajaccio, and Cauro (white and rosé), and the southern towns of Sartène, Santa-Lucia-di-Tallano, and Bonifacio (red and white). The best wine of Corsica, and the only one deserving of attention abroad, is Patrimonio Rosé, grown near Bastia. All these wines have a distinct flavour, and are higher in alcohol than the inexperienced drinker expects. Corsican wines are often compared to those of the Côtes du Rhône and the Côtes de Provence, although they are not so good. All supplies and equipment needed to care for vineyards and for wines must be brought in from France and it is one of the problems of Corsica that it has little or nothing to export in return.

Most of the vines cultivated on the island are of Italian rather than French origin; they include Moscata, Aleatico, Vermentino (a variety of the Malvasia or Malvoisie), Genovesella, Sciaccarello, Biancone, and Biancolella. The amount of Corsican wine made each year is almost impossible to estimate—so much of it is drunk on the spot—but it is something like 4,781,000 imp. gallons (5,750,000 U.S.).

Cortaillod

The best red wine of Neuchâtel—its well-known vineyard is Cru de la Vigne du Diable.
See SWITZERLAND.

Cortese

White wine grape of Italy, which produces a dry, light wine.
See PIEDMONT.

Corton

Burgundy red and white wines. District: Côte de Beaune, France. Commune: Aloxe-Corton. Official Classification: Great Growth (Grand Cru).

From the little town of Aloxe (pronounced Alosse), the vineyard road meanders down to Beaune. This small district produces the finest red wines of the Côte de Beaune, and the best of the Corton vineyards are Le Corton, Corton-Bressandes, and Corton Clos du Roi. There is some white wine also, more vigorous and perfumed than the neighbouring Meursault, but elegant and delicate; and Corton-Charlemagne is one of the great white growths of the Côte de Beaune. Corton, like most vineyards in Burgundy, is cut up into parcels, and some of the largest slices are owned by the excellent shipper, Louis Latour, and by the Prince de Mérode. Wine from five parcels in Aloxe is auctioned in the Hospices de Beaune sale as Cuvée Dr. Peste and as Charlotte Dumay, after the benefactors who gave the land to the Hospices. On the label, the great name of Corton precedes that of any other fine vineyard, such as Corton-Bressandes, Corton-Clos du Roi and Corton-Charlemagne. Great wines take the name of the famous vineyard rather than that of the commune. Le Corton covers some 193 acres. About 10% of the production is in white wine.

Corton-Charlemagne

Burgundy white wines. District: Côte de Beaune, France. Commune: Aloxe-Corton. Official Classification: Great Growth (Grand Cru).

This is one of the great white Burgundies—at its best it is in the class of the illustrious Montrachet. Since production is small, in comparison with the world-wide demand (61·5 acres), this is a rare wine, rich, with great breed, not as soft as the white Meursaults and more steely. Corton-Charlemagne, made exclusively from the noble Chardonnay grape (at one time, the lesser sections might be planted in the coarser Aligoté, but this is no longer allowed), is big and of a golden colour. The vineyard is divided into three parts: two of the principal owners are the estimable shippers, Louis Latour and Louis Jadot; the rest belongs to half a dozen or so very fine growers, the most considerable of whom produces about two hundred cases, the smallest only fourteen cases. This splendid wine, unfortunately, is slowly shrinking in quantity, mainly because the vines planted on the steep slopes must be tended by hand, and after heavy rains the workers have to haul back the soil on their own backs, since horses and oxen cannot climb here. This is a form of hard labour which does not appeal to the younger generation of *vignerons*.

See ALOXE-CORTON.

Château Cos d'Estournel

Bordeaux red wine. District: Haut-Médoc, France. Commune: Saint-Estèphe.

Owned by Pierre Ginestet, proprietor of Château Margaux, the vineyard is directly across the vineyard road—which is also the commune boundary between Pauillac and Saint-Estèphe—from Château Lafite. Classified a Second Growth (*Second Cru*) in 1855, Cos d'Estournel is discernibly one of the greatest of the great 'Seconds'. Typical of Saint-Estèphe, it is a big, hard wine which, under the able direction of Monsieur Ginestet, has become one of the most popular of the classified growths of the Médoc. According to Bernard Ginestet, the son of the present owner, the name Cos was given to the vineyard by the Templar Knights returning from the Crusades, which had taken them to Rhodes and its neighbouring island, Cos. The vineyards rise comparatively high above Pauillac, and the château itself, a charming Chinese Gothic fantasy unique in the Médoc, dominates the landscape. During the war, the little pagodas which decorate the vineyard wall served the Germans as anti-aircraft batteries. They were destroyed, but have since been restored. Monsieur Ginestet also prides himself in owning, one mile away from Cos, the charming Château Marbuzet, also in Saint-Estèphe.

Characteristics. The wines reflect the position of the vineyard—half-way between Saint-Estèphe and Pauillac. They are lighter and more supple than other important Saint-Estèphes but still full and rich, with a tendency to fatness or *gras*.

Vineyard area: 130 acres.

Average production: 18,000 cases.

Château Cos-Labory

Bordeaux red wine. District: Haut-Médoc, France. Commune: Saint-Estèphe.

The only Fifth Growth (*Cinquième Cru*) in Saint-Estèphe as the great vineyards were classified in 1855, Cos-Labory is beautifully situated on the high-rising roll of hills on the boundary line of Pauillac and Saint-Estèphe. Its two neighbours are Château Lafite, just over the line in Pauillac, and Château Cos-d'Estournel. With the latter vineyard, it was once the common property of a London owner; but it belongs now to Monsieur G. Weber.

Characteristics. The wines are big and well rounded out. A well-made, typical Saint-Estèphe.

Vineyard area: 37 acres.

Average production: 4,500 cases.

Cosecha

Spanish for 'harvest'; indicates vintage year on Spanish wines, i.e. *cosecha* 1961, *cosecha* 1962.

Cot

Another name for the Malbec grapevine; also known as Pied-Rouge, Cahors, etc.

Côte

French term for a slope with vineyards. When used to designate a wine—as Côtes du Rhône, Côte de Nuits, etc.—it will usually mean a wine of lesser quality than a Clos, Château, or other wine indicated by a specific vineyard name.

Côte de Beaune

Burgundy red and dry white wine. *District: Côte d'Or, France.*

Although 80% of the 1,440,000 imp. gallons (1,730,000 U.S.) annually produced is red, the slope is chiefly famous for its dry white wines, the greatest of which come from the southern end, the unofficial Côte de Meursault or Côte des Blancs. In actual fact, however, both red and white are made throughout, and either may be superb.

The slope, the southern or lower half of the Côte d'Or, begins at Ladoix, a long stone's throw from the end of the Côte de Nuits, and runs some fifteen miles, to just below Santenay. The name derives from its major city, ancient Beaune, the 'Capital of Burgundian Wines', which stands in the same relationship to wine-shippers as Chicago does to meat-packers. Beaune is simple even for the most stubbornly non-Gallic tongue, whereas many of the other Burgundian place-names look quite formidable. One apocryphal story is that a well-known London wine-merchant habitually introduced his apprentices to Burgundies with this terse advice: 'There are two kinds of Burgundy: Beaune and the rest. We sell Beaune.' Massive though its output may be, however, all that is Côte de Beaune is not necessarily Beaune.

The slope is composed of nineteen separate communes whose wines, ranging in quality from indifferent to incomparable, are sold under a variety of names. Some bottles have only the name of a single, exceptional vineyard, signifying that the wine is from grapes grown only in that vineyard, and that the vineyard is one which the French authorities consider among the very greatest of Burgundy (there are eight on the Côte de Beaune), and that the wine has attained the quality commensurate with the name. Slightly lower in the legal hierarchy is wine sold with the name of a commune followed by that of a vineyard. The minimum standards are rather lower than those for the greatest wines, but the difference is often impossible to detect—in many cases these wines equal or even better their more renowned cellar-mates. The lesser wines of the Côte are sold with the name of the commune of origin and nothing more. This is the skeleton of the slope's system of nomenclature, but there are always a few variations and exceptions.

Bottles will sometimes be found bearing the word 'Cuvée' followed by someone's name, signifying that it is wine from Beaune's Hospices or Charity Hospital and comes from a vineyard donated by the person indicated (*see* HOSPICES DE BEAUNE). By the time this wine gets to the consumer, it is usually higher in price than any of its peers—usually too high—in spite of the fact that the annual November auction sale of wines at the Hospices de Beaune traditionally sets the price standards for the entire Côte d'Or. To console him for the price he has paid, the buyer has the double pleasure of getting a good wine provided it has not been falsified, and contributing to a worthy charity at the same time.

Another name sometimes found on bottle-labels is Côte de Beaune-Villages, used only to indicate a blend of wines from two or more communes along the slope. Very occasionally, labels will have the name of a commune followed by Côte de Beaune, but the appendage has little real significance and the wine may be considered the same as any other bearing simply the name of the commune concerned.

As is particularly true through Burgundy, it is difficult to generalize about the wines. Most red wine is reasonably light and fast maturing, delicate, and full of perfume, but exception must be made for red Corton from the commune of Aloxe-Corton, a wine which is noble and full, of a resplendent deep red colour, and one of the longest lasting in Burgundy. White wines from the Côte de Beaune are always dry, but there is a world of difference between the great whites of Aloxe-Corton, on the northern end of the slope, and those from the Côte de Meursault to the south. Even within the Côte de Meursault, wines from Meursault itself will differ markedly from those of Puligny-Montrachet and Chassagne-Montrachet next door, the former tending to be delicate and feminine, the latter more austere. Yet all come from the same grape variety and all are vinified in much the same way, perhaps proving that if there is any justification for the abundance of wine names in Burgundy, it is simply in this very obvious truism: that two vines of the same family may be planted within less than half a mile of each other and the fruit each gives will not resemble that given by the other. If any general summary of the wines of the Côte de Beaune were to be made, it would be that, at their best, the white wines are without peer in the entire world; the reds cede top honours to their counterparts of the Côte de Nuits.

Côte de Beaune Soil

Geologically, the slope is composed of three types of soil, dating from different periods of the Jurassic age; but of these only two are important to the wines. Bathonian era soil, consisting of a base of hard rock topped with a thin layer of earth and sometimes with a whitish marl, is found to some extent in the vineyards of Beaune and Pommard. The whitish marl assumes more importance in the Côte de Meursault, where it forms the best soil for grapes grown for white wines. Soil from the Oxfordian era tends to leave an iron-rich oolite at the base of the slopes, and grapes grown in it give light red wines with a pronounced bouquet. As this soil climbs the slopes, it turns greyish, its clay content increases, and the resulting grapes ferment into red wines with enormous finesse and elegance, but full and rich and beautifully balanced. Corton is the prime example. But even where this soil is at its greyest, it nevertheless preserves the iron-imparted tinge of red, with the result that the difference between vineyards giving grapes for fine red wines and those producing white is immediately apparent: the soil colour is the exact indication. Perhaps nowhere else in the world is this difference so marked or so dramatic.

Legal Wine Standards

Côte de Beaune wine must—as is the case with all French wines of Appellation Contrôlée—attain certain minimum standards before it is granted the right to any legal place-name. These standards vary according to the vineyard where the grapes were grown. Six of them have the right to carry only vineyard name and the words Great Growth (*Grand Cru*) if the wines meet the high standards required; these are asterisked on p. 226. The other wines are communal First Growths (*Premiers Crus*) if they stem from the better vineyards, or simple communal wines. Any wine not meeting the standards for the name for which it is theoretically qualified is declassified into the highest rank for which it can qualify, but there is no advancement; no First Growth may ever be sold as a Great Growth no matter how good the wine. The standards are:

Red Wines

Great Growths (*Grands Crus*)

1. Wine must be made exclusively from Pinot Noir, Pinot Liebault, and Pinot Beurot grapes. A maximum of 15% Pinot Blanc or Chardonnay grapes may be used at the discretion of the winemaker.
2. Production must not exceed 267 imp. gallons (321 U.S.) of wine per acre of vines.
3. Wine must contain at least 11·5% of alcohol by volume.

First Growths (*Premiers Crus*)

1. Same grape varieties as for Great Growths.
2. Production must not exceed 312 imp. gallons (374 U.S.) per acre.
3. Wine must have at least 11% of alcohol.

Communal Wines

1. Same grape varieties as for other *appellations*.
2. Production must not exceed 312 imp. gallons (374 U.S.) per acre.
3. Wine must contain at least 10·5% of alcohol.

White Wines

Great Growths (*Grands Crus*)

1. Only Chardonnay (also called Beaunois and Aubaine) grapes may be used.
2. Production must not exceed 267 imp. gallons (321 U.S.) per acre.
3. Wine must have at least 12% alcohol, 11·5% for wine from the vineyards of Bâtard-Montrachet, Bienvenue-Bâtard-Montrachet, and Criots-Bâtard-Montrachet.

First Growths (*Premiers Crus*)

2. Only the Chardonnay vine may be used.
2. Production must not exceed 308 imp. gallons (370 U.S.) per acre.
3. Wine must contain at least 11·5% alcohol.

Communal Wines

1. Only Chardonnay grapes may be used.
2. Production must not exceed 308 imp. gallons (370 U.S.) per acre.
3. Wine must contain 11% of alcohol.

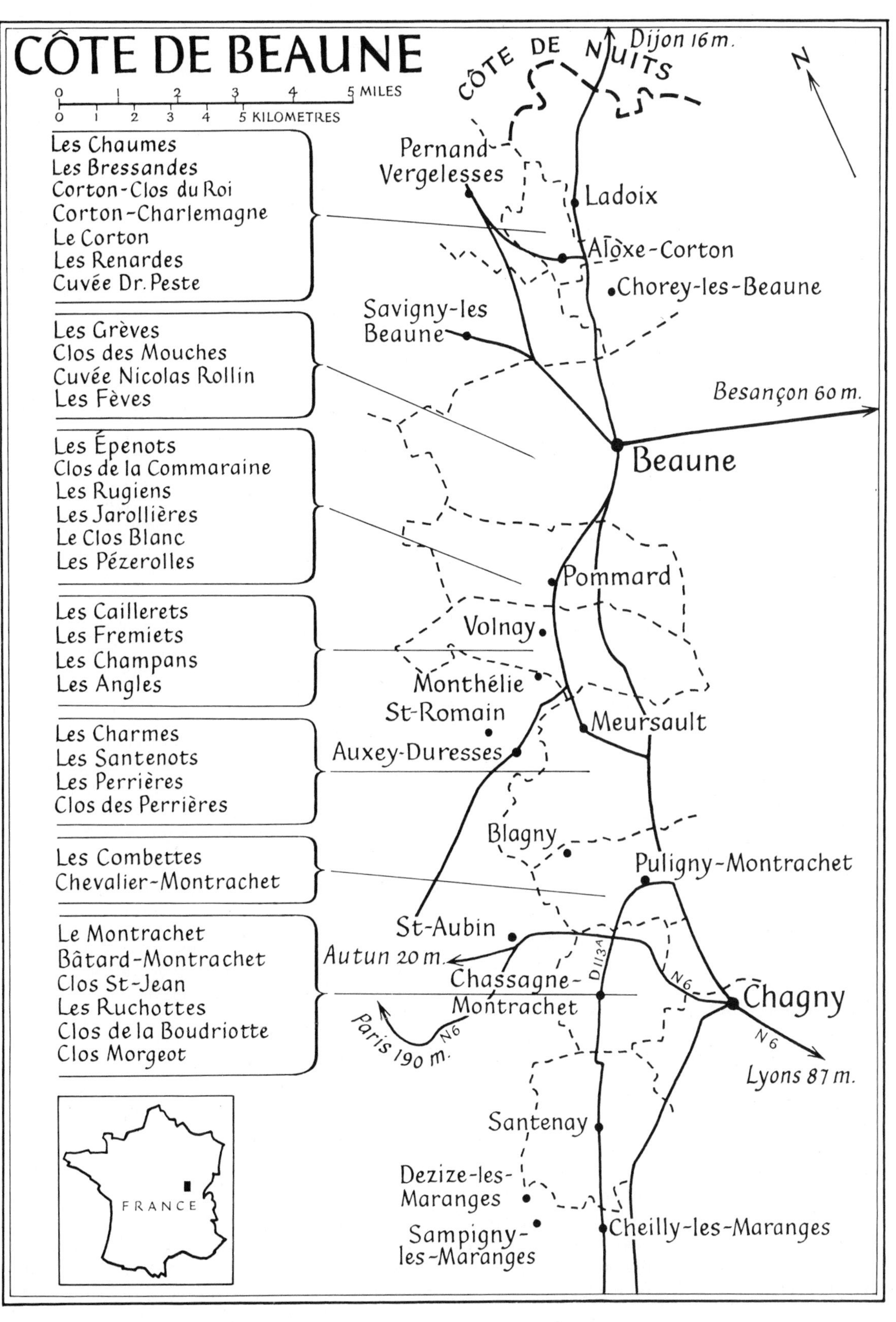
CÔTE DE BEAUNE
0 1 2 3 4 5 MILES
0 1 2 3 4 5 KILOMETRES
Les Chaumes
Les Bressandes
Corton-Clos du Roi
Corton-Charlemagne
Le Corton
Les Renardes
Cuvée Dr. Peste
Les Grèves
Clos des Mouches
Cuvée Nicolas Rollin
Les Fèves
Les Épenots
Clos de la Commaraine
Les Rugiens
Les Jarollières
Le Clos Blanc
Les Pézerolles
Les Caillerets
Les Fremiets
Les Champans
Les Angles
Les Charmes
Les Santenots
Les Perrières
Clos des Perrières
Les Combettes
Chevalier-Montrachet
Le Montrachet
Bâtard-Montrachet
Clos St-Jean
Les Ruchottes
Clos de la Boudriotte
Clos Morgeot
FRANCE
CÔTE DE NUITS
Dijon 16 m.
N
Pernand-Vergelesses
Ladoix
Aloxe-Corton
Chorey-les-Beaune
Savigny-les Beaune
Besançon 60 m.
Beaune
Pommard
Volnay
Monthélie
St-Romain
Meursault
Auxey-Duresses
Blagny
Puligny-Montrachet
St-Aubin
Autun 20 m.
D 113A
Chassagne-Montrachet
N6
Chagny
Paris 190 m.
N6
N6
Lyons 87 m.
Santenay
Dezize-les-Maranges
Sampigny-les-Maranges
Cheilly-les-Maranges

OUTSTANDING VINEYARDS—RED WINES

Vineyard	*Commune*
*Le Corton	Aloxe-Corton
Le Clos du Roi	Aloxe-Corton
Les Renardes	Aloxe-Corton
Les Chaumes	Aloxe-Corton
Les Bressandes	Aloxe-Corton
Clos Saint-Jean	Chassagne-Montrachet
Clos de la Boudriotte	Chassagne-Montrachet
Clos Morgeot	Chassagne-Montrachet
Les Vergelesses	Savigny-les-Beaune
Les Marconnets	Savigny-les-Beaune
Les Santenots	Meursault
Les Fèves	Beaune
Les Grèves	Beaune
Les Marconnets	Beaune
Les Bressandes	Beaune
Les Clos des Mouches	Beaune
Aux Cras	Beaune
Les Champimonts	Beaune
Les Épenots	Pommard
Les Rugiens	Pommard
Les Jarollières	Pommard
Le Clos Blanc	Pommard
Les Pézerolles	Pommard
Clos-de-la-Commaraine	Pommard
Les Caillerets	Volnay
Les Champans	Volnay
Les Fremiets	Volnay
Les Angles	Volnay

OUTSTANDING VINEYARDS—WHITE WINES

Vineyard	*Commune*
*Le Montrachet (*in part*)	Puligny-Montrachet
*Le Montrachet (*in part*)	Chassagne-Montrachet
*Chevalier-Montrachet	Puligny-Montrachet
*Bâtard-Montrachet (*in part*)	Puligny-Montrachet
*Bâtard-Montrachet (*in part*)	Chassagne-Montrachet
*Bienvenue-Bâtard-Montrachet	Puligny-Montrachet
*Criots-Bâtard-Montrachet	Chassagne-Montrachet
Les Combettes	Puligny-Montrachet
Les Pucelles	Puligny-Montrachet
Les Chalumeaux	Puligny-Montrachet
Blagny-Blanc	Puligny-Montrachet
Les Ruchottes	Chassagne-Montrachet
Clos des Perrières	Meursault
Les Perrières	Meursault
Les Charmes	Meursault
Les Genevrières	Meursault
Corton-Charlemagne	Aloxe-Corton

See separately under the respective communes: ALOXE-CORTON, SAVIGNY-LES-BEAUNE, BEAUNE, POMMARD, VOLNAY, CHASSAGNE-MONTRACHET, PULIGNEY-MONTRACHET, MEURSAULT. *See also these Côte-de-Beaune communes:* PERNAND-VERGELESSES, LADOIX-SERRIGNY, CHOREY-LES-BEAUNE, SAINT-ROMAIN, MONTHÉLIE, AUXEY-DURESSES, SAINT-AUBIN, SANTENAY, DEZIZE-LES-MARANGES, SAMPIGNY-LES-MARANGES, CHEILLY-LES-MARANGES.

Côte de Beaune-Villages

A very general name for Burgundian wines. To gain the use of it, wines must be a blend of two or more red wines of at least 10·5% of alcohol and must have the title to one of the place-names listed below. There will be enormous variation in the amount made in any year, following the decisions and speculations of the wine shippers who do the blending and the amount of wine to stem from the various communes concerned. This can be anything between 84,000 imp. gallons (101,000 U.S.) and 152,000 imp. gallons (183,000 U.S.). The place-names which have the right to be used for this minor Côte de Beaune wine are:

Auxey-Duresses	Meursault Blagny
Chassagne-Montrachet	Monthélie
Cheilly-les-Maranges	Pernand-Vergelesses
Chorey-les-Beaune	Puligny-Montrachet
Côte de Beaune	Saint-Aubin
Dezize-les-Maranges	Sampigny-les-Maranges
Ladoix-Serrigny	Santenay
Meursault	Savigny-les-Beaune

Côte des Blancs

A ridge of the Champagne district planted in white Pinot and Chardonnay grapes. The principal towns are Avize, Cramant, and Mesnil.

See CHAMPAGNE.

Côte de Brouilly

Côte de Brouilly red wines are from the heart or best section of Brouilly in Beaujolais, Burgundy.

See BEAUJOLAIS.

Côte de Nuits

Burgundy red and dry white wines. District: Côte d'Or, France.

The Côte de Nuits stretches for about twelve miles along the Côte d'Or, south of Fixin and ending on the verge of a stone quarry just below Nuits-

Saint-Georges, the principal town, from which it takes its name. Some of the vineyards planted on the slope are, within carefully defined limits, among the best in the world.

The natural hazards which can make wine production as uncertain as any other form of crop farming are particularly troublesome in this small area—the only district in which the Pinot Noir grape will, in favourable circumstances, give of its best. Farther north, it would yield a thinner, harder wine; farther south, one which would be softer and less robust. Even in the Côte de Nuits this delicate grape is not easy to raise; and only certain sections of the slope have the soil which favours the vine. That is why the great vineyards of this region are so small, and why one will produce a fine wine while the growth from its near neighbour will be mediocre. And so the vineyards of the whole Côte d'Or are called *climats*—each 'climate' varying, for better or worse, according to its exposure, soil, and drainage.

On the Côte de Nuits, all the *climats* face south-east, where the rising sun strikes the vineyards, drawing the moisture up through the vines. Farther south, the sun would be too hot and the vines would wither; farther north, it would not be hot enough. In such a region, where it takes so little to spoil a vintage, wine-making is a difficult and exacting art; and each *vigneron* adds something to the character of his own wine. So, tasting one against another, anyone accustomed to wine-drinking will perceive the difference between a Côte de Nuits and a Côte de Beaune, or even between a Charmes-Chambertin and the contiguous Clos de Bèze.

The soil of the Côte de Nuits is a reddish clay full of small chalky pebbles, with varying amounts of lava, fuller's earth (a type of clay rich in the silicates of calcium and magnesium), salts of lime, potassium, and phosphorus. The subsoil, which dates from the Jurassic age, is a flinty clay with iron and chalk; but the 'trenching', or deep ploughing that vineyards go through, turns it up and mixes it all together.

The 4,000-odd acres of vines are mostly Pinot Noir, but there are some Chardonnay, and a few sections are planted in Gamay, Melon, and Aligoté for wine reserved almost entirely for the workers and their families. Most of the wine is red, although a little white is grown, principally in the communes of Vougeot and Chambolle-Musigny, and the informing grape is the noble Pinot Noir. (Two other varieties may be used in wines bearing great names —Pinot Liebault and Pinot Beurot; but these vines, offshoots of the Pinot Noir they closely resemble, are planted only in small quantities.)

The wines vary in quality from the magnificent Great Growths to those bearing the names of their communes—third grade in a classification of three. The first is Great Growth (*Grand Cru*), the intermediate, First Growth (*Premier Cru*). The standards demanded by law for the wines of the Côte de Nuits are:

Great Growths (Grands Crus)

1. The harvest must not exceed 267 imp. gallons (321 U.S.) per acre, except in the vineyards of Latricières-Chambertin, Charmes-Chambertin, Mazoyères-Chambertin, Mazis-Chambertin, Ruchottes-Chambertin, Chapelle-Chambertin, and Griotte-Chambertin in the commune of Gevrey-Chambertin, where the maximum is 285 imp. gallons (342 U.S.) per acre.
2. Red wines must contain 11·5% alcohol; white wines, 12%.
3. The only permissible grape varieties are Pinot Noir, Pinot Liebault, and Pinot Beurot for red wines and Chardonnay for white. Red wines may, at the discretion of the grower, include up to 15% Pinot Blanc or Chardonnay.

First Growths (Premiers Crus)

1. The harvest must not exceed 312 imp. gallons (374 U.S.) per acre.
2. Red wines must contain at least 11% alcohol; white wines, 11·5%.
3. The grape varieties are required to be the same as for Great Growths, listed above.
4. These wines may be sold under the name of the commune and of the vineyard, or with the commune name followed by the words First Growth. If they fail to meet the necessary requirements, they are down-graded to the communal wines.

Communal Wines

1. The harvest must not exceed 312 imp. gallons (374 U.S.) per acre.
2. Red wines must contain at least 10·5% alcohol; white wines, 11%.
3. The grape varieties are required to be the same as for Great Growths.
4. Wines that fall below these standards are declassed and sold with those of more general *appellations*, such as Bourgogne.

These regulations cover all the good wines of the slope, except those named Vins Fins de la Côte de Nuits (*q.v.*). These last are superior to the more general Burgundian *appellations*, yet do not rank among the distinguished and truly fine wines of the Côte de Nuits.

OUTSTANDING VINEYARDS—RED WINES

Vineyard	*Commune*
Clos de la Perrière	Fixin
Clos du Chapitre	Fixin
Le Chambertin	Gevrey-Chambertin
Le Clos de Bèze	Gevrey-Chambertin
Latricières	Gevrey-Chambertin
Mazys (or Mazis)	Gevrey-Chambertin
Mazoyères	Gevrey-Chambertin
Charmes	Gevrey-Chambertin
Ruchottes	Gevrey-Chambertin
Griotte	Gevrey-Chambertin
Chapelle	Gevrey-Chambertin
Clos Saint-Jacques	Gevrey-Chambertin
Varoilles	Gevrey-Chambertin
Clos de Tart	Morey-Saint-Denis
Les Bonnes Mares	Morey-Saint-Denis
Clos de la Roche	Morey-Saint-Denis
Clos Saint-Denis	Morey-Saint-Denis
Clos des Lambrays	Morey-Saint-Denis

(Clos des Lambrays is a great vineyard in Morey-Saint-Denis, but it is not an Appellation Contrôlée because the owners have been bickering with the Institut National des Appellations d'Origine for the last thirty years.)

Vineyard	*Commune*
Les Musigny	Chambolle-Musigny
Les Bonnes Mares	Chambolle-Musigny
Les Amoureuses	Chambolle-Musigny
Clos de Vougeot	Vougeot
Les Grands-Échezeaux	Flagey-Échezeaux
Les Échezeaux	Flagey-Échezeaux
La Romanée-Conti	Vosne-Romanée
La Romanée	Vosne-Romanée
La Tâche	Vosne-Romanée
Les Gaudichots	Vosne-Romanée
Les Richebourg	Vosne-Romanée
La Romanée-Saint-Vivant	Vosne-Romanée
Les Malconsorts	Vosne-Romanée
Clos des Réas	Vosne-Romanée
Les Suchots	Vosne-Romanée
Les Beaux-Monts (also Les Beaumonts)	Vosne-Romanée
La Grande Rue	Vosne-Romanée
Les Saint-Georges	Nuits-Saint-Georges
Aux Boudots	Nuits-Saint-Georges
Les Cailles	Nuits-Saint-Georges
Les Porrets	Nuits-Saint-Georges
Les Pruliers	Nuits-Saint-Georges
Les Vaucrains	Nuits-Saint-Georges
Clos de la Maréchale	Prémeaux
Les Didiers	Prémeaux
Clos des Forêts	Prémeaux
Clos des Corvées	Prémeaux
Aux Perdrix	Prémeaux

OUTSTANDING VINEYARDS—WHITE WINES

Vineyard	*Commune*
Musigny Blanc	Chambolle-Musigny
Clos Blanc de Vougeot	Vougeot

See separately under the respective communes: FIXIN, GEVREY-CHAMBERTIN, MOREY-SAINT-DENIS, CHAMBOLLE-MUSIGNY, VOUGEOT, FLAGEY-ÉCHEZEAUX, VOSNE-ROMANÉE, NUITS-SAINT-GEORGES, *and* NUITS-SAINT-GEORGES-PRÉMEAUX.

Côte d'Or

Red and dry white wines. District: Burgundy, France.

The Côte d'Or is variously referred to as the 'backbone' and as the 'heart' of Burgundy, proving perhaps that the Burgundian knows his wine-making better than his anatomy. Whatever its relation to the other sections of this great region, it produces some of the most magnificent Burgundies. Some of its reds are peerless and at least one white, Montrachet, is considered by many experts to be the most perfect of all dry white wines. In good years even the secondary Côte d'Or wines are equalled only by a handful of wines the world over. Unquestionably, the 'Slope of Gold' is well named.

The slope is composed of a series of bleak, disorderly, low-lying hills stretching some forty miles between Dijon and Santenay, and taking in twenty-four communes and one hamlet. All the vineyards are remarkable, but only those in the favoured tenderloin strip—averaging 180 feet in width—are truly great by Burgundian standards; they alone can produce the superlative Burgundies—but in incredibly small quantities and often at fairly elevated prices. An authentic Côte d'Or Burgundy can never be cheap. Few are completely authentic.

These wines stem from two types of grapes—Pinot Noir for red and Chardonnay for white. Neither vine produces abundantly. (Several close relatives of these grapes are allowed as well; but they are planted in insignificant amounts; other vines may be found on the slope, but their wines are not properly Côte d'Or, and if permitted a place-name will revert to the more general Burgundy (*q.v.*).) In addition to the relatively low yields of the noble vines, the hazards of their cultivation are considerable in so northerly a climate, where inclement weather is frequent and punishing. It is just this northerly climate, however, which is responsible

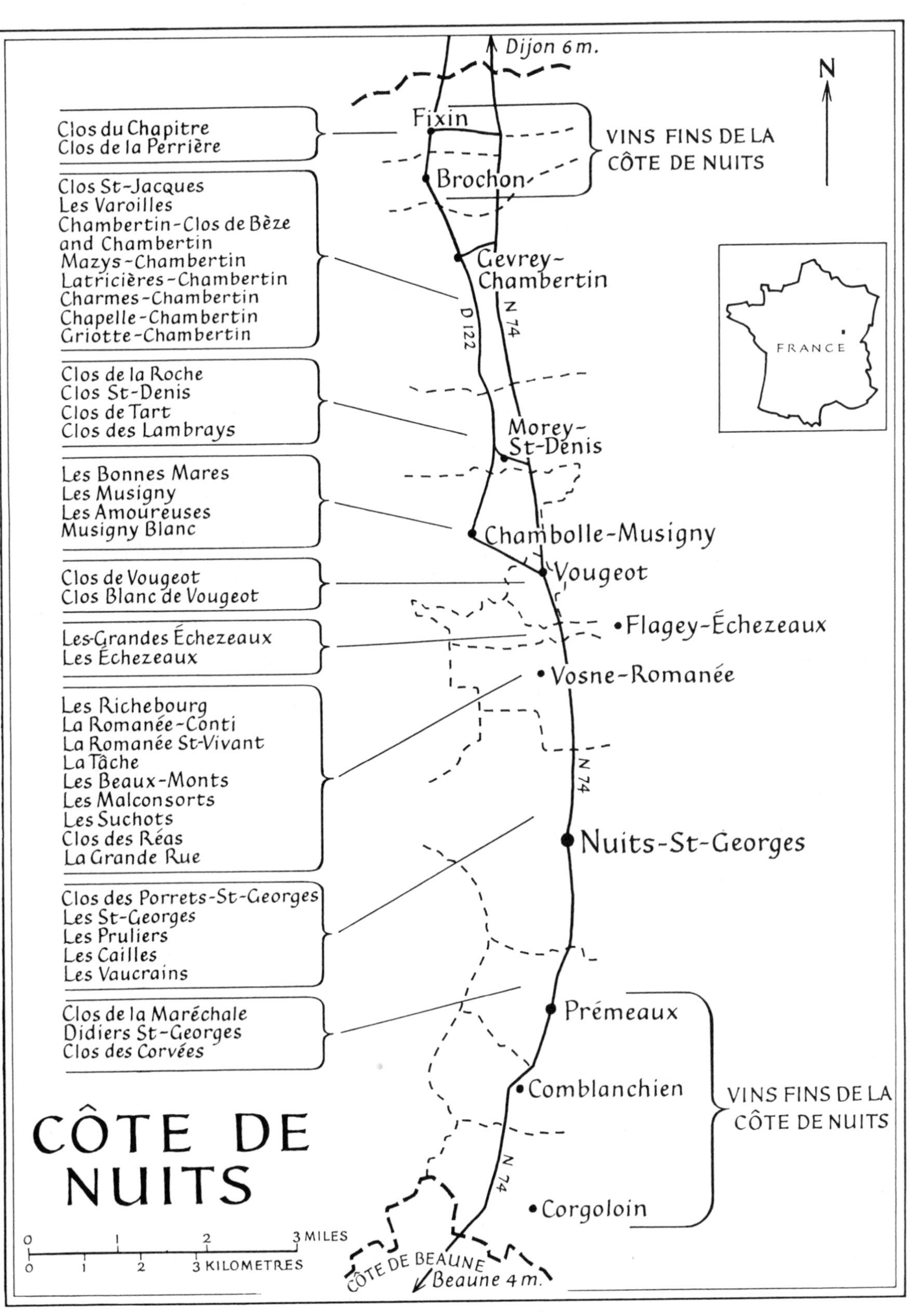
Dijon 6m.
N
Fixin
Brochon
VINS FINS DE LA CÔTE DE NUITS
Clos du Chapitre
Clos de la Perrière
Clos St-Jacques
Les Varoilles
Chambertin-Clos de Bèze and Chambertin
Mazys-Chambertin
Latricières-Chambertin
Charmes-Chambertin
Chapelle-Chambertin
Griotte-Chambertin
Gevrey-Chambertin
D 122
N 74
FRANCE
Clos de la Roche
Clos St-Denis
Clos de Tart
Clos des Lambrays
Morey-St-Denis
Les Bonnes Mares
Les Musigny
Les Amoureuses
Musigny Blanc
Chambolle-Musigny
Clos de Vougeot
Clos Blanc de Vougeot
Vougeot
Flagey-Échezeaux
Les-Grandes Échezeaux
Les Échezeaux
Vosne-Romanée
Les Richebourg
La Romanée-Conti
La Romanée St-Vivant
La Tâche
Les Beaux-Monts
Les Malconsorts
Les Suchots
Clos des Réas
La Grande Rue
N 74
Nuits-St-Georges
Clos des Porrets-St-Georges
Les St-Georges
Les Pruliers
Les Cailles
Les Vaucrains
Clos de la Maréchale
Didiers St-Georges
Clos des Corvées
Prémeaux
Comblanchien
VINS FINS DE LA CÔTE DE NUITS
N 74
Corgoloin
CÔTE DE NUITS
0 1 2 3 MILES
0 1 2 3 KILOMETRES
CÔTE DE BEAUNE
Beaune 4m.

for the fineness of the wines in years when they do succeed, since it exacts the maximum effort from the vine simply to bring its fruit to maturity and ensures that the hard-won grapes will be of superb quality. Not every year, of course, turns out to be an unqualified success—although here again the importance of vintage charts has been largely overestimated. Admittedly there will be more difference between the vintage years in the wines of Burgundy than there will be in those of comparatively sunny Bordeaux; yet a bottle of a Côte d'Or wine from a lesser year—if the wine is authentic and appropriately priced—may well provide a delightful experience. Often, an excellent wine is made even in the most 'disastrous' of years—which proves that wine refuses to obey the rules laid down by the statisticians and chart-makers. This shows that a well selected wine is a greater quality factor than the claim of a vintage year.

The important wines of the Côte d'Or fall into three categories: wines labelled with the name of a commune; those with the name of the commune followed by that of a vineyard—for instance, Nuits-Saint-Georges Les Porrets; those with only a vineyard name (e.g. Chambertin). Wines with communal place-names only (e.g. Gevrey-Chambertin) may come from virtually any vineyard in that commune and the standards they must attain are the lowest exacted along the slope. Such wines are often excellent, sometimes distinguished, but never great. The second group embraces wines from grapes grown only in the specific vineyard indicated and the minimum standards are rather higher. The wines include some of the most splendid Burgundies. The third group dispenses with everything but the name of the single outstanding vineyard where the grapes are grown, and makes up the class of the Great Growths (*Grands Crus*), of which there are only thirty-one on the Côte d'Or. The wines may generally be expected to be peerless, although some others which carry both vineyard and commune name equal, and very occasionally better, them. What is important for the buyer is to be able to distinguish commune from vineyard, on the label. This is not always so simple as it seems.

Many a beginner has inadvertently bought a bottle of 'Gevrey-Chambertin' for 'Chambertin', or 'Chambolle-Musigny' for 'Musigny'. The mistake is an honest one made possible by the peculiar Burgundian custom of adding to the name of a commune that of its most famous vineyard. The practice is by no means standard—Pommard, Volnay, and Beaune, for example, consider their names far more valuable than those of any vineyard the commune might possess—and to complicate matters further, several vineyards themselves have hyphenated names. Thus Gevrey-Chambertin is a commune but Chambertin, Latricières-Chambertin, Charmes-Chambertin, and several others are vineyards, and outstanding ones at that. Fortunately there are only twenty-four communes on the Côte d'Or, of which about thirteen are of real importance. (A list of these communes with their leading vineyards follows at the end of this entry; and they are listed with average production under the heading Côte d'Or in the entry on Burgundy—*q.v.*)

The slope of the Côte d'Or itself falls neatly into two parts: the Côte de Nuits to the north and the Côte de Beaune to the south. In general it might be said that the former is responsible for the greatest red Burgundies, the latter for the whites, but there are exceptions. In bygone times there was a Côte de Dijon extending to the north of the Côte de Nuits, but the expansion of the city of Dijon and the lesser quality of the wines it produced have combined to reduce its importance almost to nothing, despite the fact that the slope was once held in considerable esteem. In the commune of Chenôve—even today the source of a few, minor wines—there stands what is said to be the biggest wine-press in the world. 'The Duke's Wine-press' is the official name, but to the natives it is 'Big Maggie', affectionately named for Marguérite, a lusty fifteenth-century Duchess, who purportedly bestowed her favours on those pickers and wine-makers who did the fastest and the best jobs. Chenôve, Marsannay, and Couchey still produce wines in a minor way, but Fixin, at the beginning of the Côte de Nuits, is the first commune of any real importance.

The mid-section of the hills between Fixin and Santenay has become the great vineyard region of the Côte d'Or. Determining factors are the vine, the angle of the hill and the way it is struck by the sun, the amount of rainfall, and the drainage of excess water; but perhaps most important of all is the soil—the most critical element in the production of any fine wine. The Burgundian hills date from the same time (and are part of the same formation) as the easterly Jura Mountains which give their name to the period in which they were formed, the Jurassic age, some 130–155 million years ago. In the intervening 129-or-so million years between their formation and the first stumbling appearance of man, the hills were alternately baked by the sun and covered with ice, drenched with water and whipped by savage winds, and the net result is the iron-rich oolitic rubble and chalky clay at present composing the soil. The Burgundian is firmly convinced that the entire scheme was preordained, that the precise combination of factors found on his hills was planned expressly for his vines and nothing else. What else could possibly grow on the Côte d'Or? And where else can you possibly equal wines such as these?

While the Côte d'Or Burgundies are among the world's handful of great wines there are obviously some which are better than others. A classification is an ephemeral thing at best, for the men concerned have much to do with the quality of the individual wines, and men are subject to change. It is nevertheless possible to make an overall classification of the wines. The order of the following list represents a personal opinion based on the author's years of testing Burgundies and comparing them one against the other, and no wholesale agreement is anticipated. In order to give a true estimate of the quality of these vineyards, the wines should reflect the character of the soil and be estate-bottled or *Mis en bouteilles à la Propriété*.

RED WINES

Vineyard	*Commune*
La Romanée-Conti	Vosne-Romanée
Chambertin-Clos de Bèze and Chambertin	Gevrey-Chambertin
La Tâche	Vosne-Romanée
Les Richebourg	Vosne-Romanée
Musigny	Chambolle-Musigny
Clos de Vougeot	Vougeot
Les Bonnes Mares	Chambolle-Musigny
Grands-Échezeaux	Flagey-Échezeaux
La Romanée-Saint-Vivant	Vosne-Romanée
Corton-Clos du Roi	Aloxe-Corton
Les Saint-Georges	Nuits-Saint-Georges
Latricières-Chambertin	Gevrey-Chambertin
Le Corton	Aloxe-Corton
Les Bressandes	Aloxe-Corton
Cuvée Nicolas Rollin	Beaune (Hospices de Beaune)
La Grande Rue	Vosne-Romanée
Les Renardes	Aloxe-Corton
Cuvée Dr. Peste	Aloxe-Corton (Hospices de Beaune)
Clos des Porrets-Saint-Georges	Nuits-Saint Georges
Mazis-Chambertin	Gevrey-Chambertin
Les Amoureuses	Chambolle-Musigny
Clos de Tart	Morey-Saint-Denis
Les Pruliers	Nuits-Saint-Georges
Les Cailles	Nuits-Saint-Georges
Les Caillerets	Volnay
Clos de la Perrière	Fixin
Clos Saint-Jacques	Gevrey-Chambertin
Les Varoilles	Gevrey-Chambertin
Les Échezeaux	Flagey-Échezeaux
Les Beaux-Monts (also Beaumonts)	Vosne-Romanée
Les Malconsorts	Vosne-Romanée
Clos de la Roche	Morey-Saint-Denis
Les Fremiets	Volnay
Les Champans	Volnay
Les Suchots	Vosne-Romanée
Clos des Réas	Vosne-Romanée
Chapelle-Chambertin	Gevrey-Chambertin
Charmes-Chambertin	Gevrey-Chambertin
Griotte-Chambertin	Gevrey-Chambertin
Clos du Chapitre	Fixin
Clos des Lambrays	Morey-Saint-Denis
Les Rugiens	Pommard
Les Épenots	Pommard
Les Jarollières	Pommard
Clos de la Maréchale	Nuits-Prémeaux
Didiers-Saint-Georges	Nuits-Prémeaux
Clos des Corvées	Nuits-Prémeaux
Les Vaucrains	Nuits-Saint-Georges
Les Santenots	Meursault
Les Fèves	Beaune
Les Grèves	Beaune
Clos des Mouches	Beaune
Clos de la Boudriotte	Chassagne-Montrachet
Clos Saint-Jean	Chassagne-Montrachet
Clos Morgeot	Chassagne-Montrachet
Clos de la Commaraine	Pommard
Les Angles	Volnay
Le Clos Blanc	Pommard
Les Pézerolles	Pommard
Clos Saint-Denis	Morey-Saint-Denis

WHITE WINES

Vineyard	*Commune*
Le Montrachet	Chassagne and Puligny-Montrachet
Chevalier-Montrachet	Puligny-Montrachet
Clos des Perrières	Meursault
Bâtard-Montrachet	Chassagne and Puligny-Montrachet
Corton-Charlemagne	Aloxe-Corton
Les Perrières	Meursault
Les Ruchottes	Chassagne-Montrachet
Musigny Blanc	Chambolle-Musigny
Les Charmes	Meursault
Les Combettes	Puligny-Montrachet
Clos Blanc de Vougeot	Vougeot

See also CÔTE DE NUITS; CÔTE DE BEAUNE; BURGUNDY.

Côte Rôtie

Red wine. District: Rhône Valley, France.

The second most celebrated of the Rhône wines, coming after Châteauneuf-du-Pape, is the red Côte Rôtie, generous, rich in colour and tasting of truffles or raspberries. The 'roasted slope' is on a hillside, barely two miles long and terraced steeply with old stone walls. Here, in the exiguous parcels of vineyard, the grapes sun themselves on the vines all the summer long. The Côte lies on the right bank of the River Rhône at the northern end of the Côtes du Rhône region. The vineyards are split between the communes of Ampuis and Tupin-et-Semons and face south-south-east. The wines are high in alcohol and have a concentrated astringent characteristic.

The slope is in two parts: the Côte Brune and the Côte Blonde. The difference can be seen in the soil, and tasted in the wines. In the Côte Brune, the land is brownish, rich in clay, containing large amounts of iron oxide; the Côte Blonde's soil, lighter in colour, is dominated by chalk and clay. The wines of the Côte Brune are the milder at the outset, but become strong and vigorous with age, while their blond counterparts are sprightly and gay when young but fade considerably faster. Legend has it that the real reason for the difference between the two is that Maugiron—an early Lord of Ampuis—presented these vineyards to his two daughters, one blonde, the other brunette, and the slopes assumed the characteristics of their respective mistresses and have retained them ever since.

The wines of both slopes are red. Full, to a point of concentrated warmth, and long-lived, they have an assertive bouquet, and a suave, satiny finish. To avoid an excess of vigour, the *vigneron* adds to his fermenting wine a small amount—never more than 20% of the total—of white grapes. This addition rounds it out and adds a measure of finesse. Syrah is the red grape used, Viognier the white, and the two grow side by side on the plunging cliffs.

In recent years the vineyards have been shrinking. The reason is the steepness of the slopes where they are set out. Mechanization is impossible, and all the labour must be done by hand. Paradoxically enough, the wines have been gaining in reputation as the vineyards have been shrinking, and the obvious temptation to 'stretch' the wines has not, unfortunately, always been resisted. Present official figures reveal about 150 acres of vines in the Côte Rôtie, and about 40,000 imp. gallons (48,000 U.S.) of wine annually.

Coteau

French for 'hillside' (plural: *coteaux*). The word occurs in the names of certain wine districts, e.g. Coteaux de la Loire.

Coteaux d'Aix, Coteaux des Baux

Red, white, and rosé wines. District: Provence, France.

Provençal wines harvested in and around the city of Aix-en-Provence in certain delimited areas. The wines have the right to the qualification Vins Délimités de Qualité Supérieure, the secondary classification of French wines. They may be red, white, or rosé, the minimum alcoholic content of the reds and rosés being 11% and the whites 11·5%. Permissible vines are the Grenache, Carignan, Clairette, Cinsault, Ugni Blanc, Mourvèdre, Cournoise, and the Muscat vine types.

The name Coteaux des Baux cannot stand alone, but must always be Coteaux d'Aix, Coteaux des Baux. The area in which it is harvested takes in six communes, none of which may be included among the twenty-eight which may grow wines simply labelled Coteaux d'Aix. In both cases they are minor Provençal wines.

Coteaux de l'Aubance

White and some rosé wines. District: Anjou, France.

The small, lazy River Aubance flows northward into the Loire, joining it about thirty miles downstream from Saumur, running through gently sloping hillsides which support vineyards of a quality only slightly below those of Anjou's Coteaux de la Loire and Coteaux du Layon. The white wines made in Aubance are generally sweet, sometimes semi-sweet, and are among those Angevin wines most frequently encountered abroad. The rosés do not differ appreciably from any others made in the region. Chenin Blanc grapes only are allowed for white wines—the sweetest of which are allowed to attain the noble rot (*q.v.*) before they are picked—and Cabernet Franc is dominant for rosé. About 240,000 imp. gallons (300,000 U.S.) are produced annually.

See ANJOU.

Coteaux du Layon

Loire Valley white wine. District: Anjou, France.

Principally, the sweetest, richest and most mellow of all the Angevin white wines, and, when successful, the best. Although less flowery than a Sauternes, they have an inimitable bouquet and a lightness that belies their alcoholic content, often as high as 15%. They are slow to mature but long-lived. Some dry white wines, also, are made in the district.

See ANJOU.

Coteaux du Loir

Loire Valley red, white, and rosé wines. District: Anjou, France.

A small wine district north of the Loire, producing red, rosé, and white wines and easily confused with the Coteaux de la Loire. The River Loir is actually a tributary of the main stream.

As is true throughout the Loire, white wines tend to be better than reds. They come from Chenin Blanc grapes, must contain a minimum of 10% alcohol, and are dry wines, except when an exceptionally hot summer generates enough sugar in the grape for the making of sweet and semi-sweet wines. These, in contrast to the fast-maturing dry wines, sometimes require a certain amount of bottle age before they are ready to drink.

Red and rosé wines come from Pineau d'Aunis (rapidly disappearing before Cabernets), from Cabernet Franc, Gamay, and Cot grapes, and Groslot (up to 25% of grapes used) is allowed for rosé. The vines are planted in soil ranging from chalky clay (in general supporting grapevines for white wines) to a mixture of clay and flint; and the wines are occasionally semi-sparkling or crackling (*pétillant* in French). Annual production is about 8,000 imp. gallons (9,600 U.S.).

See ANJOU.

Coteaux de la Loire

Loire Valley white wines. District: Anjou, France.

Slightly harder and not quite as sweet as growths from the Coteaux du Layon across the river, these are nevertheless very agreeable dessert wines. The better ones among them have up to 12% or 13% of alcohol, and preserve a certain amount of extra sugar. The rich sweetness is achieved in the same manner as in the Sauternes region of Bordeaux—by leaving the grapes on the vine in the autumn until the noble rot (*q.v.*) sets in.

The finest vineyard plot in this area is Savennières, to which the French wine authority awarded a special Appellation Contrôlée in 1953.

Not all the wines grown on these slopes are sweet. The area extends into part of the Muscadet region, near Nantes, and here the wines, though the more robust of their kind, are light, pale, and dry.

See ANJOU.

Coteaux de Saumur

See SAUMUR; ANJOU.

Coteaux de Touraine and Coteaux de Touraine-Mousseux

See TOURAINE.

Côtes d'Agly

Slopes to the north-east of Grand Roussillon where about 3,000 acres produce grapes for fortified wine.

See SWEET FORTIFIED WINES OF FRANCE.

Côtes de Bergerac

See BERGERAC.

Côtes de Blaye

See BLAYE.

Côtes de Bordeaux

See PREMIÈRES CÔTES DE BORDEAUX.

Côtes de Bordeaux Saint-Macaire

White wine district of Bordeaux, making good secondary wines.

Côtes de Bourg

See BOURG.

Côtes Canon Fronsac, Côtes de Fronsac

Red wines. District: Bordeaux, France.

The mediæval town of Fronsac, near which Charlemagne once had a castle, set in the fork of the Rivers Isle and Dordogne, fifteen miles east of Bordeaux, has two of the Appellations Contrôlées or official place-names in Bordeaux wines. Some white wine is made, but only red is entitled to an *appellation*. Côtes de Fronsac encloses the smaller zone of Côtes Canon Fronsac, which produces the finer wines, although some of the first vineyards in the larger area are almost equally good. Côtes Canon Fronsac lies on the high rim of the Canon Hills, a great green bluff overlooking the Dordogne. The small region is proud of its name and boasts two separate Châteaux Canon, as well as eight other vineyards which include Canon in their name. These are not to be confused with *the* Château Canon of Saint-Émilion.

The wines are heavy for Bordeaux, and a delicacy formerly found only in a few of the best growths is very slowly making its way downwards among the wines, which in the past have not been as well made as they should. The heavy, hearty red wines find their main following in the countries bordering the English Channel and North Sea. In 1956, led by an industrialist from the north of France who has retired to his Fronsac vineyard with his American wife, the first organized attempt was made to bring the region up to date and into competition with famous neighbouring places such as Saint-Émilion, Pomerol, and Médoc.

In the February 1956 freeze which destroyed or damaged one-third of the Bordeaux vineyards, Fronsac was least touched of all, because of its elevated position on high bluffs which escaped the cold; and with this fresh start the growers of the region decided both to improve their wine-making and to make the wine better known abroad. Convincing an essentially peasant and parochial-minded populace of the necessity of this has been the most difficult part of the project.

The wines tend to be slow in developing. A 1934, tasted from the double magnum in 1956, was far from ready to drink. Some bottles have a thick, unpleasant, and 'cooked' taste.

Côtes de Castillon

Red wines. District: Bordeaux, France.

Pleasant secondary wines of Bordeaux (*q.v.*). Many excellent values can be found among the well selected vineyards of this district which neighbours Saint-Émilion.

Côtes de Duras

Red and white wines grown in fifteen communes around the town of Duras about seventy miles to the south-east of the city of Bordeaux, in France. The white wines are made from the Sémillon, Sauvignon, Muscadelle, and Mauzet grape varieties, and the red from the Cabernet, Merlot, and Malbec vines. The wines must have a minimum alcoholic content of 10% for red wines and 10·5% for whites.

Most of the wines produced on the 2,500 acres of vineyards are white and the total varies from about 240,000 to 640,000 imp. gallons annually (290,000 to 771,000 U.S.).

Côtes de Haut-Roussillon

The district on the eastern edge of the Pyrenees, with the most romantic history in France, is now a producer of small muscat and grenache wines, generally consumed on the spot.

See SWEET FORTIFIED WINES OF FRANCE.

Côtes du Jura or Côtes du Jura-Mousseux

See JURA.

Côtes de Montravel

See BERGERAC.

Côtes de Provence

Designation for wines of secondary guaranteed quality (V.D.Q.S.) in Provence, France.

See PROVENCE.

Côtes du Rhône

The name of a vineyard region (and its wines) bordering the River Rhône in south-east France.

See RHÔNE.

Côtes de Toul

One of the two controlled place-names in the Lorraine area of France. The qualities are classed Vins Délimités de Qualité Supérieure (delimited wines of superior quality) and most of them are *vins gris*, the traditional light pink of Lorraine (*q.v.*).

Couderc

A French hybridizer who has developed vines suitable for sound but unspectacular wines both in France and elsewhere.

Château Couhins

Bordeaux white wine. District: Graves, France. Commune: Villenave-d'Ornon.

Adjoining Château Carbonnieux and Château Bouscaut, Couhins, and the former Château Pont de Langon (now one vineyard), belong to the proprietors of Château Calon-Ségur in the Médoc. Past owners of parts of the property have been a Spanish Ambassador to France and a Bishop of Algiers. 50% Sauvignon, 25% Muscadelle, and 25% Sémillon grapes are used in making the very dry white wine from this classified vineyard.

Characteristics. Light but full of character, with a charming flavour. A very well-made, dry wine.

Vineyard area: 34 acres.

Average production: 3,200 cases.

Coulure

Vine disease: dropping of flower-clusters or berries during the initial period of development—or simply a failure to develop.

See CHAPTER EIGHT, p. 36.

Court Noué

Another name for infectious degeneration of vines. Also called fanleaf.

See CHAPTER EIGHT, p. 36.

Courtier

French term for a wine-broker—who is known in Alsace as a gourmet.

Château Coutet

Bordeaux white wine. District: Sauternes, France. Commune: Barsac.

Château Coutet is entitled to use either of the legal French place-names Sauternes or Barsac.

Barsac, an Appellation Contrôlée in its own right, is one of the five communes included in the Sauternes district. In 1855, when the wines were officially classified, Coutet, situated a mile below the town of Barsac, was made a First Growth (*Premier Cru*) of Sauternes.

A web of connexions links the vineyard with Château d'Yquem. The architecture of the oldest parts of both châteaux—dating from the thirteenth century—is identical; the well in the courtyard of Coutet has its exact duplicate in the courtyard of d'Yquem, half a dozen miles away; Château Coutet belonged until 1923 to the Lur-Saluces family, which has for two centuries owned d'Yquem.

The present proprietors are Monsieur Edmond Rolland and his wife, who was a Guy. Actual purchase in 1925 was by Madame Rolland's father, of the large firm of Guy et Mital, wine-press manufacturers in Lyons, who bought the estate from the syndicate which had purchased it from the present Marquis de Lur-Saluces's father. Few more splendidly French tables are set in south-west France than that of the Rollands in the feudal banqueting-hall of the château, where one entire wall is covered by a magnificent tapestry.

The *chais* stand across the courtyard from the château. Grapes are brought in at vintage when they have achieved the sugar-rich state of overripeness standard in Sauternes, and are pressed in one of the big electric Guy et Mital presses before being pitchforked into a suction funnel which carries them into a huge rolling tube. This carries away the stems, and then the pulp is pressed twice again, the juice dripping and gushing down through trapdoors into the vat below the floor. The juice must be run off every night into barrels, where it ferments and then remains for three years achieving maturity.

Believed by many to be the best of the Barsacs, the wine is the result of the most careful viniculture. When the proprietor feels that it does not come up to his standard, he sells it as anonymous Barsac, refusing to give it the name of the château. Most of the harvest is bottled on the estate, but a small part is sent in barrel to England to avoid the higher duties on bottled wine. Monsieur Rolland insists on presenting to the English market the same Coutet that is bottled in France, at the lower price which British bottling permits; and to this end he keeps control of the bottling of his wine in England, sometimes travelling to England himself to oversee the process. There is a constant comparison of samples, both of British bottlings sent to Coutet, and of Coutet bottlings sent to the firm which has been given bottling rights in England.

Like all other flat-lying vineyards in Sauternes, Coutet was badly hit by the February 1956 freeze. The present label is the same as that of Château Filhot, which belongs to the Lur-Saluces family.

Characteristics. The wine is more *nerveux* or more piercing than its Sauternes counterparts, and it is this particular quality which is said to have given the château its name. (Coutet comes from the French word *couteau*, or knife; and the wine takes its characteristics from its rocky, calcareous subsoil.) Although Barsacs have the same degree of sweetness or of *liqueur* as the nearby Sauternes, usually varying from 3% to 6% Beaumé, they are drier to the taste, because of this piercing quality. This wine has great breed and holds its fruit for a long time.

Vineyard area: 80 acres.

Average production: 6,000 cases.

Cradle

A wicker or wire basket designed to hold a wine bottle in a position slightly above the horizontal and theoretically to ensure that the sediment will be stirred up as little as possible when the wine is served.

If the wine is carefully transported from cellar to table in a cradle, and all poured into glasses in one smooth action—which obviously requires a number of glasses—the cradle may be of some service. Otherwise the rocking back and forth of the wine in the cradle stirs up the sediment, and it is preferable to decant.

Cramant

Village in the Épernay district of Champagne which makes one of the greatest wines of the Côte des Blancs.

See CHAMPAGNE.

Cream Sherry

Heavily sweetened Oloroso Sherry. Unknown in Spain, launched in England, the style is now highly popular in the United States.

See SHERRY.

Crémant

A white wine made of red and white grapes and only partly sparkling. This wine is found in Champagne, but the word is not to be confused with Cramant, a wine-making village of Champagne.

Crème

Literally 'cream'; on a liqueur-label, the word once designated a drink that had been sweetened, to differentiate it from a dry spirit such as a brandy. In contemporary usage it still generally means a sweet liqueur. Some of the better known Crèmes are:

Liqueur	*Flavouring*
Crème d'Ananas	Pineapple
Crème de Banane	Banana
Crème de Cacao	Cocoa
Crème de Café	Coffee
Crème de Cassis	Blackcurrant
Crème de Chocolat	Cocoa
Crème de Cumin	Caraway seeds
Crème de Fraise	Strawberry
Crème de Framboise	Raspberry
Crème de Mandarine	Tangerine
Crème de Menthe	Peppermint
Crème de Moka	Coffee
Crème de Noyau	Almond
Crème de Prunelle	Sloe
Crème de Roses	Rose
Crème de Thé	Tea
Crème de Vanille	Vanilla
Crème de Violette	Violet

Crème Yvette

Very sweet American liqueur flavoured with the Parma violet and named for Yvette Guilbert, the incomparable French diseuse who had a memorable success in the 1890s.

Crépy

Crépy is a light, white wine of at least 9·5% of alcohol from the chalky slopes on the southern side of Lake Geneva in the French department of Haute-Savoie. The wines are grown on a scant 150 acres and are dry and aromatic. Some of them are naturally *pétillant*, the semi-sparkling condition usually translated as 'crackling'. Some 25,000 imp. gallons (30,000 U.S.) are made yearly, from the Chasselas grape, and they are rarely, if ever, shipped.

Crescenz

Common misspelling of Kreszenz (*q.v.*), one of the German words indicating the grower.

Criollas

Grape descended from the vines brought to Argentina by the Jesuits and still the leading producer of white and rosé wines.

Criots-Bâtard-Montrachet

Burgundy white wine. District: Côte de Beaune, France. Commune: Chassagne-Montrachet. Official Classification: Great Growth (Grand Cru).

Yet another of the splendid Montrachets, coming from a vineyard of about three and a half acres. The wines of Chassagne have an unmistakable flavour: dry but not hard, inclined to be flowery, but with no sweetness in the aftertaste. The average production is about 1,550 imp. gallons (1,860 U.S.).

See BÂTARD-MONTRACHET; CHASSAGNE-MONTRACHET.

Château Croizet-Bages

Bordeaux red wine. District: Haut-Médoc, France. Commune: Pauillac.

One of several Fifth Growths (*Cinquièmes Crus*) in the 1855 Classification of great vineyards, this is planted in the old domain of Bages, on the hilly land surrounding Pauillac. The estate is sometimes known as Château Calvé-Croizet-Bages. Monsieur Paul Quié, the proprietor, owns the Second Growth (*Second Cru*) vineyard Rauzan-Gassies in Margaux; and Château Bel-Orme-Tronquoy-de-Lalande, a Bourgeois Supérieur growth near Saint-Estèphe.

Characteristics. Good but not outstanding.

Vineyard area: 55 acres.

Average production: 7,500 cases.

Crozes-Hermitage

French red and white wines.

See HERMITAGE; RHÔNE.

Cru

French for Growth. In French usage the word denotes a vineyard of high quality, usually considered worthy of independent recognition under the laws of classification. An officially classified vineyard is *Cru Classé*.

Crust

The deposit in old Port. It is so called because it forms a crust around a bottle.

Crusted Port

Bigger and fuller-bodied than most Tawny Ports or Ruby Ports, the style is like that of Vintage Ports, and improves in bottle. Seldom from a single vintage year and never from a great year (because in such a case a Port vintage would have been declared), it will not have quite the magnificence of a vintage-year Port. Decanting is required.

See PORT.

Cruzan Rum

Of St. Croix, Virgin Islands.

See RUM, VIRGIN ISLANDS.

Cryptogams

Fungus diseases affecting vines.

See CHAPTER EIGHT, pp. 35–6.

Culaton

This is the Piedmontese word for the bottom of the bottle, or dregs. In Piedmont, northern Italy, there is an old superstition that the dregs should be saved until the day after the bottle is opened, and then given to friends. Considering the heaviness of the deposit formed by Piedmontese wines this seems an odd, unfriendly gift.

Cumin Liquidum Optimum Castelli

Generally referred to as C.L.O.C. This is a Danish liqueur, white and flavoured with caraway seed. The name means 'The best caraway liqueur in the castle'. A form of Kummel.

Cup

A summer drink served in glass jugs and made of iced wine diluted with soda-water, with an addition of spirit or liqueur, decorated with pieces of fruit, and iced.

Curaçao

Originally a Dutch liqueur made from the skins of oranges which grow on the Dutch island of Curaçao off the coast of Venezuela. It became so popular that many distillers sell it, under different names. Cointreau and Grand Marnier are examples of proprietary types; while Triple Sec is made by many firms.

Cut

To adulterate liquor with water; or one wine with another—for example, ordinary red wines of France may be cut with Algerian.

Cuve

French term for wine vat.

Cuvée

French term for contents of wine vat; hence a vatting. The term now usually means all the wine of a vat, or all the wine made at one time and under similar conditions. In France it also means a vineyard parcel or lot. In Champagne, there are two further meanings. Vin de Cuvée is the wine of the first pressing. A cuvée is also a blend of Champagnes, or a special lot of wine.

Cyprus

The island of Cyprus, edged by its jagged beaches, lies in the most easterly part of the Mediterranean, about sixty miles from the Lebanon coast. Its plains are sun-baked, but snow lies on the mountain peaks from January until April, and most of the wine comes from the slopes. Viticulture is important in the island. Out of a farming population of some 64,000 families, about 30,000 are dependent to a certain extent on vine cultivation and the wine industry—which has expanded considerably in the past twenty years. The island's vineyards now cover more than 90,000 acres—that is, 8% of the total cultivable area.

These vineyards, which look so romantic to tourists, are for the most part divided into small plots. They are to be found mainly in the volcanic soil of the southern foothills of the Troödos Mountains, in the districts of Limassol, Paphos, and to a lesser extent in Nicosia and the region of the Makheras Mountains. With an average harvest of over 100,000 tons (112,000 short tons) of grapes, production per head of the population is relatively higher than that of various important wine-making countries in Europe.

Wine History

Cyprus, island of Aphrodite, who was worshipped in her temple at Paphos, is known to have been inhabited since the Mycenean Age, and to have traded with other Ægean peoples. Both Greeks and Phoenicians founded colonies there. In the Cyprus Museum there is a beautiful amphora believed to date from about 900 B.C. Recent excavations of mosaics and other remains bear witness to the fact that wine-making flourished in ancient Cyprus; and it is known that the wines were drunk in ancient Egypt, as well as in classical Greece and Rome. Many of the local legends are connected with the cult of Aphrodite, in whose honour great feasts were held, especially on the occasion of the annual pilgrimage to her temple at Palaipaphos. Hesiod described how the Cypriot Nama was made from the sun-dried grapes. This sweet wine was re-named Commandaria by the Knights Templar, to whom, in 1191, Richard I gave the island. Because of its superb quality, the Commanders monopolized its sale; and their Commandaria has been made in Cyprus ever since. Today's Commandaria has the oldest tradition of any individually named wine. In the Chronicle of Richard Cœur de Lion's journeys during the Crusades, it is recorded that on his first arrival on the island, there was a banquet at which were offered 'the very best wines from the vineyards of Cyprus, which, it is reported, are unlike those of any other country'. Centuries later, in 1743, Richard Pococke wrote in London of 'The rich Cyprus wine which is so much esteemed in all parts of the world and is very dear and produced only about Limassol. In some places indeed they make good red wine.' Cyprus wine was imported into Britain in the times of the Plantagenets. Commandaria was drunk at a great banquet given in London in 1352 by Henry Richard, Master of the Vintners' Company, in honour of King Peter I of Cyprus. There were five monarchs at the dinner: Edward III of England, David of Scotland, John of France, and Waldemar of Denmark, besides Peter I of Cyprus—and so the party came to be known as 'The Feast of the Five Kings'. More than two hundred years later, Queen Elizabeth I granted a profitable monopoly to Sir Walter Raleigh for the importation of Cyprus wines through Southampton, where a small colony of Cypriot merchants flourished.

There is a story that a taste for the local wine decided the Turkish Sultan Selim II to capture Cyprus in 1571. Selim, renowned for his indulgence in wine (he was nicknamed The Sot), summoned his commander-in-chief and ordered him to take the island, with the words: 'Within the island there is a treasure which only the King of Kings is worthy of possessing.'

Viticulture was not abolished under Turkish rule, but inevitably it languished, so that production of wines was reduced to a trickle. It was not until, in 1878, the English began to administer the island that new life came to the vineyards. By some miracle, the phylloxera plague did not reach Cyprus, and the old vines have gone on growing on their own roots.

Cyprus vines have played their part in the creation of some famous wines abroad. They were introduced into Madeira in the fifteenth century, for the famous Madeira wine. A similar origin has been attributed to Marsala and Hungarian Tokay.

Grape Varieties

About 80–85% of the wine-making grapes are red (Mavron), 10–15% white (Xynisteri), and about 2–3% Muscat.

The local Mavron wine is grown in most of the vineyards of Cyprus—the finest of the variety on the slopes of a hill named Afames, near the village of Platres. Some of the best red wines are made from grapes from this area.

The white Xynisteri vine is cultivated in many districts. Pitsilia and the vineyards of the Paphos area in the west are noted for this variety, which forms 90% of the production of the Famagusta and Larnaca vineyards.

Types of Wine

Red Wines

These are made mainly from the local red grapes, but other species are introduced to give acidity, colour, and a better balanced must; notably an oval grape named Opthalma; and the Maratheftika, so called because it was grown originally in the Marathassa area.

The Mavron grape also is used in the production of the rosé known in the island and in Greece as Kokkineli. It is deep in colour for a rosé, fresh to the palate, and usually quite dry. When iced, it can be drunk with almost any food. Among the better-known red wines are Afames and Othello, both dry. It is important to remember, however, that much of the wine is made to appeal to the local taste which, in reds, is for a very full, deep-coloured wine with a high tannin content. This goes well with the strongly flavoured, spicy foods of Cyprus.

White Wines

The finished white wines are full-bodied with a flavour entirely their own. Most of them are fairly dry: people like them so, and the local yeasts are capable of fermentation in the presence of even the high degree of alcohol usual in Cyprus if any free sugar is present. Among the better-known white wines are Aphrodite and Arsinoe, both dry.

Commandaria

This luscious dessert wine, the one for which Cyprus is famous, has been made for hundreds of years in the mountain villages—and especially in Kalokhorio, Zoopiyi, and Yerassa. The informing grape varieties are Mavron and Xynisteri. Now, as in ancient Greece, the growers blend white grapes with red, and some of them still mature their wine as it was aged in Homeric days: in huge earthenware jars, coated with pitch, vine-ash, and goat-hair, buried in the earth, and kept for many years. Yet, in the next property, you may see modern cement tanks; and in Limassol, the busy wine port, the big companies do everything in an up-to-date way. The Commandaria will vary from village to village, according to the methods used and the proportion of red grapes to white. The resulting wine is, after its long ageing, often so concentrated that even for domestic consumption it will be blended with certain other wines—which do not impair its characteristic flavour. The art of blending is therefore an important factor in the production of this wine.

Sherry-types

A large range of 'sherries' is made in Cyprus, for the home and export markets. It varies considerably in style. Britain, the principal market abroad, has received some wines of the same alcoholic strength as Spanish Sherry, clarified and bottled in England; wines of differing alcoholic content to be blended by the importer; and a sweet wine, lower in alcohol, and least expensive of all these moderately priced sherry-types. Lately, however, the Cypriots have been concentrating upon high-strength sherries, and the next step in the evolution of the trade is flor sherry. Stocks are being built up in the island, and it is expected that this prestige wine will break into a more highly priced market.

EXPORT

In 1964, about 3,200,000 imp. gallons (3,840,000 U.S.) of table wine and sherry were exported, with the United Kingdom taking the record figure of some 1,700,000 imp. gallons (2,040,000 U.S.). Cyprus is also, and increasingly, a source of inexpensive table wines. As a result of changes in the industry, these wines have been improving, and progress is being made in export figures, especially for restaurant carafe wines. The foundations of the island's success in the foreign market were laid by Mr. F. Rossi of London. In 1956, he drew up a report on the wine industry, recommending improvements and experiments. As a result, cuttings of new varieties were sent to Cyprus—where the Government has been vigorous in following up Mr. Rossi's recommendations, and a Wine Council, representing all sides of the industry, has been formed. Other investigations have been carried out by specialists such as Professor Branas and Mr. Marcout. Consequently, the island's wineries have been modernized and the latest production equipment installed—including controlled fermentation units. Systematic experiments and studies on viticulture, selection of sites, soils, and aspect of vines, have been carried out by the government agencies, and technical assistance is provided for those who need it. Many of the new cuttings which were originally planted at the quarantine station at Ayia Irini are now coming into commercial production and will make an important contribution to the quality of Cyprus sherry and beverage wines.

SPIRITS

The island produces about 1,600,000 imp. gallons (1,921,000 U.S.) a year of brandy, about a twelfth part of which is exported. In proportion to the sale of wines abroad, the figure for spirits has fallen of late years. Inside Cyprus, people often drink the brandy as a long iced drink or 'sour'. 'V.S.O.P.' is made by the Cognac method.

Production of brandy and other spirits on a large scale dates only from the beginning of the British administration. Pilfar, rather like Curaçao, and KEO Spécialité, which resembles Cointreau, are two of the liqueurs now being made. The Government generally buys up all the grape alcohol, or Zivania, of the island. Flavoured with gum mastic and aniseed, it becomes Cypriot spirit in the forms of Masticha and Ouzo.

Czechoslovakia

Czechoslovakia produces wine, but is mainly a wine-importing country. While all three regions—Bohemia, Moravia, and Slovakia—make wine, the total harvest does not meet the national demand. In these conditions, little of the product is seen abroad.

Viticulture is an ancient craft among the Czechs, but has had a more than usually turbulent history. Wine was certainly grown in Bohemia by the ninth century. In the second part of the fourteenth century, at the direction of Emperor Charles IV, Burgundian vines were imported and planted systematically. Cultivation, especially around Prague in Bohemia, was prolific in the sixteenth century and at the beginning of the seventeenth before the devastations of the Thirty Years War. A reviving viticulture was wiped out anew in both the eighteenth and nineteenth centuries, so that Czech wine-growing as it exists today dates only from the 1920s, when the whole national viticulture was reconstructed.

Production seems, from the somewhat conflicting figures obtainable, to fluctuate with the conditions of the vintages in the region of 18 million imp. gallons (23 million U.S.) a year, about two-thirds to three-quarters of which comes from the eastern end of the country (Slovakia). It was estimated in

Prague at the end of 1955 that by that date practically all home demand for first-class wines was being supplied from Czech sources.

Bohemian wines inevitably have an affinity with German wines. Prague is at the same latitude as the Rheingau and the Palatinate and the principal vines are the same: Rhine Riesling, Traminer, and Sylvaner for the white wines; and Blauer Burgunder, Portugieser, and Saint-Laurent for red wines. The best quality zone is that of the three towns, Litoměřice, Roudnice, and Mělník on the Elbe River not far north of Prague, and also at Brezanky and Velké Zernoseky.

The majority of Moravian wine comes from the southern central area of Czechoslovakia below Brno, and just across the border from the Krems-Vienna wine sector in Austria. Here again there are affinities which cross national frontiers. The Czech area is bounded by Znojmo in the west, Mikulov on the Czech–Austrian border, and by Hustopeče to the north-east. With Riesling, here divided into two types and called Rhine Riesling and Italian Riesling, the Veltliner is found. This produces excellent white wine along the Danube in Austria. Important also are Sylvaner, Traminer, Weiss Burgunder, and a variety the Czechs call Rulany which may be the Ruländer. The wines around Mikulov are exclusively white, and are light and aromatic, with rather high acidity.

At the eastern end of Czechoslovakia, lying to the north of Hungarian Tokaj, a 'Tokay' is made from the Furmint, Lipovina, and Muscatel grapes. The Furmint is widely used in Hungary. The best-known place-name in Czechoslovakia is Malá Trňa. Throughout the rest of the Slovakian region on the borders of the Tatra and Carpathian mountain ranges much wine is made. In the west of the region, the vineyard totals about 10,000 acres, the chief vines being Veltliner, Italian Riesling, Neuberger Sylvaner, and Muscatel. The largest wine area is north of Bratislava, the most concentrated production being at Modra and Pezinok.

D

Dalwood

Important vineyard in New South Wales.
See AUSTRALIA.

Dame-Jeanne

French term for a large glass bottle containing anything from one to ten gallons, usually covered with wicker and used for storing and transporting wines and spirits; the English equivalent is a demijohn. In Bordeaux, the name is also used for a bottle containing more than a magnum but less than a double magnum; the equivalent of 2½ litres.

Dampierre

Commune producing rosé and red wines in the Coteaux de Saumur district of Anjou (*q.v.*).

Damson Gin

A British gin flavoured with damsons—small, dark plums.

Danziger Goldwasser

White aniseed and caraway-flavoured liqueur, originally plain, later with the addition of gold flakes floating in the bottle. A Silverwasser was also made in which flakes of silver replaced the gold. Both were originally made in the old port of Danzig. A number of firms put out similar liqueurs, of which the Liqueur d'Or made in France is probably the best known.

Dão

Portuguese red wines, and some white, from the vineyards south of the Douro.
See PORTUGAL.

Château Dauzac

Bordeaux red wine. District: Haut-Médoc, France. Commune: Labarde-Margaux.

The vineyard, a Fifth Growth (*Cinquième Cru*), lies on flat gravelly soil near the southern limit of the zone allowed the place-name Margaux. Formerly owned by the Bordeaux wine firm of Nathaniel Johnston, then the property of Monsieur H. Bernet, who sold it in 1966 to A. Mialhe.

Characteristics. Undistinguished.
Vineyard area: 27 acres.
Average production: 3,500 cases.

Debröi Hárslevelü

One of the better dry, white wines of Hungary. Wine made from the grape variety Hárslevelü, which also goes into Tokay.
See HUNGARY.

Decant

To pour wine from its bottle to another container from which it will be served, in order to separate it from its deposit or to oxidate or aerate it.

Decanter

Glass vessel or container usually of attractive design used for serving old wines which have been decanted to separate them from their deposit. It is much too often used also for holding Sherries, Ports, and other wines which do deteriorate, although not rapidly, once the cork is pulled. The best decanters are made of clear crystal, to show off the colour of the wine to its best advantage. When the decanter is brought to the table, it is customary also to bring the cork from the winebottle for the inspection and approval of the master of the house and any interested guests.

Dégorgement

French term for the removal of the deposit from bottles of Champagne and other sparkling wines.
See CHAMPAGNE.

Deidesheimer Grainhübel

Best wine of Deidesheim in the German Palatinate, or Pfalz.
See PALATINATE.

Deidesheimer Herrgottsacker

Best-known wine of Deidesheim in the German Palatinate.
See PALATINATE.

Deidesheimer Leinhöhle

An outstanding wine of Deidesheim in the German Palatinate.
See PALATINATE.

Delaware

One of eastern America's better white-wine grapes, found particularly in Ohio and the New York Finger Lakes district. It yields clean, fresh, spicy but not 'foxy' wine, much of which is made sparkling.

Délicat, Delikat

French and German terms for the subtle taste of a wine of low alcoholic content, less than 12% of alcohol by volume and, as in the case of many fine German wines, sometimes as low as 8% of alcohol by volume.

Delicatessen

Unexceptional red hybrid grape developed by T. V. Manson of Texas; said to have taken its name from the large number of different grape varieties that went into it.

Demi

Literally 'half', meaning half a litre, the term to use when asking for a large glass of draught beer in France. Demie (the French feminine) refers to a half-bottle.

Demie-queue

Half a *queue*. Since a *queue* is an ancient Burgundian term for two *pièces* or barrels, a *demie-queue* would be one *pièce*. It holds 228 litres, or 50·1 imp. gallons (60·2 U.S.). The term is rarely used.

Demijohn

A large glass bottle with a wicker wrapping, holding anything from one to ten gallons. It is commonly used for storing and transporting wines. The name is a corruption of the French Dame-Jeanne (literally 'Lady Jane') and attempts to trace it back to Arabic or Persian have been largely discounted on the evidence that the Arabs seem to have developed their word from the Italian.

Demi-Sec

French for 'semi-dry'. These words appearing on the label of a bottle of Champagne do not, in fact, indicate a dryish wine, but rather one which is sweetish.

See CHAMPAGNE.

Denaturant

A substance added to alcohol to make it unfit for drinking, thus legally avoiding the heavy excise duty on potable alcohol. Denatured spirits: spirits so treated.

Denmark

Wine is not produced in Denmark, because of the cold climate.

There is considerable trade in 'fruit wines', and in 1964 the sale of such wine reached some four-and-a-half million bottles. The most popular are the Danish berry wines such as blackcurrant, blackberry, and cherry. In addition, liqueurs are made. The best-known is probably Cherry Heering, and most of the cherries for this come from the beautiful little Danish island of Sealand. Another popular liqueur is Cloc Brun, a spicy drink with a slight taste of caraway seed, and 38·5% alcohol by volume.

SPIRITS

For many years the Danes have been experimenting with the production of whisky. In 1952, Cloc Whisky, the first to be distilled in Denmark, was put on the market. The manufacturers use malt barley which has been dried over a peat fire. The whisky is distilled in pot stills and seasoned in oak barrels.

The most important of the potable spirits industries in Denmark is the making of aquavit (spelt *akvavit* in Danish). The total number of bottles produced in 1960 was nearly 6 million.

See AQUAVIT.

Denominación de Origen

Guarantee of validity on Spanish wine-labels.

See CHAPTER FIVE, p. 15.

Densimeter, Densimetry

The densimeter, used for reading the density of grape must, consists of a hollow cylindrical float with a weighted ball beneath and a graduated rod above. The instrument is based on the Archimedean law that a body displaces a quantity of water equal to its own bulk.

See MUSTIMETER.

Château Desmirail

Bordeaux red wine. District: Haut-Médoc, France. Commune: Margaux.

The vineyard, classed a Third Growth (*Troisième Cru*) in the Gironde Classification of 1855, has been absorbed by Château Palmer. The building, in the village of Margaux, belongs to Monsieur Zuger, the owner of Château Malescot-Saint-Exupéry, and no vineyards are connected with it. The *chais* are in a complete state of disrepair; and the fact that this non-existent vineyard is still included in the lists of the 1855 Classification is further proof of the obsolescence of this classification.

Dessert Wine

Full or fortified sweet wine suitable for drinking with or after dessert. In the United States, any wine fortified with brandy or spirits. The table wines in this category are Barsac, Sauternes, sweet Vouvrays or Loire, as well as Beerenauslesen and Trockenbeerenauslesen of the Rhine and Moselle.

Dézaley

Well-known white wine of Lavaux in the Canton of Vaud.

See SWITZERLAND.

Dezize-les-Maranges and Dezize-les-Maranges-Côte de Beaune

Burgundy red and white wine. District: Côte de Beaune, France.

A minor wine-growing commune at the southern end of the Côte de Beaune. The wines are very light, fast-maturing, and sometimes they have a good deal of fruitiness. They are usually blended with wines from certain other communes of the slope and sold as Côte de Beaune-Villages, but may occasionally be bottled under their own names. The difference is one of geography and quality. Dezize-les-Maranges alone refers to wine which has been grown on the 150 acres within the legally approved communal limits. If Côte de Beaune is added, it must come from 75·8 acres, comprising only the best part of the larger area.

Dhroner Hofberg

Outstanding wine of Dhron on the Moselle.

See MOSELLE.

Diamond (Moore's Diamond)

An American hybrid grape—developed by Jacob Moore—once widely used as a source for white wine, but better adapted to producing table grapes.

Diana

Early American hybrid grape, an attempt to improve the famous Catawba grape. It is still fairly widespread in Ohio and New York State for white wines, but is not ideal, since it tends to vary considerably in quality from year to year.

Diastase

A ferment which has the power to convert starch into dextrine, and then into sugar.

Die

See CLAIRETTE DE DIE.

Dimyat

White-wine grape grown on the Black Sea coast of Bulgaria.

See BULGARIA.

Dionysos

Greek god of wine. Originally a nature deity of fruitfulness and wine, he probably came from Thrace. According to Greek mythology, he was the son of Zeus and Semele, a divinity with prophetic gifts, who travelled over the then known world, spreading the knowledge of vine cultivation, as well as worship of himself with the frenetic Bacchic rites which (according to the *Bacchae* of Euripides) destroyed Pentheus, King of Thebes, who opposed them. Bacchos, another name for the wine god, was afterwards adopted by the Romans as Bacchus (*q.v.*).

Dipping Rod

Graduated measure for ascertaining contents of casks.

Distillation

The art or science of distilling. It is based on the fact that alcohol, being lighter than water, vaporizes at a lower temperature, with the result that when a slightly alcoholic liquid is heated to a temperature between the two boiling points, the vapours that rise can be caught and condensed back to form a liquid with a higher alcoholic content. Distilling is done either in single-shot pot stills or continuous patent stills, the quality and characteristics desired dictating the method.

The definition of distillation given by J. H. Perry in the 3rd edition of *The Engineers' Handbook* is as follows:

'*Distillation* is the separation of the constituents of a liquid mixture by partial vaporisation of the mixture and separate recovery of vapour and residue. The more volatile constituents of the original mixture are obtained in increased concentration in the vapour; the less volatile in greater concentration in the liquid residue. The completeness of separation depends upon certain properties of the components involved and upon the arrangements of the distillation process.

In general, *distillation* is the term applied to vaporization processes in which the vapour evolved is recovered, usually by condensation. *Evaporation* commonly refers to the removal of water from aqueous solution of non-volatile substances by vaporisation. The vapour evolved, *i.e.* the water, is discarded.

The majority of the applications of distillation are found in the separation of one or more of the components from mixtures of organic compounds.'

See CHAPTER TWO, pp. 6-8.

Dizy

Commune near Ay, in the Marne Valley, producing a First Growth Champagne.

See CHAMPAGNE.

Dolceacqua (or Rossese)

Red wine from Rossese grapes from along the Italian Riviera.

See LIGURIA.

Dolcetto

Italian grape producing red wine.

See PIEDMONT.

Dôle

Good red wine of the Valais from the Dôle or Gamay grape.

See SWITZERLAND.

Dom Pérignon

According to legend, the father of Champagne as we know it.

See CHAMPAGNE.

Domaine, Domäne

French and German terms for wine estate: *Mis en bouteilles au domaine* means bottled at the domain or vineyard; the French for estate-bottling.

Domaine de Chevalier

Bordeaux red and white wine. District: Graves, France. Commune: Léognan.

One of the few Bordeaux estates to be called a *domaine* instead of a château. The vineyard was placed among the top eleven red wine vineyards of Graves in 1953, and among the top five white wine vineyards for its lesser quantity of white wine. It is not quite what it was at the turn of the century, but Chevalier is still an outstanding Graves.

Characteristics. A very fine wine with great vigour, even in the lesser years. Among the best of the red Graves. The white is excellent.

Vineyard area: 37 acres.

Average production: red—1,440 cases; white—700 cases.

Dop Brandy

The South African equivalent of marc, or the distillation of grape husks after the wine is pressed out. Dop is of dubious quality and incredibly high taxes were put on it to make its production economically impossible, with the result that it is now seldom seen.

Dosage

French term for the addition of sugar syrup to sparkling wine before final corking and shipment.

See CHAMPAGNE.

Doubling

Redistilling spirits to improve strength and flavour.

Dousico

Heady Greek drink flavoured with aniseed.

Doux

French for 'sweet' as applied to wines, e.g. Sauternes, Barsac. On the label of a bottle of Champagne this word indicates a very sweet wine which is seldom sold in Great Britain or the United States.

Douzico

A Turkish spirit rather like Kümmel (*q.v.*).

Downy Mildew

Also called false mildew in America and mildew in Europe, to differentiate it from powdery mildew; the most crippling fungus disease of the vine.

See CHAPTER EIGHT, p. 36.

Draff

In whisky-making, the residual solid matter after fermentation of the grain.

Drambuie

A liqueur compounded from Scotch whisky, heather honey, and herbs, by a secret formula belonging to the Mackinnon family near Edinburgh. The formula is said to have been given to an early Mackinnon by Bonnie Prince Charlie, as a reward for helping him to escape to France. The derivation of the name is a corruption of the Gælic *An Dram Buidheach*, meaning 'the drink that satisfies'. One of the three most popular liqueurs in the U.S.A.

Draught

Beverage, notably beer, drawn from bulk, or supplied and taken directly from barrels or casks.

Dreimännerwein

'Three men wine', as the wine of Reutlingen in Germany is jokingly referred to. It is so called because it is said to be so bad that to make one man drink it, a second is needed to hold him fast, and a third to pour the wine into his mouth.

Dry

Opposed to sweet. A wine is dry when all the sugar in the grapes has been completely fermented into alcohol. White Burgundy, most Alsatian wines, certain Graves and Champagnes, many Moselle and Rhine wines, are dry. So also are such aperitif wines as Fino and Amontillado Sherries. In American wine parlance, the term 'dry wines' is mistakenly given to wines under 14% or table wines as opposed to 'sweet wines' which are synonymous with fortified wines. The acid content of a wine also determines the sense of dryness, unless the latter is covered up by excessive sugar.

Dubonnet

A dark red, proprietary French aperitif made of a sweetened wine base with bitter bark and quinine added to impart the characteristic taste. It is also manufactured in the United States where a white variety, seen also in England, may be found.

Château Ducru-Beaucaillou

Bordeaux red wine. District: Haut-Médoc, France. Commune: Saint-Julien.

The vineyard forms an unbroken carpet with that of Château Beychevelle. The name, given by the former owner Monsieur Ducru, means literally 'beautiful pebbles', and is very appropriate. The chief feature of the vineyard is its richness in the pebbles, or *cailloux,* which contribute to the greatness of so many of the wines of the Médoc, especially Château Latour. At Beaucaillou the gravelly soil is very deep.

The château itself is set away from the road on the lip of the slope over the River Gironde.

This vineyard became, to some extent, run down in the thirties and early forties, and many Bordeaux critics felt it no longer deserved its place as a Second Growth (*Second Cru*). In the fifties, however, it was revived by the efforts of its young owner, Monsieur Borie, and is now one of the vineyards worth watching.

Characteristics. Supple yet full-bodied, a typically fine Saint-Julien. One that is definitely to be counted on for year-in, year-out quality.

Vineyard area: 85 acres.

Average production: 10,500 cases.

Château Duhart-Milon

Bordeaux red wine. District: Haut-Médoc, France. Commune: Pauillac.

Some of the vineyard lies alongside that of Château Lafite. Duhart-Milon is the only Fourth Growth (*Quatrième Cru*), Classification of 1855, in Pauillac. It was recently sold to Château Lafite.

Characteristics. Has certain things in common with the other Pauillac wines, but the quality has not been all that it might. Its new owners have already improved the quality and the wine's reputation will certainly grow.

Vineyard area: 55 acres.

Average production: 7,000 cases.

Dumb

Wine slang, describing wines of quality which stubbornly remain hard for many years, before reaching their peak. Usually these wines have a great deal of tannin. 1937 produced such wines.

Dunder

Sugar cane lees used to promote fermentation of rum.

Dur

French for hard, used of wine.

See DUMB.

Duras

See CÔTES DE DURAS.

Château Durfort-Vivens

Bordeaux red wine. District: Haut-Médoc, France. Commune: Margaux.

The vineyard, classed a Second Growth (*Second Cru*) in the Gironde Classification of 1855, was owned by Monsieur Pierre Ginestet. Originally the property of Monsieur Durfort de Duras, the château acquired its present name when it was purchased by Monsieur de Vivens in 1924. For many years, dating from just before the turn of the century, the property belonged to the Bordeaux wine firm of Delor. It is situated at the entrance to the village of Margaux, near Châteaux Margaux, Palmer, Rausan-Ségla, and Rauzan-Gassies. In 1963 the vineyard and *chais,* without the château, were purchased by the owner of Brane-Cantenac. A most dedicated viticulturist, he has increased the vineyard area threefold from its original 25 acres.

Vineyard area: 85 acres.

Average production: 6,000 cases.

Duriff

Californian grape—another name for the Petite-Syrah (*q.v.*).

Dürkheim (Bad Dürkheim)

The *Wurstmarkt* held here in September is Germany's greatest wine festival. Dürkheim produces the best-known red wine of the Palatinate, and a great deal of white.

See PALATINATE.

Dutchess

American hybrid grape developed in Dutchess County, New York, during the mid-nineteenth century. It gives light, dry white wines and is still cultivated to some extent in New York State.

E

East India

In the days when sailing ships went round by the Cape of Good Hope, casks of Sherry and Madeira were often put aboard as ballast: the long, rocking voyage to India and back improved and aged the wines. Some merchants still use this name for their good dessert blends, and an Amoroso (sweetened Oloroso) may be so called.

Eau-de-Vie

Generic French term for brandy or spirits.

Eau-de-Vie d'Andaye

A Basque spirit from the Pyrenees near Hendaye.

Eau-de-Vie de Cidre

Calvados or apple brandy.
See CALVADOS; APPLEJACK.

Eau-de-Vie de Dantzig

French equivalent of Dantziger Goldwasser (*q.v.*); also called Liqueur d'Or.

Eau-de-Vie de Lie

Spirit distilled from lees (wine deposit) in wine casks.

Eau-de-Vie de Marc

See MARC.

Eau-de-Vie de Vin

Spirit made from wine; brandy.

Ebullioscope

Apparatus for determining the alcoholic content of wine and spirits. It is based on the fact that at 760 millimetres of atmospheric pressure, water boils at 212°F. (100°C.) while alcohol boils at 172°F. (78°C.). The boiling point of the tested liquid will indicate its proportion of alcohol and water by its position between 172° and 212°F. (78° and 100°C.).

Échezeaux

Burgundy red wine. District: Côte de Nuits, France. Commune: Flagey-Échezeaux. Official Classification: Great Growth (Grand Cru).

Échezeaux is a place-name, not a vineyard—a situation which could only happen in Burgundy. It is a place-name which takes in all or parts of eleven different vineyards (including one called Upper Échezeaux, but none called Échezeaux) and has been granted the rating Great Growth (*Grand Cru*), the highest Burgundian rating.

As though they were not satisfied with having cast their net and called everything within it Échezeaux, the French wine authorities took another step and situated their place-name in a town which has no other important vineyards (with the exception of Great Growth Grands Échezeaux). Flagey-Échezeaux is on the wrong—or east—side of the main road, between Dijon and Lyons, on the plain where no wines of note grow, and has only a small foothold on the sloping, west side of the road. The result is that if wines from the vineyards of Échezeaux do not meet the high minimum standards, they are sold as Vosne-Romanée.

In fact, little wine is sold as Échezeaux, most of it going to market as Vosne-Romanée—which is next-door to these vineyards. Another reason why little Échezeaux is sold under that name is that few people know about it, and fewer have any confidence in their ability to pronounce it.

The size and diversity of the assembled vineyards means that an Échezeaux—when found under its own name—will be subject to considerable variation. Some will be beautifully rounded-out, stepping-stone wines, bridging the gap between the full, sturdy Vougeots and the light, delicate Vosne-Romanées; others will have less distinction than they should. Their lack of worldly fame, however, makes them wines of value, for there is relatively little demand for them, and they sell for lower prices than wines of similar quality but greater repute.

The vineyards from which these wines come are:

Vineyards	*Acres*
En Orveaux	24
Les Treux	12
Clos Saint-Denis	4·5
Les Cruots (or Vignes-Blanches)	8·1
Les Rouges-du-Bas	9·9
Champs-Traversins	8·8
Les Poulaillières	12·9
Les Loachausses	9·3
Les Quartiers de Nuits	6·4
Les Échezeaux-de-Dessus	8·8

Production in an average year comes to 12,000 imp. gallons (14,400 U.S.), or the equivalent of about 6,000 cases.

Echt

A Russian or Polish Kümmel of the crystallized type.

See KÜMMEL.

Edelfäule

German term for *Botrytis cinerea* (*q.v.*) or noble rot.

Edelweiss

Proprietary Italian Fior d'Alpi, or liqueur flavoured with extracts from alpine flowers.

Edelzwicker

On an Alsatian bottle label, Edelzwicker indicates a wine that is a blend of noble grape varieties.

Eelworm

Parasite harmful to vines.

See CHAPTER EIGHT, p. 38.

Egg Nog

Hot drink of egg beaten up in rum or brandy, sweetened and flavoured with nutmeg.

An egg flip is a similar drink, made with hot spirits, ale or wine.

Égrappage

French term for the separation of stalks from grapes before they are pressed or placed in the fermenting vats. This is necessary because the stalks contain oils and tannins that would render the wine bitter and harsh. The machine used is known as an *égrappoir*.

See SEPARATION.

Egri Bikavér

Probably the best-known wine of Hungary, apart from Tokay. The wine is red and the name means 'Bull's Blood of Eger'.

See HUNGARY.

Egypt

From time to time a tomb is opened and jars are found with dried traces of what, perhaps fifty centuries ago, was wine. From the remains of Ancient Egypt we know how the grapes were picked and pressed and how wine was buried in the tombs. Except for one man, that might be all.

The twentieth-century adventure of the Egyptian, Nestor Gianaclis, is in some ways one of the most fascinating of our time. With every modern scientific help, it has been a struggle to go forward to a past lost for two thousand years.

It was well known in classical times that the wines of Egypt were very fine. Cleopatra served to Cæsar Mareotic wine, which was said to come from ancient Meröe, near the fourth cataract of the Upper Nile. There were other Egyptian wines in great vogue throughout the Mediterranean world.

At the beginning of this century, Egyptian wine, so far as it existed at all, was undeniably bad. Nestor Gianaclis set out to search for the soil on which good wine could be grown. At the same time he tried to find out how good the wine of his ancestors had really been. Would not tastes have changed greatly in two thousand years? From evidence in the works of Virgil, Horace, Pliny, and others who wrote of wines in ancient Greece and Rome he came to the conclusion their tastes were not fundamentally different from our own. If they had liked Egyptian wines, then we would like them too.

Under the sand which buried it, on the brink of the desert, he found a soil that was utterly different from the alluvial soils which came down with the river and were deposited in the delta and the valley of the Nile. Chemical analysis confirmed that the soil, chalky and free of salts, was almost identical with that of Champagne in France. This was a more than promising beginning, and the first vines were planted in 1903.

Most of the difficulty lay ahead. The ancient vine plants were barely a memory in the most weighty books on wine, hardly more than a scratch or two here and there on a pyramid or tomb. It would have been as easy to locate an ancient Egyptian as a grape of ancient Egypt.

Seventy-three known grape varieties were tried over the years, in co-operation with experts from France, Italy, Hungary, and other wine-growing countries; and twenty new types developed by Gianaclis were subjected to laboratory analysis. Great wine required the sun, the soil, the proper vine, and the right combination of all these things. Gianaclis had to do in a few years what in other lands had taken centuries of trial and error: to match the right technique and the right vine to the climate and soil.

In 1931, after more than a quarter of a century of effort, it looked as if the battle were won. In that year, wines from the Mariout vineyard west of the Nile delta presented by Nestor Gianaclis before the Chambre Syndicale des Courtiers Gourmets of Paris were optimistically judged as worthy of being classed with the wines of the Rhine and such white Burgundies as Montrachet and Meursault. Two years later, it was being said in France that the wine of the Pharaohs had been resurrected and that the world could drink again the nectar which had been praised by Virgil.

Today, some of the wines fulfil part of their promise and are very fine. Quantity, though increasing, is relatively small. But a serious effort is being made to bring these wines from what might be called a super-Californian or super-Algerian climate into the world market. Samples have been sent to world fairs and, with production expanding (some 660,000 imp. gallons (792,000 U.S.) in 1962, more wine than can be absorbed at home), the Government is seeking to increase exports.

Egypt is equipped with exemplary wine laws. The decree of 6 October 1945 makes it illegal to call any wine sold in Egypt 'champagne', 'tokay', 'port', 'sherry', 'bordeaux', 'burgundy', etc., unless it really is the foreign wine of the type and from the place designated. The use of the name 'cognac' is forbidden to Egyptian brandies.

SPIRITS

The difference in price between domestic and foreign spirits in Egypt is not great. Imported Cognac and whisky give strong competition to the domestic rum, arak, and brandy, which are taxed at 30%. The rum, distilled from the molasses of Egyptian sugar cane, is of good quality. Tafia, however, a cruder spirit also from the residue of sugar-making, is produced in about twice the volume of rum (approximately 182,000 imp. gallons (218,570 U.S.) annually against 81,000 imp. gallons (97,276 U.S.) of rum) and is alcoholically stronger, usually over 100° proof. Rum and tafia together, combined with a tafia-and-30%-brandy mixture made in about one-tenth the quantity of rum, account for an average 280,000 imp. gallons (336,000 U.S.) annually. Brandy is made (from imported raisins, or fresh grapes) in about half the volume of rum, and arak and ouzo are produced in fairly substantial amounts. A popular alcoholic beverage of Egypt is Buza, distilled from fermented dates. The distillation process is usually haphazard and poorly conducted and the dates are often half-rotten. This contributes, however, to the popularity of the beverage, which is usually the only one the fellahin, who make up most of its market, can afford.

Eitelsbacher Karthäuserhofberg

Outstanding vineyard of Eitelsbach in Western Germany.

See RUWER.

Elbling

Grape grown in Luxembourg, Lorraine, and Germany—where it is also known as Kleinberger.

Elefantenwein (Elephant Wine)

Reference to a wine from Tübingen, Germany, which is said to have been made from grapes so hard that no men could have trodden them, but only elephants. The same comment is made of the Reutlinger wine of the Neckar region.

Élixir d'Anvers

Belgian liqueur made in Antwerp by F. X. de Beukelaer. It is compounded of herbs and plants on a base of brandy, is golden in colour, moderately sweet, and very fragrant.

Elixir Longæ Vitæ

Another name for Pommeranzen Bitters.

See BITTERS.

Elongated Wine

British term for wine 'lengthened' by addition of water to reduce strength for purposes of excise duty.

Eltviller Sonnenberg

Most elegant of the Eltville wines. The other outstanding vineyard here is Eltviller Langenstück.

See RHEINGAU.

Elvira

American hybrid grape developed in the late nineteenth century in Missouri and still used for white wines, usually sparkling.

Emilia-Romagna

Red and white wines. Central Italy.

South of the River Po, running from the Apennines to the Adriatic, stretches one of the great productive plains which recur throughout the Italian peninsula. A mountain soars up from the plain, with the operetta Republic of San Marino perched on top and vines clinging to its steep sides, but most of the Emilia-Romagna is flat, and throughout the plain the dominant activity is agriculture. Wheat and maize are cultivated and vines are not neglected, although sometimes they appear to be. Solid chunks of vineyard are rare, but everywhere you will see vines. They run rampant over the countryside, twining around any available support, apparently without benefit of cultivation or the bite of the pruning knife. This haphazard growth lends a curious charm to the scenery, but does little for the quality of some of the wines, although the district produces three growths which will rate the new *Denominazione di Origine*.

Lambrusco and Albana produce the honoured fruit of Emilia-Romagna, but Sangiovese is the widespread vine. The wine it gives is variable in the extreme, sometimes slightly bitter and hard, sometimes mellow and warming. It is always, however, available, is always red, and always dry—and this last characteristic is enough to endear it to many visitors to the region. It accounts for the bulk of the annual 75 million imp. gallons (90 million U.S.) of wine the region produces.

Lambrusco di Sorbara

This has no connexion with *Vitis labrusca*, a native American vine species. It is perhaps the best-known example of the region's viticulture, the wine-name deriving from the grapevine. It is red and sometimes unpleasant: a dry or sweetish, semi-sparkling wine with a disconcerting bright red foam.

Albana di Romagna

A golden-yellow wine—which may be semi-sweet or dry (although the dry type usually retains a slight trace of sugar). Perhaps its outstanding characteristic is an almost voluptuous velvetiness—when it is well made. It is generally true in Italy that wine quality tends to vary widely, even within small areas. Galla Placidia, Regent of the Western Roman Empire (A.D. 435), is said to have been an early devotee of Albana. Travelling through the region, she stopped at a small town to quench her thirst at the local inn and was served with the wine, but in a coarse mug. Her reaction to the Albana was: 'I must drink you in gold.' And Bertinoro ('Drink-you-in-gold') has been the name of the town ever since.

English Cuvée

Very dry Champagne, specially blended for the English taste.

See CHAMPAGNE.

Entre-Deux-Mers

White wines. District: Bordeaux, France.

A light, clean, white carafe wine, tending in the last few years to be vinified dry. Traditionally it was a mellow, soft, and sometimes sweet white wine. Red wine is made in the district, but it is sold as Bordeaux and is not entitled to the place-name. There are no outstanding growths or vineyards. Much of the wine is made by the fifteen admirable modern co-operatives, with a combined capacity of 9 million imp. gallons (11 million U.S.).

Deriving its name from its location, the region lies between the two rivers—'seas'—the Garonne and the Dordogne; and lies, also, between Bordeaux and Libourne in the zones of Pomerol and Saint-Émilion wines. The range of hills along the River Garonne facing the Graves, Barsac, and Sauternes wine districts, and a small enclave of gravel soil on the Dordogne near Libourne, are the best parts, but they have been given separate place-names. Loupiac and Sainte-Croix-du-Mont on the Garonne and Graves de Vayres from the small gravel enclave on the Dordogne are wines of higher quality made within the limits of Entre-Deux-Mers.

Enveloppe

French term for the straw sheaf, now rarely used, which is put around bottles to protect them. Cardboard is used for wines entering the United States because American laws forbid straw as a possible carrier of disease, pestilential insects, and parasites.

Enzian

Spirit distilled in the alpine and adjoining countries from the yard-long roots of the yellow mountain gentian. It makes one of the most aristocratic forms of schnapps.

Enzyme

Catalytic agent responsible for alcoholic fermentation. Enzymes are chemical substances excreted by yeasts and although they are not themselves changed during fermentation, it can occur only in their presence.

See CHAPTER NINE.

Épernay

An important centre of the Champagne trade.

See CHAMPAGNE.

Épesses

White wine of Lavaux in the Canton of Vaud, Switzerland.

See SWITZERLAND.

Erbacher Markobrunn

See MARKOBRUNN; RHEINGAU.

Erdener Treppchen

Best-known wine of Erden on the German Moselle, an outstanding dry wine.

See MOSELLE.

Erinose

A very small mite, destructive to some varieties of vine.

See CHAPTER EIGHT, p. 38.

Ermitage

See HERMITAGE.

Espalier

Method of training vines. The trunk terminates in one or two arms and several canes, all in the same plane, and supported by a trellis or wire. There are several variations on this method, including the decorative trellis-trained vine; and the practical guyot pattern of a trunk and one arm.

See CHAPTER EIGHT, p. 33.

Espumoso

Spanish term for sparkling.

Est! Est!! Est!!!

The dry wine of Montefiascone, Italy.

See LATIUM.

Esters

Slow reaction between the acids of the wine and the alcohols forms esters, which have a sweet, fruity smell.

See CHAPTER NINE.

Estufades

Huge heating chambers in which wines of Madeira are 'cooked'.

See MADEIRA.

Étampé

French term for branded.

Ethers

Chemical compounds, important components of wines and spirits imparting bouquet or aroma.

Étiquette

French term for bottle label.

Étoile

One of the best white wines of the French Jura comes from this southernmost area of the region.

See JURA.

Eudemis

One of the distinctive grape-moths.

See CHAPTER EIGHT, p. 37.

Eumelan

Red-wine-giving grape of the eastern United States. It is a poor producer and not outstanding for the wine-maker.

Excise

Tax on home product as compared with customs.

Excoriose

A rare vine malady.

See CHAPTER EIGHT, p. 37.

Exportation of Wine

Figures change, inevitably, from year to year, influenced by the season's harvest and by industrial and political fluctuations. Among the half-dozen largest exporting countries, France, Italy, and Morocco increased their sales between 1958 and 1964; Tunisia fell somewhat, Spain and Portugal a good deal. Although Argentina, the U.S.A., and U.S.S.R. are big producers of wine, none of these three countries exports very much.

WINE EXPORTS IN 1964

Exporting country	*Hectolitres*	*Imp. gallons*	*U.S. gallons*
Algeria	9,150,200*	201,282,439	241,729,069
France	3,658,975	80,488,668	96,662,436
Italy	2,320,177	51,038,326	61,294,204
Portugal	2,269,835	49,930,922	59,964,274
Spain	2,079,847	45,751,642	54,945,190
Morocco	1,970,000	43,335,272	52,043,263
Tunisia	1,352,668	29,755,450	35,734,648
Bulgaria	965,170	21,231,424	25,497,765
Hungary	569,000	12,516,634	15,031,785
Rumania	424,000	9,326,982	11,201,190
Yugoslavia	397,317	8,740,020	10,496,281
Greece	269,350	5,925,054	7,115,661
Western Germany	180,851	3,978,288	4,777,704
South Africa	176,299†	3,878,155	4,657,449
Cyprus	116,900‡	2,571,519	3,088,252
Chile	70,530	1,551,491	1,863,254

Exporting country	*Hectolitres*	*Imp. gallons*	*U.S. gallons*
Australia	69,930	1,538,292	1,847,404
Luxembourg	66,980	1,473,399	1,769,471
Austria	18,654	410,343	492,799
Turkey	17,594‡	387,026	464,797
Israel	14,392	316,589	380,206
Switzerland	9,754	214,565	257,680
Albania	8,490	186,760	224,288
U.S.A.	7,890	173,561	208,437
Netherlands	5,499	120,965	145,272
Argentine	4,000*	87,990	105,672

* = Estimated   † = 1963   ‡ = 1962

Extra Sec

French for Extra Dry. These words appearing on the label of a bottle of Champagne do not, in fact, indicate an extra dry wine, but only one which is fairly dry. A really dry Champagne will be labelled Brut.

Ezerjó

White-wine variety grown in Hungary. Also the full gold-coloured wine of Mór, near Budapest.

F

Factory House

A club and club building in Oporto where the finest Ports in the world are drunk. Nowadays it is correctly called the British Association, but everyone refers to it as the Feitoria Inglesa or English Factory House. In early days the Factory system was one of British extra-territorial rights in foreign countries, which is why out of courtesy to Portugal the name of the Club has been changed. Even today, however, British Port companies have favourable rights in Portugal accorded no other nation.

Members of the 'Factory House' comprise the most exclusive British Port circle, every one being a partner in a British Port firm in Oporto.

Even so, no British partner may join the Factory House if there is a Portuguese partner in his firm.

Falerno

The vineyards where the modern Falerno is grown are on the slopes of Monte Massico (about half-way between Rome and Naples) and the wine is generally white, semi-dry, and moderately strong.

Falernian was the most famous of all the ancient Roman wines, and it too came from the vineyards of Monte Massico; but we do not now know what grapes went into it, and we have only a very imperfect idea of how it tasted.

See CAMPANIA; CLASSICAL WINES.

Falernum

A flavouring syrup, not very strong (6% alcohol by volume) made in Bermuda and the West Indies of syrup, lime, almonds, ginger, and spices. It is a popular flavouring for rum drinks.

Fan Leaf

Another name for infectious degeneration of vines.

See CHAPTER EIGHT, p. 36.

Fass

German for cask.

Fassle

A German drinking vessel rather similar in principle to the *porrón* of Spain, in that the liquid is spurted from a tube into the drinker's mouth. The *Fassle*, or little barrel, is a five-litre wooden cask into whose bung-hole cork a tube, the *Spitzle*, has been inserted. As with the *porrón*, the trick of drinking from the vessel entails a steady hand, and a quick flick of the wrist to avoid the drinker's being doused in the stream of liquid.

Fat

A big, soft wine without the hardness to give it body, and containing much natural glycerine. Typical examples are the Bordeaux Pomerols and some Saint-Émilions.

Faye d'Anjou

Commune with the right to an Appellation Contrôlée in the Coteaux du Layon district of Anjou, France.

See ANJOU.

Federweisser

New wine, milky or 'feather white', found in German inns after the vintage.

Fehérbór

Hungarian term for white wine.

Feints

Leavings of second distillation of Scotch malt whisky.

Fendant

Best white wines of Valais, Switzerland, made from the Fendant (or Chasselas) grape.

See SWITZERLAND.

Ferme

Firm or stubborn. Usually a wine of quality; but as long as it is in this condition, it is not ready to drink, being hard and tannic.

Fermentation

The decomposition of sugar chiefly into ethyl alcohol and carbon dioxide. The classic equation is given by Gay-Lussac:

$$\underset{\text{(180 grams)}}{C_6H_{12}O_6} \longrightarrow \underset{\text{(92 grams)}}{2C_2H_6O} + \underset{\text{(88 grams)}}{2CO_2}$$

Unfortunately, this is not quite accurate, careful measurement proving that whereas the alcoholic content should be the equivalent of 51% of the sugar, in reality 47% is normal and the odd 4% forms a number of side-products including higher alcohols, nitrogenous compounds, glycerin, etc. Fermentation is caused by enzymes in yeasts. There are various yeasts which have differing effects upon the sugars available for fermentation (principally, grape, cane, and milk sugar). In order that fermentation should proceed satisfactorily, temperature and aeration must be properly regulated.

See CHAPTER NINE.

Fernet Branca

The best-known Italian bitters. It is used as an aperitif and generally recommended to settle upset stomachs and hangovers.

See BITTERS.

Château Ferrière

Bordeaux red wine. District: Haut-Médoc, France. Commune: Margaux.

This excellent vineyard, in the very heart of the village of Margaux, classed a Third Growth (*Troisième Cru*) of the Médoc in the Classification of 1855, is at present leased to Château Lascombes. Each year a limited quantity of Ferrière is made by the owners of Château Lascombes.

Fiano

The grape which makes the light white, slightly tart wines of Avellino, near Naples.

Fiasco

Italian straw-covered glass flask holding about two litres of wine. It is associated particularly with Chianti.

Ficklin Vineyards

Madera County, California.

Californian winery specializing in good port-type wines made from the choicest Portuguese grapes. Four of the finest varieties are used: Tinta Cão, Tinta Madeira, Alvarelhão, and Touriga. Exceptional care goes into the making of Ficklin ports, and with the help of the Davis Œnological Station, they are producing matured wines comparable with those of Portugal.

See AMERICA: CALIFORNIA AND THE WEST.

Field Grafting

For a description of this method of grafting vines, see Chapter Eight, p. 32.

Château de Fieuzal

Bordeaux red and white wines. District: Graves, France. Commune: Léognan.

The vineyard, which once belonged to the La Rochefoucauld family, is planted on good gravelly slopes, and is very well managed by the present owner, Monsieur Erik Bocké. He is an impresario as well as a grower, and his flair for theatrical production can be assessed by visitors to his cellars and *chai*. The vineyard was made a Classified Growth (*Cru Classé*) in 1959.

Characteristics. In quality, the wines can hold their own with almost any of the Graves. The red is generous and velvety, with a charming bouquet; the white, dry and *racé*.

Vineyard area: 32 acres.

Average production: 4,650 cases.

Château Figeac

Bordeaux red wine. District and Commune: Saint-Émilion, France.

Long one of the best-known Saint-Émilions, and in 1955 classed among the First Great Growths (*Premiers Grands Crus*), Figeac must not be confused with other Saint-Émilion vineyards employing the word in various combinations of the name. Six other of these Figeac vineyards surround Château Figeac (Charles de Figeac was a nobleman of Saint-Émilion) but the unmodified name belongs to the best of the growths, one of the largest important vineyards in Saint-Émilion. Touching Cheval-Blanc, and near the Pomerol boundary, the vineyard surrounds a château and wine *chai* widely separated by the length of a broad avenue which bisects a splendid park. The young owner, Monsieur de Manoncourt, is an ardent and progressive wine-maker.

Characteristics. The wine, which declined for a time, has returned to form in the last decade or so. It is a characteristic Saint-Émilion, robust and well rounded.

Vineyard area: 62 acres.

Average production: 9,500 cases.

Château Filhot

Bordeaux white wine. District and Commune: Sauternes, France.

Owned by the Comtesse Durieu de Lacarelle (sister of the Marquis de Lur-Saluces, proprietor of Château d'Yquem), the vineyard produces somewhat drier wines than Yquem and is generally considered to have been unjustly classed a Second Growth (*Second Cru*) of Sauternes in 1855. If the wines were now re-rated it might be made a First. The château, a beautiful eighteenth-century country house set in smooth lawns, looks more English than French; and as it happens, Filhot wines have always had a large following in England.

Characteristics. High in alcohol; one of the driest of Sauternes—and, as such, an exception to most of the others.

Vineyard area: 120 acres.

Average production: 7,000 cases.

Fillette

French slang term for a half-bottle in certain parts of France, as for instance, in Anjou. Literally 'a little girl'.

Film Yeast

Another name for *flor*.

See SHERRY.

Filtering

The clarification of wine by passing it through special devices—or simply through a layer of filter paper—with the object of ridding it of any suspended particles. In many fine wine districts the older method of fining (*q.v.*) is used. Filtering, for all its ease and practicality, can rob a fine wine of some of its quality. This is also true of the much-used Seitz Filter which has layers of asbestos. Too many layers or slipshod handling can filter out all distinction, leaving the wine insipid and without character.

Fine Champagne

Not a Champagne but a Cognac brandy, properly a blend from the districts of Grande Champagne and Petite Champagne.

'*Une fine*' (pronounced 'feen') is the popular way of calling for a Cognac in France—any Cognac—but correctly it is liqueur Cognac of the Champagne (chalky and best) Cognac district.

See COGNAC.

Finesse

French term for exceptional elegance or breed (*q.v.*).

Finger Lakes

Wine-growing region in New York State. This is the most important district in the Eastern States, and some of the finest sparkling wine in America is produced here. The best vineyards are beside Lake Keuka and Lake Canandaigua; and there are others around Lake Seneca and Lake Cayuga. Some of the leading firms are established in the Pleasant Valley–Hammondsport district, and some excellent sparkling wines are made here, as well as other types.

See AMERICA: EASTERN STATES.

Fining

Fining, or *collage*, is the process by which wine is clarified of any suspended particles. This can be done either with an organic agent such as blood, casein, protein, or gelatine, which will coagulate and carry down with it the clouding particles; or with a clarifier which has a mechanical action—such as bentonite, cellulose, infusorial earth.

See CHAPTER NINE, p. 43.

Finish

Lingering aftertaste.

Fino

The driest type of Sherry (*q.v.*).

Fins Bois

One of the lesser districts in the Cognac region of France.

See COGNAC.

Fior d'Alpi

Literally, Alpine flowers. It is a sweet Italian liqueur, yellow in colour and usually containing a branch of rock-sugar crystals inside the characteristic tall, narrow bottle.

Firkin

English beer barrel of 9 imp. gallons (10·8 U.S.) capacity.

Fitou

Red wine. District: Southern France.

A French wine-growing area of more historical than contemporary importance. Fitou, which marches with Roussillon, near the Spanish border, is made up of nine communes: Fitou, Leucate, Caves-de-Treilles, Lapalme, Tuchan, Paziols, Cascastel, Villeneuve-les-Corbières, and Treilles. The hot Mediterranean sun beats down brutally on the scarcely fertile slopes, 600 acres of which are given over to vines.

The vine types are mostly Carignan and Grenache, which must—singly or together—make up 75% of any wine carrying the name of Fitou. The other 25% may be made up of one or several of the following: Cinsault, Terret Noir, Malvoisie, Maccabéo, Muscat, or Picpoule. The maximum that the French authorities allow is 260 imp. gallons (312 U.S.) of wine per acre, except in certain extraordinary years.

Fitou is one of the best wines of the Midi. It is a dark, pungent, heavy red wine, high in alcoholic content, making a good, rather common, but sound table wine. To gain the name it must be aged in the barrel for at least nine months (until 1953 the ageing period was two years in the barrel) before it is sold. The average production of Fitou is less than 100,000 imp. gallons (120,000 U.S.) and for this reason it is not often found outside its native area.

Fixed Acidity

The presence of natural and desirable acids (principally tartaric) which are the cause of an agreeable tartness in wine.

See CHAPTER NINE.

Fixin

Burgundy red wine. District: Côte de Nuits, France.

Fixin is the northernmost of the wine communes of the Côte de Nuits, the upper arm of Burgundy's famous Côte d'Or. Present-day Fixin includes the area that was, before 1850, that of Fixin and its neighbour, Fixey. In spite of the augmentation of property, the town did not gain a great deal as far as vineyards were concerned.

Most of the wines of the town are not sold under the commune name at all but are included in the Vins Fins de la Côte de Nuits. However, rather more than 100 acres within the town are allowed to be sold as Fixin, the best of which comes from the twelve-acre vineyard, Clos de la Perrière. According to the now obsolete classification of the Côte d'Or vineyards made in 1860, this vineyard was considered as an Outstanding Growth (*Tête de Cuvée*) and was the only one so honoured in Fixin. The more recent classification made by the Institut National des Appellations d'Origine des Vins et Eaux-de-Vie (the National Institute of Place-names of Wines and Spirits) has, more realistically, demoted it to First Growth (*Premier Cru*) of Fixin, a status which it shares with five other vineyards. The wines from the Clos de la Perrière are generally deep, alcoholic, and slow to mature, and while they bear a strong resemblance to those from the neighbouring commune of Gevrey-Chambertin, they have less breed and magnificence than do Gevrey's greatest wines. In some years, however, they can be better than many from the secondary vineyards which rank just behind the great Chambertin.

Within the confines of Fixin there are some 500 acres growing wines allowed to go to market only as Vins Fins de la Côte de Nuits and about 105 acres whose wines are sold as Fixin. These 105 acres include the following classified growths, all of which may be sold as Fixin Premier Cru, or with the town name followed by the name of the vineyard.

FIRST GROWTHS (*Premiers Crus*)

Vineyard	*Acres*
Clos de la Perrière	12
Clos du Chapitre	11·75
Les Hervelets	9
Les Meix-Bas	1·25
Aux Cheusots (Clos Napoléon)	4·5
Les Arvelets	8·25

Flagey-Échezeaux

Flagey-Échezeaux in Burgundy is a town but not a place-name—in the vinous sense of the word—although the two great vineyards within its confines are place-names in their own right. The town stands to the left of the main road which runs through the Côte de Nuits, and its boundaries are so staked out that they force a small passage between Vougeot and Vosne-Romanée and fan out into a beachhead on the great slope.

The two vineyards within the town are Échezeaux and Grands-Échezeaux (*qq.v.*). Both are Great Growths (*Grands Crus*)—the highest official rating given to Burgundian vineyards—and in the years when the wine does not meet the rigorous minimum standards, they are declassed either into First Growths (*Premiers Crus*)—slightly less than Great Growth—of neighbouring Vosne-Romanée, or into the more general Vosne-Romanée with no other indication of origin.

Flagon

A large bottle usually of flattened globular shape, its capacity entirely dependent upon the wishes of its user; a squat bottle similar to the *Bocksbeutel* (*q.v.*) of German Franconia used for Commonwealth (and especially Australian) 'burgundies'.

Fleurie

Only in recent years sold consistently under the communal name of Fleurie, these wines are not as well known as some other Beaujolais, but they are among the most typically Beaujolais of all, perfectly expressing the fresh, fruity charm of this French red wine.

See BEAUJOLAIS.

Fliers

Tiny, tasteless particles sometimes appearing in wine. They are caused usually by cold and disappear if the wine is warmed to normal room temperature.

Flohpeter

Waggish reference to a German wine so sour that any *Flöhe*, or fleas, which bit the drinker would be instantly killed by the acid in his bloodstream.

Flor

The white skin or layer which appears uniquely on some Sherries and on certain wines of the Jura in France. When *flor* develops on Sherry, the wine becomes Fino; when it does not, the wine is Oloroso.

See SHERRY; CHAPTER NINE, p. 53.

Floraison

French term for flowering of the vines, at the end of which very small green berries will have formed.

See CHAPTER EIGHT, p. 34.

Flowery

Taste reminiscent of flowers, found in young wines; the younger the wine the more flowery it is apt to be. Few great wines have this quality.

Fluid Ounce

In Great Britain, the volume of one standard ounce weight of pure water, measured at a temperature of 62°F. (17°C.) and a barometric pressure of 30 inches. In the United States, one-sixteenth of a standard U.S. pint. The equivalents under the metric system are 2·841 centilitres to a British fluid ounce, 2·957 centilitres to an American ounce. The American is about 4% greater than the British.

Folle Blanche

Once the principal grape for the thin white Charente wines which are distilled into Cognac, this has now been largely displaced by the Saint-Émilion vine, although a small percentage is still used. The grape is planted also in California.

Forbidden Fruit

An American liqueur perhaps better known abroad than at home. It is made from the shaddock —a citrus fruit somewhat like a large grapefruit— infused in brandy. It is reddish-brown in colour, and is sold in a round bottle, the size of a grapefruit.

Foreshots

The first crude spirit to emerge from the still in whisky-making.

Forster Jesuitengarten

Best-known of the outstanding Forster wines in the German Palatinate, or Pfalz.

See PALATINATE.

Forster Kirchenstück

Best of the outstanding Forster wines in the German Palatinate, or Pfalz.

See PALATINATE.

Fortified Wine

Wine to which brandy has been added sometimes to stop fermentation, and to increase alcoholic content. Some examples are Port, Sherry, Malaga, and Madeira. In America the term is illegal and such wines are usually called dessert wines.

See PORT; SHERRY; MADEIRA; MALAGA; SWEET FORTIFIED WINES OF FRANCE.

Forzato

Italian term for wine made from overripe grapes.

Foudre

French term for large cask for maturing, storing, and transporting wine. Used to some extent in Alsace, where the word was adopted from the German *Fuder*, and for ordinary or bulk wine.

Château Fourcas-Hostein

Bordeaux red wine. District: Haut-Médoc, France. Commune: Listrac.

The hill of Fourcas on the north edge of Listrac—really not so much a hill as the culmination of the Listrac plateau—is shared by Fourcas-Hostein and, a little further on, the equally excellent and pleasantly countrified Fourcas-Dupré. Château Fourcas-Hostein, classed *Bourgeois Supérieur* in 1855, is perhaps rated below its true position and might be considered as a classified Great Growth (*Grand Cru*) of Médoc. Up to 1951 there were two Fourcas-Hosteins, each belonging to one of two cousins; now the vineyard is united under one ownership.

Characteristics. A full, slightly hard, and yet distinguished wine.

Vineyard area: 57 acres.

Average production: 6,000 cases.

Fourtet (Clos)

Bordeaux red wine. District and Commune: Saint-Émilion, France.

One of the twelve First Great Growths (*Premiers Grands Crus*) of Saint-Émilion, as officially classified in 1955. The vineyard is planted along the wall of the eleventh-century village, one of the most picturesque in France. The cellars, cut in solid rock under the vines, are among the sights of the town.

Characteristics. Saint-Émilion is typified in this full-bodied fine wine. Recently, however, it has been criticized as having somewhat declined in quality.

Vineyard area: 50 acres.

Average production: 6,700 cases.

Fox-Grape

Popular name for grapes of *Vitis labrusca*, which runs wild in north-east and north-central America. It can be used for wines which have a very pronounced taste and aroma. Known as 'foxy', although it has nothing in common with the scent of a fox, it is a strongly flavoured grape.

Foxy

The special taste quality of the American wines—i.e. wines made from native grapes in Eastern America. It is a particular characteristic of wines made from grapes of the species *Vitis labrusca*, of which type Concord is probably the best-known example.

Fraise

French *eau-de-vie*, or white alcohol, a brandy distilled from strawberries.

Framboise

French *eau-de-vie*, or white alcohol, a brandy distilled from raspberries.

Franc-de-Goût

French term for clean-tasting.

France

Enjoyment of fine wines is one of the most civilized of pleasures; and the greatest wines in the world come from France, centre of modern civilization, not in the fine arts only, but in the minor, delightful arts of eating and drinking. Wine is a source of inspiration for her artists and the delectation of her workmen; a symbol of French *savoir-vivre* and a major French industry. The mysteries of wine-making cannot be reduced to statistics, any more than a picture can be analysed by the size of its canvas or the time it took to paint; yet statistics are striking and important.

France produces more wine than any other country (although Italy is making a concerted effort to overtake her); and the French import, export, and drink more wine (both *per capita* and *in toto*) than any other nation. There are roughly 3½ million acres of vines in France, most of which exist solely for wine—although a few produce table grapes—and their output is some 1,332 million imp. gallons (1,600 million U.S.) per year. Of this, by far the greatest proportion is *ordinaire* for everyday drinking, but about 177 million imp. gallons (213 million U.S.) are classed as Appellation Contrôlée—the fine wines of France. Since 1953, the vineyard area has diminished by nearly 250,000 acres, in consequence of a subsidized uprooting of vines for common wine as a measure against over-production. Some 6 million of the 40-odd million Frenchmen owe their livelihood directly to wine, including growers (about 1½ million of them), wholesalers and shippers, regularly employed vineyard workers, manufacturers of wine-making equipment and machinery, laboratory technicians, and a host of civil servants, part of whose task is keeping track of statistics such as these. Then, carriers transport wine, among other loads; shops sell it, among other commodities; and many other Frenchmen would be living far less well than they do were it not for wine.

France imports about 258 million imp. gallons (310 million U.S.) of wine each year, the bulk still from Algeria, but some from Morocco, Tunisia, Spain, Italy, and Greece. She exports over 80 million imp. gallons (96 million U.S.) annually, a part to the former countries of Overseas France and most of what is left to Germany, Benelux, Switzerland, Great Britain, and the United States, in that order. Wine accounts for 8% of total agricultural revenue in the country and 23% of revenue coming from the exportation of agricultural products. The average French family spends from 8% to 13% of its food budget on wine, and consumption in 1964 was 27·3 imp. gallons (32·8 U.S.) per head per year—the highest in the world. This amount only includes wine that has been taxed; considerably more is consumed on large and small vineyards without the interference of tax collector or official statistician. Wine is a huge industry, an incalculable economic asset, an invaluable source of foreign currency, and the means by which innumerable Frenchmen earn all or part of their living. But it is more than just this. It is almost a way of life.

Wine History

Wine was made in Gaul (now France) before the Roman occupation, mainly, no doubt, around the Greek colony of Massilia (Marseilles). The Romans spread the knowledge of wine further, and taught the natives to prune and tend their vines. There were two great trade routes by river and road from the early settlement of Narbonne: from Béziers to the Garonne (whence there was already a sea route to Britain); and by the Rhône and Saône to the Moselle and Loire Valleys. Goods went by water to the inland port of Chalon-sur-Saône, and from there by wagon. Wine travelled in earthenware amphoræ, and fragments of these jars have been found in the river beds and along the roads. Wrecked ships loaded with amphoræ have been retrieved from the Mediterranean—the jars, still corked, contain a liquid that, in the years before Christ, was new wine. The Gauls made barrels and as early as Roman times these were in use. Centuries later the saintly King Louis IX liked to make casks in his spare time and as he made his visits from monastery to monastery, he would stay to taste the wine the monks had made.

Gradually, as new and hardier grape varieties were discovered, the vineyards pushed farther north: to Gaillac and the Côtes du Rhône; then as far as the Loire, Brittany, and the Île-de-France. In the early Middle Ages, before the trade with Gascony had become important, Rhine wines were coming into London and *Vins de France*—the French wines from the districts near Paris, and greatly esteemed. As the demand increased, more supplies of wine came in from La Rochelle, Angers, and Saumur. Rouen was then a very busy port. Argenteuil, celebrated in the nineteenth century in the paintings of the Impressionists, was famous more than six hundred years earlier, when its wines appeared on the table of the King, Philip Augustus. Before Champagne began to sparkle, its wines probably went in with those of the Seine; towards the end of the seventeenth century, the growths of Reims, Ay, and Épernay were praised by Saint-Evremond and others.

Nor were any of the wines as strong in alcohol or as lasting as those we are accustomed to. The light red Clairet of Gascony, as it arrived in England in the fourteenth century, was drawn fresh from the cask, and drunk within a year of the harvest. In 1352 this edict was issued in London: '. . . mixing of old Bordeaux wine with young Bordeaux and passing off the blend for young Bordeaux is forbidden as an offence against the king and the people.' Since the wine was kept in porous casks at the time, there was no way of ageing it, and an old wine would no doubt have been *passé* and unpleasant.

In those days, many of the vineyards of France belonged to the Church—the monks took almost as much pains to spread the vine as they did to spread the Word, and their wines became an important source of revenue. In Burgundy, the Dukes as well as the Fathers cultivated vines, and they were good publicists for their own wines. For many years Burgundy was consumed principally in France and in Flanders (the Burgundian nobles also held court at Brussels); but when, in 1685, the Edict of Nantes was revoked, fleeing Huguenots introduced it abroad, especially in Switzerland, Holland, and Germany. About 1750, the first commercial houses and travellers in wine were set up.

In Bordeaux, the wine-making *bourgeoisie* became rich and powerful. Throughout the Hundred Years War and afterwards, England remained the chief customer, with Holland later creeping up to second place for white wines. In Tudor times the English took to drinking more of both beer and sack, and French wine did not flow so freely nor so cheaply as before. But it continued to come in, even when most of it had to be smuggled, at the time of Marlborough's wars and the heavy duties imposed by the Methuen Treaty.

Wars on French soil constantly damaged French vineyards, which were patiently reconstituted. The fortunes of the vine-grower wavered over the centuries. In spite of bitter struggles, and the passage of armies, monk and peasant (and noble as well) continued to care for the vines and to make wine, adapting their customs to local conditions. Vines were pruned short in Bordeaux, long in the Rhône Valley; grapes were left to rot on the vines in Sauternes; Dom Pérignon (they say) discovered the cork as a bottle fastener and the way to make sparkling wines; growers in Château-Chalon put their grapes on straw mats and left them to dry in the autumn sun. Other growers in other parts of the world have developed parallel systems, but in no other country have these techniques been so devotedly applied; nor has any other country been so richly endowed with variations of soil and climate. It is not surprising that France produces the widest variety of great wines in the world.

Building the tradition of quality in French wines has not been without its setbacks. The attempts by the Duke of Burgundy to ban the 'disloyal gaamez' —the productive grapevine, Gamay, that did no honour to the wines of the Côte d'Or—is one chapter in this struggle. The continual fight against fraud is another. The strict and enlightened laws of Appellation Contrôlée should provide the happy ending to the story; but the number of convictions for fraud that occur each year in France demonstrates that not all the community is motivated by the desire to strive only for the finest quality. Nevertheless, in the great wine regions the majority

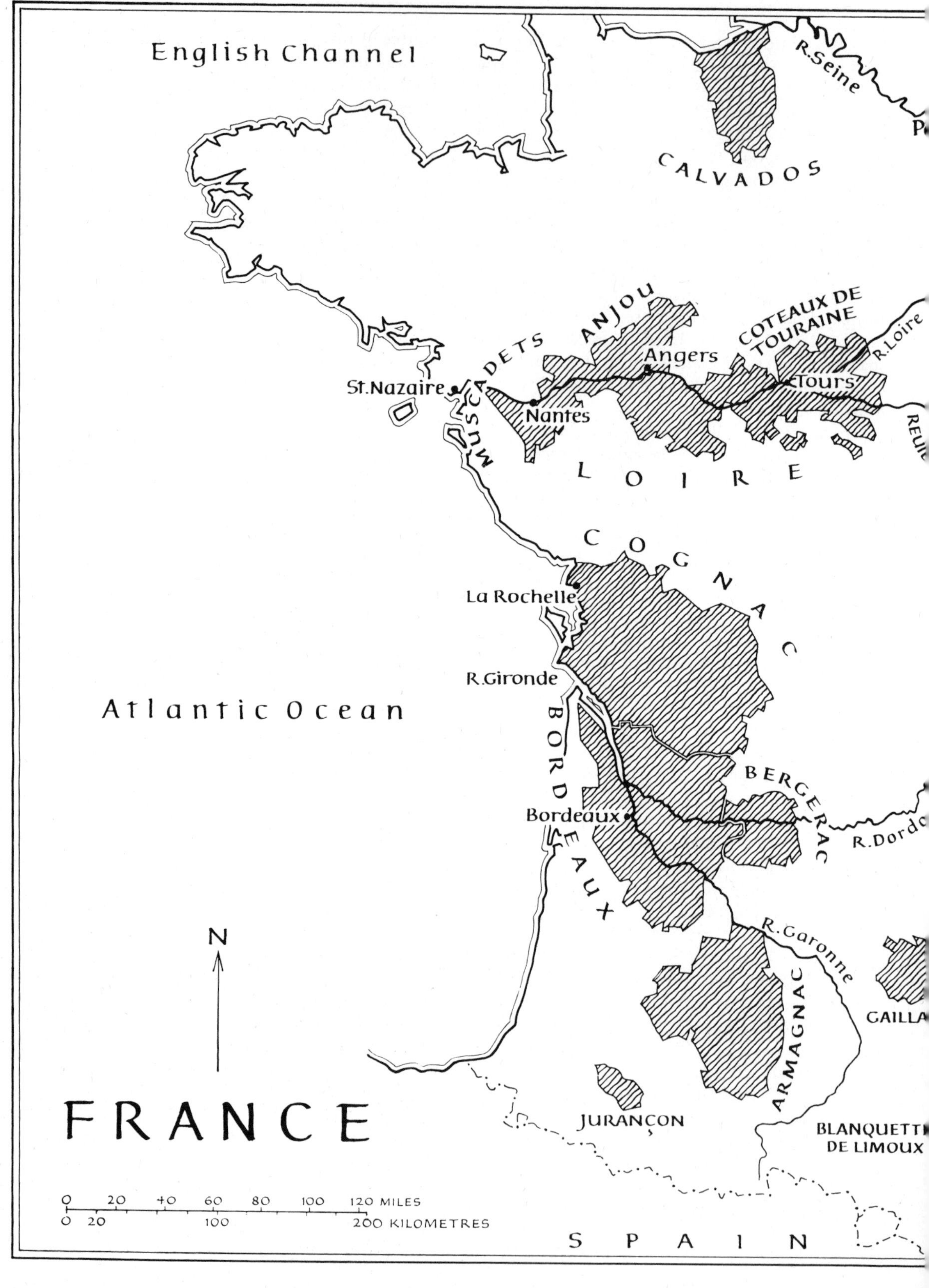
English Channel
R.Seine
CALVADOS
ANJOU
COTEAUX DE TOURAINE
R.Loire
MUSCADETS
St.Nazaire
Angers
Tours
Nantes
LOIRE
COGNAC
La Rochelle
R.Gironde
Atlantic Ocean
BORDEAUX
BERGERAC
Bordeaux
R.Garonne
ARMAGNAC
N
FRANCE
JURANÇON
0 20 40 60 80 100 120 MILES
0 20 100 200 KILOMETRES
SPAIN

Reims
HAMPAGNE
Chablis
CHABLIS
RE
Pouilly-s-Loire
Nevers
R.Loire
BURGUNDY
C.DE NUITS
C.DE BEAUNE
CHALONNAIS
Dijon
Beaune
R.Saône
MÂCONNAIS
Mâcon
BEAUJOLAIS
Lyons
R.Meuse
R.Moselle
ALSACE
Strasbourg
R.Rhine
GERMANY
R.Doubs
JURA
SWITZERLAND
AUSTRIA
Geneva
R.Rhône
SEYSSEL
CÔTE RÔTIE
ITALY
CÔTES DU RHÔNE
CLAIRETTE
DE DIE
R.Durance
Tavel
Châteauneuf-du-Pape
Avignon
Nimes
MUSCATS
Frontignan
Marseilles
PROVENCE
Nice
ROUSSILLON
Banyuls
Mediterranean Sea

of growers strain all their resources to make the best possible wine year after year, though the cards in the modern era are perhaps more heavily stacked against them than ever before.

The present cry is for more of everything, turned out faster and more cheaply. If there is anything that does not respond to this call, it is wine. It can be made inexpensively, but it will not then be fine wine; it can be made in bulk, but cannot thus be great wine. The best wines have always been those from comparatively non-productive grapevines—from vines that are deliberately pruned short in order to reduce output and channel the plant's energy into the production of superior fruit, but little of it. The grower cannot obtain quantity and quality at the same time.

Another trend working against the contemporary grower is that towards a standard product. Wines will be different in different years; they can be standardized by blending, but no blending-vat in the world is capable of turning out a standard wine of the highest quality. Ordinary wine from southern France or Algeria can be pleasant enough with a meal; but cut with finer wines they do no justice to themselves nor to the consumer.

The question is: will fine wines survive this trend? The French growers think they can continue in the traditional way; and the admirably stringent laws of Appellation d'Origine support their conviction. Many wine-drinkers, in France and abroad, support their efforts to maintain the old high standards, by taking an interest such as has never before been manifested in fine wines. Others, more pessimistic, quote the rising cost of labour and equipment, which may cause the making of fine wine to become an economic impossibility, especially since even a comparatively short stretch of unfavourable weather can devastate the greatest vineyards. Fortunately for France, the high quality of her wines—admirably maintained by the laws of Appellation Contrôlée—is so firmly established throughout the world, that she can charge the extra premium necessary for the protection of such standards.

Vine-growing Regions

France is divided into ninety departments and about two-thirds of these have commercial vineyards. Each wine is the result of the specific climate and soil from which it comes, the grape varieties from which it is made, and of the men and traditions behind it—factors which will differ in each case. The history of Burgundy would not have been the same without the Cistercians and the French Revolution; the wine trade of Bordeaux was a development of her close ties with England; Champagne is inextricably linked with the discovery—whether by Dom Pérignon or another—of the Champagne process; the wines of the Rhône valley owe much of their present success to one extraordinary man—the Baron Le Roy de Boiseaumarié. But although the wines of France are numerous, the great regions are comparatively few. These are the most important (*see also under separate headings*):

Alsace

More than most other districts, Alsace is perfecting her wines. The best of them, superior to many of Germany's lesser wines, have not yet achieved the quality of rivals from the better domains in the Rheingau, the Palatinate, and the Moselle; yet some of the Alsatian wines are quite excellent.

Bordeaux

The largest of the great wine regions of France and the most productive. The reds—or Clarets—of the Haut-Médoc, Graves, Saint-Émilion, and Pomerol, the sweet, rich whites of Sauternes and Barsac, and the drier whites of Graves have been imitated the world over—but rarely very successfully.

Burgundy

The wines vary so much that it is absurd to use the name to describe a single 'type' of wine. Reds may be austere and aristocratic as are Corton and Chambertin, or light and delicate as any fine wine from Chambolle should be. The whites are always dry; but the enormous variation between Chablis, Montrachet, and Meursault, for example, can only be appreciated by tasting.

Champagne

The name is so famous that many people don't know precisely what it is, but erroneously suppose it to be any 'bubbly' white wine. Yet Champagne is rigidly controlled and strictly defined in France, and the name, far from applying to all sparkling wine, is only legal when applied to one that is unique, and made, uniquely, in the district for which it is named.

Loire Valley

The white wines may be dry, semi-sweet, or sweet, and are usually better than the reds. All are beguiling; but many are better buys at home than abroad, because they do not always travel well.

Rhône Valley

The reds are sturdy, big, perfumed, and often magnificent. The whites also have a distinctive vigour of their own. The rosé from Tavel is probably the best-known of all rosé wines.

See also ANJOU; AUDE; BERGERAC; CORSICA; FITOU; GAILLAC; JURA; GARD; GRAND ROUSSILLON; HÉRAULT; JURANÇON; LANGUEDOC; LORRAINE; MIDI; PROVENCE; SOUTH-WEST FRANCE; SWEET FORTIFIED WINES OF FRANCE; TOURAINE; V.D.Q.S.

SPIRITS

As the greatest wines in the world come from France, so do the finest spirits: no brandy can compare with French Cognac, Armagnac, and Calvados; and in addition to these peerless brandies, the fertile French mind has developed countless cordials, liqueurs, and aperitifs, many strictly for the French palate, others equally appreciated outside France. The important ones, which will be found under their own headings in this book, are:

Armagnac

Wine brandy from the Gascon country, home of the boisterous d'Artagnan.

Calvados

Apple brandy from the old province of Normandy. When well made and properly aged it can be fabulous.

Cognac

Not any brandy, but a specific brandy. It is, perhaps, the most celebrated wine brandy in the world, and the one whose name is most commonly misused. True Cognac is made only in the Charente district.

Marc

Brandy from the pomace rather than the juice of the grape. Much of it too harsh and rough for consideration among fine spirits, but some, particularly an old marc of Burgundy, can be remarkable.

Brandies, or *eaux-de-vie,* are made from fruit as well as from wine; and many are called *alcools blancs* because of their white colour. Quetsch is distilled from purple plums, mirabelle from yellow plums, framboise from raspberries, fraise from strawberries, and kirsch from cherry-stones. These white spirits are matured slowly in crocks, and are very dry and high in alcohol. A great many of them come from Alsace and Lorraine; the Dordogne makes prune, another plum spirit.

All over France, liqueurs are made—a dazzling variety: Chartreuse, green and yellow, Benedictine, Cointreau, crème de menthe, anisette (*q.v.* under separate headings); and aperitifs both spirituous and sickly. Among the best-known of these are the dry French vermouth, Dubonnet, Amer Picon, Suze, Saint-Raphaël, Pernod and Ricard.

Franconia, Franken

White and red wines. Central Germany.

The wines vary considerably, but they can be divided roughly into four groups, corresponding to four different prevailing soil conditions. Franconian (or Franken) wines are mostly white, and the best of them grow in the eastern part of the W-shaped zigzag of the River Main, east of the Rheingau. Iphofen, Rödelsee, Castell, and Abtswind are neighbouring communities, which lie east of the last bend of the Main in Franconia, giving their names to white wines grown on what is the most reliable soil in the region. Loamy and thick, it holds the moisture; and if this is not the ideal ground for noble wines, it has the advantage of providing a fairly consistent crop, in a part of Germany where wine-growing is even more precarious than elsewhere. Sylvaner is almost the exclusive grape variety in this strip, and the wines tend to be full, round, and rather soft.

The famous Stein wines are the only ones known widely abroad, although all Franconian wines tend to attract attention wherever they are exported, because of the unusual shape of the flattish flask or *Bocksbeutel* (*q.v.*) in which they are bottled.

Steinwein, or the 'stone wine', is properly—and in Germany legally—only the wine of the Würzburger Stein, a steep slope above the town of Würzburg, with a southern aspect and a soil which is predominantly lime. So famous have the wines of this slope become that abroad all Franconian wines in the characteristic bottle are apt to be called 'Stein wines'. The true Steinweine are green-gold, with an uncompromising quality that destines them for connoisseurs.

Würzburg, along with Escherndorf and Randersacker, the other two most important towns, lies in the second of the four distinct soil areas, moving westward from the Abtswind–Castell–Iphofen region. The soil is primarily chalky. Riesling, Müller-Thurgau (the crossing of Riesling and Sylvaner), and Traminer wines are grown, as well as Sylvaner, the principal type throughout Franconia. The wines of this section often have a distinct *goût de terroir*, a taste contributed by (but not a taste of) the soil. Like the Hospices de Beaune in Burgundy, two asylums for the ailing and poor support themselves here, largely by the sale of wines, and incidentally provide a consistently high standard of bottles. They are the Juliusspital and the Burgerspital of Würzburg. Both have dealt in wines for more than three centuries. The Juliusspital cellars are vast, and it is the boast of their owners that only natural wines have ever been made there.

Due west of Würzburg, in the other deep bend of the Main, a sandy soil characterizes the third geological division of Franconia. Here the wines—the most important coming from Klingenberg and Bürgstadt, facing each other across the river—are mixed; the red wines are made chiefly from the Spätburgunder variety, which came originally from Burgundy.

The fourth district is the most westerly one, nearest the Rheingau; and perhaps for this reason, the wines are reminiscent of Rheingaus. Hörstein is the best *Gemarkung* or township.

That the Franconian wine-culture is probably the most marginal in Germany can be shown in striking figures. Before the Thirty Years War (1618–1648) the vineyard extent was slightly under 100,000 acres; in 1870 it was 24,000 acres; in 1900, 17,000 acres; in 1924 it was about 10,000 acres; and today, approximately 7,000 acres. This shrinkage has been caused by war; the Thirty Years War destroyed the whole plantation and the Second World War was devastating, especially around Würzburg. The climate has been just as disastrous; Franconia has cold winters and hot summers, with severe frost often striking in the critical blossoming time in spring or at harvest time in October. Such conditions have driven viticulture up on to the steepest slopes where nothing else will grow, and the lower, more fertile areas have been turned over to other crops. On the credit side, in this century, and intensively since 1950, experiment has developed by both chemical and botanical methods a much-improved vine, more capable of resisting frost, disease, and rot. X-ray, hot and cold shock, and chemical treatment, have been used to force beneficial mutations in Sylvaner, Riesling, and Müller-Thurgau vines. Moreover, the mere retreat of the vine to the higher, more difficult slopes has undoubtedly caused an improvement in the quality, along with the lessening in quantity, of Franconian wines. The grape is always best where the vine must struggle for life.

The Best Varieties

Town or Village (Gemarkung)	*Vineyard* (Lage)
Würzburg	Stein wines: Schalksberg, Stein, Harfe, Ständerbühl, Steinmantel, Zurück Leisten wines (often called Stein wines): Schlossberg, Innere Leiste, Roth, Felsenleiste, Äussere Leiste Neuberg wines: Abtsleite, Äusserer Neuberg, Innerer Neuberg, Alandsgrund, Klinge, Oberer Neuberg, Rössleinsweg, Stephanspfad Others of lesser importance are the Pfaffenberg, Sonstige, and Heidingsfelder wines with their various smaller parcels
Castell	Schlossberg
Escherndorf	Lump, Kirchberg, Hengstberg, Fürstenberg
Randersacker	Hohburg, Lämmerberg, Marsberg, Pfülben, Teufelskeller
Iphofen	Julius Echter Berg, Kronsberg, Burgweg, Bettenberg, Pfaffensteig
Rödelsee	Küchenmeister, Schwanleite, Hoheleite
Abtswind	Altenberg, Hasenberg, Schild
Hörstein (Riesling)	Abtsberg
Homburg	Kallmuth
Sommerach	Katzenkopf

Frappé

French term for a drink, chilled or iced, or with shaved ice as in the case of crème de menthe frappée.

Frascati

Dry white wine of the Castelli Romani, Italy. *See* LATIUM.

Frecciarossa

A good light wine made in Lombardy (*q.v.*).

Fredonia

Prolific American red grape used for red wine, especially in New Jersey.

Free-Run

Wine running freely from the residue after fermentation, or from pressed wine at the first light pressing. It is the best and in many regions it is bottled separately.

Freisa

Grape used for a sprightly red Italian wine with a delightful bouquet.

French West Indies

See RUM, FRENCH.

Frizzante

Italian term for semi-sparkling wine.

Fronsac

See CÔTES CANON FRONSAC.

Frontignan–Muscat

A Mediterranean district of southern France producing muscat wines (Muscat de Frontignan). Frontignan is a term often used in France for a 75-centilitre bottle.

See SWEET FORTIFIED WINES OF FRANCE.

Fruity

The spring-like first expression of many wines, innocent and fresh, most pronounced to the nose. The characteristic is caused by a high volatility of the esters, or flavour and perfume essences, and is likely to disappear quickly in wines not rich in sugar. The fruity dry or semi-dry wine should be drunk young, before it begins to fade. A fruity red wine will not have been fermented on the lees for a long time. It will lack tannin and will have been bottled young. Beaujolais is an example of a fruity red wine. The Moselle is known for its fruity white wines.

Fuder

German term for large cask holding 1,000 litres or 220 imp. gallons (264 U.S.) of wine.

See FOUDRE.

Fumarium

Roman hot room for 'improving' wine by exposing it to smoke.

Fumé de Pouilly

A white French wine, also known as Pouilly-Fumé.

See POUILLY-SUR-LOIRE.

Fumigation

Burning of a wick of sulphur in a vat or barrel of wine, to destroy bacteria or unwanted yeasts—to a considerable extent, by replacing the air in the container, and by bringing the wine into contact with sulphuric acid gas. Too much sulphur will spoil the taste of the wine. In Bordeaux, a quarter of a wick of sulphur to a *barrique* holding 49·5 imp. gallons (59·4 U.S.) is generally effective. The French term for the process is *méchage*, from *mèche*, meaning wick.

See SULPHUR DIOXIDE; CHAPTER NINE.

Furfural

An aldehyde present in minute quantity in wines and spirits.

Furmint

The fine white grape from which Hungarian Tokay is made. It also goes into some of the German wines.

Fusel Oil

Term generally designating the volatile, nauseous higher alcohols removed by the rectification of spirituous liquors.

Fût

One of the French terms for a cask or barrel.

G

Château Gaffelière-Naudes

Bordeaux red wine. District and Commune: Saint-Émilion, France.

Considered by some experts to have reached second place among Saint-Émilions in recent vintages, led only by Château Cheval-Blanc, the property is beautifully situated on the sharply curving short road which cuts from the main Bordeaux–Périgueux road up to the hillcrest town of Saint-Émilion. It is the property of Comte Malet-Roquefort, and was classed a First Great Growth (*Premier Grand Cru*) in 1955. The name has been shortened since 1963 by dropping the 'Naudes', and calling it simply Château la Gaffelière.

Characteristics. Superb wines, yet variable. In good years, among the very best of Saint-Émilions.

Vineyard area: 60 acres.

Average production: 9,400 cases.

Gaillac

Still and sparkling white wines. District: South-west France.

South-east of Bordeaux is the French department of the Tarn, and the River Tarn—not a big river but one of the most beautiful in France, a sparkling trout stream cutting through the rocky passes which tower in majestic cliffs above it. In the hills near the city of Gaillac, the slopes are planted in vines which give the wines called Premières Côtes de Gaillac or Gaillac Mousseux (Sparkling Gaillac).

The vineyards of Gaillac seem to have produced better wine in the Middle Ages than the sweetish and uninteresting whites they yield now. (Tastes have changed, too.) The Plantagenet kings of England were devoted to Gaillac, so was Henry VII. In his *Mémoires de Languedoc* (1633), Catel wrote that this wine, much prized by foreign princes, left a taste of roses in the mouth.

The right conditions for the making of Gaillac wine are laid down in a series of decrees dating from 1938 onwards. There are six vines which may be used: Mauzac, l'En de l'El, Ondenc, Sémillon, Sauvignon, and Muscadelle. Mauzac usually accounts for 80% to 100%, varying with the vineyards. To qualify for the place-names, under French wine law, the wines must attain 12% of alcohol for Premières Côtes de Gaillac and 10·5% for wines designated simply Gaillac. The sparkling wines must be made according to the Champagne method of secondary fermentation in the bottle, or by the Gaillac method —a slight variation of this—in which the wines are bottled while they still hold unresolved sugar, causing imprisoned fermentation, and often a fairly heavy bottle-sediment as well.

Galgenwein (Gallows Wine)

Humorous reference to a German wine so harsh and strong that after it has been drunk the gallows is unnecessary—because, they say, the *Galgenwein* trickling down the throat of the drinker can choke him so effectively that no gallows rope is needed.

Gallization

Another term, used in Germany, for *chaptalisation* (*q.v.*).

See CHAPTER NINE, p. 47.

Gallon, British Imperial

The volume of ten standard pounds of distilled water weighed in air at a temperature of 62°F. (17°C.) and a barometric pressure of 30 inches; 277·274 cubic inches. It is the equivalent of 1·20095 U.S. gallons or 4·54596 litres.

Gallon, U.S.

The former British 'wine gallon' of 231 cubic inches which was replaced in Great Britain in 1826 by the standard imperial gallon. It is the equivalent of approximately five-sixths of the volume of the imperial gallon (·83267) or 3·78531 litres.

Gamay

A red grape from which red wine is made. Undistinguished in the rest of Burgundy, it yields admirable wine in Beaujolais. It is equally temperamental in California, where it does excellently well in the mountainous vineyards of Santa Cruz, but makes very ordinary wine in the Napa Valley.

Gamza

One of the principal grape varieties in Bulgaria, producing red and some white wines.

See BULGARIA.

Gard

One of the three most important wine-producing departments of France, quantitatively speaking. The other two are Aude and Hérault. From Gard in the South of France comes a great deal of ordinary wine, as well as the robust red Costières (*see* V.D.Q.S.) and the white Clairette de Bellegarde (*q.v.*).

Garda

Name of groups of Italian wines (Chiaretto-del-Garda, Moniga-del-Garda, and Riviera-del-Garda) grown near Lake Garda.

See LOMBARDY.

Garrafeira

Term on Portuguese wine labels indicating that the wine has been matured for some years in bottle before being offered for sale. It could perhaps be equated with 'Reserve' or 'Special Reserve'.

Gay-Lussac

French chemist who produced the classic chemical formula for the process of fermentation (*q.v.*). His work on the alcoholometer and sulphuric acid were great contributions to wine-making.

Gazéifié

French term for sparkling wine where the sparkle comes from artificial carbonation.

Gean Whisky, Geen Whisky

A liqueur made in Scotland of whisky and black cherries.

Geisenheim

In this Rheingau town is the most important viticultural school in Germany. Its vineyards produce some good wines, notably Morschberg and Rothenberg.

See RHEINGAU.

Gemarkung

German town or village name of a wine. Comparable to commune name in France.

Generous

A wine is generous when it has warmth and is rich in alcohol and vitality.

Geneva

The English spelling for *Jenever* (*q.v.*), the name used in Holland for Dutch gin.

See GIN.

Gentiane

French and Swiss liqueur distilled from the root of the gentian plant. The most popular French aperitif of this style is Suze.

See ENZIAN.

Gentil

Alsatian synonym for Riesling grape (*q.v.*).

Gerk

See GRK.

Germany

'The breed of the fine German wines is the result of the struggle for life at the northernmost climate in which the vine can grow. Costs are higher, cultivation is more intensive, the fight against insects and disease sterner, fertilizing more essential.'

This statement by Professor Steinberg, Director of Germany's most important viticultural school at Geisenheim on the Rhine, sums up the story of German wines. While various German vineyard areas claim to be the farthest north in the world, the fact is that more of the German wine-belt lies in a colder and less friendly climate than any other important zone. The vine accepts the challenge and, especially if it is the Riesling, produces wines of pure gold. It demands in return to be treated like a prima donna.

Viticulture is carefully controlled. A plot may only be planted in vine if it is going to produce wine of a certain quality. All owners are obliged to declare their vineyards, and their stocks. Only about 6% of the agricultural land is in vine, but in the south and south-west of the country, where the vineyards are, the culture is economically important. Plantings are being gradually extended, but the acreage is not yet as considerable as it was in 1938. 85% of the grapes produce white wines. About 300,000 people are regularly employed in viticulture—over 500,000 at harvest time—but, directly or indirectly, some one million live off the wine industry. As wages have risen, so has domestic consumption of wine: in 1964 it averaged 12·2 litres a head (2·7 imp. gallons; 3·2 U.S.). Out of a total production in that year of over 158 million imp. gallons (190 million U.S.) almost four million imp. gallons (4,800,000 U.S.) were exported. The total revenue from wine was about 600 million Deutschmarks.

Wine History

The long and tangled story of German wines, woven deeply though it is into the Gothic tapestry of history along the Rhine, may be sketched fairly briefly.

It is probable that wine was being made in what is now Germany, at about the beginning of the

Christian era. The Romans came, and left their imprint on the people, the towns, the wines, the history and customs of the Moselle and the Rhine. Most significant, perhaps, in viticulture has been the influence of the Roman inheritance law, which decreed that estates were not to be passed on intact to a single heir, but must be handed down to descendants in equal shares. In Germany, the snipping of vineyards into postage-stamp parcels, each with its individual owner and vinous method, has created a maze of vineyard names and wines. The confusion is now recognized as detrimental and the trend is towards simplification of nomenclature and, wherever possible, consolidation.

After the Roman period, and a later phase in which vineyards were bandied about by mediæval kings and knights, wine became the domain of the Church. The consequences are apparent to anyone who visits the Moselle, the Palatinate, or the Rhine. The great estates retain the shape given them by the monasteries; and some of the monastic wine-sheds themselves may still be seen, out of use now, their giant beam presses recalling the days when cowled men were making the wines. A little anecdote told at Kloster Eberbach catches the spirit of the time. The cellar-master of this cloister above the Rhine, sampling a cask one day, detected the taste of iron. Dismayed, he ran to the cook, who, tasting in his turn, discovered not iron but a taint of leather. Both together hurried to the prior. He tasted too, to decide between them, but found them both wrong: in his opinion, the wine tasted slightly of wood. When the cask was emptied, after much sturdy drinking and disputing, a key was found at the bottom, fastened to a bit of wood by a leather strap —or so they say.

In 1803, Napoleon secularized the German vineyards. A few great holdings remained intact; and today most of these are run by the State. But for the Gall Process, small growers would probably have perished altogether: gallization of wine is the addition of sugar, now regulated by law. 'Sugar, or sugar dissolved in pure water, may be added to grape must or wines . . . provided this is done for the purpose of supplementing a natural lack of sugar or alcohol, or of counteracting a natural excess of acid, to an extent sufficient to produce in the said wines a composition equal to that of wines derived in a good year from grapes of the same kind and origin . . . and provided also that the sugar is added to the must before fermentation.' This treatment, generally known by the French name, *chaptalisation*, carried small growers over the bad years, which they might not otherwise have survived. It is important to note, however, that no estate-bottled or Originalabfüllung wine may be *verbessert*, or chaptalised. (A wine referred to on the label or on price lists as Originalabfüllung is necessarily estate-bottled and natural, though one merely branded on the cork with the name of the grower or merchant need not be either of these things.) Most of the finest German growers are joined in the Verband Deutscher Naturwein-Versteigerer, which forbids tampering of any kind. (*See under Export and Wine Laws, below.*)

In spite of this, there was, in the first years after the war, a pronounced trend towards sweeter wines—the result of wartime sugar-starvation in Germany. Since 1956, however, the Germans have been reverting to the drier wines. Years which give great vintages in France do not usually produce the wines most to the German taste; the 1959s, for example, would now be considered too sweet.

The production peak in German wines was reached before the Thirty Years War (1618–1648), a very much greater quantity of wine being made then than at any other time. War, vine plague, and other devastations have since had their way. Like the Gall Process in its time, Spätlesen wines saved the German growers at the end of the eighteenth century. The exact origin of these left-on-the-vine wines is disputed, but the Bishop of Fulda may have been the originator. He was a lazy fellow who forgot to give the order to pick the grapes one harvest-time. When he remembered, the grapes were nearly rotten and were thrown to the peasantry —for whom they produced a glorious elixir. This technique of letting the grapes reach noble rot (*q.v.*) late in the autumn produces the great Sauternes, and the German Spätlesen and Trockenbeerenauslesen wines today, but the enormous risk of early frosts and the additional cost of labour in the individual picking of the berries are gradually forcing prices too high for the market on both Rhine and Moselle.

Changing public taste plays its inevitable role in Germany. The real wine-taster prefers the older wines, the Edelfirne, in which the oils have been transformed by a beneficial maderization. 'One bottle of the young wine may have the effect of three bottles of the old—the next morning,' they say. This is because the older wine has achieved balance; yet public taste is inclining more and more towards the younger vintages.

The Wine Districts

The important areas, such as the Rheingau, the Moselle, the Palatinate, Rheinhessen, and others, are treated separately under their own headings.

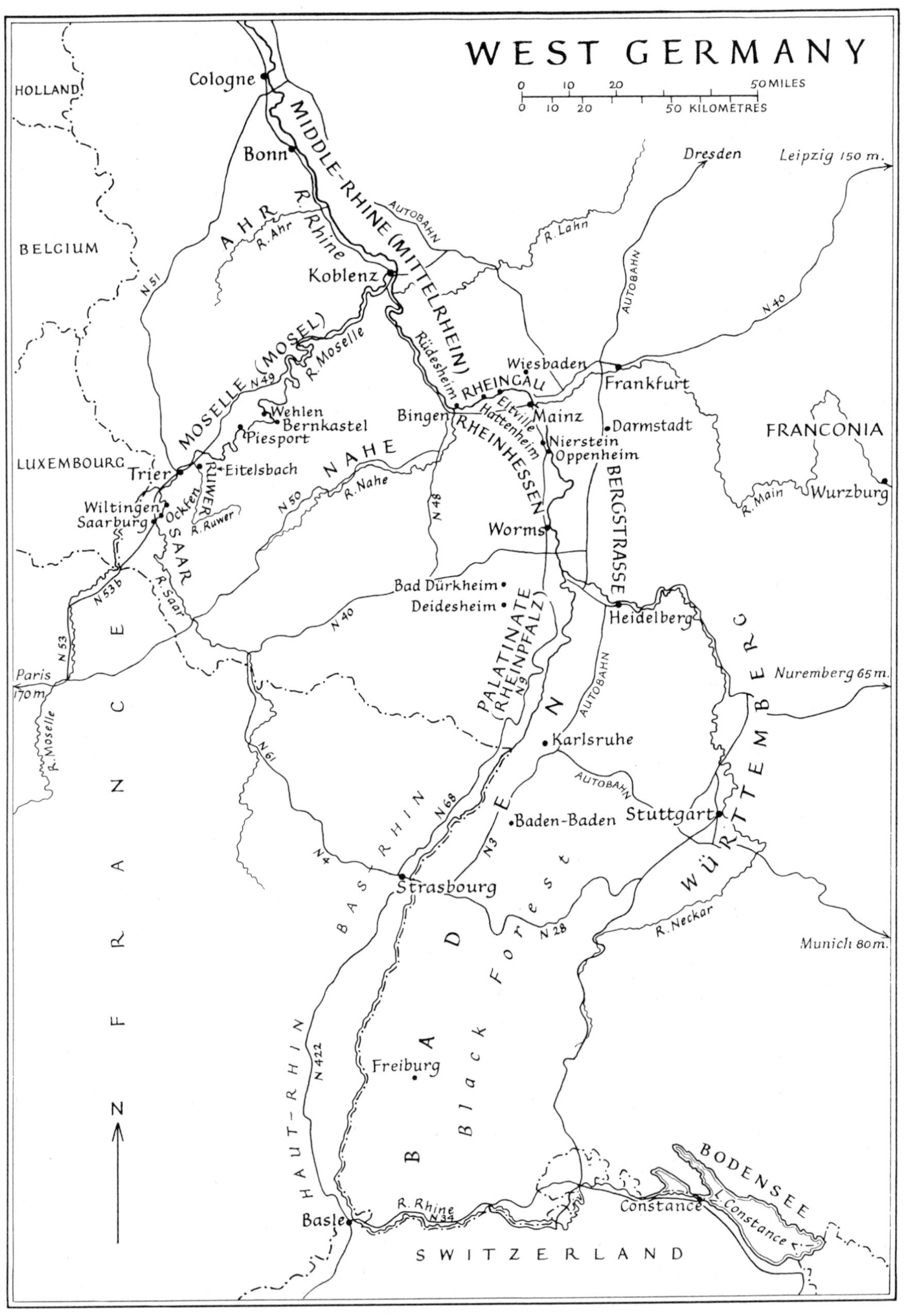
WEST GERMANY
0 10 20 50 MILES
0 10 20 50 KILOMETRES
HOLLAND
BELGIUM
LUXEMBOURG
FRANCE
SWITZERLAND
FRANCONIA
WÜRTTEMBERG
BADEN
Cologne
Bonn
Koblenz
Dresden
Leipzig 150 m.
MIDDLE-RHINE (MITTELRHEIN)
AHR
R. Ahr
R. Rhine
AUTOBAHN
R. Lahn
N 51
N 40
MOSELLE (MOSEL)
R. Moselle
N 49
Rüdesheim
RHEINGAU
Wiesbaden
Frankfurt
Eltville
Hattenheim
Mainz
Bingen
RHEINHESSEN
Darmstadt
Wehlen
Bernkastel
Piesport
Nierstein
Oppenheim
NAHE
R. Nahe
N 50
Trier
Eitelsbach
RUWER
R. Ruwer
Wiltingen
Ockfen
Saarburg
SAAR
R. Saar
N 53b
N 53
N 48
Worms
BERGSTRASSE
R. Main
Wurzburg
Bad Dürkheim
Deidesheim
PALATINATE (RHEINPFALZ)
N 9
Heidelberg
Paris 170 m.
R. Moselle
Nuremberg 65 m.
Karlsruhe
N 61
AUTOBAHN
N 68
BAS RHIN
N 4
N 3
Baden-Baden
Stuttgart
Strasbourg
Black Forest
N 28
R. Neckar
Munich 80 m.
HAUT-RHIN
N 422
Freiburg
N
BODENSEE
Constance
L. Constance
R. Rhine
N 34
Basle

But something can be said about them comparatively and as a group.

The Palatinate, or Pfalz, is the largest producer of the major districts, and the Rheingau the smallest. The Palatinate makes about nine to ten times as much wine yearly as the Rheingau, in about seven times the vineyard space. Approaching the Palatinate in size is Rheinhessen, followed by the Moselle–Saar–Ruwer area, always lumped into one by the Germans; then Baden, Württemberg, Franconia (Franken), and Rheingau.

Red Wines

Some red wine is grown in the Rheingau, in the Palatinate, in Rheinhessen, Franconia, Baden, and Württemberg—although there is more white here—but the only red wines at all well known abroad are Assmannshauser, from the Rheingau; Ahrweiler and Walporzheimer from the Ahr; Ingelheimer from Rheinhessen; and one or two wines around Bad Dürkheim in the Palatinate. No German red wine is, or deserves to be, internationally important.

White Wines

Moselle (with Saar and Ruwer)

The most delicate of them all. Light and elegant. The most important characteristic is that derived from the slate soil.

Nahe

Something between a Saar and a Rheinhessen, and in the lower reaches of the river very similar to Rheingau wines.

Rheinhessen

The easiest to understand and place. Less acid, and therefore flatter, than the Rheingaus. Mild, fruity, and elegant.

Palatinate (or Pfalz)

The common wines are the lightest of the Rhine—mellow, soft, without much alcohol, and for drinking in quantity. Yet some of the best wines can be very full, alcoholic, and sweet, having that typical and special perfume the Germans call 'the Pfalz wine character'.

Rheingau

Producing the finest characteristics of German wines and with the greatest amount of fruit acidity. More style, firmer, heavier, greater fruitiness, and more noble taste than Rheinhessens or Palatinates.

Middle Rhine

Small and quite insignificant. Lighter than Rheingaus but in many ways similar; some of the best have a flinty taste imparted by the slate soil.

Franconia (Franken)

Stronger than Rhine Valley wines, and quite pleasant when young. These are likely to be similar in taste to Baden and Württemberg wines when the same grape varieties have been used.

Baden and Württemberg

Baden wines often resemble those from Alsace, across the Rhine, which are better, however. Wines of both districts are inclined to be heavy and pungent when they come from the Ruländer grape, a descendant of the Pinot Gris, which is in wide use.

Bodensee

Inferior. Very light wines with strong acidity and little alcohol.

Ahr

Small wines. They used to be mostly red, but more white is being made now.

Bergstrasse

Inferior. Small, light, pleasant wines to be drunk on the spot.

State Domain

The State Domain is the largest vineyard owner in all Germany. Holdings in the Rheingau and along the Bergstrasse near Heidelberg total about 270 acres, producing between 1,500 and 2,000 *Halbstücke* (102,000 to 136,000 cases) each year. Made up for the most part of former Church holdings secularized in 1803 by Napoleon, the State Domain was the domain of the Dukedom of Nassau until 1866, then of the Hessian State (often miscalled the Prussian State Domain) from 1866 to 1945, and of the Hessian State Domain since that date. There are seven estates, five wine-making centres, and a major nursery. From the point of view of quality, the State Domain holdings in the Rheingau are ranked by many experts as: first, those in Rauenthal; second, Markobrunn and Hattenheim; third, Steinberg; fourth, those in Rüdesheim; fifth, those of Hochheim.

Grape Varieties

The grape used is of paramount importance in German wines.

Riesling. This is the best German white-wine grape. If the grape-variety is not named on the label of a high-quality wine, it may generally be presumed to be Riesling—for many wines made from Riesling do not carry the grape-name on the label. All great Spätlesen, Auslesen, and Trockenbeerenauslesen wines are Rieslings; all the best Rheingau vineyards, and practically the whole of the Moselle, are planted in Riesling. A steely aristocracy is the outstanding characteristic of a Riesling wine.

particularly when it has been grown in the slate soil of the Moselle. The grape is small and the yield not high, but the character and staying-power, and the incomparable bouquet which seems to be composed of mingled fruit scents, more than compensate for the lack of quantity. The vine ripens late and is resistant to cold. Once taken away from its habitat along the Rhine and Moselle (and in nearby Alsace) and planted abroad, something happens to it, and it is Riesling in name only. This vine produces 500 imp. gallons (600 U.S.) per acre.

Sylvaner. Softer and milder, the biggest producer. In some parts of Germany it is called Franken Riesling and in others Österreicher (from Austria—Österreich—whence it came). The Sylvaner yields 1,040 imp. gallons (1,250 U.S.) per acre—double the output of the Riesling.

Müller-Thurgau. The crossing of the Riesling and Sylvaner plants, producing a wine milder than the Riesling and with a taste that has something of Muscatel. This variety is having a great success; in the past fifteen years the amount of the planting has grown enormously, and there will be much more in the future. The name comes from the man who created it. The yield is up to 1,700 imp. gallons (2,000 U.S.) per acre.

Gewürztraminer or Traminer. It gives a special spicy wine which is unmistakable; but despite its fineness, the vine has had an up-and-down fate because it is hard to grow. It produces about the same quantity as the Riesling.

Muskateller. Rare; this southern type does not like the northerly climate and generally remains too acid.

Gutedel. Produces the light, sweet table wines of the Markgräfler, below Freiburg in Baden.

Ruländer. The Pinot Gris—also called Grauerburgunder or Tokaier. It gives a full, heavy, and sometimes fiery wine.

Elbling. Mediocre. Grown especially for the German sparkling wines known as 'Sekt'.

Red wines come from the following plants: Spätburgunder, all of the best; Frühburgunder; Portugieser, light and of less distinction; Trollinger in Württemberg—the same vine is called Blauer Malvasier in the Palatinate; Müller-Schwarzriesling.

Export and Wine Laws

85% of German wines—and all the important ones—are white. The cost of producing them is twice that of wine-production in France, four times as great as in Spain. France has twenty times as much vineyard as Germany; but the yield per acre in Germany is very much higher than that in such fine regions of France as Burgundy and Bordeaux. The leading customer for exported German wines, short on quantity but long on quality, is Great Britain, followed by the United States. It is a rather surprising fact that even as far back as 1909–14 this was the case; for the U.S.A. is not usually thought of as a leading wine customer.

Fortification of wine by the addition of alcohol is not allowed in Germany, but alcohol may be added in the form of spirit, up to 1% of volume in wines to be sent to tropical countries. Rhine wines grow on wires, trained to two—sometimes three—parallel strands, except in the Moselle vineyards, which are so steep that stakes are used instead. Bowed out at either side of these stakes, the Moselle vines look rather like lorgnettes.

Almost all the best vineyards face south, to get the maximum sun—or, if not south, then west, because sunshine is stronger in the afternoon than in the morning. The surfaces are carefully levelled so that one section of vine will not overshadow another—an apparently slight disadvantage which might make all the difference in such a marginal area.

Two kinds of wine are exported from the important districts: regional wines blended by the shipper; and authentic bottlings from the domain (Originalabfüllung, shortened on labels to Orig.-Abfg.). Since they are natural, unsugared, and characteristic of the districts they come from, the domain bottlings are by far the better. These are not, however, the same as French château-bottled wines. The produce of one Bordeaux vineyard is equalized by a first racking in one big vat; but in Germany, where most estates are cut up into small parcels of vineyard, the contents of separate casks, taken from different parcels, may be sold under the same domain label—which is apt, therefore, to cover wines of unequal quality, of varying degrees of dryness or sweetness, and various prices. Whereas in Bordeaux the clever buyer hopes to find himself a bargain in the cheapest château-bottled wine from one château in any given year, in the same year he might come across, in one German domain, as many as fifteen or twenty prices, and as many wines, all bearing the same label. Nevertheless, the level is high and the wines will be delightful to drink.

German wine laws forbid any picture on the label representing a geographical place unless the wine is actually from that place—or unless two-thirds of it is. For a German wine may be a blend and still carry a vineyard name, as long as it is natural and unsugared, and two-thirds of the contents of the bottle come from the place purported.

The German Natural Wine Association, or Verband Deutscher Naturwein-Versteigerer, is the chief agency in maintaining the quality of German wine. Much more strict than the wine laws, it binds its members to a rigid code. They may not sugar wine; may not buy wine (to prevent blending and adulteration). The membership, while it encompasses only about 7% of German vineyards, includes most of the leading estates. They enter voluntarily and are policed by Government inspectors. The small black eagle with the grapes on the breast and the letters VDNV therefore compose an emblem guaranteeing that the wine is natural and of a certain standard of quality.

As this is written in 1967 revolutionary new legislation is being enacted which will make obsolete many of the above-mentioned laws regarding Naturwein and Originalabfüllung.

A Wine-label Baedeker

A German wine label is one of the hardest things to find your way around. The following tips may be of some help.

Apart from special designations, the basic wine label will read: District . . . Vintage Year . . . Town or Village . . . Vineyard . . . Grape type; e.g. Rheinpfalz . . . 1953er . . . Forster . . . Ziegler . . . Riesling. The grape type is optional and does not always appear.

Fass Number on unsugared Rhine wines; Fuder Number on unsugared Moselles. These, seen on some labels, are cask numbers indicating the actual cask from which the bottle was drawn. Unlike most others in the world, German vineyards seldom vat or equalize the wines. Each wine is made alone in its own cask.

Wachstum, Kreszenz, Naturwein, Korkbrand, Rein, Naturrein, Echt, Ungezuckert, Originalabfüllung, Originalabzug, Kellerabfüllung, Kellerabzug, Schlossabzug, Originalwein, Eigengewächs are all terms telling you in one way or another that the wine is a pure natural product and has not been sugared.

Kabinett (*Cabinet*). This was originally the Rheingau nomenclature for specially reserved wines kept locked up in the cellar; but the term has gradually been stretched to include any fine growth to which a proprietor chooses to give this name, although it has a more specific meaning in some of the Rheingau vineyards. Sometimes a Kabinettwein is one sold above a certain price per cask; always, it is wine of quality. At Schloss Johannisberg it is graded higher than the Originalabfüllung, its price and quality indicated by label and capsule, or seal colour—(*see under* RHEINGAU: JOHANNISBERG for fuller details of this grading by colour, a scheme which is being adopted by other growers, in an attempt to simplify the confusion caused by the countless names and grades in German wines).

The words Spätlese, Auslese, Beerenauslese, Edelbeerenauslese, Goldbeerenauslese, Trockenbeerenauslese on a bottle label all indicate some degree of special selection. Spätlese (late-picked) and Auslese (selected) are determined in the vineyard at the time of picking. Beerenauslese, Edelbeerenauslese, Goldbeerenauslese and Trockenbeerenauslese (berry-selected) are determined in the vat-room. (At harvest-time the better and riper grapes are brought in and spread out on a big trough-like table, and experienced vintners select the berries individually—the ripe dry ones for Beerenauslese, Edelbeerenauslese, and Trockenbeerenauslese in ascending order of dry ripeness.)

After selection, these fine sweet grapes are processed for the crushing, which often takes place in huge, cylindrical, galvanized metal vats with a blown-up sausage-like inner tube called a Willmespresse. The wines are almost as rich as liqueurs in the autumn; a mould or noble rot called *Botrytis cinerea*, or Edelfäule, covers the ripest grapes, improving and concentrating them. Nearly always this extra ripeness comes late, after the vineyard has been once gone over, in which case the special grapes are called Spätlese, or late-picked. When the picking is by individual berry among bunches, some of which are overripe and some not, the wine is a Beerenauslese (berry-selected). When the berries have been left to shrivel on the vine to an almost raisin-condition and are then individually selected, the wine is the peak achievement of German viniculture, a dried-berry-selected Trockenbeerenauslese. (Goldbeerenauslese is a much less common term for the same thing.) A Spätlese is not always sweet, however; in lesser years when there is no excess sugar, late-picking does not imply extra sweetness—and in such years it is impossible to make an Auslese. German law now forbids the selling of a late-picked wine as Spätlese unless it has all the characteristic ripeness and fullness.

Hochgewächs, Spitzengewächs, and Edelgewächs (*Gewächs*, growth) indicate much the same qualities as the *lesen* terms (peak growth, noble growth). Trockenbeerenauslesen wines cost up to twenty times the price of the ordinary wines from the same vineyard. Nevertheless, they are now generally sold at a loss. The quantity of juice lost from the drying of the berries is about ten times the normal loss; and when the grapes are left so late on the vine the grower risks the destruction of his entire crop through frost—which happens in the best Moselle vineyards, for example, on an average of two years in three. Hardly any vineyard makes more than a quarter of a *Stück* (400 bottles) of such wine even in the most favourable years.

BARREL SIZES AND UNITS OF SALE

German wines are sold either at auction or in the cellars, directly to the purchasers through commission brokers, the latter being called *Freihand* sale. Cask dimensions are not uniform, although there is an increasing trend towards a change to the hectolitre measure which is the standard in international usage.

Rheingau wines are sold in the *Halbstück* (half-cask), whether *Freihand* or at auction: this contains 600 litres or 828 bottles. If an entire *Stück* (an oval cask of 1,200 litres) is sold, the price is nevertheless reckoned in terms of *Halbstücke*. The wine is usually shipped in the *Viertelstück*, a round barrel holding half as much as the *Halbstück*, or 300 litres. The finest wines are also both auctioned and sold *Freihand* in bottle.

Moselle wines are sold in the large, long barrel called the *Fuder*. It was formerly supposed to contain 960 litres; but in the last quarter of a century this has been standardized at 1,000 litres or 1,370 bottles. The finest are also sold in bottle.

Rheinhessen wines are generally sold in the *Stück* of 1,200 litres (equal to 1,656 bottles), although sometimes, and usually with the finest, the unit is 600 litres. Peak wines are also sold in bottles.

WINE CO-OPERATIVES

With the motto 'We've got plenty of wine but no bread or money,' the co-operative movement in wine-making began from force of necessity 120 years ago in Württemberg. Today there are 528 co-operatives, fairly evenly distributed. Certain wine-towns have two, one for the Catholics and the other for the Protestants. The approximately 37,000 growers affiliated with co-operatives have small or medium holdings, the average being about an acre apiece. Wines are cellared in common, and vineyard machinery is provided which would be beyond the means of the individual small proprietor.

Probably most important in raising the general level of the wines has been the combined effort to fight vine disease in the always critical marginal wine area, and the fact that the co-operatives give their members credit, saving them from the necessity of selling their wines when unfit or not ready, simply in order to maintain vineyard and homestead.

Geropiga, Jeropiga

Grape syrup used in Portugal for sweetening Port.

Gevrey-Chambertin

Burgundy red wine. District: Côte de Nuits, France.

Gevrey-Chambertin is one of the communes of Burgundy's Côte d'Or, and more specifically of the Côte de Nuits, the northern section of the Côte d'Or. Working from north to south, it is the first of the important Côte de Nuits communes. Like almost all of the other villages along the famous strip of hills, this one has capitalized on its most famous and best vineyard and has added its name to the name of the place. Until 1847, the *appellation* was legally Gevrey, but since that time it has been Gevrey-Chambertin. The town fathers were not the only ones to be impressed by the name of their celebrated Growth. At one time, practically every vineyard tried to tack 'Chambertin' on to its own name, perhaps in hopes that some of the qualities of the wine would rub off with it. In 1936 the French authorities stepped in and decided who had the right to the name and who had not, and the matter was settled.

About 630, the Duke of Burgundy endowed the Abbey of Bèze with some land in Gevrey. The monks turned the land into a vineyard and found that they could produce an extraordinary wine. According to the stories that have come down from these ancient times, the field next to the Abbey was later owned by a peasant named Bertin and was called the Champs de Bertin, or 'Bertin's field'. Thanks to the success of the Abbey vineyards, Bertin also planted vines on his field and the name was soon shortened to Chambertin. But it was not Bertin, nor even the monks of the Abbey of Bèze, who expanded the fame of the vineyard; that was left to a man named Jobert, who owned not only Chambertin but the Clos de Bèze as well, and he made the vineyards famous. Somewhere along the line, he changed his own name to Jobert-Chambertin. The vineyards are no longer united, as they were under Jobert, and today they are divided up into plots belonging to more than two dozen growers.

Chambertin has a great history and a great reputation and there can be no wonder that the other vineyards of the town have wished to capitalize on it. Under the present law, the only ones which are allowed to use the name Chambertin together with their own are several immediately adjoining it. Since the Clos de Bèze is considered on a par with Chambertin—and indeed can sell its wines as

Chambertin if it so desires—it is allowed to place the magic name before its own, while the others must add it on afterwards. Chambertin-Clos de Bèze is the full and proper name, and the vineyard is included in the special decree which covers Chambertin. The others fall under a different decree, the major difference being that the maximum permissible yield is raised from 267 imp. gallons (321 U.S.) of wine per acre to 285 imp. gallons (342 U.S.) per acre. The vineyards are the following: Latricières-Chambertin, Mazoyères-Chambertin, Charmes-Chambertin, Mazis- (or Mazys-) Chambertin, Ruchottes-Chambertin, Griotte-Chambertin, and Chapelle-Chambertin. Altogether, they comprise the Great Growths (*Grands Crus*) of the commune, and each one is treated under its own heading.

The vineyards, most of which lie between Gevrey-Chambertin and the next town to the south, that of Morey-Saint-Denis, are along the mid-section of the hill and they can be seen from *Route Nationale* (National Highway) No. 74 which runs along the plain at the foot of the slope. A re-paved, winding vineyard road, half-way up the slope, provides a better vantage point, however. If you leave Gevrey-Chambertin by this road, the first important vineyards to come into sight will be those of Mazis (the second half of the name is usually left out in any discussion of the vineyards but should always be included on the labels) with Ruchottes just above it on the slope. Both of these are on the right, and they adjoin the Clos de Bèze with Griotte and Chapelle on the left, directly across the road from it. A small tool-house stands in the Clos de Bèze, bearing the name of Pierre Damoy, one of the better growers and the largest single owner in the place, but aside from that there is nothing to distinguish one vineyard from another. After passing the Clos de Bèze, there is a large but simple sign informing the passer-by: 'Here starts the vineyard of Chambertin'. Almost before he has had time to digest this information, there is another sign to tell him: 'Here ends the vineyard of Chambertin'. The length—and it is roughly twice as long as it is wide—is barely more than 1,500 feet. Aside from these landmarks, there is no sign in the earth or in the vines that here the soil is such that the resulting wine will be a greater or a slightly lesser one. There is no way for the newcomer to identify the various vineyards at all. For that it is necessary to go to the wines.

Like most of the villages of the Côte d'Or, Gevrey-Chambertin sits in a small defile, called a *combe,* between two hills in the range that makes up the Côte d'Or. All the Chambertins are on the slope on the southern side of the village, but there are other excellent vineyards on the north side as well. In the classification made in 1860 of the vines of the Côte d'Or, only Chambertin and the Clos de Bèze were classed as Outstanding Vineyards (*Têtes de Cuvée*) and all the others, including those which have been elevated to the modern ranks of the Great Growths (*Grands Crus*), were classed below them as First Growths (*Premiers Crus*). With these vineyards, in 1860, were several others, such as the Clos Saint-Jacques, Varoilles, Fouchère, Étournelles, and Cazetiers. Today, most of these are included among the official First Growths and are allowed to add the vineyard name to the name of the commune (selling, for example, as Gevrey-Chambertin Clos Saint-Jacques) or may add the words *Premier Cru* to the name of the commune. Many experts consider it unfortunate that the vineyards of Varoilles and Clos Saint-Jacques were not included with the finest vineyards of the commune and given Great Growth status. In many years, the excellent wines from these two vineyards compare very favourably with the others, except possibly for the wines of Chambertin and the Clos de Bèze.

The communal wines of the village, those that go to market with the words Gevrey-Chambertin and no other indication of origin, are the least of the wines of the commune, although some of them may certainly be very pleasant. Most of them are grown in Gevrey-Chambertin, but some may come from the better vineyards in the neighbouring town of Brochon. The amount of wine sold as Gevrey-Chambertin or as Gevrey-Chambertin Premier Cru came to very slightly over 166,000 imp. gallons (200,000 U.S.) in the year 1954. This year is taken since it is considered to be one of 'average quantity' in French wines. The total vineyard area for Gevrey is 506·5 acres. The vineyards of note in the commune are listed below. (*See also under separate headings.*)

GREAT GROWTHS (*Grands Crus*)

Vineyard	*Acres*
Chambertin (Outstanding Vineyard)	32·5
Chambertin-Clos de Bèze (Outstanding Vineyard)	37·5
Latricières-Chambertin	15·4
Mazoyères-Chambertin	47·4
Charmes-Chambertin	30·7
Mazys- or Mazis-Chambertin	22·14
Ruchottes-Chambertin	20·89
Griotte-Chambertin	7·86
Chapelle-Chambertin	10·3
Varoilles	14·7
Clos Saint-Jacques	17·1

Vineyard	*Acres*
Aux Combottes	12·4
Bel-Air	9·2
Les Cazetiers	22·5
Combe-au-Moine	11·8
Étournelles	5
Lavaut	23·3
Poissenot	5·4
Champeaux	16·7
Les Goulots	4·5
Issarts (or Plantigone)	4·5
Les Corbeaux	7·7
Cherbaudes	5·4
La Perrière	6·1
Clos-Prieur (upper section only)	4·9
Le Fonteny	9·4
Champonnet	8·2
Au Closeau	1·3
Craipillot	6·8
Champitennois (also called Petite Chapelle)	9·8
En Ergot	2·9
Clos du Chapitre	2·4

Gewächs

German term meaning 'growth of'. Same as Kreszenz.

Gewürztraminer

A type of Traminer vine, and therefore Traminer wine, said to be even more spicy than this spiciest of grape varieties in forming many Alsatian and German wines. Actually, in usage, the two names are practically interchangeable and any real difference in meaning has been lost.

For description of Traminer and Gewürztraminer wines *see* ALSACE; GERMANY.

Gigondas

One of the best communes of the Côtes du Rhône, producing red, white, and rosé wines.

See RHÔNE.

Gill

Quartern or a quarter of a British pint.

Gin

Gin is a juniper-flavoured spirit obtained by the distillation and rectification of the grain spirits of malted barley and rye—or sometimes of corn or maize. Yet the definition 'Gin is a grain spirit' is not entirely correct. Theoretically, it can be made from any rectified spirit. During the last war, gins were, in fact, distilled in England from raw molasses spirit; and some London Dry gins for domestic consumption are still based on this, although the majority of gins are now based on grain, both for home and export markets. The price of gin in the home market is the same for practically all varieties based on grain.

The two principal types of gin are British (the gin produced in the United States is made in a similar manner) and Dutch. The latter is known in the Netherlands as Jenever and in England as Hollands, or else as Schiedam, after one of the towns where it is manufactured. The English words 'gin' and 'geneva' are corruptions of *jenever* and *genièvre* (French), both meaning juniper—nothing to do with the Swiss city. *Genièvre* is a word seldom heard in France now: *gin* (pronounced jeen) is one of the anglicisms which have crept in since the war, and which, purists complain, are ruining the French language.

Both the Dutch and the English claim, and sometimes disclaim, the invention of gin. It is certain that, in the seventeenth century, gin was being made from barley, hops, and juniper berries in England; Hogarth's famous picture *Gin Lane* shows the consequences. In 1736 the Gin Act banned gin. Like most prohibitions, this did not work, and repeal followed in 1742, because illegal gin was worse than the legal kind.

Since the discovery of redistillation, or rectification, it has been possible to remove the harmful characteristics from any raw spirit, leaving practically pure alcohol. In the making of Dutch gins (as of rums and the heavier whiskies) preliminary rectification is not part of the process, which thus preserves some of the taste of the barley, malt, and grain.

Hollands is often sold in stone jars or crocks, and the Dutch usually drink it neat, out of narrow tall glasses. It is made by infusing a mash of malted barley and rye, or, occasionally, maize. When it has cooled, this is set to ferment with yeast; in two or three days, fermentation is complete and the alcoholic liquid is then distilled. The distillation is redistilled with flavouring—juniper berries and various other ingredients, according to the recipe of the maker. (In some cases, the juniper berries are mashed in with the malt.) If the process of redistillation over flavouring is repeated, the result is what is known as Double Gin. Hollands is distilled at a lower proof than British gin; and it is generally aged in bond. By law, it must contain 35% of alcohol by volume.

In the making of British or American gins, a highly rectified—or neutral—spirit, by now colourless and tasteless, is redistilled with the juniper berries and coriander or other flavourings. If this process is repeated, the product is a gin of the London Dry variety. Dry gin is so easy to make that it may fairly be classed as an art of the kitchen: since it is merely flavoured neutral spirit, it must be a natural temptation to the home distiller. Some makers buy their spirit already distilled. (Inferior gins are made by adding essential oils to plain spirit and omitting distillation altogether.) Dry gins, being so highly distilled (or rectified) contain no fusel oil, and need not, therefore, be aged to remove this harmful taint. In fact, they gain nothing by ageing and are ready to drink at once.

Gins take their character from the flavouring recipe which is the secret of each maker. After the base spirit has been rectified, flavouring matter is added by one means or another. Sometimes alcohol, juniper berries, and such other ingredients as may be used are simply steeped together. Another technique (seen, for example, at the Burrough's Beefeater gin plant in London) is that of passing the spirit over into a 'flavour still', a box-like small still in which the vapours contact volatile juniper, angelica, coriander, etc. The flavours used by the various distillers, whilst always including juniper, are diverse. Some of the others are fennel, liquorice, orange peel, anise, caraway, calamus, orris, almond, etc.

In addition to the variations between the different brands, there are two other distinct types of gin. Old Tom Gin is one which has been sweetened by adding sugar to the dry variety. Plymouth Gin is made in Plymouth, England, by a single firm (Coates) and is intermediate in style between the ordinary English gin and Dutch gin. (Sloe Gin (*q.v.*) utilizes gin but is not properly a gin.)

In the United States, London Dry gins may be of three kinds: gin imported from England; gin made in the U.S. under licence or grant from the original British distiller; or any dry gin made in America and simply given the name as a type-name. In all cases, the general principles of preparation are the same.

Golden gin is gin which has been barrel-aged, taking its golden hue from the wood, but it is quite uncommon. The great preference in the United States is for neutral gins, because they are generally used as bases for cocktails and should harmonize with a wide range of flavours—although most gin is drunk in dry martinis, in Collinses, or with tonic water.

Lemon gin, orange gin, and so on are usually artificially flavoured gins; but they can be produced from the named ingredient.

Gin Fizz

A long, cool, effervescent drink composed of gin, lemon juice, a little sugar, ice and soda-water. There are several other fizzes, variations on this recipe and based on either gin or brandy.

Ginger

Ginger Ale

A favourite English or American mineral drink, frothy and of a ginger colour; it is often added to gin or whisky to make a long drink comparable with gin and tonic. The ale is carbonated water to which colouring matter has been added, drops of capsicum extract or essence of ginger and some glucose or sugar. 'Froth heading' may also be added to make the drink more foamy.

Ginger Beer

A pale, frothy bottled drink popular in England. It is made by the fermentation of sugar, ginger, cream of tartar, and yeast with water, and is bottled before it has finished fermenting. The carbonic acid thus generated produces an ærated drink.

Ginger Wine

A homely English beverage—but made commercially. The ingredients: ginger, yeast, sugar, lemon rind, raisins, and water. It is often fortified with spirits and a little capsicum.

Ginger Brandy

Tawny-coloured, ginger-flavoured spirit made in Great Britain.

Girò di Sardegna

Sweet red dessert wine of Sardinia (*q.v.*).

Château Giscours

Bordeaux red wine. District: Haut-Médoc, France. Commune: Labarde-Margaux.

Château Giscours had fallen completely from its traditional position of one of the best of the Third Growths (*Troisièmes Crus*) of the Médoc, as classified in 1855, when the present owner, Monsieur Tari, also a wine-maker on a large scale in the Oran Department of Algeria, took it over in 1954. A formerly fine growth had been debased by the planting of hybrid vines. By 1955–6, these were all ripped out by Monsieur Tari and the vineyard entirely reconstituted through grafting with first-class vines. The recent vintages show a great improvement, and in the hands of the present owner can be expected to continue to do so.

The records of Château Giscours go back to 1552 when a Seigneur de la Bastide sold it to Pierre de l'Horme. During the Revolution the property was confiscated from the Saint-Simon family and came into the ownership of the State. In 1793 a Monsieur Jacob acquired it on behalf of two Americans, John Gray and Jonathan Davis of Boston.

The present château was built by Count Pescatore, a banker in the time of Napoleon III. Eventually, in 1852, it was purchased by Edouard Cruse, and remained in the Cruse family until 1913. It stands, with two great wings adjoining it, at the head of one of the most magnificent parks in Bordeaux, with a lake, lily-choked canals, and a wood of rhododendrons containing at least one giant Californian sequoia.

Characteristics. Light and delicate, highly perfumed, and often elegant. The first year in barrel, Giscours never tastes as good as most of its neighbours, but during the second year of barrel-ageing, the quality begins to tell and the wine matures well. Giscours has lately made great strides as far as quality is concerned.

Vineyard area: 180 acres.

Average production: 20,000 cases.

Givry

Commune of the Côte Chalonnaise, producing mainly red wines.

See also CHALONNAIS.

Glen Elgin

Important vineyard in New South Wales, producing red table wines, and some white. The principal grape varieties are Syrah and 'Riesling' (actually Sémillon).

See also AUSTRALIA.

Glenloth

Vineyard in the Reynella district of South Australia.

See AUSTRALIA.

Château Gloria

Bordeaux red wine. District: Haut-Médoc, France. Commune: Saint-Julien.

The vineyard contains parcels from Château Léoville-Poyferré and Château Gruaud-Larose, Second Growths (*Seconds Crus*), and from Château Saint-Pierre and Château Duhart-Milon, Fourth Growths (*Quatrièmes Crus*). The *chais* were originally those of Château Saint-Pierre. The owner and manager of the vineyard is Monsieur Henri Martin, Mayor of Saint-Julien, and one of the leading figures both in Médoc and Bordeaux wines; in 1956 he became President of the Interprofessional Committee of Bordeaux Wines. Qualities of terrain, and intelligent, energetic management have raised the wine far above its official rating. At present ranked as a Bourgeois Growth (*Bourgeois Cru*) of Médoc, it amply justifies elevation to classified Great Growth (*Grand Cru*).

Characteristics. Soft, round and subtle, with, at the same time, some of the best characteristics of Saint-Julien—fullness with delicacy. Usually a well-made wine.

Vineyard area: 80 acres.

Average production: 11,000 cases.

Gluco-œnometer

An instrument to test the strength of new musts; used in making Port.

Gobelet

Method of training vines: a single trunk terminates in several arms rising in the shape of a vase or goblet.

See CHAPTER EIGHT, p. 33.

Goblet

A drinking cup or glass with foot and stem.

Goldwasser

See DANZIGER GOLDWASSER.

Gourmet

Alsatian term for a wine broker—who is known in the Bordeaux district as a *courtier*.

Goût Américain

To the American taste. The term is a misnomer, for it refers to sweet Champagne, although this is not, in fact, shipped to the United States nowadays.

Goût Anglais

To the English taste. The term refers to dry Champagne for the English market.

Goût de Pierre à Fusil

French term for the gunflint taste of a very dry white wine, such as Chablis.

Goût de Terroir

In French this means, literally, earthy taste; it denotes a peculiar flavour imparted by certain soils, and not the taste of the soil itself.

Graacher Himmelreich

Best-known of the Graach wines inside Germany,

and usually best of the wines of Graach on the German Moselle. Josephshof, second in quality to Himmelreich, is the better-known wine abroad.

See MOSELLE: MIDDLE MOSELLE.

Gragnano

Leading red wine of Campania, Italy.

See CAMPANIA.

Graisse

A disorder of wine: fatty degeneration, by which the wine becomes viscous and turgid.

See CHAPTER NINE, p. 53.

Grand Cru

French term for a great vineyard.

Grand Cru Classé

A special designation for the very best of the some 2,000 wine châteaux of the Gironde. Médoc, Sauternes, and Barsac were classified in 1855, Graves in 1953, and Saint-Émilion in 1955. In 1965, this designation was reserved by law exclusively for Bordeaux.

Château Grand-La-Lagune

See Château LA LAGUNE.

Grand Marnier

An orange-flavoured, brandy-based, very sweet proprietary French liqueur of the Curaçao type made by the Établissements Marnier-Lapostolle in Neauphle-le-Château and Château de Bourg, in France. It is made in two types, yellow and red, of which the red is stronger and the yellow sweeter.

See CURAÇAO.

Château Grand-Puy-Ducasse

Bordeaux red wine. District: Haut-Médoc, France. Commune: Pauillac.

A third of the vineyard is the portion of the old Château Grand Puy, the remainder of that vineyard now being Château Grand-Puy-Lacoste; another third lies near Château Batailley south of Pauillac; and a third to the north near Châteaux Pontet-Canet and Mouton-Rothschild.

Grand-Puy-Ducasse is rated Fifth Growth (*Cinquième Cru*) in the classification of 1855, and the château itself is on the wide street bordering the river docks of Pauillac, where it now houses a wine museum and the headquarters of the Médoc wine fraternity, the Commanderie du Bontemps.

Characteristics. Lighter, with good breed, but less well constructed than those of Grand Puy-Lacoste (*q.v.*).

Vineyard area: 20 acres.

Average production: 2,800 cases.

Château Grand-Puy-Lacoste

Bordeaux red wine. District: Haut-Médoc, France. Commune: Pauillac.

The wine is mostly exported—to England, the U.S.A. and Germany—and is served on the flights of Air France. A Fifth Growth (*Cinquième Cru*) of Médoc, the vineyard lies on one of the highest parts of Pauillac. In Old French the word *puy* meant 'high point', and the eminence on which the vines are planted is conserved in the name. Grand Puy, dating from at latest the fifteenth century, was acquired after the French Revolution by a Monsieur Lacoste who tacked on his own name. Like Château Calon-Ségur and a few others, it is one of the rare Médoc vineyards to be entirely in one section and undivided, and intact since the Classification of 1855.

Characteristics. Excellent, full-bodied wines; may start out on the rough side but they mature into sturdy and extremely pleasant wines of great breed. Monsieur Dupin, the owner since 1934, has done much to give the praiseworthy wines the increasingly good reputation they have acquired; and of this he is justifiably proud. He will long be remembered as the most gastronomically inclined Médoc owner of the post-war period. Today, Grand-Puy-Lacoste deserves a better classification than the Fifth rating it received in 1855.

Vineyard area: 52 acres.

Average production: 8,000 cases.

Grand Roussillon

Red, white, and rosé wines. District: Southern France.

A wine-growing region in southern France encompassing the districts of Banyuls, Côtes d'Agly, Côtes de Haut-Roussillon, Maury, and Rivesaltes in the departments of Pyrénées-Orientales and Aude, bordering Spain and the Mediterranean. Red, white, and rosé wines are made, but only those which are sweet and fortified with brandy and those known as *Rancio* are of any importance.

The vine is said to have been introduced by Hannibal in 217 B.C. and planted by sick, tired, or straggling soldiers who found the climatic conditions similar enough to their native Carthage to induce them to desert the famous general and settle in France. The vines were ripped out by the Arabs but replanted by Charlemagne and have since then undergone a number of calamities caused by Grand Roussillon's strategic position between France and

Spain. Each wave of conquerors and each invading army has been followed by a general replanting.

The region is a poor one, its climate hot, its soil mountainous, meagre, and peppered with rocks. Most vineyard holdings are small and the greater part of its wine is vinified in co-operative cellars. Some of Grand Roussillon's lesser output is used for the making of wine-based aperitifs.

See SWEET FORTIFIED WINES OF FRANCE.

Grand Saint-Bernard

A pale green Swiss liqueur.

Grande (Fine) Champagne

Best district of the Cognac vineyards and consequently the mark, on a Cognac label, of the finest brandy from the point of view of vineyard quality. Some say that a certain percentage of brandy derived from wine of the Borderies across the River Charente is needed to combine heartiness with the splendid finesse of Grande Champagne. Its distinction comes from the chalk in the soil; the word *champagne* in French indicates chalky soil. Similarity of sort is the only thing Grande Champagne Cognac has in common with Champagne wines.

See COGNAC.

Grands-Échezeaux

Burgundy red wine. District: Côte de Nuits, France. Commune: Flagey-Échezeaux. Official classification: Great Growth (Grand Cru).

(*Flagey-Échezeaux is not an* appellation, *and when the wines do not meet the required minimum standards they are declassed into communal wine of Vosne-Romanée.*)

The widely prevalent myth that all Bordeaux is light and all Burgundy heavy can easily be scotched by placing a bottle of Grands-Échezeaux next to a fine Saint-Émilion. Grands-Échezeaux lies between Vougeot and Vosne-Romanée, and the wines provide the logical half-step between the sturdy fullness of the former and the easy, aristocratic elegance of the latter; they balance the body necessary for a well-rounded wine with a delicacy and a finesse which prompts the Burgundian to characterize them with the words *en dentelle*, 'like lace'. Despite the fact that they are little known, they are unquestionably among the greatest of all red Burgundies.

The vineyard embraces 22·6 acres up the hill and across a road from the Clos de Vougeot—on the southern side of the vineyard—and the entire Clos is visible from it. A number of growers own sections, including the Domaine Civile de la Romanée-Conti and such able and excellent wine-makers as René Engel and the sons of Louis Gros. Average production of the entire vineyard is about 5,400 imp. gallons (6,500 U.S.) or the equivalent of just under 2,700 cases.

Granja União

Brand name for some of the best wines of Brazil. Both red and white are sold by this company.

See BRAZIL.

Granjo

A natural sweet white wine of Portugal made by letting noble rot form on late-picked grapes, as is the method in Sauternes and with the Spätlese German wines.

Grape

Fruit of the vine. Wine is made from the fermented juice of the grape, of which there are many varieties.

See CHAPTER EIGHT.

Grappa

The Italian word for marc, or spirit distilled from grape husks. The term is also used in California and in Spanish-speaking countries. Most grappa is harsh, coarse, young, and fairly mediocre.

Graves

Red and white wines. District: Bordeaux, France.

Because they have met only with mediocre blended wines of the district, Graves, to many people outside France, is simply a sweetish white wine. In fact, the better white wines of Graves are dry, the greatest wines red. This large region—forty miles long and at some points twelve miles wide—stretching from the fringe of the Médoc to the edge of Sauternes and containing a variety of sites and soils, naturally produces wines of different types.

Graves encloses the city of Bordeaux and, as the suburbs spread, the vineyard is thrust back. Only such great estates as those of Haut-Brion and La Mission-Haut-Brion are too valuable to be given up to building, and these are now islands surrounded by houses and shops and touched by the main road. In the Middle Ages, however, when the bourgeois growers of Bordeaux used to hurry back at nightfall to its sheltering walls, this closeness to the city was a great advantage, and Graves was in both senses of the word the first district of Bordeaux. Indeed, in England, where most of the wine went, the names were synonymous. This was still the case in the seventeenth century, when Pepys wrote of the good wine of Haut-Brion; but during the next hundred years the wines of the Médoc came into fashion. For some time after the Napoleonic wars even the great vineyard of Haut-Brion sank, through mismanagement, into mediocrity. The oïdium epidemic of the early eighteen-fifties struck hard in Graves, and the growers were slower than those of other districts to reconstitute their vines. Whether for this reason, or because of local politics, Graves was not included in the 1855 Classification of the Gironde wines. Yet Haut-Brion, now restored to its former glory, could not be left out: so, ignoring geography, the classifiers added it to the First Growths (*Premiers Crus*) of the great vineyards of the Médoc. In fact, all the big red wines of Graves—vigorous, full-bodied, and lasting—always had their partisans. The growers pulled themselves together, and in the splendid pre-phylloxera years of 1864–5 the shippers were again doing keen business with them.

The name Graves comes from the gravelly soil in which the red grapes (Cabernet Sauvignon, Cabernet Franc, Merlot, Malbec, and Petit Verdot) flourish. The same soil occurs elsewhere, in Pomerol, Saint-Émilion, and the Médoc. The vines, also, are Médoc vines, and there is a family resemblance between the red wines of these adjoining areas. If the Médocs (especially the Margaux) are more feminine and delicate, the Graves have more body, a distinct character, and a pleasing frankness.

The white Graves actually outnumber the red. In the southern part of the district towards Sauternes, and in a soil which contains a proportion of sand, white wine grapes (Sémillon, Sauvignon, and a very little Muscadelle) predominate. The same vines grow in Sauternes. These white wines are mainly dry, especially in the north of Graves (the best of all is the small production of Haut-Brion Blanc); but some, near Sauternes, are suave, soft, and *moelleux*. Down here, the land is well wooded and crossed with little streams, the country of the most romantic Bordeaux châteaux: Olivier, mirrored in the still waters of its moat, once the hunting lodge of the Black Prince; and the Château de la Brède, moated too, and even more beautiful. Montesquieu lived here and cultivated his vineyard. It is more famous now for its library than its wines.

In 1953, the best vineyards of Graves were classified in both red and white wines. This rating was much criticized, and was revised in 1959. Only two vineyards were added in red wines, three in white, and the revision brought little satisfaction. In each, Château Haut-Brion is classified a red wine of Graves, while remaining a First Growth of the Médoc. A glaring error in the original Graves Classification was its failure to include among the whites Château Haut-Brion Blanc, one of the finest dry white wines in the world. This error was rectified in 1960.

GRAVES 1959 OFFICIAL CLASSIFICATION

(*For the individual classified growths, see under separate headings, and for the list of all Graves Growths, see Appendix* A, *VII.*)

CLASSIFIED VINEYARDS MAKING BOTH RED AND WHITE WINE

Vineyard	*Commune*
Château Bouscaut	Cadaujac
Château Carbonnieux	Léognan
Domaine de Chevalier	Léognan
Château Malartic-Lagravière	Léognan
Château La Tour-Martillac	Martillac
Château Olivier	Léognan

CLASSIFIED VINEYARDS MAKING RED WINE

Vineyard	*Commune*
Château de Fieuzal	Léognan
Château Haut-Bailly	Léognan
Château Haut-Brion	Pessac
Château La Mission-Haut-Brion	Pessac
Château La Tour-Haut-Brion	Talence
Château Pape-Clément	Pessac
Château Smith-Haut-Lafitte	Martillac

CLASSIFIED VINEYARDS MAKING WHITE WINE

Vineyard	*Commune*
Château Couhins	Villenave-d'Ornan
Château Laville-Haut-Brion	Talence

See BORDEAUX.

Graves de Vayres

White and red wines. District: Bordeaux, France.

Facing Libourne on the River Dordogne in south-west France, an enclave of gravel soil juts into the predominantly clay soil of the large wine region of Entre-Deux-Mers (carafe white wine). The quality on the gravel terrain is definitely superior and merits the individual wine *appellation*, Graves de Vayres. Vayres is the chief village, and *graves* is the regional term for the type of gravel. This place-name is famous beyond all reason in Germany where the cheap Graves de Vayres are sold as the wines of Graves, although the resemblance is remote.

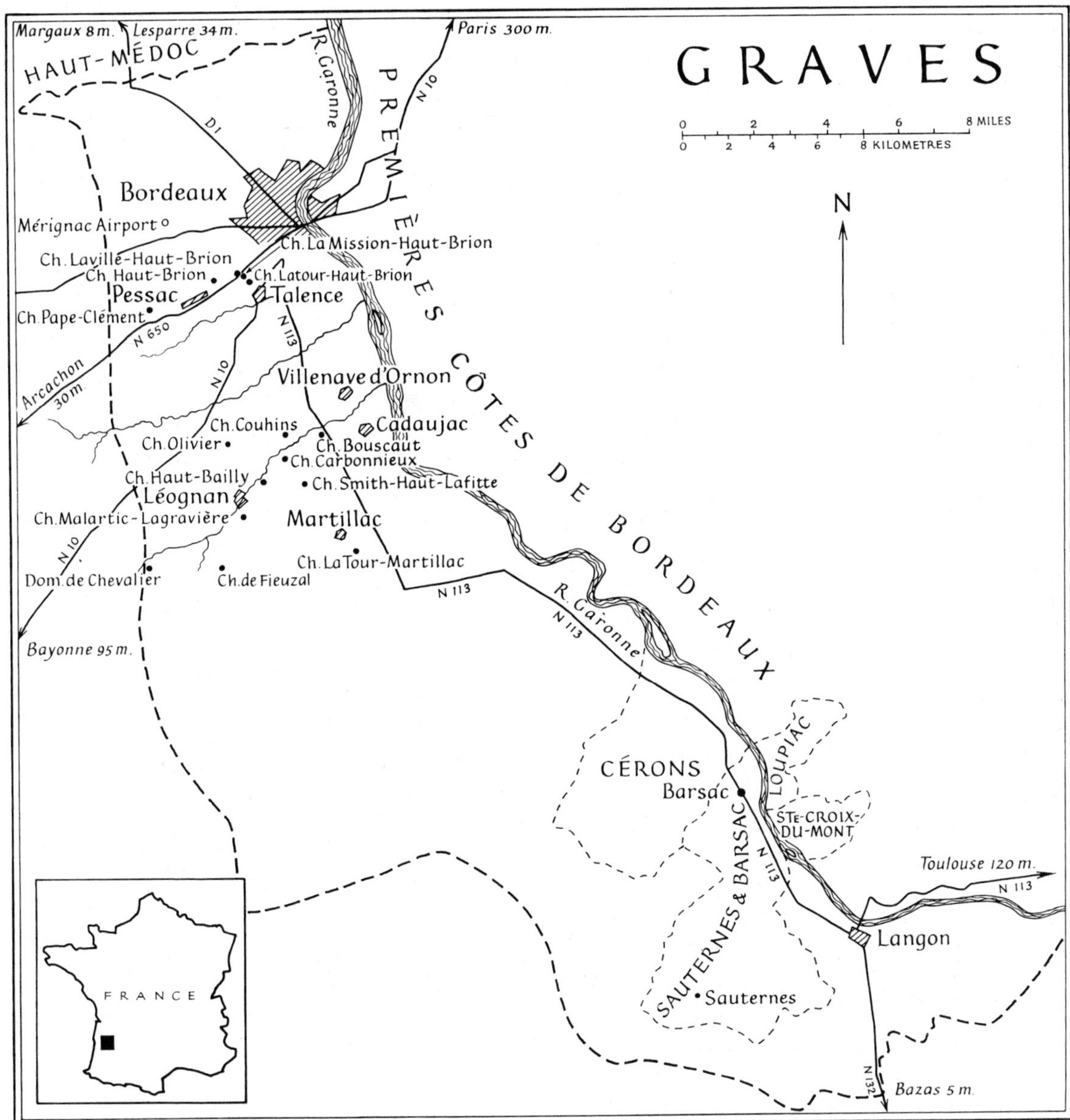

The red wines mature quickly and are very attractive and supple, standing comparison with all but the best of the Pomerols and Saint-Émilions from across the Dordogne, but the quantity in an average year is tiny (14,000 imp. gallons; 16,800 U.S.). The white wines (466,000 imp. gallons; 560,000 U.S.) are suave and mellow, distinguished by their quantity of natural fatness.

Graves Supérieures

White wines. District: Bordeaux, France.

An official French wine designation which means a white wine of the delimited Graves district surrounding Bordeaux in south-west France, which has obtained 12% or more of alcohol by natural fermentation. While Graves produces both red and white wines, only white are eligible for this designation. It is often correctly pointed out that, in French, Supérieures does not indicate a better Graves but merely one higher in alcohol; yet it is true that most of the classified and best-known and best Graves white wines are Graves Supérieures.

See also GRAVES.

Greco

The grape used in Greco di Gerace, in some of the wines of Calabria and elsewhere in Italy.

Greco di Gerace

One of the best wines of Calabria, sweet and golden, with a flowery bouquet.

See CALABRIA.

Greece

The cultivation of the vine ranks among the first of the products of Greek agriculture. A grower of wine from ancient times (there are many references to it in the *Iliad* and the *Odyssey*), Greece was destined to be so by her soil and climate. The chalky soils of the Greek mainland, Crete, and other islands, and the volcanic soils of important vine-growing islands such as Santorin, are favourable to viticulture. Of the 544,176 acres planted in vines in 1960, 341,894 acres were devoted to wine grapes. (There were some 6,118 acres given up to young vines which had not yet started to produce.) Because the climate is so dry, the grapes grow sweet and the wines have a characteristic, fresh flavour—best of all are the luscious sweet varieties. Those destined for export are made by up-to-date methods at the plants of big manufacturers. For their own use, the peasants are apt to go about their wine-making as their ancestors did in the old days when Dionysos was still worshipped.

After the First World War, refugees coming in from wine-growing regions in Asia Minor increased the vineyard area of Greece, and a great deal of wine was exported, particularly between 1926 and 1929. In the years after the Second World War, general conditions, allied to outbreaks of phylloxera and mildew, did a great deal of harm. Anti-phylloxera measures were introduced, and vineyards reconstituted, so that the area in vine is now equal to the pre-war vineyards; but export figures are not. Ranking seventh in European wine production, and twelfth in world production, Greece does not take a comparable place in the world market. In 1959 she made 84,457,000 imp. gallons (101,372,000 U.S.), of which 2,085,000 imp. gallons (2,502,000 U.S.) were exported. In 1962, after a slightly larger harvest, export figures rose to 5,537,840 imp. gallons (6,645,408 U.S.). Her principal customers are Germany, Switzerland, Sweden, Benelux, and the United States, in that order. By 1964 her production had fallen to 77,565,000 imp. gallons (93,151,000 U.S.) though export figures had risen to 5,925,000 imp. gallons (7,116,000 U.S.).

Even of late years, there have been few attempts to control quality or enforce the laws of appellation, and the easy-going Greek consumer has made no demand upon the producer, with the result that vineyards have not maintained an even character.

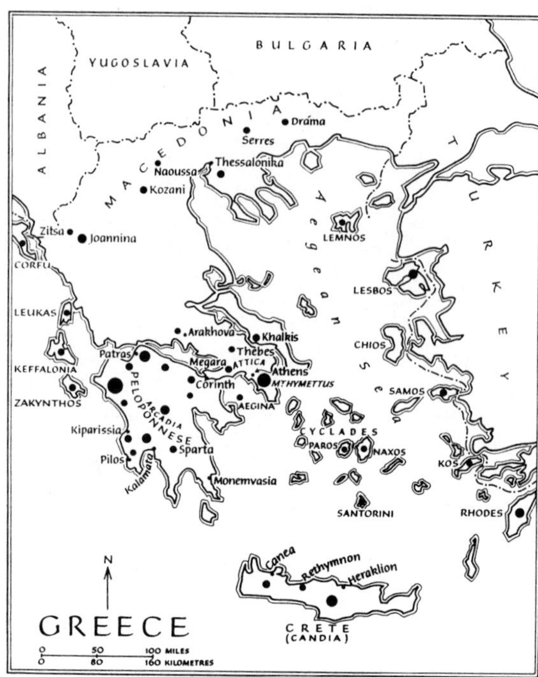

In general, wine is taken for granted as something plentiful and often cheap, most of which is not even bottled but is aged in huge vats. This has meant that there has been no luxury trade to speak of, with the minimum of estate-bottling among small growers. However, legislation was set up to bring in certain controls, which were made law in 1963, and now should gradually become effective. Moreover, an Institute of Tasters was founded in 1962—a non-profit-making concern comparable to the *Consorzi* in Italy. So far, it has little authority but, since it is devoted to the promotion of better wines, it may yet be instrumental in improving overall quality.

As it is now, the Greek wine business can be divided into three main groups: (1) The co-operatives; (2) large private companies; (3) the smaller individual producers.

The important private bottling firms are: Société Hellenique des Vins et Spiritueux; A. Cambas, S.A.; and Achaia-Clauss.

Wine Regions

The Peloponnese

The peninsula is the largest wine-growing district in Greece, producing about 25% of the total quantity; and one of the most important firms is the Co-operative of Patras in the extreme north, across the straits from Missolonghi where Byron died of fever—since those days, the place has been cleared of mosquitoes. The town of Patras, reached by the lovely coast road along the shores of the Corinthian Gulf, or by the railway which runs parallel with it, nestles at the foot of a steep mountain. The vineyards, five miles wide, cover the beautiful slopes. The principal grape varieties are Mavrodaphne, Muscat, Aghiorghitico and Phileri. There are no neat rows of trimmed vines—they grow everywhere, like bushes, basking in the full heat of the sun. Some of the best Greek wines come from this district—a few red, but mainly dry white, like the clean-tasting Santa Laura, and Santa Helena. But a sweet white Muscat is made here, too, and more important, the luscious Mavrodaphne (grown also on the island of Cephalonia): Mavrodaphne is one of the few dessert wines which seems to express itself best when it is not chilled but is served at room temperature. It is an expensive, heavy, sweet red wine with 14% to 16% of alcohol by volume. Other wines of the region are the light pinkish Tegea; the supple Mantinea; and Nemea, dry but very dark, almost black, in colour.

Attica

Attica is the second most productive region, accounting for about 15% of the wine. In this country, south of Athens, bordered by splendid beaches and a well-paved coast road, the vineyards yield a great deal of the ordinary wine for domestic consumption. The white Savatiano grape appears here; Mandilaria and Mavroudi for red wines, and some Rhoditis for rosé. Here also the dry Hymettus is made, near Mount Hymettus, a wine that should be drunk between two and four years old; and Marco. The best white wine of Greece is a carefully made wine from a small estate called Pallini.

Macedonia

The west and central parts of this region are particularly favourable to viticulture, producing satisfactory red wines. And on the southern slopes of Mount Vilia a sweet wine is made from the red Muscat.

Island of Rhodes

This island, already civilized in Mycenean times, once famous for its Colossus, then as the stronghold of the Hospitallers, has been making wine for many centuries. The principal company is the Co-operative, C.A.I.R.; while the best-known wine, the dry white Lindos, is grown around the city of that name, where the ruins of the Parthenon stand.

Island of Samos

The island, divided from Turkey by a narrow strip of the Ægean Sea, was denuded of vines when it was conquered by the Turks at the time of the fall of Constantinople (1453). Yet, when the Greeks regained it in 1912, they found the vines replanted and the wines as good as ever. Laws were passed in the following twenty-five years which made Samos one of the very few guaranteed place-names in Greece. No wine not grown on the island may take the name; nor may the Samos wine be blended with any other—most Greek wines are allowed an admixture of up to 30%. In order to enforce this rule, wines from other parts of Greece are forbidden in Samos. The sweet Muscat of Samos is one of two Greek wines most often seen abroad and most liked (the other is Mavrodaphne). The white Muscat grape, resembling the Muscat de Frontignan, produces the bulk of Samos wines. The island is mountainous, and the steep slopes, often terraced, are well suited to the vine. The yellow-gold grapes flourish in the mild climate, but there is considerable variation in the times of ripening in different parts of the vineyard: on the plain, harvesting starts in August, but it does not begin until October in the high mountain vineyards.

In addition to the natural sweet wine, dry and fortified sweet wines are made on Samos, and nearly all have the distinct, heavy flavour and bouquet of the Muscat.

Island of Santorin

Both dry and sweet wines are made from a variety of vines which flourish in the volcanic soil, and sometimes they are very pleasant. A good, dry wine will always be labelled Santorin; the sweet may be either Santorin or Vino Santo. On the sun-parched hills of this beautiful island the grapes achieve such a high degree of sugar that the wines often run 15% of alcohol per volume.

Island of Crete

This large island is an important centre of Greek viniculture. The hilly country gets a great deal of sun, and production is fairly prolific. Among the vines planted are Romeiko, Kotisphalo, Mandilari and Liatico; and the resulting table wines are big and fleshy, rich in alcohol, developing in finesse as they mature. Here, as on Samos, a serious effort is made to protect the appellation of the wines. Some of these may be labelled Candia—or Archanes. The big co-operative is Chania. A small area of the vineyard is owned by A. Cambas S.A. and Achaia-Clauss, but little of what they sell comes from their own land.

Other Greek Wines

Retsina

This is the most popular name in Greek wines, yet it is not an individual type but a generic one. It is simply any wine which has been flavoured with pine resin—and that means about 50% of the wine made in Greece. White and rosé wines may be treated in this way, but red are not. In the southern and central parts of the country, almost everyone—especially amongst the peasants—prefers his wine with this piny, resinous taste. More than 80% of the Savatiano wines of Attica are treated with resin.

There are many stories of how the use of resin came about. One theory is that the ancient Greeks preserved the wine with the pine gum and, incidentally, liked to add a flavour they had soon grown accustomed to. Another suggestion is that it happened accidentally, when a shortage of oak forced growers to store their wine in barrels made of pine—this is unlikely, since discoveries in Egyptian tombs have proved that, before the days of classical Greece, the bottoms of wine jars were smeared with resin and bitumen to preserve the wine. It was considered even then that the resin improved the flavour. The ancient Romans also added pitch and other ingredients to their wine, but the use has not, in Italy, persisted into modern times. Retsina should be drunk cool. The Greeks say that the best of it comes from around Athens. The peasants who make it for their own consumption do so in the old-fashioned way and often drink it quite soon after fermentation. The usual alcoholic content of Retsina is 12·5%–13% by volume. Unlike most wines, it does not improve with age.

Monemvasia or Malmsey

Nowadays, the name Monemvasia merely refers to wines that are more or less characteristic of the Malmsey type produced in any part of Greece. In the old days, however, Monemvasia, lying in a deep harbour in the south of Greece, was a busy port, from which this wine was exported—it gave its name to a type of wine it shipped but did not grow, and which was produced on Naxos and others of the smaller Cyclades—and also on the island of Crete, or Candia. Monemvasia spread through the Mediterranean world, appearing in Spain under the name Malvagia, in Italy as Malvasia, in France as Malvoisie—while in the English-speaking countries to which it was imported, it was known as Malmsey. It was famous in England in Shakespeare's day and earlier—everyone remembers that the Duke of Clarence was drowned in a butt of Malmsey. Some confusion has been caused by a general failure to realise that Malmsey has long denoted not a place-name but a style of wine, or a wine from the Malvoisie grape variety, and that it is not restricted to Spain, Madeira, or Crete.

Other Greek wines occasionally seen abroad include Mantineia, a pinkish dry wine from the uplands of Arcadia, at its best at around five years of age, and well cooled; and Mavro Naoussis, a deeply-coloured dry red wine from the Naoussa district in central Macedonia.

Spirits

Brandy

The better Greek brandies are made from the Savatiano and other white and red grape varieties generally grown on the mainland or on the island of Samos. They are now being produced in three styles: the youngest, five years old; the Five Star, about twenty-five years; the Seven Star, over forty. The colour and aroma are the natural results of ageing in cask. Other brandies may be sweetened and flavoured for use as aperitifs or liqueurs. Metaxa, Botrys, Cambas, and Lizas are the popular dry, light-coloured brandies.

Ouzo and Mastika (*or Masticha*)

These are the principal aperitifs. Ouzo, an anise-flavoured liquid, is usually taken cold, with water or 'on the rocks'. It turns cloudy when water is added, and thus resembles absinthe or French pastis or Pernod. Mastika, which has a brandy base to which gum mastic is added, is made on the island of Chios, but both drinks originated on the mainland of Greece.

Raki

This is an arrack-type spirit, usually made on the east coast, from a neutral wine base with a maceration of figs and other fruits. It is clear white in colour, strong and fiery in character, and usually consumed without any significant ageing period. It is a rustic drink, not one for export.

Grenache

A sweet grape which gives wines high in alcohol and distinctive in bouquet. It is used for the sweet Grenache dessert wine of Banyuls in the Roussillon region, and is planted elsewhere in France, where it is known as Alicante, Carignane Rousse, Tinto, etc. In Spain it appears as Alicantina or Garnacha. It is grown also in northern California, where it makes excellent rosés.

Grenadine

Sweet red syrup, usually non-alcoholic but sometimes with a very slight alcohol content, used as a sweetening agent. Originally made from pomegranates.

Grey Riesling, Grey Dutchess

A white Californian grape which is not, in fact, a Riesling at all, but a descendant of the French Chauché Gris.

Grey Rot

Ignoble rot, a disease of the grape. In certain conditions this rot forms, causing stains on the leaves and alterations within the fruit.

See CHAPTER EIGHT, p. 37.

Grignolino

An Italian grape which in Piedmont produces a red wine—dry and rather heady or semi-sweet and *pétillant*. Cultivation of the vine is, unfortunately, on the decline in Italy. Transplanted to California, it is yielding some pleasant wine.

Grillet

See CHÂTEAU-GRILLET.

Grinzing

Wine-making slopes and suburb of Vienna. Here the new Heurige wine is drunk.

See AUSTRIA.

Griotte-Chambertin

Burgundy red wine. District: Côte de Nuits, France. Commune: Gevrey-Chambertin. Official Classification: Great Growth (Grand Cru).

A full wine which can produce splendid bottles, but few of them appear under their proper names. The number of growers in the vineyard is small—for Burgundy—and the wines are generally sold to various shipping-houses, some of which engage in the practice of stretching the wines of better-known place-names. Despite this regrettable habit, 1958 production of Griotte's 13·5 acres amounted to 1,473 imp. gallons (1,770 U.S.) of wine or the equivalent of about 800 cases, and 1958 was average for quantity.

Grk, Gerk

White Dalmatian wine, dry, pale yellow in colour, with an individual aftertaste.

See YUGOSLAVIA.

Grog

Originally a diluted rum, said to be called after the nickname (Old Grog) of Admiral Vernon who first ordered the dilution of the Navy's rum. The name is sometimes used for undiluted rum and for spirits in general; but is usually applied to hot rum, with or without lemon and spices.

Grolleau (Groslot)

Grape used in France, notably in the rosé wine of Anjou. It is also known as Pineau de Saumur.

Grombalia

Region which produces 90% of Tunisian wines.

Château Gruaud-Larose

Bordeaux red wine. District: Haut-Médoc, France. Commune: Saint-Julien.

Labels of years before 1934 will show either Gruaud-Larose-Sarget or Gruaud-Larose-Faure. The vineyard, originally one, was divided a little more than a hundred years ago when the Sarget heirs, then the sole owners, sold the larger part to a Monsieur Faure. In 1934, Gruaud-Larose was re-united by the present owner, Monsieur Cordier, also owner of Château Talbot. Since then Gruaud-Larose has been making consistently good wines. Monsieur Cordier is also to be congratulated on the way he keeps his cellars. Unfortunately, however, in June 1965 the *chais* containing half the 1964 vintage were burnt down. Gruaud-Larose is a Second Growth (*Second Cru*) of Médoc by the Classification of 1855.

Characteristics. Relatively light and fast maturing, typical of the best Saint-Juliens, with considerable finesse and a light perfume.

Vineyard area: 136 acres.

Average production: 15,000 cases.

Grumello

Red wine of Valtellina, Italy, made from the Nebbiolo grape.

See LOMBARDY.

Grünberg

A small, isolated German wine district in Silesia, surrounding the town of Grünberg, in East Germany.

Grüner Veltliner

Chief grape variety of Lower Austria.

Guebwiller

Alsatian wine town near Colmar.

Guignolet

Black cherry liqueur brandy found mostly in France in the Anjou and Touraine districts and the department of the Vendée.

Château Guiraud

Bordeaux white wine. District and Commune: Sauternes, France.

Château Guiraud and Château d'Yquem are the only first-classified Sauternes (Official Classification of 1855) actually in Sauternes. This is because the commune of Sauternes was considered too small to provide enough wine to earn world-wide reputation, and the designation was extended to four adjoining communes, in which all the twelve best vineyards are situated except those of Yquem and Guiraud. In early days, the Guiraud vineyard was known as Château Bayle. The characteristic French pepperpot turret, capped with a black conical roof, is attached not to the château but to the wine *chai*; the château is a box-like nineteenth-century-style dwelling in a nest of trees, in front of which the L-shaped, long, low *chai* with its unexpected turret at one end extends along the rim of a beautifully kept vineyard.

Characteristics. Rather sweet without great breed, with some remarkable vintages.

Vineyard area: 130 acres.

Average production: 10,250 cases.

Gumpoldskirchner

A delicate white wine, one of the best in Austria, made in the vineyards of Gumpoldskirchen.

See AUSTRIA.

Gunflint Taste

A special taste in white wines from chalky subsoils. Chablis is the prime example of a wine with this quality.

Gutedel

German variant of the Chasselas family of grapes, found also in California.

Gutsname

German term for wine estate. The same as château or clos in Bordeaux and Burgundy.

Guyenne, Connétablie de

Wine fraternity devoted to the promotion of white wines in a district of Bordeaux in France.

See PREMIÈRES CÔTES DE BORDEAUX.

Guyot

A variation of the espalier method of training vines. This consists of a trunk and one arm and is largely used in such fine-wine regions as the Médoc.

See CHAPTER EIGHT, p. 33.

Gyöngyös

The white sparkling wines of Gyöngyös are among the best in Hungary. Red wines are grown in this district too and in greater quantity.

See HUNGARY.

H

Halbrot

Swiss term for rosé wine.

Half-bottle

A bottle holding about half the contents of a standard bottle. The British half-bottle holds roughly 12 British fluid ounces; the American, 12·5 U.S. fluid ounces.

Half-on-half

Tawny-coloured Dutch liqueur, half Curaçao and half orange bitters.

Hallcrest Vineyards

The Hallcrest Vineyards are near Felton in the Santa Cruz Mountains, California. Since they were planted on the crest of a hill, they were named Hallcrest by their owner, Chaffee E. Hall. Hallcrest specializes in Cabernet Sauvignon and White Riesling, with indication of vintage year. The bottles carry an elegant label designed by the Grabhorn Press in San Francisco, and they are dressed with lead-foil caps imported from the Netherlands and with wire-mesh covering fabricated in France.

See AMERICA: CALIFORNIA AND THE WEST.

Hallgartner Schönhell

Outstanding vineyard of Hallgarten, producing one of the best Rheingau wines. Another important Hallgarten vineyard is Deutelsberg.

See RHEINGAU.

Hard

Excessive tannin in a wine gives hardness which may disappear with age. This is a drawback which later becomes an asset, for it preserves the wine and changes with age to firmness. Usually hardness is a sign of youth and quality, but 1945 Bordeaux red wines were hard until the middle sixties.

Harriague

Grape grown in Uruguay, and elsewhere.

See TANNAT.

Hárslevelü

A Hungarian variety of grape used in making Tokay and other wines.

Hattenheimer Nussbrunnen

One of the greatest Rheingau wines.

See RHEINGAU.

Hattenheimer Wisselbrunnen

With Hattenheimer Nussbrunnen and with Steinberg, one of the great Rheingaus, and in the triumvirate of the greatest Hattenheimers.

See RHEINGAU.

Haut

French for 'high', in the feminine, *haute*. This word affixed to a regional name on a wine label is erroneously believed to imply 'higher in quality'. What it actually means is 'higher' in the geographical sense—more northerly, up-river, etc. Example: Haut-Médoc, so named because it is above Médoc on the River Gironde. That it makes better wine is mere coincidence. As for the designation Haut-Sauternes, geographically there is no Haut-Sauternes, and from the point of view of quality, the term is meaningless.

Château Haut-Bages-Libéral

Bordeaux red wine. District: Haut-Médoc, France. Commune: Pauillac.

Lying near Pontet-Canet, the vineyard has been classed a Fifth Growth (*Cinquième Cru*) of the Médoc. The name derives from the high slopes of Bages, where it is situated, and a Monsieur Libéral, an early owner.

Characteristics. Fairly full-bodied but sometimes on the common side. The wines seem to be improving, however.

Vineyard area: 35 acres.

Average production: 3,300 cases.

Château Haut-Bailly

Bordeaux red wine. District: Graves, France. Commune: Léognan.

Unlike most of the great Graves vineyards, Haut-Bailly makes no white wine; but the red wine is among the eleven classified growths (1953 and 1959) of the district.

Replanted after the devastation by the vine-louse phylloxera three-quarters of a century ago by Ballot des Minières, whose fame at the time caused him to be called King of Vine Growers, the vineyard was excellent for a period, but then fell on bad times. The successor of Minières, a little too eager to rival his predecessor, carried 'improvements' in wine-making so far that the wine was being bottled only eight months after vintage, instead of the former four years, and was pasteurized. Having abandoned such 'progressive' practices, Haut-Bailly has recovered its early prestige and the wines are balanced and full, distinct among Graves red wines, and rather resembling certain Médocs.

Characteristics. A full, well-rounded wine with great finesse.

Vineyard area: 21 acres.

Average production: 2,500 cases.

Château Haut-Batailley

Bordeaux red wine. District: Haut-Médoc, France. Commune: Pauillac.

A part of Château Batailley until 1942, the vineyard shares with that estate its position of Fifth Growth (*Cinquième Cru*) of Médoc as classed in 1855.

Characteristics. Much like Château Batailley, with a certain robust strength.

Vineyard area: 34 acres.

Average production: 5,200 cases.

Château Haut-Brion

Bordeaux red and white wines. District: Graves, France. Commune: Pessac.

The name of the vineyard, which is today owned by the American financier, Clarence Dillon, and his son Douglas Dillon, formerly Secretary of the Treasury of the United States, is spelled in various ways in a history that dates back about five hundred years. We know that in 1509 the property was bought by Jean de Ségur. In 1525 it passed into the possession of the Admiral, Philippe de Chabot, whose career is said to have astonished even the Abbé Brantôme—Chabot was with King François I when he was taken prisoner at Pavia. He did not keep Haut-Brion long: before the end of the century it went, in the dowry of Jeanne de Bellon, to the Pontac family, and remained until, through the marriage of a female Pontac, it became in the eighteenth century the property of the Fumel family—who at one time owned Château Margaux also. In the same way, the Pontacs had had another vineyard at Blanquefort, producing white wine. 'Pontack' wines were famous in seventeenth-century England, and the name was sometimes used on the white wine, though more often on the red of Haut-Brion. There was a tavern in the city of London, kept by a French cook—the Royal Oak in Lombard Street, where Pepys went to drink 'a sort of French wine called Ho Bryen that hath a good and most particular taste'. A member of the Pontac family was said to have an interest in this tavern. In 1683 John Evelyn noted in his diary that he had had a talk with Monsieur Pontac, son of the famous President of Bordeaux, owner of the excellent vineyard of Haut-Brion, whence came the greatest of the Bordeaux wines. Dryden, Swift, and Defoe also dined at the same place in their turn, and Swift found the wine dear at seven shillings a flagon. In 1677 Locke, the philosopher, had visited Haut-Brion and remarked that prices had risen 'thanks to the rich English who sent orders that it was to be got for them at any price'.

It was during the prosperous years of the eighteenth century that the wines of the Médoc gained in popularity on those of Graves. But Haut-Brion was never outshone. In 1770, the Comte de Fumel divided the estate in half. He kept the château and part of the vineyard; the rest, known as Chai Neuf, he sold to the Marquis de Latresne. At the time of the Revolution, the owner of the château was his fifth son, Joseph, Mayor of Bordeaux. In 1794, Joseph was guillotined; part of the château property was seized by the Government, part remained with the family, who afterwards bought back the State's share—and in 1801 sold it to Talleyrand, who kept it only until 1804.

There is no record of Talleyrand having lived there, but no doubt he found a use for the wines. His success in diplomacy depended not only on his quick wit, the charm of his conversation and the talents of his cook, but also on the excellence of his wines. At the Congress of Vienna he got the better of everyone, and one of the ways in which he influenced people was by inviting them to his splendid dinner-parties.

After 1804 Haut-Brion saw one of its least glorious periods under a succession of businessmen until, in 1836, Monsieur J. E. Larrieu bought the château. Four years later he was able to buy back the Chai Neuf, too, and so restored the property to its true state. Before long he had done the same for the wine; and when in 1855, the Classification of the Great Growths of the Gironde was made, although other leading wines of Graves were omitted, Haut-Brion was rated a First Growth (*Premier Cru*) with the three great Médocs, Lafite, Latour, and Margaux.

When the rest of the Graves were at last classified, in 1953 and again in 1959, the great red wine of Haut-Brion was, of course, listed First Growth and is now a First Growth of both Graves and Médoc. The white wine did not do so well. Haut-Brion Blanc, less famous than the red (mainly because only one-tenth the quantity is made), is usually the most characteristic and one of the finest dry white wines of the whole region of Bordeaux. Yet, in the classification of the white Graves it was not placed among the five First Growths. Finally, however, this omission has been repaired. The wine is now classified with the white wines of Graves.

The vineyard is situated on the outskirts of Bordeaux, with suburbs encroaching upon it both from the city and from the sizeable village of Pessac.

The large walled vineyards of Haut-Brion and La Mission-Haut-Brion, facing each other across the main road, are surrounded by a conglomeration of petrol pumps, grocers' shops, and ironmongers.

The red wine is grown on the great breast of the vineyard, swelling above the main *chais* and the château; while at the top of the rise, where the land is levelled, there is a smallish patch of Sémillon and Sauvignon vine, giving the white wine, with a rather desolate-looking little building to house it. A better *chai* for white wine could hardly be found, however, than this, with its cooling earth floor and the windowless walls giving dark shelter.

The soil where the white wines grow is inclined to be clayey, while the vines for the red wine flourish in the famous soil of deep *graves*—the regional word for gravel. This gravel, which has given the Graves district its name, is nowhere so prevalent as at Haut-Brion, where in places it is fifty and sixty feet deep. The porous soil, with its pebbles which reflect the sun and retain the heat, is said to be the factor that causes Haut-Brion to be good even in lesser years. The excess water drains away quickly, giving the vine the semi-aridity it likes.

Characteristics. The red wine is great and often very full, with a special taste imparted by the gravelly soil of its native Graves. It achieves great elegance, and even in the lesser years it is apt to succeed better than others of the district because, owing to its situation, the grapes mature a little earlier at Haut-Brion than in most of the other quality vineyards. Also, the recruiting of harvest workers is easier in the suburbs of Bordeaux where large crews are available and can easily be suspended during rain.

The white wine is one of the best dry wines of Bordeaux.

Vineyard area: 92 acres.

Average production: white, 800 cases; red, 10,000 cases.

Haut-Médoc

Red wine. District: Bordeaux, France.

The finest part of the Médoc red wine region, near Bordeaux in south-west France, and an official wine place-name or Appellation Contrôlée. The name designates the upper Médoc, in the sense that it is up-river. The famous districts of Margaux, Pauillac, Saint-Julien, and Saint-Estèphe, and all the famous Médoc châteaux, are in Haut-Médoc.

See MÉDOC.

Haut-Montravel

See MONTRAVEL.

Haut-Peyraguey (Clos)

Bordeaux white wine. District: Sauternes, France. Commune: Bommes.

The sloping vineyard surrounds a 'château' that looks like a white farmhouse. The vines grow in a clayey and gravel soil. The wine was classed a First Growth (*Premier Cru*) of Sauternes in the Official Classification of 1855.

Characteristics. Carefully made, sweet, rich wine of breed and distinction.

Vineyard area: 18 acres.

Average production: 1,900 cases.

Hectare

Metric measure of area containing 10,000 square metres or 2·471 acres.

See APPENDIX D.

Hectolitre

French unit of measure equalling 100 litres, or 21·9976 imp. gallons (26·4179 U.S.). All ordinary French wines are sold by the hectolitre. Abbreviation: Hl, or colloquially, Hecto.

Heidelberg Tun

A barrel in Heidelberg Castle constructed in 1751 by the cellarmaster, Jakob Engler the Younger, for the Elector Karl Theodor. It holds 220,000 litres (48,400 imp. gallons; 58,100 U.S.) (about 300,000 bottles) but has only been filled three times and long ago sprang a leak. The pump by which wine used to be drawn out of the cask may be seen in the Königsaal, or Great Hall, of the castle.

Hérault

One of the three most important wine producing departments of France, quantitatively speaking. The other two are Aude and Gard. From Hérault, in the Montpellier-Béziers district of southern France, comes a great deal of ordinary wine, as well as the superior dry wine Clairette du Languedoc (*q.v.*) and the sweet Muscat de Lunel (*see* SWEET FORTIFIED WINES OF FRANCE).

Hermitage, Ermitage

Rhône Valley red and white wines. District: Rhône Valley, France.

The big, long-lived Hermitage wines are grown on the slopes above Tain, a little town by the Rhône, fifty miles south of Lyons and twelve miles north of Valence. Small, terraced vineyards, divided by stone walls into parcels known locally as *mas*, climb the hill which rises abruptly behind the town. At the summit, a local landmark is the ruined chapel of Saint-Christophe, built on the site of a Roman temple of Mercury. According to some stories, Saint Patrick planted vines here during his first sojourn in Gaul. On this hillside lived the hermit from whom the wines take their name: the knight Gaspard de Stérimberg, who turned penitent after the Crusade of 1224 against the Albigensian heretics, and chose to spend in this beautiful spot the rest of a life which was to be divided between religious meditation and the cultivation of his vineyard. To the many visitors who came to see him he offered wine—all he had—and so the fame of Hermitage was spread.

The soil is meagre—a thin layer of chalky limestone on a hard granite subsoil—and the whole extent of the vineyards is 375 acres, yielding some 356 imp. gallons (428 U.S.) to the acre. When they are bearing, the vines are susceptible to *coulure* (*q.v.*). It is not surprising, therefore, that genuine Hermitage is a comparatively rare and expensive wine.

The red-wine grape is the Syrah, variously reported to be the Shiraz of Persia, brought home by Crusaders (some say by Stérimberg himself); or to have been introduced by the Romans. In any case, the vineyards here are said to be among the oldest in France. The white-wine grapes, cultivated in the centre of the slope, are Marsanne and, to a small extent, Roussanne. Less than 30,000 cases is the average yield of this distinctive white wine—full, with a flinty flavour and a character so definite that it can hold its own with such highly seasoned foods as curry. This is among the longest-lasting of all dry white wines and will sometimes be good after twenty years. But it maderizes eventually and is usually at its best at somewhere between six and fifteen years old.

Both white and red wines incline, in youth, to harshness. The red may be rough at first, but in maturity it is soft and velvety, big and generous, forming a heavy sediment. In age, it develops a rich aroma and aftertaste, a bouquet redolent of raspberries and wallflowers, and a glowing *robe* which shifts in colour from deep purple to the brownish cast known as *pelure d'oignon*. In nineteenth-century England, Hermitage was much esteemed, and Professor Saintsbury described it as 'the manliest of wines'.

Twice as much red wine is made as white. In addition to the predominant Syrah, other grape varieties are permitted, in small quantities, and these add their own qualities to the wine. The best vineyards for red are: Les Bessards, Le Méal, L'Hermitage, La Varogne, Les Diognières, Les Greffieux, and La Pierelle.

Chante-Alouette is the most celebrated of the white Hermitages, which are dry and delicate, yet have body as well as bouquet. This is the name of a vineyard, and also the trade-mark of the firm of Chapoutier, and the wine is usually a blend from the better vineyards, such as Beaumes, Les Murets, Les Rocoules, La Chapelle, Maison-Blanche—and, of course, Chante-Alouette itself. Some of the growers, aware of the value of publicity, have painted their names in whitewash on the dividing walls between the *mas*—Chapoutier, Paul Jaboulet Aîné, and Jaboulet-Vercherre—these three are shippers as well as important growers. Production is in the neighbourhood of 66,000 imp. gallons (79,000 U.S.) a year.

L'Hermitage is just below that group of vineyards which produce wines that are sold as Crozes-Hermitages: agreeable wines, but not to be compared with those permitted the distinguished name Hermitage.

Heurige

New light wine served, and sometimes made, in the vine-covered houses of Grinzing on the outskirts of Vienna. The literal translation is 'wine of this year' but it is more generally known as May wine.

Highball

A long, iced drink, usually whisky and soda.

Hippocras

An aromatized wine, popular in the Middle Ages. It was made, probably, from sour wine sweetened and spiced and then filtered through wool, the filter being known as Hippocrates' Sleeve.

Hochheimer-Domdechaney

This big, fruity wine is probably the best of the Hochheimers from the River Main beyond Wiesbaden; but owing to great similarity in quality, it is always classed with the Rheingau wines nearby on the Rhine. This Hochheimer contributed the name Hock used in England for Rheingaus and loosely for all Rhine wines.

See RHEINGAU.

Hock

British term which applies accurately to the wines from the Rheingau section of Germany and loosely to all wines of the Rhine type. The word derives from Hochheim, a town in the Rheingau.

See RHEINGAU.

Hogshead

A cask of varying capacity; the most commonly used container for shipping wines and spirits in bulk. The name is said to be a corruption of the Scandinavian *ox-hoft*, which itself varies from 56 to 58 imp. gallons (67–79 U.S.). Some of the more widely used hogshead capacities are:

	gallons	
	imp.	*U.S.*
Burgundy and Bordeaux	49·5	59·4
Beer and cider	54	64·8
Sherry	54	64·8
Whisky	55	66
Port	57	68·4
Brandy	60	72

See BARRIQUE.

Holland

See NETHERLANDS.

Hollands

The style of gin usually seen in Holland, where it is called Jenever, and distinguished by the stone jar or crock in which it is frequently sold. It differs from London Dry gin, the basic British and American type, by being less thoroughly distilled. In common with Scotch whisky, Cognac, and Jamaican-style rum, it is distilled lightly enough to permit the original taste-factors to pass over into the final product. (London Dry gins are made colourless and tasteless in distillation and flavoured afterwards.) Hollands is not a neutral cocktail ingredient like London Dry types, but a spirit which the Dutch take neat.

See GIN.

Homeburn

In Norway, spirit distilled at home; 'homebrew'.

Honey Brandy

A distilled mead.

See MEAD.

Hops

A climbing perennial with rough lobed leaves like those of the vine. The ripened cones of the female plant are used in brewing, to give flavour to the beer. Cultivated in Europe, Central Asia, and America.

Hospices de Beaune

The ancient façade of the Charity Hospital rises in the centre of Beaune; and the sale of its wines each year sets the prices for those of the entire Côte d'Or, dictates the value of the harvest which is the life-blood of Beaune, and ushers in the *Trois Glorieuses*—the three lavish banquets at which Burgundians congregate to glorify and drink their favourite wines.

The Hospices were founded in 1443 by Nicolas Rollin, Chancellor to the Duke of Burgundy, and his wife Guigone de Salins. Beaune at that time seems to have been entirely populated by beggars (only twenty-four of its families were considered to be solvent) and so it was undoubtedly a wise choice as a site for the charity hospital. There were those who said that Rollin—who was, among other things, a collector of taxes—could well afford to build a hospital for the poor he had helped to grind down; but his charity has been perpetuated, and grants, often in the form of vineyards, have been coming in through the centuries.

In the high outer wall of the Hospices is an arched doorway leading into a cobbled court dotted with groups of visitors and crossed now and again by members of the Dames Hospitalières, the lay organization which, from the start, has cared for the sick. Since they were members of this lay organization, the Hospices did not fall into the hands of the State during the French Revolution, when anticlerical feeling was high and Church property confiscated. Inside the court the architecture is mediæval, with peaked, carved-wood dormers rising from the superb roof of multicoloured tiles. Pillars hold up a balcony which runs around the court, in the middle of which is a massive stone well. There are other courts behind this one, rarely seen by visitors, and off one of the last of these the wine is made.

The auction sale of the wines of the Hospices de Beaune is one of the biggest events of the Burgundian year and the wine merchants who come to take part are mainly French and Belgian, but others come from all over the world. The city begins to get crowded a few days before the sale—usually the third Sunday in November—and the day before they all troop into the *chais* to taste the wine. At the end of the day, the first banquet of the *Trois Glorieuses* is held in the ornate hall of the Clos de Vougeot.

The actual auction of the wines takes place in one of the outer courts, or in one of the halls leading off it, and is always presided over by some public figure. Prince Bernhardt of the Netherlands, the British and American Ambassadors to France have been among recent presidents. All bidding is done in true mediæval manner 'by the candle'; three small tapers are placed in a holder, and as the auction starts one of them is lit; when it dies, the second is lit and then the third, and the last bid heard before the third has snuffed itself out takes the dubious prize. Competition is keen, because ownership of even a small amount of Hospices de Beaune wine carries considerable prestige, both for wine merchants and restaurateurs, and prices frequently soar far above value. (However, the buyer always has the consolation that he is contributing to a worthy cause.) A slight defect in the system is that all wines are carted off in barrel within a month of the sale, and buyers do not always take the proper care of it. With prices so high and demand so great, the temptation to stretch these wines is strong.

The vineyards owned by the hospital are scattered throughout the Côte de Beaune and all wines are sold under the name not of a vineyard but of the original donor. Cuvée Dr. Peste, for example, is made from grapes grown in the vineyard of Corton, in the section of Aloxe-Corton called Maréchaude; but since this parcel of land was donated by Dr. Peste, the wine is always sold under his name. The Hospices have a total of some 128 acres of vines and make an annual 41,600 imp. gallons (50,000 U.S.) of wine, 85% of it red.

In addition, they distil a marc de Bourgogne, and when the wines are auctioned off, the marc of the previous year is sold with them. About 6,650 imp. gallons (8,000 U.S.) of marc is average for any year and, as is the case with the wines, prices run slightly higher than for comparable spirits distilled elsewhere in Burgundy. At the conclusion of the auction, the second of the *Trois Glorieuses*—a dinner held in the cellars of the Hospices—begins. The following day the trinity is brought to a close with La Paulée, a banquet in the village of Meursault, where growers are supposed to bring a bottle of their best and rarest wine and pass it around the table. At the end of this, everyone goes home to recover.

The results of the 1962 Sale were as follows (a *pièce* is the equivalent of a barrel, a *feuillette* is half a *pièce*):

Red Wines

(1) Corton—Charlotte Dumay, 17 *pièces*; (2) Beaune—Estienne, 15 *pièces*; (3) Pommard—Billardet, 28 *pièces*, 1 *feuillette*; (4) Savigny-les-Beaune et Vergelesses—Fouquerand, 12 *pièces*, 1 *feuillette*; (5) Beaune—Guigone de Salins, 16 *pièces*, 1 *feuillette*; (6) Beaune—Virely, 20 *pièces*, 1 *feuillette*; (7) Volnay—Général Muteau, 17 *pièces*; (8) Savigny-les-Beaune—Arthur Girard, 19 *pièces*; (9) Beaune—Brunet, 11 *pièces*, 1 *feuillette*; (10) Volnay—Blondeau, 20 *pièces*; (11) Beaune, Maurice Drouhin, 19 *pièces*; (12) Volnay-Santenots—Gauvain, 13 *pièces*; (13) Corton—Docteur Peste, 16 *pièces*; (14) Monthélie—J. Lebelin, 6 *pièces*; (15) Beaune—Hugues et Louis Bétault, 17 *pièces*; (16) Volnay-Santenots—Jehan de Massol, 9 *pièces*, 1 *feuillette*; (17) Auxey-Duresses—Boillot, 3 *pièces*; (18) Beaune—Clos des Avaux, 24 *pièces*; (19) Beaune—Nicolas Rollin, 18 *pièces*; (20) Beaune—Rousseau-Deslandes, 17 *pièces*; (21) Pommard—Dames de la Charité, 21 *pièces*, 1 *feuillette*; (22) Savigny-les-Beaune et Vergelesses—Forneret, 20 *pièces*; (23) Beaune—Dames Hospitalières, 9 *pièces*.

White Wines

(24) Corton-Charlemagne—François de Salins, 2 *pièces*, 1 *feuillette*; (25) Meursault-Genevrières—Baudot, 20 *pièces*; (26) Meursault—Jehan Humblot, 4 *pièces*; (27) Meursault-Charmes—Albert Grivault, 7 *pièces*; (28) Meursault—Loppin, 10 *pièces*; (29) Meursault-Genevrières—Philippe le Bon, 7 *pièces*; (30) Meursault—Goureau, 7 *pièces*; (31) Meursault-Charmes—de Bahèzre de Lanlay, 14 *pièces*.

Hotte

French term for a longish back-basket for carrying grapes.

Houghton

Outstanding vineyard in Western Australia, owned by the Emu Wine Company.

See AUSTRALIA.

Houx

Alsatian holly spirit.

See ALSACE: SPIRITS.

Hudson River Valley

A wine-producing region on the west bank of the Hudson, between Newburgh and Kingston, in New York State. Principal vineyards are High Tor, and those of the Hudson Valley Wine Company. American vines are grown, of which the favourites are the Catawba and the Delaware. Red, white, and rosé wines are produced.

See AMERICA: EASTERN STATES.

Huelva

Province of Spain which produces strong, heavy wines.

See SPAIN.

Hungary

The most famous Hungarian wine, the wine of kings and emperors, is Tokay (*q.v.*) and other wines of Hungary suffer the fate of younger brothers. Yet, eclipsed though they may be in fame, some of

them are excellent. Hungarian wine-making standards are claimed to be among the highest of all; strict controls have been the rule, and Hungary was one of the pioneers of place-name and grape-variety regulations. The peaks of quality, however, are less apparent since the economy became 'Socialistic'.

Wine has always been made in Hungary. Three-quarters wiped out by the vine-louse phylloxera in 1875 and by the vine fungus pernospora in 1891, the industry was rebuilt on grafted American root-stocks and with the most modern methods. 100,000 acres of 'sand' vineyard were created, the sandy soil being practically immune to phylloxera. Statistics show that in 1964 production had risen to 121,977,000 imp. gallons (146,487,000 U.S.).

Classified wines are either First Great Growths (wines of 'Appellation d'Origine Contrôlée') or Great Growths (wines of 'Appellation d'Origine', controlled but not as stringently). The vines must be close-pruned to induce the highest possible quality and no wine not entitled to the appellation may be introduced into the rest.

With only one or two exceptions, and the exception in the case of the Tokays, wines of Growth carry first the name of the place from which they come and second the name of the grape variety.

FIRST GREAT GROWTHS

Tokaji Aszu
Tokaji Szamorodni Dry (száraz)
Tokaji Szamorodni Sweet (Édes)
Badacsonyi Szürkebarát
Badacsonyi Kéknyelü
Badacsonyi Rizling
Badacsonyi Furmint
Balatonfüredi Rizling
Csopaki Rizling
Móri Ezerjó
Debrői Hárslevelü
Somlói Furmint
Pécsi Furmint
Egri Bikavér (Bull's Blood)
Villányi Burgundi
Soproni Kékfrankos
Villányi Kadarka
Szekszárdi Kadarka
Gyöngyösi Kadarka

Grape Varieties

The leading white variety is the Furmint and the leading red variety is the Kadarka.

Although it produces wine elsewhere, for instance in Austria, the Furmint may be considered characteristically Hungarian. It is used in Tokay, but not only in Tokay. The gold-yellow grape, thick-skinned, makes several other noble wines.

Quality white wines are also made from the Ezerjó (notably at the village of Mór), Veltelini (or Pirosveltelini) Rizling (Hungarian spelling of Riesling), French-derived Pinot Gris, and Kéknyelü vines.

The red grape Kadarka produces most of the quality red wine. In the sole First Great Growth—Egri Bikavér—where it is not the exclusive variety, it participates with others.

Bottle Types and Markings

Tokay Aszu and Tokay Szamorodni are marketed to the trade in special white half-litre bottles (for a description of the labelling by grades, *see* TOKAY). Most other Hungarian export wine, including the other styles of Tokay, is sold in the tall slender bottles usually identified with German wines. But Egri Bikavér and one or two others are in the short-shouldered Bordeaux bottle.

The wines carry the guarantee of authenticity—the words 'Magyar Állami Export Pincegazdaság' forming a circle which encloses the word *Budafok*. Anyone who finds this emblem stamped on the body label knows he has the real thing. Monimpex, Budapest, are the only persons entitled to export wines from Hungary.

One or two tips on deciphering the Hungarian labels. The possessive is formed by the addition of 'i'. Thus Debrői Hárslevelü is the wine of Debrő from the Hárslevelü grape. Tokaji Aszu is Tokaj (Hungarian spelling) of the Aszu style, etc. The word *bor* means 'wine'.

The Best Hungarian Wines

The finest wines are produced on the middle heights of the slopes where the Hungarian central plain begins to rise into the mountains, or in the warm 'sea' climate of Europe's largest lake. The foothill exposures usually have the advantage of catching the most sun and the drainage benefits the vineyards, as is always the case with slope wines. So definite is the difference that in the Hegyaljai district, where Tokay is made, the wines of the Hegyaljai plain are ordinary and, except in a strip above a height of 300 feet, the Furmint grape is no longer subject to the mould which forms the sugar-rich dried berry responsible for the Aszu and Essence Tokays. The wines of the shores of Lake Balaton profit also from slope locations and generally south exposure, as well as from the heat-reflecting influence of the lake. Here, as on large rivers such as the Rhine, mirrored sunshine helps the grapes to ripen.

Tokay is the farthest north and farthest east of the vineyards, being in the extreme north-east of the country in the foothills rising steeply to the Carpathian Mountains in Russia and Rumania. Down along the edge of the plain leading to Budapest and on to Lake Balaton other important vineyards are dotted.

To the south, on the facing extremity of the plain, another intermittent string of choice zones includes nearly all the rest of the good vineyards. The only important area not in the two files slanting across Hungary on either side of the central plain is that of Sopron on the Neusiedler Lake.

Egri Bikavér and other wines of Eger

These are wines grown on the slopes of the Bükk Mountains surrounding the old baroque town of Eger. About 5,000 acres in the Kadarka vine produce Egri Kadarka. The wine tends to be a little more delicate and a little lighter than the other First Great Growth of the region, Egri Bikavér.

Egri Bikavér ('Bull's Blood of Eger') is probably the best-known Hungarian red wine, perhaps because of its dramatic name. The dark heavy wine, which tends to be mildly dry and can, in time, attain a luscious velvet, is worthy of its fame. It has fire in it, and is big. In the Bordeaux-style bottle with the large bull's head on both the label and the neck label, it is easy to identify. Unlike most Hungarian wines of quality, it is a vatting. Bull's blood of Eger is a blend of three kinds of grapes: Kadarka, Médoc Noir, and Burgundi.

Eger—more accurately the fifteen villages entitled to use the name on wines—is in the north of Hungary, about midway between Budapest and Tokaj. Eger was once known by the German name Erlau; the well-known Erlauer red wines came from there, as well as from the neighbouring districts of Visonta and Gyöngyös.

Sparkling Gyöngyös

The Gyöngyös and Visonta wine districts lie across a wide valley to the west of and really forming a unit with Eger. The wines of the region are chiefly red, but there are some white ones. The white sparkling wine of Gyöngyös is usually considered the best of this style in Hungary. In general, the red wines, mostly based on Kadarka, approach or may surpass the Egers in smoothness or even delicacy, especially in the early years; but they lack the distinction and breed of such a wine as Egri Bikavér at its best.

Móri Ezerjó

The name is sometimes spelled as a single word. It is the wine of the Ezerjó ('a thousand good things') grape from the village of Mór—and five neighbouring villages with the right to use the wine name.

Mór is one of the oldest wine-growing regions in Hungary; mountainous, with vineyards on slopes of clay soil or a brownish-yellow loam. The wine is of a pale green hue and is found in the tall, slender 'Rhine-shaped' bottles. It tends to be very dry, and there is usually a little bite from the natural acidity which accompanies it.

Debrői Hárslevelü

This is made from the distinctively Hungarian grape variety Hárslevelü, one of those also producing Tokay. The wine achieves a very great deal of residual sugar, and can resemble a cheap Sauternes. It is golden, and comes in the 'Rhine-shaped' bottle.

The Wines of Balaton

Some of the very best wines of the country come from the shores of Lake Balaton in south-west Hungary. This is the largest lake in Europe. Thanks to its excellent position on the north shore of the lake, with the vineyards facing south over the reflector-shield of the water, and its soil of decomposed lava, the district of Badacsony numbers even more noble Growths than does Tokaj. Mount Badacsony is an extinct volcano.

The best known of the Badacsonys is Badacsonyi Kéknyelü, a dry greenish-white dessert wine which can achieve a firmness and breed reminiscent of the fine Rhine wines and the slate-Moselles. Its nearest competitor in popularity, and over on the sweet side, with a pleasant roundness and mellowness, is the golden Badacsonyi Szürkebarát. In this wine, unlike all the other Badacsonys, the second term in the nomenclature is not that of a grape variety; *szürkebarát* means 'Grey Friar'. The wine is made from the Pinot Gris.

The Olaszrizling vine produces a rather steely Badacsonyi Rizling and also the Balatonfüredi Rizling.

The First Great Growth wines are produced from the Furmint grape, the best of them Balatoni (or Badacsonyi) Furmint. The other first great growth Furmint is the Somlói Furmint from Somló near the head of the lake. The wines of the Somló and Ság hills in this region are typically greenish and demand a very long time to mature.

The Hungarian names 'Badacsonyi Rizling' and 'Balatoni Furmint' have been anglicized to 'Balatoni Riesling' and 'Balatoni Furmint' respectively for the United Kingdom.

Kadarka Wines of the South

Three full-bodied Kadarka wines are made in the regions of Szekszárd, near the Danube, and Villány and Pécs, close together and nearer the Yugoslav border. All are slope wines in mountainous country peppered with hamlets and villages with unpronounceable names, which fortunately are grouped for wine purposes under one or the other of the two First Great Growths: Szekszárdi Kadarka, and Villányi Kadarka. Of the three, Szekszárdi is the best known—no doubt ustifiably—as generally it will be subtler, with a greater nose than the others. The Szekszárdi soil, usually clayey and sometimes with a thick loam, also has some chalk in it. All the wines are fermented on the skins for a week or slightly longer.

SPIRITS

Hungary produces a wide range of liqueurs and brandies. The most famous is Barack Pálinka (apricot brandy), an unsweetened spirit distilled from fresh apricots which come from the orchards of Kecskemét. This is sold in the standard 70 cl. and 35 cl. bottles (24·6 and 12·3 British ounces, 23·7 and 11·8 U.S.) and in the traditional *Fütyülős* (flask) of 50 cl. (17·6 British ounces, 16·9 U.S.), which has a very long neck. From the same area comes Kecskeméti Barack Liqueur, a mellow apricot, rich with the fragrance of the fruit.

The best of the rest of the fruit liqueurs are the cherry brandy and the golden pear liqueur (Császárkorte in Hungarian). Another interesting liqueur is Hubertus, based on herbs and slightly more bitter in taste.

Of the other unsweetened spirits, the most renowned are Szilva Palinka or Szilvorium (plum brandy), Vodka, Kirsch or Eger, and Casino Rum. All of these are more or less known in Great Britain, Canada, the United States, and South America.

Hunter River Valley

Wine district of New South Wales, Australia. The vineyards here are the oldest in the country, and among the few that produce almost entirely table wines. They centre around Pokolbin and Cessnock.

See AUSTRALIA.

Hybrid

A cross between two different vine varieties, usually one of *Vitis vinifera* stock and one from an American species. The ultimate aim of the experimental hybridizer is to develop a vine with the hardiness and resistance to disease of American vines but bearing fruit of *Vitis vinifera* quality. A number of sound hybrids exist, and a few are very good for certain localities; but the field is still uncrowded. Hybridization is carried on in the United States (in New York, Maryland, and California), in Canada, and in European countries, notably Germany and France. The vines developed by French hybridizers usually bear the name of the hybridizer and a number. Some of the better-known names are Baco, Couderc, Siebel, and Seyne-Villard. Philip Wagner in Baltimore is contributing greatly through his hybrids to the improvement of Eastern American vineyards. Having found many hybrids that are indigenous to the climate and soil of the Eastern States, he is beginning to reduce the 'foxy' taste in the vines of this region.

See CHAPTER EIGHT, p. 30.

Hydromel

See MEAD.

Hydrometer, Sikes

In Great Britain, the hydrometer is legally recognized for measuring the strength of alcoholic beverages.

For comparison with French and American measures, *see* APPENDIX C.

Hymettus

Light wines, both red and white, produced near Mount Hymettus in Attica.

See GREECE.

I

Illinois

Wine-growing region in the United States. *See* AMERICA: EASTERN STATES.

Immiscible Liquids

Liquids which do not mix: the classic example, oil and wine. For this reason, wine was sealed by a thin film of olive oil before corks came into use.

Imperial (Impériale)

An outsized bottle, used for fine French Bordeaux wines put down for long keeping. The capacity of the imperial is approximately eight ordinary Bordeaux bottles or six litres.

Importation of Wine

The largest importers are not wineless countries (England or Scandinavia, for instance) but those which themselves produce wine on a considerable scale: France heads the list, Germany comes second, Switzerland third. The Portuguese possessions buy two-and-a-half times as much wine as does the United States. It is significant that certain countries which produce and export large quantities of wine also import a great deal.

IMPORTS OF WINE IN 1964

Importing country	*Hectolitres*	*Imperial gallons*	*U.S. gallons*
France	11,739,586	258,242,717	310,135,209
Germany	4,112,595	90,467,220	108,646,123
Switzerland	1,457,369	32,058,620	38,500,629
Portuguese Overseas territory	1,346,926	29,629,139	35,582,956
U.K.	1,230,635	27,071,016	32,510,792
Belgium and Luxembourg	816,932	17,970,543	21,581,628
Franc zone territory	660,000	14,518,416	17,435,814
East Germany	647,100*	14,234,647	17,095,023
U.S.A.	588,800	12,952,187	15,554,860
Netherlands	347,837	7,651,579	9,189,123
Czechoslovakia	334,269	7,353,116	8,830,685
Sweden	306,800	6,748,864	8,105,012
U.S.S.R.	304,200†	6,691,670	8,036,325
Austria	279,711	6,152,971	7,389,377
Canada	148,780	3,272,803	3,930,455
Denmark	146,800*	3,229,248	3,878,148
Italy	84,604	1,861,085	2,235,060
Finland	55,010	1,210,088	1,453,249
Norway	47,795	1,051,375	1,262,644
Eire	32,600*	717,122	861,224
Venezuela	31,078*	683,641	821,015
Hungary	30,000†	659,928	792,537
Mexico	11,362	249,937	300,160
New Zealand	10,670	234,714	281,879
Brazil	7,300†	160,582	192,851
Japan	6,497	142,918	171,637
South Africa	4,237†	93,204	111,933
Australia	4,100†	90,190	108,313
Malta	2,900†	63,793	76,612
Libya	2,700*	59,394	71,328
Syria	1,207	26,551	31,886
Portugal	1,056	23,229	27,897
Argentina	500	10,999	13,209

* = 1962 † = 1963

Incrustation

The formation of a crust in wines, specifically Ports.

India

The history of wine in India is sporadic, but it is known to have been made there two thousand years ago, and was still enjoyed in the era of the Moguls—Kashmir was then a wine region. In 1628, the monarch Jahangir was pictured on a coin with a goblet of wine in his hand. There were vineyards, then, at Golconda, Kandahar, and Surat. A century ago, the wines which had survived were those of Kashmir—some were shown at the Calcutta Exhibition of 1888. But the vines, which had been imported from Bordeaux, were attacked by phylloxera, and had to be grafted on to American root-stocks.

Today, there are a few vineyards near Madras. Started by French missionaries, about 1889, they have been enlarged in recent years around Kodaikanal, Dharmapuri, and Penukanda. Even so, this growing of vines is more of a hobby than a serious business, and the Madras market absorbs the harvest. At the other end of the sub-continent, in Kashmir, the surviving vines, which now show some of the characteristics of American species and grow half-wild, are used for table grapes. There is not much demand for wine among a people who do not much care for alcoholic drinks, or are forbidden, by their religion, to taste them.

Spirits, nevertheless, are manufactured in India. Not only fermented palm and rice drinks, but brandy, gin, rum, and whisky. In 1960 the following quantities were made:

	gallons imp.	*gallons U.S.*
Brandy	72,044	86,520
Gin	89,964	108,042
Whisky	168,377	202,210
Rum and bitter	243,114	291,968

Infectious Degeneration

A virus, or virus-like, vine disease, also known as fan leaf and court noué.

See CHAPTER EIGHT, p. 36.

Inferno

Red wine of Valtellina, in Italy, made from the Nebbiolo grape.

See LOMBARDY.

Ingelheimer

With Assmannshauser, this is one of the best—perhaps the best—of German red wines, but certainly not among the world leaders. For even at their best, German red wines are mediocre by world standards.

See RHEINHESSEN.

Inglenook Vineyards

Napa Valley, California

These vineyards were founded in 1879 by Captain Gustav F. Niebaum, on the slopes of Mount St. John. He kept the vineyards up until his death in 1908, when Inglenook was passed on to his nephew John Daniel, who directed operations throughout the Prohibition era. From the days of Repeal to the present time, John Daniel Jr. has successfully carried on the family tradition of growing fine grapes; and at present there are 225 acres in vines, the best of which are the Cabernet Sauvignon, Pinot Noir, Pinot Chardonnay, Pinot Blanc, Traminer, and Sémillon. Additional acres are planted in the Gamay of Beaujolais and the Merlot from Bordeaux.

The production at Inglenook is almost entirely in table wines; the sale of generic wines has been given up for the sake of concentrating on producing six white varietals, five red varietals, and a Gamay rosé. Inglenook was the first Californian vineyard to restrict output to varietal wines, although this did not happen until the late thirties. In 1964 the vineyard was sold to United Vintners (Petri).

See AMERICA: CALIFORNIA AND THE WEST.

Inspissated Wine

Boiled-down 'must' or unfermented grape juice used in flavouring or colouring certain wines.

Institut National des Appellations d'Origine

Commonly known as I.N.A.O.

See APPELLATION D'ORIGINE CONTRÔLÉE.

Iona

Native American hybrid grape, developed in New York where it is cultivated today mostly for sparkling white wine. The fruit is sweet and dark red, and it ferments into a clean, distinctive dry wine—one of several examples of white wine made from red grapes. The name comes from Iona Island, in the Hudson River near Peekskill

Iran (Persia)

The fame of Iran as a wine-making country is in the past, when it was one of the earliest lands to practise viniculture. According to one legend, wine was discovered accidentally by a Shah of Persia, and Herodotus says the Persians were deep drinkers. There are many other references to the wines, and to the size and prodigality of the vines, in classical literature. And even after the Moslem interdiction Omar Khayyam continued to sing the praises of his native wine. Shiraz was the celebrated wine, and there was a theory that the Syrah grape, grown now in the Rhône Valley and other places, was originally brought to western Europe from Shiraz, by returning Crusaders. Ancient vines, stout as trees, still grow there. Other famous wines (according to Mr. L. W. Marrison) were Khorasan and Mazandaran.

Today, vines grow in Iran mainly in the foothills of the mountains and especially in the north, in Alborz. Some are planted, also, in the hilly country in the centre and south-east. But most of these vines yield table grapes, the majority for domestic consumption, and grapes to be dried as raisins—some of these are exported. The quantity of wine is insignificant (between 40,000 and 42,000 imp. gallons (48,000 and 50,400 U.S.) a year). Principal centres are Khorasan, Fars, East Azerbaijan, Teheran, and Mazandaran.

Spirits

Arak is the principal spirit, and some 1,100,000 imp. gallons (1,321,000 U.S.) are made each year. Sometimes wine is reinforced with raki and sugar.

Irancy

Rather ordinary red and rosé wines produced in the department of Yonne, some ten miles south of Chablis in northern Burgundy.

Isabella

A prolific American grape, once highly thought of but now used almost exclusively for blending in the production of sparkling wine in New York State. The grape is blue, but it gives a pale, slightly 'foxy' wine with no pronounced characteristics. Unfortunately, it can also be found under the name 'Americano' in southern Switzerland.

Ischia

An island in the Bay of Naples which produces dry white wines, many of which are sold under 'Capri' labels.

See CAMPANIA.

Isinglass

A whitish, semi-transparent gelatinous substance obtained from the bladders of certain freshwater fishes, especially the sturgeon, and used for fining or clarifying wines and beers.

See CHAPTER NINE, p. 45.

Island Belle

North American grape for red wine of mediocre quality, planted notably in the State of Washington. Also known as Campbell's Early.

Islay

An island in the Inner Hebrides, off Scotland, which, with the near-by peninsula of Kintyre, produces all of the West Highland malt whisky distilled. There are about twice as many distilleries on Islay as at Campbeltown, the centre of the industry in Kintyre.

See WHISKY, MALT.

Israel

Wine of almost every type is made in Israel: red and white table wine; medicinal wine; sparkling wine for every palate—*brut*, extra dry, semi-dry, sweet—made by the Champagne method of secondary fermentation in bottle. All those designed for export are prepared under religious supervision, since for Jewish communities abroad they may be sacramental as well as beverage wines. Aperitifs, also, are produced, as are brandy and liqueurs.

The mainstays of Israel's production were, until recently, full-bodied, sweet red wines, golden muscatels and a sweet wine of the Tokay type. Now, however, dry and semi-dry table wines, both red and white, are gaining in popularity. In 1960, about 60% of the production was in table wine. In the past, appellations were often borrowed from other countries, and bottles might be labelled Carmel Malaga or Carmel Port. This practice is gradually being abandoned, and most of the wines have new Hebrew names. Some of the most important are as follows:

Sweet Dessert Wines

Muscatel. Partom and Vered (formerly Port). Topaz, Tokeah, Tivon, and Savion (formerly Tokay). Almog, Gilon, and Nalagenia (formerly 'Malaga'). Sharir ('Sherry'). Yakeneth ('Alicante'). Yashan Noshan. Yenon. Moriah. Atzmauth.

Dry and Semi-Dry Table Wines

Red. Adom Atic. Primor (formerly Pommard). Vin Rouge Supérieur. Château Windsor. Carmelith. Atzmon. Mont Rouge.

White. Carmel Hock. Mont Blem. Massadah. Château Montagne. Levanan. Doron.

Red and white. Avdad. Ashkalon. Ben-Ami.

Sparkling Wines

President.

Aperitifs

Vermouth (red, white, dry).

The main centres of production are near Tel-Aviv and south of Haifa. Other districts are Gederah, Northern Negev, the hilly region bordering the road to Jerusalem, and Galilee in the north.

Wine History

Palestine must have been among the earliest countries to enjoy wine. It is generally assumed that the first known vineyards were those of Anatolia, Persia, Mesopotamia, and Egypt, all of them growing vines over three thousand years ago. At an early date there was communication between Palestine and Egypt. A letter written about 1800 B.C. reported that Palestine was blessed with figs and with vineyards producing wine in greater quantity than water —in fact, 'the children of Israel sit each beneath his vine and his fig'. Another correspondent wrote that all the gardens of Palestine were full of fruit-giving vines, and the wine flowed from her cellars like waterfalls—this was about 1500 B.C.

The many references to wine in the Bible need not be repeated here. One of the first things Noah did, when the flood was over, was to begin 'to be a husbandman, and he planted a vineyard and he drank of the wine'. According to one theory, there actually was a flood and the approximate date was 2800 B.C. During the 18th Dynasty (1580–1450 B.C.) the Egyptians conquered Palestine, and again, about 925 B.C., Jerusalem was taken. When the Egyptian soldiers destroyed Israelite cities, they tore up the vineyards, but these were replanted and soon flourished again. As for Canaan, the land flowing with milk and honey flowed also with wine. In the Book of Numbers, ch. xiii, the story is told of how the two men Moses sent to spy out the land came back with a great cluster of grapes which they tied to a staff and carried between them. The place where they cut it down was named the brook Eshcol.

The vintners of biblical times were knowledgeable about wine-making (as was Mago of Carthage) and many of their customs are still known and respected today. In a country where there was sometimes more wine than water, the wine was used for all kinds of things as well as for drinking and as a medicine: houses were washed out with it, clothes were dyed in it—it has been estimated that the population used as much as 3–4 litres a head, every day.

Vines grew all over the country—on the hills, in the valleys, on the plain, even on the shores of the Dead Sea. Grapes were carefully selected for picking—the whole process was not unlike that in use in parts of Cyprus (*q.v.*). There were many different types: white; red or 'pretty' wine; dark coloured 'negro' wine; sultana wine; milk wine (a posset, perhaps); and asparagus wine, boiled with the vegetable. Various mixtures were prepared, also—honey and peppers with sweet wines, herbs and peppers with sharp wines. There was wine to be drunk at one year of age, at three years, or after long storage in cellars. Before big festivals, the wine was racked three times; and at the Feast of the Tabernacles, the booths were decorated with wine jars. Wines from Lebanon were highly thought of; and famous Helbon, to be bought in Damascus (Ezekiel, ch. xxvii) was a cooked white wine. It is probable that there were more white wines than red.

Wine production was at its peak in Palestine in the time of the Second Temple—destroyed in A.D. 70 in the war with the Romans. Many famous vineyards were then torn up. Some were reconstituted, but although the Jewish people continued for some time to cultivate the vine in a desultory way, production did not flourish again until modern times. Yet in the first four centuries of this era, Roman writers described various Palestine wines—Shechem, Lydda, Cæsarea, Ashkelon, and Gaza—which were highly esteemed and exported, to Syria, to Egypt, and even to England. After the Arab conquest (A.D. 600–1,000) most of the vineyards were uprooted; so strict was the Moslem prohibition that even table grapes were destroyed in case they should be pressed for wine.

In the Middle Ages, however, Crusaders found a few vineyards near the Mount Carmel range, near Bethlehem and Nazareth. Some of them stayed long enough to cultivate vines on their own account. In 1280 it was reported that 'Near Bethlehem there are still magnificent vines. The Moslems do not tend them, but the Christians make very good wine.' It seems that the Christians had to pay heavy taxes for the privilege; and that some Moslems living near the Christian settlements made wine to sell to their neighbours.

Wine of Modern Israel

Modern wine history in Palestine began in 1870, with the foundation of the first agricultural school. This started with a vineyard at Mikveh, bearing a few eating grapes, but mainly wine grapes, all of *Vitis vinifera*: Alicante, Bordeleau, Carignan, Petit Bouchet, and others. There were at this time some Christian monastic holdings, also planted in *Vitis vinifera*, but these were small. In 1880 the German Templars planted sizeable areas in the Carmel district. They brought their vines from the Rhine Valley, and made some good wine.

In 1882, at the time when the earliest Zionists were arriving in Israel, the first vineyards, under the patronage of Baron Edmond de Rothschild, were planted, again with *Vitis vinifera*. Soon there were large cellars in use, and vineyards at Shomron and in different parts of Galilee. In 1890 the area under Jewish cultivation was 7,000 acres, there was beginning to be a surplus of wine, and growers were considering problems of marketing and export when the phylloxera plague arrived, destroying many plants and putting an end to the surplus for some time. Rothschild advised the growers to replant with vines grafted on to American root-stocks.

By 1906 the industry was able to stand on its own, and Rothschild handed over to the growers the cellars at Rishon-le-Zion, near Tel-Aviv, and at Zikhron-Yaacov, south of Haifa. These are still the main centres. The name given to the co-operative which was then formed was Société Coopérative Vigneronne des Grandes Caves Rishon-le-Zion et Zikhron-Yaacov. It still functions today, producing 75% of the wine of Israel. The viticultural methods were French, introduced by Baron de Rothschild. These have been kept up-to-date and nowadays million-gallon concrete storage tanks are used, and all the latest processes for stabilizing the wines and for mechanized bottling.

To begin with, Israel's wine industry was run at a loss. Once the Jewish State was established (in 1948), with thousands of immigrants arriving, many from wine-growing countries, cultivation began to flourish. In the first five years, acreage doubled, and approximately 3,700 acres have since been added. Today, domestic consumption of wine is some 2,558,000 imp. gallons (3,072,000 U.S.) and there is a surplus of about 317,000 imp. gallons (380,000 U.S.) for export.

With so much of the land in new vine, the quality of the wine has not yet declared itself. Certain wines produced from European grape varieties grown in different regions of Israel are showing themselves to be pleasant and satisfactory; and a few of the Israel wines have lately won prizes at international competitions and exhibitions. They will undoubtedly continue to improve with the technical help and good equipment that is prevalent, thus making Israel into a good wine producer as regards both quality and quantity. In 1957, the Israeli Wine Institute was established for the purpose of scientific and market research, and the testing, for quality, of all wines for export.

RECENT PRODUCTION

For the years 1949–55, the average annual production was 1,600,000 imp. gallons (1,900,000 U.S.). In 1960 the yield was 3 million imp. gallons (3,600,000 U.S.) of wine and 500,000 imp. gallons (600,000 U.S.) of brandy. By 1964 production had shot up to 8,500,000 imp. gallons (10,300,000 U.S.). About 70% of this figure was made by the Co-operative Society of Wine-Growers, Rishon-le-Zion, and Zikhron-Yaacov. Other important wineries are Eliaz, Friedman-Tnuvah, and Carmel Zion. About 500 growers are today members of the Co-operative Society, which is responsible for some 90% of the export trade in wine. In 1952 the Society established in the U.S.A. a company called Carmel Wine Co. Inc., New York, and this is their representative for wines exported anywhere in the United States or Canada. There is also a branch in Great Britain—The Carmel Wine Company. This is almost as old as modern viticulture in Israel, for it was founded in 1897, only fifteen years after the revival of the Palestine vineyards. Wines and spirits are imported partly in bottle, and partly in bulk for London bottling. Great Britain and America are Israel's principal customers, but wine is exported in smaller quantities to twenty-six other countries.

Château d'Issan

Bordeaux red wine. District: Haut-Médoc, France. Commune: Cantenac-Margaux.

Before the disruption of the Austro-Hungarian Empire during the First World War, Château d'Issan was the favourite wine of the Royal Court of Vienna. The Emperor refused to drink any other, and everyone else followed his lead.

'For the Table of Kings and the Altar of God' is the proud motto of the vineyard, and may be seen carved in the stone of the gate. The beautiful seventeenth-century château, itself a replacement of a fortress-castle of the thirteenth century, had begun to collapse by 1952–3 when restoration was begun.

Lying across the vineyard road from Château Prieuré-Lichine on the north of the village of Cantenac, Château d'Issan, owned by Madame M. E. Cruse, approaches Château Palmer and is entitled to the place-name of Margaux. It is a Third Growth (*Troisième Cru*) in the Classification of 1855. Unfortunately, label and name have suffered near-oblivion. The wine is now bottled in the *chais* of the Cruse firm, and is therefore not château-bottled.

Characteristics. While the delicacy and the typical taste of a Margaux are present, the wines have a body and fleshiness slightly reminiscent of those farther to the north of the Médoc, the Pauillacs, for example.

Vineyard area: 37 acres.

Average production: 6,000 cases.

Italy

The Italian likes his wines heady, robust, and, above all, plentiful. He is the most natural wine-drinker in the world, downing his annual 23 imp. gallons (28 U.S.) a head of wine—good, bad, or indifferent—with the greatest satisfaction. The ordinary wine may be rough, incompletely fermented, thick, lacking in finesse; but it will always be a welcome accompaniment to the meal.

Italy has been described as one vast vineyard—and the description is apt. Vines spill out everywhere: climb trees and drape their branches, run along roads and hang festooned from fences, flourish in glorious disorder beside olive-trees, and in fields of grain. The vine grows easily, flowering into great bunches of grapes. One does not see nearly so many of the serried ranks of disciplined, close-trimmed vineyards here as in France and Germany. And Italian viniculture is sometimes as easy-going as its viticulture. Indeed, in some vineyards it seems that the vintner's main concern is with getting wine from fermenting vat to mouth in the shortest possible time. Wines splash constantly from one end of the country to the other.

In 1964 Italy became the world's largest producer of wine: the country is also the third largest wine exporter in the world. Italy makes some 1,454,570,000 imp. gallons (1,746,857,000 U.S.) of wine yearly (these in fact are the figures for 1964) and exports some 51,038,000 imp. gallons (61,294,000 U.S.). In the list of wine-importing countries, Italy comes seventeenth, importing 1,861,000 imp. gallons (2,235,000 U.S.). Yet the total vineyard acreage is beginning to shrink, and steep mountain plots are being abandoned in favour of those on the plains or the easy slopes; the reasons, that the young men are leaving the land for the cities, that wages are rising, and as much as possible of the work must be done where machinery can be used. The decrease in acreage in 1962 was 0·72%. There are about two million vineyard workers registered in Italy—28% of the agricultural labour force; but peasant owners of small parcels might bring the number up to four million. In 1960–1 the money made by wine represented 11% of the whole agricultural revenue.

Some of the wines are excellent—among the best of them, the Barolos and Barbarescos of Piedmont, the Valpolicellas and Soaves of Veneto, and Tuscany's celebrated Chianti—and, indeed, the traveller may discover an exceptional bottle almost anywhere along the road. But, unfortunately, these fine wines are not always to be found. Many of the best wines of Italy are made, for their own consumption, by the smaller growers who sell what surplus they have to old-established customers, often inherited along with the vineyard—and the casual tourist is unlikely to meet with such a cultivator or his wine. What he will normally drink will be the output of the large companies—standardized wine, its quality depending entirely upon the firm which makes it.

Wine Controls

Italian wines have suffered not only from the haphazard methods of the vinicultor but also from an easy-going attitude to nomenclature which has made it possible for wines which did not even deserve the name Tuscan to be sold under the label of Chianti. The root of the trouble was the Government's failure to safeguard the place-names of the fine wine regions—and this in spite of repeated attempts to bring in legislation, along the lines of the French Appellation d'Origine, for the control of these place-names. (The most important contribution was made by Dr. Fignoletto.) The same struggle occurred, of course, in France, but was brought much earlier to a satisfactory conclusion.

The French Government, afraid of having its market flooded with cheap Italian wines as the tariff barriers were constantly lowered to comply with the Common Market agreements, urged the Italian Government to set up control laws, somewhat along the lines of the Appellations d'Origine Contrôlée.

Denominazioni di Origine

Hence at last, in July 1963, regulations for controlling place-names, or denomination of origin, were made law. There are three different denominations, graded as follows:

(a) Simple
   e.g. Rosso Toscano, a wine from the vinestock Rosso anywhere inside Tuscany.

(b) Controlled
   e.g. Barolo, a fine wine of Piedmont, produced only in Barolo, Castiglione Faletto, Serralunga d'Alba, and parts of Monforte d'Alba, La Morra, Verduno, Monchiero, and Diano d'Alba.

(c) Controlled and guaranteed
   e.g. a true Barolo sealed and labelled with the official insignia. Wine for export may bear the red seal of the I.C.E., or Institute for Foreign Trade.

Although regulations stipulate, for any controlled wine, the name of the exact place of origin (e.g. Marsala), a wine with the requisite qualifications which has been made in the surrounding district for ten years or more may also be allowed the place-name (e.g. Marsala, produced in the neighbourhood of Marsala).

Simple denomination (*Denominazione di Origine Semplice*) is allowed to ordinary wines made from grapes traditionally cultivated in an area—the zones are determined by decree of the Ministry of Agriculture and Forestry. But such wines carry no official guarantee of quality; no provision is made for special control, and only in doubtful cases of territorial complication does the law demand that the zone of production be defined by ministerial decree.

Controlled denomination (*Denominazione di Origine Controllata*) is an appellation reserved for wines which have achieved the stipulated standards for quality. Vineyards producing such wines are inscribed in an official register.

Controlled and guaranteed denomination (*Denominazione di Origine Controllata e Garantita*) is awarded only to fine wines attaining qualities and prices established after the recommendation of the Ministry of Agriculture and Forestry. Such wines must be sold in containers not exceeding 5 litres (1·1 imp. gallon; 1·3 U.S.). The labels must state that the origin of the wine is controlled and guaranteed, the net content of the bottle, the name of the grower and bottler, the place of bottling, and also the alcoholic strength. Growers who wish to have their wine classified in this top category must send in a request to the Ministry of Agriculture and Forests, for a government inspector, who will have the wine analysed. Such applications must be backed by copious documentation as to region, average annual production, details of vine variety, characteristics of wines, etc. For wines of controlled and guaranteed origin the application can only be recognized if it has the support of a fair percentage of the growers concerned. The recognition of these two higher denominations is finally effected by the President of the Republic on the advice of the Ministries concerned. From that time forth, the wine-makers must adhere strictly to the following rules:

1. Inscription of the vineyards in the appropriate register, with compulsory declaration of production and stocks.
2. Correct labelling of bottles and flasks.
3. Inspection by members of voluntary organizations delegated by the Ministry of Agriculture.
4. Co-operation in preventive steps taken to repress fraud and assert the controls of the denomination of origin.
5. Paying of penalties for infraction of the regulations.

The National Institute for the Inspection of Denomination of Origin (*Istituzione del Comitato Nazionale per la Tutela delle Denominazioni di Origine*) is nominated by the Ministry of Agriculture and Forestry in association with the Ministry of Industry and Commerce. It is composed of a President and twenty-eight members, representing the ministries involved, and including one from the I.C.E. The function of this committee is to promote and watch over the controlled and guaranteed Italian wines, and to initiate studies for their improvement. Although membership of this class of denomination is voluntary, it is considered that all the better producers are anxious to win the certificate of guarantee for export, and very ready to submit their wines for inspection and analysis.

Because membership is voluntary, not all wine for export is so controlled—it is up to the customer to read the label before he buys a bottle of Italian wine. Some of the controlled wine (in particular, that shipped to Great Britain) is exported in casks. These will be sealed with the official seal—but it has been suggested by the I.C.E. that, if this control is to mean anything, its officials should also inspect the wine after it has been bottled by the importer to prevent the prevailing abuses in the United Kingdom.

Following what was undoubtedly a regrettable lack of controls, these new laws are certainly to be commended. Assuming the Common Market becomes effective, it will still take many years for the lesser wines to achieve the desired quality. First, everyone concerned in the Italian wine trade will have to be persuaded that it is worth sacrificing quantity of production to quality. The law of 9 October 1964, amending and replacing earlier regulations which had become out of date and ineffective, requires the Government to issue a decree controlling the production of musts, wines, and vinegars, and establishing regulations to prevent fraud in the preparation and sale of these products.

The Consorzi

Inside Italy, any of the local *consorzi* may, if they wish, check up on the control of their wines and help to safeguard the regulations. Before the introduction of the Denomination of Origin laws, the only wine which carried any guarantee of quality was that wearing the seal of a local wine society or *consorzio*. The system is voluntary. Some regions have a *consorzio*, others do not; and where one exists, some firms and growers may be members, others may not. Both members and non-members, unfortunately, had equal right to the local appellation, although members alone could receive the *consorzio* seal. One consequence of this vague arrangement (in the years before the regulations of 1963) was the predicament of Chianti.

True Chianti is a specified red wine made in a specific area and, moreover, in fairly small quantities—roughly 2,200,000 imp. gallons (2,640,000 U.S.) of Classico, and 6,600,000 imp. gallons (7,900,000 U.S.) for all *consorzi*, annually. Yet estimated sales were, a few years ago, anything from 41 million imp. gallons (50 million U.S.). Some of the wine came from Tuscany and bore some resemblance to the real thing. Much more was concocted from Chianti or other Tuscan wine, stretched and blended with inferior growths from elsewhere. It is hoped that the *Denominazioni di Origine* laws will succeed in protecting these fine wines and controlling the sales.

As for the *consorzi*, the standards for each are drawn up by its members and are thus subject to wide variation. Sometimes they are so high that their wines will always be excellent; sometimes they settle for a fairly low average. They generally dictate the permitted grape varieties, the limits of the district, the minimum alcoholic content, and whether or not wines may be imported from outside the area. A universal rule is that all wine must be tasted by a select committee and approved before the seal is given—and affixed in such a way that the bottle cannot be opened without the seal's being broken. Each *consorzio* has its own apparatus for enforcing rules, and in cases of gross or repeated

ITALY
BEST-KNOWN WINES
Aglianico del Vulture — 1
Albana — 2
Aleatico di Portoferraio — 3
Asti Spumante — 4
Barbera — 5
Barbaresco — 6
Bardolino — 7
Barolo — 8
Capri — 9
Castelli Romani — 10
Chianti — 11
Cinque Terre — 12
Cirò — 13
Est! Est!! Est!!! — 14
Frascati — 15
Gattinara — 16
Gragnano — 17
Lacrima Christi — 18
Lago di Caldaro — 19
Lambrusco — 20
Marsala — 21
Moscato di Pantelleria — 22
Orvieto — 23
Sangiovese — 24
S. Maddalena — 25
Soave — 26
Valpantena — 27
Valpolicella — 28
Verdicchio — 29
SWITZERLAND
AUSTRIA
HUNGARY
FRANCE
YUGOSLAVIA
ADRIATIC SEA
TYRRHENIAN SEA
IONIAN SEA
VALLE D'AOSTA
PIEDMONT
LIGURIA
LOMBARDY
TRENTINO ALTO ADIGE
FRIULI-VENEZIA-GIULIA
VENETO
EMILIA ROMAGNA
TUSCANY
UMBRIA
MARCHES
ABRUZZI
LATIUM
CAMPANIA
BASILICATA
APULIA
CALABRIA
SICILY
MARSALA
L. Maggiore
L. Como
L. Caldaro
L. Trasimeno
R. Dora Baltea
R. Ticino
R. Po
R. Adige
R. Arno
R. Tiber
R. Volturno
Turin
Asti
Gattinara
Milan
Bergamo
Bolzano
Trento
Verona
Padua
Venice
Genoa
Bologna
Ravenna
Forli
Florence
Pisa
Leghorn
Siena
Montepulciano
Perugia
Portoferraio
ELBA
Montefiascone
Rome
Foggia
Naples
ISCHIA
CAPRI
Potenza
Brindisi
Taranto
Palermo
Messina
Reggio
MT. ETNA
Syracuse
PANTELLERIA
N
MILES
KILOMETRES

violation the penalty may be expulsion. A degree of collaboration between the *consorzi* and the Institute for Inspection of Denomination of Origin could result in a great improvement in the overall standard of Italian wines.

Wine Regions

The Italian peninsula is characterized by its ever-changing landscape. The Alps give way to the Apennines, and plains and mountains alternate, all the way down to the rugged hills of the 'arch' and 'toe' of the Italian 'boot'. In general the finest wines are made in the north, but the south has several that are entrancing, particularly when drunk on the spot. The Italians have divided their nation into regions, or administrative sub-sections, and it is convenient to discuss the wines under these categories. The regions and their wines (*see the principal districts also under separate headings*) include:

Abruzzi

This region on the Adriatic seaboard gives way to central Italy. It produces some unpretentious and often pleasant wines. Red Montepulciano di Abruzzo and Cerasuolo di Abruzzo, and white Trebbiano di Abruzzo are all names for the dominant contributing grape variety, and are all agreeable at home, but would almost certainly lose some of this charm were they to be shipped.

Apulia

The great, southern, bulk-producing plain of Italy. The output is generally used for making vermouth, for blending, or for ordinary wines.

Basilicata (Lucania)

This southern region, once known as Lucania, is a jumble of forbidding mountains and inaccessible valleys. Some wine is made. The best known is Aglianico del Vulture; the first part of the name is that of the vine; the second of the mountain on which it is cultivated. Fairly large amounts of Muscat and Malvasia vines are also grown.

Calabria

The extreme southern tip of Italy. Sweet white Greco di Gerace (from Greco grapes) and deep red Cirò di Calabria (mainly from Gaglioppo grapes grown in Cirò) are the best-known wines; lovers of Muscats may also find the region to their liking.

Campania

The most popular wines in this region around Naples are the red and dry white Falerno, red Vesuvio, mainly from the Aglianico grape and grown on the volcanic foothills of Mount Vesuvius, and the red and white Ravello grown near the charming village of that name on the Amalfi coast. Also from this region comes Lacrima Christi, generally a soft and fairly dry white wine, though a little red is also produced. Close to Amalfi is made the red Gragnano which is so delicious to drink on a flower-laden terrace over the Bay of Naples; and from the islands of Capri and Ischia come the gay light wines known as Capri.

Emilia-Romagna

A vast agricultural area in central Italy, not outstanding for wines. Red, usually slightly sweet, Lambrusco is often recommended to newcomers, and Albana accommodates those who like their wines white and not too dry. Neither is an outstanding prospect for export. A large amount of Sangiovese (red) is also made on the hills of Romagna.

Latium

The wines of the Castelli Romani (Castles of Rome), among the country's best, are generally dry and white, and are almost invariably captivating on their native ground—the best-known is Frascati. Many withstand the rigours of ocean travel. Est! Est!! Est!!! from Montefiascone is the white, dry, and semi-sweet wine with the best wine legend of Italy (*see* EST! EST!! EST!!!).

Liguria

The Italian extension of the French Riviera is not famous for wine. Dry and slightly sweet white Cinque Terre is about the best-known, although there are others, such as Dolceacqua (red), etc.

Lombardy

The Valtellina reds, Sassella, Grumello, Valgella, Fracia, and Inferno are highly prized; and the wines from the banks of Lake Garda are often delightful; they come in all three colours, but the rosés are probably the best, especially the Chiaretto.

The Marches

No wines of great distinction are made in this area between the Apennines and the Adriatic. The principal red wine is Rosso Piceno; and Verdicchio dei Castelli di Jesi is white, usually well made, often found abroad.

Piedmont

The home of Italy's two finest red wines, Barolo and Barbaresco, and also of the sparkling, sweet Asti Spumante. Other good still wines are Freisa,

Barbera, Gattinara, Grignolino d'Asti, and Nebbiolo Piemontese.

Sardinia
Most of the noteworthy wines on this rugged island are Muscats and Malvasias, sweet, sometimes fortified dessert wines.

Sicily
Sicilian Marsala could have been imitation Port, but quite properly chose its own style, and its own name. When authentic, it can be superb, and the Moscato di Noto and Moscato di Siracusa are sweet, strong dessert wines with a distinctive taste. Although one is inclined to associate Sicily with sweet fortified wines, some agreeable table wines are produced here, too; white Mamertino, red Faro, straw-yellow and red Corvo di Casteldaccia, and the red and white wines of Etna, grown at the foot of the still active volcano, Mount Etna.

Trentino-Alto Adige
The wines from Riesling and Traminer grapes generally go flooding into Austria (which once owned the Alto Adige) and Switzerland, and might stand shipment elsewhere. Santa Maddalena is a red wine much appreciated by Italy's northern neighbours.

Tuscany
The best—and most famous—wine is Chianti. There are a number of different Chiantis, but the growers of the 'Classical' Chianti district maintain that only they have a real right to the appellation. Under different names, some of the others would be wonderful wines, but they are not always true Chiantis.

Umbria
This section north of Rome is the home of Orvieto. Traditionally sweet, this beguiling wine is now being made dry as well, and conservative drinkers are not wholeheartedly in favour of the trend. The dry is becoming the rule rather than the exception.

Veneto
The wines of the Verona district are the best of this region and include dry red Valpolicella, Valpantena, and Bardolino, and dry white Soave.

Friuli-Venezia Giulia, Valle d'Aosta, and Molise
The three remaining regions of Italy are not very important as far as wine production is concerned.

Ives

Native American variety of grapes, hardy and vigorous but inconsistent. The red coarse-skinned grape yields a strong 'foxy' red wine.

Izarra

A Basque attempt to reproduce Chartreuse, made in Bayonne in south-west France. Like its more famous prototype, it is fabricated in two styles, yellow and green, of which the green is the more highly alcoholic.

J

James

American muscadine grape sometimes used in the south for making a strongly flavoured, not very agreeable wine.

Japan

From Kyushu in the south to northernmost Hokkaido, the Japanese islands count some 41,000-odd acres of vines producing both table and wine grapes. By 1963 production had risen to over 10 million imp. gallons (12 million U.S.), yet for every Japanese who picks up a glass of wine there are a hundred who reach for sake or beer. Consumption of sake (brewed from rice), beer, and other grain beverages has reached enormous proportions and the public has been warned that this consumption must be reduced to conserve the dwindling grain supply. Wine is being presented as a possible alternative.

The wine-growing regions of Japan are the Yamanashi and Osaka districts and to a lesser extent those of Yamagata and Nagano—equally large but producing still more mediocre wines. All are on the principal island of Honshu which is the only island producing any considerable amount of wine. The combination of high humidity and acid soil makes grape growing difficult and the vines selected must be early ripeners to mature before the torrential September rains destroy the labour of an entire summer. About 100 vines to the acre are planted at distances of roughly 20 feet. They grow on trellises, or in among vegetables. The total acreage of vineyards is something like 24,700.

Japan is one of the few countries in the world where the three families of vine—European, American, and Asian—are able to flourish. Yet none of the three produces with any quality in Japanese soil. Varieties of the American *Vitis labrusca* and some of the hybrid vines are about the only ones which yield adequate and occasionally agreeable wines. The Japanese Koshu vine and Delaware Campbell's Early account for a good percentage, although the European Sémillon is increasingly used for white wines, and Cabernet Sauvignon, with some Merlot, accounts for 75% of the reds. In general, European vines are particularly susceptible to such fungus diseases as mildew and oïdium, both of which run rampant in the humid climate of Japan.

Although the history of the Japanese vine goes back to the twelfth century, the story of Japanese wine is as recent as the nineteenth. Vines have always been used as decoration, and grapes for medicinal purposes, but wines had to await the influx of Europeans and Americans. The Japanese, agriculturally inquisitive by nature, responded to the new idea and sent people to France and to California to study the wine industry. The twentieth century has seen this industry grow and prosper in Japan but it has yet to come into its own.

Too many of the Japanese vineyards are small and hindered by inexperienced personnel and poor handling. There are many co-operatives, but these are generally no better equipped or managed than the others. A shining exception is the Sado-ya in the Kofu Valley of the Yamanashi district where some quite pleasant wines are made from such European grapes as Merlot, Cabernet Sauvignon, Sémillon, Malbec, and Pinot Blanc. However, the general run of Japanese wines is poor and table wines lag well behind dessert wines, sparkling wines and 'port'- and 'sherry'-types. A commentary on quality has been given by a Japanese scientist writing on Japanese 'port'. According to Isama Yokosuka, in the *American Journal of Œnology*: 'Natural production of Port wine by fermentation is not performed. Instead Port wine is made by blending 1–15% wine with ethyl alcohol, tap water, dye, perfume, sugar, and organic acids, and the resulting product is unduly poor in quality.'

Japanese Beetle

A parasite which attacks American vines.

See CHAPTER EIGHT, p. 38.

Jasnières

Loire Valley white wines. District: Anjou, France.

A tiny Loire vineyard district in the Coteaux du Loir, north of the main stream. The wines are white and *moelleux*, or semi-sweet, and come from Chenin Blanc grapes grown in predominantly chalky soil. The vineyards are in the twin parishes of Lhomme and Ruillé-sur-Loir, and their output is not high.

Jenever

The name used in Holland for Dutch gin; which in English-speaking countries is usually called Hollands. Jenever is a combination of the French and Dutch words for juniper, on which the gin taste is based, and has no connexion with the Swiss city.

Jerez de la Frontera

Andalusian town which is the centre of the Sherry trade.

See SHERRY.

Jeriñac

A registered name (also occasionally spelled Xereñac and Cherinac) for the brandy of Jerez de la Frontera, Spain. A little-used and unsuccessful substitute for the improper designation Coñac for Spanish brandy (because Cognac, however spelled, may correctly only be the brandy of Cognac in France).

See SPAIN.

Jeroboam

An outsize bottle, the capacity of which is open to variation. In Champagne, it holds the equivalent of four bottles; in Bordeaux, five. In England it is normally (but not necessarily) six.

Jeropiga

See GEROPIGA.

Jigger

American term for shot-glass, or small measure of spirits. It equals 1½ fluid ounces.

Johannisberg

1. Great growth of the Rheingau. The best-known of these wines is Schloss Johannisberger.

See RHEINGAU.

2. Swiss wine from the Sylvaner grape which probably owes its renown to the fact that it shares the name of the great German Johannisberger.

See SWITZERLAND.

Johanniswein

From as early as *Minnesinger* records of the thirteenth century, St. John, who sat next to Christ at the Last Supper, and to whom legend ascribes the drinking of a goblet of poisoned wine without harm, after he had made the sign of the Cross over it, has been connected in a special way with the blessing of wine in Germany. In Deidesheim, on St. John's day, 27 December, the folk of the community take an especially fine bottle from their vineyards to Mass for blessing. This St. John's Wine, as it is called, is considered not only beneficial to health and fertility, but a bringer of peace as well, and it is often drunk as a loving-cup. Johanniswein is also much in demand for a wedding drink, and in many parts of Germany farewell drinks of 'one for the road' are often served in St. John's Wine. It is known that Martin Luther himself served these.

Jordan

Although in the distant past vineyards flourished in this part of the world and wine was regarded as a good familiar thing, some 45,000 acres of land now planted in vine are devoted almost entirely to table grapes.

The inhabitants of Jordan are not wine-drinking people; here, as elsewhere in the area, more arrack is made than wine—for which, in 1960, the total production figure was 33,000 imp. gallons (39,000 U.S.).

Josephshof

Throughout the world (except in Germany where Himmelreich is more famous) this is the best-known vineyard of the Graach district of the German Moselle. Inclined, like the other Graach wines, to be long-lasting and mouth-filling, for a Moselle, this is almost the only one known by the vineyard name alone. It is called simply Josephshof; the township name of Graach does not appear.

See MOSELLE.

Julep

A long, cold drink made with spirits, sugar, mint, and crushed ice.

Juliénas

Widely-known wines of the French Beaujolais. They tend to be obvious and seldom come quite up to the reputation of the other more famous villages, Fleurie, Brouilly, or the wine of Moulin-à-Vent.

See BEAUJOLAIS.

Jura

Red, white, and rosé wines. District: Jura Mountains, France.

From the slopes of the Jura Mountains, lying midway between the Côte d'Or of Burgundy and the Swiss border to the east, come a number of wines which make up in variety what they lack in quantity. Still and sparkling wines, red, white, and rosé wines, *vins de paille* or 'straw wines', and the curious *vins jaunes*, or yellow wines, are all made under the inclusive *appellation* Côtes-du-Jura or Côtes-du-Jura Mousseux. Arbois, Château-Chalon, and L'Étoile are more specific: L'Étoile wines may only be white or *jaune*; the best white wines of the region are made at Arbois.

A landscape of sunny plains and steep cliffs, the Jura region has a wide variety of soil. Ranging from the almost pure clay of the lowlands, through the pebbly marl which has eroded the base of the cliffs, to the limestone-rich silt at the top, these slopes were once producers of wine in great quantity. The advent of phylloxera caused the vineyards to shrink drastically, and they have never been reconstituted. From about 46,000 acres planted in 1836, the figure has dropped so far that today there are less than 1,500 acres devoted to fine vines in the whole Jura area.

Perhaps the most characteristic wine of the Jura is the *vin jaune*. Coming exclusively from the grape variety known as the Savagnin, thought to be of Hungarian origin, this wine is one of the longest-lived—drinkable bottles aged fifty years or more are by no means rare. To obtain *vin jaune*, the grapes are harvested late and are pressed in the same manner as for white wine. The juice is then sealed up in barrels and remains there for a length of time which varies from six to ten years—six years is the legal minimum. Shortly after the wine is put into the barrels, a film forms on the top, effectively sealing it off from the air. This film, which is made up of micro-organisms, lives on oxygen from the air and contributes the peculiar yellow colour and nutty fragrance that mark *vin jaune*. The film, or 'flower', is the same as is found in the making of Sherry, where it is called *flor*. It is related to a disease of wine caused by the vinegar microbe which combines oxygen and alcohol to make vinegar. The difference is that the vinegar microbe spoils the wine completely, whereas the microbe which appears on the wine of the Jura changes it slightly, with beneficial effect, and remains the same white colour as long as it is allowed to stand.

Another type of wine made in the Jura is the *vin de paille*. It derives its name from the time-honoured process of allowing the grapes to dry out on beds of straw before pressing, as well as from the straw colour of the wine. Actually, *vin de paille* is usually made today by hanging the grapes up in well-ventilated rooms. The long drying process, which by law must be at least two months, provides a wine of richness and longevity. Because of the difficulties of making this wine, and particularly because of the high price at which it has to be sold, the growers of the Jura are turning away from it, and there is some reason to fear that *vin de paille* may disappear from the area.

Very few of the wines of the Côtes-du-Jura are exported or shipped. Some is sold to Alsace and Switzerland, both in the vicinity of the Jura, but for the most part it is drunk in the area where it is made. One reason for this is that the wine is much appreciated by those who make it; and another is that, distinctive and unusual though they may be, the wines of the Jura are generally considered among *vins de pays*, excellent when drunk on native ground, but unable to stand comparison with the great wines of France. The wine of lesser quality, sold under the inclusive *appellation* Côtes-du-Jura, accounts for less than 166,000 imp. gallons (200,000 U.S.) a year, and the balance is sold under the more exclusive names Arbois, Château-Chalon, and L'Étoile.

Arbois

Perhaps the best-known of the wines of the Jura. Made in thirteen towns in the lower foothills of the Jura Mountains, centring around the charming town of Arbois, it includes all the types described above.

The Savagnin grape variety, in addition to making *vin jaune*, also goes into the white wine to augment the Melon d'Arbois (as the Chardonnay variety is called in that area) and the Pinot Blanc *vrai*. The Poulsard, the Trousseau, and the Gros Noiren (the Pinot Noir of Burgundy) are the varieties that go into the red and rosé wines. Some of the white wines can be extremely pleasant. The red wines are not considered distinctive, but many Frenchmen, particularly around the Arbois area, maintain that the Rosé d'Arbois is on a par with Tavel. Expert opinion, however, ranks it lower than this famous rosé wine of the Rhône.

The town of Arbois, besides being famous for its wines, is also known as the birthplace of Louis Pasteur, and as the place where he performed his famous experiments on wine. These experiments were made when the growers became concerned about the way their wines were spoiling on ocean voyages. The work had world-wide repercussions.

Château-Chalon

To the south and slightly to the west of the Arbois area is the small town of Château-Chalon, which gives its name to the wine grown there and in three adjoining towns. Under the Appellation d'Origine laws, only *vin jaune* is allowed to be sold under the name. This wine remains in the barrel for as long as six years; an excessive period for a white wine. At the end of this period the wine must—by law—be bottled. Less than 200 hectolitres (4,400 imp. gallons; 5,200 U.S.) is made each year.

The name is derived from an old castle which overlooks the area but which has nothing to do with the vineyards. (Note, therefore, that this is *not* a château wine.) Always bottled in wide, rather square bottles called *clavelins*, the only wine allowed to be put into such bottles, the *vin jaune* of Château-Chalon is considered to be the best example of this unique wine.

L'Étoile

Some of the best white wines of the Jura come from the southernmost area, that of L'Étoile, which comprises a small region of three communes. With an average production of less than 21,000 imp. gallons (25,000 U.S.), L'Étoile produces within its small area all the white wine types allowed in the Jura—white, yellow, *vin de paille*, and sparkling wines.

Jurançon

White wines. District: South-West France.

The vines are grown on the extremely steep hillsides in the foothills of the French Pyrenees—hillsides which are, for the most part, too steep to be cultivated by anything except the hand of man, although in some places animal and tractor power may be used. A limited amount of wine is grown along these slopes and among the foothills, the best towards the Atlantic—in the Jurançon region, near the city of Pau. The deep golden-white wines are usually sweet and have a flowery perfume uniquely their own. Only white wines are made.

At one time the vineyards of Jurançon were vast and important, but since the scourge of the phylloxera, they have never reached their former productiveness. Some of the local growers are said to have shown a strong prejudice against grafting their vines on to American root-stocks—the only effective way of restoring the vineyards.

The spring frosts have a deadly effect upon the young shoots—and to combat this the vines are grown very tall. Stakes with cross-arms, making them look like fields of crosses—the unusual aspect of the region—support the vines, which are anywhere from four to six feet high. The productive parts of the vines are those trained on wires running from three to four feet from the ground, along which the vine shoots are trailed after the danger of frosts has passed.

The noble vines of the Jurançon area are the Gros Manseng, Petit Manseng, and Courbu, all of them old and all peculiar to the region. The wine made must be 85% from these vines and no more than 15% from the Camaralet and Lauzet, the permissible secondary varieties. The vines are trimmed to carry from one to four long shoots, cut to yield from nine to fifteen cluster-producing buds or eyes. Short pruning (leaving only two or three eyes) is forbidden, and if a vine overproduces at the expense of its growth, it is regulated by leaving less shoots the next year. The fourth year after planting, the vines can produce grapes which may be included in the making of Jurançon wine. The maximum legal yield is 216 imp. gallons (260 U.S.) per acre.

The harvest in the Jurançon region is an extremely late one, the growers usually waiting for the *pourriture noble*, or noble rot, to form on their over-ripe grapes—this dries the liquid from them and leaves only a small amount of honey syrup. Sometimes the grapes are left on the vines until after Hallowe'en. The rich, sweet wine is kept for four years in the barrel before it is bottled—and would probably be much better if it were bottled younger. Too much rather poor dry wine is produced—which has given this district a bad name. Less than 34,000 imp. gallons (40,000 U.S.) is made each year—and much of it is consumed in the region of the Pyrenees, although the wine can be bought in Paris and elsewhere.

K

Kabinettwein

German term for Cabinet Wine, or a special reserve, denoting wines from the better selected barrels. This is more than just a term, and can be considered as a reliable line of quality demarcation, mainly based on price.

See GERMANY

Kadarka

The leading red variety of grape in Hungary, known also in Rumania as Codarcă.

Kæfferkopf

Important vineyard in Ammerschwihr, Alsace.

See ALSACE.

Kafir, Kefir

A Caucasian alcoholic beverage made from fermented cows' milk (*see* KOUMISS). Kefir grain is added.

Kaiserstuhl

Best vineyard area in German Baden (*q.v.*).

Kallstadt

Wine town in the district of Bad-Dürkheim.

See PALATINATE.

Kamptal, Kamp Valley

Wine region of the River Kamp in Lower Austria. Some of the best slopes for vineyards are those of the Heiligenstein and the Gnisberg.

See AUSTRIA.

Kanyak

Turkish brandy whose name, to the suspicious, seems remarkably close to Cognac.

Karthäuserhofberg

Outstanding vineyard in the German town of Eitelsbach.

See RUWER.

Kasel

Most important village of German Ruwer wines. The best vineyard is Kaseler Nies'chen.

See RUWER.

Kava, Ava-Ava

A native wine of the South Sea Islands prepared from the root of the Polynesian kava shrub.

'The liquor which they make from the plant called the ava-ava is expressed from the root. The manner of preparing this liquor is as simple as it is disgusting to a European. It is thus: several people take some of the root, and chew it until it is soft and pulpy: then they spit it out into a platter or other vessel, every one into the same: when a sufficient quantity is chewed more or less, water is put to it according as it is to be strong or weak: the juice thus diluted is strained through some fibrous stuff like fine shavings: after which it is fit for drinking, and this is always done immediately. It has a pepperish taste, drinks flat, and rather insipid.'—Captain Cook 1774, at Tahiti.

Nowadays kava is usually made in a screw-type press.

Kaysersberg

Wine town in Alsace (*q.v.*).

Keg

Small wood or metal cask usually of less than 10 imp. gallons (12 U.S.) capacity.

Kéknyelü

A white wine, best-known of the Badacsony growths in Hungary (*q.v.*).

Kellerabfüllung, Kellerabzug

German term for bottled at the estate where the wine was grown. Literally, 'bottled in the cellar'.

Kintyre

A peninsula on the west coast of Scotland which, with the island of Islay, produces all West Highland malt whisky. Well into the eighteenth century, Kintyre was still considered a main island of the Inner Hebrides.

See WHISKY, MALT.

Kirsch, Kirschwasser

Brandy distilled from cherries complete with stones. After distillation, it is matured in paraffin-lined casks or earthenware, to prevent it taking on the colour that wood would impart; true kirsch is always pure white.

Kirsch is made notably in Alsace, Germany, and Switzerland; the German kirsch often goes under the name Schwarzwalder. Much Swiss kirsch is made in the vicinity of Basle and carries the name Basler Kirschwasser.

Château Kirwan

Bordeaux red wine. District: Haut-Médoc, France. Commune: Cantenac-Margaux.

The vineyard lies on slightly rolling land behind Cantenac, one of the first important villages one encounters along the Médoc wine road. Kirwan is between Château Brane-Cantenac, a Second Growth (*Second Cru*) vineyard, and Château Prieuré-Lichine, a Fourth Growth (*Quatrième Cru*). Since February 1956, all Cantenac vineyards have had the right to the place-name Margaux, the famous wine town only a mile away, which produces a very similar type of great wine.

Kirwan is rated a Third Growth (*Troisième Cru*) in the Classification of 1855. British owners gave it its name in the fifteenth century. About 1880, the vineyard became the property of the city of Bordeaux, and in the first year of this century the wine shippers Schröder and Schyler acquired a monopoly of the produce. In 1924 they bought the vineyard. Kirwan is not château bottled but is bottled at the Schröder and Schyler cellars in Bordeaux.

Characteristics. It is difficult to ascertain the qualities of this wine as it is not château bottled and varies considerably from bottle to bottle, depending on where you drink it, but it can sometimes be very good.

Vineyard area: 52 acres.

Average production: undetermined as not château-bottled.

Kislav

A Russian spirit made from water-melons.

Kloster Eberbach

Once a Cistercian monastery, now owned by the State. The vineyard, near Hattenheim, produces the fine Steinberg wine.

See RHEINGAU.

Knipperlé

A white-wine grape used in Alsace. Among other local names for it are Kipperlé, Kleinergelber, and Kleiner Rauschling.

Königsbacher

One of the outstanding wines in the Mittelhaardt region of the Palatinate.

See PALATINATE.

Konsumwein

German term for ordinary wine.

Kontuszowka

A Polish liqueur with the flavour of oil of lavender.

Korbel Vineyards

Sonoma County, California, U.S.A.

This winery specializes in sparkling wines.

The Korbel brothers came from the small town of Behine in Czechoslovakia to settle down in Guerneville in the Russian River Valley of Sonoma County. They made their first 'champagnes' in the Nineties, and after the Second World War they dropped their table wines and devoted their skill exclusively to the production of sparkling champagnes. Early in 1954 Anton and Leo Korbel sold the corporation to Adolph and Paul Heck. The Hecks, originally from St. Louis, were formerly president and production manager of Italian Swiss Colony of Asti, California; Adolph became the president and wine-maker of Korbel and Paul Heck the executive vice-president.

Some of the important varieties used at the ranch for the production of sparkling wines are Pinot Noir, Pinot Blanc, Sémillon, and White Riesling. The winery produces Korbel Brut and Korbel Extra Dry (for eastern markets mainly), and Korbel Sec (medium dry), Korbel Rouge, and Korbel pink champagnes.

See AMERICA: CALIFORNIA AND THE WEST.

Kornbranntwein

A liquor made in Germany and Holland from fermented cereal grains. As rye is the usual ingredient, it is almost a continental equivalent of rye whiskey.

Kornschnapps

A European liquor made of fermented corn.

Kosher Wine

In its strictest sense, wine made according to Rabbinical law for use during Jewish religious services. The term also covers what is essentially Passover Wine, which is, by a considerable margin, the largest-selling in the United States today.

Jewish ritual calls for wine at the Friday evening service, on the eve of a festival, on Holy Days, and during the Passover Season. The wine must be pure, natural, unmixed, and sound, and must be made according to rigid standards of purity under the supervision of a rabbi, but otherwise, it is not different from wine for domestic consumption. Kosher wine can serve both purposes. Passover wine—once home made for the most part—differs in that it is thicker and sweeter than is usual, and it has become synonymous with Kosher wine in most of America.

It comes almost entirely from Concord grapes grown in the vineyards of New York State—where Concord is now commanding such a good price that it is pushing out finer grape varieties. Figures given by a New York wine-maker in 1956 are a good indication: for Delaware (an excellent grape for white wine), 165 dollars (£58 18*s.* 6*d.*) per ton; Concord, before the upsurge of Kosher wine, 35 dollars (£12 10*s.*) per ton, afterwards 95 dollars £33 18*s.* 6*d.*); but Concord production is triple that of Delaware.

American Kosher wine-centres are New York City and Chicago, neither of which is noted for vines. As a general rule, grapes grown in upper New York are bought by fruit-packers who freeze them and ship them as needed to the wineries where they are thawed, allowed to ferment, dosed with cane sugar (partly to increase sweetness, partly to counteract the otherwise unpleasantly high acidity of the Concord grape) and doctored with sulphur to prevent fermentation after bottling. Wine-making is thus a year-round occupation, no longer dependent upon such old-fashioned matters as time of harvest.

Producers of natural table wines in America are of two minds about the enormous sales of Kosher wines. The hopeful outlook is expressed by one California grower who feels that a step in the right direction has been made when a new consumer buys a bottle with 'wine' on the label, and that eventually he will demand something better, and turn to table wines. The opposite reaction characterizes the trend as 'disastrous' for two reasons: the Concord grapes which are replacing finer varieties in New York's vineyards will be extremely hard to uproot; the advertising campaigns which are largely responsible for the popularity of Kosher wines are based on a counter-snobbery that extols Kosher wines at the expense of all others. It is the conviction of most of the wine trade in the United States—the truth of which has been demonstrated by experience—that once a customer has been persuaded to buy wine (assuming that he drinks it under moderately favourable conditions) he will become a consistent buyer.

Koumiss, Kumiss

A Siberian or Caucasian beverage of fermented mare's, cow's, or sometimes camel's milk.

See KAFIR.

Krajina

Yugoslav wines, mainly red but some white, grown on the borders of Rumania and Bulgaria. Krajina means 'borderland'.

See YUGOSLAVIA.

Krampen

A section of wineland around Cochem on the lower River Moselle in Germany, so called because of the sharp bend or cramp taken by the Moselle to accommodate itself to the increasing hardness of the slate cliffs. The wines are not among the best of the Moselle because the soil is too hard.

See MOSELLE; LOWER MOSELLE.

Kreszenz

One of the German words indicating the grower of a wine. Kreszenz Hans Muller on a label would mean vine from the vineyard, or parcel, of Hans Muller. This is important in Germany where each barrel may be harvested individually and most vineyards have many owners, often handling their wines differently and getting widely different results.

Kriska

West African palm wine.

Charles Krug Winery

Napa Valley, California, U.S.A.

Established in 1861, this is the oldest operating winery in Napa Valley. It is now owned and family operated by C. Mondavi & Sons, who produce and bottle at Charles Krug Winery, St. Helena, fine generic and varietal wines.

Charles Krug, one of the great names in California wine history, was a worthy pupil of Colonel Haraszthy in Sonoma. In 1858 he made the first commercial wine in Napa County using a small cider press. He built his first winery and planted his first vines on the present St. Helena site in 1861; and soon his wines were famous throughout America and in Europe. During his lifetime he trained C. H. Wente, Jacob Beringer, C. J. Wetmore and many other leading Californian wine-makers, and was a prominent figure in California wine circles until his death in 1892.

Since 1943, when the Mondavis acquired the Krug winery buildings and vineyards, the size, scope, and efficiency of the cellars have been enlarged. They are among the best equipped and most efficient in California. The family has also pioneered winemaking innovations and techniques. The vineyards are planted to such fine white grapes as Chardonnay, Chenin Blanc, Gerwürztraminer, Johannisberg Riesling, Sémillon and Sauvignon Blanc, and red varieties which include Cabernet Sauvignon, Gamay, and Pinot Noir.

In 1962 the Mondavis purchased approximately 500 acres in nearby Oakville of the historic To Kalon vineyard, considered to be the finest in all Napa Valley. Other sources of fine Napa Valley wine grapes contribute to the vineyard programme.

The premium wines of C. Mondavi & Son bear the label Charles Krug. Other labels are Napa Vista and CK. In 1966, Charles Mondavi dissociated himself from his brother and started a winery under his own name in Napa.

See AMERICA: CALIFORNIA AND THE WEST.

Kümmel

Both Germany and Holland claim to have invented the liqueur, but Russia, Poland, and the Baltic countries have always been among its staunchest admirers. It is distilled from grain alcohol and is flavoured with caraway seeds; it is sweet and pure white. Sugar is sometimes allowed to crystallize in the bottle, in which case it is known as Kümmel Crystallize. One of the most famous types of Kümmel is Allasch Kümmel, made in Allasch near Riga, now in the U.S.S.R.

See LIQUEURS.

Kvass

A refreshing Russian beer home-brewed from rye, barley, and malt and flavoured with mint or cranberries.

L

La Brède (Château de la Brède)

See BRÈDE.

Château La Lagune

Bordeaux red wine. District: Haut-Médoc, France. Commune: Ludon.

(*Ludon is not a place-name and the wine has the place-name of Haut-Médoc.*)

A Third Growth (*Troisième Cru*) as classified in 1855, La Lagune is the first of the classified vineyards reached on the wine road of the Médoc going north from Bordeaux. The wines were both great and famous at the turn of the century. At that time, in order to distinguish the vineyard from others known as La Lagune, the name was changed to Grand-La-Lagune. In recent years the wine had fallen from its former high standard, and the vineyard then suffered so severely in the frosts of 1956 that considerable replanting was necessary. The vineyard was until recently the property of the Société Civile Agricole du Château Grand-La-Lagune, which embarked upon the boldest present-day planting programme in the Médoc: a scheme which calls for enlarging and improving the vineyard, modernizing the installations and restoring the château as it was when it was built in the reigns of Louis XIII and Louis XIV. It is now owned by Monsieur Chayoux of Champagne fame.

Characteristics. Potentially a wine of great quality, and it is expected that as a result of the efforts now being made, it will regain its former high position. This wine, full, with a depth of flavour, has much of the breed found in Margaux, some seven miles north, with some of the character of Graves.

Vineyard area: 150 acres.

Average production: 19,000 cases.

Château La Mission-Haut-Brion

Bordeaux red wine. District: Graves, France. Commune: Pessac.

The château, placed behind symmetrical vines and directly across the main road from Haut-Brion, is less than a mile out of Bordeaux on the road to the seaside resort of Arcachon. The red-wine vines surround the château and border the tracks of the Bordeaux to Spain railway, running in a cutting a hundred paces from the *chais*. The red wine was classified in 1953 among the eleven best in Graves.

The vineyard was founded in the seventeenth century by the priests of the Mission of Saint Vincent de Paul. A gem of monastic art remains to commemorate the founders, a tiny peaked chapel, on the inner roof of which the years of the great vintages used to be lettered in gold—until the gold was given to the Government, during the war.

When the grapes are brought in, they are pitched into a sixteenth-century wooden trough; but the wines ferment in immaculate modern glass-lined vats which give the *chai* something of the look of a prosperous confectioner's kitchen. Mr. Woltner, the owner, sells wines at a high price, often justified as the vineyard produces some remarkable bottles. He is also the owner of Château La Tour-Haut-Brion and Château Laville-Haut-Brion which produce good white wines.

Characteristics: A superb red wine. Many knowledgeable brokers classify the wine as having the same character as Château Haut-Brion across the road. It achieves full big roundness with considerable breed.

Vineyard area: 55 acres.

Average production: 10,000 cases.

La Rioja

Wine-producing province of Argentina (*q. v.*).

La Tâche

Burgundy red wine. District: Côte de Nuits, Vosne-Romanée, France. Official Classification: Great Growth (Grand Cru).

La Tâche means 'the task' in French and is associated with the concept of piecework. It is not known, however, whether the early workers in this vineyard were paid by work accomplished rather than by the hour, or whether the name is a corruption of some other unknown word.

The legal place-name actually embraces more than just the vineyard of La Tâche. This comprises some three-and-a-half acres, but the name has been extended to take in 14·9 acres by giving the franchise to adjoining plots such as Les Gaudichots and La Grande Rue, which stand between La Tâche and the twin Romanée and Romanée-Conti. This enlargement took place in 1936, when the laws covering Burgundy were drawn up, and it was decided that the quality of these neighbouring vineyards was such that they merited the name.

La Tâche, like Romanée-Conti, is a vineyard that has but one owner: the Société Civile de la Romanée-Conti. The wines resemble those of the Society's more famous growth, but are more delicate, yet they are full-bodied, with an amazing depth of flavour. In recent years, La Tâche has frequently come forth with better wines than those of Romanée-Conti, although neither is largely made. Production in 1960, an average-quantity year, was 3,422 imp. gallons (4,121 U.S.) or the equivalent of about 1,700 cases.

Château La Tour-Blanche

Bordeaux white wine. District: Sauternes, France. Commune: Bommes.

The vineyard has been the property of the French Government for half a century, the wine being made by tenants, who pay to the State a rent of about twenty barrels every year. The estate has slipped from the position that caused it to be placed high among the Sauternes First Growths (*Premier Crus*), second only to Château d'Yquem in the Classification of 1855. On the other hand, the wine now being made, definitely lighter and less sweet than its neighbours in the Bommes-Sauternes district, has its followers. The château itself is the site of an important viticultural school, which is the reason for the gift of the estate to France by Daniel Osiris in 1907. Since 1955 the French Ministry of Agriculture has operated this vineyard.

Characteristics. Light and less sweet for a Sauternes, tending very slightly to be dry, and with a typical vigour or nerve.

Vineyard area: 65 acres.

Average production: 4,000 cases.

Château La Tour-Carnet

Bordeaux red wine. District: Haut-Médoc, France. Commune: Saint-Laurent.

(*Saint-Laurent is not a place-name and the wine carries the* appellation *Haut-Médoc.*)

Classified a Fourth Growth (*Quatrième Cru*) of the Médoc in 1855. The square tower—the donjon of a thirteenth-century castle—that gives the wine its name overlooks one of the most beautiful properties of the Médoc, and the vineyard was famous and commanded leading prices as far back as 1354. Today, unfortunately, cow pastures seem to have become more important to the owner than are vines. The vineyard, greatly curtailed by recent freezes, could only regain some of its former fame if the owners would spend considerable amounts to buy vineyards from neighbouring châteaux.

Characteristics. Undistinguished. Seldom does it attain the standards expected of a Classified Growth.

Vineyard area: 25 acres.

Average production: 1,800 cases.

Château La Tour-Haut-Brion

Bordeaux red wine. District: Graves, France. Commune: Talence.

Latour-Haut-Brion is one of the three Haut-Brion suffix wine châteaux on the outskirts of Bordeaux—the others are La Mission-Haut-Brion and Laville-Haut-Brion. The last of these is one of five vineyards classed as Firsts among Graves white wine vineyards in 1953, and the other two were classed among the First red wine vineyards. None of the latter châteaux should be confused with Château Haut-Brion, in Pessac, the great First Growth (*Premier Cru*) belonging to the Dillon family.

Characteristics. Full, rather hard wines, similar to those of La Mission-Haut-Brion but less fine.

Vineyard area: 10 acres.

Average production: 1,000 cases.

Château La Tour-Martillac (Kressmann La Tour)

Bordeaux red and white wine. District: Graves, France. Commune: Martillac.

In front of the long, low, farmhouse-like château on the slope of Martillac, south of Bordeaux, is the vine-covered tower which gives the wine its name. It is all that remains of a château destroyed in the French Revolution.

Red and white wines are made in about equal quantities. In recent years, some of the white wine has been aged in big barrels, the size of the German Rhine and Moselle *Halbstück*, instead of the usual Bordeaux barrel of 225 litres—an experiment conducted to see if fruitier wines might not be obtained from the greater mass of liquid in proportion to the wood surface through which the wine breathes—which would mean a lesser oxidation, and a wine which would stay young longer. The experiment has rightly had time to prove itself and the owners believe they are developing an improved dry white wine. The excellent whites are accompanied by a red wine rated, in 1953, as one of the eleven Graves red wines worthy of classification (not château-bottled) as outstanding.

For thirty years, La Tour-Martillac has belonged to the Kressmann firm of Bordeaux, which bought it outright when the last owner died and they were threatened with the loss of the wine which had been a favourite of their clientèle for several generations.

Characteristics. A very good shipper's wine, not château-bottled, but pleasant to drink.

Vineyard area: 25 acres.

Average production: red—3,750 cases.
white—700 cases.

Château La Tour-de-Mons

Bordeaux red wine. District: Haut-Médoc, France. Commune: Soussans-Margaux.

Owned by the proprietor of Château Cantemerle, La Tour-de-Mons has for years had the benefit of the careful viticultural treatment which has raised

Cantemerle far above its position as a Fifth Growth (*Cinquième Cru*). Château la Tour-de-Mons, ranked a Bourgeois Growth (*Cru Bourgeois*) in the 1855 Médoc Classification, also justifies a higher rating. The vineyard is today managed by Monsieur Bertrand Clauzel, mayor of Soussans. The estate has an old ruined tower tangled in vine, and was founded in 1289 by Jehan Colomb of Bordeaux, one of whose Italian relatives was two centuries later to discover America. Subsidiary vineyards are Château La Tour-de-Bessan and Château Richeterre.

Characteristics. A very fine, round wine with all the delicacy of Margaux. Although a Bourgeois Growth, it is one of the best in this old-fashioned category. It deserves a better rating as it produces wines finer than many Classified Growths. Its excellent ownership guarantees that the wine will be well made.

Vineyard area: 75 acres.

Average production: 6,000 cases.

Labrusca

A species of grapevine (*Vitis labrusca*) found in North America.

See CHAPTER EIGHT, pp. 29, 71.

Lacrima (or Lacryma) Christi

A soft and fairly dry white wine made from grapes grown along the southern slopes of Mount Vesuvius—not to be confused with the Lágrima of Málaga. A red wine is also produced.

See CAMPANIA.

Ladoix-Serrigny

Burgundy red and white wine. District: Côte de Beaune, France.

Little wine is sold under the place-name Ladoix-Serrigny. Wines are made, but the bulk may be sold as Côte de Beaune-Villages, and the best with those of next-door Aloxe-Corton. Because of the option, the amount of Ladoix-Serrigny varies from 10,000 imp. gallons (12,000 U.S.) in one year to less than 830 imp. gallons (1,000 U.S.) the next. Most of the wines are red; but there is a little white—rarely more than 250 imp. gallons (300 U.S.).

The town is the northernmost on the Côte de Beaune and is bisected by the Route Nationale (National Highway) No. 74 which runs from Dijon south to Lyons and on to the Côte d'Azur. The name comes from the Celtic *doix*, 'fountain': for besides being a source of wine, the town has a spring. Serrigny, the other half of the commune, is an ancient hamlet which sits on the east—and, viticulturally speaking, the wrong—side of the National Highway. Throughout the Côte d'Or, vines growing on the slopes west of the Highway have the right to the great place-names, while those to the east can do no better than the general name 'Burgundy'.

The vineyards Les Vergennes and Le Rognet, bordering on Aloxe-Corton, are officially allowed the place-names of Corton and Corton-Charlemagne, and those immediately adjoining are Aloxe-Corton (for list *see* ALOXE-CORTON). These wines tend to resemble their neighbours in all respects, and the lesser wines of the town are light-bodied and fast-maturing, often with an entrancing bouquet. The grapes are grown on about 335 acres.

Château Lafaurie-Peyraguey

Bordeaux white wine. District: Sauternes, France. Commune: Bommes.

Placed on a slightly lower hill-top opposite that of Château d'Yquem, the Moorish-looking walled castle, built in the thirteenth century, looks out through its fortified gates over the sloping sea of its vines. The *chai* is inside the courtyard, and there one of the most full-bodied of the Sauternes may be tasted, excellent when very young from the barrel, as fine Sauternes always are. The vineyard was classified a First Growth (*Premier Cru*) in 1855.

Characteristics. If the 1855 Classification were to be revised, these wines might be downgraded. Not as rich as many of the better Sauternes, yet distinguished wines.

Vineyard area: 40 acres.

Average production: 3,000 cases.

Château Lafite

Bordeaux red wine. District: Haut-Médoc, France. Commune: Pauillac.

Château Lafite, one of the best red wines of Bordeaux—which is to say, one of the most elegant wines in the world—has eight centuries of history behind it. In 1234 it was the property of Gombaud de Lafite; and a hundred years later the wines were already famous. In the eighteenth century, Madame de Pompadour served them; and Madame Dubarry said that since Bordeaux was the king's favourite, she would drink nothing else. Lafite claims to have been in each case the chosen wine, and it may very well have been so.

The vineyard was at one time owned by Alexandre de Ségur, proprietor also of Château Latour and Château Calon-Ségur. It became public property in 1794, after the owner (the President of the Parliament of Guyenne) had been guillotined in the

Revolution; and afterwards it was bought, first by a Dutchman (in whose time the first bottles of vintage wine were laid down in the cellar) and then by the English banker, Sir Samuel Scott. The Rothschild family acquired Lafite when it was put up for auction in 1868. The bidding was so extraordinarily high that it was said only a Rothschild could triumph; and, indeed, the château went to Baron James de Rothschild for what, today, would be slightly more than £4,200,000 (1,500,000 dollars). By an odd coincidence—or perhaps it was the association that whetted his interest—the Rothschild bank in Paris is in the Rue Laffitte.

Lafite will be found on early labels spelled with two t's or two f's, or both; and the name itself is said to derive from an old Médoc word *lahite*, which was a corruption of *la hauteur* (the height). Lafite is the highest knoll of the Pauillac area, which merges into the adjoining commune of Saint-Estèphe. The château sits high above the marshland bordering the Gironde. Great ocean-bound vessels can be seen from the windows, throwing up feathers of smoke into a clear sky; or can be heard hooting their way through the mist.

One of the present owners of Lafite, Élie de Rothschild, is the cousin of Philippe de Rothschild of Château Mouton-Rothschild, and between their wines—the vineyards actually touch—a kind of competition has developed. Lafite is made from the grape varieties Cabernet Sauvignon and Franc, Petit Verdot, and much Merlot which imparts the softness for which this wine is famous. Mouton, however, having very little Merlot, is 70% Cabernet Sauvignon, and so is harder.

Lafite is proud of its great name, and no wine which is not of the first quality (the wine from young vines, for instance) is allowed to bear it, but is sold instead as Carruades de Château Lafite-Rothschild. In most years, this secondary wine averages from one-third to one-half of the total production. It has been said that the management of Lafite plans using, instead, the Duhart-Milon label for its Carruades. This fourth-classed vineyard which adjoins Château Lafite was bought by the Rothschild Bank in 1962.

The estate consists of some 300 acres, half of them devoted to viticulture. There, as in other vineyards of the Médoc, the vines are planted about a yard apart and are carefully trained along two or three rows of thin sticks, to keep them from damage by contact with the earth, with the plough, or even with a brisk wind. Here, as everywhere in the Médoc, the trellises are fifteen inches from the ground, and each vine runs horizontally along a wire. The owners of Lafite say that the north–south exposure of the vineyard is conducive to early ripening, and that the misty atmosphere gives the grapes their thin skins. They ripen in August, becoming glassily transparent; and from this time onwards, nobody is allowed in the vineyard, in case the grapes should be bruised. The last ploughing takes place in July.

The *chais* cluster round the château; and in the great *cuverie*, or vat-house, are twenty-four Bosnian oak vats, each holding 2,750 imp. gallons (3,300 U.S.). The château itself, set on a handsome eighteenth-century terrace, is shown on the labels. Vines grow right up to the garden walls; the house is built of pale stone, throwing into relief the green of two magnolias and an ancient cedar tree.

The cellars of the château are heavily vaulted, their four long galleries lit by wrought-iron chandeliers, each holding six electric candles. Here is the most impressive sight in Lafite: a rank of bins, each with its wooden vintage plaque. The walls are black with mould and the bottles seem to be covered with fur. The earliest is 1797; others still have their labels 1801, 1805, and 1811, the year of the comet, said to be the best vintage of the early nineteenth century. 1870 was a famous year in the history of Lafite. Other great classical vintages were 1893, 1895, 1900, 1906, 1923, and 1926. Fine years were 1874, 1875, 1878, 1899, 1904, 1911, 1916. In 1905 the wine was light but had an exquisite flavour; in 1934 it was full-bodied and mellow. 1945, although slow-maturing, will be a classic of all time; 1949 and 1952 are excellent; while 1953 was one of the greatest of recent decades, exemplifying Lafite at its very best. Since then, the superb 1955 has been overshadowed by the fabulous 1959 and the 1961, which reached ridiculously high prices, but will nevertheless be regarded as classics.

Since wine ages more slowly in large bottles, there are many magnums and double magnums in the Lafite cellars, as well as Imperials, which hold eight bottles, and Nebuchadnezzars (ten bottles), and the stone staircases leading to the cellars are lined with Jeroboams (five bottles). The bottles are recorked every twenty-five years. When the cork deteriorates, so that the wine begins to evaporate, the bottle is 'leaky'—*bouteille couleuse*—and is then filled up again; this happens to about 5,000 bottles every year.

Characteristics. In great years, when Lafite is successful, it can be supreme. It has great finesse and a particular softness imparted by the Merlot grape. The wine tends to be firm yet delicate and supple, with an eventual lightness developed in age. Lesser vintages are still excellent wines, lighter than those of great years, but always showing breed, fragrance, and depth of flavour.

Vineyard area: 150 acres.

Average production: 12,000 cases of Lafite and 6,000 cases of Carruades.

Château Lafon-Rochet

Bordeaux red wine. District: Haut-Médoc, France. Commune: Saint-Estèphe.

The only Fourth Growth (*Quatrième Cru*) Classification of 1855 in Saint-Estèphe. Lafon-Rochet is in the possession of the Cruse family. The wine is seldom seen on the Bordeaux market and demand for it abroad is negligible.

Characteristics. Not outstanding, but may improve as the vines get older. At present the wines barely deserve their 1855 status. This may be why the owner is so opposed to a new classification.

Vineyard area: 37 acres.

Average production: 4,000 cases.

Lager

See BEER.

Château Lagrange

Bordeaux red wine. District: Haut-Médoc, France. Commune: Saint-Julien.

The large estate spread over the high slopes a mile back from the Gironde looks down over vineyards, among them Château Beychevelle and the Léovilles. Improved and developed by the wealthy wife of the French minister who held it just before 1855, it was classed a Third Growth (*Troisième Cru*) of Médoc in that year. Its present inferiority is another indication of how obsolete the 1855 Classification is.

Characteristics. Slow-maturing wines of average quality, rather coarse and lacking in distinction. But they have shown a marked tendency to improve lately.

Vineyard area: 89 acres.

Average production: 9,000 cases.

Lágrima

A sweet, fortified Málaga wine, not to be confused with the Lacrima Christi grown near Naples, although both wines are golden in colour and the name of each means 'Tears'.

See MÁLAGA.

Lake Erie

Important wine district in the eastern United States. Vineyards are established on the mainland, centring around Sandusky but also on the islands Kelley, North Bass, South Bass, and Middle Bass. Good American grape varieties are used of which the favourites are the Catawba and the Delaware. Both red and white wines are produced and some interesting sparkling wines.

See AMERICA: EASTERN STATES.

Lalande de Pomerol

Bordeaux red wine. District: Bordeaux, France.

The commune, which now includes Néac, adjoins the famous region of Pomerol in south-west France, but the wines, although similar to Pomerols, have a distinct taste of their own. Several of them compare well with all but the finest Pomerols. Château Bel-Air, just across the line from Pomerol, is outstanding.

See POMEROL.

Lambrusco

1. A sweetish semi-sparkling red wine of little virtue, made in the Emilia-Romagna region of Italy. It has no connexion with the *Vitis labrusca* of America.

2. Grape grown in Italy for red wine, especially in Emilia and Alto Adige.

Château Lanessan

Bordeaux red wine. District: Haut-Médoc, France. Commune: Cussac.

(*Cussac is not a place-name and the wine carries the place-name Haut-Médoc.*)

Ranked a Bourgeois Growth of the Médoc in 1855, the large vineyard produces wine which sells well above its class and ought to be elevated to a higher position. The museum of horse-trappings, coaches, carriages, and carts draws numbers of visitors.

Characteristics. The very good wines are carefully made by the owner of Château Pichon-Longueville-Baron and manager of Château Palmer, Monsieur Bouteiller. The wine is full and round, with a pleasant amount of finesse, and at the same time a delicacy which has astounded the Bordeaux merchants whenever they have tasted old bottles of this fine vineyard. Severe spring frosts in 1956 and 1957 have curtailed production.

Vineyard area: 45 acres.

Average production: 3,000 cases.

Château Langoa-Barton

Bordeaux red wine. District: Haut-Médoc, France. Commune: Saint-Julien.

Glimpsed between gates a little back from the vineyard road as it prepares to wind steeply through the town of Saint-Julien, Langoa houses not only the cellars and *chais* of its own Third-Growth (*Troisième Cru*) vintages but also those of the Second Growth (*Second Cru*) Château Léoville-Barton. The two estates adjoin. Ronald Barton, the great-great-grandson of the Hugh Barton who bought Langoa in 1821, and a third of the great Léoville vineyard in 1826, lives in Château Langoa and makes both wines in his cellars.

Characteristics. Lighter but very similar to neighbouring Léoville-Barton, yet not attaining quite the same degree of excellence. The wine is not château-bottled but is taken to the cellars of Barton & Guestier, where it is bottled by this well-known shipping firm.

Vineyard area: 42 acres.

Average production: Undetermined as not château-bottled.

Languedoc

A vast plain in southern France embracing the Department of Hérault where quantities of wines are made, mostly mediocre. One of the better ones is Clairette du Languedoc (*q.v.*).

Château Lascombes

Bordeaux red wine and rosé wine. District: Haut-Médoc, France. Commune: Margaux.

A feudal holding of the Dukes of Duras, Lascombes may have acquired its name from the Chevalier de Lascombes who owned it early in the eighteenth century; or he may have taken his title from the estate. The local people say that the derivation was *La Côte—Lascote—Lascombes*, a corruption over the centuries of the original designation, meaning the hill, knoll, or slope. In any case, the vineyard spreads over the knoll of Margaux, the highest elevation of the commune. This outstanding situation caused the wines to be ranked equal with those of the adjoining vineyard of Château Margaux on many occasions in the past; and in 1855 the estate was classified a Second Growth (*Second Cru*) of Médoc.

By unwise selling of parcels, the vineyard had dwindled to forty acres and become a patchwork when the Ginestets, present owners of Château Margaux, acquired it in the early twenties. The reconstruction and improvement of the vineyard begun then has been continued by the author and a group of American friends who bought Château Lascombes in 1952; and today the vineyard has been reunited in an expanse of 125 acres on the north-east of Margaux.

The grey stone château, on the edge of the village and the chief landmark in the village itself, was built by a nineteenth-century owner, Monsieur Chaix d'Est-Ange, who was at the time President of the French Bar—and famous for having won the case of the Suez Canal for France against Egypt. The Sèvres coffee service given him in gratitude by Napoleon III may still be seen in Margaux, profusely decorated with portraits of the mistresses of Louis XIV.

Château and *chais* have been altered, enlarged, and improved by the American ownership and today Lascombes is considered a Médoc show-place. The atmosphere is international: flags of all the member countries of the United Nations, once the flags of Rockefeller Center in New York, fly from twenty tall poles at the side of the vineyard; and many visitors come each year from various parts of the world to see the exhibition of paintings on the theme of Vine and Wine. The barrels rest in a new, modern *chai* lighted by brands made of gnarled vine trunk.

A rosé wine first made experimentally in 1953 has proved extremely popular in the United States where it keeps up with the growing reputation in the English-speaking countries of the red Lascombes wine. The rosé is sold under the name of Rosé de Lascombes.

Characteristics. Excels in finesse and has an indefinable light Margaux bouquet epitomizing the 'feminine' qualities of the Médoc—a bouquet that many have defined as reminiscent of violets. The wine matures relatively rapidly and has great staying power, too, so that it is very fine when young or old. The most popular château-bottled wine in the U.S.A.

Vineyard area: 125 acres.

Average production: 14,000 cases.

Latium

White and red wines. District: around Rome.

If the Castelli Romani wines ever lose their place among the eternal wonders of Rome, there is no justice in Heaven. These bright, dry or semi-sweet white wines from the Alban hills just south of the city provide the finest single means of diverting the mind from aching feet after a touristic morning in Rome and, judging by the amount sold, the Roman loves them as much as the visitor. The sources are the towns of Frascati, Colonna, Castel Gandolfo, Grottaferrata, Montecompatri, and Marino, although Velletri, Colli Albani, and Colli

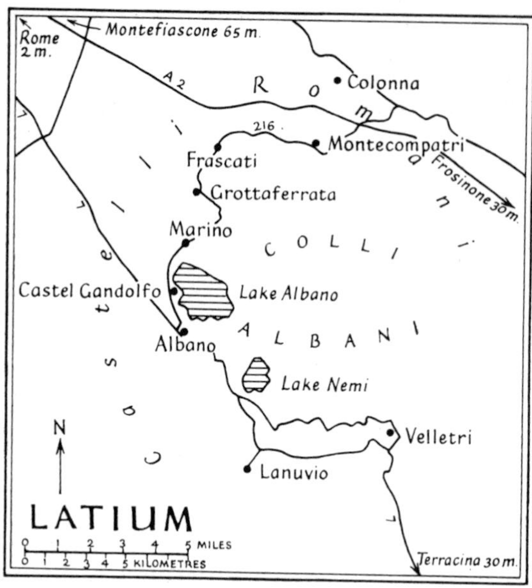

Lanuvini are names which may also be found—but the wise visitor seldom bothers to specify his wine. Every self-respecting *trattoria* keeper has his own supplier, and whether you ask for Frascati, Colonna, or *vino bianco*, the chances are that the waiter will agree, and then bring you whatever he happens to have. In any case, it is almost certain to be eminently drinkable. (The best is probably Frascati which tends to be sturdier and longer-lasting than the others. Its light texture should be viewed with suspicion, however, as it has an alcoholic content that makes it extremely insidious.)

The Castelli Romani wines come mainly from Trebbiano grapes; they run from about 11% to 13% of alcohol, have a yellowish tinge, and are usually slightly sweet, unless 'extra dry' is specified. Almost 12,500,000 imp. gallons (15 million U.S.) are made annually and most of this is gulped down in Rome, although a certain amount is shipped abroad. Red wines also are produced in this Roman province.

Perhaps even more famous than these Roman offerings is *Est! Est!! Est!!!* (*q.v.*), the white wine of Montefiascone near Lake Bolsena. Labels sometimes appear without exclamation points, sometimes with one following each 'Est', and sometimes as given above, and there seems to be no approved formula. The name is credited to the German Bishop Fugger, who made a trip to Rome in A.D. 1111. The Bishop was a drinker of discrimination, and since he did not wish to risk inferior wines on his long journey, he sent a trusted servant ahead with instructions to taste those along the route and to mark on the wall of each inn and tavern 'Est' (It is) where the wine was good and 'Non Est' (It is not) on the others. All went normally until the servant reached Montefiascone, where he tasted the wines, then rushed forth to scrawl the triple epithet on the wall before returning to settle comfortably into the wine cellar. According to the legends, both master and man passed the rest of their lives there, drinking themselves contentedly to death.

The wine itself is sometimes dry, more often slightly sweet. It is small and tinged with yellow, a darkness in shade which actually offers little to the cultivated palate, but is certainly worth trying at its source if only in deference to the Bishop, remembering that the story is better than the wine.

Cesanese di Piglio is Latium's best red wine. The grapes are Cesanese (or Cesanese di Affile), grown in this district between Rome and Cassino. The wine may be dry or semi-sweet, but it usually verges toward dryness. It tends to be deeply coloured, with a distinctly strong character and is often high (up to 15%) in alcohol.

Among lesser wines are Muscats and Malvasia (the best comes from Grottaferrata—which also makes a dryish, fairly light wine), a sweet white wine sometimes sold fresh out of the fermenting vat. Terracina, a city some seventy-five miles south of Rome on the fabled Appian Way, is known for a Muscat which tends to be slightly lower both in alcohol and sugar content than is normally expected. It is often recommended to accompany the exquisite Roman pastries—and with good reason.

Château Latour

Bordeaux red wine. District: Haut-Médoc, France. Commune: Pauillac.

Château Latour, already famous, was discussed in his *Essays* by Montaigne, himself a vine-grower in Bordeaux in the sixteenth century. It was near the end of the seventeenth century that the estate passed, by marriage, from de Chavanas, counsellor-secretary to King Louis XIV, to the Ségur family, ancestors of the recent proprietors. The second Ségur to own it was known as the Vine Prince, celebrated as the possessor at one and the same time of Château Lafite, Château Latour and Château Calon-Ségur. In the French Revolution the property was divided and it was not until 1841 that the family succeeded in regaining the lost half. In 1842, the Société Civile de Château Latour was formed, at that time unique but since widely copied: only members of the family could belong. In 1963, the de Beaumont family sold their interest to Lord Cowdray. The firm of Harveys then bought one-fifth of this. Monsieur Henri Martin, the Mayor of Saint-Julien, who is also the President of the Bordeaux Wine Association, administers the estate.

The tower—La Tour—stands alone at the edge of the vineyard. It was once part of a wall raised against pirates by the Médoc people of the Middle Ages. The actual stones stand as they were placed in a reconstruction, ordered by Louis XIII, from the debris of a levelled fortress. The fort itself, which stood where the *chais* are now placed, was razed during the Hundred Years War. It is said that a great quantity of gold pieces was thrown into the moat, thus starting the legend of buried gold at Château Latour. In fact, the story may not be altogether a myth, since a map found not long ago in the Tower of London affirms the presence of the gold, and corporations have been formed in England—so far unsuccessfully—to recover it.

The principal contribution to the quality of Château Latour wine is made by the soil, half of which is composed of egg-sized stones. Strain two pounds of it and a pound of stones will remain in your sieve. The ploughs of Latour have to be sharpened twice a day, and the soil itself has so much body that two oxen are required to draw a plough through it. A former Marquis de Ségur stunned the Court of Versailles with his glittering waistcoat, and King Louis XV announced: 'Messieurs, here is the richest man in my kingdom. His soil produces nectar and diamonds.' The gleaming stones sewn on to the Marquis de Ségur's silk waistcoat were cut and polished quartz from the vineyard of Latour. A few such stones can still be seen today in the entrance hall at Latour and in the wine museum of the Maison du Vin in Pauillac.

Latour still partly employs the method of vine replacement called *jardinage*. Every vine is allowed to live to its maximum age and is then torn out and replaced individually, although in most vineyards plants are now uprooted in sections at a set retirement age—usually thirty-five or forty years. The result is that, until recently, Latour had one of the oldest average plantations, and consequently greater body, higher alcoholic content and extra fulness in the wine. In very old vines, quality increases but quantity decreases. Latour makes about 100 cases per acre, whereas 125–130 is normal for some of the lesser vineyards. Seven-tenths of Latour's one hundred acres are in Cabernet Sauvignon grapes, the remainder in Malbec, Merlot, Cabernet Franc, and Petit-Verdot.

The grape must, or fermenting juice, of Château Latour is left in the new, gleaming, stainless steel vats from fifteen to twenty days, depending on the characteristics of the vintage; this is almost twice the time allowed in most of the other Médoc vineyards. This method creates a harder, slower-maturing wine, which will finally achieve great heights but which must be waited for. Only the grower of an aristocratic wine commanding a very high price can afford this expensive process. Château Latour is classed a First Growth (*Premier Cru*) with Château Lafite, Château Margaux, and Château Haut-Brion.

Characteristics. Full-bodied and hard when young, Latour develops into something firm, rich, and noble. Needing long ageing to reach its peak, it is well worth waiting for. The vineyard often succeeds in years when the others are inclined to falter.

Vineyard area: 140 acres.

Average production: 16,200 cases.

Latricières-Chambertin

Burgundy red wine. District: Côte de Nuits, France. Commune: Gevrey-Chambertin. Official Classification: Great Growth (Grand Cru).

Latricières is officially rated a Great Growth (*Grand Cru*) of the Côte d'Or (for the significance of this and the standards demanded *see* CÔTE DE NUITS). It is in all respects the closest vineyard to Le Chambertin.

Chambertin and Latricières lie to the right of the vineyard road as you move south from Gevrey-Chambertin to Morey-Saint-Denis and only a tiny, rutted track divides them. At the top of the vineyard, a tumble-down stone wall separates it from the matted and tangled undergrowth and the woodland which extend to the top of the hill, and below this stone wall is a small section of which the author is part-owner. As is true of most great Burgundian vineyards, a number of growers own sections of Latricières.

After Chambertin and the Clos de Bèze, Latricières produces the best wines in the commune. While not generally having all the fulness and nobility of the two top Growths (*Crus*), it will share much of the same strength, the deep and virile colour, and especially the breed; for its main attribute is that it excels in finesse, often to a greater degree than Chambertin and Chambertin-Clos de Bèze. The area of the vineyard is seventeen acres and the grapes which are grown in it were made into just over 4,100 imp. gallons (5,000 U.S.) of wine in

1966—average for quantity—or the equivalent of just over 2,000 cases.

Laudun

One of the best communes of the Côtes du Rhône, producing red, white, and rosé wines.

See RHÔNE.

Lavaux

Terraced vineyards in the canton of Vaud, which produces one-third of the wines of Switzerland. The white wines of Lavaux come from the Chasselas grape.

See SWITZERLAND.

Château Laville-Haut-Brion

Bordeaux white wine. District: Graves, France. Commune: Talence.

This is one of three Graves vineyards bearing the suffix Haut-Brion. It makes only white wine and is among the five First Growths (*Premiers Crus*) for Graves white wines.

Characteristics. A typical, pleasant dry Graves.

Vineyard area: 10 acres.

Average production: 2,400 cases.

See CHÂTEAU LATOUR-HAUT-BRION.

Layon

See COTEAUX DU LAYON; ANJOU.

Lazio

Italian spelling of the region of Latium (*q.v.*).

Leaf Reddening (Rougeau)

A malady of the vine.

See CHAPTER EIGHT, p. 36.

Leaker

A bottle with wine oozing from the cork, indicating that air is reaching the wine, which is likely to spoil due to premature oxidation.

Lebanon

See SYRIA AND LEBANON.

Lees

The sediments or dregs, consisting of tartrates, left at the bottom of a wine cask. These are left after racking a wine from one barrel to another.

Château Léoville-Barton

Bordeaux red wine. District: Haut-Médoc, France. Commune: Saint-Julien.

Léoville-Barton, with the other two Léoville vineyards a Second Growth (*Second Cru*) in the Classification of 1855, forms a quarter of the original Léoville estate, now divided into three. There is neither château, *chais*, nor cellars on the property. The owner, H. R. Barton of the wine firm of Barton and Guestier in Bordeaux, lives at the nearby Langoa-Barton estate and makes both Langoa and Léoville-Barton there. Langoa-Barton was bought by the present owner's great-great-grandfather in 1821, and Léoville-Barton five years later. This vineyard, although it has one of the least attractive labels among the Classified Growths, has recently been producing one of the best Saint-Juliens of all.

Characteristics. One of the best of the Léovilles, with excellent body and breed.

Vineyard area: 62 acres.

Average production: 6,000 cases.

Château Léoville-Las-Cases

Bordeaux red wine. District: Haut-Médoc, France. Commune: Saint-Julien.

Léoville-Las-Cases comprises half the old estate of Léoville, the other half being divided between Châteaux Léoville-Barton and Léoville-Poyferré. It extends from the edge of the town of Saint-Julien to the borders of Château Latour, and in the past the combined Léoville vineyard stretched from Château Beychevelle to Château Latour. One of the most notable landmarks along the Médoc vineyard road is the Las-Cases gateway just past Saint-Julien, which appears on the wine label.

Las-Cases, with the other Léovilles, is a Second Growth (*Second Cru*) in the 1855 Classification, but one which had a temporary setback in quality during the early fifties. In 1959, 1961, and 1964, however, it was repeatedly one of the best Médoc wines. The vineyard is now run by M. Delon, but until 1900 it belonged to the Marquis de Las Cases, from which comes both the name of the principal Growth and also a secondary bottling under the label of Clos du Marquis, into which approximately one-fifth of the production was diverted.

Characteristics. At one time the wines were too light and were slightly thin. There has been a marked improvement lately—the 1959 was superb, the 1961 was a classic, and the 1964 excelled. This is an example of a vineyard that was replanted. The young vines produced thin hard wines; but in 1959 the comparative maturity of the vines was combined with a change in the methods of vinification—brought about by Dr. Peynaud, the Professor of Œnology at the University of Bordeaux—to create a metamorphosis in this wine.

Vineyard area: 135 acres.

Average production: 18,500 cases.

Château Léoville-Poyferré

Bordeaux red wine. District: Haut-Médoc, France. Commune: Saint-Julien.

A Second Growth (*Deuxième Cru*) of Médoc as classified in 1855, Poyferré once formed a single vineyard with the two other Léoville Growths, Léoville-Barton and Léoville-Las-Cases. The wine can be the best of the Léovilles and the 1929 in particular was considered one of the finest bottles of this century in the Médoc, though it is now little more than a memory. Poyferré is now perhaps the least good of the Léovilles. A secondary mark, Château Moulin Riche-Poyferré, is popular in England.

Characteristics. Not so good as neighbouring Léoville-Las-Cases, the wine is more supple and lacks the breed of its neighbours. It has slipped considerably from what it was, partly losing distinction because of the youth of the vines.

Vineyard area: 85 acres.

Average production: 13,000 cases.

L'Étoile

See ÉTOILE; JURA.

Levure

French term for yeast.

Liebfrauenstift

The wine of the Liebfrauenkirche vineyards near Worms, in the Rheinhessen. In the days before the name became almost meaningless these wines could have been labelled Liebfraumilch, and were considered as the best of what is now a vague place-name.

Liebfraumilch

One of the most misleading names in wine. It may mean anything—and therefore nothing. Today, by German law, Liebfraumilch, originally the wine of Liebfrauenkirche and Worms, may be applied to any wine of Rheinhessen. Rheinhessen wines, distinctive in their own right, are so named; the remainder call themselves Liebfraumilch.

See RHEINHESSEN.

Liechtenstein

The wine of the 'postage stamp' principality on the Swiss–Austrian border is light red—almost rosé—and two-thirds of it comes from around Vaduz, the capital.

See VADUZER.

Light

In red wines this will mean a small, inconsequential wine, low in alcoholic content and in tannin, though it may be very pleasant. But a light white wine such as a Moselle can be great.

Liguria

Red and white wines. District: Italian Riviera.

Liguria forms a slim half-moon along the Mediterranean, a block of mountains rimmed with beach, its flanks formed by the Alps to the west, the Apennines to the east, with Genoa in the centre. It is an extension of the French Riviera, and in keeping with the atmosphere of this lovely region, wine-making is romantic. The grapes have to be lowered down forbidding cliffs from practically inaccessible vineyards, to be carried to the press in skiffs. But however much he may enjoy watching the harvest here, the wise visitor will generally drink wines from somewhere else. Liguria makes 9,200,000 imp. gallons (11 million U.S.) annually, but most of it is quite ordinary wine.

Dolceacqua or Rossese

This red wine (the names are interchangeable), comes from western Liguria, from the flower-laden slopes behind Ventimiglia and Bordighera, mainly from the vineyards of Dolceacqua, and from Rossese grapes. Not low in alcohol (12%–14%), it makes an adequate table wine.

Cinque Terre

This famous white wine is often highly praised. It means 'five lands' and comes from the five towns of Vernazzi, Campiglia, Riomaggiore, Monterosso, and Biassa. It is usually semi-sweet, less frequently fully sweet, is made from Vernaccia grapes and is a sound but not inspiring wine.

Vermentino Ligure, Coronata, and Polcevera

Thin, light white wines similar in characteristics, all mainly from Vermentino grapes (although Bosco and Brachetto vines are also grown, particularly in the Coronata district) and should not be expensive. Vermentino Ligure may sometimes be slightly sparkling.

Likörwein

German term for dessert wine.

Lillet

Semi-dry French aperitif made of white wine and brandy. It is pale in colour and slightly resembles vermouth, but leaves a sweetish aftertaste.

Limoux

A small town near Carcassonne in south-west France, which makes a little-known still wine (Vin de Blanquette) and a slightly better-known, but rather peculiar, sparkling wine (Blanquette de Limoux).

See BLANQUETTE DE LIMOUX.

Liqueur d'Expédition

French term, used in Champagne for a solution of sugar, wine, and sometimes brandy added to sparkling wine after extracting the cork just before shipment.

See CHAMPAGNE.

Liqueur Jaune

Name often given to imitations of yellow Chartreuse.

See CHARTREUSE.

Liqueur d'Or

Pale yellow French herb liqueur with gold flakes floating in the bottle; a variation of Danziger Goldwasser.

Liqueur de Tirage

French term for the solution of sugar and old wine added to Champagne and other sparkling wine to ensure a second fermentation.

See CHAMPAGNE.

Liqueur Verte

Name often given to imitations of green Chartreuse.

See CHARTREUSE.

Liqueurs

These sweet, usually strongly alcoholic drinks which are served in very small glasses after dinner are made of sugar, syrup and spirits, flavoured with plants, fruit or herbs, and are often an aid to digestion. The white fruit-brandies or *eaux-de-vie* produced in Alsace and elsewhere—framboise, quetsch, kirsch, slivovitz, etc.—sometimes referred to as liqueurs, do not really come into this category; nor do the excellent, old, dry Cognacs and Armagnacs which are drunk, undiluted, after meals, although these are commonly known as 'liqueur' brandies.

History

Although the distillation of water and aromatic liquids was known in earlier times and mentioned by Hippocrates, Galen, and Pliny, alcoholic spirits were not distilled until, probably, about A.D. 900, by the Arabs; unless, indeed, they were made from cereals in northern Europe somewhat earlier. Liqueurs, a still later invention, began with the mollification of crude spirits by sweet syrups, and continued with the addition of sweet herbs, to enhance the flavour—and also to improve the health of the drinkers. In the Middle Ages, as we know, wine (and later spirits) was the principal antiseptic for dressing wounds, while plants, roots, and herbs provided the remedies for most diseases. The monks grew these in their monastery gardens and experimented with their use; the alchemists carried their researches further. Arnáu de Vilanova, Catalan physician and chemist, born *c.* 1240, was 'the inventor of modern tinctures in which the virtues of herbs are extracted by alcohol'. He and his pupil, Raimundo Lulio, were the first to write about alcohol and to make known their recipes for healing liqueurs. Beginning with sweetened spirit, they were soon introducing lemon, rose, and orange-flower. Afterwards, they might add particles of gold, then considered to be a universal panacea. Arnáu, whose advanced ideas brought him into trouble with the Inquisition, was protected by the Pope, whose life he had saved with potions of wine mixed with herbs and gold. When the Black Death came to Europe, liqueurs mixed with vegetable balms and tonics were treasured medicines.

By the fifteenth century the Italians had become the leading liqueur makers, and Catharine de' Medici took some of their receipts to France with her. Montpellier was a famous centre of manufacture; a liqueur that Louis XIV liked very much is said to have contained amber, aniseed, cinnamon, and musk. Other spirit bases besides wine brandy were brought into use, including rum from the new colonies. Housewives often concocted their own liqueurs and then, as now, they were used as flavouring in the kitchen. But during the last century the industry made such progress in most of the countries of Europe, and such a variety was put on sale, that home-made ratafias and liqueurs began to disappear.

Manufacture

One system—a simple mixing of spirits, sugar-syrup, and bottled essence of peppermint or some other flavour—would be comparatively easy to carry out in the kitchen. In a rather more complicated form, this method is sometimes used commercially. The result, in either case, is a crude liqueur.

The finest are generally those that have been distilled; but some fruits and delicate herbs which cannot be submitted to distillation will merge very satisfactorily with the spirit through the processes of maceration or infusion. The purpose of distilling liqueurs is the opposite of that obtaining in the distillation of pure alcohol. There, the vegetable matter constitutes the impurity which must be separated from the spirit; whereas in the liqueur the flavouring substances must be extracted and blended with the spirit base. Of the fruit-rinds, kernels, seeds, flowers, leaves, and roots which are used in the mysterious blends, a large number can be distilled. The usual process is to steep the materials in alcohol for varying lengths of time and then, when the spirit is well impregnated with the flavour, to distil it. Afterwards comes the sweetening with sugar-syrup. The distilled liquid is normally colourless. Some liqueurs, such as Kümmel and Cointreau, will remain so; but since many brands of liqueur are traditionally green, amber, red, or yellow, harmless colouring matter will then be added to the majority. All liqueurs, whether coloured or clear, are filtered to ensure perfect clarity. In the varying intervals before bottling they repose in modern stainless steel or brass-lined vats.

Of the alternative methods, infusion is suitable for substances which are soluble in water and not very volatile. The slower cold infusion, or maceration, is resorted to when the ingredient is easily soluble in water and would be injured by heat; in such a case, the fruit or plant is steeped in spirit until this is thoroughly permeated with the taste and perfume. After maceration, the liquid may well be thick and in need of preliminary straining; and, although fruity liqueurs made without distillation often retain their natural colour, the maceration of more than one substance may produce a muddy colour which must be corrected. As a rule, an innocuous dye, tasteless and without scent, is added, in an alcohol solution, before filtration. A fine crimson, for instance, can be produced with cochineal, powdered alum, cream of tartar, water, and alcohol.

When sugar is added, the mixture gains in suavity and body as well as in sweetness. Sometimes the sweetener is simple sugar-syrup, sometimes a blend of sugar and glucose or, occasionally, honey. When one of the ingredients is the juice of a sweet fruit, the dose of sugar is, of course, proportionately smaller.

It is upon the choice of flavouring substances that will blend harmoniously and easily, and on the balance of sugar and alcohol, that the success of the finished liqueur depends. Every manufacturer guards the secrets of his recipes. In some cases, the prevailing ingredients are known. Cointreau, for example, is made with orange-peel steeped in wine-brandy—but there are other, unnamed components. Aniseed, clearly, is the principal flavouring in the anis liqueurs, caraway in kummel, peppermint in crême de menthe. The Italian mentuccia is known also as centerbe, after the hundred herbs that go to its making. The famous Benedictine, of Normandy, on the other hand, is made to a secret formula. Among the flowers, fruits, spices, and plants which have their savour extracted for liqueurs are lavender, rose, orange, lemon, juniper, vanilla, angelica, thyme, fennel, mint, orris-root, camomile, cinnamon, almonds, curaçao bark, cloves, and ginger.

See also under individual headings: BENEDICTINE, GRAND MARNIER, etc.

Liquor

The most widely employed word for 'spirit' or 'alcoholic spirit' in America; in some isolated instances, the word still retains its original meaning of liquid.

Liquoreux

French term meaning 'rich and sweet'.

Lirac

Rhône Valley rosé, and some white, wine. District: Rhône Valley, France.

Lirac lies near Tavel and its vineyards resemble the more famous growths of its neighbour. The difference is that white wines—albeit in small quantity—are made in Lirac, only rosé in Tavel. Lirac has sandier soil than Tavel, with the result that its rosé is less full, less distinctive. The white wine is enjoyable but not extraordinary. About 54,000 imp. gallons (65,000 U.S.) of rosé are made annually, 1,250 imp. gallons (1,500 U.S.) of white.

See RHÔNE.

Lisbon Port

A port-type wine from the Lisbon area which sought to capture some of the export market for legitimate Port before this was made illegal by Portuguese wine laws early in the century.

Listofka

A Russian aperitif flavoured with blackcurrants.

Listrac

Bordeaux red, and some white, wines. District: Haut-Médoc, France.

Listrac is a commune of Haut-Médoc, important

in wine production although none of the Classified châteaux stands within its boundaries. The 755 acres of vineyard, planted on a good stretch of gravelly soil, rising into hummocks with a favourable exposure, yield full-bodied wines—a good deal of respectable *vins fins*, and some good red classed as *Bourgeois Supérieurs* and *Crus Bourgeois*. Among the *supérieurs* are Château Fonréaud, Château Fourcas-Dupré, and Château Fourcas-Hostein. There is also a co-operative cellar. In 1959, the total harvest was 119,885 imp. gallons (143,989 U.S.).

See BORDEAUX.

Litre

Standard metric liquid measure; the volume of one kilogramme of pure water measured at a temperature of 40°F. (4°C.) and an atmospheric pressure of 760 millimetres. It is equal to 1·5980 British pints, 1·90810 U.S. quarts, 35·1961 fluid ounces (33·8146 U.S.), and 100 centilitres.

Livermore Valley

Californian wine region producing, notably, very good white wines in Alameda County.

See AMERICA: CALIFORNIA AND THE WEST.

Ljutomer

Yugoslavian spelling of Yugoslavia's best-known wine. On labels destined for English-language countries, the 'j' is customarily omitted. Lutomer white wines are of several styles identified by the grape variety, also indicated on the wine label.

See YUGOSLAVIA.

Lodge

The word *loja* in Portuguese refers to a warehouse above the ground. However, it is the English who have made Port, in respect of its wealth, its renown, and even the wine itself, and the English tongue is notoriously unwilling to bend itself around words in other languages. *Loja* was transformed into lodge, and the warehouses of Port wine along the River Douro in Portugal are referred to as lodges.

Logroño

Important wine town and district in Rioja-Alta, the best table-wine region of Spain.

See RIOJA.

Loir

A tiny French river, a tributary of the Loire, on the banks of which several pleasant wines are grown.

See LOIRE; COTEAUX DU LOIR; JASNIÈRES.

Loire, The

Red, white, and rosé wines. District: Loire Valley, France.

The title in itself is almost a misnomer. No wine—excepting a small quantity of Muscadet de Coteaux de la Loire and Anjou, Coteaux de la Loire—is actually sold under the label Loire, and in fact a number of the vineyard areas along the river—Vouvray, Anjou, Sancerre, Pouilly, Muscadet, and Saumur—are far better known.

Yet, the wines are almost invariably considered as a group and as Loire wines. This nomenclature is justified by the fact that all of them share certain characteristics—all have a stamp that indelibly marks them Loire.

They can best be defined as 'charming'. If they lack some of the magnificent breed of the great Bordeaux and Burgundies, they have nevertheless a special style, a grace and gaiety which makes them wonderfully refreshing. All manner of wines are made—dry red and sweet white, rosé and dry white, sparkling, *pétillants* and still, and the better ones are found abroad in fair quantity. It is usually best to drink them fairly young—red as well as white—since they tend to decline after three to five years in bottle, especially after a voyage. This does not apply to the sweet whites, for the extra increment of sugar and increased alcoholic content helps to preserve the wine and allows it to age gracefully and withstand shocks which might be fatal to one of less robust constitution. Here, more than in almost any other district of France, good vintage years are of paramount importance, for if there has not been enough sun, there will be excessive acidity, throwing the wines out of balance.

The Loire comes down from the Massif Central in south-central France, flows due north, turns through a right angle, and then flows west to Nantes where it empties into the Atlantic to finish a journey of some 668 miles. Almost half this journey is completed before the first vineyards with controlled place-names—those of Pouilly-sur-Loire and Sancerre—spring up on the gently sloping banks; but from this point on, vine and vineyards abound. Quincy and Reuilly are skirted (they are drained by a tributary, the Cher) but near Tours the twin districts of Anjou and Touraine stand back to back, with the Coteaux du Loir and tiny Jasnières close by on the small River Loir (*le* Loir, not to be confused with the greater *la* Loire, of which it is a tributary) and vines continue all the way to the Muscadet district, around Nantes.

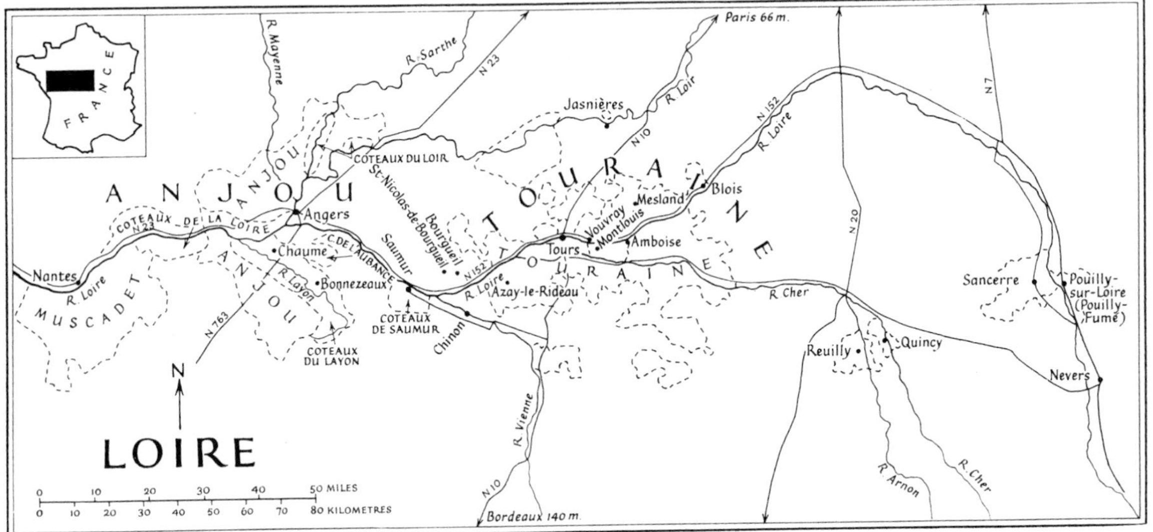

Wine History

It is not clearly established whether vines existed before the Roman invasion, or whether they were introduced by Cæsar's wine-drinking legions. Certainly the Romans developed and extended the vineyards of Gaul. What is well established is that the early Church was instrumental in advancing viticulture and viniculture in the Loire, as elsewhere, and that the Church of St. Martin at Tours had considerable vineyard holdings at various periods, some as far afield as Burgundy, but considerably more along the banks of the Loire. The local growers, as a matter of fact, declare that the art of pruning was discovered by that saint's donkey.

The story goes that in A.D. 345, St. Martin was making one of his periodic vineyard tours: he was an early wine enthusiast, aiding growers throughout the valley and bringing them up to date with what viticultors elsewhere were doing. Early one morning, he came riding into Anjou, heading for a vineyard which belonged to the Church. When he got there, he tethered his mount at the end of a row of vines. The inspection was a thorough one, St. Martin stopping here and there to ask questions or advise the monks who were tending the vines—and perhaps he went into the cellars to taste the last year's vintage. When, some time later, he returned, he was horrified to discover that his donkey had been munching the leaves, and that some of the tender young shoots had been nibbled right down to the trunk of the vine. But the next year those same shoots were the ones which grew back the most abundantly and produced the best fruit. The lesson was not lost on the monks, who quickly developed a more efficient method of pruning than donkey-tethering.

During the turbulent Middle Ages the vineyards of Touraine and Anjou assumed a considerable importance in Anglo-French trade, for the English Plantagenet kings were also Counts of Anjou; but before England lost all her French possessions, English taste veered towards the wines of Bordeaux. Ships from the Netherlands still sailed up the Loire to buy stocks of wine; but this trade too was curtailed when France and Holland went to war in 1672—a war in which the famous song *Auprès de ma Blonde* was first sung. Having lost two of their best markets, the Loire growers were forced to start building up a trade inside France—much more difficult than shipping wines down to the coast, in those days of poor roads, high tolls, and constant danger from thieves and highwaymen. Yet they succeeded. And now, as then, France and Belgium remain the most important customers for Loire wines, although recent advances in viniculture have made it possible to send them overseas without damage, and they can be found in fair quantities in England, the United States, and elsewhere.

Types of Wine

All the important types of still table wines are made along the Loire, as well as a substantial amount of sparkling and some semi-sparkling, or *pétillant*—a word that has become all but synonymous with Vouvray. The sparkle was introduced in the nineteenth century, when Champagne and other bubbly wines became the fashion. Most Loire sparkling wines are white and most come from Saumur and its environs, but there are others as well.

The best of the Loire wines are the still whites, both sweet and dry. The dry varieties should be consumed fairly young—nine months to five years old as a general rule—while the sweet may sometimes take as many as fifteen years to please the exacting palate of the local *vignerons*. These sweet wines are best bought young (although they must be stored until they are ready to drink) because for them, as for all good wines, the price is considerably lower when they are newly bottled. Rosé wine is something of a Loire speciality, and there are two types: a light rosé, and another fuller in colour and character, and sweeter, made entirely from Cabernet grapes. This Rosé de Cabernet, somewhat sweet, is the better wine of the two. Red wines are generally dry, fairly soft, fruity, and quick to mature, and when drunk young can be perfectly delightful.

Vine Varieties

Loire Valley wines do not always carry the name of the grape variety from which they come, as do those from Alsace, for example; but the names do guarantee that they were made from specific types of grapes. Those used are:

Cabernet Franc. The dominant grape (called Breton in Touraine) for red wine makers who also employ it in making vin rosé. This vine is said to have been brought to the Loire in the twelfth century. In the seventeenth the Abbé Breton planted a new vineyard for Cardinal Richelieu; hence the local pseudonym Breton for the grape. The vines came originally from the Gironde, where the grape is grown for the red wines of Bordeaux. Other local names for the grape are Véron, Bouchy, Bouchet, etc.

Cabernet Sauvignon. Some Sauvignon is found, mostly in Anjou, where plantings have increased of late years, and even in 1954 production had risen to some 1,320,000 imp. gallons (1,585,000 U.S.). Most of the grapes are pressed for pink wine.

Chasselas. A grapevine used for about three-quarters of the production of dry white Pouilly-sur-Loire, the minor wine of the district of the same name. The best wines of Pouilly are Blanc Fumé de Pouilly, or Pouilly-Fumé, and are made with the Sauvignon Blanc, also known as Blanc Fumé.

Chenin Blanc. Despite its restriction to the districts of Anjou, Touraine, and Jasnières, this is the most widely-planted grapevine for white wines along the banks of the Loire. It is called Pineau de la Loire in Touraine. The vine is known to have grown in Anjou from very early times. It is no doubt a selection of once wild plants. The fruit is used both for sweet and for dry white wines, the main factor being in many cases the weather—hot summers give sweet wines, chill rainy ones give dry wines. The other factor is the method of fermentation used by the wine-grower at will. Dry wines can be made in hot summers if all the sugar is allowed to be converted into alcohol.

Cot. A minor vine cultivated in the valley of the Cher in Touraine. The red wines it produces are uninteresting. Other names for this grape are Pied-Rouge, Malbec or Malbeck, Cahors.

Gamay. The vine of Burgundy's Beaujolais district is planted to a slight extent in the Coteaux de la Loire and in the Touraine. It is used for rosé wines rather than red, except in the Ancenis district.

Groslot. This grape is used for rosé wine in Anjou.

Gros Plant du Pays Nantais. Planted around the Muscadet district, it produces fresh white wines. Sometimes on the acid side, these wines are only consumed locally along the Atlantic coast.

Muscadet. Actually Melon de Bourgogne, but when transplanted, in 1639, from its native Burgundy to the vineyards at the mouth of the Loire, the vine took on a new name. The dry white wines made from its grapes are light, fresh, slightly hard and acid, and excellent with sea-food.

Noble. This is used in small quantities for red wine in the Touraine, synonymous with Pinot.

Pineau d'Aunis. Once the important grapevine for red wines but now almost entirely replaced by Cabernet Franc. It is still found in limited amounts in Anjou where it has been growing since the twelfth century.

Pinot Noir. This grape variety was cultivated in abundance in Sancerre up to the beginning of the twentieth century. Since then, little by little, it has been replaced by the Sauvignon. Recently, there has been a strong tendency to replant certain vineyards of Sancerre in Pinot Noir, as in good vintages it produces very good rosés. The red wines, because of their quality, are acquiring a noteworthy following.

Sauvignon Blanc. The white grape of Bordeaux does exceptionally well in the upper Loire where it is used exclusively for the dry white wines of Sancerre, Quincy, Reuilly and the best wine of Pouilly-sur-Loire, the Blanc Fumé.

Loire Wine Districts

There are nine major districts of the Loire of which three—Anjou, Muscadet, and Touraine—are huge and contain a number of sub-districts, while the rest are small and of lesser importance. These districts are:

Anjou

Makes red and white wines (the latter both sweet and dry, of which the sweet are the better) and dry and semi-sweet rosé. It includes the sub-districts of Anjou-Coteaux de la Loire, Savennières, Bonnezeaux, Coteaux de l'Aubance, Coteaux du Layon, Quarts de Chaume, Saumur, and Coteaux de Saumur.

Coteaux du Loir

A minor and very small district taking its name from the tiny River Loir and producing red, white, and rosé wines. The white are sweet, the rosé quite charming, the red sometimes not very good. It must be repeated that the Loir, a tributary of the Loire, is not to be confused with the greater river.

Jasnières

A small district making up the heart of the Coteaux du Loir and producing the superior wine. The wines are entirely white and are usually described as *mœlleux*: slightly sweet, velvety and rich in texture.

Muscadet

The vineyards at the mouth of the Loire produce a fresh and delightful dry white wine which once served the dubious purpose of stretching the limited supply of Burgundy's Chablis. Now sold under its own name, the wine is building a substantial reputation for itself both in France and abroad. Muscadet is divided into three place-names. The most famous is Muscadet de Sèvre et Maine, some ten miles south of Nantes, deriving its name from two small rivers running through the vineyard area. The second is Muscadet Coteaux de la Loire; and the third is referred to simply as Muscadet.

Pouilly-sur-Loire

A district of the upper Loire where Sauvignon Blanc grapes are pressed to make the excellent dry white Pouilly-Fumé, otherwise known as Blanc Fumé de Pouilly, and Chasselas grapes to make the similar but less distinctive Pouilly-sur-Loire.

Quincy

Although thirty miles from the Loire and adjoining a tributary, the output of Quincy is always considered as Loire wine. Dry and white, it is much like Sancerre, Pouilly-Fumé, and Reuilly, with a slightly distinctive *goût de terroir*.

Reuilly

Dry white wine—often thin, harsh and acid—from Reuilly on the Arnon, a tributary of the Cher. It resembles the wine from nearby Quincy.

Sancerre

One of the best-known growing districts of the upper Loire, famous for its dry white wine made entirely from Sauvignon grapes. There is also a very good dry rosé and occasionally, a red wine—both made from Pinot Noir.

Touraine

The second of the two largest districts of the Loire. The wines may be red, white, or rosé and the whites may either be sweet or dry. The sub-districts of the Touraine include: Bourgueil and Saint-Nicolas-de-Bourgueil, Chinon, Montlouis, Touraine-Amboise, Touraine-Azay-le-Rideau, Touraine-Mesland, and the world-renowned Vouvray.

See also under separate headings.

Lombardy

Red, white, and rosé wines. District: Northern Italy.

From the towering Alps along its northern boundary to the pleasure resorts of Lake Garda and almost to the city limits of Milan, Lombardy is a region of wines and vines. There are stretches, of course, where no vine is seen: northern reaches where the land is too forbiddingly mountainous, or central lowlands where the soggy valleys are given over to the culture of rice. In general, however, the vine is found throughout. It does best in the Valtellina section, an Alpine corner near the Swiss border, some fifteen to twenty miles due south of Saint Moritz, but the wine from grapes grown near Lake Garda is also popular with the Italians. In addition, Lombardy can boast of the well-known vineyard Frecciarossa, dealing in something almost unheard of in Italy—estate-bottled wines.

Valtellina

In this district, centred around the town of

Sondrio, the three almost identical red wines are Sassella, Grumello, and Inferno, all from Nebbiolo grapes grown on the more manageable Alpine slopes. A similar but lesser growth is the red Valgella. Perhaps the mountaineer is a different type from the plainsman, but wine, and even life, in the Valtellina does not seem to have changed for centuries. The peasant who pours you a glass of wine and warns you not to stay out too late (werewolves inhabiting the upper slopes are still dangerous at night) might well be from another age entirely, and it is difficult to conceive of his changing his wine-making techniques. Mechanization is rare and even animals often find the slopes too steep, leaving man to struggle alone to till the land. For this reason, and because the Nebbiolo is always a shy bearer, the amount of wine made is small—less than 580,000 imp. gallons (700,000 U.S.) a year for the combined four wines. Once made, they seem to epitomize not only the virtues but the faults of Italy's wines. All are lighter in alcohol (11% to 12%) than the Nebbiolo wines of Piedmont. All fit neatly into an Italian meal with its amazing ability to reduce the pungent harshness so often found in the wines, and bring out unsuspected characteristics, although they may develop these virtues to a fault, becoming rough, coarse, sometimes common; yet at their best they have an agreeable freshness, and occasionally, as is true throughout the country, they have a light sparkle, as unexpected to the wine-maker as to the drinker. When these wines succeed, they are hearty and good.

Lugana

This, Lombardy's leading white wine, is made from Trebbiano grapes with some Vernaccia not infrequently added. For all the fuss made about it, this is a small wine, generally yellowish in colour, running to about 11% to 12·5% of alcohol. It is regrettable that Italian wine-makers—contrary to their general practice—usually age their white wines too long; if it were brought young out of the barrel, Lugana would probably be delightful.

Frecciarossa

The district is in the province of Pavia, bordering on Piedmont. The carefully-made wines come strictly from a seventy-acre vineyard on a castle-topped hill near Casteggio and are of four types: Bianco (dry, white), Ambrato (semi-sweet, white), Rosso (dry, red), and Saint George (dry, rosé). The white wines are made from Riesling and Pinot Noir grapes, the others from Pinot Noir, Bonarda di Gattinara, Barbera, and Croattina. Something under 41,500 imp. gallons (50,000 U.S.) are made annually, split into almost equal parts among the four, and the wines are distributed widely throughout the world. Estate-bottled wines are to be found here—something very rare in Italy. Other wines of the region are the red Barbacarlo and Buttafuoco.

Lombardy also makes a muscat and a sparkling muscat in commercially important (but fortunately not significantly large) quantities, selling them as Moscato di Casteggio and Moscato di Casteggio Spumante. The former is a typically sweet muscat wine, the latter something like Asti Spumante (*see* PIEDMONT).

London Dry Gin

One of the two basic styles of gin—the other is Hollands. This is the gin of both the United States and England. The base spirit is distilled until neutral and flavouring, from a number of different herbs but chiefly juniper, is added afterwards. Less totally distilled, Hollands (or Dutch gin) retains flavour characteristics from the original spirit.

See GIN.

Lorraine

Red, white, and rosé wines. District: North-East France.

Since 1951 the wines of Lorraine, which had practically ceased to exist, have been making a small comeback. This north-eastern province of France had, at one time, been well known for its *Vin gris* (a type of rosé made from Gamay) and for its sparkling wines. Three wars, phylloxera, and the passing of rigid control laws in Champagne, all but wiped Lorraine off the wine map. Two controlled place-names exist today, both established in 1951 and both of them having the right to the name of *Vins Délimités de Qualité Supérieure*, the secondary French classification of wines. They are the Côtes de Toul and Vins de la Moselle.

Lorraine has always been one of the more troubled parts of France. After the war of 1870 the province was split in two, half going to France and half to Germany. During this period, the wines of Lorraine probably enjoyed as much renown as they have ever had. Those grown on the German side were made into Sekt, or German sparkling wine; and those on the French side became either Vins gris or were made sparkling and sold as Champagne; the Champagne shippers did this with Lorraine wine, until in 1908 Champagne had a disastrous year and virtually all the wine had to be brought in from Lorraine. The Champagne growers objected so violently, such riots and havoc broke out in the region, that a rigid delimitation law was passed in 1908, strengthened further in 1911. Henceforth, Lorraine wines would have to find another outlet.

Before the growers could get back on their feet, the First World War came. Such vineyards as survived in the battleground area fell victim to phylloxera. Hybrid vines were planted for the making of very ordinary wine to be drunk in Lorraine by the inhabitants. Only after the Second World War did the growers of Lorraine start replanting their finer vine types with any consistency.

The better wines of Lorraine are today much what one would expect from a vineyard area so cold and so far north. Low in alcohol and high in acid, the grapes are harvested late—the end of October. The red wines which result are far less pleasant than the white and rosé. High acidity in red wines is a definite defect.

Côtes de Toul

Most of the wines are Vins gris, the traditional light rosé wine of Lorraine. They come from parts of the communes of Lucey, Bruley, Pagney-derrière-Barine, Ecouvres, Dongermain, Mont-le-Vignoble, Charmes-la-Côte, Blénod-les-Toul, and Bulligny. The permitted vines are the Gamay de Toul, Gamay de Liverdun, Pinot Noir, and Pinot Meunier (all of these either separately or together must comprise at least 80% of the wine); and Aubin Blanc, Blanc d'Euvézin, and Aligoté (these three comprise up to a maximum of 20%). The vines are allowed to yield no more than 346 imp. gallons (416 U.S.) per acre.

The alcoholic content of the Côtes de Toul will only run about 8·5% in an average year, but may go as high as 10% or even 11% in years that are particularly hot, and acidity is markedly high. Only about 66,500 imp. gallons (80,000 U.S.) are made each year. The vineyards of the Côtes de Toul are in the process of being expanded, and this figure may rise.

Vins de la Moselle

The Vins de la Moselle are made in three separate areas and each of the wines has its own characteristics. The wines from around the city of Metz are mostly light rosé wines often found under the name of Clairet de Moselle. Those which come from around Sierk are generally white. The traditional *vin gris* is made principally around Vic-sur-Seille. All must derive from the same vines, which are the Gamay (30%), Auxerrois Blanc, Auxerrois Gris, Meunier Blanc, Meunier Gris, Pinot Noir, Pinot Blanc; Elbling (20% maximum, but has not been allowed at all since 1961), Sylvaner (30% maximum), Riesling, and Gewürztraminer. Like the wines of the Côtes de Toul, these tend to be extremely acid but are often pleasantly fruity when young. For the *appellation* Vins de la Moselle, the harvest must not exceed 303 imp. gallons (364 U.S.) per acre and the amount made averages about 8,300 imp. gallons (10,000 U.S.) yearly. As in the Côtes de Toul, this figure is rising.

Spirits

Among the colourless eaux-de-vie that are made from fruits here, as elsewhere, the Mirabelle de Lorraine is the best known. It is made from small yellow plums.

Los Hermanos Vineyard

A well-known Napa Valley Winery, in California, owned by the Beringer family.

Loupiac

White wine. District: Bordeaux, France.

This is the continuation northward of Sainte-Croix-du-Mont on the right bank of the River Garonne, and facing Sauternes across the river. It produces approximately the same quantity as Sainte-Croix-du-Mont and under identical conditions, the sole difference being that these vineyards are in the commune of Loupiac. The wines may be considered with those of Sainte-Croix-du-Mont, as there are no important differences.

See SAINTE-CROIX-DU-MONT.

Low Wines

Whisky after first distillation and before redistillation.

Lower Moselle

See MOSELLE.

Lugana

Principal white wine of Lombardy, made from Trebbiano grapes, with sometimes an addition of Vernaccia.

See LOMBARDY.

Lunel—Muscat de

See SWEET FORTIFIED WINES OF FRANCE.

Lussac-Saint-Émilion

Commune with an Appellation Contrôlée, making red wines, in the region of Bordeaux (*q.v.*).

Lutomer

English spelling of Yugoslavia's best-known white wine. There are different styles identified as Lutomer Riesling, Lutomer Sylvaner, etc.

See YUGOSLAVIA.

Luttenberger

The German name for the wines of Ljutomer in Yugoslavian Slovenia during the Austrian occupation before the First World War. The white wines became famous under this name, by which they are still occasionally called. They are now correctly Ljutomer wines, or Lutomer on English-language labels.

See YUGOSLAVIA.

Luxembourg

The white wines grown on the rolling, pretty Luxembourg bank of the Moselle are very similar to those of Alsace. Light and fruity, they are stay-at-home wines for the most part, since few of them are ever seen outside the Benelux Union.

Each year the 3,000-acre strip of vineyard produces a rough average of 3 million imp. gallons (3,600,000 U.S.) of wine, though there can be considerable variation. In 1950, for instance, 3,750,000 imp. gallons (4,500,000 U.S.) were made, while in 1949 only 416,000 imp. gallons (500,000 U.S.). This is a consequence of the northerly climate, a constant risk for the producer of wine in this region.

Of the wines, 75% are consumed in the Grand Duchy itself, amounting to two bottles in three of all the wine the Luxembourgers drink, the odd bottle being made up by importation, mainly from France and Italy. The *per capita* consumption is twenty-seven or twenty-eight bottles per year, far down the list for a European nation. Most of the wine not used up at home goes to Belgium. Holland and Germany receive a token quantity, and the amount exported to the rest of the world is a statistical drop in the bucket. To taste Luxembourg wine you must go to Luxembourg itself, or at least to Belgium.

Wine History

At the time of the French Revolution Luxembourg was a part of France and the Revolution drove the monks from the vineyards they had tended. The vineland was broken up into small parcels, a condition which has survived to this day, when there are 2,067 vineyards. The size of the average plot is just under $1\frac{1}{2}$ acres, only a half-dozen being from eight to fifteen acres in size. This extreme tendency to division is counteracted by the co-operatives, one existing in each main town of the wine belt; between them they account for 65% of total production.

At the turn of the century Luxembourg wine went almost entirely into blends called vaguely Moselblümchen—mixtures of low-quality German Palatinate and Lower Moselle wines with the Luxembourg product. When this practice was ended by the First World War and severance from Germany, Luxembourg had no sale for the characterless bulk wine that was being produced. A long crisis extended from 1914 to 1925. Then the Government Viticultural Station was founded at Remich on the Moselle. Premiums were paid for uprooting second-class vineyards. Luxembourg viticulture had accepted the principle, in force to this day, that wine is a quality—not a quantity—product. The Viticultural Station is the teacher and policeman of this movement. There is a department of analysis, free instruction and help for growers, a scientific campaign against vine disease, and supervision of the laws governing place-names on bottle labels.

Vines have grown here from the time of the Romans. Luxembourg vintage records extend as far back as 809 (when the wine was a failure). In 1866, again, it was so sour that, as a joke topical at the time, the people named it Bismarck. One of the worst setbacks occurred in 1944, when the Moselle was caught in the von Rundstedt Counter-offensive, finishing with the Battle of the Bulge; but the following year the vineyards were flourishing again.

What the Wines are Called

The Luxembourg vineland faces east, across the Moselle to the German bank. Wine is grown nowhere else in the tiny country. The advantage of catching the early sun on the east-facing slope is augmented by the forest protection crowning the hills, cutting off a wind which usually blows from the west all the year round. The whole gentle length of the Moselle is an alternating patchwork of vineyard and orchard. The cherry and plum trees provide the fruit for the kirsch, quetsch, and mirabelle distilled in the Duchy.

Luxembourg wine labels carry, according to law, name designations of the following four types:

Vin de la Moselle Luxembourgeoise. Seldom used and limited to wine exported in cask and to the ordinary wine, known as *grâchen*.

Vin de la Moselle Luxembourgeoise used in combination with the grape variety. This is what appears on most common wines, e.g., Vin de la Moselle Luxembourgeoise Riesling.

Locality name, with or without vineyard site, and grape variety, e.g., Wormeldange Riesling, Riesling from the Elterberg vineyard near Wormeldange.

Appellation Complète, sometimes also called Appellation Contrôlée, and corresponding to the French designation of that name. This is the category of fine wines. Labels must indicate vintage year, locality, vineyard site, grape variety, name of grower, and his domicile. Wines of one of the first three types may or may not be vintage-dated, but those of the fourth must be. There are also strict regulations governing treatment and the type of vine, and wines must pass official tasting tests of the Commission of the Marque Nationale.

Since its establishment by the Government in 1935, the Marque Nationale has begun to appear on more and more Luxembourg wine. A small label prominently lettered Marque Nationale and indicating that the wine is from Luxembourg is affixed to the neck of the certified bottles. Marque Nationale wines are bottled under Government observation and control, subjected to blind tasting tests.

Grape Varieties: Best Wines

The best vineyards are found on the chalky marl soil of Remich and the stony chalk-and-clay soil of Grevenmacher. A chalky soil with scattered stones and a marly subsoil is considered to be good Riesling soil, while the peculiar clay soil varying in hue from green to red is the soil for the Pinot varieties.

The grape varieties of Luxembourg are:

	Acres planted
Riesling	408
Traminer	37
Ruländer	104
Pinot Blanc	44
Auxerrois	204
Sylvaner	59
Riesling + Sylvaner	844
Elbling	969
Muscat Ottonel	4

From these, the best wines are the following:

Riesling+Sylvaner. A light table wine with a slight Muscat taste. Best locality: entire Moselle.

Pinots. Auxerrois, Pinot Blanc and Ruländer (or Pinot Gris). Fuller, more generous and with more body than the Riesling+Sylvaner, though often with less bouquet. Best localities: Wellenstein, Remerschen, Schengen.

Riesling. Elegant and full of distinction, tending to be acid in the wet years. Best localities: Wormeldange, Stadtbredimus, Wintrange, Schengen, Remich, Grevenmacher, Ehnen.

Traminer. Velvety, big, and with the typical spicy perfume and taste. Best localities: Ahn, Wellenstein, Schwebsingen, Schengen, Machtum.

Spirits

Kirsch, quetsch, and mirabelle are produced from the cherry and plum orchards. The number of distilleries in operation varies but is usually around 950, making an annual average of 41,600 imp. gallons (50,000 U.S.) of the fruit spirit.

Château Lynch-Bages

Bordeaux red wine. District: Haut-Médoc, France. Commune: Pauillac.

Classified a Fifth Growth (*Cinquième Cru*) of Médoc in 1855, Lynch-Bages actually commands prices equal to those of some Second Growths (*Seconds Crus*). It is located at Bages, hardly a quarter of a mile south of Pauillac, and is plainly seen on the left of the wine road approaching Pauillac. Originally the property of an Irishman, Mr. Lynch—who was mayor of Bordeaux—the vineyard has been, since 1933, in the Cazes family, and in recent years in the hands of the young and energetic mayor of Pauillac, Monseiur J. C. Cazes. With this capable management the growth has come rapidly into its own. In both 1955 and 1956, at blind tastings held at Château Prieuré-Lichine in Cantenac-Margaux, with leading vineyard owners, wine brokers and Bordeaux shippers participating, Lynch-Bages took first place among the leading Médoc classified growths. That this fine vineyard is still classed as a Fifth Growth indicates the obsolescence of the 1855 Classification.

Characteristics. Can produce rich, full, round, beautiful wines. It is flattering to the taste in its youth, but in ageing it does often show a lack of breed.

Vineyard area: 160 acres.

Average production: 13,000 cases.

Château Lynch-Moussas

Bordeaux red wine. District: Haut-Médoc, France. Commune: Pauillac.

The output of this small vineyard, which was classified a Fifth Growth (*Cinquième Cru*) of the Médoc in 1855, is principally sold in Holland and Belgium. In common with its large neighbour, Château Lynch-Bages, the estate was once the property of Mr. Lynch, an Irish mayor of Bordeaux. Classified Fifth Growth (*Cinquième Cru*) in 1855.

Characteristics. To be drunk young.

Vineyard area: 16 acres.

Average production: 1,600 cases.

M

Macadam, Vin de

An old Parisian term for a sweet white wine brought right out of the fermenting vat and rushed to the boulevards of Paris. Much of this wine was drunk in the open-air cafés, overlooking the macadam-paved streets and squares. The most famous of these wines came from the area around Bergerac (*q.v.*).

Mâché

French term for a wine which tastes tired, either from racking or from travel. It is as though it had been mashed up by chewing.

Mâcon

Market town and wine centre for Lower Burgundy.

See MÂCONNAIS.

Mâcon Supérieur

An Appellation Contrôlée of the Mâconnais region (*q.v.*).

Mâconnais

White wines, some red and rosé. District: Southern Burgundy, France.

The southern Burgundy section of the Mâconnais adjoins that of the Beaujolais. It occupies one corner of the department of Saône-et-Loire, and its south-east corner overlaps the wine district of the Beaujolais, specifically the commune of la Chapelle-de-Guinchay. The wines made in this corner are usually sold as Beaujolais if they are red and as Mâconnais if they are white, this being one of the rare cases where the vintner can make the best of both worlds.

The best, and the most famous, of the Mâconnais is the dry white Pouilly-Fuissé, a wine which has commanded a place on many good tables over the years and is still growing in popularity. It is not, however, the only Pouilly to be made. Nearby are the vineyards of Pouilly-Loché and Pouilly-Vinzelles; and in the valley of the Loire there is another dry white wine made in the town of Pouilly-sur-Loire. The Pouilly-Fumé (*q.v.*) from this last town is similar in colour and in name, but the grapes used are different—and so are the wines.

Pouilly-Fuissé is to the white wines of southern Burgundy what the Beaujolais is to the red. Neither of them is ever a very great wine, either may often be an excellent wine, both are usually extremely pleasant wines. The public affection for Pouilly-Fuissé and the wines of the Mâconnais is far older than for those of Beaujolais, which has only gained its wide circle of admirers during comparatively recent times.

The Mâconnais has been sending its wines to clamouring markets since the seventeenth century, thanks, so they say, to an imaginative grower named Claude Brosse. About 1660, Brosse decided that it was high time that someone outside the region knew about the excellence of the Mâconnais wines. A man of enormous stature, and evidently fearless as well, he loaded his cart with two barrels of his finest wine and started off for Paris. Trips to Paris were rare in those days, for there were some 250 miles of muddy and nearly impassable roads, and highwaymen in waiting. But Brosse managed to arrive safely with his wine in Paris—it took him thirty-odd days. His imposing stature caught the attention of the King who wanted to know what he was doing so far from home, and since the business was wine, he wanted to taste it. When the King had sipped the wine, Brosse got an immediate order for the royal cellars. What the King happened to like was also exactly what the court had always wanted, and Brosse and the wines of the Mâconnais were launched.

The present Mâconnais growers produce more than white wines. A large amount of red is also made, and the makers could add rosé, although there is comparatively little of this at present. Being next to the Beaujolais, where the noble vine is the Gamay, the growers of the Mâconnais tend to plant the same vine, but the results are less happy. The traditional red-wine vine has always been the Gamay à Jus Coloré (Gamay with coloured juice), sometimes called Gamay-Teinturier. It produces large grapes in vast quantities and these, unlike those of most vines, give a dark juice. This particular vine, of all the varieties of Gamay, has come in for an enormous amount of abuse. It is the 'disloyal plant' of Duke Philip the Bold and it has been condemned and forbidden in Burgundy over and over again. In the Mâconnais, however, the red wines may still include up to 15% Gamay-Teinturier.

The reason why the Gamay vine does so much better in the neighbouring Beaujolais than in the Mâconnais is the soil. Nowhere in the Mâconnais does one find the granite soil which gives Beaujolais its special appeal. By the same token, the chalky hills of the Mâconnais permit the Chardonnay vine, Burgundy's only noble white-wine vine, to produce, with delightful results. Actually there are three areas of soil, the best that of Pouilly-Fuissé, slightly to the south-west of Mâcon. Here there is a series of dips and rises where the soil is limestone mixed with slate, dating back to the Jurassic age some 150 million years ago. To the north-west of Mâcon there is a slightly different formation, this time a long valley where the disintegration of the chalky oolite has allowed enough top soil for the planting of vines. Both of these sections are excellent for growing grapes for white wines. Towards the northern end of the district the terrain gets more varied and confused. At one point there is a preponderance of chalk, and at another of slate, and the wines tend to follow the lead given by the soil. Some are good, some not so good, the characteristics depending upon the particular soil in which they were grown.

The soil of certain parts of the Mâconnais has always had a fascination for geologists and diggers in the earth. Not only are there several layers of rock formation underlying the district, each one dating from a different period, but the area has proved a good place for digging up relics of the distant past. Fossils dating back 6,000 years have been excavated from the vicinity of Solutré—one of the communes making Pouilly-Fuissé—and there is hardly a ploughman in the region who has not at one time or another turned up some ancient bit of equipment, often dating back to Roman days. But the history of the Mâconnais is written not only in the soil. The great mediæval monastery of Cluny was built at the town of that name, some ten miles north-west of Mâcon. Its monks did a great deal to keep learning alive during the Dark Ages, and Cluny was once the most powerful arm of the Church in France. The monks also helped to forward the knowledge and practice of vine-growing and wine-making and to inspire the local peasants to increase their vineyards and care for them properly. It is not recorded whether the monks inspired the wine or whether the wine inspired the monks, but it is certain that Burgundian viniculture virtually owes its existence to the industry of the inhabitants of Cluny.

In this corner of southern Burgundy they have their own methods of viniculture. The sun is warmer than it is further north, on the Côte d'Or, and the warm seasons are slightly longer. The Chardonnay vine, in particular, is allowed to grow much higher here than elsewhere in Burgundy. Because of the stronger sunshine, the growers say that the grapes need not be pruned close to the ground where the stony soil will reflect heat on to them. Furthermore, in the Mâconnais they can often afford to wait as much as two weeks longer than in the Côte d'Or for the grapes to ripen.

Most of the wine sold is Mâcon Supérieur, or Mâcon, followed by the name of the commune where the wine was grown. A slightly lesser amount will be sold simply as Mâcon with no other indication of source, while the best, of course, is sold under one of the three Pouilly *appellations*. As is usual with French wines, the names include more than simply place of origin.

PLACE-NAMES OF THE MÂCONNAIS

Pouilly-Fuissé

Pouilly-Fuissé is the king of the Mâconnais white wines, and the very finest rank high among white Burgundies. In general, these wines are fairly light and very dry. The better ones have a forthright, round fulness that distinguishes them from the lesser, light wines which are lacking in character and are over-acid. They are less hard than the Chablis and not so fruity, with a slight *gout de terroir*, the taste imparted by the soil in which they are grown. They tend to have a very light, fine bouquet, and at their youthful best are of a pale golden colour with overtones of green. They are definitely wines to be drunk when they are young, reaching their peak after about six months in bottle and holding it for from three to five years. Some of them have enough alcoholic content to last longer than that, but there will be no improvement and little point, therefore, in keeping them.

To be a real Pouilly-Fuissé, the wine must have been grown in one of the communes of Solutré-Pouilly, Fuissé, Chaintré, or Vergisson. It must be made only from the Chardonnay vine, the amount harvested not to exceed 400 imp. gallons (481 U.S.) of wine per acre. The content in the must—or unfermented grape-juice—should amount to 187 grammes (6½ ozs.) of natural sugar per litre, and the finished wine must have a minimum alcoholic strength of 11%. The sugar is always stated to be natural, since the growers here, as elsewhere in Burgundy, are allowed to add a certain amount of extra sugar to the wine, a process known as *chaptalisation*. The purpose of this practice is to raise the sugar content in years when the sun has been too weak to instil enough natural grape-sugar into the fruit, and what is added gets converted into alcohol with the grape-sugar. *Chaptalisation* is a tricky business, for when it is practised to excess it tends to diminish the finesse and elegance of the wine, making it fuller, heavier, and sometimes very much coarser than it should be.

Within the area of the four towns allowed the use of the name of Pouilly-Fuissé, there are about 1,100 acres of vines. From these come on an average about 350,000 imp. gallons (420,000 U.S.) of wine each year. The best is sold as Pouilly-Fuissé with the name of the vineyard added, and to qualify for this the sugar content of the must is elevated to a minimum of 204 grammes (7¼ oz.) and the alcoholic content must be 12%. The better vineyards, and those apt to be found on a bottle label, are: (in the town of Solutré-Pouilly) Les Chailloux, Les Boutières, Les Chanrue, Les Prâs, Les Peloux, Les Rinces; (in the town of Fuissé) Château Fuissé, Le Clos, Clos de Varambond, Clos de la Chapelle, Menetrières, Versarmières, Les Vignes-Blanches, Les Châtenets, Les Perrières, Les Brûlets.

In general, the wines from Solutré-Pouilly tend to be more feminine and delicate than those from the other communes, while those from Fuissé are apt to be the strongest. The wines of Chaintré and Vergisson are not so consistent in quality as are the others.

Pouilly-Loché and Pouilly-Vinzelles

These are the two lesser Pouillys of the Mâconnais. Although the legal restrictions—exclusive of growing area—are exactly identical with those of Pouilly-Fuissé, they never attain quite the same degree of excellence. As a rule, they are lighter, with less breed that the Pouilly-Fuissé, although they often have more fruitiness.

The geographical distinction is simply that Pouilly-Loché must be harvested within the town of Loché, nearest to Fuissé, and Pouilly-Vinzelles comes from Vinzelles, directly south of Loché. Together they account for about 58,000 imp. gallons (70,000 U.S.) of wine per year.

Mâcon Supérieur or Mâcon

This *appellation*, followed by the name of the commune, could include red, white, and rosé wines, but in practice slightly more than half are white, and most of the rest, red. The red wines are small, generally not of outstanding quality, and even in the headquarters for the area, the town of Mâcon, the red wines drunk are often from the neighbouring district of the Beaujolais. The whites are perhaps less distinctive than those of Pouilly-Fuissé, but every now and then one of the better growers will come up with one which will be their equal or even better than some of the lesser Pouillys.

The wine must be grown in the delimited area that lies within the *arrondissement* of Mâcon, or within the communes of Boyer, Bresse-sur-Grosne, Champagny-sous-Uxelles, Champlieu, Etrigny, Jugy, Laives, Mancey, Montceaux-Ragny, Nanton, Sennecey-le-Grand, or Vers. It must be made from a certain selection of grapes. For red wines, only the Gamay Noir à Jus Blanc, Pinot Noir, and Pinot Gris are allowed, with up to 15% Gamay Noir à Jus Coloré and also up to 15% of Pinot Blanc or Chardonnay, the allowable vines for white wines. The normal production of any wine may not exceed 400 imp. gallons (481 U.S.) per acre. In the red there must be a minimum of 180 grammes of sugar per litre and 10% of alcohol when that sugar has fermented; and for white wines there must be at least 187 grammes (6½ oz.) of sugar per litre fermenting into 11% of alcohol.

The white wines could be sold as Burgundy, if so desired, and if the reds came only from the Pinot plants, they too could be sold as Burgundy; but there is small incentive for this to be done. As it now stands, about 1,700,000 imp. gallons (2 million U.S.) per year are sold as Mâcon Supérieur.

Mâcon; Pinot-Chardonnay-Mâcon

At the bottom of the Mâconnais scale are those wines which are sold simply as Mâcon-Rouge, Mâcon-Blanc, or Pinot-Chardonnay-Mâcon (something of a misnomer since the wines can be made from the Pinot Blanc as well as the Chardonnay, the same as the less cumbersome Mâcon-Blanc). All told, the *appellation* covers the lesser red and white wines, but mostly the red.

To earn this place-name, these wines must be harvested in a quantity not exceeding 446 imp. gallons (535 U.S.) per acre, as opposed to the 400 imp. gallons (481 U.S.) figure for the other wines of the district. It is always important to remember that quantity and quality seldom if ever coincide in wines. The same growing area is prescribed as for Mâcon Supérieur; but in the wines themselves, the differences are that red wines for this *appellation* need only have a sugar content in the grape of 162 grammes (5¾ oz.) of sugar per litre, giving 9% of alcohol, and the white wines must have 170 grammes (6 oz.) of sugar, giving 10% of alcohol.

Under this *appellation*, about 560,000 imp. gallons (675,000 U.S.) of red wine are made each year, and about 140,000 imp. gallons (170,000 U.S.) of white.

Madagascar

This island lying off the coast of Africa makes a certain amount of rum.

See RUM, FRENCH.

Madeira

Until the turn of the eighteenth century, Madeira

—like its cousins, Port and Sherry—was exported as an unfortified beverage wine. It is known that brandy was distilled from surplus grapes on the island of Madeira as early as 1704. However, it is not until 1753 that we have the first indication that 'a bucket of brandy was added to each pipe of shipping wine', and so gave Madeira its present character, a distinctive wine with its own unique excellence. It was about this time also that the wine became most popular in the United Kingdom and the American Colonies.

Some great Madeiras were, and still are, made, but the markets built up during the days of sailing ships and exploration have passed. Madeira is no longer primarily produced for Britain and the United States (although these are still good markets) but is now also sold largely in Scandinavia, France, Germany, Belgium, Holland, and Canada. This has come about partly as the result of easier communication, partly because of political and economic changes, but chiefly in consequence of two vine diseases which nearly did away with the wines entirely.

Wine History

The history of the island is almost the history of its wines. Madeira is politically an integral part of Portugal, and geographically an island in the Atlantic, 360 miles from the coast of Morocco and 530 miles from Lisbon. It is thirty-six miles long and fourteen and a half miles wide, a holiday-maker's paradise of steeply-sloping, intricately-terraced, hillside vineyards and shady flower-filled valleys.

Madeira and its tiny volcanic neighbours, Porto-Santo and The Desertas, were islands known to the ancient Phoenician, Genoese and Portuguese as the 'Enchanted Isles'. But none was so audacious as to penetrate the thick woods and see what was there until Prince Henry the Navigator sent his intrepid Captain João Gonsalves Zarco to claim them for Portugal in 1418. Zarco apparently landed near where modern Funchal stands, but found it impossible to move further. Madeira, 'Isle of Trees', was aptly named. Trees intertwined and woven together claimed the entire island and defeated all attempts to hack through them. Zarco solved the problem. He set the island on fire and sat back to wait.

According to legend he waited a long time. It is said that the fire raged for seven years . . . and when it had finally gutted itself out the trees were gone and the centuries-old humus and leaf-mould volcanic soil had been enriched into the most fertile in the world.

Settlers arrived from Portugal, Spain, Holland, and Italy; sugar cane and the Malvoisie vines were planted. The rich soil and sub-tropical climate made Madeira a lush garden in the midst of the Atlantic. Mariners called in at Funchal in search of fresh water, fresh food, and to replenish wine casks. Treaties between Portugal and Britain helped Madeira as well as Port wines. Englishmen who departed to establish colonies in America took their tastes with them, and Madeira began to be shipped to the new world as well as the old. As the American colonists moved towards rupture with England, Madeira became more and more the wine of America . . . almost, in fact, a patriotic duty. In drinking Madeira, the rebellious colonist could feel he was thumbing his nose at a tyrannical King and Parliament who had established a ruling that European goods going to the American Colonies could only be carried in British ships. Naturally, British ship-masters were not above charging a premium price for the exercise of this monopoly; but, geographically, Madeira is in Africa, and under the terms of the law its wines could arrive on ships bearing any flag. The idea was quickly grasped by the Americans, and Madeira was a common sight on American sideboards. The popularity of Madeira along the Eastern Seaboard lasted for the period of the Clipper ships.

The English writer, Captain Frederick Marryat, remarked in his *Diary in America* (1839, Vol. I, Part II, pp. 102–3): 'Claret and other French wines do very well in America, but where the Americans beat us out of the field is in their Madeira, which certainly is of a quality which we cannot procure in England. This is owing to the extreme heat and cold of the climate, which ripens this wine; indeed, I may almost say that I never tasted good Madeira until I arrived in the United States. The price of wines, generally speaking, is very high, considering what a trifling duty is paid, but the price of good Madeira is surprising. There are certain brands which if exposed to public auction, will be certain to fetch from twelve to twenty, and I have been told, even forty dollars per bottle.'

During the eighteenth and early nineteenth centuries, the fortunes of Madeira were probably at their peak. The Napoleonic Wars had cut into French wine exports, but Madeira was untouched and business boomed. Fortification had put strength into the wines, and the long sea voyage aged and ripened them. Shipments to England and America were heavy, with the ports of the Southern States—

Savannah and New Orleans, Charleston and Baltimore—handling the bulk of the trade.

Disaster fell on Madeira in 1852, when oïdium struck the vines. They were just recovering from the attack of this fungus blight when they were again attacked, by phylloxera, in 1872. This time, weakened by the ravages of the oïdium, they succumbed to the *Phylloxera vastatrix* which attacked their roots and killed the vines. Many of the old-established British shippers left the island and it is to the courage, endurance and persistence of a handful who remained that we owe the present Madeira wine. They imported American rootstocks which had become immune to the disease (phylloxera having originally spread from America to Europe). It was many years before these American vines were in full production and when there was enough wine to ship, this was found to be coarse, although plentiful, since the American plants are prolific. The vines had to be cut down and grafted with the pre-phylloxera European vine.

Wine-making

The vintage is probably as picturesque in Madeira as anywhere in the world, and is certainly the longest. Starting at sea level in mid-August it continues as the grapes ripen on the slopes until October. The crushing of the grapes is still done in *lagares*, or large wooden troughs, by bare-footed men. The 'dance' of the grapes is followed by a more rigorous pressing, after which the grape juice or *mosto* is brought to shippers' lodges in Funchal in goat skins, or in casks on sledges drawn by oxen.

The *mosto* ferments and turns itself into wine or *vinho claro*, which is fortified and put into an *estufa* to go through a process, peculiar to Madeira, known as *estufagem*. This process is a relic of the old days when all Madeira was sent round the world, or to India and back, in order to mature. The rolling of the ship and the heat of the tropics obviously hastened the maturing of the wine, but during the Napoleonic Wars, when freights were difficult to obtain, the process of *estufagem* (or bringing the wine up to a warm temperature in a sort of heating chamber) was invented.

The *estufa* today is a large store with central heating in which pipes of wine are placed for six months. The temperature of the wine is gradually brought up to 104°–114° F (40°–46° C.) and then allowed to drop to normal in the sixth month, thus producing much the same effect as would a voyage round the world.

Wine which has never been *estufado* is known as *canteiro*, meaning a scantle. When the wine comes out of the *estufa*, it goes through an *estagio*, which is an eighteen-months' rest to recover from the treatment. Then it is blended into 'lots', known as *soleras*, where it is given time to rest and marry before it is finally blended for shipment.

Madeira wine lives longer than any other and there are still some priceless old pre-phylloxera vintages in existence. Tasting them is not only a pleasure but an exciting and memorable experience.

Wine Types

There are four distinct types of Madeira, named after the grapes from which they are produced, dry and full rich, with intermediate steps between. The leading types are named after the grape variety from which they are made. These are:

Sercial. The best of the dry Madeiras, excellent with soups, and the proverbial companion to turtle soup; sometimes pale, sometimes golden, often slight in body but always dry with an overwhelming nose. André Simon, the famous writer on wines, has described one of them as 'a soul with a nose'.

Verdelho. Sweeter and softer than a Sercial; leaves a dry, clean taste in the mouth.

Bual (*Boal*). Fuller and sweeter than either of the preceding, russet-brown to dark in colour, with a distinctive bouquet.

Malmsey. From the Malvoisie grape. A rich, luscious, generous wine with considerable body, balance, and bouquet. This type of Madeira is excellent after dinner and extremely good with a bite (especially a sweet one) between meals—in Victorian days, mid-morning callers were habitually entertained with a slice of cake and a glass of Madeira.

Other names to be found on bottles of Madeira are:

Rainwater. A blend. Originally a trade-mark, it has now become almost a generic name. The wine may be dry or medium rich, but is always pale and light as the name implies.

Dated Soleras. Many dated *soleras* are offered for sale; the word *solera* before or after the date denotes that these wines are not only of that date, but have from time to time been topped up with specially chosen younger wines, of equal quality and similar characteristics. The average age of a *solera* is estimated to be some eighty years. These are always particularly fine wines. For a fuller account of the solera system, *see* SHERRY.

Maderization

Owing to age or poor storage, white wines may lose their freshness and fruitiness and acquire a brown tinge. This browning or oxidation has been named maderization, from the Madeira taste, which is connected with the presence in the wine of ethylic aldehyde—the result either of oxidation of alcohol, or of the dissociation of aldehyde-sulphurous acid through progressive oxidation of sulphurous acid. Maderization also results from leaving white wines in the barrel too long before bottling. In the Madeiras, Marsalas, Sherry and the Château-Chalons of the French Jura, maderization adds to the greatness of the wines, producing a taste called *rancio*. In other white wines it is a flaw. It is particularly unpleasant in the Montrachets and Meursaults of the Côte de Beaune; and is more unpleasant in Graves than in Sauternes, because the sweetness of a Sauternes hides the flat, musty, brownish taste.

By combining the action of sulphur dioxide with that of casein, it is possible to protect wines against maderization; and the flat taste can be corrected with sulphurous acid.

Madiran

Red wine from the Hautes-Pyrénées district of south-west France. The wine, full in body and of a pronounced bouquet, is made from Tannat (30%–70%), Cabernet-Sauvignon, Bouchy, and Pinenc grapes and attains 11% of alcohol. The white wine made in this area in the valley of the Adour is Pacherenc du Vic Bilh (*q.v.*).

Château Magdelaine

Bordeaux red wine. District and Commune: Saint-Émilion, France.

Particularly well-known in England and Belgium, the wine was classified a First Great Growth (*Premier Cru*) of Saint-Émilion in 1955. The vineyard lies alongside those of Ausone and Belair on the heights of Saint-Émilion village.

Characteristics. The well-tended vineyards produce a pleasant wine which is full and velvety with distinctive aftertaste.

Vineyard area: 18 acres.

Average production: 3,200 cases.

Mailly

Village near Reims producing a first-quality Champagne (*q.v.*).

Maipo Valley

One of the best wine regions in Chile (the other is the Aconcagua Valley) specializing in Cabernet and Malbec grapes and making long-lasting wines of finesse and balance.

See CHILE.

Maître de Chai

French term for the man in charge of vinification and ageing of all the wine made on an estate in Bordeaux. The name, which may be shortened to *maître*, is used especially in Bordeaux, of the head cellarman at the château or at the shipper's *chais*. He is of necessity an experienced wine-maker and a good taster. In other districts, the *maître de chai* will be called a *caviste*.

Málaga

Spanish sweet wine. District: Andalusia.

Málaga—important though it was even in the recent past—is no longer seen in any great quantity abroad. Germany, the one considerable customer, takes two-thirds of the total which flows each year over the Spanish borders; Switzerland comes next and the remainder is divided among the rest of the world. England—a great customer from Elizabethan times, when the wine was famous as 'Mountain'—now imports only a small amount; the United States buys only a token quantity of a wine which, before the war, was very popular. The total production, in 1958, for eastern Andalusia, of which Málaga is the principal wine, was 1,100,000 imp. gallons (1,321,000 U.S.).

The typical Málaga is sweet. Dry wines are made from the more mountainous vineyards, but, as on the Douro River in Portugal—where dry wines are being pushed by some vintners as a means of regaining their dwindling Port wine market—the true tendency of the climate and viticultural conditions is to produce sweet wines. The dry Málagas, like the dry Ports, are produced by efforts against nature. No other wine has suffered more from the present swing away from sweet to dry wines.

In Málaga itself, it seems doubtful that the growers realize the full extent of their difficulties. Perhaps the soft climate, thickening the blood like syrup even in winter, is responsible. The heat, the sun, the intense radiation of light on Spain's warmest seaside resort make the wines what they are—and probably the wine-makers too. The men in the little bars do not drink Málaga (they like dry wines, they say, and besides Málaga wine is expensive); even in the *bodegas* the vintners can be seen drinking and serving other wines. With the Malagueños showing such lassitude and indifference, the wine trade may never pull out of its slump.

Grape Varieties and Wine Types

It is interesting that Málaga grapes do not produce Málaga wine. One-third only—about 23,000 acres—of the vineyard produces wine. A special loophole in the wine law lets in grape-must from outside the Province of Málaga, whenever it is necessary to maintain the level of the wine stocks. Otherwise, the wine is required to come from a limited area which includes the greater part of the province, and must be matured in the cellars in and within a ten-mile radius of the town of Málaga. The humidity and the micro-organisms established during centuries are considered as necessary to the character of the wine as the soil itself.

The grape varieties going into the typical Málagas are Pedro Ximénez, Lairén, Moscatel, Moscatel Morisca, Jaén Blanco, Jaén Tinto, and Jaén Doradillo. The Roma grape, small and harsh-tasting, is said to be used in making faked Port, and this is very possibly true as the wine has resemblances to the Douro product. A Muscatel wine is made—about 10% of the total production—but this is not a true Málaga.

The better and better-known of the dessert wines are the white Lágrima (meaning 'tear') and Málaga Negro or Dulce Negro, sometimes called *color*, or simply Málaga. The Spaniards claim that the more famous Lacrima Christi from near Naples is named after their Lágrima, and not the other way round. The wine is made from the Lairén grape, and is usually no more than average in quality. Pedro Ximénez, from the grape of that name, is a sweeter wine than the Lágrima, sometimes reaching 13% of sugar and 20% of alcohol. It is dark brown in colour.

Other wines entitled to the official place-name and the right to exportation with a certificate of origin include Málaga Golden White (actually rather dark in hue and not a true white wine); Málaga Dry White, more alcoholic than the sweet style and attaining as much as 22%; Pajarete; and Rome, a red wine. Pajarete is sweet and comes from the Pedro Ximénez and Lairén varieties, but it is never very interesting or distinguished. Among the dry Málagas, there are some bearing a faint family resemblance to dry Finos and to dry Olorosos—to the latter a certain amount of Pedro Ximénez is added to sweeten the wine.

Method of Wine-making

The characteristic treatment of the sweet brown wines is the mixing in of *color*, a concentrate of essence made by cooking down wine, and the halting of fermentation by the addition of wine brandy. This prevents some of the sugar from being converted to alcohol and keeps it as sweetness. The grapes have previously been exposed in the sun for up to a week after picking, a treatment which causes them to dry almost to raisins, increasing proportionately in sugar as they lose in water.

The vats, holding sometimes 100,000 litres, are reminiscent of vats in California, but the maturing process after fermentation—for the better wines—is like that of Sherry. The tiered barrels (or *botas*) form a true *solera* system. Having gone through an early education of about three months, during which they are racked, filtered, and cleared, the wines enter the solera—a school of barrels graduating upwards like a series of classrooms. The virtue of the *solera* and its secret, as in Sherry, is that each younger wine, promoted a grade up as the older wine is drawn off, takes on some of the characteristics of its seniors.

See SHERRY.

Château Malartic-Lagravière

Bordeaux red and white wine. District: Graves, France. Commune: Léognan.

The reputation of the red wine is very old, and it was included among the eleven Classified red wines of Graves in 1953. An excellent dry white wine is made, which is less well known than the red.

Characteristics. A big, mouth-filling wine with a distinctive taste, derived probably from the preponderance of Cabernet Sauvignon grapes.

Vineyard area: 25 acres.

Average production: red—2,300 cases.
white—280 cases.

Malbec

One of the lesser grapes contributing to the red wines of Bordeaux, prolific and light in character. It is grown in other places too, and is sometimes known as Cot.

Château Malescot-Saint-Exupéry

Bordeaux red wine. District: Haut-Médoc, France. Commune: Margaux.

The vineyard name derives from the Counts of Saint-Exupéry, who purchased the vineyard in 1827, and the château itself, a substantial grey-stone manor-house, is right in the town of Margaux. The building, nothing but a shell, after being gutted by the Germans, was repaired in 1964 by the son of the present owner.

In recent years, until 1955, the estate belonged to

Seager Evans, British distillers, who sold it in that year to Paul Zuger—up to that time their administrator in the vineyard and one who has always been an able wine-maker. Zuger is the president of the association of the official wine place-names of Margaux which came into being in 1956.

The vineyard was classified Third Growth (*Troisième Cru*) in the Médoc Classification of 1855. Half of the output is reserved for sale in France; half is exported to England, Belgium, and the U.S.A.

Characteristics. Quite full for a Margaux wine, very elegant and sometimes slightly hard at the outset. The wines reflect the high proportion—50%—of Cabernet Sauvignon grapes used.

Vineyard area: 45 acres.

Average production: 5,000 cases.

Malmesbury

Wine region in the coastal belt of Cape Province.

See SOUTH AFRICA.

Malmsey

English corruption of the name of a vine which started out as Monemvasia in Greece, became Malvasia in Italy, Malvoisie in France, and Malvagia in Spain. Malmsey is also used to refer to the wines from this vine, the most famous of which—during the present day—come from the island of Madeira (*q.v.*), a Portuguese possession in the Atlantic.

Malmsey was famous in the England of Shakespeare's day and the references to it are numerous. Perhaps the best-known fact about Malmsey is that the Duke of Clarence was drowned in a butt of it. It is likely that the wine in which the unfortunate Duke found his end came from the island of Crete rather than from Madeira.

Malolactic Fermentation

Secondary fermentation, caused by the conversion of malic acid into lactic acid and carbon dioxide. When this occurs while the wine is in barrel, the result is simply a reduction in acid strength; but in bottle, the malolactic fermentation causes the wine to become turgid and gassy. This happens much more frequently in Burgundy than it does in Bordeaux, and may be the result of premature bottling.

See CHAPTER NINE, p. 50.

Malta

Vines are grown mostly along the southern coastal strip of the island, but since the climate changes from torrential early rains to scorching heat, the resulting wine is generally harsh and rough, an ordinary wine, either red or white. An attempt is being made to produce sweet, rich dessert wine from Muscat grapes, principally for exportation to the United Kingdom. About 3,000 acres are under vine, but the greater part of production is devoted to table grapes. Production of wine is estimated to be about 900,000 imp. gallons (1,100,000 U.S.) a year.

Malvasia

Originally Monemvasia in its native Greece, the grape Malvasia has spread throughout the viticultural world, sometimes with modifications in name. In France it is Malvoisie, in Spain Malvagia, and the sweet, heavy wines it gives long ago became famous in England as Malmsey.

Mandarine

Sweet, gold-coloured liqueur with the flavour of tangerines.

Manganese

This is present in almost all wines, in quantities never large but varying with the different vineyard soils. More of the mineral is found in Beaujolais than in Bordeaux, more in red wine than in white. Most of the manganese in a grape is contained in the pips.

Mannitic Fermentation

When the temperature of the fermenting vat rises above 95°F. (35°C.) and when the wines are lacking in acidity then the good yeasts die and other bacteria take over. The wine then throws a deposit, and becomes cloudy, with a bitter-sweet, 'mousy' taste.

See CHAPTER NINE, pp. 48, 52.

Manzanilla

The dry fine wine, fortified and unfortified, of Sanlúcar de Barrameda, Spain, sold as a type of Sherry.

See SHERRY; MONTILLA.

Maraschino

A liqueur made from the sour cherry Marasca which only grew in Dalmatia. Before the Italian enclave in Dalmatia was incorporated in Yugoslavia, Maraschino was not made anywhere except in Zadar (sometimes known by its former name, Zara). Maraschino, 50% proof, is sold in wicker half-litre bottles. Luxardo is the largest distiller. After the war the company moved from Trieste to Padua; to ensure their supply they planted 200 acres of marasca cherries. Drioli, a lesser firm, is the other well-known Italian maraschino distiller.

Marc, Eau-de-Vie de Marc

Spirit distilled from the pomace which remains when the grapes have been pressed and the juice run off. It is usually distilled at a high strength and has a distinctive taste—grapey, almost leathery—when it is well aged. Most districts have their own marcs; those from Burgundy are the best-known, and excellent marcs come from Romanée-Conti, Musigny, Chambertin, Nuits-Saint-Georges, Meursault, and Montrachet. Marcs from the white wine Burgundy districts are lighter and have a little more finesse than those from the red wine areas. The most expensive is the Marc des Hospices de Beaune; one of the lightest, and one with great finesse, comes from Champagne. Another of repute is the Marc d' Auvergne.

In Italy and California, this spirit is known as grappa.

The Marches

Red and white wines. District: East-Central Italy.

Like the rest of the peninsula, this Italian state is steeped in history—even the name is said to date from the days when the area was a frontier province in the empire of Charlemagne. Here, as elsewhere in Italy, the countryside is covered with vines and some 67 million imp. gallons (80 million U.S.) of wine are made annually, but most of them are only fit for local consumption.

Exception might be made for the Verdicchio dei Castelli di Jesi, a light, dry or semi-sweet white wine, pale gold or straw-coloured, which can be surprisingly high in alcohol (up to 14%). It is made at Cupramontana, Monteroberto, and Castelbellino, in the province of Ancona, and is one of the few lesser wines of Italy which travels.

The principal red wine of the Marches is Rosso Piceno, from the Piceno Hills on the fringe of the Apennines. The grapes are Sangiovese and Montepulciano (nothing in common with the Vin Nobile di Montepulciano, made from entirely different grapes in Montepulciano in Tuscany (*q.v.*)) and the wine is small and unexceptional.

Marcottage or Layering

Traditional method of propagating vines.

See CHAPTER EIGHT, p. 32.

Mareotic Wine

A fine wine of Ancient Egypt, very well known in classical times. Cleopatra is said to have served it to Cæsar.

See EGYPT.

Mareuil-sur Ay

A village in the department of the Marne and the commune of the Champagne district, near Épernay, producing very fine wines.

See CHAMPAGNE.

Margaux

Bordeaux red wines. District: Haut Médoc, France.

Margaux wines form a royal family. The Great Growths (*Grands Crus*), and the least among the modest vineyards, all share the same characteristics. No other commune of Bordeaux and the Médoc contains such a distinct gradation of similar vineyards.

It is the summer of great sun that brings Margaux to its prime. In the best years, the greater Growths of the fine districts a little to the north, in Saint-Estèphe and Pauillac, may overreach themselves; in any case, it will be a long time before they are ready to drink. But in Margaux, the strong sun will have awakened the subtle, hidden virtues which lie in the vines. In such years, Margaux vineyards are likely to surpass all others in the Médoc. The wines they give are the most feminine, the most delicate, the most elegant; and it is the bolder Saint-Estèphe or, characteristically, a Pauillac which will sometimes excel in the lighter years.

The name is said to derive from Marojallia, so called by Ausonius, the fourth-century Latin poet after whom the Château Ausone, in Saint-Émilion, was also named.

The village of Margaux itself lies twenty miles north of Bordeaux, and it is a sleepy place. A poster outside a tiny cinema which opens three times a week and is heated by a giant pot-bellied stove; occasional sheep droves, the clatter of sabots, old men in cafés—that is about all, except for the wine. In the season of fermentation the smell of the wine is everywhere in the air, as thick as burning leaf-smoke. Tall châteaux with steep roofs stand right in the village, and plots of vine encroach on the dwellings and shops. Beyond, everything is vine—a calm ocean, brown in winter and green in summer, but always ruffled by a breeze. An occasional château rises in the distance, with its park around it like a froth of waves.

Five villages, not one, have the right to the place-name of Margaux. A quarter of a century ago, the wine of all five was considered as one—Margaux itself, Arsac, Soussans, Cantenac, and Labarde produced similar wines, and shared the same light gravelly Margaux soil. Then, the mayor of Margaux, a wine man himself, brought a suit against a certain proprietor in Soussans. This grower had a strip of land along the river bank where the soil, a muddy alluvial deposit, is not the true soil of Margaux, and its wine had no right, therefore, to the place-name. The legal process was fought and won, but the result was hardly what had been intended. The court ruled that neither the wine from this one vineyard nor any other made in Soussans could be called Margaux.

Within a few years, similar rulings denied the Margaux name to Arsac, Labarde, and Cantenac. There was consternation, for only a single important Margaux vineyard had all its vines in Margaux, and every other overlapping into the outcast communes by even an acre now had no right to the name, since some of its wine did not come from within the permitted circle. Margaux was almost in a state of civil war—because certain rather undistinguished growers safely within the commune now had a vested interest in resisting change.

For twenty years nothing could be done. Even when the Appellation Contrôlée, or officially-controlled place-name, was established, the authorities were obliged to respect the earlier rulings of the courts. Then in 1953 someone had a bright idea. If Margaux could not mean what it ought to, why have any Margaux at all? At last action could be taken; and the place-name Margaux, which could not be extended back to its rightful limits, was totally suppressed: not even Margaux wine could now call itself Margaux. Again there was consternation, and this time the sit-tight Margaux growers found that they could not sell their wines, could not get the proper documents, could not export. They demanded a decision, and the Appellation Contrôlée authorities suggested that perhaps the whole problem ought now to be reconsidered.

As a result, new regulations laid down that Margaux wines are those from the communes of Margaux, Soussans, Arsac, Cantenac, and Labarde; that they must be grown from soils ascertained by the experts of the Appellation Contrôlée to be typically Margaux; they may not yield more than 302 imp. gallons (363 U.S. gallons) to the acre, and in type of noble grape variety, in methods of pruning, cultivation, and wine-making, they must come up to high quality standards and must satisfactorily pass an anonymous taste test.

The first of the tastings for the Appellation Contrôlée Margaux took place in 1956, and the subsequent banquet and festivities were held in the great salon of Château Lascombes.

It is rarely that the leading vineyard of an area epitomizes and brings to the highest perfection the district characteristics, rather than standing out for excellences more peculiarly its own, but this is the case with Château Margaux. The Margaux vineyards rated as Classified Growths (*Cru*) in the 1855 Classification are:

First Growth (Premier Cru)
Château Margaux

Second Growths (Seconds Crus)
Château Rausan-Ségla
Château Rauzan-Gassies
Château Lascombes
Château Durfort-Vivens
Château Brane-Cantenac

Third Growths (Troisièmes Crus)
Château Kirwan
Château d'Issan
Château Giscours
Château Malescot-Saint-Exupéry
Château Boyd-Cantenac
Château Cantenac-Brown
Château Palmer
Château Desmirail
Château Ferrière
Château Marquis d'Alesme

Fourth Growths (Quatrièmes Crus)
Château Prieuré-Lichine
Château Pouget
Château Marquis-de-Terme

Fifth Growths (Cinquièmes Crus)
Château Dauzac
Château du Tertre

(For the individual Classified Growths, see listed under individual châteaux names.)

Château Margaux

Bordeaux red wine, some dry white. District: Haut-Médoc, France. Commune: Margaux.

Château Margaux, with its colonnaded portico, and an interior which is pure Empire, stands in a large park beside a magnificent magnolia tree. In the fifteenth century the wine, under such names as Margou and Margous, was already known, and the site was occupied by a fortified castle known as Lamothe. It is interesting to note that one of the owners of Lamothe was the Seigneur de Durfort; whereas, until recently, the proprietor of Margaux owned the nearby Château Durfort.

The vineyard was greatly improved by replantings in 1750 and the present château was built at the beginning of the nineteenth century—by a pupil of Victor Louis, architect of the Bordeaux opera-house. In 1836 the Vicomte d'Aguado bought the property. His son sold it in 1879 to the Comte Pillet-Will, who introduced various vinicultural improvements. By 1925 the château had come into the possession of the Duc de la Trémoïlle, from whom a corporation (including Fernand Ginestet, then owner of the adjacent Château Lascombes), acquired it. Between the years 1935 and 1949 Ginestet bought out his partners, and in 1949 he became sole owner. It was generally considered that, owing to too rapid treatment after the phylloxera scourge at the end of the last century, the wine had declined; but opinion, now unanimous, is that in the last years the Ginestets have restored it magnificently. The present owner is Monsieur Pierre Ginestet, son of Fernand.

With Château Lafite, Latour, and Haut-Brion, Margaux has been ranked first among Médoc wines since 1855. There is also a small amount of dry white wine, a rarity in Médoc, not carrying the grand name of Château Margaux but known as Pavillon Blanc du Château Margaux.

No other commune of Bordeaux has a château of the same name—there is no Château Sauternes or Château Pauillac. All the wine of Château Margaux is château bottled.

Characteristics. At its best, the most elegant and delicately feminine of the region. Perfectly balanced, and quick to develop, for a Médoc. Finesse is synonymous with its name. In 1965, Pierre Ginestet instituted the controversial policy of affixing a vintage only to great vintages; the lesser years will be sold as non-vintage wines as is done in Champagne.

Vineyard area: 155 acres.

Average production: 13,000 cases.

Markobrunn, Marcobrunn

From Erbach on the German Rhine, Markobrunn is occasionally labelled Erbacher Markobrunn—but it is one of the few German wines so great in its own right as to eliminate the town or village or district name in most cases. Not perhaps the greatest of the Rheingau, although easily the best of the Erbachers, it is certainly one of the liveliest, heartiest, spiciest, and deservedly best-known Rhine wines.

See RHEINGAU.

Château Marquis d'Alesme-Becker

Bordeaux red wine. District: Haut-Médoc, France. Commune: Margaux.

Originally planted in 1616, the estate was acquired in 1803 by a Monsieur Becker, which accounts for some confusion about the name of the wine. For a long time Becker attached his name to that of Marquis d'Alesme, and Becker being the simpler name, the wine began to be called simply Becker in Bordeaux. Bottles labelled up until a few years ago are likely to carry the name Marquis d'Alesme-Becker; but Becker has now been dropped.

The small vineyard occupies one of the finest positions in Margaux, the knoll of Margaux, or La Combe, which it shares with the Second Growth (*Second Cru*) vineyard, Château Lascombes. Thirty-five years ago, Château Marquis d'Alesme was bought by Comte Chaix-d'Est-Ange, then owner of Château Lascombes, who meant to combine the two vineyards. This plan was not carried out, and today Marquis d'Alesme is run jointly with Château Malescot-Saint-Exupéry by Paul Zuger.

This Third Growth (*Troisième Cru*), according to the 1855 Classification of Médoc wines, has two secondary vineyards: Cru La Fleur-Margaux, place-name Margaux; Domaine du Balardin, place-name Bordeaux Supérieur.

Characteristics. A minor and not well-known wine with the typical finesse of Margaux.

Vineyard area: 29 acres.

Average production: 3,000 cases.

Château Marquis-de-Terme

Bordeaux red wine. District: Haut-Médoc, France. Commune: Margaux.

This Fourth Growth (*Quatrième Cru*) of Médoc, Classification of 1855, is in the opinion of many the best-kept vineyard in the Médoc. If the wine fails to come quite up to the expectation of the marvellously handled vines, it is perhaps because, through forcing, the plants are made to produce too great a quantity, losing proportionately in essential elements such as the tannin and glycerine needed for the finest wine. The vinification has not been so well cared for as the vineyard.

Characteristics. Relatively full for a Margaux, and although not among the top wines of this commune, despite its large production it sometimes attains finesse and perfume.

Vineyard area: 104 acres.

Average production: 11,000 cases.

Marsala

The principal dessert wine of Italy is made in

north-west Sicily, where the town of that name is situated. In the late eighteenth century it was introduced into England by Mr. John Woodhouse, whose family soon built up a flourishing trade. The dark wine, which has a taste of burnt sugar, is a blend of an aromatic white wine, of *passito* made from dried grapes and fortified, and of grape-juice syrup. It is matured in cask for from two to five years.

Marsala all'uovo, or Marsaluovo, is a smooth, warming winter drink of Marsala combined with egg yolk and spirit—a development, perhaps, of zabaglione, the frothy sweet made from egg and Marsala.

See SICILY.

Marsanne

White wine grape planted in Provence, Algeria, Savoy, and elsewhere.

Louis Martini Company

Napa-Sonoma, California, U.S.A.

Louis M. Martini, the founder of this fine wine firm, was born in Pietra Ligure, Italy, in 1887 and came to the United States at the turn of the century. For many years his dream had been to produce excellent wines, and when Prohibition was repealed in 1933, he built a large winery at St. Helena, some forty miles from San Francisco. Over the next ten years he acquired three important, well-situated vineyards and planted them with fine grape varieties. In 1941, the author and his then associate Frank Schoonmaker started selling American wines under American names. It was then that Louis Martini wines, amongst others, were for the first time offered east of the Rockies.

The company has 200 acres in Napa, 280 acres in Sonoma County, and 80 acres in St Helena. These vineyards form almost an equilateral triangle, within twenty miles of each other. In St. Helena the vines are mainly Gamay, Cabernet Sauvignon, and Petite Sirah; in Napa Valley, the Pinot Noir, Cabernet, and Zinfandel predominate. The Sonoma Vineyard has many great varieties, including the Cabernet Sauvignon, Pinot Chardonnay, and Sémillon. As a general rule, the Sonoma Vineyard contains the white grape varieties and the Napa Vineyard the red varieties.

See AMERICA: CALIFORNIA AND THE WEST.

Mascara

Important Algerian wine region, near Algiers. Red, white, and rosé wines are grown here. This dark red wine is often used as a base for many of the better-known wines of France, especially in Burgundy, where it is a favourite part of a 'shipper's blend'.

See ALGERIA.

Mash

In whisky-making, grain which has been steeped in hot water. During the mashing process, the starch in the grain is converted to fermentable sugar.

Mastika (or Masticha)

A favourite Greek aperitif, made on the island of Chios, from a brandy base with gum mastic added.

See GREECE.

Maury

Small area of Grand-Roussillon producing fortified sweet wines.

See SWEET FORTIFIED WINES OF FRANCE.

Mavrodaphne

This heavy, sweet, red dessert wine is one of the two best-known wines of Greece (*q.v.*).

Mavroud

One of the grapes widely used in Bulgaria. It produces wines of about the same acidity and alcoholic strength as those made from the Gamza; but this wine has a dark ruby colour.

See BULGARIA.

Maximin Grünhäuser Herrenberg

One of the best wines of the Ruwer. Herrenberg is the top vineyard of Mertesdorf-Grünhaus.

See RUWER.

May Wine

Traditional preparation of a light Rhine wine into which the aromatic leaves of the herb Waldmeister (woodruff) have been infused. May wine is served chilled and ladled from a bowl, usually with strawberries or other fruit floating in it. A gay and refreshing drink, it can actually be prepared almost anywhere with either a Rhine wine or any light, dry, white wine.

Mayacamas Vineyards

Napa-Sonoma, California, U.S.A.

The beautiful terraced Mayacamas Vineyards are

high on the upper crests of the Mayacamas Mountains some twelve miles north-west of Sonoma in Napa County, California. The owner, Jack F. M. Taylor, a former oil executive, began to make wine in 1945. He and his family are devoting the greater part of their time and interest to the Chardonnay grape, grown in France, for Chablis and Pouilly-Fuissé; and plantings of white Pinot are being reduced to make way for it. In 1951 the Taylors harvested 760 pounds of this grape—not yet enough to be a commercial proposition: but in 1955, they increased their harvest to 8 short tons (7 long tons), a healthy start on the road to the goal of 60 short (53·6 long) tons which they have set themselves. Mayacamas Vineyards is one of the twenty-six Premium Wine Producers of the approximately 350 California bonded wineries, and this excellent group produces less than 4% of the wine in the state. The Taylors add to the small percentage of fine wines, not only with their excellent Chardonnay, but with an agreeable rosé made from the Napa Valley Gamay. They also age and blend unfinished Napa wines that bear the Lokoya White label.

See AMERICA: CALIFORNIA AND THE WEST.

Mazis-Chambertin

Burgundy red wine. District: Côte de Nuits, France. Commune: Gevrey-Chambertin. Official classification: Great Growth (Grand Cru).

Mazis (sometimes Mazys) is only slightly below Latricières-Chambertin in the hierarchy of wines which add Chambertin to their names, and to achieve this place is no mean accomplishment. The two giants of the commune of Gevrey-Chambertin are Le Chambertin and Chambertin-Clos de Bèze. Latricières is generally conceded to come next.

The vineyard adjoins the Clos de Bèze on the south side of Gevrey-Chambertin and its wines often have much in common with those from the ancient Clos, although they are generally lighter and with enormous finesse, perhaps lacking some of the austere strength of the Clos wines. There are 22·4 acres planted exclusively in Pinot Noir grapevines and production in 1960—an average year for quantity—amounted to about 4,974 imp. gallons (5,970 U.S.) or the equivalent of some 2,500 cases.

Mazoyères-Chambertin

Burgundy red wine. District: Côte de Nuits, France. Commune: Gevrey-Chambertin. Official classification: Great Growth (Grand Cru).

Mazoyères is a vineyard listed as Great Growth (*Grand Cru*) in the official classification of the wines of the Côte d'Or of Burgundy. The ruling reads Mazoyères or Charmes, and in practice it means that Mazoyères may be sold as Charmes although Charmes may not be sold as Mazoyères. Most of the growers take advantage of this ruling, feeling that Charmes is both easier to say and better-known than Mazoyères. In theory, under the existing laws, some 13,300 imp. gallons (16,000 U.S.) of wine could be made with the name Mazoyères in an average year; in practice, there has been none declared as such since 1958. The combined acreage for Mazoyères and Charmes is 65·3.

See CHARMES-CHAMBERTIN.

Mead

The drink of ancient Anglo-Saxons, made from fermented honey. It is a clear, pale golden liquid tasting of honey, with usually about 8% alcohol by volume. Hydromel (honey-water) was the Roman equivalent and Metheglin (from the Welsh) is a spiced mead. When mead has been distilled it is called honey brandy.

Mealie Beer

A native grain beverage drunk in southern Africa.

Meal-Moth

The meal-moth, or *Pyralis*, feeds on the foliage and fruit of the vine.

See CHAPTER EIGHT, p. 38.

Medford Rum

Name given to virtually all rum made in colonial America.

See RUM, NEW ENGLAND.

Medicated and Medicinal Wines

Wines enriched with spices and/or drugs have long been used by physicians in treating diseases. Dioscorides, Galen, and others, through the ages, have given various recipes. Medical use of wine is mentioned in all mediæval régimes for health. In modern times, cheap, red, fortified wines often have meat extract or extract of malt and other substances added, purportedly to render them more health-giving. In some instances, wines are treated with ipecacuanha or pepsin, in which case they cease to be wines and become medicines.

Médoc (Haut-Médoc)

Red wine. District: Bordeaux, France.

The Médoc, first in importance of the great

Bordeaux districts, is rated by many experts as the greatest in the world for fine red wines. Considering the bulk of good wine produced, and the incomparable vintages of some of the châteaux, this is probably a fair assessment.

A Médoc is a typical Claret, possessed of a subtle bouquet in age which suggests the scent of rose or violet, or an indefinable smell of woods in springtime and clean earthiness. The wines are feminine and delicate, compared with the fuller, heartier Clarets of Saint-Émilion; they have often been described as the 'queens' of the world's red wines. Médocs have tremendous finesse, when properly aged; even the lesser Growths (Crus) respond to some ageing, and the greatest can be drunk when they have been sixty (or even more) years in bottle and still be found full of life, mellow, and magnificent.

With a few exceptions, only red wines are made in this region, and no white wine has the right to be called Médoc. The wines from the Margaux vineyards, nearest Bordeaux, are most feminine of all: heartiness increases on a gradually rising scale to the other end of the zone at Saint-Estèphe, a village forty miles north of Bordeaux. This is the range of Haut-Médoc (the best part of the region), a place-name in its own right which will appear on labels. Médoc is the name given, in this sense, to the wines north of Saint-Estèphe, the point of the peninsula gradually narrowing to Soulac, where the Gironde flows into the sea. The region beyond Saint-Estèphe produces high-quality table wines, and there are many co-operatives—one of them at Bégadan, thirty miles north of Pauillac, with a capacity of 625,000 imp. gallons (750,000 U.S.)—but all the famous wines are in Haut-Médoc. In addition to the two place-names, or Appellations Contrôlées, Haut-Médoc, and Médoc, which will appear on labels, five communes within Haut-Médoc have official place-names of their own: Margaux, Saint-Julien, Saint-Estèphe, Pauillac, Moulis, and Listrac, of which the first four are the best-known (*see under individual headings*). The more precise the designation, the more distinguished the wine—a Margaux will generally be more individual, and will have submitted to higher wine-making requirements, than the wines of a broader designation, such as Médoc. All but five of the sixty-two vineyards are within the four communes.

This district has the advantage over all others in that vintage years, although important, mean less here than elsewhere in France because, although the wines sometimes reach great peaks, they never sink much below their normal standard—even in the lesser years a well-made Médoc will be an agreeable wine, because the great châteaux always make good wines. The vintages of the best years will be slow in maturing; the others will be ready to drink much sooner.

The Médoc takes its name, a corruption of the Latin *in medio aquæ*, from its geographical position, almost in the middle of the water, for the eighty-mile strip of peninsula, with its gravelly, sandy soil is seldom more than fifteen miles in width as it stretches between the Atlantic and the Gironde. The vineyard strip is far narrower. Only lands on the Gironde side, a belt hardly two miles wide, produce the great wines. The rest of the Médoc westward to the giant dunes rimming the ocean is a region of pinewoods interspersed with a few fields, and an occasional vineyard, and its wines are simply called Bordeaux. Along the best strip of land, the vineyards are in clusters. In the wine centre in Pauillac, a map thirty feet by six feet shows in microcosm the panorama of the Médoc with all the classified châteaux, and a few others, superimposed; and a glance reveals how the vineyards group thickly around Margaux, Saint-Julien, Pauillac, and Saint-Estèphe, with gaps between. The reason for this is plain: the land rises moderately at Margaux, most steeply at Pauillac and Saint-Estèphe. The moist lower land, through which the little creeks furrow to the river, is unfit for fine wine. Study of the geological chart explains the phenomenon. The ancient Quaternary land—a very gravelly, pebbly soil in modern times—appears islanded by the newer river soil which has eddied in around it in all the lower parts. The newest of all, the alluvial soil, is forbidden any of the important Médoc place-names. The Médoc's previous gravel dates from the end of the Tertiary and the beginning of the Quaternary Eras. It is said that glaciers, slowly moving down from the distant Pyrenees, followed the course of the nearby river, pushing back its high right bank. When the glaciers thawed the small pebbles remained in the soil. These pebbles give the Médoc gravel its special virtue of holding the heat of the sun during the day, and reflecting it back to the low-pruned grapes at night.

With the qualities of the soil—the *cailloux* or small stones which give *race* to the wine—the elements of weather, of vine variety, viticulture, and wine-making are necessary to the formation of a characteristic Médoc. The Atlantic climate is distinctly softer and damper here than in the other Bordeaux districts. The Médoc is the closest wine zone to the sea, and the Gironde, formed by the

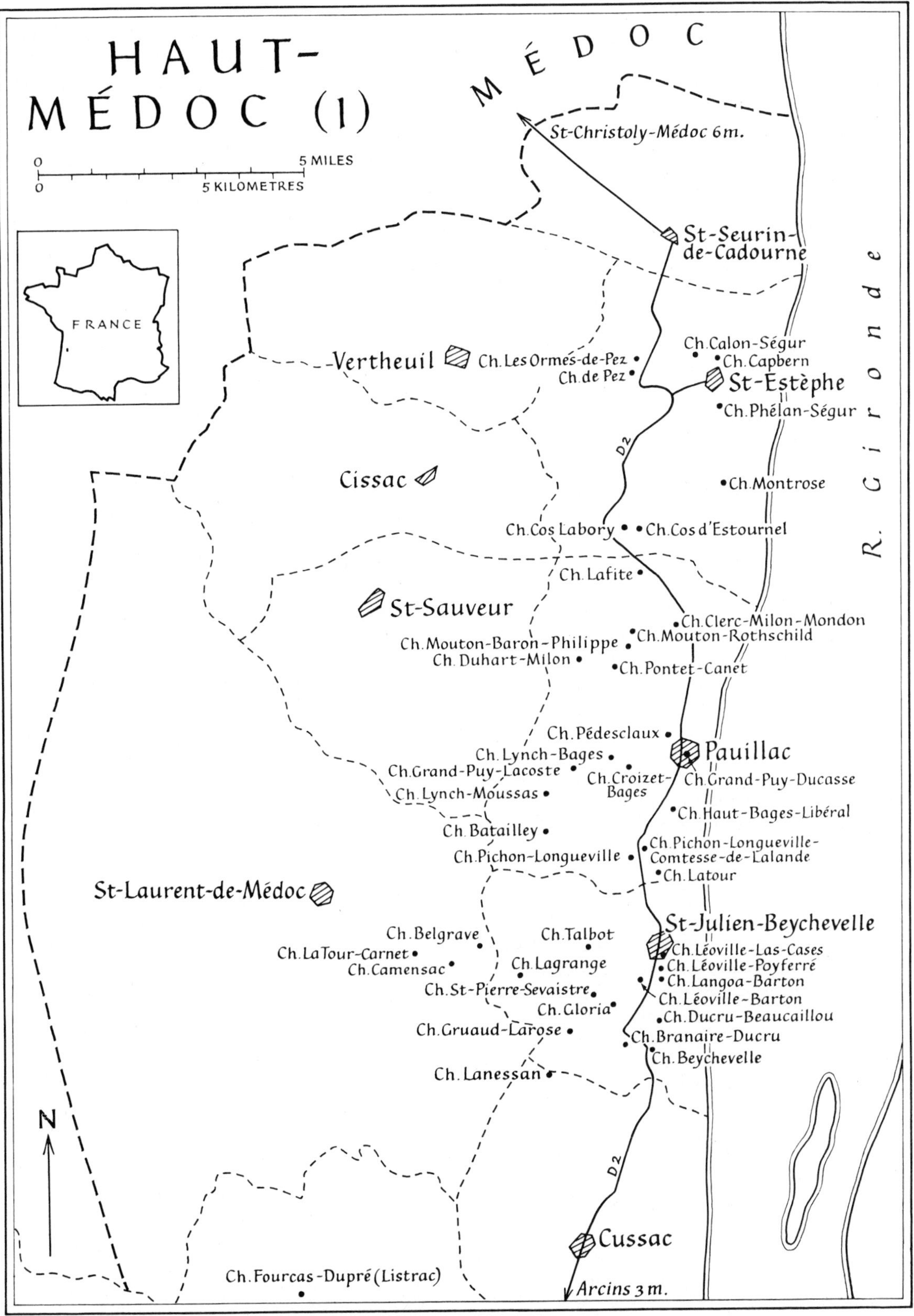

HAUT-MÉDOC (1)
MÉDOC
0 5 MILES
0 5 KILOMETRES
FRANCE
St-Christoly-Médoc 6m.
St-Seurin-de-Cadourne
R. Gironde
Vertheuil
Ch. Les Ormes-de-Pez
Ch. de Pez
Ch. Calon-Ségur
Ch. Capbern
St-Estèphe
Ch. Phélan-Ségur
D2
Cissac
Ch. Montrose
Ch. Cos Labory
Ch. Cos d'Estournel
Ch. Lafite
St-Sauveur
Ch. Clerc-Milon-Mondon
Ch. Mouton-Rothschild
Ch. Mouton-Baron-Philippe
Ch. Duhart-Milon
Ch. Pontet-Canet
Ch. Pédesclaux
Pauillac
Ch. Lynch-Bages
Ch. Grand-Puy-Lacoste
Ch. Croizet-Bages
Ch. Grand-Puy-Ducasse
Ch. Lynch-Moussas
Ch. Haut-Bages-Libéral
Ch. Batailley
Ch. Pichon-Longueville
Ch. Pichon-Longueville-Comtesse-de-Lalande
Ch. Latour
St-Laurent-de-Médoc
St-Julien-Beychevelle
Ch. Belgrave
Ch. Talbot
Ch. La Tour-Carnet
Ch. Camensac
Ch. Lagrange
Ch. Léoville-Las-Cases
Ch. Léoville-Poyferré
Ch. Langoa-Barton
Ch. St-Pierre-Sevaistre
Ch. Léoville-Barton
Ch. Gloria
Ch. Ducru-Beaucaillou
Ch. Gruaud-Larose
Ch. Branaire-Ducru
Ch. Beychevelle
Ch. Lanessan
N
D2
Cussac
Ch. Fourcas-Dupré (Listrac)
Arcins 3 m.

confluence of the Dordogne and the Garonne, is as wide, when it passes Pauillac and Saint-Estèphe, as is the great Mississippi.

The Cabernet Sauvignon is the characteristic grape variety, contributing different proportions to the various Médocs, but generally making up about 60% of the grapes used. Cabernet Franc, Merlot, Malbec, and Petit Verdot are used in smaller amounts, and Carménère is included infrequently and contributes a fraction. No other grapes are permitted. The wines with the most Cabernet Sauvignon will be the hardest when young, but will last very long. Merlot is generally included, up to about 20%, to give a suppler balance, and these wines will be at their best in the sunnier years, the harder ones holding up better in the lighter years.

Vines are generally allowed to achieve about thirty-five years, after which they are torn up and replanted. A few fine vineyards still cling to the old method of letting each vine reach its maximum age and die, before replacing it individually. Most vineyards, however, use the system of rotative planting—tearing up and replanting smaller parcels at different times. Most owners try to keep their older vines for as long as possible, thus improving the wine, since the vine gives better and better quality as it ages; but it is expensive both in added labour and in lost quantity, the latter dropping sharply in the older years of the vine.

Harvesting usually starts in the last days of September; or, about one year in six, in October; and one year in fifty, in August. The hotter the summer, the earlier the harvest. Separation of the stalk from the grapes, juice, and pips is obligatory, and is done by either of two methods. The new device is a revolving perforated metal sleeve: grapes and juice fall through the holes, and stems are carried off down the cone. Smaller and more old-fashioned vineyards separate by hand-scrubbing over a grid; grapes and juice fall through it, stems remain on top. In the course of great discussions, no one has ever demonstrated that either method is better than the other in producing wine of quality.

After separation from the stalks, the hulls and juice ferment together in vats and the wine acquires its colour (the pigment lies just inside the skins), and the tannin which contributes longevity. At most vineyards the wines are now vatted from ten to twelve days, after which they are drawn off the skins into barrels, where they spend the twenty-two to twenty-eight months before they are bottled. A handful of aristocratic vineyards still vat from three weeks to a month, the traditional Médoc method, by which they achieve a wine with the maximum of tannin. Big wines of this style demand longer ageing, which they will finally repay in extra long life; the slower process is possible only for growers able to command the prices their wines will eventually cost.

In 1855, for the World Fair in Paris, the wines of Médoc (and Sauternes) were classified by a commission of Bordeaux brokers basing their judgements principally on the verdict of the previous hundred years. The listing, from First to Fifth Growths, requires considerable overhauling, but is completely valid for the First Growths (*Premiers Crus*). The three great First Growths of the Médoc are Château Lafite, Château Margaux, and Château Latour. To these, Château Haut-Brion was added in 1855, rightly from the standpoint of wine, if not of geography; because although geographically it is situated in Graves, its wine ranks with the great three of Médoc. Because of its quality and the high prices at which it is sold, Château Mouton-Rothschild, classified first of the Second Growths (*Seconds Crus*) in 1855, really belongs with the First Growths, too. And, incidentally, a Second, Third (*Troisième*), Fourth (*Quatrième*), or Fifth Growth (*Cinquième Cru*) is not a second-, third-, fourth-, or fifth-*rate* wine. (For a fuller treatment of this subject, *see* BORDEAUX: CLASSIFICATION.)

Exceptional Growths (*Crus Exceptionnels*)—it is easy for Anglo-Saxons to make the mistake of supposing these to be *better* than the Great Growths (*Grands Crus*), *which they are not*—Bourgeois Growths (*Crus Bourgeois*) and Artisan Growths (*Crus Artisans*) were classified after the sixty-two greatest in 1855. Among these are many fine wines, and some which deserve elevation to the greater Growths. The Classification of 1855 will be found in the Appendix. A suggested reassessment of the Bordeaux Growths, as graded by the author in 1958 and later in 1966, follows the general entry on the Bordeaux Growths Classification. From this it will be seen that classification of Growths no longer represents the truth in a number of cases. For the individual Classified Growths, *see Château Lafite, Château Latour, Château Margaux, etc.*

CLASSIFIED MÉDOC WINES

Classification of 1855

FIRST GROWTHS (*Premiers Crus*)

	Commune
Château Lafite	Pauillac
Château Margaux	Margaux

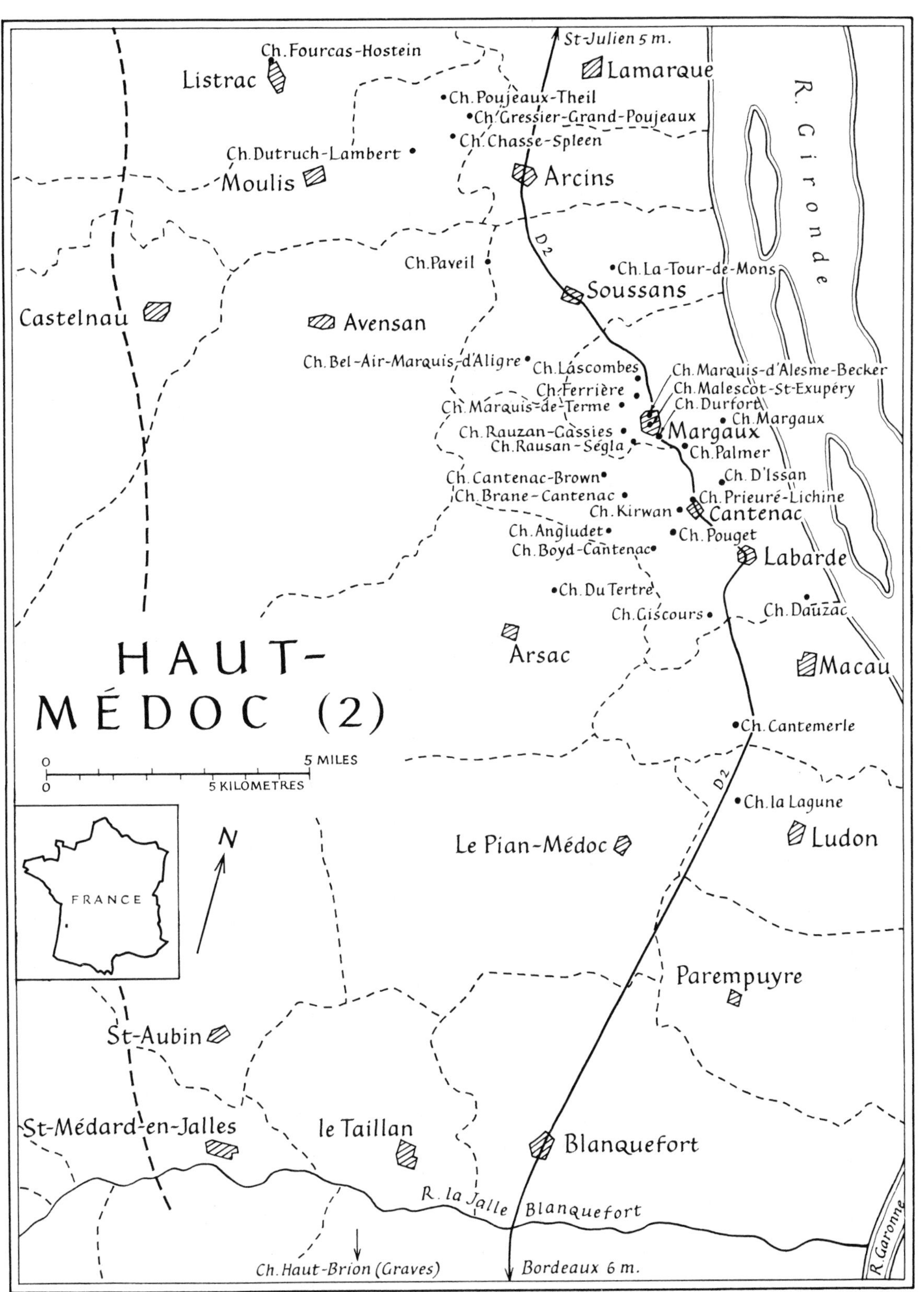

St-Julien 5 m.
Ch. Fourcas-Hostein
Listrac
Lamarque
Ch. Poujeaux-Theil
Ch. Gressier-Grand-Poujeaux
Ch. Chasse-Spleen
Ch. Dutruch-Lambert
Moulis
Arcins
R. Gironde
D2
Ch. Paveil
Ch. La-Tour-de-Mons
Soussans
Castelnau
Avensan
Ch. Bel-Air-Marquis-d'Aligre
Ch. Lascombes
Ch. Marquis-d'Alesme-Becker
Ch. Ferrière
Ch. Malescot-St-Exupéry
Ch. Marquis-de-Terme
Ch. Durfort
Ch. Margaux
Ch. Rauzan-Gassies
Margaux
Ch. Rausan-Ségla
Ch. Palmer
Ch. Cantenac-Brown
Ch. D'Issan
Ch. Brane-Cantenac
Ch. Prieuré-Lichine
Ch. Kirwan
Cantenac
Ch. Angludet
Ch. Pouget
Ch. Boyd-Cantenac
Labarde
Ch. Du Tertre
Ch. Dauzac
Ch. Giscours
Arsac
HAUT-
MÉDOC (2)
Macau
Ch. Cantemerle
0
5 MILES
0
5 KILOMETRES
D2
Ch. la Lagune
N
Le Pian-Médoc
Ludon
FRANCE
Parempuyre
St-Aubin
St-Médard-en-Jalles
le Taillan
Blanquefort
R. la Jalle
Blanquefort
R. Garonne
Ch. Haut-Brion (Graves)
Bordeaux 6 m.

	Commune
Château Latour	Pauillac
Château Haut-Brion	Pessac (Graves)

SECOND GROWTHS (*Seconds Crus*)

	Commune
Château Mouton-Rothschild	Pauillac
Château Lascombes	Margaux
Château Rausan-Ségla	Margaux
Château Rauzan-Gassies	Margaux
Château Léoville-Las-Cases	St.-Julien
Château Léoville-Poyferré	St.-Julien
Château Léoville-Barton	St.-Julien
Château Durfort-Vivens	Margaux
Château Gruaud-Larose	St.-Julien
Château Brane-Cantenac	Cantenac-Margaux
Château Pichon-Longueville	Pauillac
Château Pichon-Longueville, Comtesse de Lalande	Pauillac
Château Ducru-Beaucaillou	St.-Julien
Château Cos-d'Estournel	St.-Estèphe
Château Montrose	St.-Estèphe

THIRD GROWTHS (*Troisièmes Crus*)

	Commune
Château Giscours	Labarde-Margaux
Château Kirwan	Cantenac-Margaux
Château d'Issan	Cantenac-Margaux
Château Lagrange	St.-Julien
Château Langoa	St.-Julien
Château Malescot-Saint-Exupéry	Margaux
Château Cantenac-Brown	Cantenac-Margaux
Château Palmer	Cantenac-Margaux
Château La Lagune	Ludon (Haut-Médoc)
Château Desmirail	Margaux
Château Ferrière	Margaux
Château Calon-Ségur	St.-Estèphe
Château Marquis d'Alesme Becker	Margaux
Château Boyd-Cantenac	Margaux

FOURTH GROWTHS (*Quatrièmes Crus*)

	Commune
Château Prieuré-Lichine	Cantenac-Margaux
Château Saint-Pierre-Bontemps	St.-Julien
Château Saint-Pierre-Sevaistre	St.-Julien
Château Branaire-Ducru	St.-Julien
Château Talbot	St.-Julien
Château Duhart-Milon	Pauillac
Château Pouget	Cantenac-Margaux
Château La Tour-Carnet	St.-Laurent (Haut-Médoc)
Château Lafon-Rochet	St.-Estèphe
Château Beychevelle	St.-Julien
Château Marquis-de-Terme	Margaux

FIFTH GROWTHS (*Cinquièmes Crus*)

	Commune
Château Pontet-Canet	Pauillac
Château Batailley	Pauillac
Château Grand-Puy-Lacoste	Pauillac
Château Grand-Puy-Ducasse	Pauillac
Château Haut-Batailley	Pauillac
Château Lynch-Bages	Pauillac
Château Lynch-Moussas	Pauillac
Château Dauzac	Labarde-Margaux
Château Mouton-d'Armailhacq (now called Mouton du Baron Philippe)	Pauillac
Château du Tertre	Arsac-Margaux
Château Haut-Bages-Libéral	Pauillac
Château Pédesclaux	Pauillac
Château Belgrave	St.-Laurent (Haut-Médoc)
Château Camensac	St.-Laurent (Haut-Médoc)
Château Cos Labory	St.-Estèphe
Château Clerc-Milon-Mondon	Pauillac
Château Croizet-Bages	Pauillac
Château Cantemerle	Macau (Haut-Médoc)

EXCEPTIONAL GROWTHS (*Crus Exceptionnels*)

	Commune
Château Villegeorge	Avensan

	Commune
Château Angludet	Cantenac-Margaux
Château Chasse-Spleen	Moulis (Haut-Médoc)
Château Poujeaux-Theil	Moulis (Haut-Médoc)
Château la Couronne	Pauillac
Château Moulin-Riche	St.-Julien
Château Bel-Air-Marquis-d'Aligre	Soussans-Margaux

Meleto

A good classical Chianti of the firm of Ricasoli.

See TUSCANY.

Mendoza

Province of Argentina producing 75% of the wine of that country.

See ARGENTINA.

Mentuccia

In Italian, 'small piece of mint'; a liqueur made by the Aurum Distillery of the Centerbe type.

See CENTERBE.

Mercurey

Burgundy red and white wines. District: Chalonnais, France.

One of the four leading wines of the district. The Chalonnais wines bear a resemblance to those of the Côte de Beaune, perhaps because the Pinot Noir is the grape used. The best wines of the slope are the reds of Mercurey.

See CHALONNAIS.

Merlot

The blue-black, thick-skinned grape which imparts softness and roundness to the red wines of the Médoc district in Bordeaux. This grape is grown also in Italy, Switzerland, Chile, a little in California, and elsewhere.

Mersin

White liqueur flavoured with oranges and herbs; the Turkish Curaçao.

Mescal, Mezcal

One of the names for the Mexican cactus plant from which pulque and tequila are made. Also another name for tequila (*q.v.*).

Mesnil

Village in Champagne which produces one of the best wines of the Côte des Blancs.

Metaxa

A slightly sweet, deep-coloured brandy made in Greece (*q.v.*).

Metheglin

A word meaning 'spiced drink', derived from the Welsh; it was generally used for mead.

Methuselah, Methusalem

A giant bottle used—if at all—in Champagne. It has the capacity of eight standard bottles.

Meursault

Burgundy white, and a very little red, wine. District: Côte de Beaune, France.

Meursault is the 'Capital of the Slope of the Great White Wines', and although the 'Côte de Meursault' does not exist in official terminology, it does in popular fancy, which is, in a large measure, justified. This section of the Côte de Beaune includes the communes of Meursault and Puligny-Montrachet, and the hamlet of Blagny, ranged along a cluster of hills distinct from the rest of the slope. On the north, a defile cuts it off from Auxey-Duresses and Monthélie; to the south, another separates it from Saint-Aubin; the west side terminates at the top of the slopes; and the east is set by the main road from Beaune to Chagny which marks the beginning of the Burgundian plain and the end of the fine vineyards. A further unifying factor on the Meursault slope is the chalky, coarse-grained subsoil which predominates and provides the perfect base for the Chardonnay grapevine. Some of the Meursault vineyards fall on the wrong side of the northern divide and grow, mainly, Pinot Noir grapes; and the resulting red wines borrow the name of adjoining Volnay (*q.v.*) or are sold as Volnay-Santenots.

Meursault means 'mouse-jump' and it is said the vineyards for red wines and those for white were once only a mouse-jump apart. Today it would take a pretty herculean mouse to bridge the gap in most places, although throughout the vineyards Pinot Noir vines can still be found, and the wine-makers of Meursault annually produce anywhere from 11,000–13,200 imp. gallons (13,200–15,900 U.S.) of red.

As Côte d'Or places go, Meursault is fairly large, qualifying either as an overgrown village or a stunted town. The hills roll gently around it, rising to the hamlet of Blagny—set off in the south-west corner—where wines are sold as Blagny, Meursault-Blagny, or occasionally as Blagny-Côte de Beaune. They are both red and white; and wines having the right to the last-mentioned place-name are sometimes blended with those from certain other communes of the Côte de Beaune and sold as Côte de Beaune-Villages. Meursault itself is prosperous and has several interesting monuments. The delicate spire which rises from the rather squat church reminds Burgundians of a 'beaver hat on a peasant'; and nearby is a grim, grey edifice which served as a leper colony during the Middle Ages. The Hospices de Beaune have been given several vineyards in Meursault; and as is customary with the Hospices, the wines are sold under the name of the donors: Loppin, Jehan Humblot, Baudot, Goureau, Albert Grivault, and Behèzre de Lanlay. Meursault also has a smaller Hospice of its own, older than its neighbour of Beaune, whose gate adjoins the main road leading up to the village.

Most Meursault is white and the wines are soft, round and feminine in texture, with a bouquet that eludes description, bordering now on the scent of violets, now on the aroma of almonds. Dry, but not so dry as the steely Chablis, they have a quiet luxuriousness, and a lasting and marvellous aftertaste. They reach their peak fairly quickly, and only the best respond to ageing at all happily—the lesser ones tending to maderize fairly quickly. The finest of the Meursault whites is Perrières and those from the heart of the vineyard—the Clos des Perrières—are superb wines, often fit to challenge the incomparable Montrachet. After Perrières come Charmes and Genevrières and La Goutte d'Or, the appropriately named 'drop of gold', all of which incorporate the same seductive grace and elegance but are apt to have a shade less finesse. Meursault reds are sturdy and require a certain ageing before they open up and reveal a fiery strength and excellent bouquet, but they do not quite come up to the qualities of the reds of the Côte de Nuits.

In slight contrast to the white wines of Meursault, those of tiny Blagny are long-lasting, becoming ready to drink after about two years in the bottle and holding for as long as twenty. Blagny white is, understandably enough, very close to Meursault in taste characteristics, but will be, if anything, a little firmer, and slightly more assertive. The reds are much the same, and Blagny red is apt to be slightly better than Meursault red.

If you include the hamlet of Blagny, Meursault has more surface area devoted to vines than any other commune of the Côte d'Or, and it ties with Pommard and Beaune each year for first place in amount of production. The official figures for Meursault are 1,188 acres of vines (wines from five hundred of which may add Côte de Beaune to the communal name), and production for an average-quantity year is 178,900 imp. gallons (214,800 U.S.), all but 200 imp. gallons (240 U.S.) in white. The best vineyards of the commune are given the designation First Growth (*Premier Cru*) and the right to produce wines that will carry both commune name and vineyard name on the label. These vineyards are:

In Meursault

FIRST GROWTHS (*Premiers Crus*)

Vineyard	*Acres*
Clos des Perrières and Les Perrières	42·2
Les Charmes-dessus	38·3
Les Charmes-dessous	30·8
Les Genevrières-dessus	19·3
Les Genevrières-dessous	13·0
La Goutte d'Or	13·8
Le Porusot-Dessus	4·4
Le Porusot	4·0
Les Bouchères	10·5
Les Santenots-Blancs	7·3
Les Santenots du Milieu	19·8
Les Caillerets	3·3
Les Petures	27·0
Les Cras	11·7

In Blagny

La Jennelotte	11·9
La Pièce-sous-le-Bois	27·8
Sous le Dos d'Ane	13·3

Meursault-Blagny

See MEURSAULT.

Mexico

Wine is made, mainly in the north of the country, in vineyard areas extending altogether over some 33,000 acres: in the northern part of Lower California; in the State of Coahuila, just south of central Texas; in Chihuahua and Quesétaro, and around the town of Aguascalientes.

The first vineyard was planted by Don Francisco de Urdiñola, at.Parras, in 1593. It was one of the earliest to be cultivated in America, although wild vines had been growing freely in the gulleys and on the hillsides of the region. The name of the city means vine-trellises and Parras, situated between Monterrey and Torreón, in south Coahuila, is still a centre of viticulture, with the ancient plantation of Don Francisco always in vine. It now belongs to the Bodegas of the Marqués de Aguayo. The leading firm of Casa Madero also has its headquarters in Parras.

Among the most important wine producers in Mexico are the Compañia Vinicola de Saltillo, which operates near the town of that name and in Aguascalientes; and, best-known if not best, the Bodegas de Santo Tomás in Lower California. The Santo Tomás label is surprisingly familiar at home and abroad, for the wines it covers are fairly ordinary port-type, sauternes-type, moselle-type, sherry-type, and so on. The Bodegas del Marqués de Aguayo is a big producer; so also is Vergel, if the quality is somewhat uneven—a failing not unusual in Mexican wines.

Other leading firms include, in Parras, the Bodegas del Delfin, owned by Aguirre Benavides; Bodegas del Rosario, by Señor Antonio Benavides and Señor Elías T. Tejada; Bodegas de Perote, the property of Señor Arturo Perez de Yarto; Bodegas del Vesubio, which belongs to Señor Nicolás Milonás; and, in Chihuahua, the famous Bodegas de Delicías. Most of the important proprietors are united in the Vine Growers' Association, Asociación Nacional de Vitivinicultores.

Mexican wines tend to be low in acidity. The industry has suffered from the fact that, after an excellent beginning in the days of the Spanish conquest, most of the vine was uprooted because the Mexican product was considered to be in competition with the wines imported from Spain. This setback has never been overcome. The vineyard acreage has indeed increased in recent years, but it could undoubtedly be expanded and improved.

The Mexicans themselves are not great drinkers of wine, although it flows at fiestas and on other special occasions. In order to promote the habit, the Vine-Growers' Association began a campaign, some years ago, to encourage the use of inexpensive table wines. The 2,500,000 imp. gallons (3 million U.S.) now produced annually are largely of this kind. There is, moreover, a good deal of adulteration of the common wines—due, no doubt, to the immature development of the industry, and to lack of co-operation and control, especially where the many small proprietors are concerned. A large quantity of wine spirit, or *aguardiente*, is made also.

It is to be regretted that Mexico is one of a number of countries which appropriate for some of their wines the place-names properly applicable only to specific geographical areas of the world. At present, the names appearing on wine and wine-spirit labels are:

Aguardiente, Jerez (sherry-type), Vino de Fruta, Vino Dulce, Vino Quinado (bitter quinine), Vermouth, Coñac, Oporto (port-style), Moscatel, Vino Blanco, Vino Tinto, Soleras, and Vino Aromatizado.

SPIRITS

The characteristic Mexican spirits are Tequila (*q.v.*), Pulque, and Mezcal made from the juice of the century plant. Others are obtained from sugar cane. Among other spirits produced in Mexico are ron (rum), anis, and brandy.

Michigan

Wine-growing district in the United States. The principal vineyards are situated in the southern part of the state. Sweet and sparkling wines are made there, but unfortunately they are of poor quality.

See AMERICA: EASTERN STATES.

Midi

The vast stretch of land west of the mouth of the Rhône in southern France, which supplies the greatest quantity of ordinary wine in France. The Midi includes the departments of Aude, Hérault, Gard (*qq.v.*), and part of the Eastern Pyrenees.

Mildew

The European name for Downy Mildew, a vine disease of American origin.

See CHAPTER EIGHT, p. 36.

Millefiori

Pale gold Italian liqueur said to have been made from the extracts of a thousand Alpine flowers. The bottles usually contain a small twig, around which sugar has crystallized. Made by Vigevanese.

Millerandage or Shot Berries

Vine disease; clusters with grapes of varying sizes. An aftermath of Coulure, following unsatisfactory flowering or insemination.

See CHAPTER EIGHT, p. 36.

Millésime

French term for vintage year.

Mirabelle de Lorraine

The *eau-de-vie* or spirit distilled from the mirabelle or yellow plum is made in both Lorraine and Alsace in the east of France, but only spirit from the plums of the region of Nancy and of Metz have the right to the place-name of Mirabelle de Lorraine. This is an official Appellation d'Origine, or controlled place-name, under French law.

Of the two, Metz plums are the better. Mirabelle

Fine du Val de Metz is the designation to look for. The plums are picked in dry weather, fermented by specially selected yeasts, kept in the wood for approximately two months and then double-distilled in exactly the manner of Cognac. The liquor is afterwards aged in casks.

See also ALSACE.

Mis en Bouteille au Château

French term for château bottled. This description on the label means that the wine has been bottled at the vineyard where it was grown and made. It guarantees the authenticity of the wine. The term is general in Bordeaux wines.

Mis en Bouteille au Domaine

French term for estate bottled. Same as *Mis en Bouteille au Château*. The term generally used in Bordeaux; but the practice is much less general in Burgundy, where many of the vineyards are split up into small parcels, than it is in Bordeaux. *Mis en Bouteille à la Propriété* is another term for estate bottled. It guarantees the authenticity of the wine.

Mistelle

A fortified 'wine' made by adding spirit to grape juice before it ferments. The excess of alcohol prevents fermentation and all the natural sugar is retained in the juice. It is used mainly as a base for vermouth and other wine aperitifs. Huge amounts of Mistelle were made in, and shipped from, Algeria every year.

Mittelhaardt

Part of the Palatinate district in Germany, where the best of these wines are made.

See PALATINATE.

Moelleux

Literally 'marrowy'. A French term used of soft, sweet, fruity white wines, especially in Sauternes.

Mohammedan Prohibition

The tenet of Mohammed denying the use of alcoholic drink to his followers in Islam. With the decrees of early emperors in China, it is the only prohibition which has had a lasting effect. The consequence has been the almost total death of viniculture throughout the Islamic world, though isolated vineyards have held out among non-believers enclosed within Islam and among Mohammedans for table grapes. In modern times, Europeans, notably the French in North Africa, have restored wine-making in Mohammedan lands.

Monbazillac

A sweet white dessert wine from the Bergerac region in south-west France.

See BERGERAC.

Monemvasia

Original Greek name for the style of wine anglicized as Malmsey (*q.v.*).

Monica di Sardegna

Sweet fortified wine of Sardinia (*q.v.*).

Monimpex

The Hungarian State Export Agency for wines and spirits.

Monopole

This designation, frequently found on wine labels, literally means 'an exclusive'. Blank Monopole would be the proprietary brand of the wine shipper whose name would occupy the blank. The wines are blends and are seldom if ever sold by the vintage year. The shipper attempts to produce a uniform wine year after year, sacrificing the high points which individual growths or years might achieve in order to be able to provide a consistent, reliable wine.

Montagne-Saint-Émilion

A large commune in which lie some respectable vineyards of Saint-Émilion (*q.v.*), in the Bordeaux region of south-west France.

Montagny

A commune of the Chalon slope in Burgundy which is allowed the Appellation Contrôlée.

See CHALONNAIS.

Montagu

Wine region in the Little Karoo district.

See SOUTH AFRICA.

Montefiascone

White wine grown in the foothills of the Volsini Mountains, Italy. It is concerning this wine that the story about Est! Est!! Est!!! is told.

See LATIUM.

Montepulciano

Known as Vino Nobile di Montepulciano. This light red wine achieved some literary fame in the eighteenth century.

See TUSCANY.

Montepulciano di Abruzzo

Light, red Italian wine.

See ABRUZZI.

Monthélie and Monthélie-Côte de Beaune

Burgundy red and white wine. District: Côte de Beaune, France.

Monthélie is the *frère bâtard* of Volnay. It is one of the most picturesque wine communes of Burgundy with steep streets and tiny houses, venerable with age, many of which still maintain their centuries-old wine presses and equipment. But the wines are seldom distinguished.

Red, white, and some sparkling wines are made, although the balance is heavily weighted towards still reds. The grapes are Pinots, as they are throughout the Côte d'Or, and are grown in soil so poor that Burgundians claim: 'A chicken, in Monthélie, would starve during the harvest.' Within the ancient commune—the remains of a Gallic cemetery testify to its age—are about 250 acres of vines, and production in 1960, an average quantity year, was 42,600 imp. gallons (51,200 U.S.) of red, 1,210 imp. gallons (1,450 U.S.) of white. Wines may be sold indiscriminately as Monthélie or as Monthélie-Côte de Beaune-Villages. A standard, and generally accurate, rule of thumb is that Monthélie should cost about three-quarters the price of a Volnay of the same year. The best vineyards are given the rating First Growth (*Premier Cru*) and may add vineyard name to commune name on labels. Although these vineyards have not yet been finally established, interim right is granted to the following:

FIRST GROWTHS (*Premiers Crus*)

Vineyard	*Acres*
Sur la Velle	15·2
Les Vignes Rondes	6·7
Le Meix-Bataille	5·9
Les Riottes	1·8
La Taupine	10·7
Le Clos-Gauthey	3·5
Le Château-Gaillard	2·3
Les Champs-Fulliot	21·6
Le Cas-Rougeot	1·4
Duresse	25·6

Montilla

Still and fortified wines. District: Southern Spain.

Montilla and Manzanilla, close relations of Sherry, but not always in the Sherry family, vie with each other as the two favourite bar wines in Spain—after the common red, which owes its great popularity to the fact that its price is about a penny a glass. A *copa* of Manzanilla or Montilla costs little more. Surely nowhere else is it possible to drink so much wine of real style and character for so little money.

Half a century ago, when the demand for Sherry was at its height, most Montilla made the journey of 250 miles, as the wine cart rolls, down to Jerez-de-la-Frontera. Even today, much Montilla becomes Sherry in Jerez. Now, however, Montilla, with certain other wines, mostly from the province of Huelva, may enter Sherry only as a poor relation, with the permission of the Jerez shippers after they have made an examination of samples. It is allowed in only to make up shortages which still occur, although they are much less frequent since the heavy planting in Jerez after the Spanish Civil War. Even so, Montilla may only amount to a third of the content of the wine *bodegas*.

Because it was profitable to capitalize on the great name of Sherry, Montilla acquiesced in this arrangement. But by 1944, local pride had become stronger than expediency—and an official place-name Córdoba or Montilla-Moriles was launched. Since then, the growers have been promoting the wines under their own name.

Most of the region is situated in the southern part of the province of Córdoba—its heart, a countryside of hills and plateaux north of the Sierra on the slopes of which the vines are planted. To the north of the vineyards lie the grain-producing plains of Córdoba, to the south the olive groves of Southern Andalusia.

The two choice sections—Montilla Sierra and Moriles—do produce light, dry finos of an excellent character and breeding, wines which can be compared with Sherry Finos but with a subtle though definite taste of their own. They are not, and cannot be, Sherries in the proper sense, since the name is restricted to the wines of Jerez. But if there ever was a justification for the breaching of the rule of place-names, it is probably in the case of Montilla and the Manzanilla Finos. At the present time, Manzanillas are officially Finos of Jerez even though Sanlúcar de Barrameda whence they come is, like Montilla, some distance from Jerez, though much nearer than Montilla. All wines of Sanlúcar de Barrameda, and certain wines of Jerez and Montilla, are true Finos—characteristically light, crisp, bone-dry, and produced by the action of a unique micro-organism called *flor*. The tendency is to lump them together as Sherry Fino, the name which has world-wide renown.

In the Montilla Sierra and Moriles districts—about twenty miles apart and a little over an hour's run south of Córdoba—in parts of Jerez and in Sanlúcar de Barrameda, the conditions exist which create Fino. A type of chalky soil called *albariza* is essential. As far as quality of the wine is concerned, the *albariza* patches of Montilla and Jerez, separated by 110 miles, are nearer neighbours than are patches of *albariza* and plots of the commoner soils, *barro* or *arena*, which lies next to them in Jerez.

The baked white *albariza* crust, wrinkled, seamed, and crow's-footed like the skin of a very old man, protects the moisture at the roots of the vine all through the scorching, rainless Andalusian summer, and the grape-musts achieved are destined to produce Fino—for if they are not allowed to develop *flor*, the film of white micro-organisms which covers the surface like snow, they will be Olorosos. In Montilla, the musts are fermented in small vats and frequently racked from one vat to another. This seems to have some beneficial influence on the *flor*, which develops quickly. Here as in Jerez, the higher quality wines are first kept in a nursery until they are ready to be promoted into a *solera* system. In the *solera*, each barrel is older than the grade below, and the wines, moved upwards from one to another in small quantities, take on the characteristics of the older wines in each cask.

In both Manzanilla and Montilla, the bottled wine—which is seen outside Spain—is not quite the same as the Manzanilla or Montilla usually drunk in Spain. The basic virtue of both wines is a frail, light freshness in extreme youth. The quality is diminished by bottling, and the best of both types never leaves the barrel until it goes into the glass. Extremely pleasant Manzanillas and Montillas are, however, available in the bottle, and once opened, they should be drunk, for the very dry sherries deteriorate if they are kept too long after the bottle has been uncorked. Very dry Finos do not improve in bottle and the younger they are consumed, the better.

In Spain, Montillas are usually sold from the barrel and in their first year. In this condition they can be incomparable, even when very cheap; they are the only wines capable of competing with Manzanillas and some of the Finos of Jerez as the best and freshest of all aperitifs. The name itself, from the town of Montilla, is the inspiration of Amontillado, which literally means Montilla-ed wine; but in one sense this is somewhat misleading, as it implies that the Montilla style is the browner and more aged stage of Fino wine—Amontillado as the term is used in Sherries now. This is the opposite of the truth, for the best Montilla is light and pale.

Two other grape varieties (Baladí and Lairén) are cultivated to a small extent, but in effect all Montilla comes from the Pedro Ximénez grape. Curiously enough, this variety, which is used as a sweetener in wines in Jerez, Malaga, and elsewhere, gives a dry wine in Montilla. Here it is not sun-dried on straw mats—to increase its proportionate sugar content—as is the practice in other districts. The mountainous vineyards have a primitive atmosphere, and great earthenware jars not unlike those of Valdepeñas may still be seen, although in Montilla they are used for fermentation, not for storage.

A very palatable red wine comes from Doña Mencía, a few miles east of Montilla; and at the larger village of Rute, toward the mountains ranging up behind Málaga, the making of Montilla is combined with a considerable industry of aguardientes and anisados.

Montilla Sierra

Like Sherry Fino. One of the two best Montillas, from Spain.

See MONTILLA.

Montlouis

Loire Valley white wine; still and sparkling. District: Touraine, France.

This is known as the unsophisticated younger brother of Vouvray, because of its resemblance to the district which faces it across the Loire, and because the wines are so similar that sometimes even experts cannot distinguish between them. But while the finest Montlouis can often be classed with fine Vouvray, the bulk cannot compete. Most of the annual 416,000 imp. gallons (500,000 U.S.) of Montlouis is not up to Vouvray standards.

The wine is entirely white, from Chenin Blanc grapes grown in Montlouis, Lussault, and Saint-Martin-le-Beau, and it usually remains in the twilight zone where wines are never really sweet nor really dry. A certain amount is made sparkling; but the still and semi-sparkling—or *pétillant*—are best and the most beguiling. Still wines must have 10% of alcohol; sparkling, only 9·5%.

Montrachet

Burgundy white wine. District: Côte de Beaune, France. Communes: Puligny-Montrachet and Chassagne-Montrachet. Official classification: Great Growth (Grand Cru).

Little known as late as the seventeenth century, these wines began to achieve renown in the mid and late eighteenth century, and are now considered by many connoisseurs to be the greatest of all dry white wines. 'Divine', 'magnificent', 'formidable', 'to be drunk on one's knees with head bared', 'gorgeous with martial pageantry'—this and much more has been said about Montrachet, with only Professor Saintsbury demurring slightly with his 'very great, but the best makes the veins swell like whipcord'. It is a wine of exceptional elegance and breed, quite dry, yet it has depth, and a seductive bouquet.

The vineyard stands at mid-slope, straddling the line dividing Puligny-Montrachet from Chassagne-Montrachet. At this point, nothing is to be seen but seedy wild grass and outcroppings of the meagre, chalky subsoil, in direct contrast to the dense underbrush and foliage which crowns the slopes in other parts of the Côte d'Or. Around it are such other famous Growths as Chevalier-Montrachet and Bâtard-Montrachet, and the vineyard once called Les Demoiselles, now Caillerets. All produce exceptional wines; all are rightfully placed among the greatest of the world's dry white wines.

The vineyard of Montrachet contains just over nineteen acres and produces a wine that is as rare as it is magnificent. The average yearly production is 4,165 imp. gallons (5,000 U.S.). In the past, the harvest was often reserved for years in advance and prices were so high as to be almost meaningless. A bottle of authentic Montrachet is still a great rarity and will always be so. In 1962 the French Government paid £429,000 (1,201,000 dollars) to preserve the nineteen acres of Montrachet—the cost of diverting the new Paris-Lyons motor road, which would otherwise have passed by Puligny and affected the vineyards.

The sad fact is that infectious degeneration (sometimes called *court-noué*) has been detected in the vineyard. So little is known of this lethal disease that it is referred to as a virus or virus-like malady, of which even the cause is obscure. What is certain is that it kills vines. It also lives in the soil, and the life-span of vines planted consecutively in the same spot becomes progressively shorter. Unfortunately, no cure has yet been discovered and, unless one is forthcoming (the foremost vine pathologists in many countries are working together to overcome the menace), the world's finest and most famous dry white wine may become only a memory.

Little is known of the early history of the vineyard, and nothing of the geniuses who first started making the white wines and later perfected them. Montrachet was for many years largely in the hands of the Marquis de Laguiche, and the present Marquis still has nearly a quarter of the vineyard, making about eight *pièces*, or barrels, a year. The Baron Thénard is another relatively large owner, with slightly less than the Marquis de Laguiche; and although he has other important holdings, both in vines and in outside interests, the Baron declares that he is proudest of his slices of Montrachet.

The best section of Montrachet is that lying in the commune of Puligny-Montrachet, comprising 9·8 acres, just over half the vineyard. Perhaps it is the fact that this slope faces more to the east than in the south-exposed section which falls into Chassagne, or perhaps it is some subtle combination of imponderables that makes the wines what they are, but they have always had the finer reputation. Yet, nowadays, a few of the well-made wines from the surrounding vineyards sometimes rival the Montrachet.

See CHASSAGNE-MONTRACHET; PULIGNY-MONTRACHET.

Montravel

Semi-sweet wine of Bergerac, France.

See BERGERAC.

Château Montrose

Bordeaux red wine. District: Haut-Médoc, France. Commune: Saint-Estèphe.

Buried in the vineyard and far from the main roads, Montrose is a pleasant villa with an unusual galleried annexe that looks rather like a Swiss châlet. The grounds run down to the river, past rows of small numbered houses tenanted by the workers. A peculiar touch is given by the 'street names' here: rue d'Alsace, rue Mulhouse, and so on, commemorating the homesickness of a former Alsatian owner. The vineyard, classified Second Growth (*Second Cru*) in the Classification of 1855, is divided into square plantations, separated by alleys, and it is owned and worked by Madame Charmolue and her son.

Characteristics. Hard, slow maturing, with a bigness and fulness that characterizes so many of the wines of Saint-Estèphe—although it is with Latour in neighbouring Pauillac that it is sometimes compared. Its deep fullness gives Montrose its distinctive character. A very even quality is maintained over the years. This full-bodied wine is very popular in England.

Vineyard area: 120 acres.

Average production: 11,000 cases.

Morey-Saint-Denis

Burgundy red, and some white, wine. District: Côte de Nuits, France.

The wines of Morey-Saint-Denis vary slightly

more than do those from most Côte d'Or communes. Some reflect the position of the vineyards, providing a half-step between the austere majesty of Gevrey-Chambertin and the delicate elegance of Chambolle-Musigny; others, excelling in sturdy masculine strength, are acknowledged as the most *corsés* wines of the slope. Either way, one thing is certain: the wines are little known.

In bygone days hardly any wine was sold as Morey, although a considerable quantity was made. The output of the commune was usually blended with that of its neighbours or sold outright as Gevrey-Chambertin or Chambolle-Musigny. As a result, Morey never became famous, and even today relatively few wine-lovers are familiar with the commune or its wines—which are thus seldom demanded and often exceptional value.

The village has little to offer in the way of attractions, and few visitors see more than the dusty main square through which the sloping vineyard road winds, and the vineyards on both sides. Beside the square—enclosed in a great wall—is the domain of the Clos des Lambrays (one of Morey's outstanding vineyards), and next to it is the Clos de Tart. The other top vineyards are on the outskirts.

In 1860, and again in 1936, the best vineyards of Burgundy were rated. By the earlier classification, the finest wines of Morey were considered to be Clos de Tart, Clos des Lambrays, and Bonnes Mares —although Bonnes Mares has but a small foothold in Morey, most of it falling into Chambolle-Musigny. This has been altered slightly and the new official list counts the commune's finest wines as: Clos de Tart; Clos de la Roche; Clos Saint-Denis; Bonnes Mares (*see under individual headings*).

The Clos des Lambrays is omitted from this list and has been given a slightly lesser status, and many critics feel that this was a grave mistake, for the wines that come from Lambrays are always impeccably made and in good years are among the very greatest of the slope. At the time the classification was drawn up, however, the owner of Lambrays did not prove herself so adept at advancing the claims of her property as did some others, and the prestige of the wines has suffered accordingly.

Lambrays and the Clos de Tart are the sturdiest of the commune's wines, followed generally by the Clos de la Roche. Bonnes Mares often verges on the delicacy of the Chambolle, yet maintains a firm strength and considerable stamina, and the Clos Saint-Denis is the lightest and most fragile. In addition to these wines are others sold each year as Morey-Saint-Denis or as that followed by the name of the vineyard. The latter come from the First Growth (*Premier Cru*) vineyards of the commune—specially selected for the superior quality of the wines they produce—and are usually excellent wines, although without the magnificence of the greatest Growths which are identified on labels only by vineyard name. Apart from the four top-rated Growths, there are 251 acres of vineyard in the commune, and production in 1960, an average year for quantity, was 61,520 imp. gallons (73,880 U.S.) of red wine. Usually Morey will also produce up to 830 imp. gallons (1,000 U.S.) of white wine.

GREAT GROWTHS (*Grands Crus*)

Vineyard	*Acres*
Bonnes Mares (*see also* CHAMBOLLE-MUSIGNY)	4·6
Clos de la Roche	37·9
Clos Saint-Denis	16·2
Clos de Tart	17.8

FIRST GROWTHS (*Premiers Crus*)

Vineyard	*Acres*
Clos des Lambrays	14·8
Les Ruchots	6·5
Les Sorbet	7·3
Clos Sorbet	8·2
Les Millandes	10·6
Le Clos des Ormes (in part)	12
Meix-Rentiers	2·9
Monts-Luisants	7·7
Les Bouchots	5
Clos Bussière	7·4
Aux Charmes	3·1
Les Charnières	6
Côte Rôtie	1·3
Calouères	3·3
Maison Brûlée	4·6
Chabiots	5·4
Les Mauchamps	6·2
Les Froichots	1·6
Les Fremières	5·8
Les Genevrières	2·2
Les Chaffots	3
Les Chénevery (in part)	8
Aux Cheseaux	6
La Riotte	6·1
Clos Baulet	2·1
Les Gruenchers	1·5
Les Faconnières	4·3

Morgon

Heartiest of the good French Beaujolais red wines, sometimes so much so that it resembles the Burgundies grown a few miles to the north.

See BEAUJOLAIS.

Móri Ezerjó

The wine of the Ezerjó grape, made in the village of Mór, it is sometimes written as one word.

See HUNGARY.

Moriles

A section of the Montilla vineyard not far from Córdoba in the south of Spain. The wine produced is a dry Fino.

See MONTILLA.

Morocco

The wine industry of the not very long established state of Morocco is at one and the same time very young and very old. Indigenous vines were grown in Morocco in classical times and some of them were sent to Rome. But wine-making died out under the Moslems, with their strict prohibition of alcoholic beverages, and cultivation of wine-grapes, as distinct from dessert-grapes, was only re-established after the French took control of the region in 1912. Little was done in the prospective vineyards until 1919, and the real expansion of Moroccan viticulture was fostered by the French settlers between 1929 and 1935, an expansion that has largely resulted in the present 185,000-odd acres planted in vines.

There are no very important place-names. A few will be found on Moroccan wines as indications of superiority, but they are not to be classed with the French system of Appellation d'Origine Contrôlée. Wines, with or without these place-names, do account for one-quarter of the agricultural revenue of the country, however. Most of these are red, or rosé. A smaller quantity of white wines is made, too, in spite of the fact that in the hot climate these tend to maderize, or oxidize, too quickly; the makers have somewhat the same trouble with the rosés, although in this case they are more successful. *Vin gris*, also, is produced in the districts south of Casablanca and east of Marrakech; sweet dessert wines of a deep ruby colour are made and exported; and sparkling wines are produced by the Champagne method.

The Moroccan Ministry of Agriculture has inaugurated controls of vineyards, of quality of vines as well as wines; and regulation of the wine market. All wine must be sound, healthy, and saleable, and must contain at least 11% of alcohol (not very difficult in this semi-tropical country) or Moroccan law, initiated by the French, will not permit it to be exported. Most of the controls of wine were formerly in the hands of French nationals, and Moslems had very little to do with the industry, beyond providing most of the manual labour. Nevertheless, some 40% of the annual 57 million imp. gallons (68 million U.S.) are consumed in the country, and a little over 100,000 imp. gallons (120,000 U.S.) are imported. Exports of wine from Morocco amount to about 44 million imp. gallons (53 million U.S.) yearly, with a tendency to increase. Since Morocco became independent, internal consumption has decreased enormously.

The wines are, on the whole, rough, heady reds, much like those of Algeria and Tunisia. Just under half of them are grown in the region around Meknes, although some also come from Rabat-Rharb, Casablanca, Fez, Oujda, and Marrakech. The vines used are mostly the bulk-giving types, such as Cinsault, Carignan, Grenache, and Alicante-Bouschet, for red. The first two are the best, and give also a rosé which can be very pleasant when it is young, and is probably the most popular type inside Morocco. The principal white wine grapes are Clairette, Maccabeo, Ximénez, Plant X, and Grenache. Native grapes, still grown in the traditional vineyards, are mainly for the table, although the Rafsai white grape of the Riff mountain region is now being used in wine-making. These vines are not, unfortunately, resistant to phylloxera, which has been ravaging the vineyards of the north.

The other ancient vineyards bearing table grapes are situated on the northern (Zerhoun) and southern (Atlas) mountain slopes. The existence of all these old vineyards, divided into small parcels and peasant-owned, is menaced by the phylloxera louse. The modern vineyards, planted in imported vines, are to be found in the flat regions of Meknes-Fez, Oujda-Taza, and Rabat-Casablanca. Cultivation is intensive here, and mechanization has largely replaced animal-drawn ploughs. From the north-east come the best rosés, comparable with those of west Algeria; and the muscats of Berkane. Taza, in the centre, produces a red wine good for blending; red and rosé, as well as a straw-coloured white, are made around Fez; and the most important red-wine production of Morocco, a growth with colour, body, and a distinctive flavour, is at Meknes, south-west of Taga. Red wine comes also from the Daiet or Roumi slope vineyards east of Rabat; while to the north of these, round Sidi Slimane, richly coloured Dar Bel Hamri is the principal wine. The wines of the Casablanca region are not, regrettably, allowed to come to full maturity, so quickly are they consumed; and the rosés from here resemble in colour the *pelure d'oignon* (*q.v.*). South of Casablanca, in the old vineyards of El Jadida and Demnate, are made the dry, fruity *vins gris* which are considered very special in Morocco.

Moscatel de Setúbal

Fortified wine made near Lisbon.
See PORTUGAL.

Mosel

German version of Moselle (*q.v.*).

Moselblümchen

'Little Flower of the Moselle'. The wine name, akin to Liebfraumilch from the German Rheinhessen, refers to a common, enormously overrated wine, upon which the additional sin of adding sugar is usually wreaked. When you see this wine you can be certain that the individual vineyard growth sold under this generalized invented name had nothing to recommend it in its own right.
See MOSELLE.

Moselle, Mosel

German white wines.

The secret of Moselles can be told in two words: slate and Riesling. Like the linked syllables of a sorcerer's spell, they produce the variety that makes each wine different even from its nearest neighbour, and the light, delicate quality, full of incomparable bouquet, which proclaims it inimitably Moselle.

In prehistoric times, the Devonian Sea covered the area where today the deep cleft of the Moselle runs from the French Vosges Mountains down to meet the Rhine. The sea sank away, and the sea-life and the sea-flowers fossilized and became a kind of slate or shale. The Germans call it *Schiefer*.

Caught between the walls of slate, the River Moselle cut deeper and deeper. When the Romans arrived, bringing vines (though vines may or may not have been planted by the people who were there before them), the river canyon was already deep enough to be below the wind. The river twists like a snake, and the countless bends screen it from the wind. The wide river in the narrow valley tempers the air and reflects and intensifies the sun. The slate itself has given way slowly to the water and the elements until the banks are worn and steep; where the vines are rooted it holds moisture and heat, and

reflects this heat upwards when the sun is shining. These elements of the secret of the Moselle explain why for two thousand years wine has been made without interruption in the northernmost of the important vineyards of the world. The Moselle lies on a parallel a little north of Newfoundland, but frosts do not reach the protected valley until late November. Long before this, the winter has numbed the crowns of the hills and the surrounding country.

The people who work single-mindedly in their remote, precipitous vineyards are of mixed stock, and even today distinct types can be recognized, such as pure Celts, or Roman heads which might have been cut on ancient coins. In their isolation, they have remained conservative, religious, and hard-working, dedicated, throughout the centuries, to the terrific task of bringing the fruit down from the nearly perpendicular cliffs of vineyard, where the sticks which support each vine shine like steel ranks of bayonets high above the bend of the river. Moselle growers tell how no machine or animal can labour on these sheer slopes—only a man, carrying everything up and down on his back. Fortunately, a certain amount of mechanization is now developing year by year: washed down earth, fertilizer, cylinders of spray, and even cutting plough-blades can be hauled slowly to the top by cables wound on to the drums of engines, and often suspended cable cars carry the workers up like mountaineers.

Slate is half the key to the Moselle. The vineyard names frequently end in '-lay' (or '-ley'): this means simply that the soil is slaty. The Middle Moselle, from roughly around Trier to just below Zell, is the best section. The clue again is slate, which crumbles here at just the right rate to renew the soil, keeping it constantly virgin. Below Zell, the slate is harder: too hard for the vine to develop fully. In the Upper Moselle, the soil is not slaty but chalky, and an inferior wine results. 'The slate is the *race* of the wine,' they say on the Moselle. They mean that the breed of the wine comes from the peculiar and beneficial working of the Riesling vine with the slate. The grape is the other half of the secret.

Riesling was not always grown on the Moselle. The Romans planted *Vitis elvenea*, a vine like the Elbling, which still produces common wines on the Upper Moselle today. The Riesling probably began as a grape for red wine (growth of red-wine types is prohibited by law on the Moselle now), and even today the Riesling variety occasionally reverts and produces dark grapes. White Burgundy grapes were prevalent in the fifteenth and sixteenth centuries; in the seventeenth century, Riesling began to appear. In 1787 Prince-Bishop Clemens Wenzeslaus of Trier made the planting of Riesling obligatory.

It is not Riesling, however, which makes it possible to track down the special characteristics and worth of almost every individual vineyard parcel. Except in the Upper Moselle, Riesling is universal in this region. The third largest German vineyard area (after the Palatinate and Rheinhessen), the Moselle is the most extensive Riesling vineyard of all. A few small plots test out various early-ripening varieties, and there is some Müller-Thurgau (the crossing of Riesling and Sylvaner) which is gaining in most German sections but does not seem very suited to the steep slate slopes, dry and full of stones; the rest is all Riesling. What does vary is the slate.

The infinity of differences among the wines, one of the things which makes the drinking of Moselles so delightful, comes from the exposure to the sun of the slope and the side of the river on which it is found. Since the character of the slate has made the character of the river, in the long run everything can be traced back to that one single factor.

They explain this very interestingly in the half-timbered wine taverns along the banks of the river, when they bring out a map of the Moselle and chart the individual curves. Wherever the river has encountered the hardest shale, it has had to bend; and at the same time it has silted the facing shore. The result is that the inside of the bend is steep, hardish shale or slate, and the outside is always a low promontory of heavier earth deposited by the eddy of the river. The noblest wines, with the great breed, fight for life on the sheer shale slopes. Directly opposite, a lazier, fuller wine will grow on the alluvial soil. Piesport, Bernkastel, Graach, Wehlen (the village itself is on the other shore facing the vineyards), Zeltingen, Ürzig, they are all on the inner bends of the river. By happy chance the excellent sections face a few points either east or west of south—Piesport, south-east; the strip from Graach to Zeltingen, south-west; Ürzig, south-east; so they get the maximum sun exposure, too. The single exception to this would seem to be Bernkastel, the most famous of all. The town lies in the mouth of a small valley running back between two hills and forking out around the base of a third. The Doktorberg, on the down-river side above the town, curves in from the Moselle edge in such a way that Bernkasteler Doctor grows on a slope turned only a little west of south. This is the most costly piece of vineyard in Germany, and perhaps in the world, although its real value is not quite up to its fame.

The great events in Moselle wines have been well spaced out—the founding of the vineyards at about the beginning of the Christian era: the spreading of vine and wine by the Cistercian monks who came to cultivate huge areas after their arrival on the Moselle in 1134; the establishment of Riesling as the universal variety by the end of the eighteenth century; and finally the great and significant increase of production, particularly in the last fifty years. Yield per acre varies so much (the yield of 1934 was over twelve times that of 1923, for example) that no average figure can be struck that would not be deceptive. Nevertheless, the amount of Moselle produced each year is much greater than it used to be. Improvement in growing methods and the use of commercial fertilizer, along with the pressure of increasing demand, accounts for this. Today, about 22,000 acres are in vine: of this total, approximately two-thirds are free of disease, while in the remaining third, the battle against vine diseases and the grape-louse phylloxera is intensive. The Saar and Ruwer, flowing into the Moselle and viticulturally reckoned with it, and the district around Trier, are most heavily attacked.

The precarious struggle accounts for the high price of good Moselle wines: the grower must make up in his best years for all the other years when the northerly climate prevents him from making any wine to speak of. The approximately 20,000 Moselle vineyards are divided into 163 townships, 93% of the growers having less than two-and-a-half acres, and only half of one per cent having more than twelve acres. There are fifty-nine wine co-operatives. The Moselle wine cask is called the *Fuder* and originally held 960 litres—211 imp., 254 U.S. gallons—although today for purposes of reckoning it is almost always considered a lot of 1,000 litres—220 imp., 264 U.S. gallons.

In this most dramatic of all wine areas—in the timbered mediæval inns of Bernkastel, or in over-exploited Cochem—where the towers are like a toy-maker's fantasy—one of the most spectacular German vinicultural achievements is probably beginning to die out. This is the amazing golden, mouth-filling, Trockenbeerenauslesen wine. This incomparably rich concentrate of all that is the Moselle's truest gift to the drinker is gradually becoming too costly. It can only be obtained by the repeated picking over of the sheer slopes to select each individual berry on the very point of maximum overripeness. In a country where the rising cost of labour is the most significant factor in the economy this is becoming impossible. Sebastian Prüm of Wehlen still sells his Moselles under the name of his father, Johann Josef Prüm, and he has what may well be the finest private cellar in existence for the range and quality of wines grown within the family. He says that Trockenbeerenauslesen Moselles, at today's prices, are losing propositions for the grower and are produced only as a matter of pride in the art and tradition of wine-making.

All the outstanding wines come from the Middle Moselle and the tributaries Saar and Ruwer (the German wine label lumps the three rivers together and carries the designation Mosel–Saar–Ruwer). The secondary districts are Upper Moselle and Lower Moselle.

Middle Moselle

The middle section of the Moselle begins below Trier, Germany's oldest city—just where seems to be a matter of dispute—and by general consent ends below the great bend at Zell, where the villages of Alf and Bullay face each other across the water. The boundaries can be more exactly defined. No wine of any real importance, and only one with a widely-known name, grows either above or below the Middle Moselle which begins at Piesport and ends at Erden. The greatest wines, going down-river, are the Piesporters, Braunebergers, Bernkastelers, Graachers, Wehleners, Zeltingers, Ürzigers, and Erdeners. The best parts of the Middle Moselle are so valuable that parcels may cost sixty to seventy, and in rare cases as much as two hundred times the price of similar parcels in the Upper Moselle. £14,000 (40,000 dollars) an acre is reached, and more than double this in Bernkasteler Doctor. A Lower Moselle wine which sometimes claims to be Middle Moselle and which is famous without deserving to be so is the Zeller Schwarze Katz. The label with the black cat on a barrel seems to be responsible for the reputation of this wine, a very ordinary one originally from a single vineyard in Zell, but now—such is the power of celebrity and high sales—a wine far more abundant than the Schwarze Katz vineyard or even all of Zell could produce. This must be classed with the Liebfraumilch of the Rheinhessen and with Little Flower of the Moselle, made from a variety of nameless wines with sugar added. (*See* LIEBFRAUMILCH under RHEINHESSEN for discussion of umbrella-type wine names.)

Vineyards and Place-names

Bernkastel-Kues

Numbering 6,000 inhabitants today, Bernkastel

was founded as a city in 1291, receiving city rights from Barbarossa. Nestled down between the Doktorberg and the Schlossberg, crowned by the ruin of Landshut Castle, the town, with its mediæval square, half-timbered houses and wrought-iron signs, is almost too neat and new-painted, like a film set, yet it is an authentic, if carefully preserved, old town, kept spick and span for the thousands of tourists—the greatest concentration arrives for the vintage festival on the first week-end in September, when the baroque fountains actually flow with wine. The mixed soil of earth and shale gives the wines their special character. In some ways, the earthy terrain imparts something of the roundness and mouth-fillingness of a typical Pfalz wine, but with this, and outweighing it, is the characteristic Moselle nuttiness and spicy flavour imparted by the slate. The Bernkastel slate is harder than any other—this has been proved by the oaks of Bernkastel. Oak is used for tanning shoe-leather: the Bernkastel oak for the tanning of sole leather, the oak of Wehlen and other neighbouring zones for the uppers. This same influence declares itself in the *race* of the wines. Some Bernkastelers, and especially Bernkasteler Doctor, have a slight smoky under-taste, like the wines of Bingen on the Rhine. This may come from the soil; or the smoke of the town, lying up over the Doctorberg when the wind is from the west, may have something to do with it.

Area: 450 acres in white wine.

Bernkastel Vineyards

Bernkasteler Doctor. The most famous Moselle wine, unquestionably first-rate, but nowadays ridiculously over-priced. In the fourteenth century Prince-Bishop Bœmund II of Trier is said to have been cured of illness by the wine: hence the name, and countless jokes, rhymes, and poems ever since. The slope faces south and a little west above the town, and the wines are said to profit by the sun's heat reflected from the roofs as well as from the broad surface of the river. Bernkasteler Doctor Feinste Auslese was chosen by Dr. Adenauer for his State gift to Eisenhower—fifty bottles of what he considered to be Germany's greatest. The owners are the widow of Dr. Hugo Thanisch, Lauerburg, and Deinhard and Co., Thanisch and Deinhard having nearly all of it. When the Deinhard share was purchased in 1902 from Herr Kunst, the Mayor of Bernkastel, payment was in gold, the highest price ever paid for a vineyard up to that date.

Graben. Thanisch is the principal owner and the vineyard is beside the town: there is little difference in quality between Graben and Doctor and many people prefer the former.

The other principal vineyards are Badstube; Lay; Rosenberg; Schwanen.

The lesser vineyards of Bernkastel are: Altenwald, Held, Königsstuhl, Matheisbildchen, Pfaffenberg, Bratenhöfchen, Pfalzgraben Schlossberg. Braunes is a regional name, not that of a vineyard; never an estate or original bottling.

Kues Vineyards in Bernkastel

Kues, across the river, became part of Bernkastel in 1905. The famous sight, where the broad bridge from Bernkastel touches shore, is the St. Nikolaus Hospital, founded in 1448. Thirty-three old, poor men were to be taken in and cared for, never more nor less; and it has been done from that time to this. Kues is not as charming as Bernkastel, and the wines grown on the outer bend of the river, and therefore on a heavier soil deposited by the river eddy, are less distinguished.

Weissenstein is generally the best of these, having the same south exposure, although across the river, as Bernkasteler Doctor; but it is a fuller wine, with less breed because it grows on the heavier soil of the promontory shore.

Other vineyards worth mentioning are Herrenberg, Kalbrech, Lay, Rosenberg.

Brauneberg

The great wines are elegant, feminine, and exceedingly flowery. In 1806, when Moselle vineyards were classified, Brauneberg was placed first. For centuries the slope, the Braune Berg, facing the village of Brauneberg across the river, was known as Dusemond, deriving from the Roman term for Sweet Mountain. It is the largest unbroken stretch in the heart of the Moselle (about two miles) and averages approximately 900 feet in height.

Area: 126 acres of outstanding white wine.

Vineyards: Juffer and Falkenberg are best, and of the two Juffer is more famous. Bürgerslay, Hasenläufer, Kammer (or Kammerhof), an exclusive holding of the Bergweiler estate, produces very good wines; also Lay, Obersberg.

Erden

The Erden slope is called Moselle's Gold Mountain, and the tribute is justified. After the Doktorberg, this gives the best returns of any Moselle area. The wines are particularly fruity and have great breed, coming from slate harder than usual, as is the case at Bernkastel. Along the Moselle they have a saying that the wines of Wehlen are more *Mädel* (girl) and the wines of Erden are more *Bube* (boy). They are certainly fuller than the delicate Wehleners.

Area: 155 acres of white wine.

Vineyards: Prälat is perhaps one of the best of these excellent vineyards; it is almost exclusively held by the brothers and sisters of the Berres family. Treppchen, or earthen steps, accurately describes the high terraced vineyard, the best-known of Erden, producing an outstanding dry Moselle. Bussley, Herrenberg, Herzley (now sold as Bussley). Hötley, Kaufmannsberg. (These are the main names authorized by the Erden Council in 1934.)

Filzen

Filzen, of lesser importance than the above, lies just up-river from Brauneberg but the vineyards are on the promontory (alluvial soil) side of the river.

Area: 112 acres of white wine.

Vineyards: Klostergarten is the most important, followed by Nonnenberg, Rosenberg, Schieber.

Graach

The wines are long-lasting and strong, and they fill the mouth. Even so, grown on slaty soil, they have the characteristic breed or steely *race*. When there is no rain in September and October, Graach makes wonderful wines; in general they are at their best in the dry years. Practically all the vineyard once belonged to the Church; today, Prüm, Thanisch, Deinhard, and Kesselstatt are the main owners, and they, not the Graach vintners, have the best parts.

Area: 256 acres of white wine.

Vineyards: Himmelreich, lying very high up on a pure slate soil, is first in quality and the best-known Graacher within Germany. Josephshof is the best-known Graacher abroad. It is one of the few Moselles sold without the township name, simply as Josephshofer. Originally called St. Martinshof after the St. Martin Monastery, it was renamed for Joseph Hain who acquired it after the secularization of Church property; he sold it to Count Kesselstatt in 1858 and it is entirely owned by the Kesselstatt Domain today. The other principal vineyards are Domprobst and Abtsberg. The lesser ones are Bistum, Goldwingert, Kirchlay (the wines now take the name of Domprobst); Lilienpfad (good but small); Pétrus, Rosenberg; Stablay (good but small); Tirley (not seen on labels—takes name of Himmelreich). Münzlay is a regional name (*see* Wehlen *below*).

Kesten

The wines are grown on a small plain, in mixed cultivation with fruit orchards.

Area: 170 acres in white wine of lesser importance.

Vineyards: Paulinsberg, Herrenberg, Niederberg.

Lieser

Located between the Braune Berg and Kues. Some of the wines are quite sprightly, though generally of lesser importance.

Area: 270 acres of white wine.

Vineyards: Niederberg, Kirchberg, Paulsberg, Pfaffenberg, Rosenberg, Schlossberg. Several of the other vineyard names are often used in combination with Niederberg.

Maring

Adjoins Lieser, in Middle Moselle.

Area: 263 acres in white wine of lesser importance.

Vineyards: Brauneberg, Rosenberg, Schwarzlay, Sonnenuhr.

Mülheim

The best-known vineyard, Sonnenlay, lies inland on the alluvial side of the river.

Area: 150 acres in white wines of lesser importance.

Vineyards: Sonnenlay, Elisenberg, Johannesberg, Kloster.

Osann

Area: 190 acres in white wines of lesser importance.

Vineyards: Hahnenberg, Hofberg, Rosenberg.

Piesport

The wines are round, with great breed and spiciness. They tend to be long-lived and are especially distinguished by their fruitiness and a particular piquancy. They show at their very best in dry years, while in wet years they may be poor. The Moselle makes a sharp bend at Piesport and the sun is caught in a land-locked amphitheatre facing south-east. The slope is 1,500 feet high, and above the vineyard are rocks and oak forest. In a wet summer, the forest holds too much moisture and the vineyard cannot dry out.

Area: 150 acres in white wine.

Vineyards: Goldtröpfchen (1st), Schubertslay (2nd, exclusive holding of City of Trier), Falkenberg, Grafenberg, Günterslay. The better ones are

Bildchen, Hohlweit, Pichter, Taubengarten. Michelsberg is a regional name, never an estate bottling.

Ürzig

The vines, growing on a very sheltered, and in some places incredibly steep, southern exposure have a soil structure different from that in any other part of the Moselle—a deep-strata volcanic soil of mixed slate and croppings of coloured sandstone, giving a special taste. The wines, as male as any, are spicier than others and have great fruitiness; in the opinion of some experts, their overall quality is better than that of Bernkastelers. In hot years these wines are magnificent.

Area: 170 acres in white wines.

Vineyards: Würzgarten, Kranklay, Urglück (part of Würzgarten). *Schwarzlay:* Often mistakenly believed to be a leading Ürziger vineyard, this is a regional name which may be applied to any wine of Ürzig, Zeltinger or any other vineyard within an 8-mile radius of these townships. The name is only used by wine merchants, never by growers, and therefore the wine is never estate bottled. A common wine.

Veldenz

Extremely picturesque with a ruin-crowned little mountain, but well inland from the Moselle.

Area: 170 acres of white wine of lesser importance.

Vineyards: Bitsch, Carlsberg, Geisberg, Kirchberg, Neuberg.

Wehlen

A plain unassuming village compared to some of its neighbours, Wehlen nevertheless looks across the Moselle to what, in Germany, is commonly considered the best Moselle vineyard. Wehlener Sonnenuhr does not reach quite the fabulous prices commanded by Bernkasteler Doctor but Germans say it is the better wine. The distinguishing character of the Wehleners is their extreme elegance and finesse, unsurpassed in any other wine.

Area: 240 acres of white wine.

Vineyards: Wehlener Sonnenuhr, a wine of enormous elegance and bouquet. The best parts are held by the Prüms of Wehlen: Sebastian Alois Prüm, Peter Prüm, and, best sections of all, the wine estate (Wachstum) Johann Josef Prüm, now actually owned and run by the nephew of Sebastian and Peter—another Sebastian Prüm, son of Johann Josef Prüm, deceased. Lay (2nd), Nonnenberg (3rd), Feinter, Klosterlay, and Rosenberg.

Münzlay is a regional name which may be used for the wines of Wehlen, or from anywhere else within a 6-mile radius. The name is used by wine merchants only, never by growers, and therefore the wine cannot be estate bottled.

Wintrich

Area: 240 acres of white wines.

Vineyards: Geiersley, Ohligsberg, Geyerskopf, Grosser Herrgott, Neuberg, Rosenberg, Simonsberg, Sonnenseite.

Wittlich

More significant historically than for the present-day wines. It was from here that the Cistercian monks, arriving from an establishment in nearby Himmerode in 1134, spread viticulture over much of the Moselle and Ruwer.

Area: 94 acres of white wines of lesser importance.

Vineyards: Klosterberg, Pichtern, Portnersberg.

Zeltingen

These outstanding wines have the widest range of any Moselle village, and this is not always to their advantage. In a good year, Zeltingen will produce about 2½ million bottles of wine. No other Moselle area approaches this. As a result, many ordinary bottles of Zeltinger are seen, obscuring the fact that some splendid ones are also made. It is hard to pin down Zeltinger as to type, for there is a considerable range, from light, flowery wines to others with as much body as is likely to be found in a Moselle. The very finest have a charming feminine quality.

Area: 522 acres of white wine.

Vineyards: Sonnuhr (best, 90% owned by Wachstum Johann Josef Prüm, marked by and named after one of the many sundials set in the rocks above the Moselle vines); Rotlay; Schlossberg (perhaps more body than the other two best); Herzlay, Himmelreich, Kirchenpfad, Kirchlay, Stefanslay, Steinmauer. *Schwarzlay*—regional, never estate bottled—is discussed under Ürzig.

Less Important Regions—Values

No wine (except Zeller Schwarze Katz) outside the heart of the Middle Moselle can be said to be really well known. The greatest names are great because the vineyards are held in part or in entirety by the big owners; most active in the wine auctions, these men have made their wines famous. Few renowned wines are found outside the region between Piesport and Erden; but, simply because they are less famous and therefore cost less, certain wines from outside the area are excellent value. While space forbids discussion of the following villages and vineyards, those where the wines have been found to be of really high quality, though relatively unknown and low-priced, are designated by the capitalized word VALUE. Town or village (or *Gemarkung*) names are italicized; better vineyards of each *Gemarkung* are named within brackets.

Cröv or *Kröv*; famous vineyard Nacktarsch (Halsbach, Niederberg, Paradies, Petersberg).

Detzem (Königsberg, Maximiner Klosterlay, Stolzenberg, Würzgarten).

Dhron VALUE (Dhronhofberg VALUE—if from the parcel owned by the Bischöfliches Priesterseminar it will be known as Dhronhofberger; if from parcels of other growers it will be called Dhronerhofberg; Kandel, Pichter, Roterd, Sangerei).

Enkirch, very large production, up to 1,750,000 bottles in the best years (Edelberg, Herrenberg, Steffensberg, Weinkammer).

Kinheim (Eulenlay, Hubertushofberg, Löwenberg, Petrusberg, Rosenberg).

Klüsserath (Brüderschaft, Königsberg, St. Michael).

Leiwen (Klostergarten, Ohligsberg).

Lösnich (Försterlay, Petersberg, Rosenberg).

Longuich (Herrenberg, Kirchberg, Maximiner Herrenberg).

Mehring (Blattenberg, Goldkupp, Heidenkupp, Huxlay, Kuckuckslay, Zellerberg).

Neumagen VALUE. Probably the oldest wine community in Germany. Much of the ancient viticultural equipment displayed in the famous Trier Museum was excavated here (Rosengärtchen VALUE, best Neumagener; Laudamusberg VALUE, Engelgrube, Hengelberg, Layenberg, Pichter, Pfaffenberg, Thierlay).

Reil (Falklay, Goldlay, Mäuseberg, Mulley-Hofberg, Pfefferberg, Sorrent, Staaden, Weingrube).

Thörnich VALUE (Schiesslay VALUE, Ritsch VALUE, Enggass).

Traben-Trarbach—linked villages across Moselle, wine-trade centre; a restaurant surprisingly set in the ancient portal of the bridge; wines are strong, do not always last long, and have the quality Germans call 'steel'. (Königsberg, Kräuterhaus, Würzgarten, Burgberg, Halsberg, Hühnerberg, Schlossberg, Ungsberg).

Trier—oldest city in Germany, wine-trade centre, some of the ancient buildings survived the bombs of the Second World War (Augenscheiner, Geisberg, Johannisberg, Neuberg, Retzgrube).

Trittenheim VALUE (Altärchen and Apotheke VALUE, two excellent but scarcely-known wines, thus outstanding buys; Clemensberg, Fahrfels, Falkenberg, Laurentiusberg, Neuberg; Sonnteil, Vogelsang, Weierbach.

Wolf (Goldgrube, Herrenberg, Sonnenlay).

Zell (Burglay, Dommherr, Nussberg). *See* Zeller Schwarze Katz discussed under MIDDLE MOSELLE; a greatly over-inflated name.

Principal Moselle Estates

Bergweiler

Wehlen/Moselle. Property consists of thirty-five acres distributed among the towns of Wehlen, Graach, Bernkastel, and Brauneberg. Holdings comprise principal parts of the Wehlener, Graacher, Bernkasteler, and Brauneberger vineyards, including Brauneberger Kammer or Kammerhof in its entirety.

Geschwister Berres

Ürzig/Moselle. Domain of slightly more than nine acres which includes the Würzgarten vineyard in Ürzig, the major portion of the Prälat vineyard in Erden, as well as parcels of the other Erdener vineyards, Busslay, Herrenberg and Treppchen.

Richard Josef Berres (Joh. Berres Jr. Erben)

Ürzig/Moselle. Holdings comprise approximately ten acres and include sections of Würzgarten and Treppchen in the towns of Ürzig and Erden respectively.

Bischöfliches Konvikt

Trier. The preparatory school for the Catholic seminary in Trier whose entire domain consists of some fifty-four acres in eight towns and villages on the Moselle, Saar, and Ruwer. Moselle properties include parcels of the Piesporter vineyards, Falkenberg, Goldtröpfchen, Pichter, and Lay, as well as parcels of the following lesser vineyards often sold as Piesporter growths: Niederemmel, Piesporter Schubertslay, Taubengarten, and Güntherslay; Minheim: Piesporter Lay; Dhron: Piesporter Grafenberg.

Bischöfliches Priesterseminar

Trier. The Catholic seminary in Trier. Aggregate holdings comprise sixty-nine acres in eight towns and villages on the Moselle, Saar and Ruwer.

Moselle properties include portions of the Erdener vineyards Hödlay, Himmelreich, Kaufmannsberg, Treppchen, and Filiusberg; portions of the Ürziger vineyards Hofberg and Würzgarten; sections of the Trittenheimer vineyards Neuberg, Clemensberg, Laurentiusberg, and Sonnteil; and a part of the Dhron vineyard Dhronhofberger.

Dr. Weins Erben (S. A. Prüm Erben)

Wehlen/Moselle. A member of the Prüm family whose domain of approximately eleven acres takes in sections of the choicest of vineyards of Sonnenuhr, Nonnenberg, Lay, Rosenberg, and Klosterlay in the towns and villages of Wehlen, and of Himmelreich, Kirchlay, Domprobst, Abtsberg, and Stablay in the town of Graach.

Ferdinand Haag (Vorm. Conrad Fehres Erben)

Brauneberg/Moselle. Holdings comprise slightly more than six acres and include excellent shares in the vineyards Hasenläufer, Lay, Falkenberg, Juffer, Bürgerslay, and Juffer-Sonnenuhr in the town of Brauneberg. Often makes superb wines.

Kesselstatt Domain

Moselle. The Counts von Kesselstatt came to the Moselle from Austria two hundred years ago. Since 1858 the domain has owned the Josephshof vineyard in Graach in entirety, and has augmented its holdings with choice parcels in Piesport since 1847.

Josef Milz, Jr.

Trittenheim/Moselle. Property consists of nearly six acres in the town of Trittenheim and includes sections of Laurentiusberg, Laurentiusberg-Felsenkopf, Altärchen, Apotheke, Leiterchen, and Weierbach.

Johann Josef Prüm (Wachstum)

Wehlen/Moselle. Probably first among all Moselle estates for stupendous range of wines all of superb quality. Total domain comprises twenty-seven acres in Zeltingen, Wehlen, Graach, and Bernkastel, producing about 15,000 imp. gallons (18,000 U.S.) a year. Sebastian Prüm, heir of his father, Johann Josef, owns and manages the estate; cellars under the house and wine sheds on the bank of the Moselle stream with moisture like a cave under a waterfall. Inside these dripping walls he keeps what must be one of the finest collections of Auslesen and Trockenbeerenauslesen wines in the world. J. J. Prüm holdings include: almost exclusive ownership of Zeltinger Sonnuhr and sections of Zeltinger Schlossberg and Zeltinger Rotlay; the choicest parcel of Wehlener Sonnenuhr as well as portions of the other Wehlener vineyards, Nonnenberg, Lay, Rosenberg, Wertspitz, Feinter, and Klosterlay; major sections of the Graacher vineyards of Stablay, Himmelreich, Abtsberg, Domprobst, Goldwingert, and Lilienpfad; and parcels of Lay, Bratenhöfchen, Rosenberg, Schwanen, Pfaffenberg and Pfalzgraben in Bernkastel.

Peter Prüm (S. A. Prüm Erben)

Wehlen/Moselle. Wines definitely challenge those of the J. J. Prüm estate but the quantity is less, Peter Prüm's holdings comprising about ten acres. Peter Prüm, an uncle of the Sebastian Prüm who owns the J. J. Prüm estate, inherited his properties from his father and now owns choice parcels in Wehlener Sonnenuhr, Lay, Klosterlay, Nonnenberg, and Rosenberg; and, in addition, holds substantial portions of the Graacher vineyards of Himmelreich, Domprobst, and Heiligenhaus.

Sebastian Alois Prüm (S. A. Prüm Erben)

Wehlen/Moselle. Brother of Peter Prüm and the other uncle of Sebastian, the present owner of the J. J. Prüm estate, Sebastian Alois likewise inherited an excellent domain from his father. Consisting of nearly eight acres, it includes a very select part of Wehlener Sonnenuhr as well as other choice Wehlener morsels in Lay, Nonnenberg, Feinter, Rosenberg, and Klosterlay. Sebastian A. Prüm's Graacher holdings are composed of superior parcels in Stablay, Himmelreich, Domprobst, Abtsberg, and Kirchlay.

Freiherr von Schorlemer

Lieser/Moselle. A noble domain which includes some of the best Zeltingen and Brauneberg growths: Zeltinger Rotlay and Brauneberger Juffern; as well as other properties in the towns of Graach, Wintrich, and Lieser.

Dr. Hugo Thanisch Ww.

Bernkastel-Kues/Moselle. The present owner is the granddaughter of Dr. Thanisch, whose most famous vineyard was Bernkasteler Doctor. The estate, now managed by Frau Thanisch, consists of over twelve acres distributed between the towns of Bernkastel and Graach. Bernkasteler properties include outstanding portions of Doctor, Graben, Lay, Rosenberg, Pfalzgraben, and Theueren Kauf. Graacher holdings comprise major sections of Domprobst, Stablay, and Himmelreich.

Oscar Tobias

Müstert/Niederemmel-Piesport/Moselle. A principal owner in the town of Niederemmel-Piesport with nearly four acres, Tobias's properties include sizeable parcels in Goldtröpfchen, Lay, Güntherslay, Taubengarten, and Bildchen.

Vereinigte Hospitien

Trier. A public hospital in Trier with total holdings of over seventy-two acres in five towns and villages on the Moselle and Saar. In addition to parcels in the Augenscheiner, Neuberg, Thiergärtner, and Maximiner Pichter vineyards of Trier, the hospital owns the largest share of the well-known vineyard Piesporter Schubertslay as well as sections in the other Piesporter vineyards of Goldtröpfchen, Dompichter, and Pichter-Treppchen.

Lower Moselle

The Lower Moselle is usually considered as beginning at Alf-Bullay, although the vineyards of Zell, Briedel, and Pünderich in the tortuous bend of the river just above are in a kind of no-man's-land, named now as Middle Moselle, now as Lower Moselle. It might be more accurate to make the division at Eller, the next bend below Alf-Bullay, because after Eller the slate grows noticeably harder and this is the significant characteristic of the Lower Moselle.

Except for a small amount of Müller-Thurgau in the section called Krampen, the vine is the same as that of the great wines of the Middle Moselle Riesling. But the slate soil structure below Eller is too hard to crumble. This restricts the area in which the vine can grow; nor is the earth constantly refreshed by the decay of the shale as it is in Middle Moselle. This makes all the difference, and the wines incline to be ordinary.

The following are the principal towns and villages or *Gemarkungen* and their better-known vineyards or *Lagen*:

Town or Village (Gemarkung)	*Acres*	*Vineyards* (Lagen)
Aldegund	170	Hötlay, Klosterkammer, Palmberg, Rosenberg
Alf	150	Herrenberg, Kapellenberg, Kronenberg
Beilstein (Krampen) (Krampen, German for 'cramp', refers to the tremendous contortion of the Moselle from Eller to Cochem)	45	Hahn, Herrenberg, Schlossreich, Kalmond, Herl, Kirchberg, Sonnteil
Bremm (Probably the steepest vineyard in Europe, parcels terraced, no cable lift, and everything carried upwards on shoulders)	180	
Briedern (Krampen)	89	Rüberg
Bruttig (Krampen)	131	Brandenberg, Johannisberg, Kreuz, Kuckucksberg, Rathausberg
Cochem (Krampen) (as pretty as a Swiss clock, but spoiled by tourists, being on the main route from Bonn)	375	Langenberg, Schloss, Schlossberg
Ediger (Krampen)	266	Elzoberg, Feuerberg, Hasensprung, Osterlämmchen, Pfaffenberg
Ellenz-Poltersdorf (Krampen)	100	Born, Goldbäumchen
Eller (Krampen)	125	Bienenlay, Kalmond, Kapplay, Rotkäppchen
Klotten	275	Burgberg, Kapellenberg, Rosenberg
Kobern	100	Pfarrberg, Uhlen, Weissenberg
Moselkern (Below Burg Eltz, one of the most amazing castles on the the Moselle and property of Count Eltz, one of the best wine-growers in the Rheingau)	82	Heberеltz
Pommern (Krampen)	142	Goldberg, Greismund, Kapellenberg, Rosenberg
Senheim (Krampen)	185	Bienengarten, Kirchenreich, Lay, Rosenberg, Schwarzberg, Wahrsager
Treis	200	Bienenberg, Elslay, Sonnenberg, Kappellenberg
Valwig (Krampen)	180	Herrenberg, Schwarzenberg
Winningen	450	Hamm, Rosenberg, Uhlen

Upper Moselle

The vineyards of the Moselle above Trier are considered to belong to the Upper Moselle, but they are really linked in name only since they lack all the essential elements which go to make up true Moselle wines: slate soil and Riesling. Most of the vine on the Upper Moselle is Elbling, related closely to the variety brought to the Moselle by the Romans 2,000 years ago; there is a little Müller-Thurgau, a crossing of Riesling and Sylvaner; and recently some Ruländer has been planted. The soil is of chalk substance, not slate. Yet Upper Moselle wines often have a particular charm of their own, and, taken on average, they are probably better than the Lower Moselles, although neither can challenge the wines of the middle strip. Many Upper Moselles, good wines in their own right, are sound value, being little known and therefore not driven up in price.

The best vineyards lie opposite Luxembourg, where the river runs between the two countries just before joining with the Saar and plunging towards Trier.

Nittel is the biggest, best-known, and best of the *Gemarkungen.* Good vineyards are Gipfel (1st), Leiterchen, Rosenberg.

Wincheringen: Second town in importance.

Wellen vineyards: Altenberg, Scharzenberg, Steinkaul.

Mother Wine

Wine concentrated by boiling, used to strengthen young wines. A mural in the tomb of Menopth in Egypt shows that this process is at least 4,000 years old.

Mou

French term for flabby.

Mouillage

French term for reduction by addition of water.

Moulin-à-Vent

Fullest in body and in some markets the best-known of the red Beaujolais wines, France.

See BEAUJOLAIS.

Moulis

Bordeaux red wine. District: Haut-Médoc, France.

A commune of Haut-Médoc which has its own Appellation Controlée.

Mountain

Old English name for Málaga wine (*q.v.*).

Mourisco

Important grape in the making of Port (*q.v.*).

Mourvèdre

Red-wine grape grown in the Midi and elsewhere in France, in Algeria and in Spain. Among its many synonyms are Négron, Espar, Mataro, Catalan, Beni Carlo, and Tinto. Elsewhere it is known as Mataro (*q.v.*).

See PROVENCE.

Mousseux

This designation found on a French label means that the wine is sparkling. In France it is the term used for all sparkling wines except those grown in the geographical district of Champagne. (Only sparkling wine of that area may be called Champagne.)

Château Mouton-du-Baron Philippe (Château Mouton-d'Armailhacq)

Bordeaux red wine. District: Haut-Médoc, France. Commune: Pauillac.

Until about two hundred years ago, Château Mouton-d'Armailhacq and the present Château Mouton-Rothschild formed one estate. In 1855 Mouton-Rothschild was classified first among the Second Growths (*Seconds Crus*) of Médoc, a position it would undoubtedly surpass if the vineyards were reclassified today; and Mouton-d'Armailhacq was classified a Fifth Growth (*Cinquième Cru*), and is today better-known than some Third (*Troisièmes*) and Fourth Growths (*Quatrièmes Crus*). Mouton-d'Armailhacq lies between the famous vineyards of Mouton-Rothschild and Pontet-Canet to the north of Pauillac. The wines are excellent, and much of the credit must be given to Baron Philippe de Rothschild, owner of Mouton-Rothschild, who since 1930 has also been making Mouton-d'Armailhacq and in 1951 gave this vineyard his first name—it is now generally known as Château Mouton-du-Baron-Philippe. He has proved to be one of the most intelligent growers and promoters in the modern history of Médoc and Bordeaux wines. Although the two vineyards join, the wines are made separately.

Characteristics. A very good Pauillac, lighter than Mouton-Rothschild. While not officially a second wine of Mouton-Rothschild, many experts consider it to be exactly that, and the quality seems to bear them out.

Vineyard area: 85 acres.

Average production: 11,000 cases.

Château Mouton-Rothschild

Bordeaux red wine. District: Haut-Médoc, France. Commune: Pauillac.

There are at least five explanations of why the vineyard is called Mouton, which is French for 'Sheep'. Two are suggested by the owner, Baron Philippe de Rothschild: it seems that in Old French the hilly land was called *Mothon*, and moreover, the series of little rises and hills composing the vineyard suggest the backs of a flock of sheep. But round Pauillac they say that Mouton is simply the place where the *moutons* grazed in the old days. Until the time of that predecessor of the Rothschilds who was Baron de Brane and Seigneur de Mouton (this was the eighteenth century and his title supplies a logical explanation for the name), the property was called Château Pouyallet; and between the fourteenth century and 1853—when the Rothschilds bought it—there was a succession of owners including the Duke of Gloucester (1430), Jean Dunois, and Gaston de Foix. For four generations now, and more than one hundred years, the vineyard has been held by Barons de Rothschild—Nathaniel, James, Henri, and today the great-grandson, Philippe—and the quality and reputation of the wine have been constantly improving. Mouton was already highly rated in 1855 when Médoc wines were classified and since at that time it was neither selling quite with the First Growths (*Premiers Crus*) nor with the Second Growths (*Seconds Crus*) it was placed first of the Seconds. This compromise did not please Mouton and the famous motto of the vineyard originated: *Premier ne puis, Second ne daigne, Mouton suis*. Translated as 'First I cannot be, Second I do not deign to be, I am Mouton,' the motto has been made into a practical reality by the Rothschilds. Today, Mouton-Rothschild sells with the four First Growths, Margaux, Haut-Brion, Lafite, and Latour, and in many years surpasses them.

This eminent position is due to the high quality of the wine itself, and to the brilliant publicity and promotion given the name, especially since, in 1926, Philippe de Rothschild took over the administration and later the ownership. He was assisted in the running of the estate by the able Monsieur Marjary. A production of an average 500 barrels is exclusively in Cabernet Sauvignon grapes, and is long-vatted. Pierre and Raoul Blondin, cellar-masters at Mouton, whose father, still pottering about the place, was cellar-master before them for nearly half a century, insist that great wine cannot be made except by long vatting. The practice of leaving the grape juice in contact with the hulls and residue of the grapes in the fermentation vats for only nine to twelve days is now almost universal throughout the Médoc. But at Mouton, juice and grape residue macerate together for a full month; that is, for a fortnight or more after fermentation has ceased. This, and the exclusive use of Cabernet Sauvignon, are designed to produce a big, hard wine, which requires long bottle-ageing, but matures finally into a splendid, very long-lasting wine. The demand for old vintages of Mouton justifies this practice, and the price commanded makes it possible.

The great *chai* of new wines at Mouton-Rothschild is the most spectacular in Bordeaux. Double doors are thrown open at the side of the room where the baron gives his banquets, and neatly aligned barrels stretch away for a hundred yards in five or six rows. The *chai* is at ground level; but down below, in moss-blackened cellars, are tunnels storing 80,000 bottles of Mouton at a constant temperature of 52°F. (11·1°C.). Here, too, is the fabulous wine 'library' of which the show-pieces are cobweb-covered bottles a hundred and more years old. Along the rear wall there is a bin of bottles made up from every vintage since the Rothschild ownership began. Showmanship is not restricted to the estate. Bottle labels, for example, carry each year an original illustration by a different celebrated artist; in 1947 it was Jean Cocteau; another year, Marc Chagall. For years Baron Philippe, expertly aided by his wife Pauline, has been collecting paintings, goblets, tapestries, vases, and any other objects connected with wine. These were assembled in a superbly lit museum, which was opened in 1962, and form a collection for which every wine-lover should be grateful.

Rothschild has been criticized by some of the more conservative growers in Bordeaux; yet he has done as much for the promotion of Bordeaux châteaux wines as all the rest of the proprietors together—if owners of the great First Growths and the author are excluded. His vineyard unquestionably deserves to be classified a First Growth, and its position as a Second is an outstanding proof of the obsolescence of the 1855 Classification.

Characteristics. Always heavy, full, and almost fleshy, with a special taste that natives of Bordeaux refer to as a *goût de capsule* or 'taste of the capsule' from its distinctive, hard and almost metallic flavour. The high percentages of Cabernet Sauvignon grapes used make it very slow to mature and very full-bodied.

Vineyard area: 175 acres.

Average production: 11,000 cases.

Mulled Wine

Diluted red wine, brought to the boil, spiced and sweetened, and served very hot. It has an extraordinary ability to discourage a cold in the early stages.

Müller-Thurgau

The grape and the wine derived from the crossing of the Riesling and Sylvaner vine varieties and rapidly increasing in popularity in Germany. There is also a certain amount of it in Alsace. The name is not likely to appear on bottle labels, except in the case of a few Alsatian wines.

See GERMANY; ALSACE.

Munson, Thomas V.

American hybridizer who developed several

hybrid vines, notably Delicatessen. Munson set up his experimental vineyards in Denison, Texas, and all but revolutionized hybridization by his zealous efforts to bring in new families of grapes as 'blood lines'. His own work, however, is of somewhat limited importance to the wine-maker since it was oriented towards table grapes rather than wine.

Münster-bei-Bingerbruck

Better wine district of the two Münsters of the Nahe Valley, Germany.

See NAHE.

Murray River

Vineyards on the boundary between Victoria and South Australia. They produce fortified wines and brandy, and also grow Palomino and Pedro Ximénez grapes for sherry-type wines.

See AUSTRALIA.

Murrumbidgee

Irrigated vineyard region on the Murrumbidgee River, New South Wales, producing mainly fortified wines.

See AUSTRALIA.

Muscadel

Another name for sweet, usually fortified wine from the Muscat grape (*q.v.*). It should not be confused with Muscadet (*q.v.*).

Muscadelle

A white-wine grape grown in the Bordeaux region, where it contributes to both sweet Sauternes and dry Graves.

In the last century, an excellent Muscadelle was grown in South Africa where it produced the good Cape wine called Constantia.

Muscadet

White wines. District: Brittany, France.

The Muscadet vineyards, the only ones in Brittany to be classified, lie far down the River Loire, near the city of Nantes. The vines grow around the town, almost encircling it, and the pale, light wine with a trace of musk in the bouquet is the perfect accompaniment to sea-food caught and eaten on the shores of the Atlantic. The grape is the Melon of Burgundy rechristened. The light, fresh wine, most of it charming only when it is young, used to be known in its own region alone. Later on, Paris discovered it and took it up; and since the last war it has made its way abroad, and gradually become popular.

The region divides into two—the Coteaux de la Loire, and a group of villages south of Nantes, in Sèvre-et-Maine. Although most of the grapes need to be picked in good time, to avoid overripeness, some on slopes facing north mature slowly and give full-bodied wine that holds up well. As a rule the wine is not vatted, but is fermented in barrels in the cellars. Some is bottled while it still contains carbonic gas, producing a wine with a slight prickle or *perlé*.

Coteaux de la Loire

The vineyards are confined to small plantings on the rocky shores of the river, and the wines incline to be drier and more robust than those of the other district, with a higher acid content. This is a virtue—the Muscadet to avoid is that which is flabby because it lacks acid. Some of the best wines are those of Saint-Herblon (which has a taste of gunflint), Oudon, and Saint-Géréon, with Drain and Liré on the left bank.

Sèvre-et-Maine

The wines vary a good deal from commune to commune, but on the whole they are supple and fruity, and should be drunk rather young. Noteworthy names are Vallet, Mouzillon, Le Pallet, Saint-Fiacre, La Haie-Fouassière, Vertou, Monnières, Gorges.

See ANJOU; COTEAUX DE LA LOIRE.

Muscadine

Vines native to southern sections of North America, the best-known example of which is the Scuppernong—the others are the James and the Mish.

The grape is not popular with the wine-maker, partly because of its low sugar content and high acidity, and partly because of its very pronounced and unattractive aroma when vinified.

See CHAPTER EIGHT, p. 29.

Muscat

1. A sweet grape, usually white, subdivided into many varieties. The wines tend to be heavy, strong in scent and flavour, and to produce sweet dessert wines or to be eaten as table grapes. In California, the Muscat d'Alexandrie is extensively cultivated for wine, but this is not a grape of good quality.

2. Muscat de Beaumes-de-Venise, Muscat de Frontignan, Muscat de Lunel, Muscat de Saint-Jean-de-Minervois.

See SWEET FORTIFIED WINES OF FRANCE.

Muscat d'Alsace

A dry, fruity Muscatel of Alsace.
See ALSACE.

Muscat of Samos

See SAMOS; GREECE.

Muscatel

Wine made from Muscat grapes. These may be red or white, dessert or sparkling wines. Two of the better-known are Muscat de Frontignan and Muscat de Samos.

In California a regrettable quantity of fortified wine known as 'Muscatel' is sold as a substitute for spirits.

Muselage

In French, literally 'muzzling'; the wiring which clamps the corks on to Champagne bottles.

Les Musigny

Burgundy red and white wine. District: Côte de Nuits, France. Commune: Chambolle-Musigny. Official classification: Great Growth (Grand Cru).

The remark 'If our slope were not the richest in the world it would be the poorest' was prompted by a view of Musigny. The vineyard lies along a small dirt road and across it is nothing but underbrush and rubble. On one side, the land is virtually worthless. On the other, it has been known to bring up to approximately £10,700 (30,000 dollars) per acre.

The vineyard is in three parts: Les Musigny, Les Petits Musigny, and La Combe d'Orveau. The three stretch out along the slope, with Les Petits Musigny between the other two, and on a plateau below stands the château of the Clos de Vougeot surrounded by its vineyards. Pinot Noir is the dominant vine, but there is also some Pinot Blanc and Chardonnay, not all for making white wine.

In general, the vintners who own parts of Musigny make red wine. White is produced sporadically, and rarely if ever exceeds 165 imp. gallons (200 U.S.). The reds, however, are noted for their delicacy, their elegance and, above all, their finesse. Burgundians claim that a slight addition of Pinot Blanc or Chardonnay grapes to the must heightens these qualities considerably. The law allows 15% of the vines to be of white variety, but the growers usually feel that 10% is sufficient.

In a good year the wines, in addition to their matchless feminine delicacy, have an incomparable bouquet reminiscent of violets or raspberries. They become ready to drink after two years or so, but a fine estate-bottled Musigny can be expected to develop for years and to profit enormously from imprisonment in the bottle.

The vineyard covers 16 acres. The amount of wine made in an average year for quantity is 5,236 imp. gallons (6,288 U.S.) or the equivalent of less than 3,000 cases.

Must

Grape juice before it ferments completely and becomes wine. The French word is *moût*.

Mustimeter or Saccharometer

The mustimeter or saccharometer is defined in the *Dictionnaire du Vin* as a densimeter brought into popular use by Salleron and bearing the Gay-Lussac centesimal scale; it shows the weight in grammes of a litre of the liquid into which it is immersed. This instrument of paramount importance in wine-making is used in almost every vineyard in France.

The division in the centre of the scale and marked 1,000 represents the weight of distilled water (1,000 grammes per litre); the divisions above measure lower densities and those below measure higher densities, i.e. the weight in grammes of a litre of the must or liquid being tested.

To determine the density of a must, a few bunches of grapes are crushed into a container, the juice being filtered through a cloth into a test-tube. The mustimeter and a thermometer are immersed one after the other in this juice and the readings taken, e.g. 1065 on the mustimeter scale and 18°C. on the thermometer. Reference is made to the correction table below to see what adjustment is necessary to the mustimeter reading to arrive at what it would be if the must temperature were 15°C.

For example:
The must is tested at a temperature of 18°C.; the mustimeter shows 1065; the correction table shows that 0·5 must be added to the mustimeter reading so that the weight of the must at the normal temperature of +15°C. is 1065·5. If the temperature were 12°C. instead of 18°C., the correction—0·4—would have to be deducted from 1065, the reading then being 1064·6.

Taking the corrected density of 1065·5 we refer to Table 1 opposite to see what is the weight of sugar contained in a litre of the must and what will be the alcohol content which the wine will have after fermentation.

1. EQUIVALENT DENSITY TABLE FOR WINES AND ABNORMAL AND NORMAL GRAPE-MUSTS OF LESS THAN 10% PROSPECTIVE ALCOHOL.

with their sugar and probable alcohol content and the weight of sugar which must be added to raise them to 10% (according to Salleron)

Mustimeter density or degree	*Areometer degree Baumé*	*Grammes of sugar per litre of must*	*Alcoholic content of the wine to be made*	*Weight of crystallized sugar to be added to 1 litre of must to get a wine of 10° alcoholic strength in volume (in grammes)*
1,000	0			
1,001	0·1			
1,002	0·3			
1,003	0·4			
1,004	0·6			
1,005	0·7			
1,006	0·9			
1,007	1·0			
1,008	1·1			
1,009	1·3			
1,010	1·4			
1,011	1·6			
1,012	1·7	2	0·1	168
1,013	1·8	5	0·2	166
1,014	2·0	7	0·4	163
1,015	2·1	11	0·6	159
1,016	2·3	13	0·7	157
1,017	2·4	15	0·9	154
1,018	2·6	18	1·1	151
1,019	2·7	21	1·2	149
1,020	2·8	23	1·4	148
1,021	2·9	26	1·5	146
1,022	3·1	29	1·7	142
1,023	3·2	31	1·8	139
1,024	3·4	34	1·9	137
1,025	3·5	37	2·1	134
1,026	3·7	39	2·3	130
1,027	3·8	42	2·4	127
1,028	3·9	45	2·6	124
1,029	4·1	47	2·8	122
1,030	4·2	50	3·0	120
1,031	4·3	53	3·1	119
1,032	4·5	55	3·2	115
1,033	4·6	58	3·4	112
1,034	4·7	61	3·5	110
1,035	4·9	63	3·7	107
1,036	5·0	66	3·9	104
1,037	5·2	69	4·0	102
1,038	5·3	72	4·2	99
1,039	5·4	74	4·4	95
1,040	5·5	76	4·5	93
1,041	5·7	80	4·7	90
1,042	5·8	82	4·8	88
1,043	6·0	84	5·0	85
1,044	6·1	87	5·1	83
1,045	6·2	90	5·3	80
1,046	6·3	92	5·4	78
1,047	6·5	95	5·6	75
1,048	6·6	98	5·7	73
1,049	6·7	100	5·9	70
1,050	6·9	103	6·0	68
1,051	7·0	106	6·2	65
1,052	7·1	108	6·3	63
1,053	7·3	111	6·5	59
1,054	7·4	114	6·7	56
1,055	7·5	116	6·8	54

Mustimeter density or degree	*Areometer degree Baumé*	*Grammes of sugar per litre of must*	*Alcoholic content of the wine made*	*Weight of crystallized sugar to be added to 1 litre of must to get a wine of 10° alcoholic strength in volume (in grammes)*
1,056	7·7	119	7·0	51
1,057	7·8	122	7·2	48
1,058	7·9	124	7·3	46
1,059	8·0	127	7·5	42
1,060	8·2	130	7·6	41
1,061	8·3	132	7·8	37
1,062	8·4	135	7·9	36
1,063	8·6	138	8·1	32
1,064	8·7	140	8·2	31
1,065	8·8	143	8·4	27
1,066	8·9	146	8·6	24
1,067	9·0	148	8·7	22
1,068	9·2	151	8·9	19
1,069	9·3	154	9·0	17
1,070	9·4	156	9·2	13
1,071	9·6	159	9·3	12
1,072	9·7	162	9·5	8
1,073	9·8	164	9·6	7
1,074	9·9	167	9·8	3
1,075	10·0	170	10·0	

2. Equivalent Density Table for Grape Musts of More than 10%.

with their sugar and probable alcoholic content and the volume of water that must be added to reduce them to 10% (according to Salleron)

Mustimeter density or degree	*Areometer degree Baumé*	*Grammes of sugar per litre of must*	*Alcoholic content of the wine made*	*Volume of water which must be added to 1 litre of must to bring it to a density in litres of 1,075*
1,076	10·2	172	10·1	0·01
1,077	10·3	175	10·3	0·02
1,078	10·4	178	10·5	0·04
1,079	10·6	180	10·6	0·05
1,080	10·7	183	10·8	0·06
1,081	10·8	186	10·9	0·08
1,082	10·9	188	11·0	0·09
1,083	11·1	191	11·2	0·10
1,084	11·2	194	11·4	0·12
1,085	11·3	196	11·5	0·13
1,086	11·4	199	11·7	0·14
1,087	11·6	202	11·9	0·16
1,088	11·7	204	12·0	0·17
1,089	11·8	207	12·2	0·18
1,090	11·9	210	12·3	0·20
1,091	12·0	212	12·5	0·21
1,092	12·2	215	12·6	0·22
1,093	12·3	218	12·8	0·24
1,094	12·4	220	12·9	0·25
1,095	12·5	223	13·1	0·26
1,096	12·6	226	13·3	0·28
1,097	12·7	228	13·4	0·29
1,098	12·9	231	13·6	0·30
1,099	13·0	234	13·8	0·31
1,100	13·1	236	13·9	0·33
1,101	13·2	239	14.0	0·34
1,102	13·3	242	14·2	0·36
1,103	13·5	244	14·4	0·37
1,104	13·6	247	14·5	0·38
1,105	13·7	250	14·7	0·40

CORRECTION TABLE

Temperature °C.	*Correction*	*Temperature* °C.	*Correction*
10°	−0·6	21°	+1·1
11°	−0·5	22°	+1·3
12°	−0·4	23°	+1·6
13°	−0·3	24°	+1·8
14°	−0·2	25°	+2·0
15°	0	26°	+2·3
16°	+0·1	27°	+2·6
17°	+0·3	28°	+2·8
18°	+0·5	29°	+3·1
19°	+0·7	30°	+3·4
20°	+0·9		

The first column of the above table shows the density of the must, i.e. the mustimeter reading. The second column shows the corresponding values for the Baumé areometer (or gluco-œnometer) and of the Gay-Lussac densimeter or saccharometer. The third column gives the weight of grape sugar contained in a litre of the must. The fourth corresponds to the probable alcohol richness which the wine will have after fermentation, presuming all the sugar is fermented—which does not always occur, particularly beyond 14% to 15%. The fifth column indicates the weight of pure crystallized sugar which must be added to a litre of must for the wine to contain 10% of alcohol after fermenting. By pure crystallized sugar is meant white sugar standardized at 100°. When using less pure sugars, white or brown, the table figures would be too low; they would have to be raised proportionately to the degree of impurity of the sugar used. In Table 2 there will be found, conversely, the amount of water which each litre of must exceeding 10% will have to have added to bring it down to the normal density of 1075.

If we refer to the example given earlier we find:

1. That a must of 1065 density corresponds to 8·8° Baumé;

2. That it contains 143 grammes of grape sugar per litre;

3. That, after fermentation, this sugar will give 8·4% of alcohol, which means that the wine will contain 8·4 litres of alcohol per hectolitre.

4. That 27 grammes of crystallized sugar per litre must be added in order to bring the alcohol content up to 10%.

Mutage

French term for artificial interruption of fermentation. Often this is achieved by the addition of sulphur dioxide, leaving unfermented sugar in the wine; and it used to be done in the Entre-Deux-Mers district of Bordeaux, producing a white wine with a very sweet finish.

Mycodermi Aceti

Bacterium which forms vinegar, or vinegary wines. Today usually called Acetobacter.

Mycodermi Vini

The yeast commonly believed to be responsible for the formation of a film on certain wines.

See FLOR; SHERRY.

N

Nackenheimer Rothenberg

Best of the Nackenheimers in the German Rheinhessen (*q.v.*).

Nahe

White, and some red, wines. District: North-West Germany.

The wines of the valley of the River Nahe, a tributary of the Rhine, have been showing a distinct improvement since the local method of mixed cultivation (in which different grape varieties grew more or less side by side) has been almost entirely eradicated. Today, the less favoured sites are planted in Sylvaner vines (in the Nahe they are called Franken), accounting for about 60% of the total; and of the best sites producing the *Spitzenweine* or 'peak wines', about 30% are in Riesling. There is some Müller-Thurgau, the fairly recent crossing of Riesling and Sylvaner, which is proving to be a success and producing very spicy, tasty wines; and there is a little more than 1% of red wine.

The best wines come from the section of the river between Bad Kreuznach and Schloss Böckelheim. Farther upstream, they are extremely light, usually Riesling, and rather suggestive of the Saar wines (although they never attain the same finesse). This is not surprising, as a glance at the map will show. Saar and Nahe are close to each other in this section, and in earlier times it used to be customary to lump the Saar wines with those of the Upper Nahe, instead of with the Moselles as they are classed now.

The Nahe empties into the Rhine at Bingen opposite Rüdesheim. For the same reason that the wines of the Upper Nahe are Saar-like, these wines down-river from Bad Kreuznach are like Rheingaus. They come into the same climatic belt. These divisions are not to be taken as hard and fast, however; in anything as capricious and various as wine that would be impossible. In a recent tasting in the Nahe, some of the Roxheimers and Gutenbergers were lighter than Moselles.

The Nahe district includes two smaller river valleys. These are the Alsenz and the Glan, neither producing especially interesting wines.

Modernization of wine-growing methods all along the Nahe is the consequence of vine disease which destroyed whole areas. The Government came to the aid of the ruined growers—otherwise viticulture on the Nahe might have ceased. Today, methods are much improved, but this has turned out to be a mixed blessing. The cost of wine-making has risen in proportion to the gain, one result of which is that only the State Domain and a relatively small number of fairly large owners can afford the risks implicit in making wine of quality. May frosts, common enough in the Nahe, may wipe out the entire crop of the year. The problem has been solved in part by the wine co-operatives, now making about one-fifth of the total annual production, equivalent to some 7 million bottles.

Vineyards

The best wines come from Schloss Böckelheim, Bad Kreuznach, and Niederhausen, followed by Norheim, Rüdesheim, and Roxheim. (Rüdesheim-Nahe must not be confused with Rüdesheim in the Rheingau.)

Schloss Böckelheim and Niederhausen

Technically, Schloss Böckelheimer wines belong to the township or *Gemarkung* of Niederhausen, although even here there is some confusion, arising from the fact that there is a small village of Schlossböckelheim, and a recent listing of all German districts classes them separately. What is primarily important is that the wines are known independently as Schloss Böckelheimers, and this is the way in which it is most convenient to deal with them.

Schloss Böckelheimer Kupfergrube and Niederhauser Hermannshöhle (the latter growing on a slate soil rare in this part of the Nahe) are the best and the best-known Nahe wines, the former perhaps a little the better. Hermannshöhle, however, can have great elegance and breed. Both vineyards are on the terraced Kupferberg, or Copper Mountain, and both are owned chiefly by the State Domain, which, by use of convict labour, has cleared and planted the slopes within the past fifty years. One of the most familiar sights here, during the First World War, was Hindenburg sitting at a table on one of the terraces, sipping his favourite wines and brooding over the Western Front.

Schloss Böckelheimer Kupfergrube, Felsenberg, Mühlberg, and Königsberg are among the most important Nahe wines.

The best Niederhausen vineyards are Hermannshöhle, Rosenheck, Rosenberg, Klamm, Kerz, Steinwingert.

Bad Kreuznach

The principal vineyards are: Narrenkappe (one of the outstanding Nahes), Kronenberg (outstanding), Krötenpfuhl, Kahlenberg, Brückes, Hinkelstein, Mönchberg, St. Martin.

Rüdesheim-Nahe

The principal vineyards are: Rosengarten (Rüdesheimer Rosengarten is a very important name and frequently used as if it were a regional name, thus covering wines not from the Rosengarten vineyard); Wiesberg, Kesselberg.

Norheim

The vineyards are: Kafels, Hinterfels, Kirscheck, Dellchen.

Roxheim

Wines are usually sold under other names and, therefore, are not well known. The main vineyards are: Neuerberg, Birkenberg, Hollenpfad, Wiesberg.

Other Vineyards

Heddesheim: Honigberg, Kilb, Hipperich.

Laubenheim (well known and of fair quality, resemble Rheingaus): Löhr, Vogelgesand, Karthäuser.

Altenbamberg (Alsenz wines, not very interesting).

Bad Münster or *Bad Münster am Stein* (better-known of the two Münsters of the Nahe, but the other Münster has the better wines): Felseneck, Höll, Rotenfels, Kronenmauer.

Dorsheim: Goldloch, Honigberg, Burgberg.

Ebernburg (landmark, picturesque; wines ordinary): Erzgrub, Fuckern, Köhlen.

Langenlohnsheim (second largest area after Bad Kreuznach but the Rheingau-like wines are not very outstanding): Rodenberg, Steinchen.

Münster-Sarmsheim or *Münster-bei-Bingerbrück* (better wines of the two Münsters of the Nahe): Kapellenberg, Pittersberg, Langenberg, Mühlen, Dautenpflänzer.

Waldböckelheim: Königfels.

Winzenheim: Honigberg, Rosenhecke, Auf dem Berg, Manik, Metzler.

Other communities sometimes with interesting wines are Bretzenheim, Burgsponheim, Gutenberg, Meddersheim (light wines), Merxheim (light wines), Waldhilbersheim, Windesheim.

Napa-Solano

Californian wine region producing finest red table wines. Many good white wines also come from the Napa valley.

See AMERICA: CALIFORNIA AND THE WEST.

Natur

German term for natural wine. By German law, *Naturwein* is pure, unblended, and unsugared. All the great Rhine and Moselle wines are in this category and the producers belong to a Natural Wine Society which forbids the adding of sugar or any other taste-giving materials to wine. Often encountered on labels, there are several terms in German for natural wine, all meaning the same thing: *Natur, Naturrein, Naturwein, Ungezuckert, Unverbessert* (i.e. Natural, Natural-pure, Natural Wine, Unsugared, Unimproved).

Natural Wine

Wine to which nothing has been added which can influence the taste or strength.

Nature

In France *Vin nature* is natural, unsweetened wine. A special meaning applies in Champagne, where it denotes still wine.

Néac

Bordeaux red wines. South-West France.

Previously a very small district adjoining Pomerol, Néac ceased to exist in 1954 when it was joined to that of Lalande de Pomerol. The move was a wise one, for it did away with a place-name that served no purpose since the two wines are similar in every respect.

See LALANDE DE POMEROL.

Nebbiolo

A grape used in Italian red wines; e.g. in Lombardy for Sassella, Inferno, etc.

Nebuchadnezzar

An oversize bottle containing the equivalent of twenty ordinary bottles.

Nectar

The drink of the ancient Greek gods. The name was later used for wines of special quality, and even today bottles of Nectar may be found in Greece.

Negus

An old-fashioned hot drink made with Port, sugar, lemon and spice.

Nerveux

French definition of an assertive, rigorous wine not complicated by any subtle overtones.

Netherlands Spirits

In the Netherlands, the making of spirits is generally referred to as the 'old national industry' and dates back to about 1500. Originally alcohol was distilled from wine, but in the second half of the sixteenth century the processing from cereals was started. It was not until the Government imposed a high import duty on German brandy in 1670 and prohibited the importation of French brandy that the Netherlands distilling industry could reach its full development. In the eighteenth century, distilleries flourished, the greatest advances being made on the River Meuse, particularly at Rotterdam, Delfshaven, and Schiedam. At least forty of the 140 distilleries in the Netherlands today are established in Schiedam. In 1964 the total production of spirits amounted to 193,972 hectolitres, 100% by volume. The total value of exports was more than £3 million ($8,400,000) in 1964.

The percentage of the different spirituous liquors exported in 1953 (based on the price of each) is as follows:

Jenever	22·2%
Liqueurs	30·5
Advocaat	35·9
Whisky	4·7
Dry gin	1·8
Other distilled beverages	4·9
	100%

Jenever

This is the original distillation of the Netherlands. It is often supposed to be identical with gin, but in fact there are considerable differences in the taste as well as the ingredients of the two products.

The original Jenever type is made by distilling malt-wine, or a mixture of malt-wine and spirit, over juniper berries, and possibly over other aromatic vegetable ingredients, with or without the addition of sugar. Jenever is traditionally drunk neat, slightly cooled, and sipped rather than swallowed, though young Dutchmen often take it in long drinks.

Brandewijn

One of the oldest forms of the drink, it is popular in some districts of the country. The essential factors in its preparation are ripening on charcoal and the addition of certain flavours. The brandewijn is also used as the raw base for Advocaat, and for putting various fruits in—cherries, plums, etc.; and for the characteristic raisins and apricots in brandewijn.

Bessenjenever or Blackcurrant Gin

This is another typically Dutch product, processed on a neutral alcohol base and flavoured with an extract of blackcurrants.

Advocaat

This drink, so thick that it has to be taken with a spoon, is made of brandewijn, eggs, sugar, and vanilla, and it has an alcoholic content of 15% to 18%. A somewhat thinner type of Advocaat is exported to England.

Raisins in Brandewijn

Sugar candy and cinnamon are added to the raisins and the spirit. The alcohol content is approximately 15%.

Liqueurs

The favourite Dutch distillations are Anisette, apricot brandy, cherry brandy, Curaçao, crème de cacao, kümmel, maraschino and persico (this last is distilled from peach stones).

Whisky

Holland manufactures a certain amount of whisky. The barley, maize, and rye are dried on peat fires, for the sake of the smoky flavour.

Elixirs (Bitters)

These are made by the infusion of herbs, seeds, and peels in alcohol, sometimes to be distilled, sometimes not. There is usually a good deal of colouring matter and very little sweetening. Elixirs are not as much in favour as they were forty or fifty years ago; the best liked are red and green Pommeranz, which have a higher alcoholic content than most—particularly important for red Pommeranz when it is used in cafés for home-made Schilletje or Voorburg. Other elixirs or bitters are Longae Vitae, Catz bitters, Angostura, Boonekamp, and so on.

See ADVOCAAT; GIN.

Neuberger

Grape cultivated for Austrian wines.

Neuchâtel

Swiss canton which produces dry, light, sprightly wines, mostly white.

See SWITZERLAND.

Neutral Brandy

Brandy distilled at a very high proof. Completely neutral brandy would be distilled 200° proof, or

100% alcohol, and would lack any distinctive characteristics save those of pure alcohol. In practice, anything over 170° proof is considered neutral. The same applies to neutral spirit used as a blending agent in whiskies.

New Jersey

Wine-producing region in the United States, with Egg Harbor as its centre.

See AMERICA: EASTERN STATES.

New Zealand

Vines have been cultivated in New Zealand since 1833 when James Busby—an ardent viticulturist—brought some from Australia; but until recent years wine production has been small and entirely consumed at home. It increased considerably during the Second World War, when import restrictions cut off the flow from abroad. By 1964 imports had risen to 234,000 imp. gallons (289,000 U.S.) and production to 1,600,000 imp. gallons (1,900,000 U.S.). Attempts are being made to improve wine quality and build an export market.

New Zealand wines bear no exact resemblance to European, but are nevertheless sold as madeira, port, sherry, hock, claret, sauternes and the like. Many are made from hybrid grapes, since the New Zealand climate is generally too moist for the success of *Vitis vinifera*—sensitively prone to fungus diseases under conditions of high humidity.

Growing areas comprise about 863 acres in wine grapes confined to the North Island. The important districts are the Auckland-Northland area, planted largely in hybrid vines, and the land around Hawke's Bay where the less humid climate permits the growing of *Vitis vinifera* vines.

Generally speaking, white New Zealand wines are better than red, both for fortified wines (a very high percentage of total production) and unfortified table varieties. Reds tend to have too much acidity and are often thin, harsh, and astringent—even after ageing. This same acidity adds a fresh crispness to white wines, giving them a special New Zealand character. Because of its somewhat chilly weather, New Zealand is situated at the climatic limit for successful cultivation of the vine and so the sun rarely generates enough sugar in the grapes for the making of naturally sweet wines. Sugar—up to two pounds for each gallon of must—has to be added, with the result that the sweet wines are mediocre.

Wine consumption is small. The annual consumption *per capita* of alcoholic beverages comes to: 18 imp. gallons (21 U.S.) beer, 0·66 imp. gallons (0.8 U.S.) spirits, 0·69 imp. gallons (0·84 U.S.) wine.

In 1960, a peak year for production, 774,850 imp. gallons (930,600 U.S.) of fortified wines were made, and 143,450 imp. gallons (172,280 U.S.) of unfortified table wines. This was an increase of nearly 11% on the output for 1959.

Niagara

1. Wine-growing region in New York State. The important vineyard is Chateau Gay and its best wine is an unblended, sparkling Delaware.

2. One of the older American hybrid grapes, yielding white wine of pronounced 'foxiness'.

See AMERICA: EASTERN STATES.

Niederhäuser Hermannshöhle

One of the best-known wines of the Nahe Valley in Germany.

See NAHE.

Niersteiner

Best Rheinhessen wines, with great nose and elegance. All the finest are Rieslings.

See RHEINHESSEN.

Nip

British term for a quarter-bottle; reputed to be half a pint.

Noah

Green-coloured grape giving white wine; an American hybrid first recorded in Illinois. After the phylloxera disaster in Europe in the late nineteenth century, Noah was taken to France but was soon discarded by French growers because of the 'foxiness' of its wine. It may still be found here and there, however.

Noble Rot

A grape fungus which in sweet white-wine grapes becomes a virtue.

See BOTRYTIS CINEREA.

Noblejas

Wines of Toledo, usually sturdy reds somewhat comparable with those of the lesser Côtes du Rhône in France.

See SPAIN.

Noggin

A gill or a quarter of a British pint.

Norheim

Wine district of the Nahe Valley, Germany.
See NAHE.

Norton

Perhaps the best of the native American vines for red wine. It yields wines that are full, well balanced, agreeable, and not 'foxy'.

Norway

In the old days, lasting through the Middle Ages almost into the seventeenth century, the popular alcoholic beverages in Norway were beer and mead. Although they were, at an early stage, in contact with wine-drinking people, the Norwegians did not take much to wine until centuries later. The revolution in drinking habits came with the introduction of spirits. This was a comparatively late innovation, for not until the seventeenth century could spirits be bought on a commercial scale. Then they came very much into use. Except in the years between 1756 and 1816, every householder was allowed to make his own liquor—Aquavit being favourite. In 1830 about 11,000 stills were active.

In 1845 the change came. By then the potato had emerged as the foremost raw material for the production of spirituous drinks; and potatoes are awkward for amateur distillers to handle. In this year (1845) a law was passed to prohibit the use of stills with capacities of less than 200 litres (44 imp. gallons; 52·8 U.S.). These two factors combined to diminish the attractions of spirit-making as a home industry.

Gradually most of the trade came into the hands of the two large firms of distillers: Jørgen B. Lysholm, Trondheim; and Løiten Brænderis Destillation, Kristiania. In 1927, however, the wine monopoly A/S Vinmonopolet took over the distilleries, and still controls the sale of all potable spirits in Norway. The board of this institution is appointed by its managing director, the King. The object of the monopoly is to control sales and thus control alcoholism. A/S Vinmonopolet is responsible for the rectification of locally produced alcohol, for the importation of wines and spirits and for their wholesale as well as retail sale. Even alcohol destined for medical and industrial use is controlled. The wholesale importation of beer is similarly controlled, although this is allowed to be sold in certain licensed shops. The total amount of wine sold in 1961 was 1,040,786 imp. gallons (1,249,815 U.S.). There is no duty on wines and spirits, but fiscal taxes are fairly high.

In 1961 sales of spirits were 248,416,675 imp. gallons (298,334,676 U.S.), made up as follows:

Foreign bottled spirits	4·9%
A/S Vinmonopolet bottling of imported spirits	15·2%
Imported spirits mixed with Norwegian alcohol	33%
Norwegian-produced alcohol	46·9%

According to the official statistics, every adult over fifteen years of age in the country consumed 3·6 litres (·79 imp. gallon; ·95 U.S.) of pure alcohol in that year.

The Løiten and Lysholm varieties of Norwegian Aquavit are exported on a large scale to most markets in the world.

Norway also produces 'Linie Aquavit', which is a unique 'crossed' speciality. 'Linie Aquavit' is Aquavit that has crossed the Line, i.e. the Equator. To uphold an ancient tradition, Aquavit that has already been aged in oak is sent to Australia and then back to Norway on the Wilhelmsen cargo liners, thus crossing the Line twice. During this journey the Aquavit undergoes an extra maturation process influenced by the movement of the ship. The salt sea air and the changes in temperature also assist this maturation. The A/S Vinmonopolet guarantees on the label that the trip was made, when, and aboard which ship. 'Linie Aquavit' is excellent with hors d'œuvres and spicy foods.

Noyau

Colourless or slightly pink sweetened liqueur with the flavour of oil of almonds, or of peach or cherry kernels.

Nu

In France, the price of wine given *nu* is the price without the cost of cask or bottle.

Nuits, Côte de

See CÔTE DE NUITS.

Nuits-Saint-Georges

Burgundy red, and some white, wines. District: Côte de Nuits, France.

The ancient town of Nuits, which in 1892 incorporated the name of its most cherished vineyard to become Nuits-Saint-Georges, lies close to the southern end of the slope to which it gives its name. Unlike most others of the Côte de Nuits, the official place-name covers vineyards in Nuits and in nearby Prémeaux, a little to the south, these two making up the last of the important communes before the soil changes to emerge as the Côte de Beaune. Actually the Côte de Nuits extends slightly farther to the south, through the towns of Comblanchien and Corgoloin, but neither of these two is outstanding and their wines benefit only from the name *Vins Fins de la Côte de Nuits* (*q.v.*).

No vineyard in Nuits was included among the thirty-one Great Growths (*Grands Crus*)—the top-rated vineyards of the Côte d'Or, as classified by the I.N.A.O. (Institut National des Appellations d'Origine); nevertheless some very great vineyards are to be found there. Entering the town from the north, one sees the first of them on the right of the old vineyard road and on the lower slope descending from Vosne-Romanée. This slope drops gently to the River Meuzin—only a dried-up trickle most of the year—and another begins on the other side, rising steeply in a great rock-strewn bluff topped with trees and underbrush. Only the lower third of this slope is planted in vines, but along it are the best of the vineyards of Nuits: Les Pruliers, Les Porrets, Les Cailles, Les Saint-Georges, and, slightly above Saint-Georges, Les Vaucrains. Les Saint-Georges lies along the town-line and to its south are Didiers, Clos des Forêts, and the Clos de la Maréchale, the best growths of Prémeaux.

Nuits, largest town on the slope named after it, is nevertheless not very big. The population is slightly less than 5,000 and virtually every man, woman, and child is engaged in the wine business in one way or another, although Nuits is also famous for its Marc de Bourgogne (*see* MARC), its Cassis, a sweet black-currant liqueur (*q.v.*), its grape juice, and its sparkling Burgundy. Despite all these extras, the true fame of Nuits will always rest where it belongs, on its natural wines. The I.N.A.O. may not have considered any of the vineyards of the commune to be worthy of the highest rank among Burgundian vineyards, but the earlier 1860 Classification recognized no fewer than nine as Outstanding Vineyards (*Têtes de Cuvées*), the top rung of the ladder. Les Saint-Georges, Aux Boudots, Les Cailles, Aux Cras, Aux Murgers, Les Porrets, Les Pruliers, Aux Thorey, and Les Vaucrains were the nine; all of them are now officially First Growths (*Premiers Crus*) of the commune, and all produce superb wines. (Throughout Burgundy, First Growths are labelled with both name of vineyard and town name, e.g. Nuits-Saint-Georges Les Porrets, while the Great Growths carry *only* vineyard name, e.g. Chambertin.)

The outstanding distinction of the wines of Nuits is their firmness. Fuller in body than most Burgundies, they are apt to take years to mature. The firmest is generally Vaucrains, one of the finest of the commune and indeed of the whole Côte de Nuits; it is a wine to be laid down rather than drunk young. Bouquet is also a Nuits characteristic, and the wines are sometimes quite pungent. Les Saint-Georges will, because of its finesse, in most years take the honours in this field and in addition will be deeper in colour and more 'winey' than the others. Les Pruliers often starts out with a slightly metallic taste, but this passes and the wine ages wonderfully. Les Porrets, and the Clos des Porrets in particular, are the fruitiest. Clos des Porrets is a small section of the larger vineyard, and is the best part. It is owned entirely by Henri Gouges, one of the staunchest advocates of authentic Burgundian wines, and one of Burgundy's most respected growers. Gouges also makes a good white wine, but only in small quantities and most of it is sold in Paris. Boudots is another good vineyard, and Cailles combines the Nuits characteristics with a special velvety quality all its own.

The vineyards of Nuits-Saint-Georges total about 536 acres. In 1960, an average quantity year, they produced 187,143 imp. gallons (224,749 U.S.) of red wine. About 500 imp. gallons (600 U.S.) of white wine are usually made.

In Nuits-Saint-Georges

FIRST GROWTHS (*Premiers Crus*)

Vineyard	*Acres*
Les Saint-Georges	18·6
Les Vaucrains	15
Les Cailles	9·4
Les Porrets or Porets	17·5
Les Pruliers	17·5
Aux Boudots	15·8
Les Haut-Pruliers	11·2
Aux Murgers	12·4
La Richemone	5·5
Les Chabœufs	7·2
La Perrière	10
La Roncière	5·4
Les Procès	4·7
Rue-de-Chaux	7·7
Aux Cras	7·7

Vineyard	*Acres*
Aux Chaignots	13·8
Aux Thorey	15·3
Aux Vignerondes	8·4
Aux Rousselots	11·2
Les Poulettes	5·8
Aux Crots	21·2
Les Vallerots	24
Aux Champs-Perdrix	5·3
En La Perrière-Noblet	5·4
Aux Damodes	32·5
Les Argillats	18·5
En La Chaine-Carteau	6·6
Aux Argillats	6·3

In Prémeaux

FIRST GROWTHS (*Premiers Crus*)

Vineyard	*Acres*
Clos de la Maréchale	23·6
Clos des Arlots	10
Clos des Corvées	12·7
Clos des Forêts	16·6
Les Didiers	7
Aux Perdrix	8·3
Les Corvées-Paget	3·9
Les Clos Saint-Marc	2·2
Clos des Argillières	10·4
Clos des Grandes-Vignes	5·2

O

Oast House

A building containing a kiln for drying hops.

Oberemmeler

Fine wines of the Saar, in Germany. Karlsberg, Raul, Rosenberg, Hütte and Scharzberg are well-known vineyards.

See SAAR.

Obscuration

In brandy, the difference between actual alcoholic strength and that shown by measuring its specific gravity. The difference comes from the addition of colouring matter, changing specific gravity but not strength; and its amount will sometimes, but very rarely, be noted on labels.

Ockfener Bockstein

Always one of the best, and in certain years *the* best, of the wines of the German Saar. Big and full-bodied for one of the Saar wines, which tend to be light.

See SAAR.

Octave

Small cask of one-eighth of the capacity of a pipe. As the pipe varies considerably in capacity, so does the octave, which may range from 12 to 18 imperial gallons (14–21 U.S.), but is usually given as 14 (17 U.S.).

Œil de Perdrix

French for 'Partridge Eye'. A term derived from the pinkish tint in a partridge's eye and appplied to a pinkish tinge in white wines. It is found in some of the white Burgundies and in Champagnes. This term has been dying out since vin rosé began to be popular.

Œnology

The science of wine. In their *Traité d'Œnologie*, J. Ribéreau-Gayon and E. Peynaud define it also as the science which deals with the preparation and preservation of wine and its elements, by the application of the rules of chemistry. The authors of the treatise have also stated that the function of œnology is to prevent wine sickness and, in general, to aid the production of the best possible wines with the minimum of waste and of unnecessary expense. There is no question of making a good wine out of a bad one: quality is governed by the soil, the weather, and the grape variety. Wine should be a natural product. But the best of wines, left to mature on its own and according to the whims of nature, would be spoiled. Man must intervene to arrange for the developing wine the conditions in which its natural characteristics and bouquet can come to perfection.

An œnologist is a technician who has gained his diploma in the science of vinification.

Oesterreicher

The Sylvaner or Franken Riesling grape.

Off-Licence

In England, a licence permitting sale of wine, beer, and spirits to be consumed off the premises, and by extension, the shop department of the public-house itself, usually referred to as an 'off-licence'. There is a corresponding term 'on-licence' in the trade for public-houses and wine-shops, and the permit they require is an on-licence. The American term is off-premises.

Oggau

Wine town in Burgenland. This is one of the important place-names in Austria (*q.v.*).

Oïdium

Powdery mildew; a fungus disease of the vine.

See CHAPTER EIGHT, p. 37.

Okolehao or Oke

Hawaiian beverage distilled from a mixture of molasses, rice lees and juice of baked ti-root (the root of the taro or kalo plant). It is dark and smoky, and usually bottled at 80° proof.

Old Tom Gin

Gin which has been sweetened with sugar.

Oldest Bottled Wine in Existence

The Wine Museum in Speyer, German Palatinate, boasts of the oldest bottled wine in existence. It is estimated to be approximately 1,600 years old, and is tightly sealed by the hardened oil used in Roman times to provide a protective film which floats upon the wine surface. Sealed amphoræ dating from Roman days have also been found in the Mediterranean.

Oleron's Disease

Vine malady found to some extent in South Africa, rarely elsewhere.

See CHAPTER EIGHT, p. 36.

Château Olivier

Bordeaux red and white wine. District: Graves, France. Commune: Léognan.

Although both the red and white wine are rated among the top Graves Growths as classified in 1953, the dry white wine is generally the favourite. The thirteenth-century château itself, turreted and buttressed, and enclosed by a moat, is no longer concerned with wine; but *chais* and vineyard have for many years been controlled by the firm of Eschenauer in Bordeaux. The castle was the hunting lodge of the Black Prince in the fourteenth century.

Characteristics. Not château bottled, but pleasant; wine of character; and there are some outstanding bottles.

Vineyard area: 57 acres.

Average production: red—1,150 cases; white—3,900 cases.

Oloroso

A nutty, pungent Sherry, richer than Fino. For comparison and discussion of Oloroso and Fino, *see* SHERRY.

Opimian Wine

One of the half-dozen great wine names of antiquity and unlike all the others—Pramnian, Falernian, etc.—not the name of the geographical place from which the wine came, but the name of a vintage. During the Consulship of Opimius in the year 121 B.C., the Roman summer was one of such splendour that great wines were made; chiefly Falernian and others, which were said (probably with some exaggeration) to have retained their full quality for a hundred years.

Oporto

A city at the mouth of the River Douro in northern Portugal. According to Portuguese law, any fortified wines that are to be labelled Port must be shipped from Oporto.

See PORT.

Oppenheimer

In certain hot, dry years this will surpass Niersteiner as the best German Rheinhessen wine.

See RHEINHESSEN.

Orange

Orange Bitters

Popular in England as an addition to mixed drinks. The flavouring ingredient is the peel of sharp Seville oranges.

See BITTERS.

Orange Brandy

Made from brandy and oranges. The recipe, according to André Simon, is 1 gallon best brandy; the rinds of 8 Seville oranges and 2 lemons, cut very thin; 2 lb. loaf sugar. Put it into a stone jar and cork down. Shake the bottle for a few minutes every day for twenty-one days. Strain it, bottle, and cork.

Orange Wine

Made in Brazil from fermented orange-juice.

Ordinaire

French term for the common wine the people drink every day.

Oregon

Wine-producing region of the United States, one of the few where *Vitis vinifera* will grow.

See AMERICA: CALIFORNIA AND THE WEST.

Orgeat

Flavouring syrup originally made from barley, but now an emulsion of almonds.

Originalabfüllung

A term for estate bottled in German. For full description of this, and other terms of the same meaning, *see* GERMANY.

Originalabzug

A term for estate bottled in German. For full description of this, and other terms of the same meaning, *see* GERMANY.

Orvieto

One of the most consistently delightful white wines of Italy.

See UMBRIA.

Osaka

One of the main vine-growing districts of Japan (*q.v.*).

Ouillage

The topping up of wine barrels to compensate for evaporation. This is done repeatedly during the initial period of ageing.

See CHAPTER NINE, p. 42.

Ouzo

A spirit popular in Greece, sometimes seen in the United States, England and elsewhere. Ouzo is a close cousin to pastis, absinthe and French Pernod.

It is drunk cold with water, in which, like pastis, Pernod, and absinthe, it turns milky.

See GREECE: SPIRITS.

Oxhoft

Scandinavian liquid measure, 56–58 imp. gallons (67–69 U.S.).

Oxidation

Term most generally seen as a synonym for maderization, i.e. a flaw in white wine which, usually after too long a time in cask or bottle, becomes brownish in colour and flat in taste.

A substance is oxidized when it fixes oxygen or when it gives up hydrogen, or, more basically, when it accepts electrons from another source, e.g. the oxidation of sulphurous into sulphuric acid; or of sulphuretted hydrogen, where sulphur is freed. Wine embodies such oxidizable substances as tannins, colouring matter, iron, or sulphurous acid added during ageing.

See MADERIZATION; CHAPTER NINE, p. 43.

P

Paarl

River Valley in Cape Province, South Africa; a region of light table wines.

See SOUTH AFRICA.

Pacherenc du Vic Bilh

White wine of the French Pyrenees which is made in virtually the same general area as red Madiran (*q.v.*), that is, the valley of the Adour. The principal grapes used are Ruffiat, Mansenc, Courbu, Sémillon, and Sauvignon.

País

A grape and wine of Spanish origin which has been in Chile long enough to be considered a native.

Palatinate (Pfalz, Rheinpfalz)

German white and red wines. District: Southern Germany.

The Palatinate, or Pfalz, is one of the more charming provinces of Germany, and the sunniest. The picture-book villages, bright with painted shop-signs and flowery window-boxes, are set among orchards and the wine-garden, as the people call it here. The winters are so mild and the summers so hot that figs and lemons flourish; the fruit-trees are heavy with cherries, apricots, and peaches, and the grapes ripen early, to produce soft, full-bodied wines. Lying west of the Rhine and north of the French frontier and Alsace, the Pfalz is covered with great woods, rising with the fringe of the Haardt Mountains at the edge of the plain of the Rhine. The province derives its name from the Latin *palatium*, palace, in German, *Palast* or *Pfalz*. The first palace of the Emperors was on the Roman Palatine Hill; but afterwards, every royal residence was called a 'palace', and the officer in charge became the *comes palatinus* or *Pfalzgraf*—a title which was later to be handed down from one ruler of the Palatinate to another.

The beautiful bouquet and characteristic taste of the Pfalz wines come as much from the soil, which is a mixture of chalk, lime, and basalt, as from the climate. In fact, most of the wine is pleasant rather than distinguished; but, since the autumns here are long and mild, there is a great deal of rich, sweet dessert wine—Spätlesen and Trockenbeeren-auslesen made from specially selected, late-gathered grapes. The Palatinate is the largest wine district of Germany, contributing about one-fifth of the national total; but the greater part of this is kept for domestic consumption.

There are said to be more than 3,500 individual vineyard place-names in the Pfalz, and some 25,000 vineyard parcels, 87% of them of two-and-a-half acres or less. Only the middle section of a strip of vineyard sixty or seventy miles long, and three or four miles wide, produces wines worthy of export to the world market. Even so, the confusion of names is tangled enough.

Most of the wine grows along the Weinstrasse, a wine road beginning on the French border at the Weintor—a high stone-roofed gate topped with a gigantic figure of the German eagle—and reaching north to the edge of Rheinhessen. The countryside is lightly broken, flattish, and sunny, with the hills of the Haardt on the one hand and the Rhine sometimes visible at a distance on the other; the old villages are very South German, with twisting, narrow, cobbled streets and half-timbered houses, often decorated with vine motifs worked into stone—the whole Weinstrasse lives almost solely by wine and great is the rejoicing in a good year, great the sorrow in a bad one.

80% of Palatinate wine is white. Of the remaining red wines some of those from Bad Dürkheim—the largest single wine community in Germany—are best; but they do not equal the quality of Bad Dürkheim white wines. The Palatinate label indicates wine district, vintage year, village, vineyard parcel and grape variety, e.g. Rheinpfalz 1959er Forster Ziegler Riesling. The term Auslese or Spätlese or Trockenbeerenauslese added to this will mean that the wine has been specially selected and usually late-gathered. Quite standard in the German districts, this labelling will usually include as well the name of the wine estate, or *Weingut*; and the word *Originalabfüllung* guarantees that the wine is the estate bottling of the grower. German wines bearing on the label the device of an eagle with grapes on the breast and the letters V.D.N.V. are made by members of the German Natural Wine Association, including practically all the best growers in the Verband Deutscher Naturwein-Versteigerer which enforces special standards on its membership higher than the requirements of the German Wine Laws.

England and the United States are the chief importers of high-quality Palatinate wines, followed by Belgium, Holland, Switzerland, Scandinavia, and some of the South American countries—especially Brazil where the sweeter, richer wines are particularly liked. The great wines, coming from the Mittelhaardt section of fifteen or eighteen communities out of a Palatinate total of more than 250,

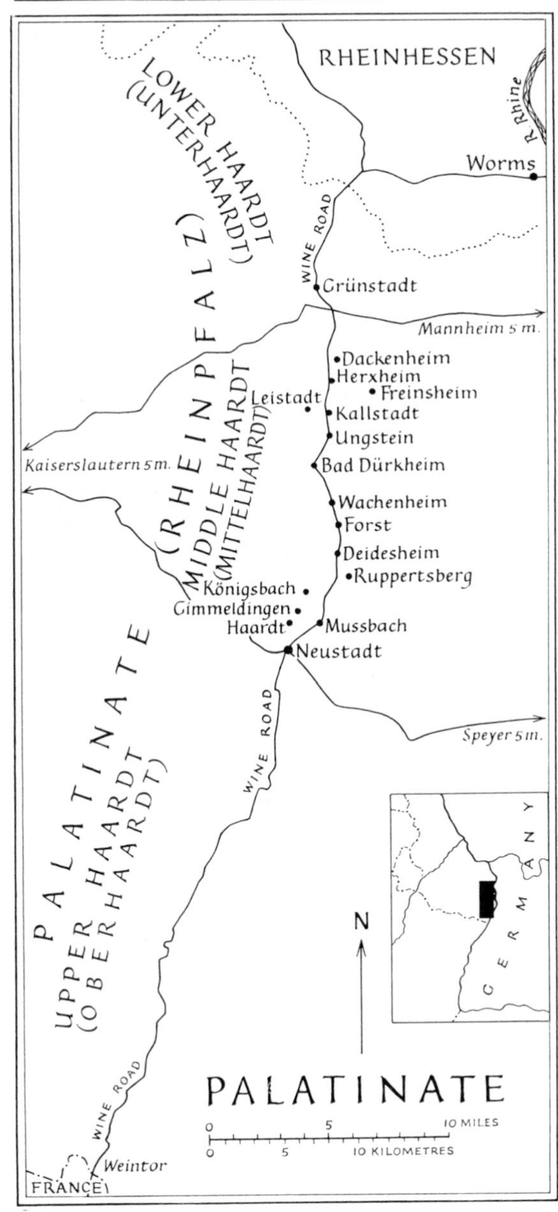

are from the Riesling grape variety, and this will nearly always be indicated on the label. The Rieslings, with their fine bouquet and great breed, producing sometimes the fine, rich Spätlesen, Auslesen, Beerenauslesen and Trockenbeerenauslesen wines, comprise, however, only about 15% of the Palatinate total of white wine. More than half is from the Sylvaner grape, which generally goes into commoner wine. Excellent wines, spicy and with great bouquet, but in small quantity, are made from the Gewürztraminer. In the south, which somewhat confusingly is called the Upper Haardt, there is some Gutedel, Muskateller, white Burgunder, and Tokayer, the Palatinate name for the Ruländer or Grauer Burgunder grape. Some Müller-Thurgau, the crossing of Riesling and Sylvaner, is grown; and around the village of Maikammer a light wine, drunk very young, is made from the Malenga grape. Practically all the red wine comes from the Blauer Portugieser variety, and only the Dürkheimer Feuerberg and Königsbacher are of any interest.

Generally, the Palatinate wines, owing to the milder climate, have more body than any others in Germany; and a larger proportion of natural wine is produced, since there is less temptation to use sugar here than there is in the colder areas. Much of the common wine, because it provides a soft base, is used by shippers for blending in the Rheingaus and Moselles. For many years, the Palatinate has been afflicted by vine maladies. As recently as the summer of 1955 it was necessary to use 20,000 gallons of spray a day in the region of Wachenheim alone.

The Important Palatinate Vineyards

Of the three areas into which the Palatinate is divided—Upper Haardt, Middle Haardt, and Lower Haardt—only the Middle Haardt produces interesting wines. The soil of the other two sections is heavier. The Upper Haardt, in the south, is a vast sea of vineyard. An occasional superior wine is produced, such as some Maikammerer and the very sweet Edenkobener; but the emphasis is on quantity. The yield frequently reaches 1,250 imp. gallons (1,500 U.S.) an acre (as against 433–474 imp. gallons (520–570 U.S.) per acre in the great vineyards) and quality and quantity do not go together.

Mittelhaardt

The strip of the Weinstrasse producing what the Germans call *spitzen* or 'peak' wines begins at the resort town of Neustadt and extends northward, like the broadening course of a river of vine, to the area around Herxheim, Dackenheim, and Freinsheim. A little more than half of the thirty-two villages are important, and the villages of Deidesheim, Forst, Königsbach, Ruppertsberg, and Wachenheim, producing the Deidesheimer, Forster, Königsbacher, Ruppertsberger, and Wachenheimer wines, are outstanding.

65% of all growers vintage their wines at the co-operatives, of which there are two in each village, one for the Catholics and one for the Protestants—or, occasionally, the division may be Conservative–Liberal. The co-operatives generally undersell the big estates in price. They make estate-bottled and occasionally Auslesen wines, but the Beerenauslesen and Trockenbeerenauslesen wines come only from the big estates.

Rain is held off by the east-lying Haardt hills, and the zone has less rain and more sun than any other part of Germany.

Forst

A hill of volcanic basalt called the Pechstein or Basaltsteinbruch, lying to the west of the village, provides a special soil which holds the sun's heat and releases it upwards on to the vines during the night. The equalization of temperature permits the grapes to ripen more completely than anywhere else in Germany, and many late-gathered wines are produced. The best sites are in the vicinity of the Basalt Mountain, often dressed with the rubble from the quarries, and one of these, Forster Kirchenstück, has been valued under the German Valuation Law at £607 (1,700 dollars) an acre, the highest rating given to any site. The sale price, however, is considerably higher than the price it is valued at.

Vineyard area: 510 acres white; a trace of red.

Grape varieties: Riesling 70%, Sylvaner 25%, Traminer 5%.

Most important vineyards: Forster Kirchenstück. Forster Jesuitengarten, perhaps best-known, is the exclusive holding of the Bassermann-Jordan wine estate. 200 years ago, owing to world demand for Jesuitengarten, the Mayor of Forst allowed the four vineyards surrounding Jesuitengarten to use the name; Basserman-Jordan sued the village of Forst, and lost the first stage of a legal process which still continues. Freundstück. Ungeheuer.

Other vineyards: Alser, Altenburg, Elster, Fleckinger, Hahnenböhl, Kranich, Langenacker, Langenböhl, Langkammert, Linsenstück, Musenhang, Neuberg, Pechstein, Schnepfenflug, Stift, Süsskopf, Walshöhle, Ziegler.

Deidesheim

The competition between the Forster and Deidesheimer wines is very close, but the two communities certainly lead all others in the Pfalz in most years. Deidesheim itself is an old, attractive place; and Gasthaus zur Kanne, founded in 1160, is well worth a visit. Each May, in a famous wine festival, a prize goat is auctioned at the baroque town hall. The custom has been in force for nearly 600 years; the little village of St. Lambrecht has had to pay this forfeit for grazing its goats on Deidesheim land ever since the fifteenth century. The Bassermann-Jordan estate, with holdings in many towns and villages, is located in Deidesheim, as is Reichsrat von Buhl, and the two estates together have the largest Deidesheim holdings.

Vineyard area: 870 acres white; 37 acres red.

Grape varieties: Riesling 60%, Sylvaner 30%, Gewürztraminer 5%, Portugieser 5%.

Important vineyards: Generally first in quality, although less well known than Herrgottsacker, and on a steep south-facing slope, is Grainhübel. Herrgottsacker is first-class but in most years not quite up to Grainhübel. Leinhöhle, a deservedly very famous vineyard. Kalkofen. Kieselberg. Mäushöhle.

Other vineyards: Buschweg, Dopp, Erdner, Geheu, Grain, Hahnenböhl, Hohenmorgen, Kränzler, Langenböhl, Langenmorgen, Linsenbusch, Martenweg, Mühle, Neuberg, Nonnenstück, Reiss, Rennpfad, Schnepfenflug, Thal, Tiergarten, Vogelsgesang, Waldberg, Weinbach. (Any Deidesheimer may call itself Hofstück, a name which is therefore likely to mean little and will never be applied to wines entitled to the better place-names.)

Ruppertsberg

Strong, fruity wines with a great deal of breed come from the best vineyards of this ancient wine-town, founded before the birth of Christ, and an important junction in Roman days. It lies on the south border of Deidesheim and shares two vineyards with that village.

Vineyard area: 270 acres white; 107 acres red.

Grape varieties: Riesling 20%, Sylvaner, 50%, Portugieser 30%.

Vineyards: Hoheburg (first in quality), Goldschmidt, Linsenbusch (also in Deidsheim), Nussbien, Achtmorgen, Diedel, Gaisböhl, Helbig, Kreuz, Mandelacker, Mühlweg, Quelle, Reiterpfad, Spiess.

Königsbach

Königsbach is famous in its province for having contributed the stone from which the Reichstag in Berlin was built. The vineyards lie quite high up against the pine-crowned hills, and the best wines are white. Red wines, however, are of considerable local interest. Sold generally as Königsbacher Rotwein, and made from the Spätburgunder and Frühburgunder variety (Pinot Noir), they share with some Bad Dürkheimers the name of the best Palatinate red wine.

Vineyard area: 170 acres white, 44 acres red.

Grape varieties: Equal amounts of Riesling and Sylvaner; some Gewürztraminer; best red wines from Spätburgunder and Frühburgunder; bulk of red wines from Portugieser.

Vineyards: Bender, Idig, Reiterpfad (red), Falbert (red), Mückenhaus (red), Mühlweg, Rolandsberg, Weissmauer.

Wachenheim

The tale they tell in Wachenheim is that generations ago the mayor of the town challenged the Abbot of Limburg to a drinking bout to the finish. Both had strong heads; but it was the mayor who was still under full sail when the Abbot, overcome by good Wachenheim wine, slipped under the table. As a mark of his esteem, he freed Wachenheim from paying the tithe of one-tenth of its wealth to Kloster Limburg. For the last half-century, Wachenheim has concentrated entirely on high-quality wine, some of it from Dr. Bürklin-Wolf, the President of the German Wine Growers' Association, and the owner of one of the three leading estates of the Pfalz. Schloss Wachenheim makes quantities of *Sekt* (sparkling wine) from Riesling and Burgunder vines.

Vineyard area: 750 acres white; 150 acres red.

Grape varieties: Riesling 25%, Sylvaner 50%, Portugieser 20%, Traminer 5%.

Most important vineyards: Gerümpel (most important; the Riesling Trockenbeerenauslese 1949 of Bürklin-Wolf fetched 14 dollars (£5) per bottle at the vineyard); Altenburg, Bächel, Rechbächel, Luginsland, Rennacker, Wolfsdarm.

Other vineyards: Böhlig, Dreispitz, Fuchsmantel, Goldbächel, Goldberg, Hellholz, Odinstal, Letten, Mandelgarten, Myrrhe, Römerweg, Schenkenböhl, Schlossberg, Silberbach, Süssbuckel, Weinhorn.

Second-rating Mittelhaardt Towns

Bad Dürkheim

Dürkheim Feuerberg is the best-known Pfalz red wine; but about three times as much white is made as red. The Dürkheim Wurstmarkt (Sausage Market) in the second and third weeks of September has been held for more than 500 years and is Germany's greatest wine festival, just as Dürkheim, with 2,000 acres, is the biggest wine town in Germany; the wine barrel on the northern outskirts of the town (it is now a restaurant) is said to be the largest in the world, holding two million bottles.

Vineyard area: 1,500 acres white; 500 acres red.

Grape varieties: Riesling, 15%, Sylvaner 55%, Portugieser 25%, Gewürztraminer and other 5%.

Vineyards: Feuerberg (red), Michelsberg, Spielberg, Eichenböhl, Fasanengarten, Forst, Frohnhof, Fuchsmantel, Gerth, Haidfeld, Halsberg, Heiligenhäuschen, Hochbenn, Hochmess, Klosterberg, Letten, Mandelgarten, Nonnengarten, Proppelstein, Rittergarten, Schenkenböhl, Steinberg.

Dackenheim

Some good wines from a chalk and lime soil on the border of the Middle Haardt and Lower Haardt; the best of them incline to be long-lasting.

Vineyard area: 132 acres white; 66 acres red.

Grape varieties: Riesling 20%, Sylvaner 40%, Portugieser 40%.

Vineyards: Liebesbrunnen, Kapellengarten, Vogelsang.

Freinsheim

A very great range of wines, from ordinary to excellent, both red and white. The village has a Gothic church, a baroque town hall, and is quite lovely, especially in cherry-blossom time, when visitors crowd to see the 'sea of blooms'.

Vineyard area: 250 acres white; 200 acres red.

Grape varieties: Riesling 10%, Sylvaner 50%, Portugieser 37%, Traminer 3%.

Vineyards: Musikantenbuckel (most important); Hannen, Liebfrauenberg, Gottesacker, Hochgewann, Kreutz, Oschelskopf, Rosenbühl.

Gimmeldingen

On two rolling hills at the foot of the Haardt range; white wines are mostly Sylvaner and are rather soft, full and sweet.

Vineyard area: 320 acres white; 62 acres red.

Grape varieties: Riesling 20%, Sylvaner 65%, Portugieser 15%.

Vineyards: Meerspinne (most important); Bienengarten, Kieselberg, Hahnen, Hofstück, Hölle, Kapellenberg, Schild, Teichwiese, Vogelsang.

Haardt (Haardtherzchen)

Since 1953 the name Haardtherzchen has begun to supplant all Haardt vineyard names. Every vineyard of the Haardt township may use it, and the purpose is to make it famous as a trademark. Kalkgrube is the best site; Herzog has produced some quite elegant wine in good years; Bürgergarten has developed full-bodied and very sweet wines. These and other individual vineyard names (Aspen, Herrengarten, Hofstück, Kirchpfad, Letten) will in most cases be found only in vintages prior to 1953, while more and more Haardtherzchen will be encountered.

Vineyard area: 370 acres, nearly all white.

Grape varieties: about one-third Riesling and two-thirds Sylvaner.

Herxheim (Herxheim am Berg)

Wines here are familiarly known as Herxheimer Oil. Some have the hardness and character the Germans call 'steel'.

Vineyard area: 300 acres white; 170 acres red.

Grape varieties: In white, Sylvaner 75%, Riesling 25%; reds, Portugieser.

Vineyards: Honigsack (most important); Blume, Felsenberg, Goldberg, Grass, Himmelreich, Kanzel, Kirchtal, Kirschgarten, Mahlstein, Sommerseite, Steinberg.

Kallstadt

The wines are usually rather full-bodied and heavy, grown on a peculiar chalk hill, the soil of which is classed as 'hot'; and for some reason they are particularly popular in England. The small village with the vines sloping away below is very peaceful; a beautifully simple war memorial embossed with grapes and leaves marks its centre.

Vineyard area: 600 acres white; 200 acres red.

Grape varieties: Riesling 40%, Sylvaner 35%, Portugieser 20%, Gewürztraminer 5%.

Vineyards: Saumagen (most important); Horn, Kobnert, Nill, Steinacker; Annaberg, Benn, Hessel, Hasenlauf, Hühneracker, Kreidekeller, Kreuz, Kronenberg, Rudelstein, Trift.

Leistadt

Not very interesting wines, half white and half red. All the whites are Sylvaner; all reds Portugieser.

Vineyards: Felsenberg, Herrenmorgen, Jesuitengarten, Kalkofen.

Mussbach

White and red wines.

Grape varieties: Sylvaner; small amount of Riesling, Portugieser.

Vineyards: Eselshaut, a new vineyard which in the last two decades has become the best. Bischofsweg, Glockenzehnt, Hundertmorgen, Pabst, Stecken, Vogelgesang.

Neustadt

Middle point on the Weinstrasse, the southern boundary of the Mittelhaardt and the largest town of the Pfalz wine country, Neustadt is more deservedly renowned as a centre, wine market, and resort than for usually unexciting produce of its vines.

Vineyard area: 370 acres white; 75 acres red.

Grape varieties: Riesling 40%, Sylvaner 30%, Portugieser 25%, Traminer 5%.

Vineyards: Grain, Vogelsang, Böhl, Guckinsland, Kies, Ziegelberg.

Ungstein

'Ungsteiner awakens the dead' is the motto of Ungsteiner wine. Whether it does or not, the quite heavy white wines from the south and east-facing slopes tend to be fiery.

Vineyard area: 515 acres, about equally white and red.

Grape varieties: Riesling 20%, Sylvaner 40%, Portugieser 40%.

Vineyards: Honigsäckel (most important); Weilberg; Bächel, Diemert, Herrenberg, Hühneracker, Kobnert, Kreuz, Kreuzmorgen, Michelsberg, Osterberg, Spielberg, Vogelsang.

Wine Estates

Palatinate wines are sold either at the vineyard (Freihand sale) in 1,000-litre lots, at auction in 100-litre lots, or in bottle. The largest individual growers auction their own wines exclusively, and there are numerous group auctions where wines from smaller vineyards as well as some of the big ones are sold.

The three most important estates are known in the Pfalz as the Three Bs (Bassermann, Buhl, and Bürklin), and there is little to choose between them; one or the other may be slightly in the lead, depending on the year. Dr. Deinhard, Fitz-Ritter, Stumpf-Fitz of Annaberg, and Georg Siben Erben are also very important.

Practically all the best growers in Germany belong to the Verband Deutscher Naturwein-Versteigerer or German Natural Wine Association, identified on bottle labels by the emblem of a black eagle with grapes on its breast. The membership of the V.D.N.V. in the Palatinate follows:

Estate	*Headquarters*	*Acreage*	*Location of Holdings*
Bassermann-Jordan (Some of the vineyards date from before 1360; the present-day estate has been built up by the Bassermann-Jordan familys ince it came into their hands at the end of the eighteenth century. In the half a mile of low, black-walled cellars under Deidesheim are some of the most wonderful Pfalz wines; for example, the	Deidesheim	100	Forst: Forster Kirchenstück, Forster Jesuitengarten, Pechstein, Ungeheuer, Ziegler, Langenacker, etc.

Estate	*Headquarters*	*Acreage*	*Location of Holdings*
almost unbelievable Forster Jesuitengarten Trockenbeerenauslese 1900—or the 1950er Forster Jesuitengarten Riesling Trockenbeerenauslese, which has commanded the highest post-war price for a Pfalz at £5 10*s.* (15 dollars) a bottle to the vineyard before all mark-ups. At the 1955 German Quality Wines Auction, the 1952er Deidesheimer Hohenmorgen Riesling Trockenbeerenauslese fell only 5*s.* 9*d.* (·80 dollar) below this mark. The historic estate, the guest book signed by celebrities —from Mendelssohn to Max Schmeling—belongs to the grand old man of Pfalz wines, Dr. Friedrich von Bassermann-Jordan, now an octogenarian and formerly president of the German wine growers. His gigantic book in three volumes is the authority in the language of the history of wine.)			Deidesheim: Deidesheim Hohenmorgen. Grainhübel, Geheu, Kalkofen, Leinhöhle, etc. Ruppertsberg: Ruppertsberg Goldschmied, Hoheburg, etc. Bad Dürkheim Ungstein
Josef Biffar	Deidesheim	22	Deidesheim; Ruppertsberg
Johann Breiling & Sons	Deidesheim	13	Deidesheim; Ruppertsberg
Reichsrat von Buhl	Deidesheim	180	Deidesheim: Deidesheimer Leinhöhle, Kieselberg, Rennpfad, etc. Forst: Forster Freundstück, Kirchenstück, Ungeheuer, etc. Wachenheim: Wachenheimer Goldbächel, Luginsland, etc. Ruppertsberg: Ruppertsberger Hoheburg, Hofstück, etc. Königsbach: Königsbacher Rolandsberg, Idig, etc.
Dr. Albert Bürklin-Wolf (Bürklin-Wolf properties have been in the same family since 1790. A tall, oval, carved cask of even earlier vintage stands at the bottom of steep stairs down into one of the two great cellars in Wachenheim. Within are more contemporary touches in the moist, dripping dankness; each cask is named with its vineyard parcel and a cartoon in white paint also depicts the wine's origin; a cemented-up bomb hole gapes in one wall and Dr. Bürklin-Wolf tells how his cellars served as shelters in the war. The single direct hit killed no one, but exploded a lot of Pfalz wine. Dr. Bürklin-Wolf is one of Germany's most energetic wine defenders and promoters. In 1964 he became the President of the German Wine Growers' Association. His name is synonymous with the quality that he demands and himself produces.)	Wachenheim	185	Wachenheim: Wachenheimer Gerümpel, Goldbächel, Odinstal, Böhlig, Rechbächel (exclusive), Langebächel (exclusive), Luginsland, etc. Forst: Forster Kirchenstück, Pechstein, Ungeheuer, Ziegler, etc. Deidesheim: Deidesheimer Hohenmorgen, Kalkofen, Reiss (exclusive), etc. Ruppertsberg: Ruppertsberger Hoheburg, Spiess, Geisböhl, Reiterpfad, Nussbien, Goldschmitt, Schlossberg, etc. Bad Dürkheim
Dr. Deinhard	Deidesheim	63	Deidesheim: Deidesheimer Leinhöhle, Rennpfad, Kieselberg, Grainhübel, Herrgottsacker, Geheu, etc. Forst: Forster Kirchenstück, Ungeheuer, etc. Wachenheim: Wachenheimer Goldbächel, Gerümpel. Ruppertsberg: Ruppertsberger Hofstück, Spiess, Nussbien, Goldschmitt, etc.
Dietz-Matti	Deidesheim	20	Deidesheim; Ruppertsberg

Estate	*Headquarters*	*Acreage*	*Location of Holdings*
Karl Fitz-Ritter	Bad Dürkheim	40	Bad Dürkheim; Ungstein
Friedrich August (heir of J. W. Friedrich)	Freinsheim	12	Freinsheim; Herxheim
Herbert Giessen	Deidesheim	11	Ruppertsberg; Deidesheim; Forst
Norbert Görg (heir of)	Deidesheim	12	Deidesheim; Forst; Ruppertsberg
Heinemann	Forst	17	Forst; Deidesheim; Ruppertsberg
Hellmer	Mussbach	30	Mussbach; Gimmeldingen, Königsbach; Ruppertsberg
Herberger	Deidesheim	8	Deidesheim; Forst; Ruppertsberg
Ferdinand Kimich	Deidesheim	30	Deidesheim; Forst; Ruppertsberg
Karl Kimich	Deidesheim	13	Deidesheim; Ruppertsberg
Koch-Herzog	Deidesheim	27	Deidesheim; Ruppertsberg; Forst
Köhler Ruprecht	Kallstadt	10	Kallstadt
Karl Koster	Friedelsheim	13	Friedelsheim; Deidesheim; Bad Dürkheim
Gustav Kramer	Deidesheim	16	Deidesheim; Forst; Ruppertsberg
Lehmann-Hilgard	Freinsheim	32	Freinsheim; Herxheim
Emil Magin (heir of)	Forst	12	Forst; Deidesheim; Wachenheim
Mönchhof-Winzingen	Neustadt	15	Neustadt; Gimmeldingen
Georg Mosbacher (heir of)	Forst	10	Forst; Deidesheim
Pfarrgut (Town holding)	Deidesheim	8	Deidesheim; Ruppertsberg; Forst
Pfarrgut (Town holding)	Forst	8	Forst
Pfarrgut (Town holding)	Ruppertsberg	5	Ruppertsberg
Pfarrgut (Town holding)	Wachenheim	2	Wachenheim; Forst
Joseph Pioth	Forst	37	Deidesheim; Forst
Jos. Reinhardt II	Deidesheim	22	Deidesheim; Ruppertsberg; Forst
Karl Ruprecht	Kallstadt	8	Kallstadt; Herxheim
Friedrich Ruprecht	Kallstadt	10	Kallstadt
Georg Siben (heir of)	Deidesheim	30	Deidesheim; Forst; Ruppertsberg
Dr. Jul. Siben	Deidesheim	8	Deidesheim; Forst; Ruppertsberg
Heinrich Spindler	Forst	12	Forst; Deidesheim; Ruppertsberg
Wilhelm Spindler	Forst	65	Forst; Deidesheim; Ruppertsberg; Wachenheim
Staatl. Lehr- und Versuchsanstalt für Wein- und Obstbau (Government Viticultural School)	Neustadt	30	Neustadt; Haardt; Ebernburg
Stumpf-Fitz	Annaberg near Bad Dürkheim	30	Kallstadt; Bad Dürkheim
Tiemann	Deidesheim	34	Deidesheim; Ruppertsberg; Forst
Wallbillich	Forst	7	Forst; Deidesheim; Wachenheim
L. Werle (heir of)	Forst	5	Forst; Deidesheim
Hubert Wiss	Forst	7	Forst; Wachenheim; Deidesheim

In addition to the private holdings, given above, the V.D.N.V. includes twenty-two of the fifty-eight wine co-operatives in the Palatinate. The member co-operatives, located in the various towns, hold a total of 4,205 acres scattered in all areas. The first Pfalz co-operative was founded in Bad Dürkheim in 1898.

Palestine

The wines of the Holy Land are treated under Israel (*q.v.*).

Palette

Controlled place-name in the wines of Provence (*q.v.*).

Palm Wine

Spirit obtained by fermenting palm sap.

Palma

An export term for a very clean, delicate Sherry Fino. (*See* SHERRY.)

Château Palmer

Bordeaux red wine. District: Haut-Médoc, France. Commune: Cantenac-Margaux.

Lying between the vineyard road and Château Margaux and directly across the road from Château Rausan-Ségla and Château Rauzan-Gassies, Palmer is one of the two or three best-known and most sought-after Third Growths (*Troisièmes Crus*) as classified in 1855. Its name, taken from General Palmer, the English general who owned it early in the nineteenth century, may contribute, by its easy pronunciation, to its fame in English-speaking countries, but the reputation is deserved. Then known as Château de Gasq, the vineyard, along with Château Lafite, was popular at the court of Versailles in the time of Louis XV.

The owners are international: French, Dutch, and British. They combine to sell this excellent wine in the markets in which they are strong, hence Palmer fetches deservedly high prices. Before the Second World War, the owners of Palmer bought Château Desmirail, another Third Classified Growth in Margaux. In 1963 the wines of Palmer were sold under the name of Desmirail; except for this, however, the name has disappeared.

Characteristics. Full and big, often resembling the wines of adjoining Château Rausan-Ségla, although in recent years Palmer is apt to be finer and harder. In the past two decades, on account of its excellent qualities, it has become one of the most popular of the château-bottlings of the Médoc and with Calon-Ségur one of the two most popular Third Growths.

Vineyard area: 64 acres.

Average production: 10,000 cases.

Palo Cortado

Rare Sherry wine combining the characteristics of an Oloroso and a Fino.

See SHERRY.

Palomino

The dominating white grape in the making of Sherry at Jerez, Spain; used also for lesser wines in other parts of Spain. It has been planted in California, where it is used both for dry table wines and for the best of the sherry-types; and it is known there as the Golden Chasselas.

Palus

Vineyard land adjacent to the Rivers Dordogne, Garonne, and Gironde in the Bordeaux region of France; also the islands in the Gironde. The land is too heavy and moist for grapes to produce fine wine, but considerable quantities of *vin ordinaire* are made there, part of which becomes the everyday wine of the Bordeaux vineyard worker.

Pamid

An ancient and prolific grape variety grown in Bulgaria and used for the ordinary red wine.

Château Pape-Clément

Bordeaux red wine. District: Graves, France. Commune: Pessac.

Founded in 1300 by Bertrand de Goth, Archbishop of Bordeaux, the vineyard acquired its name when he became Pope Clement V. The vineyard was not ranked when the Graves Growths were classified in 1953, and controversy rages in Bordeaux as to whether or not this was just. The wines had fallen off and only in recent years have they regained their earlier quality. Yet Pape-Clément easily commands prices higher than several of the other Graves red wines and the wine itself is often much better.

Characteristics. An up-and-coming vineyard. The owner deserves great credit for the good wines he manages to produce in the off years.

Vineyard area: 62 acres.

Average production: 10,000 cases.

Parfait Amour

A very sweet spiced liqueur, either red or violet, from France and Holland.

Paris

Paris once counted her own wines among her attractions. Vineyards existed in numerous quarters of the city, the most famous in Montmartre where there is still a street named rue de la Goutte d'Or, or 'street of the drop of gold', in memory of the reputed excellence of Montmartre white. In the Passy section, warm springs once provided cures for disordered city-dwellers and the route led to the rue des Vignes, 'street of the vines', for a sip of wine afterwards. The heyday of Parisian viticulture was the thirteenth century, but most of the vines were afterwards destroyed. Those that were not have been swallowed up by the city—with the exception of a few in Montmartre, kept for the sake of tradition. Their wines are auctioned off each year at foolishly high prices.

Parras

Centre of Mexican viticulture, site of the Bodegas del Marqués de Aguayo.

See MEXICO.

Parsac-Saint-Émilion

Bordeaux red wine. District: Saint-Émilion.

Commune whose vineyards, planted on chalky slopes, produce full-bodied wines of rich colour.

See SAINT-ÉMILION.

Passes

French for strip, or small label, affixed to bottles giving subsidiary information not covered on the neck or on the main label.

Passe-Tout-Grains

Decent red Burgundy wines made from a blend of Pinot with Gamay or other lesser grapes.

See BURGUNDY.

Passion Fruit Liqueur

Deep golden, very sweet Australian liqueur from the passion fruit.

Passito

Italian wine made from dried grapes. Usually it is a dessert wine, although such grapes are sometimes added to dry wines.

Passover Wine

The wine of the great Jewish festival.

See KOSHER WINE.

Pasteur, Louis

The great French chemist of the Jura, eastern France, discovered pasteurization while experimenting with the local wines. Before his time (1822–1895), wine-making methods were mainly practical, owing little to scientific theory. Pasteur isolated the micro-organisms which make grape juice ferment; but surprisingly, the practice of centuries has been little changed by this discovery. Quantity production of wine has definitely been influenced by Pasteur; quality production only very slightly.

Pasteurization

The process, named after Louis Pasteur, of sterilizing wine (or other liquids) by heat.

Stabilization of wine, milk or other liquid by heating it briefly and rapidly to a temperature usually 140° to 150°F (60° to 66°C), thus ridding it of most micro-organisms. It is sometimes effective in the case of ordinary wines but is not recommended for fine wines. Not only are the bacteria destroyed, but the wine also becomes dead to evolution. The process may be carried out before or after bottling.

See CHAPTER NINE, p. 47.

Pastis

The aperitif of Marseilles. Pastis is made on an alcohol base with herb flavourings, notably liquorice. It bears a strong resemblance to anis but is slightly less distinctive in taste; and when diluted with water, it clouds and turns milky, with none of the green tinge of anis. Both pastis and anis have certain characteristics in common with absinthe. They are lower in alcohol, however, and wormwood, the ingredient which caused absinthe to be banned in most civilized countries, is omitted. Three of the better-known brands of pastis are those produced by Pernod, Ricard, and Berger in France; and a certain amount is illicitly home-made in southern France and Corsica.

Patent Still

Continuous distilling apparatus. It is more economical than the older pot still in that the pot still is basically a copper pot which has continually to be opened and refilled. The patent still is sometimes called the coffey still, because it is based on a patent taken out by Aeneas Coffey in 1832. Coffey's patent is an improvement on one by Robert Stein of Scotland, who patented the first design for a still of this type in 1826. Most of the finest rums and whiskies are always pot-distilled, this method allowing more of the taste and aroma to pass over with the distillate. Except for those favouring light-style liquors, pot-distilled remains synonymous with highest quality in most brandies and spirits.

Patras

Region of Greece producing good, mainly white wines. The town of Patras contains many of the large wine companies and co-operatives.

See GREECE.

Patrimonio Rosé

Wine produced between Bastia and Île Rousse. This is the best of the Corsican wines.

See CORSICA.

Patron Saints of Wine in Germany

The Germans have borrowed a French saint: Urban, the Bishop of Autun, between the Saône and the Loire, is one of their most honoured patrons of the grape. His day, 25th May, is fêted in many of the German wine districts, and a vast number of chapels and statues of St. Urban are to be found in the wine-growing areas of the country.

St. Kilian, the Frankish saint, is the patron of the vintners and their product in the wine districts of

Franconia. And the vineyards bordering the Lake of Constance boast of Otmar, Abbot of the monastery of St. Gallen, to whom legend ascribes a barrel which replenished its store of miraculously healing wine as quickly as its contents were drunk. Common sense should have told the vintners of Lake Constance that the potential threat of this never-ending source would in time have made their product and themselves unnecessary, yet they have chosen to commemorate the Abbot as their patron.

Other saints and holy figures connected with wine in Germany include St. Cyriakus in the Palatinate, St. Genoveva and St. Magdalena, St. Walter, St. Werner, the holy Elizabeth, and even the saintly Mary, as well as St. Peter connected with the grape through many stories and legends.

See also SAINT MARTIN; SAINT VINCENT.

Pauillac

Bordeaux red wine. District: Haut-Médoc, France.

Most important of the four great wine communes —Margaux, Saint-Julien, Pauillac, and Saint-Estèphe—of the Médoc peninsula jutting out from the mouth of the Gironde, Pauillac is paradoxically the least known. This is because the fame of the individual vineyards overshadows that of the town. Château Lafite, Château Latour, Château Mouton-Rothschild, and others are known as themselves, not as Pauillac wines, though all are in the commune. Consequently, with so much château-bottling, there is little regional wine to be sold as Pauillac.

Vineyard grading in this district is curiously uneven. Counting Mouton-Rothschild as a First Growth (*Premier Cru*), which it is in quality though not in name, Pauillac has three First Growths; a single Second Growth (*Second Cru*) now divided into two Pichon-Longueville vineyards; no Third Growths (*Troisièmes Crus*) at all; a little-known Fourth Growth (*Quatrième Cru*), Château Duhart-Milon; and then, suddenly, twelve Fifth Growths (*Cinquièmes Crus*)—out of the eighteen in the entire Médoc. The absence of Pauillac Seconds, Thirds, and Fourths illustrates the present considerable inaccuracy of the 1855 Official Classification, since several of the Fifths would be placed higher on any realistic scale drawn up now.

The wines do not possess much generic similarity, tending rather to be individual, except that all share the characteristic of being fairly full-bodied for Médocs. They are bigger than the more delicate Margaux, and, with one or two exceptions, less hearty than the Saint-Estèphes. On the other hand, no very accurate generalization can be made about wines as different as, for example, Lafite and Mouton-Rothschild, where special selection of grape variety gives the former an added finesse and the latter an advantage of stamina.

Beginning in the south at Château Latour, which touches Saint-Julien, the land is gently rolling, with vineyards placed along the soft ridge which slopes down into inferior marshy land beside the Gironde. At the old enclave of Bages, just before the town of Pauillac, there is a more pronounced rise; after Pauillac, the highest land holds Pontet-Canet, Mouton-d'Armailhacq (now known as Mouton du Baron Philippe), and Mouton-Rothschild, side by side on a plateau; and then Lafite, bordering Saint-Estèphe on the most sloping vineyard land of Pauillac. This is the only part of the first-class land in the Médoc which is almost hilly.

For centuries Pauillac itself was an important port. Even today there is a customs post, and a few ships arrive from America and Africa. But with the coming of steam and the shortening of the distance up to Bordeaux, Pauillac went to sleep. The few cafés with their untenanted pavement tables facing the grassy quay, the bleached, empty hotels, the neglected stack of the sunken ship jutting out of the brown water, all contribute to a Rip Van Winkle atmosphere. Few remember that this was where La Fayette set sail for the American Revolution.

The Commanderie du Bontemps de Médoc, the local selling organization, composed of growers, shippers, and various dignitaries interested in wine, has its headquarters in the river port, and today ceremonies of the wine society are the most vivid events in the place where once river pirates met with a hot reception and engagements of the Hundred Years War were fought.

The Pauillac vineyards rated as Classified Growths (*Crus*) in the 1855 Classification of Médoc wines are:

First Growths (Premiers Crus)
Château Lafite-Rothschild
Château Latour

Second Growths (Seconds Crus)
Château Mouton-Rothschild
Château Pichon-Longueville, Baron de Pichon
Château Pichon-Longueville, Comtesse de Lalande

Fourth Growth (Quatrième Cru)
Château Duhart-Milon

Fifth Growths (Cinquièmes Crus)
Château Batailley
Château Haut-Batailley
Château Croizet-Bages
Château Clerc-Milon-Mondon
Château Grand-Puy-Ducasse
Château Grand-Puy-Lacoste
Château Haut-Bages-Libéral
Château Lynch-Bages
Château Lynch-Moussas
Château Mouton du Baron Philippe (Mouton-d'Armailhacq)
Château Pédesclaux
Château Pontet-Canet

See also under separate headings.

Château Pavie

Bordeaux red wine. District and Commune: Saint-Émilion, France.

Considerably subdivided in recent years, Château Pavie is still the largest of the outstanding Saint-Émilion vineyards. It is beautifully situated on the completely vine-covered flank of hill which faces, from the south, the other flank on which Ausone and the village of Saint-Émilion stand. All the vines are south-exposed. It may be the frequent change of ownership which caused the Pavie wines to fall off for a time, but for the last decade or so they have been back in form, and in 1955 Château Pavie was classified one of the twelve First Great Growths (*Premier Grands Crus*), while the split-off vineyards, Château Pavie-Decesse and Château Pavie-Macquin, in the lower category, were classed Great Growths (*Grands Crus*) of Saint-Émilion.

Characteristics. A big production and a good, typical Saint-Émilion—generous wine with a big nose.

Vineyard area: 153 acres.

Average production: 16,200 cases.

Pays, Vins de

See VINS DE PAYS.

Peach Brandy

Properly, brandy distilled from peaches, but often used for peach liqueur, obtained by steeping peaches in sweetened brandy.

Pécharmant

The best of the red wines of Bergerac, in South-west France, bearing a resemblance to the lesser wines of Saint-Émilion.

See BERGERAC.

Pecsenyebór

Hungarian term for dessert wine.

Château Pédesclaux

Bordeaux red wine. District: Haut-Médoc, France. Commune: Pauillac.

Classified a Fifth Growth (*Cinquième Cru*) in 1855, the small estate now belongs to Monsieur Lucien Jugla.

Characteristics. A small uneven wine. The vinification is not always what it might be.

Vineyard area: 25 acres.

Average production: 3,000 cases.

Pedro Ximénez

A very sweet grape grown in Andalusia and elsewhere in Spain. It is used mainly in the making of sweet wines; or as a sweetener for sherries.

Pelin

Iced Rumanian wine drink with an infusion of herbs.

Pelure d'Oignon

'Onion-skin'. The term applies to the brownish tinge which marks some old wines. It was once used, also, for many pink wines before *rosé* became the popular term; and it is still sometimes so used.

Perlant

French term for mildly sparkling wine.

See PÉTILLANT.

Perlwein

A sparkling wine made by artificial carbonation, and popular in Germany.

Pernand-Vergelesses and **Pernand-Vergelesses-Côte de Beaune**

Burgundy red and white wines. District: Côte de Beaune, France.

The village of Pernand-Vergelesses is one of the most ancient and is certainly the most primitive of all the wine communes of Burgundy. It lies on the back slope of the 'mountain'—the high hill that rises behind Aloxe-Corton, and is skirted by Ladoix-Serrigny and Savigny-les-Beaune. A small, rutted dirt-track leads up to the tiny, jumbled-together houses and in these buildings live many of the growers of Corton-Charlemagne, one of Burgundy's greatest white-wine vineyards. Few of these growers own more than a handkerchief-sized portion of the vineyard and their annual production varies from upwards of a dozen down to three or four barrels, or even less.

There are no great or famous vineyards entirely within the communal limits. Portions of vineyards allowed the place-names Corton, Corton-Charlemagne, and Charlemagne (*q.v.*) fall within the commune but this is an accident of geography and the wines are rightly considered with those of Aloxe-Corton. Wines sold under the commune name are predominantly red and are minor Côte de Beaunes. They are light, sometimes have considerable bouquet, and are often very fruity. Some Burgundians say they are wines that burn with a hot and intense flame, but burn out reasonably quickly. The whites are simultaneously soft and heavy, without the breed of the great whites of Aloxe.

About 1,250 imp. gallons (1,500 U.S.) of white wine are made annually, but the amount of red varies from 8,300 imp. gallons (10,000 U.S.) to 25,000 (30,000 U.S.) since it may be sold as Pernand-Vergelesses, Pernand-Vergelesses-Côte de Beaune (there is no difference in the wines of these two names), or, after blending with others from specified communes of the slope, as Côte de Beaune-Villages. There are about 250 acres of the finer vineyards.

The French authorities have not yet finished the task of selecting the First Growth (*Premier Cru*) vineyards—those that may (if the wine meets slightly higher than normal qualifications) be sold with both commune name and vineyard name on bottle labels. While this work is in progress, the following vineyards have been given this rating provisionally.

FIRST GROWTHS (*Premiers Crus*)

Vineyard	*Acres*
Île des Vergelesses	23·1
Les Basses Vergelesses	43·3
Creux de la Net	12·4
Les Fichots	27·5
En Caradeux	49·8

Pernod

A popular, anis-flavoured aperitif made by the firm of Pernod Fils in France. Like others of this family it becomes cloudy when water is added.

See PASTIS.

Perry

A kind of pear cider, which is made both still and sparkling.

Persia

See IRAN.

Peru

Peru is one of the oldest South American wine-producing countries, but is not one of the largest or most important. Vines have been grown in Peru at least since 1566, when Francesco de Carabantes planted some in the vicinity of Ica, south of the capital city of Lima.

The terrain and climate of Peru is such that it will not support vines in all of its regions. The snow-capped Andes are generally too cold and too rugged, and the northern part of the country is suitable for other types of cultivation but not for the vine. In these parts of Peru, mining and the rearing of livestock—in particular, the llama—are the important occupations. Most of the vines are of European stock and many wines are natural, both red and white, although some are fortified and modelled on Sherry, Port, and Madeira. The table wines somewhat resemble those of Spain. Only about 2,000,000 imp. gallons (2,600,000 U.S.) of wine are made and the 20,000 acres of vineyard are found around Ica, around Lima itself, and around the ancient Inca cities of Cuzco and Arequipa. In the south, the vineyards of Moquega are also fairly important.

SPIRITS

While the Spanish population habitually drinks wine, the Indians prefer *chicha*, brewed from corn and molasses, or one of the alcohols distilled in the country. The best of the Peruvian alcohols is the Pisco brandy (*q.v.*) which they distil from Muscat wine. This brandy is the base of the Pisco Sour which is made with the white of an egg, and Angostura Bitters.

Pessac

Fine wine commune of the Graves district of Bordeaux. This is the village of Châteaux Haut-Brion and Pape-Clément.

See GRAVES.

Pétillant

French term for wine which is slightly sparkling or crackling—an alternative term being *perlant*. This is used only of wines which owe their sparkle simply and naturally to unfermented sugar still present in the wine when it is bottled. The maximum pressure admitted in France for *pétillant* types is 2 atmospheres at 68°F. (20°C.).

Petit-Chablis

Pleasant but lesser wines of Chablis produced in Lignorelles, Ligny-le-Châtel and other places allowed the *appellation* Chablis.

See CHABLIS.

Petit Verdot

Grape grown in the Bordeaux region.

See VERDOT.

Petite Champagne

Not a Champagne, but the second best of the regions producing Cognac, which will bear its name or be called Fine Champagne.

See COGNAC.

Petite-Sirah (Syrah)

A grape planted in California, and yielding a fairly good red wine. It is also known as the Duriff. Some authorities say that this grape descends from the Syrah from which French Hermitage is made. Others maintain that it is not.

Château Pétrus

Bordeaux red wine. District and Commune: Pomerol, France.

The outstanding wine of Pomerol and one of the top eight Bordeaux red wines, Pétrus commands prices comparable with those of the First Growths (*Premiers Crus*) of the Médoc. On gravelly soil covering a smooth rise of land higher than the surroundings but not steep enough to be called a hill, the vineyard lies about a mile from Libourne and two miles or so from Saint-Émilion, on the road linking those historic vinous villages. The attractive small house in which the *chai* is to be found is decorated with the symbols and keys of St. Peter (Pétrus), and he is also the venerable gentleman carved in wood who guards the portals. Until her death a year or two ago, the owner was Madame Loubat, a lady of great energy and character, in her eighties and still a car driver and active *vigneronne*. Tasting the wine in the *chai* with her was a double delight; her old-fashioned French courtesy was as charming as the wine she made. The vineyard is now the property of Monsieur Moueix and Madame Loubat's heirs.

Pétrus unfortunately suffered severely in the freeze of February 1956, and Château Pétrus 1956, 1957, and several of the later vintages will never appear on the market in any quantity.

Characteristics. Superb, well-rounded and fruity—sometimes velvety. A wine that can be drunk before it is very old.

Vineyard area: 16 acres.

Average production: 2,500 cases.

Château de Pez

Bordeaux red wine. District: Haut-Médoc, France. Commune: Saint-Estèphe.

Traditionally one of the leading *Bourgeois Supérieur* wines of the Médoc, but actually deserving of a higher classification. The vineyard is directly across the road from Château Calon-Ségur in the village of Saint-Estèphe.

Characteristics. Less full than many of its neighbours, it has the characteristic hardness and slow-maturing qualities of Saint-Estèphe. It is one of the lesser vineyards of the Médoc consistently producing wines which are at the same time inexpensive and good.

Vineyard area: 55 acres.

Average production: 8,000 cases.

Pfalz

Alternative name for the Palatinate (*q.v.*) in Germany.

Phylloxera

A parasitic disease of the vine. The *Phylloxera vastatrix* is a burrowing plant louse of the Aphididæ family, probably indigenous to the native vines of eastern America, and certainly less harmful to them than to any other vines. In the second half of the last century, phylloxera caused considerable damage in Californian vineyards. Then, on vines sent from the United States, it was brought to Europe, where it devastated the vineyards of most of the wine-making countries. It was extremely destructive in France, where it was active in the 1870s, and elderly connoisseurs of wine are still debating the respective merits of pre-phylloxera and post-phylloxera Clarets. The remedy for the disease is the grafting of *Vitis vinifera* varieties on to the native American root-stocks which are naturally resistant to this root-eating grub. The grafting does not change the nature of the *Vitis vinifera* grape, but it does affect its longevity.

Vines no longer live as long as they did. Old vines give quality—but few grapes. Young vines give more grapes, but less quality. Another consequence, not yet proven, but graver if it is a fact, is this: only since phylloxera has the vine disease fanleaf, or infectious degeneration, been found. Leading scientists have come to the conclusion that phylloxera may spread the disease.

See CHAPTER EIGHT, p. 37.

Pichet

French term for a pitcher, sometimes of wood or earthenware, for wine or cider.

Château Pichon-Longueville, Baron de Pichon

Bordeaux red wine. District: Haut-Médoc, France. Commune: Pauillac.

More than a century ago, the two Pichon-Longueville vineyards, nowadays facing each other across the vineyard road, were one. The Pichon-Longueville (Baron) bottle will sometimes be found labelled simply Pichon-Longueville; the wine of the Comtesse de Lalande portion will always be labelled Pichon-Longueville-Lalande, or Pichon-Longueville, Comtesse de Lalande.

The château of Pichon-Longueville-Baron, built in the nineteenth century, is probably the most striking of its period in Bordeaux, with its 'renaissance' turrets soaring up like spires. The outline of the château is perfect for a label, but unfortunately it is not used for this purpose. The vineyard is a Second Growth (*Second Cru*) of Médoc, and is most expertly managed by Monsieur Bouteiller, the present owner.

Characteristics. This fine, full-bodied wine is consistently producing excellent wines each year.

Vineyard area: 55 acres.

Average production: 6,000 cases.

Château Pichon-Longueville, Comtesse de Lalande

Bordeaux red wine. District: Haut-Médoc, France. Commune: Pauillac.

The vineyard comprises about three-fifths of the old united estate of Pichon-Longueville, separated a little more than 100 years ago, and is entirely enclosed within the semi-circle of the Château Latour vineyard behind it. The character of the wine from some parts of the estate is very close to that of Château Latour. A Second Growth (*Second Cru*) Classification of 1855, the wine will always be labelled Pichon-Longueville-Lalande or Pichon-Longueville, Comtesse de Lalande. Pichon-Longueville found without qualification will mean the wine is Pichon-Longueville-Baron (*q.v.*). Monsieur Mialhe, owner of Pichon Comtesse, as the vineyard is called in Bordeaux, is also the owner of Château Siran (a *Cru Bourgeois* in Margaux) and a part-owner of Château Palmer, also in Margaux.

Characteristics. Lighter and more supple than Pichon-Longueville-Baron, this excellent wine seems, in the nineteen-sixties, to be gaining an edge of popularity over Pichon-Baron, which in its turn was more popular in the fifties. The quality of the 1964 Pichon-Lalande is so good that it should still further increase the demand.

Vineyard area: 100 acres.

Average production: 12,000 cases.

Picpoule, Picpoul

A white-wine grape grown extensively in southern France. It produces a rather thin white wine, and is used also for vermouth. Catalonians call it Avillo.

Piedmont

Red and white wines. District: North-west Italy.

Piedmont, 'foot of the mountain', is the extreme north-west corner of Italy. Its capital is the prosperous city of Turin, centre of the vermouth industry, and the region produces two of Italy's finest red wines: Barolo and Barbaresco. White, and sometimes sickly sweet, sparkling Asti Spumante and the rather less popular Moscato d'Asti are also products of the province. They all have controlling organizations—or *consorzi*—to define and administrate their quality and authenticity.

Piedmont is a vast plain spreading out from the sinuous valley of the upper Po and surrounded by Alps to the north and west, Apennines to the east and south-east, and the Monferrato Hills to the south. In spite of the precipitous slopes of some of its mountains and the unsuitability of part of its plain, Piedmont is third—after Apulia and Sicily—in wine production in Italy, making more than 150 million imp. gallons (180 million U.S.) annually, 80% of it from the southern section of the tumbled-together Monferrato Hills. These are fairly low but often incredibly steep, resembling somewhat the hills of the Beaujolais district in France, but far less orderly. Yet in this region the tall vines are everywhere, sometimes sharing their plots with olive trees and wheat or other crops. Vines also extend into the rest of Piedmont, but the wines—while sometimes pleasant—are inferior to those from the Monferrato district. Piedmont's chief grapevine is Nebbiolo but there are also significant numbers of Muscats and of Barbera, Bonarda, Freisa, Brachetto, Cortese, Dolcetto, Erbaluce, and Grignolino grapevines scattered from the low river valley to the

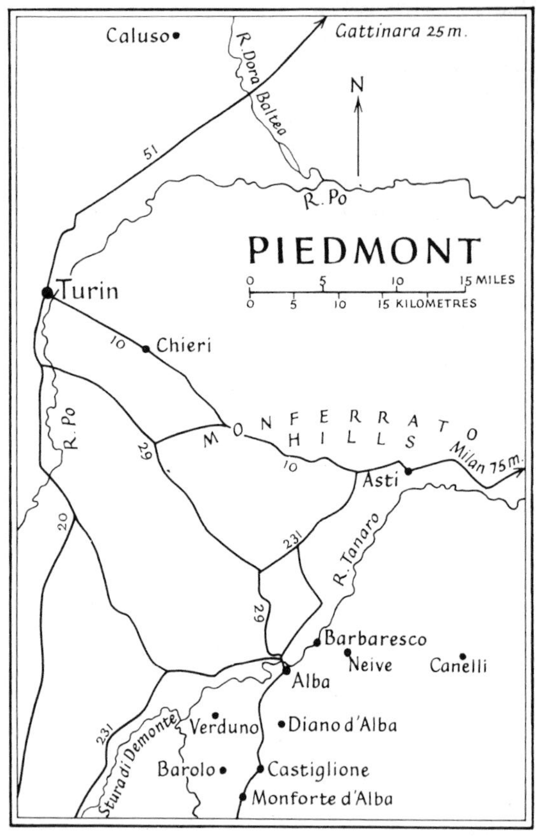

austere heights of the Valle d'Aosta—the mountainous corner which climbs to the Swiss border.

Barolo and Barbaresco

These two were placed among the country's top three red wines (Vini di Categoria Extra) by an Italian governmental rating in 1941 and their selection has met with almost universal approval. (The qualifications of the third—Santa Maddalena from Trentino-Alto Adige—have, on the other hand, been severely criticized.) Both are big, strong, enormously robust wines with powerful depth and a heavy pungency. Barolo, which is slower to mature, reaches the greater heights of the two, but because of its pungency and uncompromisingly masculine aftertaste (so strong that it is often characterized as 'the aftertaste of tar') it is not always so well liked as the lighter Barbaresco. The colour of both is deep red—in a fine Barolo, almost black—fading slightly with age and assuming the brownish 'onion-skin' hue around the edge when poured into a glass.

Both wines are offspring of the Nebbiolo grapevine whose temperament is ideally suited to the climate of Piedmont and its steep, rocky slopes. Both are fermented for fifteen to eighteen days before the juice is drawn off the must, to be run into huge oak vats to age—Barolo for four to seven years, Barbaresco not so long. These vats range in size from fairly small to enormous and the best are made from time-blackened Slovenian oak from the forests of Czechoslovakia. During the long ageing process, the wines settle, rid themselves of much of their heavy deposit, and lose their harshness. Bottle-age is necessary—particularly for the finest wines—to soften them; but even after considerable ageing they will still be heavy wines which go best with red meat, pasta, or game. At best they lack the finesse and breed of better French wines.

The growing areas for the wines are almost adjacent in the depths of the Monferrato Hills—Barolo covering some 25,000 acres in the towns of Barolo, Castiglione, Monforte d'Alba, Verduno, and Diano d'Alba; the smaller Barbaresco area slightly to the north-east in Barbaresco and Neive—and sales of both are at least double production figures. Some bottles will bear the seal of the local *consorzio*, which has approved the wine, and the seal bears the name of the organization (Consorzio per la Difesa dei Vini Tipici Barolo e Barbaresco): in the case of Barolo, this seal is a golden lion in a field of blue; in Barbaresco, the imprint of an ancient tower which stands in the town.

Asti Spumante and Moscato d'Asti

The bottle is tilted at the proper angle, the white towel wrapped around the neck, the cork eased, but suddenly it comes out of the bottle with a vigorous 'pop' and the opener will be told to 'go back to Asti', no matter what the sparkling wine, nor where it is opened. For there is no doubt that Asti Spumante makes a small explosion when the cork is pulled.

When Charles Gancia brought the secrets of its manufacture back to his firm in Canelli in the late 1850s the wine was sold as Asti champagne, Muscat champagne, or Italian champagne; but the reaction of the French combined with national pride to advocate a more original name, and Asti Spumante was finally chosen. Curiously enough, this name is now sometimes taken by growers in distant parts of the world when they wish to differentiate their sweet sparkling wine from one which is nearer to Champagne or sparkling Burgundy.

Asti Spumante is a sweet, slightly flowery, sparkling Muscat. With its very low degree of alcohol (9% to 10%), large content of sugar, and its gay bubbles, it is the perfect wine for unsophisticated festivity, and is a particular favourite in its own country. For one thing, it is cheap inside Italy—compared with sparkling wines in other parts of the world—but once import duties are added, in other countries, it jumps out of its price class. Moscato d'Asti is a similar wine, but lower in alcohol (7% as a rule) and made by the bulk process rather than the regular Champagne process employed by the better houses for their good wines. (*See* CHAMPAGNE, *and particularly 'Champagne Process' within it.*) The wines are made in forty-four communes near the small city of Asti in the Monferrato Hills, entirely from Muscat grapes.

In spite of its fame Asti Spumante is not selling as it once did. Popular taste is turning from sweet wines, and vintners are slowly overtaking the trend with dry variations on their traditional themes. In Asti, almost all the large houses are now diverting a part of their production to dry sparkling wines, mostly from Riesling and Pinot grapes, but seldom from those grown in the immediate vicinity. The better firms have special vineyards where their grapes are grown and vinification is accomplished as soon after picking as possible. Some other houses are apt to import grapes from anywhere, depending upon where they happen to be able to buy them in that particular year. Asti's dry sparkling wines do not usually carry the name of the city—that is reserved for the more famous sweet ones—but are usually sold as Pinot, Pinot Spumante, Gran Spumante, or some similar name; and a few are sent abroad as 'Lacrima Christi'—an appellation which belongs to Campania. These dry wines are generally thin, usually undistinguished, but in Italy their low cost makes them fairly good buys.

Of the sparkling wines, only Asti Spumante and Moscato d'Asti enjoy Consorzio protection. Bottles guaranteed by the Consorzio as being worthy of the name they bear will carry a seal portraying San Secondo, the patron saint of Asti, on horseback, and the name of the organization: Consorzio per la Difesa dei Vini Tipici Moscato d'Asti e Asti Spumante.

Minor Wines

The minor wines of Piedmont are almost entirely named from the grape variety from which they are made. As a rule these wines can be considered variable in the extreme, depending largely upon where they come from (which will seldom be known) and the skill of the wine-maker. They have, however, certain more or less typical characteristics. Wines named after grapevines are marked with an asterisk.

*Barbera**

Heavy, very deep, often harsh red wine made in quantity throughout the region and indeed, all Italy, but principally in the provinces of Asti, Alessandria, and Cuneo.

*Bonarda**

Dark red wine mostly from around Asti; it is sometimes rendered sparkling.

*Brachetto**

Undistinctive, almost invariably sparkling, red wine, and rather sweet.

Caluso (Passito di Caluso)

A *passito*—or wine from dried grapes—made from Erbaluce vines grown in Caluso forty miles from Turin. The wine is sweet and white and made in only small quantities.

Carema

Light and fresh red wine from Nebbiolo grapes grown in the Valle d'Aosta along the banks of the Dora Baltea.

*Cortese**

Still and unexceptional, dry white wine, sometimes made sparkling. It should be taken very young.

*Dolcetto**

In Piedmont the wine from this grape is not sweet, as its name suggests. It is dark red in colour, rather light in body.

*Freisa d'Asti and Freisa di Chieri**

Sprightly red wine with a charming fruitiness and a delightful bouquet. The best is from Chieri (near Turin) or the Monferrato Hills. Perhaps the best of the lesser wines of Piedmont. Some Freisas are sold as *frizzante* or with a slight sparkle which the French would call pétillant.

Gattinara

Light, dry red wine from Nebbiolo grapes grown in the town naming the wine, slightly to the north of Turin.

*Grignolino d'Asti**

Dry, slightly bitter, pinkish-red wine lacking some of the depth and density usually found in most Piedmontese reds, but with its own attraction.

*Nebbiolo Piemontese**

Piedmont's noble vine, when planted in districts other than the great ones, gives a light red wine varying considerably in quality but pleasant enough as a general rule.

Pierce's Disease

A disease that afflicts vines in California.

See CHAPTER EIGHT, p. 36.

Piesporter Goldtröpfchen

Usually the best of the very great wines of Piesport, German Moselle. The Piesporter are incomparable when produced in a dry summer.

See MOSELLE.

Pimm's Cup

There are four Pimm's Cups, and it is said that they were originated by a bartender at Pimm's Restaurant in London and so delighted the customers that the staff was continually being asked to put some up for people to take home. As a result, they began to be made commercially. When bottled, each resembles a heavy cordial; but once mixed with fruit juice, cooled, garnished with borage and cucumber rind, and served in tall glasses, they become refreshing summer drinks. The four types are:

Pimm's No. 1	Gin-based
Pimm's No. 2	Whisky-based
Pimm's No. 3	Rum-based
Pimm's No. 4	Brandy-based

Pineau d'Aunis

A grape used in rosé wines of Anjou, and in red wines of the Loire Valley, where it is gradually being replaced by Cabernet Franc.

Pineau des Charentes

Fortified wine of Cognac region, drunk as an aperitif.

See SWEET FORTIFIED WINES OF FRANCE.

Pineau (Pinot) de la Loire

Another name for the grape Chenin Blanc (*q.v.*).

Pinot, Pineau

One of the most distinguished families of wine grapes responsible alone or in part for the greatest Burgundies and Champagnes and for many other fine wines. Pinot is a temperamental vine, however, and is not well adapted to areas outside northern France. The outstanding member of the family is Pinot Noir or 'Noirien', the red-wine vine of Burgundy. Pinot Liebault and Pinot Meslier contribute to Burgundian wines, but are, for all practical purposes, identical with the Noirien. Pinot Gris and Pinot Blanc, eminently noble vines, contribute to white Burgundies. All Pinots abound also in the finer Champagne vineyards. Pinot Chardonnay is actually a misnomer, for it is not a Pinot. Current usage is simply to call it Chardonnay.

Pinot Blanc

The white grape of the famous Pinot vine, used in making the fine white wines of Burgundy; and, mixed with Pinot Noir, it goes into Champagne. In Germany, it is known as Klevner, and sometimes as Weissburgunder.

Pinot Gris

A grape of the Pinot family which yields good wine in Alsace, where it is also known as Tokay d'Alsace. In other parts of France, it appears as Pinot Beurot; Fauvet; Malvoisie; and Auxerrois Gris. In Germany, it changes its name to Ruländer.

Pinot Noir

The Pinot Noir is one of the greatest of fine-wine grapes. It makes the fabulous red wines of Burgundy, and it is largely responsible for Champagne. The vine is difficult, only moderately prolific, but in the right soil and the right climate it produces with splendour. The Pinot Noir is planted, to a lesser extent, in other parts of Europe and in California. Here it is sometimes confused with the Pinot Meunier, and with the Pinot St. Georges, which is not a real Pinot grape. In Germany, under the name of Spätburgunder, it produces the best of that country's red wines. Synonyms: Pineau; Savagnin; Cortaillod (Switzerland); Klevner (Alsace).

Pint

Standard liquid measure, one-eighth of a gallon. The British pint contains 34·677 cubic inches or the equivalent of 0·568 litres or 20 British fluid ounces; the American pint, 28·875 cubic inches, equal to 0·473 litres, or 16 U.S. fluid ounces.

Pipe

A large cask with tapered ends and of varying capacity, used especially for Port. Some of the more widely used are:

Madeira	92 imp. gallons (110·5 U.S.)
Marsala	93 imp. gallons (111·7 U.S.)

Wine	105 imp. gallons (126·1 U.S.)
Port and Tarragona	115 imp. gallons (138·1 U.S.)
Lisbon	117 imp. gallons (140·5 U.S.)

Piquant

French term for wine which is sharp, acid, and biting on the palate. This is entirely derogatory.

Piqué

French term for vinegary wine.

Piquette

French term for wine made by adding water to the husks and skins of grapes, the juice of which has already been pressed out. This is low in alcohol, tart, and fresh, and has made up the wine ration of the European vineyard worker since Roman times at least. By extension, the term is used in a derogatory sense for any poor or mediocre wine.

Piqûre (or Acescence)

A disorder of wine which produces a grey film.
See CHAPTER NINE.

Pisco Brandy

Brandy distilled from Muscat wine in Peru, Chile, Argentina, and Bolivia. Originally Peruvian, the best comes from the Ica Valley, one of Peru's better wine districts, near the port of Pisco. After distillation, the brandy is placed in clay containers and is usually drunk young. It is used as a base for the Pisco Punch which has been put on the market by a firm in San Francisco.

Pitching

Adding yeast to a solution to cause fermentation.

Plastering

Addition of plaster of Paris (gypsum or calcium sulphate) to low-acid musts to induce the necessary degree of acidity. In all but a very few instances, the practice is not conducive to high wine quality, but it is an accepted step in the process of Sherry-making.

Plavac

Native Yugoslavian species of grape used extensively in red Dalmatian wines.
See YUGOSLAVIA.

Plum Brandy

A white *Eau-de-vie* made from plums.
See QUETSCH; MIRABELLE; SLIVOVITZ.

Plummer

A medium-bodied type of Jamaican Rum.
See RUM, JAMAICA.

Plymouth Gin

Made in Plymouth, England, the style is intermediate between Dutch gin or Hollands, and London Dry gin, the type seen almost universally in Britain and the United States.
See GIN.

Poiré

French for perry or fermented pear juice. *Eau-de-vie de poire*, made in Switzerland and some parts of France, is pear brandy, which can be superb.

Poland

Vodka, the drink associated with Poland, has been made there for hundreds of years. Indeed, the people say that Vodka was originally Polish, not Russian. In the Middle Ages, the Poles made the spirit, first as a medicine, then as a drink, in monasteries and small manors all over the country. As it became popular, the word *woda* (water) achieved the affectionate diminutive and the spirit its name, wodka, or vodka. Different makers had, naturally, their various recipes, handed down as family secrets; and some of these formulae are still in use as bases for modern processes of manufacture.

Vodka is now seldom made from potatoes, although there is a Wodka Luksusowa, or luxury vodka, which is still obtained from potato spirits, doubly rectified and purified. Generally, the spirit comes from grain—often rye. This is filtered repeatedly, is stored for a considerable time in tall steel vats, and afterwards pumped out into mixing machines, diluted with a special soft distilled water, then refined by filtering. A finished product, such as the well-known Vyborova, or Wyborowa, should be neutral, mild and crystal clear. The Polish vodka, unlike the Russian, is all bottled at home. In the last decade or so, export figures have risen by about 800%. For western countries, there is a system of labelling according to alcoholic strength: blue for 79% British (90% U.S.) Vyborova; red label for 66% British (75.5% U.S.). Polish vodka, probably because it is expensive, is considered to be a very chic drink in France. The recommended way to drink it is freezing cold: a Pole will probably take the bottle from the ice compartment of his refrigerator and have it brought to the table in an ice bucket; and he may serve it not only at the beginning of a meal, but throughout. (For this purpose,

Krakus, a high-quality vodka made according to traditional recipes, is held to be the best.)

Several types of vodka are manufactured in Poland, some of them flavoured with fruit, flowers, or herbs. Among these are Żytnia, a pale spirit which retains the taste of the rye; Soplica, a dry brandy vodka to which wine distillates and matured apple spirit have imparted the aroma; Jarzębiak, rowan vodka, its rather tart sorb apple flavour sometimes mellowed with a little sugar and softened by distillates of wine; Tarniówka, a sloe spirit. Especially characteristic of Poland and much liked abroad is the Żubrówka vodka with the bison on the label. This, when it is the genuine high-quality spirit, is flavoured with the wild, 'holy' grass which the *żubra*, or Polish bison, love to eat in the forests of eastern Poland. This vodka, pale olive green in colour, has an odd, subtle taste and scent; and in each bottle there is a blade of grass. A glass of Żubrówka is traditionally offered to returning hunters in the region of the Białowieża Forest. The State has now taken over the monopoly of distilling all the well-known vodkas exported or drunk locally.

Liqueur Vodkas and Brandies

Starka, a very old type of vodka, is made from rye, distilled at lower proof than the Vyborova, aged in oak wine-casks, and afterwards blended with wine. The resulting drink is dry with a characteristic flavour and a pale brown colour. Poland also produces its own brand of Śliwowica (Slivovitz or plum brandy); and a Winiak Luksusowy, or brandy, from pure rectified spirit and imported wines.

Other Liqueurs and Cordials

Wiśniówka, a cordial made from black cherries, is the most popular abroad. Poland exports other fruit cordials: cherry liqueur and honey cherry brandy; a goldwasser, or Złota Woda; a strong herbal liqueur called Likier Ziołowy; and—a speciality—old Krupnik Honey Liqueur, made from rectified spirit, honey and spices. This drink, handed down from the Middle Ages, has the peculiarity that it is served hot. The legend goes that Giedymin, a Lithuanian prince of the fourteenth century, was saved from freezing to death by one of his knights who, just in time, brought him a cup of the hot liqueur.

Polcevera

Thin, light, white Italian wine.

See LIGURIA.

Polychrosis

One of the grape-moths.

See CHAPTER EIGHT, p. 37.

Pomace

Crushed or pulped grapes or fruit after the juice has been extracted. In French, *marc*. The spirit distilled from it is also known as *marc* (*q.v.*).

Pomace Brandy

California 'Grappa' from pulp of grapes.

Pombo, Pombe

A beverage of the Bantu people of Africa made from millet or sorghum.

Pomerol

Red wines. District: Bordeaux, France.

The red wines are like sturdier Médocs or Saint-Émilions with the finesse and subtlety of Médocs added. For this reason, they are often said in Bordeaux to be intermediate between the two other great red-wine types of that region. Pomerol, situated next to Saint-Émilion, uses the grape varieties which produce the Médocs, and this is sufficient to account for the transitional wines. It is true that the Pomerols on gravel soil, bordering on the Saint-Émilion vineyards on gravel soil (of which the greatest is Cheval-Blanc), greatly resemble their neighbours. Pomerol wines, however, are distinct and individual, having a velvety fatness, or *gras*, among the red Bordeaux. To liken them either to Médocs or to Saint-Émilions is to give a false impression. Intermediate in fullness of body between the other two, they nevertheless derive a special taste from the iron in the subsoil of the small Pomerol district, with the result that the wine is one of the most characteristic of the red Bordeaux.

The district of 1,500 acres, nearly all of it in the commune of Pomerol but a fraction in the commune of Libourne, is situated on a plateau above and behind the river town of Libourne. Like Saint-Émilion, not half a dozen miles away, the region was important and a junction in Roman times, when most travel and transport was along the waterways.

The vine flourished in Pomerol in those days, as it did in Saint-Émilion. Templars had come to Pomerol in the twelfth century to carry forward and enlarge the viticulture of the Romans. The fighting in the Hundred Years War destroyed some of the vineyards, but these were afterwards re-established. Thereafter, the growers of Pomerol did their wines no permanent good by parading them as Saint-Émilions; and not until the nineteenth century did these begin to be known abroad. Today, however, more and more connoisseurs are discovering the virtues of Pomerol.

The ground varies from vineyard to vineyard,

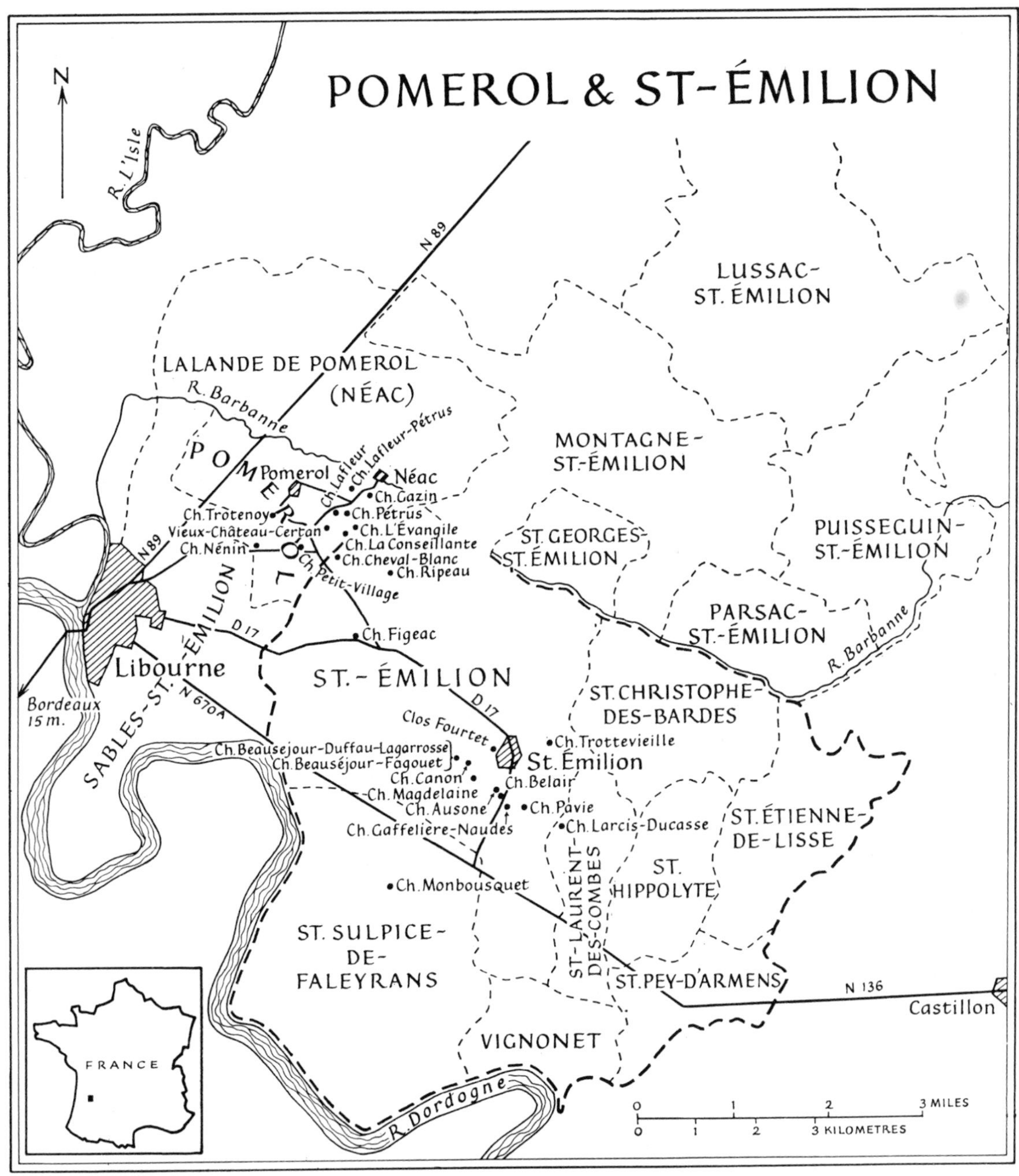

and with it the wines. Soils are gravelly, clayey or sandy, sometimes all three in a single vineyard; a little clay in a gravelly soil seems to produce wines of the greatest suppleness, while those from predominantly gravel soil may be less fine. The best-known vineyards are not found in the sandy terrains.

In comparison with the manorial Médoc and such regions as Sauternes where mediæval fortresses still stand, Pomerol is almost homely. Its 'châteaux' are often villas, their gardens necessarily small in a region where space is at a premium, since the great vines demand every inch. After the February 1956 freeze, which struck hardest of all in Pomerol, the area took on a blighted look, and the following summer thousands of dead vines could be seen lying in the churned soil from which they had been uprooted. It was like a battlefield.

No Pomerol 1956 and little 1957 and 1958 were seen. Where the vine was blighted but not killed, wine was made again in 1958 and 1959 vintages.

Pomerol vineyards are not classified. The best of them, and one of the eight best red Bordeaux, is Château Pétrus (*q.v.*). Similar in type are Château La Conseillante, Château Vieux-Château-Certan, and Château Trotanoy. Château Petit-Village (belonging to the owner of Château Margaux in the Médoc) is on an entirely gravel soil, and produces very full-bodied wines with a splendid nose and the gleaming, dark ruby colour typical of Pomerols.

While not classified, the outstanding Pomerol vineyards are considered to be the following:

OUTSTANDING GREAT GROWTH

Château Pétrus

FIRST GREAT GROWTHS

Château l'Évangile	Château Lapointe
Château Gazin	Château Nénin
Château La Conseillante	Château Petit-Village
Château Lafleur	Château Trotanoy
Château Lafleur-Pétrus	Vieux-Château-Certan

Pommard

Burgundy red wine. District: Côte de Beaune, France.

Pommard ranks second among Côte de Beaune wine communes, producing something over 166,000 imp. gallons (200,000 U.S.) annually. Before the laws of Appellation d'Origine brought a measure of control into the wine business, a Burgundian writer estimated that the amount of Pommard sold throughout the world each week was more than the commune could make in ten years. Its amazing popularity still makes it one of the most abused place-names, and experts are slightly at a loss to explain it. Pommard, they maintain, even when it comes from Pommard, is almost always an extraordinarily pleasant wine, but hardly ever among the greatest Burgundies.

Just south of Beaune the main highway forks, one road heading for Chagny, the other swinging into the hills past Pommard, Volnay, and Monthélie, and on to Autun. The road curves sharply, skirting the town, with vineyards on both sides of it, many of them enclosed in walls bearing the names of various shippers. If you take this road, the vineyard of Les Petits Épenots starts on your right at the fork, followed by Les Grands Épenots, Le Clos Blanc, and finally the town itself. Pommard is sleepy and small with a curious belfry standing in the main square, and a sluggish stream divides the town approximately in half. Almost before you have entered it, you are out again in the midst of a sea of vineyards, this time leading up the hill to Volnay.

There is less difference between wines of different vineyards in Pommard than is usual in Burgundy, although Les Épenots is generally extremely soft and round with a good bouquet, Les Rugiens the firmest, and Les Argillières the lightest. Another outstanding vineyard is Les Chaponnières. All the wines share the characteristics of firmness, fairly deep colour and bouquet. Sturdier than those of Beaune, they fill the mouth, leaving a pleasant after-taste; but when set aside, most of the red wines of the Côte de Nuits show themselves much fuller both in body and in texture. *Chaptalisation*, or the addition of sugar to the fermenting must, will raise both body and alcoholic content and it is unfortunate that some shippers tend to overdo a good thing, producing a sturdier but coarser wine.

Pommard emerged better from the first of the important Côte d'Or vineyard classifications than the second. In 1860 three of the village's vineyards were ranked among the finest of the Côte d'Or, but the official list drawn up in 1936 has set them back, giving them a right only to the designation First Growth (*Premier Cru*). In practice, this means that all the wines of Pommard will carry the town name, and the better bottles are sold with both the name of the town and the vineyard, such as Pommard-les-Épenots, or Pommard-Rugiens.

One reason why Pommard has become so well known is that the vineyards are huge and production high. There are 837 acres of vines in Pommard for fine wines, considerable areas of which are owned by the large shipping houses who have kept the name well before the public.

The First Growths of Pommard have not yet been officially established. Until they are, the following vineyards have interim right to the designation:

FIRST GROWTHS (*Premiers Crus*)

Vineyard	*Acres*
Les Rugiens-Bas	14·5
Les Rugiens-Hauts	18·8
Les Épenots	25·6
Les Petits-Épenots	50·1
Clos de la Commaraine	9·8
Le Clos Blanc	10·6
Les Arvelets	20·9
Les Charmots	8·9
Les Argillières	9·0
Les Pézerolles	15·6

Vineyard	*Acres*
Les Boucherottes	4·1
Les Saussilles	9·4
Les Croix-Noires	3·1
Les Chaponnières	8·2
Les Fremiers	12·2
Les Bertins	9·1
Les Jarollières	7·9
Les Poutures	10·9
Le Clos Micot	9·8
La Refène	6·1
Clos du Verger	6·2
Derrière Saint-Jean	3·0
La Platière	14·3
Les Chanlins-Bas	17·7
Les Combes-Dessus	6·9
La Chanière	24·7

Pommeranzen Bitters

Bitters that derive their flavour from the fruit of the Pommerans (a type of orange) tree. Sometimes called *Elixir Longæ Vitæ* (Elixir of Long Life).

Ponsigue

Venezuelan cordial flavoured with the Ponsigue cherry on a base of rum.

Château Pontet-Canet

Bordeaux red wine. District: Haut-Médoc, France. Commune: Pauillac.

Classified a Fifth Growth (*Cinquième Cru*) in 1855, and traditionally at the head of the Fifths, Pontet-Canet actually sells with the Seconds and Thirds. It is one of the best-known and the largest of the Médoc vineyards. The wine is made principally from the Cabernet-Sauvignon and Merlot grapes. The huge plantation, sloping down rolling hills towards the port of Pauillac, is patchworked intermittently with areas not in grape. Vines are uprooted in sections after thirty-five years and the plot allowed to rest for five years, planted in alfalfa. The roots are left in the earth when the section is again ploughed for vine, to provide nitrogen. Production on the approximately 190 acres of total plantation sometimes reaches 1,500 hogsheads or barrels in a year. The wine, at the end of nine months, is transported to the Cruse *chais* in Bordeaux where it is bottled.

It is regrettable that the important Cruse firm of Bordeaux, owner of the château since 1864, does not bottle the wine at the château. Pontet-Canet possesses underground wine-cellars capable of holding 1,200 barrels; Châteaux Mouton-Rothschild, Lafite, and Beychevelle are among the few others with deep cellars, rare in the Médoc. The Pontet-Canet *chai* of first-year wines is unique in the height of its roof and its airiness, since the owners believe, in opposition to most others in the Médoc, that the wines require a free and constant flow of fresh air to carry off carbonic gas in the initial year of ageing.

Characteristics. Never château-bottled and apt to be variable. Sometimes very distinguished and slow to mature; in other years, rather common.

Vineyard area: 190 acres.

Average production: Impossible to determine as not château-bottled.

Pony

Spirit measure of one fluid ounce; a small glass containing about four fluid ounces, used especially for brandy.

Porrón

A spouted glass drinking vessel used in Spain and derived from the leather *bota*, or Spanish wine skin. One of the sights of Spain is the skill and good humour of the expert *porrón* drinker as he shoots a thin stream of wine through the air from spigot to mouth. This is not to be recommended to the wine-taster, however, because the wine must be gulped down to keep up with the arching stream. In Spain, the method is claimed to multiply the effect of the wine.

Port

Portuguese fortified wine.

By Portuguese law, Port is the wine of the Upper Douro (Cima de Douro, Alto Douro), fortified by the addition of Portuguese grape brandy, and shipped from Oporto, the city at the mouth of the Douro which has given Port its name. By British law, Port proper is exactly the same thing. This law permits, however, the use of the designation port-style for Australian port, South African port and even British port.

In the United States, port-type wines are allowed the name port if they carry the modification of the name of their place of origin, which generally means Californian port. While some growers try to make a 'real port', and do perhaps produce a good fortified wine, the American laws are so loose that the designation may go on the label of wine from any area, made in practically any manner—and therefore guarantees nothing. Whatever they may be, the ports made in South Africa, Australia, California, and in North and South America are not Port.

Only about 8% of the yearly production of Port is drunk in Portugal, where lighter wines are preferred. Port is predominantly a wine for the cold climates. White Port, made from white grapes but otherwise the same as red, although usually drier, is popular in France, where all Port is drunk as an aperitif. It is found to some extent in other markets, especially Scandinavia, Belgium, and Holland.

In 1962, *per capita* consumption of Port outside Portugal was highest in Scandinavia, with Norway heading the list with 0·27 litres (9·1 imp. oz.; 9·5 U.S. oz.). Frenchmen drank 0·16 litres; Englishmen, 0·15, and, least of all, the Americans—0·001. Export figures for that year (5,927,000 imp. gallons; 7,119,000 U.S.) showed an improvement, and were the best for ten years, small though they were when compared to the average 42,200,000 (9,283,000 imp. gallons; 11,148,000 U.S. gallons) of pre-war days. Yet Port earns 42% of the country's total export revenue, topped only by the figures for cork and tinned fish or other preserves.

What is meant when Port, *tout court*, is discussed, is, or ought to be, Port from Portugal, and generally red. A certain type of rock called schist is probably the factor which, in conjunction with the climate and with methods of treatment worked out carefully over a long time, gives the wine its character. The Upper Douro has only half the rainfall of Oporto, and the lowest rainfall in Northern Portugal.

Originally, Portuguese wine was not fortified (as most of it is not today) but it was harsh and raw and did not travel well. When the relationships of two seafaring nations, England and Portugal, had grown close, the wine often went to England, where it was not much liked. Then it began to be treated with brandy, probably to help it travel, possibly to make it more appealing. The brandy arrested the fermentation of the sugar into alcohol, retaining some of the sweetness. It is interesting to know that Port is fortified up to 20%, so that today, 20% of a bottle of Port is brandy.

The history of the actual development of the Port region shows what a role the schist plays. Like the slate of the Moselle, it contributes breed, and the wine would not be the same without it. Two hundred years ago the area of the Douro was first marked out, a much smaller plot than it is today. It was gradually enlarged until it came to include the present officially delimited zone of Port Wine—the region of Upper Douro, stretching about sixty miles along the river from Ŗégua towards the Spanish frontier. This is the terrain of the schist, a soft kind of crystalline rock which easily splits and crumbles, and which is set down in the midst of a tumbled, wild country otherwise almost entirely granite. These granite soils produce wine, for instance the table wines of the Lower Douro or neighbouring Dão, but not Port.

Port is also a consequence of British enterprise and climate, and of the British palate too. English merchants played a leading part in the development of Port, and their wine lodges hold nearly half of the maturing wine at the mouth of the Douro today. They also own many of the biggest *quintas,* or wine estates, some of which are very large. Before the war, Britain bought half of all the Port produced. The abrupt decline in the British market for Port, probably due in part to high duties but apparently also indicating a real change in taste, has by now lost the traditional Port-drinking nation its first place: but a drop in importation of nearly half has brought the Port Wine industry face to face with hard facts. Surveys seem to indicate that instead of sitting over the Port after the ladies have withdrawn, some Englishmen now tend to leave the dining-room with their wives for coffee and liqueurs. Therefore, far-sighted wine merchants are beginning to promote Port as an agreeable feminine after-dinner drink.

The Making of Port

The vines grow on stepped or terraced levels on the sometimes very steep cliffs of the Douro. If it were not for the terracing, built up laboriously over generations, nearly the whole of the vineyard would wash into the river during the violent rains falling between October and May. The climate is hard—blazing in summer and iron-cold in winter—and life is primitive.

The vines are planted, often by blasting, so that the roots can find their way deep enough to secure moisture during the dry summers. Before the scourge of the phylloxera the wine was made from any number of grape varieties, almost at random. To a considerable extent, this is still the case. Nowadays all vines are grafted on phylloxera-resistant American root-stocks, and while the types are not quite so various, the chief grapes still number over a dozen. It is a truly tragic sight to see the 'mortuaries' as they are called—the terraces left abandoned since the phylloxera and crumbling to ruin along much of the Douro, after they were created with such enormous human effort. Often it has been considered easier to begin new terraces than to try to salvage the old ones—and the tendency is to avoid the old south-facing slopes and plant on north-facing ones to escape the heat, too extreme for men to work in.

Every Port is, at least to some extent, a blend, for it is universally considered that certain plants do better in some weather conditions, some in others, and that different types contribute different qualities, no one vine being able to produce the best wine. Touriga, similar to the French Cabernet Franc, Bastardo, and Mourisco are very important, and four or five dark red types are considered to give deep colour. These are called the Tintas. Important among these are Tinta Cão and Tinta Francisca, the latter probably very close to the French Pinot Noir. White Ports are produced from the Verdelho, Rabigato, and others.

The bunches of grapes are cut and heaped by the picker into a tall wicker basket which he balances at the back of his neck on a roll slung from a forehead band. In this manner the grapes are carried to the treading-troughs by a single file of men; or, if the distance is long, they are tumbled from the tipped baskets into tubs on ox carts. The troughs, called *lagares*, are usually made of large granite slabs. In them the fun—and the wine—begins. Barefooted men jump in, grasp one another by the arms, in a chain, to keep upright on the slippery mass, and begin to tread the grapes. While they do this, a few instruments give them a tune, and they chant in a lament which sounds Arabian. In four-hour shifts, they trample out all the juice, which has already begun to ferment from the heat and the action—no invention has yet succeeded in replacing the human foot for this work. Today most of the work is done by mechanized crushers; this modern process is less colourful but more efficient.

At the moment when the overseer considers that fermentation has reached the proper point, and his saccharometer tells him that just the desired amount of sugar remains unconverted into alcohol, the juice, now raw wine, is let off into large containers called *toneis*. Portuguese brandy is waiting to be introduced in proportion of about one part to five parts of the wine. Since wine cannot ferment at over 16% of alcohol, fermentation stops. The sugar, which would have fermented out, remains in the wine—that is why most Ports are sweet. The degree of sweetness is determined by the point at which fermentation is checked and, of course, by the later marryings and blendings.

In the early spring of the year following the vintage, the blended wine and brandy, a young crude Port, is put into Port pipes (casks of 115 imp. gallons; 138 U.S.) and either sent to Oporto by rail or loaded on to a *rabelo*, a single-sailed boat like a longish scow, guided by a giant sweep. If it goes by *rabelo*, the wine has a dizzy trip down to the mouth of the Douro; in the spring, the river is high and swift-flowing after the rains, and boils over the rapids.

It is not actually in Oporto but at Vila Nova de Gaia, just across the river, that the wine finds a home. This is where the wine lodges are.

Vintage Port

If it has been a great year, the maker will set the best of his wine aside to make Vintage Port. A vintage is often declared by agreement among most of the shippers, but not always. For one thing, the non-vintage Ports are blends of the wines of the various vintages; and if a shipper has a heavy demand for excellent Ports from the wood, he will be reluctant to divert his wines into a Vintage. On an average, a vintage is declared roughly three or four times in a decade. The greatest year among vintage Ports now obtainable is usually considered to be 1927, and it has practically disappeared. Typical of great years since are 1934, 1935, 1942, 1945, 1947, 1948, 1950, 1955, and 1960. Years still talked about over a glass of Port, but rarely a Port of the year in question, are 1878, 1896, 1908, 1912. All these can, in fact, still occasionally be found—even, with great difficulty, the 1878s and 1896s.

A wine selected for Vintage Port is shipped, almost invariably to England, two years, or sometimes a little longer, after its vintage, and almost immediately bottled. Vintage Port is aged in glass. The rest is aged in wood.

During the war, Vintage Ports were bottled in Portugal, but generally they are bottled at their destination and are then laid down. Port always throws a heavy deposit as it matures; when thrown in the bottle, it is called the 'crust'. If the deposit, or crust, is disturbed, it will not always settle down again, and the wine will be spoiled. Thus, shipping in bottle is not advisable.

Vintage Ports require from ten to fifteen years to mature, and in some cases longer. Their true prime, in the great wines, lies years further on, for they improve in the bottle for a long time.

Port should be served at room temperature, which it should achieve gradually by being brought to the room several hours before use. A bottle of Vintage Port (which should be drunk after dinner) will suffer if it is open to the air very long, though a Ruby Port or Tawny will survive better. (Some people in Vila Nova de Gaia maintain that they will keep ten days, providing the decanter is full or nearly so.) When the lighter Ports are drunk as aperitif wines they may be served chilled.

The small 'Port glasses' do not give the wine a chance, and this is especially true of Vintage Port, which has a much bigger bouquet than any other and must have room within the glass to realize it. There is, in fact, no reason not to use the tulip-shaped clear wine glass which serves so well for most other wines, and there are good reasons for doing so. In the chimney of the tulip glass, the nose of the wine will develop fully and not be dispersed, and the colour will be seen at its best through the crystal.

Vintage Port must be carefully decanted in order to bring the clear wine safely off the crust, which will have formed on the inner underside of the bottle. It is not too difficult to pour the wine without disturbing it. For some vintages, for instance 1935 as bottled by Sandeman, a granite-shotted bottle is used, because granite chips roughen the inside and anchor the deposit.

Crusted Port

A wine which is not necessarily that of a single vintage, but which is handled in the same way as Vintage Port and develops in the same way, is called Crusted Port—because of the sediment which forms in the bottle.

It can be very excellent and will be more full-bodied and, in particular, have more nose than one of the Ports aged in wood; but it will not reach the heights of Vintage Port simply because it will have been made from a slightly lesser wine.

Tawny Port

In the *armazems,* or wine lodges, of Vila Nova de Gaia, wine which has not been set aside to become Vintage Port is blended and matured in oak. Each shipper tries to achieve a uniform wine year after year, and does this by blending the vintages of various years together, and by blending differing wines to reach an orchestration he considers right. This is why the Ports of this style differ from trade-mark to trade-mark but run true to type. The term often used in Vila Nova de Gaia—and suggestive of the care and art used—is 'bred': they breed the wines, not blend them, they say.

As the wine ages, it turns in colour from purple to ruby, and then, gradually, brown-golden, the shade called tawny. Ruby Port is the younger version of the wine. It is bottled while it is still red, it has more freshness and it ought to be fruity. The Tawny Port takes a long time to age in the wood; years elapse before it can be bottled and sold, and therefore it is not cheap. It should be drunk soon after it has been bottled, when, if it is an old Tawny, it will have acquired a great elegance. It will never have the majestic power of a grand Vintage Port, but can have extreme finesse. A great Vintage Port is more suited to a cold climate; a splendid, but lighter, old Tawny to a warmer climate. Unfortunately, there is another method of producing Tawny Port which results in a wine which may be good, but certainly will not have the refinement of an old Tawny: Ruby and White Ports are frequently blended together to make 'Tawny'. Incidentally, if you must keep your Tawny Port any length of time in bottle, the expert opinion is that you will have better luck with it if you stand it up.

Tawny Port is never cheap, and if you are in one of the big *armazems* in Vila Nova de Gaia you will see why it cannot be. More than 2% of the wine evaporates each year. You glance along the three-tiered rows of casks and may see a thousand of them. Shudder then, because, from those 1,000 pipes, 15,000 bottles of good Port will vanish into the Portuguese air before you can return to the same spot a year later.

The Future of Port

The post-war drop in sales to Great Britain caused a swing to dry Port. Since the amount of sweetness in any Port is determined by the residue of unfermented sugar left at whatever point fermentation is arrested, it is perfectly possible to make it dry. It is only necessary to let the sugar ferment out. The resultant wines are completely natural. The only question is, whether or not they are fully realized Ports; and it is a question hotly debated today in Oporto and on the Douro.

The motive behind the change was simply that public taste was veering more and more towards aperitif and lighter wines—dry wines suited to drinking before or during a meal rather than after. If, they argued in Oporto, people would not linger after a meal to sip old Port, then they would show the world that they were capable of producing dry Ports of the first quality. The opposite view was that Port, the finest after-dinner wine ever devised, cannot excel as a dry wine, and should, therefore, meet the market crisis by being even more its true self. The crisis will be properly understood for what it is—a national one—when you consider that while in bulk Port is a mere 10% of Portuguese wine, it exceeds all other Portuguese wine and brandy together in annual value. The news, however, is encouraging. In the past three or four years there have been increases in the sales of traditional Port Wines.

For the present, while there is increasing experimentation in dry Ports, the long-term effort to produce the finest possible wines by rigid quality controls is being intensified. Port was the first strictly delimited wine area in the world—the original zone was marked out by the Marques de Pombal in 1756. Vila Nova de Gaia—originally selected because the empty codfish sheds already there promised to make excellent warehouses—has always been a tightly guarded *entreposto*. Until very recently, watchmen patrolled with guns with the order to shoot at sight if anyone was found in the restricted areas out of hours. The Port Wine Institute—the Instituto, as everyone refers to it in Oporto—conducts blind tastings in what must be one of the finest tasting rooms in the world. Running water effectively blots out all smells; tasters may not answer the telephone during sessions so there can be neither disturbance nor briefing. All Ports are tasted 'blind' by experts who must pass examinations and then serve as assistant tasters for four full years before acquiring a vote. Only about one-third of the approximately 100,000 pipes submitted annually win the right to be called Port Wine. (Most of the remainder becomes brandy for fortifying Port; some is drunk in Oporto and the district, but not as Port.)

It remains to be seen whether such stringency—and strict controls of areas, along with budding controls of dating as to vintage—will really serve to stop the swing away of popular taste. Where the wine as wine is concerned, market considerations aside, the answer probably lies in the summary of what gives Port wine its special character, expressed by José Joaquim da Costa Lima, the vigorous and optimistic ex-director of the Instituto. He said Port must strive to be more 'Port' than ever. It needs brandy, he said, because the greatest Port wines have the greatest body and the greatest *dis*equilibrium. Were it not for this, the wine could not assimilate 20% of brandy, would go out of balance; but a wine in *dis*equilibrium like a great Port accepts the brandy and is put *into* balance. So what will happen to the great Port if the fermentation-stopping dose of brandy is left out of the equation in order to make a dry wine is uncertain.

See WHITE PORT.

Porter

A very dark brown British beer with a bitter taste. It is brewed from malt which has dried at such a high temperature that it has become browned or charred. This is the drink to which Elizabeth Barrett Browning had such an objection.

See BEER.

Portland

A moderately productive American hybrid vine yielding both table grapes and those for wine-making. The grapes are green, the wines white.

Portugal

Wines of Portugal divide naturally into three groups: the common wine; table wines, so called, from certain legally marked-out areas and grown and produced under wine controls; and the famous fortified wines, Port and Madeira.

In the fifteenth and sixteenth centuries, Portuguese navigators carried the flag and the name of Portugal to most parts of the world. They also carried Portuguese wine. Before this, beginning at least as early as the middle of the fourteenth century, the wines were known in England. These were not Ports as we know them now, but unfortified beverage wines. In 1353 England and Portugal signed a treaty permitting Portuguese fishermen the right to fish off the English coast; this and the later traffic in salt cod led to the establishment of wines as a part of the trade with Britain. Port can hardly be considered apart from England. The soil and climate of the upper part of the River Douro above Oporto may make the wine, but the English climate has formed the taste and habits of those who drink it.

By 1578 the wine traffic had grown so large that a British Consul had to be settled in the chief port to oversee it. This was not Oporto, from which today all Port Wine must be shipped according to Portuguese law. The port was Viana do Castelo, fifty miles to the north, a tiny place in the region of what are now called the Vinhos Verdes, or the green wines. The evidence that the thin, rather harsh wines were not popular is found in the history of the beginning of the eighteenth century. England was quarrelling with France, and in 1703, to strike a blow against French wines, Portuguese wines were given preferential entry into England by the terms of the Methuen Treaty. Yet it was not until after the middle of the century when fortification began that the wine became an English favourite.

The export wines of Portugal are all influenced by the success story of Port, and many try to copy it. This was more common before the wine laws became strict, and until a few years after the beginning of this century there were certain Portuguese wines, not from the Upper Douro, which were labelled 'port'.

Most Portuguese wines, Port apart, reach a good average standard. They are not to be compared with the fine wines of France and Germany; but a considerable improvement has been made in the last ten years. Of the million gallons of Portuguese still wines shipped to England in 1961, some commanded a fair price; and the cheaper ones are good value compared with the not quite so cheap blended regional wines of France and the cheaper hocks.

The Common or Local Wines

Portugal is one of the leading wine countries of Europe and the Portuguese account for 125 bottles per person per year. In 1964 total production was 304,650,000 imp. gallons (365,866,000 U.S.), divided as follows: 212,290,000 (254,950,000 U.S.) of ordinary wines; 90,050,000 (108,140,000 U.S.) of controlled wines; and 1,620,000 (1,943,000 U.S.) other wines. There was more red than white, and an increase in the quantity of legally controlled wine. The figures for the fine fortified wines were: Port, 6,010,000 imp. gallons (7,220,000 U.S.); 957,000 imp. gallons (1,150,000 U.S.) of Madeira. The total area of vineyard is 795,000 acres, about 70% planted on the slopes. This is divided into some 300,000 plots with an average production of roughly 267 imp. gallons (321 U.S.) per acre, and around 240,000 people are permanently engaged in this branch of agriculture, while some 1¼ million (or 15% of the population) depend directly or indirectly on the wine trade for their living. Wine brings in just over 4% of the national revenue, and 9% of the export returns, thus playing an important part in the economy of the country. And the Portuguese themselves drink about 25·1 imp. gallons (30·1 U.S.) a head.

A great deal of the common wine comes from the coastal district of the province of Estremadura, just north of Lisbon. The vineland is gently rolling, intensely green, and traversed by winding roads which seem designed to visit every corner rather than to reach any destination.

One of the main centres is Torres Vedras, where the wines are mostly strong, heavy reds. The large co-operative is the focal point, rising in the dusty town. Tasted from the vat a year before it is going to be sold, the red wine is coarse and common. The white is low in acidity and flat. In Ribatejo, Cartaxo wines are full-bodied reds; Almeirum, inland, produces dry white wines lacking in acidity. Alcobaça, near the coast, makes a fairly good white wine which is rather soft. All these, and the dessert wines of the same regions, will generally carry the name Estremadura.

A Bairrada Ruby is also commonplace: it is made near Coimbra, one of Europe's oldest university towns, where the students still wear flowing capes from the hem of which they tear away a ragged strip every time they kiss a girl or are lucky in love.

Lafões is one of the better-known of the more ordinary wines within Portugal, and is fresh and crackling, like a Vinho Verde. For the last three-quarters of a century, sparkling wine has been made by the Champagne method of secondary fermentation in the bottle, mainly at Lamego near the Douro.

Wines With Certificate of Origin

Most of the better Portuguese wines carry official certificates of origin and are produced under controlled conditions in designated districts. Of these, Port is by far the most important.

Port apart, the principal Portuguese wines of Appellation d'Origine, the French term for place-name and the one in general use throughout the wine world, are: Bucelas, Carcavelos, Colares, Verde, Dão, and Moscatel de Setúbal. The first two and the last are seldom seen abroad. Carcavelos, a sweet dessert wine from just outside Lisbon, is hardly ever exported.

Bucelas

The wine from Bucelas, from immediately north of Lisbon, used to be very well known and a century ago was widely exported, but today little of it is seen abroad. A Bucelas Velho (Old Bucelas) sipped in the typical Portuguese tasting glass, shafted like a lantern chimney, had the characteristic astringency of the Arinto grape, from which about 70% of Bucelas is made, and at ten years of age had become a rich gold. Tasted beside it, a Branco Sêco, literally 'Dry White', a commoner wine from the Arinto grape from outside the Bucelas district, was out of balance, at the same time thick, heavy, and acid, yet it lacked nose, and the colour was a watery, pale gold.

Colares

The true wine of Colares profited by the scourge of phylloxera. When, towards the end of the last century, the vine pest was imported into Europe on American vines, it devastated practically all the continental vineyards. The soil of Colares is of two types: heavy earth and sand. In the loamy area, phylloxera took the same course as everywhere else, and today all vines are grafted on phylloxera-resistant American root-stocks. But the grub could not penetrate to the deep roots in the sandy soil.

The result is one of the most unusual vineyards

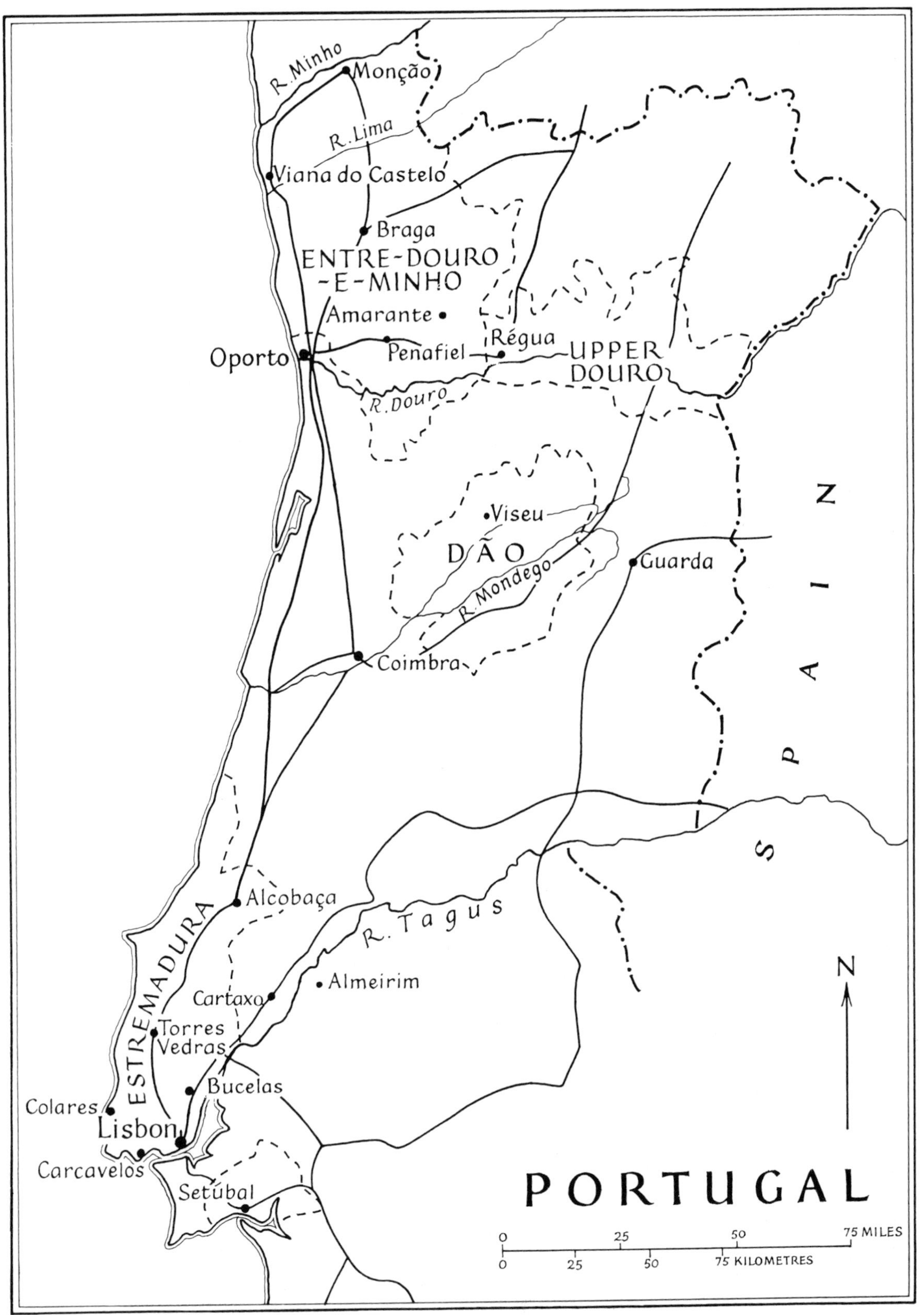
R. Minho
Monção
R. Lima
Viana do Castelo
Braga
ENTRE-DOURO
-E-MINHO
Amarante
Oporto
Penafiel
Régua
UPPER
DOURO
R. Douro
Viseu
DÃO
R. Mondego
Guarda
Coimbra
SPAIN
Alcobaça
R. Tagus
ESTREMADURA
Almeirim
Cartaxo
Torres
Vedras
Bucelas
Colares
Lisbon
Carcavelos
Setúbal
N
PORTUGAL
0
25
50
75 MILES
0
25
50
75 KILOMETRES

in Europe. Twenty miles from Lisbon, across the thick neck of a headland which rises to its apex in the mountain of Sintra, is the dune-and-sea-coast vineyard of wind-shifted sand, divided by screens of reed woven together with willow and briar. The work of vine planting is appallingly hard. A trench more than man-high must be dredged with the mattock, and the vine shoot put down in the bottom of it so that the root can grip in firm soil. In the years before phylloxera, there was little incentive to endure this hard labour and the area was mostly a ridge of sand and scrub pine; when the plague sliced Europe's wine production by half, it became profitable to work the arid Colares terrain.

The happy days of rocketing prices did not last in Colares, once it was found that grafting on American roots largely solved the phylloxera crisis, and the dune vineyards were threatened with extinction. But in the meantime a special and unexpected advantage had been discovered, which was that the vines not only resisted phylloxera but that they had a peculiar and attractive quality of their own. It was an advantage many of the growers promptly set themselves to wipe out.

All Colares dune-wine comes from the Ramisco grape, a variety believed originally to have come from Bordeaux, whereas the loam-soil vineyards, which are terraced and fringe the mountain of Sintra high above the sea, are planted principally in a blue-black grape called the João Santarem. The yield is greater, there is no need to dredge down to find a soil capable of holding both the roots of the vine and the moisture and necessary fertilizers which the sand cannot retain; almost from the first, loam-soil wine was mixed in with the sand soil to amplify the quantity. The trouble was that the wines are unlike, and the loam wines common.

A substantial improvement came about in 1931 with the founding of the wine co-operative, the Adega Regional de Colares, situated on a eucalyptus-lined street near the sea, and in the two dozen huge vats of which all Colares wine must now be made. Sand-soil and loam-soil wines are placed in two categories, the latter being required to be aged six months, the former eighteen months; in addition to which they must be at least 80% from the Ramisco grape. (In practice, they are wholly Ramisco.) Sand wines are bottled but loam wines are sold in large *fiascos* or straw-covered flasks.

The Ramisco grape produces a wine slow to develop, and wines are sometimes left in the large casks of Angola mahogany or American redwood for as long as fourteen years. The practice is unfortunately very irregular, which accounts for the fact that a range of Colares shows great inconsistency. The peculiarity of the taste is at first a shock to the palate: a 1948 was distinctly musty while a 1945 was strong, tannic, and smoky.

Of all the various companies vatting in the Adega Regional de Colares, only one produces a vintage wine in the true sense. Bottles of other firms will be found to carry the designation Vindima or Colheita, followed by the year, but the wines are blends, containing some wine of that year. It is supposed to be the informing or predominating year, but this is very dubious and vague.

Peculiar also to Portuguese wines generally, and to Colares wines in particular, is the term and usage *Garrafeira,* or *Reserva.* A bottle carrying the designation *Garrafeira* on the label is one which has been kept a certain number of years before sale. A Vindima will generally have been sold as soon as bottled, unless otherwise indicated.

Moscatel de Setúbal

Produced on untrained, irregular vines like black, twisted arms rising from the earth, and seldom planted in rows, the wine is produced in very small quantities in a region across the bridge from Lisbon, where nowadays a common red wine is the major yield. It is a fortified wine, lighter and less concentrated than a Malaga. From bottles that are young, it is perfumed and fruity and very grapy.

Dão

The Dão wines come from south of the Douro in the north-central area of the country. The landscape is extremely wild and mountainous, and much of the vineyard is terraced, as on the Upper Douro where Port is made. In much of the region, the granite crops to the surface and cultivation of any kind is impossible, the best vineyard areas lying in the valleys where the soil is composed of weather-crumbled granite. Wine has been made around the city of Viseu for at least seven centuries; but only within the last forty years has the Dão region been officially marked out within a triangle, the points of which are Viseu, Guarda, and Coimbra.

Several hundred times as much red wine is produced as white. About half the white grapes suffer the fate of being thrown in with the red to make a bright ruby wine. The leading red grapes are the Tourigo and Preto Mortágua—and a variety in wide use called Tinta Pinheira is probably a Portuguese strain of the French Pinot. The most important white varieties are the Dona Branca and the Arinto, the latter supposed to be close in origin to the German Riesling.

Unlike the vines to the north in Vinhos Verdes, Dão vines are almost invariably pruned low. Cultivation is very difficult, the planting often involving blasting. The rugged nature of the countryside has, as might be expected, enforced a continuance of primitive life. Gathered grapes are still carried to the vats in baskets on the women's heads, and except in rare cases, the wine is no longer trodden out by the naked feet of the *trabalhadores*.

The chief characteristic of Dão wines, taken as a whole, is their smoothness and suavity, a quality which shows up in analysis, where the wines prove to have an unusually rich glycerine content. There is frequently a hint of yeast in the nose, and in this region yeasts are customarily forced. Some dark red 1947s tasted had a distinct Pinot Noir flavour.

Vinhos Verdes

The district in the north-west of Portugal directly south of Spanish Galicia, designated under the wine laws as Verde, lies south of the River Minho and north of the Douro, and forms the province of Entre-Douro-e-Minho, a name which the wines occasionally carry.

The Vinhos Verdes vineland dates from Roman times, and probably earlier. One of its peculiar features is that over many centuries there has been little change in the wine: this is because the factors creating it are firmly rooted in the nature of the region. It is the most densely populated part of Portugal. Small farmers (55,000 wine growers produce 210 imp. gallons (250 U.S.) or less each per year) intensively cultivate tiny plots, and in the normal sense there are no vineyards. The vines are trained on trees or trellises bordering roads and fields. No space is wasted.

The land presents a smiling face, but a wrinkled one. In shape it is a huge bowl sloping gradually away from the Atlantic and slowly rising. The bowl form buttressed by higher ranges holds the wet onshore winds and Minho is both mild and rainy. It is cut and furrowed by many rivers—the creases of the face. As a result, even though the terrain is not rough, it is divided into numerous zones, seven of which were considered distinct enough to be made sub-regions by the wine laws of fifty years ago.

Of these, in a general way the wines of Lima, Basto, Braga, Amarante, and Penafiel can be taken to be characteristic Vinhos Verdes. The white wines of Monção, however, are fruity and possessed of a powerful nose, a quality lacking in the Vinhos Verdes, and are richer and more alcoholic (12% to 14%). This is the result of their being made from the Alvarinho grapes. The more usual white-wine varieties in Minho are Azal Branco and Dourado; and in the red wines Barroçal, Vinhão (also called Tinto or Tinta) and Espadeiro (also named Espadeiro do Basto Padeira).

The distinguishing character of all Verdes wines—including Monção white wines which possess this factor too—is a crackling or slightly biting or prickling quality. It is produced intentionally in wines which are destined in any case to be very light. These are bottled when only four or five months old, and all care is taken to suppress the fermentation of the malic acid during the fermentation of the alcohol. But in the bottle the malic acid ferments, changing to lactic acid, and giving the wines their special sprightliness, and a light prickle caused by the trapping of a certain amount of carbonic gas. They are wines designed for summertime drinking. Possessing, generally, about 9% to 10% alcohol, they are heavily exported to Brazil—which seems to contradict the common theory that, owing to their lightness, they cannot travel. Tasted in Portugal, a Penafiel Verde Branco proved to be fresh and attractively lively, with high acidity, and of a light greenish colour. Not to be forgotten are the rosé wines of Portugal, outselling all others in the United States and in England. These come largely from the Vinhos Verdes region, on the outskirts of the Douro. These wines account for exports of several hundreds of thousands of cases a year. Of these Lancers and Mateus are the most popular.

Pot

1. An attractive and much-needed small wine bottle in southern Burgundy, notably the Beaujolais, of about a half-litre capacity (approximately 17 ounces) into which wine is run from the cask to be served in restaurants and cafés. Larger than a half-bottle, smaller than a whole one, the Pot Beaujolais has become very popular in France since 1958; and as a result of the author's efforts it has been taken up in the United States also; and is likewise to be found in England.

2. A French wine measure, now obsolete.

Pot Still

Old and simplest form of still, used in the distillation of Cognac, etc.

See CHAPTER TEN, p. 56.

Poteen, Potheen

Illegal Irish whiskey.

Pottle

An obsolete English wine measure equivalent to a half-gallon.

Château Pouget

Bordeaux red wine. District: Haut-Médoc, France. Commune: Cantenac-Margaux.

A Fourth Growth (*Quatrième Cru*) as classified in 1855. The vineyard is now worked co-operatively with Château Boyd-Cantenac, Third Growth (*Troisième Cru*), by Monsieur Guillermet who owns the two estates. Both wines are made at Château Pouget but they are distinctly different. Pouget has never had a great reputation and there is no reason to change this status.

Characteristics. Generally uninteresting and on the common side.

Vineyard area: 20 acres.

Average production: 2,500 cases.

Pouilly-Fuissé

The finest dry white wine of southern Burgundy and one that has now for some years received the renown which it deserves in England and the United States. Pouilly-Fuissé has made great inroads into the market once controlled by Chablis. It is made from Chardonnay grapes grown in four communes of the Mâcon slope.

See MÂCONNAIS.

Pouilly-Fumé

Excellent dry, white, Loire Valley wine.

See POUILLY-SUR-LOIRE.

Pouilly-Loché

A minor dry white wine from southern Burgundy's Mâcon slope bearing a considerable resemblance to the more famous and better Pouilly-Fuissé.

See MÂCONNAIS.

Pouilly-sur-Loire

Loire Valley white wines. District: Loire Valley, France.

At Pouilly, below Nevers in the Loire Valley, the land rises gently, almost imperceptibly, from the often sluggish river, but sufficiently for vines to grow—they are always happier on hillsides than on plains. Two types of grapevines are grown and two types of wine made, both white, both dry, but otherwise entirely different.

Pouilly-Fumé is the better wine. It comes from Sauvignon grapes and is light yet round, crisp, and eminently pleasing and refreshing. Similarities both in style and name cause it to be confused with Pouilly-Fuissé from the Mâcon district, but in truth the two are entirely different. The Loire's slightly lesser offering is marked by what is usually called a 'gunflint' dryness and an indescribable flavour often compared to truffles. But although the flavour can be delightful, the wines usually lack breed.

The lesser wine is Pouilly-sur-Loire from Chasselas grapes which are mostly grown in clay soil. The wine is almost as dry as its more impressive neighbour but has far less staying power and tends towards commonness; a respectable carafe wine in its native habitat, but of little interest elsewhere.

Some 2,000 acres are devoted to Pouilly's vineyards, on which there is more Chasselas planted than Sauvignon. The yearly output is close to 166,000 imp. gallons (200,000 U.S.) of Pouilly-sur-Loire, and only 33,000 imp. gallons (40,000 U.S.) of Pouilly-Fumé.

Pouilly-Vinzelles

Dry white wines from the Mâcon district which, in very good years, resembles, though it never quite equals, the wine of Pouilly-Fuissé near which it is made.

See MÂCONNAIS.

Pourriture Noble

French for 'noble rot' caused by the fungus or mould *Botrytis cinerea* under favourable conditions.

See BOTRYTIS CINEREA.

Powdery Mildew

Also called true mildew and oïdium—a widespread and damaging disease of the vine.

See CHAPTER EIGHT, p. 37.

Pramnian Wine

Famous Greek wine of antiquity.

See CLASSICAL WINES.

Precipitation

A deposit of bitartrate of potassium (cream of tartar) may appear in the form of small crystals in young wine, either red or white, which has been subjected to the cold. The remedy is to warm the wine bottles and turn them about until all the crystals have dissolved and the germ is destroyed.

Premières Côtes de Blaye

A district of Bordeaux producing white and red wines. The white wines are the best of the Blayais.

See BLAYE.

Premières Côtes de Bordeaux

White and red wines. South-West France.

The official place-name or Appellation Contrôlée accorded red and white wines from a district on the

Garonne opposite Graves, Barsac, and Sauternes. Beginning just above the city of Bordeaux and running southward up the river for thirty miles, the zone is never more than a mile or two wide. In its southern part, it encloses the good sweet white-wine communes of Loupiac and Sainte-Croix-du-Mont.

White wine surpasses the red in volume by six or seven times, and is finer in quality. While it is not an absolute rule, red wine generally grows in the downriver half of the region nearer Bordeaux, and white wine upriver. Specified vines for red wine are the same as for Médoc: Cabernet, Merlot, Malbec, Petit Verdot, and Carménère—and for white wine are the same as those used in Sauternes and in Loupiac and Sainte-Croix-du-Mont: Sémillon, Sauvignon, and Muscadelle. White wines range from dry through semi-sweet to sweet. They do not quite come up to those of Loupiac and Sainte-Croix-du-Mont, but it must be remembered these compare well with all but the finest Sauternes.

The right side of the river, if a little less important in wine production, is unquestionably the prettier. The slope is steep, whereas on the Graves–Barsac–Sauternes side the land is flat. Frequent cuttings into the bluff reveal the white chalk and clay soils which contribute to the character of the Premières Côtes de Bordeaux wines. The exposure is generally south.

Cadillac, in the white-wine part of the region, houses one of Bordeaux's great wine fraternities, the Connétablie de Guyenne, devoted to the promotion of white, sweet wines. Descended from the Connétables or constables of Bordeaux who, in the Middle Ages, judged the wines passing on the river and decreed whether or not they could go to market, the society is housed in Cadillac's gigantic mediæval château of the Dukes of Épernon.

Preuve

A small glass vessel like a test tube lowered on a chain into Cognac barrels to obtain some of the liquor, to taste or 'prove' it. Called, in the local slang, a *taupette*.

Pricked Wine

Sour wine with an excess of volatile acidity.

Château Prieuré-Lichine

Bordeaux red wine. District: Haut-Médoc, France. Commune: Cantenac-Margaux.

Originally the priory of Benedictine monks, early spreaders of the gospel of the vine in Bordeaux, the vineyard was bought by the author and a group of American friends, in 1952. Since that date the property has been grouped and reconstituted on the best slightly-rising ground in Cantenac. Some of the recent vineyard acquisitions included the lands known as 'La Bourgade' which were owned by the La Chapelle family from the fifteenth century to 1867. In 1667 Guy de La Chapelle presented wines from his vineyard to Louis XIV. They were placed in competition with Burgundies recommended by Fagon, the king's doctor. Nevertheless, the wines from 'La Bourgade' remained among the favourites of Louis for many years. By exchanging two metres of land for one and sacrificing quantity for quality, the poorer, lower, and sandier plots have been bartered for higher, gravelly, and better-drained land. These exchanges brought into the Prieuré-Lichine vineyard portions of Châteaux Palmer, Ferrière, Kirwan, Giscours, d'Issan, and Boyd-Cantenac, Third Growths (*Troisièmes Crus*) and of Châteaux Durfort-Vivens and Brane-Cantenac, Second Growths (*Seconds Crus*). Prieuré-Lichine was classified a Fourth Growth (*Quatrième Cru*) in the Médoc Classification of 1855, and it is the hope of the owners that by the acquisition of these excellent plots, and by extensive replanting and improvements in vinicultural methods and equipment, they are creating a wine well above its classification.

Since the change of ownership, the wine has become very popular in America, and the château itself (which contains many mementoes from the world's wine countries acquired by the author during the preparation of this book) has become a kind of Anglo-American club in south-west France. As they drive along the vineyard road to Margaux, visitors are welcomed to the château by signs elegantly lettered in both French and English. As a vineyard situated in Cantenac, Château Prieuré-Lichine is now entitled to the place-name Margaux, a privilege accorded to Cantenac wines in 1954 on account of the proximity of the famous commune of Margaux and the great similarity between wines of the two places. The vineyard was previously known as Château Le Prieuré.

Characteristics. Soft, fast-maturing, relatively full-bodied yet with all the delicacy for which the wines of the commune of Margaux are so justly renowned.

Vineyard area: 47 acres.

Average production: 5,500 cases.

Production of Wine

It is safe to estimate that almost half the total production of wine in the world is supplied by France, Italy, and Spain, although quantities vary

World Wine Production in 1964

Producing Country	*Hectolitres*	*Imperial gallons*	*U.S. gallons*	*Acreage planted in vines*
Italy	66,124,000	1,454,569,302	1,746,857,220	4,169,790
France	60,563,000	1,332,240,649	1,599,947,278	3,440,918
Spain	32,845,776	722,528,242	867,716,426	4,182,761
Argentina	19,533,393	429,687,766	516,031,223	669,678
Portugal	13,849,174	304,648,590	365,866,094	844,512
U.S.S.R.	11,279,000[3]	248,110,930[3]	297,967,494[3]	2,627,719
Algeria	10,477,025	230,469,405	276,780,999	889,579
West Germany	7,185,349	158,060,433	189,821,831	196,548
U.S.A.	7,148,250	157,244,344	188,841,754	624,855[3]
Rumania	6,500,000[1]	142,984,400[1]	171,716,350[1]	747,247
Yugoslavia	5,900,000[3]	129,785,840[3]	155,865,610[3]	649,887
Hungary	5,545,000	121,976,692	146,487,256	632,590
Chile	4,837,097	106,404,525	127,785,945	276,486
South Africa	3,734,580	82,151,797	98,659,761	184,746
Greece	3,526,000	77,563,538	93,149,515	559,372
Bulgaria	2,901,850	63,833,736	76,660,783	468,445
Austria	2,871,169	63,158,827	75,850,256	99,168
Morocco	2,458,623	54,083,805	64,951,657	172,974
Tunisia	1,834,836	40,361,988	48,472,514	127,983
Australia	1,706,388	37,536,441	45,079,188	135,799
Brazil	1,262,500	27,771,970	33,352,599	170,503[2]
Switzerland	917,605	20,185,108	24,241,197	29,289
Uruguay	836,730[2]	18,406,052[2]	22,104,649[2]	46,261[2]
Czechoslovakia	749,078	16,477,918	19,789,068	63,958
Japan	457,640[3]	10,066,982[3]	12,089,888[3]	53,745
Cyprus	410,000[2]	9,019,016[2]	10,831,339[2]	94,394[6]
Canada	396,000[2]	8,711,050[2]	10,461,488[2]	20,819
Israel	389,050	8,558,166	10,277,884	25,946
Turkey	370,000	8,139,112	9,774,623	1,935,567[2]
Luxembourg	165,000	3,629,604	4,358,954	3,042
Mexico	114,160	2,511,246	3,015,867	33,359
Peru	97,704[3]	2,149,254[3]	2,581,135[3]	20,633[3]
New Zealand	72,937	1,604,439	1,926,842	1,396
Egypt	45,000[3]	989,892[3]	1,188,806[3]	24,389[3]
Malta	40,000[1]	879,904[1]	1,056,716[1]	2,965[1]
Lebanon	38,500[2]	846,908[2]	1,017,089[2]	61,776[2]
Albania	30,692	675,150	810,818	29,702
Syria	25,000[1]	549,940[1]	660,448[1]	172,504
Jordan	14,700[4]	323,365[4]	388,343[4]	44,973[4]
Netherlands	6,400[5]	140,785[5]	169,075[5]	635
Bolivia	6,000[1]	131,986[1]	158,507[1]	4,695[1]
Belgium	3,900	85,791	103,030	1,122
Iran	3,600[1]	79,191[1]	95,104[1]	185,329[1]
Colombia	100[1]	2,200[1]	2,642[1]	494[1]

[1] = estimation [2] = 1962 [3] = 1963 [4] = 1959 [5] = wine arising from imported grapes and from home-grown grapes unsuitable for consumption [6] = 1961

from country to country each season, as a result of climatic changes and diseases affecting the vines—and this in spite of modern scientific discoveries which have solved many of the problems of both viticulture and viniculture. In 1957 the world harvest was remarkably small: in 1959 and 1964 very large. Wine, a natural phenomenon, is always unpredictable. Politics also contribute to the variation. Algeria, for example, lately a part of metropolitan France and an enormous producer, is now an independent, mainly Moslem country. Production figures have dropped there, although not yet very greatly.

Prohibition

Prohibition of wines, spirits, and other alcoholic beverages has been tried at various times by varying groups and nations. With the sole exceptions of a period in ancient China and of the successful edict prohibiting alcohol to the Moslem, none of them has been in the slightest way a success. Probably the most spectacular attempt was that of the United States Government between the years 1920 and 1933 with the 18th Amendment to the Constitution.

The 18th Amendment to the Constitution read, in part, that 'the manufacture, sale or transportation of intoxicating liquors within, the importation thereof into or the exportation thereof from the United States and all territory subject to the jurisdiction thereof for beverages purposes is hereby prohibited.' It was eventually ratified by forty-six states and it went into effect on 16 November 1920. It had been preceded slightly by the Volstead Act (October 1919) which had been passed over the veto of President Wilson and which had prohibited the manufacture, sale, or transportation of any beverage over 1% of alcohol by volume. The general result was chaos.

Throughout the nearly fourteen years of Prohibition speakeasies flourished, 'bathtub gin' became the national drink (although the name was more colourful than accurate), bootleggers made fortunes, and products were sold under labels advising the purchaser that he should under no conditions add so much water to the contents or leave the solution at such and such a temperature for a certain length of time, or an illegal alcoholic beverage might result. The cellars of the country resounded with the explosions of bottles of home-made beer and many a solid and otherwise law-abiding citizen considered it a duty to smuggle some sort of spirit home with him when he went abroad. The supreme act of illogicality was the opening in New York of a speakeasy operated by the Federal Government on the theory that by breaking the laws they might better catch the lawbreakers.

The matter was resolved on 5 December 1933 when the 21st Amendment to the Constitution declared the whole dismal experiment a failure and repealed the 18th Amendment. Since that time the system of local option has prevailed whereby states are allowed to choose for themselves (Mississippi was the last dry state to vote wet in 1961), and counties, townships, and villages within states often decide for themselves. The consequences of a town remaining 'dry' often recall the phrase of George Bernard Shaw referring to a dry town in Ireland: 'The inhabitants neither swear nor get drunk, and look as though they would very much like to do both.'

Prokupac

The 'national vine of Serbia', an important producer in Yugoslav wines.

Proof Gallon

A gallon of spirit at proof strength; the basis for most customs and excise charges.

See WINE GALLON.

Proof Spirit

'I must explain for the information of Mr. Snowden that when we speak of these degrees, what we mean is degrees of proof spirit; and when we speak of degrees of proof spirit, what we mean is degrees.' This was Sir Winston Churchill's clarification when asked in the House of Commons what proof spirit was. The confusion was justified. When Clark invented the hydrometer late in the eighteenth century, he knew nothing of 100%, or absolute, alcohol. He only knew that if he dropped his weighted float into spirituous liquor, he could determine its density, and calculate the amount of alcohol, by the depth to which the float sank. A certain concentration he arbitrarily named proof; anything over the mark was O.P., over proof; anything under was U.P., under proof. Thirty years later a hydrometer was developed (by Bartholomew Sikes—sometimes spelled Sykes) which has remained in use from 1816 to the present day. By Sikes's measurement, proof, in the United States, is 50% of alcohol by volume at 60°F. (16°C.). In England, proof is 49·28% of pure alcohol by weight or 52·10% by volume, at 60°F. (16°C.). Each 0·5% of alcohol over or under proof is reckoned as one degree O.P. or U.P. Alcoholic content in a spirit is usually stated as so many degrees proof: 70° proof (or, correctly, *of* proof, though it is seldom so stated) means the same as 30° under proof, in either case seventy parts of proof being present and thirty lacking. It must always be remembered that 100% pure alcohol is not at proof, but 75·35° O.P.

Provence, Côtes de Provence

Rosé, red, and white wines. District: South of France.

Provence is the old province of the troubadours and the Courts of Love in south-east France, and traditionally the land of gaiety and sunshine. It faces the Mediterranean Sea, and from Marseilles, which secures its western corner, it moves east through the great naval seaport of Toulon and on to Cannes and Nice. The vine grows, not far away from sun-bathing crowds, in meagre soil that is rich in sand, limestone or slate—and little else.

The first vines brought into France are said to have been planted in Provence by Phocæans, plying their routes from Italy, Greece and Asia Minor. Cæsar is recorded to have chosen these wines to give to his returning legions as they made their way back to Rome laden with spoils of the Gallic Wars. One village, still growing vines, is reputed to have been named by Cæsar himself: this is La Gaude, which stands just above Cannes; and Cæsar, tasting the local wine, is said to have smacked his lips together and proclaimed, *Gaudeamus!* (Let us rejoice!)

Officially, Provence no longer exists but is divided into the French departments of Bouches-du-Rhône, Var, Vaucluse, Basses-Alpes, and Alpes-Maritimes. To the tradition-loving French, however, and everyone else as well, it will always be Provence. With its clear, blue sea, its sun and its Mistral—the dread wind that blows from the north always for three, six, or nine days—Provence will never change its character. And an essential part of its character is the Provençal wines.

The region produces annually almost 125 million imp. gallons (150 million U.S.) of wines, all of which maintain a certain Provençal character. They are wines to be taken in gulps rather than sips. While they often have a certain roughness, they manage to combine with it considerable liveliness and gaiety and their alcoholic content is such that the drinker is apt soon to take on the same characteristics.

The greatest quantity of wine made in Provence is rosé, but white and red are produced here too—the reds sometimes resembling the wines of Italy. The rosés are among the finest of France—and the perfect accompaniment to the regional specialities, most of which are sea foods fresh from the Mediterranean. These wines should be drunk when fairly young. Some of the better red wines can be aged for a few years but rarely is any Provençal wine at its best after more than five years.

On a quantity basis, red and rosé wines outrun the whites. These white wines, rarely found outside France, have a strength which has prompted one grower to describe them as 'tarpaulin edged with lace'. The rosés are fresh, clean and heady, and the best of them (now that they are better made than once they were) have no orange cast.

Place-names

Bandol

Some twenty miles to the east of Marseilles, along the Mediterranean coast, an area of about 300 acres has been marked off and given the right to grow wines bearing the place-name Bandol. The area falls into the communes of Bandol, Sanary, La Cadière d'Azur, Le Castellet, and several portions of the communes of Ollioules, Evenos, Saint-Cyr-sur-Mer, and Beausset, in soil that is predominantly a flinty limestone.

One of the more confusing aspects of Provence is the large number of vine types allowed to be used for the various wines. In Bandol, there are sixteen different grapes, seven for white wines and nine for red and rosé. To complicate matters further, red and rosé are permitted to include up to 20% of their volume of grapes allowed for white wines, providing they are all vinified together. The result is then a lighter wine but not an inferior one.

Clairette and Ugni Blanc are the primary vines allowed for the whites, of which at least 50% must be Clairette; Grenache, Cinsault, Mourvèdre, and Mourvaison are the principal grapes for red and rosé. (Accessory vines are Columbeau, Frontignan, Malvoisie, Doucillon, and Sauvignon for white wines; and Carignan, Pécoui-Touar, Tibouren, Syrah, and Pinot for the others.)

For the place-name Bandol, the wine must have an alcoholic content of at least 11%. Here in the sunny south of France the limits are usually higher than the legal minimum. Wine can be sold as Bandol after an ageing period in the barrel amounting to eight months for white and rosé and a minimum of eighteen months for the red.

The name on a wine label may be Bandol or Vin de Bandol, either one meaning the same thing. Production is just under 83,000 imp. gallons (100,000 U.S.) of wine annually, of which more than two-thirds is red and rosé and the remainder white. Although some export is beginning, most of the wine is sold in Provence or in the restaurants of Paris.

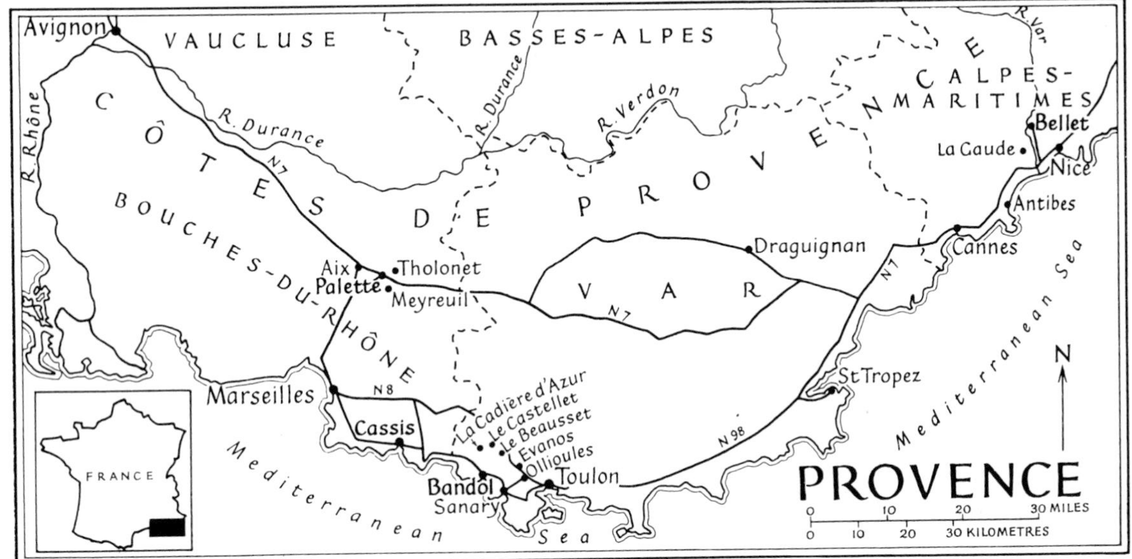

Bellet

Bellet, with Bandol and Cassis, is grown along the Riviera. What there is of it is usually drunk on the spot. The wine is made in a number of localities standing behind and slightly to the east of Nice, and in Nice itself.

The soil for the wines of Bellet is made up of pudding-stone, a curious formation composed of innumerable small pebbles which have been rounded and worn down by the action of wind and water. They are rich in flint and perhaps it is this that causes the wines to be among the very best in southern France. The pudding-stone soil which falls in the communes of Les Séoules, Le Pilon, Le Grand-Bois, Golfan, Cappan, Saint-Romain-de Bellet, La Tour, Candau, Saquier, Saint-Sauveur, Gros-Pin, Serre-Long, Crémat, Mont-Bellet, Puncia, and Lingesteria has been delimited as the growing area. Here, as in the rest of Provence, a fairly large number of vines are allowed, divided into primary and accessory types.

Folle (or Fuella) and Braquet are primary for red and rosé Bellet, and the whites come from Rolle, Rousanne, Clairette, and Espagnol. These must make up at least 60% of the grapes going into the wines. (Accessory vines are Cinsault, Carignan, Bourboulenc, and Grenache for red and rosé, and Sauvignon, Moscatelle, Sémillon, Listan, and Pignerol for whites.)

The fermented wine must have an alcoholic content of 10·5% for white, red and rosé wines. The wines of Bellet average 8,000 imp. gallons (10,000 U.S.) per year, mostly red and rosé, the white accounting for just over one-tenth of the harvest.

Cassis

One of the best of the Provençal rosés is that of Cassis, a little seaport town about fifteen miles to the east of Marseilles and one of the main supply points for the fish sent into that city. Fish and wine, in Cassis, are a perfect combination—for the sturdy dry rosé, or the full, heady white make magnificent companions for *bouillabaisse,* the succulent rock-fish and lobster stew which most Frenchmen rightly maintain can only properly be made in Marseilles.

The vineyards growing grapes for Cassis are all in the single commune. The growers maintain that the gentle breezes from the Mediterranean are so constant that the temperature rarely changes. This, they say, explains the annual harvest which also varies very little from year to year, amounting to about 83,000 imp. gallons (100,000 U.S.). In Cassis white wines predominate over red, a situation which is not typical of Province. The principal vines are Ugni Blanc, Sauvignon, Doucillon, Clairette, Marsanne, and Pascal Blanc for white wines; and Grenache, Carignan, Mourvèdre, Cinsault, and Barbaroux for red and rosé.

Wine must have a minimum alcoholic content of 11%. This applies equally to all Cassis wines, regardless of colour.

They are often served too cold, even in Cassis—a practice that ruins their flavour—but are wonderful wines. The whites and rosés are the best. They are strong, fine, heady, and robust.

Palette

Near the ancient city of Aix-en-Provence, the hills start rising in a steep, rocky cliff leading up to the growing area of Palette. This is the only superior wine area in Provence that is not along the coastal strip. It lies in the communes of Meyreuil, Tholonet, and Aix-en-Provence. The white wines made here are among the best in Provence; the red wines are good and keep well.

Palette wines have only come under strict controls lately, and some of the practices from earlier and more haphazard days continued into the nineteen-sixties. Vine growers who had olive trees in their vineyards were ordered to uproot them by 1963. The new laws decree, however, that Palette has more permissible vine types than are usually found even in Provence, the total coming to twenty-five or more. For white wines, the growers are allowed to use Clairette, which must comprise at least 55% of the final mixture, and in addition any combination of the following: Grenache Blanc, White Muscats (most types), Terret-Bourret (limited to less than 20% of the total), Picpoule, Pascal, Araignan, Colombaud, and Ugni Blanc or Ugni Rosé. Red and rosé wines must be made from more than 50% of a combination of Grenache and Cinsault and under 10% Mourvèdre, and the rest from a dozen different varieties.

This jumble means that the wines will vary considerably, depending on the grapes the maker decides to use and how much of each he employs. Wines of Palette are tasted and approved by a committee of experts set up by the I.N.A.O. They display the same virtues and the same faults as the other wines of Provence. Very enjoyable when drunk in the old city of Aix-en-Provence, they lose most of their sprightly charm and gaiety when shipped.

Côtes de Provence (V.D.Q.S.)

A status granted in 1953 allows the wines that meet the proper standards to be sold as Côtes de Provence with the letters V.D.Q.S. on the label. This is a French secondary quality guarantee. Some of the wines may be sold as Côtes de Provence, Classified Growths (*Cru Classé*); many of these are the more renowned vineyards well established before the 1953 decree. Any vineyard today may be given the right to the status Classified Growth if the owner asks for it and the wine deserves it.

The vineyards of the Côtes de Provence are split into five different areas extending from Marseilles inland to the city of Draguignan and on to the River Var just before Nice. Grenache, Cinsault, Carignan, Mourvèdre, Tibouren, Clairette, Ugni Blanc, and Rolle are the principal grape varieties. The resulting wines are not always of the calibre of the four Provençal wines already discussed, but they are often extraordinarily pleasant. The total annual quantity of V.D.Q.S. wine produced in the departments of the Var and Bouches du Rhône amounts to 13,200,000 Imp. gallons (15,840,000 U.S.). This is approximately 10% of the total production of Provence.

Côtes de Provence wines are becoming known on the markets of the world, thanks to a group of growers who have formed the Syndicat de Défense des Vins des Côtes de Provence (Syndicate for the Protection of the Wines of the Côtes de Provence). One of the many ideas the group is promoting is the use of special bottles designed to catch the eye of the Riviera tourist; now most of the companies connected with the organization are beginning to sell their wines in shapely bottles that mark a departure from tradition. This group of growers owes much of its energy to its president, the Comte de Rohan-Chabot, himself the owner of one of the better Classical Growths, the Château de Saint-Martin.

Provignage

Method of propagating vines.
See CHAPTER EIGHT, p. 32.

Prunelle

A green French liqueur made from the kernels of sloes. It is produced by the firm of Garnier.

Prunellia

A green liqueur made from the kernels of sloes by the French firm of Cusenier.

Puglia

See APULIA; ITALY.

Puisseguin-Saint-Émilion

A commune of Saint-Émilion producing full-bodied red wines.
See SAINT-ÉMILION.

Puligny-Montrachet and Puligny-Montrachet-Côte de Beaune

Burgundy red and white wine. District: Côte de Beaune, France.

Puligny is near the southern end of the Côte de Beaune, in the unofficial sub-district locally called the Côte de Meursault—the slope that takes its name from the nearby commune of Meursault and lays claim to the greatest white wines of the world. The claim is not without justification. The wines which come from the vineyards of Puligny-Montrachet and Chassagne-Montrachet are certainly among the very greatest of the dry white wines of France, and that from one vineyard (the fabulous Montrachet) is considered by many experts as undeniably the world's greatest dry white wine.

In Puligny, everyone makes wine. The mayor himself—a powerful, heavily-set man—is a leading grower and he maintains a cordial but deep-rooted rivalry with his genial counterpart in Chassagne. The village priest is another respected grower, and between Masses he is apt to be out in the vineyard, supervising work or just inspecting his vines. At harvest time, the entire village may be found in the vineyards on the slope behind the town. This slope has a slightly different appearance from the rest of the Côte de Beaune. In Puligny and Chassagne, the rolling hills are bare of trees; areas not planted in vine are covered not in the tangled underbrush found elsewhere along the slopes but in close-cropped, sickly-looking grass punctuated with rock and slabs of calcareous outcropping. The low-lying vines, however, share none of this unprepossessing appearance.

The vineyard of Montrachet is so outstanding that it is a case completely apart from the other wines of Burgundy and is treated separately under its own heading. In addition to Montrachet, Puligny shares another Great Growth with Chassagne—Bâtard-Montrachet—and has other incomparable vineyards that it owns outright. Chevalier-Montrachet and Bienvenues-Bâtard-Montrachet are two of the greatest, and all these vineyards are ranked by the French authorities as Great Growths (*Grands Crus*). In theory, this means that the authorities consider the wines among the thirty-one most magnificent of the Côte d'Or of Burgundy, and in practice, that the wines—when they meet the high minimum requirements—will be labelled simply with the name of the vineyard instead of (as is the case otherwise) with commune name and vineyard name or simply with commune name. (*See all Great Growths as individually entered.*)

Although the Great Growths are generally accepted as being the finest, some of the others are also superb and in the hands of a talented wine-maker may turn out equal to the topmost. One of them is Pucelles, just north of Bienvenues-Bâtard-Montrachet; and above Pucelles is Le Cailleret, adjoining the Chevalier. Cailleret was once called Les Demoiselles, but its position next to the Chevalier was responsible for the change in name—the jokes were too frequent and too bad. On the opposite side of town—bordering on Meursault—is the excellent Les Combettes divided by the road that forms the town line from Charmes in Meursault. Higher up the slope, towards the tiny hamlet of Blagny—which spills over from the upper corner of Meursault to the upper corner of Puligny—is Les Chalumeaux, another exceptional vineyard.

All of Puligny's white wines share approximately the same characteristics. They are eminently dry, not so soft or so luxurious as Meursaults, and are apt to have a full, rich, flowery, or sometimes fruity, bouquet. The green-gold colour takes on different highlights and hues, and the wine has a strength and a masculinity rare in white wines. It leaves the mouth fresh and full of varying sensations and the better the wine is, the more lingering will be the aftertaste.

In addition to white wines, a small amount of red is made—but not generally from grapes grown in the highest ranking vineyards—and it is seldom the equal of the reds made in neighbouring Chassagne, although it often has good body and a distinctive and expressive bouquet.

Throughout the commune there are about 580 acres devoted to vines. Wines that stem from 345 acres within this larger area have the right to add the designation Côte de Beaune to the commune name and are often of superior quality. The best wines, of course, are those which carry simply vineyard name (Great Growths) or vineyard name and commune name (First Growths or *Premiers Crus*). The amount of wine produced in Puligny in 1959 was 50,504 imp. gallons (60,660 U.S.) of white, and 3,954 imp. gallons (4,750 U.S.) of red.

GREAT GROWTHS (*Grands Crus*)

Vineyard	*Acres*
Montrachet (*in part*)	9·9
Bâtard-Montrachet (*in part*)	14·9
Chevalier-Montrachet	17·7
Bienvenues-Bâtard-Montrachet	9·4

FIRST GROWTHS (*Premiers Crus*)

Vineyard	*Acres*
Les Combettes	16·6
Les Pucelles	16·8
Les Chalumeaux	17·3
Le Cailleret	13·4
Les Folatières	8·5
Clavoillens	13·7
Le Champ-Canet	11·4
Le Refert	32·6
Sous le Puits	17·1
Garenne	0·9
Hameau de Blagny	9·8

Pulque

A Mexican spirit obtained from the juice of the cactus known variously as the agave, century plant, American aloe, and mezcal. Pulque is a fermented beverage, usually drunk when it is freshly made, and very popular among the Mexicans.

See TEQUILA.

Punch

1. A hot, strong winter drink made with spirits, fruit and spices and traditionally served in a bowl.

2. Norwegian Punch: a sweetened after-dinner liqueur based on Batavia Arrack and running about 26%–27% alcohol by volume. It is made by the Norwegian State-controlled wine and spirit company, A/S Vinmonopolet.

Puncheon

A large cask of varying capacity, formerly 58 imp. gallons (70 U.S.), but now usually about 83 imp. gallons (100 U.S.). Used in the West Indies for rum.

Punsch (Punch), Swedish

Swedish liquor on a base of rum. It dates from the eighteenth century when Swedish merchants began trading with the East Indies, importing, amongst other things, the rice and sugar cane spirit which is the foundation. Originally the punch was served hot; but since the nineteenth century it has generally been taken cold.

Punt (or Kick)

Indentation in bottle bottoms, originally to reinforce them and to hold the sediment, thus preventing it from spreading throughout the bottle.

Pupitre

French term for a hinged rack for holding sparkling wines neck down while they are prepared for the *dégorgement* or ejection of the deposit accumulated during the second fermentation.

See CHAMPAGNE.

Puttonyos

Hungarian buckets used for measuring quantity of specially selected grapes used in Tokay wine. Thus the collar label on every bottle of Tokaji Aszu will state: 3 Puttonos, 4 Puttonos, etc.—the export agency simplifies the spelling by removing the 'y'.

See TOKAY.

Pyralis

Meal-moth which feeds on the vine.

See CHAPTER EIGHT, p. 38.

Q

Quart

A quarter of a gallon, whether imperial or U.S. A British quart equals 1·136 litres, an American 94·6 centilitres. (In France the term 'quart' is used in restaurants and cafés for a small carafe, reputedly a quarter of a litre; also in Champagne for a small bottle used in bars for Champagne cocktails or for one glass.) The standard American quart equals 32 U.S. fluid ounces; the British quart, 40 British fluid ounces.

Quart de Chaume

Section of Coteaux du Layon, in Anjou.
See ANJOU.

Quarter-Cask

Originally a cask of one-fourth the capacity of a Pipe (*q.v.*). In practice, quarter-casks vary from 25 to 35 imp. gallons (30–42 U.S.).

Quetsch

Blue plum spirit made in Alsace and in Lorraine.
See ALSACE: SPIRITS.

Quincy

Loire Valley white wines. District: Loire Valley, France.

Minor dry white-wine district classed with those of the Loire, although Quincy is drained by the River Cher some thirty miles away. The vineyards are in the communes of Quincy and Brinay. They are planted in a chalky soil, and the wines resemble those of neighbouring Reuilly, of Sancerre and Pouilly-sur-Loire, and, like the output of these towns, come only from Sauvignon grapes. About 550 acres are devoted to vines; output averages an annual 83,000 imp. gallons (100,000 U.S.).

Quinquina

A French aperitif with a base of fortified wine and quinine added to impart a slightly bitter taste.

Quinta

The word means, literally, 'agricultural estate' in Portuguese, and, by extension, has come to mean vineyard.

R

Château Rabaud-Promis

Bordeaux white wine. District: Sauternes, France. Commune: Bommes.

Originally the single estate of Rabaud, one of the oldest Sauternes properties; known to have been an enormously productive vineyard of more than 200 acres by 1660. The present château was built by Victor Louis, the architect of the Bordeaux theatre. The holding, having come into the hands of Monsieur de Sigalas in 1864, was sold in part to Monsieur Promis in 1903. In the 'thirties, the vineyards of Rabaud-Promis and Rabaud-Sigalas were reunited, only to divide again in 1952. When they were constituted as the single vineyard of Rabaud in 1855 the wine was classified a First Growth (*Premier Cru*) of Sauternes, and this classification extends to both Rabaud-Promis and Rabaud-Sigalas.

Characteristics. Not one of the greatest. Sweet, and a certain lack of breed.

Vineyard area: 74 acres.

Average production: 17,500 imp. gallons or about 8,700 cases.

Château Rabaud-Sigalas

Bordeaux white wine. District: Sauternes, France. Commune: Bommes.

Property of the Comte and Comtesse de Lambert—the Comtesse is a descendant of the Sigalas family. *See* Château Rabaud-Promis for an account of the Rabaud estate; originally a single vineyard.

Characteristics. Better than its neighbour; rather distinguished.

Vineyard area: 13 acres.

Average production: 3,000 cases.

Rabigato

One of the principal grape varieties used in making white Ports.

Rablay-sur-Layon

Wine commune with the right to an Appellation Contrôlée in the Coteaux du Layon district of Anjou.

See ANJOU; COTEAUX DU LAYON.

Race

French word for distinction and breeding in a wine.

Racking

The draining or pumping of wine off its lees from the barrel in which it has been maturing into a new, clean one. This process is repeated several times during the ageing of wine.

See CHAPTER NINE, pp. 42, 44.

Rainwater

Originally a trade-mark, now a type denoting a light, dry Madeira.

Ramisco

A grape variety which makes the dune wines of Colares in Portugal.

Rancio

This term is applied in Spain to the nutty flavour in Sherry. In California it applies to the taste brought about by cooking in sweet dessert wines. In somewhat the same sense it is used to describe a pungent taste in Madeiras, Marsalas, Málagas, and others. In France the adjective is applied particularly to the characteristic taste of the sweet dessert wines of Banyuls when they are well aged, and also to the wine of Château-Chalon.

Raspail

French herb liqueur, yellow in colour, said to be made from a formula devised by François Vincent Raspail in 1847.

Ratafia

It is claimed that the name was applied to any liqueur drunk at the ratification of a treaty or agreement. It now applies to sweetened aperitifs made from wines. Examples: Ratafia de Bourgogne; Ratafia de Champagne.

Rauchbier

In Germany literally 'smoke beer'—a beer made there from smoked malt.

Rauenthaler

The different Rauenthalers such as Langenstück and others taken together are probably the greatest of the German Rheingaus and certainly, with the exception of Schloss Johannisberg, command the highest prices. Practically no inferior wine is made in this district, which is not always true of the other great Rhine sections.

See RHEINGAU.

Château Rausan-Ségla

Bordeaux red wine. District: Haut-Médoc, France. Commune: Margaux.

Adjoining Rauzan-Gassies, with which it originally formed a single vineyard, Rausan-Ségla lies across the Médoc vineyard road from Château

Margaux and Château Palmer, on the south side of the village of Margaux. It is classed a Second Growth (*Second Cru*) in the Classification of 1855.

Acquired by Pierre des Mesures de Rausan in 1661, it remained in the Rausan family for two hundred years. Thomas Jefferson wrote: '. . .Rozan-Margau, which is made by Madame de Rozan . . . this is what I import for myself . . .'. In addition to the vineyard carrying their name, the Rausans—or Rozans—for a time hired Château Margaux and Château Latour, also making those wines. In 1866, Rausan-Ségla was sold to the maternal grandfather of the Cruse family, Bordeaux wine merchants, who sold it again in 1956 to Monsieur de Mesnon, who in 1962 resold it to British Holt group, the owners of Eschenauer, the Bordeaux wine shippers.

Characteristics. Very fine, perfumed, and perhaps slightly fuller than the other Margaux wines. The best of them usually require a good deal of ageing. If the wines have a fault, it is that they are not as consistent as they might be.

Vineyard area: 75 acres.

Average production: 10,000 cases.

Château Rauzan-Gassies

Bordeaux red wine. District: Haut-Médoc, France. Commune: Margaux.

Once a single vineyard with Rausan-Ségla, now adjoining it on the south of Margaux, Rauzan-Gassies was already well known in 1530. Of the many proprietors over more than four centuries, none could have been more eccentric than a Chevalier de Rauzan who, when he could not get the price he expected for his wines, put them aboard ship and sailed to London. Proclaiming that he was going to sell his wines himself from the deck of the boat, he awaited customers. Still not getting his price, he announced that he would pour one barrel into the Thames each day until he got a better offer—or had no more wine. The story goes that by the third day all London was crowding to watch this unheard-of performance; and the fame of it spread so that he was soon offered a high price for every barrel left aboard.

The vineyard is now owned by Monsieur Paul Quié, owner also of Château Croizet-Bages. Quié lives in Paris and the wines were tended by the same manager who took care of Château Marquis de Terme. Like the latter growth, the vineyard is excellently kept, but perhaps the vines are a little forced. Rauzan-Gassies is a Second Growth (*Second Cru*) in the Classification of 1855. Today critics feel that the character of the wine is not equal to the quality of the vineyard as it is at present being cultivated. Hence prices paid on the Bordeaux market make Rauzan-Gassies one of the cheapest Second Growths (*Seconds Crus*), and its reputation has fallen accordingly.

Characteristics. In the past decade, many Bordeaux critics have remarked that Rauzan-Gassies has slipped considerably in quality. Some vintages have even been marked by an excess of volatile acidity.

Vineyard area: 52 acres.

Average production: 8,000 cases.

Ravat

A French hybridizer whose greatest achievement was probably the vine Ravat 262, giving, in the United States, a light red wine akin to a Beaujolais. Ravat 6 is his best white-wine grape, but is of questionable value in the United States because of its susceptibility to cold winters.

Château de Rayne-Vigneau

Bordeaux white wine. District: Sauternes, France. Commune: Bommes.

Classified a First Growth (*Premier Cru*) of Sauternes in 1855. The vines grow in a large vineyard sloping away from the dark turreted château. The wine is not the only treasure produced by the soil. For some reason which experts have never solved, in this patch of earth alone in the whole region, precious and semi-precious stones appear. Sapphires, opals, jasper, onyx, and topaz have been found, and are collected in the museums of France and many other countries.

Characteristics. This potentially great vineyard is capable of improvement.

Vineyard area: 120 acres.

Average production: 7,700 cases.

Martin Ray Vineyards

Santa Clara, California, U.S.A.

The Martin Ray Vineyards are advantageously planted on the eastern and southern slopes of Mount Eden, rising over 2,000 ft. above the Saratoga foothills in California. On the site overlooking the Santa Clara Valley, Martin Ray skilfully attends to the production of some of the finest and certainly the most expensive of Californian wines.

In 1936 he purchased the Paul Masson Vineyards and winery, and had great success with his wines; but in 1943 he sold those vineyards and purchased his present property, near by but on higher ground.

The hillside vineyards, with excellent exposure and an underground drainage system, are planted with three varieties: Pinot Noir, Cabernet Sauvignon, and Pinot Chardonnay. Martin Ray is a dynamic and very much discussed personality, who follows European traditions of viniculture. His excellent varietal wines are labelled by vintage years, and any not up to his high standard are sold in bulk. Martin Ray specializes in champagne-type and table wines, which are all marketed in champagne bottles with champagne corks for better ageing. The wines are often more expensive than the French importations of Bordeaux and Burgundy.

See AMERICA; CALIFORNIA AND THE WEST.

Rebate Brandy

South African trade term for brandy made under fairly rigid conditions imposed by the Government and aged at least three years in wood. The measure was initiated to encourage distillers to increase brandy quality, the government giving a tax rebate of 4*s.* 6*d.* ($0.63) per bottle on any brandy which contains at least 25% of 'rebate'. Lesser and harsher spirits, on the other hand, are very heavily taxed.

Récolte

French for wine harvest. It may be either the harvesting or the crop, but generally *récolte* is used to refer to the crop, and *vendange* to the harvest.

Rectification, or Rectifying, of Spirits

In distillation (the object of which is to separate or purify substances, making use of the differences in their volatility), the components of a mixture are vaporized in order of their boiling points, so that one part can be drawn off from another. If the substance is already purified, or of constant composition (i.e. all components with equal boiling points), then the operation is rectification. A rectified spirit is one which has undergone purification by distillation at a licensed rectifier's premises.

The definition of rectification given by J. H. Perry in *The Engineers' Handbook* (3rd ed.) is as follows:

> *Rectification* is a distillation carried out in such a way that the vapour rising from a still comes in contact with a condensed portion of vapour previously evolved from the same still. A transfer of material and an interchange of heat result from this contact, thereby securing a greater enrichment of the vapour in the more volatile components than could be secured with a single distillation operation using the same amount of heat. The condensed vapours, returned to accomplish this object, are termed *reflux*.
>
> The generally used devices, in which vapours from a still on their way to a condenser can flow countercurrently to a portion of the condensate returned as reflux, are called *rectifying columns* or *towers*.

See CHAPTER TEN, pp. 56–7; GIN.

Rehoboam

An outsize bottle sometimes used for Champagne. It holds the equivalent of six normal bottles.

Reims

This ancient French cathedral city is also one of the principal centres of the Champagne trade—the other is Épernay.

See CHAMPAGNE.

Remuage

Remuage (moving around) is a term used in the process of making Champagne. Bottles placed in specially built racks are turned or shaken a little every day for about four months before they are shipped, so that the sediment may move down towards the cork. Finally, sediment and cork will be removed in one skilful movement in the process of *dégorgement*.

See CHAMPAGNE.

Repeal

To Americans, Repeal refers to 5 December 1933, when the 21st Amendment to the Constitution of the United States was passed, repealing the 18th (Prohibition) Amendment and allowing alcoholic beverages once again to be sold legally in the United States.

See AMERICA.

Reputed Pint

British half-bottle; there are twelve to the imperial gallon (1·2009 U.S.).

Reputed Quart

British regular bottle for wines and spirits; one-sixth of an imperial gallon, or about 75 centilitres.

Reserva

Indication on Rioja (Spain) wine labels that the wine has been aged; sometimes indicates quality, sometimes enfeeblement.

See RIOJA.

Retsina

Greek wine, ordinary white and rosé, which has been treated with pine resin. This means a considerable quantity of the wine consumed in Greece. In the southern and central parts of the country almost everyone—especially among the peasants—prefers his wine with this piny, resinous taste.

See GREEK WINES.

Reuilly

White, rosé, and red wines. District: Loire Valley, France.

Small, little-known Loire wine district lying along the Arnon, a tributary of the River Cher, and producing a small quantity of dry white wine from Sauvignon grapes. Some vines giving grapes for red and rosé wines are also grown, but their output does not receive an Appellation Contrôlée. About 250 acres of Sauvignon produce about 16,600 imp. gallons (20,000 U.S.) of Reuilly annually, the wine resembling that of Sancerre and Pouilly-sur-Loire—although it is usually more acid, and lighter.

Réunion Island

Rum-making island in the Indian Ocean, formerly a French colony.

See RUM, FRENCH.

Rhein

German spelling of Rhine.

See PALATINATE; RHEINGAU; RHEINHESSEN; RHINE—MIDDLE-RHINE.

Rheingau

Mostly white and a few red wines. District: German Rhineland.

The Rheingau wines are, if a choice must be made, the best in Germany when they are at their finest. As such they become, with their peers of the Moselle, and the great white Burgundies, the finest white wines in the world for their variety in taste characteristics.

In an average or poor year, the lower Rheingau wines from the Rüdesheim district and the Hochheimers in the upper Rheingau region will be better than the wines from the greater areas, which will be too light; but in the big years, the famous Spätlese and Trockenbeerenauslese Riesling wines from the strip of the Rhine front between Eltville and Winkel will be incomparable. Wonderful as the loveliest Moselles may be, they will never quite touch the character and breed of the greatest Rheingaus. A few white Burgundies have the character and strength to challenge the dry Rheingaus and it can be argued that in one sense such a wine as Château d'Yquem in Sauternes is their superior in sweet wines, for, owing to the milder climate in the Bordeaux district, the productivity, comparable in quality, is infinitely greater in quantity. Yet the long-lived, late-gathered Rheingau great growths are true kings in the royalty of wines. Rich and with exquisite breed after a sunny summer and a hazy autumn, blessed with the river mist the Rheingau peasants call the 'Wine-Maker', they will last for thirty or forty years.

Wine is the only important product from Eltville to Rüdesheim and Assmannshausen, the town of red wines a little farther around the river bend where the water races. Because of this, everyone is dependent on the weather as it bears on the grape, and the area has its crises. Manuring is standard procedure in German vineyards, and a further problem of the Rheingau is that, unlike most German growers, these have too little domestic husbandry to provide their own dung, which must therefore be bought—an expensive matter. The slopes facing due south are guarded from the north wind by the heavily-treed ridge of the Taunus hills, and further protected because the river bends enough to cut off most of the wind from east or west. The vineyards are broken and steep, rolling in green waves parallel to the river. 'If the plough can go there, the vine should not,' is a Rheingau proverb, and in a rough way it is true. The steepness, the southern exposure, and the sheltered slopes make possible the production of the late-gathered wines, the grapes sometimes being left on the vines until the noble rot of the *Botrytis* has set in, sometimes as late as December. The Rhine itself, at its widest at the Rheingau (two-thirds of a mile), serves to warm the vines by reflecting back the sun-rays during the day, thus doubling their effectiveness; and by holding the day's warmth in the night, causing a greater equality of day and night temperature, very beneficial to the vine. In the early spring, and particularly in the late autumn when the grape must hang long on the vine, through the critical days of falling temperature, the soft Rhine mist keeps off the frost.

The Rheingau extends along the north bank of the river from a little below Wiesbaden to Lorchhausen, a short distance downriver from Assmannshausen. Viticulturally, it also includes Hochheim, on the other side of Wiesbaden and on the River Main, where the wines are of the same type. It is Hochheim which gives the name Hock, used properly in England for all Rheingau wines and loosely for all wines of the Rhine area.

The total planted area is a little less than 6,000 acres, a very small piece of the vineyard area of the world considering its reputation. A little red wine is grown at Niederwalluf, Hattenheim, and much more at Assmannshausen, only the latter of which merits any attention; but the Rheingau is a kingdom of white wines—and a kingdom of the Riesling grape, also. In other Rhine districts, the Riesling grows only in the finest plots, always outstripped numerically by the Sylvaner variety; but in the Rheingau, 72% of all the vine is Riesling, 15% Sylvaner, and 8% Müller-Thurgau, which is a crossing of the Sylvaner and Riesling; while the red wines of Assmannshausen come from the Spätburgunder Pinot Noir variety, brought a long time ago from France. The Riesling grape of the Rheingau has a very small, very aromatic, late-ripening berry with a tough hide. It is this tough skin which makes the Riesling chief of all Rheingau varieties in resistance to the late-autumn cold; and it is the final penetration of the thick skin by the noble rot *Botrytis* which causes the intense sugaring and mysterious chemical changes of the great peak wines.

Out of 2,820 Rheingau growers, well over one thousand own less than an acre of vineyard each; another thousand own between one and five acres; only 220 growers own more than five acres. These figures, however, are deceptive if taken to mean that there are no large estates in the Rheingau. There are. The great owners, few though they may be, hold a fair proportion of the whole acreage, and a very much higher proportion of the best parts. These large holdings are nowadays suffering severely from labour shortage. The big Opel automobile plant, the chemical industries in Ludwigshafen, Frankfurt, and Mainz (the Rhine–Main triangle), the jobs in Wiesbaden, siphon off the Rheingau working force; and in Germany, as elsewhere, the higher the standard of living rises, the fewer land-workers there are. In spite of the difficulties of large ownership, since about 1935 the tendency has been to concentrate holdings by exchanges. Areas parcelled up and divided by inheritance, and by the practice of holding small bits of vineyard in various sections, as a protection against losses from frost or hail (which may be extremely localized) are gradually being consolidated.

At the great vineyard of Schloss Johannisberg above the village of Geisenheim, it is the custom to shoot off a gun at the completion of the harvesting of each 100 barrels. In days past a single shot would be heard in the crisp autumn, but today there will be two or three; the production has been doubled. Taking an average across the whole Rheingau, production has been 100% to 150% more per vineyard acre since the turn of the century. In 1900 an average of 25 imp. gallons (30 U.S.) was obtained per acre; today, 60–90 imp. gallons (70–110 U.S.). This striking change, achieved by improved methods of fertilizing and spraying, by greater knowledge of vine selection and fighting of vine disease, has been a necessary means of combating the rising cost of labour and the generally uncertain conditions of a single-crop area so entirely dependent on the weather. Another factor is that the growers transplant grafts of Riesling and unite them with phylloxera-resistant wild vines. Yet the quantity and quality of the grapes is higher.

Has the quality of the wine been hurt? Recent experiments conducted by Professor Birk of the Viticultural School and Research Station in Geisenheim, the finest wine school in Germany, have established that certain strains of the Riesling can be made to yield three to four times more in quantity without loss of quality. (This is a new development, going counter to the age-old rule that in viticulture quantity can only be obtained at the expense of quality.) However, experience in the Rheingau seems to prove that close-pruning of the vine—the method of ensuring high quality in, for example, the Bordeaux region of France—causes the Riesling to cast off its flower (the eventual grape cluster) in order to give all its strength to the development of the leaf. When it is allowed to grow taller, the vine flowers fully and develops well. Despite the general German practice of growing the vine tall, and the highly-developed methods at Geisenheim in the Rheingau by the State Domain and by other leaders, some connoisseurs maintain that Rheingau wines are falling off as a result of the stepping up of quantity. Perhaps the real truth is that this must be done if economically the Rheingau wines are to survive at all. In fact, in the last decade or so, a move has been made to plant the rows wider apart, following the method of Lenz Moser of Austria, to permit machine cultivation and so to reduce labour. The vines must then be trained even higher if the level of quantity production is to be maintained.

Three different types or classes of names appear on Rheingau wine labels. (1) By far the greatest number identify the wine by the vineyard name, preceded by the town or village name: as Hattenheimer Nussbrunnen from Hattenheim; Rauenthaler Herberg from Rauenthal, etc. (2) Markobrunn and Steinberger usually stand alone, although they may occasionally be preceded by the town or village name: Hattenheimer Steinberg; Erbacher Markobrunn. (The alternative Marcobrunner will be found on the labels of two estates, Frh. Langwerth von Simmern and Graf Schönborn, which own the best parts of the district. Erbacher Marcobrunn is used by Schloss Reinhartshausen Prinz

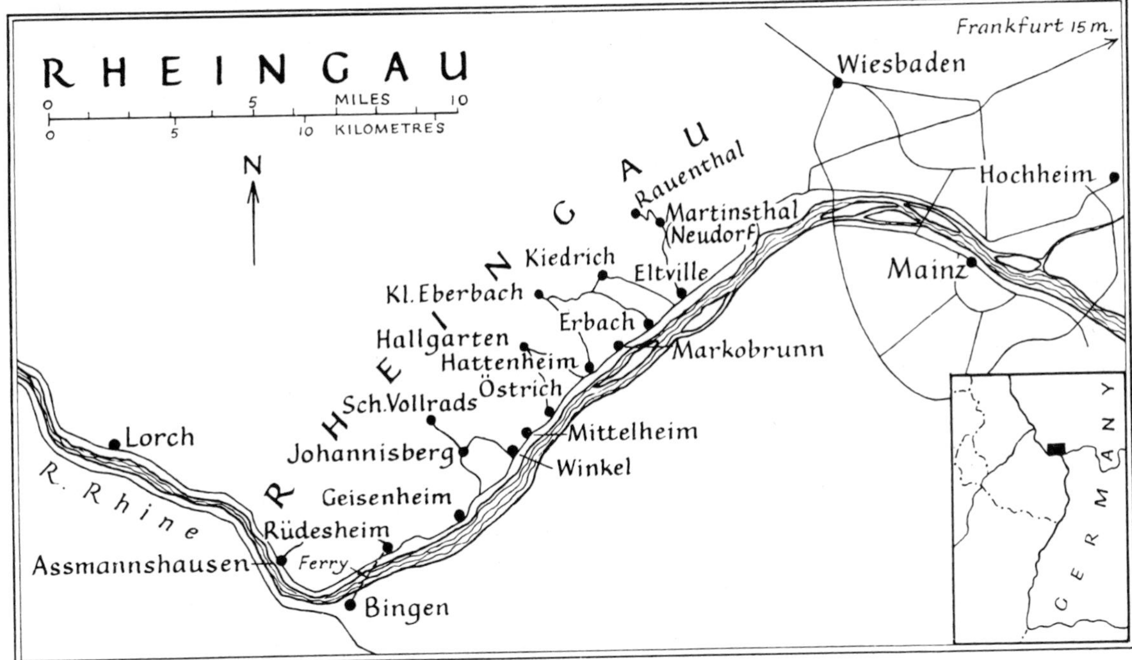

Friedrich von Preussen, State Domain, von Oetinger and Kohlhaas.) (3) Four of the great wines are the Schloss wines (Schloss means castle). They are Schloss Johannisberg, Schloss Vollrads, Schloss Reinhartshausen, and, very recently, Schloss Eltz.

The huge number of vineyard names plagues the Rheingau as it does other German districts, making it impossible for anyone but a professional to know what is actually in a good many bottles simply from the label; but, fortunately, there is now a pronounced trend to unify small parcels under one name when the differences are not great. The German wine laws make it possible for the grower to be a little evasive as to just what is in his bottle. If a wine is a blend from adjoining vineyards of similar type and quality, it is perfectly legal to call it by the place-name of either vineyard. Moreover, a wine can take the place-name of a vineyard if 66% of what is actually in the bottle comes from that vineyard, the rest coming from any other vineyard or vineyards of the same type, quality and ownership which may be anywhere within the town area.

The Important Rheingau Vineyards

There are a little over two dozen Rheingau wine *Gemarkungen* or towns and villages, of which a scant dozen are in the top class. Many experts feel the best towns and villages, in terms of quality in the great years, run from east to west and are: *First,* best vineyards of Rauenthal. *Second,* best vineyards of Erbach-Hattenheim-Hallgarten. *Third,* best vineyards of Johannisberg, with Schloss Vollrads and Winkler Hasensprung, in Winkel. *Fourth,* best vineyards of Rüdesheim. The latter rise in medium years to the top of the list in relation to the other vineyards.

Assmannshausen

Assmannshausen is often said to produce the best red wine in Germany, although others favour Ingelheimer, from farther upstream on the other side of the Rhine. No red wine of Germany is outstanding, particularly if measured against German white wine or French red wine. The Rhine is extremely swift at Assmannshausen and as you stand in the steep vineyards you see the river steamers form in line, cabled together, for the stubby tug to pull them around the bend to Rüdesheim. When a stiff wind blows upriver through the narrows, all the flags fly forward from the sterns as if the boats were backing up. The red-wine vine growing in the characteristic bluish-red shale is the Spätburgunder, so called because it was brought from Burgundy by the Cistercian monks in the twelfth century. The wine it makes is mild and velvety, with a slight undertaste of almonds—something like a middling Burgundy but without any of its powerful characteristic aroma. The same vine, called Pinot Noir in France, produces the red Burgundies today. During the centuries, the Spätburgunder has grown poorer in quality in its transplanted home and the Assmannshausen vineyards had shrunk considerably by the time of the First World War. Since then, the State Domain, now holder of 80% of the total acreage, has developed the vineyards intensively and they are again improving.

In the years when the wines do not come up to standard, the State Domain sells them to be made into Sekt (sparkling wine). A peculiar wine of Assmannshausen bears the jaw-breaking name, Rotweiss Edelbeerenauslese, because its colour is between white and rosé. Assmannshausen is unique in being a wine at once sweet and red and nearly great —but in the last respect, it never quite succeeds.

Vineyard area: 140 acres: 90 acres red; 50 acres white.

Grape varieties: Spätburgunder, Sylvaner, Riesling.

Most important vineyard: Höllenberg (very early records show this vineyard was already in cultivation in 1108).

Eltville

The Eltville wines tend to be better in years when the more important sections fall off. In 1953, for example, these were among the best in the Rheingau, because the finer vineyards had too much sun, causing a loss of freshness. The name of the village on the Rhine bank is of Roman origin: *alta villa.* Until the end of the fifteenth century it was the summer seat of the Prince-Electors of Mainz, and ruins and palaces of the period still stand. Almost adjoining on the river bank are the picturesque and highly important wine estates of Graf Eltz and Frh. Langwerth von Simmern.

Vineyard area: 335 acres white.

Grape varieties: Riesling, Sylvaner, Müller-Thurgau.

Most important vineyards: Taubenberg (near Steinmächer—a better wine and with more character than Steinmächer); Sonnenberg (lively and elegant).

Very important vineyards: Langenstück (generally more full-bodied than Sonnenberg, grown on heavy loam); Kalbspflicht (resembles Langenstück, a full, heavy wine); Klümbchen (exclusive holding of Schloss Eltz); Mönchhanach (light, somewhat resembles lesser Sonnenbergs); Sandgrub (on border of Kiedrich and better part is in Kiedrich); Steinmächer (good location, near Rauenthalerberg); Bunken is a section of the Sonnenberg now generally coming to be called Sonnenberg; Grimmen the same. Freienborn, largely owned by Langwerth von Simmern, is a large vineyard but not of first quality.

Erbach

Generally full-bodied wines of masculine character, of which the best and the most famous is Markobrunn.

Markobrunn

Sometimes written Marcobrunn, sometimes Markobrunn (*see* p. 345), the wine is one of the greatest and best-known Rheingaus. It does not reach the superb elegance of a top Rauenthaler but it has more body and is characterized by a spicy, lively quality. It was preferred to all other Rheingaus by Thomas Jefferson on his Rhine journey in 1788. The name derives from an ancient spring (*Brunnen* means spring or well) which may still be seen, with a neglected wall bearing the name Markobrunnen, the spring of Saint Mark. The fact that this well and the famous vineyard lie on the boundary-line of Erbach and Hattenheim has given rise to a story legendary along the Rhine. For generations the two villages contested the right to claim the site as theirs. Finally, ancient records were unearthed which proved that the well was on the Erbach side of the communal boundary. Great was the rejoicing among the Erbachers. But on the fourth or fifth morning they fell silent and became very glum. During the night some wit from Hattenheim had gone to the well and scrawled in huge letters:

So ist es recht und
So soll es sein,
Nach Erbach das Wasser,
Nach Hattenheim den Wein.
(All is right, all is fine,
Now Erbach has the water,
But Hattenheim has the wine.)

Perhaps the best Markobrunn is made by Graf von Schönborn (Graf von Schönborn-Wiesentheid'sches Rentamt), and by Frh. Langwerth von Simmern, who between them own the heart of the vineyard, which is first both in quality and quantity. Other owners of excellent parcels are Schloss Reinhartshausen, State Domain, Frh. von Oetinger, and a little owner named Kohlhaas who has three rows of vines.

Vineyard area: 260 acres, white wine.

Grape variety: Riesling.

Most important vineyards: Markobrunn (see above). Hohenrain (mainly owned by Schloss Reinhartshausen; heavy, full-bodied wines). Siegelsberg, situated just above Markobrunn (these wines, usually quite full-bodied, are owned mainly by State Domain and Schloss Reinhartshausen).

Other vineyards: Bachhell, Brühl (these strong, powerful wines, mainly owned by Schloss Reinhartshausen and von Oetinger, are not widely known abroad but are among the better-known growths within Germany). Gemark. Herrenberg. Michelmark (good medium-class wines). Honigberg (lies just below Kloster Eberbach and is the highest-lying site in Erbach, produces medium-quality wines). Rheinhell (exclusive holding of Schloss Reinhartshausen). Seelgass (very ordinary wines). Steinmorgen (a good section but much divided up among numerous owners). Steinchen (good full-bodied wines). Kränzchen is the name given to blended wines of Erbach.

Geisenheim

The district, lying between Rüdesheim and Johannisberg, is not as well known as the wines deserve. There are some famous domain holdings besides that of Graf von Schönborn, there are the estates of Frh. von Zwierlein Erben, of Erbslöh'sches Weingut, of Staatl. Lehr- und Forschungsanstalt, and some smaller growers, such as Philipp Graf, A. Vollmer and Theo Soherr. It is these estates which by concerted promotion have made the vineyard names now famous throughout the Rheingau. The castle of one of the important wine growers, Graf von Schönborn, stands in the town and has a considerable historical importance of its own. Inside it, in 1648, an ancestor of the present count drafted the treaty which ended the Thirty Years War. Opening out of a small back street in the town are the spacious grounds of the Geisenheim Viticultural School, which is the highest-ranking viticultural and vinicultural institute in Germany. In the ugly red brick buildings in the parklike grounds, in the greenhouses, vineyards, experimental nurseries, laboratories, and classrooms, techniques have been worked out which fundamentally influence vine growing and wine-making in Germany. The Rheingau growers send in samples for study, analysis, and suggestions as to how to improve the wines; and the school adjudicates court trials based on wine fraud. Students must have had four years of practical experience before they can enter the school. One of the recent Geisenheim projects has been the attempt to stamp out fraudulent sugaring of wine, always the main problem in northerly vineyards. Radioactive sugar is put into wine and then traced with a geiger counter. By this method it is possible to see how the added sugar acts in contrast to the natural sugar; which ferments first, which remains longer, and so on. Future wines will be measured against the graphs obtained, and it will be possible to see if they have been doctored.

Vineyard area: 190 acres, white wine.

Grape varieties: Riesling, Sylvaner, Müller-Thurgau.

Most important vineyards: Rothenberg (a very full-bodied rich wine), Kläuserweg, Morschberg.

Very important vineyards: Decker, Lickerstein, Mauerchen, Katzenloch, Kirchgrube.

Other vineyards: Altbaum, Backenacker, Fuchsberg, Hoher Rech, Kapellengarten, Kosackenberg, Rosengarten, Schlossgarten, Steinacker.

Hallgarten

Some important wines and many small wines. The plantations are high-lying, just opposite the great Steinberg vineyard. At the time of the Boer War three co-operative associations were formed. The most flourishing was nicknamed 'The English'; the poorer group called itself 'The Boers'. Later on a third was added, with the name of 'The Germans'; and finally, a fourth co-operative, 'The Boxers' was installed at the time of the Boxer Rebellion. These association names have gradually become official, and now may even appear on labels, e.g.: *Buren*, meaning Boers. The best and largest individual growers are Prinz von Löwenstein and Karl Franz Engelmann.

Vineyard area: 375 acres, white wine.

Grape varieties: Riesling, Sylvaner.

Important vineyards: Deutelsberg (great wines are made by this vineyard, actually in Hattenheim, although the wines are usually known as Hallgartener). Schönhell (in big years this is among the best in the Rheingau), Hendelberg (full-bodied wine, very sweet in the big years).

Other vineyards: Jungfer, Kirschenacker, Mehrhölzchen, Rosengarten, Würzgarten.

Small vineyards: Biegels, Deez, Egersberg, Geyersberg, Neufeld, Reuscherberg, Sandgrub.

Hattenheim

The home of great wines—Steinberger, Hattenheimer Nussbrunnen, Hattenheimer Wisselbrunnen, and Hattenheimer Mannberg, owned mainly by Frh. Langwerth von Simmern and in part by the State Domain. The wines are very similar to the Markobrunner. The twisted Gothic village lies a little back from the Rhine, with the vineyards above. In the old-world *Weinstuben*, or on a hotel terrace on a sparkling day, the wonderful wines taste better than they do anywhere else. The biggest of them are typically great Rheingaus.

Vineyard area: 406 acres white.

Grape varieties: Riesling, Sylvaner, Müller-Thurgau.

Kloster Eberbach and *Steinberg*

Steinberg, a few miles out of Hattenheim, is associated with that town, but does not bear its name. Steinberger is among the best Rheingau wines in a great year. The variation in quality from year to year is enormous, and a *Halbstück* (equivalent to 68 cases) may reach 30,000 German marks in a great year and sell for only 800 marks in a small one. 300 bottles of Steinberger Trockenbeerenauslese 1921 were sold on the spot for 172 marks a bottle and to the consumer for between 300 and 380 marks each. The vineyard, a long narrow strip extending up a steepish rise, lies sixty or seventy yards west of Kloster Eberbach, where all Steinberger is vintaged and stored (there is no Kloster Eberbach wine as such). Along the wall higher up are rows producing a superior wine known as Steinberger Mauerwein. The monastery, nearly a thousand years old, was first established by Augustinian monks; with the change-over to the Cistercians, the first of this order in Germany, the real success began. By 1135 they were planting vines in the tract which is today the Steinberg. With their motto 'By Cross and Plough', with the aim of opening up areas to farming and viticulture, and with their knowledge of wine from Burgundy, it is not surprising that they cut away the forest, put in vines, and prospered. By the thirteenth century, their wine fleets were sailing the Rhine to Cologne and in its greatest day Kloster Eberbach held 25,000 acres in the Rheingau and Rheinhessen. Today, the vast church built between 1150 and 1200 is a huge empty shell, the rows of mediæval screw wine presses gather dust, and interest has shifted to the ultra-modern wine-making plant, one of the finest in Germany. (The fourteen giant wooden wine presses of the fifteenth, sixteenth, seventeenth, and eighteenth centuries, in the chamber of the Lay Brothers, were in use until 1925.) At different times a lunatic asylum, a prison, and (during the First World War) a military hospital, Kloster Eberbach is now State-owned, making not only Steinberger but also State Domain wines such as Rüdesheimer Markobrunn and the State Domain Hattenheimers. The Steinberg vineyard itself is completely State-owned. In 1803 the property was secularized by Napoleon; in 1806 it fell into the hands of the Duke of Nassau; in 1866 it was taken over by the Prussian State, and in 1945 by the Hessian State. The private cellar of the Duke of Nassau may still be seen. It was this special 'Kabinett' of his that originated the term *Kabinettwein* (the spelling 'Cabinet' is now more general).

Area: The total area of the Steinberg vineyard is 70 acres. It produces about 20,000–22,000 cases in an average year, of which 25% is sold direct and 75% auctioned, always at Kloster Eberbach.

Grape variety: Riesling.

Vineyards: Steinberg, Mannberg (owned by Langwerth von Simmern), Nussbrunnen (a typically great Rheingau), Wisselbrunnen (a typically great Rheingau). Deutelsberg (lies in Hattenheim but usually sold as Hallgartener—see Hallgarten). Boxberg (poorest part of Hattenheim). Engelmannsberg (big, powerful, masculine wines, 95% State Domain). Hassel and Hinterhaus (adjoining and very similar, soft wines). Klosterberg (small wines). Pfaffenberg (excellent and extremely dry, exclusive holding of Graf von Schönborn). Schützenhaus (among the better Hattenheimers, *spritzig* or fresh, medium-bodied). Stabel (may still be encountered but is now part of Nussbrunnen). Willborn (resembles Schützenhaus). Heiligenberg (good medium quality).

Hochheim

The wines are fruity, mellow, well balanced, with a characteristic taste derived from the soil that varies almost from parcel to parcel. In some of the vineyards there is an unmistakable smoky characteristic reminiscent of certain Moselles. While the Hochheim wines, situated eastward on the Main and not on the Rhine, share something with the Rheingaus, Rheinhessen, and Franconian wines, they are invariably classed with the Rheingaus. The name Hock from Hochheim has become the English name for all Rheingau and often all Rhine wines. The State Domain, Aschrott, Schönborn, and Werner are the largest growers and have the best parcels.

Vineyard area: 390 acres, white wine.

Grape variety: Riesling.

Vineyards: Domdechaney (best vineyard—fruity, strong, full-bodied wines). Kirchenstück (lighter than Domdechaney, elegant). Rauchloch (means 'smoke-hole', and, as the name indicates, distinctly smoky taste in many years). Stein, Bettelmann, Daubhaus, Gehitz, Hölle, Kohlkaut, Neuberg, Sommerheil, Stielweg. Viktoriaberg (a light, elegant wine from pure sand soil, named after Queen Victoria whose favourite it was). Wandkaut, Weid, Weisserd.

Johannisberg (*Schloss Johannisberg*)

The town is outstripped by the name of its great vineyard Schloss Johannisberg. To the village of that name belong 208 acres of the big vineyard—and of this area, Schloss Johannisberg owns 74 acres. Some Rheingau brokers and growers considered it to be consistently one of the best of the Rheingaus, even if its greatness did not justify its high price, highest on the Rheingau and often twice that of wines which almost equal it. Today, however, many German buyers feel that the neighbouring vineyards are producing better wines. The huge block-form Schloss up on the hill-top above the countless rows of symmetrical vines is unquestionably the most imposing sight on the right bank of the Rhine. Originally called the Mons Episcopi, the hill was given to the Benedictine monks by the Archbishop of Mainz at the end of the eleventh century. After the secularization decreed by Napoleon in 1803, the vineyard was in turn the property of the Prince of Orange, of Napoleon, and the Emperor of Austria—who gave it to Metternich in 1816, for services rendered at the Congress of Vienna, and with the Metternich family it remains today. The castle was partially destroyed by bombs during the Second World War, but it has now been rebuilt.

The estate-bottled (*Originalabfüllung*) Schloss Johannisberg is divided into three grades of quality and price by label and seal in red, green, or pink—red being lowest and pink highest. (Similar schemes have long been used by other growers.) Red seal Originalabfüllung Schloss Johannisberg is the most ordinary grade of the wine; green seal Originalabfüllung includes Spätlese; pink seal includes Auslese, Beerenauslese, and Trockenbeerenauslese. The wine which is not considered up to standard is made into Sekt, the German word for sparkling wine, and sold as Schloss Johannisberger Cabinet-Sekt Fürst Metternich.

Higher on the scale of quality than the Originalabfüllung are the Cabinet Wines, and these also are graded in price and quality by label and capsule colour. For bottles of the years up to 1953 the scale, from lowest to highest quality, is the following: yellow, orange, violet, white, lilac, sky-blue, dark-blue, gold-blue, gold. This is now simplified, and for bottles beginning with the 1953s the colour designations are: orange label and capsule; white label and capsule (better wines); sky-blue label and capsule (next higher grade); gold label and capsule (Beerenauslesen and Trockenbeerenauslesen). (In lesser years there will be none of the highest grades of the wines; therefore, there are not pink seal Originalabfüllung or gold label Cabinets for every vintage. In 1954 no Cabinet or Originalabfüllung Schloss Johannisberger was made in any grade.)

The only other important owner in the village of Johannisberg was the von Mumm family of French Champagne fame, which has since sold the property to the German baking-powder king Oetker. But the estate still bears the name Von Mumm'sche Domäne.

Other vineyards: Erntebringer, Hansenberg, Hölle, Kerzenstück, Vogelsang, Klaus, Kahlenberg, and Goldatzel.

Kiedrich

The vineyards lie high up at the foot of the Taunus Mountains behind Erbach. Some of the wines have undoubted distinction and character.

Vineyard area: 230 acres, white wine.

Grape varieties: Riesling, Sylvaner, Müller-Thurgau.

Important vineyards: Gräfenberg, in good years unquestionably one of the best Rheingaus. Sandgrub (or Sandgrube), a vineyard partly in Eltville but the Kiedrich portion is the better. Wasserrose (or Wasserros).

Other vineyards: Heiligenstock (fair quality in some years). Klosterberg (small). Langenberg (a little better than Klosterberg). Turmberg. Weiersberg.

Lorch

The largest quantity producer of the Rheingau, which only in the best years comes up to the average in quality. A characteristic *goût de terroir* is much liked by some people, however. Count Kanitz has the largest holdings and produces far and away the best wines.

Vineyard area: 560 acres, white wine.

Grape varieties: Riesling, Sylvaner.

Vineyards: Bodenthal (best and largest). Honigberg. Krone. Pfaffenwies.

Martinsthal

Until twenty years ago this was called Neudorf. The wines are rarely, if ever, exported.

Vineyard area: 90 acres, white wine.

Grape varieties: Riesling, Sylvaner.

Vineyards: Geisberg. Langenberg. Sand.

Mittelheim

Average quality wines, adjoins Johannisberg on the east.

Vineyard area: 300 acres, white wine.

Grape varieties: Riesling, Sylvaner, Müller-Thurgau.

Vineyards: Edelmann (best). Gottestal. Honigberg. Magdalenenacker. Oberberg.

Neudorf

Since 1935 this has been called Martinsthal—*see* above.

Östrich

The wines both here and in adjoining Mittelheim are disappointing in comparison with their great neighbours.

Vineyard area: 500 acres, white wine.

Grape varieties: Riesling, Sylvaner, Müller-Thurgau.

Important vineyards: Eiserberg is the best vineyard, though Lenchen is better-known. Eiserpfad and Eiserweg are parts of the Eiserberg vineyard. Magdalenengarten is one of the few cases of a fairly important name being made by a vineyard entirely divided up among small growers.

Other vineyards: Aliment, Doosberg (has a fair name within Germany), Hölle, Kellerberg, Klostergarten, Mühlberg, Rheingarten.

Rauenthal

With the exception of Schloss Johannisberg, these wines are the most expensive of the Rheingau; and, with Johannisberg, Steinberg, and the best parts of Hattenheim and Erbach they are, in good years, some of the greatest. Generally throughout the Rheingau the best lands are held by the big wine estates; they have the best viticultural methods and go to the most pains, and they make the finest wines. It is a special characteristic of Rauenthal that even the small growers produce excellent wines. The largest holder is the State Domain (60 acres), followed by Graf Eltz with 10 acres, and Frh. Langwerth von Simmern with 7 acres, but Eltz has some of the very choicest bits. On an average, the Rauenthal vineyards produce about one-third less wine per acre than is grown in other districts—but they gain in quality what they lose in quantity. The greatest section has always been the Rauenthalerberg, a slope under cultivation for 700 years, but vineyard area consistently pushes back the rim of the forest above. The wines have great bouquet and elegance.

Vineyard area: 180 acres, white wine.

Best Vineyards: Baiken, Gehrn, Rothenberg, Wieshell (the Wieshell Blümchen section is an exclusive holding of Graf Eltz), Wülfen, Steinhaufen, Kesselring, Langenstück, Burggraben, Eisweg, Ehr, Geierstein, Grossenstück, Hilbitz, Hühnerberg (or Herberg), Maasborn, Nonnenberg, Pfaffenberg, Siebenmorgen, Steinmacher, Wagenkehr.

Rüdesheim

The situation of the Rüdesheimer vines on the steep slopes rising up from the Rhine makes the wines quite dependable in all but the worst years, and inclined to be below the general high level in the best years. The slopes have maximum sun exposure, and the benefit of reflected rays from the river; the grapes are therefore riper than elsewhere in cool summers. On the other hand, the sun burns the slopes, which drain very quickly, and in a hot summer the wines will be lacking in fragrance and roundness. While Rüdesheim is a well-known Rhine wine town in Germany, it is less famous there than abroad, where it shares with Nierstein in the Rheinhessen the honour of being the most celebrated of all. It is a great haunt of tourists cruising along the Rhine; and the concentration of shippers in the town means that many a non-Rüdesheim wine carries 'Rüdesheim' on the shipper's label. No other vineyards in Germany suffered so badly from the war; 200 bomb craters were blasted in the forty-five acre area of the State Domain alone. A peculiarity of Rüdesheim viticulture is that a little Orleans vine, the variety brought originally to the Rheingau in the time of Charlemagne, can still be found there. Even on the well-exposed slopes of Rüdesheim, it is only in the best years that the variety ripens enough to give good wine. What is perhaps the world's best collection of drinking vessels is housed in a half-ruined castle called the Brömserburg, or Niederburg, the oldest castle of the whole Rhine area, dating in parts from the ninth, tenth, and twelfth centuries. You may see implements used in Rheingau viniculture at the time of Christ, tiny clay cups of the Stone Age and all their descendants, as the typical high-stemmed German drinking glasses evolves before your eyes. The evolution of the German bottle is also shown, reaching its present form about 1790.

Vineyard area: 350 acres, white wine.

Grape variety: Riesling.

Best vineyards: those of the Rüdesheimerberg are best. They may be identified either as Rüdesheimer/Berg or Rüdesheimerberg, followed by the site name. Berg Bronnen, Berg Lay, Berg Burgweg, and Berg Rottland are the finest, followed by Berg Roseneck, Berg Zinngiesser, and Berg Zollhaus.

Important vineyards: Bischofsberg, Hinterhaus, Pares, Schlossberg, Stumpfenort, Wilgert.

Other vineyards: Bienengarten, Dickerstein, Engerweg, Hellpfad, Kiesel, Klosterkiesel, Mühlstein, Platz, Wüst.

Winkel

The town on the bank of the Rhine, with its several excellent vineyards and the Grey House, said there to be the oldest house in Germany, cannot compete in interest with the famous estate lying within its boundaries a five-minute drive up the vineyard slopes. This is the renowned Schloss Vollrads.

Vineyard area: 395 acres.

Grape varieties: Riesling and Sylvaner.

Best vineyard: Hasensprung, Jesuitengarten.

Important vineyards: Dachsberg, Ansbach, Honigberg, Steinacker.

Schloss Vollrads

The actual castle, a five-storey tower, stands up out of a green sea of vineyards across the courtyard from the wine-sheds. It is almost as inaccessible as it was until 1920 when the drawbridge was still in use. Today you may walk across a permanent bridge to the base of the tower and watch the swans in the moat; and if you are lucky you can go farther. Graf Matuschka-Greiffenclau keeps in the castle the private museum of the family, which has been arranged in the library of the ancient tower. It is not always possible to penetrate to the tower; but there is a good deal to be seen in the wine sheds and in the large house, built in the seventeenth century and partly rebuilt in 1908; and you may taste the superb wines too. Graf Matuschka-Greiffenclau, the former President of the Union of German Wine Growers, was, until 1964, the most influential man in German viticulture, and his estate at Schloss Vollrads is one of the only unified tracts on the Rhine, where the vineyards tend to be so much parcelled out. The Greiffenclau family has been at Vollrads since the fourteenth century, and is the oldest of the wine clans of the Rhine. The late-gathered wines of Schloss Vollrads, heady, and heavy with perfume, are always exquisite. The wines are entirely from the Riesling grape and the approximately seventy-five acres where they are grown constitute one of the three largest privately-owned Rheingau vineyards. The best area, roughly a fourth of the total, is the Schlossberg–Marienberg plot.

The estate-bottled wines are in four groups, mounting in quality:

(1) Originalabfüllung, but without any further distinguishing name; (2) Originalabfüllung Schlossabzug; (3) Originalabfüllung Kabinett; (4) the selectively-picked wines Originalabfüllung Auslese, Beerenauslese, and Trockenbeerenauslese. The Beerenauslesen and Trockenbeerenauslesen wines are only produced in the greatest years.

A sparkling wine (i.e. Sekt) is made from the lesser wine grown, and sold as Schloss Vollradser.

Vineyard area: 370 acres, white wine.

Grape variety: Riesling.

Wine Estates

German wines bearing on the label the device of an eagle with grapes on the breast and the letters V.D.N.V. are made by members of the German Natural Wine Association, including nearly all the best growers in the Verband Deutscher Naturwein-Versteigerer, which enforces on its members standards higher than the requirements of the German wine laws (*see* GERMANY; EXPORT AND BOTTLE LABEL).

Below is a list of the important domains in the Rheingau; those marked with an asterisk are members of the V.D.N.V.

Estate	*Headquarters*	*Acreage*	*Location of holdings*
*Graf zu Eltz (Since 1953 all the Eltz wines have carried the designation Schloss Eltz, although the individual vineyard names also still appear on the labels. Schloss Eltz in Eltville is one of the largest privately-owned Rheingau estates and has been in the Eltz family since 1625. The castle contains a fine collection of paintings. The Burg Eltz, one of the most romantic-looking castles on the Moselle, is also the property of Graf zu Eltz.)	Eltville	83	Eltville: Eltville Grimmen, Engerweg, Bunken, Sonnenberg, Mönchhanach, Langenstück, Grauer Stein, Kalbspflicht, Klümbchen (exclusive) Kiedricher Sandgrub Rauenthal: Rauenthaler Hilbitz, Rothenberg, Burggraben, Pfaffenberg, Gehrn, Steinhaufen, Baiken, Herberg, Wieshell
Frh. Langwerth von Simmern (The huge enclosed castle with its wine sheds on the bank of the Rhine is the most impressive of the great houses remaining from the days when Eltville was the summer seat of the Prince-Electors of Mainz.)	Eltville	62	Eltville: Eltviller Sonnenberg, Taubenberg, Freienborn Rauenthal: Rauenthaler Rothenberg, Herberg Erbacher Markobrunn Hattenheim: Hattenheimer Nussbrunnen, Mannberg

Estate	*Headquarters*	*Acreage*	*Location of holdings*
*Jakob Fischer (Owners since 1464)	Eltville	20	Eltville
Stadtpfarrgut (Church holding)	Eltville	7	Eltville
*Carl Belz	Eltville	7	Eltville
*Weinbauschule der Landesbauernschaft Hessen-Nassau (Hessen-Nassau Viticultural School)	Eltville	17	Eltville
*Franz Boltendahl	Eltville	7	Eltville; Rüdesheim; Erbach; Rauenthal
*Dr. R. Weil	Kiedrich	30	Kiedrich; Eltville
*Schloss Reinhartshausen (Owned by Prinz Friedrich of Prussia.)	Erbach	94	Erbach: Erbacher Markobrunn, Siegelsberg, Honigberg, Herrnberg, Hohenrain, Rheinhell, Brühl, Steinmorgen Hattenheim: Hattenheimer Wisselbrunnen, Stabel, Heiligenberg, Willborn, Hassel, Hinterhaus
*C. A. & H. Kohlhaas	Erbach	12	Erbach (including a small piece of Markobrunn)
*von Œttinger	Erbach	12	Erbach: Erbacher, Markobrunn, Brühl, Gemark, Kahlig, Hohenrain, Pellet, Rheingarten
*Graf von Schönborn (One of the Rheingau's greatest estates for its variety of holdings, and great quality.)	Hattenheim	41	Hochheim: Hochheimer Domdechaney, Stein, Rauchloch Erbacher Markobrunn Hattenheim: Hattenheimer Wisselbrunnen, Engelmannsberg, Pfaffenberg (exclusive), Hassel, Johannisberger Klauser Berg Geisenheimer Rothenberg Rüdesheim: Rüdesheimer Berg, Zollhaus, Hinterhaus, Berg Bronnen, Berg Roseneck Lorch: Lorcher Schlossberg, Krone
*Town of Hattenheim	Hattenheim	5	Hattenheim
Prinz Löwenstein	Hallgarten	22	Hallgarten: Hallgartener Schönhell, Deutelsberg, Hendelberg, Egersberg, Kirschenacker, Jungfer, Mehrhölzchen, Reuscherberg
*Carl Franz Engelmann	Hallgarten	10	Hallgarten; Östrich
*Ulrich von Stosch	Östrich	10	Mittelheim; Östrich
*Julius Wegeler (owned by Deinhard & Co.)	Östrich and Rüdesheim	50	Östrich; Hallgarten; Geisenheim; Rüdesheim
*Pfarrgut (Church holding)	Östrich	7	Östrich
*Reitz'sches Weingut	Mittelheim	8	Mittelheim; Winkel; Östrich
*Dr. Julius Mülhens-Berna (Haus Mülhens)	Mittelheim	8	Winkel; Östrich
*Geromont'sche Gutsverwaltung	Winkel	12	Winkel; Johannisberg
*A. von Brentano	Winkel	30	Winkel; Mittelheim; Östrich
*Graf Matuschka-Greiffenclau	Winkel	85	Schloss Vollrads (Winkel)

Estate	*Headquarters*	*Acreage*	*Location of holdings*
*Prince Metternich	Johannisberg	65	Schloss Johannisberg
Landgraf von Hessen	Johannisberg	30	Johannisberg; Winkel; Geisenheim
*Staatl. Lehr- und Forschungsanstalt für Wein- Obst- und Gartenbau (Geisenheim Viticultural School)	Geisenheim	45	Rüdesheim; Geisenheim
*Theo. Scherr	Geisenheim	10	Geisenheim
*Weingut Zobus (heir of)	Geisenheim	3	Geisenheim
Ritter zu Groenesteyn	Rüdesheim and Kiedrich	27	Rüdesheim: Rüdesheimer Berg-Mühlstein, Berg-Stoll, Berg-Bronnen, Berg-Paares, Berg-Hellpfad, Berg-Platz, Berg-Rottland, Wilgert, Bischofsberg, Hinterhaus, etc. Kiedrich: Kiedricher Gräfenberg, Turmberg, Wasserrose, Steeg, Langenberg, Sandgrub, etc.
*Julius Espenschied	Rüdesheim	8	Rüdesheim
*Graf von Kanitz	Lorch	40	Lorch
*Aschrott	Hochheim	30	Hochheim: Hochheimer Weiler, Daubhaus, Steinern Kreuz, Hochheimer Berg, Raaber, Neuberg Stielweg, Weishaus, Wiener, Hölle, Sommerheil, Stein, Domdechaney, Kirchenstück
*Domdechaney Werner	Hochheim	30	Hochheim: Hochheimer Daubhaus, Steinern Kreuz, Reichestal, Neuberg, Hangelstein, Weiler, Wandkaut, Mummhans, Sommerheil, Kohlkaut, Gehitz, Stielweg, Weid, Hölle, Kirchenstück, Domdechaney, Rauchloch
*Weingut of Frankfurt-am-Main	Hochheim	37	Hochheim

State Domain

This, the largest vineyard owner in Germany, with some 325 acres, holds some of the best vineyards of Rauenthal, Kiedrich, Erbach (Markobrunn), Hattenheim (all of Steinberg), Rüdesheim, Assmannshausen (red), and Hochheim. It is everywhere a member of the V.D.N.V. except at Assmannshausen where, in small years, the red wine has to be chaptalised, which is against the rules of V.D.N.V. The State Domain owns another 50 acres or so on the Bergstrasse between Darmstadt and Heidelberg. Its headquarters are at Eltville. Each holding is managed by an inspector.

The quality varies each year: in medium years, Rüdesheim and Hochheim are favoured; in hot years (the great ones), the Rauenthalers, Steinbergers, and Markobrunners come out on top.

The holdings of the State Domain are, in detail:

Township or village	*Vineyards*
Rüdesheim	Berg Rottland
	Berg Burgweg
Rüdesheim (*cont'd.*)	Berg Bronnen
	Berg Roseneck
	Berg Paares
	Berg Zollhaus
	Berg Stumpfenort
	Schlossberg
	Bischofsberg
	Klosterkiesel
	Klosterlay
	Hinterhaus
	Wilgert
	Engerweg
	Wüst
Hattenheim	Engelmannsberg
	Mannberg
	Willborn
	Schützenhaus
	Hassel
	Hinterhaus
Assmannshausen	Höllenberg
Erbach	Markobrunn
	Siegelsberg
Kiedrich	Gräfenberg
Eltville	Taubenberg

Township or village	*Vineyards*
Hochheim	Domdechaney
	Stein
	Kirchenstück
Rauenthal	Gehrn
	Baiken
	Wieshell
	Pfaffenberg
	Langenstück
	Wagenkehr
	Grossenstück
	Wülfen
	Steinmächer
	Steinhaufen
	Hühnerberg
Steinberg (belongs to the township of Hattenheim)	Steinberg

Rheinhessen

German white and red wine.

Rheinhessen provides soft wines without pronounced character, the most obvious and easy to know of all German growths. Owing probably to their straightforwardness and sweetness, the best of them have always been popular abroad. They are not wines to lay down, for they improve very little in bottle and tend to fade after eight or ten years. With the exception of the tiny quantity of specially selected Auslese and Trockenbeerenauslese, a Rheinhessen over ten years of age will seldom be interesting.

The German province of Rheinhessen, which gives its name to the wines (all produced inside the province are Rheinhessens and none grown outside may claim the name), is the Hesse which provided the Hanoverian kings of England with their Hessian troops of mercenaries, and it lies in the middle of the German wine country in a crook of the Rhine. The river, bending sharply at Mainz, washes it on two sides. Westward, the region is bounded by the River Nahe; on the south, the border with the Palatinate is a purely arbitrary political division, the two areas flowing into each other without any perceptible change.

Going up the Rhine, however, through Rheinhessen and into the Palatinate, there is a visible difference. The Palatinate is more romantic, more open, and the timbered houses have an old-fashioned look. In the heart of Rheinhessen, at Nierstein and Oppenheim, the strangled grimy streets with their rows of brick houses might be in Pittsburgh or Newcastle. It is surprising that people who can build such towns and live in them should also make the lovely Niersteiner and Oppenheimer wines.

There is a saying in Rheinhessen: 'If you are not a wine grower, then you're not a Rheinhessen man.' For a thousand years wine has been produced in the district, and today 176 of the 186 towns have vineyards. Most are tiny. Except around Nierstein, Oppenheim, and Bingen, the choicest areas, there are no large holdings, and 80% of Rheinhessen growers have no more than a two and a half acre plot each. They live partly by wine and partly by other farm pursuits—which is a fundamental strength of the Rheinhessen economy, enabling the district to offset bad vintage years. Making up for the weakness inevitable in vineyards cut up into such small parcels, and the consequent inability of the smallholders to purchase large-scale equipment and expensive machinery, there are fifty-nine wine co-operatives, with a total membership of 3,820 growers. On the way up-river from Oppenheim towards Worms, each of the little villages in between the expanses of gently rolling vineyard has its clean, new-looking co-operative.

The important wine centres stand at either side of the bent arm of the Rhine, at Bingen, Oppenheim, and Nierstein. Most of the best vineyards lie on what is called the Rhine front, a strip going back a mile or two from the river edge. The centre of the inland area is the town of Alzey, focus of a district bearing the same name. The Alzey wines are good, clean-tasting common wines, but they are seldom, if ever, exported. The 36,000 acres of Rheinhessen vineyard are divided almost equally among the four official districts, each called a Landkreis; Landkreis Alzey, Landkreis Bingen, Landkreis Mainz (including Oppenheim and Nierstein), and Landkreis Worms—although Worms has about 2,000 acres less than the others. Worms is not in the select first rank of Rheinhessen wines, with Bingen and the Niersteiners and Oppenheimers of Landkreis Mainz, and its dubious passport to fame is that of being the original home of Liebfraumilch. This is now a generic term which can enclose any Rheinhessen wine like a plain wrapper, giving little or no indication of the contents inside (*see* LIEBFRAUMILCH). Of the 35,000 acres providing highly variable amounts of wine from year to year (note the difference between 1949 and 1950 on the following chart), 87% are in white wine and 13% in red wine. The proportions of red and white are about the same in the four districts, although Bingen, because it includes the famous red Ingelheimers from farther east along the Rhine, has a larger amount of red than the others.

Soil, vine, weather, and man always combine to create the qualities of a wine. The climate in Rheinhessen is mild and dry, with a good deal of sunshine,

Wiesbaden
54
RHEINGAU
R. Main
42
R. Rhine
Mainz
455
9
Rüdesheim
FERRY
Bingen
Ingelheim
Gau-Algesheim
40
Büdesheim
Laubenheim
Ockenheim
Bodenheim
41
Dromersheim
Elsheim
Nackenheim
Gau-Bischofheim
Harxheim
RHEINHESSEN
Hahnheim
Nierstein
Schwabsburg
Bosenheim
Oppenheim
Dexheim
420
Wörrstadt
Friesenheim
Dienheim
Dalheim
Ulversheim
Ludwigshöhe
Guntersblum
Alzey
GERMANY
Mettenheim
Bechtheim
40
Westhofen
R. Rhine
271
Osthofen
Dalsheim
47
Worms
N
RHEINHESSEN
0 5 10 MILES
0 5 10 KILOMETRES
E 12
PALATINATE
(RHEINPFALZ)
Saarbrücken 50m

and comparative freedom from the killing spring and autumn frosts which terrorize the neighbouring growers, especially on the Moselle. The rule of Nature being what it is, the wines lack the character they would develop in a more precarious climate—where the vines have to fight for their lives; instead, they reflect the comparative softness of Rheinhessen weather. 65% of the wine comes from the Sylvaner grape variety, and this fortifies the tendency to a rich mildness which may find its highest expression in roundness and 'full-mouthedness' (as they say in Rheinhessen) but never in 'steel' (another excellent Rheinhessen expression) and distinction. The 10% of Rheinhessen wine from the Riesling grape, usually found on the south faces of hillside vineyards, provides the small quantity possessing *race* and steel. About two-thirds of the district is planted in Sylvaners; there is now about as much Müller-Thurgau as Riesling; and a trace of Gewürztraminer, a variety which used to be widespread but has died out and is being re-established here and there around Bingen and below Oppenheim. Red wines are made from the Burgunder, Portugieser, and St. Laurent plants, the well-known reds from Ingelheim coming from the first two varieties.

The Rheinhessen soil, composed of chalk, marl, and quartz (often a chalk decking with marl beneath), varies considerably. The facings along the Rhine around Bingen are slate, like the slate of the Moselle, while from Nackenheim to Nierstein, and a little farther on, a peculiar red sandstone is found, a deposit from the Ice Age. Its water-shedding property accounts for the fact that Niersteiners, Nackenheimers, and Schwabsburgers are likely to suffer less than most vines in very wet years.

Production

The vineyard acreage has remained fairly constant, around 35,000 acres for the last thirty years. The fluctuation of production since 1945, however, is typical. 22,064,000 imp. gallons (26,500,000 U.S.) were made in 1935, the biggest quantity year of the quarter-century, from a little less vineyard than is in vine today. In 1945 there were 4,833,200 imp. gallons (5,805,000 U.S.); in 1950, 17,210,000 imp. (20,670,000 U.S.), and in 1955, 9,947,200 imp. (11,946,680 U.S.).

The Important Rheinhessen Vineyards

The following are the most important Rheinhessen wines, including all that are to be found in England and the United States. The Rheinhessen wine label identifies the wine by town or village (*Gemarkung*) and vineyard (*Lage*). As an example, wine of the Daubhaus vineyard in the township of Oppenheim is Oppenheimer Daubhaus. The town or village name as listed below, placed before the name of the vineyard, and with *-er* added, will always give the name of the wine as it appears on the label—except for the wines of Bingen which are not Bingener but Binger wines.

Towns and villages of Landkreis Bingen lie south of the Rhine, between Bingen and Mainz. Towns and villages of Landkreis Mainz lie west of the Rhine, north and south of Oppenheim. Landkreis Worms is centred around Worms in south-east Rheinhessen. Thus the Landkreis given in brackets after the town or village establishes its general location. Towns and villages of Landkreis Alzey are not included, because the wines are not exported.

The best vineyards are in Landkreis Mainz and Landkreis Bingen. In a further attempt to sort out the confusion resulting from the countless names in German wine, the towns or villages are rated I, II, and III, to indicate their general importance. Vineyards usually producing the best wines come first, in alphabetical order, not in order of quality; other good vineyards follow.

The names of growers, running into many hundreds, cannot be listed here. In the better wines, however, the grower's name or name of the wine estate appears on the label, indicated by *Wachstum, Weingut*, or a similar term, and is an index of quality. An attempt has been made to list some of the best growers, but the list is not exhaustive.

Grape varieties indicate the type of the wines. White: Sylvaner (soft), Riesling (more character), Müller-Thurgau (Riesling + Sylvaner), Gewürztraminer (spicy). Red: Burgunder (red aromatic). A bottle of white Rheinhessen wine without indication of the grape variety will almost certainly be Sylvaner.

Alsheim (Landkreis Worms) II

Low ridge of hills one mile from Rhine, half-way between Worms and Oppenheim. Largest producer in Worms, among four largest in Rheinhessen. Large quantity of Riesling.

Vineyard area: 920 acres: 845 acres white; 75 acres red.

Grape varieties: Riesling, Sylvaner, Müller-Thurgau, Gewürztraminer, Portugieser, St. Laurent.

Vineyards: Fischerpfad, Friedrichsberg, Goldberg, Römerberg, Rosenberg, Brechtel, Hahl, Kälbchen, Karstweg, Ohligstück, Rüst, Sandhöhle, Sonnenberg, Sommerhäuschen.

Bechtheim (Landkreis Worms) II

Slope wines, two-and-a-half miles back from low vineless flat land bulging into the Rhine.

Vineyard area: 800 acres: 750 acres white; 50 acres red.

Grape varieties: Riesling, Sylvaner, Portugieser.

Vineyards: Geyersberg, Hasensprung, Löwenberg, Pilgerpfad, Rosengarten, Wölm, Bende, Gotteshilfe, Haferberg, Katzenloch, Stein.

Wine estates: Dr. Blum'sches Weingut, Ferdinand Kœhler, Weingut Wilhelm Schœneck.

Bingen (Landkreis Bingen) I

Lying directly across the Rhine from Rüdesheim and the Rheingau, at the point where the Nahe flows into the Rhine, Bingen sprawls up a mountain famous since Roman times for its vineyards. Bingen-Kempten, on the town's outskirts, and Bingen-Büdesheim, behind it, where rolling hills fringe the Nahe, form a unit with Bingen and can be considered as such. The connexion with Rüdesheim is a ferry which whirls like a feather in the powerful current when it docks at either bank. Steep, tangled Bingen qualifies for its name Wine Town, Rhine Town: surviving the plague, the Thirty Years War, and other disasters, it had provided its 6,000 citizens with 130 wine bars and 120 wine merchants by the end of the last century. Population has tripled today, and the fun goes on. When a past Bishop of Mainz, addressing the Bingen clergy, asked to borrow a pencil, everyone reached under his cassock and brought out a corkscrew, which was then dubbed the 'Bingen pencil', a name which has stuck. Distinctly Rheinhessen wines, though separated from the Rheingaus only by the width of the river, Bingen wines derive a liveliness from the slate soil. Those grown right along the Rhine front sometimes have a smoky taste, said to come from the smoke of the busy railway and the river boats.

Vineyard area: 625 acres: 550 acres white; 75 acres red.

Grape varieties: Riesling, Sylvaner.

Vineyards: Eisel, Rochusberg (great breed, grown on slate and quartz slope), Rosengarten, Schwätzerchen, Anberg, Bienengarten, Hinter Eisel, Ohligberg, Rheinberg, Rochusweg, Schlossberg.

Wine estate: Villa Sachsen.

Bingen-Büdesheim (Landkreis Bingen) I

See Bingen for description.

Vineyard area: 260 acres: 195 acres white; 65 acres red.

Grape varieties: Riesling, Sylvaner, Gewürztraminer, Burgunder, Portugieser.

Vineyards: Scharlachberg (the reddish tinge of the clayey-slate soil gives 'Scarlet Hill' its name. Wines are sold as Scharlachberg, with or without the town name. They are sound white wines and are likely to come from any of the vineyards in the region where the Bingen and Büdesheim towns meet).

Other Vineyards: Kieselberg, Osterberg, Rosengarten, Steinkautweg.

Outstanding wine estate: Jung auf Junghof.

Bingen-Kempten (Landkreis Bingen) I

See Bingen for description.

Vineyard area: 170 acres: 158 acres white; 12 acres red.

Grape varieties: Riesling, Sylvaner.

Vineyards: Pfarrgarten, Gänsberg, Hinterhäuser, Kirchberg, Lies, Rheinberg, Schnack.

Bodenheim (Landkreis Mainz) I

Monastery holdings of the Middle Ages produce spicy, full wines with much bouquet, but they never reach the peaks attained by the Niersteiners and Oppenheimers three or four miles south.

Vineyard area: 710 acres: 500 acres white; 210 acres red.

Grape varieties: Riesling, Sylvaner, Müller-Thurgau, Portugieser.

Vineyards: Bock, Ebersberg, Kahlenberg, Neuberg, Braunloch, Burgweg, Hoch, Leidhecke, Leimen, Leistenberg, Rettberg, Silberberg, St. Alban, Westrum.

Wine estates: Peter Kerz III, Oberstleutnant Liebrecht'sche Weingutsverwaltung, Anton Riffel.

Bosenheim (Landkreis Bingen) II

In flat land bordering the Nahe.

Vineyard area: 260 acres: 210 acres white; 50 acres red.

Grape variety: Sylvaner.

Vineyards: Bosenberg, Galgenberg, Honigberg.

Dalheim (Landkreis Mainz) III

Rather strong wines, quite clean-tasting.

Vineyard area: 240 acres: 235 acres white; 5 acres red.

Grape varieties: Sylvaner, Portugieser.

Vineyards: Altdörr, Gänsberg, Sommerthal.

Dalsheim (Landkreis Worms) III

A great deal of trouble with phylloxera is causing extensive replanting with American vine stocks at a cost estimated at £90,000 (250,000 dollars) over the next twenty years. Sylvaner was always the main producer, but Müller-Thurgau introduced in the last quarter-century suits the clayey soil.

Vineyard area: 480 acres: 460 acres white; 20 acres red.

Grape varieties: Riesling, Sylvaner, Gewürztraminer, Müller-Thurgau, Spätburgunder, Portugieser, St. Laurent.

Vineyards: Steig, Brünnchen, Rodenstein.

Dexheim (*Landkreis Mainz*) *II*

Since the Middle Ages considered equal with Oppenheim, Schwabsburg, and Nierstein, which it adjoins, but nowadays not quite up to the peak wines of its neighbours.

Vineyard area: 180 acres white; trace of red.

Grape variety: Sylvaner.

Vineyards: Doktor, Hölle, Ostertal.

Wine estates: Adolf Dahlem, August Dahlem, Sander.

Dienheim (*Landkreis Mainz*) *I*

The village adjoins the town of Oppenheim on the south and the vineyards, on the Rhine front, produce first-quality wines.

Vineyard area: 875 acres white.

Grape variety: Sylvaner.

Vineyards: Falkenberg, Guldenmorgen, Krötenbrunnen, Silzbrunnen, Tafelstein, Ebenbreit, Goldberg, Gumben, Kandelweg, Langweg, Modern, Neuweg, Pflänzer, Rosswiese, Zwölf Morgen.

Wine estates: Willi Göttmann, Ludwig V. Stark.

Dromersheim (*Landkreis Bingen*) *II*

In a protected inner valley. One of the oldest wine areas in Rheinhessen, formerly a holding of Kloster Fulda.

Vineyard area: 500 acres: 375 acres white; 125 acres red.

Grape varieties: Sylvaner, Müller-Thurgau, Portugieser.

Vineyards: Laberstall, Honigberg.

Elsheim (*Landkreis Bingen*) *II*

Chiefly famous as the location of the biggest annual viticultural celebration of Rheinhessen, bringing together many hundreds of growers and picturesquely named 'Little Green Week of the Selz River Valley'.

Vineyard area: 240 acres: 187 acres white; 53 acres red.

Grape varieties: Sylvaner, Riesling, Gewürztraminer.

Vineyards: Blum, Bockstein, Rosengarten, Spielberg.

Friesenheim (*Landkreis Mainz*) *III*

Vineyard area: 73 acres white.

Grape varieties: Müller-Thurgau, Sylvaner.

Vineyards: Altdörr, Goldgrube, Knopf.

Gau-Algesheim (*Landkreis Bingen*) *II*

On the Rhine front between Bingen and Ingelheim, facing the Rheingau. A famous New Wine Festival takes place during the second week-end in October in the historic market place, formerly the scene of one of the great annual wine markets of the Middle Ages.

Vineyard area: 375 acres: 250 acres white; 125 acres red.

Grape varieties: Sylvaner, Riesling, Burgunder, Portugieser.

Vineyards: Rothenberg, Stolzenberg, Goldberg, Hasensprung.

Wine estate: Avenarius'sche Gutsverwaltung.

Gau-Bischofheim (*Landkreis Mainz*) *I*

South-facing on hill slope just north of Nierstein.

Vineyard area: 150 acres white.

Grape variety: Sylvaner.

Vineyards: Gauberg, Glockenberg, Herrnberg, Pfaffenweg, Brühl, Hinterhaus, Kircheck, Kreuzwingert, Vikarei.

Guntersblum (*Landkreis Mainz*) *I*

Usually fruity wines. On the Rhine front; third largest producer in Rheinhessen with much small parcelling in the shallow-slope vineyards, forming a solid stretch of vines extending about a mile on either side of the vineyard road.

Vineyard area: 880 acres white; trace of red.

Grape varieties: Sylvaner, Riesling, Müller-Thurgau, Gewürztraminer.

Vineyards: Autental, Bornpfad, Steig, Vogelsgärten, Eiserne Hand, Hasenweg, Himmelthal, Kehl, Kreuz, Steinberg, Wohnweg.

Wine estates: Emil Schätzel, Schlossgut Schmitt.

Hahnheim (*Landkreis Mainz*) *II*

South-facing slope vineyards in centre of Rheinhessen.

Vineyard area: 240 acres: 228 acres white; 12 acres red.

Grape varieties: Sylvaner, Riesling, Müller-Thurgau, Burgunder, Portugieser, St. Laurent.

Vineyards: Dachsberg, Knopf, Moosberg, Monchberg, Paffenröder.

Wine estate: Walter Heinz.

Harxheim (Landkreis Mainz) II

Steep-slope wines from vineyards adjoining the Nierstein area, but not coming up to the peak wines of the Rhine front hills at Nierstein.

Vineyard area: 200 acres: 187 acres white; 13 acres red.

Grape varieties: Sylvaner, Müller-Thurgau, Portugieser.

Vineyards: Osterberg, Schlossberg, Hartenberg, Kichelberg.

Wine estates: August Böll, Peter Lotz.

Ingelheim (Landkreis Bingen) I

Here the red wines surpass the whites, the reverse of the usual order, both in Rheinhessen and in Germany generally. The white wines are good table wines but are not distinguished. The red wines from the Frühburgunder and Spätburgunder grape varieties have real quality; some experts say that the finest red growths are the best red wines of Germany and the only ones in a class with the world's great red wines. Nieder-Ingelheim, Ober-Ingelheim, Frei-Weinheim and half a dozen other such names of small nearby communities or parts of Ingelheim are being absorbed into the single name Ingelheim, owing to its fame; and Ingelheim wines will be from anywhere in the hilly area of the mediæval town overlooking the Rhine.

Vineyard area: 860 acres: 530 acres white; 330 acres red.

Grape varieties: Frühburgunder, Spätburgunder, Portugieser, Sylvaner, Riesling, Müller-Thurgau.

Vineyards: Horn, Pares, Rheinhöhe.

Wine estate: J. Neuss (reds).

Laubenheim (Landkreis Mainz) II

The wines which grow on the slopes up over the factory areas on the southern outskirts of Mainz lack the distinction of their neighbours farther down the Rhine.

Vineyard area: 330 acres: 280 acres white; 50 acres red.

Grape varieties: Sylvaner, Riesling.

Vineyards: Seckergrund, Silberglöckchen, Steig, Edelmann, Hitz, Klosterneck, Neuberg, Rettberg.

Wine estates: Otto Dettweiler, Eugen Haffner (Erben), Hans Göhlen.

Ludwigshöhe (Landkreis Mainz) I

By the time the tiny village below Oppenheim is reached, the slope has levelled to a broad plain. A good deal of Ludwigshöhe wine goes into Liebfraumilch.

Vineyard area: 140 acres white.

Grape varieties: Sylvaner, Riesling.

Vineyards: Kellerweg, Modern, Teufelskopf, Geyerscheid, Rheinpfad.

Wine estates: Weingut Brüder Dr. Becker, Johann Gräf.

Mettenheim (Landkreis Worms) II

Wines grow on the edge of the flat land in a wide bend of the Rhine, a little south of the excellent stretch from Bodenheim up to Guntersblum. Good average wines. No peak wines.

Vineyard area: 294 acres: 266 acres white; 28 acres red.

Grape variety: Sylvaner.

Vineyards: Liebfrauental, Michelsberg, Schlossberg, Goldberg, Feuerberg, Fuchsloch, Hellborn, Kandelberg, Platte, Römerstein.

Wine estate: Gerhard Koch.

Nackenheim (Landkreis Mainz) I

On the red, clay and slate soil just above Nierstein, some really first-class white wines are grown. Nackenheimers used to be used for blending, but their high quality has become recognized. In some years Nackenheim produces the lowest quantity yield per acre in Rheinhessen, always an index of high quality. The town, dominated by a baroque church, is pushed almost into the Rhine by the steep vine-covered mountain; the moderating influence of the river on the climate aids the wines. Nackenheim has the largest wine-bottle capsule factory in Europe.

Vineyard area: 170 acres: 158 acres white; 12 acres red.

Grape varieties: Riesling, Sylvaner.

Vineyards: Engelsberg, Fenchelberg, Fritzenhöll, Kapelle, Langentag, Rothenberg (outstanding), Schmitts-Kapelle, Dieterkapp, Hahlkreuz, Kahlenberg, Platte, Rheinhahl, Sommerwinn, Spitzenberg.

Wine estates: Gunderloch-Lange, Gunderloch-Usinger.

Nierstein (Landkreis Mainz) I

The most important area, giving the best Rheinhessen wines. Everyone in Nierstein is an owner in the vineyards that have been famous for hundreds of years. Of some 550 parcels, about two dozen produce the soft, elegant, full-bodied, peak wines known around the world as Niersteiners. Look for Riesling on the label: the best Niersteiners are from the Riesling grape and are so identified. The wines have a marvellous bouquet. Nierstein derives its name from the mineral springs the Romans called

Neri, and from the boundary stone which once marked the division between German and Frankish territories. The town came to be called Neri am Stein, which was corrupted to Nierstein. Driving from Mainz with the Rhine on your left, you see the fairly steep *Weinberg*, solid with vine, sloping back from the road, the chief areas indicated by large white block letters spelling out HIPPING, FOCKENBERG, etc. It is the largest wine *Gemarkung* on the Rhine, and much the largest in Rheinhessen.

Vineyard area: 1,620 acres white.

Grape varieties: Riesling, Sylvaner. (A trace of the Orleans grape variety, once widespread in France but now vanished, is found here. It was brought to Germany in the Middle Ages from Orleans, then an important French wine zone, supposedly by Charlemagne.)

Vineyards: Generally Niersteiners are now known under their collective names. This is part of the attempt to simplify the confusion arising in all German wines from the overwhelming number of names resulting from the great number of small vineyard parcels—there were once 50,000 different wine names. Niersteiners may, however, still use the individual parcel names, and some do. In the following list, collective names (capitalized) are followed by some of the individual parcel names still found on labels.

AUFLANGEN (Hinter Saal, Pfuhlweg, Rohr)
HEILIGENBAUM (Orbel)
HIPPING (Fläschenhahl, Fuchsloch, Kehr, Pfütze, Tal)
ÖLBERG (Steig, Streng, Warte)
REHBACH (Floss, Pettental)
BILDSTOCK (Bleiche, Muhl, Neunmorgen, Rossberg)
FOCKENBERG (Brudersberg, Fritzenhölle, Steig, Rosenberg, Schmitt, Schnappenberg, Weissenberg)
PATERBERG (Burgweg, Galgenberg, Hölle, Hummertal, Monzenberg)
ST. KILIANSBERG (Granzberg)
SPIEGELBERG (Domtal, Findling, Hessbaum, über der Rehbacher Steig)
(*Note:* Also producing excellent Niersteiner: Brudersberg, Glöck, Taubennest, Zehn Morgen)

Wine estates: Emil Förster, Frh. von Heyl zu Herrnsheim, Gustav Gessert, Weingut Louis Guntrum, Georg Harth, Fritz Hasselbach, Weingut Friedrich Kehl, Franz Karl Schmitt (widow of), Georg Schmitt'sches Weingut, Georg Albrecht Schneider, Reinhold Senfter, Weingut Heinrich Schlamp Jr.

Ockenheim (Landkreis Bingen) II

Can be very good in years with plenty of sunshine, when quite a lot of Spätlese is made on the best south-facing slopes. The Müller-Thurgau grape variety is being used more and more, owing to the public taste for the aromatic wines produced.

Vineyard area: 480 acres: 320 acres white; 160 acres red.

Grape varieties: Sylvaner, Riesling, Müller-Thurgau, Portugieser.

Vineyards: Hölle, Laberstall, Affenberg, Fullknopf, Neuberg, Rechweg.

Wine estate: Wilhelm Merz.

Oppenheim (Landkreis Mainz) I

Generally, Oppenheimers are fuller and softer than Niersteiners, while Niersteiners have more elegance. In dry, hot years Oppenheimers are likely to surpass Niersteiners; in wet, cool years Niersteiners will be better. The Oppenheimer soil retains water whereas the Niersteiner slope is steeper and water runs off. After two or three glasses of the splendid wine, the town may take on the virtue of its famous product. Seen coldly, it is an ugly scar of brick and dirty grey stucco along a sooty railway line. In the stark interior of St. Katherine's Church there are a few tombstones decorated with vineyard motifs from the fifteenth and sixteenth centuries.

Vineyard area: 710 acres white.

Grape varieties: Sylvaner, Riesling, Müller-Thurgau.

Vineyards: Brünnchen, Daubhaus, Goldberg, Herrenberg, Kreuz, Krötenbrunnen, Kugel, Reisekahr, Sackträger, Steig, Herrenweiher, Kette, Rohrgasse, Saar, Schlossberg, Zuckerberg.

Wine estates: Friedrick Baumann, Adam Becker, Franz Josef Gallois, Louis Guntrum, J. A. Harth & Co., Ernst Jungkenn, Karl Koch (Erben), Franz Josef Senfter, Carl Sittmann, Weingut der Stadt Oppenheim, Dr. L. Winter.

Osthofen (Landkreis Worms) II

Vineyard area: 610 acres: 580 acres white; 30 acres red.

Grape varieties: Müller-Thurgau, Riesling, Sylvaner.

Vineyards: Goldberg, Kirchberg, Hasenbiss, Herrenberg, Klosterberg, Rheinberg, Wölm.

Schwabsburg (Landkreis Mainz) I

With its windowless tower and castle built by Frederick Barbarossa, Schwabsburg is a pretty village and vineyard lying in a little valley a mile west of Nierstein. The vineyards have south and south-west exposure, and they share the reddish, slate and clay soil of the usually greater vineyards on the Rhine front.

Vineyard area: 240 acres white; trace of red.

Grape varieties: Sylvaner, Riesling.

Vineyards: Domtal, Ebersberg, Kirschplatt, Orbel, Federberg.

Selzen (Landkreis Mainz) II

Vineyard area: 220 acres white.

Grape variety: Sylvaner.

Vineyards: Osterberg, Gottesgarten, Rosengarten.

Wine estate: Weingut Schätzel (Erben).

Ülversheim (Landkreis Mainz) II

Wines usually strong and full-bodied, grown almost entirely on the south face of the Rhine front.

Vineyard area: 235 acres white.

Grape varieties: Sylvaner, Riesling, Müller-Thurgau.

Vineyard: Farrenberg.

Westhofen (Landkreis Worms) II

Vineyard area: 900 acres: 810 acres white; 90 acres red.

Grape varieties: Sylvaner, Riesling, Müller-Thurgau, Gewürztraminer, Portugieser, St. Laurent.

Vineyards: Brunnenhäuschen, Hackgraben, Kirchspiel, Liebfrauenberg, Bergkloster, Klausenberg, Kelterstein, Pilgerborn.

Worms (Landkreis Worms)

An occasional tiny vineyard may be found right in among the ancient buildings and war ruins of the city—one (a Valckenberg property) is in the shadow of the Cathedral where Martin Luther was condemned as a heretic in 1521, but nothing in Worms is of viticultural importance, except the Liebfrauenstift and Liebfraumilch.

LIEBFRAUMILCH AND THE LIEBFRAUENSTIFT

On 29 April 1910, a fatal day in German wine history, the Chamber of Commerce of Worms ruled that the name Liebfraumilch could now be used by any Rheinhessen wine of good quality. It was like staking out a tired old horse in the public park and saying that any child of good quality could mount it. Today, Liebfraumilch is likely to be any Rheinhessen wine at all, usually one with no claim to a distinctive appellation of its own. The meaninglessness of the name is finally proved by the German wine law which specifically says Liebfraumilch may carry no picture of a district, village or church (particularly not the Liebfrauenkirche in Worms) on the label. It is officially wine from nowhere.

It can never have been very good, for the soil of the Liebfrauenstift vineyards around the tall, bleak church on the outskirts of Worms is flat, river-deposit earth which gives a special taste to the wines. Nevertheless, arising in the sixteenth and seventeenth centuries, before vineyard place-names had come into being, the name Liebfraumilch gradually became world famous. The production of the original vineyards around the Liebfrauenkirche, never more than 2,000 cases in the best years, was entirely inadequate for the demand, and the name spread over other wines.

Ironically, of all Rheinhessen wines today, those which specifically may *not* carry the name of Liebfraumilch are the wines of the Liebfrauenstift vineyard. They are known as Liebfrauenstift Kirchenstück (the best), Liebfrauenstift Klostergarten, or simply Liebfrauenstift. Most of the parcels behind ten-foot brick walls on all sides of the church are owned by the Valckenberg and the J. Langenbach estates, though small holdings are in the hands of Eberhard, W. Mahler, and E. Rieth. Visited on a May day in 1955, new vines were being planted in one of the biggest Langenbach parcels and there was much very young vine to be seen in most sections. The grape variety is principally Riesling, and Liebfrauenstift wines are often used for blending.

Rheinriesling

Variety of Riesling cultivated in Austria.

Rhenish

English term formerly used for Rhine wines and extended to all German wines. It has dropped out of currency in favour of Hock.

Rhine (Middle Rhine)

White and a few red wines. District: German Rhineland.

With craggy shores, crumbling castles, the racing Rhine, and its legend of the siren Lorelei, the section of the river from below Bingen down to Coblenz and beyond is the most interesting to travel by steamer, but not, unfortunately, by palate. The wines are ordinary, as varied as the quartz, clay, and lime soils in which they grow, and are hardly ever exported. Some of the best Rieslings can be suggestive of Moselles; Sylvaner and Müller-Thurgau vines also produce the copious white wines. Red wine was once fairly common here, but now what remains is for local consumption only.

Wine grows not only on the slopes along the Rhine, which in certain places (Boppard, for example) are favoured by a south-facing exposure, but also in the side valleys branching into the hills, where conditions are particularly unfavourable. The cold winds coming down from the Hunsrück Mountains meet the warm air rising from the Rhine and cause sudden frosts in late spring and early autumn. On the other hand, the Middle Rhine, below St. Goarshausen, is one of the few sections of the world's vineyards where phylloxera has not yet struck.

The Boppard Hamm, facing south in the deepest bend of the Middle Rhine, is the best Middle Rhine vineyard.

Viertälerwein (Four Valleys Wine) comes from the district on the left bank of the river below Assmannshausen and Lorch where the Rheingau ends. The term Viertälerwein used to be looser but now it embraces only the wines of the Oberdiebach, Manubach, and Steeg valleys. These are Rieslings, very light in character. Probably the best of the vineyards are Bocksberg and Flur in the Steeg Valley. Other good vineyards in Steeg are Mühlberg, St. Jost, and Schlossberg; in Manubach, Langgarten, and Retz; in Oberdiebach, Teich, Schlossberg, Pützengrub, Hub.

Bacharach, down on the river in front of Steeg, is often included with the Viertäler wines. The Bacharach wines are at least as good as the others, and the best are from the Dell and the Untere and Obere Wolfshöhle vineyards.

The fourth of the four valleys is Engehöll, and adjoining it, Oberwesel, with the Rheinhell and Lauerbaum vineyards. All the wines of this section grow on a slate soil, like that which imparts their steely character to the rather similar Moselles.

Rhine Wines

General name for wines grown along the River Rhine.

See RHEINGAU; RHEINHESSEN; RHINE (MIDDLE RHINE); PALATINATE.

Rhône (Côtes du Rhône)

Red, white, and rosé wines. District: Southern France.

The Rhône is a river of wine; it drains vineyards on its broad delta plain, along the steep cliffs above Avignon, in the Cévennes and the Jura Mountains, and around the lake of Geneva. Yet the only wines to bear the name are those which come from the central section—the Côtes du Rhône.

Lyons, with its great gastronomic tradition, stands at the head of the Rhône Valley; east of the river is the land of the fat Bresse chickens; to the west, Périgord, rich in truffles and *foie gras*; from the south come the plentiful fruit and fish of the valley—and the great restaurants excel in *poulet en vessie,* in *quenelles Nantua*, and all the rest of the famous regional dishes and *charcuteries*. The inhabitants eat heartily and wash down their meals with the robust Rhône wine—and with Beaujolais.

The vineyards of the Côtes du Rhône extend for 140 miles from Lyons to Avignon, stretching precariously over sheer, high cliffs on both sides of the sun-baked river. Their touchstone is granite—the soil's dominant element. Drawing their character from the steep, sun-drenched granite cliffs they come from, the wines are not subtle; they are big, rough and heady, with a strong almost pungent perfume, and they are tamed only by long imprisonment in the bottle. They compare seldom in quality, never in quantity, with the greatest Clarets and Burgundies; but at their best they can be superb. Yet it has been the fate of these distinctive wines often to be classed as Burgundies—a practice which does justice to neither region. The reason perhaps was the proximity of the upper Rhône vineyards to those of southern Burgundy; or the sturdy Burgundy bottle in which Rhône wines also are sold.

Except for Tavel, Châteauneuf-du-Pape, and Hermitage, Rhône wines have not hitherto been well known. The situation has changed, however. As a result of the efforts of the Baron LeRoy du Boiseaumarié the wines are often seen outside their own region. The Baron, one of the few men to have a statue erected to him during his own lifetime, is himself a grower in Châteauneuf-du-Pape; and was President of the International Wine Office, he holds the rank of Commandeur of the Légion d'Honneur, and he heads the syndicate of growers of the Côtes du Rhône. Baron Le Roy was instrumental in formulating and obtaining the controls that brought honest wines back into Châteauneuf-du-Pape which had been fraud-ridden, and he later extended his activities to embrace first all Rhône wines, then all of France.

The area over which the Côtes du Rhône extend is long and narrow, and the wines produced there show considerable variation. Some sections of the Côtes are more advanced than are others, and are apt, therefore, to produce better wines. Overall quality has risen enormously in recent years, but it is uneven; many growers still need help, especially those in the lesser-known districts. The entire region produces something over 16,500,000 imp. gallons

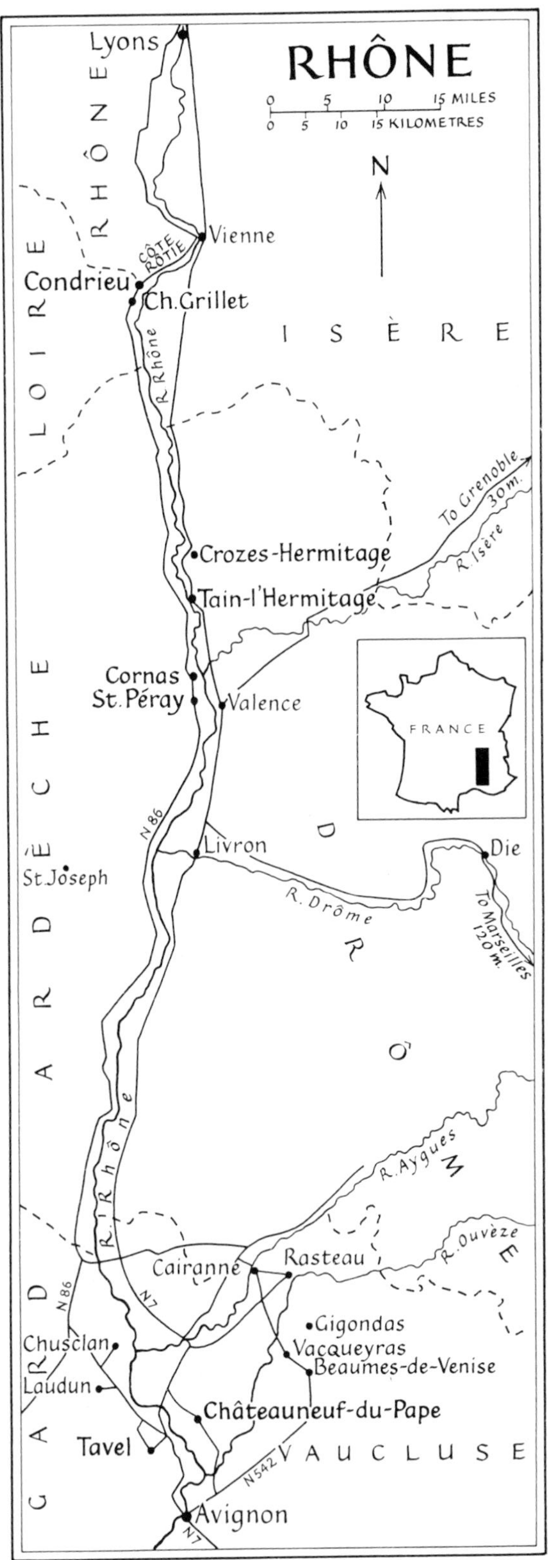

(20 million U.S.) of wine annually, some under the name Côtes du Rhône, some—superior in both quantity and quality—under more specific headings.

The better wines include:

Name	*Average production (imp. gallons); U.S. gallons shown in parentheses* red and rosé	*white*
Côte Rôtie	44,700 (53,700)	
Condrieu		2,500 (3,000)
Château Grillet		290 (350)
Cornas	28,300 (34,000)	
Saint-Joseph	44,000 (52,836)	4,600 (5,521)
Saint-Péray		27,000 (33,000)
Hermitage	49,600 (59,600)	25,800 (31,000)
Crozes-Hermitage	84,282 (101,229)	31,500 (37,850)
Châteauneuf-du-Pape	1,087,000 (1,305,000)	8,900 (10,700)
Tavel (rosé only)	400,000 (475,000)	
Lirac (rosé and white)	54,000 (65,000)	1,250 (1,500)

See under individual headings.

The region's lesser wines are sold either as Côtes du Rhône, or with that name followed by some addition. While it is generally true in French wines that the more specific name denotes the better growth, this is not strictly so along the Rhône. When the general name is followed by that of one of the four better communes—Cairanne, Chusclan, Gigondas, Laudun—the wines will have met higher than normal standards and are often delightful. If, on the other hand, the general name is followed by the name of a department—Ardèche, Drôme, Loire, Rhône—the standards are more relaxed and the wines may be inferior. One important consideration in this question of standards is the minimum required alcoholic content—always stipulated for fine French wines. Although alcoholic content is always a question of importance, it is vital to Rhône wines. Alcohol adds body and strength, two characteristics that are closely identified with these wines. If the label says simply, Côtes du Rhône, the wine must have at least 10·5% alcohol by volume. If this name is followed by the name of a department (Côtes du Rhône—Drôme, for example), only 9·5% is required, sapping the wine of some of its robust strength. Those wines that come from the four communes mentioned above have alcoholic contents ranging from a minimum 12% to 12·5%.

Most of the finer Côtes du Rhône wines are pressed from one kind of grape, sometimes two or three—with the exception of Châteauneuf-du-Pape, where thirteen are allowed. The principal variety is the Syrah, which gives firm, robust wines of fine colour and bouquet, but is sometimes inclined to be hard. The introduction of the white Viognier imparts the qualities of softness and freshness. Other leading white-wine varieties are Roussanne which, grown on a sunny slope, gives fine soft wines, and Marsanne, a sturdier and more productive grape planted more often than Roussanne. For the general name Côtes du Rhône, growers may include grapes from any or all of the following varieties: Grenache, Clairette, Syrah, Mourvèdre, Picpoule, Terret Noir, Counoise, Muscardin, Bourboulenc, Carignan, Ugni Blanc, Roussanne, Marsanne, and Viognier.

Rhône summers are long and consistently warm. As a result, there is not as much variation between the vintage years as elsewhere in France. There is, however, some difference. The best years of the present century are: 1929, 1934, 1937, 1942, 1943, 1945, 1947, 1949, 1950, 1952, 1955, 1957, 1960, 1961, 1962, 1964, and 1966.

Characteristics of Rhône Wines

Côte Rôtie. These robust and heady wines stand up well. The colour is rich; there is a hint of violet in the bouquet; and, some say, of raspberry in the taste.

Condrieu. White wine with a tinge of colour; robust and perfumed. Both dry and semi-sweet styles are produced, and all are at their best when young and fresh. Condrieu is a favourite of the Lyonnais.

Château Grillet. The wine, which shows some resemblance to Condrieu, is robust and vigorous, with perhaps a little more finesse than the latter. Since the production is very small, this wine is not much seen outside its own district.

Hermitage. The red wine is full-bodied and vigorous, with a certain delicacy and softness in maturity, and a fragrance of iris-root in the bouquet. It ages well. The white wine has a golden tinge, is dry yet fruity, with a characteristic perfume. It will last a long time without oxidizing.

Crozes-Hermitage. Red wine with a rather violet tinge, not so deep in colour as Hermitage, nor with so much softness. It has a faint *goût du terroir*.

Saint-Joseph. The red wines are delicate and perfumed, with less body than the Hermitage, but of a fine ruby colour. They are ready after a few years in bottle. The white wines are supple and *moelleux*, lighter than the white Hermitage.

Cornas. Red wine, sometimes a bit hard to begin with, of a fine garnet colour. It ages well, becoming soft and velvety in maturity, but never so perfumed as Hermitage.

Saint-Péray. White, spirited wines with body, a tinge of colour, and a definite bouquet. In ageing, they sometimes maderize. Some of these wines make dry or semi-sweet *mousseux*.

Clairette-de-Die. A semi-sparkling white wine from the Clairette and Muscat grapes, made near the village of Die on the River Drôme.

Châteauneuf-du-Pape. A full-bodied wine, deep in colour, softer and quicker to mature than most Rhône growths. There is also a white wine, pleasant but of less importance.

Tavel, one of the best rosés of France, comes mainly from the Grenache grape. It has a clear, pink colour, without any trace of orange flaw. It is light, refreshing, and at its best when chilled.

Vaucluse and Gard. The wines, planted in a variety of soils in these two departments, are of widely varying types. In general, the terraced, gravelly, clayey vineyards are planted for rosé. Lirac and Chusclan produce pink wines which are not far behind those of Tavel. Laudun makes white as well as pink and red. Gigondas, Cairanne, and Vacqueyras wines are supple, and rather high in alcohol; red, white and rosé are made. Beaumes-de-Venise and Rasteau are dessert wines—*see under* SWEET FORTIFIED WINES OF FRANCE.

Ribeauvillé

Wine town in Alsace (*q.v.*).

Ricard

Very popular French liquorice-flavoured aperitif. Because of its strong taste and reasonably high alcoholic content, it is generally diluted with water before drinking, whereupon it turns milky and cloudy. This is a commercial pastis.

Rice Wine

A Japanese fermented liquor made from rice. *See* SAKÉ.

Riceys, Rosé de

A still, pink wine of Champagne (*q.v.*).

Richebourg

Burgundy red wine. District: Côte de Nuits, France. Commune: Vosne-Romanée. Official classification: Great Growth (Grand Cru).

Richebourg is one of the giants of its commune, partly since it is rated Great Growth (*Grand Cru*)—as high as a Burgundian vineyard can get—and partly since its 19·8 acres (part in Richebourg, part in Les Verroilles) make it one of the largest of the great vineyards of Vosne. Only Romanée-Saint-Vivant, among the top vineyards of Vosne, is larger.

The vineyard lies well up the slope with La Romanée and La Romanée-Conti to the south of it and Romanée-Saint-Vivant just across the road and is considerably larger than its traditional size. In the 1930s, a decree of the Minister of Agriculture permitted the vineyard slightly above it on the slope, known as Verroilles or Richebourg, to be included in the controlled place-name. This made legal a practice that was actually a long-standing custom. It added, however, some 7·6 acres to the *appellation* Richebourg. Unlike some of the other Great Growths of Vosne, this one is not a monopoly of any grower but is, at the time of writing, in the hands of eight different owners. Only three of these have sizeable holdings: Domaine Louis Gros, Domaine de la Romanée-Conti, and Charles Noellat.

Needless to say, the fact that eight different growers make the wine means that there will be some variation between any two Richebourgs of a given year. In general terms, however, it is the 'velvet wine' of Vosne. All the commune's wines have this velvety quality, but in Richebourg it is more pronounced than in the others. Beneath this veneer is a robust fullness and the wine acquires a superb perfume with age. The amount of wine averages about 4,800 imp. gallons (5,750 U.S.) annually or the equivalent of some 2,406 cases.

See VOSNE-ROMANÉE.

Riesling

A grape variety producing the most distinctive and noble wines of Alsace, the Moselle and the Rhine. The fruit is small, yellowish, not very juicy; but it is one of the great grapes of the world. Alsatian Rieslings are generally sold as such and the varietal name usually, but not always, appears on the label of the great German Rhine and Moselle Rieslings. Riesling is also grown in Austria, California, Chile and Switzerland.

Château Rieussec

Bordeaux white wine. District: Sauternes, France. Commune: Fargues.

After changing hands a number of times and acquiring sections which had formed adjoining small vineyards, Rieussec was consolidated in its present situation. Making a wine quite different from its neighbour, fuller-bodied but less subtle, it is contiguous with Château d'Yquem, and the property is about half in vine. The wine was officially classed a First Growth (*Premier Cru*) Sauternes in 1855.

Characteristics. Very *liquoreux*, or rich in unconverted sugar—but not one known to age well.

Vineyard area: 105 acres.

Average production: 7,000 cases.

Río Negro

Wine-producing province of Argentina (*q.v.*).

Rioja

Red wines. District: Northern Spain.

Within the last half-century the best Riojas have established themselves as incontestably the best red table wines in Spain. Even so—and in spite of the fact that they head Spanish wine-lists and are good value—these often tend to be only average wines. Yet an occasional bottle from one of the better firms shows how outstanding the Rioja can be, equal to any red wine except the finest Bordeaux and Burgundies. The trend, however, is to equalize quality in the large companies which dominate the market and comprise, with a few specified exceptions, the only firms allowed to produce those Rioja wines entitled to certificates of origin. On the other hand, the rise in the tide of overall quality can be expected to go on. As to quantity, the yield from 201,465 acres of vineyard is 31,400,000 imp. gallons (37,700,000 U.S.).

The beginnings of the industry in this region along the River Ebro are obscure, and it can be assumed that its northerly climate caused it to lag behind the more apparently vinous Mediterranean districts of Spain. Yet Rioja did take part, at least to some degree, in the flowering of Spanish wines during the period of the discovery of the Americas and the opening up of vast markets to Spanish export.

A difficulty peculiar to Rioja was the lack of any good road by which the wines could be sent out to the rest of Spain, and the world. For more than half a century, beginning in 1790, the achievement of this road was the goal of a wine industry's attempt to regain the splendour of the days of Spanish power.

The success story of Rioja starts with the founding, sixty-five years ago, of the viticultural station in Haro, heart of the kidney-shaped vineyards along the Ebro; and the more or less simultaneous beginning of the fight to eliminate all outside wine from Rioja and prevent any other Spanish wines from using the name—a fight not yet completely won.

History has come full circle and it is now generally recognized that Rioja owes its unique place among Spanish table wines to its geographical position. The region divides into two zones as it goes downhill with the steep Ebro Valley, and only Upper Rioja—Rioja Alta—is northerly and Atlantic in type. It is significant that Rioja Baja produces nothing but common wines, never bottled and little exported.

Denominations of Origin and the Making of the Wine

Two dozen companies have the right to make Rioja—wine of Rioja entitled to the place-name, the certificate of origin, and the small, square, mill-edged stamp of authenticity on the bottle label. The number is not officially limited to two dozen; but to qualify, a producer must have 400 hogsheads in his stores—this is a big investment and the ordinary man cannot afford the price of the wood for so many barrels. The system is admittedly hit-and-miss, not devised to keep anyone out but to permit supervision and control in a developing and improving yet still imperfect situation. Already a few growers and producers, not big enough to have the 400 barrels, have been allowed in because of the excellence of their wines.

Not to be compared with the tight wine laws of France, or those governing Sherry, the Rioja controls are far beyond anything in any other table-wine region within the country. The denomination Rioja, or the place-name of one of the villages within the zone, may only be used for wines combining certain specified characteristics and standards of quality. Where wines genuinely produced in the district do not quite come up to standard, the village name may appear on the label only according to this formula: 'This wine was made in the village of X, but has not achieved the quality demanded for Rioja.'

The legal zone for the production of Rioja falls within the limits of the province of Logroño, and in the following villages: Baños de Ebro, Barriobusto, Cripán, Eliego, El Villar, Labraza, Labastida, Laguardia, Lanciego, Lapuebla de Labarca, Leza, Moreda, Navaridas, Oyon, Páganos, Salinillas, Samaniego, Villabuena, and Yécora in the region of Alava; and Viana San Adrian, Azagra, Mendavia, Andosilla, and Sartaguda in Navarre. Wines which have been aged or 'elaborated' outside the zone are not allowed to carry the name Rioja.

The making of the wines follows French methods—not surprisingly since French hands and heads did the work some three-quarters of a century ago when phylloxera had destroyed the vineyards of Bordeaux but had not yet reached Rioja.

The flood of the French into Rioja in those days has left its mark: wines are vatted and fermented in much the same way as in France, and those not sold within a year as light, common wines are matured in oak casks, some of the Bordeaux size. Kept in cellars which, in certain *bodegas* (or wine-making establishments), resemble those of France to the last detail, the wines are racked two or more times a year. Nothing else is done to them apart from fining.

In one essential, the method differs from the one now used in France, and this is apparent in the finished wines. Riojas are generally kept far too long in the wood—up to fifteen years, as was sometimes done eighty years ago in Bordeaux—and then are sold immediately after being bottled, achieving no bottle-age at all. There are a few notable exceptions to this rule; the main one is to be found at the *bodega* of the Marques de Riscal in Elciego, where the French treatment is followed rigorously and the wines are bottled after three years and aged in the bottle. There is possibly a taste among Spaniards for weakened, over-oxidized, frail wines, based on their difference from most Spanish wines, which are generally big and hard. In any case, barrel-ageing of the wines is badly overdone. When this practice is corrected—and there are signs that it will be—the potentially splendid Rioja red wines will come even more into their own.

Rioja Wine Types: Bottle Labels

The Rioja wine district, officially delimited along the two sides of the River Ebro, is almost entirely in the province of Logroño in the north of Spain, a little east of Burgos. The small part not in Logroño province bulges like a bubble into the province of Alava—where the marked difference is that the Ebro, a narrowish thin stream at this point, cuts through the land, which now begins to rise. The important difference in the wines themselves is that here in Alava the Riojas are heavier and full-blooded, while in the plain of the Ebro they are lighter, more Claret-like.

The region is finely subdivided for local purposes, but in the present state of the development of the wines, three divisions are important.

Rioja Alta

Upper Rioja, the north-west end of the zone, above, and including, the city of Logroño. The climate is the same here as it is around the Basque coast and the Bay of Biscay, and so not unlike that of Bordeaux. The autumns, mild and long, are favourable to harvesting; spring is pleasant. There are hard frosts and some snow in winter but the season is not violent. Yet two dangers challenge the vines: late spring frosts, usually occurring at the end of April or the beginning of May after warmer weather has brought the sap up the plant; and the *solano*, a roasting, local wind coming out of the east.

Rioja Baja

Lower Rioja. The wines are rarely bottled. As the Rio Ebro drops towards the Mediterranean, below the town of Logroño, the climate changes; here, it is more like Aragón than the Bay of Biscay. Autumns and springs are violent, the weather is hotter; while Rioja Alta is moderately dry, Rioja Baja is classified as arid. Because of the greater heat, the season here is always two weeks in advance, yet in the vast stretch of vineyard along the Ebro, the grapes are harvested later than they are upriver—and, as a result of this extra maturing time, they produce a wine markedly higher in alcoholic content, reaching up to 15% or 16% as compared to 11% or 12·5% in Rioja Alta.

Alavesa

Wines in Alava are listed in the high-quality group, with those of Rioja Alta. Bottle labels sometimes state that the wine is an Alavesa. Generally, it will be heartier than Rioja Alta; it is habitually compared with Burgundies but, tasted on the spot, is reminiscent rather of a good Rhône wine.

Riojas are kept one year and then bottled and sold; or sold in barrel; or they are matured in American oak casks either of 600 litres (*bocoyes*) or 225 litres (*barricas bordelesas* or Bordeaux barrels). These maturer wines are the ones which generally reach both the foreign market and the better restaurants in Spain.

Vintage wines are labelled Cosecha (harvest) followed by the year (i.e. Cosecha 1964, Cosecha 1962), or Reserva or Reserva Especial, the latter designations sometimes followed by the year and sometimes not. Reserva is a wine which has been kept longer than a Cosecha (almost invariably in wood, not in bottle); and a Reserva Especial will generally have been kept longer still. It is not always easy to choose between them: the older wines are sometimes over-aged and flat from too long a life in the wood; on the other hand, the best wines of the greatest years are usually the ones set aside for this maltreatment. Vintage date, incidentally, is to be taken as more approximate than definite. It is now considered to be of a certain vintage if 'most' of the wine in the bottle or barrel is of that vintage. The greatest years of this century in Rioja are 1904, 1920, 1922, 1924, 1925, 1934, 1935, 1942, 1948, 1954, 1955, 1957, 1958, 1960, 1964 and 1965.

White wines are sweet (dulce) or dry (seco). The white wines cannot compete with the reds, and are too often *pasado* (maderized). Red wines are graded by age as Finos de mesa (fine table wines) or Reservas, and by degree of colour: rosado, clarete, ojo de gallo, and tinto, ranging from pale pink to deep red. Clarete and tinto are the types most often to be met with; the clarete is sometimes made by mixing white and red wines, but fortunately this is not general practice in Rioja—as it is in La Mancha—and most clarete is an honest pink wine produced by short contact with the colour-imparting skin of the red grape from which it comes. Tinto is simply the Spanish word for red wine—which is never called *rojo*, although the literal word *blanco* is used for the white.

Here, as in California, the wines are usually known by the names of the shippers and not by vineyards. It is freely admitted in Rioja that the various vineyards differ widely: it matters considerably whether the plot has a southern or a northern exposure; the soil of the hill slopes is primarily slate and very much more ancient than the alluvial soil of the valley bottom and the river edge, and this influences the wines. Nevertheless, separate vatting of musts according to vineyard is in its infancy. If a wine *does* carry the name of a vineyard—a few names, such as Zaco, Tondonia, and Paceta have become widely known—this will be largely symbolic. Standing at the edge of the town of Haro, for instance, and looking out over Viña Zaco or one of the other noted vineyards lying inland like the spread of a canvas tarpaulin folding towards the Ebro, you will learn that though originally the wine was entirely or almost entirely of the vineyard in question, as fame and demand grew the usual miracle was performed. A quantity equal to the demand was produced, regardless of the physical capacity and size of the vineyard.

In the past, Riojas were known as Cepa (vine variety) Sauternes, Cepa Chablis, Cepa Rhin, Cepa Barsac, Cepa Medoc, and so on; or sometimes as Estilo Sauternes, Especial Sauternes (or Graves, or Barsac), or even simply as Chablis, or Sauternes. This imitative labelling has recently been outlawed by an agreement with France. However, most Spanish restaurants continue the billings on their wine lists. The wines often do resemble the types they copy—but only approximately at best.

Vine Varieties

The rolling Rioja Alta, sheltered from rough

weather by high mountains—which are out of sight—has a khaki-coloured, parched look, something like Arizona, or North Africa. The patchwork hills striped and quilted by the vine plots might be in Chablis. Statistically, this is a wine country of about 100,000 acres of vine, producing yearly about 21,600,000 imp. gallons (26 million U.S.) of wine. The calcium soil, with its important slope deposits of slate, and the temperate climate, help to make Rioja wine what it is today—one of the best buys in red wine in the world, considering the price; and potentially a red wine which might rise to a high level.

Wine-making in the important growths is modernized. Even the many small growers who produce the ordinary wines sold everywhere in the north of Spain (but not entitled to the place-name Rioja) now plough the earth instead of chopping it by hand. At the same time, the backward corners of the province are primitive and picturesque. The ancient villages tucked into the hills are all off the main roads—an isolation which has safeguarded their character—and countless houses are distinguished by ornate coats-of-arms in stone. The district taking its wine name from a slurred-over pronunciation of one of the little rivers tributary to the Ebro, the Rio Oja, is poor, one of the poorest in all Spain. The general look of desolation in Rioja has comparatively little to do with the wine. Every large producer swears that while he buys grapes from small individuals when his own vineyard yield is insufficient, he never buys must or wine. All Rioja, from the export point of view, is made at least in theory in the two dozen big *bodegas*.

The principal wine producers in the Rioja area are as follows:

La Rioja Alta, S.A.
R. Lopez de Heredia, Viña Tondonia, S.A.
Bodegas Gómez Cruzado, S.A.
Carlos Serres, Hijo
Andrés de la Torre
Bodegas Lacuesta
Bodegas Franco Españolas
Bodegas Bilbao
Rioja Santiago, S.A.
Compañía Vinícola del Norte de España
Bodegas Bilbainas
Bodegas Riojanas
Bodegas El Montecillo
Vinos de los Herederos del Marqués de Riscal, S.A.
Vizconde de Ayala
Savin, S.A.
Federico Paternina, S.A.
Bodegas Berberana
Bodegas del Romeral-Felix Azpilicueta Martínez, S.A.

The red wines are produced from the grape varieties: Garnacha, Tempranillo, Graciano, Mazuelo, Miguel del Arco, and Monastrel. No Rioja vine, either red or white, is capable of making a satisfactory wine alone; all lack some essential ingredient—acidity, richness, finesse—and all the good wines are blends.

Garnacha, which resembles French Grenache, is the big common producer, weak in bouquet, and not a variety which ripens fully in the Rioja Alta, except in the hottest years. It yields the mass of wine in Rioja Baja—and other parts of Spain, especially around Madrid, where it is generally called Aragón or Tinto Aragonés, because it came originally from Aragón. Its wide use in Rioja is due mainly to its ability to resist *oïdium*, which, with mildew, is the great menace there.

The must of the Tempranillo is high neither in sugar nor in acid and is quite neutral, the other elements in a blend with this grape always informing the taste. But it matures quickly—although it does not keep particularly well—and it is valued for its contribution of colour. Graciano has a marked and quite individual perfume; Mazuelo, a variety close to the Carignan of the Rhône and Provence in France, would be more widely grown if it were not for its susceptibility to *oïdium*.

The white wines are usually a blend of Malvasía, Viura, Calagraño, Garnacha, Moscatel, and Turruntés. An increasing amount of white Garnacha (Garnacha Blanca) is being planted, but this variety is low in acidity—the chief flaw in Rioja white wines. The result is that a lot of sulphur dioxide (SO_2) is put into the musts, and, although volatile, leaves a residue of sulphurous taste.

Château Ripeau

Bordeaux red wine. District and Commune: Saint-Émilion, France.

Recently combined with Château Jean-Faure, adjoining it and long under the same ownership, Ripeau is now one of the largest producers among the best Saint-Émilion vineyards. Lying next to Château Cheval-Blanc, near the boundary of Pomerol, the vineyard suffered as badly as Cheval-Blanc and the Pomerol vineyards did in the February 1956 freeze, and there was little 1956, 1957, 1958, or 1959 Château Ripeau wine. Other later vintages, however, are in the market in quantity. The property is owned by Michel de Wilde, the son-in-law of Madame Loubat, who with her husband established both of the vineyards now combined.

Characteristics. A generous wine with an individual bouquet. Typical of a good Saint-Émilion.

Vineyard area: 45 acres.

Average production: 10,000 cases.

Ripley

American hybrid grape developed by the New York State Agricultural Station to be used as a table grape and for wine. The wine is white and dry, but by itself tends to be flat; the grape might contribute to a very superior blend if the proper partner could be found.

Riquewihr

Wine town in Alsace (*q.v.*).

Rishon-le-Zion

One of the main wine centres in Israel (*q.v.*).

Rivesaltes

Sun-baked district of Haut-Roussillon, France, famous for its Muscat wines.

See SWEET FORTIFIED WINES OF FRANCE.

Robertson

Wine district in the Little Karoo region of the Cape Province.

See SOUTH AFRICA.

Roche

See CLOS DE LA ROCHE.

Rochefort-sur-Loire

Wine commune in the Coteaux du Layon district of Anjou (*qq.v.*).

Roditis

One of the principal grape varieties used for Greek spirits.

La Romanée

Burgundy red wine. District: Côte de Nuits, France. Commune: Vosne-Romanée. Official classification: Great Growth (Grand Cru).

La Romanée is the smallest (2·1 acres) of the great vineyards of Vosne. It stands directly above La Romanée-Conti, from which it is divided by a footpath, and despite their proximity and the similarity between the names and the wines, the two are separate and distinct.

It is generally conceded in Vosne that the wines which come from this plot often lack some of the elegance and finesse of those from La Romanée-Conti; but it is also affirmed that the two are difficult to tell apart, even by the most expert tasters. La Romanée is perhaps the more robust of the two, gaining in fullness and body what it cedes in finesse.

The vineyard is owned entirely by the Abbé Just Liger Belair, and in 1959 he made 350 imp. gallons (422 U.S.) of wine, or the equivalent of a mere 180 cases. But as the sale and distribution of the wine is now entrusted to a shipper, the wine is never estate bottled, and this is regrettable.

See VOSNE-ROMANÉE.

La Romanée-Conti

Burgundy red wine. District: Côte de Nuits, France. Commune: Vosne-Romanée. Official classification: Great Growth (Grand Cru).

The vineyard of the Romanée-Conti, one of the most famous in the world, is contained in a scant four-and-a-half acres. The fabulous prices paid for the wine that trickles out are as high as any and the wine-drinker who manages to get a bottle considers himself lucky indeed. If the wine has become over-priced it is largely the fault of the wine snobs who order it to impress and so send up prices.

Contrary to usual Burgundian practice, *all* wine from the Romanée-Conti is estate bottled, and every bottle carries on label and cork the seal of the Société Civile de la Romanée-Conti, owners of this vineyard and the renowned La Tâche, as well as of parts of others. The property has been in the same family since 1869, when it was bought by Monsieur Duvaut-Blochet, and that was only the ninth time it had changed hands since the thirteenth century. The vineyard has been passed down within the family and is owned today by Monsieur de Villaine, a bank manager in Moulins. Among previous owners have been the Government of France, which seized the vineyard during the French Revolution; and the Prince de Conti, from whom it was seized. The Prince acquired it in 1760, in spite of the protests of Madame de Pompadour who wanted it for herself.

Because it is estate bottled, the only significant collection of older vintages of Romanée-Conti is at the Domain, and a visit to its cellars is a mouth-watering experience. These cellars are primitive and modest, but stacked with bottles, the contents of which have been described by P. Morton Shand as 'a mingling of velvet and satin'.

Actually, the wines fall into two distinct categories: the pre-1945 vintages, and those thereafter. Until that year the owners of the vineyard kept it planted in French vines, rather than graft their

French plants on to American root-stocks as did the other growers when phylloxera first hit France. The vines had been allowed to reproduce by *provignage*—burying the old vine in the ground with only one shoot emerging to become a new one—and thus were direct descendants of the vines planted by the monks more than twelve centuries earlier. But phylloxera, the devastating vine louse, is a constant menace and the vines had to be treated with enormous care and expensive chemicals. The latter were, of course, non-existent during the war years, manpower was desperately short, and the vines deteriorated until they were giving a meagre fifty cases a year. In 1945 the owners gave up the old ways and tore up their vineyards, replanting with vines grafted on to phylloxera-resistant American root-stocks.

The result is that the quantity of Romanée-Conti has risen sharply since 1945, but the quality is at present below that of the nectar once made.

At their best, the wines of the Romanée-Conti have perfect, rich balance combined with extraordinary breed and finesse, and local experts maintain they are the most 'virile' of the wines of Vosne—meaning, perhaps, that there is an iron hand beneath the velvet glove. The wines have an aftertaste that stays in the mouth an amazingly long time. While quantity is definitely higher than it was once, it is still not considerable. An average harvest may come to only 1,188 imp. gallons (1,425 U.S.) or less than six hundred cases.

See VOSNE-ROMANÉE.

La Romanée-Saint-Vivant

Burgundy red wine. District: Côte de Nuits, France. Commune: Vosne-Romanée. Official classification: Great Growth (Grand Cru).

The vineyard is a Great Growth (*Grand Cru*), one of the thirty-one outstanding great vineyards of the Côte d'Or, five of which are in Vosne. Occupying 23·6 acres, it is the largest of the Great Growths of Vosne and takes its name from the long-since destroyed Abbey of Saint-Vivant, its owner for a considerable period.

Romanée-Saint-Vivant is just down the hill from Romanée-Conti and Richebourg, above the village of Vosne, and despite its large size there are only four growers who share it. The wines have the qualities and characteristics of the other Great Growths of Vosne: the same velvety grace, and the expansive perfume. They are undoubtedly among the great wines of Burgundy. In 1960 the amount of wine made was 5,634 imp. gallons (6,763 U.S.).

Rosato

Italian term for pink wine or rosé.

Rosé

In French, pink or rose-coloured wine. When properly made it comes from red grapes fermented for two or three days on the colour-imparting skins and husks, but drawn off at the delicate moment when just enough colour has been absorbed to give the wine its attractive pink cast. In France, the best rosé is from Tavel near the mouth of the Rhône but some excellent ones are now being made in Bordeaux, in Anjou, and in most wine-producing regions. In America, where rosé is tremendously popular, some good examples come from California.

Rosé des Riceys

A still pink wine of Champagne (*q.v.*).

Rosette

White wines, semi-sweet and rarely distinguished, from Bergerac, France.

See BERGERAC.

Rosolio

A red Italian liqueur with a taste of roses. The French used to make their own version of this liqueur, which they called Rossolis.

Rossese or Dolceacqua

Red wine from Rossese grapes, grown along the Italian Riviera.

See LIGURIA.

Rosso Piceno

Red Italian wine from the Piceno Hills, on the fringe of the Apennines.

See THE MARCHES.

Rotgipfler

Grape variety cultivated in Austria.

Rouge

French term for red wine.

Rougeau (or Leaf Reddening)

Vine disease, caused by a wound which prevents the sap returning to the roots.

See CHAPTER EIGHT, p. 36.

Rough

A big red wine, with a considerable amount of tannin, will be rough before it has had time to mature, which in the biggest years may take well over a decade. This roughness is not to be confused with the coarseness of wines from poor grapes and poor vineyards—a common, harsh flavour which will never disappear with age.

Round

To be round, a wine must be harmonious but also big. It will be in perfect balance, and it gives a sense of 'roundness' in the way it fills the mouth.

Roussette

The principal wine of Seyssel, in Haute-Savoie, France. It is white, flinty-dry, and made from Roussette grapes.

See SEYSSEL.

Roussillon

See GRAND ROUSSILLON; SWEET FORTIFIED WINES OF FRANCE.

Ruby Port

Blended Port wine which has been aged in barrel but not as long as Tawny Port, which, if left alone, it will in time become. This is a younger, fresher Port.

See PORT.

Ruchottes-Chambertin

Burgundy red wine. District: Côte de Nuits, France. Commune: Gevrey-Chambertin. Official classification: Great Growth (Grand Cru).

Many excellent and even outstanding bottles can be found, although this wine is one of the lesser of the Chambertin family. Some severe critics have called the wine common, and lacking in breed, but while it is not generally the equal of the magnificent Chambertin, a well-made Ruchottes should be neither of these things.

The vineyard adjoins the Clos de Bèze, to the south of the village of Gevrey-Chambertin, and is fairly high on the slope for exceptionally great wines. It covers 7·9 acres, and production in 1960—an average-quantity year—amounted to 1,761 imp. gallons (2,113 U.S.) or the equivalent of about 850 cases.

See GEVREY-CHAMBERTIN.

Rüdesheimer Berg, Rüdesheimerberg

The Rüdesheimerberg, or Rüdesheimer Mountain, a steep slope rising up from the Rhine, produces the best Rüdesheim wines. The label will carry Rüdesheimerberg, written as either one or two words, followed by the name of the actual vineyard spot, as Rüdesheimer Berg Bronnen, or Rüdesheimer Berg Lay. Owing to the steepness of the cliff-like vineyards, drainage is excellent and in the wet years Rüdesheimer Berg wines are among the best Rheingaus. The grapes roast in the sun in the hot years, producing wine frequently below Rheingau average.

See RHEINGAU.

Ruländer

Greyish-coloured Burgundy grape (Pinot Gris) introduced into Germany by one Ruhland; it is also planted in Alsace and Switzerland. Also called Grauerburgunder or Tokaier.

Rully

A commune in the Chalon Slope of Burgundy which produces both red and white wines and has its own Appellation Contrôlée.

See CHALONNAIS.

Rum

Rum is the distillate of products of fermented sugar cane. Of all spirits, it retains the most of those natural taste factors which come to it from its product of origin. Starch-derived spirits, such as vodka from potatoes, or whisky from grain, must be cooked, or malted. In the case of rum, based on sugar, the processes by which starch is turned into sugar are not necessary: rum does not have to be distilled at very high proof, as gin and vodka do: it receives the minimum of chemical treatment, and can be aged in casks which have already been used for spirit-ageing, because it does not need the tannin which such a spirit as Cognac will absorb from the oak. Rum may be flavoured or adulterated by other processes than the essential reduction of its proof strength with pure water—but it need not be; and if it is a decent rum, it should not be. Its colour varies from water-white, the natural hue, through amber to mahogany. The only colouring matter used is sugar caramel, which does not affect the flavour. A rum's real character will be determined by the following factors:

The Material of which it is Made

Rum is made principally from molasses, which is the uncrystallizable mass remaining after the formation of sugar; sometimes directly from the sugar-cane juice; or from second-grade molasses and other residues. The last type is usually called *tafia*, not rum, and it is seldom worth exporting, or even bottling. The majority of fine rums come from molasses, but a few do not: one of the best of

Haiti is made directly from cane juice; and the most famous rum of Martinique comes from cane juice concentrated into a syrup.

Changing Tastes in Rum

Full body and a distinctive richness of flavour used to be the qualities most appreciated in rum; but in the last twenty-five years tastes have been gradually changing. Many people now prefer a lighter rum, subtler in flavour and more delicate in aroma. The greater demand for the light style has led to a more general use of the continuous column patent still.

Slow or Rapid Fermentation

The rapid fermentation *of a rum of the light type* can be completed in as little as twelve hours, and a day to a day and a half is general practice. Although Jamaica and other countries are now making a good deal of this style, Puerto Rican and Cuban are the usual examples of typical light rums. Slow fermentation, reinforced by the addition of *dunder* (the residue left in the still after distillation), produces a heavier type; men who prefer their rum distinctive and pungent say that any other kind is like skimmed milk. Slow fermentation may take up to twelve days. The Wedderburn and Plummer types, traditional Jamaican rums of the old style, are so identified with slow fermentation; and Martinique produces slowly-fermented heavy rums of *Grand Arôme*. High ester rums are made in much the same way as are the Wedderburn rums except that a much higher ester content is aimed at.

Yeast Types

The yeasts used in fermentation are cultured or natural. When they are cultured, it is said that they are likely to be bred in secret, like Derby runners, everything staked on their individuality. An important Haitian maker is convinced that the secret of his rum is in the harmony between cane and yeast, which come from the same place; whereas Puerto Rican distillers believe to a man that the taste of their product owes its virtue (very great, they say) to the private strain of yeast they cultivate.

Pot or Patent Still

As in the making of whisky, either the pot still or the continuous-operation patent still may be used. The patent still is more suitable for the increasingly popular light rums. Pot-still spirits retain more of their natural character; the rums are heavier and not, therefore, to all tastes. The old Jamaican style rum is the prototype for pot-distilled rums of greater body.

Proof at which Distilled

Lighter rums are distilled at higher proof. In Jamaica, for instance, distillation strength may rise to 96° (Gay-Lussac), whereas the fuller pot-still rums will be distilled at about 86° (Gay-Lussac).

Place of Origin

A somewhat confusing question. The U.S. Federal Alcohol Administration regulation puts it this way: 'Puerto Rico, Cuba, Demerara, Barbados, St. Croix, St. Thomas, Virgin Islands, Jamaica, Martinique, Trinidad, Haiti, and Santo Domingo rums are not distinctive types of rum. Such names are not generic but retain their geographical significance. They may not be applied to rum produced in any other place than the particular region indicated in the name.' The fact is that each main centre makes differing types of rum, but the distinct rum types *are* identified with certain areas. Jamaica is even now associated with a heavy, pungent rum although today it is producing lighter types; and conversely, light rums are attributed to Cuba or Puerto Rico, although each island makes a certain amount of rum in other styles. Differences in the rums are the result of differing methods of preparation, and of the influences of soil, climate, and especially water.

Origin of Rum

Rum is initially the essentially West Indian product of cane and water—sugar cane perhaps brought from the Azores by Columbus on his second voyage; and the pure West Indian water which tumbles down from the mountains. First records of rum are from Barbados in 1600; and here is a description of a rum punch-bowl of the West Indies in the spacious days of the eighteenth century:

'A marble basin, built in the middle of the garden especially for the occasion, served as the bowl. Into it were poured 1,200 bottles of rum, 1,200 bottles of Málaga wine, and 400 quarts of boiling water. Then 600 pounds of the best cane sugar and 200 powdered nutmegs were added. The juice of 2,600 lemons was squeezed into the liquor. Onto the surface was launched a handsome mahogany boat piloted by a boy of twelve, who rowed about a few moments, then coasted to the side and began to serve the assembled company of six hundred, which gradually drank up the ocean upon which he floated.'

Rum was overwhelmingly popular in the American colonies before 1775. Twelve million gallons (10 million imp. gallons) a year were downed, four gallons (3 imp.) per person; whereas one-and-a-quarter gallons a year per person for all spirituous liquors combined is the best that can be done today. One historian declares that the British law of 1763, designed to make the Americans give up Spanish West Indian rums in favour of the British product, caused the Revolution—and a revolution might just as well be fought over rum as over tea.

An apparently authentic story about Paul Revere tells that he set out on his ride in morose silence, and did not begin to shout that the English were coming until he had stopped at the home of a rum distiller—one Isaac Hall, Captain of the Minute Men—for two drafts of Medford rum. (Medford was the name for all the rum along the Atlantic Coast in those days.) George Washington, at any rate, was launched on rum. He was elected to the Virginia House of Burgesses in 1758 not by campaigning but by distributing among the voters 75 gallons of rum; and it was the Virginia House of Burgesses which later sent him to the Continental Congress.

Rum was used in the slave trade, boats loaded with the spirit going to Africa to trade, and bringing back Negroes. Dead Man's Chest, a tiny West Indian island, roistered its way into history—'Fifteen men on Dead Man's Chest—yo-ho-ho, and a bottle of rum.' In the 1920s, rum revived a kind of piracy, when the speed launches were running rum from Cuba to the Florida Keys.

After Prohibition, the United States developed a fad for drinking concoctions of rum mixed with slices of fruit and chunks of ice. This still goes on, although excellent brands of rum are now available.

The distillation process is approximately the same for rum as for whisky—except that rum need not be malted. (*See* DISTILLATION; GIN; WHISKY.)

By and large, the British drink British West Indian rum and the French the rums of the French West Indies. United States imports are principally from Puerto Rico, followed by the Virgin Islands, with Jamaica and Haiti a long way behind, and a still smaller amount from the French West Indies, Barbados, and other islands.

See RUM, PUERTO RICO; RUM, JAMAICA; RUM, BRITISH WEST INDIES; RUM, FRENCH WEST INDIES; RUM, HAITI; RUM, MARTINIQUE, etc.

Rum, Barbados

The beautiful garden-like island of Barbados in the British West Indies is composed largely of sandstone, coral, and volcanic ash deposits, a mixture which gives the soil a porous character very suitable to the cultivation of sugar cane. Although the warm climate is ideal, the island has no rivers and all the water used for irrigation as well as for other purposes must be pumped from subterranean caverns.

Since sugar cane is the island's major product, much rum is made; production has been increasing slowly while export has been rising more rapidly. Latest figures show a jump upwards in exports of one-third to about 720,000 proof gallons annually.

Barbados rum is distilled from molasses, the by-product of the sugar cane; and distillation is carried out both in pot stills and in patent stills. Semi-light in body and colour, Barbadian rums generally have a soft, almost smoky or leathery flavour. Only three distilleries operate on the island; the West India Rum Refinery, Barbados Distilleries, and Mt. Gay Distilleries. Certain of the old rums of the latter company can be drunk neat, like a fine brandy.

Rum, British Guiana

Two types of rum are made, pot still and continuous still.

The distinguishing characteristic of British Guiana rum is its exceedingly rapid fermentation—usually completed in from thirty-six to forty hours.

In addition to export rum, there is made for domestic consumption in this country of some 400,000 souls situated close to Venezuela a 'fruit' rum made by steeping various spices and fruits in the distillation from Coffey continuous stills. The product is then lightly tinted with caramel and bottled at a strength of 25° under proof or 85·7° U.S. proof. The resulting rum is lighter-bodied than the better-known Demerara variety. Courantin, one of the 'fruit' rums, is occasionally seen in England; it has a pleasant and quite noticeable scent of spices and fruit.

Demerara, named after the river along which the sugar cane grows, is the important rum of British Guiana (Guyana). Most is exported. Both continuous and pot-still processes are used. Made from molasses, not directly from cane juice, the rum is fermented spontaneously in wooden vats. A trace of sulphuric acid is added to kill bacteria and a little ammonium sulphate to feed the yeast. The rum is generally quite darkly coloured by the addition of caramel obtained by burning cane sugar. Demerara is not as heavy as might appear from its colour. Because of the very rapid fermentation process, it is not likely to have quite the pronounced flavour of rums which are obtained by slower fermentation. Among

Demeraran rums themselves, those distilled in pot stills will have up to a third more of the taste-giving esters than the Coffey-still varieties, and more than twice the amount of the higher alcohols. Demerara is exported at approximately 43° over proof, or 163·4° U.S. proof. British Guiana leads the other British-influenced countries of the Caribbean in rum export.

Rum, British West Indies

Barbados, Jamaica, British Guiana (Guyana), and Trinidad form this group in the Caribbean; the first, second, and fourth are islands, the third a small country on the north-east coast of South America. Together they produce about 7 million proof gallons of rum annually, Barbados and Jamaica making roughly 1½ million gallons each, while Trinidad and British Guiana make some 2 million gallons each. The leading exporter, with about 1½ million gallons, is British Guiana, followed by Jamaica with 1 million gallons, Barbados with 700,000 gallons, and Trinidad with 300,000 gallons.

Rum is the traditional drink of the British Navy. There are records of the ship's crew of Sir George Summer taking refuge from a hurricane at Bermuda in 1609 and seeking consolation in drinking rum, referred to as 'comfortable waters'. Hundreds of thousands of gallons of rum were included in the British supplies during the American Revolution. From the eighteenth century to the present day, rum has been rationed out daily to the men of the Royal Navy.

See RUM, JAMAICA; RUM, BARBADOS; RUM, BRITISH GUIANA; RUM, TRINIDAD.

Rum, Cuba

The light, delectable rum of Cuba is the natural drink of the Cubans, to whom the lightness of the type is all-important—and the rum is distilled and aged with that end in view, and treated with charcoal to make it even lighter.

Cane sugar, yeast, and the crystalline torrent water of the volcanic West Indian islands are the dominant ingredients of good rums. The Cuban and Puerto Rican types are generally distilled from molasses—a by-product of refined cane sugar—and fermented with cultured yeast and pure water. Cuban rum is often processed by blending or transforming newer spirits with older ones, and is sand-filtered during ageing.

There are two leading styles of rum in Cuba: Carta Blanca (White Label), which is the base for Daiquiris; and Carta Oro (Gold Label), to which some caramel is added to mellow the colour—this is, therefore, a little darker as well as sweeter than the Carta Blanca. The best rums come from the vicinity of Santiago, at the south end of the island. The principal producers prior to Castro's take-over were: Compañía Ron Bacardi, Alvarez Camp y. Co., Santiago; Arechabaia, Cadenas, Matanzas. Now all exports have ceased.

Rum, Demerara

The export rum of British Guiana.

See RUM, BRITISH GUIANA.

Rum, French

Rum is rapidly increasing in popularity in France, imported mainly from the French West Indies, and to a lesser extent from Réunion Island. The rums are not very often seen outside France and, except for two or three from Martinique, cannot be considered to figure in the world market.

French West Indies

A considerable quantity of full-bodied rum, some of it high grade, is made in the islands of Martinique and Guadeloupe. It must be remembered that the islands are not possessions or territories of France but are actual French departments, like the Gironde or Basses-Pyrénées. In this preferential situation, it is natural that the rums gravitate to the French mainland, where they are widely sold. Of the two islands, Martinique is more important.

See RUM, MARTINIQUE.

Réunion Island

The sole spirituous product of this former French colony in the Indian Ocean off the coast of Madagascar is rum. Like Martinique and Guadeloupe, Réunion is actually a department of France. About 833,000 imp. gallons (1 million U.S.) annually are distilled from molasses. Most of this is white rum, very little aged; but a small quantity of cask-matured rum is also produced.

French Guiana

Prévot and Mirande, the two distilleries, produce annually a little less than 165,000 imp. gallons (200,000 U.S.) of undistinguished white rum. No other spirit is made.

Madagascar

The rum production of this now independent territory off the African coast is small in comparison with the island's size; about 415,000 imp. gallons

(500,000 U.S.) annually have been made just recently, but generally the total is less than that. The rums come both from molasses and direct from cane juice. The methods of cask-ageing and of artificial colouring by the addition of caramelized sugar are each in use. Rum is the only spirit made.

Rum, Haitian

Although sugar cane is grown on all parts of the island of Haiti, it is in the north, behind the small port of Cape Haitian, that the best cane for rum-making is found. A rim of mountains runs along the north coast, and behind, in the valleys, the rainfall is not as abundant as it is elsewhere. The mountain Citadelle of the Black Emperor, Henri Christophe, who went dramatically mad and killed himself with a silver bullet, soars into the sky, high above the cane-cutting crews, rhythmically swinging their machetes while the chanter calls out his rising and falling phrases to set the pace.

A century and a half ago Haiti revolted and freed itself from France. Nevertheless, traditions, attitudes, and customs are still predominantly French; and the French skill in making fine brandy continues to influence the making of Haitian rum—which is double-distilled in pot stills, the first run, or raw rum, being redistilled. This is the same method used in the production of Cognac brandy. First-run Haitian rum, however, is often sold as a low-priced island product, although never exported. It is completely colourless: hence its name—clairin. On the Haitian feast days, this rum is sold raw by the glass, from small folding stands placed along the streets and roadways, each stand lit with a flickering lamp which gleams like a yellow star. Clairin is considered to have the special virtue of propitiating the powerful gods of Voodoo. For this reason, or perhaps only because it is cheap, it is the libation spirit poured on the ground at the Voodoo ceremonies (90% of the country still worships in the religion brought by the slaves from Africa), and the gods have their taste before the celebrants begin to drink.

The best known of Haitian rum, and one of the fine rums of the world, is Rhum Barbancourt. This is medium-bodied and has an exquisite balance. According to Monsieur Jean Gardère, maker of Barbancourt, this is to some extent due to the fact that a certain yeast found in the area where the cane grows is used to ferment the juice. This common origin, with the same soil ingredients and conditions, has a subtle influence on both yeast and cane juice, producing the harmony which does undoubtedly exist in the rum. The juice, which is pasteurized in order to seal in the natural vitamins throughout distillation, is processed as soon as it has been crushed from the cane, and there is no secondary fermentation. The Barbancourt plant, founded in 1862, now has a capacity of 416,000 imp. gallons (500,000 U.S.). One-star, three-star and five-star rums are made, the former originally limited to Haitian sale, but both are now exported.

Until a century and a half ago, France was the market for Haitian rums, import of which sometimes reached 15 million imp. gallons (18 million U.S.) a year. Today, Martinique rum dominates the French market. Jean Gardère says that the persistent link between France and Haiti is the kinship of soils; the calcareous soil underlaid with lime, which yields rum in Haiti, is practically identical with that which gives two of the greatest vinous products of France—brandy in Cognac and wine in Champagne.

The following are the principal rum distillers of Haiti:

Proprietor	*Name of rum*	*Distillery*
Jean Gardère	Rhum Barbancourt	Damien (Port-au-Prince)
René Audain	Rhum Tropical	Manègue (Port-au-Prince)
Hermann Colas	Rhum Marie Colas	Cazeau (Port-au-Prince)
Guy Séjourne	Rhum Champion	Croix des Bouquets
Max Nazon	Rhum Nazon	Port-au-Prince
Armand Tesserot	Rhum Tesserot	Port-au-Prince

Rum, Jamaica

No centre of rum-making has been so much affected by recent changes in taste as Jamaica has been. Traditionally, a heavy, rich flavoured, almost pungent rum was made here—slow-fermented, strengthened with dunder and distilled in pot stills at low proof.

Nowadays, although Jamaican rums still tend to have a more characteristic flavour and aroma than do most others, they are definitely lighter than they used to be, and the slow-fermentation method has been abandoned. The rums made can be divided into four types: light continuous-still rum—or common clean; light and medium-bodied, pot-still rum; Wedderburn and Plummer heavier types; high ester rum.

For the first type, molasses is the raw material, and distillation is carried out in a continuous still of two or three columns—distillation strength may be as high as 96° (Gay-Lussac). Great care is taken not to remove the true rum constituents of the fermented wash.

Light and medium pot-still rums are made from a wash obtained by mixing cane juice, high-grade molasses, water and acid. In the pot still, characteristic taste and smell are retained.

Wedderburn and Plummer rums have more body than the previous types—in these the tradition of the past is preserved, and anyone who wants to sample an old, robust Jamaica rum should taste one of them. Most of the pot-still rums are distilled at around 86° (Gay-Lussac).

High ester rums are fermented and distilled in much the same way as are Wedderburn—but the ester content must be higher.

The bulk of the Jamaican (and of other West Indian) rum is taken to London to be aged and bottled there.

Rum, London Dock

British West Indian rum taken in bulk to London and aged and bottled there.

Rum, Martinique

The large production of 3,500,000 imp. gallons (4,200,000 U.S.) annually divides to approximately 2 million imp. gallons (2,400,000 U.S.) distilled from molasses and about 1 million imp. gallons (1,200,000 U.S.) distilled directly from the juice of the sugar cane.

There are nearly 100 principal growers of cane sugar and about fifty rum-makers. The capital, Fort-de-France, is as much a town of rum as any other in the world. The dusty savannah with its statue of Josephine, who left the island to become in time the bride of Napoleon, is fringed all along one side by the dingy rum offices, piled up to the roofs with crates awaiting shipment. The port is at the side of the town, not along the main quay but on an inlet, where the trans-oceanic vessels rear over the houses, their stacks poking up incongruously along what appears to be a marine avenue, a little lazy smoke appearing as they get up steam to carry the rum out to the world. At one time, Martinique was the proud owner of a rum capital quite different from the rather tawdry and crowded town of Fort-de-France. This was St. Pierre, richest city of the Caribbean. The ruins may still be seen—handsome cobbled streets along the sides of which pure mountain water bubbles and sings. The buildings are crushed, empty skulls overgrown with wild banana, vine, and mango: in a few seconds, early in the century, a blast from the nearby volcano obliterated the town, killing 40,000 people. Despite the desolation, there are several rum companies established in the strip of St. Pierre which is coming to life again along the coal-black, volcanic beach; and one of the best known of all the rums, Saint James, has its plantations nearby.

While about fifty proprietors make the rum, it is said in Martinique that at the head of the industry are ten families. This led, in the early fifties, to a strike probably unique in history—'the strike of the ten families'. When the sugar cane is ripe, it must be cut and treated at once. Since a Communist government was then in control of the island, the rum and sugar owners considered that they were being taxed out of existence. The cane ripened and the sole crop of the island was ready to be made. 'Now,' said the ten families to the Communist deputies, 'we go on strike. *We* can hold out over a year of no profits. Do you think you can? Without sugar and rum there will be no crop to tax, and no income for you. Don't you think we ought to sit down and have a reasonable discussion?'

The rums made directly from cane juice are sometimes strengthened by the addition of dunder for the fermentation and sometimes not. (Dunder is the residue left in the still after distillation and is generally used in processes of slow fermentation.) When the rums are uncoloured by cask-ageing and remain white they are called Grappe Blanche. Such spirits are mainly consumed on the island, forming the base for the inevitable Martinique Punch.

Punch Martiniquais, of early West Indian origin, is probably British. The recipe is: rum, cane-sugar syrup, and a slice of lemon peel. In the happy days just before inflation, the cost was 7 francs (now 1½*d.* or 2 cents) and they gave a customer the sugar-syrup bottle, the rum bottle, a tumbler, and left him to himself. By bringing in a sugar-cane syrup usually made in Martinique, the firm of Duquesne has introduced the punch in France.

A single Martinique rum is made by the fermentation of dunder, about 60%, with concentrated cane-juice syrup. This is the well-known Rhum Saint James, sold in its squarish tall bottle. Its darkness and its aroma distinguish it from most other rums.

Rums made from molasses are fermented with dunder and coloured with caramelized sugar. The premium rums of this style are called Grand Arôme and are slow fermented over a period varying from eight to twelve days. The heavy, rich rums compare with the Wedderburn-type rums of Jamaica, the prototype for the style.

Many consider Rhum Clément, made both white and tawny, to be the aristocrat of Martinique rums. The distillery near the village of François is unpretentious. The canes are trundled on threading railway lines, pushed by the black workers or pulled by a tiny engine, and are then carried up into the jaws of the crushing rollers on belts like greatly enlarged tyre-chains. Juice drips stickily into the vats; bled, smashed cane slides off down a chute. The juice achieved by this process is converted into several grades of rum, the finest of which, one is told by Monsieur Charles Clément himself—small, dapper, and the most charming of men—are aged upwards of a dozen years. Rhum Duquesne, another good type, is made in the south of the island. Part of the production is distilled as white rum, sold under the trade mark 'Genippa'; the rest is aged in warehouses, to be sold as 'Grand' Case' (silver label, three years old) and 'Val d'Or' (gold label, ten years old). The whole enterprise is a family business managed by Monsieur O. des Grottes.

Rums utilizing molasses are almost always made at distilleries connected with the large sugar refineries. There are not so many of these, the important ones being at Vive—run by Fernand Clerc, whose three hundred pounds make him in at least one sense the biggest rum man on the island—at Galion, Rivière Salée, François and Lareinty. The distilleries making rum direct from cane juice are much more numerous.

Several other spirituous drinks are made in Martinique, some of them based on rum. They include the native rum punch, bottled by the firm of Dogue; anisette, triple-sec, crème d'orange, and other liqueurs. Orange is the most common flavouring. Maduva, messica, and maitina are all concocted with essence or juice of orange.

Rum, New England

Rum, of a particularly strong, heavy, and hearty sort, was among the factors which shaped New England. Blackstrap molasses came in from the West Indies to Connecticut, Rhode Island, and Massachusetts, and went out again as rum—to the taverns of the northern colonies, by ship to the southern ones to be traded for cotton and tobacco, and to Europe for the goods the New World was not yet prepared to make for itself. The most important aspect of the rum business, however, was the 'triangular trade' which made the fortune of many a New England sea-captain. Rum, shipped from New England to Africa, bought slaves. Slaves, carried to the islands of the West Indies, filled the ships with molasses and the molasses was brought back to New England to make rum. The unsuccessful efforts of George III to tax molasses added as much heat to the cause of the American Revolution as did the more renowned Stamp Tax, and 'taxation without representation' was denounced over many a glass of New England rum in many a wayside tavern.

Perhaps the first of the important spirit industries of the United States, New England rum is still being made in Massachusetts, where about 166,000 imp. gallons (200,000 U.S.) of it are sold each year. It is still a heavy rum, dark, pungent, and full-bodied. Distilled at no more than 160° proof, it is aged in charred oak barrels; and it is from this ageing that it takes its characteristic dark colour. There are only three firms making New England rum today.

In addition to those still being made and sold, there are some superb old rums to be found in the private cellars of New Englanders—which, once tasted, stand with certain fine old American Bourbons in the same class as fine French Cognacs.

Although their populations are small, the New England states of Maine and New Hampshire have the highest present *per capita* consumption of rum in the United States.

Rum, Panay

See RUM, PHILIPPINE ISLANDS.

Rum, Philippine Islands

Two leading brands of rum are made: Tanduay and Panay. These have different flavours and Tanduay is by far the better seller of the two; it is also the higher priced. Present average monthly production of the Tanduay Distillery Inc. of Tanduay and Panay is 41,000 imp. gallons (50,000 U.S.).

Rum, Puerto Rico

Puerto Rico is the foremost world producer of rums and its products dominate the United States market, accounting for 70% of the rum consumption there. The two main types are White Label (very light-bodied) and Gold Label (slightly less light). In the United States, White Label outsells the Gold by about three to one, while in Puerto Rico itself the proportion is reversed—although there is not such a large demand for it among the inhabitants of Puerto Rico as there is for such cheaper varieties as Palo Viejo and Ron Llave.

Cuba (*q.v.*), the other island which is famous for its light rums, also produces White Label and Gold Label.

Puerto Rico has always depended upon its rich and abundant crop of sugar cane as a vital means of support and it is from this sugar cane that the rum industry draws its existence. Ponce de Leon, who headed the first government of the island, is known to have distilled the cane, and a despatch writer in

1526 reports that the natives were getting tipsy on sugar-cane rum. Ponce de Leon was a commercially-minded man, and one authority goes so far as to state that his search for the fountain of youth was nothing more than a quest for a sound distillable water.

The refining of raw sugar cane results in fine sugar and a by-product called black-strap molasses. Puerto Rican rums are distilled from this molasses, fermented with cultured yeast and mountain water, aged under Government control, and required to be shipped in bottle. During the war years when whiskey was short, rums of every description were made and many a bad Puerto Rican rum or purported Puerto Rican rum found its way into the United States. After the war, these could no longer be sold and they remained a glut on the market; and Puerto Rico established strict export laws to assure high-quality rums under the island imprint. The Government now operates a rum pilot plant through the University of Puerto Rico—the only instance in which a project of this nature is Government sponsored.

Puerto Rican rum is a characteristic type and is usually light-bodied and dry in contrast to the thicker aromatic rums of Martinique. Generally, Puerto Rican-type rums are fermented with cultured yeast and distilled in patent stills.

Puerto Rican rums are made on widely scattered points of the island, which have sharp differences in climate, ranging from almost perpetual rainfall to almost constant drought. The soils vary too; and, finally, each distiller cultivates his own yeast from a single yeast cell, producing the type which is peculiarly identified with his own brand name. Yeast is continually manufactured by every distiller in order to provide a sufficient amount for the carrying on of fermentation from day to day, and the yeast strain is never allowed to die. It is considered in Puerto Rico to be the secret of the rum. Something in these yeasts and soil and climatic conditions indelibly marks the rums, and as there are intuitive wine-tasters, so there are rum connoisseurs who boast that when they taste a glass of rum they can say exactly where it came from.

Many of the old distillers who made rum before Prohibition were forced out of business during that period. An exception is the Puerto Rican Distilling Company, maker of Ronrico, which is generally light, although some 151° heavier-bodied rum is made. Fourteen distiller permits are at present granted in Puerto Rico. The Destilería Bacardi claims to have the largest capacity of any distillery in the world. The principal exported brands (arranged alphabetically) are: Bacardi, Boca Chica Carioca, Don Q, Maraca, Merito, Ronrico.

Rum, Tanduay

One of the leading types made in the Philippine Islands.

See RUM, PHILIPPINE ISLANDS.

Rum, Trinidad

The rums, which are medium light in type, are distilled from molasses in continuous stills. Before fermentation, the molasses is diluted with water and clarified—which makes the following fermentation easier to control. Yeast is added, and the quick fermentation will be over in anything from thirty-six to forty-eight hours. The resultant rums, clean but not as distinguished as some of the other styles, are distilled at strengths varying between 83° and 96° (Gay-Lussac).

Rum, Virgin Islands

The rums tend to be medium-style, generally somewhat heavier than the light rums of Puerto Rico. Much of the product is exported in bulk.

Of the three islands, St. Thomas, St. John, and St. Croix, the last is much more suited to the growing of sugar cane, and therefore to the production of rum. St. Thomas is small, hardly more than a few mountains rearing up out of the Caribbean Sea; while St. Croix is much more extensive, with many stretches of flat land, almost the whole of its surface consisting of beautiful beaches surrounding a vast field of cane. The rums of St. Croix are called Cruzan, and this name will frequently appear in one form or another on the label. The local Government owns and operates the distillery.

Rumania

Vines were grown in Rumania long before our era. There were vineyards in Scitia Minor (today's Dobrudja) even before the Greeks founded their Black Sea colonies, early in the seventh century B.C. And on the foothills of the Carpathians there long existed such large plantations as those at Cotnari and Uricani, Huşi, Odobeşti, Panciu, Nicoreşti, Dealul-Mare and Drăgăşani. The Greeks sent the wine in amphoræ throughout the civilized world of their day. Later on, the merchants of the northern ports carried away great casks of the wine to their big fairs, which would not have been complete without the barrels of Cotnari, Odobeşti, and Drăgăşani.

Planted recently, and now developing well, are the vineyards of Tîrnave, Sîmbureşti, and Segarcea. The extension of the vineyards over most of the country is due first and foremost to the fact that Rumania is situated almost entirely in the vine-growing zone (towards the northern limit) and the country has the favourable features of rolling hills, with sunny, sheltered slopes and southern exposure, and a wide range of suitable soils.

Principal Regions

The Cotnari Vineyard

In north-east Rumania, near the historic town of Iassy, these vineyards cover the lower slopes of the Carpathians and enjoy splendid conditions of climate, soil, and exposure. Cotnari is one of the oldest wine-producing districts in the country—in 1646 it was mentioned by the Jesuit monk, Mareus Bandinus, in an account of his sojourn in Moldavia. Old as it is, the vineyard still flourishes. Its new plantations, the result of modern scientific knowledge, promise a great development in the near future.

Grape varieties: Grasă de Cotnari, Fetească Albă, Tămîioasa Romînească, Frîncuşa.

Type of wine. Cotnari is a natural dessert wine, with 13%–15% alcohol and more than 50 grammes in a litre of residual sugar. It is well balanced, with a particularly fine flavour and bouquet.

The Murfatlar Vineyard

Situated close to the Black Sea, on the Murfatlar hills, the vineyard has a character all its own: the other plantations in the country are, in general, more scattered; here they form an unbroken vineyard of more than 1,730 acres on sunny slopes fanned by a mild sea breeze, and the wine-making plants are run according to up-to-date methods by qualified technicians. There exists, also, in this region, an experimental station of the Institute of Horticultural and Viticultural Research.

Grape varieties. The prevailing grape here is Pinot Chardonnay. Other types, such as Pinot Gris, Muscat Ottonel, Pinot Noir, and Cabernet Sauvignon, are also grown, with satisfactory results.

Type of wine. Murfatlar is a dessert wine, with a fine bouquet in which a faint, unique nuance of orange-flower is detectable.

The Tîrnave vineyard

Extending along the banks of the River Tîrnave, the vineyards, although not very old and regarded as relatively new, are already well known for the quality of their wines. The more important areas are: Mediaş, Richiş, Jidvei, Seuca, Valea-Lungă, Aţel, Tigmandru, Vorumloc—to mention only a few of the more outstanding.

Grape varieties to be found in the vineyard area are: Italian Riesling, Fetească, Ruländer, Furmint, Traminer, Sauvignon, Neuburger, Muscat Ottonel.

Type of wine. The vintners have succeeded in preserving the formula for the old and famous Perla de Tîrnave. This is a well-balanced blend of the main grape varieties grown in the vineyard and comprising in its complex bouquet the whole character of the Tîrnave region.

The Dealul-Mare Vineyard

Where the lower slopes of the Carpathian hills imperceptibly meet the plain and the hillocks bask in the hot rays of the sun, the vines produce such Rumanian favourites as the wines of Valea Călugărească, Tohani, Săhăteni, Urlaţi, Istrita, Pietroasele.

Grape varieties: Italian Riesling, Fetească Albă, Tămîioasa Romînească, Muscat Ottonel.

Type of wine. The pride of the Valea Călugărească vineyard is the red wines from the Pinot Noir and the Cabernet Sauvignon. These are big wines of a rich, dark colour, with a pleasant flavour, harmonious, and velvety, yet full of character. The white table wines of Tohani and Săhăteni are well known and well liked.

The Focşani Vineyard

This is the largest stretch of vineyard in Rumania, extending over such varied country and types of soil, and subject to climatic conditions so diverse, that the wines produced in the region are correspondingly various. The principal types are:

Odobeşti. White table wines, and quality wines from Riesling, Fetească, Muscat Ottonel, and Aligoté grapes.

Coteşti. White and red table wines and quality wines from Riesling, Fetească, Muscat, Pinot Noir, and Cabernet Sauvignon grapes.

Panciu. White table wines, especially appreciated for their freshness.

Nicoreşti. Red table wines and quality wines from Băbească de Nicoreşti.

The Banat Vineyard

There are two centres of production: the vineyards of the plain—Teremia Mare, Tomnatec—which produce large quantities of pleasant table wines of a greenish-white colour and of a consistent quality, and the hill vineyards, such as Buziaş, Recaş, Miniş, Ghioroc, Baratke, Pîncota, and Şiria.

Grape varieties used in the white wines of Teremia and Tomnatec are: Creaţa (Riesling de Banat), Majorca, and Steinschiller.

Type of wine. From the stony terraces of Miniş comes the famous Kadarka de Banat—a red wine appreciated for its characteristic flavour and aroma.

The Other Vineyards

The white wines of Drăgăşani, the white and red wines of Segarcea, the semi-dry white wines of Alba Iulia, Aiud, Lechinţa, and Bistriţa complete the wide range of wine production in Rumania.

It has been estimated that by the development of the nurseries and by the application of modern scientific methods of viticulture and viniculture Rumania's vineyards should, by 1968, extend over more than 740,000 acres. The present plan is to plant large areas with varieties which will ensure the basic production necessary for the big vinicultural combines which are being created in order to turn the country's great wine potential to the best account.

WINE EXPORTS

Wine has become an important export only in recent years. In 1960 more than 8,800,000 imp. gallons (10,600,000 U.S.) were sent abroad—different varieties to suit the tastes of different markets. Thus, to the German Federal Republic are exported white and red table wines from Riesling, Fetească, Kadarka, Cabernet Sauvignon, and Rotburgunder grapes. To Austria, besides ordinary white wines, Rumania sells quality wines of the Riesling, Fetească, Ruländer, Muscat Ottonel, Tămîioasa Romînească varieties, as well as red wines such as Rotburgunder and Cabernet Sauvignon. Rumanian wines are also exported to Switzerland, Belgium, Holland, Sweden, Denmark, France, and Great Britain—and, of course, in great quantities to Poland, Czechoslovakia, and East Germany.

The following are the principal varieties of wine bottled for export by the Focşani Fructexport:

White Table Wines

Perla de Tîrnave	Aligoté
Fetească de Tîrnave	Riesling de Dealul-Mare
Riesling de Tîrnave	Ordinary white table wine
Grünsilvaner	Superior white table wine
Rulända	
Furmint	
Sauvignon	

White Dessert Wines

Cotnari
Murfatler
Muscat Ottonel

Red Wines

Pinot Noir	Cabinet
Cabernet	Băbească de Nicoreşti
Kadarka	

In 1959, Rumania entered wines for the competition organized by the French at Montpellier. According to an enthusiastic French report these wines: '. . . were a pleasant surprise . . . a sumptuous Merlot de Nicoreşti, ruby-coloured and with a delicate flavour . . . Cabinet de Ploieşti, light and with a pleasing finesse. The dry and semi-dry white wines of Coteşti remind one of our Alsatian growths, and can be classified among the best in the world. The Riesling, with its freshness, and the Fetească with its delicate yet definite aroma has met with unanimous approval. In the same group, the Fetească de Tîrnave lived up to its name—The Pearl of Tîrnave. . . . The thick Chardonnay de Murfatlar with its taste of honey . . . and the subtler Cotnar . . . delighted the tasters.'

Rumbullion, Rumbustion

Two seventeenth-century English West Indian terms for rum. The exact origin of the words is obscure, although it has been suggested that they come from the dialect of Devonshire.

Ruppertsberger

Good wines of Mittelhaardt in the German Palatinate. The best vineyards are Hoheburg, Goldschmidt, Linsenbusch, Nussbien.

See PALATINATE.

Russia

Wine production in the U.S.S.R. is rapidly increasing and a yearly output of 250 million imp. gallons (300 million U.S.) is being aimed at—the 1962 figure reached 186,120,000 imp. gallons (23,344,000 U.S.); whereas in the ten-year period before the devastation of the Second World War it averaged 110 million imp. gallons (132 million U.S.). While wine, especially on the borders of the Black Sea, has always been important in Russia; it was in the 1930s that the Government undertook a rapid expansion of viticulture in the naturally favoured areas, particularly the Soviet Republics of Armenia, Azerbaijan, and Georgia, in the neck between the Black and the Caspian Seas, and in the Crimea. By 1948 the acreage in vine tripled the pre-Revolution figure and had passed a million acres;

in 1962 it had risen to some 2,567,500 acres, many of them planted in hybrids. Over 2 million imp. gallons (2,400,000 U.S.) were exported in that year. In England, for instance, six Russian table wines were on sale: red—Mukuzani and Saperavi, from Eastern Georgia, and the heavier Negru De Purkar from Moldavia; white—Tsinandali and Ghurdzhani from Georgia, and Riesling called Anapa.

Increase of production is partly due to territorial acquisitions, notably in the present Moldavian Soviet Socialist Republic—formerly Bessarabia and a part of Rumania. Bessarabia has always produced a large quantity of wines, especially around Kishinev, now the capital of the Moldavian S.S.R.; much of this wine, formerly known as Bessarabian, also comes from around the mouth of the River Dniester, in the region of what is Belgorod Dnestrovskiy, but was Akkerman—a name by which the wines were frequently known. This district is now actually in the Ukraine.

Very important in the Soviet scheme of wine expansion is the making of sparkling wines. By 1960 25 million bottles were being marketed annually. Probably the best is Kaffia, from the Crimea. A close second, if not equal, is that made at the Abraou Dursso Collective at Krasnodar in the region of the Kuban Valley near the Sea of Azov, a section always important in Russian viticulture. The wine is the same as the white wine of Abran (sometimes wrongly attributed to the Crimea) which lies to the west.

Important Districts

With a few mediocre exceptions, all the wine of the Soviet Union is produced in the vast arc of southern Russia, beginning at the Rumanian border on the west and stretching across the north of the Black Sea, the Caucasus, the Caspian Sea, and finally the north of Iran and India to the frontiers of China and Mongolia. The whole of this huge region produces wines in larger or smaller quantities but all the important ones come from west of the Caspian Sea—from the lower River Don, from around the Sea of Azov, and especially from the Crimea. Good wines are produced in the Caucasian republics of Azerbaijan, Georgia, and Armenia.

From earliest times, vines flourished in these regions, and wines are known to have been made long before our era. Traces of viticulture have been found in the ancient kingdom of Van which, about a thousand years before Christ, extended as far as the Armenian plain and the southern part of Transcaucasia. By the time of Herodotus (*fl.* 460 B.C.), the wines of Armenia had won great renown. When, some 250 years earlier, the Assyrians descended on the cities of Van, they found and pillaged great cellars of wine. Sulphur was already in use, and some of the wine is believed to have been pressed from sun-dried grapes. The Georgians, also, learned very early to cultivate their vines. Archæologists have discovered painted wine jars and large amphoræ dating from, at latest, the second millennium B.C.; in the *Odyssey*, Homer praised the 'perfumed, sprightly wines of Colchis (western Georgia), land of the golden grape'. And Xenophon related that the inhabitants of the Black Sea shores made robust wines, pleasant and aromatic when mixed with water.

Crimea

The sweet wines and the dessert wines, both red and white, are the most important, though dry wines and fortified wines are made, as well as sparkling wines, which include the good Kaffia. Production is not large, but the small area of the Crimean peninsula thrusting into the Black Sea is the finest wine region of Russia. The southern and eastern sections are best, and important vineyards lie along the coasts and near the cities of Sevastopol and Simferopol. Crimean viticulture was originally developed at the beginning of the last century, under the direction of Pallas, a French expert who brought many workers and managers from France to create or improve the vineyards. The chief estate, which gave its name to the most famous wine, was Massandra, the property of Prince Woronzow. Today Massandra is the name used for a combine of a number of Crimean wine collectives, and there is a red Massandra and a dry white one. But the most famous of these wines, still being made, is the rich amber, fortified Madeira-type, sometimes considered the best wine of Russia. Other outstanding Crimean wines are the white Livadia, made from the Muscat (there is also a red Livadia from the Cabernet grape); the dry white Sémillon Oreanda (usually called Orianda outside Russia); the Saperavi or, nowadays, the Saperavi Massandra, a dry red wine not to be confused with the great golden dessert Massandra, but a very flavourful wine on its own account; the pink dessert Alupka, and the Ay-Danil dessert wines. A number of grape varieties known in Europe are used here—for example, Riesling, Cabernet, Pinot Gris, and, most extensively, Muscat.

River Don

The lower Don, as it descends to empty into the Sea of Azov below Rostov, produces red and white wines and a relatively small quantity of sparkling wine, the best-known of which is Donski. The viticultural centres are Tsimliansk, Constantinovka, and Novocherkassk. Grape varieties are of local type: Siberian, Krasnotop, Pukhliakovski, and others.

Moldavia

Formerly Bessarabia and part of Rumania, Moldavia produces the largest quantity of wine in the U.S.S.R., but much of the region is planted in hybrid vines which give ordinary wines. There are also, however, some Pinot, Aligoté, Riesling, Traminer, and other European varieties.

Ukraine

After the scourge of the vine louse phylloxera in the last century, a great percentage of the area was replanted in hybrids. These are now being systematically replaced. Centres are Odessa and Nikolayev on the Black Sea, and Dniepropetrovsk on the Dnieper.

Stavropol

Dessert and sparkling wines from the north slopes of the Caucasus Mountains.

Krasnodar

A region, and also its principal city, lying east of the Black Sea and the Sea of Azov. Good red and white dry wines are made along the Black Sea, near Anapa and Novorossiysk, from the Riesling and the Cabernet grapes. There are some very large collective farms, one of which, with about 2,500 acres, was called Molotov. The Kuban Valley in this district has always been famous for its large production of sparkling wine, including that from the Abrau-Dursso Collective, one of the best in the U.S.S.R. Two sparkling wines that are exported from this area are Krasnodar itself and Isimljanskoje Igristoje.

Georgia

With about 200,000 acres, the Georgian Republic is much the largest producer among the first-quality wine districts, containing some of the oldest vineyard sites in Russia. Some Georgian wines seen abroad are white Myshako Riesling and Ghurdjurni. The Takhetia region is the most successful, and the best wines include the white Napureouli and Tsinandali; the red Mukuzani, and Mzvane or Mtzvane. A quite good red wine is made from the Saperavi grape variety, which also produces one of the finest red table wines of the Crimea. Mzvane, making the white wine of the same name, is also a grape variety; and another local type of importance is the Rka-Ziteli, giving the white wine Rka-Ziteli.

Azerbaijan

Table wines are produced in Russian Azerbaijan on the border of Persia. Kirovabad is the centre, with Kurdamirsk, Chemakhinsk, and Geokchai. Dessert wines and fortified wines are also made in this region.

Armenia

Wine has always been a fundamental product in the Armenian economy and the region is called 'Fatherland of the Vine'. Natural wines, fortified wines, and brandy are made in large quantities. The wine centres are Echmiadzin, Achtarak, Vedin, and Oktemberian.

In addition to the foregoing important districts, expanding wine production by means of irrigation is under way in Turkmenistan where fortified wines, a so-called Tokay, and Yasman-salik and Kara-Isium are made. In Uzbekistan, north of Turkmenistan, three-quarters of the grape culture is devoted to the locally famous Iziun table grape, but the remainder goes principally to dessert wines; in Daghestan, adjoining Georgia and Azerbaijan, a certain amount of fairly good wine is made; in Tadzhikistan, on the north of Pakistan and Kashmir, dessert wine is now being produced from about 22,000 vineyard acres; and in the vast stretches of Kazakhstan, which reaches from the Caspian Sea to Mongolia, vine planting has been introduced in recent years.

The following are the authorized Soviet wine place-names or Appellations d'Origine. These were extracted from a bulletin of the International Wine Office, to which acknowledgement is also due for some of the other material on Soviet wines. Certain wines are designated by the Soviet wine industry as port, madeira, tokay, etc. *This can never be correct*, as only a wine from the banks of the Upper Douro River in Portugal can fulfil all the conditions necessary to Port; only a wine from the island of Madeira can fulfil the conditions for a Madeira, etc. But in the situation prevailing at the time of writing, of very limited information from the Soviet Union, the terms port-type, madeira-type, etc., will be used to indicate the approximate style of the wines.

Grape varieties and Place-names	*Degree of alcohol*	*Sugar*	*Wine district*	*Type*
	(WINES OF ABRAU-DURSSO COMBINE, KRASNODAR)			
Riesling Abrau	10–11·5		Abrau-Dursso	Dry white
Cabernet Abrau	9·5–11		Abrau-Dursso	Dry red
Riesling Anapa	9·6–11·5		Anapa	Dry white
	(WINES OF MASSANDRA COMBINE, CRIMEA)			
Sémillon Oreanda	10·5–12		Crimea	Dry white
Riesling Massandra	10·5–12		Crimea	Dry white
Aligoté Ay-Danil	10·5–12		Crimea	Dry white
Cabernet Livadia	10·5–12		Crimea	Dry red
Saperavi Massandra	10·5–12		Crimea	Dry red
Bordo Ay-Danil	10·5–12		Crimea	Dry red
White Muscat Massandra	12·5	23	Crimea	Sweet dessert
White Muscat Livadia	12·5	30	Crimea	Sweet dessert
Pink Muscat Gourzouf	12·5	27·5	Crimea	Sweet dessert
Black Muscat Kuchuk-Lambat	12·5	25·5	Crimea	Red dessert
White Muscat Kastel	16	20–21	Crimea	Red dessert
Pink Muscat Alupka	16	20–21	Crimea	Pink dessert
Tokay Ay-Danil	12·5–13·5	30	Crimea	Dessert
Tokay Alouchta	16	20–21	Crimea	Dessert
Pinot Gris Ay-Danil	12·5–13·5	23	Crimea	Dessert
Aiou-Dag	16	18–20	Crimea	Red Muscat
Sou-Dag	17·5	9·5	Crimea	White port-type
Alupka	17·5	9·5	Crimea	White port-type
Livadia	18·5	8	Crimea	Red port-type
Kuchuk-Lambat	18	10·5	Crimea	Red port-type
Alouchta	17·5	9·5	Crimea	Red port-type
Massandra	18·5	6	Crimea	Red port-type
Kuchuk-Uzen	18·5	6	Crimea	Madeira-type
Massandra	19·5	4	Crimea	Madeira-type
		(BESSARABIA COMBINE)		
Pinot	10–11·5		Moldavia	White
Aligoté	10–11·5		Moldavia	White
Bordo (presumably Cabernet)	10–13		Moldavia	Red
	(WINES OF TEMPELHOF COLLECTIVE)			
Riesling	11–12		Tempelhof	White
Sylvaner	11–12		Tempelhof	White
		(UKRAINIAN S.S.R.)		
Riesling	11–12		Ukraine	White
Aligoté	11–12		Ukraine	White
Cabernet	11–12		Ukraine	Red
		(AZERBAIJAN S.S.R.)		
Matrassa	11–13		Azerbaijan	Red
Akastafa	18	13	Azerbaijan	White port-type
Kara-Tachanakh	16	18	Azerbaijan	White dessert
Chemakha	16	20	Azerbaijan	Red dessert
Kurdamir	16	23	Azerbaijan	Red dessert
		(GEORGIAN S.S.R.)		
Napureouli	10·5–12		Georgia	White
Tsinandali	10·5–12		Georgia	White
Mukuzani	10·5–12		Georgia	White
Mzvane	10·5–12		Georgia	White
Manadis	10·5–12		Georgia	White
Gurdjurni			Georgia	White
Myshako Riesling			Georgia	White

SPIRITS

The Russian national drink is traditionally vodka, which has for some time now been most popular also west of the Iron Curtain.

See VODKA.

Russian River Valley

Californian wine district in Sonoma County on the coast 50 miles north of San Francisco.

See AMERICA: CALIFORNIA AND THE WEST.

Ruster Ausbruch

A very sweet Austrian wine, made from late-picked grapes in the vineyards of Rust, Burgenland.

See AUSTRIA.

Rutherglen

Celebrated region in Victoria, Australia, producing some of the best fortified and dessert wines, and some full, red table wines as well, now, however, all in smaller quantities than formerly.

See AUSTRALIA.

Ruwer

White wines. District: Western Germany.

The Ruwer wines, at their best, are the lightest of Germany—lighter than those of the Saar or of the Moselle. In the best years they have a bouquet suggesting cinnamon, but in poorer years they may be too acid for most tastes. In general, the nearer the Moselle the wine grows, the better it is likely to be. Ruwer (and Saar) wines are always classed with the Moselles, and the German wine label simply lumps them as Mosel-Saar-Ruwer. Both Saar and Ruwer are tributaries of the Moselle, but while the Saar is a substantial river, the surprising thing about the Ruwer is that it is a stream almost narrow enough to jump across. It boils down out of a narrow valley through the little town of Ruwer on the Moselle edge and enters the broad river not far below Trier. Upstream the valley widens. It is there, and in a small side valley devoted to the Avelsbach vineyards, that the Riesling vine grows and the wines are made.

WINE AREAS

Kasel

This is the most important *Gemarkung* or town. With 185 acres at the mouth of the valley, it has about double the vineyard of its peers; and the only town equalling it in quantity—Waldrach farther up the valley—makes only small wines. Probably the best Kaseler is Kaseler Nies'chen, a splendidly soft light wine when at its best.

Important vineyards. Nies'chen (or Niesgen), Kehrnagel, Steininger, Hitzlay, Dominikanerberg, Katharinenberg, Käulgen, Kohlenberg, Lorenzberg, Paulinsberg, Taubenberg.

Mertesdorf

Maximin Grünhaus will be a very good wine in a dry year. It is the outstanding growth of the *Gemarkung* Mertesdorf and derives its names from the fact that before the secularization of Church property in Germany by Napoleon, it belonged to the St. Maximin Abbey of Trier. It is now owned by von Schubert.

Important vineyards: Maximin Grünhauser Herrenberg, Lorenzberg, Spielberg, Treppchen.

Eitelsbach

Karthäuserhofberg is the remaining outstanding Ruwer vineyard. A property of 34 acres, it is probably the largest single vineyard in the whole of the Moselle area. It was given to the Carthusians by the ecclesiastic Baldwin, in the middle of the fourteenth century, and passed intact into the hands of the Rautenstrauch family at the time of the secularization of Church lands in 1802. Hans Wilhelm Rautenstrauch is the owner today. The vineyard is in the town of Eitelsbach and the wine is called Eitelsbacher Karthäuserhofberg.

Important vineyards: Karthäuserhofberg, Marienholz, Rothenberg, Sonnenberg.

Avelsbach

The vineyards lie in the jagged triangle between the Moselle and the Ruwer, sometimes classed with one group, sometimes with the other. Convict labour cut away the forests about ninety years ago; consequently the soil is new, the slate not as matured as in vineyards where vine may have grown as long as 2,000 years, and the wines have a rougher taste, which some do not like. In very hot summers they may have quality, but in general they lack breed.

Important vineyards: Altenberg, Dom Avelsbach and Dom Herrenberg (both owned by Cathedral of Trier), Hammerstein (State Domain), Herrenberg, Tielslay.

Waldrach

This *Gemarkung* has about 180 acres in small wines.

Important vineyards: Ehrenberg, Jesuitengarten,

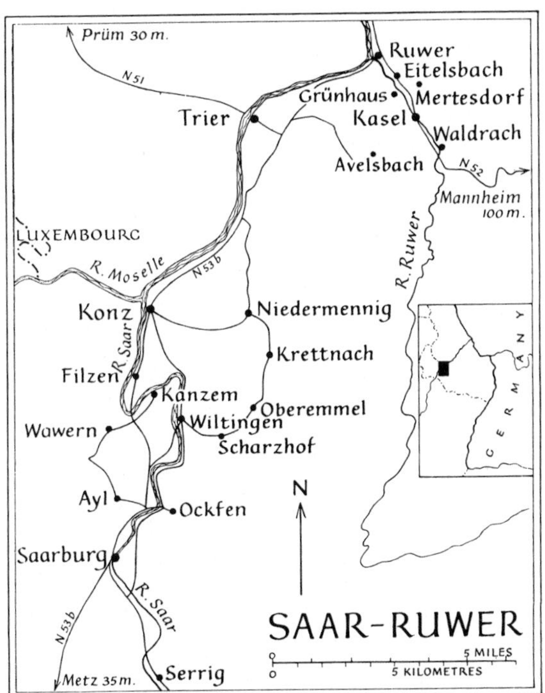

Krone, Klosterberg, Meisenberg, Schloss Marienlay.

Principal Ruwer Estates

Bischöfliches Konvikt

The preparatory school for the seminary in Trier. Total domain composed of approximately fifty-four acres in eight *Gemarkungen* on the Ruwer, Moselle, and Saar. Ruwer properties in Eitelsbach comprise parcels in Grossenberg, Marienholz, Wäldchen, and Schlicht; and in Kasel they include sections of Held, Kupp, Käulgen, Niesgen, Steininger, and Kernagel.

Bischöfliches Priesterseminar

The seminary in Trier, whose holdings consist of sixty-nine acres in eight *Gemarkungen* throughout the Ruwer, Moselle, and Saar. A principal owner in Kasel on the Ruwer, the seminary's properties include sizeable parcels in the vineyards of Hitzlay, Kernagel, Niesgen, Käulgen, Steininger, Kohlenberg, Taubenberg, and Herrenberg.

Fritz Patheiger Erben

Proprietor of twelve acres in Kasel. Kasel holdings include portions of Kernagel, Kohlenberg, Käulgen, Niesgen, Steininger, and Herrenberg.

Kesselstatt Domain

An outstanding domain established by the Austrian Counts von Kesselstatt in the late eighteenth century which at present includes sections of the best Kasel vineyards.

Hans Wilheim Rautenstrauch Erben

Property composed of approximately thirty-eight acres within the *Germarkung* of Eitelsbach. Holdings include the entire vineyard of Eitelsbacher Karthäuserhofberg, as well as portions of the vineyards Orthsberg, Kronenberg, Stirn, Sand, and Burgberg.

Von Schubert

Sole owner of Maximin Grünhaus, a vineyard of major importance in Mertesdorf.

S

Saar

White wines: District: Western Germany.

The Saars can outclass the Moselles in the best years. A hot, dry summer brings great wines along this tributary that leads into the Moselle—light, spicy, unique in flavour, with a special taste like that of blackcurrants, and a bouquet resembling Muscatel. The wines are generally longer-lasting and slower to age than the Moselles. The vine is entirely Riesling and the soil characteristics in the lower Saar are the same as on the Moselle—a slate which crumbles slowly and replenishes the earth. Above Saarburg there is less of this slate characteristic. From Serrig to Konz-Karthaus, where the River Saar enters the River Moselle, the banks are almost solid vineyard. Saar wines, which in the great years are in some respects almost super-Moselle in their development of the characteristic elements of *race* and steely elegance, are always classed with the Moselles.

Ockfen probably has the highest average of good wines, but the general opinion is that the best individual vineyard is the famous Scharzhofberg, lying a little farther down the river behind the village of Wiltingen.

BEST VINEYARDS

Ayl. The quality of the wines closely rivals the Ockfeners. Ayler Herrenberg, Ayler Kupp (a connoisseur's wine, exquisite in a hot year, from a perpendicular vineyard mainly owned by Bischöfliches Priesterseminar, Trier); Ayler Neuberg, Ayler Scheiderberg.

Falkenstein. A vineyard within the *Gemarkung* of Konz-Karthaus; but the wines are known simply as Falkensteiner, without the town name.

Filzen. Neuberg, Pulchen, Urbelt.

Kanzem. Very delicious wines, heavier, fuller, rounder than most Saars, less *race* but charming when drunk young. Altenburg (probably best), Unterberg, Berg, Kelterberg, Sonnenberg, Wolfsberg.

Konz. Kelterberg, Zuckerberg (*see* Falkenstein above).

Krettnach. Euchariusberg, Silberberg.

Niedermennig. Euchariusberg, Herrenberg, Junkerberg, Sonnenberg.

Oberemmel. Fine wines. Altenberg, Agritiusberg, Eltzerberg, Hütte, Junkerberg, Karlsberg, Lauterberg, Raul, Rosenberg, Scharzberg (sometimes called Oberemmeler Scharzberg but more often simply Scharzberger).

Ockfen. The best wines of the Saar. Bockstein is the best vineyard and rivals Scharzhofberger from Wiltingen as the finest Saar wine; it is fuller than Scharzhofberger but less elegant, and in certain years it may be the better wine. Geisberg, Herrenberg (State Domain), Heppenstein, St. Irminer.

Saarburg. Antoniusberg, Antoniusbrunnen, Klosterberg, Leyenkaul, Schlossberg.

Serrig. Kupp, Vogelsang, Würzberg, Antoniusberg, Kindenburglay.

Wawern. Goldberg, Herrenberg, Ritterpfad.

Wiltingen Scharzhofberg is the finest vineyard, and in most years finest on the Saar. The wines have a superb elegance. The vineyard faces south and west on a large hill behind Wiltingen and the story of its ownership is a curious one. It was planted 200 years ago by the monastery of St. Maria of Trier. At the beginning of the nineteenth century when Napoleon was secularizing Church property, a priest named Muller enrolled the vineyard under his name, to protect it. Napoleon came and went; Muller held on to the vineyard, married a young woman, and founded a family. His descendant, affable Egon Muller, with Koch probably the best grower on the Saar, has the main part of the vineyard today. Domscharzhofberger is Scharzhofberger from the portion of the vineyard belonging to the Dom (Cathedral) of Trier.

Wiltingen vineyards: Scharzhofberg, Braune Kupp, Gottesfuss, Scharzberg. The last higher up than Scharzhofberg, has less slate in the soil and consequently less *race*, a rougher wine than Scharzhofberg. Braunfels, Johannislay, Klosterberg, Kupp, Neuberg, Rosenberg, Schlangengraben, Schlossberg.

PRINCIPAL SAAR ESTATES

Bischöfliches Konvikt, Trier.

The Catholic refectory in Trier. The total domain comprises about fifty-four acres in eight *Gemarkungen* on the Saar, Ruwer, and Moselle. Saar vineyard properties in Avelsbach include Wolfsgraben, Häusgen, and Hex, and in Ayl include Ayler Herrenberger (registered mark).

Bischöfliches Priesterseminar, Trier

The Catholic seminary in Trier whose aggregate holdings cover some sixty-nine acres in eight *Gemarkungen* on the Saar, Ruwer, and Moselle. Saar holdings include major portions of the Ayler Kupp vineyard in Ayl, of the Wiltinger Kupp vineyard in Wiltingen, and of the vineyards Altenberg, Wolfsberg, and Unterberg in Kanzem.

Hohe Domkirche, Trier

Domain composed of approximately thirty-three acres in the two Saar *Gemarkungen* of Avelsbach and Wiltingen. Hohe Domkirche parcels in Avelsbach are Dom-Avelsbacher Altenberg and Dom-Avelsbacher Herrenberg; and in Wiltingen they are Dom-Scharzberg, Dom-Scharzhofberg, Dom-Wiltinger Braunfels, and Dom-Wiltinger Rosenberg.

K. Weissebach Erben (von Othegraven), Kanzem/Saar

Holdings consist of 11 acres in the Kanzemer Berg vineyard in Kanzem.

Le Gallais, Kanzem/Saar

Approximately six acres distributed between the *Gemarkungen* of Wiltingen and Wawern. Properties in Wiltingen include Kupp and Braune Kupp; and in Wawern Le Gallais owns Goldberg.

Gebert, Ockfen/Saar

Total domain of twenty-six acres comprises portions of the vineyards Bockstein, Herrenberg, and Geisberg in Ockfen.

Forstmeister Geltz (Bes. Krick-Geltz), Saarburg.

Holdings of nearly nine acres in the *Gemarkungen* of Saarburg and Ockfen. Saarburg properties include parcels in Leyenkaul and Antoniusbrunnen, and Ockfen holdings include sections of Bockstein and Geisberg.

Forstmeister Geltz (Bes. Zilliken-Haring), Saarburg-Beurig

Proprietor of sections in Rausch, Antoniusbrunnen, Leyenkaul, and Mühlberg in Saarburg, and Bocksteiner and Geisberger in Ockfen. Approximately eight acres in all.

Graf zu Hoensbroech, Rauhof/Wiltingen (Saar)

Property of six acres composed of shares in the vineyards of Kupp, Dohr, Braunfels, and Gravels in Wiltingen.

Von Hövel (Friedrich Von Kunow), Oberemmel/Saar

Total holdings of approximately twenty-eight acres spread between the two *Gemarkungen* of Oberemmel and Wiltingen. Oberemmel properties comprise portions of Rosenberg, Agritiusberg, Lautersberg, Hütte, Junkerberg, Eltzerberg, and Altenberg. Wiltingen properties include portions of Scharzberger and Scharzhofberger.

Max Keller, Saarburg, Bes. Saar

Domain consists of nearly thirteen acres and is composed of parcels in Bockstein, Bockstein Neuwies, and Geisberg in Ockfen; and in the vineyard of Stirn in Niederleuken.

Lintz, Wawern/Saar

Proprietor of nineteen acres in Wawern. Principal holding is the vineyard Alleinbesitzer des Wawerner Herrenberg (registered name, Wawerner Herrenberger).

Egon Müller, Scharzhof/Wiltingen/Saar

Holdings comprise seventeen acres and include the largest portions in the vineyards of Scharzhofberg, Scharzberg, and Runenfels in Wiltingen.

Adolf Rheinhart, Saarburg

Total domain consists of thirty-four acres. Rheinhart properties include sections of Bockstein, Herrenberg, Geisberg, and Oberherrenberg in Ockfen; a parcel of Feils in Schoden; a section of Scharzberger in Wiltingen; and a portion of Saarburg in Saarburg.

Vereinigte Hospitien, Trier

An eleemosynary hospital in Trier whose entire holdings comprise over seventy-two acres in five *Gemarkungen* on the Saar and Moselle. Saar properties include portions of the Kanzem vineyards of Altenberg, Wolfsberg, and Kelterberg; portions of Wiltingen vineyards of Wiltinger Kupp and Wiltinger Braune Kupp and portions of the Serrig vineyards of Serriger Schloss Saarfelser Schlossberg and Serriger Schloss Saarfelser Vogelsang.

Otto van Volxem, Oberemmel/Saar

Proprietor of approximately fifteen acres distributed between the two *Gemarkungen* of Wiltingen and Oberemmel. Wiltingen holdings include Klosterberg, Braunfels, Scharzhofberger, and Scharzberger. Oberemmel holdings include parcels in Altenberg and Falmet.

The State Domain owns wine-producing properties in the Saar, but the lands were cleared only ninety years ago and the wines do not achieve real finesse in soils not thoroughly matured.

Note: Wines in Avelsbach and Wiltingen to which *Dom* is prefixed are wines of the Hohe-Domkirche, or Cathedral of Trier.

See MAP on p. 473.

Sables-Saint-Émilion

Part of the village of Libourne, between Pomerol and Saint-Émilion, is allowed this place-name.
See SAINT-ÉMILION.

Saccharometer

See MUSTOMETER.

Saccharomyces Ellipsoïdeus

The yeast of wine, found on the skins of grapes.
See YEASTS; CHAPTER NINE, p. 41.

Sack

Early name for Sherry wine (see, for example, Shakespeare, *Henry IV*, *Part* 2, Act IV, Scene 3). It was believed at one time to come from the Spanish *seco*, dry; but as the wine at that time was probably sweet (not at all the Sherry we know) it is easy to accept Mr. H. Warner Allen's theory that the word came from the Spanish *sacar*—to take out, to export. The name of this sweet export wine was afterwards attached to other, comparable wines, such as Canary Sack and Málaga Sack.

Sacramental Wines

Used in the sacraments of the Christian Church. The need to keep up the supply of these wines caused the monasteries to take an active part in the viticulture of the Middle Ages. The term also applies to wines used during the Passover and other Jewish holidays.

Sacramento Valley

Californian wine region.
See AMERICA: CALIFORNIA AND THE WEST.

Saint-Amour

Red wines of Beaujolais, in south Burgundy.

The vineyards are the farthest north in the region, touching the area of Pouilly-Fuissé in the Mâconnais. The red wine is one of the fullest of the Beaujolais.
See BEAUJOLAIS.

Saint-Aubin and Saint-Aubin-Côte de Beaune

Burgundy red and white wines. District: Côte de Beaune, France.

Saint-Aubin stands back in the Côte d'Or hills behind Puligny-Montrachet and Chassagne-Montrachet, but its wines are not equal to those of its famous neighbours. For one thing, it is slightly too high above the favoured strip of the slope's midsection for really first-rate wines. Because of the quality difference, the Saint-Aubins should be considerably less expensive than others of the Côte de Beaune and, if bought fairly young, can be excellent value.

Wines may be sold as Saint-Aubin, Saint-Aubin-Côte de Beaune, or, after blending with growths from other communes, as Côte de Beaune-Villages—any wine with the right to one of these names has the right to them all. There are almost 350 acres devoted to vines and production in an average year for quantity is 21,000 imp. gallons (25,000 U.S.) of red wine, 10,000 (12,000 U.S.) of white and more sold under the Villages name. Some of the better vineyards have been made First Growths (*Premiers Crus*) and labels may carry both commune name and vineyard name.

These vineyards are:

	Acres
La Chatenière	24·7
Les Murgers-des-Dents-de-Chien	7·4
En Remilly	4·9
Les Frionnes	2·5
Sur-le-Sentier-du-Clou	29·7
Sur Gamay	34·6
Les Combes	37·1
Champlot	19·8

Saint-Aubin-de-Luigné

Dry, white wines of the Coteaux du Layon district of Anjou (*q.v.*).

Saint-Denis

See CLOS SAINT-DENIS; MOREY-SAINT-DENIS.

Saint-Émilion

The vine, a variety of Ugni Blanc, which yields the greater part of the Charente wines used in making Cognac (*q.v.*). It is grown in other districts of France, where it is also known as Clairette à grains ronds, Clairette de Vence, Graisse, Queue de Renard, Roussan, etc. In Italy, this grape is called Trebbiano; in Corsica, Rossola.

Saint-Émilion

Red wine. District: Bordeaux, France.

The wine is the fullest and heartiest of the red wines of Bordeaux, and is often compared with Burgundy. Some of the vintages require a considerable amount of time to develop; the 1945, for example, was not ready to drink before 1965. This, however, is exceptional, and the 1945 has been very slow-maturing throughout Bordeaux.

The vineyards can be conveniently divided into two types: those of the plain and those of the slopes. But within the groups, and across them, there is considerable variation, owing to the differences in soil and the different exposures of a terrain which, rising up into a crown around the town of Saint-Émilion itself, is very hilly except where it flattens out on the borders of the neighbouring district of Pomerol. This distinction between plain and hill played a drastic role in late February 1956, when Bordeaux viticulture experienced its second most disastrous winter since 1709. The frost settled in the lowest areas and all the vineyards of the plain, including Château Cheval-Blanc, finest of the Saint-Émilions, lost their 1956 and 1957 crops, and in many cases crops for years after, since either the productive branches or the whole vines were frozen. (Three years later, various growers reported that vines were suddenly dying from the after-effects of this frost.) Hill vineyards survived, and Château Ausone, probably the best of the slope wines, was, for example, unhurt.

Saint-Émilion itself is believed to be the oldest wine town in France, and certainly it is the most picturesque. Placed on a hill of soft, easily hewn stone, it is uniquely all of a piece; the wine cellars of many of the châteaux are the old quarries from which the rock itself was cut in the Middle Ages, and blocks of the rock provide the tawny, sun-ripened stone of which the town is built. There can be no more romantic setting for drinking a great wine than in sight of the vineyard where it is grown. The terrace of the town's leading restaurant, the Hostellerie de Plaisance, is erected on the dome of a church—the grey, dim Église Monolithe, hollowed out of the solid rock underneath the inn. This ninth-century chapel is the largest in the world to be cut out of a single rock. An unforgettable sight is a ceremonial installation of the wine society, the Jurade, conducted in guttering taper light in the crypt. From the Plaisance belvedere, sipping your wine, you have a view across the mellow, red roofs of the King's Tower, built by Louis VI in 1124, of the ruined arches over the Cloister of the Cordeliers, and of vineyard spilling down the Saint-Émilion slopes and spreading out over the plain.

Ausonius, who wrote an epic poem about the Moselle, lived in a luxurious Roman villa which may or may not have been near the present site of Château Ausone. In his time, the third century, vineyards already girdled Saint-Émilion. The saint himself came in the eighth century, on his way to Santiago de Compostela in Spain, then an important goal of mediæval pilgrims. If you go down into his hermitage near the church, and stand by his bed and seat carved out of the stone, they will tell you that he found the place a wilderness and, attracted by a miraculous spring, established a colony. It may not be irreligious to think this spring may have been Saint-Émilion wine, for the city was bustling and had already known and was forgetting the Roman grandeur. In any case, the saint lingered, and never went to Santiago de Compostela.

An Appellation Contrôlée, or legally-controlled wine place-name in its own right, Saint-Émilion is also a Bordeaux, in the wine area of that name. The city of Bordeaux is about eighteen miles to the west.

In addition to Saint-Émilion itself, seven surrounding communes have the right to the place-name Saint-Émilion. They are Saint-Laurent-des-Combes, Saint-Christophe-des-Bardes, Saint-Hippolyte, Saint-Étienne-de-Lisse, Saint-Pey-d'Armens, Saint-Sulpice-de-Faleyrens and Vignonet. Lying in a semi-circle on the south and west of Saint-Émilion, none produces a wine of the high level of the first-rate growths; but Château Larcis-Ducasse in Saint-Laurent-des-Combes, which is a continuation of the slope beyond Pavie, is worthy of mention. Château Monbousquet, set back from a small country road across the Bordeaux–Périgeux road, on the flat land of Saint-Sulpice-de-Faleyrens, is an estate where wines and horses of breed are raised by Saint-Émilion's great promoter, Daniel Querre, certainly one of the largest growers of wine. He is a beaming man of 300 pounds, whose trumpet voice issues the call to grape harvesting from the top of a twelfth-century tower each year during the Jurade ceremony of the *Ban des Vendanges*.

Five communes lying to the north of Saint-Émilion and to the west of Pomerol have the right to add Saint-Émilion to their names, the Appellations Contrôlées of this district being: Saint-Georges-Saint-Émilion, Montagne-Saint-Émilion, Lussac-Saint-Émilion, Puisseguin-Saint-Émilion, and Parsac-Saint-Émilion. Château Saint-Georges, and to a somewhat lesser extent the other wines of Saint-Georges-Saint-Émilion, are only divided from the Saint-Émilions proper by tradition and usage; and from the quality standpoint, they have the same characteristics of longevity and splendour developing after sufficient age in bottle.

Sables-Saint-Émilion is an Appellation Contrôlée given to the wines of a small district touching Saint-Émilion on one border, but lying between Pomerol and the River Dordogne. Grown from sandy soil, as the name implies, these lesser wines are actually closer in type to the lesser Pomerols than to the Saint-Émilions.

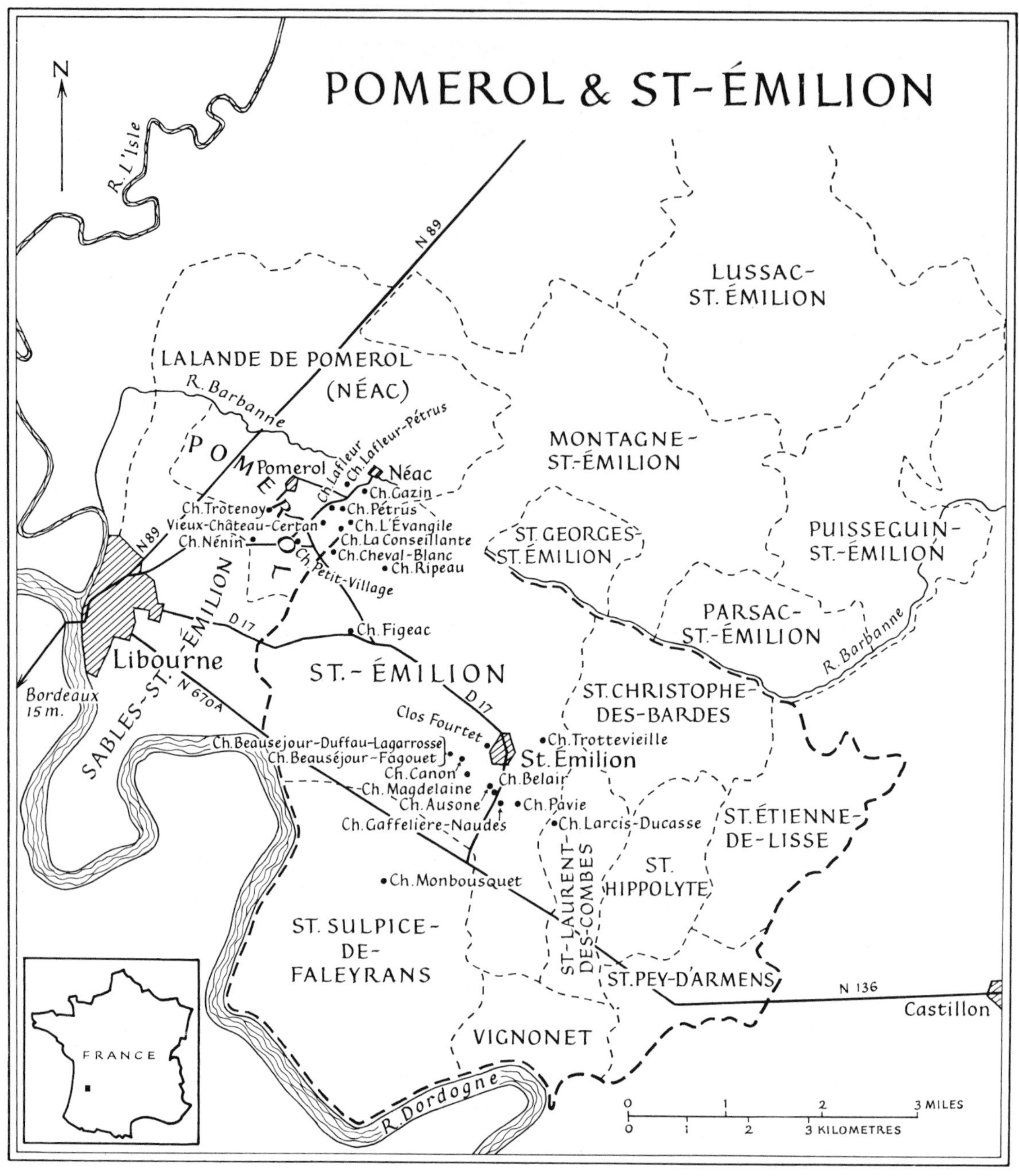

The wines of Saint-Émilion were officially classified in the summer of 1955 by the French Institut National des Appellations d'Origine, the body that controls wine place-names. Before that date, Château Cheval-Blanc and Château Ausone had always been considered as the leading and exceptional growths, with the others following after. In 1955 they were accorded the right to stand at the head of the First Great Growths (*Premiers Grands Crus*), but were not otherwise distinguished from ten more which were also rated Firsts, and listed in alphabetical order after Ausone and Cheval-Blanc. Learning from the difficulties that had been encountered in the classification of Médoc wines exactly a century earlier, the officials who set up the Saint-Émilion classification did not make the mistake of dividing the Classified Growths (*Crus*) into Firsts (*Premiers*), Seconds (*Seconds*), Thirds (*Trois-*

ièmes), Fourths (*Quatrièmes*), and Fifths (*Cinquièmes*), thereby running the risk that a Third Growth might be mistaken for a third-rate wine. The vineyards of Saint-Émilion were placed in two groups only: First Great Growths (*Premiers Grands Crus*), of which there are twelve; and Great Growths (*Grands Crus*), which total about seventy.

FIRST GREAT GROWTHS (*Premiers Grands Crus*)

Château Ausone	Château Figeac
Château Cheval-Blanc	Clos Fourtet
Château Beauséjour-Duffau-Lagarrosse	Château La Gaffelière-Naudes
Château Beauséjour-Fagouet	Château Magdelaine
Château Belair	Château Pavie
Château Canon	Château Trottevieille

The entire classification will be found in the Appendix. For the individual First Great Growths, see under their names. Cheval-Blanc is unanimously elected best of all Saint-Émilions and, with Château Pétrus in Pomerol, equal to the four Médoc Greats —Lafite, Latour, Margaux, Haut-Brion (Graves); and Mouton-Rothschild, classified a Second Growth, but acknowledged equal of the Firsts. The position of Château Ausone is not so secure, but most people feel it follows Cheval-Blanc, and also deserves a place in the upper hierarchy. A few contend that, in recent years, Gaffelière-Naudes, just below it on the same slope, has equalled and sometimes surpassed Ausone.

Saint-Estèphe

Bordeaux red wine. District: Haut-Médoc, France.

Saint-Estèphe is the northernmost and fourth in order of the great red-wine communes on the famous Médoc peninsula jutting north from Bordeaux in south-west France. Of the annual 768,376 imp. gallons (922,777 U.S.) entitled to the official place-name (the largest volume of the communal wines), not all is of the very high average quality of the wines of Margaux, Pauillac and Saint-Julien. Some of the lesser Saint-Estèphe wines are transitional between the Bas-Médocs and the more aristocratic Haut-Médocs. This is not surprising as the village stands on the boundary of the two regions.

While the lesser wines may lack something in finesse, in Château Cos d'Estournel, Château Montrose, and Château Calon-Ségur Saint-Estèphe has three of the most distinguished Médoc vineyards. The span of the quality range is broader than in the other three famous communes, and a certain care is needed in selecting the wines.

Characteristically full and with a big nose, the wines vary within the region, and a Calon-Ségur at the northernmost extremity will be the most 'Saint-Estèphe' of the Saint-Estèphes. At the opposite end of the scale from the delicate and feminine wines of Margaux, Saint-Estèphes are frequently likened in Bordeaux to Saint-Émilion wines, generally heavier than the Médocs. When young, they will be distinguished for their fruity fullness.

Saint-Estèphe has five vineyards rated as Classified Growths (*Crus*) in the 1855 Classification of Médoc wines, fewer by far than the other leading communes. They are:

Second Growths (Seconds Crus)	*Third Growth* (Troisième Cru)
Château Cos d'Estournel	Château Calon-Ségur
Château Montrose	

Fourth Growth (Quatrième Cru)	*Fifth Growth* (Cinquième Cru)
Château Lafon-Rochet	Château Cos-Labory

(For individual Classified Growths, *see* CHÂTEAU COS D'ESTOURNEL, CHÂTEAU MONTROSE, CHÂTEAU CALON-SÉGUR, etc.)

Sainte-Foy-Bordeaux

Bordeaux white wine. District: South-West France.

Sweet white wines made according to the Sauternes method of select picking of overripe grapes, and from the Sauternes varieties Sémillon, Sauvignon, and Muscadelle. The wines come from the easternmost part of the Bordeaux wine region and are more properly linked with the adjoining area of Monbazillac sweet white wines. A small quantity of red wine also bears the name, but it generally amounts only to about 3% of the production.

Saint Gall

Fortified French aperitif on a red wine basis.

Saint-Georges-Saint-Émilion

One of five communes in the north of Saint-Émilion which share the right to the Appellation Contrôlée Saint-Émilion (*q.v.*).

Saint-Jean-de-Minervois, Muscat de

See SWEET FORTIFIELD WINES OF FRANCE.

Saint-Joseph

Red and white wines of the French Côtes du Rhône.

See RHÔNE.

Saint-Julien

Bordeaux red wine. District: Haut-Médoc, France.

One of the four leading Médoc red-wine communes in the Bordeaux region in south-west France—the others are Pauillac, Margaux, and Saint-Estèphe—Saint-Julien is smallest in production, making about 333,000 imp. gallons (400,000 U.S.) a year of wine entitled to the official place-name or Appellation Contrôlée. As a regional wine it is probably the best-known of the four in the world market.

The wine, from vines grown in a gravelly soil marked by the presence of a considerable amount of clay, has affinities with both those of Pauillac immediately to the north, and those of Margaux, grown eight or nine miles to the south, the other side of a stretch of land too low and moist for fine wines. Slightly darker in colour and fuller-bodied than the typical Margaux, the wines in this respect tend to resemble the Pauillacs; but they are less full and quicker to mature than a characteristic Pauillac, and have more of the finesse, delicacy, and femininity identified with Margaux.

The community, a small village lying in among the famous Léovilles, on a curve of the vineyard road running north from Bordeaux, is also known as Saint-Julien-Beychevelle, signifying the link with the ancient Beychevelle estate. After crossing pasture-land, the vineyard road suddenly climbs, and on the higher ground Saint-Julien begins, with Château Beychevelle and then Château Ducru-Beaucaillou on the river side, and Château Branaire-Ducru facing them across the road. At the turning, a thirty-foot-high wine bottle, an eyesore in the corner of the vineyard of Beychevelle, takes the visitor's eye. Entering the region, a large billboard announces:

PASSERS-BY!
You are now entering the ancient and
celebrated vineyard of Saint-Julien.
Bow low!

The ancient fame of Saint-Julien has been revived by its mayor, Monsieur Henri Martin, owner of Château Gloria, and in the late fifties and middle sixties the President of the C.I.V.B., the official Bordeaux wine association.

In an average year, approximately sixty different wines carry the Saint-Julien place-name, to which they are entitled if grown in the delimited region, cared for according to certain quality restrictions, and approved in annual taste testings.

The Saint-Julien vineyards rated as Classified Growths (*Crus*) in the 1855 Classification of Médoc wines are:

Second Growths (Seconds Crus)	*Third Growths* (Troisièmes Crus)
Château Léoville-Lascases	Château Lagrange
Château Léoville-Poyferré	Château Langoa-Barton
Château Léoville-Barton	
Château Gruaud-Larose	
Château Ducru-Beaucaillou	

Fourth Growths (Quatrièmes Crus)

Château Saint-Pierre	Château Branaire-Ducru
Château Talbot	Château Beychevelle

Saint-Julien has neither first nor fifth growths.

(For individual Classified Growths, *see Château* LÉOVILLE-LASCASES, *Château* LÉOVILLE-POYFERRÉ, *Château* LÉOVILLE-BARTON, etc.)

Saint-Lambert-du-Lattay

Commune making sweet white wines in the Coteaux du Layon district of Anjou (*q.v.*)

Saint-Laurent

Red-wine grape used in Austria, Czechoslovakia, etc.

Saint Martin

Saint Martin (*c.* 345) was an early patron of wine in the Loire Valley, and to him is attributed the discovery that wines do better when they are pruned.

See LOIRE.

Saint-Nicholas-de-Bourgueil

Red and rosé wines from a sub-district of the Touraine in the French Loire Valley. The total area of 35,000 acres is planted in Cabernet Franc

See BOURGUEIL; TOURAINE.

Saint-Péray and Saint-Péray Mousseux

Dry and sweet still wine; also sparkling wine. District: Rhône Valley, France.

The wines were highly appreciated in France during the Second Empire (1852–70) but fell from grace shortly afterwards, and are only beginning to come back into favour. Now, as then, the full-bodied sparkling wine seems to be the more sought after.

The vines (Roussanne and Marsanne) are grown on cliffs overlooking the Rhône, on the river's right bank. Sometimes the growers will wait until the grapes are overripe and let the *pourriture noble,* or noble rot, form on them, drying the skin and leaving a sugar-rich grape for making an ultra-sweet wine. Generally, however, the grapes are picked at maturity and vinified into a dry wine. Much of the output is subjected to a secondary fermentation in the bottle to render the wine sparkling. About 200 acres of vines exist, and production amounts to nearly 27,000 imp. gallons (33,000 U.S.) annually.

Château Saint-Pierre

Bordeaux red wine. District: Haut-Médoc, France. Commune: Saint-Julien.

About three-and-a-half centuries old, the vineyard is a Fourth Growth (*Quatrième Cru*), 1855 Classification. For a time it was split into two vineyards, Château Saint-Pierre-Bontemps and Château Saint-Pierre-Sevaistre, but it has been reunited under Dutch ownership. The wines have been in need of considerable improvement. Some of the best sections of this vineyard were purchased by Henri Martin who incorporated them into his Château Gloria.

Characteristics. Rather light and generally undistinguished. Improved vinification would heighten quality.

Vineyard area: 36 acres.

Average production: 3,200 cases.

Saint-Raphaël

Delicate red, bitter-sweet French aperitif based on fortified red wine and flavoured principally with quinine. It is highly advertised throughout France where it is very popular.

Saint-Romain

Burgundy red and white wine. District: Côte de Beaune, France.

Lying far back in the hills, behind Meursault and Auxey-Duresses, Saint-Romain makes a little wine, of reasonably little note, although it may often represent good value as against other growths of the famous slope. Some of it—both red and white—is sold under the communal name, and some is blended with wines of other specified communes of the Côte de Beaune and sold as Côte de Beaune-Villages. There are about 250 acres allowed for the growing of the finer vines and production in a good year for quantity is about 832 imp. gallons (1,000 U.S.) of red wine and 2,100 imp. (2,500 U.S.) of white with an unspecified further amount sold as Côte de Beaune-Villages.

Saint Vincent

Patron saint of French wine growers. According to legend, he became thirsty in Heaven and asked permission to return to Earth for a little while, so that he might taste the good wines of France again. He was granted leave of absence and no doubt he meant to go back when his time was up. But the red wine of Graves was his undoing; he was found in the cellar of La Mission-Haut-Brion, lost to the world and to his appointment in Heaven, and as a punishment he was turned to stone.

His statue is still to be seen there, clutching a dilapidated bunch of grapes and wearing his mitred cap awry. The Saint Vincent holiday is widely celebrated in Burgundy. Processions honouring this wine saint are held in many villages of the Côte d'Or on 22 January each year.

Sainte-Croix-du-Mont

Bordeaux white wine. District: South-west France.

A small district south of Bordeaux and divided from Sauternes by the River Garonne. The white wines are sweet and are very reminiscent of their neighbours across the river, made from the same grape varieties—Sémillon, Sauvignon, and some Muscadelle—and produced from late-picked and overripe grapes which have achieved a concentrated sweetness, as in Sauternes. If the wines lack the very great elegance and finesse of some Sauternes, they are nevertheless the best of the white sweet wines of the right bank of the Garonne and priced far below the famous Sauternes, are excellent buys.

The bluff or slope of Sainte-Croix-du-Mont carries solid vine like a cape over its sloping shoulders. At the top thrusts out the church of Sainte-Croix-du-Mont with its delicate spire and, a hundred yards away, the mediæval fortified castle; these landmarks are illuminated in the summer and they shine for miles over the Sauternes and Graves vineyards.

Production averages around 290,000 imp. gallons (350,000 U.S.), about half that of Sauternes, and to achieve the place-name the wines must attain 13% of alcohol. In fact they frequently reach 15%. No better place for tasting them can exist than the outdoor terrace built just below the castle in 1955 and 1956. From the tables placed on the grassy ledge of the bluff, vineyard tumbles away in a rush below, until it is checked by the low-lying land bordering the river. Across the river, shrouded with willows, Sauternes extends and on the horizon the form of Château d'Yquem can be dimly made out.

Saké

A Japanese fermented liquor, from 12% to 16% alcohol by volume. It is made from rice which is cleansed and steamed and allowed to ferment. Towards the end of the fermentation period more rice is added, then the saké is drawn off, filtered, and put into casks for maturing.

The saké is colourless and rather sweet, with a bitter aftertaste. The Japanese serve it warm, in porcelain cups. Natives of Okinawa also make a saké, but it is harsher and usually served cold.

Salmanazar

A large glass bottle usually for display purposes. When filled it contains 9·6 litres or 338 fluid ounces (325 U.S.). The equivalent of twelve regular bottles.

Salta

Wine-producing province of Argentina (*q.v.*).

Saltillo

Wine-producing town in Mexico, site of the Compañia Vinícola de Saltillo.

See MEXICO.

Samogon

Bootleg vodka in Russia.

Samos

The muscat of Samos is one of the best-known wines of Greece, and the place-name is controlled.

See GREECE.

Sampigny-les-Maranges and Sampigny-les-Maranges-Côte de Beaune

Burgundy red and white wines. District: Côte de Beaune, France.

Sampigny is a minor wine commune at the southern end of the Côte de Beaune. Its wines are normally blended with those from other Côte de Beaune communes and sold as Côte de Beaune-Villages, but may also sometimes be found under their own name. The vineyards cover 108 acres, and wines from the seventy-two-acre heart may add the designation Côte de Beaune to the commune name. In exceptionally rare cases, wines may be seen with the label Sampigny-les-Maranges, or Sampigny-les-Maranges-Clos du Roi, in both cases the added names being those of the better vineyards within the commune. Les Maranges and the Clos du Roi are the only two that have this right.

Samshu

The Chinese saké (*q.v.*).

San Joaquin Valley

Warm Californian region producing raisins and sweet fortified wines. The principal districts are: Madera, Fresno, Kings, Tulare, and Kern counties.

See AMERICA: CALIFORNIA AND THE WEST.

San Juan

Province of Argentina extensively planted in vines.

See ARGENTINA.

San Marino (Sangiovese)

The smallest country in the world, only twenty-three square miles and half of that nearly perpendicular, produces a red table wine called Sangiovese and a sparkling, sweet, dessert Moscato. The total production of wine is some 440 imp. gallons (528 U.S.) annually. Every drop of the rather hard Sangiovese, all of the Moscato, and a dessert liqueur named Titanium, are consumed by the approximately one million tourists who, every year, visit the toy state enclosed within Italy. Titanium takes its name from Monte Titano, the sheer peak that thrusts up from the Italian plain ten miles inland from Rimini and the Adriatic. On top of this the town of San Marino is perched. The liqueur is made from the wild flowers of the mountain, as it has been for over a century. To sip it or drink the wine in an outdoor café in the spotless little stone town, looking out to the Adriatic or to the dim blue Apennines, is a bibulous experience never to be forgotten —and you are sure to hear from some native of how San Marino has kept its independence against such would-be conquerors as Cesare Borgia and Napoleon and remained a dot of freedom for 1,600 years.

San Michele

Danish liqueur flavoured with tangerine.

Sancerre

Loire Valley white wines. District: Loire Valley, France.

A small, well-known district of the upper Loire producing an annual 130,000 imp. gallons (156,000 U.S.) of slightly greenish-tinged white, very dry wines. The town from which the district takes its name commands a sweeping view of the river from the top of a hill, on the slopes of which (and on those of the hills of twelve surrounding towns) are planted about 700 acres of Sauvignon vines. No other grape is allowed in wine labelled Sancerre. The best vineyards are Bué, Champtin, and Chavignol.

This wine derives a special flavour from the district's limestone soil—markedly dry and apt, in wet summers, to have too much acidity. In warm summers, however, this acidity is balanced by sufficient alcohol and the wine has a crisp and refreshing tang. Never great, Sancerre is nevertheless one of France's very pleasant and popular white wines.

Sandweine

The 'Sand wines' of Burgenland in Austria get their name from the sandy soil in which the vines grow—soil which the phylloxera louse avoids. These wines are among the few in Europe which need not be grafted on to American root-stocks. They are labelled *Seewinkel* followed by the informing grape variety.

See AUSTRIA.

Sangiovese

Red wine grape used in Chianti, Montepulciano, and other Italian wines.

Sansevero

Dry white Italian wine.

See APULIA.

Santa Clara-San Benito-Santa Cruz

Californian wine region, centred in Santa Clara county.

See AMERICA: CALIFORNIA AND THE WEST.

Santa Maddalena

Red wine of Alto Adige, sometimes referred to as Sankt Magdelener.

See TRENTINO-ALTO ADIGE.

Santa Rosa

Centre of Californian wine district in Sonoma county.

See AMERICA: CALIFORNIA AND THE WEST.

Santarem-João Santarem

Blue-black grape used in the hill-slope wines of Colares, Portugal (*q.v.*).

Santenay and Santenay-Côte de Beaune

Burgundy red, and some white, wines. District: Côte de Beaune.

Santenay is the last important wine commune of the Côte de Beaune before it tails off into the southernmost Cheilly-les-Maranges, Dezize-les-Maranges, and Sampigny-les-Maranges. The wines —which have equal right to the name of the commune or communal name with Côte de Beaune added—are predominantly red and are light, fast-maturing, sometimes extraordinarily fruity, and often very good if priced below those from some of the other Côte de Beaune wine communes. Authentic red Santenay of a good year often rivals wines from Chassagne-Montrachet or Volnay, although it never gets into a position to challenge the exceptionally great Burgundies. Some of it is blended with the output of other Côte de Beaune communes and sold as Côte de Beaune-Villages, and some is sold under the more specific commune names. Quantities go to Switzerland and the Low Countries where, being fairly low in price, the wine is highly appreciated. There are almost a thousand acres of vineyard within Santenay's boundaries, and in an average-quantity year production amounts to about 148,000 imp. gallons (177,500 U.S.) of red wine and 2,500 imp. gallons (3,000 U.S.) of white.

Santorin

A Greek wine, from the island of the same name, which may also, when it is sweet, be labelled Vino Santo.

See GREECE.

Sapindor

Green, spicy-tasting French liqueur flavoured with plants from the Jura Mountains and put up in an imitation pine-tree bottle.

Sardinia

Red and white wines. District: Italian island in the Mediterranean.

The mountainous island of Sardinia, in the Tyrrhenian Sea, off the coast of central Italy is, after Sicily, the largest island in the Mediterranean. It has been inhabited since prehistoric days and it seems probable that even the earliest dwellers must have cultivated the vine—virtually nothing else will grow there. The island has a strange, wild air and is populated by a short, individualistic people to whose mysterious origins huge stone monuments may be the undeciphered clues. Giants' tombs, witches' houses, and the even more mysterious Nuraghi—conical stone towers which seem to have served early Sardinians both as dwellings and as defences—pepper the island, and around them the inhabitants go about their business. Wine is a fairly big part of this business, amounting to about 12,400,000 imp. gallons (15,000,000 U.S.) annually, the greatest part of it sweet, with a marked taste (from the granite soil of the vineyards), and extraordinarily strong.

Vernaccia

Sardinia's best-known wine. Most of the vines grow around Oristano, in the valley of the Tirso which runs from central Sardinia westward to the Gulf of Oristano, midway along the coast. The dry, amber-coloured wine is high in alcohol (16% or higher), has a light bouquet, and a quick, slightly bitter aftertaste.

Nuragus

This, one of the better table wines, is made from grapes of that name grown around Cagliari. Nearly 4 million imp. gallons (4,800,000 U.S.) of the straw-coloured, heady wine (12%–14%) are made annually.

Vermentino

The wine comes from the vineyards spreading south from Santa Teresa di Gallura, the northernmost town. From grapes grown on the unpromising mountain slopes, about 13,000 imp. gallons (15,600 U.S.) of wine are made annually, but it lacks distinction. It is dry, amber-coloured, and has 13%–14% of alcohol.

Malvasia di Bosa

This is produced in small quantities—2,600 imp. gallons (3,100 U.S.) in an average year—from Malvasia and Seberu grapes grown near Bosa, on the west coast of the island, slightly to the north of centre. The wine has a nutty flavour, a deeper, richer colour, and is slightly less dry than Vernaccia.

Oliena

The dryish, garnet-red wine is made from Cannonau and Monica grapes grown in the district of Nuoro.

Dessert Wines

The bulk of the vinicultural efforts of the islanders probably go into the making of dessert wines, and it is undeniable that the hot climate favours vines giving grapes rich in sugar for strong, sweet wines. Girò di Sardegna is sweet and red, slightly reminiscent of Port, and is made from Girò grapes grown in the general vicinity of Cagliari. Monica di Sardegna is similar, but deeper in colour—almost a deep purple. Both wines generally contain about 17% of alcohol or more. Nasco is white—or rather a deep, golden colour—and is famed partly for its bouquet (said to have the perfume of orange blossoms) and partly for its slightly bitter tang. Muscats may also be found, notably Moscato di Tempio (from Tempio in northern Sardinia), most of which is made sparkling; and its still counterpart, Moscato di Campidano.

See ITALY.

Sassella

Red wine of Valtellina, Italy, made from the Nebbiolo grape.

See LOMBARDY.

Saumur and Coteaux de Saumur

Still, semi-sparkling, and particularly sparkling white wines, usually dry. Some rosé and red. District: Anjou, France.

The difference between the two names has never been clearly established and may never be, and for the moment they have substantially the same meaning. The wines are red, white, and rosé (although in actual practice red wines are rarely, if ever, seen abroad) and may be either still or sparkling, the production of the latter taking up a goodly proportion of each year's harvest. Sparkling Saumur is presentable, is slightly heavier and more common than sparkling Vouvray, but is certainly no match for Champagne.

Most sparkling Saumur is vinified and aged in huge caves, which burrow back into the chalky cliffs surrounding the ancient city. French law insists that all such wines be made by the Champagne process (*see* CHAMPAGNE) of secondary fermentation in the bottle, and 40% of the wines must come from the juice of Chenin Blanc grapes; the rest is ordinarily made up of Groslot with some Cabernet.

Non-sparkling white Saumur will sometimes be about the finest of its type in the region of Anjou. It is generally dry—sometimes, however, preserving a slight trace of sweetness—and often proves more robust than the dry wines from the rest of the district. Rosé (both ordinary and that made exclusively from Cabernet grapes) is quite frequently encountered, but it does not differ markedly from good Angevin rosés. Some of the whites are *pétillants* or semi-sparkling. About 457,000 imp. gallons (550,000 U.S.) are made annually.

Saussignac, Côtes de

White wines (not very important) of the Dordogne region in south-west France. Wine-producing villages are Gageac-et-Rouillac, Monestier, and Razac-de-Saussignac. Since 1955 the name Saussignac can be replaced by Bergerac, provided the wines come from the above-mentioned communes, and attain the prescribed degrees of sugar and alcohol.

Sauternes

White wine. District: Bordeaux, France.

The suspense in the final moment of harvesting a Sauternes is worthy of a Hitchcock film. To make

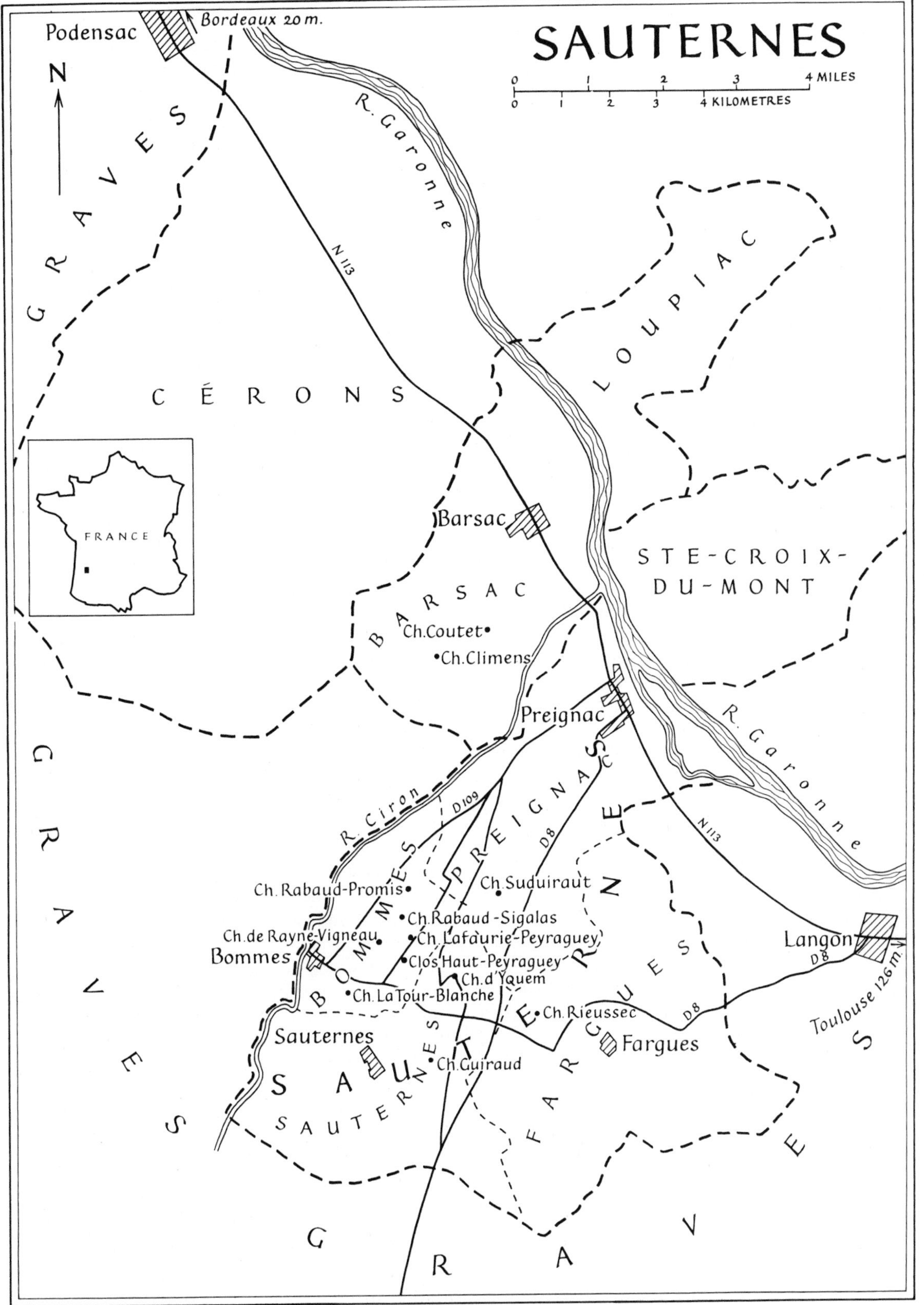
SAUTERNES
0 1 2 3 4 MILES
0 1 2 3 4 KILOMETRES
N
Podensac
Bordeaux 20 m.
R. Garonne
N113
GRAVES
LOUPIAC
CÉRONS
FRANCE
Barsac
STE-CROIX-DU-MONT
BARSAC
Ch.Coutet
Ch.Climens
Preignac
PREIGNAC
R. Ciron
D109
D8
Ch. Suduiraut
Ch. Rabaud-Promis
Ch. Rabaud-Sigalas
Ch. de Rayne-Vigneau
Ch. Lafaurie-Peyraguey
Bommes
Clos Haut-Peyraguey
Ch. d'Yquem
BOMMES
Ch. La Tour-Blanche
Ch. Rieussec
Sauternes
Fargues
FARGUES
Ch. Guiraud
SAUTERNES
Langon
Toulouse 126 m.

the entirely natural sweet wine, the grape must achieve the state of overripeness the French call *pourriture noble*. Failing this, the wine will lack the extra richness, sugar, and alcohol sometimes reaching 16% and even 17% with 6% of sugar; in fact, it will not even be entitled to the legal designation of Sauternes. But if, on the other hand, the beneficial overripening is allowed to go too far, the bouquet is lost in the increased suavity and richness of the wine. Add to this the fact that the overripening occurs very late in the season when frost may strike down the vines any day, and it is easy to understand the nervous pacing of the grower in Sauternes, inspecting his vines several times a day as he decides whether to pick or not.

No other wine in the world is made on such a scale by this delicate and nerve-racking process, though a portion of the crop from certain great vineyards along the Rhine and Moselle in Germany is produced identically. Trockenbeerenauslese, the German word for the process and the resultant wine, perhaps best describes it. 'Dried-grapes-specially-selected'—a child's Meccano-set word built up with German literalness.

The Sauternes process is the only one by which a wine of such richness may be produced without human interference in the form of extra sugar, of fermentation arrested by the addition of brandy, or any of the other methods used in the production of various wines. A mould or fungus, *botrytis cinerea*—the French picturesquely, and with botanical correctness, call it a mushroom—attacks the grapes late in the autumn, and the skins shrivel. No sugar is *added* by this process, but the proportion of sugar becomes greater as the water grows less. At the same time, the mould causes transformation within the grapes, of a nature not yet defined, that increases the glycerines and pectins which will give the wine its suavity and smoothness. The 'legs' of a great Sauternes are celebrated. They are the slow streams which descend with unctuous richness down the inner side of the glass after the wine has been tipped away.

The bunch of grapes, ready for the selected picking, is dried and folded and (while it is not a pleasant comparison) has a marked resemblance to the wizened, leathery, folded-in appearance of a hanging bat. Covered over with the *pourriture noble*, it hardly gives promise of the golden nectar it is to produce. With much of the juice dried out, the quantity is reduced. To this loss of volume must be added the greatly increased cost of picking. The mould develops haphazardly over a vineyard, and the rows must be picked through as many as six times. For these reasons, true Sauternes can never be cheap.

True Sauternes. For no other wine is more widely flattered by the theft of its name. 'Sauternes' is not merely a white sweet wine, but the white sweet wine of Sauternes, France. The wines to be met with in many other places in the world which call themselves sauternes—or even sauterne, as if to justify bad practice by bad spelling—are not what they claim to be.

The character of a wine is determined by several factors, among which are the influences of a specific soil and climate in a given geographical place; for grapevines do not behave in the same way in different soils and climates. When the right vine or vines have been found for a certain wine-favouring area, a famous wine will result, over decades of development. Nowhere else will exactly the right combination of factors exist to produce the same wine.

The Sauternes district is composed of five communes: Sauternes, Barsac, Bommes, Preignac, and Fargues. In all sections the wine is made identically, and mainly from the Sémillon grape, with about 20% of Sauvignon. Muscadelle is used in very small amounts in the blends. Because a Sauternes vineyard is not picked section by section but according to the degree of overripeness, there is a difference in quality between early-season pickings and very late pickings. When brought in, the bunches first enter a long revolving tube. This *fouloir*, or beater, extracts the first juice. Then, after destalking, the grapes are pressed three times. In the past all these different grades of juice were made into separate wines; but about the end of the last century this practice largely ceased. Today the general custom is to mix the yield. This is done in large tanks, where the day's pick remains only a few hours, and is then let off into casks, where it ferments and matures. Differences in the different days' harvesting cause differences in the wine in cask, and when it becomes apparent that a wine is not up to standard, it is the practice of every fine château to exclude it from that which will be bottled under its name. Instead, it is sold to the Bordeaux shippers, to be bottled simply as Sauternes. (In such cases, shippers are strictly forbidden to let it be known that the bottle is really from one of the Classified Growths (*Crus*), being sold at the much lower price for regional wine.)

Yielding on an average only 300 bottles to the acre, the entire region produces the equivalent of 2½ million bottles a year. Sauternes tend to differ from one vineyard to another, but the only generalization to be made is that the Barsacs, which are entitled to the separate name Barsac as well as that of Sauternes, are likely to be less sweet. They come from a flatter land, and a less stony, more chalky soil in the northern portion (*see* BARSAC). It is Sauternes proper, the rolling, hilly region around the tiny village of Sauternes and the towns of Bommes and Fargues, which is the most picturesque. The vineyard road, hardly more than a lane, runs between old stone walls. The great vineyards clothe the slopes, the crown of which will usually display the château. Lower-lying vineyards were severely damaged in the freeze of February 1956, and from these, and to a lesser degree the slope vineyards, no 1956 or 1957 vintage was seen, and very little of vintages for several subsequent years.

Sauternes should be served cold, but not so iced that the taste will be numbed. It can be brought to serving temperature in an ice bucket or in the refrigerator. Some French people will serve an old Sauternes which has oxidized as an aperitif; the oxidation will have reduced some of the sweetness but not all.

Sauternes are best served at the end of the meal when they go well with a dessert and even better with fruit, and some knowledgeable people serve a glass of sweet Sauternes *as* the dessert. Counter to all this, however, is the opinion of the owner of Château d'Yquem, who maintains the nineteenth-century tradition that Sauternes should be drunk not with the dessert only but also with certain fish.

CLASSIFIED VINEYARDS OF SAUTERNES AND BARSAC, 1855 CLASSIFICATION

FIRST GREAT GROWTH (*Premier Grand Cru*)

Château d'Yquem (Sauternes)

FIRST GROWTHS (*Premiers Crus*)

Château La Tour-Blanche (Bommes)
Château Lafaurie-Peyraguey (Bommes)
Clos Haut-Peyraguey (Bommes)
Château de Rayne-Vigneau (Bommes)
Château de Suduiraut (Preignac)
Château Coutet (Barsac)
Château Climens (Barsac)
Château Guiraud (Sauternes)
Château Rieussec (Fargues)
Château Rabaud-Promis (Bommes)
Château Rabaud-Sigalas (Bommes)

SECOND GROWTHS (*Seconds Crus*)

Château Myrat (Barsac)
Château Doisy-Daëne (Barsac)
Château Doisy-Védrines (Barsac)
Château d'Arche (Sauternes)
Château Filhot (Sauternes)
Château Broustet (Barsac)
Château Nairac (Barsac)
Château Caillou (Barsac)
Château Suau (Barsac)
Château de Malle (Preignac)
Château Romer (Fargues)
Château Lamothe (Sauternes)

For First Great Growth and First Growths, *see* CHÂTEAU D'YQUEM, CHÂTEAU LA TOUR-BLANCHE, CHÂTEAU LAFAURIE-PEYRAGUEY, etc. *See also* BARSAC.

Sauvignon Blanc

An exceptionally fine white grape used for some excellent white wines. With Sémillon (and some Muscadelle) it produces all of Bordeaux's finest whites, from the sweetest Sauternes to the driest Graves. Some marvellously pleasant Loire Valley white wines come solely from this grape, notably those of Sancerre, and the best wine of Pouilly-sur-Loire where the wine is known locally as Blanc Fumé, 'white smoke', or rather, white Sauvignon taste. In California the Sauvignon Blanc is considered among the finest grapes for white wine, especially in the Livermore, San Benito, and Santa Clara valleys. The wine varies, of course, according to the soil and climate of the vineyard and the manner in which grapes and wine are treated; but whenever conditions are favourable, the wine will have considerable breed and distinction. Among other names for this vine are Surin, in parts of the Loire valley, and Muskat Sylvaner in Germany.

Sauvignon, Cabernet-Sauvignon

The finest of the Claret grapes grown in the Médoc; small and blue-black in colour, thick skinned and juicy. The wine they yield is very full and slow in maturing. The other regional names for this grape include Bouchet and Vidure.

See CABERNET.

Savagnin

The dominant grape variety in the golden-white wines of Château-Châlon. Savagnin Rose is another name for the red Traminer of Alsace; Savagnin Noir is none other than the Pinot Noir.

Savatiano

One of the principal grape varieties used for Greek liqueurs and also for table wines—often those which have been doctored with resin—it is found in central Greece and in the Peloponnese.

Savennières

The best part of the Anjou-Coteaux de la Loire district in France.

See ANJOU.

Savigny-les-Beaune and Savigny-les-Beaune-Côte de Beaune

Burgundy red and white wines. District: Côte de Beaune, France.

In the early Middle Ages the vineyards were

owned by Cistercians and Carmelites, but the French people and many of the nobility were not far behind in establishing their claims. A great moated castle, built in 1340, totally destroyed in 1468, and rebuilt in 1672, still stands to the side of the main square, surrounded by a rambling and slightly dishevelled park. During the eighteenth century this was the home of the Duchesse de Maine. Today its opulence has declined, its windows are closed, and a few chickens scratch in what was once the main court.

Within the confines of present-day Savigny there are about 900 acres of vines, and production in an average year for quantity is 112,400 imp. gallons (135,000 U.S.) of red wine, 4,400 (5,300 U.S.) of white. This wine was greatly appreciated in the distant past (a Duke of Burgundy wanted to elevate one grower to the rank of a demi-god for the quality of his wine) but its reputation has diminished considerably. It is distinctly light and fragrant with considerable finesse but definitely not a wine to keep for any length of time.

The town stands between Pernand-Vergelesses and Beaune and the wines of all three are fairly similar, although those of Beaune are far and away the best. Savigny sells its wines either under the commune name or under commune name with Côte de Beaune added, but if a wine qualifies for either name it is qualified for both. Wines may also be blended with those from certain other communes along the slope and sold as Côte de Beaune-Villages. The best vineyards of the commune are rated First Growths (*Premiers Crus*)—higher minimum standards and better wines—and their wines may be sold with both commune name and vineyard name. These vineyards are Vergelesses, Marconnets, Dominode, Jarrons, and Lavières.

Savoy (Haute-Savoie)

In this region of France, two white wines are permitted Appellations Contrôlées. These are Crépy and Seyssel (*q.v.*).

Scharlachberg

Excellent white wine from near Bingen on the German Rhine.

See RHEINHESSEN: BINGEN-RÜDESHEIM.

Scharzhofberg

Generally the finest wines of the German Saar. These wines frequently attain an incomparable elegance.

See SAAR.

Schaumwein

A German term for sparkling wine.

Schiave

A red grape grown in Italy, particularly in the vineyards of the Alto Adige.

Schiedam

Term sometimes used for Hollands gin because Schiedam in Holland is one of the chief places of its manufacture.

Schiller Wine

A pinkish wine from red and white grapes, which once comprised half the wine made in the German Württemberg district; during the last thirty years, however, it has gradually been dying out.

Schloss Böckelheimer Kupfergrube

Good wines of the Nahe Valley in Germany, grown on the slopes of the Kupfergrube or 'Copper mine'.

See NAHE.

Schloss Johannisberg

Most expensive of the Rheingaus (German Rhine wine). The best-informed brokers and growers on the river consider it one of the finest Rheingaus consistently over the years, though not always first in any given year. (For a full explanation of the different types of capsuling, indicating the different grades and qualities of Schloss Johannisberg, *see* RHEINGAU: JOHANNISBERG.)

Schloss Vollrads

Best of the wines of the Winkel section of the German Rhine, and one of the best Rhine wines, Schloss Vollrads is bottled and sold in four grades or qualities. These are—in ascending order—Originalabfüllung, Schlossabzug, Kabinett, and the specially-selected, super-rich Auslese and Trockenbeerenauslese. (For a full description of these grades and the wine *see* RHEINGAU: SCHLOSS VOLLRADS.)

Schlossabzug

The same as Originalabfüllung—a natural, unsugared wine, bottled on the estate; in this case a *Schloss* or castle.

See RHEINGAU.

Schnapps

In Germany and Holland, any strong, dry spirit; in Scandinavia, usually Aquavit. An aromatic schnapps is made from a base of Dutch-style gin flavoured with aromatic herbs.

Schooner

A tall drinking glass most suitable for beer; usually about 15 fluid ounces.

Schwarzwalder

German name for kirsch or cherry brandy.

See KIRSCH.

Scotch Whisky

See WHISKY, SCOTCH.

Sec

French for 'dry'. This word appearing on the label of a bottle of Champagne does not, in fact, indicate a very dry wine, but rather one which is inclined towards sweetness.

See CHAMPAGNE.

Secco

Italian term for dry wine; as French *sec*.

Séché

A term widely used in France for harsh, flat wines with an astringent aftertaste. This is usually the result of excessive oxidation.

Sediment

Lees or solid matter deposited by a wine while it is ageing. Such deposit does not necessarily affect the taste of the wine but because of its bitter consistency and the fact that it spoils the look of the wine, it should be separated from it by decanting before serving.

See CHAPTER NINE.

Seeweine

Pleasant little wines of Lake Constance (or Bodensee) in the south of Germany.

See BADEN.

Seewinkel

See SANDWEINE.

Seibel

French hybridizer who developed hundreds of vines of varying characteristics. Some of his most notable achievements were described by Philip Wagner in *A Wine Grower's Guide*.

Sekt

German term for sparkling wine. Ludwig Devrient, a Berlin actor famous in the nineteenth century, invented a popular joke by calling for his Sekt—cup of sack—when he played Shakespeare's Falstaff. He began to use the same term when calling for his favourite drink, Champagne, in restaurants and the name Sekt for German champagne-type wine was established.

Sémillon

White-wine grape used in the Sauternes and Graves districts of Bordeaux, and fairly widely throughout the Dordogne and south-west France. It is grown also in California.

La Senancole

A liqueur resembling yellow Chartreuse, made originally by Cistercian monks of the Abbey of Senanque, in Provence. The yellow, aromatic, herb-based liqueur was named after the River Senancole which flows near the Abbey. It is now made by a commercial distiller, but under the supervision of the monks.

Separation

In the making of wine, grapes are usually separated from their stalks before fermentation by a machine known in France as an *égrappoir* or *foulo-grappe*. Agreement with this practice, first adopted in the fine red wine regions of Burgundy and Bordeaux, is not unanimous, but there are strong arguments in its favour. In the case of red wines, separation increases the degree of alcohol by about 0·5 as a result of changes which take place between the must and the stalk. It makes the wine less astringent and gets rid of foreign substances. The wine will be clearer, suppler, and ready sooner than those which have absorbed extra alcohols and tannins from the stems; and the process saves labour, since the marc which remains after pressing will be less bulky if there are no stalks in it.

The *égrappoir* has not been much used in making white wines, but nowadays it is often employed before the pressing of finer wines.

Seppeltsfield

Famous vineyard in Barossa Valley, South Australia.

See AUSTRALIA.

Sercial

A white grape variety producing one of the best Madeira wines; dry, sometimes pale, sometimes golden, with a tremendous 'nose'.

See MADEIRA.

Sève

Literally 'sappy' (from the French word for sap). The term as used in France suggests a feminine charm, elegance, and a distinction which is graceful and not assertive in a masculine way. It is employed also to describe Sauternes which have that deep, luscious quality.

Seyssel

White still and sparkling wines. District: Upper Rhône Valley, France.

Near the source of the Rhône is the butterfly-shaped district of Seyssel, made up of the communes of Seyssel (department of Haute-Savoie), Seyssel (department of Ain), and Corbonod. The dividing line between the twin cities of Seyssel and between the two departments is the Rhône. The wines are white, and some of them are made sparkling.

The area consists of a series of hills and depressions cut out by some ancient glacier that also left in its path the flinty-clay and flinty-chalk deposits which compose the present soil. These hills provide a number of southerly and south-easterly slopes, on which the vines are planted. For the still Seyssel, the only grape planted is the Roussette. Whether or not this was the vine that was grown in antiquity at Saint-Cornas and Hermitage along the lower Rhône and transported to Seyssel by boats trading in salt; or whether it was imported from Cyprus—or is the Hungarian Furmint brought in by one of the Princes of Savoy—is still a matter for discussion. Whatever its origin, the vine produces a light, flinty-dry, white wine that is best when drunk young and is, for that reason, usually bottled in the April following the harvest. The Roussette also goes into the sparkling Seyssel in a proportion of at least 10%, the rest being made up of Molette and Chasselas. This last vine is called, in Seyssel, Bon Blanc.

The delimited area of Seyssel has about 100 acres planted in vines, and the average production is less than 48,000 imp. gallons (58,000 U.S.) yearly.

Seyve-Villard

Contemporary French hybridizer who has developed a number of hybrid vines mostly for warm or hot climates, including some of the best available to the wine-maker. For red wines, S-V13359, S-V 18315, and S-V 23657 have had a certain success, as have his white S-V 5276 and S-V 19287 which resembles the Muscat grape.

Shandy or Shandygaff

A long drink popular in England; beer mixed with ginger beer or lemonade.

Shebeen

In Ireland and Scotland, a place where taxable liquors are sold without a licence; also, a low tavern or public house.

Shekar

Hebrew term for 'intoxicating drink', later applied only to cider.

Sherry

Sherry, celebrated since Shakespeare's time, tends to eclipse, for most people, the fame of all other Spanish wines. It is a fortified wine: grape brandy has been added to bring up the alcoholic content to between 15·5% for the Finos and 18% for the Olorosos. The Spaniards themselves are much fonder of Sherry than are the Portuguese of Port, but the English drink a great deal more: in one fairly recent year, they consumed three-fifths of the total production. The taste is growing in America, too. Most connoisseurs agree that, before a dinner at which fine wines will be served, a dry Sherry is the perfect aperitif. Outside Spain, Amontillado, which has a nutty flavour peculiarly its own, is the favourite before-dinner Sherry; but returning travellers often prefer the dry Finos and Manzanillas.

The Sherry vineyards lie around the town of Jerez-de-la-Frontera, south of Seville, in the most romantic part of Spain. Here, a great horse-fair is held each spring: just as Seville is a city of wine and of bulls, Jerez (which once traded in gold and in Barbary apes) is a town of horses and of wine. The great bulls and bullfighters come here, too, from Seville, and young *caballeros* in grey Córdoba hats ride with the beautiful girls on horseback, or drive them in open carriages. But the Féria is not the only thing which draws travellers to Jerez: there is also the Sherry itself, and the mystery of its ageing.

The wine, which plays an essential part in the life of the town, takes its name from the Latin Xeres and the Arabian Sherrisch. Vines have grown in the region ever since the Phœnicians founded the town, over a thousand years before Christ. The Greeks came and then the Romans, who ruled the city for four hundred years. It was from the later invaders, the Vandals, that the whole province took the name Andalusia. Then, in 711, the Moors arrived. Until the reconquest of Jerez, about 1264, it lay on the border between the warring Christian and Moslem kingdoms, and so was known as Jerez-de-la-Frontera. Much later—in the nineteenth century—the export of Sherry wine reached its peak,

and the town enjoyed great good fortune. Towards the end of the century, however, Sherry was declining in popularity, and in the eighteen-nineties phylloxera reached Andalusia. The vine disease—which at that period destroyed most of the vineyards of Europe—and the change in fashion, menaced the prosperity of Jerez, and for some years exports were sadly reduced. Fortunately, the trade was to revive.

Sherry is known neither by vintage nor by vineyard. Vintage identity is lost in the *solera* system, by which an old, fine Sherry is used to discipline a raw, young one. Vineyard names do not exist for two reasons: (1) nearly all Sherry is blended from several different *pagos* (Spanish for area); (2) the important *pagos* are divided into many different vineyards and, therefore, between many owners, so that no one has the exclusive right to the name.

Nevertheless, place of origin is important. 40% of the stocks of any firm must be purchased from the Zona de Jerez Superior (Zone of Superior Sherry), or 'the triangle', as it is called—an irregular triangle lying inside the points of the three important towns, Jerez de la Frontera, Sanlúcar de Barrameda, and Puerto de Santa María. This zone is comprised of the finest soil, named *albariza*. The vineyards are composed of the white chalk soil which nourishes the vine with its lime content and protects it from summer heat by forming a naked crust beneath which moisture is retained. The famous *pagos* of Macharnudo, Carrascal, Añina and Balbaina; and Miraflores in the east, producing the finest Manzanilla, are inside the triangle. Secondary soils are the *barro* and the *arena*. The former contains some chalk, with a considerable admixture of clay and sand; the latter is sandy, containing alumina and silica. These soils are found in other parts of the Sherry-producing zone, in which the Superior Zone produces the best wine. All Sherries are produced within the Sherry zone which covers the towns of Jerez de la Frontera, Puerto de Santa Maria, Sanlúcar de Barrameda, Trebujena, Chipiona, Rota, Puerto Real, and Chiclana de la Frontera (all in the province of Cadiz).

Vineyards, Vines, and Vintaging

There is a saying in Jerez—*Niñas y viñas son malas de guardar*—which might be translated 'It's hard to keep watch over vineyards and young girls.'

This is another way of saying that the Palomino, the grape which gives 90% of Sherry, is one of the few great wine grapes in the world which is also delicious to eat. A result is the curious *bien-te-veo*, which literally means 'I can see you'—a small hut or look-out set up on stilts in the vineyards so that an overseer may watch out for whoever might steal the grapes.

There are other varieties of grape in Jerez (Pedro Ximénez, Mantúo, Albillo, Cañocazo) but the Palomino is predominant. An apparent abundance of grape varieties may confuse the amateur, because Palomino is known in the area by no less than seven other names. Listán is the most common of these, and is in wide use in the Sanlúcar Manzanilla vineyards. Horgazuela is the name for Palomino in Puerto de Santa María, and elsewhere are encountered Tempranilla, Palomina, Ojo de Liebre, Temprana, and Albán. Whatever it is called, the vine produces thick clusters of pale, fat grapes, hanging like swarms of bees and ripening as much from the reflection of heat off the hard shield of the *albariza* as from the direct sunshine. Pruning removes all but a single branch of the vine, supported in a forked stick against the weight of fruit to come. The production of the vine is limited, in order to extend its life: two-thirds shorter (giving it a total of about thirty years) than it was before the replanting, on grafted American roots, after phylloxera. The effort to preserve the vines is based on the high cost of replanting. The vineyards themselves are patched here and there in rolling country otherwise given over to grain and cotton; but from the main roads and the railways, they cannot be seen at all. The whitewashed houses up the narrow dirt tracks that lead from the vineyards are attached, like unimportant outbuildings, to the great sheds within which the vintaging is carried out. In the spring, when the plants are being treated against disease, the mules plod along the rows, their panniers burdened with earthen Arab urns stained brilliant blue by copper sulphate. At harvest time, the grapes are carried in the woven wicker *canastas* or wooden *tinetas* and dumped in gleaming heaps on esparto grass mats the size of large, round trays. In an hour or two the whole yard of the wine shed is given over to this sunning of the grapes, which lasts until the sunshine has brought the sugar-content of the grapes into proper balance; and bees and wasps drone over what appear to be mounds of molten honey.

The grapes are trodden out during the night in vast wooden troughs called *lagares*, not by naked feet but by a peculiar kind of shoe with nailheads driven slantways in rows into the sole. The studs catch the grape pips and prevent them from being crushed with the pulp, which would give the juice a slightly bitter taste. Men in shorts, the treading shoes on their bare feet, Spanish berets or caps on their heads, stamp in rows, each supporting himself on the slippery mass by the use of a wooden spade which he holds like a staff in one hand. The juice pours out through a wooden pipe into a smaller tub placed beneath the *lagar*. It is collected in jugs, filtered, and taken into the *bodega* in butts. From time to time, forming and slapping with the flats of the spades, as if patting up small mountains of butter, the treaders reshape the grape mass in the trough round an axle. The final process is the piling up of the pulped grape remnant into a cake, and winding it round with esparto grass—this primitive method of holding the mass in form has never been bettered. A bar on the axle is screwed down on to the cake by two or more men revolving it slowly, and the last juice is wrung out.

The first fermentation of Sherry, lasting three days to a week, is extremely violent. The barrel bungs foam over like the mouths of newly opened Champagne bottles. After this, there is a slow fermentation of about three months, during which time the bung stoppers are left loose so that the wine is in free contact with the air. At the end, the Sherry is totally dry—i.e. every bit of fermentable sugar has been converted into alcohol, and the tumult dies down to a long slow fermentation. In January or February the wine is racked and tested (with the nose, not by tasting) for quality and for the type it may finally become. (The microscopic yeasty flowers that form a scum on the wine—the *flor*—are thicker on a must going to Fino than on one going to Oloroso.) Each cask is marked with chalk. Then, towards the end of the first year (which is passed in the *añada*, or the first-year casks), the Sherry is again racked and tested for the character it is definitely going to develop. When the wine is transferred to fresh casks, wine brandy is added—a smaller quantity to the Fino type than to the Oloroso type. Again the *capataz* (cellar-master) will mark the butts with chalk. One downward stroke—or *raya*—means that the wine is good, with a clean bouquet and sufficient body; two, the wine is quite good; three strokes, there is some slight flaw; and two strokes with a cross-bar (grid) means that the wine is only fit for burning, i.e. distilling into brandy. When the Sherry has declared itself to be potentially a Fino or an Oloroso, it is put into four or five *criaderas*, or nurseries; and when its time comes, it progresses to a *solera*.

Solera

The most interesting thing about Sherry (apart from the mysterious *flor*) is the peculiar system by which it is kept at its best. A very old, very fine Sherry has the power to educate and improve a younger one. Because of this, the old wines are kept in the oldest barrels of what the growers call a *solera*. This is a series of casks graduated by age. A series is made up of identical butts. The oldest class in a *solera* is the one called the Solera. The next oldest is the first Criadera, the next the second Criadera, and so on. When the wine is drawn from the Solera, it is drawn in equal quantity from each butt. Then starts a progressive system by which the Solera is refilled by the first Criadera and that in turn by the second Criadera, etc. The magic result of this system is that the oldest casks remain eternally the same in quality. A cask of 1888, for instance, may retain hardly a spoonful of its original vintage; but each replacement poured back into it over the years will have been educated to be 1888, and replacements still to come will be schooled to the same standard. By this system, it is possible not only to preserve the same quality and character of wine over the years, but also, by constantly refreshing the Fino types with younger wine, to keep these from losing their freshness.

In the Sherry Bodegas

The wine is stored in dim, cool sanctuaries at ground level, all facing south-east to the sea. These are the *bodegas* of the great wine firms, to which everyone is welcome. Nothing is asked of the guest but a love for Sherry or the willingness to learn. He will be invited to taste a vast range of wines, and the *capataz*, or perhaps the owner himself, will take up and wield deftly the willowy *venencia*, or sherry dipper—a narrow silver cup at the end of a whalebone, flexible spine. He is given a hint of the deep mystery of the *flor* as the *venencia* is plunged into the wine. The white scum of *flor* must be penetrated by a stabbing thrust, the bullet-like cup plunging through the creamy layer to reach the wine; the cup disappears into the barrel bung, and with a sudden motion that causes a distinct *pock* of sound, the whalebone wand is flicked sharply down. Pouring the wine, once it has been brought out in the silver *venencia* cup, is an art that looks simple—and is not. The expert grips the flexible shaft between his thumb and forefinger and, holding a glass with his free hand, he lets a long stream of wine cascade through the air and into the glass. The amateur tries it—and with unerring accuracy the Sherry goes up his sleeve.

The *flor*—the Spanish for 'flower'—is the white yeast that grows on the surface of the wine, magically increasing at the budding of the vine in spring and at its fruiting in the autumn. At first thin and flaky, like the snow in a glass paperweight, *flor* becomes in time a skin like old cream. After its period of flowering it settles to the bottom of the wine.

Air turns most wine acid. Sherry—and the wines of the Jura in France—thrive, however, on air. Deprived of it, they do not produce their characteristic taste. The towering vaulted *bodegas* of Jerez are open to the passage of the air on which the *flor* feeds. Two different microscopic organisms (they are technically a bacterium *Acetobacter*, which turns wine into vinegar, and a yeast of the group responsible for fermentations) feed on air. In normal situations, it is the former that appears, and it is for this reason that other wines deteriorate when they come in contact with the air. Somehow, in the region around Jerez (and in Jura) at a concentration of alcohol from 11·5% to 15·5% and at a temperature of 58° to 68°F. (14° to 20°C.), it is the second of these two incomparable growths which succeeds, transforming the wine into that dry, light, crisp condition called Fino in Sherry. The Spaniards believe that this yeast is the *Saccharomyces*, the yeast that forms a *flor* veil on the surface, consuming whatever sugar is left in the wine after fermentation.

The Types of Sherry

All Sherries stem either from the Fino or the Oloroso type. Fino is Sherry on which *flor* has developed fully. Oloroso is a wine which has not shown a disposition to have plentiful *flor* and the small or nearly non-existent 'flowering' of which has been suppressed by the addition of a stronger dose of fortifying wine brandy than that given a Fino. No one can influence this first basic decision taken by the wine itself, and no one knows why one cask wants to become Fino while a barrel of what appears to be the same wine, from the same harvest and vineyard, wants to become Oloroso. There is nothing to do but watch and wait, and when the wine has made up its mind, treat it accordingly.

Fino

This is a very pale, light gold wine; the lightest in colour of the Sherries. The nose of the wine is not pronounced but characteristic—like the scent released by a freshly picked apple. There is a hint of almond, too. Ideally, Fino should never be bottled —for, when it is drunk from the wood, there has never been any interval when the wine was not in beneficial contact with the air. Less fortified than Oloroso, Fino is more alive. Once bottled, it may keep up to two years—depending on weather and cellaring conditions—but it will not improve at all and will eventually lose its freshness. Because of its delicate constitution, Fino is exported at higher alcoholic strength to help it travel (18% to 20%, while domestic Fino is 16% to 17%) and this diminishes the bouquet.

There is no way of knowing just how old your bottle of Fino is when you buy it, since the Sherry (which is always bottled just before shipping) is not dated, although some shippers feel that labels should bear the date of bottling. Under the circumstances, Fino should be bought shortly before it is to be drunk, and from a supplier who can be trusted not to have kept it too long on the shelf. Once opened, Fino is inclined to fade away; and for this reason, the practice in Jerez is rather to buy the wine in half-bottles.

Manzanilla

This is both a Sherry Fino—the Fino of Finos—and a separate and individual wine in its own right. This comes about because it is produced in *soleras*, develops *flor*, and comes from the Palomino grape grown on the same kind of chalky, limy soil which produces Fino; but it does these things eleven or twelve miles from Jerez, around the sea-coast town of Sanlúcar de Barrameda. It is the sea that makes the difference, giving the special tang or bitterness, especially in the aftertaste, which distinguishes Manzanilla. This is the palest of the Finos, a fresh, incredibly light, tart wine—usually sold from the barrel in Spain. It is the unchallenged favourite of many Spanish people, and at any bar, along with the inevitable *tapas*—onions, olives, shrimps speared on toothpicks—one will hear calls for Manzanilla.

A peculiar proof of the relationship between Manzanilla and Fino wines of Jerez is that if young Manzanilla is taken to a *bodega* in Jerez for storing it becomes Jerez Fino; whereas, if a young Jerez Fino is taken to Sanlúcar de Barrameda and kept in the Manzanilla *bodegas*, it becomes Manzanilla. This mysterious behaviour is explained by the influence of the sea air. Blowing through the Sanlúcar *bodegas*, it creates Manzanilla, with its own unmistakable, salt-sharp tang.

In the small, whitewashed town of Sanlúcar de Barrameda, they classify their Manzanillas into five types: (1) Manzanilla Pasada; (2) Manzanilla Olorosa; (3) Manzanilla Fina; (4) Manzanilla; and (5) Amanzanillado. In fact, Manzanillas are graded in exactly the same way as Sherries are in Jerez.

Palma

A name often used interchangeably with Fino in Spain, Palma has recently come into use in export for Fino of a particularly clean, delicate quality. Palmas may be graded 1, 2, 3, or 4, the higher numbers indicating greater age.

Entre-Fino

This is a coarser Fino of lesser quality.

Vino de Pasto

A medium pale, dry, young Entre-Fino. The term is not used in Spain.

Amontillado

This is a darker-coloured Sherry, from one to three degrees stronger in alcohol than a Fino. It averages 18% of alcohol by volume, though with age it may reach 24% and 25%. A Fino which is kept in cask and not refreshed from time to time by younger wine may become an Amontillado. Since there is a great demand for Amontillado, the practice is to watch for a darkening of the *flor* and an increasing nuttiness in the taste of Finos. If this is found, the cask is marked to indicate that it should not be refreshed: in one *bodega*, where English influence predominates, the simple word 'no' is chalked on the barrelhead.

Amontillados as sold are not always pure Amontillado. Many of those seen abroad have been somewhat sweetened. They may have Fino or other wines blended in, although there must be some Amontillado or the characteristic nuttiness of flavour will disappear. Generally speaking, the nuttier the taste, the truer the Amontillado. These wines are dry, clean, and brisk both to the nose and palate. There are some Amontillado-Finos which lie on the borderline. It should be remembered that Sherry types shade one into the other; the demarcations are somewhat arbitrary, and necessitated by commercial considerations. In one of the largest Jerez *bodegas*, special visitors are sometimes shown a scale of thirty-four glasses in which are Sherries ranging in colour from straw to mahogany, in alcohol from 15·2% to 22·8%, and in taste from light and fresh to pungent. Every one of these will be dry. No Sherry is sweet in the natural state.

Oloroso

This is a more full-bodied wine than Amontillado. As its name implies, the wine is strong in bouquet—nutty and pungent in the finest bottles. But its most distinctive characteristic is *gordura*—a rich vinosity and opulence that can literally be translated as 'fatness'. Oloroso leaves a lingering sensation of richness on the palate which produces an illusion of sweetness. In fact, while there are many sweetened Olorosos sold as such—or Amoroso, Cream, and so on—the natural Oloroso is dry.

It was not until about a century and a half ago that a taste began to develop with the public for the lighter Sherry derived from the *flor*. Previously, Oloroso was the only style shipped and the *flor*, which must have existed as it does today, was dosed out of existence with brandy. The consequence of the taste for Fino was the division of the wines according to whether or not they showed a marked tendency to develop *flor*. Once a wine has declared its tendency to become Oloroso, it receives a heavier brandy fortification than that given to a Fino. The alcohol in the brandy suppresses such *flor* as it may have.

In a true Oloroso, the nose of the wine must be absolutely clean. The average alcoholic strength will be 18% to 20% of the volume, although with age 24% and 25% may be reached. The Olorosos are beautifully golden, the gold darkening with the years and indicating the wine's age in the barrel. Having more body than Finos, Olorosos will survive better in the bottle but, like other Sherries, they do not improve in glass.

Palo Cortado

This is a rare type: an Oloroso with the characteristics of the Fino group. In different *bodegas* Palo Cortado tends to mean different things. At one of the most important firms, a Palo Cortado is an Oloroso with a Fino nose. A true Palo Cortado is a vintage wine, very rare in Sherry, and something which simply 'happens'—it cannot be achieved by blending. It is admitted, however, that the real thing must be matured for at least twenty years and is commercially not practicable, and that wines of the style actually on the market are *like* Palo Cortado.

Raya

Very common in Jerez, this designation will not be found abroad. It means a lesser and coarser Oloroso, relating to Oloroso as Entre-Fino does to Fino. There is also an in-between grade called Raya Olorosa.

Amoroso

This is a sweetened Oloroso, of a dark colour. The style was created for the English taste and is unknown in Spain. (Although in Spain Sherry is taken dry, it is the practice to add sweetener before shipping for many export styles. The best of such sweeteners is Pedro Ximénez, or P.X.)

The full-bodied Amoroso, known as East India, gets its name from the practice in the days of sailing vessels of sending casks of Sherry aboard ship to the East Indies and back. The airing of the wine and the constant rolling at sea was considered beneficial, and the saying was that 'the sea-sick wines of Jerez are worth double'. Brown Sherry is a very dark, sweet Amoroso, likely to be cheaper than East India. Sherries are sometimes darkened by the addition of *color* (a blend of fresh and concentrated grape must) to produce styles demanded in certain markets. Brown Sherry is usually a blend of old Oloroso, P.X., and a touch of *color*.

Cream Sherry

This is a heavily sweetened Oloroso. It was developed in Bristol, England, and is now extremely popular in the United States also. Some Cream Sherries are bottled in Bristol from Oloroso sent in cask from Jerez; and Creams are now produced in Jerez also to meet the growing demand—although Bristol Cream and Bristol Milk are of course bottled in Bristol.

In England, dark, sweet Sherries may be served, not as aperitifs, but as alternatives to Port at the end of a meal.

Tio Pepe

This is not a type, but a brand name for a dry Sherry, just as Dry Sack is for a medium Sherry.

Most Sherry wine is served at room temperature; but a dry Amontillado can be slightly cooled, and Finos and Manzanillas may be chilled.

Sherry Butt (or **Bota**)

This storage butt contains 600 litres (132 imp. gallons; 158·5 U.S.). The shipping butt contains 500 litres (110 imp. gallons; 132 U.S.). For buying purposes, the butt is reckoned as holding 516 litres (112 imp. gallons; 134 U.S.), allowing 16 litres (3 imp. gallons; 3·6 U.S.) for evaporation, clarification, etc.

See SHERRY.

Shiraz

A city in south-west Iran, near the Persian Gulf, which gave its name to the best-known Persian wines. Before the Mohammedan prohibition, wine was freely drunk in Persia; and viticulture persists on a small scale in the mountainous regions. Shiraz is mentioned by Marco Polo, and classical writings carry fabulous accounts of it, in one case telling how the vine was trained by pulleys and weights to grow up one side of the house and down the other.

See IRAN.

Shot Berries

The formation of grape clusters of varying size; this failure of the vine normally follows *coulure* or dropping of the flower, in late spring and early summer.

See CHAPTER EIGHT, p. 36.

Sicily

Red and white wines. Region: Italian island.

Sicily, divided from the toe of Italy by the Straits of Messina, is the largest and most romantic of the Mediterranean islands. It has beautiful beaches, the volcanic Mount Etna, and stretches of wild maquis. Oranges, lemons, and vines grow there; and in nearly 3,000 years of occupation, men have left classical ruins, baroque towns and palaces, sun-baked villages, and a few scabrous slums. Summers are hot and vines prolific: Sicily's contribution to the total wine production of Italy is between six and seven million hectolitres a year.

Phœnicians, Greeks, and Saracens have ruled Sicily, Norman and Spanish kings have reigned there. In 1860, Garibaldi arrived with a straggling troop of volunteers and freed the island from the

Bourbons. He landed at Marsala, and is said to have found the wine shop of the English merchant, Woodhouse, open, and to have refreshed himself with the sweet Marsala wine which he preferred.

TYPES OF WINE

Marsala is the most important—a dessert wine in great favour all over Italy, and one which can be ordered by the glass in almost any café or bar. Marsala, dark amber in colour, is a blended wine made from grape-juice syrup (must), from aromatic white wine, and from *passito* of dried grapes, fermented with brandy. The wine is matured in cask from two to five years.

Corvo di Casteldaccia. Red and white wine produced in the neighbourhood of Palermo. It is dry, with a delicate bouquet.

Etna. There is red and white wine, made from grapes grown on the volcanic slopes of the mountain. Both are high in alcohol—the red a rich jewel colour, the white, a pale straw.

Mamertino. None of the Sicilian wines is really dry, but this golden white wine from the slopes around Messina is semi-sweet and very strong, with an aromatic bouquet.

Moscato di Siracusa. The vineyards of this province yield a rich, sweet, golden wine from the Muscat grape.

Malvasia di Lipari. A sweet yellow wine from sun-dried grapes, produced in the islands of Salina, Stromboli, and Lipari.

Moscato di Pantelleria. An amber coloured, perfumed, dessert wine from the island of Pantelleria.

Faro. A red wine produced in the neighbourhood of Messina: quite a good table wine, usually not too high in alcohol, but sometimes reaches 14%.

Eloro. The red and white wine made in the country around Ragusa and Noto is dryish and brilliant in colour; the white wine is deep yellow.

Frappato di Vittoria. A cherry-red dessert wine, sometimes very sweet, sometimes not so sweet, always alcoholic, produced near Ragusa.

GRAPE VARIETIES

These include Calabrese, Carricante, Cataratto, Frappato, Greco, Grillo, Insolia, Albanello, Malvasia, Minnella, and Nerello, cultivated in vineyards many of which are cut up into small parcels.

See ITALY.

Silent Spirit (Cologne Spirit or Neutral Spirit)

British distillers' term for rectified spirit, colourless, odourless, and tasteless, used in making gin and other spirituous drinks.

Silvestro

Italian liqueur into which go a number of different herbs, dominated by mint. It is said to have been invented by Fra San Silvestro.

Singlings

Brandy after the first distillation and before re-distillation.

Šipon

Slovenian grape variety which may be found on the labels of Ljutomer (or Lutomer) white wines, e.g. Lutomer Šipon. The word is pronounced Shee-pon, and sometimes spelled Chipon.

See YUGOSLAVIA.

Sirah

Red wine grape.

See SYRAH; PETITE-SYRAH.

Sitges

Sweet dessert wine of an unusually pale type.

See SPAIN.

Skhou

Distilled koumiss (*q.v.*).

Sling

A mixed iced drink in a long glass. The ingredients are spirits (usually gin), cordials, and fruit juice.

Slivovitz

Slivovitz (pronounced Shleevovits) is the most common name for Serbian and Bosnian plum brandy from Yugoslavia. Sometimes Slivovica, or Slivovitza, or Šljivovica (Šljiva means plum in Serbian), it is made from a blue plum in the second largest plum-growing area in the world. Slivovitz is the national drink in Bosnian and Serbian Yugoslavia, where it is called rakija. The spirit is double-distilled, and in export, in West Europe, Britain, the United States, Australia, and other countries, it is sold at 70° proof and 87° proof, in tall bottles, or in round, flat bottles, the shape of the traditional Yugoslav wooden flask. Famous since the Middle Ages, it comes from the fruit of trees never less than twenty years old, and is fermented three months in 1,665 imp.-gallon (2,000 U.S.) casks. Distilled twice, it matures in the wood in 416 imp.-gallon (500 U.S.) casks; when it is one year old, hand-selected fresh plums are added. The brandy is then bottled, and should be given about five more years. Variants of

Slivovitz are made in other Balkan countries, but Yugoslavia is the most important producer.

Sloe Gin

A cordial made from the small, bitter, black plum-like fruit of the blackthorn, steeped in gin (*q.v.*).

Smash

A long, iced drink made with spirits, sugar, and mint.

Château Smith-Haut-Lafitte

Bordeaux red wine. District: Graves, France. Commune: Martillac.

The magnificent château stands untenanted in the midst of beech woods. The red wine, classed one of the first of Graves in 1953, is a monopoly of the Louis Eschenauer firm of Bordeaux.

Characteristics. A white wine with less character than most of the Graves in the first class, but rewarding when it is allowed to attain its full age.

Vineyard area: 17 acres.

Average production: 1,300 cases.

Soave

Italian white wine grown in the neighbourhood of Verona. It is dry, with an agreeable bouquet and a smooth texture.

See VENETO.

Sochu

Chinese spirit distilled from saké.

Soft

A wine which is not firm, not hard, and not rough. Wine of certain grape varieties matures rapidly and quickly achieves softness; in other cases, age is the determining factor. Once softness is attained, it is unlikely that a wine will keep long afterwards.

Solera System

Method by which Sherry wine, Málaga wine, and some Spanish brandies are produced.

See SHERRY.

Som

Most Rumanian wine is made from the Riesling, Leanyka, and Furmint, which is known by its Rumanian name of Som.

Somlói Furmint

A white wine from Somló, near Lake Balaton.

See HUNGARY.

Sommelier

French term for wine waiter.

Sonnenglanz

Important vineyard at Beblenheim, Alsace, France.

See ALSACE.

Sonoma-Mendocino

Californian wine region, north of San Francisco, which provides some excellent table and sparkling wines.

See AMERICA: CALIFORNIA AND THE WEST.

Sorbino

Finnish cherry liqueur.

Sour

An American mixed drink made with fruit juice (usually lemon), spirits, and ice, i.e. whisky sour, brandy sour, etc.

South Africa

South Africa with its dry, hot climate and its viticultural tradition of three centuries is a wine-producing country, but unfortunately not yet a wine-drinking one. Although, happily, the trend towards the civilized habit of taking a glass of wine with a meal becomes more general every day, excessive drinking of hard liquor—whisky, brandy, (the largest per capita consumption in the world) and gin—still presents a problem that the authorities are anxious to solve. The great improvement in the quality of sherry-type and table wines is no doubt contributing largely to the slow change for the better in drinking tendencies. Not so many years ago, the so-called sherries were extremely harsh, and the table wines rough and indistinguishable; but this is no longer the case. There has, moreover, been a tremendous improvement in the presentation—that is, the labelling—of the better table wines, even in the last few years.

How long it will take to turn South Africans into beverage wine drinkers, as distinct from those who drink to celebrate, it is difficult to say; but the outlook is not unhopeful. Now that the cheap, rough wine of early days is on its way out, growers are making table wines which are, in some cases, attaining a higher average quality than some of their European counterparts. It is significant that the consumption of table wines in South Africa has, according to a reliable estimate, trebled in the years since the end of the war. These wines are today gaining a following on the competitive London market.

The south-western Cape is one of the most reliable wine-growing districts in the world. The climate is seldom erratic, and heavy rain just before the grape picking is a rarity, so that there is scarcely ever a poor vintage. Depending upon the area, the picking season, or vintage, begins in February or March and when a farm has several grape varieties this may go on for as long as six weeks.

Wine History

In 1955 the South African wine industry celebrated its tercentenary. It was at the end of the year 1654 that the first cuttings from Holland arrived at the Cape, and probably they were short, three-inch-long slips of young vines from the Rhineland. The following year another consignment was sent out from Holland, and they were probably all Muscat, Green Grape (Grœndruif), Muscatel and the Steen grape known as Steendruif in Afrikaans.

On 2 February 1659, wine was pressed for the first time at the Cape, and Johan van Riebeeck wrote in his diary: 'Today, praised be the Lord, wine was made for the first time from Cape grapes.'

Credit should be given to the Co-operative Wine Growers' Association of South Africa for a chronological history of events since, in 1679, Simon van der Stel became Governor of the Cape of Good Hope, established his farm at Groot Constantia, and set an example to the colonists by making fine wines. Significant dates were as follows: *1688* French Huguenots arrived and settled in Franschœk, Paarl, Drakenstein, and Stellenbosch; they extended the vineyards and improved the quality of Cape wines. *1711* South African wines were becoming known and an early traveller in his writings spoke of the 'world-famed Constantia wines', which were then being made at Wynberg. These were sweet wines. *1805* The English took possession of the Cape and, because of the Napoleonic wars, encouraged the export of South African wines to Great Britain. *1811* The first official wine taster was appointed, by Sir John Cradock, to keep an eye on the quality of the wine exported. *1826* Export trade to Britain flourished and wine growers and merchants invested considerable capital in the industry. *1861* With the abolition of preferential tariffs by the Gladstone government, the export trade to Britain collapsed. *1885* Phylloxera ravaged Cape vineyards and wine growers faced complete ruin. To combat the disease, they grafted their vines on to disease-resistant American root-stocks. The vines flourished, but soon the industry was faced with an even greater danger—over-production. *1917* Over-production meant ridiculously low prices for wine, and the growers decided to form a central organization to look after their interests. This led to the founding in 1918 of the Co-operative Wine Growers' Association of South Africa Ltd., today better known as the K.W.V. *1924* Parliament passed Act 5 of 1924, the Wine and Spirit Control Act. The K.W.V., under its constitution, annually fixes the minimum price to be paid for distilling wine; this Act made the transactions of non-members subject to the same provisions as those of members, and changed the face and character of the South African wine industry. *1926* The export trade with Britain and Holland was resumed. *1931* The South African Wine Farmers' Association (London) Ltd. was established in the United Kingdom, with the K.W.V. holding a half interest. The purpose of this company was to effect distribution, maintain continuity of supplies, uniformity of quality and stability of prices. *1940* The Wine and Spirit Control Amendment Act, No. 23 of 1940, was passed and provided for the fixing of the price for good wine sold by producers; it also empowered the K.W.V. to limit the production of wine alcohol in the Cape. *1950* K.W.V. acquired full control of the South African Wine Farmers' Association (London) Ltd.

Wine Regions

As an important form of agriculture, viticulture is limited to the south-western districts of the Cape, between latitudes 33° and 34° S. The areas with summer rainfall are not favourable for vine growing; but vines grown at a high altitude in the Transvaal and Northern Cape produce table grapes, raisins, and sultanas. Good Sauternes grapes (Sémillon and Sauvignon Blanc) are grown in the Cape and compare with vines grown in Sauternes near Bordeaux, but the legal requirement to fortify this type of wine beyond the 16% mark means that a pure, natural, medium-sweet table wine cannot be obtained.

The viticultural area may be divided into two distinct regions, the Coastal Belt and the Little Karoo. The former stretches from the coast to the first mountain range, and the districts of Stellenbosch, Paarl, Malmesbury, Ceres, Tulbagh, and the Constantia Valley lie in this area. The latter extends

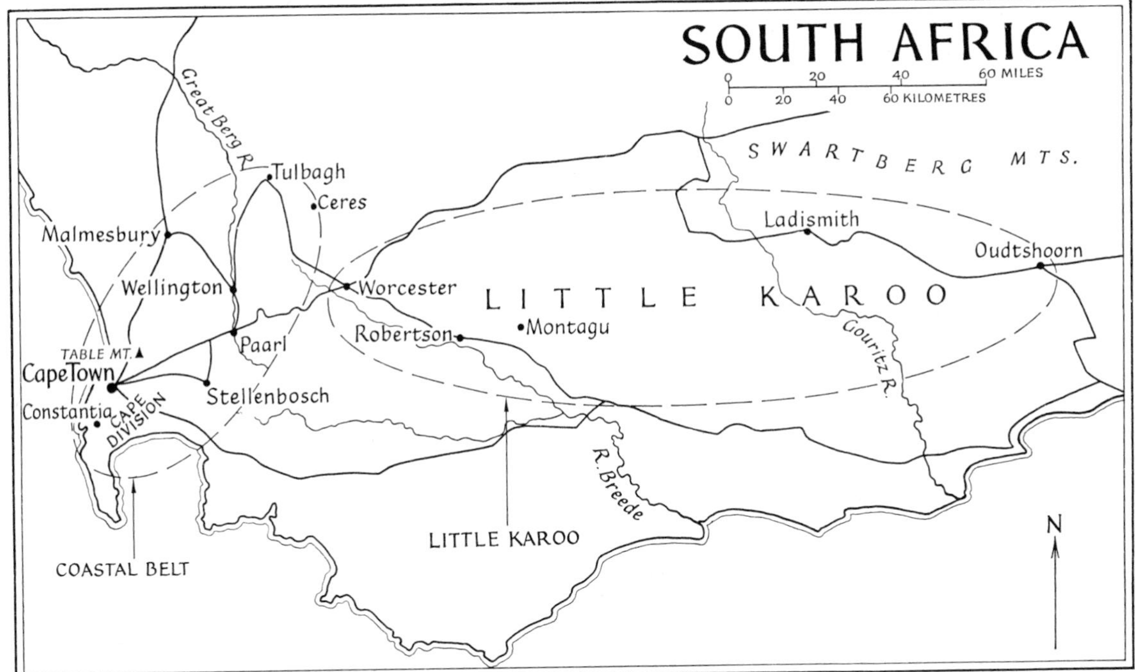

from beyond the Drakenstein Range to the Swartberg Mountains, and embraces the districts of Worcester, Robertson, Montagu, Oudtshoorn, and Ladismith.

The Cape Division (in which lie the wine farms to the south-east of the Table Mountain range that runs across the Cape Peninsula) is the oldest wine-growing area in the country.

The Coastal Belt vines are grown mainly on mountain slopes, the yield being three to six tons (3·36 to 6·72 short tons) per acre, from which dry white and red wines are produced, as also are good sherry- and port-types. As a result of the slight variation in climatic conditions, there is likewise very little variation in the quality of these wines from year to year. The grape varieties grown are Hermitage, Steendruif (very like Sauvignon Blanc), Grœndruif, Riesling, Cabernet Sauvignon, Clairette Blanche, and the Port varieties.

In the Little Karoo, where the rainfall is less than half that in the Coastal Belt and where the vines are grown under irrigation, the yield is six to ten tons (6·72 to 11·2 short tons) per acre, and the grape varieties are Hermitage, Steendruif, Hanepoot, Muscadel, and Sultana. From these grapes sweet wines, sherry-types, and brandies are produced.

In the Coastal Belt the soil varies from sandy to heavy loam, while in the Little Karoo the soils are deep, rich alluvial. Some wine growers claim a considerable variation in origin of the soils on their farms. 51,077 morgen (1 morgen = 2·09 acres) in this region are planted to 127 million vines, while in the Little Karoo 24,000 morgen are planted to 90 million vines.

The seasons in South Africa are not as in Europe. Spring lasts from September to November, summer from December to February, autumn from March to May, and winter from June to August. The grapes reach full ripeness between February and April, and the harvesting begins before the onset of autumn.

Types of Wine

The Constantia wines already mentioned as being exported in the late eighteenth and early nineteenth centuries were dessert wines, and these are still of good quality. They include port-type and Muscadel wines, the former produced from Hermitage and Portuguese variety grapes grown at Paarl, Stellenbosch, and adjoining areas; and the latter from Muscadel grapes grown at Robertson, Montagu, Bonnievale, and the Nuy district of Worcester.

Sherry-type production in South Africa started about thirty years ago, and only as recently as 1942 were these wines produced by the *solera* system, the traditional method of Sherry manufacture in Spain. It is interesting to note the resemblance geographically and climatically between Paarl, centre of the South African wine industry, and the Sherry-producing areas of Andalusia in Spain. Jerez de la

Frontera has a latitude of 34°41′N. and Paarl is situated at 33°45′S.

Both light-bodied and full-bodied red natural wines are produced at the Cape—the light from Cabernet, Hermitage, and Shiraz grapes grown in the Constantia Valley, and in the districts of Stellenbosch and Somerset West nearest to the coast; the fuller wines from Hermitage, Shiraz, Pontac, and Gamay grapes grown at Paarl, Stellenbosch, and Durbanville. Rosés have been produced at the Cape for some years now and are gaining in popularity.

Dry and semi-sweet white table wines, which must contain less than 2% sugar, are made from Riesling, Stein, and Clairette Blanche grapes grown at Paarl, Stellenbosch, and Tulbagh.

Sparkling wines are made from Riesling and Clairette Blanche grapes by natural fermentation, and also by artificial impregnation of the wine with carbon dioxide.

There is some difficulty in giving the total vintage return for South Africa, a figure that has to be compiled from the returns of growers which include both alcoholic products and non-alcoholic products such as table grapes and grapes for the making of raisins and sultanas. They do not, however, include returns from the main sultana-producing areas. Based on the returns of growers as supplied by the Co-operative Wine Growers' Association, the wine production for the year 1965, district by district, was as follows:

District	*Tons/Leaguers*
Caledon	10,535
Cape Peninsula	14,080
Ceres and Tulbagh	29,899
Malmesbury	89,059
Montagu	39,946
Paarl	105,577
Robertson	144,167
Stellenbosch	92,614
Worcester	179,346
Total	705,223

One leaguer equals 127 imp. gallons (152 U.S.) of wine, and is equivalent to one short ton (2,000 lb.) of grapes. An analysis of the above figures shows that wine produced on farms totalled 189,235 leaguers, and grapes delivered by farmers to co-operative wineries and others amounted to 273,476 long tons (306,290 short tons).

Spirits

Liqueurs with an alcoholic content of 55° to 78° proof spirit, or 32% to 44% by volume, are made in ever-increasing variety, based upon European counterparts; but the legendary liqueur named by early Cape settlers, Van der Hum, is typically South African. It was produced in days gone by in the Old Cape homes with a flavouring made from *nartjie* (tangerine) peel, but now, unfortunately, a synthetic flavouring is employed.

Brandy was first made in the Cape in the year 1672. It is now distilled and matured under strict Government supervision. The alcoholic content is 75° proof spirit or 43% by volume. The grapes from which distilling wines are produced are the 'French' and 'Green' varieties grown in the areas around Worcester, Montagu, and Robertson. Only the best quality distilling wines are allowed to be used for distillation into brandy and these must be approved by the Government Brandy Board. All types of South African brandy must contain a minimum of 25% brandy distilled in a pot-still, matured for a minimum period of three years in casks of imported oak approved by a Government Commissioner. If certified by the Government Brandy Board to be pure wine brandy, it qualifies for an excise duty rebate of 4*s.* 6*d.* (63 cents) per proof gallon, and provision has now been made for higher rebates for brandies matured for four and five years.

Organization of the Wine and Spirit Industries

At the producer's level, the wine industry is highly organized, largely as a result of the monopolistic powers of the Co-operative Growers' Association of South Africa—the K.W.V. already referred to. This was founded in 1918, its main object being: 'To so direct, control and regulate the sale and disposal by its members of their produce, being that of the grape, as shall secure or tend to secure for them a continuously adequate return for such produce.'

Early opposition from wine growers who preferred to withhold support from this Co-operative was overcome in 1924, when Parliament passed the Wine and Spirit Control Act in terms of which the transactions of non-members were made subject to the same conditions and obligations as were imposed by the Constitution of the K.W.V. Since that time, no person may sell, acquire, or utilize wine in the Cape Province for distilling or conversion into spirits except through or with the consent of the Association; nor may any wine grower sell or distil or otherwise dispose of brandy or spirits distilled from his own wine except through and with the consent of the K.W.V.

Under its constitution, the Association annually fixes a minimum price for distilling wine, declares the surplus (i.e. that portion of the vintage which it considers cannot be absorbed by the local market) and indicates what portion of a member's vintage must be held by him and delivered as a surplus, free of charge, to the Association. If the member cannot deliver the specified surplus, owing to his having sold his entire crop, then he must contribute cash instead. Co-operation is compulsory. The K.W.V. is debarred from selling its products for use in Africa south of the Equator except to distilling co-operative societies, and to the wholesale trade. In the South African wine industry a clear distinction is made between what is called Good Wine and Distilling Wine. The former is intended for consumption as wine, while the latter is intended for distillation into brandy or wine spirits.

The Surplus Declaration by the Association under its constitution for the year 1959 was 35% of the total crop, and in handling the surplus it found its greatest outlet in the Cape's traditional market, Great Britain. In South Africa, the K.W.V. has five wineries situated in Paarl, Stellenbosch. Robertson, Montagu, and Worcester, with a total storage capacity of almost 40 million imp. gallons (48 million U.S.). Membership of the Association increased from 1,940 in 1918 to 4,444 in 1959—evidence of successful organization under the co-operative system. Uncontrolled surpluses before 1918 resulted in wine growers being barely able to obtain a penny per bottle for their best wines.

In the year 1938, South African exports of wine and brandy amounted to 1,891,700 imp. gallons (2,271,800 U.S.) and 91,646 imp. gallons (110,000 U.S.) respectively, while in 1965 the figures were respectively 4 million imp. gallons (4,800,000 U.S.) and 458,900 imp. gallons (551,000 U.S.). This successful development may be ascribed to two factors—organized marketing and quality control; and today almost 90% of all South African wine and brandy exports to overseas countries come from the cellars of the K.W.V. No longer is South Africa's wine trade based on preferential tariffs but on quality. Cape wines have to pass a Government quality control before they may be exported, and the excise control of brandy in the Union is among the strictest in the world. All brandies shipped from South Africa carry with them certificates of age, method of maturation, and distillation.

The difficulties of nomenclature of wines are great, indeed almost insurmountable, and there is not space here for a thorough analysis of the subject. The salient point is that under a trade agreement between France and South Africa, the latter does not use Appellations d'Origine such as champagne, burgundy, claret, or sauternes; moreover, South Africa may not use the name sherry at all in the Netherlands and Germany; while in Great Britain she may not employ the words sherry or port without qualification. To use the word 'type' is to stigmatize the wine before it reaches the consumer, and consequently South African wine growers have been obliged to resort to such names as Paarlsack for their sherries, and to descriptive adjectives such as Paarl Ruby and Paarl Tawny for their ports. In the opinion of certain authoritative South African wine men, such restrictions, necessary as they may be, present a great handicap to their wine growers, and no adequate solution of the problem has yet been found. But, so far as table wines are concerned, they cannot do better than name the wine from the grape variety (e.g. South African Riesling) as is done in Alsace and already, to some extent, in South Africa.

South-West France

Apart from the great region of Bordeaux, there are several more wine-growing provinces in this part of France, stretching from the Dordogne to the Pyrenees. Some of these wines are entitled to Appellations Contrôlées and they will be found under individual headings: Bergerac, Côtes de Saussignac, Côtes de Duras, Côtes de Montravel, Gaillac, Jurançon, Madiran, Monbazillac, Pacherenc de Vic Bilh, and Pécharmant.

A second group of lesser wines, agreeable to drink in their own part of the country, is listed under the Vins Délimités de Qualité Supérieure. These are: Béarn (Basses-Pyrénées), red, white, and rosé. Cahors (Lot), red. Côtes du Buzet (Lot-et-Garonne), red and white. Côtes du Marmandais (Lot-et-Garonne), red and white. Côtes de Fronton (Haute-Garonne), red, white, and rosé. Irouléguy (Basses-Pyrénées), red and white. Lavilledieu (Tarn-et-Garonne), red and white. Rousselet de Béarn (Basses-Pyrénées). Villaudric (Haute-Garonne).

See V.D.Q.S.

Spain

About 11% of the country is planted in vines, and two million people or 15% of the population work for the wine-makers. Some four million acres produce over 500 million imp. gallons (600 million U.S.) of which nearly 39 million (46 million U.S.) are exported.

The greater part of the country is a vast tableland, or *meseta,* with outbreaks of jagged mountain ranges and snow-covered peaks. Its climate is harsh and continental, with dry, torrid summers and biting winters. Seen from the air, it is like a brown relief map wrinkled into dry creeks and valleys, with sudden gleams of water. For the traveller by road or train, however, the monotony is broken: after an expanse of arid grass come umbrella pines, cork oaks, a sweet-smelling scrub of rosemary and lavender, or a patchwork of olive groves. Arriving at one of the great rivers, you are in a landscape of cornfields and poplar trees. Once through the Sierra Morena, into the province of Córdoba, the sharp air softens. In the spring, all Andalusia is green; and figs, oranges, and lemons grow in season. The winters are mild here, and around the Mediterranean coast the weather is tempered by the sea and the narrow strip of land bordering the shore is planted like a garden with fruit, and olives, and vines. Vines grow most prolifically near the Mediterranean, or on the sheltered slopes of some of the mountain valleys. The most productive areas are in New Castile, La Mancha, Catalonia, and along the east coast.

The best wines come not from these parts but from western Andalusia, the Sherry country, which provides 6% of Spanish wine; and from the Rioja vineyards in Logroño, Alava, and Navarre, which contribute 8% as against 30% from New Castile and 19% from Catalonia.

History

The vineyards of Andalusia are very old. In about 1100 B.C. the Phœnicians founded Gadir (Cadiz) and planted vines, presumably brought from the east. Then came Greeks, Carthaginians, and Romans, spreading both the vines and the science of viticulture through Spain. Wine was supplied to Rome, and Cicero praised the growths of Tarragona and Catalonia. When Rome fell, the barbarians invaded—Vandals, leaving their name to Andalusia, followed by Goths. They must have trampled down the vineyards, but the vine persisted; and when the Arabs landed, in 711, they protected and increased the grapevines for the sake of the fruit. Gradually, the wine-drinking Christian kings won back the land until, in 1492, the last Moorish kingdom of Granada was retaken.

Early in the fourteenth century Spanish wines were coming to England. By the time of Spain's ascendancy, when the Emperor Charles V was ruling the Netherlands from Spain, Sack (Sherry), Tent (Alicante), and Canary wines were familiar drinks in northern Europe.

At the beginning of this century, Spain, less affected by the phylloxera epidemic than were many European countries, was doing a flourishing export trade. But the French laws against the entry of foreign wines in the early nineteen-thirties, and the crisis of over-production to which importations from Algeria into France contributed, hit Spain hard. Then came the Spanish Civil War. Neglected vines developed phylloxera; whole vineyards, especially those near Madrid and Toledo, were destroyed. Wine became scarce, and the price doubled. The Second World War made conditions worse, and in the nineteen-forties there were outbreaks of mildew and a prolonged series of droughts to contend with. Not until 1952–3 did wine production really improve and prices begin to drop. Since 1959, the vineyard area has been spreading, mainly in New Castile.

Within the last few years exports of Spanish wine to England and Belgium have increased. Wine brings in just over 5% of the national revenue. Spain is particularly dependent on foreign trade because, unlike most Latin countries, it does not use up enough of the harvest at home. Many of the people are so poor that they cannot afford to drink much wine, and so the annual consumption per head is only 11 imp. gallons (13 U.S.) a year, compared with 23·5 imp. gallons (28 U.S.) in Italy, and 31 imp. gallons (37 U.S.) in France. Yet the growers are often obliged to sell at a loss. The vineyard land is much parcelled out. Many of the plots are too small for mechanization, and the number of these little properties is beyond official calculation. Attempts have been made to promote the co-operative system, and this has been developing gradually in Navarre, Catalonia, and the eastern littoral—often allied to olive oil production. There are now about 600 co-operatives. Although the overseas trade in fine Sherry wines continues to flourish, the bulk of the export business is in ordinary wines shipped in cask.

Wine Laws

It is too soon to accept the claims of all Spanish wine labels, but control and regulation of wine and vine in the country are progressing steadily. Sherry already has one of the strictest and best functioning wine controls in the world. Rioja, the leading table wine, not so long accustomed to these high standards, is becoming much more reliable—and after Sherry, Rioja is, in quality if not in quantity, the most important wine abroad (*see* SHERRY, RIOJA).

Denominación de Origen

An ambitious programme for establishing official

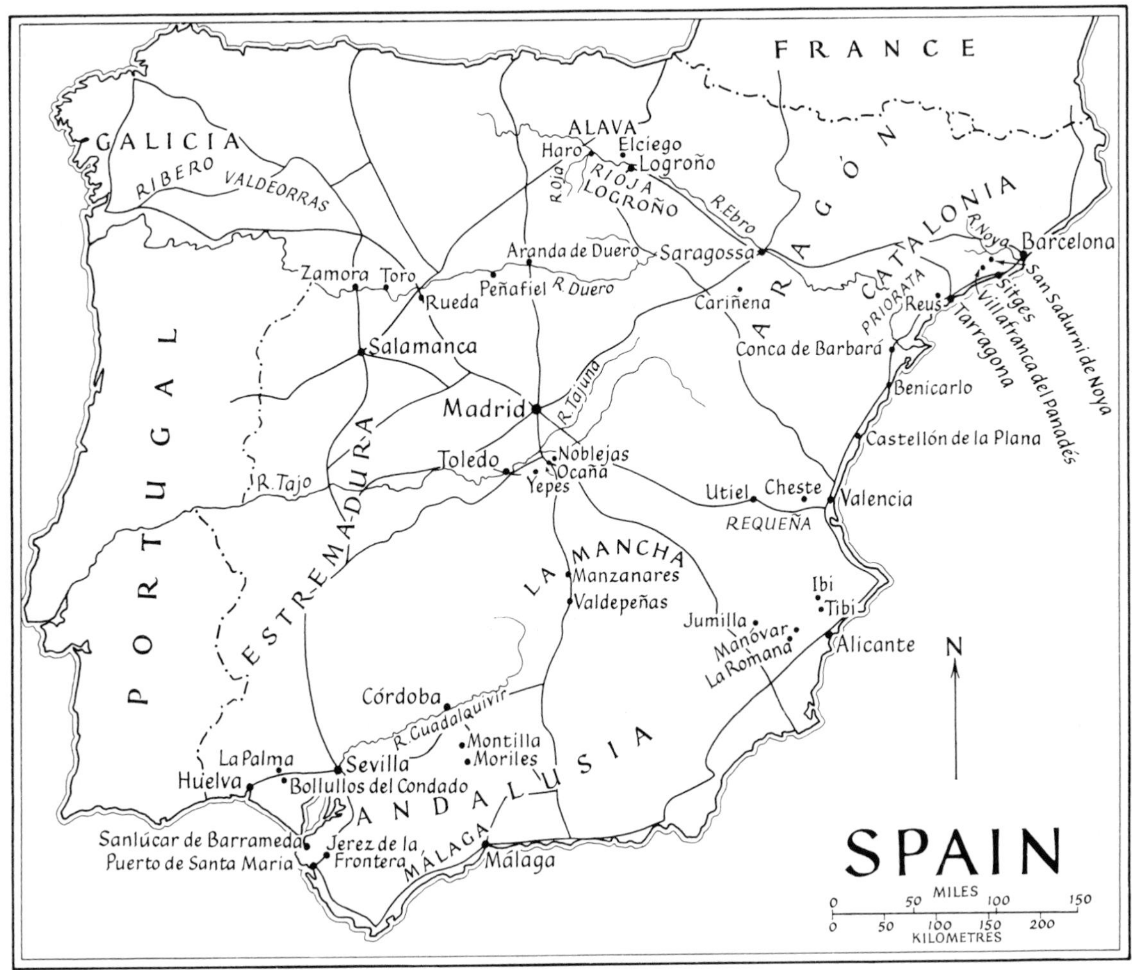

place-names (Denominación de Origen), with excellent standards and quality controls, was devised some years ago. So far, the following controls of place-names are already functioning:

Andalusia. Sherry (Jerez or Xeres). Montilla-Moriles (in Córdoba province); Málaga.

Catalonia and Alicante (east coast). Tarragona, Priorato, Panadés, Alella, Alicante, Valencia, Utiel-Requeña, Cheste.

Northern Spain. Rioja, Navarra, Cariñena.

Galicia (north-west). Ribero, Valdeorras.

The following place-names are on the list, but are not yet effectively controlled:

Andalusia. Huelva, Manzanilla, Sanlúcar de Barrameda.

East Coast. Malvasía de Sitges, Conca de Barbará, Barcelona.

Central Spain. La Mancha, Manzanares, Noblejas, Valdepeñas.

Western Spain. Estremadura, Rueda, Toro.

Inside Spain, Rioja dominates every first-class wine list—with the result that some of the sound Valdepeñas and other respectable wines are apt to be ignored. Customers have come to think of Rioja as being the only wine fit to accompany a good meal. In general, the white wines are not up to the standard of the red ones, although there are naturally exceptions to this rule—Alella, for one, a very agreeable white wine.

Spain, with its mountains and violent contrasts of scenery, is a land of widely differing wines; but individual characteristics are very much ironed out by the vintner's steady hand. Not only are crops from various vineyards vatted together within an area, but there is a good deal of blending across country. Except in districts like Rioja, neither the principle of vintages nor that of individual vineyard names has taken hold. The average goal is plateau, not peak—although this does not apply to the celebrated wines of Málaga, nor to the dry and sweet fine wines of Montilla-Moriles, south of Córdoba.

See MÁLAGA; MONTILLA-MORILES; RIOJA; SHERRY.

Regions of Lesser Wines

Alicante

The red wine (Alicant, or Tent) was famous in the old days. Modern Alicante is one of Spain's wine kitchens, and a central port for shipments. Much of the harvest from the vast vineyards of La Mancha, and of Murcia, flows in to be blended and rechristened—an art known in Spain as 'elaboration'.

The hinterland of Murcia is poor, though long ago the province was rich in mines, but in the *huerta*, the garden-land where the Arab system of irrigation has been maintained, palms grow, figs and olive-trees, cotton, and vines. Then comes Alicante and another rim of fertile littoral stretching north to the city of Valencia. There are maize and rice fields here, orange groves, and more vines. The wine region of Alicante divides into two. The first extends from the coast to the western border of the province. Partly encircled by sheltering mountains, the vineyards are planted high, on thin soil, chalky and pebbly. The principal vines struggling in these arid patches are Monastrel, Garnacha Tintorera (red Grenache), and Bobal. The second district is in the *huerta*, lying between the coast and the first of the mountain ranges. The soil varies considerably—some of it is red and light. The leading grape variety is the Moscatel Romano.

A highly alcoholic and long-lived red wine used to come from vineyards to the north of the town of Alicante; but the district has never quite recovered from its phylloxera epidemic, and the best place-names today, farther inland and north, are Biar, Benejama, Monóvar, La Romana, Tibi, and Castalla—although they are often lumped together under the general appellation Montaña. All in the mountain area are red or pink wines, and those which do not lose their identity in the blending vats have a high acidity and a characteristic bouquet.

Valencia

The coastal country, still rich, still sheltered from the winds of the plateau by mountain ranges, is a region of small farms and vineyards. There are three distinct sections of vineland: one on the coastal plain, one high up in the hills, and the third in the rolling landscape between. The leading grape varieties are Moscatel, Malvasía, Planta Nova, Pedro Ximénez, and Planta Fina for white wines; Garnacha and Monastrel for red.

Valencia, like Alicante, has seen its wines outrivalled by the Tarragonas. Once it was famous for the robust red Benicarlos from the district of Castellón de la Plana and Benicarló northward along the coast.

The red wines of Utiel-Requeña sometimes achieve great perfume. They come from the grape varieties Bobal, Garnacha, and Crujidera. Cheste is produced north-west of Valencia from Messeguera, Planta Nova, Macabeo, Pedro Ximénez, Moscatel Romano, and Planta Fina. The red wines are inclined to be sweet, the rosés are drier—in Spain these are called *claretes*.

Tarragona

Around Tarragona, the Catalan port where such excellent fish dishes are to be eaten, the country is harsher again, and the mountains closer. The wine region covers the plain, upper and lower Priorato, part of Ribera Alta del Ebro, and part of Gandesa. To the east flows the River Ebro, to the east, also, the River Gaya.

Controls function better here than they do in many places, and both inside and outside Spain shipments carry certificates of origin, and genuine bottles wear authentic seals and bands of guarantee. The wine actually named Tarragona is sweet, and therefore not as widely seen as it used to be, although a lot goes to South America, to Germany, and a few other places. The appellation is restricted to the dessert and fortified red and white wines produced within a delimited area and matured or prepared in the cellars of Tarragona, or of Reus close by.

Some good bottles may be found among the pink wines and, especially, the white table wines of Conca de Barbará in the south of the province near the delta of the Ebro.

Tarragona comes from two very different types of terrain, and the wines would differ more in style were it not for the practice of blending to an average standard. Mountain vineyards, almost inaccessible to man and sometimes quite inaccessible to ploughs, produce on the chalky heights musts that are aromatic and rich in sugar. If they were left in their natural state, they would outstrip the more ordinary growths of the plain. The white dessert Tarragonas, most of which do come from the lower land, are not as sweet as Málaga, the Spanish wine they most nearly resemble. They differ, too, in having a noticeable *goût de terroir* imparted by the sandstone and clay soil. The fortified wines are often frank attempts to imitate Port. Until 1916, when the importation was stopped by British law, much of this wine was sold in England as 'Tarragona Port'; and illicit bottles bearing this name are to be met with today in too many markets, including that of the United States. The wine is not as a rule bad—but it is not Port.

The principal grape varieties are Garnacha Negra and Picpoule for red wines; Macabeo, Malvasía, Moscatel, and Xarello for white. Sometimes the vines are planted among olives and almond trees. Only the best of the wines made have the right to the appellation Tarragona.

Other Wines of Catalonia

Priorato. The vineyards, west of the port of Tarragona, produce a good table wine with a properly controlled *Denominación de Origen.* The principal grapes are Garnacha and Corifiena for red wine; and, for the smaller quantity of white, Garnacha Blanca, Macabeo, and Pedro Ximénez. Some of the wine is sweet, but the dry is better.

Alella. The vineyards, north of Barcelona, cover two slopes of a steep massif, one facing the sea, the other inland. The vines combine well—those with a northern outlook being high in acidity, to counteract the low acidity of the south-facing grapes. The pleasant white table wine of this Denominación de Origen comes from Garnacha Blanca, Garnacha Rosada, Picpoule, Macabeo, and Malvasía. Red wine also is made, from Garnacha Negra and Tempranillo.

Sitges and Panadés. The Catalonians are the most vital of Spanish people and Barcelona one of the richest, most modern, and vibrating of its cities. In this province, viticulture and viniculture are carried out with energy and application, and the 1 million imp. gallons (1,200,000 U.S.) of wine produced each year attain a high average of quality. Panadés and Sitges are well known. The best of the Panadés are dry, good to drink with shellfish, and sometimes called Villafranca del Panadés. Half-way between Barcelona and Tarragona, about an hour's journey along a coast white with Roman ruins, the resort town of Sitges dominates a stretch of shore with something of the look of the Florida Keys. The light pale dessert wines come from the Malvasía grape—hence the proposed place-name Malvasía de Sitges.

Cariñena

The name comes from the town in Aragón, south of Saragossa. Most of the wines, both red and white, are sweet, heavyish dessert wines. There is also a *clarete.* Neither Aragón nor Navarre growths can compare (although the vineyards of Navarre are admirably kept) with Rioja, the leading wine in northern Spain.

Ribero

In this district the vines grow on the slopes and in the valleys of the Miño, Avia, Arenteiro, and Barbontino. The plants are allowed to grow tall, supported on espaliers. Both red and white wines are made. The principal grapes are Garnacha, Tempranillo, Muncia, Caino, and Brancellao (red); Teixadura, Jerez, Godelho, Macabeo, and Albillo (white).

Valdepeñas

In La Mancha a sea of short-pruned vines, miles of them, breaks the monotony of the sun-baked plain, punctuated by villages and windmills. In the arid red soil, the vines are planted three metres apart, and olive-trees sometimes grow among them, casting a little shade. From plot to plot the yield varies—a plant may give anything from two pounds to seven pounds of grapes. Valdepeñas itself is pre-eminently a wine town, sharing the half-forgotten reputation of its vintages—heavy and fiery, dangerous wine. Often, these were the characteristics of common wines in other places which had borrowed the name of the famous Valdepeñas. Both red and white wines are made, and the dominant grapes are Cencibel (Tinto Fino), Tinto Basto, and Garnacha for red, and Airén (Lairén), Pardillo, and Cirial for white. They are pleasant to drink, some rather light, and flat in taste because of their low acidity. The white wines are dry. Harvested at the beginning of October, they are all kept in giant earthenware jars, twice as tall as a man, and in these graceful amphoræ the wine may mature for five or six years—though most of it is aged for one year only. Valdepeñas, 136 miles south of Madrid on the road to Granada, considers itself *the* wine town of the world. With a population of less than fifty thousand, it has fifty *bodegas.* On a Sunday afternoon these will be jammed with men drinking and discussing wine.

Noblejas (Toledo)

The stern city of Toledo inside the curve of the yellow River Tagus, where El Cid came riding in, and El Greco lived, has a wine aptly named Noblejas. But although great claims are made for it, the wine itself is not as noble as the city. Bitter winters and brazen summers are supposed to produce big, sturdy wines like those of the sun-roasted Côtes du Rhône in France. It is even alleged that the soils of the two regions are exactly alike. Yet, judged by nose and palate, the wines are common. Methods of cultivation might well be improved, but the soil will never produce a great growth.

The vineyard region to the south and east of

Madrid is enclosed by the Tagus and the Tajuña. Noblejas is the wine proposed for the official Denominación de Origen. Two white wines of interest are Yepes and Ocaña.

Valdeorras

In the greener north-western corner of Spain, south-west of Santander where King Alfonso used to take his holiday, is a vineyard area clustered about the valleys of the rivers Sil and Bibey. Both red and white wines are made, principally from the Garnacha, Alicante, Jerez, and Godelho grapes.

Toro and Rueda

The western province of Spain, marching with Portugal, is Estremadura. Zamora, to the north of this land of merino sheep and handsome towns, makes thick, dark, alcoholic wines, which are grown north of Salamanca. Rueda whites, produced a little to the east, are the counterparts of these honest commoners.

(In this region, Dr. Maynard Amerine, America's leading professor of œnology, came upon one of those rare finds that sometimes bless the explorer of vineyards: the wine of Vega Sicilia, at Quintanilla de Abajo, west of Peñafiel. On this Spanish reach of the River Duero, which becomes the Douro of Portugal, the wine was too high in acidity and had been kept too long in the wood. Even so, it was outstanding.)

Huelva

At the southern end of the Spanish/Portuguese border is Huelva, making more heavy wines, principally from vineyards planted around the towns of Bollullos del Condado, Palma, and Manzanilla, halfway between the cities of Huelva and Seville. At different times, they have had good reputations, usually as Condado de Niebla or Palma del Condado; and it is probable that the original Manzanilla (now the name of the great aperitif wine made a hundred miles south, at Sanlúcar de Barrameda), was developed in or near the town.

The Canary Islands and Majorca

Canary Sack, Palma Sack (the latter from Las Palmas, port of Gran Canaria), made the Spanish islands off Africa wine-famous in the Elizabethan age. The colour was named from the bird, the bird from the islands, and the islands were once overrun with dogs (*canes*). The coincidence of the bird and the wine having the same name provided many puns in old plays ('Never in your life . . . unless you see canary, put me down'—Shakespeare, *Twelfth Night*, Act. I).

The importance of Canary wine in the world diminished with the oïdium plague of a century ago, although some two million gallons of common wine (*corriente*) are still produced for local consumption, most of it white, a little *clarete*.

Majorca

The largest of the Balearic islands has a good deal of its surface planted in vines, from which it makes a very dark red wine, quite a lot of ordinary wine, and some dessert wine of the Malmsey type.

See MÁLAGA; MONTILLA-MORILES; RIOJA; SHERRY.

Spirits

Spain produces a good wine brandy; a strong, white *eau-de-vie* known as *aguardiente*; and, among other liqueurs and spirituous drinks, two to which the Spaniards are partial: anis and absinthe. *Aguardiente,* primarily a generic term for spirits, is sometimes applied to brandy.

Brandy

From the Arab conquerors of their country, the Spaniards learned the art of distillation. Arnaldo de Vilanova (1240–1311), who wrote the much-quoted treatise on the subject, was Spanish, as was his pupil, Raimundo Lulio.

In Spain, as elsewhere, distilled spirit was taken at first only as medicine, and rather poor wines were used for the purpose—sometimes sick wine, or lees of wine. That Jerez, now the first district for brandies, had a distillery in the sixteenth century is proved by the records of the Jesuit college founded there in 1580. We do not know how good the product was. Two-and-a-half centuries later, Cyrus Redding wrote that Spanish brandy was second only to French Cognac.

Early shipments of the brandy may have been rather crude. The story goes that orders, mainly from the north of Europe, were not always despatched at once. Waiting for *mañana* in their oak casks, inside the *bodegas*, the spirits developed in maturity and aroma. The makers, noticing the good results of inadvertent ageing, began deliberately to mature their brandy. Even so, their export trade did not grow very much until the late nineteenth century. The expansion of the trade at that time was largely due to Mr. O'Neale and Señor Juan Hernández Rubio, who set out to study the methods of Cognac—where Señor Rubio spent some time learning the trade. He then set up for himself in

Jerez and in 1884 established the firm of Riva y Rubio. Since 1905 their trademark has belonged to Diéz Hermanos.

Since wine brandy is used in the fermentation of Sherry, it was natural that the Sherry firms should lead the way in the distillation of brandy for export. Soon, most of the big *bodegas* were joining in. Later on, in 1931, they formed the official syndicate of the wine and spirit makers and exporters (*Fabricantes Exportadores de Aguardientes, Compuestos y Licores*).

Pure grape brandy is made, also, in other parts of Spain: in La Mancha, Catalonia, and Valencia. But the centre of the trade is Jerez, with its wines grown in chalky white soil; and the next best brandy comes from the strong, perfumed wines of Montilla-Moriles (*q.v.*).

To begin with, the Jerez distilleries used an old-fashioned alembic heated directly by the flame; but latterly they have developed a more complex type in which graduation is regulated by a system of discs that can be cooled by an outside flow of water, until the desired degree of alcohol is obtained.

Two methods of ageing are used in Jerez. (1) A combination of the French and the Spanish systems is followed for high-quality brandies: the heart of the run is matured in oak casks and acquires the marked characteristics of the young wood. It is then reduced to about 44°, a little sugar syrup is added, and the spirit continues its ageing in a *solera* system similar to that developed in the maturing of Sherry (*q.v.*). As a rule, a few barrels are kept apart to be subjected to long ageing in the original wood—this is for special brands. (2) The process for more ordinary brandies is to reduce with water, immediately after distillation, the hearts and alcohols to 44°, to add the syrup and, if necessary, a little caramel for colour, and to age the spirit entirely in the *solera* system of blending, in which the brandy passes from one to another of a dozen or more large casks, to finish in the oldest cask which will contain some very old brandy. In the process of decanting spirit from one cask to another, no butt loses more than half its contents, so that there is always enough of a maturer blend to 'educate' the raw young brandy. The *solera* system, therefore, is quite unlike the method employed in Cognac, where the brandy remains always in the same cask of new oak, from which it absorbs, in less time, more colour and more taste of tannin and resin than would be possible in barrels already used for wine. For more than twenty-five years, the Jerez growers have been making casks of Spanish oak, which is more knotted than the American and harder to work, but lasting and practical. Unfortunately, there is not enough of it to supply the demand for new casks, and some wine barrels must be employed.

Jerez brandy is very much to the taste of the Spaniards, and has more or less replaced French Cognac, of which it is not an imitation—there are perhaps points of comparison with Armagnac. It is a pity that the makers did not, from the first, find an original name for it, instead of the derivative Coñac. The authorities for the Denominación de Origen afterwards tried to introduce the appellation Jereñac or Zereñac, but these did not catch on, and the product is now more generally known as Brandy.

This brandy is sometimes sold, inside Spain, in glass demijohns covered with esparto grass, more often in bottles. It is sold under a system of marks: One, Two, or Three Stars; or the classes Extra, Superior, or Reserve, on the label, with its name and registered mark. The age of good Jerez brandies varies between five and twenty-five years, its degree between 40% and 45% of alcohol by volume. But sometimes brandy is exported in barrel at the higher degree of 58% or 60%, and reduced when it arrives at the importing country.

Aguardiente

The white, strong spirit which has no other name than the generic *aguardiente*. By Spanish law this may not be made from grain. Alcohol is allowed to be distilled from wine, rectified from the residues of wine, or obtained from beet or cane sugar. Simple *aguardiente* is likely to be cane-sugar spirit.

Absinthe

Unlike France and Switzerland, Spain has not yet forbidden the use of wormwood (*ajenjo*), which is a principal ingredient of absinthe, with other such plants as anis, fennel, hyssop, etc. In the last century one of the best sources for wormwood was Orly, near Paris. The herbs are macerated together before distillation, which has to be carried out very slowly and carefully. Synthetic absinthes are made from essences dissolved in alcohol (*see* ABSINTHE).

Anis

The best variety of anis is made from seeds of the star anis plant, with alcohol, sugar, and other aromatics. This is known as Manchego (La Mancha is the best district for the domestic herb—a good deal of anis is, however, imported from France, Malta, and elsewhere). The Andalusians are particularly fond of strongly flavoured anis, which turns cloudy in water (*see* ANIS).

Spanish Earth

Silicate of aluminium—used in fining or clearing wines.

Sparkling Burgundy

Red, rosé, or white Burgundy wine rendered sparkling either in huge vats or in bottle, according to the Champagne method. Since the region's fine wines are never used in its production, sparkling Burgundy is almost without exception undistinguished, sometimes downright bad.

See BURGUNDY.

Sparkling Wines

Wines made effervescent by the presence of carbon dioxide in the bottle. The best of these wines are made by the Champagne method of secondary fermentation in bottles (*see* CHAMPAGNE). The others are made either by the bulk process—fermenting the wine in big tanks and bottling under pressure (*see* CHARMAT); or by the less commendable method of adding carbon dioxide in much the same way as it is pumped into gassy fruit drinks (*see* CARBONATED WINES).

Spätburgunder

German descendant of the Pinot Noir grape, brought there from Burgundy. It comprises 60% of the vine in the Ahr Valley.

See AHR.

Spätlese

Late-selected, naturally sweet wines.

See GERMANY.

Spätrot (Grape)

See ZIERFANDLER.

Spent Liquor

The left-over residue after distillation.

Spirits

Potable alcoholic liquids obtained through distillation. Examples: brandy, whisky, gin, vodka.

See CHAPTER TEN, p. 56.

Spiritus Vini Gallici

'Spirit of French wine'—British pharmaceutical term for brandy.

Spritzer

German term for Rhine wine and soda, one-third wine to two-thirds soda, i.e. the Byronic hock and seltzer. It is a cool and refreshing summer drink, when taken in a tall glass with plenty of ice. Any sound wine can be used, but white or rosé are the favourites.

Spritzig

German term for the light prickle caused by a very slight secondary fermentation in the bottle.

Spruce Beer

This black beer, sometimes called Danzig spruce beer, is fermented at Danzig from young shoots and sap of the spruce tree.

Spumante

Italian term for sparkling wine, of which the most celebrated example is Asti Spumante.

Stalky

Hardness in wine from the tannin in the stalks. Usually the stalk is separated from the grapes and pressed independently for the juice it yields. It is also used in the distillation of marc or grappa.

See GRAPPA; MARC.

Stein Wines

Steinweine are the green-gold, 'stone' wines of Franconia in Germany, and of Styria, Austria. In the famous oval, flat Franconian flask they are nevertheless of such special character that they are generally destined for the connoisseur.

See FRANCONIA; AUSTRIA; BOCKSBEUTEL.

Steinberger

In the finest wine years along the German Rhine this is one of the best Rheingaus. A small quantity of superior wine produced along the surrounding wall on a higher rise is known as Steinberger Mauerwein. A Steinberger 1921 attained the fabulous price of £32 (90 dollars) a bottle. The vineyard lies not far from Wiesbaden, beyond the ancient Cistercian monastery, Kloster Eberbach, renowned for its wines—and sometimes the wine is spoken of as Kloster Eberbach. In fact, Steinberger is made in the Kloster Eberbach cellars, but there is no Kloster Eberbach wine as such.

See RHEINGAU.

Steinhaeger

A Westphalian (German) gin resembling Hollands.

See HOLLANDS; GENEVA.

Stellenbosch

Wine district in the Cape Province.

See SOUTH AFRICA.

Still Wines

Non-sparkling table or beverage wines. U.S. law stipulates that still wines must contain less than 14% of alcohol. The term is sometimes used for the non-sparkling wines of Champagne.

Stinger

An iced drink made with brandy and crême de menthe and flavoured with a twist of lemon.

Stoup

An obsolete term for a drinking vessel, cup, flagon, or tankard; and also for a draught of wine.

Stout

A strong black, heavy, British beer.

See BEER.

Stravecchio

Italian term for very old wine.

Straw Wines

Wines from grapes that have been picked at maturity and dried on straw mats in the sun or suspended in lofts, before vinification. A notable example is the *vin de paille* from the Jura Mountains in France.

Strega

An Italian liqueur, sweet, and yellow in colour.

Stück

German Pfalz and Rheinhessen cask of 1,200 litres (264 imp. gallons; 317 U.S.), or 1,656 bottles. The usual Rheingau measure is the *halb-Stück* or half *Stück*, containing 828 bottles.

Stuck Wine

One which stopped fermenting before all the sugar had been converted to alcohol.

Styria

Wine region of Austria; not a large producer. White and rosé wines are made here; Graz, the capital, has, like Vienna, its *heurige*, or May wines; and another interesting growth is the pale gold *Steinwein*.

See AUSTRIA.

Château de Suduiraut

Bordeaux white wine. District: Sauternes, France. Commune: Preignac.

Once famous and classed as a First Growth (*Premier Cru*) in 1855, the vineyard almost disappeared from existence in the first part of this century. It has been reconstituted, and in the last decade has produced good wines. Formerly known as Cru du Roy, the vineyard adjoins Château d'Yquem along one strip.

Characteristics. A rather soft Sauternes—the wines have a tendency to oxidize rapidly because of an excess of muscadelle vines.

Vineyard area: 168 acres.

Average production: 9,600 cases.

Sugar Wine

'Wine' made by adding sugar and water to grape husks and allowing the mixture to ferment.

Sugaring

A 'sugared' wine is one whose grapes received additional sugar before fermentation. Sugaring is usually done to compensate for under-ripeness in the grapes. Permitted sugaring during fermentation is in France called *chaptalisation*.

Sulphur Dioxide

The use of sulphur to sterilize wine is almost as old as wine itself: in the *Iliad*, Achilles fumigates his cup with sulphur before pouring a libation to Zeus. In modern wine-making, sulphur dioxide (SO_2) is sprayed on newly-picked grapes to stop premature fermentation; is added to newly fermenting wine, put into barrels in which wine will be stored, and is given in discreet doses to wine to keep it healthy. Used in moderation, it imparts no taste or aroma; but if overdone it is apt to produce both—a fairly frequent fault with mediocre sweet and semi-sweet white wines where massive doses are added to ensure that the unfermented sugar will not be attacked by yeasts after the wine is bottled.

The action of the sulphur is to kill unwanted yeasts. Those microbes and bacteria which are harmful to wine are the first affected, but *Saccharomyces* yeasts are only attacked if a considerable quantity of sulphur is present. The traditional method of releasing sulphur dioxide, which is a gas, is by burning sulphur wicks; but compressed liquid SO_2 is also available, and tablets of potassium metabisulphite ($K_2S_2O_5$) when dissolved in wine give sulphur dioxide, water and unimportant quantities of cream of tartar, one of wine's normal constituents.

Sulphurization

The purpose of dosing must or wine with sulphur dioxide (SO_2) or sulphurous acid (H_2SO_3) is to slow down fermentation where necessary; to kill unwanted micro-organisms; and to aid in the production of a sound wine. It is very important that sulphurization should not be overdone, a fault which leads, in carelessly made wines, to an unpleasant smell, and even a taste, of sulphur. The amount of sulphurous acid which will become bound will increase slightly with increasing sugar content. The pH determines the amount of SO_2 in the active form (H_2SO_3). As the pH goes up, more SO_2 must be added to have an equivalent amount in the active form. The quantity which may be used is regulated by law, the maximum varying in each wine-making country, since the necessity for sulphurization depends to some extent upon the climate. Yeasts are most resistant to SO_2 when they are most active (which happens in the tumultuous fermentations which take place in very hot weather), and at such times an unusually high dose may be permissible—as it is also when there is some disorder in the wine or must. Where fermentation is slow (as when there have been heavy rains at the beginning of the harvest, or in a cold climate), less than 100 milligrammes of sulphur dioxide per litre will be sufficient to sterilize the wine-making processes. Where the temperature of the atmosphere is 68°F. (10°C.) or over, the dose may be as high as 150 milligrammes per litre. Sulphurous anhydride added to red wine grapes or to the must of white wine in carefully calculated doses helps to destroy biological disorders, while leaving the true alcoholic yeasts free to develop.

PURIFYING ACTION OF SULPHUROUS ANHYDRIDE

Sulphurous acid per itre (in grammes)	*Volatile acidity (sulphuric acid in grammes)*	*Condition at tasting*	*Microscopic examination*	
			Liquid	*Deposit*
trace	16·10	Sour and affected by *casse*	Bacteria of *tourne* and *aigre*	Yeast and bacteria
0·050	0·76	Yellow, brown, fairly clear, slight musty taste	Some bacteria	Fairly pure yeast
0·100	0·52	Slightly roseate, sparkling (*droit de goût*)	Free from bacteria	Pure yeast
0·150	0·47	bright pink,		
0·200	0·45	sparkling		—
0·250	0·36	(*droit de goût*)		

The above table shows how SO_2 acts as a purifier: how it kills the bacteria; and how it acts as a preventative of brown *casse* by destroying oxidases. Wines which have been treated with sulphur dioxide are apt to be better balanced and richer in certain elements than are those which have not been so treated. The alcoholic content may rise from one-tenth to four-tenths per degree—this is a fairly general phenomenon, confirmed by the diminution of volatile acid. This increase is the result of a purer fermentation and thence a better utilization of the sugar. The use of sulphur dioxide does not cause a permanent fading in colour, although it is indeed added to red grapes which are being made into white wine. In red wine, loss of colour will be temporary, and the wine will regain its hue when action ceases. Under the right conditions, the final colour will not only be improved, but will be free of any brown or yellowish cast. When the time comes to rack the wine, it will be found that the quantity of SO_2 present will decrease with each racking.

See SULPHUR DIOXIDE: CHAPTER NINE, pp. 50–1.

Süssdruck

Swiss term corresponding to the German *auslese*.

See AUSLESE; GERMANY.

Suze

A very popular yellow, bitter, French aperitif based on gentian.

Sweden

Sweden's northerly climate provides cold comfort for grape vines and wines must be—and are—imported from elsewhere. Like her Scandinavian neighbours, Sweden manufactures various spirits, consumes most of what she manufactures, and imports more. Imports, like all other aspects of the wine and spirits trade, are in the hands of the State Monopoly, the Aktiebolaget Vin & Spritcentralen, and it is interesting that half of the huge inventory of this well-run organization consists of wine.

Sweden's liquor industry was nationalized in 1917, a step taken to keep the country from 'going dry'. In the years leading up to this date, the Swedish distilleries—175,000 of them—were producing about 21,650,000 imp. gallons (26 million U.S.) of spirits per year—and the scant population (3 million) was soaking this up with alarming results. The situation was fairly critical when the Swedish legislature took the matter up. Temperance movements were applying full pressure on the law-makers, and only as a result of the foresight and ability of Dr. Ivan Bratt was the State Monopoly introduced as a compromise, controlling sales of spirits and putting them on a rationed basis. The control was lifted in 1955.

Present sales of wines (imported) and spirits amount to about 17 million imp. gallons (20,400,000 U.S.) yearly, but Sweden's population has more than doubled; and more than a third of this figure represents wine rather than spirits. The most popular drink is, of course, Aquavit—the national spirit—followed by Swedish Punch, a rice and sugar-cane liqueur (*q.v.*). On the Monopoly shelves may be found, in addition to wines, about twenty different brands of Aquavit and Brännvin, four of punch, two of gin, and some two dozen assorted liqueurs including anisette, cacao, orange liqueur, apricot brandy, and 'Christmas Wine' or Vinglögg.

Imported into Sweden annually are about 3,350,000 imp. gallons (4 million U.S.) of wine, split in fairly equal parts between table wines and fortified wines, with perhaps a little more of the fortified. Vermouth, Sherry, and Port—in that order—are the most important fortified wine imports while the major table wines are—again in order of importance—Spanish red wines, Algerian wines, red Bordeaux, Spanish white wines, and red Burgundies. Sparkling wines are almost negligible with an annual import total of about 41,500 imp. gallons (50,000 U.S.).

Swedish Punch

A spicy cordial based on rum. It is sometimes drunk in a small glass as a liqueur, sometimes mixed with hot water to make a punch.

Sweet

High sugar content makes wines sweet. Sweetness may be added by sugaring or liqueuring, or by artificially halting fermentation before all sugar has been converted to alcohol. The great natural sweet wines are made from overripe grapes in which the sugar has concentrated. These include the Sauternes and Barsacs of Bordeaux and the great Rhine and Moselle wines designated Auslese, Beerenauslese, or Trockenbeerenauslese (i.e. selected berries; individually picked, and overripe, dried almost to a raisin condition).

Sweet Fortified Wines of France

The sun-drenched Mediterranean coastline of France, particularly the corner next to the Spanish border, has long proved its suitability for growing those grape varieties that produce wines as sweet as they are potent. These wines, which are of little interest in countries where Port and Sherry are available, are known in France as *vins doux naturels* and *vins de liqueur*, or sweet natural wines and fortified wines. In both cases, the wines are strengthened by the addition of pure alcohol or brandy—a process known as 'fortifying'. The term 'sweet natural wine' is apt to be confusing, since it could apply equally to these fortified wines, and to sweet but unfortified wines like those made in the Sauternes district of Bordeaux. The difference between a *vin de liqueur* and a *vin doux naturel* is slight, and the terms are often used imprecisely and synonymously. The main difference is that in the case of a *vin de liqueur* the fortifying spirit is added before any fermentation can take place and the result is thus simply grape juice and spirits. As such, it is in the class of a high grade *mistelle*, except that the latter is used as a base for aperitifs and the former comes from better grapes and is designed to be drunk as it is. The *vin doux naturel* must be at least 90% from one grape variety, or be a blend of the varieties Muscat, Grenache, Maccabéo, or Malvoisie grapes, and the fortifying alcohol (5% to 10% of the volume to be treated) is added in the course of fermentation—not to prevent, but to arrest it. Both systems revolve around the fact that the sugar will not ferment after the wine has reached a certain strength; and both allow the wine to retain its sweetness, while providing it with a high alcoholic content. The legal alcoholic limits are 14% minimum and 21·5% maximum; and most of these wines are sold at about 18%. (These limits do not apply to the *vin de liqueur* made in the region of Cognac and known as Pineau des Charentes, where they are changed to 16% and 22%.)

The sweet wines are made in small and widely scattered areas, ranging from Grand Roussillon in the extreme south-west corner on the Mediterranean, eastward to Frontignan, Lunel, Mireval, and Saint-Jean-de-Minervois, and across the Rhône to Rasteau and Beaumes-de-Venise. Somehow the vines in these areas have managed to survive, in spite of the fact that they have been trampled on by armies—Romans, Arabs, French, and Spanish are among the many that have either crossed the area or settled in it—and in spite of the phylloxera epidemic. Modern economy seems to be succeeding where ancient armies and insects failed, however, and the present production of these wines is less than 4 million imp. gallons (5 million U.S.) per year—a mere drop in the barrel.

Areas producing Fortified Wines

Grand Roussillon

Grand Roussillon is a collective name for the five

legally delimited districts of Banyuls, Maury, Rivesaltes, the Côtes d'Agly, and the Côtes-de-Haut-Roussillon in the French departments of Pyrénées-Orientales and Aude. The vines grown in this area, principally the Muscat, Grenache, Maccabéo (or Maccabeu), and Malvoisie, produce a variety of wines, including red, white, and rosés of all types and a diminishing quantity, fortunately, of those known as *rancios*. Rarely will any two people agree on how to describe the taste of a *rancio*, but everyone seems to be able to identify it. The wine is, in a sense, 'rancid', although it is not nearly so unpleasant as the word suggests. The French refer to this flavour as *goût de terroir*, or taste imparted by the soil—in fact it is only imparted by alluvial soil; and to get the taste, the wines must age for a long time, and must become oxidized. Ageing is the secret of a *rancio* and, combined with oxidation, it brings forth the characteristic tang and heavy fragrance.

The credit for the introduction of wines into Grand Roussillon is given to the army of Hannibal which passed through in 217 B.C. According to local legend, Hannibal left here his sick, tired, and straggling soldiers who found the climate enough like their native Carthage in North Africa to settle down and plant vines. The vines were pulled up when the Arabs, with their Moslem prohibition against alcohol, moved in, but were replanted after the area had been reconquered. Hot and dry, mountainous and peppered with rocks, the land of Grand Roussillon is an arid, unwelcoming place, but vines often thrive in the most unlikely soil. Most of the holdings are small and so is production, and one sees everywhere that friend of the small grower, the co-operative cellar. Here the member-growers bring their grapes in the autumn, and here the wine is made. This system saves each grower the expense of buying individual presses and all the other equipment needed for making wine.

Banyuls

The wines of Banyuls in the extreme south-east corner of Grand Roussillon are generally considered to be the best that the province has to offer. A desolate, rocky land cut by steep ravines and baked by the hot sun that throws its early morning beams on the steep, vine-covered slopes, Banyuls is known for its sweet, heavy fortified wines, although it produces other wines as well. A natural red wine and a rosé, both called Grenache after the informing grape variety, have won some renown in their home country, but are rarely found elsewhere in France and are almost never exported. At harvest time (late in the autumn) the grapes are brought down the steep slopes on mule back and about four-fifths of the production—total production averages between 624,000 (750,000 U.S.) and 666,000 gallons (800,000 U.S.) each year—is taken to the nine co-operative cellars to be made into wine. The 7,000 acres of vineyard are tended by some 1,600 growers and their workers.

Côtes-de-Haut-Roussillon

Adjoining Banyuls and lying slightly to the east and north of it is what is perhaps the most romantic section of the region. The history of the Côtes-de-Haut-Roussillon can still be read today from the many ruins on its steep slopes—monasteries and hermitages as well as the fallen estates of the Knights Templars who, after the Crusades, established one of their headquarters in this area. However, as Roussillon's importance in international politics has declined, so has the reputation of its vineyards. What were once the favourite wines of kings are now reduced to a small quantity, most of which are consumed locally. The *rancio* of Haut-Roussillon, once held in high esteem, has been more or less abandoned, because the cost of storing the wine while it ages makes it too expensive to produce. The Côtes-de-Haut-Roussillon produces more wine than does Banyuls—its average yield per acre comes to more than 215 imp. gallons (260 U.S.) as against less than 85 imp. gallons (100 U.S.) for Banyuls—but it devotes less acreage to the production of fine wines. Here again, a good deal of the harvest is sent to co-operative cellars to be vinified. On 3,750 acres, the 1,100 growers produce an average of just under 1 million gallons a year, and about half of this is made into wine in the fourteen co-operatives.

Rivesaltes

Farther away from the Spanish border, and lying next to the Côtes-de-Haut-Roussillon, is the area known as Rivesaltes. Here the sun-baked alluvial soil also produces wines that were better known in the past than they are today, and more honoured. The famous wines of Rivesaltes have always come from the Muscat grape—it is said to be one of the best Muscat wines in France. The 'Muscat de Rivesaltes' is a natural sweet wine produced throughout the Roussillon region. It is controlled by severe tasting tests. In the past half-century or so, however, the growers have been slowly neglecting the Muscat and replanting more and more in Grenache and Malvoisie. The reason for this is that the wine from the Muscat grape is one

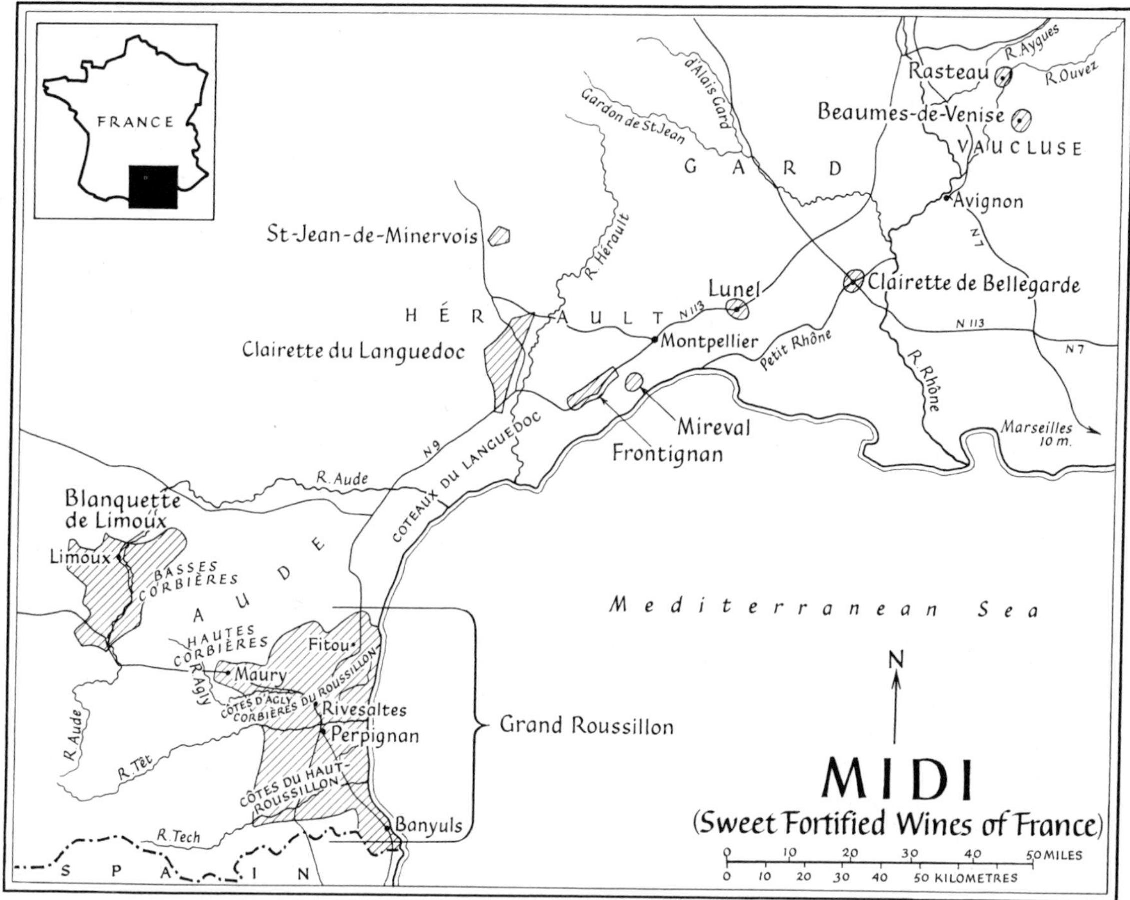

that must be tended with great care and the yield is very low. But the sweet, amber wine of the Malvoisie still thrives in Rivesaltes and is much appreciated by the inhabitants. Here again, production is small. The area planted in fine vines (the Muscat, Grenache, Maccabéo, and Malvoisie) is about 5,000 acres, and average production comes to between 710,000 (850,000) and 750,000 imp. gallons (900,000 U.S.) per year. On these 5,000 acres are some 2,000 growers, and they take about three-quarters of their crops to co-operative cellars to be vinified.

Côtes d'Agly

The harsh, grey, rocky soil of this large area, in the north-east of Grand Roussillon, is cut by the upper arm of the River Agly, before it runs down through Rivesaltes. The land is also watered, now and then, by streams which run swiftly after the infrequent downpours and then dry up for the rest of the year. The most extensively grown vines are those of the Grenache variety, although none of the wines is considered to equal those of the other sections of Grand Roussillon. Approximately 580,000 imp. gallons (700,000 U.S.) of wine each year come from about 3,000 acres, and the 1,560 small growers make about two-thirds of their wine in co-operative cellars.

Maury

The small area of Maury, in the north-east corner of Grand Roussillon, has had the unfortunate destiny to be in a militarily strategic position and has thus been almost totally destroyed, time after time. But whenever the new wave of conquerors settled down or left, the peasant growers would again replant their vines in the unpromising stony soil. Mostly planted in vines of the Grenache Noir variety, the wines are sweet, and the red ones are extremely dark in colour. This darkness fades with age, and the wines of Maury take on the brownish tinge that the French refer to as the *pelure d'oignon*, or onion skin. Maury accounts for an average of well under 580,000 imp. gallons (700,000 U.S.) per year. Its 3,500 acres are tended by about 530 growers and virtually all of the production is vinified in the three co-operative cellars.

Frontignan

Once again the origins of the vines here are lost in the mists of time, but growers in the Frontignan area—facing the Mediterranean Sea, some distance west of the delta of the River Rhône—say that the famous Muscat wines of Frontignan date from Roman times, or that the vines were brought back from the Crusades, or that they were planted to celebrate a royal marriage, in 1204. It is widely believed that returning Crusaders did bring back grapevines from the Near East and so altered the course of viticulture in these regions and in the Pyrenees. At the present time, less than 110,000 imp. gallons (130,000 U.S.) of wine are grown annually by some 350 growers on 875 acres of land around the ancient city of Frontignan in the department of Hérault.

The Muscat de Frontignan, so called because only the vine of that name is allowed, is made according to one of three methods. The first is for natural wine not enriched by any addition of alcohol, and it is the same as the process for any other natural wine, except for one stage, known as *passerillage*. This originated in Spain, and was designed to increase sugar content: the stalks of the grapes are pinched just above the clusters, and just before the grapes are picked in the late autumn. This cuts off the passage of sap between the grapes and the vine. The grapes are then allowed to ripen thoroughly in the hot Mediterranean sun, and, since no sap can get to them, they dry out, leaving the grapes extra-rich in natural sugar. This system allows the wine to attain the legal minimum of 15% alcohol.

The other two types of wine, *vin doux naturel* and *vin de liqueur*, are the more common, and the difference between the processes of production has already been explained. Both systems allow this powerful wine to retain at least a part of its natural sugar, and in both cases the wine must have an alcoholic content of at least 15%.

In an attempt to preserve the integrity of the wine, it has been decreed that all genuine Muscat de Frontignan must be sold in bottles bearing a special seal, which is given by a group of experts, only after they have tasted a sample of the wine and approved its quality.

In the area adjacent to Frontignan a lesser-known Muscat is produced, called Muscat de Mireval.

Saint-Jean-de-Minervois (Muscat de)

A tiny pocket in the department of Hérault in southern France, Saint-Jean-de-Minervois makes *vin doux naturel* and *vin de liqueur* following the same customs and regulations as its neighbour, Frontignan. Production here is rarely as high as 3,000 imp. gallons (3,500 U.S.) per year, however.

Lunel (Muscat de Lunel)

Like the Muscat wines of Frontignan, those of Lunel are made into *vin doux naturel* and *vin de liqueur*; no unfortified wines are produced here. Another district whose importance is more historical than contemporary, Lunel now embraces about forty acres and its four growers make some 3,330 imp. gallons (4,000 U.S.) of wine a year.

Beaumes-de-Venise (Muscat de)

On the eastern side of the Rhône in the department of Vaucluse, Beaumes-de-Venise makes *vin doux naturel* and *vin de liqueur* exclusively from the Muscat grape, as does Frontignan. With seven acres of vines and two growers, the area produces only about 1,650 gallons (2,000 U.S.) per year.

Rasteau

Slightly to the north of the region of Beaumes-de-Venise is the delimited area known as Rasteau. This enjoys the peculiar advantage of being able to grow and sell fortified wines, made in the same way as those entitled to the name Grand Roussillon; and of making, also, other wines in the same manner as those wines entitled to the name Côtes du Rhône. The result is that the production of the 875 acres varies from no fortified wines in one year to almost 125,000 imp. gallons (150,000 U.S.) in another. The deciding factor is the weather—and which type of wine it happens to favour. The fortified wines of Rasteau must come at least 90% from the Grenache grape and the others from any vine allowed in the making of Côtes du Rhône. No matter which type of wine they choose to make, the 130 growers take virtually all of the harvest to the one co-operative cellar.

Pineau des Charentes

At some time towards the end of the sixteenth century, a worker in one of the cellars in the Cognac region of France made the mistake of putting some newly-made wine into a barrel already containing a small amount of Cognac. The result of this error has come to be known as Pineau des Charentes and has been made ever since. First produced in very small quantities, the output was increased after the First World War and the wine was put on to the commercial market.

Pineau des Charentes must be made by producers of Cognac in the two French departments of Charente and Charente-Maritime, and only from their own grapes. The new wine is taken and, within twenty-four hours, a little Cognac, a year or two old, is added to it. The colour may be either rosé or white: the rosé variety comes from the Cabernet Sauvignon, Cabernet Franc, Malbec, and Merlot Rouge grapes; the white from the Saint-Émilion, Folle Blanche, Colombard, Blanc Ramé, Jurançon Blanc, Montils, Sémillon, Sauvignon, or Merlot Blanc grapes. It can only be sold after receiving the seal of approval of a committee of tasters which has wide powers. These include the right to approve, to disapprove, to demand further ageing or blending with the same product from another part of the area and to specify the quantities to be used. This last rule was added to improve the quality of some wine that comes from a seaside area and may, when unblended, have a slightly salty taste. All Pineau des Charentes, which is a popular aperitif in France, must contain from 16·5% to 22% of alcohol. Something over 550,000 imp. gallons (660,000 U.S.) are made each year.

Switzerland

Switzerland is largely a wine-drinking, wine-growing country; and as it is divided into three parts—French-speaking, Italian-speaking, German-speaking—so the vineyards tend to follow, with vines of French, Italian, or German types. There are, however, a few notable exceptions: Johannisberger is grown from the green Sylvaner grape in the French canton of the Valais, and the Bordeaux Merlot has been imported, very successfully, into the Ticino. So the striking general characteristic of Swiss wines is their infinite diversity; the vast difference, for instance, between the sunny Dézaley that grows on the slopes above Lake Geneva and the Vispertermin wines harvested up in the mountains of the Valais, not far from the Matterhorn and 3,600 ft. above sea level. Hillside vineyards are steeply terraced, existing only by the hard labour of their owners; most of the vineyards are divided into small parcels whose proprietors now tend to join co-operatives and share equipment. Every year, in November, there is a big auction of the year's vintage, and buyers come from all around.

The total area of vineyards in Switzerland is 25,000 acres. Only three cantons out of the twenty-two plant no vines, but the most important wine production is in the French parts—Vaud, Valais, and Neuchâtel. Vines flourish on the shores of the lakes of Geneva and Neuchâtel, along the right bank of the Upper Rhône, and in the Italian Ticino or Tessin. Cultivation is sparser in east and central Switzerland, and here, as well as in the Ticino and around Geneva, most of the wines are drunk locally. In 1960 the country as a whole produced 24 million imp. gallons (29 million U.S.), of which the Swiss consumed 17,600,000 imp. gallons (21 million U.S.). The idea that Swiss wines do not travel is giving way now that they are to be seen in the windows of wine merchants in England and in other countries abroad. It is generally agreed that these wines can be very agreeable but a bit short, i.e. not lasting on the palate. In comparison with French wines, they are not cheap.

French Switzerland

La Suisse Romande is a pleasant place, a sunny country of hills sloping down to lake shores, of orchards and castles.

Vaud

This is the largest wine-producing canton in the country. In 1960, 9,239,000 imp. gallons (11,095,000 U.S.) came from the vineyards planted east and west of Lausanne, along the shores of Lake Geneva. The wine region divides into two—Lavaux to the east of the city, and La Côte to the west.

Lavaux

The region stretches for ten miles, from Lausanne to Montreux, with Vevey almost exactly in the centre (*see* VEVEY FESTIVAL). It faces south over the lake, getting the best exposure to the sun and protected from extremes of temperature. It is said that wines were made here in Roman times, and this is probably true. It is certain that the Bishop of Lausanne, who was active *c.* 1137, took a serious interest in the cultivation of the vine, commanded the Cistercian monks to tend the grapes and thus established them as the first important growers in the area—which begins at Lutry and ends at Pully. To the traveller, this is one of the most charming wine districts in Switzerland. The Castle of Chillon broods over the lake; the vineyards climb up from the shore in a progression of steep terraces; vines grow in every crevice of the rocks, and the grapes ripen in the double heat of the sun and of the sunshine reflected from the water. But the proprietors lead a hard life; machines cannot be taken up the steep inclines, harvesters have to climb precipitous paths with their *hottes* full of fruit, and when the soil is washed down the slopes by the rain, they must carry it up again on their backs.

Principal vineyards: Dézaley, which produces a golden, still growth, described by many of the Swiss as their finest wine; Saint-Saphorin, Rivaz, Epessés, Riex, Villette, Lutry, Cully. In the neighbourhood of Lausanne are the Clos des Abbayes and the Clos des Moines, owned by the city and reserved for official receptions.

Grape variety: principally, the Chasselas. This grape variety adapts itself well to the soil and climate, producing very dry robust wines quite different from those grown in France.

La Côte

The pastoral charm of these vineyards on the western shore of Lake Geneva is unspoilt, in a country of orchards, fields, and of vines planted mainly on the upper slopes, above the farmland. The wine road passes some charming villages—Féchy, Mont-sur-Rolle, Vinzel, Luins. Others of the lively, pleasant wines grown in this district are Bougy, Begnins, Bursins, Perroy.

Vaudois Chablais

These rather heady, smooth white wines are produced in the district of Aigle, on the foothills of the Alps. The growths of Bex, Ollon, Yvorne, Villeneuve, and Aigle have race, acidity, tang, and the true gunflint flavour.

Northern Vaud

In this little area, which stretches as far as Concise near the southern end of Lake Neuchâtel, grow the white and red wines of Orbe, Grandson, Bonvillars, and Concise. A few miles to the east, divided between the Cantons of Fribourg and Vaud, the *pétillant* white wines of Vully are planted along the shore of the Murtensee. Some red wines, little known but quite drinkable, are also produced in this area.

Neuchâtel

This is the most northerly part of French Switzerland. The wine region begins a little way up the lake, at Vaumarcus, and continues in an uninterrupted plantation as far as Le Landeron, at the opening of the neighbouring Lake Bienne—a less important group of vineyards extends along the farther shores of this lake, their best growths the lively wines of Schafis and Twann. The Neuchâtel white wines, grown in a chalky soil, are light and sprightly. For over a century, vintners have been practising French methods of secondary fermentation in bottle and they say that a good Neuchâtel makes stars in the glass. The town of Neuchâtel, capital of the canton, stands at the north-west corner of the lake. Looking down at it from the hills, you see the formidable castle, and the church of Notre-Dame. Vines surround the town. Neuchâtel is the most widely exported wine of Switzerland.

Principal vineyards: Auvernier, Cormondrèche, Cressier, St.-Blaise—the wines are sold sometimes under the label of a *clos* or village, oftener as Neuchâtel. Red wines, also, are grown in this district and one, Cortaillod, is considered to be among the best in Switzerland.

Grape varieties: Chasselas and Pinot Noir. The Cortaillod Œil de Perdrix, made from Pinot Noir and short-vatted, has a special charm.

Valais

This is the *vieux pays*—the old land—on the banks of the Rhône as it flows, from its source, between Italy and France. The river is bordered by fruit trees and, on its right bank, vineyards climb the mountainside. On the lower slopes, the sheltered terraces bask in the sun. Higher up, you may catch a glimpse of peasants perched at a dizzy height above the water, breaking up the soil by hand or tying vines to the tall stakes. Here, where the autumns are long, mild and mellow, vines have been in cultivation since Roman days, and old traditions persist. At times, the peasants of Anniviers will come down from their mountains, with fife and drum, to enjoy a fête day between their long, hard spells in the vineyards. When the harvest is over and the new wine made, eight-gallon barrels are dragged up to these settlements above the clouds and stored in the cellars, for the wine to mature in its larchwood casks for ten or fifteen years. This is known as the Vin du Glacier, and it is usually a rather hard white wine.

Between Loèche and Martigny, some 8,900 acres are planted in vine—about one-fifth in red, the rest in white. Old vines and young ones march up the slopes and straggle into the gullies. Little aqueducts, or *bisses*, cut into the dry land, bring their glacier water, and walls separate the terraced vineyards. Most Valais wines take their names from the grape, not the place.

Principal growths and grape varieties: Fendant, or Chasselas, makes a soft, fruity, rather heady white wine with a pleasing bouquet. The vine may have been imported originally by mercenaries returning home from France—since the land was too poor to support all the inhabitants, many hired themselves out as soldiers abroad and later returned with money, honours, and vine plants. A general who

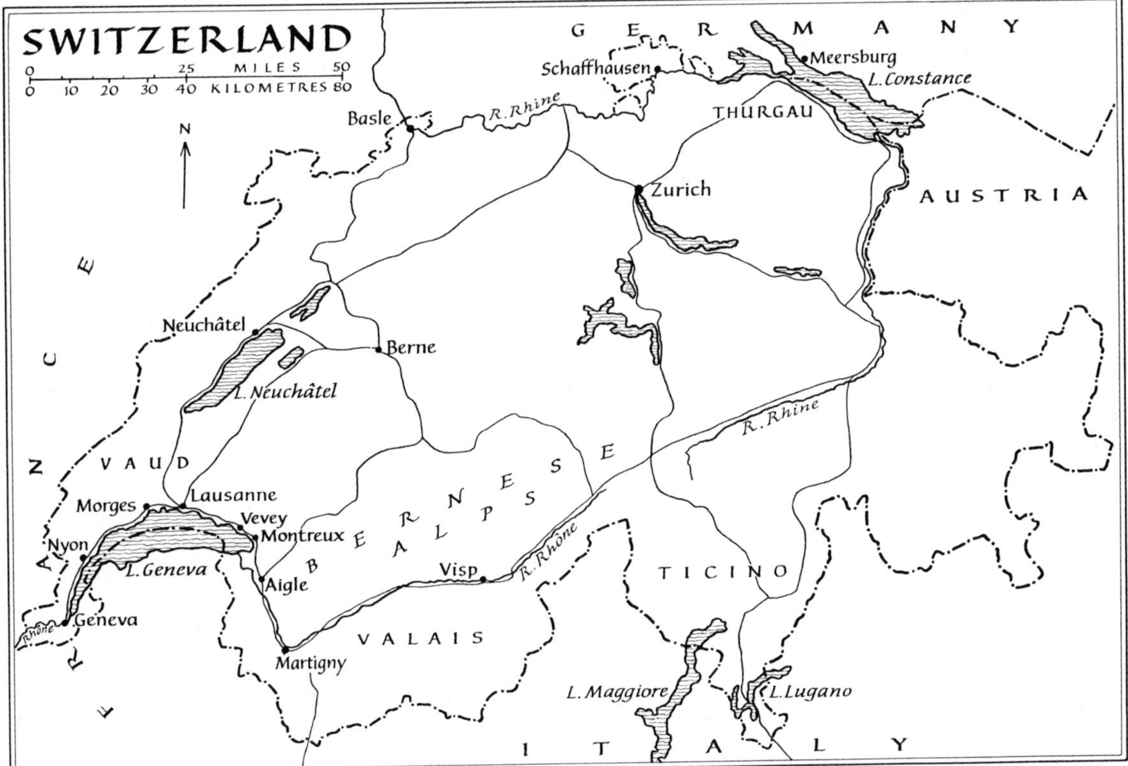

fought for Louis XV is actually believed to have brought in the Chasselas-Fendant, with one of the king's gardeners to supervise its planting. The French Gamay produces Dôle, a powerful, perfumed red wine, which some connoisseurs consider to be the best of all the Swiss vintages. It is a noble, generous wine of a fine ruby colour. There is also a Petite Dôle from the Pinot Noir grape. The Pinot plant was imported in 1848, and Dôle was first produced about 1851. Johannisberg, from the green Müller-Thurgau, is a wine of a character not dissimilar to that of the Rhine, elegant and delicate, with a fine bouquet. It is the only vintage that goes well with the local asparagus; and in years when the grapes are harvested late, it achieves a *pointe de douceur* and makes an agreeable dessert wine. Riesling, from the Rhine vine, is a pleasant little wine as is white Hermitage. Colonel Dénéréaz brought in the white grape about one hundred years ago; and quite recently, Dr. Wuilloud managed to acclimatize in his domaine at Diolly, the red Syrah of Hermitage. The grey Pinot, gathered late, makes, in the Valais, Malvoisie, a sweet soft dessert wine with a lingering aroma. Arvine, Amigne, Humagne, and Rèze are the old vines of the Valais. Amigne may have been the *Vitis aminea* of the Romans and Muscat, which also grows here, their *Vitis apiana*. It is certain that Rèze and Humagne were current at the beginning of the fourteenth century. Arvine is a noble, spirited wine, Amigne is pleasantly perfumed, Humagne is a sound wine with body and spirit. The Rèze has almost, but not quite, disappeared. Fendant is the wine that flows most plentifully. The red *vin de pays*, or Vieux Rouge du Valais, is gradually vanishing, and is well worth tasting before it is too late.

Geneva

The vineyards of this smallest canton in Switzerland, planted in a horseshoe around the city of Geneva, produce charming, light wines that are little known abroad. They are mostly rather dry and slightly *pétillants*, with a fine bouquet.

Principal vineyards: best-known are the growths of the district of Mandement, on the western shore of the lake. The wine that bears this name is light and dry with a trace of hazel-nut in the bouquet. Villages which give their names to Geneva wines are Peissy, Russin, and Satigny—in a small region, the largest Swiss wine parish. Here stands the Priory of Satigny, dating from A.D. 50. In the year 912, the Prior gained possession of the vineyards.

Grape varieties: Chasselas for white wines. Lately there have also been plantings in Pinot and Gamay, since the soil reveals distinct potentialities for red wines.

ITALIAN SWITZERLAND

In the Ticino, the sun shines, the lakes are blue, the stalls in the arcaded streets of the towns are piled with ripe fruit and, although wine-making is not a major occupation, the vineyards bear well, both red and white wines. The native Nostrano, from Bondola and other grapes, are inclined to be harsh, yet, when they are drunk cool in the shade of an arbour —as Keats liked to drink Claret—they have a distinctive, agreeable flavour. In the past few years, the Bordeaux Merlot has been planted here: it gives a soft, fruity red wine, sold under the official label Viti, and promises well for the future of Ticino wine growing.

GERMAN SWITZERLAND

Zürich

The leading district in the wine-making of German Switzerland is not so favoured in soil and climate as are the warmer western cantons, yet it produces some pleasant wines. Klevner (Pinot Noir) is now being planted and production has improved.

Principal vineyards: Herrliberg, Meilen, and Erlenbach produce rather sweet red wines. There are white wines, grown mainly along the shores of the lake of Zürich, whereas some red ones come from Weinland.

Grape varieties: Klevner, Riesling + Sylvaner and Rauschling.

Schaffhausen

In this northern canton the most important district is Stein-am-Rhein. There is a splendidly situated vineyard here, and a fresh and very agreeable wine is made from Klevner. A good deal of it is made, also, at Hallau, in Klettgau. From Stein come the Blaurock and the Kefersteiner; and a good Malvoisie, from Pinot Gris, is made near the town of Schaffhausen.

Other cantons—Aargau, St. Gallen, Thurgau, the Grisons, and Basle—produce wine in a smaller way, but it is mostly consumed within the regions.

Sylvaner

A productive white grape grown in Alsace, Austria, Switzerland, and Germany. The wines it gives are light and pleasant. It is also called Oesterreicher or Franken in German-speaking countries.

See ALSACE, AUSTRIA; GERMANY; SWITZERLAND.

Synthetic Wine

A concoction of concentrated fruit-must, yeast, and water.

Syrah, Sirah

The grape grown in the Rhône Valley for red Hermitage—it is said to have been brought back, either from the Middle East by Crusaders, or to have come from Syracuse with the earlier legions of Probus. In any case, the grapes will flourish in warmer climates, and they have been transplanted to other parts of the world, such as Switzerland, California, Australia, and South Africa.

Syria and Lebanon

In ancient times vines flourished on the shores of the eastern Mediterranean, and this was probably the earliest wine-making region of the world. Damascus was a great centre, mentioned in the Bible, and the wines of Helbon and the famous Chalybon were exported all over the then known continents. (*See* CHAPTER ONE.)

Nowadays, vineyards are found mainly in the mountainous country away from the coast. In Syria, apart from the district of Latakia, vines grow in the hilly regions of Aleppo, Homs, and Damascus—some 180,000 acres in all. In Lebanon, the acreage, which has doubled in the past twenty years, is now about 58,750. Three-quarters of the vineyard is planted in the valley of Bekaa. In both countries, the bulk of the harvest is intended for table grapes, dried raisins, and grape juice, leaving an inferior quantity of grapes to be pressed for wine. Arak also is made. Spirit-making is generally in the hands of Christians, and it is they who produce and use the wines—ordinary table wines with 9%–10% of alcohol, from French grape varieties. A little sparkling wine is made as well.

During the war, French troops stationed in Syria naturally demanded wine, and production increased, and the wine-making processes improved. When the French troops left, production fell a great deal, and is now lower in Syria than it is in the Lebanon. Figures for 1962 were: Lebanon, 777,000 imp. gallons (925,000 U.S.); Syria, 453,200 imp. gallons (543,800 U.S.).

Szekszárdi Kadarka

One of the best of the full-bodied red wines of southern Hungary.

See HUNGARY.

Szemelt

Hungarian wine term for Auslese.

See AUSLESE; GERMANY.

T

Table Wine

In one sense, this is the ordinary wine commonly drunk at table. The term is being used more and more to describe still natural wines, differentiating them from sparkling wines. U.S. Federal Law specifies that the term 'table wine' applies only to wines having less than 14% of alcohol per volume.

Tafia, Taffea

The early French West Indian Negro word for rum, and therefore one of the first names in general use for the spirit. In the original Creole it was spelt 'taffia'. Today tafia is a second-quality spirit made from impure molasses or cane left-overs, while rum proper is made from the first-grade molasses or cane sugar.

See RUM; EGYPT.

Taglio

Italian term for blended wine.

Tahbilk

A vineyard in Victoria making most white, and a few red, table wines, all sold under the name of the informing grape variety.

See AUSTRALIA.

Château Talbot

Bordeaux red wine. District: Haut-Médoc, France. Commune: Saint-Julien.

Classified a Fourth Growth (*Quatrième Cru*) in 1855, Talbot commands equal prices with some of the Second Growths (*Seconds Crus*). The wine is made mainly from the Cabernet Sauvignon and Petit-Verdot vines, and takes its name from the English Lord Shrewsbury who was killed in the region at the end of the Hundred Years War; but it is uncertain whether Talbot himself ever owned the property. Monsieur Cordier, the present owner, has made a great success of his *chai*, which is dramatically modern, neat, and clean; big vats and huge barrels have taken the place of the traditional hogsheads or *barriques*.

Considering its good wine, and the many less good wines with a better classification, Château Talbot can be said today to be definitely under-classified.

Characteristics. Big, full-bodied, and yet supple wines, which are usually well made.

Vineyard area: 119 acres.

Average production: 14,000 cases.

Tannat

Important grape vine in Madiran, in the French Pyrenees. This is considered to be the same as the Harriague, extensively used in Uruguayan viticulture.

Tannin

An important component of wine, drawn from grape skins, pips, and stems and dissolved in the liquid during fermentation. It is an essential constituent of wine, giving character and long-lasting quality. It also combines with the aldehydes to precipitate a deposit. Tannin is an astringent substance found also in tree-bark and some nuts; it has certain antiseptic qualities.

See CHAPTER NINE, p. 52.

Tarragona

One of the half-dozen or so official wine place-names in Spain.

See SPAIN.

Tarragona Port

A thick, heavy, red wine made near Tarragona south of Barcelona in Spain, which incorrectly professes to be Port wine. True Port wine comes only from specially delimited vineyards on the Douro in Portugal. This imitation port from Tarragona has been excluded by law from Britain since 1916. It is still sold in the United States and some other countries.

Tart

See CLOS DE TART.

Tartar

This important by-product of wine comprises the greater part of the crystalline deposit left in wine casks and vats. In a relatively pure state, this is cream of tartar; but where there has been contact with lime, some neutral tartrate of calcium will be present also. Remedies against precipitation of tartars in the wine are antitartrates, such as citrate of sodium, or freezing.

Tartaric Acid

The most important of the fixed acids found in wine, and one particularly associated with the grape rather than other fruits.

See CHAPTER NINE, p. 50.

Tartrates

Salts of tartaric acid; a component of wine.
See CHAPTER NINE, p. 50.

Tastevin

A small silver cup for tasting wine used principally in Burgundy, but also in the Midi. It is flat with raised indentations to reflect the colour of the wine.

Tatachilla

Large vineyard in McLaren Vale, South Australia; its wines are sold in England as Keystone burgundy.
See AUSTRALIA.

Taupette

Slang in the Cognac region for *preuve*, the little glass tube let down into the Cognac barrel on a chain in order to obtain some of the liquor to test or 'prove' it.

Tavel

Rosé wine. District: Rhône Valley, France.

Vintage years mean less along the Rhône than in other fine vineyard regions of France, and probably least of all at Tavel. The reason is that Tavel makes only rosé and rosé owes far more to soil and grape variety than to weather. The ratio between alcohol and acidity will vary slightly over the years, but the skill of the *vigneron* in making wines from properly matured grapes—picking early in hot years, late in cool ones—does much to regulate it. Furthermore, vintage differences seldom mean a great deal until the wine has attained some age. By its very nature, rosé is a wine to be drunk in its first blush of youth—vintage years can therefore be overlooked. (The only qualification to this rule is that checking the year marked on the bottle will tell you whether or not the wine is still young and fresh. A one-year minimum, five-year maximum is a good rule.)

As rosés go, Tavel is full-bodied and sturdy. It is also unquestionably the world's best-known pink wine. Legally, it must contain 11% of alcohol, but usually it reaches 12% or more. The dominant grape in its make-up is Grenache, but several others are also allowed in varying amounts.

The vines grow in a varied soil made up predominantly of cretaceous marl and chalk. The permitted growing area, roughly 1,560 acres, includes almost the entire commune of Tavel—about five miles from Châteauneuf-du-Pape and the same distance from Avignon, on the right bank of the Rhône—and a tiny section of neighbouring Roquemaure. Almost 400,000 imp. gallons (475,000 U.S.) of wine are produced annually from Tavel's 4,500 acres, and they are shipped not only throughout France, but all over the world as well.

Tawny Port

Port wine matured in wood for anything from four to ten years, and blended before it is bottled. Not as heavy and splendid as a great vintage Port, it will, however, have more finesse. Ruby Port is the younger version of this wine, fresher, fruitier, but lacking the attained elegance. Tawny Port should not be laid down, but should be drunk soon after it is bottled.
See PORT.

Tent

Spanish red wine from Alicante. The term was once common in England.

Tequila

Of all the three drinks fermented from the juice of the Mexican century plant—tequila, mescal, and pulque—tequila is the most civilized. White as water, tossed down in the style of the Mexican adept, after a lick of salt from the back of the hand, it is like liquid fire in the throat. Popular in the U.S.
See PULQUE.

Terlano, Terlaner

White wine of South Tyrol.
See TRENTINO-ALTO ADIGE.

Teroldego

Widespread grapevine in Trentino, Italy, producing red wines, especially in the districts of Mezzolombardo and Mezzocorona.

Château du Tertre

Bordeaux red wine. District: Haut-Médoc, France. Commune: Arsac-Margaux.

For some years the château in the country lane joining Arsac and Margaux and, since 1956, entitled with other Arsac wines to the place-name Margaux, was abandoned. It has now been replanted under the supervision of Philippe Gasqueton of Château Calon-Ségur and makes a small quantity of wine. A Fifth Growth (*Cinquième Cru*) in the Classification of 1855, Château du Tertre, in its present state, is an indication that the 1855 Classification no longer represents the truth.

Characteristics. The quality of the wine slipped almost out of sight, but in 1966 it made a small recovery and will hereafter improve.

Vineyard area: 42 acres.

Average production: 2,000 cases.

Thermometer

No vat-house or *chai* should be without a thermometer, and one is invaluable also in a cellar or any room where wine is stored. A *maître de chai* who constantly takes the temperature of the fermenting must will, in very hot weather, probably be able to moderate fermentation where this is excessive and so save the wine—hence, in an unusually hot summer, one vineyard will produce a better wine than another in the same district. A thermometer must be used, too, in conjunction with such instruments as mustimeters and alcoholmeters, in registering the degree of spirits. In Great Britain, Holland, and the United States, the Fahrenheit type is employed; in Germany, the Fahrenheit and the Réaumur; while in France and most of South America, the thermometer in use is the Celsius, based on the Centigrade system.

The variations in their scales are as follows: Centigrade, or Celsius, shows the freezing-point of water as 0° and its boiling-point as 100°; Réaumur shows 0° as the freezing-point of water and its boiling-point as 80°; Fahrenheit shows 32° as the freezing-point of water and its boiling-point as 212°.

To ascertain the temperature of a liquid the thermometer should be kept in the liquid for some minutes; the thermometer is quick to respond and the division on the scale at which the mercury stops indicates the temperature of the liquid. Tables showing the respective scales of the three thermometers are given in Appendix D, but below are shown the calculations necessary to convert from one scale to another.

To convert Centigrade into Réaumur, multiply the Centigrade temperature by $\frac{4}{5}$. To convert Réaumur into Centigrade, multiply by $\frac{5}{4}$.

To convert Centigrade into Fahrenheit, multiply the Centigrade temperature by 1·8 and add 32. To convert Fahrenheit into Centigrade subtract 32 from the Fahrenheit temperature and divide by 1·8.

To convert Fahrenheit into Réaumur subtract 32 from the Fahrenheit temperature and multiply by $\frac{4}{9}$. To convert Réaumur into Fahrenheit multiply the Réaumur temperature by $\frac{9}{4}$ and add 32.

See CHAPTER NINE.

Thief

A *pipette* or tube for withdrawing wine or liquor from a cask or other container; usually made of glass, sometimes of silver.

Three-Star

A designation used in Cognacs and Armagnacs and frequently believed to indicate an exact age of three, five, or some other number of years. Actually, Three-Star is a type, and while it may average roughly an age of five years in Armagnacs, and somewhat younger in Cognacs, it does not necessarily do this. The system was probably devised because of the ease of drawing a star symbol—at the time the use of stars arose in Cognac, the trick of drawing a star without lifting pen from paper was in vogue—and subsequently it became famous. While a Three-Star brandy need not be of any given age, it will always be younger than a V.S.O.P., X.O., or Reserve, and will be less expensive. Star styles and other designations are considered fully under Cognac (*q.v.*).

Tia Maria

A proprietary West Indian liqueur based on rum and flavoured with Jamaican spices and coffee.

Tinta

A grapevine family—Tinta Cão, Tinta Francisca, etc.—used in making Port. Some of these Tintas have now been planted also in California.

Tintara

Vineyard in McLaren Vale, South Australia.

See AUSTRALIA.

Tirage

French term for the act or process of drawing wine from barrels.

Tischwein

German term for common wine, or *vin ordinaire*.

Toddy

A hot drink made with spirits, sugar, lemon slices, cloves, and hot water. In certain tropical countries, it is also a cold drink, made from the liquor of the fermented sap of palm trees.

Tokaier

See RULÄNDER.

Tokaji

This is one of the label words for Tokay, and it will be followed by an indication of the type of Tokay, e.g. Tokaji Edes Szamorodni.

See TOKAY.

Tokay

Down into the river town of Tokaj, the two streams Bodgrog and Hernád rush from the Carpathian Mountains; they converge and flow to the Danube and thence into the Black Sea.

Nobody knows how long vines have grown on the volcanic soil in the fork of the rivers; they were already there when the Magyar (Hungarian) tribes arrived a thousand years ago. In the corner of Hungary near Slovakia and the Ukraine, the wine was famous at least by the time of the Crusades. The eighteenth-century writer Szirmay de Szirma says that the real fame of Tokay arrived with the discovery of the Aszu method only half a century before his time. Modern writers date it earlier, but probably the contemporary report is right. It is Aszu Tokay we know today.

There are people in Hungary who will say that the steely wines of great breed from Lake Balaton are the best in the country, but the world will not agree. Tokay, the most concentrated of all, seems to capture more than any other the romance of wine. Even Champagne cannot quite approach this golden aristocrat, once guarded by an entire troop of Cossacks for the table of Catherine the Great. The most superb Trockenbeerenauslese Rhine or Moselle, or a Château d'Yquem of the greatest year, will lack at least one of the elements that ennobled Tokay. Voltaire said of it: 'This wine invigorates every fibre of the brain and brings forth an enchanting sparkle of wit and good cheer from the depths of the soul.'

The process by which the more concentrated grades are made has a good deal in common with the method used for Sauternes or the German Trockenbeerenauslesen wines, but in some ways it is unique. Twenty-nine villages have the right to the name for their wines—Tokaji as it appears on the labels, 'wine of the Tokaj', the *i* being the Hungarian possessive. All are grown on a volcanic soil with feldspar, porcelain clay, and porphyry in it, a fundamental contribution to the character of the wine. The originality of Tokay, however, derives from a condition of the weather, a grape which profits from this, and a method of wine-making.

The soil contributing to the character of Tokay is zealously guarded; and as a guarantee that there will be no foreign mixture with the native wine, no one from outside is admitted into the delimited area.

The Aszu Method

The Tokaj-Hegyalja district, where Tokay wines are made, is hilly, the slopes rather gentle. This is in north-east Hungary, with the Hegyalja Mountain, once a volcano, rising up out of the plain. The vineyard slopes are protected from the north, and autumn remains a long time.

The Tokay-Furmint grape, a dull yellow fruit with a thick skin, becomes overripe in the warm rays of the autumn sun, and achieves the condition of *aszu* or *Botrytis cinerea* (*q.v.*). The dried, extra-rich berries, which in some years are not picked until after snow has fallen and will thus have become immune to cold, are prepared to give a concentrated dessert wine.

So far, the process is the same as that used in Sauternes or on the Rhineland slopes and Moselle terraces where a late-gathered, dried-berry wine will be made. In France and Germany the essential process is to pick over the vineyard repeatedly, selecting only the overripe or dried-up berries each time. In Hungary, the Furmint grape cluster, too, ripens unevenly, some berries being ready days before others. But the method devised is different, and different styles of wine result. In picking over a Tokay vineyard, the dried grapes are separated from the others and put into containers, the Hungarian name for which is *puttony*. In making the characteristic Aszu Tokay, a certain number of buckets or *puttonys* of the overripe berries are added to the general run. The wine is thus a blend from the two sources. Then, in Hungary, but not in France or Germany, a lesser wine is made by simply picking over the entire vineyard, taking ripe and overripe grapes indiscriminately. A richer wine, of course, results in the big years than in the small ones; and the nature of the vintage depends on the stage of ripening of the vineyard on the day of picking.

The Great Names in Tokay

It must be mentioned that in addition to the special names giving the style of the Tokay, some of this wine is exported with the usual label nomenclature used in Hungary; the place of origin followed by the grape variety.

Tokaji Aszu

The character of a Tokaji Aszu will be indicated by the *puttonys* content stated on the neck label. The buckets or *puttonys* of raisin-dry, concentrated grapes added to the fermentation of the pick-of the-vineyard run are shown on each bottle of the vatting. Thus the neck label on every bottle will state: 3 Puttonys, 4 Puttonys, or 5 Puttonys, etc. The more *aszu* berries that have been put in, the more concentrated the wine will be.

The overripe, dried, shrivelled berries, picked separately and put into the little *puttony* pails, are worked in a trough into a kind of dough. This pulp is mixed with ordinary Tokay (Furmint and Hárslevelü grapes) and the whole is trodden in canvas bags. Afterwards, it is put into a small cask of 26 to 33 imp. gallons (32–40 U.S.) and rests in the special low Tokay wine vaults.

Alcoholic content and other characteristics of course vary with the *puttonys* content, but alcohol is generally between 14% and 15% by volume. The Furmint grape does not achieve the proper condition for making Aszu below one hundred metres of altitude, and all the best wine is made on the slope vineyards ranging between an altitude of 426 and 820 feet. It has been estimated that the *Aszu* berry proportion of the entire Tokay crop averages about one part in 3,000, although in many years no *Aszu* can be made at all.

Tokaji Szamorodni

The character of the wine will tend to follow the vintage year. If the year has produced a large proportion of *Aszu* berries the wine will approach the style of a Tokay Aszu, because it is obtained by vatting together dried and normal berries alike, after picking over the whole vineyard. It is more important to know the Tokay years for Szamorodni than for Aszu, as on the former there is no indication of *puttonys* strength. On the other hand, considerable help has been given to British and American buyers by the labelling of export bottles of Szamorodni as either dry or sweet; the indications are given in the English language both on the body and neck label. Szamorodni Sweet will, of course, be from the pickings which included more *aszu* berries and can have a tremendous nose. If the designation Tokaji Édes Szamorodni should be encountered, this also indicates that the Szamorodni is sweet.

Tokaji Aszu and Tokaji Szamorodni are sold only in white bottles of 17·6 oz., with long throats, shaped not unlike Indian clubs. The other varieties of Tokay wine, such as Tokay Furmint, are sold in the tall, slender Rhine-style bottle usual for Hungarian wines.

Tokaji Máslás

After an Aszu or Szamorodni has been racked, Tokay wine is poured into the little 120 (26 imp. gallons; 31 U.S.) or 150 (32 imp. gallons; 38 U.S.) litre *Gönci* barrel and for several months left to stand on the lees. The result is Tokaji Máslás.

Tokaji Forditás

Tokaji Forditás is made by performing a second time the making of Aszu. The used pulp after the Aszu has been made is revived by the addition of fresh must, and a second fermentation is obtained.

Other Tokay Terms

Tokaji Pecsenyebor: Tokay dessert wine of at least 11% of alcohol.

Édes: sweet Tokay.

Száraz: dry Tokay.

In a part of the world which has so often changed hands, and consequently languages, variations in terms and spellings are to be expected. In most cases the connections are recognizable—viz. Eszencia, Essenz, Essence (Hungarian, German, English). Ausbruch might not be recognized as Aszu, but it was the term during the time of the Austro-Hungarian Empire and is still used sometimes. An example of the range of names is found in the Furmint: Io Formint, Furmint Szigeti, Som (Transylvanian language); Moslavina (Croatian); Mosler, Moslerrebe, or Zapfner (German).

First Great Growths
(Appellation d'Origine Contrôlée)

(Tokay nomenclature refers first to the town, second to the district, third to the type of wine-making, not grape variety.)

Tokaj Hegyaljai Szamorodni
Tokaj Hegyaljai Forditás
Tokaj Hegyaljai Eszencia
Tokaj Hegyaljai Máslás
Tokaj Hegyaljai Aszu

Tokay d'Alsace

Another name for the Pinot Gris grape.

Tom Collins

An iced drink made of gin and sugar mixed with lime and lemon juice and filled up with soda-water.

Tom and Jerry

A drink made of eggs, hot milk or water, sugar, brandy, and rum.

Tonneau

In France, 1. Any large barrel. 2. The standard wine measure in Bordeaux. Although no container

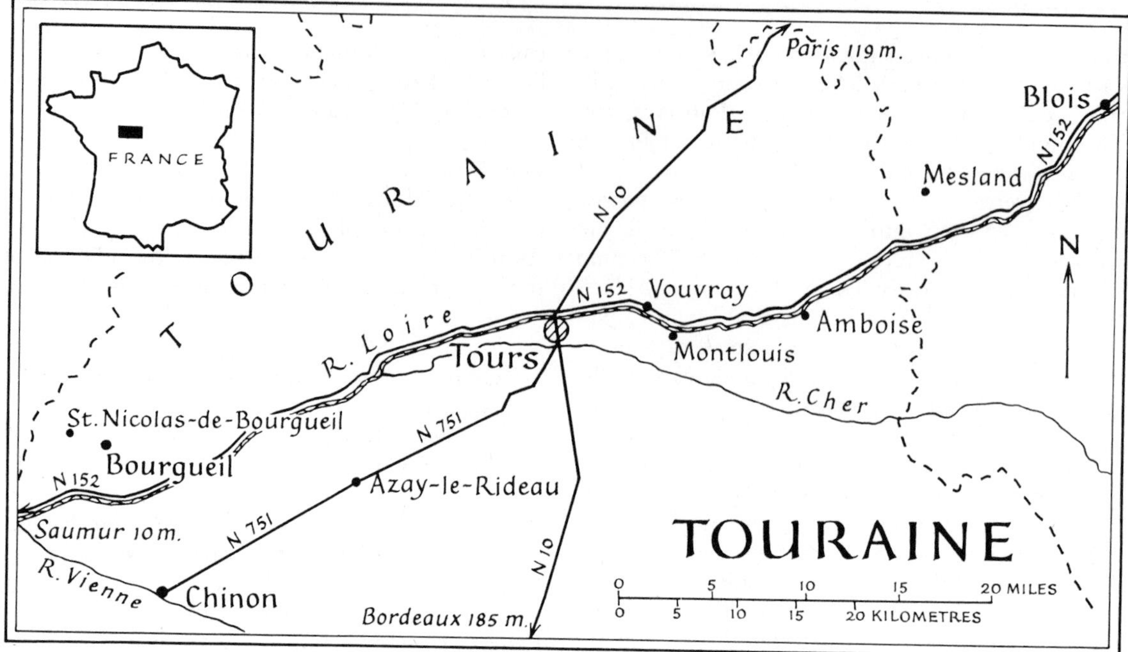

of this size actually exists, a Bordeaux tonneau is equal to four *barriques* or barrels and contains 900 litres, equivalent to 198 imperial gallons or 237 U.S. gallons. One tonneau yields ninety-six cases of twelve bottles each.

Toro

Red wine of Zamora.
See SPAIN.

Toul

See CÔTES DE TOUL; LORRAINE.

Touraine and Coteaux de Touraine

White, red, and rosé wines. District: Loire Valley, France.

The large district spreads over both banks of the Loire around Tours and is famous both as 'the garden of France' and the 'château country' of such magnificent palaces as Blois, Amboise, Chenonceaux, and Azay-le-Rideau. It is celebrated also as the region where the inhabitants speak the purest and clearest French of all. Something over 3,330,000 imp. gallons (4 million U.S.) of wines is made annually in the Touraine, some fairly ordinary but a few in the front rank of French wines.

Tours is on the Loire's left bank, an old city not without charm. The best vineyards are across the river and slightly to the north, but you will hardly realize that Indre-et-Loire and Loir-et-Cher (the departments in which Touraine lies) is wine country until you leave the valley. The winding river road threads its way beneath high cliffs, and roadside advertisements inform you that wines may be obtained, but a vine is a rare sight indeed. Most of the vineyards are on the other side of the bluffs which rise steeply from the river, planted on the back sides. These slopes are important, for tunnelling back into them are long cellars whose limestone walls maintain a constant temperature and humidity, where the wines age under excellent conditions. There is hardly a house without its deep cellar running back into the hill on which it stands, and hardly a cellar where wines are not quietly sleeping, waiting for the 'moment of truth' when the cork is pulled and the wine turned gently into the clear glasses.

To most people, Touraine wines mean Vouvray, yet the district produces red and rosé wines as well as white. Touraine white is the finest. Still and sparkling wine, red, rosé, and white, stem from this rich and fertile section of the valley and some have the great vigour the others lack. Many, however, are too low in alcohol—in general the measure of a wine's stamina—to travel, but are decidedly pleasant when sipped in the shadow of a soaring castle wall overlooking the river.

A lot of the Touraine soil is too heavy with clay, and too moist, to be suitable for wine; but as you climb the slopes you find a coarse-grained limestone topped with a chalky clay, a formation known as *aubuis*, which Loire growers say is ideal for the Chenin Blanc vine, the most widespread variety here; and Vouvray is the best example of the wines it produces. In other localities, the soil is flintier and and has less limestone; and Cabernet Franc and lesser amounts of Gamay, Cot, Pinot Noir and Pinot Gris, and a minute amount of Groslot are planted for rosé wines. This is the type of soil prevalent in Chinon.

Wine is named either from the district or from one of the more specific sub-districts. The general name is Touraine—Touraine Mousseux if sparkling—applied to wines from the specified area which attain from 9% to 10·5% of alcohol, and which have been harvested in no more than 390 imp. gallons (468 U.S.) per acre. Wines with more specific names must meet more stringent standards. The Touraine sub-districts (*see under individual headings*) are: Bourgueil and Saint-Nicolas-de-Bourgueil, Chinon, Montlouis, Touraine-Amboise, Touraine-Azay-le-Rideau, Touraine-Mesland, Vouvray.

Touraine-Amboise

Loire Valley red, white, and rosé wine. District: Touraine, France.

A minor subdivision of the Touraine, making a small quantity of wine generally slightly better than that simply called Touraine but not in the class of the more famous Touraine sub-districts. Red and rosé wines come from Cabernet Franc, Cot, and Gamay grapes; white from Chenin Blanc; red wines must have 9·5% of alcohol, rosé 10%, and white 10·5%.

See TOURAINE.

Touraine–Azay-le-Rideau

Loire Valley white wines. District: Touraine, France.

Azay-le-Rideau, with its magnificent château, was given the right, in 1953, to sell its dry wines under its own name, one that applies equally to the output of the seven surrounding communes. The wines must be made from Chenin Blanc grapes, must have at least 10% of alcohol, and are good but not exceptional Touraine wines.

See TOURAINE.

Touraine-Mesland

Loire Valley red, white, and rosé wines. District: Touraine, France.

A minor subdivision of the Touraine given its own controlled place-name in 1955. Red and rosé wines come mainly from Gamay grapes; white from Chenin Blanc and Sauvignon; rosé and white wines must have 10·5% alcohol, red only 10%.

See TOURAINE.

Touriga

Leading red grape in the Dão region of Portugal. It is used also in making Port.

Tourne

A disorder of wine, in which it becomes gassy and disagreeable to nose and taste, hazes, and loses colour.

See CHAPTER NINE, p. 53.

Traben-Trarbach

White-wine villages on opposite banks of the German Moselle, each possessing some good vineyards.

See MOSELLE.

Traminer

The vine variety distinguishing the spiciest wines of Alsace. Known also as Gewürztraminer, it appears frequently on the labels of the German wines derived from this grape. This grape is also planted in the South Tyrol.

See ALSACE; GERMANY; GEWÜRZTRAMINER.

Trappistine

A very pale yellow-green, herb-flavoured, Armagnac-based liqueur made at the Abbaye de Grâce de Dieu in the French department of Doubs.

Trebbiano

The Italian name for Ugni Blanc, one of the most widespread white-wine grapes from Italy. This vine also flourishes in France where it is known by various names, notably Saint-Émilion des Charentes (*q.v.*).

Trebbiano di Abruzzo

Italian white wine.

See ABRUZZI.

Trentino-Alto Adige

White and red wines. District: Italian Tyrol. (*Known also as Tridentine Venetia.*)

The Alto Adige is potentially Italy's finest growing area for dry white wines, but at present the potential is only realized in isolated instances. Soil, climate, and vines in this Alpine north-east corner are capable of producing inexpensive wines to rival those of Austria or Alsace, but the grower has been the inhibiting factor, generally preferring to stick to the traditional methods of keeping wine too long both in fermenting vat and barrel and consequently sacrificing the fresh, clean sprightliness that more modern methods of vinification could produce.

With a few exceptions, the wines give the impression of having once been delightful before they were allowed to get slightly tired.

Before 1919 the Alto Adige was part of the Austrian Tyrol. The Treaty of Saint-Germain, at the end of the First World War, transferred it to Italy; but the inhabitants remain Germanic, and Austria continues to drink the wines. What the Austrians do not import goes mostly to Switzerland and this division of the spoils predates the coming of the Italians by a considerable time. Most of the 21 million imp. gallons (25 million U.S.) made annually are red; but good though some of them may be, they are outclassed by the best of the whites. It is a general rule that the finer whites are from the northern Alto Adige section, the reds from Trentino—extending south around the city of Trento to the sunny shores of Lake Garda.

Grapevines

The vines cultivated in Trentino-Alto Adige are a cosmopolitan group. The Austrian influence is reflected in Rieslings and Traminers, the French in Pinots, Cabernets, and Merlots; and the Italians have introduced—among others—Schiave, Lambrusco, Teroldego, and Garganega (known locally as Terlano). Riesling is the most interesting vine. When cultivated on the chilly slopes, it gives grapes capable of fermenting into marvellous wine. Much the same can be said of Traminer, although it is a general rule that Riesling will always produce the finer fruit under the same conditions. Schiave is common in the northern part of the region, producing sound, sometimes thoroughly delightful red wines; and Merlot seems to be on the increase. The Italian discovery of the Merlot is an important event in modern viniculture, for the result is a wine in the hearty Italian manner but one with the rough edges considerably smoothed.

In Trentino, the most widespread vine is Teroldego (or sometimes Teroldico) producing largely red wines of ordinary quality. Lambruscos and Merlots are abundant also, but the grapes of these and other vines are usually crushed together or blended after crushing to give a wine with more balance than any one seems able to produce alone.

Best Wines

Riesling

Potentially the queen of the Alto Adige but nowadays too often aged in cask until it is yellowish and oxidized. Some exceptions must be allowed (although not to the extent claimed by the Italians) and these give one reason to think that while the wines will never have all the breed of the finest German Rieslings, they could conceivably stand with anything below this level.

Santa Giustina

Alto Adige red wine from slopes near the city of Bolzano (formerly Bozen), but one which seems to be disappearing. It has a fresh, clean fruitiness mingled with the typical Italian heartiness, and is usually reasonably high in alcohol (perhaps 12%–14%). Its growing area is said to be merging gradually with that of the more famous Santa Maddalena.

Santa Maddalena

Alto Adige red wine, sometimes referred to—even today—as Sankt Magdelener. It is made from Schiave and some Lagrein grapes grown on slopes near Bolzano and, together with Barolo and Barbaresco from Piedmont, was rated in 1941 as one of the three finest red wines of Italy. While Santa Maddalena is a clean, smooth, pleasant, red wine, it does not deserve such an honour, particularly when placed next to a really fine Chianti or Valpolicella. Yet there is now a tendency to improve the quality.

Teroldego

Red wine from Trentino made in such quantity that it bears the reputation of being the backbone of Trento. Dry, ruby red, and full-bodied, it is pungent and sturdy, tending towards harshness, sometimes with a slight trace of tannic bitterness. Good, sound wine on its native ground, it is not a bright prospect for export.

Traminer (Gewürztraminer)

Dry and white and imbued with the typical spicy perfume. The best in Italy comes from the Alto Adige and although it is not yet outstanding, it may well be one of the excellent and reasonably priced wines of tomorrow.

Val d'Adige (Valdadige)

Red wine from Schiave, Lambrusco, Pinot, and Teroldego grapes grown on the banks of the lower Adige in the Trentino section of the region. The river is long and passes through a wide variety of soils, rendering the wines variable in the same measure. The best is perhaps comparable to Teroldego.

Vino Santo (Trentino)

Sweet dessert wine from grapes (usually Malvasia and Trebbiano) which are dried before vinification. It is similar to Tuscan Vin Santo but without all the latter's excellence.

LESSER WINES

Cabernet

Both Cabernet Franc and Cabernet Sauvignon are cultivated, but neither to a great extent. The grapes are usually added to those of other vines, and an unblended Cabernet would probably not be very distinguished. Most of the grapes do not achieve sufficient ripeness at harvest time to make a good wine.

Caldaro (Lago di Caldaro)

Pleasant, garnet-red wine with a trace of almond in the bouquet; from Schiave and Rossara grapes grown around Lake Caldaro (formerly the Kalterersee) about ten miles south of Bolzano. It is light and enjoyable, but gains little with age.

Colline di Caldaro

Red wine from Schiave and Pinot Noir, grown along slopes in the general vicinity of Lake Caldaro.

Küchelberger

Pleasant red wine from the Küchelberg, a mountain near Merano. Schiave grape vines predominate.

Lagarino Rosato

Pink wine from Lagrein grapes. Before 1919 it was Lagreinkretzer.

Marzemino

A grapevine, the fruit of which is responsible for a considerable amount of the ordinary red wine of Trentino. Best when young.

Meranese di Collina

Light red wine from Schiave grapes grown along the hills near Merano, about ten miles north of Bolzano.

Merlot

These Bordeaux grapes are used for both red and rosé wines, and both can be extremely pleasant.

Moscato Atesino

Neither so heavy nor so sweet as most Muscat wines and thus an interesting change for Muscat lovers.

Pinot Noir

The grapevine—sometimes called by its old Austrian name, Blauburgunder—is cultivated in scattered sections of the region, but the wine rarely appears in unblended state. It is sometimes made *spumante*, or sparkling.

Sorni

Red wine from Merlot, Teroldego, and several sub-varieties of Schiave grapes. The town of Sorni is slightly north of Trento.

Sylvaner

A small, dry white wine, but perfectly adequate in carafe at or near its source. Bressanone (formerly Brixen) is its headquarters.

Terlano

A well-known and quite presentable greenish-white wine of the Alto Adige. Terlano is the local name for the Garganega vine, but the wine is more often a blend of Terlano, Riesling, and Pinot Noir.

Termeno d'Avio

Unspectacular rosé wine from southern Trentino. It is made from Lambrusco, Merlot, Teroldego, and Marzemino grapes.

Rosso Vallagarina

Ordinary red wine pressed from Schiave, Merlot, Teroldego, and Marzemino grapes and usually running about 12% of alcohol.

Trier

Ancient wine city of the German Moselle. There is a famous museum here, and fair white wines are produced.

See MOSELLE.

Trinidad Rum

See RUM, TRINIDAD.

Triple Sec

Triple Sec white curaçao was originally the name used by the makers of Cointreau, but so many other firms started using the designation that the originators ceased putting it on their labels and called their liqueur simply Cointreau. Triple Sec is now used by a number of manufacturers in various countries for liqueurs of the curaçao type.

See CURAÇAO.

Trittenheim

Wine town of the German Moselle. Among the good vineyards are Falkenberg, Laurentiusberg, Apotheke, and Altärchen.

See MOSELLE.

Trockenbeerenauslese

Literally 'dried-berry-selected' in the block-building German language, the elephantine word describes the process whereby the finest sweet wine of the Rhine and Moselle, and some of the most elegant wines in the world are obtained. The grapes are allowed to dry and shrivel on the vine until the ultimate in concentrated sugar-sweetness is achieved; the berries are then individually selected, in this state of super-maturity, by the pickers. Increasing labour costs in a prosperous post-war Germany are rapidly pricing the exquisite type of wine out of the market. Trockenbeerenauslese is the German equivalent of the Sauternes-style wine of France, with the difference that in the warmer south-western France, it is still possible to produce a naturally sweet wine by individual selection of grapes at a price which, though very high, is still not prohibitive.

See MOSELLE.

Château Trottevieille

Bordeaux red wine. District and Commune: Saint-Émilion, France.

Always one of the leading Saint-Émilions, it was rated a *Premier Grand Cru* when the vineyards were officially classified in 1855. Trottevieille sells well abroad, and particularly in Belgium. The property belonged to Marcel Borie, who also owned Château Batailley, a classified vineyard in the Médoc.

Characteristics. A carefully made wine with body and bouquet and a fine colour.

Vineyard area: 17 acres.

Average production: 3,250 cases.

Tuica

A plum spirit made in Rumania. It varies in colour from greenish to yellow. It is sometimes taken hot with sugar and peppers.

Tun

A wine cask containing 210 imperial gallons (252 U.S.), or 954 litres. A tun filled with water or wine weighs approximately one ton avoirdupois.

Tunisia

The vine was established, especially in the vicinity of Carthage, in Punic and Roman times. Afterwards, under the rule of the Moslems, wine-making was forbidden for more than a thousand years. The modern history of wine in Tunisia, now an independent country, began when it came under French control.

Viniculture along French lines was developed in the Cape Bon region, on the peninsula enclosing the Gulf of Tunis on the east; around Tunis itself; and in the Medjerdah and Oued Miliane valleys. Wines were made in quantity, a peak of nearly 1,200,000 hectolitres (26,375,000 imp. gallons; 31,680,000 U.S.) annually being maintained in the 1930s. Phylloxera, the deadly vine louse which half a century earlier had ruined Europe's vineyards, reached Tunisia in 1936. In ten years the vineyard area had dropped by half, and wine production by nearly two-thirds.

Replanted on grafted, phylloxera-immune American vine stocks (as were the post-epidemic vineyards of Europe), the Tunisian vine plantation now covers some 124,000 acres, not all of which are yet in full production. Quantity stands at about 32 million gallons (39 million U.S.). This means that the 1932–42 maximum has now been surpassed, although when the vineyards were first reconstituted, an attempt was made to obtain quality at the expense of quantity.

Tunisia produces red, white, and rosé natural wines, fortified Muscat wines, and *eaux-de-vie*. All wine growing is confined to a narrow area near the coast, forming a crescent around and behind Tunis, but at some distance from the town. The leading districts are Grombalia and the section formed by the triangle Tunis-Mateur-Bordj-Toum, producing quantitatively more than 90% of the total. Growths (*Crus*) are not particularly important in the present state of Tunisian viticulture; however, names of some repute include Carthage, Tébourba, Coteaux du Khanguet, Saint-Cyprien, Cap Bon, and Sidi-Tabet. Important names of fortified wines are Byrsa and Rancio.

The traditional grape varieties in Tunisia have always been, for the red, Carignan, Alicante-Bouschet, and Cinsault; for white wines, Clairette de Provence, Beldi, and Ugni; and for the rosé, Alicante-Grenache. The wines have characteristically shown a tendency to maderize: the reds, particularly, which are based exclusively on Alicante-Bouschet, matured too rapidly in the climate, showing a feeble colour and then quickly developing the onion skin hue and a bitterish taste. In an attempt to correct this, Pedro Ximénez vines from Spain, and Sémillon and Sauvignon from France, have been introduced for the white wines; and for the red

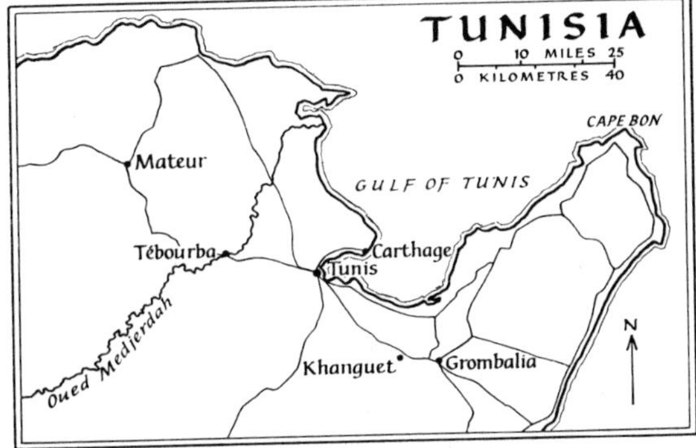

wines, the Nocera, Pinot Noir, and Cabernet varieties. The rosés, based on Alicante-Grenache, have proved the most successful of the types, making one of the best rosés of North Africa, provided that they are bottled as soon as they fall clear and are drunk young. Otherwise they will maderize.

Two quality controls have been established in Tunisian wines. Hemmed in as it is by desert, restricted by the necessity of remaining within the small zone where Europeans are settled, the vineyard is not considered to be sufficiently diverse to justify the large-scale use of place-names, or Appellations d'Origine Contrôlées. At the same time, controls are wanted, as an incentive to make wines of quality by guaranteeing that such wines will be identified and therefore command premium prices.

In 1942 the classification Vin Supérieur de Tunisie was established. It includes no restriction as to place of origin within Tunisia nor limitation as to grape varieties. Wines submitted by growers for the classification are analysed chemically to establish their purity and are then blind tasted by a committee of experts chosen by the Commission of Classification. Vins Supérieurs de Tunisie are sold in bottle. The bottle dressing carries a numbered insignia showing that it belongs to a classed lot, and the vintage must be indicated. The wines must be at least one year old. (It is interesting that the technique parallels almost exactly that set up in 1955 in Bordeaux for wines to be exported to the U.S.)

In 1947, the Appellation Contrôlée 'Vin Muscat de Tunisie' was established. In place of origin, wines are not restricted except to Tunisia, but they must be of the Alexandrian Muscat, Muscat de Frontignan, or Muscat de Terracina grape varieties. The wines are fortified by one of two means: tasteless, rectified spirit may be added before fermentation has begun, thus preventing fermentation and retaining the entire sugar content of the must as sugar; or the fermenting must may be stopped by the addition of either spirits of wine or completely rectified spirit, resulting in a wine of a minimum of 17% of alcohol and of 70 grammes of sugar per litre. The wines made by the first method should properly be called mistelles, as they are actually grape juice with added alcohol, never having undergone fermentation. It is illegal to mix the two types. The better quality results from the use of wine spirits rather than of completely rectified spirit.

In 1958 the following Appellations d'Origine also were controlled: Muscat de Thibar; Radès; Muscat de Radès or Vin Muscat de Radès; Kelibia, Muscat de Kelibia, or Vin Muscat de Kelibia.

Turkey

At the turn of the century Turkish wines were seen in some quantity in western Europe. But exports ceased with the First World War, and by the late twenties that war and the Turco-Greek conflict which followed had almost put an end to wine-making. The prolific, grape-producing regions of Thrace and the Ægean had been devastated, and most of the non-Islamic population had disappeared. The land was left to cultivators who liked eating grapes, were forbidden by their religion to drink wine, and were often persuaded that to sell their grapes to wine-making plants was sinful. It was the task of the new Republic to revive the country's viniculture.

When, in 1927, the State Monopolies wine industries were started, total production had fallen to about 440,000 imp. gallons (528,000 U.S.) a year. Since the middle thirties, however, it has been expanding gradually, and the State has been making a serious effort to raise quality as well as quantity without putting up prices: in order to win customers, Turkey must sell more cheaply than the established wine-producing countries. Up-to-date machinery has been installed in the Government plants, employees have been trained in modern techniques of viticulture and viniculture; and the decree of 1928 that the Moslem faith was no longer the official religion has helped to overcome the scruples of some of the growers.

In comparison with the West, Turkey now seems to be a late-comer in wine production; yet the vine flourished in this region long before Greek colonists planted the first vineyards in Gaul. The earliest vines of all are believed to have grown wild in Anatolia and around the shores of the Caspian Sea; and in Mesopotamia the Sumerians are said to have been making wine as long ago as the third millennium B.C. This long start was lost in the Middle

Ages when the Turks themselves (ardent converts to Islam) began their conquests, which culminated in the fall of Constantinople in 1453. Grapes went on growing, but most of them were (and are) kept for the table, or made into vinegar or the *miel de raisin* which many of the peasants use instead of sugar. In the early years of the Ottoman Empire there was a must tax on the production of wine in the vineyards of non-Moslems. In 1564 a new tax was levied on all alcoholic drinks—but this proved so difficult to enforce that it was afterwards repealed. By the late nineteenth century, although indigenous wine-drinkers were still rare, something like 75 million imp. gallons (90 million U.S.) of wine were produced, largely for export.

The types of wine made in Turkey are dry, semi-dry, sweet, fortified, and sparkling. The grapes for the sweet wine are late-picked; the fortified wines are sweet Muscatels; the sparkling wines are carbonated. The best growths come from central and south-eastern Anatolia; others of very good to medium quality are produced in the Thracian and Ægean regions. The districts divide conveniently as follows: (1) Thrace and Marmara; (2) Ægean; (3) Middle Anatolia; (4) South and East Anatolia. Officially approved grape varieties are:

WHITE WINE VARIETIES

Region	*Grape*	*Place*	*Quality of Wine*
Thrace and Marmara	Beylerce	Bilecik	Very good
	Yapincak	Tekirdağ—Mürefte	Good to medium
	Altintaş	Erdek	Good to medium
Ægean	Muscat	Izmir (Bayrakli—Bornóva)	Very good
	Seedless	Ægean region	Good to medium
Middle Anatolia	Hasandede	Ankara (Keskin)	Very good
	Narince	Tokat	Very good
	Emir	Nevşehir—Ürgüp	Very good
South and East Anatolia	Kabarcik, Döbülgen	Gaziantep—Maraş	Good to medium

RED WINE VARIETIES

Region	Grape	Place	Quality of Wine
Thrace and Marmara	Papazkarasi	Kirklareli	Very good
	Karalahna	Tekirdağ—Bozcaada	Good to medium
	Kuntra	Çanakkale—Bozcaada	Good to medium
	Adakarasi	Tavşanadasi	Good to medium
	Karasakiz	Çanakkale	Good to medium
Ægean	Irikara, Tokmak	Izmir	Good to medium
Middle Anatolia	Kalecik	Ankara (Kalecik)	Very good
	Çubuk	Ankara (Çubuk)	Very good
	Dimrit	Niğde—Kayseri—Konya.	Good to medium
South and East Anatolia	Sergikarasi	Gaziantep	Very good
	Öküz Gözü	Elâziğ	Very good
	Horozkarasi	Gaziantep—Maraş	Good to medium
	Boğazkere	Elâziğ	Good to medium

METHODS OF WINE-MAKING

Turkish growers rarely make their own wine, although a few do so in places such as Bozcaada and Mürefte. They usually sell their grapes to the townsmen who operate the plants. These fall into two categories: on the one hand, the Government-controlled Monopolies established in 1927 and the Atatürk Farm Administration; on the other, private enterprises. The State wineries are operated with modern industrial machinery by technically-qualified personnel; the private concern, often housed in a shop or shed, may be quite seedy and makeshift, the machinery is usually rather primitive and the makers are unlikely to be trained viniculturs. Some of these men make trouble with the peasants by offering for their grapes—already very cheap—a price which is absurdly low.

In pressing the fruit, both hand-operated and

hydraulic basket presses are used—the latter in the big plants. The pomace is first pressed by hydraulic processes, afterwards by hand presses; only in making wines of better quality is the must of the second pressing processed independently. In well-run plants, the juice ferments in concrete tanks in rooms where the temperature is kept low, and is transferred after about a week to more concrete tanks, for ageing. Most of the wines are rather light and are aged only for from eight to twelve months; a few bigger wines will be left for two or three years. Since most Turkish wines are low in acidity, it is necessary to add sufficient sulphur dioxide—the quantity is controlled by the regulations drawn up in 1953—and to rack the wine earlier than is usual. The first racking generally takes place fifteen to twenty-one days after ageing begins, and then sulphur is added; the second racking comes in four to six months; the third, six months later. Those wines which are allowed longer ageing are afterwards racked only once a year. The wine is fined before bottling, mainly with gelatine—blue finings are not permitted—and is sometimes filtered. Most plants blend their wines to achieve consistency of style, and sell it in bottle—but some is marketed in cask. The product of the State Monopolies is generally cheaper than wine made by private firms.

Production

In spite of the efforts of the State, output is still small. The habit of wine-drinking is being urged on the people, and as the old religion loses its hold the custom is indeed growing. Yet most Turks would rather eat their grapes—and these grow luxuriantly over most of the country and are cheaper to buy than most other fruits. In 1958 annual domestic consumption of wine was reckoned at 1·4 pints (1·69 U.S.) per head. In 1950 Turkey came fourth among the countries listed by the Office International du Vin for vineyard acreage—but wine production was by no means proportionate. About 3% only of the grapes was being diverted to this end. The situation improves slowly:

Year	*Vineyard acreage*	*Wine production in gallons*	
		imp.	*U.S.*
1936	852,505	1,175,775	1,412,003
1955	1,747,791	5,433,844	6,525,879
1962	1,787,726	7,468,868	8,962,642

Average yearly production is reckoned as about 4,400,000 imp. gallons (5,284,140 U.S.); here, as elsewhere, harvests are at the mercy of frost and storms.

The principal objective of the State wine industry is, naturally, to increase its export trade. In 1950 the value of wine imported amounted to 25,724 Turkish lire, that exported to 238,184 Turkish lire. In 1956 the import figures were 2,843,340 Turkish lire and the export 700,000 Turkish lire. (Imported wine is almost entirely Champagne. The chief customers for Turkish wines are England, Sweden, Denmark, and, heading the list, Germany: Turkish wines are high in alcohol, German wines are low; one needs the other.) Before these figures can substantially be improved upon, the Government department concerned is well aware that certain reforms must be made, primarily in standards of viticulture and the selection of grape varieties. In order to encourage half-hearted growers, regulations were at first only leniently enforced; now peasants must be made to learn modern methods of tending their vines, and private manufacturers obliged to model themselves on the State monopolies. Moreover, Turkey is growing too many varieties of grapes, and although permissible vines for each region have been listed, standardization has not yet been enforced. Then phylloxera, which reached Turkey towards the end of the last century, still lingers in some districts: cultivators have not yet mastered as thoroughly as have the *vignerons* of western Europe the art of grafting their vines on to disease-resistant American root-stocks. Finally, the Government is hoping to find domestic substitutes for the corks and wooden staves (for barrels) which are so expensive to import. With so many improvements planned, it is to be expected that Turkish wine will soon become familiar abroad.

Tuscany

Red and white wines. District: Central Italy.

Tuscany is the home of Chianti, so famous that it is sometimes mistakenly assumed to be synonymous with Italian wine. Tuscany is also the source of a great deal of other wine which is sold as Chianti, as well as a certain amount actually *not* sold as Chianti. It is perhaps superfluous to add that several oceans of this renowned wine spring from elsewhere in Italy (and the world), but that all true Chianti comes from Tuscany. And some of it is excellent.

Chianti

The Chianti district comprises about 173,000 acres between Florence and Siena and is as steep, rocky, and unpromising a vineyard area as any. You leave Florence by the busy main road and the

Porta Romana, pass the quiet, well-tended, American military cemetery, then turn off to the left and find yourself virtually in another world. The hills are bleak, low-lying but steep, peppered with vines, cypresses, and harsh rocks. The road is no longer a highway but a winding, narrow lane where few cars may be seen, only an occasional ox cart or horse ambling slowly along in the summer heat. Weather-beaten signposts point the way to the historic but dusty and deserted-looking centres: Greve, Radda, Castellina, and Gaiole. From the tops of the higher hills frown massive fortresses; this is the area which once served as a buffer state between warring Florence and Siena. The castles were built by the Florentines to stop raiders from Siena; and in 1376 the châtelains combined to form the Chianti League to deal with attackers and hold them off long enough for Florence to arm. The conflicts of bygone times are the province of the historian, but the student of wine can also profit from a glance at this background: it is one of the claims of the area—now known as the Classical Chianti district—to have sole right to the name Chianti. Historically, the Classical Chianti growers say no one else within or without Tuscany is entitled to the name. They reinforce their historical argument by pointing out that geologically the district differs from surrounding areas. The ancient clay schist soil, the layers of covering flint and limestone, and the thin top of pebbly sand are not duplicated elsewhere. Since soil is an essential—perhaps the most essential—factor in deciding the characteristics of any wine, it follows that nothing grown outside the Classical Chianti district is really Chianti. Logic to the contrary, most Chianti is grown outside.

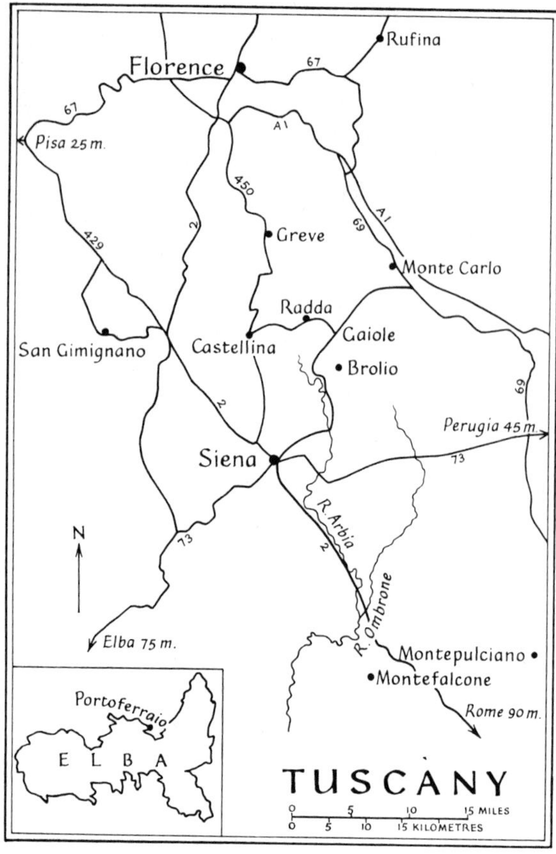

Perhaps the name is too famous. Perhaps the gay, round-bottomed flask—the ubiquitous *fiasco*—drew too much attention to it. The fact remains that growers in half a dozen surrounding areas became attracted by the sweet smell of success and began selling their wines as Chianti—admittedly qualifying it by some other term, but calling it Chianti nonetheless. Each, in addition, has formed its own *consorzio* to protect the name it has appropriated, and each arrogantly proclaims its right to go on using the name, as they have for years.

It must be admitted that some of the subsidiary Chiantis are wonderful wines. Chianti Rufina (not Ruffino, which is a trade-mark) is often considered to be a better balanced wine than the Classical variety; but some of the other offerings are not in the same class. Fortunately, despite the confusion and proliferation of names, real Chianti is available and easily recognizable: the authenticity of any bottle or *fiasco* may be verified by checking to see if it has the seal of the Classical Chianti *consorzio* (Consorzio per la Difesa del Vino Tipico di Chianti) portraying a black cockerel on a gold background with a surrounding red circle bearing the name of the organization. The following wines are allowed the Appellation d'Origine: Chianti Colli Aretini, Chianti Colli Fiorentini, Chianti Colli Senesi, Chianti Colli Pisane, Chianti Montalbano, Chianti Rufina.

Contrary to popular conception, Chianti is apt to come either in the normal tall bottles or a *fiasco*—in general, the finest ones are run off in regular bottles, the better to age them. (The straw wrapping of a *fiasco* has a tendency to rot; and furthermore, only the true wine bottle has the indented punt in the bottom to catch the sediment thrown by an old wine.) Some Chianti firms never put their finest wine in a *fiasco*, while others confound confusion by using both styles for both qualities; yet it can be accepted as a general rule that Chianti in *fiasco* must be drunk young, while in bottle it may be kept and aged. It is an interesting sidelight on the *fiasco* that today it is not as cheap in comparison with a bottle as it was fifty years ago. At that time it was possible to blow the round-bottomed flasks, and hire women to weave straw around them, for practically nothing. Today labour is more expensive and mass-produced bottles cost less per unit, even if they lack the customer appeal of a *fiasco*.

True Chianti, even after years of ageing, is never a very subtle wine. A great part of its charm lies in the heady strength, the sturdy vigour, and slight trace of bitterness—even harshness—which is so characteristic of it. In the better wines, this bitterness disappears to some extent and the wine mellows and softens; but it never goes entirely away. Some young Chianti may have a prickly, *frizzante*, semi-sparkling bite, caused by adding the fermenting juice of late-maturing grapes to the wine after it is made, and this heightens the refreshing characteristics and adds to its gaiety. Only in very rare cases will Chianti be a great wine, but it can almost invariably be counted on to be pleasant.

The wine is traditionally made from five types of grapes used in a set formula. Sangiovese (70%) is said to impart body and alcoholic content; Canaiolo (20%) gives bouquet and tempers the hardness; and Trebbiano and Malvasia (5% combined)—both being white grapes—lighten the intensity of the colour. Finally, Colorino (about 5%) helps in giving true Chianti its usually bright ruby-red colour.

The large firms have unfortunately set a very low standard of quality in the wines they export. As in most of Italy, the really outstanding wines are made in small quantities and one is apt to find them only in some Italian hotels or restaurants where the proprietors are willing to pay the price for quality. In such a case it is a pleasure to drink Chianti—which is too often just an ordinary wine in a Chianti flask.

Vin Santo

The name, it is said, means 'wine for the Saints'. Fortunately, some is reserved for sinners, too, but it is doubtful if it will ever be enough. The real Vin Santo is a sweet, golden wine made by farmers in Tuscany—in fact throughout Italy—but never in any quantity. Some firms in and around Florence are beginning to put small amounts on the market, but as yet good ones are rarely sent for export.

Vin Santo is a pleasant dessert wine, albeit one that is not as sweet as most others in this category. It is vinified (in Tuscany, at any rate) from carefully dried Trebbiano and Malvasia grapes—which are dried by suspending them from hooks along the rafters of a loft or attic. The drying takes several months, and at the end about two-thirds of the juice has gone, leaving the rest comparatively richer in sugar. This juice is then pressed and put in small barrels, of never more than 125 imp. gallon (150 U.S.) capacity which are filled about three-quarters full, then closed and left in a warm place for four years. Heat, as a rule, is death to wine, but in this case a special maderization is wanted, the wine changing in colour from white to deep amber and taking on a nutty, almost Sherry-like taste and aroma. At the end of its ageing, it is filtered and is then ready to drink. The grapes are selected more for taste than sugar content and the wine is distinctive—sweet, but the sweetness masked and balanced by its austere, elevated alcoholic content.

Other Wines of Tuscany

Aleatico di Portoferraio

Sweet, red dessert wine from the capital of Elba, the island that was not quite big enough to contain Napoleon. Its Aleatico (made from grapes of that name) is a full, warm, rich wine and one that can be excellent. Its fame, however, seems to be outrunning it, and there are grounds for suspicion today that not all the wine so labelled is what it claims to be.

Arbia

Dry white wine from Trebbiano grapes grown along the River Arbia at the southern end of the Classical Chianti district. It is pleasant wine, especially when young. One of the better wines is sold as Torricella, both a place-name and a mark of the firm of Ricasoli.

Bianco dell'Elba

Light straw-coloured wine from Procanico grapes grown on the Isle of Elba. Italian wine enthusiasts like to compare this to Chablis, but they should not be taken too seriously.

Bianco Vergine Colli Aretini

'Virgin white', partly on account of its colour, partly since only free-run grape juice is used, not juice extracted in the press. About 11% of alcohol, dry, and pleasantly fresh, in consequence of an acidity slightly higher than is customary in Italy.

Brolio

An excellent Classical Chianti of the firm of Ricasoli, named after the huge mediæval fortress where the wine is always made. The best is never put in *fiasco* and will not always have the name Chianti on the label.

Brunello di Montalcino

Red wine from the hillsides near Montalcino, some twenty-six miles south of Siena. The Brunello grape is a variety of Sangiovese.

Meleto

A good classical Chianti of the firm of Ricasoli.

Montecarlo

Red or white wine from a town in eastern Tuscany. Trebbiano grapes are dominant in the white; Sangiovese, Trebbiano, and Canaiolo go into the red.

Moscatello di Montalcino

Tuscan sparkling Muscat wine, but generally closer to *frizzante* (semi-sparkling) than *spumante* (sparkling). It is produced in small quantities by a co-operative cellar.

Vernaccia di San Gimignano

White wine from Vernaccia grapes usually vinified to be dry, more rarely sweet. The better-known dry variety is a light amber colour with a small bouquet and a slightly bitter aftertaste, and the sweet is still much used as an altar wine—its original purpose.

Vino Nobile di Montepulciano

A red wine that achieved some literary fame in the eighteenth century when the poet Francesco Redi apostrophized it in his *Bacchus in Tuscany* as *Montepulciano d'ogni vini è il Re* (Montepulciano, of all wines it is king). Perhaps in deference to contemporary republican Italy, the 'king' has become something of a commoner. It is made mainly from the Sangiovese grape.

U

Ugni Blanc

Widespread vine giving grapes for dry white wine. It is cultivated in southern France; in the region of Cognac—where it is called Saint-Émilion (*q.v.*)—and elsewhere; also in California and throughout Italy where, under the name Trebbiano, it contributes to most of the better Italian dry white wines.

See TREBBIANO.

Ullage

The air space in a bottle or cask between the top and the level of the wine. In bottled wine it is usually brought about by a faulty cork or by over-exposure to heat and should be approached with caution if not suspicion—the wine may well be bad.

See OUILLAGE.

Umbria

White wines. District: Central Italy.

The vines are pruned short, their branches frequently draped over the lower limbs of small trees which are kept in shape and cut down to size simply for that purpose. Umbrian growers do not share the apparent lack of concern shown by cultivators in some Italian vineyards, and theirs are apt to be remarkably well kept.

This region, south of Florence and north of Rome, produces some 20 million imp. gallons (24 million U.S.) of which Orvieto is the best known.

Orvieto is white, and one of Italy's most consistently delightful wines, some of it semi-sweet, some of it dry. The latter is the result of the modern taste for drier wines. Orvieto was early aware of the new trend, many of the growers began to vinify their wine dry—and there was a great outcry. Conservative wine-drinkers, such as Tuscany's austere Baron Ricasoli, have felt that sweet Orvieto is one of the finest examples of Italian viniculture; vinified to be dry, it becomes a pleasant, reputable wine, but no longer Orvieto. The growers reply that the market for Orvieto *amabile* or *abboccato* (as the semi-sweet is designated) has fallen off to the point where it is no longer possible to specialize in it. 'Our traditional wine is as good as it was,' they maintain, 'but, in addition, we are putting out a dry wine under the same name. It may have slightly different characteristics, but it is still of Orvieto quality.'

Sweet Orvieto has a particular charm and special delicacy. The grapes are mainly Trebbiano, Malvasia, Verdicchio, Verdello and Procanico. In the dry wine, Trebbiano is the dominant grape.

Orvieto is aged in deep cellars dug back into cliffs, resembling those found in Vouvray, and these play an important part (the growers say) in giving the wine its characteristics. Dry Orvieto is usually considerably higher in alcohol than is the sweet type where some of the sugar has been prevented from fermenting (up to 13% as against 11%), but it manages to preserve the charm of its counterpart. It is rarely perfectly dry, but seems to balance a trace of residual sugar against a faintly tart after-taste. About half of the million-odd gallons produced annually are dry.

Upper Moselle

See MOSELLE; UPPER MOSELLE.

Uruguay

The smallest of the South American countries achieves a vinous importance incommensurate with its size by producing between 19 and 20 million imp. gallons (22–24 million U.S.) of wine annually; but the Uruguayan is a wine-drinking man and little of it is exported. Small amounts sometimes trickle into neighbouring Brazil, but, in general, if you want to drink Uruguayan wines you must go to Uruguay.

Red, white, and rosé wines are made. The pink is considerably deeper in colour than is usual, verging more towards Spanish *clarete* than French rosé. Vermouth is also produced, and some fortified and sparkling wines. Contrary to the general rule, fortified wines are often sold as port and sparkling wines as champagne, but in other respects, Uruguayans tend to prefer wines with local names; or wines named from the dominant or informing grape used. The most widespread vine is Harriague, and it is reasonably established that this is the Tannat of Madiran in the French Pyrenees. Vidiella, of obscure origin, and Cabernet from the Bordeaux region of France are also fairly widely planted; and when wine from the two is blended together the result is well balanced and agreeable. Some Barbera and Nebbiolo—imported from Italy and keeping their original names—are also to be found. White wines are made, notably from Sémillon and Pinot Blanc grapes. Some hybrids and the American Isabella vine are planted, but the increased production of these varieties is accompanied—as it always is—by a marked decrease in quality.

Uruguayan viticulture was established in the 1890s near Montevideo and today extends over the low hills and plains of the departments of Montevideo, Canelones, San José and Maldonado (along the

River Plate), Soriano and Paysandú (next to Argentina), and Florida (in central Uruguay). The country is actually an extension of the Brazilian plain, and the gently rolling, volcanic hills—*cuchillas*—never rise above 2,000 feet. Climate is temperate and mild—maintaining an average high of 71°F. (22°C.) in the summer months of January and February, and an average low of 50°F. (10°C.) in the winter months of July—and rainfall is sufficient but not excessive. The vineyards cover about 50,000 acres.

Spirits

The Uruguayans distil quantities of brandy—most of which is miscalled cognac—and some Grappa, distilled from pomace after the grapes have been pressed. Caña—a type of rum—is popular, as is amara (or amargo), an aperitif. Anisette, gin, and guindado (fermented cherries reinforced with alcohol) are also fairly common. A popular Vino Seco is made by adding a large quantity of white wine to red, then enriching the mixture with wine alcohol and letting the whole maderize in the sun, a process which sounds somewhat distressing to conservative amateurs of wine. All wines and spirits are controlled by the State, and various schools at the University of Uruguay are attempting to improve knowledge, and thus wines, by sending students to study abroad, particularly in Italy and France.

Ürziger Würzgarten

White wine. Middle Moselle.

The best wine-producing vineyard of Ürzig produces a spicy and fruity wine, from volcanic and slate soil of such steepness that vintaging becomes a death-defying mountain sport. The best vineyards are Würzgarten, Schwarzlay and Kranklay.

See MOSELLE.

Usquebaugh

The anglicized form of *Uisge beatha*, original Celtic name for whisky.

U.S.S.R.

See RUSSIA.

V

Vacqueyras

One of the best communes of the Côtes du Rhône, producing white, red, and rosé wines.

See RHÔNE.

Vaduzer

Red wine of Liechtenstein.

Two-thirds of the wine which is grown in the little principality on the Swiss-Austrian border is called 'Vaduzer', after Vaduz, the capital. The remaining third is produced in Schaan, Triesen and Balzers, and known as Schaaner, Triesner and Balzner.

Vineyards were probably established in Liechtenstein by Roman invaders and later, by monks, in the first centuries of the Christian era. At this time the country was not Liechtenstein, but a part of the Roman Empire (and later of Germany). In 1699 and 1712, the Princes of Liechtenstein purchased the Rhine plains and towering mountains over which they have ruled ever since. All the vines were cultivated by monks until 150 years ago when the vineyards were secularized. Today, about 17,000 imp. gallons (20,000 U.S.) are made annually.

Vaduzer is a light wine, bordering on a rosé. It is made exclusively from the Blauburgunder grape, although in earlier times white Elbling was the dominating grape there. Riesling-Sylvaner was tried, too; but both varieties were abandoned. The small growers have a co-operative and a single domain, Bockwingert, comprises about half the vineyard area in Vaduz. The most interesting estate is the Abtwingert, the vineyard of the Rotes Haus.

In 1525, this Red House already belonged to the Benedictines of the order of Saint Johann in Toggenberg. It was probably a hundred or more years old then. A visit to the massive Gothic wine-press still in operation in the cellars shows why the Rotes Haus is classed second to the castle of the Prince of Liechtenstein among the sights of the Principality. In the middle of the nineteenth century, Alois Rheinberger—the Rheinbergers are the present owners—took the methods of Vaduzer wine-making to Illinois and planted the well-known vineyard of Masberg Mansion at Nauvoo.

Val d'Adige

Common red wine grown on the banks of the River Adige, in Trentino.

See TRENTINO-ALTO ADIGE.

Valdepeñas

Favourite wine of the cafés of Madrid, grown in vineyards south of the capital in La Mancha. Strong red wines and dry white wines. Until the great popularity of Rioja, this was the best-known Spanish non-fortified wine.

See SPAIN.

Valgella

Red wines of Valtellina, Italy, made from the Nebbiolo grape.

See LOMBARDY.

Valpantena

A wine somewhat similar to Valpolicella.

See VENETO.

Valpolicella

The best wines of Veneto, in Italy—ruby red, fragrant and fruity, with a delicate bouquet and a rich texture.

See VENETO.

Valtellina

Name of a series of red Italian wines made from Nebbiolo grapes.

See LOMBARDY.

Van der Hum

A South African liqueur of which the principal ingredient is the peel of the *nartjie*, a type of South African orange. The subsidiary ingredients vary according to the producer, each one of whom has his own closely guarded formula. The liqueur is tawny in colour and has a strong taste of orange. Van der Hum means 'what's his name'; a variation, known as Brandy-Hum, is made by diluting Van der Hum to half quantity with brandy, thus reducing the sweetness.

See SOUTH AFRICA.

Varietal Wine

American term for wine made wholly or predominantly from the grape variety named on the label such as California Pinot Noir, New York State Riesling, etc. Legally, such wine must be made of at least 51% wine from the grape named. The rule was established in an attempt to break away from meaningless generic names such as Californian burgundy and is now followed by most of the best wine-makers. The day when American producers cease entirely to use misappropriated and misapplied European place-names, and adopt varietal names for wines that are strictly American, will be a bright day indeed for American wine lovers.

Vat

A container for wine varying in size; the name is derived from the Dutch word for 100 litres (1 hectolitre, or 22 imperial gallons, 26·4 U.S. gallons). It is the usual translation for the French *cuve*—a vessel of oak, stainless steel or cement (sometimes lined with glass) in which wines are fermented and blended.

V.D.N.V.—Verband Deutscher Naturwein-Versteigerer

This is the Natural Wine Association of Germany. Its purpose is the maintenance of quality in German wines. Only a fairly small percentage of the country's vineyards belong, but the principal estates are members. These usually (but not always) incorporate in their labels the emblem of the society: a black eagle with grapes on its breast.

See GERMANY.

V.D.Q.S.

These letters stand for Vins Délimités de Qualité Supérieure, or delimited wines of superior quality. They are found on wines from certain sections of France—wines which are considered good enough to be quality-controlled, but not of the calibre of the wines of Appellation d'Origine Contrôlée. In effect, they make up a secondary classification of the better wines of France.

Although the classification only dates back to 1949, it includes a number of wines, some of them extremely good. Many of the better—but none of the best—wines of France are included, and previously all of the best wines of Algeria. In the decrees covering the various V.D.Q.S. wines, the growing area, the vines permitted, and the minimum limits of alcohol are always stipulated. In most cases, the wines must be tasted by a committee of experts set up for that purpose and only after approval has been given have they the right to the name. V.D.Q.S. wines carry these initials as well as the name of the place of origin on their labels, and in the case of estate-bottled wines, the name of the grower will also be included. They are likely to be good buys, if they can be found, and provided most of the price goes for the wine and not for duties and transportation, for they are sound and do not carry the high price that may go with a greater reputation.

V.D.Q.S. Place-name Wines

Béarn
Cabrières
Cahors
Chambord
Châtillon-en-Diois
Chautagne
Corbières
Corbières du Roussillon
Corbières Supérieur
Corbières Supérieur du Roussillon
Costières du Gard
Coteaux d'Aix et des Baux
Coteaux d'Ancenis
Coteaux du Giennois
Coteaux de Saint-Christol
Coteaux de Vérargues
Côtes d'Auvergne
Côtes du Buzet
Côtes du Forez
Côtes de Gien
Côtes du Lubéron
Côtes du Marmandais
Côtes de Provence
Côtes de Toul
Côtes de Ventoux
Côtes de Vérargues
Faugères
Fronton
Côtes de Fronton
Gros Plant de Pays Nantais
Haut-Combat
La Clape
Minervois
Mont Près (Chambord-Cour-Cheverny)
Picpoule de Pinet
Pic-Saint-Loup
Quatourze
Rosé de Béarn
Rousselet de Béarn
Roussillon des Aspres
Saint-Chinian
Saint-Drézéry
Saint-Georges-d'Orques
Saint Saturnin and Montpeyroux
Villaudric
Vins d'Auvergne
Vin de Béarn
Vins d'Irouléguy
Vins de Lavilledieu
Vins du Lyonnais
Vins de la Moselle
Vins de l'Orléanais
Vins de Renaison Côte Roannaise
Vins de Saint-Pourçain-sur-Sioule
Vins de Savoie-Roussette de Savoie and nine sub-districts:
Vins de Savoie Abymes, etc.

(V.D.Q.S. wines are treated in various portions of this book, under various headings. In some cases they are treated under their own proper names—Corbières, Minervois are examples—and in others are placed under regional headings: e.g. Provence.)

Veldt

One-time unit of measure used in Cognac, now extinct: 27 veldts equalled a Cognac cask of 205 litres, 35 veldts equalled 60 British imperial gallons (72 U.S.).

Veltliner

White-wine grape grown in Austria and Czechoslovakia, and also to a small extent in California.

Velvety

Used of a wine which, through ageing, has reached sufficient maturity to conserve body, yet produces a sensation of great smoothness.

Vendange

French term for the grape harvesting; also the vintage season.

Venencia

In Spain, especially Jerez de la Frontera, a bullet-shaped silver cup on a pliable whalebone handle usually about two-and-a-half feet long. This is used for taking samples from Sherry casks.

Veneto (Venetia)

Red and white wines. District: North-East Italy.

The wines of Veneto are about the most charming and consistently good in Italy, although rarely if ever could one of them be classified as great. The region around Venice produces some 80 million imp. gallons (96 million U.S.) per year and is considered fifth in importance among Italian wine districts. Soave is dry, white, and—as the name implies—distinctly suave, while Valpolicella, Valpantena, and Bardolino perform graceful variations on a theme, the dominant notes of which are dry, red, and light. The typically Italian pungency and harshness seem to be absent from these wines, which come from the vineyards around Verona, city of Romeo and Juliet. Wander round Verona's Roman amphitheatre or listen to the opera on a summer evening; amble through the ancient streets or into one of the mediæval courtyards—and the Veronese wines, pleasant to drink anywhere, here seem perfectly delicious. It is true that wines always taste best in their own district; but these, fortunately, are able to travel—and seem to carry a bit of Verona with them.

The Best Wines of Veneto

Valpolicella

This is unquestionably the best. It is ruby-red, of medium alcoholic content (perhaps 10%–13%), has a delicate bouquet and a rich, mouth-filling texture. Every now and then a bottle will emerge with a slight trace of residual sugar, and this will start working in the bottle, giving the wine a *frizzante* or prickling taste that is by no means unpleasant. As is the case with other Veronese wines, the best bottles can be expected to come from the smaller houses—because of the unfortunate predilection many firms have for labelling wines according to demand rather than supply.

The principal grapevines cultivated in the vineyards of Valpolicella are Negrara, Corvino, Rossara, and Molinara; Barbera, Lambrusco, and Sangiovese vines may also be found in the area.

Valpantena

A red wine similar to Valpolicella, coming from a nearby valley. The grapevines are predominantly Corvino, Molinara, and Negrara, but others creep in from time to time. The wine lacks some of the elegance of Valpolicella and has a tendency to mature faster. It also fades faster.

Bardolino

This is grown in the place of that name, and in the neighbouring territories on the south-eastern shore of Lake Garda: a dry wine, clear ruby-red in colour. When very young, it has a beguiling charm, which it tends to lose after a very short time. The 'new look' in Italian viniculture is very much in evidence here, for Bardolino is now being fermented a considerably shorter time than is traditional, resulting in a wine which is lighter, fresher, cleaner, and distinctly more pleasant than it would otherwise be, with an alcoholic content of 10·5%–13%. It is made from a variety of grapes, with Corvino, Molinara, and Negrara in the lead.

Soave

Like its red counterparts, Soave is not great but almost always good for an Italian wine. It has, at its best, a light straw colour with greenish highlights, a small but pleasant bouquet, and a dry, very slightly acid taste. Like so many Italian white wines it comes from the Trebbiano grapevine (although Garganega is also important), in this instance cultivated in the towns of Soave and Monteforte d'Alpone, about ten miles east of Verona. Care should be taken when buying the wine because its increasing popularity has not been accompanied by a comparable increase in output. A Soave Spumante (sparkling Soave) is very occasionally seen, but it has little to offer and its export future is dubious. The high iron content of Soave's soil leads to problems in wine clarification which are increased when the wine is made sparkling.

Minor Wines of Veneto

Colli Euganei

Small Veronese white and red wine from the Euganean Hills, twenty miles south-east of Soave. It is normally used as a carafe wine.

Colli Trevigiani

Light, rather flat, acid-deficient white wine mostly from Prosecco and Verdiso grapes. The Prosecco of Valdobbiadene is the most highly thought of.

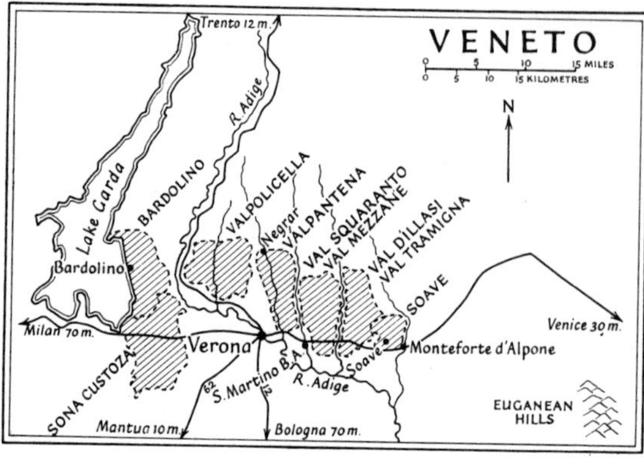

Garda

The wines from the banks of Lake Garda—from the so-called Brescian Riviera—are of slightly lesser cast than their northern neighbours; the reds are lighter and not so good and the whites are simply not distinguished. Rosé wine, known as *vino rosato,* or *chiaretto,* is a fairly recent development, and when young is perhaps the best. To sit in the twilight overlooking the great, tranquil lake while the Alps seem to move closer as the sun sinks is a glorious experience, and a glass of pink Garda wine certainly takes nothing from it. In character, these wines closely resemble some made along the French Mediterranean coastline, and like them are best when seen at home. Sangiovese, Groppello, and Moniga are the important grapevines and some of the more frequently encountered names are Chiaretto del Garda, Moniga del Garda, Riviera del Garda, and Valtanesi. Everyone will have his own choices among them.

Garganega di Gambellara

Light, dry, white wine resembling Soave and sometimes labelled as such, although it is higher in alcohol. Gambellara is about five miles from Soave; and Garganega and Trebbiano are the grapes used in the vineyards. A sweet dessert wine is made here, too.

Recioto Veronese

Sweet, full-bodied red dessert wine from grapes dried on the vine and specially selected as they attain the proper degree of sweetness. Sometimes made sparkling. It is produced in the same district as the Valpolicella and Valpantena.

Vino Veronese

Light and pleasant carafe wines from the Verona district. The Sona-Custoza sub-district south of Bardolino, Squaranto-Mezzane east of Valpantena, and Val d'Illasi-Val Tramigna between Valpantena and Soave, are the principal sources. Corvino, Molinara, and Rossignola vines are predominant.

Venezuela

Venezuela has no vineyards. The country does produce spirits, but not many of them and only in small quantities.

The leading spirit is probably cocui (sometimes cocuy) from the agave cocui plant, the equivalent of the Mexican tequila/mescal spirits. It varies in proof from 80° to 100°, depending upon the still used and the purity desired, and is drunk neat rather than complemented with lime and salt, as tequila is. The taste of cocui is a special one, somewhat similar to that of tequila but slightly harsher.

Rums—and some excellent ones are made—are popular, as are *aguardientes*; beer is on the increase and a few liqueurs are produced in the vicinity of Caracas. In addition to these, a beverage fermented from corn and called *chicha* is popular with the Indians. *Chicha* is coarse, acid, unusually high in alcohol and altogether far too rough to be widely appreciated.

Vente sur Souches

French term for advance sale of wines made before the harvest, 'on the vinestock'. When the agreement is based on a certain degree of alcohol in the wine, the price can be fixed under a reserve for an increase or decrease of this price, according to whether the wine, when it is made, has an unexpectedly higher or lower degree of alcohol. Every contract for a *vente sur souches* must include a declaration that the consenting parties are aware of this rule (art. 320–332, Code du Vin). Any infraction of the law is subject to indirect taxation and to a fine (art. 1760, Code du Vin). Sometimes in recent years there have been advance sales of classified growths of Bordeaux. The quotations have then been given in tonneaux, or tons.

Véraison

French term for the maturing of the grape, when it changes from green to a reddish hue, or a translucent greenish-white.

See CHAPTER EIGHT, p. 34.

Verdelho

A leading grape variety used in making white Port, and grown elsewhere—in Australia, for example.

Also the designation of a sweet, soft Madeira wine.

Verdicchio dei Castelli di Jesi

Light, dry or semi-sweet, white Italian wine.
See THE MARCHES.

Verdot

The grape, also known as Petit Verdot, is used plentifully in the ordinary red wines of Bordeaux, and sparingly in the better Médocs.

Vergennes

American grapevine whose fruit yields a pleasant, light, dry wine. Originally from Vermont, the vine is most widely cultivated in New York State.

Verjus

In French, grapes resulting from a late or second flowering of the vine. Such grapes do not mature and they retain a high acid content; they are used by the wine-maker in very hot summers when the ripe grapes are deficient in acid.

Vermentino

This grape produces a good white wine in Liguria, the Italian Riviera, and is grown also in Corsica.

Vermentino Ligure

Thin, light, white Italian wines, sometimes slightly sparkling.
See LIGURIA.

Vermouth

Vermouth is not a wine. It is wine-based, but it undergoes so many additions and manipulations that it ceases to be recognizable as the product of the vine. It is, however, a popular and excellent aperitif, and is indispensable in some cocktails—principally, of course, in the dry martini.

The name is derived variously from the German *Wermut* or the Anglo-Saxon *wermod*, both meaning wormwood. Vermouth was certainly being made in Italy in the seventeenth century, and now it is produced all over the world and the two main types are 'French' and 'Italian'. Vermouth is also made in California and many of the wine-producing countries.

Vermouth-making is a complicated but not a great art. It requires wine, sugar syrup or mistelle (unfermented grape juice fortified with brandy), alcohol, assorted herbs and plants, a pasteurizer, refrigerating vats, vast filters, and a table of ingredients, weights, and measures. When these essentials are collected, the process becomes a production-line affair.

The essential matter is the wine, usually white and fairly insipid. The transformations in taste will be such that the use of distinctive or fine wine would be a needless expense; and much Italian vermouth is based on the product of the southern Italian plains, that of France on the output of the Midi. Next in importance are the herbs and flavourings. These will include wormwood, hyssop, quinine, coriander, juniper, cloves, camomile, orange-peel, and sometimes even rose petals, but the exact ingredients and their proportions are jealously guarded by each manufacturer. The wine may be aged as much as two years or it may not be aged; but the first step will be the addition of sugar syrup or mistelle. After this come alcohol and flavourings.

The flavouring herbs which give vermouth its character are macerated and steeped in alcohol. They are sometimes heated, so that the flavour may pass into the spirit in the same manner as in an infusion of tea. When the alcohol is sufficiently flavoured, it is added to the sweetened wine and the whole mixture agitated to blend it together. Even in the most modern plants, wooden paddles are generally used for blending, so that any extraneous tastes may be kept out of the eventual vermouth. Tannin is added, then gelatine to clarify it; and, finally, the mixture is pasteurized. After pasteurization, it is refrigerated, falling sometimes as low as 14°F. (−10°C.) for a period of two weeks or so. During this time any tartrates in the wine form crystals and drop to the bottom of the vats, and from there the vermouth is put through a huge Seitz filter to remove any last impurities and tartrate particles that might remain. After this rigorous treatment, the vermouth is stored for a few months, bottled, and shipped. It can now be reasonably expected to survive in tropical heat or arctic cold; but manufacturers say that prolonged periods of excessive temperature will turn even this hardy creature, oxidizing it and giving it a musty and unpleasant taste. Such an occurrence, however, takes considerable heat.

French vermouths are generally held to be dry, Italian sweet. This is to some extent true, but both types are made in each country, although the very sweet are all Italian. The very dry French Chambéry is allowed the *appellation d'origine*. This is a special type, lighter than those from Sète in Southern France. Chambéry is made from lighter wines, many coming from surrounding Alpine hillsides—the herbs are not the same as those used by the manufacturers of the heavier vermouths. Another popular dry type is Noilly-Prat. The Italian Cinzano may be red or white, sweet or fairly dry—as also may Martini and Gancia.

Vernaccia

White-wine grape used in Italy for wines of the Marches, Sardinia, etc.

Vernaccia di Sardegna, or **Dicampidano**

One of the best-known wines of Sardinia (*q.v.*).

Verveine du Vélay

French liqueur made in Puy, Central France, on a brandy base, flavoured with herbs. There are two varieties, one yellow and one green; the green is the stronger.

Verzenay

Village near Reims producing a first-growth Champagne.

See CHAMPAGNE.

Verzy

Commune of the mountain of Reims district producing a first-growth Champagne.

See CHAMPAGNE.

Vevey Festival

The world's most important wine festival, given since the seventeenth century, in the town of Vevey, Switzerland, a development of the activities of the mediæval Wine-Growers Guild. The official name is Fête des Vignerons. The fête has taken place in this century in 1905, 1927, and 1955. The 1955 festival, which took five years to prepare, was one of Europe's biggest tourist events that year. The performances, sometimes by as many as 3,300 participants including 950 children, celebrated the wine before daily audiences of 15,000 for two weeks.

See SWITZERLAND.

La Vieille Cure

A very popular French liqueur made at Cenons near Bordeaux according to a formula which includes various brandies and fifty-two different herbs. It is golden in colour and somewhat similar to Benedictine.

Vigneron

French term for a wine-maker and wine grower; a skilled vineyard worker.

Vignoble

French term for vineyard.

Vila Nova de Gaia

A village lying opposite the city of Oporto, on the River Douro in northern Portugal. Most of the Port lodges, or warehouses, are in Vila Nova de Gaia and all Port wine which is legally Port is shipped from Oporto.

See PORT.

Villafranca del Panadés

Wines from the province of Barcelona. The best types are dry.

See SPAIN.

Vin

French term for wine.

Vin Blanc

French for white wine.

Vin Bourru

French term for wine still on the original lees, or just drawn from the barrel. It is a praiseworthy term in such wines as Beaujolais, which are to be drunk young.

Vin de Coule

French term for wine from first pressing.

Vin de Cuvée

Term used in Champagne for wine of first pressing.

Vin Doux Naturel

In France sweet wine which has been fortified with brandy, added to stop fermentation and ensure both a high alcoholic content and a residue of unfermented sugar. The yeasts cease their activity when approximately 17% of alcohol is present. Most of the French *vins doux naturels* come from the Grand Roussillon region on the Mediterranean near the Spanish border; the bulk of the rest, from Frontignan nearer the mouth of the Rhône. This may be red or white, and contains from 14% to 17½% of alcohol by volume (although the great bulk is sold at 18%) and has little attraction for wine-drinkers where Sherry and Port—to which it bears some small resemblance—are available.

See also VIN DE LIQUEUR; SWEET FORTIFIED WINES OF FRANCE.

Vin Fin

A much-abused French term meaning wine of quality. The inference is that the wine so called is superior. This is sometimes true—as in the case of Vins Fins de la Côte de Nuits—but is much too loosely used when it appears on a label with a commercial trade name.

Vin de Garde

A great French wine with high alcoholic content and much tannin. Worth laying down until maturity has subdued all early excesses.

Vin du Glacier

Hard white wine of Valais, so named because after the harvest it is stored in high Alpine villages.

See SWITZERLAND.

Vin de Goutte

French wine from last pressing.

Vin Gris

Pink wine frequently attributed to Alsace but really pertaining to nearby Lorraine.

See LORRAINE; ALSACE.

Vin d'Honneur

French for Wine of Honour. Since, from earliest times, wine has been poured in libation to the Gods and has graced the tables of kings, it was natural that men should serve it to those whom they wished to honour. Even today, *vins d'honneur* are offered on certain occasions. Historic wine ceremonies recalled by Messieurs Renouil and Traversay in their *Dictionnaire du Vin* are:

Vin de Bourgeoisie offered in the Middle Ages to the Mayor and any citizen who was made burgher of a town.

Vin de Coucher (nuptial wine) offered before they retired by newly married couples to the guests who had honoured their wedding feast.

Vin de l'Étrier (stirrup cup) offered to a parting guest.

Vin du Curé offered to the priest after baptism.

Vin de Veille (night-cap) which courtiers used to place beside the king's bed in case he should want a drink in the night.

Vin du Clerc offered by defendants to the clerk of the tribunal after a verdict in their favour.

Vin Jaune

Yellow wine of the Jura region in France. This is made from late-picked grapes and kept for an unusually long time; when it is in the barrel it forms a white film, known in Sherry-making as *flor*.

See JURA.

Vin de Liqueur

This French term has two meanings. 1. A very sweet wine, such as a rich Sauternes. 2. Wine of approximately 18% of alcohol caused by the addition of brandy and added to Champagne prior to shipment.

Vin de Marc

Wines made in France from a pressing of the residues with added water and sugar.

Vin Mousseux

Sparkling wine.

Vin Ordinaire

The French term for common wine.

Vin de Paille

'Straw wine', made in the Jura region of France, and elsewhere. It derives its name from the time-honoured process of drying the grapes on beds of straw before pressing, as well as from the colour of the wine.

See JURA.

Vin de Presse

In France, wine made from the pressing of the residues after the regular wine has been made. Taken by itself, it is very harsh.

Vin de Primeur

In French, young wine. Often used as a synonym for Vin Bourru (*q.v.*).

Vin de Queue

French term for inferior wine made from the pressing of the stalks.

Vin Rosé

French term for pink wine, made from red grapes by fermenting the juice on the skins (which give the colour) a shorter time than is taken for red wine. Rosé should never be a mixture of red and white wines—although it sometimes is; it should be served quite cool.

Vin Rouge

French for red wine.

Vin Santo

See TUSCANY.

Vin de Tête

In Sauternes, wine from the first crushing; the best. Château d'Yquem, 1921, had a *crême de tête.*

Vinage

French term for adding alcohol to wine to raise its strength. In some districts, and for cheap wines, a moderate addition of alcohol improves the product; but the practice can only be condemned in the case of fine wines.

Vinasse

Residual liquor. In French, the residue of wines and fermented liquors after distillation, also a derogatory term for ordinary wine.

Vine

Woody-stemmed climbing plant of the Ampelidaceæ family which includes virginia creeper and other varieties as well as the grape-producing *Vitis* (with its sub-genera *Euvites* and *Muscadiniæ*) which alone is of importance to the wine-maker.

See CHAPTER EIGHT, p. 29.

Vine Species

For classification of the species of genus *Vitis*, *see* CHAPTER EIGHT, pp. 29–30.

Vinello, Vinettino

Various forms of the diminutive applied to the Italian word for wine, to express contempt for its poorness or thinness. Therefore, a little, thin wine.

Vinho Liquoroso

Portuguese for fortified wine.

Vinho do Rodo

Portuguese for sparkling wine.

Vinho Trasfugado

Portuguese term for Madeira, after it has been racked, or drawn off its lees.

Vinhos Verdes

Light, crackling or slightly sparkling, these wines from the north of Portugal, just below Spanish Galicia, are extremely popular in their homeland and make charming hot-weather drinks.

See PORTUGAL.

Vinifera

Species of genus *Vitis* (sub-genus *Euvites*) which embraces those native European vines responsible for the greatest wines of the world. *Vitis vinifera* has been transplanted to Australia, South Africa, California, and South America.

See CHAPTER EIGHT, pp. 29–30.

Vinification

Wine-making.

Vino da Arrosto

Italian term for wine of breed.

Vino de Color

In Spain, concentrated grape juice for colouring and sweetening wines.

Vino Corriente

Spanish term for common wine.

Vino Dulce

In Spain, very sweet wine for blending.

Vino Espumoso

Spanish for sparkling wine.

Vino de Pasto

Spanish for table wine. It is also a type of Sherry of no great distinction.

Vino Santo

Sweet white dessert wine made in Greece and in the Venetian region of Italy where the golden wine comes from white grapes left to dry on the plant.

Vino Tierno

Spanish term for heavy, sweet wine, used in blending.

Vino de la Tierra

Spanish term for *vin de pays* or ordinary wine of the region.

Vino Tinto

Spanish term for red wine.

Vinosity

The essential quality or heart of the wine, a strong personality achieved by the accentuation of the best characteristics of the particular type. The term is often used to suggest high alcoholic content, an error arising from the failure to realize that alcohol is only one among the ingredients contributing to the character of the wine.

Vinprom

The State Enterprise for handling wine-growing and the wine trade in Bulgaria (*q.v.*).

Vins Délimités de Qualité Supérieure

See V.D.Q.S.

Vins Fins de la Côte de Nuits

A name that is found on certain Burgundian bottles. It signifies that the wine is one of the lesser ones of the Côte de Nuits in France. In quality, these stand between wines bearing the name of a commune and those which have a more general name, such as Burgundy (*Bourgogne* in French). While both red and white wines could be made, in practice they are all red, from Pinot Noir grapes, and all have a minimum alcoholic content of 10·5% (white wines would have to contain at least 11%). Production amounts to about 55,000 imp. gallons (66,370 U.S.) in an average year for quantity, and the vineyards are divided among several communes in the following manner: Fixin 500 acres; Brochon 118; Prissey 30; Comblanchien 135; Corgoloin 200.

Vins de la Moselle

One of the two controlled place-names in the Lorraine area in France. The growths are classed Vins Délimités de Qualité Supérieure (delimited wines of superior quality). Some are rosés, some white.

Vins Natures de la Champagne

See CHAMPAGNE.

Vins de Pays

The term is one used in France for wines which are strictly local and regional in character, which are grown, made, and consumed in one particular region, and are rarely, if ever, found outside it. In some cases, these have acquired an exaggerated and even a snobbish following among travellers who like to show their familiarity with native ways.

These regional wines often have a low alcoholic content, and so are sometimes not fit to travel, yet, drunk young and in the region where they are made, they may be very pleasant. For example, a restaurant in the Savoie recommends a Roussette d'Apremont, the *vin de pays*. This small white wine is taken by at least 70% of the customers—and they are quite right. The same may be said of many of the small wines of Anjou and the Jura (particularly around the region of Arbois), although the same wines would be disappointing if they had to undergo ageing and shipment.

Vintage and Vintage Charts

The vintage is the *vendange* or gathering of the grapes, and hence the wine from grapes of a specific harvest, the date of which will be shown on the label.

Champagne and Port have given the word vintage a special connotation, namely, 'a very good year'. The lesser years are blended to give a non-vintage wine and it is only in the great years that a vintage is stated on the label. Bordeaux, Burgundies, Rhine wines etc.—any wine from a good vineyard—will bear a vintage date on the label irrespective of whether the year was good or poor.

The vintages of different years are rated on a scale (usually from 1 to 10); and the system is a useful one in countries of temperate climate where in spite of careful viticulture, variations in the weather may so affect the harvest that one year's yield may be excellent, the next only average, and the third quite poor. But these ratings, printed on charts and circulated among consumers, may lead to a certain amount of confusion, because they do not tell enough.

Charts are based on the fact that wine-makers can judge, roughly, at the time of the harvest how good the wine is going to be. The statisticians then come along and summarize the consensus of opinion into ratings. But these estimates of its quality apply to the wine at its peak, which may be in five years' time, or in fifteen. The charts stated that 1945, for instance, was a great year; but not that a slow-maturing red wine, such as Bordeaux, would not reach perfection for some twenty years because an excess of tannin makes it slow to mature, and so a great deal of this wine was drunk prematurely.

For the same reason, of two young wines, the pleasanter to drink now may very well be the one which has received the lower vintage mark, simply because it is not going to last so long, and will, therefore, have developed better in its first two or three years than the wine of the greater vintage.

Moreover, there are endless exceptions to vintage ratings. Several poor red wines were made in Burgundy in the great year of 1947, but the chart cannot tell you this. On the other hand, there is always a vineyard which comes up with something magnificent, even in the worst years. These wines will be good bargains, because they cannot be so highly priced as an equal wine of a 'good' year. On the whole, red wines from leading vineyards in the finest districts seldom fall below a certain standard, even in a poor summer.

In countries where the summers are always unbearably hot, the weather will not seriously affect the quality of the wine, and vintage ratings are, therefore, of little importance.

Vintage Port

Along the River Douro in Portugal, where the only true Port wine is made, not every year is considered worthy of being called a vintage year. Only eight or nine vintage years have been universally declared in the last quarter of a century, although a vintage may be declared by an individual Port-wine maker for his wine, and so the practice is not uniform. Vintage Port, selected from the best years, is always the wine of a single year, which will be indicated. Any Vintage Port should be aged in bottle at least a decade; it goes on improving in glass for many, many years.

See PORT.

Vintage Wines

Of a particular vintage or year, which is marked on the label.

Virginia

Wine-producing region in the United States. The vineyards, few but good, are situated principally in Albemarle and Clack counties, with Charlottesville at the centre.

See AMERICA: EASTERN STATES.

Vitis vinifera

The species of vine from which most of the wine in the world is made. For a fuller account of this and other types of vine (*Vitis*) as, for example, *Vitis labrusca, Vitis riparia, Vitis coignetiæ, see* CHAPTER EIGHT, pp. 29–30.

Vodka

Vodka, once the traditional Russian drink, taken neat and tossed off quickly before, during and after meals, is now an international one consumed and indeed made over most of the Western World. (It still shows at its best with caviar.) The neutrality of the spirit has made it popular: many people who like to drink do not really care for the taste of alcohol. The lack of smell is another virtue. The fashion for vodka-drinking in the West started in California and soon spread over America and then Europe. Some people like to dilute it with mineral water or tomato juice, others to take neat vodka and follow it with a chaser. And it is, of course, a remarkably good base for martinis and other cocktails.

Vodka, which was native to Poland, Latvia, Lithuania and Estonia, as well as Russia, was popularly assumed to be a spirit made from potatoes. Now it is more likely to be produced from grain. Like gin, it is distilled at very high proof, rectified into a spirit with neither the taste nor the aroma of the materials used. Unlike gin, it remains unflavoured—although some individual vodkas are infused with herbs and aged for more than three years—sometimes in barrels that have contained wine.

Different vodkas range from about 65° proof to more powerful types at 98° proof.

Volatile Acidity

In wine, the state caused by the presence of acetic acid—the acid of vinegar, which is the principal cause of vinegary wine.

See CHAPTER NINE, pp. 50, 51–52.

Volnay

Burgundy red wine. District: Côte de Beaune, France.

The Volnays are rather delicate wines for Burgundy, quick to mature, with less depth of colour than the Beaunes and Pommards, and greater elegance. They are suave, rounded, well balanced, with a particularly fine bouquet. The commune lies south of Pommard, on rather high ground. Some of the vineyards are more exposed than others, and as a measure against the disasters of frost and hail, they are much parcelled out. The total area is about 527·5 acres; the average yield, approximately 143,000 imp. gallons (172,000 U.S.).

In the Middle Ages, Volnay had a light, *œil de perdrix* colour which was much relished and the wine was popular. The dukes of Burgundy made presents of Beaune and Volnay to kings and to the papal court at Avignon. Louis XI, who kept his prisoners in cages, defeated the Burgundian dukes, annexed their land, and got possession also of the vines of which they were so proud. Volnay seems to have been a special favourite: the entire harvest of 1477 was taken, by his orders, to his château at Plessis-les-Tours. The white wines can be legally sold as Meursault.

Volnay is only a jump away from Meursault, and there is an old jingle which runs:

Entre Pommard et Meursault
C'est toujours Volnay le plus haut.

Topographically, this is undisputable. Set between two hills, the village dominates its vineyards and is itself dominated by the church—most of the vineyard paths lead down, the village streets climb up to the church. Caillerets, the highest of the vineyards, close to the cemetery, is also the best. Up the slopes, you can see across the great Burgundian valley, sometimes as far as the snow-capped Jura peaks. Just south of Volnay, off to the right and up a lane, is the small village of Monthélie. Its wines lesser and less known than the Volnays, are also less expensive.

Another local jingle is:

Qui n'a pas de vignes en Caillerets
Ne sait ce que vaut le Vollenay.

which means that no *vigneron* can really know what Volnay means unless he owns a strip of vines in Caillerets, *les cailles du roi.* The Volnay vineyards are as follows:

FIRST GREAT GROWTHS (*Premiers Grands Crus*)

Vineyard	*Acres*
Les Caillerets	6·64
Les Caillerets-dessus	36·35
Clos des Ducs	6·00
Les Brouillards	16·84
Les Mitans	9·85
L'Ormeau	10·72
Les Angles	8·54
Les Pointes d'Angles	3·07
Les Fremiets	16·05
Les Champans	28·00
Les Chevrets	14·96
Le Clos des Chênes	40·17
La Barre	3·19
La Bousse d'Or	4·84
TOTAL	205·22

The difference between this total and the overall figure of 527·56 acres represents the area producing wine entitled to the general *appellation* Volnay.

Vöslau

One of the regions near Baden producing red wines and Roten Sekt, or red sparkling wine.

See AUSTRIA.

Vosne-Romanée

Burgundy red wine. District: Côte de Nuits, France.

No vineyards have ever been praised so highly and so consistently as the best of Vosne-Romanée. In good years the wines are unquestionably magnificent and are among the most expensive in the world.

The five greatest vineyards of Vosne are minuscule, even by Burgundian standards. Their combined area is sixty-five acres and the annual output is only slightly more than 11,600 imp. gallons (14,000 U.S.), the equivalent of less than 6,000 cases. Demand for the largest of them—Romanée Saint-Vivant—is so insistent that the grower could never hope to approach it, and wines from La Romanée and Romanée-Conti are so rare that drinking one of them must always be an event.

Romanée-Conti is the great wine of the commune in spite of the small size of the vineyard—just four-and-a-half acres. The pre-war vintages—hardly more than a memory now—were the most magnificent, for replanting and the large number of young vines in the vineyard have, since the fifties, brought the quality slightly down from its former height. While the Romanée-Conti is the 'central jewel in the necklace of Burgundian wines', La Romanée, La Tâche, Richebourg, and Romanée Saint-Vivant are worthy companions for it. (*See individually under separate headings.*)

The great unifying factor in the wines of Vosne is their velvety softness and finesse. All of the wines of the commune share these characteristics, and in addition they are light and delicate and beautifully balanced; they are feminine wines, not assertive, and they age most gracefully. This is true not only of the greatest vineyards, but also of those classed just slightly below—such as Grande Rue, Gaudichots, Beaumonts, and Malconsorts, all of which produce wonderful wines.

The vineyards which produce the wines that go to market with the words Vosne-Romanée on the label are mostly in that commune, but some are in adjoining Flagey-Échezeaux. Wines from Flagey's two greatest vineyards—Grands-Échezeaux and Échezeaux—may carry their own names or may be declassed into First Growth of Vosne-Romanée (Vosne-Romanée *Premier Cru*). Since the names are not well known, and rather difficult for the non-Gallic tongue to pronounce, growers often use the lesser name for these wines despite the general rule that the more specific the name the better the wine and therefore the higher the price. These two vineyards alone increase the Vosne-Romanée vineyard area by 180 acres and there are fifty-one more acres in Flagey, producing wines that carry the name Vosne-Romanée, geography to the contrary. Vineyard acreage actually within Vosne amounts to about 425 acres and the combined amount of wine made in 1960, an average year for quantity, amounted to 144,932 imp. gallons (173,962 U.S.). The classified vineyards of Vosne are:

In Vosne-Romanée

GREAT GROWTHS (*Grands Crus*)

Vineyard	*Acres*
La Romanée-Conti	4·5
Les Richebourg	19·8
La Tâche	14·9

Vineyard	*Acres*
La Romanée	2·1
La Romanée Saint-Vivant	23·6
Les Gaudichots	14·3
Les Malconsorts	14·7
La Grande Rue	3·3
Les Beaux-Monts (also Beaumonts)	6
Les Suchots	32·4
Clos des Réas	5·3
Aux Brûlées	9·6
Aux Petits-Monts	9·2
Aux Reignots	4·2
La Chaume	17·9

In Flagey-Échezeaux

GREAT GROWTHS (*Grands Crus*)

Vineyard	*Acres*
Grands-Échezeaux	22·6
Échezeaux	104·7

Vougeot

Burgundy red and white wines. District: Côte de Nuits, France.

Stand on the vineyard road on the bluff to the south of Chambolle-Musigny and you can see the land pitch sharply down in front of you, revealing on the plateau below the famous castle of the Clos de Vougeot (*q.v.*) surrounded by vineyards, the whole enclosed by a weatherbeaten stone wall.

Excepting the Clos—the largest single vineyard in Burgundy and one of the most famous in the world—there is not a great deal to Vougeot. A tiny settlement nestles to one side of the low wall with its small arched entries, and outside this wall lie several vineyards whose wines are sold—if they conform to the proper minimum standards—as Vougeot followed by the name of the vineyard.

Commune and Clos take their name from the River Vouge, a tiny stream that comes bubbling down the hill separating Vougeot from Chambolle-Musigny. The settlement is an ancient one and its vineyards have been in continuous cultivation for centuries, for when the Cistercians arrived at the beginning of the twelfth century these were among the lands given to them by local squires. The monks pieced together the vineyard which lies within the walls of the Clos, built the château and made the name famous; and they left their stamp on the other vineyards of the area as well. No single group in history has done so much for the cause of fine wines as the Cistercians and their crowning achievements are the Clos de Vougeot and Kloster Eberbach in the Rheingau. The vineyards outside the walls are Les Petits-Vougeots and Les Cras (both planted in Pinot Noir and producing red wines) and La Vigne-Blanche or Clos Blanc de Vougeot (planted in Chardonnay and Pinot Blanc and giving white wine). The Clos Blanc is owned entirely by the Dijon shipping firm of Héritiers Guyot.

The Clos is, of course, the great wine of the commune. The others, however, are pleasant and often entrancing. Red Vougeot is generally full-bodied, filling the mouth, yet it always manages to preserve a certain delicacy, and often has an assertive bouquet all its own. The white is dry, sometimes quite fruity, and very much like one of the white wines from Aloxe-Corton on the Côte de Beaune, without having all the great breed of the finest from Aloxe.

Within the walls of the Clos are 124 acres of vines, but outside are only about thirty. From these thirty, approximately 8,000 imp. gallons (10,000 U.S.) of red wine and 1,000 (1,200 U.S.) of white are produced in an average year for quantity.

GREAT GROWTHS (*Grands Crus*)

Vineyard	*Acres*
Clos de Vougeot	124

FIRST GROWTHS (*Premiers Crus*)

Vineyard	*Acres*
Clos Blanc de Vougeot	4·6
Les Petits-Vougeots	14·4
Les Cras	10·6

The other vineyards have the right to the place-names of Vougeot Village and Vougeot 'Premier Cru'.

Vouvray

Loire Valley dry white wine; still, semi-sparkling or sparkling. District: Touraine, France.

Vouvray is the famous wine of Touraine, the peaceful, park-like Loire Valley region in the heart of the château country. The vineyards climb the slopes, upstream and across the river from Tours, once the centre of the courtly life of the Valois. The wine is produced by eight communes—Chançay, Noizay, Parçay-Meslay, Reugny, Rochecorbon, Sainte-Radegonde, Vernou, and Vouvray itself—and even in lesser years it is a light, delightful wine, excellent to drink with the local blood sausage and *rillettes* (little pots of pork *pâté*) on the terrace of the restaurant of Pont de Cisse which looks out over the sloping vineyards.

These vineyards date from the eighth century, and they have been in continuous production, except for a few years at the end of the last century, when they were devastated by phylloxera. The vines were reconstituted with grafts from sturdy, phylloxera-resistant American root-stocks, and the first harvest from the new plants was gathered about 1900. In 1936 it was laid down that the bearing portions of the vine must be Chenin Blanc or Arbois, and no other grapes are legally permitted.

The vines thrive in a clay and limestone *aubuis* soil on the chalky hills of the district, which also provide cellars for the wines to mature in. The casks are stored in caves cut into the cliff—caves in which people also lead a troglodyte existence. Driving along the river bank towards Vouvray, you can see houses which, often, are merely façades, with rooms dug back into the hillside. The high-vaulted, deep caverns make splendid cellars; in Marc Bredif's, there is a vast, circular tasting room, with an old grindstone set in the middle as a table, and niches cut out of the chalky walls for the bottles.

The wines are characteristically soft and dry, but with a tendency towards sweetness which may become pronounced in a year when the sun has been strong or the picking late: the extra sunshine generates more grape sugar, which ferments into a higher alcoholic content. The sweet wines keep longer than their drier counterparts, and usually travel better; but both types are found abroad. Although Vouvray rarely suffers a poor vintage, the wines are apt to have an acid finish when there has been insufficient sun. Once or twice in a decade, there is a great vintage year, and then the sweet, sunny wines are produced in abundance. Yet most Vouvrays, whether still, sparkling or *pétillants*, are dry, although the driest usually conserves a trace of sugar; unlike the Sauternes, most of the Vouvrays produced from the Chenin grape are short-lived and their chief characteristic is a fruity freshness, although, in the few rich years, exceptions can be found. Some of the more sugary wines are made *mousseux* (sparkling) or *pétillants* (semi-sparkling or crackling); and to many drinkers *pétillants* is synonymous with Vouvray, although a much greater quantity of still table wine is produced.

Vouvray labels rarely carry vineyard names, because wines are generally blended by local firms and sold under their names, although the town or commune of origin is sometimes included. The better bottles, of course, carry the vintage year, the best of which are 1947, 1949, 1955, 1957, 1959, 1961 and 1964. Most of the older vintages, belonging to the occasional great years, are unobtainable today.

All Vouvray must contain at least 11% alcohol (9·5% if it is sparkling); and sparkling wine must be made by the Champagne process (*see* CHAMPAGNE). On an average 1,040,000 imp. gallons (1,150,000 U.S.) of wine are produced annually in this region.

Vrac

Wine sold *en vrac* includes the wine bottle and cork, and may or may not include the capsule and label, but never the price of the case.

V.S.O.

Of Cognacs, this means Very Special Old.

V.S.O.P.

Very Superior Old Pale. This designation used in Cognacs and Armagnacs indicates a brandy in type —but not in actual vintage in the sense of wines— about twelve years old. Market demands being greater in Cognacs, the V.S.O.P.s are sold more quickly, and are now on an average younger than V.S.O.P. Armagnacs. Age in brandy is fully discussed under COGNAC (*q.v.*).

V.V.S.O.P.

Of Cognacs, Very Very Special Old Pale.

Wachau

Important wine zone in Lower Austria. Among the wines from this district are Kremser and Dürnsteiner.

See AUSTRIA.

Wachenheim

Good wine town of the German Palatinate. The best vineyards are Gerümpel, Wolfsdarm, Altenburg, Bächel, Rechbächel, Rennacker, Luginsland.

See PALATINATE.

Wacholder

German beverage resembling gin.

Wachstum

In German, this means the same as *Kreszenz* (*q.v.*).

Waldmeister

German name for woodruff, a wild herb which is essential in May Wine—a popular wine punch made in Germany from a young wine base.

Walporzheim

Region of the German Ahr Valley producing red wine.

See AHR.

Wash

Whisky after fermentation and before distillation.

Washington

Wine-growing state in United States. This is one of the few regions outside California where the *Vitis vinifera* will flourish.

See AMERICA: CALIFORNIA AND THE WEST.

Wassail

English traditional custom of preparing a special punch for Christmas Eve. The name comes from the Anglo-Saxon *wes hál*, 'be in good health'.

Wawern

German white wine of the Saar region. The best-known vineyards are Herrenberg and Goldberg.

See SAAR.

Wedderburn

The heaviest style of British West Indian rum. Pot-distilled and slow-fermented, it used to be the style identified with Jamaica, in contrast to the lighter rums of Puerto Rico and Cuba. Nowadays, however, the different centres make rums of both types, and Jamaica is producing an increasing quantity of the lighter style in addition to Wedderburn and Plummer.

See RUM, BRITISH WEST INDIES; RUM, JAMAICA.

Weeper

British term for leaker (*q.v.*).

Wehlener Sonnenuhr

German wine exports are unanimous in naming Wehlener Sonnenuhr as the best Moselle wine and this in spite of the fact that Bernkasteler Doctor is better-known. No other Moselle, and no other wine in the world, has greater elegance, greater finesse than Sonnenuhr at its best. J. J. Prüm is the greatest name in this wine.

See MOSELLE.

Weibel Vineyards

Alameda County, California, U.S.A.

A company specializing in champagne-type wines; a late-comer among the finer Californian wineries. Rudolph Weibel Sr. had worked with wines in Switzerland and with Champagnes in France since 1906, and afterwards settled in San Francisco in the wine importing business. He and his son, Frederick, founded the Weibel Champagne Vineyards in 1939 at Mission San José in southern Alameda County. The property was once owned by Josiah and Leland Stanford, and wine was sold under the label of Stanford.

The Weibels specialize in bottle-fermented champagne-type and for their Grand Cru Select they use a blend of the very fine Pinot Chardonnay.

See AMERICA: CALIFORNIA AND THE WEST.

Wein

German term for wine.

Weinbauer

German term for wine-grower.

Weinberg

German term for a hillside vineyard.

Weingut

German term for wine estate.

Weinviertel

Important valley and region of Austria lying north of the Danube.

See AUSTRIA.

Weissbier

German name for a sour beer popular in Berlin.

Weissburgunder

The chief grape variety cultivated in Styria, Austria.

Welschriesling

The chief grape variety cultivated in Burgenland, Austria.

Wente Brothers Vineyard

White, red and rosé wines. Livermore, Alameda County, Northern California, U.S.A.

An old-established property in the Livermore Valley, producing good varietal wines—in particular, the finest graves-type and sauternes-type in America. Carl Wente, the founder, came to the U.S.A. from Germany in 1880, and owed his early training in Californian wines to Charles Krug of Napa Valley. Wente put his experience into practice when he purchased, in the latter part of 1883, a few vineyards in the Livermore Valley. The firm has long specialized in top-quality table wines—thanks partly to the excellent soil.

Carl Wente enlarged his property, and his two sons, Ernest and Herman, until recently owners, added to it the valuable El Mocho Vineyards. On the El Mocho property, Louis Mel, the former owner, planted cuttings of Sémillon, Sauvignon Blanc, and Muscadelle du Bordelais from the famous Sauternes vineyard of Château d'Yquem. Today, these fine plants are in the capable hands of the Wente growers and their Château Wente sauterne is perhaps the finest sauternes-type in America.

At the present time the estate has 480 acres of vineyard, of which 90% is planted in such choice white varieties as Chardonnay, Grey Riesling, Sylvaner, Sémillon, Sauvignon Blanc, Muscadelle. Among the 10% of red grape varieties, there are Pinot Noir, Gamay, and Zinfandel.

Most of the Wente wines are very probably labelled with varietal names rather than the misused place-names borrowed from Europe.

Whiskey, American

American whiskey and the American people grew up together. The pioneer needed a drink as sturdy as himself, as rugged as the land he grappled with; something to cure snakebite, ward off disease, something to enjoy when he returned from the lonely plains and forests to the honkytonk saloons. Young whiskey, rough and 'green', helped to sustain the men who conquered the young American continent; and still holds undisputed sway over the tastes of their descendants. Sixteen bottles a year pour down the throat of the average American adult; altogether more than 60 million cases, almost 133 million imp. gallons (160 million U.S.) of whiskey, ranging from well-matured, often magnificent spirit to harsher 'spirit blends', are consumed. Another vast quantity, estimated variously at from 30 million to 80 million U.S. gallons (25 million to 66 million imp.) is sold each year as 'moonshine' or 'bootleg' at a loss to the Government of about 300 million dollars (£107 million) in uncollected excise taxes—and sometimes at a loss to the drinker of his life, to the bootlegger of his liberty. One out of every four drinks of hard liquor consumed in the United States is bootleg—the untamed spirit of the plains still prevails.

Whiskey was originally spelt whisky and was made in the mists and moors of Scotland. Probably at the same time it was whiskey among the peat bogs and lake country of Ireland. Today it is spelt whiskey in the United States and in Ireland. It is made in various parts of the world, but the largest single producer is the United States. American whiskeys differ from their European counterparts not only in taste and aroma but in general nature, too. They are not regional in character; Scotch whisky is inimitably Scotch, Irish whiskey the unique product of Ireland, but American whiskeys are classed by type, not origin. Bourbon, rye, or other styles can be made anywhere in America, and as long as they meet the Government's specifications and pay their taxes, they have the Government's blessing.

Whiskey's Rise to Popularity

The Founding Fathers of the American Republic were not whiskey-drinkers. The pilgrims of the North and the Virginia gentlemen of the South had tastes which turned towards beer and wine, rum and applejack. Whiskey had to await the settlement of Pennsylvania by Scotch-Irish immigrants and the great surge of Westering; and its original production owed much—as is the case with applejack—to poor roads and lack of communication. The settlers had brought over with them the secrets of distilling and the land was fertile—perfect for grain, the base of whiskey. But transport was another problem. The roads that existed were poor, and in rainy seasons impassable, and if the farmer failed to get his crop to market he was ruined. But if he let the grain ferment, distilled it either at his own home in small pot stills or in that of a neighbour, the problem was solved. With the grain turned into whiskey, he had a less bulky cargo and a lighter one—a product that was easier to sell. In Pennsylvania and over in Kentucky, distilling was built up at the small farms into an important industry. The rum-makers of New York tried to have the spirit banned from the state, but in spite of their efforts whiskey won the competition and replaced rum as the common drink. The industry grew and prospered until a famous commotion forced it to move farther west.

In 1791 the government of President Washington was having financial difficulties. To raise money, it established an excise tax on whiskey—and the makers protested. The violence of the Whiskey Rebellion, or insurrection, has been greatly exaggerated, although the President felt called upon to send troops of the militia to ensure the maintaining of peace and order—and the proper collection of excise taxes. The farmers grumbled, declared that the Government was meddling in their private affairs, and moved west, to southern Indiana and Illinois, deeper into Kentucky and farther west in Pennsylvania. Hostile Indians were easier to face than friendly tax collectors. What the farmers looked for—and found—in these areas was pure, clear, distiller's water, with little organic material but rich in sulphate of lime and earthy carbonates; the kind of water found over veins of chalk or limestone. In the eastern United States, a deep base of limestone runs through western Pennsylvania, through Kentucky, Indiana, and southern Illinois, then ducks underground and reappears in Maryland. Today 80% of America's licensed distillers are to be found in these five states, where American distilling came of age.

From these early beginnings, whiskey became a business—and big business at that. In 1911 the nation produced over 100 million U.S. gallons (83 million imp.), a figure which was not to be exceeded until 1935. In between these dates fell the Dark Age of American spirits, when distilleries were closed and padlocked, and bootlegger and smuggler reigned. On 16 November 1920 the Volstead Act became the Eighteenth Amendment to the Constitution of the United States, thus proclaiming Prohibition; and not until 5 December 1933 was the politician ready to admit officially that the noble experiment was in reality a dismal failure. It took the distillers a little while to dust their equipment and get back into production, but by 1935 they were in full swing. Since Repeal—excepting the years of the Second World War—the industry has followed a strong albeit slightly erratic course. Peak production was in 1951, when the amount distilled was over 205 million U.S. gallons (170,600,000 imp.). Since then the industry has stabilized, producing approximately 100 million U.S. gallons (83 million imp.) annually and withdrawing about the same amount from the warehouses where the spirit ages.

Whiskey-making

Whiskey is made from grain. Any grain may be used, but in America the important ones are corn (maize) and rye with some millet, sorghum, and barley. The grain is 'mashed' (diluted with water and cooked in huge pressure cookers) then left to ferment into 'beer' or 'distiller's beer'. Sweet mash whiskey is made by adding selected yeasts to start the fermentation; sour mash by triggering it with some left-over 'spent beer' or 'draff'—the residue of a previous fermentation. Both 'beer' and 'draff' are then pumped into huge patent stills for distillation and rectification. By American law, all whiskey must be distilled at less than 190° proof U.S. (166° British), or about 95% alcohol. Above that figure, the spirit loses all the characteristics or congeners of the grain used and becomes merely neutral or 'silent' spirit. Most whiskey is distilled from 140° to 160° proof, and some as low as 125°, notably some of the better Bourbons and ryes. After distillation, it is diluted and aged (the Bourbon in new, charred oak barrels), is diluted again—to between 80° and 100° proof—and bottled.

The origin of the charred barrel for ageing whiskey is unknown. According to one legend, it began in the West Indies in the making of rum. A fire in a warehouse charred some of the barrels which were used as they were, and the spirit was so improved by the experience that it became general practice to use charred barrels for rum, and later for whiskey. Another story attributes the origin to Kentucky: here the practice of steaming barrel staves to make them bend more easily was overdone and the wood charred; but it is hard to believe that a Kentuckian would be so careless in a matter so important as whiskey. Whatever the origin, the practice improves and softens the taste of the spirit and imparts body and colour to it.

Whiskey Types

American whiskey types are fairly rigidly defined by law. Some definitions have little interest for the consumer, since the types concerned are never on sale and serve merely as the base from which others are developed. The more important (*see also under individual headings*) are:

Bourbon Whiskey

Originally the corn whiskey made in Bourbon County, Kentucky; now any whiskey distilled at no more than 160° proof, stemming from a mash of at least 51% corn, and aged for not less than four years in new charred oak barrels. It may be made by the sour mash process and most bottles will be Straight Bourbon or Blended Straight Bourbon.

Corn Whiskey

Different from Bourbon, corn whiskey must be made from a mash of at least 80% corn, and may be aged in used or uncharred barrels.

Rye Whiskey

The mash must contain at least 51% rye, distillation must be no higher proof than 160°, and ageing accomplished in new charred oak barrels. Some Straight Rye and Blended Straight Rye are found, but not to the same extent as in Bourbon.

Other definitions include:

Whiskey

The most general name of all, never found alone on bottles. A label which carries any other term—Straight, Blended, Bourbon, etc.—must, of course, fulfil the requirements for whiskey as well as for the other terms it carries. According to the Government, whiskey is 'an alcoholic distillate from a fermented mash of grain distilled at less than 190° proof in such a manner that the distillate will have the taste, aroma, and characteristics generally attributed to whiskey, and withdrawn from the cistern room of the distillery at not more than 110° proof and not less than 80° proof and is further reduced before bottling to not less than 80° proof'. Since no ageing period is specified, a bottle simply labelled whiskey would be reasonably raw and undrinkable.

Straight Whiskey

Whiskey distilled at no more than 160° proof and aged at least two years in new charred oak barrels. Straight corn whiskey may be aged in used or uncharred barrels. Straight whiskies found on the market are usually Straight Bourbon or Straight Rye; they comprise about 27% of total whiskey sales.

Blended Straight Whiskey

A blend of two or more straight whiskies. This type makes up only about 1% of whiskey sales, but serves as a base for one of—blended whiskey.

Blended Whiskey

A blend made of at least 20% 100°-proof straight whiskey either with other whiskey or neutral spirit or both, bottled at no less than 80° proof. About 25% of all whiskies sold are blended. The advantage is that they are lighter and less expensive than straights, and the leeway of 80% (which can be made up of any combination of whiskies or plain spirit) allows the distiller to make a consistent standard whiskey, one that will not vary from year to year. It also permits the making of some very poor excuses for whiskey. One to which a large proportion of neutral spirit is added is known as a spirit blend and offers little to the civilized palate. The secret of a blended whiskey at any distillery is in the art of a master blender, who can distinguish what characteristics are needed to produce the replica of the firm's previous whiskey, determine the amounts of each component, and ensure that all the ingredients blend or 'marry' properly. A small amount of Sherry—up to 2½%—may be added as a blending agent.

Bottled-in-Bond Whiskey

The words do not necessarily guarantee a superior whiskey, but in fact this is what is usually indicated. The term is allowed only for straight whiskies, at least four years old, bottled at 100° proof, the product of a single distillery by the same distiller and from a single season or year. The whiskey is aged in Government-controlled warehouses (although control is fiscal, not qualitative) and taxes are paid on withdrawal.

Whiskey, Bourbon

Early in the colonial history of America, a Baptist minister, Elijah Craig, established a still in Georgetown, Kentucky, and began producing whiskey from a base of corn. The still is said to have been the first in Kentucky and the minister christened his product Bourbon County Whiskey, from the county of origin. It was considerably later that Kentucky became the unchallenged headquarters of the American whiskey industry.

Kentucky today has more than half of the nation's licensed distilleries and remains the major source for Bourbon, but the whiskey has long since jumped the county lines. By American regulation the name applies to any whiskey distilled from a fermented mash of grain containing at least 51% corn (the other grains vary, but a good balance is achieved with corn, rye, and malt); distilled at not more than 160° proof (in practice somewhere between 125° and 140° is more common); and aged in new charred oak barrels. Whiskey aged two years in wood and unblended is Straight Bourbon Whiskey;

blended only with other Straight Bourbons, it is Blended Straight Bourbon or Bourbon—A Blend of Straights.

Blended Bourbon is a mixture of Bourbon and other spirit, either whiskey or grain neutral spirit. A Straight Bourbon is usually a heavy, dry, mellow and full-bodied spirit, while a blended one will be lighter, from the addition of neutral spirit. In the United States, Straight Bourbon and Blended Straight Bourbon are the largest selling whiskeys, with some 77 million U.S. gallons (64 million imp.) or approximately 29 million cases sold annually, mostly in the south and west.

When the ground corn has been weighed and prepared for mashing, it is mixed with limestone water and steamed. The other ingredients (as rye and barley malt) are then added. The yeast, sour wine in character, takes about five days to grow; this, with the mash, is pumped through coolers into the fermenters, at a temperature of about 70°F. (21°C.) and left for the necessary period, while the yeast is being nourished by maltose sugars—and so the whiskey is made. Part of the mixture produced while the temperature rises is called new beer, and in distillation this has to be separated from the whiskey by heating—alcohol has a lower boiling point than new beer, therefore the whiskey forms vapours, which are condensed for further distillation. The new whiskey passes into a cistern where the proof is reduced, and is then poured into barrels to mature in a Government bonded warehouse. Every six months characteristics are tested and graded. When it is ready for bottling, it is checked against standard samples of its brand, regauged for tax payment, and then bottled.

Whiskey, Corn

Whiskey distilled from a mash of fermented grain containing at least 80% corn. It is aged, if at all, in used containers, but usually gets little ageing, since the demand for it is in rural areas where fiery, young 'corn likker' sets standards of taste. Corn whiskey, unaged, is raw, colourless, and—to say the least—unsubtle. It differs from Bourbon in many respects; legally, in that Bourbon must be from a mash 51% of which is corn, and must be aged in new, charred cooperage.

See also WHISKEY, AMERICAN.

Whiskey, Irish

'Of all wine, Irish wine is the best' was the ingenuous statement of Peter the Great of Russia; and it simply confirmed what generations of Irish had always believed. Just how many generations is a disputed point, for some maintain that the making of whiskey goes back at least a thousand years; others put it at a mere 500 or so. Unquestionably, long before either whiskey or brandy was commercially remunerative, the Gael—both Irish and Scot—was distilling his fermented barley malt for his own pleasure. The Irish claim that brandy—a comparative newcomer—came about thanks to Irish missionaries taking the secret of distillation into France. How else, they ask, can you explain the similarities in the methods of distilling and the coincidence of *uisge beatha* and *eau-de-vie*, both of which mean 'water of life'?

Until a century ago, Scotch whisky was for Scotsmen and Irish was the stuff which enjoyed popular favour. Then the Scots learned how to blend their brews and still keep them inimitably Scotch, and made them known with brilliant salesmanship. After a period of doubt as to whether these blends could in fact be legally called whisky, after these doubts were resolved by a Royal Commission, the world came clamouring to their door. The world is still there, and the Irish, in spite of improving prospects and faithful adherents all over the globe, are having some trouble in finding an expansion of the markets for their austerely dry pot-still, unblended spirit of distinctive flavour. A further burden on the Irish distiller is high taxation, so that the Irishman cannot afford a fair share of his natural drink, and the moonshiner is attempting to provide a beverage made without the benefit of the excise officials. The popular name for this beverage is 'poteen'—illegal whiskey named from the little—and easily dismantled—pot still in which it is made. Back in the bogs and around the lakes, poteen-making is popular and profitable, and the police rarely catch up with a bootlegger before he has packed his equipment and moved on. If, in his hurry, he were to leave some behind him, the lucky finder would be saved up to *22s. 6d.* (3 dollars) a bottle.

In spite of taxes, the Irishman loves his whiskey. Even horses, they say, hardly know how to leave the stuff alone. It happened some time ago, but they still talk about it in Dublin. Back in a small agricultural town a farmer, after a long night journey, stopped to water his horse at the local trough. The horse drank deep, and when his thirst was quenched, he moved away from the trough, staggered slightly and collapsed—dead drunk. The trough was found to be full of fine, old whiskey, pure and ready to drink. Rejoicing was general until someone called the police who, in turn, called in the local excise people. Their enquiries showed that a nearby distillery was using convenient local waterpipes to drain its whiskey out of an excise-free warehouse for bottling, but someone had got it on the wrong circuit. The fine was large, and horses are staying sober in that part of Ireland now.

The excise officials are not always so fortunate. In spite of their efforts, poteen-making persists in certain areas, and in those parts, it is said that no self-respecting cattle or sheep dealer would consider doing business with a man who didn't offer him a small *deoch* to ward off early morning chill in the winter animal fairs. This may or may not have an effect upon the price, depending presumably upon the quality of poteen offered.

The making of quality Irish whiskey, such as Old Bushmills', follows much the same principles as the making of Scotch. (*For full details of the distilling process, see* WHISKY, SCOTCH.) There are, however, some important differences in procedure. The popular and prestige Irish whiskeys are pure pot-still, containing no grain whiskeys as in the average Scotch. Also, they are three times distilled against twice in Scotland. Next, the mash is all of Irish grain—mostly barley, malted and unmalted, with a little wheat, oats, and rye. The malted barley is not, as it is in Scotland, dried directly over peat, so it lacks the 'smoky' or 'peaty' taste so common in Scotch. The wash, or whiskey before distillation, is placed in great stills, much larger than the Scottish type, sometimes capable of holding up to 16,600 imp. gallons (20,000 U.S.); and distilling is done to bring out the whiskey at about 50° over proof (roughly 86% alcohol by volume or 172° by American standards) instead of 20° over proof (70% or 140° American) preferred by the Scot. As in all pot-still spirits, the middle section of the distillate is the only part drawn off, and the 'heads' and 'tails' are held over to be redistilled. The Irish calculate that a mere 10% of the wash comes over as whiskey, and much of this will evaporate as the spirit ages.

An Irishman, writing on his native whiskey, says it takes seven days of a man's time to make whiskey and seven years of its own. The man may spend a greater or lesser amount of time making the preparations, but the whiskey will not really be worth the name unless it gets the full time, although by Irish law it is mature at five. Some is aged for ten years, and the very best for twelve or fifteen—always in the wood; for once out of the cask whiskey will age no more.

Scotch whisky is a blend of heavy malt whisky with grain whisky which changes the characters of both ingredients and produces what the world knows as Scotch. On the other hand, Irish whiskey blends, in the mash, the ingredients of malt and grain and, after pot-still distillation, the addition of grain whiskey or grain spirit has no syllogistic effect but merely weakens the flavour. Irish whiskey will have caramel added—to give it the proper colour—and water, so that it will be within reasonable limits. Most is sold at 30° under proof in Britain and Ireland (80° proof American), but this is subject to minor variations. Furthermore, most of the whiskey is the traditional pot-still whiskey. Irishmen have been pushing Irish punch (Irish whiskey, lemon peel, sugar, and boiling water) and Irish coffee (Irish whiskey, coffee, and sugar with a layer of cream floating over the top) in promoting their product—and there are now several blended whiskies on the market. While they have been criticized for not adapting their ideas earlier to changing world taste their critics are perhaps unaware of the true nature of the product. There can be no doubt that a characteristic pot-still Irish whiskey properly aged is a magnificent spirit.

Whiskey, Rye

Most American rye whiskey is made in the states of Pennsylvania and Maryland, and is consumed generally in that region. Straight Rye accounts for less than 500,000 U.S. gallons (332,000 imp.) of whiskey per year and many consumers switched from it during and after the war when several well-known brands changed from making straight to making blended whiskey.

According to Government regulations, rye must be distilled from a mash of fermented grain containing at least 51% rye, at a proof not to exceed 160°, and must be aged in new charred oak barrels. Straight Rye has at least two years' barrel-age and is unblended; Blended Straight Rye—as the name implies—is a blend of two or more Straight Ryes. Bottles labelled simply Blended Rye will have neutral spirit or sometimes other whiskeys added, resulting in a lighter, less distinctive, less expensive spirit. Ryes are generally heavier and slightly more austere than Bourbons, with some affinity to Irish whiskey, although they are made in patent stills instead of Irish-style pot stills.

Whisky, Canadian

The most distinctive characteristic of Canadian whisky generally speaking is its lightness of body. All Canadian whisky, Canadian rye whisky, must, by Federal law, be produced from cereal grain only. The combination of grains used, their treatment, and the special and rigid control exercised by the distiller during the entire production process, set Canadian whisky apart from any other grain distillate.

Canadian whisky is well known outside its own country and its good reputation has been built up over 130 years by one company, over 100 years by each of four others, and by several distillers not so long established who are yet maintaining the traditions of their elders.

This is how Canadian whisky is made.

The Grain

No amount of ageing will make good whisky out of an inferior batch of grain. Therefore, when the grain is moved to the distillery, none is accepted until it has been thoroughly tested and approved by the distiller's chemist. When the grain, which consists of corn and rye and barley malt, has been milled into a fine meal or coarse flour, it is fed into a large cooker containing a fixed amount of water. This mash is heated with live steam in order to get the starch into solution and when this has been accomplished, barley malt is added to convert the starch into grain sugar. This step, saccharification, produces the grain sugar which is later fermented into alcohol by the introduction of yeast.

The Yeast

The culture and development of the yeast is a full-length story in itself. Each distillery carefully develops in test-tube bottles an isolated, pampered culture. One of the most critical points of control is the development of the living yeast cells. Since these *are* alive, sterile techniques and extreme caution are employed to prevent contamination.

Fermentation

The mash which has been saccharified is pumped from the cookers through large cooling coils into fermentation vats or tanks, which are then inoculated with the living yeast cells. The cells convert the sugar in the mash into alcohol and carbon dioxide, and this process takes about three to four days.

Distillation

When fermentation is complete the fermented mash is pumped into a continuous-operation, temperature-controlled, multiple-column patent still, usually cylindrical in shape and several storeys high. This complex modern equipment allows many variations in the distilling procedure and consequently many variations in the final product. Thus the distiller is able to control the concentration of those components which contribute the flavour to the whisky.

Ageing

The next major step is the ageing of the whisky. Canadian distillers have found nothing that can do the job of mellowing and maturing their product better than nature itself. The unmatured whisky from the still is reduced to barrelling strength and put into wood casks or barrels which may be charred on the inside, and this young whisky now faces a four-, six-, eight-, or twelve-year wait, in temperature-controlled warehouses. During the ageing process, a number of slow chemical reactions occur, the more volatile components of the whisky evaporate and the wood brings out a mellowing process. Certain wood sugars and tannin are extracted from the wood and it is these extracts which give the whisky its golden colouring. When sufficiently aged, various batches of whisky are 'married'—an art in itself. The resulting product is tasted and tested for quality, and when approved, the whisky is filtered many times, bottled, labelled, and ready for the market.

Canadian whisky for consumption in Canada is bottled at 70° proof (Sikes) or 39·9% of absolute alcohol by volume. Canadian whisky bottled in Canada for export is usually bottled at the proof strength permitted or used in the country of destination. It is exported to 154 different countries and territories throughout the world.

The Canadian distiller is subject to more Government supervision and control than any other manufacturer or privately-owned enterprise in the nation. Some 200 excise officers are stationed in Canadian distilleries and their control extends from the receipt of grain at the distillery, all through the production process, bottling, and shipment, and terminates with the payment of excise duty.

There is no Government interference, however, with the distilling techniques employed by individual distillers. Each has complete control over the quality and character of his products.

The label on a bottle of Canadian whisky which states distilled, aged, blended, bottled under Canadian Government supervision is no idle boast, it is a statement of fact.

Whisky, Malt

This is Scotch whisky made in Scotland entirely from malted barley (with yeast and water), to be distinguished from grain whiskies in which some maize (corn), wheat, oats, or rye will be used.

Malt whisky is distilled in pot stills, grain whisky in patent stills. For this reason, grain whisky distilleries can turn out many times more than malt whisky distilleries in the same length of time.

There are three types of Scotch malt whisky: Highland Malt, West Highland Malt now known as Islay malt, and Lowland Malt. The first is produced widely throughout the Highlands in some eighty distilleries, half of them in the vicinity of the River Spey. This is considered the best. West Highland, from Islay in the Inner Hebrides and the peninsula of Kintyre, is usually stronger-flavoured. The comparatively few distilleries in the south making Lowland Malt Whisky produce it generally for blending. West Highland Malts are often referred to as Islay or Campbeltown. There are seven distilleries on the island of Islay and one on the island of Jura producing Islay malts with the characteristic 'smokiness' which has made them famous. They are Ardbeg, Eowmore, Bruichladdich, Bunnahabhain, Caol Ila, Lagavulin and Laphroaig, and Isle of Jura.

See WHISKY, SCOTCH.

Whisky, Scotch

Scotch whisky is imitated everywhere. At one time the Japanese made it in a town they renamed Aberdeen for the benefit of their bottle labels. The Germans, thorough if not successful, imported the actual water from Speyside in Scotland, but they did not get Scotch, which was, and remains, inimitable.

Just why it is that Scotch can be made only in Scotland is one of the mysteries—akin to the unanalysable combination of known ingredients that is the true virtue of great wines. Supposedly, Scotch is merely the product of barley, yeast, Scottish water and Scottish air, and a distilling process which holds no mystery at all.

The barley, it appears, can come from anywhere. It has been imported from as far away as Australia or California, or grown at home in Scotland or England. The foreign barley used to be considered the better, because the drier—an important factor—but now, as a result of sterling restrictions, most of it is domestically grown. What makes Scotch 'Scotch' is another matter. Blending—these days—has something to do with it. Until a century ago, Scotch was for Scotsmen, a straight, high-proof beverage. Blending began, and it is this trick which has carried the fame of the drink around the world—only in Scotland is unblended 'singles' Scotch whisky to be found in any quantity. The secret of the blending lies in the fact that all the components are Scottish, with Scotch malt whisky as the irreplaceable base. To produce their unique malt whiskies, the Scottish distillers themselves rely on techniques which are more like magic than science. It is an authentic story that the actual physical shape of the pot still can have something to do with the whisky distilled in it; and one distiller, having built a new still and never being able to recapture the lost beauty of his spirit, was compelled to have his worn-out still recopied—including the patches.

The whisky runs through quite a history—and several identities—before it becomes the Scotch we know. Arrived at the distillery, barley is screened to get rid of extraneous seeds, etc. Following, generally, a period of storage, there is the steeping: the barley is plunged into water in large vats and left for a predetermined saturation period. Then it goes to the broad cement floors where the maltmen spread and tend it. In two to three days it germinates; rootlets spring forth, and when, four or five days later, these wither and the grain becomes modified, the maltmen consider that the barley is 'malted'.

The malt is conveyed to the kiln floor, where it lies on sheets of perforated metal until thoroughly dried by warm air from peat fires burning below. Towards the end of this process, when it is considered that the green malt has absorbed so much of the peaty flavour that it will retain it till liquor meets palate, coke or anthracite is added to bring the temperature to 160°F. (71°C.). Devised to let the controlled heat pass off, the kiln roofs are cowled with 'pagoda tops', the air escaping under the ruffled eaves nowadays aided by extractor fans which lend a strange Chinese grace to the sturdy blunt, Scottish stone buildings.

After its trial by fire, the malt is allowed to rest for about two months, then it is screened, and the withered rootlets, or malt culms, are strained off to become useful cattle food. The malt itself is ground or crushed in a roller mill of appropriate design.

The ground malt is then poured into the mash tun, a great claw-armed, circular tub, with a sprocket rod, splashing endlessly around, stirring the crushed malt through the seething water. Four waters, each hotter than the one before, are used in this extracting of the solubles from the malt. This solution is called 'wort'—pronounced wurt. The first two waters, which have been saved from an earlier extraction, are known as the 'sparge'. The infused waters passing off from the tun stream through the cooling machine which cools them down by 72% to 75°F. (24°C.), an appropriate temperature for adding yeast. After this, they are lodged in the fermenting vats, usually called the backs. The third and fourth washings of waters become the new sparge, to be saved and used as first and second waters in a later extraction. The residue after the wort is drawn is the draff, or cattle food.

Yeast is added to the wort in the backs—fermenting vats sometimes of larch or pine but nowadays often of steel—and fermentation begins. The active element of the yeast changes the sugary wort into alcohol and carbon dioxide; the carbon dioxide escapes into the air and the alcohol remains at about a gallon of proof spirit per ten gallons of wort. Once again the name of this product we are following through its conversion from barley to whisky changes. What was once malt, and then wort, is now 'wash'.

The wash flows into the copper pot stills—dully-gleaming affairs which in the great distilleries can dwarf the size of a man—and is distilled. It passes through a phase after the first distillation when it carries still another name, 'low wines' (because it has not yet reached the height of full strength); but during redistillation the clear and stronger fractions are collected in the Spirit Receiver Vat and are now classified as whisky. This new whisky will be about 16° over proof or about 58% alcohol by volume, and will require to be reduced a little by pure spring water. At around 11° over proof or 55·5% alcohol by volume, it enters the cask. The distiller will have expected to get a range of from two-and-a-half to three gallons from his bushel of barley, but he will lose something of both strength and volume while his whisky lies for the maturation period in cask. In a damp climate he will lose more strength and in a dry one more volume. It is something to think about that each year 2,500,000 imp. gallons (3 million U.S.) of Scotch whisky evaporate into the soft Scottish air.

The cask itself is the final contribution to the beauty of the whisky. This improves greatly with age—in barrel, not in bottle—and it matures usually in casks made from American oak. The casks must be oak. When wine-steeped casks are not obtainable, the distiller will have to add a little caramel or burnt-sugar colouring to give his whisky the tawny tinge the public expects.

Whisky casks are known as butts if they hold over 80 imp. gallons (96 U.S.); as hogsheads if they hold from 45 to 80 imp. gallons (54–96 U.S.); barrels if they hold 35–45 imp. gallons (42–54 U.S.) and as quarters if their capacity is less than 30 imp. gallons (36 U.S.). Octaves hold between 9 and 15 imp. gallons (11–18 U.S.). The butts are of three different types, varying in shape; puncheons, pipes, and one called simply a butt.

The blenders are the great artists of the whisky trade, and it is fascinating to see these men at their work, going more by sense of smell than taste, their nostrils dilating sensitively in the tall, narrow, tulip-shaped, nose-ing glasses with their short two-finger-wide stems. When a blender has made his selections, the ingredients are mixed together by paddle stirrers in colossal vats, then left to 'marry'. The proportions will be about 40% malt whisky and 60% grain whisky, though occasionally these will be approximately reversed. It is the blending which creates the infinite scale of whiskies; it is not uncommon for a blend to be made up from as many as fifty types. Most experts agree that the best Scotch blends usually consist of about half Highland and Lowland malts, a little Islay or Campbeltown, and the remainder, unmalted grain whisky. On the whole, the Highland malts are light in body and full-flavoured; the Lowland malts are also light, but less distinctly smoky; while the Campbeltowns and Islays are noted for heavy body and plenty of smoke.

Before bottling, whisky is reduced by the addition of soft water from the Scottish lochs—and it is filtered.

The shortage of Scotch in the nineteen-forties was mainly the result of the wartime ban on distilling and the limited ration of barley allowed the industry in the first years after the war (the quota of barley 1945–1950 covered one year's distillation), combining with the long period necessary for ageing. Another factor has been the great increase in world sales, especially in the United States. At the present time, when supplies are fortunately adequate, Americans are drinking thirteen million—or more—cases a year of this most popular of all the grain spirits—which has now become the most fashionable aperitif and nightcap drink in France and other European countries. The present trend shows an increase in the consumption of single malts.

The rise in excise on Scotch whisky has been astronomical. A hundred years ago it was 10*s.* (1.40 dollars) a proof gallon. The two great upward leaps were after the two world wars—to £1 10*s.* (4.20 dollars) after the First; and to £11 11*s.* 11*d.* (32.47 dollars) after the Second. In 1967 it is £16 1*s.* 3*d.* (45 dollars).

White Port

Port wine (Oporto, Portugal) made from white grapes. Generally, it inclines to be a little sweeter than red Port and finds its great market in France; but there is a growing tendency also to manufacture a dry white Port which is served as an aperitif in Portugal and is beginning to be known and appreciated abroad.

See PORT.

White Rot

A blight of vines.

See CHAPTER EIGHT, p. 37.

Wienerwald-Steinfeld

A good vineyard region in Austria, embracing Gumpoldskirchen and Baden.

See AUSTRIA.

Wiltingen

A town in the Saar Valley, south-west of Trier. The 350 acres of surrounding vineyards produce excellent white wines of which the best-known is Scharzhofberg.

See SAAR.

Wine

The word should apply only to the naturally fermented juice of the grape, although it is extended too often to 'wines' made from vegetables, berries, and other fruits. The term is abused especially in reference to drinks made from cherries. True wine produced from grapes can be divided into three main types:

1. Still beverage, or table wines to accompany a meal. These divide again into red, white, and rosé (according to the grapes used and the length of time the skins have been left to ferment with the juice); and into dry or sweet wines, depending on whether all the grape sugar has been allowed to ferment into alcohol, or whether some residual sugar has been left.
2. Sparkling wines, of which Champagne, made by the process of secondary fermentation in bottle, is the finest example.
3. Fortified wines, such as Port, Sherry, and Madeira, to which brandy has been added.

The different wine-growing countries make, from a variety of grapes, numerous wines in each category—every one of importance is to be found under its own heading.

For an analysis of the nature of wine and an account of how it is made, *see* CHAPTER NINE, pp. 39–55.

Wine Counterfeiters and Grape Thieves

Throughout history the growers of the grape have not dealt lightly with those who pilfered or tampered with their products. In Germany, grape thieves were led through the villages with their hands held up before them and locked in a fiddle-shaped, wooden vice. This was equipped with a bell which clanged above their heads, so that all the villagers might turn out to mock them. Alternatively, the thief might be forced to ride backwards through the town on a donkey, the stolen goods in his hands, the legend emblazoned on his back and breast: 'He stole grapes!' It was in Germany also that wine counterfeiters and wine adulterators were severely punished during the Middle Ages, being sentenced to death for falsifying the honest product of the grape.

Wine Fountains

For hundreds of years the wine fountains, from which wine flowed in place of water, brightened the scene at harvest and other festivals in many countries. Old German chronicles tell of the wine fountain of Urach (claiming to be the oldest in Germany with its date of 1474) where the wine flowed for three days and nights in alternating jets of red and white, to celebrate a royal wedding. Wine fountains were known to the Egyptians, the Greeks and the Romans. Today the custom has been revived and the wine fountains flow at many European harvest festivals.

Wine Gallon

A gallon of 160 British (128 U.S.) fluid ounces of wine or spirits irrespective of proof or alcoholic strength; also known as bulk gallon.

See PROOF GALLON.

Wine Societies

Different wine-making districts of France have each their own society or *confrérie*, part mediæval relic, part sales promotion. Growers and shippers take part, dressed in the historic costumes with which they have been invested at a long ceremony of inauguration, followed by a feast. Among the more famous of these associations are the Commanderie du Bontemps du Médoc et de Graves (*q.v.*), La Connétablie de Guyenne, La Jurade de Saint-Émilion, Les Chevaliers du Tastevin at Nuits-Saint-Georges, Les Compagnons du Beaujolais, La Commanderie de Champagne de l'Ordre des Coteaux, La Confrérie des Chevaliers de la Chantepleure de Vouvray, and La Confrérie Saint-Étienne in Alsace. There are societies, also, in honour of the great French brandies: La Confrérie des Alembics Charentais, at Cognac; and La Compagnie des Mousquetaires d'Armagnac (*q.v.*) at Condom.

Winkel

Town with several good vineyards on the bank of the Rhine.

See RHEINGAU.

Wintrich

Good white-wine district of the German Middle Moselle.

See MOSELLE.

Winzer

German term for wine grower. Winzerverein on a label indicates that the wine has been produced by a co-operative.

Wood

The cask. Wine is 'in the wood' when it is in the cask.

Woody

This can indicate two conditions in a wine or spirit, usually curable: (1) a smell from wholesome oak when the liquor has been too long in the cask; (2) a taint from defective wood.

Worcester

Wine district of the Cape Province.

See SOUTH AFRICA.

Wort

The extract from malt which is fermented to make malt whisky. The word is pronounced wurt.

See WHISKY.

Württemberg (Germany)

The Württemberg region is the valley of the River Neckar, flowing north and then north-west from above Stuttgart to its confluence with the Rhine at Mannheim and the valleys of the five smaller rivers that enter it. These are the Rems, Enz, Zaber, Kocher, and Jagst.

After numerous setbacks, Württemberg wines began to improve in quality during the last century, mainly under the influence of the Association for the Betterment of the Wine founded in 1824 and later the basis of the co-operatives; and by means of the replanting of the vineyards with Riesling and other noble vines. Although Württemberg is still one of the largest German producers, replanting, conversion of vineyards to other farm uses, the invasion of the vine-louse phylloxera at the end of the last century, and the expansion of city and industrial areas, have reduced the total vine plantation considerably. The wines are not among the most interesting in Germany, and in at least one way Württemberg seems unsuited for wine production: the area is a meeting point for the warmth coming from the sea zones and for the continental land-mass cold. This causes sudden and violent changes of weather, storms and, worst of all for the wine, sharp, unexpected frosts in spring and autumn. Offsetting the generally unfavourable weather, to some extent, is the warming influence of the rivers along which most of the vineyards are situated.

The important red-wine grape variety from the point of view of quantity is the Trollinger, which gives a rather harsh wine from exceptionally large grapes. Better red wines, as elsewhere in Germany, come from the Spätburgunder plant, originally the Pinot Noir of Burgundy.

Best white wines are Riesling, followed by Sylvaner, and to a lesser extent Traminer and Ruländer (an adaptation of the French Pinot Gris).

Würzburg

Centre of the German Stein wines of Franconia (*q.v.*).

Wynberg

First district in Cape Province to produce wine.

See SOUTH AFRICA.

Xérès

French for Sherry (*q.v.*). Xeres was the name given by the ancient Romans to the Sherry city of Jerez.

X.O.

The oldest style of Cognac found on the general market. The designation is used mainly by the Cognac firm of Hennessy. While, except in the exceedingly rare vintage brandies, age designations in brandy indicate a style rather than an exact number of years, X.O.s often claim, and frequently have, about forty years of barrel-age. (Brandies, like other spirits, do not age in bottle.) Age in brandy is fully discussed under Cognac (*q.v.*).

Xynisteri

One of the dominating grapes in Commandaria, the famous dessert wine of Cyprus. The other is the Mavron.

Yakima Valley

Wine region in Washington State, one of the rare districts outside California where European grape-vines have flourished.

See AMERICA: CALIFORNIA AND THE WEST.

Yalumba

Famous vineyard in Eden Valley, South Australia, from which comes a dry white wine called Carte d'Or.

See AUSTRALIA.

Yam Wine

Beverage fermented from yam roots in Africa and South America.

Yamanashi

One of the main vine-growing districts of Japan (*q.v.*).

Yawa

West African palm wine.

Yayin

Biblical term for wine, evidently related to *vinum, wein*, etc.

Yeasts

Natural, microscopic, unicellular organisms found on the skins of grapes, and responsible for alcoholic fermentation. One of these, *Saccharomyces ellipsoïdeus,* is the true wine-maker, which gives the wine its character and its main constitution. As the last grammes of sugar are fermented out, this yeast disappears and dies. A lesser variety, *Saccharomyces oviformis*, important in the white wines of Bordeaux, as well as in the Pomerols and Saint-Émilions, is more resistant to alcohol than *S. ellipsoïdeus,* and increases as fermentation advances. *Saccharomyces acidifaciens*, yet another variety of fermenting yeast, is often found to be a cause of trouble in white wines. In many modern wineries yeast selections or cultures are chosen with great care.

Undesirable yeasts may also be found in ripe grapes. These can be destroyed by sulphuring of the must, and by adding cultured yeasts.

See CHAPTER NINE, pp. 41–2.

Yeso

In Spain, gypsum-rich dust used for 'plastering' (*q.v.*).

Château d'Yquem

Bordeaux white wine. District and commune: Sauternes, France.

Château d'Yquem is the greatest natural sweet white wine, the only wine which can always, without fear of argument, be claimed to be the best of its kind—although a few Trockenbeerenauslesen of Germany may in great years be compared with it. This was recognized in ratings of Bordeaux in the eighteenth century; and in 1855, when Sauternes and Médoc were classified on the basis of their known excellence and sales, d'Yquem was the only wine classed a First Great Growth (*Premier Grand Cru*).

Distinguished even among the finest of the other Sauternes by an extra suavity and full richness and vinous luscious depth, and a more beautiful gold in colour, d'Yquem is the result partly of the highest possible wine-making standards, partly of the magnificent exposure of the terrain on a hill commanding the whole Sauternes district, and also of something almost magical which must be in the soil itself. In every great wine zone there are one or two plots which somehow manage, year in and year out, to produce wines better even than those of vineyards touching their borders. There is no more remarkable example of this than Château d'Yquem.

The property, which had produced wine for two or three centuries before that, came into the family of the Marquis de Lur-Saluces, by marriage, in 1785. It is owned and directed today by the Marquis Bertrand de Lur-Saluces, who was a great campaigner for all French wines and was the head both of the French wine promotional organization and the Association of the Classified Growths of Bordeaux. A century and a half ago, Thomas Jefferson had already written: 'Sauterne. This is the best white wine of France and the best of it is made by Monsieur de Lur-Saluces.' Add an *s* to Sauterne, and place the word 'sweet' in front of white wine to avoid controversy about the excellence of some dry whites, and the statement is true today.

Château d'Yquem is and always has been expensive. Today, it is generally sold to Bordeaux shippers *en vrac*—that is to say, at the château with no charges added for casing, etc.—at about 35 francs (approximately £2 10s or 7 dollars) per bottle. It achieved what was probably the highest price paid for any wine in the last century when the brother of the Emperor of Russia bought four barrels of the 1847 vintage for 20,000 francs (about £3,646 or 10,200 dollars nowadays). Costly as it is, the high price of the wine is justified not only by market demand, but by two special factors. In 1904, Château d'Yquem, first of all the Sauternes vineyards, introduced the practice of using only hyper-rich, half-rotted grapes attacked by the so-called noble rot (*pourriture noble*). This process—requiring the vineyard to be picked over many times because the bunches reached the desired maturity at different intervals—has made the production of all Sauternes expensive and is now the practice in all Sauternes vineyards. Château d'Yquem, in addition to this, sells under its own name only the best; the wine of poor years or from lesser sections in mediocre years is sold to the trade simply as Sauternes, at a financial loss. In 1954, for example, the vineyard declared 336 barrels of fine wine and 172 barrels of district Sauternes; and in 1955, 480 barrels with 100 barrels of Sauternes. 'All the wines of Château d'Yquem are château bottled. But the vineyard gives its name only to wines very rigorously selected . . .'—Marquis Bertrand de Lur-Saluces. Until 1876, different segments of the pressing were sold separately in differing grades, but since that date the harvest has been equalized by the vatting together of the pick of different days. The wine has an extremely long life, and bottles of 100 years and older can still be found in excellent condition, if they have been properly kept. Although this great sweet wine is properly appreciated, the present fashion for dry wines is so irresistible that Château d'Yquem is now making some fair dry white wine called Château Y.

The castle itself, a turreted and walled château-fort on its high hill, is one of the landmarks of south-western France; and one of the most charming evenings to be spent in Europe is at the annual concert given in the great courtyard by some internationally-known string quartet as part of the May Bordeaux Music Festival. The floodlit château gleams like a fairy-tale castle, its battlements and towers visible over miles of the dark Sauternes countryside.

Hail is the great enemy of the vineyard, and in both 1951 and 1952 the crop was wiped out.

Characteristics. Full-bodied and luscious with superb finesse, this expensive wine is well worth the price. It ages exceedingly well, for maderization acquired through ageing becomes an asset and is not offensive. The great sweetness offsets any overlay of excessive oxidation.

Vineyard area: 213 acres.

Average production (varies greatly): between 7,200 and 11,000 cases d'Yquem. Between 3,000 and 4,000 cases downgraded to be sold as Sauternes.

Yugoslavia

Yugoslavia, the state of the Southern Slavs, which now embraces the Croatian and Slovene provinces of the Austro-Hungarian Empire, Serbia, Montenegro and Macedonia, has the eighth largest vineyard area in Europe.

In few places does wine better fulfil the truism that it never tastes as good as where it is grown. In Macedonia and Montenegro, almost self-contained and inaccessible parts of the world which have kept their native characteristics even today, the wines, when you drink them there, are enhanced by the local costumes, the hardy romance of the surroundings, and sometimes by the very vessels in which they are kept. The carved, round, wooden brandy- and wine-flasks, ornate canteens with their leather bindings and carrying-straps of braid, are among the most attractive in the world. It is not necessary to visit the rugged regions to experience the charm of Yugoslav wines. Many thousands of tourists taste the red wines of Dalmatia in the white, walled city of Dubrovnik. A very different experience from drinking such full, red, alcoholic (15–16%) southern wines as Dingač (pronounced Dingach) or Bol in their place of origin is that of drinking the white wines of Slovenia in the Alpine north.

At the present time, Dalmatian wines are probably not at their potential best, and the wines of Slovenia are more fully realized. Slovenian white wines, Serbian white, red, and rosé, some of the wines of Istria, and lately the dry white wines and red wines of Macedonia are frequently to be met with in Great Britain and the United States. The countries to which Yugoslavia chiefly exports her wines are Germany, both East and West, Czechoslovakia, Poland, and Britain.

History

Wine is of very ancient origin in Yugoslavia, as it is in all the Mediterranean and Balkan countries. Some historians say it came from Thrace, up through the Macedonian mountains and into what is now Yugoslavia, about four thousand years ago. It is certainly true that the Dalmatian and Istrian wines flourished under the Greeks, and Slovenian wines under the Romans. Slovenia and the Danube Plain (Croatia) are full of Roman remains, decorated very often with wine and grape motifs; the several languages of Yugoslavia have common words for various aspects of vine care and wine-making, taken direct from the Latin; and the museums in towns as far apart as Dubrovnik in Dalmatia and Ptuj in Slovenia, not fifty miles south of the Austrian border, have many Greek and Roman wine amphoræ and implements dug up in the environs.

Here as in other countries of Europe, wine culture was carried on by the feudal lords and the great monasteries in the Middle Ages. We hear of the wines of Ohrid, far in the south, and of Albania, being in great favour in Europe at the time of the Crusades.

It must be remembered, however, that for centuries part of Yugoslavia was overrun by the Turks. Sarajevo, in the centre of the country, is even today the most Turkish city west of Istanbul. The needle-minarets of its seventy or eighty mosques remind us of the Moslem influence; and the Moslem is forbidden to drink wine. Thus where the Turk dominated, viticulture was abandoned until these regions were liberated from Moslem influence—a slow process of emancipation lasting from 1804 until 1912.

On the other hand parts of what is now Yugoslavia belonged to Austria. Ljutomer, for instance, was for centuries in Styria and thus was Austrian. The consequence was that northern Yugoslav wines and methods of viticulture are typically Austrian. Even today, confusion is caused by the fact that certain of these wines gained a world reputation under German names, which are now being replaced by Yugoslav appellations. Ljutomer, one of Yugoslavia's most famous wines, named after the town near which it grows, in the northernmost tip pressed into Austria and Hungary, first became known as Luttenberger, its Austrian name, and was frequently supposed to be a wine from Austria. It is seldom realized that Luttenberger and Ljutomer are different names for the same wine.

Vines and Statistics

Yugoslavia has something over 600,000 acres of vineyards and produces roughly 104,250,000 imp. gallons (125 million U.S.) of wines yearly, thus taking its place approximately in the same category as the United States, Greece, Hungary, and Rumania. Some ten different agencies handle the export of these wines, and exports have risen considerably in recent years. Between 1953 and 1955 the increase was from some 1,665,000 imp. gallons (2 million U.S.) to more than 4,580,000 imp. gallons (5,500,000 U.S.), much of which was accounted for by the reopening of trade relations between Yugoslavia and the Iron Curtain countries.

The vines grown are numerous and varied. Particularly in the north of the country, where the Austrian influence was most felt, there are imported vines such as Riesling, Traminer, Sylvaner, Merlot, and Sauvignon. However, a number of native vines are also used—as are hybrids, many of which were planted at the time of the phylloxera crisis which hit Yugoslavia about the turn of the century.

Wine-growing Districts

Yugoslavia was created just after the First World War out of six separate Slavonic-speaking states: Serbia, Croatia, Slovenia, Bosnia-Herzegovina, Montenegro, and the northern part of Macedonia. While they make up a harmonious whole, each state still clings to its ancient habits and customs, and the wines grown in each are different from the others. The proportional amounts of wine by state are as follows: *Serbia* 45%; *Croatia* 35%; *Slovenia* 9%; *Macedonia* 9%; *Bosnia-Herzegovina* 2%; *Montenegro* negligible.

Serbia

Serbia is the great bulk-wine producing section of Yugoslavia and most of the wines grown there will be more likely to be served in the place of their origin, often as carafe wines, than found abroad. They are named after the general district from which they come (example: wines from the huge region of Župa will sell as Župa Red). Most of the Serbian wines are made from the Prokupac vine, which is commonly known as the 'national vine of Serbia'. Some of the following names are the best known:

Župa (pronounced Zhoopa). Here, in the centre of Serbia, the warm, sun-bathed hills produce a vast amount of red wine which is full, heavy, and rich, but not particularly noted for its breed or distinction. A pink, or rosé wine is also made, and both types stem from the Prokupac vine. The vineyards are extensive, with the city of Aleksandrovac as the central wine town. (The ending 'ac' in Yugoslav names is pronounced as if written 'ats', e.g. Prokupats, Aleksandrovats.)

Krajina (pronounced Krayina). Centred around the city of Negotin, this district lies on the borders of Rumania and Bulgaria. The wines are almost entirely red, made from a blend of the Prokupac, Skadarka, and Začinak vines. They were once fairly well known in France where they were sent at the time of the worst of the phylloxera crisis at the end of the last century. A white wine is also made, known as Bagrina of Krajina, after the vine used.

Vlasotinci (pronounced Vlasotinsi). From the south of Serbia. Most of the wines are pink and are made from the Prokupac vines with some Plovdina.

Venčac-Oplenac (pronounced Ventchats-Oplenats). Up the Morava River from Župa, this region is the heart of the part of Serbia called Šumadija (Shumadiya) where the insurrection against Turkish

rule started at the beginning of the last century. Wines are grown—the main headquarters being the city of Topola—mainly from the Prokupac, Pinot Noir, and Gamay vines; both red and rosé wines are made. The rosé of Oplenac is well known.

Smederevo. An enormous region lying on the rolling hills on the south side of the Danube near the Rumanian border. A rather ordinary white wine is produced here; and a good white wine comes from the Smedervka grape.

Fruška Gora; *Subotica*; *Čoka*; and *Vršac.* These three regions lie in the great Danubian plain near the Hungarian and Rumanian borders and produce mostly white wines. The major vines used are the Traminer, Riesling, and Ezerjo. The white wines of Fruška Gora, softer and not quite so fresh as the Slovenian growths, have latterly shown a marked improvement in quality.

Kosmet. A district in the extreme south of Serbia near the Albanian border. Kosmet makes good red wine from new vineyards.

Croatia

The wines of Croatia can most conveniently be divided into two major types: those which are grown in the inland section stretching from the broad Danubian plain to the mountains above Zagreb, and those which come from the Adriatic coast, including the wines of the once Italian portion of the Istrian Peninsula and of the fabulous Dalmatian coast.

The inland vine-growing districts include the valleys of the Danube, Drava, and Sava rivers and extend to the alpine slopes which lead into Slovenia, adjoining the famous wine district of Ljutomer, perhaps the best in Yugoslavia. The flatter vineyards produce wines more like those in Serbia, however; most of them are light, slightly acid but agreeable wines with no particular breed but without pretence. The wines most frequently met with include those from Plješevica (pronounced Plyeshivitsa), Vinica (Vinitsa), Varaždin (Varajdeen), and Medjugorica (Mejugoritsa).

In the north-east part of Croatia, the vineyards start climbing the slopes and the Austrian influence begins to make itself felt. Traminers and Rieslings, Sauvignons and Sémillons make their appearance in the vineyards and these white wines, when they are well made, are numbered amongst the best of the country, having a richness in alcohol, a trace of unfermented sugar and a perfume that may be expected in wines from such vines. The important vine-growing towns are Kutjevo (pronounced Kutyevo), Erdut, Ilok, Vukovar, Belji, Djakoro, and Slavonski Brod.

Along the coast are the vineyards of Istria and Dalmatia. Hills recede inland from the broken coastline and the land is covered with huge rocks. The hills themselves are shaved bare by the constant Adriatic wind, the *borra*. Yet in spite of this, vines grow and produce wines of the Mediterranean style—typically big, full, and deep red, with lots of tannin and very little acid. Often the Dalmatians cut them with water before drinking—in much the manner of the French with the heady wines of Algeria. White wines are also made.

The vines are various. There appear to be some not known as named varieties elsewhere. This would seem to indicate a very early introduction of the vine into the region. In fact, some Yugoslavian viticulturists believe that one type of vine is native to Yugoslavia.

Among the least 'Dalmatian' of the wines grown are those of Polja (pronounced Polya) which form a bridge between the wines of the inland vineyards and those grown along the coast. Lighter, and lighter-coloured than most Dalmatian wines, the white wines of Imotski and Promina are the most typical.

Most of the red Dalmatian wines (red wines lead white by a ratio of about two to one) are grown from the Mali Plavac vine, a native Yugoslav variety. The best are cultivated around the regions of Bol, Pitovske Plaže (pronounced Pitovsky Plaza), Sveta Nedelja (Sveta Nedelya), Vis, Brela, Lastovo, Postup, and Dingač (Dingach). More often than not the wines will be sold with the name of the vine and the place of origin ('Plavac of Vis' or wine from the Plavac grown around Vis). Sometimes they will carry only the place-name.

Some pink, or rosé wines grown along the coast go under the name of Opol, and the best are found around the villages of Vis, Šibenik, and Kaštel.

The better white wines of Dalmatia resemble the reds in that they are heavy, deep in colour, and are distinctly mouth-filling wines. The best-known come from the Grk (pronounced Gerk), Pošip (Poship), Bogdanuša (Bogdanoosha), Vugava, and Maraština (Marashtina) vines. Grk is pale yellow and dry, with an odd aftertaste all its own, and is grown mostly on the island of Korčula and near the city of Split. Pošip is also grown on the island of Korčula; and the other vines are most successfully cultivated on the islands of Hvar and of Vis and near Šibenik and Žadar respectively.

A curious type of sweet wine called Prošek (pronounced Proshek) is made from semi-dry grapes, or by use of concentrated wine and grape juice, or by cooking the must; but this is mostly for Dalmatians and the Dalmatian palate.

The wines of the Istrian Peninsula are grown more in the Italian manner than the Yugoslavian. Various other plants are found in the same plots of land growing alongside the vines, which are often trellised or draped over trees. Teran accounts for a small part of the production here and extends into the Slovenian part of the Istrian Peninsula, where it is better known. One of the better-known wines is the Malvazÿa, grown from the vine called Malvasia in Italy, Malvoisie in France, and Monemvasia in its native Greece. It makes one of the better and more agreeable wines of Yugoslavia. Also grown are Cabernets, the vine of France's Bordeaux region, and some members of the Pinot family imported from Burgundy.

Slovenia (Ljutomer)

The whole wine region of Slovenia is influenced by the nearness of the Adriatic on the west and the enormous Danube plain on the east, moderating the alpine climate and providing fairly mild, moist winters and temperate summers. The towering mountains of the Julian Alps break up into limestone *karst* towards the Adriatic, and this is the characteristic stony vineyard soil.

Actually, the region can be broken down into three parts: the Adriatic shore, the basin of the River Drava, and the basin of the River Sava. The most important is the basin of the Drava, with the famous Ljutomer. Important growths of hereabouts include Ormož (pronounced Ormoj), Pohorje (Pohorye), Kozjak (Kozyak), Gornie Slovenske Gorice (Gornye Slovenske Goritse), and Kapela Radgona.

The Ljutomer white table wines are readily available in England, the United States, and other markets. Often spelled 'Lutomer', the wines are identified by the regional name followed by the informing grape variety: i.e. Lutomer Riesling, Lutomer Sylvaner, Lutomer Sauvignon, Lutomer Traminer, Lutomer Šipon (pronounced Shee-pon). The Sauvignons and Rieslings are dry, the Sylvaner has a slight sweet tendency, the Traminer is fairly sweet—along with, of course, the spiciness always characterizing the wines of that grape variety. The colour varies in the wines from a full gold tinged with green; while German—and sometimes French, according to the grape variety—in style, the wines are never as subtle and delicate as the comparable German and French wines; they are less highly developed and individual. On the other hand, they can have a very full bouquet and distinctive taste that may be just a little excessive. The Riesling often achieves 14–15% of alcohol, and most of the others are only a little less strong. Šipon—also sometimes spelled Chipon—is a native grape variety. The wine is either dry or sweet, depending upon how it has been vinified, and tends to keep a light freshness even when aged a considerable time.

The other two wine sections of Slovenia are of lesser importance. The best-known wine of the River Sava is the pink Cviček (pronounced Tsveechek), a light, fresh rosé that is much sought after by local Yugoslavs during the heat of the summer. The most important of the Adriatic wines is the red Kraški Teran (Krashki Tayran) from the northern part of Istria, a wine with a wide and ancient reputation for having curative powers, perhaps because of its richness in lactic acid, in iron, and in tannin but it is an acquired taste.

Macedonia

Red, white, and pink wines are grown in Macedonia and a certain amount of dessert wine as well. Macedonia is now one of Yugoslavia's important wine regions. The Turkish invasion was responsible for doing away with the vineyards for a considerable period, and these were never reconstituted after the phylloxera epidemic. However, the Yugoslav Government has made a great and successful effort to rebuild the vineyards since the end of the Second World War; and a large amount of wine intermediate in character between the Mediterranean and more northerly type is grown. The Prokupac, Kavadarka, and Stanusina vines are important for red wines, Žilavartea and Smederevka for white. Districts growing wines today include Tikveš (pronounced Tikvesh), Demir Kapija (Demeer Kapiya), and such towns as Tetovo, Ohrid, Bitola, Štip, Djeudyjelÿa, and others. Yugoslav wine experts are watching the progress of Macedonian wine with satisfaction.

Other Yugoslav Wines

Bosnia-Herzegovina and Montenegro are the smallest of the wine producers of Yugoslavia, together accounting for hardly more than 2% of the wines produced. Montenegrin wines are almost entirely confined to those grown from the Vranac (pronounced Vranats) vine and very little of this ever sees the market-place. Of the wines of Bosnia-Herzegovina two are somewhat known: Žilavka and Blatina. The best is white Žilavka, and particularly the Žilavka grown around the city of Mostar, a big, rich, alcoholic (13%–14%) wine with a profound perfume. It is generally made by vinifying grapes from the native Yugoslav Žilavka vine with about 30% of other varieties.

Vintages

According to the Institute of Viniculture in Maribor there were only two outstanding vintages in the 1800s, those of 1834 and 1890. In general, vintage is of small importance in Yugoslavia owing to the fact that most of the wine is blended. While it is true that export is restricted to a few authorized exporters and there are some large domaines and co-operatives, the actual grape-growing is still astonishingly 95% in the hands of the peasant growers—each at present limited by law to owning a maximum of 25 acres. The fortunes of the Yugoslav grower have been varied since 1950. In 1954, for example, up to two-thirds of the crop was destroyed by vine disease in certain parts of Serbia and elsewhere; while in Istria, and along the Adriatic, in the best wine areas the production was above average.

Spirits

See MARASCHINO; SLIVOVITZ.

Z

Zamora

Spanish province, north of Salamanca. Here the thick, dark Toro wines are grown; and, at Quintanella de Abajo, the Vaga Sicilia.

See SPAIN.

Zeller Schwarze Katz

The 'Black Cat' wine of Zell on the German Moselle is a good deal more famous than it deserves to be. This is due to the name, and the publicity, but not the wine, which is often a blend of poor wines.

See MOSELLE.

Zeltinger Sonnuhr

A lovely feminine Moselle, frequently the best in the district of Zeltingen, where wines run a wide gamut of variety for Moselles.

See MOSELLE.

Zierfandler

Grape variety cultivated in Austria. It is also known as Spätrot.

Zikhron Yaacov

Important centre of Israel's wine industry.

See ISRAEL.

Žilavka

Native Yugoslav grape from which a white wine of this name is grown near Mostar in Bosnia-Herzogovina: it is big, rich, and alcoholic, with a distinctive perfume.

See YUGOSLAVIA.

Zinfandel

Perhaps the most popular red wine grape variety in California.

See AMERICA: CALIFORNIA AND THE WEST.

Żubrowka (Zubrovka)

A type of Polish vodka much appreciated abroad. Pale green in colour, it is flavoured with a wild grass, favourite food of the *zubra*, or Polish bison, which figures on the label. In each bottle of genuine Żubrowka a blade of the grass is enclosed.

See POLAND.

Župa

Prolific region for red and pink wines in the Serbian part of Yugoslavia (*q.v.*).

Zwicker

On an Alsatian bottle label, the term indicates the blending of noble and common wines. Alsatian wines bearing trade-names are usually Zwickers.

Zymase

The ferment, or enzyme, in yeast which converts the sugar of the grape to alcohol and carbon dioxide.

Appendixes

Appendix A **Bordeaux Wines**

I. *The Official Classification of the Great Growths of The Gironde: Classification of 1855*

The official production is given in tons (tonneaux), the Bordeaux standard measure, consisting of four barrels. A tonneau averages around ninety-six cases when it is bottled.

The following figures of production are approximate, varying from year to year, and an estimate has been attempted by deducting the ullage or evaporation, which usually consists of 15%.

HAUT-MÉDOC WINES

First Growths (*Premiers Crus*)

	COMMUNE	*Tonneaux*	*Average Production Cases* (12 BOTTLES)
Château Lafite	*Pauillac*	180	14,600
Château Latour	*Pauillac*	200	16,200
Château Margaux	*Margaux*	150	12,100
Château Haut-Brion*	*Pessac. Graves*	120	10,000

* This wine, although a Graves, is universally recognized and classified as one of the four First Growths of the Médoc.

Second Growths (*Seconds Crus*)

Château Mouton-Rothschild	*Pauillac*	135	11,000
Château Lascombes	*Margaux*	175	14,000
Château Rausan-Ségla	*Margaux*	120	10,000
Château Rauzan-Gassies	*Margaux*	100	8,000
Château Léoville-Las-Cases	*Saint-Julien*	225	18,500
Château Léoville-Poyferré	*Saint-Julien*	160	13,000
Château Léoville-Barton	*Saint-Julien*	70	6,000
Château Durfort-Vivens	*Margaux*	70	6,000
Château Gruaud-Larose	*Saint-Julien*	185	15,000
Château Brane-Cantenac	*Cantenac-Margaux*	250	20,000
Château Pichon-Longueville	*Pauillac*	70	6,100
Château Pichon-Longueville (Comtesse de Lalande)	*Pauillac*	150	12,000
Château Ducru-Beaucaillou	*Saint-Julien*	130	10,500
Château Cos-d'Estournel	*Saint-Estèphe*	210	18,000
Château Montrose	*Saint-Estèphe*	125	11,000

Third Growths (*Troisièmes Crus*)

Château Giscours	*Labarde-Margaux*	245	20,000
Château Kirwan	*Cantenac-Margaux*	60	undetermined
Château d'Issan	*Cantenac-Margaux*	75	6,000
Château Lagrange	*Saint-Julien*	110	9,000
Château Langoa	*Saint-Julien*	75	undetermined
Château Malescot-Saint-Exupéry	*Margaux*	60	5,000
Château Cantenac-Brown	*Cantenac-Margaux*	90	7,100
Château Palmer	*Cantenac-Margaux*	110	10,000
Château La Lagune	*Ludon*	230	19,000
Château Desmirail	*Margaux*	0	0
Château Calon-Ségur	*Saint-Estèphe*	250	20,000
Château Ferrière	*Margaux*	10	850

	COMMUNE	*Tonneaux*	*Average Production Cases* (12 BOTTLES)
Château Marquis-d'Alesme-Becker	*Margaux*	35	3,000
Château Boyd-Cantenac	*Margaux*	22	1,800

Fourth Growths (*Quatrièmes Crus*)

Château Prieuré-Lichine	*Cantenac-Margaux*	60	5,500
Château Saint-Pierre	*Saint-Julien*	40	3,200
Château Branaire-Ducru	*Saint Julien*	120	10,000
Château Talbot	*Saint Julien*	75	14,000
Château Duhart-Milon	*Pauillac*	60	5,000
Château Pouget	*Cantenac-Margaux*	30	2,400
Château La Tour-Carnet	*Saint-Laurent*	20	1,800
Château Lafon-Rochet	*Saint-Estèphe*	50	4,800
Château Beychevelle	*Saint-Julien*	230	19,200
Château Marquis-de-Terme	*Margaux*	130	11,000

Fifth Growths (*Cinquièmes Crus*)

Château Pontet-Canet	*Pauillac*	200	undetermined
Château Batailley	*Pauillac*	60	5,500
Château Grand-Puy-Lacoste	*Pauillac*	100	8,000
Château Grand-Puy-Ducasse	*Pauillac*	35	2,800
Château Haut-Batailley	*Pauillac*	60	5,200
Château Lynch-Bages	*Pauillac*	160	13,000
Château Lynch-Moussas	*Pauillac*	20	1,600
Château Dauzac	*Labarde-Margaux*	40	3,500
Château Mouton-d'Armailhacq (now known as Château du Baron Philippe)	*Pauillac*	125	11,000
Château du Tertre	*Arsac-Margaux*	25	2,000
Château Haut-Bages-Libéral	*Pauillac*	40	3,300
Château Pédesclaux	*Pauillac*	35	3,000
Château Belgrave	*Saint-Laurent*	90	7,100
Château Camensac	*Saint-Laurent*	25	2,100
Château Cos Labory	*Saint-Estèphe*	55	4,500
Château Clerc-Milon-Mondon	*Pauillac*	30	2,100
Château Croizet-Bages	*Pauillac*	90	7,500
Château Cantemerle	*Macau*	70	6,200

Exceptional Growths (*Crus Exceptionnels*)

	COMMUNE		COMMUNE
Château Villegeorge	*Avensan*	Château la Couronne	*Pauillac*
Château Angludet	*Cantenac-Margaux*	Château Moulin-Riche	*Saint-Julien*
Château Chasse-Spleen	*Moulis*	Château Bel-Air-Marquis d'Aligre	*Soussans-Margaux*
Château Poujeaux-Theil	*Moulis*		

See author's suggested revised classification on pp. 145–8.

II. *The Crus Bourgeois and Crus Artisans of the Haut-Médoc*

The following figures of production are approximate, and indicate average annual output, as given by the communes and taken from their Déclarations de Récoltes records.

MINOR GROWTHS OF THE HAUT-MÉDOC

	COMMUNE	*Hectares*	*Acres*	*Tonneaux*
Château Andron-Blanquet, Château St.-Roch	*St.-Estèphe*	13	32·5	52
Château Aney	*Cussac*	2	5	5
Château Angludet	*Cantenac-Margaux*	15	37·5	27
Château Antonic	*Moulis*	5	12·5	13
Château d'Arches	*Ludon*	2	5	5
Château d'Arcins	*Arcins*	19	47·5	20
Château Arnauld	*Arcins*	3	7·5	8
Cru Arnaud, Château du Brassat	*St.-Julien*	2	5	7
Château Balogues-Haut-Bages	*Pauillac*	6	15	7
Château Barateau	*St.-Laurent*	4	10	5
Cru Barraillot	*Margaux*	3	7·5	9
Château Barreyres	*Arcins*	11	27·5	26
Château Beaumont	*Cussac*	22	55	14
Château Beauregard	*St.-Julien*	2	5	6
Château Beauséjour	*Listrac*	2	5	6
Château Beauséjour, Château Picard	*St.-Estèphe*	17	42·5	41
Château Beau-Site-St.-Estèphe	*St.-Estèphe*	20	50	58
Château Beau-Site-Haut-Vignoble	*St.-Estèphe*	12	30	52
Château Bel-Air	*St.Estèphe*	4	10	14
Château Bel-Air Lagrave	*Moulis*	4	10	11
Château Bel-Air-Marquis-d'Aligre	*Soussans-Margaux*	8	20	18
Château Belgrave	*St.-Laurent*	29	72·5	70
Château Bellegrave	*Listrac*	4	10	7
Château Bellevue	*Cussac*	3	7·5	7
Château Bellevue-les-Hautes-Graves	*Soussans-Margaux*	2	5	5
Château Bel-Orme	*St.-Seurin-de-Cadourne*	22	53	100
Cru Bibian Darriet	*Listrac*	2	5	9
Château Biston Brillette	*Moulis*	4	10	11
Château Bonneau	*St.-Seurin-de-Cadourne*	3	7·5	9
Château Bontemps-Dubarry	*St.-Julien*	2	5	5
Cru Bontemps	*St.-Estèphe*	2	5	6
Château Bouqueyran	*Moulis*	2	5	8
Château Bourgade de La Chapelle (*see* Château Rosemont)				
Château Bournac	*St.-Estèphe*	3	7·5	8
Château Branas	*Moulis*	3	7·5	4
Château du Brassat (*see* Cru Arnaud)				
Château du Breuil	*Cissac*	15	37·5	70
Château Brillette	*Moulis*	15	37·5	40
Château Bryette	*St.-Seurin-de-Cadourne*	2	5	8
Cru des Cachères	*St.-Estèphe*	2	5	6
Château Cadillon	*Lamarque*	4	10	7
Château Caillevet	*Lamarque*	3	7·5	14
Château Cambon	*Blanquefort*	2	5	5
Château Cambon-La-Pelouse	*Macau*	8	20	19
Domaine de Campion	*Margaux*	2	5	8
Château Canteloup	*St.-Estèphe*	15	375	50

	COMMUNE	*Hectares*	*Acres*	*Tonneaux*
Château Capbern, Château Capbern-Gasqueton, Château La Rose-Capbern, Château Grand Village Capbern, Château La Tour Lichine, Château Moulin-de-Calon	*St.-Estèphe*	32	80	95
Château Capdeville	*Listrac*	3	7·5	4
Château Cap du Haut	*Moulis*	4	10	10
Château Capléon-Veyrin	*Listrac*	5	12·5	12
Château Caronne	*St.-Laurent*	20	50	45
Carruades du Château Lafite-Rothschild	*Pauillac*	—	—	64
Château du Cartillon	*Lamarque*	5	12·5	7
Clos Castets, Château St.-Seurin	*St.-Estèphe*	1	2·5	4
Château Chambert (Marbuzet)	*St.-Estèphe*	2	5	6
Cru Charmant	*Margaux*	6	15	20
Château Chasse-Spleen, Château Franquet	*Moulis*	42	105	120
Château Châteaufort de Vauban	*Cussac*	2	5	6
Château Chaux	*Moulis*	3	7·5	8
Château Chevalier d'Ars (Coopérative)	*Arcins*	50	125	122
Château Cissac	*Cissac*	2	5	12
Château Citran-Clauzel	*Avensan*	30	75	63
Château Clarke	*Listrac*	7	17·5	10
Château Clauzet	*St.-Estèphe*	4	10	21
Château de Côme	*St.-Estèphe*	2	5	5
Coopérative	*St.-Sauveur*	—	—	—
Coopérative (Grand Listrac)	*Listrac*	130	321	380
Coopérative 'Grands Vins de St.-Estèphe'	*St.-Estèphe*	186	460	536
Coopérative 'Cru La Paroisse St.-Seurin-de-Cadourne'	*St.Seurin-de-Cadourne*	130	325	400
Coopérative La Rose Pauillac	*Pauillac*	210	525	700
Cru Cougot	*Arsac-Margaux*	2	5	5
Château Coutelin-Merville	*St.-Estèphe*	11	27·5	41
Château Curé-Bourse	*Margaux*	2	5	7
Château Deux Moulins	*Lamarque*	2	5	5
Château Deyrem-Valentin	*Soussans-Margaux*	4	10	9
Château Dillon	*Blanquefort*	9	22·5	29
Château Domeyne	*St.-Estèphe*	2	5	9
Château Donissan-Veyrin	*Listrac*	12	30	33
Château Duplessis Hauchecorne	*Moulis*	14	35	34
Château Dutruch Grand Poujeaux	*Moulis*	10	25	37
Domaine d'Esteau (*see* Château Fontesteau)				
Château Eyquem	*St.-Estèphe*	4	10	10
Château Fatin (*see* Château Le Crock)				
Château Felletin	*Lamarque*	5	12·5	9
Château Fellonneau	*Macau*	3	7·5	5
Clos de Ferrand	*St.-Estèphe*	1	2·5	10
Château Ferrey Gros Caillou, Cru Le Bécasse du Ferrey	*St.-Julien*	6	15	24
Cru des Fines Graves	*St.-Estèphe*	2	5	7
Château Fonbadet	*Pauillac*	30	75	100
Château Fonréaud	*Listrac*	25	62·5	60
Château Fontanet	*Le Taillan*	1	2·5	5
Château Fontesteau, Domaine d'Esteau	*Cissac*	11	27·5	15
Château Fourcas-Dupré	*Listrac*	12	30	38

	COMMUNE	Hectares	Acres	Tonneaux
Château Fourcas Hostein	*Listrac*	23	57·5	66
Château Foureau	*Listrac*	27	67·5	88
Château Gaciot	*Avensan*	4	10	10
Château Glana	*St.-Julien*	40	100	150
Château Gloria, Château Haut Beychevelle Gloria	*St.-Julien*	32	80	140
Château Gobineau-Graves-de-Lafon	*Listrac*	8	20	12
Domaine du Gona	*Cussac*	3	7·5	6
Cru Gramond	*Listrac*	2	5	5
Château du Grand-Clapeau	*Blanquefort*	5	12·5	9
Château Grandis	*St.-Seurin-de-Cadourne*	3	7·5	8
Château Grand-Jaugueyron	*Cantenac-Margaux*	3	7·5	7
Château Grand-Poujeaux-Theil	*Moulis*	32	80	100
Cru du Grand Rullong	*St.-Estèphe*	3	7·5	11
Château du Grand St.-Julien	*St.-Julien*	4	10	8
Château Grand-Soussans	*Soussans-Margaux*	3	7·5	4
Château Grand Village Capbern (*see* Château Capbern)				
'Grands Vins de St.-Estèphe' (*see* Coopérative)				
Château Granins	*Moulis*	3	7·5	10
Cru Granins	*Moulis*	1	2·5	5
Château Graves	*Moulis*	5	12·5	5
Cru des Graves	*Moulis*	1	2·5	5
Cru des Graves	*Listrac*	3	7·5	6
Château Cru du Gravier	*Arsac-Margaux*	2	5	6
Cru des Gravières	*Cussac*	2	5	6
Château Gressier Grand Poujeaux	*Moulis*	24	60	70
Château Guitignan	*Moulis*	3	7·5	9
Château Hanteillan	*St.-Estèphe*	20	50	65
Château Haut Bellevue	*Lamarque*	2	5	6
Château Haut-Carmail	*St.-Seurin-de-Cadourne*	4	10	13
Cru Haut Coutelin	*St.-Estèphe*	4	10	12
Château Haut Daubos, Château Mongrand Milon	*Pauillac*	3	7·5	4
Château Haut Hagna	*St.-Estèphe*	4	10	12
Cru Haut La Tour de Coutelin	*St.-Estèphe*	2	5	5
Château Haut Marbuzet	*St.-Estèphe*	12	30	24
Château Haut Plantey	*Listrac*	2	5	6
Château Haut Sieujean	*St.-Laurent*	3	7·5	8
Château Haut Verdon	*St.-Estèphe*	3	7·5	15
Château Héby	*Moulis*	2	5	5
Cru Hennebelle, Cru Landarey	*Lamarque*	3	7·5	7
Château Hortevie	*St.-Julien*	3	7·5	8
Château Hostein	*St.-Estèphe*	3	7·5	9
Château Houissant	*St.-Estèphe*	14	35	70
Château l'Abbégorsse-de-Gorsse	*Margaux*	4	10	11
Château La Bécade	*Listrac*	3	7·5	7
Cru La-Bécasse-du-Ferrey	*St.-Julien*	6	15	24
Château Labégorce	*Margaux*	4	10	11
Château Labégorce-Zédé	*Soussans-Margaux*	15	37·5	50
Cru La Chappelle	*St.-Estèphe*	3	7·5	7
Cru La Clidère	*Listrac*	2	5	6
Château La Closerie	*Moulis*	7	17·5	23
Château La Colonilla	*Margaux*	6	15	16
Château Laconfourque	*St.-Julien*	1	2·5	4
Château La Couronne	*Pauillac*	3	7·5	7

	COMMUNE	*Hectares*	*Acres*	*Tonneaux*
Château La Croix (*see* Château Phélan-Ségur)				
La Dame Blanche	*Le Taillan*	5	12·5	10
(The white wine of Château du Taillan, which has only the Appellation Bordeaux Blanc Supérieur)				
Château Ladouys	*St.-Estèphe*	4	10	10
Château Laffitte-Carcasset	*St.-Estèphe*	20	50	48
Château La Fleur	*St.-Laurent*	3	7·5	8
Château La Fleur Milon	*Pauillac*	7	17·5	16
Château Lafon	*Listrac*	6	15	10
Château La Galiane	*Soussans-Margaux*	4	10	9
Château La Gombaude	*Margaux*	5	12·5	15
Château Lagorce	*Moulis*	3	7·5	7
Château Lagravette-Peyredon	*Listrac*	5	12·5	10
Château La Gravière-Haut-Bages	*Pauillac*	1	2·5	4
Château La Gurgue	*Margaux*	8	20	30
Château La Haye	*St.-Estèphe*	5	12·5	12
Château Lalande (*see* Château Tronquoy)				
Château Lamothe-de-Bergeron	*Cussac*	10	25	21
Château La Mouline	*Moulis*	4	10	18
Château de Lamourous	*Le Pian*	4	10	16
Château de Lamouroux	*Margaux*	4	10	16
Cru Landarey (*see* Cru Hennebelle)				
Château Lanessan	*Cussac*	18	45	48
Cru Langa	*Cussac*	3	7·5	4
'Cru La Paroisse St.-Seurin-de-Cadourne' (*see* Coopérative)				
Château La Rose-Capbern (*see* Château Capbern)				
Château La Rose de France	*St.-Julien*	2	5	8
Château La Rose (Coopérative de Pauillac)	*Pauillac*	210	525	700
Château La Rose	*St.-Seurin-de-Cadourne*	2	5	6
Château de Laroze	*Margaux*	2	5	7
Cru Larragay	*Listrac*	2	5	6
Château Larrieu-Terrefort-Graves	*Macau*	3	7·5	5
Château Larrivaux	*Cissac*	5	12·5	19
Château Lartigue	*St.-Estèphe*	2	5	13
Château La Tour d'Anseillan	*Pauillac*	9	22·5	20
Château La Tour l'Aspic	*Pauillac*	4	10	7
Château La Tour-de-Bessan (*see* Château La Tour-de-Mons)				
Château La Tour Brana	*St.-Estèphe*	2	5	5
Château La Tour Coutelin	*St.-Estèphe*	3	7·3	11
Château Latour-Dumirail	*Cissac*	10	25	16
Château La Tour du Haut Moulin	*Cussac*	7	17·5	15
Château La Tour du Haut Vignoble (*see* Château Les Ormes-de-Pez)				
Château La Tour du Haut Vignoble	*St.-Estèphe*	12	30	52
Château La Tour de Leyssac	*St.-Estèphe*	3	7·5	12
Château La Tour Lichine (*see* Château Capbern)				
Château La Tour de Malescasse	*Lamarque*	5	12·5	9
Château La Tour de Marbuzet	*St.-Estèphe*	13	32·5	32
Château La Tour Marcillannet	*St.-Laurent*	6	15	9
Château La Tour-de-Mons, Château Richeterre, Château La Tour-de-Bessan	*Soussans-Margaux*	24	60	65
Château La Tour Pibran	*Pauillac*	5	12·5	18
Château La Tour du Roc-Grand Poujeaux	*Arcins*	12	30	31
Château La Tour du Roch Milon	*Pauillac*	18	45	20
Château La Tour des Ternes	*St.-Estèphe*	12	30	13

	COMMUNE	Hectares	Acres	Tonneaux
Château Le Boscq	*St.-Estèphe*	13	32·5	39
Château Le Crock, Château Fatin, Château St.-Estèphe 'La Croix'	*St.-Estèphe*	27	67·5	97
Château Lemoyne-Lafon-Rochet	*Le Pian*	3	7·5	10
Château Le Raux	*Cussac*	4	10	7
Château Le Roc	*St.-Estèphe*	1	2·5	5
Château Lescarjeau	*St.-Sauveur*	5	12·5	13
Cru Lescourt	*Listrac*	2	5	5
Château Les Graves de Germignan	*Le Taillan*	3	7·5	8
Château Les Ormes-de-Pez, Château Moulin Joli, Château La Tour Haut Vignoble	*St.-Estèphe*	21	52·5	80
Château Lestage	*Listrac*	29	72·5	43
Château Lestage	*St.-Seurin-de-Cadourne*	1	2·5	5
Château Lestage Darquier	*Moulis*	4	10	8
Château Lestage Darquier Grand Poujeaux	*Moulis*	4	10	13
Château L'Hôpital	*St.-Estèphe*	5	12·5	17
Château Liversan	*St.-Sauveur*	32	80	130
Domaine du Lucrabey	*Cissac*	5	12·5	7
Château Mac-Carthy	*St.-Estèphe*	4	10	15
Château MacCarthy Moula	*St.-Estèphe*	6	15	12
Château Malécot	*Pauillac*	7	17·5	21
Château Malescasse	*Lamarque*	4	10	11
Château Malmaison	*Moulis*	4	10	5
Château Marbuzet	*St.-Estèphe*	11	27·5	31
Château Marque	*St.-Seurin-de-Cadourne*	1	2·5	6
Clos du Marquis	*St.-Julien*	8	20	11
Château Marsac-Seguineau	*Soussans-Margaux*	3	7·5	9
Château Martinens	*Cantenac-Margaux*	19	47·5	14
Clos du Mas	*Listrac*	5	12·5	9
Château Maucaillou	*Moulis*	11	27·5	33
Château Maucamps	*Macau*	5	12·5	13
Château Médrac	*Moulis*	5	12·5	3
Château Meyney	*St.-Estèphe*	44	109	182
Château Milon-Mousset, Cru Milon	*Pauillac*	2	5	6
Château Mongrand Milon (*see* Château Haut Daubos)				
Château Monpelou	*Pauillac*	8	20	5
Château Montbrun	*Cantenac-Margaux*	5	12·5	25
Château Morin	*St.-Estèphe*	8	20	18
Clos du Moulin	*St.-Estèphe*	5	12·5	7
Cru du Moulin	*Cussac*	1	2·5	5
Château Moulin-à-Vent	*Moulis*	6	15	9
Château du Moulin du Bourg	*Listrac*	6	15	31
Château Moulin de la Bridane	*Pauillac*	4	10	13
Château Moulin-de-Calon (*see* Château Capbern)				
Château Moulin Joli (*see* Château Les Ormes-de-Pez)				
Cru du Moulin de Laborde	*Listrac*	4	10	10
Château Moulin-Riche	*St.-Julien*	11	27·5	19
Château Moulin Rose	*Lamarque*	3	7·5	9
Château Moulin de la Rose	*St.-Julien*	4	10	11
Château du Moulin Rouge	*Cussac*	4	10	6
Château Moulis	*Moulis*	6	15	16
Clos Muratel	*Blanquefort*	1	2·5	4
Cru Muscadet	*St.-Estèphe*	1	2·5	5

	COMMUNE	*Hectares*	*Acres*	*Tonneaux*
Château Nexon-Lemoyne	*Ludon*	2	5	10
Château Pabeau	*St.-Seurin-de-Cadourne*	24	60	100
Cru du Paléna	*Listrac*	2	5	5
Château Palmier	*St.-Estèphe*	5	12·5	18
Château Parempuyre-Cruse	*Parempuyre*	4	10	4
Château Parempuyre-Durand-Dassier	*Parempuyre*	3	7·5	10
Château Paveil	*Soussans-Margaux*	11	27·5	33
Château Pelon	*St.-Laurent*	3	7·5	8
Château Peyrabon	*St.-Sauveur*	9	22·5	16
Château Peyredon	*Moulis*	3	7·5	9
Château de Pez	*St.-Estèphe*	22	55	93
Château Phélan-Ségur, Château La Croix	*St.-Estèphe*	44	109	175
Château Pibran	*Pauillac*	7	17·5	22
Château Picard (*see* Château Beauséjour)				
Château Pierre Bibian	*Listrac*	11	27·5	45
Château Piton Richebon	*Moulis*	5	12·5	14
Château Plaisance	*Pauillac*	7	17·5	13
Château Plantier-Rose	*St.-Estèphe*	7	17·5	23
Château Pomeys	*Moulis*	5	12·5	16
Château Pomiès-Agassac	*Ludon*	9	22·5	20
Château Pomys	*St.-Estèphe*	7	17·5	18
Cru Pontet-Chappez	*Arsac-Margaux*	1	2·5	4
Château Pontoise-Cabarrus-Brochon	*St.-Seurin-de-Cadourne*	7	17·5	20
Château Poujeaux-Theil	*Moulis*	16	40	47
Cru Poumarin	*St.-Estèphe*	3	7·5	5
Cru des Pradines	*St.-Estèphe*	2	5	5
Domaine des Pradines	*St.-Estèphe*	1	2·5	6
Château Renouil Franquet	*Moulis*	4	10	8
Château Reverdi	*Listrac*	3	7·5	7
Cru Ribeau	*St.-Estèphe*	2	5	6
Château Richeterre (*see* Château La Tour-de-Mons)				
Cru Richet-Marian	*Margaux*	2	5	8
Château Robert Franquet	*Moulis*	4	10	9
Château Robert Renouil-Grand Poujeaux	*Arcins*	2	5	8
Château Roland	*Pauillac*	5	12·5	19
Château Rosemont, Château de Bourgade de La Chapelle	*Labarde*	1	2·5	9
Château Rose Ste.-Croix	*Listrac*	5	12·5	13
Château Ruat	*Moulis*	4	10	5
Château St.-Estèphe	*St.-Estèphe*	3	7·5	9
Château St.-Estèphe 'La Croix' (*see* Château Le Crock)				
Château St.-Louis-Dubosq	*St.Julien*	1	2·5	4
Château St.-Martin	*Listrac*	2	5	8
Clos St.-Martin	*Pauillac*	3	7·5	6
Château St.-Paul	*St.-Seurin-de-Cadourne*	5	12·5	16
Cru St.-Pierre	*Margaux*	2	5	4
Château St.-Seurin (*see* Clos Castets)				
Château Saransot-Dupré	*Listrac*	4	10	18
Château Ségur-Bacqué	*Parempuyre*	5	12·5	10
Château Ségur-Fillon	*Parempuyre*	5	12·5	4
Château Sémeillan	*Listrac*	13	32·5	53
Château Sénéjac	*Le Pian*	10	25	22
Château Sénhilac	*St.-Seurin-de-Cadourne*	4	10	11

	COMMUNE	Hectares	Acres	Tonneaux
Château Siran	*Labarde-Margaux*	21	52·5	70
Château Sociando-Mallet	*St.-Seurin-de-Cadourne*	5	12·5	20
Château du Taillan	*Le Taillan*	5	12·5	10
(The white wine is called Château La Dame Blanche)				
Cru Taste	*St.-Estèphe*	3	7·5	6
Château Tayac-Plaisance	*Soussans-Margaux*	2	5	6
Château du Terrey	*St.-Sauveur*	12	30	10
Château Terrey-Gros-Caillou	*St.-Julien*	12	30	50
Château de Testeron	*Moulis*	2	5	5
Château Teynac	*St.-Julien*	4	10	10
Château Teynac, Clos St.-Julien	*St.-Julien*	4	10	12
Château Tourelle	*Listrac*	2	5	5
Château Tronquoy-Lalande	*St.-Estèphe*	16	40	60
Cru du Troupian	*St.-Estèphe*	2	5	5
Cru Vallière	*Margaux*	2	5	6
Château Verdignan	*St.-Seurin-de-Cadourne*	15	37·5	67
Château Villegeorge	*Avensan*	5	12·5	12
Château Vincent	*Cantenac-Margaux*	2	5	4

MINOR GROWTHS OF THE MÉDOC (OR BAS-MÉDOC)

	COMMUNE	Hectares	Acres	Tonneaux
Domaine des Anguilleys (*see* Château Vieux Robin)				
Clos Beau Rivage	*Bégadan*	2	5	8
Château Bégadanet	*Bégadan*	4	10	12
Cru Bel Air Mareil	*Ordonnac-et-Potensac*	3	7·5	6
Château Belfort	*St.-Germain-d'Esteuil*	4	10	8
Château des Bellegraves	*Ordonnac-et-Potensac*	5	12·5	17
Château Bellerive	*Valeyrac*	9	22·5	35
Château Bellevue	*Valeyrac*	3	7·5	17
Château Bensse (*see* Coopérative de Prignac)				
Cru de Bert	*Couquéques*	3	7·5	8
Château Blaignan	*Blaignan*	4	10	11
Château Buscateau	*St.-Germain-d'Esteuil*	2	5	6
Château de By (Château Greysac)	*Bégadan*	7	17·5	28
Domaine de By	*Bégadan*	10	25	28
Cru Canteloup	*Blaignan*	2	5	6
Château Carcanieux-les-Graves	*Queyrac*	4	10	13
Château Castéra	*St.-Germain-d'Esteuil*	18	45	39
Cave Coopérative 'St.- Jean'	*Bégadan*	560	1,384	1,200
Cave Coopérative 'Belle Vue'	*Ordonnac-et-Potensac*	87	215	224
Cru Chantegric	*Prignac*	3	7·5	6
Château Chantelys	*Prignac*	4	10	11
Château des Combes	*Bégadan*	4	10	11
Coopérative	*Vertheuil*	—	—	300
Coopérative de Gaillan (Grand Vin du Vieux-Clocher)	*Gaillan*	15	37·5	26
Coopérative de Prignac, Château Bensse	*Prignac*	97	240	220
Coopérative de Queyrac, Château St.- Roch	*Queyrac*	15	37·5	50
Coopérative de St. Yzans, Cave St.-Brice	*St.-Yzans*	96	238	220
Château Côtes de Blaignan, Cru Hontane	*Blaignan*	5	12·5	14
Cru Cruscaut-Graves-du-Pin	*Blaignan*	4	10	8

	COMMUNE	*Hectares*	*Acres*	*Tonneaux*
Cru des Deux-Moulins	*St.-Christoly*	13	32·5	48
Château Gaillais-Bellevue (*see* Château Potensac)				
Grand Vin du Vieux-Clocher (*see* Coopérative de Gaillan)				
Domaine et Clos des Graves	*Ordonnac-et-Potensac*	2	5	6
Château Haut-Blaignan	*Blaignan*	5	12·5	16
Cru de Haut Château Malendrin	*Couquéques*	2	5	6
Cru Haut-Garin	*Prignac*	3	7·5	8
Château Haut-Giras	*St.-Germain-d'Esteuil*	6	15	7
Château Haut-Graville	*Civrac*	8	20	16
Château Haut-Miqueu	*St.-Germain-d'Esteuil*	4	10	11
Clos Haut-Pouyzac	*St.-Christoly*	2	5	6
Cru Hontane (*see* Château Côtes de Blaignan)				
Château La Cardonne	*Blaignan*	34	85	98
Cru La Colonne	*St.-Yzans*	3	7·5	10
Château Lafitte	*Bégadan*	3	7·5	11
Domaine de Lafon	*Prignac*	3	7·5	7
Clos Laforest	*St.-Christoly*	4	10	11
Château La France	*St.-Yzans*	3	7·5	9
Château La Gore	*Bégadan*	5	12·5	17
Château l'Aiglon	*St.-Germain-d'Esteuil*	2	5	4
Château La Lagune	*St.-Germain-d'Esteuil*	1	2·5	6
Domaine de la Lagune	*Bégadan*	2	5	6
Château La Privera	*St.-Christoly*	2	5	8
Château La Roque de By	*Bégadan*	5	12·5	8
Château La Rose Garamay (*see* Château Livran)				
Château Lassalle	*Ordonnac-et-Potensac*	4	10	10
Château La Tour-Blanche	*St.-Christoly*	7	17·5	28
Château La Tour de By	*Bégadan*	31	77·5	62
Château La Tour Cordouan	*Bégadan*	2	5	6
Château La Tour du Haut-Caussan	*Blaignan*	3	7·5	10
Château La Tour-St.-Bonnet	*St.-Christoly*	15	37·5	52
Château Laujac	*Bégadan*	4	10	19
Château Le Bourdieu	*Vertheuil*	40	100	150
Château Le Clou	*Blaignan*	4	10	16
Château Le Grand-Trepeau	*St.-Christoly*	2	5	4
Château Les Lesques	*Lesparre*	11	27·5	11
Clos Les Moines	*Couquéques*	4	10	13
Château Les Ormes-Sorbet	*Couquéques*	8	20	27
Cru Les Tourelles	*Blaignan*	3	7·5	11
Château Le Tertre-de-Caussan	*Blaignan*	5	12·5	18
Château Le Tréhon	*Bégadan*	7	17·5	22
Château L'Hermitage	*Couquéques*	4	10	10
Château Livran, Château La Rose Garamay	*St.-Germain-d'Esteuil*	10	25	27
Château Loudenne	*St.-Yzans*	9	22·5	26
Château Lugagnac	*Vertheuil*	3	7·5	10
Clos Mandillot	*St.-Christoly*	3	7·5	5
Château Monthil	*Bégadan*	4	10	8
Clos Morteil	*Bégadan*	4	10	11
Clos du Moulin	*St.-Christoly*	4	10	15
Château Panigon	*Civrac*	8	20	16
Domaine de Patache	*Bégadan*	25	62·5	110
Château Pay-de-Lalo	*St.-Germain-d'Esteuil*	2	5	7
Château Plagnac	*Bégadan*	2	5	7

	COMMUNE	*Hectares*	*Acres*	*Tonneaux*
Château Potensac, Château Gallais-Bellevue	*Ordonnac-et-Potensac*	9	22·5	35
Château Reysson	*Vertheuil*	34	85	65
Cru du Roc	*Couquéques*	2	5	6
Cru du Roc	*St.-Christoly*	6	15	15
Château Roquegrave	*Valeyrac*	5	12·5	19
Château de Roquetaillade	*Ordonnac-et-Potensac*	3	7·5	12
Château St.-Anne	*St.-Christoly*	4	10	7
Château St.-Bonnet	*St.-Christoly*	13	32·5	37
Cave St.-Brice (*see* Coopérative de St.-Yzans)				
Château St.-Christoly	*St.-Christoly*	4	10	28
Château St.-Germain	*St.-Germain-d'Esteuil*	2	5	8
Cru St.-Louis	*Couquéques*	3	7·5	11
Château St.-Roch (*see* Coopérative de Queyrac)				
Château St.-Saturnin	*Bégadan*	6	15	14
Cru Verdon	*Valeyrac*	3	7·5	12
Cru du Vieux-Château Landon	*Bégadan*	10	25	35
Château Vieux Robin, Domaine des Anguilleys	*Bégadan*	4	10	14

III. *Saint-Émilion: 1955 Official Classification*

In mid-1955 the best Saint-Émilion wines were officially classified by the French Institut National des Appellations d'Origine as First Great Growths and Great Growths.

The following figures of production are approximate, and indicate average annual output, as given by the communes and taken from their Déclarations de Récoltes records, minus approx. 15% in ullage.

First Great Growths (*St.-Émilion-Premiers-Grands-Crus-Classés*)

	Tonneaux	*Cases*
Château Ausone	35	2,800
Château Cheval Blanc	150	12,000
Château Beauséjour-Duffau-Lagarrosse	25	2,000
Château Beauséjour-Fagouet	30	2,500
Château Belair	90	7,500
Château Canon	90	7,200
Château Figeac	120	9,500
Clos Fourtet	80	6,700
Château Gaffelière-Naudes	110	9,400
Château Magdelaine	40	3,200
Château Pavie	200	16,200
Château Trottevieille	40	3,250

Great Growths (*St.-Émilion-Grand-Crus-Classés*)

(Acreage and production figures are given in the next section.)

Château l'Arrosée
Château Balestard-la-Tonnelle
Château Bellevue
Château Bergat
Château Cadet-Bon
Château Cadet-Piolat
Château Canon-la-Gaffelière
Château Cap de Mourlin
Château Chapelle Madeleine
Château Chatelet
Château Chauvin
Château Corbin
Château Corbin-Michotte
Château Coutet
Château Croque-Michotte
Château Curé-Bon
Château Fonplégade
Château Fonroque
Château Franc-Mayne
Château Grand-Barrail-Lamarzelle-Figeac
Château Grand-Corbin
Château Grand-Corbin-Despagne
Château Grand-Mayne
Château les Grandes Murailles
Château Grand Pontet
Château Guadet-St.-Julien
Clos des Jacobins
Château Jean Faure
Château La Carte
Château La Clotte
Château La Cluzière
Château La Couspaude
Château La Dominique
Clos La Madeleine
Château La Marzelle
Château l'Angélus
Château Larcis-Ducasse
Château Larmande
Château Laroze
Château Lasserre
Château La Tour-Figeac

Château La Tour-du-Pin-Figeac
Château Le Couvent
Château Le Prieuré
Château Mauvezin
Château Moulin-du-Cadet
Château Pavie-Decesse
Château Pavie-Macquin
Château Pavillon-Cadet
Château Petit-Faurie-de-Souchard
Château Petit-Faurie-de-Soutard
Château Ripeau
Château St.-Georges-Côte-Pavie
Clos St.-Martin
Château Sansonnet
Château Soutard
Château Tertre-Daugay
Château Trimoulet
Château Trois-Moulins
Château Troplong-Mondot
Château Villemaurine
Château Yon-Figeac

Principal and Lesser Growths of St.-Émilion and Surrounding Villages

	COMMUNE	*Hectares*	*Acres*	*Tonneaux*
Domaine Allée-de-Lescours	*St.-Sulpice-de-Faleyrens*	4	10	11
Château Ambois	*St.-Georges-St.-Émilion*	1	2·5	4
Clos d'Armens	*St.-Pey-d'Armens*	2	5	7
Domaine d'Arriailh	*Montagne-St.-Émilion*	4	10	6
Château d'Arthus	*Vignonet*	5	12·5	13
Clos d'Arthus	*Vignonet*	12	30	23
Château Austerlitz	*Sables-St.-Émilion*	5	12·5	18
Château Badette	*St.-Christophe-des-Bardes*	8	20	40
Château Badon (*see* Château Vieux-Ceps)				
Domaine de Badon-Patarabet	*St.-Émilion*	2	5	12
Château Baleau	*St.-Émilion*	12	30	41
Château Balestard-la-Tonnelle	*St.-Émilion*	7	17·5	45
Château Barbe-Blanche	*Lussac-St.-Émilion*	8	20	22
Château Barbey	*St.-Étienne-de-Lisse*	2	5	9
Château Barbeyron	*St.-Laurent-des-Combes*	4	10	13
Château Barde-Haut	*St.-Christophe-des-Bardes*	12	30	43
Château Bardoulet	*St.-Étinne-de-Lisse*	2	5	7
Domaine de Bardoulet	*St.-Étienne-de-Lisse*	3	7·5	15
Château Barraud	*Montagne-St.-Émilion*	4	10	21
Domaine de Barraud	*Montagne-St.-Émilion*	4	10	11
Château du Basque	*St.-Pey-d'Armens*	8	20	35
Château Bayard	*Montagne-St.Émilion*	7	17·5	39
Clos Bayard	*Montagne-St.-Émilion*	5	12·5	22
Domaine de Bayard	*Montagne-St.-Émilion*	8	20	19
Château Béard	*St.-Laurent-des-Combes*	5	12·5	22
Clos Beaufort-Mazerat	*St.-Émilion*	2	5	9
Château Beau-Mazerat (*see* Château Grand-Mayne)				
Château Beauséjour	*Montagne-St.-Émilion*	6	15	30
Château Beauséjour	*Puisseguin-St.-Émilion*	14	35	58
Château Beausite	*Vignonet*	4	10	15
Château Beausite	*Lussac-St.-Émilion*	3	7·5	10
Château Bel-Air	*Montagne-St.-Émilion*	8	20	29
Château Bel-Air	*Puisseguin-St.-Émilion*	11	27·5	55
Château Bel-Air-Lussac	*Lussac-St.-Émilion*	12	30	46
Château Belair-Sarthou	*St.-Étienne-de-Lisse*	5	12·5	19
Château Bel-Horizon	*Vignonet*	2	5	5
Château Belle-Assise	*St.-Sulpice-de-Faleyrens*	5	12·5	22
Château Bellefond-Belcier	*St.-Laurent-des-Combes*	11	27·7	42
Château Bellegrave	*Vignonet*	8	20	40
Château Belles-Plantes	*Vignonet*	3	7·5	9
Château Bellevue	*St.-Émilion*	6	15	28
Château Bellevue	*Lussac-St.-Émilion*	11	27·5	32
Château Bellevue	*Montagne-St.-Émilion*	4	10	19
Clos Bellevue-Figeac	*St.-Émilion*	3	7·5	12

	COMMUNE	*Hectares*	*Acres*	*Tonneaux*
Cru Bellevue-Mondotte	*St.-Laurent-des-Combes*	2	5	7
Clos Bellevue-Peyblanquet	*St.-Étienne-de-Lisse*	3	7·5	7
Château Bellile-Mondotte	*St.-Laurent-des-Combes*	4	10	11
Cru Béouran	*St.-Émilion*	1	2·5	7
Château Bergat	*St.-Émilion*	3	7·5	8
Cru Berlière	*Parsac-St.-Émilion*	4	10	15
Domaine de Berlière	*Parsac-St.Émilion*	3	7·5	5
Château Berliquet	*St.-Émilion*	7	17·5	19
Clos Bernachot	*St.-Sulpice-de-Faleyrens*	2	5	8
Clos Berthoneau (*see* Château du Roy)				
Château Bertineau-Goby	*Montagne-St.-Émilion*	9	22·5	28
Château Bézineau	*St.-Émilion*	13	32·5	53
Cru Bibey	*St.-Émilion*	6	15	18
Château Bicasse-Lartigue	*St.-Sulpice-de-Faleyrens*	3	7·5	11
Château Bigaroux	*St.-Sulpice-de-Faleyrens*	5	12·5	11
Château Billeron	*St.-Hippolyte*	8	20	27
Château Binet	*Parsac-St.-Émilion*	9	22·5	19
Cru Biquet	*St.-Hippolyte*	4	10	19
Château Bois-Grouley	*St.-Sulpice-de-Faleyrens*	3	7·5	14
Château Bois-Rond-Grand-Corbin	*St.-Émilion*	4	10	16
Château Bonneau, Château des Rochers	*Montagne-St.-Émilion*	9	22·5	43
Domaine de Bonneau	*Montagne-St.-Émilion*	4	10	12
Château Bord-Fonrazade	*St.-Émilion*	4	10	14
Château Bord-Lartigue	*St.-Émilion*	2	5	11
Château Boulerne	*St.-Sulpice-de-Faleyrens*	9	22·5	32
Château Bouquey	*St.-Hippolyte*	4	10	19
Domaine du Bourg	*St.-Christophe-des-Bardes*	2	5	13
Château Boutisse	*St.-Christophe-des-Bardes*	16	40	77
Château Branne	*Montagne-St.-Émilion*	6	15	35
Château Brisson	*Vignonet*	4	10	13
Château Brisson, Château Destieux	*St. Sulpice-de-Faleyrens*	9	22·5	30
Château Brun	*St.-Christophe-des-Bardes*	6	15	20
Clos Brun	*St.-Sulpice-de-Faleyrens*	3	7·5	13
Château Cadet-Bon	*St.-Émilion*	3	7·5	19
Château Cadet-Piolat	*St.-Émilion*	18	45	75
Château Calon	*Montagne-St.-Émilion*	20	50	71
Château Calon-Montagne	*St.-Georges-St.-Émilion*	3	7·5	11
Château Calon-St.-Georges	*St.-Georges-St.-Émilion*	3	7·5	12
Château du Calvaire	*St.-Étienne-de-Lisse*	6	15	23
Clos du Calvaire	*St.-Étienne-de-Lisse*	2	5	7
Château Canon-la-Gaffelière	*St.-Émilion*	18	45	61
Château Cante Merle (*see* Château Ripeau)				
Château Cantenac	*St.-Émilion*	7	17·5	42
Clos Cantenac	*St.-Émilion*	5	12·5	27
Château Canteranne	*St.-Étienne-de-Lisse*	6	15	26
Château Cap de Mourlin	*St.-Émilion*	13	32·5	66
Château Cap-d'Or	*St.-Georges-St.-Émilion*	5	12·5	26
Château Caperot (*see* Château Monbousquet)				
Clos Caperot	*St.-Sulpice-de-Faleyrens*	3	7·5	10
Château Capet-Guiller	*St.-Hippolyte*	12	30	50
Château Cardinal Villemaurine	*St.-Émilion*	7	17·5	35
Château Carteau-Bas-Daugay	*St.-Sulpice-de-Faleyrens*	4	10	18
Château Carteau-Côte-Daugay	*St.-Émilion*	3	7·5	12

	COMMUNE	*Hectares*	*Acres*	*Tonneaux*
Château Carteau-Pin-de-Fleurs	*St.-Émilion*	3	7·5	16
Domaine de Cassah	*Puisseguin-St.-Émilion*	6	15	12
Château Cassevert (*see* Château Grand-Mayne)				
Clos Castelot	*St.-Émilion*	4	10	22
Domaine de la Cateau	*St.-Émilion*	3	7·5	11
Château Cauzin	*St.-Christophe-des-Bardes*	10	25	43
Clos de la Cavaille-Lescours	*St.-Sulpice-de-Faleyrens*	1	2·5	7
Cave Coopérative				1,760
Royal St.-Émilion	*St.-Émilion*	775	1,920	600
Côtes Rocheuses				270
Cave Coopérative des Côtes-de-Castillon	*St.-Étienne-de-Lisse*	3	7·5	14
Cave Vinicole de Puisseguin	*Puisseguin-St.-Émilion*	570	1,408	3,200
Château Champion	*St.-Christophe-des-Bardes*	5	12·5	16
Château Chante-Alouette	*St.-Émilion*	6	15	23
Château Chantecaille	*St.-Émilion*	3	7·5	17
Château Chantegrive	*St.-Émilion*	5	12·5	
Clos Chante-l'Alouette, Domaine Haut-Patarabet	*St.-Émilion*	4	10	24
Château Chapelle-de-la-Trinité (*see* Château Laniotte)				
Domaine du Chatain	*Montagne-St.-Émilion*	3	7·5	10
Château Chatelet	*St.-Émilion*	3	7·5	11
Château Chauvin	*St.-Émilion*	12	30	59
Cru Chêne-Vert	*Parsac-St.-Émilion*	7	17·5	32
Château Chêne-Vieux	*Parsac-St.-Émilion*	8	20	34
Château Cheval-Brun	*St.-Émilion*	5	12·5	14
Château Cheval-Noir	*St.-Émilion*	4	10	11
Château du Clocher	*St.-Émilion*	3	7·5	13
Domaine de la Clotte	*St.-Hippolyte*	5	12·5	15
Domaine de la Clotte	*Montagne-St.-Émilion*	5	12·5	14
Château du Comte	*St.-Hippolyte*	3	7·5	5
Coopérative de Montagne	*Montagne-St.-Émilion*	145	358	706
Clos des Corbières	*Montagne-St.-Émilion*	2	5	8
Château Corbin	*St.-Émilion*	10	25	58
Château Corbin	*Montagne-St.-Émilion*	13	32·5	65
Château Corbin-Michotte	*St.-Émilion*	8	20	29
Clos Cormey	*St.-Émilion*	7	17·5	29
Château Cormey-Figeac	*St.-Émilion*	10	25	43
Domaine de Corniaud	*Montagne-St.-Émilion*	5	12·5	15
Domaine de Corniaud-Lussac	*Lussac-St.-Émilion*	3	7·5	10
Château Côte de Bonde	*Montagne-St.-Émilion*	7	17·5	14
Château Côte de Rol-Valentin	*St.-Émilion*	3	7·3	9
Cru Côte-Migon-la-Gaffelière	*St.-Émilion*	1	2·5	6
Château Côtes-Bernateau	*St.-Étienne-de-Lisse*	8	20	50
Cru Côtes-du-Fayan	*Puisseguin-St.-Émilion*	8	20	23
Cru Côtes-Pressac	*St.-Étienne-de-Lisse*	2	5	8
Cru Côtes-Roland	*St.-Étienne-de-Lisse*	2	5	9
Clos Côtes-Roland-de-Pressac	*St.-Étienne-de-Lisse*	2	5	9
Cru Côtes-Veyrac	*St.-Étienne-de-Lisse*	3	7·5	19
Château Coucy	*Montagne-St.-Émilion*	11	27·5	45
Château Coudert	*St.-Christophe-des-Bardes*	3	7·5	12
Château Coudert-Pelletan	*St.-Christophe-des-Bardes*	9	22·5	36
Château Couperie, Château Dassault	*St.-Émilion*	16	40	52
Château du Courlat	*Lussac-St.-Émilion*	9	22·5	40
Château Coûtet	*St.-Émilion*	12	30	50

	COMMUNE	*Hectares*	*Acres*	*Tonneaux*
Château Couvent-des-Jacobins	*St.-Émilion*	9	22·5	33
Domaine Croix-de-Grézard	*Lussac-St.-Émilion*	2	5	9
Château Croix-de-Justice	*Puisseguin-St.-Émilion*	5	12·5	14
Domaine de la Croix-Mazerat	*St.-Émilion*	2	5	5
Château Croix-du-Merle	*St.-Hippolyte*	3	7·5	8
Château Croix-Figeac	*St.-Émilion*	3	7·5	12
Château Croix-Peyblanquet	*St.-Étienne-de-Lisse*	4	10	9
Château de la Croix-Simard	*St.-Émilion*	1	2·5	7
Château Croix-Villemaurine	*St.-Émilion*	1	2·5	5
Château Croque-Michotte	*St.-Émilion*	10	25	75
Château Cruzeau	*Sables-St.-Émilion*	3	7·5	14
Château Curé-Bon	*St.-Émilion*	5	12·5	15
Clos Daupin	*St.-Émilion*	2	5	10
Clos Daviaud	*Parsac-St.-Émilion*	5	12·5	13
Château des Demoiselles	*St.-Christophe-des-Bardes*	1	2·5	5
Domaine des Dépendances Cru Jaugueblanc	*St.-Émilion*	3	7·5	13
Domaine Despagne	*St.-Sulpice-de-Faleyrens*	7	17·5	15
Château Despagnet	*St.-Sulpice-de-Faleyrens*	3	7·5	13
Château Destieu	*Vignonet*	4	10	15
Château Destieux	*St.-Émilion*	9	22·5	30
Château Destieux	*St.-Sulpice-de-Faleyrens*	7	17·5	25
Château Destieux (*see* Château Brisson, *St.-Sulpice-de-Faleyrens*)				
Château Destieux-Verac	*St.-Christophe-des-Bardes*	11	27·5	36
Château des Tours	*Montagne-St.-Émilion*	59	147·5	275
Château Divon	*St.-Georges-St.-Émilion*	4	10	19
Domaine des Escardos	*Vignonet*	7	17·5	12
Château Fagouet-Jean-Voisin	*St.-Émilion*	6	15	35
Château Faizeau	*Montagne-St.-Émilion*	7	17·5	32
Château Faleyrens	*St.-Sulpice-de-Faleyrens*	5	12·5	12
Château de Ferrand	*St.-Hippolyte*	30	75	148
Château Ferrandat	*St.-Laurent-des-Combes*	4	10	16
Cru Ferrandat	*St.-Laurent-des-Combes*	1	2·5	9
Château Figeac, Château Pont-de-Figeac, Château Grangeneuve	*St.-Émilion*	25	62·5	79
Clos Fleurus	*St.-Émilion*	1	2·5	8
Clos Fleurus	*St.-Sulpice-de-Faleyrens*	1	2·5	5
Château Fombrauge	*St.-Christophe-des-Bardes*	38	94	150
Château Fond-de-Rol	*St.-Émilion*	1	2·5	5
Château Fond-Razade	*St.-Sulpice-de-Faleyrens*	4	10	8
Château Fongaban (*see* Château Mouchet)				
Château Fonplégade	*St.-Émilion*	10	25	33
Château Fonrazade	*St.-Émilion*	4	10	14
Clos Fonrazade	*St.-Émilion*	4	10	25
Château Fonroque	*St.-Émilion*	16	40	100
Clos Fontelle	*St.-Étienne-de-Lisse*	1	2·5	5
Château Fontmurée	*Montagne-St.-Émilion*	5	12·5	18
Domaine de Fontmurée	*Montagne-St.-Émilion*	10	25	39
Château Fougères	*St.-Étienne-de-Lisse*	9	22·5	45
Château Fougueyrat, Cru La Tour-Laroze, Cru Le Châtelet	*St.-Émilion*	5	12·5	34
Domaine de Fouquet	*St.-Sulpice-de-Faleyrens*	6	15	5
Clos Fourney	*St.-Étienne-de-Lisse*	4	10	14
Château Fourney (*see* Vieux-Guinot)	*St.-Pey-d'Armens*	19	47·5	87

	COMMUNE	*Hectares*	*Acres*	*Tonneaux*
Château Franc (*see* Château Franc-Patarbet)				
Cru Franc-Baudron	*Montagne-St.-Émilion*	5	12·5	23
Domaine Franc-Baudron	*Montagne-St.-Émilion*	6	15	20
Château Franc-Beau-Mazerat	*St.-Émilion*	3	7·5	11
Château Franc-Cantenac	*St.-Émilion*	1	2·5	5
Château Franc-Cormey	*St.-Émilion*	2	5	4
Château Franc-Cros	*St.-Émilion*	4	10	14
Château Franc-Laporte	*St.-Christophe-des-Bardes*	9	22·5	50
Clos Franc-Larmande	*St.-Émilion*	3	7·5	9
Château Franc-la-Rose	*St.-Émilion*	4	10	20
Château Franc-Mayne	*St.-Émilion*	6	15	40
Cru Franc-Mazerat	*St.-Émilion*	2	5	8
Château Franc-Patarabet, Château Franc	*St.-Émilion*	4	10	20
Château Franc Peilhan	*Vignonet*	3	7·5	9
Château Franc-Petit-Figeac	*St.-Émilion*	3	7·5	22
Château Franc Pipeau	*St.-Hippolyte*	3	7·5	17
Château Franc Pourret	*St.-Émilion*	11	27·5	49
Cru Franc-Rozier	*St.-Laurent-des-Combes*	3	7·5	15
Château Froquard	*St.-Georges-St.-Émilion*	3	7·5	15
Château Gadet-Plaisance	*Montagne-St.-Émilion*	4	10	12
Château Gaillard	*St.-Hippolyte*	8	20	11
Château Gaillard	*Sables-St.-Émilion*	4	10	16
Château Gaillard-de-Gorse	*St.-Étienne-de-Lisse*	3	7·5	10
Château Garderose	*Sables-St.-Émilion*	5	12·5	20
Château Gastebourse (*see* Château Pontet Clauzure)				
Château Gaubert, Clos des Moines	*St.-Christophe-des-Bardes*	16	40	55
Château Gay-Moulins	*Montagne-St.-Émilion*	7	17·5	27
Clos Gerbaud	*St.-Pey-d'Armens*	1	2·5	7
Clos Gilet	*Montagne-St.-Émilion*	3	7·5	13
Château Gironde	*Puisseguin-St.-Émilion*	4	10	5
Château Godeau	*St.-Laurent-des-Combes*	3	7·5	8
Clos Gontey	*St.-Émilion*	2	5	13
Château Goujon	*Montagne-St.-Émilion*	3	7·5	5
Domaine du Gourdins	*Sables-St.-Émilion*	1	2·5	6
Château Grand-Barrail-Lamarzelle-Figeac	*St.-Émilion*	23	57·5	123
Château Grand-Berc	*St.-Sulpice-de-Faleyrens*	4	10	13
Domaine du Grand-Bigaroux	*St.-Sulpice-de-Faleyrens*	2	5	9
Château Grand-Caillou-Noir	*Vignonet*	3	7·5	16
Domaine des Grands-Champs	*Montagne-St.-Émilion*	4	10	10
Château Grand-Corbin	*St.-Émilion*	13	32·5	71
Château Grand Corbin-Despagne	*St.-Émilion*	25	62·5	182
Grand Domaine Jean-Voisin	*St.-Émilion*	2	5	7
Clos Grand-Faurie	*Puisseguin-St.-Émilion*	4	10	24
Domaine du Grand-Faurie	*St.-Émilion*	4	10	17
Château Grand-Gontey	*St.-Émilion*	4	10	16
Clos Grand-Gontey	*St.-Émilion*	4	10	17
Domaine du Grand-Gontey	*St.-Émilion*	2	5	9
Château Grand Jacques	*St.-Christophe-des-Bardes*	11	27·5	46
Château Grand-Mayne, Château Cassevert, Château Beau-Mazerat, Château Grand-Mazerat	*St.-Émilion*	17	42·5	85
Château Grand-Mazerat (*see* Château Grand-Mayne)				
Château Grand-Mirande	*St.-Émilion*	6	15	32
Clos des Grandes-Murailles	*St.-Émilion*	2	5	10

	COMMUNE	*Hectares*	*Acres*	*Tonneaux*
Domaine des Grands-Pairs	*Lussac-St.-Émilion*	2	5	8
Château Grand-Peilhan-Blanc	*Vignonet*	7	17·5	34
Château Grand Pey-de-Lescours	*St.-Sulpice-de-Faleyrens*	24	60	112
Château Grand-Pontet	*St.-Émilion*	13	32·5	65
Château Grand-Rivallon	*St.-Émilion*	3	7·5	9
Château Grangeneuve (*see* Château Figeac)				
Château Grangey	*St.-Christophe-des-Bardes*	5	12·5	22
Château Graves-d'Armens	*St.-Pey-d'Armens*	3	7·5	5
Château des Graves	*St.-Pey-d'Armens*	4	10	24
Cru des Graves	*Vignonet*	2	5	6
Château Graves d'Arthus	*Vignonet*	5	12·5	21
Château des Graves-de-Mondou	*St.-Sulpice-de-Faleyrens*	4	10	14
Château Gravet	*St.-Sulpice-de-Faleyrens*	9	22·5	48
Clos Gravet	*St.-Sulpice-de-Faleyrens*	11	27·5	51
Domaine de Grimon	*St.-Georges-St.-Émilion*	5	12·5	20
Clos du Gros	*St.-Pey-d'Armens*	1	2·5	6
Château Gros-Caillou	*St.-Sulpice-de-Faleyrens*	8	20	32
Clos Gros-Caillou	*St.-Sulpice-de-Faleyrens*	3	7·5	8
Clos des Gros-Chênes	*Vignonet*	5	12·5	27
Cru Grotte-d'Arcis	*St.-Laurent-des-Combes*	3	7·5	14
Château Guadet-le-Franc-Grâce-Dieu	*St.-Émilion*	5	12·5	19
Château Guadet-St.-Julien	*St.-Émilion*	5	12·5	20
Château Gueyrosse	*Sables-St.-Émilion*	4	10	15
Château Gueyrot	*St.-Émilion*	6	15	27
Château Guibeau	*Puisseguin-St.-Émilion*	11	27·5	76
Château Guibot-Lafourvieille	*Puisseguin-St.-Émilion*	13	32·5	59
Château Guillemot	*St.-Christophe-des-Bardes*	7	17·5	17
Château Guillou	*St.-Georges-St.-Émilion*	13	32·5	59
Château Guinot	*St.-Étienne-de-Lisse*	4	10	16
Clos Guinot	*St.-Étienne-de-Lisse*	6	15	40
Domaine du Haut-Badon	*St.-Émilion*	3	7·5	8
Domaine de Haut-Barbey	*St.-Étienne-de-Lisse*	2	5	7
Château Haut-Barbeyron	*St.-Laurent-des-Combes*	4	10	5
Château Haut-Bastienne	*Montagne-St.-Émilion*	4	10	20
Château Haut-Benitey	*St.-Laurent-des-Combes*	5	12·5	13
Château Haut-Berthonneau	*St.-Émilion*	1	2·5	7
Clos Haut-Bibey	*St.-Émilion*	2	5	11
Clos Haut-Cabanne	*St.-Émilion*	1	2·5	6
Château Haut-Cadet	*St.-Émilion*	13	32·5	36
Domaine Haut-Caillate	*St.-Georges-St.-Émilion*	2	5	10
Château Haut-Chéreau	*Lussac-St.-Émilion*	2	5	5
Domaine Haut-Corbière	*Sables-St.-Émilion*	2	5	11
Château Haut-Corbin	*St.-Émilion*	4	10	21
Domaine de la Haute-Faucherie	*Montagne-St.-Émilion*	3	7·5	12
Château Hautes-Graves-d'Arthus	*Vignonet*	9	22·5	47
Château Haut-Fonrazade, Cru La Tour-Fonrazade	*St.-Émilion*	11	27·5	43
Château Haut-Grâce-Dieu (*see* Château Peyrelongue)				
Château Haut-Grand-Faurie	*St.-Émilion*	4	10	21
Cru Haut-Grand-Faurie	*St.-Émilion*	1	2·5	5
Château Haut-Gueyrot	*St.-Émilion*	2	5	6
Domaine Haut-Guillennay	*Sables-St.-Émilion*	2	5	10
Château Haut-Guitard	*Montagne-St.-Émilion*	4	10	20
Clos Haut-Jaugueblanc	*St.-Émilion*	1	2·5	5

	COMMUNE	*Hectares*	*Acres*	*Tonneaux*
Château Haut-Jean-Faure, Clos La Fleur-Figeac, Clos La Bourrue, Château Tauzinat-l'Hermitage	*St.-Émilion*	7	17·5	49
Château Haut-Jeanguillot	*St.-Christophe-des-Bardes*	4	10	17
Château Haut-Langlade	*Parsac-St.-Émilion*	4	10	14
Château Haut-Larose	*Lussac-St.-Émilion*	5	12·5	19
Château Haut-Lartigue	*St.-Émilion*	3	7·5	15
Château Haut-Lavallade	*St.-Christophe-des-Bardes*	4	10	23
Domaine Haut-Lavallade	*St.-Christophe-des-Bardes*	3	7·5	12
Clos Haut-Listrac	*Puisseguin-St.-Émilion*	4	10	14
Domaine de Haut-Marchand	*Montagne-St.-Émilion*	4	10	6
Château Haut-Mauvinon	*St.-Sulpice-de-Faleyrens*	8	20	28
Clos Haut-Mazerat, Vieux Château Mazerat	*St.-Émilion*	8	20	35
Clos Haut-Montaiguillon	*St.-Georges-St.-Émilion*	5	12·5	24
Château Haut-Musset	*Parsac-St.-Émilion*	5	12·5	17
Château Haute-Nauve	*St.-Laurent-des-Combes*	3	7·5	8
Château Haut-Panet-Pineuilh	*St.-Christophe-des-Bardes*	2	5	9
Domaine Haut-Patarabet (*see* Clos Chante-l'Alouette)				
Château Haut-Peyroutas	*Vignonet*	2	5	6
Château Haut-Piquat	*Lussac-St.-Émilion*	9	22·5	34
Château Haut-Plaisance	*Montagne-St.-Émilion*	7	17·5	29
Château Haut-Poitou	*Lussac-St.-Émilion*	2	5	9
Château Haut-Pontet	*St.-Émilion*	5	12·5	25
Château Haut-Pourret	*St.-Émilion*	5	12·5	30
Château Haut-Pourteau	*Lussac-St.-Émilion*	2	5	8
Château Haut-Rabion	*Vignonet*	5	12·5	17
Château Haut-Renaissance	*St.-Sulpice-de-Faleyrens*	3	7·5	19
Domaine Haut-Rimoulet	*St.-Émilion*	5	12·5	20
Clos Haut-Robin	*St.-Christophe-des-Bardes*	4	10	14
Château Haut-Rocher	*St.-Étienne-de-Lisse*	5	12·5	15
Domaine Haute-Rouchonne	*Vignonet*	4	10	16
Château Haut-St.-Georges	*St.-Georges-St.-Émilion*	2	5	9
Château Haut-Sarpe	*St.-Christophe-des-Bardes*	18	45	56
Château Haut-Segotte	*St.-Émilion*	7	17·5	42
Château Haut-Simard	*St.-Émilion*	5	12·5	29
Château Haut-Touran	*St.-Étienne-de-Lisse*	3	7·5	8
Château Haut-Troquard	*St.-Georges-St.-Émilion*	3	7·5	16
Clos Haut-Troquard	*St.-Georges-St.-Émilion*	1	2·5	6
Château Haut-Troquart	*St.-Émilion*	4	10	19
Domaine Haut-Vachon	*St.-Émilion*	4	10	18
Château Haut-Veyrac	*St.-Étienne-de-Lisse*	7	17·5	30
Clos des Jacobins	*St.-Émilion*	8	20	42
Château Jacqueblanc	*St.-Étienne-de-Lisse*	20	50	100
Clos Jacquemeau	*St.-Émilion*	1	2·5	5
Château Jacqueminot	*St.-Christophe-des-Bardes*	4	10	15
Château Jacquenoir	*St.-Étienne-de-Lisse*	4	10	20
Château Jaubert-Peyblanquet	*St.-Étienne-de-Lisse*	5	12·5	11
Château Jaugueblanc	*St.-Émilion*	5	12·5	21
Clos Jaumard	*Vignonet*	2	5	8
Château Jean Blanc	*St.-Pey-d'Armens*	6	15	33
Château Jean Faure (*see* Château Ripeau)				
Clos Jean Guillot	*St.-Christophe-des-Bardes*	1	2·5	5
Cru Jeanguillot	*St.-Christophe-des-Bardes*	2	5	8
Domaine de Jean-Marie	*St.-Émilion*	2	5	6

	COMMUNE	*Hectares*	*Acres*	*Tonneaux*
Château Jean-Marie-Cheval-Brun	*St.-Émilion*	2	5	8
Château Jean-Voisin	*St.-Émilion*	5	12·5	14
Clos Jean-Voisin	*St.-Émilion*	3	7·5	9
Château Joly	*Vignonet*	6	15	27
Cru Jubilé	*St.-Christophe-des-Bardes*	2	5	9
Château Jupille	*St.-Sulpice-de-Faleyrens*	2	5	5
Château Jura-Plaisance	*Montagne-St.-Émilion*	8	20	34
Château Justice	*St.-Étienne-de-Lisse*	3	7·5	15
Château La Barde	*St.-Laurent-des-Combes*	3	7·5	6
Clos La Barde	*St.-Laurent-des-Combes*	4	10	13
Château La Barthe	*St.-Pey-d'Armens*	4	10	17
Clos-Domaine-Château-La-Bastienne	*Montagne-St.-Émilion*	12	30	54
Domaine La Beillonne	*St.-Émilion*	2	5	14
Château La Blanque-Pinson	*St.-Sulpice-de-Faleyrens*	3	7·5	8
Clos La Bourrue (*see* Château Haut-Jean-Faure)				
Château La Bouygue	*St.-Émilion*	3	7·5	17
Clos Labrit	*St.-Sulpice-de-Faleyrens*	3	7·5	19
Clos La Cabanne	*Puisseguin-St.-Émilion*	4	10	22
Château La Carte	*St.-Émilion*	5	12·5	18
Château La Chapelle	*St.-Étienne-de-Lisse*	4	10	20
Château La Chapelle	*St.-Sulpice-de-Faleyrens*	2	5	9
Cru La Chapelle	*Parsac-St.-Émilion*	7	17·5	13
Domaine de la Chapelle	*St.-Étienne-de-Lisse*	3	7·5	15
Château La Chapelle-Lescours	*St.-Sulpice-de-Faleyrens*	3	7·5	18
Château La Clotte (*great growth*)	*St.-Émilion*	4	10	14
Château La Clotte	*Puisseguin-St.-Émilion*	2	5	4
Château La Clotte-Grande-Côte	*St.-Émilion*	4	10	11
Château La Cluzière	*St.-Émilion*	2	5	5
Château La Côte-Daugay	*St.-Sulpice-de-Faleyrens*	1	2·5	6
Château La Couronne	*Montagne-St.-Émilion*	4	10	21
Château La Couspaude	*St.-Émilion*	5	12·5	16
Clos La Croix	*St.-Pey-d'Armens*	9	22·5	49
Château La Croix-de-la-Bastienne	*Montagne-St.-Émilion*	2	5	12
Cru La Croix-Blanche	*Montagne-St.-Émilion*	2	5	7
Château La Croix-de-Blanchon	*Lussac-St.-Émilion*	5	12·5	16
Château La Croix-Chantecaille	*St.-Émilion*	6	15	32
Clos La Croix-Figeac	*St.-Émilion*	3	7·3	18
Château La Croizille	*St.-Laurent-des-Combes*	4	10	9
Château La Dominique	*St.-Émilion*	17	42·5	63
Château La Fagnouse	*St.-Étienne-de-Lisse*	5	12·5	37
Château La Faucherie	*Montagne-St.-Émilion*	3	7·5	6
Château La Fleur	*St.-Émilion*	5	12·5	28
Château La Fleur-Cadet	*St.-Émilion*	4	10	14
Clos La Fleur-Figeac (*see* Château Haut-Jean-Faure)				
Château La Fleur-Perruchon	*Lussac-St.-Émilion*	5	12·5	17
Château La Fleur-Pourret	*St.-Émilion*	3	7·5	6
Château La Fleur-St.-Georges (*see* Château St.-Georges)				
Château La Fortine	*St.-Émilion*	2	5	6
Château Lagaborite	*St.-Émilion*	2	5	8
Domaine de la Gaffelière	*St.-Émilion*	2	5	9
Château La Garelle	*St.-Émilion*	12	30	48
Cru La Garelle	*St.-Émilion*	1	2·5	8
Clos La Glaye	*St.-Pey-d'Armens*	4	10	17

	COMMUNE	*Hectares*	*Acres*	*Tonneaux*
Château La Gomerie	*St.-Émilion*	2	5	12
Château La Grâce-Dieu, Château l'Étoile-Pourret	*St.-Émilion*	13	32·5	35
Château La Grâce-Dieu-les-Menuts	*St.-Émilion*	10	25	51
Château La Grande-Clotte	*Lussac-St.-Émilion*	5	12·5	19
Château Lagrave-Figeac	*St.-Émilion*	3	7·5	17
Château La Grenière	*Lussac-St.-Émilion*	5	12·5	16
Domaine de Lamaçonne	*Montagne-St.-Émilion*	3	7·5	12
Clos La Madeleine	*St.-Émilion*	2	5	8
Château La Marzelle	*St.-Émilion*	6	15	19
Château La Mauléone (*see* Château Pontet Clauzure)				
Château La Mayne	*Sables-St.-Émilion*	3	7·5	8
Château La Mélissière	*St.-Hippolyte*	10	25	11
Domaine La Mélissière	*St.-Hippolyte*	1	2·5	6
Château La Méllisière	*St.-Sulpice-de-Faleyrens*	9	22·5	9
Château La Mouleyre	*St.-Étienne-de-Lisse*	7	17·5	19
Domaine de la Mouleyre	*St.-Étienne-de-Lisse*	5	12·5	19
Château La Nauve	*St.-Laurent-des-Combes*	9	22·5	31
Clos La Nauve	*St.-Hippolyte*	2	5	5
Château l'Angélus	*St.-Émilion*	23	57·5	130
Château Langlade	*Parsac-St.-Émilion*	6	15	12
Château Laniotte, Château Chapelle-de-la-Trinité	*St.-Émilion*	5	12·5	26
Château La Paillette	*Sables-St.-Émilion*	3	7·5	10
Château Lapelletrie	*St.-Christophe-des-Bardes*	9	22·5	54
Château La Papeterie	*Montagne-St.-Émilion*	9	22·5	55
Château La Perrière	*Lussac-St.-Émilion*	5	12·5	20
Château Lapeyre	*St.-Étienne-de-Lisse*	8	20	35
Château La Picherie	*Montagne-St.-Émilion*	6	15	13
Domaine de Laplaigne	*Puisseguin-St.-Émilion*	7	17·5	31
Château La Plante	*Sables-St.-Émilion*	1	2·5	5
Château Larcis-Bergey	*St.-Émilion*	1	2·5	8
Château Larcis-Ducasse	*St.-Laurent-des-Combes*	11	27·5	57
Château Lardon-Jacqueminot	*St.-Christophe-des-Bardes*	15	37·5	74
Château Larmande	*St.-Émilion*	6	15	30
Clos Larmande	*St.-Étienne-de-Lisse*	4	10	15
Domaine Laroque, Château Nardon	*St.-Christophe-des-Bardes*	3	7·5	19
Clos Larose	*St.-Christophe-des-Bardes*	2	5	10
Cru La Rose	*Puisseguin-St.-Émilion*	5	12·5	17
Domaine de la Rose	*St.-Émilion*	2	5	12
Château La Rose-Côte-Rol	*St.-Émilion*	4	10	19
Château La Rose-Pourret	*St.-Émilion*	14	35	79
Château La Roseraie-du-Mont	*Puisseguin-St.-Émilion*	4	10	9
Château La Rose-Rol	*St.-Émilion*	4	10	19
Château Laroze	*St.-Émilion*	25	62·5	134
Château La Rouchonne	*Vignonet*	4	10	8
Château Larques, Château Châtelet	*St.-Christophe-des-Bardes*	19	47·5	36
Château Lartigue	*St.-Émilion*	3	7·5	9
Clos Lartigue	*St.-Émilion*	1	2·5	5
Cru Lartigue	*St.-Émilion*	3	7·5	11
Clos Lartigues	*St.-Pey-d'Armens*	2	5	8
Château Larue	*Parsac-St.-Émilion*	4	10	13
Château La Sablière	*St.-Émilion*	6	15	28

	COMMUNE	*Hectares*	*Acres*	*Tonneaux*
Château La Sablonnerie	*St.-Sulpice-de-Faleyrens*	10	25	35
Château Lassègue	*St.-Hippolyte*	13	32·5	54
Château Lasserre	*St.-Émilion*	6	15	17
Château La Tête-du-Cerf	*Montagne-St.-Émilion*	6	15	15
Château Latour	*Montagne-St.-Émilion*	5	12·5	21
Château La Tour	*St.-Christophe-des-Bardes*	7	17·5	27
Château La Tour-Baladoz	*St.-Laurent-des-Combes*	3	7·5	12
Château La Tour-Ballet	*Montagne-St.-Émilion*	1	2·5	5
Château La Tour-Berthoneau	*St.-Émilion*	2	5	8
Château La Tour-Blanche	*Parsac-St.-Émilion*	3	7·5	19
Château Latour Blanche	*St.-Hippolyte*	1	2·5	4
Château La Tour-des-Combes	*St.-Laurent-des-Combes*	5	12·5	25
Château La Tour-Cravignac	*St.-Émilion*	3	7·5	16
Château La Tour-Figeac	*St.-Émilion*	5	12·5	27
Château La Tour-Fonrazade	*St.-Émilion*	4	10	17
Cru La Tour-Fonrazade (*see* Château Haut-Fonrazade)				
Château La Tour-Gilet	*Montagne-St.-Émilion*	6	15	34
Château La Tour-de-Grenet	*Lussac-St.-Émilion*	16	40	90
Château La Tour-Guillotin	*Puisseguin-St.-Émilion*	6	15	24
Château La Tour-Laroze (*see* Château Fougueyrat)				
Château Latour-Musset	*Parsac-St.-Émilion*	10	25	35
Château La Tour-Paquillon	*Montagne-St.-Émilion*	8	20	35
Château La Tour-Peyblanquet	*St.-Étienne-de-Lisse*	6	14	21
Château La Tour-du-Pin-Figeac	*St.-Émilion*	17	42·5	111
Château Latour-Pourret	*St.-Émilion*	6	15	16
Château La Tour-St.-Émilion	*St.-Émilion*	4	10	18
Château La Tour-St.-Georges (*see* Château St.-Georges)		15	37·5	62
Château La Tour-St.-Pierre	*St.-Émilion*	6	15	30
Château La Tour-de-Ségur	*Lussac-St.-Émilion*	5	12·5	15
Château Latour-de-Ségur	*Lussac-St.-Émilion*	8	20	9
Château La Tour-Vachon	*St.-Émilion*	4	10	21
Château La Vaisinerie	*Puisseguin-St.-Émilion*	8	20	27
Château Lavallade	*St.-Christophe-des-Bardes*	11	27·5	56
Clos La Vallée-du-Roi	*Montagne-St.-Émilion*	3	7·5	8
Château Lavergne	*Vignonet*	2	5	15
Clos Lavergne	*St.-Pey-d'Armens*	9	22·5	46
Château Le Basque	*Puisseguin-St.-Émilion*	18	45	47
Château Le Bon-Pasteur	*St.-Émilion*	3	7·5	9
Clos Le Bregnet	*St.-Sulpice-de-Faleyrens*	5	12·5	22
Château Le Castelot	*St.-Sulpice-de-Faleyrens*	5	12·5	21
Château Le Cauze	*St.-Christophe-des-Bardes*	20	50	130
Château Le Chapelot	*Montagne-St.-Émilion*	4	10	8
Cru Le Chatelet (*see* Château Fougueyrat)				
Château Le Chay	*Puisseguin-St.-Émilion*	13	32·5	58
Château Le Couvent	*St.-Sulpice-de-Faleyrens*	3	7·5	12
Cru Le Franc-Rival	*Lussac-St.-Émilion*	2	5	9
Château Le Freyche	*St.-Pey-d'Armens*	4	10	13
Clos Le Freyche	*St.-Pey-d'Armens*	4	10	9
Clos de l'Église (*see* Château St.-Georges)				
Clos l'Église	*Montagne-St.-Émilion*	4	10	17
Clos de l'Église	*Parsac-St.-Émilion*	13	32·5	46
Château Le Grand-Barrail	*St.-Sulpice-de-Faleyrens*	3	7·5	11
Château Le Grand-Corbin	*St.-Émilion*	5	12·5	22

	COMMUNE	*Hectares*	*Acres*	*Tonneaux*
Château Le Grand-Faurie	*St.-Émilion*	4	10	17
Château Le Gravier-Gueyrosse	*St.-Émilion*	3	7·5	12
Château Le Gueyrot	*St.-Émilion*	4	10	15
Château Le Jurat	*St.-Émilion*	9	22·5	39
Clos Le Loup	*St.-Christophe-des-Bardes*	6	15	5
Château Le Mayne	*Puisseguin-St.-Émilion*	3	7·5	9
Château Le Merle	*St.-Hippolyte*	6	15	12
Château Lenoir	*Sables-St.-Emilion*	4	10	13
Domaine du Léonard	*Puisseguin-St.-Émilion*	9	22·5	40
Clos Le Pas-St.-Georges	*St.-Georges-St.-Émilion*	6	15	31
Château Le Peillan	*St.-Laurent-des-Combes*	13	32·5	20
Château Lépine	*Sables-St.-Émilion*	2	5	7
Château Le Pont-de-Pierre	*Lussac-St.-Émilion*	3	7·5	15
Château Le Poteau	*St.-Christophe-des-Bardes*	4	10	17
Château Le Prieuré	*St.-Émilion*	5	12·5	15
Château Le Puy-St.-Georges (*see* Château St.-Georges)				
Château Le Roc-de-Troquard	*St.-Georges-St.-Émilion*	3	7·5	10
Château Le Rocher	*St.-Laurent-des-Combes*	3	7·5	10
Château Le Sable-Villebout	*St.-Laurent-des-Combes*	4	10	11
Château Les Bardes	*Montagne-St.-Émilion*	3	7·5	13
Château Les Bazilliques	*St.-Christophe-des-Bardes*	6	15	30
Château Les Carrières	*Montagne-St.-Émilion*	2	5	5
Château Les Côtes-de-Gardat	*Montagne-St.-Émilion*	5	12·5	24
Château Lescours	*St.-Sulpice-de-Faleyrens*	27	67·5	125
Château Les Eyguires, Château Haut-Sarpe, Clos du Vieux	*St.-Christophe-des-Bardes*	10	25	35
Domaine Les Genêts	*Montagne-St.-Émilion*	3	7·5	9
Château Les Grandes-Plantes-Haut Béard	*St.-Laurent-des-Combes*	3	7·5	6
Château Les Grandes-Vignes	*Montagne-St.-Émilion*	2	5	10
Clos Les Graves	*Vignonet*	4	10	12
Château Les Jacquets	*St.-Georges-St.-Émilion*	5	12·5	22
Domaine Les Jouans	*St.-Sulpice-de-Faleyrens*	3	7·5	15
Château Les Laurets	*Puisseguin-St.-Émilion*	43	106	165
Château Les Moulins	*St.-Sulpice-de-Faleyrens*	4	10	19
Château Les Moureaux	*St.-Étienne-de-Lisse*	4	10	23
Château Lespinasse	*St.-Pey-d'Armens*	4	10	19
Château Les Renardières	*St.-Georges-St.-Émilion*	4	10	14
Château Les Roquettes-Mondottes	*St.-Laurent-des-Combes*	3	7·5	10
Château Lestage	*Parsac-St.-Émilion*	8	20	47
Château Les Templiers	*St.-Émilion*	3	7·5	14
Château Les Tuileries	*St.-Étienne-de-Lisse*	3	7·5	18
Château Les Tuileries-de-Bayard	*Montagne-St.-Émilion*	8	20	29
Château Les Vieilles-Nauves	*St.-Laurent-des-Combes*	2	5	7
Château Les-Vieilles-Souches-La-Marzelle	*St.-Émilion*	4	10	18
Château Les Vieux-Rocs	*Lussac-St.-Émilion*	3	7·5	5
Château Le Tertre	*St. Laurent-des-Combes*	4	10	13
Château Le-Tertre-de-Perruchon	*Lussac-St.-Émilion*	3	7·5	7
Château Le Thibaut	*St.-Étienne-de-Lisse*	9	22·5	33
Château Le Thibaut-Bordas	*St.-Étienne-de-Lisse*	3	7·5	13
Château l'Étoile-Pourret (*see* Château La Grâce-Dieu)				
Cru Le Vignot	*St.-Hippolyte*	1	2·5	7
Château l'Hermitage	*Montagne-St.-Émilion*	6	15	26
Château l'Hermitage-Mazerat	*St.-Émilion*	4	10	17

	COMMUNE	*Hectares*	*Acres*	*Tonneaux*
Domaine de Liamet	*St.-Étienne-de-Lisse*	2	5	8
Château de Lisse	*St.-Étienne-de-Lisse*	13	32·5	32
Domaine du Logis-de-Moureaux	*St.-Pey-d'Armens*	1	2·5	6
Domaine de Longat	*St.-Sulpice-de-Faleyrens*	3	7·5	6
Château de Long-Champ	*St.-Sulpice-de-Faleyrens*	4	10	26
Clos l'Oratoire (*see* Château Peyreau)				
Château L'Ormeau-Vieux	*Puisseguin-St.-Émilion*	7	17·5	23
Château Lucas	*Lussac-St.-Émilion*	9	22·5	37
Château de Lussac	*Lussac-St.-Émilion*	20	50	88
Château Lyonnat	*Lussac-St.-Émilion*	49	121	218
Château Lyon-Perruchon	*Lussac-St.-Émilion*	4	10	11
Château Macureau	*Montagne-St.-Émilion*	6	15	26
Château Magnan-la-Gaffelière	*St.-Émilion*	8	20	40
Clos des Magrines	*Puisseguin-St.-Émilion*	3	7·5	6
Clos du Maine	*St.-Laurent-des-Combes*	2	5	10
Château Maison-Blanche	*Montagne-St.-Émilion*	25	62·5	134
Château Maisonneuve	*Parsac-St.-Émilion*	7	17·5	6
Clos Maisonneuve	*Parsac-St.-Émilion*	2	5	8
Domaine de Maison-neuve, Château St.-Georges-Macquin	*St.-Georges-St.-Émilion*	17	42·5	54
Château Malineau	*St.-Émilion*	4	10	14
Château Marrin	*St.-Christophe-des-Bardes*	6	15	33
Château Martinet	*Sables-St.-Émilion*	12	30	56
Château Matras	*St.-Émilion*	7	17.5	25
Château Maugot	*St.-Étienne-de-Lisse*	20	50	66
Clos Maurice	*St.-Sulpice-de-Faleyrans*	1	2·5	6
Château Maurillon	*St.-Christophe-des-Bardes*	1	2·5	7
Château Mauvezin	*St.-Émilion*	5	12·5	26
Château Mayne-Vieux	*St.-Étienne-de-Lisse*	5	12·5	17
Château Menichot	*St.-Hippolyte*	5	12·5	18
Clos des Menuts	*St.-Émilion*	2	5	8
Domaine des Menuts	*St.-Émilion*	1	2·5	5
Château du Merle	*St.-Hippolyte*	6	15	18
Clos Meylet-la-Gomerie	*St.-Émilion*	2	5	10
Château Meynard	*Sables-St.-Émilion*	6	15	11
Château Millery-Lapelletrie	*St.-Christophe-des-Bardes*	2	5	10
Château Milon-Feuillat	*St.-Christophe-des-Bardes*	3	7·5	10
Château Mitrotte	*St.-Laurent-des-Combes*	1	2·5	6
Château des Moines	*Montagne-St.-Émilion*	4	10	21
Château des Moines	*St.-Émilion*	4	10	23
Clos des Moines (*see* Château Gaubert)				
Château Monbousquet, Château Caperot	*St.-Sulpice-de-Faleyrens*	31	77·5	144
Château Mondotte-Bellisle	*St.-Laurent-des-Combes*	6	15	16
Château Mondou	*St.-Sulpice-de-Faleyrens*	4	10	16
Clos Mondou	*St.-Sulpice-de-Faleyrens*	2	5	9
Château Monlot-Capet	*St.-Hippolyte*	8	20	37
Clos Monplaisir	*St.-Étienne-de-Lisse*	2	5	8
Château Montaiguillon	*Montagne-St.-Émilion*	23	57·5	128
Château Montaiguillon	*St.-Georges-St.-Émilion*	3	7·5	16
Château Montbelair	*St.-Étienne-de-Lisse*	2	5	8
Château Montesquieu	*Puisseguin-St.-Émilion*	14	35	63
Clos Montesquieu	*Montagne-St.-Émilion*	3	7·5	12
Château Montlabert	*St.-Émilion*	10	25	40

	COMMUNE	*Hectares*	*Acres*	*Tonneaux*
Domaine de Montlabert	*St.-Émilion*	2	5	10
Château Montremblant	*St.-Émilion*	5	12·5	25
Château Morillon	*St.-Christophe-des-Bardes*	2	5	8
Château Mouchet, Château Fongaban	*Puisseguin-St.-Émilion*	10	25	35
Château Mouchique	*Puisseguin-St.-Émilion*	4	10	17
Château du Moulin	*Puisseguin-St.-Émilion*	6	15	30
Château Moulin-Bellegrave	*Vignonet*	5	12·5	13
Château Moulin du Cadet	*St.-Émilion*	6	15	22
Château Moulin de Cantelaube	*St.-Émilion*	3	7·5	6
Château Moulin-du-Jura	*Montagne-St.-Émilion*	3	7·5	10
Château Moulin-de-Pierrefitte	*St.-Sulpice-de-Faleyrens*	3	7·5	14
Château Moulin-St.-Georges	*St.-Émilion*	11	27·5	48
Château Moulin-St.-Georges, Château Pin-du-Fleur	*St.-Émilion*	13	32·5	65
Cru Mourens	*St.-Hippolyte*	2	5	7
Château Musset	*Parsac-St.-Émilion*	7	17·5	28
Château Myosotis	*St.-Émilion*	3	7·5	10
Château Naguet-La-Brande	*Parsac-St.-Émilion*	5	12·5	12
Cru Napoléon	*St.-Laurent-des-Combes*	2	5	7
Château Nardon (*see* Domaine Laroque)				
Clos de Naudin	*St.-Christophe-des-Bardes*	2	5	6
Château Négrit	*Montagne-St.-Émilion*	9	22·5	41
Château de Neuville	*St.-Christophe-des-Bardes*	1	2·5	7
Château Pailhas	*St.-Hippolyte*	12	30	51
Clos Pailhas	*St.-Hippolyte*	3	7·5	8
Clos du Palais-Cardinal	*St.-Sulpice-de-Faleyrens*	5	12·5	6
Château Panet	*St.-Christophe-des-Bardes*	22	55	80
Château Paradis	*Montagne-St.-Émilion*	5	12·5	28
Château Paradis, Château Patarabet	*Vignonet*	19	47·5	64
Château Parans	*St.-Étienne-de-Lisse*	7	17·5	35
Clos Pasquette	*St.-Sulpice-de-Faleyrens*	3	7·5	15
Domaine de Pasquette	*St.-Sulpice-de-Faleyrens*	5	12·5	26
Château Patarabet	*St.-Émilion*	3	7·5	11
Château Patarabet (*see* Château Paradis, *Vignonet*)				
Clos Patarabet	*St.-Émilion*	1	2·5	5
Cru Patarabet	*St.-Laurent-des-Combes*	1	2·5	4
Domaine Patarabet-la-Gaffelière	*St.-Émilion*	2	5	8
Clos Patarabet-Lartigue	*St.-Émilion*	2	5	9
Château Patris	*St.-Émilion*	5	12·5	29
Clos Patris	*St.-Émilion*	1	2·5	5
Château Pavie-Decesse	*St.-Émilion*	6	15	25
Château Pavie-Macquin	*St.-Émilion*	12	30	50
Château Pavillon-Cadet	*St.-Émilion*	6	15	11
Château Pavillon-Figeac	*St.-Émilion*	4	10	9
Château Pavillon-Fougailles	*St.-Émilion*	1	2·5	5
Château Peillan-St.-Clair	*Vignonet*	6	15	18
Château Pelletan	*St.-Christophe-des-Bardes*	5	12·5	16
Château Pérey	*St.-Sulpice-de-Faleyrens*	8	20	30
Domaine de Pérey	*St.-Sulpice-de-Faleyrens*	2	5	10
Domaine Petit-Basque	*St.-Pey-d'Armens*	2	5	6
Château Petit-Bigaroux	*St.-Sulpice-de-Faleyrens*	5	12·5	15
Château Petit-Bois-la-Garelle	*St.-Émilion*	3	7·5	14
Château Petit Bord	*St.-Émilion*	1	2·5	4

	COMMUNE	*Hectares*	*Acres*	*Tonneaux*
Château Petit-Clos	*Montagne-St.-Émilion*	8	20	27
Domaine du Petit Clos	*St.-Hippolyte*	4	10	18
Petit Clos Figeac	*St.-Émilion*	3	7·5	15
Château Petit-Cormey	*St.-Émilion*	6	15	25
Château Petit-Faurie	*St.-Émilion*	1	2·5	5
Château Petit-Faurie-de-Souchard	*St.-Émilion*	10	25	52
Château Petit-Faurie-de-Soutard	*St.-Émilion*	8	20	43
Château Petit-Faurie-Trocard	*St.-Émilion*	4	10	21
Clos Petit-Figeac, Clos Pourret	*St.-Émilion*	3	7·5	16
Château Petit-Fombrauge	*St.-Christophe-des-Bardes*	2	5	6
Cru Petit-Gontey	*St.-Émilion*	2	5	9
Domaine du Petit-Gontey	*St.-Émilion*	3	7·5	9
Château Petit-Gravet	*St.-Émilion*	5	12·5	10
Domaine du Petit-Gueyrot	*St.-Laurent-des-Combes*	2	5	12
Château Petit-Mangot	*St.-Étienne-de-Lisse*	5	12·5	33
Château Petit-Refuge	*Lussac-St.-Émilion*	4	10	13
Château Petit-Val	*St.-Émilion*	5	12·5	27
Château Peygenestou	*St.-Émilion*	2	5	10
Château Peymouton	*St.-Christophe-des-Bardes*	3	7·5	10
Château Peyreau, Clos l'Oratoire	*St.-Émilion*	18	45	75
Château Peyrelongue, Château Haut-Grâce-Dieu	*St.-Émilion*	11	27·5	52
Château Peyrou	*St. Étienne-de-Lisse*	5	12·5	24
Château Peyrouquet	*St.-Émilion*	1	2·5	7
Château Peyroutas	*Vignonet*	8	20	42
Clos Pezat	*Vignonet*	1	2·5	6
Château Picon-Gravignac	*St.-Émilion*	4	10	12
Château Pidoux	*St.-Émilion*	2	5	10
Clos Piganeau	*St.-Émilion*	1	2·5	8
Château Pin-du-Fleur (*see* Château Moulin-St.-Georges)				
Château Piney	*St.-Hippolyte*	6	15	13
Cru Piney	*St.-Hippolyte*	1	2·5	4
Château Pipeau	*St.-Laurent-des-Combes*	19	47·5	112
Château Pipeau-Menichot	*St.-Hippolyte*	6	15	22
Château Piron	*Parsac-St.-Émilion*	6	15	17
Château Plaisance	*St.-Sulpice-de-Faleyrens*	6	15	29
Château Plaisance	*Montagne-St.-Émilion*	11	27·5	46
Clos Plaisance	*Parsac-St.-Émilion*	9	47·5	90
Cru Plaisance	*St.-Sulpice-de-Faleyrens*	4	10	20
Cru Plateau-Jappeloup	*St.-Étienne-de-Lisse*	3	7·5	6
Clos Plince	*Sables-St.-Émilion*	1	2·5	6
Château Pointe-Bouquey	*St.-Pey-d'Armens*	4	10	19
Château du Pont de Bouquey	*St.-Hippolyte*	3	7·5	11
Château Pont-de-Figeac (*see* Château Figeac)				
Château Pont-de-Mouquet	*St.-Pey-d'Armens*	12	30	40
Château Pontet	*St.-Émilion*	4	10	17
Château du Pontet	*St.-Étienne-de-Lisse*	3	7·5	12
Château Pontet Clauzure, Château La Mauléone, Château Gastebourse	*St.-Émilion*	8	20	43
Clos Pourret (*see* Clos Petit-Figeac)				
Château Pressac	*St.-Étienne-de-Lisse*	24	60	90
Clos Pressac	*St.-Étienne-de-Lisse*	7	17·5	32
Château du Puy	*Parsac-St.-Émilion*	6	15	24

	COMMUNE	*Hectares*	*Acres*	*Tonneaux*
Château Puy-Blanquet	*St.-Étienne-de-Lisse*	25	62·5	84
Château Puy-Bonnet	*Parsac-St.-Émilion*	5	12·5	10
Château du Puynormond	*Parsac-St.-Émilion*	7	17·5	24
Domaine du Puynormond	*Parsac-St.-Émilion*	5	12·5	21
Château Quentin	*St.-Christophe-des-Bardes*	35	87	93
Château Quercy	*Vignonet*	4	10	22
Château Queyron	*St.-Émilion*	4	10	17
Château Queyron-Pin-de-Fleurs	*St.-Émilion*	4	10	27
Château Quinault	*Sables-St.-Émilion*	12	30	58
Château Rabat	*St.-Étienne-de-Lisse*	3	7·5	10
Château Rabion	*St.-Pey-d'Armens*	5	12·5	19
Domaine Rabion-Pailhas	*St.-Laurent-des-Combes*	4	10	14
Domaine de Rambaud	*Lussac-St.-Émilion*	3	7·5	6
Château Régent	*St.-Émilion*	4	10	20
Château Reine-Blanche	*St.-Émilion*	5	12·5	16
Château des Religieuses	*St.-Christopher-des-Bardes*	2	5	9
Clos des Religieuses	*Puisseguin-St.-Émilion*	3	7·5	8
Château Renaissance	*St.-Sulpice-de-Faleyrens*	5	12·5	24
Domaine de Rey	*St.-Émilion*	4	10	19
Château Reynard	*St.-Pey-d'Armens*	4	10	14
Château Rigaud	*Puisseguin-St.-Émilion*	3	7·5	10
Château Ripeau, Château Jean Faure, Château Cante Merle, Château Troquart	*St.-Émilion*	28	70	115
Château Rivallon	*St.-Émilion*	8	20	24
Domaine de Rivière	*St.-Pey-d'Armens*	5	12·5	21
Château Robin	*St.-Christophe-des-Bardes*	4	10	14
Château Robin-des-Moines	*St.-Christophe-des-Bardes*	5	12·5	7
Château Roc	*St.-Sulpice-de-Faleyrens*	4	10	20
Clos du Roc	*St.-Étienne-de-Lisse*	3	7·5	8
Château Roc-de-Puynormond	*Parsac-St.-Émilion*	6	15	10
Château Roc-St.-Michel	*St.-Étienne-de-Lisse*	4	10	18
Château Rochebelle	*St. Laurent-des-Combes*	3	7·5	7
Château du Rocher	*St.-Étienne-de-Lisse*	9	22·5	39
Château Rocher-Bellevue-Figeac	*St.-Émilion*	8	20	14
Château Rocher-Corbin	*Montagne-St.-Émilion*	6	15	37
Château des Rochers (*see* Château Bonneau)				
Côtes Rocheuses (*see* Cave Coopérative)				
Domaine des Rocs	*Lussac-St.-Émilion*	8	20	40
Château Rocs-Marchand	*Montagne-St.-Émilion*	9	22·5	9
Château de Rol	*St.-Émilion*	5	12·5	24
Côtes de Rol	*St.-Christophe-des-Bardes*	4	10	26
Domaine de Rol	*St.-Émilion*	3	7·5	13
Château Rol-de-Fombrauge	*St.-Christophe-des-Bardes*	4	10	20
Clos Rol-de-Fombrauge	*St.-Christophe-des-Bardes*	5	12·5	23
Cru Rol-de-Fombrauge	*St.-Christophe-des-Bardes*	4	10	15
Château aux Roquettes	*St.-Laurent-des-Combes*	2	5	7
Château Roucheyron	*St.-Christophe-des-Bardes*	6	15	28
Clos Roucheyron	*St.-Christophe-des-Bardes*	1	2·5	5
Château Roudier	*Montagne-St.-Émilion*	20	50	104
Château Roudier	*St.-Georges-St.-Émilion*	3	7·5	17
Domaine de Roudiėr	*Montagne-St.-Émilion*	7	17·5	9
Domaine du Rouy	*Vignonet*	2	5	9
Château du Roy, Clos Berthoneau	*St.-Émilion*	3	7·5	20

	COMMUNE	*Hectares*	*Acres*	*Tonneaux*
Royal St.-Émilion (*see* Cave Coopérative)				
Château Roylland-Matras	*St.-Émilion*	8	20	34
Château Rozier	*St.-Laurent-des-Combes*	10	25	43
Château Rozier	*St.-Sulpice-de-Faleyrens*	3	7·5	17
Château Rozier-Béard	*St.-Laurent-des-Combes*	6	15	22
Château des Roziers	*Montagne-St.-Émilion*	4	10	14
Clos du Sable	*St.-Christophe-des-Bardes*	2	5	5
Château Sablons	*Montagne-St.-Émilion*	5	12·5	20
Château St.-Christophe	*St.-Christophe-des-Bardes*	7	17·5	29
Château St.-Christophe	*St.-Sulpice-de-Faleyrens*	3	7·5	7
Clos St.-Émilion	*St.-Émilion*	8	20	44
Château St.-Georges, Château La Tour-St.-Georges, Château Le Puy-St.-Georges, Château La Fleur-St.-Georges, Clos de l'Église	*St.-Georges-St.-Émilion*	35	87	140
Château St.-Georges-Côte-Pavie	*St.-Émilion*	6	15	21
Château St.-Georges-Macquin (*see* Domaine de Maisonneuve)				
Château St.-Jacques-Calon	*Montagne-St.-Émilion*	6	15	22
Domaine St.-Jean-de-Béard	*St.-Laurent-des-Combes*	4	10	11
Château St.-Julien	*St.-Émilion*	3	7·5	9
Château St.-Lô	*St.-Pey-d'Armens*	8	20	38
Château St.-Louis	*St.-Georges-St.-Émilion*	4	10	18
Château St.-Martial	*St.-Sulpice-de-Faleyrens*	2	5	9
Clos St.-Martin	*St.-Émilion*	1	2·5	7
Château St.-Michel	*Montagne-St.-Émilion*	2	5	9
Château St.-Paul	*Montagne-St.-Émilion*	5	12·5	23
Château St.-Pey	*St.-Pey-d'Armens*	9	22·5	59
Château St.-Pierre	*St.-Pey-d'Armens*	4	10	11
Château St.-Roch	*St.-Christophe-des-Bardes*	3	7·5	9
Clos St.-Valéry	*St.-Émilion*	3	7·5	13
Domaine de la Salle (*see* Château Sansonnet)				
Château Samion	*St.-Georges-St.-Émilion*	9	22·5	35
Château Sansonnet, Château La Couspaude, Domaine de la Salle	*St.-Émilion*	9	22·5	27
Château de Sarenceau	*St.-Émilion*	5	12·5	26
Château de Sarpe, Château Vieux-Sarpe	*St.-Christophe-des-Bardes*	6	15	12
Clos de Sarpe	*St.-Christophe-des-Bardes*	3	7·5	10
Clos des Sarrazins	*St.-Hippolyte*	6	15	14
Château Saupiquet	*St.-Émilion*	1	2·5	9
Domaine Saupiquet	*St.-Émilion*	2	5	8
Domaine de Sème	*St.-Hippolyte*	4	10	20
Clos Sicard	*St.-Pey-d'Armens*	4	10	15
Château Simard	*St.-Émilion*	15	37·5	74
Clos Simard	*St.-Émilion*	3	7·5	13
Château Soleil	*Puisseguin-St.-Émilion*	5	12·5	21
Château Soutard	*St.-Émilion*	18	37·5	74
Château Soutard-Cadet	*St.-Émilion*	3	7·5	11
Château Tarreyre	*St.-Émilion*	2	5	11
Château Taureau	*Lussac-St.-Émilion*	3	7·5	11
Château Tauzinat	*St.-Christophe-des-Bardes*	3	7·5	5
Domaine Tauzinat	*St.-Christophe-des-Bardes*	3	7·5	10
Château Tauzinat-l'Hermitage (*see* Château Haut-Jean-Faure)				
Château Teillac	*Puisseguin-St.-Émilion*	7	17·5	31
Château Terrien	*Lussac-St.-Émilion*	3	7·5	11

Château Tetre-Daugay	*St.-Sulpice-de-Faleyrens*	15	37·5	70
Château Tetre-de-la-Mouleyre	*Parsac-St.-Émilion*	2	5	8
Clos Teynac-Rival	*Lussac-St.-Émilion*	3	7·5	14
Château Teyssier	*Puisseguin-St.-Émilion*	28	70	120
Château Teyssier	*Vignonet*	4	10	16
Château Toinet-Fombrauge	*St.-Christophe-des-Bardes*	8	20	36
Château Tonneret	*St.-Christophe-des-Bardes*	2	5	10
Château du Touran	*St.-Étienne-de-Lisse*	4	10	25
Château des Tours	*Montagne-St.-Émilion*	32	80	130
Château Touzinat	*St.-Pey-d'Armens*	7	17·5	40
Château Trapaud	*St.-Étienne-de-Lisse*	11	27·5	94
Château Trapeau	*St.-Sulpice-de-Faleyrens*	8	20	47
Domaine de Trapeau	*St.-Sulpice-de-Faleyrens*	3	7·5	20
Château Trianon	*St.-Émilion*	5	12·5	21
Château Trimoulet	*St.-Émilion*	13	32·5	74
Clos Trimoulet	*St.-Émilion*	4	10	21
Château Trois-Moulins	*St.-Émilion*	4	10	15
Château Troplong-Mondot	*St.-Émilion*	24	60	120
Château Troquart (*see* Château Ripeau)				
Château Truquet	*St.-Émilion*	4	10	18
Domaine Vachon	*St.-Émilion*	3	7·5	16
Château du Val-d'Or	*Vignonet*	3	7·5	19
Clos Valentin	*St.-Émilion*	4	10	21
Clos Verdet-Monbousquet	*St.-Sulpice-de-Faleyrens*	5	12·5	11
Clos Vert-Bois	*St.-Émilion*	4	10	10
Château Veyrac	*St.-Étienne-de-Lisse*	3	7·5	25
Domaine de la Vieille-Cloche	*St.-Émilion*	4	10	20
Château Vieille-Tour-La-Rose	*St.-Émilion*	3	7·5	16
Clos du Vieux (*see* Château Les Eyguires)				
Château Vieux-Bonneau	*Montagne-St.-Émilion*	4	10	14
Vieux-Château-Calon	*Montagne-St.-Émilion*	5	12·5	24
Château Vieux-Castel-Robin	*St.-Christophe-des-Bardes*	4	10	17
Château Vieux-Ceps, Château Badon	*St.-Émilion*	6	15	28
Vieux-Château-Chauvin	*St.-Émilion*	4	10	18
Vieux-Château-Fortin	*St.-Émilion*	5	12·5	16
Château Vieux Garouilh	*St.-Sulpice-de-Faleyrens*	5	12·5	27
Vieux-Château-Goujon	*Montagne-St.-Émilion*	2	5	7
Château Vieux-Guillou	*St.-Georges-St.-Émilion*	4	10	17
Château Vieux-Guinot, Château Fourney	*St.-Étienne-de-Lisse*	5	12·5	32
Vieux-Château-La-Beysse	*Puisseguin-St.-Émilion*	4	10	6
Château Vieux-Larmande	*St.-Émilion*	4	10	11
Château Vieux-Logis-de-Cazelon	*Montagne-St.-Émilion*	2	5	8
Vieux Château Mazerat (*see* Clos Haut-Mazerat)				
Vieux-Domaine-Menuts	*St.-Émilion*	3	7·5	7
Château Vieux Montaiguillon	*St.-Georges-St.-Émilion*	3	7·5	13
Château Vieux-Mouchet	*Montagne-St.-Émilion*	1	2·5	6
Château Vieux-Moulin-du-Cadet	*St.-Émilion*	3	7·5	16
Domaine du Vieux-Moulin-de-Calon	*Montagne-St.-Émilion*	1	2·5	6
Vieux-Château-Négrit	*Montagne-St.-Émilion*	10	25	54
Vieux-Château-Palon	*Montagne-St.-Émilion*	5	12·5	17
Vieux-Château-Peymouton	*St.-Christophe-des-Bardes*	9	22·5	37
Vieux-Château-Peyrou	*St.-Étienne-de-Lisse*	1	2·5	7
Clos Vieux-Pontet	*St.-Émilion*	2	5	6
Château Vieux-Pourret	*St.-Émilion*	4	10	19

	COMMUNE	*Hectares*	*Acres*	*Tonneaux*
Vieux Château St.-André	*St.-Georges-St.-Émilion*	3	7·5	7
Château Vieux-Clos-St.-Pierre	*Montagne-St.-Émilion*	4	10	19
Château Vieux-Sarpe (*see* Château de Sarpe)				
Château Vieux-Taillefer	*Vignonet*	3	7·5	7
Clos Vieux Troquard	*St.-Georges-St.-Émilion*	1	2·5	5
Vieux-Château-Vachon	*St.-Émilion*	3	7·5	15
Domaine du Vieux-Vachon	*St.-Émilion*	3	7·5	8
Clos Vilet	*St.-Étienne-de-Lisse*	3	7·5	13
Château Villebout	*St.-Émilion*	2	5	10
Château Villemaurine	*St.-Émilion*	6	15	28
Clos Villemaurine	*St.-Émilion*	1	2·5	5
Château Viramont	*St.-Étienne-de-Lisse*	5	12·5	19
Château Yon	*St.-Christophe-des-Bardes*	7	17·5	27
Château Yon-Figeac	*St.-Émilion*	21	52·5	110
Château Yon-la-Tour	*St.-Émilion*	4	10	17
Clos Yon-St.-Martin	*St.-Émilion*	3	7·5	9
Clos Yveline	*Montagne-St.-Émilion*	2	5	5

IV *Pomerol*

The wines of Pomerol are not officially classified. Château Pétrus is recognized as being the outstanding Great Growth, followed by the eighteen other wines italicized below.

The following figures of production are approximate, and indicate average annual output, as given by the communes and taken from their Déclarations de Récoltes records.

Principal Growths

	Hectares	*Acres*	*Tonneaux*
Clos des Amandiers	2	5	11
Clos Barrail-du-Milieu, Clos du Pellerin	2	5	5
Château Beauchêne (*see* Clos Mazeyres)			
Château Beaulieu	1	2·5	7
Château Beauregard	11	27·5	51 (*3,800 cases*)
Clos Beauregard (*see* Château Taillefer)			
Château Beauséjour	2	5	6
Château Beau-Soleil	3	7·5	15
Château Bel-Air, Vieux-Château-Boënot	10	25	35
Clos Bel-Air (*see* Domaine La Pointe)			
Château Bellegraves	4	10	24
Château Bellevue	5	12·5	23
Château Boënot, Château Trintin	4	10	19
Clos Bonalgue	3	7·5	11
Château Le Bon-Pasteur	6	15	25
Domaine de Bourg-Neuf	1	2·5	6
Château Bourgneuf	9	22·5	36
Château Brun-Mazeyres	3	7·5	13
Domaine de Cantereau	1	2·5	6
Château du Casse	2	5	8
Clos du Castel	2	5	9
Château Certan-Giraud	2	5	12 (*1,150 cases*)

	Hectares	*Acres*	*Tonneaux*
Château Certan-de-May	4	10	13 (*750 cases*)
Château Certan-Marzelle	4	10	15
Château Clinet	6	15	39
Clos du Clocher, Château Monregard-Lacroix	5	12·5	28
Domaine des Clones	2	5	7
Clos du Commandeur	1	2·5	5
Cru Côte-Gazin	1	2·5	5
Clos du Fagnard	2	5	9
Château Ferrand	11	27·5	45
Château Feytit-Clinet	6	15	15
Château Franc-Maillet	4	10	22
Château Gazin	24	60	86 (*8,250 cases*)
Château Gombaude-Guillot, Château Grandes-Vignes-Clinet	6	15	30
Château Gouprie	3	7·5	15
Château Grandes-Vignes-Clinet (*see* Château Gombaude-Guillot)			
Cru Grand-Mazeyres	2	5	7
Château Grand-Moulinet	1	2·5	5
Clos Les Grands-Champs, Château Guillot	5	12·5	23
Clos des Grands Sillons	3	7·5	20
Château Grange Neuve	4	10	16
Château Grate-Cap	4	10	19
Château Guillot (*see* Clos Les Grands-Champs)			
Château Haut-Cloquet	2	5	11
Domaine du Haut-Cloquet	1	2·5	5
Cru Haut-Groupey	2	5	6
Château Haut-Maillet	5	12·5	19
Clos Haut-Mazeyres	9	22·5	27
Domaine de Haut-Pignon	2	5	7
Domaine de Haut-Tropchaud	1	2·5	6
Château des Jacobins	1	2·5	5
Château La Cabane	9	22·5	35
Château La Chichonne	2	5	5
Clos Lacombe	2	5	6
Château La Commanderie	5	12·5	20
Château La Conseillante	10	25	34 (*3,260 cases*)
Château La Croix	8	20	23 (*2,000 cases*)
Château La Croix-de-Gay	6	15	34
Château Lacroix-St.-Georges	4	10	21
Château La Croix-Taillefer	2	5	7
Château Lacroix-Toulifaut	1	2·5	11
Château Lafleur	4	10	12 (*1,150 cases*)
Château Lafleur-Gazin	4	10	13
Château Lafleur-Pétrus	8	20	31 (*3,000 cases*)
Château La Fleur-des-Rouzes	4	10	13
Château La Ganne	5	12·5	15
Château Lagrange	9	22·5	15 (*1,500 cases*)

	Hectares	*Acres*	*Tonneaux*
Château Lagrave	7	17·5	16
Château l'Angélus	1	2·5	5
Château La Patache	2	5	6
Château La Pointe	20	50	77 *(6,500 cases)*
Domaine La Pointe, Clos Bel-Air	4	10	9
Château La Renaissance	1	2·5	5
Clos La Rose	3	7·5	13
Clos La Soulatte	2	5	8
Château Latour-Pomerol	8	20	27 *(2,400 cases)*
Château La Violette	2	5	10
Château Le Caillou	5	12·5	30
Château Le Carillon	4	10	22
Château Le Gay	8	20	25
Clos l'Église	5	12·5	24
Domaine de l'Église	5	12·5	21
Clos de l'Église-Clinet	4	10	21 *(1,700 cases)*
Château l'Enclos	7	17·5	34
Château Les Bordes	2	5	13
Château Les Grandes-Vignes	1	2·5	5
Château Les Grands-Sillons	2	5	14
Château Les Hautes-Rouzes	2	5	9
Château l'Évangile	13	32·5	36 *(3,450 cases)*
Château Margot	1	2·5	5
Château Mayne	3	7·5	11
Château du Mayne	2	5	11
Château Mazeyres	10	25	47
Clos Mazeyres, Château Beauchêne	6	15	26
Château Monregard-Lacroix (*see* Clos du Clocher)			
Château Moulinet	13	32·5	50
Château Nénin	20	50	76 *(7,300 cases)*
Cru de la Nouvelle-Église	2	5	6
Clos du Pellerin (*see* Clos Barrail-du-Milieu)			
Château du Petit-Moulinet	3	7·5	12
Château Petit-Village	9	22·5	42 *(4,030 cases)*
Château Pétrus	7	17·5	26 *(2,500 cases)*
Château Pignon-de-Gay	2	5	10
Clos Pleville	1	2·5	5
Château Plince	7	17·5	34
Château Plincette	1	2·5	5
Château La Providence	3	7·5	7
Clos René	10	25	55
Domaine de René	3	7·5	8
Château Rève-d'Or	5	12·5	19
Domaine de Robert	4	10	13
Château Rocher-Beauregard	2	5	8
Château Rouget	10	25	35 *(3,400 cases)*

	Hectares	*Acres*	*Tonneaux*
Clos du Roy	3	7·5	12
Clos St.-André	2	5	12
Clos St.-Anne (*see* Château Taillefer)			
Château de Sales	31	77·5	110
Château Tailhas	9	22·5	54
Château Taillefer, Clos Beauregard, Clos Toulifaut, Clos St.-Anne	21	52·5	102
Château des Templiers	3	7·5	17
Clos des Templiers	1	2·5	10
Château Thibéaud-Maillet	2	5	16
Château Toulifaut (*see* Château Taillefer)			
Château Tristan	1	2·5	5
Château Trintin (*see* Château Boënot)			
Château Trotanoy	7	17·5	23 (*2,200 cases*)
Château de Valois	6	15	28
Domaine de la Vieille-École	1	2·5	5
Vieux-Château-Boënot (*see* Château Bel-Air)			
Vieux-Château-Bourgueneuf	3	7·5	18
Vieux-Château-Certan	14	35	56 (*5,370 cases*)
Vieux-Château-Cloquet	2	5	7
Vieux-Château-l'Angélus	1	2·5	10
Vieux-Château-Tropchaud	2	5	6
Château Vieux-Maillet	1	2·5	5
Clos Vieux-Maillet	2	5	7
Château Vraye-Croix-de-Gay	4	10	13

Appellation Lalande de Pomerol

Commune de Lalande de Pomerol

Clos des Arnaud
Château de Bel Air
Château Bourseau
Petit Clos de Brouard
Château de la Commanderie
Château les Cruzelles
Clos de l'Église
Clos l'Étoile
Domaine de Grand Moine
Château Grand Ormeau
Clos Haut Cavujon
Château Laborde
Château des Moines
Château Templiers
Clos de Moines
Château de Musset
Château Perron
Sabloire du Grand Moine
Château de Viaud
Domaine de Viaud
Clos de la Vieille Forge

Commune de Néac

Domaine du Bourg
Château Canon Chaigneau
Clos du Casrel
Château Chatain
Clos du Chatain
Domain du Chatain
Château les Chaumes
Château Chevrol Bel Air
Château Drouilleau Belles Graves
Château Fougeailles
Château Gachet
Château Garraud
Domaine des Grands Bois Chagneau
Domaine du Grand Ormeau
Château Haut Ballet
Château Haut Chaigneau
Château Lafaurie
Château Lavinot la Chapelle
Château Les Grandes Versaines
Château Moncets
Château Moulin à Vent
Château Siaurac
Domaine de Surget
Château de Teysson
Château Tournefeuille

V Côtes de Fronsac

The following figures of production are approximate, and indicate average annual output, as given by the communes and taken from their Déclarations de Récoltes records.

Principal Growths

	COMMUNE	*Hectares*	*Acres*	*Tonneaux*
Clos du Alem	*Saillans*	10	25	24
Château Arnauton	*Fronsac*	11	27·5	20
Château Bardon-Ferrand	*St.-Aignan*	2	5	7
Château Bicot (Lambert)	*St.-Aignan*	1	2·5	3
Château Bicot (Rodier)	*Fronsac*	3	7·5	6
Château Bicot Latour	*St.-Aignan*	3	7·5	16
Château Cantelouve	*Fronsac*	10	25	25
Cru Cardeneau (Durand)	*Saillans*	4	10	12
Cru Cardeneau (Godicheau)	*Saillans*	6	15	15
Domaine du Cardneau (Barraud)	*Saillans*	4	10	8
Domaine du Cardneau (Boussaye)	*Saillans*	2	5	7
Château du Carles	*Saillans*	13	32·5	28
Château Chadène	*St.-Aignan*	6	15	36
Domaine du Couprat	*Saillans*	5	12·5	9
Château du Fronsac	*Fronsac*	4	10	8
Château Gagnard	*Fronsac*	11	27·5	20
Château Gros Jean	*St.-Aignan*	4	10	22
Château Hauchat	*St.-Aignan*	1	2·5	5
Château Haut Rey	*Fronsac*	8	20	17
Château Jendeman	*St.-Aignan*	9	22·5	52
Domaine La Borie	*Saillans*	6	15	10
Domaine du Labrande	*Saillans*	5	12·5	12
Château La Croix	*Fronsac*	11	27·5	33
Château La Croix Gandineau	*Fronsac*	5	12·5	12
Château La Dauphine	*Fronsac*	6	15	14
Château La Faure	*Saillans*	13	32·5	27
Château La Fontaine	*Fronsac*	9	22·5	24
Château La Graves	*Fronsac*	3	7·5	7
Château Lague Bourdieu	*Fronsac*	4	10	14
Château Lambert	*St.-Aignan*	3	7·5	15
Château La Valade (Rupied)	*Fronsac*	11	27·5	20
Château La Valade (Roux)	*Fronsac*	4	10	13
Château La Venelle	*Fronsac*	4	10	13
Château La Vieille Curé	*Saillans*	14	35	32
Domaine Les Bernard	*Saillans*	4	10	12
Château Les Troix Croix	*Fronsac*	12	30	36
Château Magondeau	*Saillans*	9	22·5	38
Château de Malgarni	*Saillans*	3	7·5	6
Château Mayne-Vieil	*Galgon*	16	40	40
Château Moulins	*Saillans*	16	40	35
Château Musseau de Haut	*St.-Aignan*	2	5	12
Domaine Normand	*Saillans*	13	32·5	26
Château Pay de Pie	*Fronsac*	4	10	10
Château Peguilhem	*Saillans*	7	17·5	21
Château Peychez	*Fronsac*	4	10	8
Domaine Pillebourse	*Saillans*	3	7·5	6
Château Placette du Rey	*Fronsac*	4	10	7

	COMMUNE	*Hectares*	*Acres*	*Tonneaux*
Château Plainpoint	*St.-Aignan*	12	30	45
Château Richautey le Haut	*St.-Aignan*	2	5	6
Château Richodey	*St.-Aignan*	3	7·5	26
Château du Tasta	*St.-Aignan*	12	30	45
Château des Tonnelles	*St.-Aignan*	6	15	46
Clos des Tonnelles	*St.-Aignan*	4	10	18
Cru des Tonnelles	*St.-Aignan*	3	7·5	12
Clos Vieux Capot	*Fronsac*	2	5	5
Château Vieux Moulin	*Fronsac*	5	12·5	19
Château Vignes	*Fronsac*	2	5	5
Château Villars	*Saillans*	12	30	43
Château Vincent	*St.-Aignan*	4	10	27
Château Vincent (Rigaud)	*St.-Aignan*	3	7·5	9
Château Vincent (Sudra)	*St.-Aignan*	5	12·5	32
Domaine de Vincent	*St.-Aignan*	4	10	17
Château Vincent La Mouleyre	*St.-Aignan*	2	5	14

VI *Côtes Canon Fronsac*

The following figures of production are approximate, and indicate average annual output, as given by the communes and taken from their Déclarations de Récoltes records.

Principal Growths

	COMMUNE	*Hectares*	*Acres*	*Tonneaux*
Château Barrabaque	*Fronsac*	7	17·5	14
Château Belloy	*Fronsac*	5	12·5	10
Château Bodet	*Fronsac*	10	25	38
Château Canon	*Fronsac*	5	12·5	10
Château Capet-Bégaud	*Fronsac*	3	7·5	7
Château Cassagne	*St.-Michel*	4	10	15
Château des Combes-Canon	*St.-Michel*	2	5	7
Château Coustolle	*Fronsac*	12	30	37
Château Gaby	*Fronsac*	6	15	12
Château du Gazin	*St.-Michel*	25	62·5	58
Château Gombeau	*Fronsac*	4	10	13
Château Grand Renouilh	*St.-Michel*	6	15	11
Château Haut-Caillou	*Fronsac*	3	7·5	9
Clos Haut-Caillou	*Fronsac*	3	7·5	8
Château Haut-Mazeris	*St.-Michel*	6	15	16
Château Junayme	*Fronsac*	13	32·5	34
Château La Chapelle-Lariveau	*St.-Michel*	5	12·5	16
Château La Marche	*Fronsac*	27	67·5	58
Clos La Marche	*Fronsac*	2	5	4
Château La Mausse	*St.-Michel*	7	17·5	17
Château Lariveau	*St.-Michel*	7	17·5	18
Château Larchevêque	*Fronsac*	5	12·5	10
Château Les Vignes	*Fronsac*	2	5	5
Château Mazeris	*St.-Michel*	7	17·5	15
Château Mazeris Bellevue	*St.-Michel*	6	15	12
Domaine du Mouchez	*Fronsac*	7	17·5	14
Château Moulin-à-Vent	*St.-Michel*	6	15	18
Château Moulin-Pey-Labrie	*Fronsac*	4	10	13

	COMMUNE	Hectares	Acres	Tonneaux
Clos Nardin	*St. Michel*	1	2·5	4
Château Panet	*Fronsac*	4	10	8
Château Perron	*Fronsac*	3	7·5	4
Château Pichelebre	*Fronsac*	5	12·5	15
Château Roulet	*Fronsac*	3	7·5	5
Château Roullet	*Fronsac*	3	7·5	7
Château du Tasta	*St.-Aignan*	2	5	11
Clos de Toumalin	*Fronsac*	2	5	5
Domaine de Toumalin	*Fronsac*	6	15	12
Domaine de Trepesson	*St.-Michel*	2	5	6
Château Vincent	*St.-Aignan*	7	17·5	12
Château Vrai Canon Bouché	*Fronsac*	5	12·5	13
Château Vrai Canon Bourret	*Fronsac*	2	5	6
Château Vrai Canon Boyer	*St.-Michel*	7	17·5	22

VII *Graves 1959 Official Classification*

The vineyards of the Graves district were officially classified in 1953 and in 1959. Château Haut-Brion, the greatest of all Graves, is also officially classified with the great Médocs.

The following figures of production are approximate, and indicate average annual output, as given by the communes and taken from their Déclarations de Récoltes records.

CLASSIFIED RED WINES OF GRAVES

	COMMUNE	Tonneaux	Cases
Château Haut-Brion	*Pessac*	125	10,000
Château Bouscaut	*Cadaujac*	75	6,000
Château Carbonnieux	*Léognan*	45	3,700
Domaine de Chevalier	*Léognan*	15	1,400
Château Fieuzal	*Léognan*	55	4,600
Château Haut-Bailly	*Léognan*	30	2,400
Château La Mission-Haut-Brion	*Pessac*	125	10,000
Château La Tour-Haut-Brion	*Talence*	12	1,000
Château La Tour-Martillac (Kressmann La Tour)	*Martillac*	45	3,750
Château Malartic-Lagravière	*Léognan*	28	2,300
Château Olivier	*Léognan*	14	1,150
Château Pape-Clément	*Pessac*	125	10,000
Château Smith-Haut-Lafitte	*Martillac*	15	1,300

CLASSIFIED WHITE WINES OF GRAVES

	COMMUNE	Tonneaux	Cases
Château Bouscaut	*Cadaujac*	35	3,000
Château Carbonnieux	*Léognan*	90	7,000
Domaine de Chevalier	*Léognan*	9	700
Château Couhins	*Villenave-d'Ornon*	33	3,200
Château La Tour-Martillac (Kressmann La Tour)	*Martillac*	9	700
Château Laville-Haut-Brion	*Talence*	15	1,700
Château Malartic-Lagravière	*Léognan*	3	280
Château Olivier	*Léognan*	47	3,900

Other Principal Growths

wh = WHITE; r = RED

	COMMUNE		*Hectares*	*Acres*	*Tonneaux*
Château André-Lamothe	*Portets*	wh	2	5	11
		r	4	10	15
Domaine Andron	*St.-Selve*	wh	3	7·5	5
Château d'Arbanats	*Arbanats*	wh	6	15	10
Clos d'Armajan	*Budos*	r	2	5	4
Château d'Arricaud	*Landiras*	wh	12	30	49
Château des Arrocs	*Langon*	wh	3	7·5	10
Domaine Arzac	*St.-Selve*	wh	2	5	5
Clos L'Avocat	*Cérons*	wh	3	7·5	10
Château Bahans (minor growth of Château Haut-Brion)	*Pessac*	r	—	—	22
Château Bardins	*Cadaujac*	wh }	2	5	2
		r }			5
Château Baret	*Villenave-d'Ornon*	wh }	12	30	17
		r }			9
Domaine du Barque	*St.-Selve*	wh }	6	15	3
		r }			2
Clos Barreyre	*Virelade*	wh	3	7·5	8
Cru Barrouet	*Pujols*	wh	3	7·5	7
Domaine du Basque	*Pujols*	wh	3	7·5	12
Château Batsères	*Landiras*	wh	4	10	15
Château Beauchêne	*Beautiran*	wh	3	7·5	7
		r	2	5	5
Domaine du Beau-Site	*Portets*	wh	0·3	0·8	2
		r	3	7·5	9
Château Bel-Air	*Portets*	wh	2	5	6
Château Bel-Air	*St.-Morillon*	wh	4	10	7
Château Bellefontaine	*St.-Pierre-de-Mons*	wh	3	7·5	7
Domaine Bellevue	*Toulenne*	wh	1	2·5	7
Domaine de Bellevue	*St.-Selve*	wh	4	10	13
Château Belon	*St.-Morillon*	wh	3	7·5	6
Domaine de Bequin	*Portets*	wh	5	12·5	11
		r	3	7·5	7
Château Bernard-Raymond	*Portets*	wh	3	7·5	13
		r	2	5	11
Cru du Bérot	*Arbanats*	wh	2	5	6
Cru Bichons	*La Brède*	wh }	5	12·5	11
		r }			2
Domaine de Biot	*Arbanats*	wh	2	5	5
		r	2	5	4
Domaine de la Blancherie	*La Brède*	wh }	4	10	6
		r }			2
Château Boiresse	*Ayguemortes*	wh	4	10	6
Domaine du Bonat	*St.-Selve*	wh	5	12·5	14

	COMMUNE		*Hectares*	*Acres*	*Tonneaux*
Clos de la Bonneterie	*Portets*	wh	2	5	6
		r	2	5	4
Domaine de Borderie	*Portets*	wh	3	7·5	9
		r	2	5	8
Cru Boritz	*St.-Pierre-de-Mons*	wh	4	10	12
Domaine du Boscq	*St.-Morillon*	wh	2	5	5
Cru Bouyon	*Pujols*	wh	2	5	5
Château Boyrin	*Roaillan*	wh	6	15	16
Domaine de Brochon	*Arbanats*	wh	3	7·5	7
		r	2	5	3
Domaine de Brondelle	*Langon*	wh	2	5	4
Domaine de Brouillaud	*St.-Médard-d'Eyrans*	wh	7	17·5	19
Château Bruhaut	*St.-Pierre-de-Mons*	wh	2	5	4
Château de Budos	*Budos*	r	9	22·5	31
Clos Cabanes	*St.-Pierre-de-Mons*	wh	4	10	11
Clos Cabannes	*St.-Pierre-de-Mons*	wh	1	2·5	5
Château Cabannieux	*Portets*	wh	3	7·5	7
		r	3	7·5	6
Cru de Cadenne	*Pujols*	wh	5	12·5	12
Cru du Caladis (*2 proprietors*)	*Portets*	r	3	7·5	9
		wh			7
			4	10	
		r			5
Cru Calens	*Beautiran*	r	7	17·5	17
Cru Camegaye	*Landiras*	wh	2	5	9
Château Cantalot	*St.-Pierre-de-Mons*	wh	7	17·5	22
Cru de Cap-de-Hé	*Pujols*	wh	2	5	6
Cru Capet-à-Corne	*Beautiran*	wh	3	7·5	5
Château Carmes-Haut-Brion	*Pessac*	r	2	5	8
Domaine Carros	*St.-Selve*	wh	2	5	9
Domaine de Casseuil	*Langon*	wh	4	10	6
Cru Castagnet	*Virelade*	wh	3	7·5	9
Domaine Castelnaud	*St.-Pierre-de-Mons*	wh	2	5	5
Château Catalas	*Pujols*	wh	6	15	17
Cru de la Cave	*Preignac*	wh	2	5	5
Château Cazebonne	*St.-Pierre-de-Mons*	wh	7	17·5	12
Cru Chanteloiseau	*Langon*	wh	5	12·5	12
Clos Charamel	*Castres*	wh			2
			4	10	
		r			4
Château Chaviran	*Martillac*	r	4	10	6
Clos Cherchy	*Pujols*	wh	4	10	11
Cru Cherchy	*Pujols*	wh	2	5	9
Château Chicane	*Toulenne*	wh	3	7·5	12
Domaine du Ciron	*Pujols*	wh	5	12·5	19
Domaine de Clare	*Landiras*	wh	3	7·5	8
Cru Coudillet	*Virelade*	wh	1	2·5	5
Cru du Couet	*St.-Pierre-de-Mons*	wh	2	5	5
Domaine de Courbon	*Toulenne*	wh	4	10	11
Domaine du Courreau	*St.-Médard-d'Eyrans*	wh			5
			3	7·5	
		r			3
Domaine du Courreau	*St.-Morrillon*	wh	3	7·5	11

	COMMUNE		*Hectares*	*Acres*	*Tonneaux*
Château Crabitey	*Portets*	wh	7	17·5	7
		r	8	20	13
Domaine de la Croix	*Langon*	wh	4	10	10
Château Cruzeau	*St.-Médard-d'Eyrans*	wh	12	30	19
Clos Darches	*St.-Pierre-de-Mons*	wh	4	10	9
Clos Darrouban	*Portets*	wh	2	5	3
		r			3
Domaine de Darrouban	*Portets*	wh	3	7·5	15
		r	2	5	3
Château Despagne	*St.-Pierre-de-Mons*	wh	4	10	14
Clos Despagne	*St.-Pierre-de-Mons*	wh	4	10	16
Château Doms et Clos du Monastère	*Portets*	wh	15	37·5	29
		r			12
Domaine du Druc	*Landiras*	wh	2	5	6
Domaine du Durce, Domaine de Papoula	*Portets*	wh	2	5	7
		r	1	2·5	7
Domaine Étienne	*St.-Morillon*	wh	2	5	6
Cru Eyquem	*La Brède*	wh	5	12·5	12
Domaine de Faye	*Portets*	wh	1	2·5	6
		r	2	5	7
Château Fernon	*Langon*	wh	4	10	8
Château Ferran	*Martillac*	wh	3	7·5	11
		r	0·5	1·2	1
Château Ferrande	*Castres*	wh	10	25	33
Château Fieuzal	*Léognan*	wh	11	27·5	2
		r			20
Château Foncla	*Castres*	wh	13	32·5	21
		r			3
Château Foncroise	*St.-Selve*	wh	7	17·5	10
		r			4
Château des Fougères	*La Brède*	wh	2	5	5
Clos des Fougères	*Virelade*	wh	4	10	11
Château de France	*Léognan*	wh	8	20	6
		r			9
Domaine des Gaillardins	*St.-Selve*	wh	4	10	8
Cru Galand	*Cérons*	wh	1	2·5	4
Clos du Gars	*La Brède*	wh	2	5	5
Château Gazin	*Léognan*	wh	7	17·5	1
		r			10
Clos de Gensac	*Pujols*	wh	4	10	16
Domaine de la Girafe	*Portets*	wh	5	12·5	22
		r	2	5	11
Domaine de la Gleyre	*Pujols*	wh	2	5	9
Cru de Gonthier	*Portets*	wh	1	2·5	5
		r	2	5	7

	COMMUNE		*Hectares*	*Acres*	*Tonneaux*
Château Gorre	*Martillac*	wh	1	2·5	1
		r	2	5	3
Domaine du Grand-Abord	*Portets*	wh	5	12·5	18
		r	2	5	6
Château Grand Bourdieu	*Beautiran*	wh	6	15	10
Château Grand Chemin	*Cérons*	wh	2	5	8
Domaine de la Grande-Ferrade	*Villenave-d'Ornon*	r	4	10	8
Château Grandmaison	*Léognan*	wh			5
		}	5	12·5	
		r			5
Domaine de la Grave	*St.-Selve*	wh	3	7·5	6
Cru des Graves	*Portets*	wh	3	7·5	6
		r	1	2·5	4
Domaine de Gravette	*St.-Morillon*	wh	15	37·5	33
Château Graveyron	*Portets*	wh	6	15	18
		r	4	10	13
Château de la Gravière	*Toulenne*	wh	7	17·5	25
Château des Gravières	*Portets*	wh	3	7·5	12
		r	2	5	10
Clos des Gravières	*Portets*	wh	2	5	5
		r	1	2·5	5
Domaine des Gravières	*Portets*	r	2	5	6
Domaine de Guérin	*Castres*	r	4	10	6
Château Guillaumot	*La Brède*	wh	13	32·5	41
Château des Guillemins	*Langon*	wh	8	20	28
Domaine de Guirauton	*St.-Morillon*	wh	4	10	9
Cru des Guizats	*Pujols*	wh	2	5	8
Clos Harquey	*Langon*	wh	4	10	7
Château Haut-Bergey	*Léognan*	wh			2
		}	4	10	
		r			6
Cru du Haut-Blanc	*Pujols*	wh	1	2·5	4
Domaine du Haut-Blanc	*Pujols*	wh	4	10	12
Domaine Haut-Callens	*Beautiran*	wh	5	12·5	9
Cru du Haut-Claron	*St.-Morillon*	wh	3	7·5	7
Domaine de Haut-Courneau	*Portets*	wh	5	12·5	13
		r	5	12·5	13
Cru Haut-Gravette	*St.-Morillon*	wh	3	7·5	6
Château Haut-Madère	*Villenave-d'Ornon*	r	2	5	3
Château Haut-Nouchet	*Martillac*	wh			9
		}	9	22·5	
		r			6
Cru Hautes Plantes	*Landiras*	wh	3	7·5	8
Cru Haut-Reys	*La-Brède*	wh	3	7·5	7
Château Jamnets	*St.-Pierre-de-Mons*	wh			5
		}	2	5	
		r			4
Clos Jamnet	*La Brède*	wh	8	20	18
Cru Janot-Bayle	*Budos*	r	8	20	16
Domaine du Jau	*St.-Morillon*	wh	3	7·5	5
Château des Jaubertes	*St.-Pierre-de-Mons*	wh	6	15	15
Clos Jean Dubos	*Pujols*	wh	2	5	4

	COMMUNE		*Hectares*	*Acres*	*Tonneaux*
Château Jean-Gervais, Clos Puyjalon	*Portets*	wh	10	25	38
		r			3
Clos Jean-de-Maye	*Portets*	wh	5	12·5	6
		r			11
Clos de l'Abbaye-de-la-Rame	*Mazères*	wh	6	15	12
Domaine de Labeillon	*St.-Pierre-de-Mons*	wh	2	5	5
Cru La Cabane	*Pujols*	wh	4	10	11
Cru La Camuse	*St.-Morillon*	wh	3	7·5	7
Château Côtes de Lacapère	*Landiras*	wh	2	5	6
Cru Lacapère	*Landiras*	wh	4	10	15
Domaine de Lacapère	*Landiras*	wh	2	5	7
Cru Lafon	*St.-Pierre-de-Mons*	wh	2	5	9
Château La Garde	*Martillac*	r	13	32·5	40
Château Lagénie	*St.-Morillon*	wh	3	7·5	6
Château Lagueloup	*Portets*	wh	2	5	3
Cru La Hounade	*Pujols*	wh	2	5	9
Château La Louvière	*Léognan*	wh	28	70	45
		r			19
Clos Lamagine	*St.-Pierre-de-Mons*	wh	6	15	14
Cru La Mainionce	*Pujols*	wh	3	7·5	13
Cru La Médecine	*St.-Pierre-de-Mons*	wh	2	5	5
Cru de Lamoigon	*Pujols*	wh	3	7·5	5
Château Lamothe	*Cadaujac*	r	4	10	10
Château Lamothe	*St.-Médard-d'Eyrans*	wh	1	2·5	4
Clos Lamothe	*Portets*	wh	3	7·5	9
		r	2	5	11
Château Lamouroux	*Cérons*	wh	8	20	37
Château Laouilley	*Roaillan*	wh	3	7·5	3
Domaine La Payrère	*St.-Selve*	wh	5	12·5	8
		r			2
Château La Prade	*St.-Médard-d'Eyrans*	wh	4	10	9
Cru Lardite	*Arbanats*	wh	2	5	13
		r	2	5	5
Domaine de Larnavey	*St.-Selve*	wh	4	10	9
Château Larrivet-Haut-Brion	*Léognan*	r	10	25	14
Cru Larroucat	*Pujols*	wh	2	5	8
Château La Salle	*Martillac*	wh	3	7·5	8
Domaine de Lassalle	*La Brède*	wh	6	15	26
Domaine La Solitude	*Martillac*	wh	2	5	4
		r	4	10	7
Cru La Terce	*Budos*	r	2	5	3
Château La Tour	*Léognan*	wh	5	12·5	9
		r			2
Château La Tour Bicheau	*Portets*	wh	3	7·5	9
		r	5	12·5	17
Château La Tour-de-Boyrin	*Langon*	wh	13	32·5	20
Clos La-Tour-Cluchon	*Portets*	wh	2	5	3
		r	2	5	5

	COMMUNE		*Hectares*	*Acres*	*Tonneaux*
Château La Tourte	*Toulenne*	wh	6	15	16
Cru Le Bourut	*Pujols*	wh	2	5	9
Château Le Brouillaud	*St.-Médard-d'Eyrans*	wh	5	12·5	16
Cru de l'Église	*Virelade*	wh	2	5	5
Cru Le Hiladey	*Portets*	wh	2	5	4
		r	4	10	4
Clos Léhoul	*Langon*	wh	4	10	8
Château Le Mayne	*Preignac*	wh			9
Château Le Méjean	*Ayguemortes*	wh	6	15	13
Château Le More	*St.-Selve*	wh	2	5	8
Château Le Pape	*Léognan*	wh }	4	10	3
		r }			2
Château Les Charmettes	*Budos*	wh	2	5	4
Domaine Les Cluchets	*Langon*	wh	4	10	12
Cru Les Graves	*Toulenne*	wh	4	10	12
Cru Les Guizats	*Pujols*	wh	2	5	4
Cru Les Mengets	*Pujols*	wh	2	5	4
Château Lespault	*Martillac*	wh	4	10	3
		r	0·5	1·2	2
Château de l'Espérance	*La Brède*	wh	4	10	10
		r	—	—	1
Cru Les Pinsas	*Pujols*	wh	2	5	5
Cru Les Rocs	*Pujols*	wh	2	5	5
Cru Lestage	*Landiras*	wh	4	10	9
Domaine Lestang	*St.-Selve*	wh	5	12·5	8
Château Le Thil	*Léognan*	r	3	7·5	4
Cru de l'Hermitage	*Budos*	r	8	20	12
Domaine de l'Hôpital	*Castres*	r	6	15	5
Château de l'Hospital	*Portets*	wh }	5	12·5	2
		r }			9
Clos Liché	*St.-Pardon-de-Conques*	wh	3	7·5	7
Château Limbourg	*Villenave-d'Ornon*	wh }	10	25	5
		r }			6
Château Liot-Moros	*Pujols*	wh	5	12·5	17
Cru Lioy	*Budos*	r	3	7·5	4
Château Lognac	*Castres*	wh }	14	35	9
		r }			2
Domaine de Louisot	*Virelade*	wh	4	10	13
Clos Louloumet	*Toulenne*	wh	3	7·5	8
Cru de Lubat	*St.-Pierre-de-Mons*	wh	8	20	14
Château des Lucques	*Portets*	wh }	5	12·5	12
		r }			6
Domaine des Lucques	*Portets*	wh }	7	17·5	7
		r }			6
Château Ludeman-Lacôte	*Langon*	wh	7	17·5	20

	COMMUNE		*Hectares*	*Acres*	*Tonneaux*
Cru des Luques	*Portets*	wh	2	5	6
		r	2	5	8
Château Lusseau	*Ayguemortes*	wh	8	20	5
		r			6
Château Madélis	*Portets*	wh	2	5	6
		r	2	5	12
Château Madran	*Pessac*	r	3	7·5	4
Château Magence	*St.-Pierre-de-Mons*	wh	11	27·5	27
Cru Magnaud	*La Brède*	wh	5	12·5	11
Château Maillard	*Mazères*	wh	5	12·5	13
Clos de la Maison Blanche	*Budos*	wh	2	5	5
Château Malleprat	*Martillac*	wh	3	7·5	5
Domaine de Maron	*Landiras*	r	2	5	9
Domaine Martin	*Roaillan*	wh	2	5	6
Cru Massiot	*Martillac*	wh	2	5	6
Domaine du May	*Portets*	wh	3	7·5	6
		r	2	5	5
Domaine du Mayne	*Langon*	wh	3	7·5	8
Cru Mayne d'Eyquen	*La Brède*	wh	5	12·5	14
Domaine de Metivier	*Ayguemortes*	wh	3	7·5	6
Château Millet	*Portets*	wh	10	25	17
		r			20
Château Mirabel	*Pujols*	wh	3	7·5	14
Château du Mirail	*Portets*	wh	5	12·5	16
		r	3	7·5	14
Château Moderis	*Virelade*	wh	5	12·5	10
Domaine de Mongenan	*Portets*	wh	5	12·5	13
		r			2
Clos de Mons	*La Brède*	wh	3	7·5	8
Cru Morange	*Virelade*	wh	2	5	7
Cru du Moulin-à-Vent	*Cérons*	wh	3	7·5	12
Cru du Moulin-à-Vent	*Landiras*	wh	3	7·5	9
Clos du Moulin-à-Vent	*St.-Pierre-de-Mons*	wh	5	12·5	18
Domaine le Mouniche	*Ayguemortes*	wh	5	12·5	7
		r			5
Château Mouteou	*Portets*	wh	2	5	6
		r	1	2·5	4
Château Moutin	*Portets*	r	1	2·5	5
Château Mouyet	*Budos*	r	2	5	11
Château Neuf	*Léognan*	wh	6	15	4
		r			4
Cru Nodoy	*Virelade*	wh	3	7·5	7
Clos Nouchet	*Castres*	wh	7	17·5	1
		r			6
Château de Nouguey	*Langon*	wh	2	5	6
Clos du Pape	*La Brède*	wh	6	15	19

	COMMUNE		*Hectares*	*Acres*	*Tonneaux*
Domaine de Papoula (*see* Domaine de Durce)					
Cru Patiras	*Toulenne*	wh	2	5	4
Château du Pavillon	*Roaillan*	wh	6	15	8
Château Pédebayle	*St.-Pierre-de-Mons*	wh	8	20	20
Château Péran	*Langon*	wh	8	20	17
Cru Perran	*Landiras*	wh	3	7·5	12
Domaine Perrin de Naudine	*Castres*	wh }			1
			5	12·5	
		r }			6
Château Perron	*Roaillan*	wh	14	35	37
Château Pesilla	*Landiras*	wh	4	10	16
Château Pessan	*Portets*	wh	6	15	14
		r	6	15	12
Château Péyran	*Landiras*	wh	4	10	11
Château des Peyrères	*Landiras*		4	10	14
Cru Pezeau	*Beautiran*	wh }			5
			5	12·5	
		r }			1
Cru Pierret	*Castres*	wh }			8
			6	15	
		r }			3
Cru Pinaud	*Cérons*	wh	2	5	5
Château Pingoy	*Portets*	wh	5	12·5	21
		r	3	7·5	12
Château Pique-Cailloux	*Mérignac*	wh	7	17·5	13
Château Piron	*St.-Morillon*	wh	7	17·5	27
Clos de Places	*Arbanats*	wh	1	2·5	4
Domaine des Places	*Arbanats*	wh	2	5	9
		r	1	2·5	6
Domaine de Plantat	*St.-Morillon*	wh	9	22·5	16
Cru des Plantes	*Landiras*	wh	14	35	56
Domaine des Plantes	*Landiras*	wh	4	10	11
Domaine du Plantey	*Castres*	wh }			2
			2	5	
		r }			7
Château Pommarède	*Castres*	wh }			5
			4	10	
		r }			5
Château Pommarède-de-Bas	*Castres*	wh }			11
			5	12·5	
		r }			4
Château Pontac	*Villenave-d'Ornon*	wh }			20
			14	35	
		r }			15
Cru du Portail	*Landiras*	wh	2	5	7
Château de Portets	*Portets*	wh	7	17·5	18
		r	8	20	38
Cru de la Poste	*Virelade*	wh	4	10	6
Château Poumey	*Gradignan*	wh }			4
			4	10	
		r }			12
Clos Puyjalon (*see* Château Jean-Gervais)					
Château Queyrats, Clos d'Uza	*St.-Pierre-de-Mons*	wh	34	85	77

	COMMUNE		*Hectares*	*Acres*	*Tonneaux*
Château Rahoul	*Portets*	wh	2	5	5
		r	5	12·5	26
Château Respide	*Langon*	wh } r	34	85	55 / 15
Château Respide	*St.-Pierre-de-Mons*	wh	4	10	5
Château Respide	*Toulenne*	wh	5	12·5	13
Château La Rocaille	*Virelade*	wh	9	22·5	13
Domaine Roland	*Langon*	wh	3	7·5	6
Château Roquetaillade	*Mazères*	wh	3	7·5	9
Château Rosario	*Eyzines*	wh	1	2·5	4
Château Rostang-Haut-Carré	*Talence*	wh	1	2	2
		r	3	7·5	6
Château Roubinet	*Pujols*	wh	8	20	32
Cru Roudet	*Pujols*	wh	5	12·5	17
Cru Sadout	*Virelade*	wh	6	15	19
Château Saige-Fort-Manoir	*Pessac*	r	5	12·5	11
Château St.-Gérôme	*Ayguemortes*	wh	4	10	7
Clos St.-Hilaire	*Portets*	wh	3	7·5	12
		r	3	7·5	8
Clos St.-Jean	*Pujols*	wh	8	20	23
Clos St.-Robert	*Pujols*	wh	26	65	54
		r	4	10	8
Domaine du Sapeur	*Portets*	wh } r	4	10	9 / 10
Cru Sarraguey	*Virelade*	wh	2	5	7
Domaine des Sarrots	*St.-Pierre-de-Mons*	wh	2	5	5
Clos Sentouary	*St.-Pierre-de-Mons*	wh	2	5	5
Cru Terrefort	*Pujols*	wh	3	7·5	10
Domaine de Teycheney	*Virelade*	wh	2	5	4
Domaine de Teychon	*Arbanats*	wh	4	10	16
Château Toumilon	*St.-Pierre-de-Mons*	wh	5	12·5	9
Cru Toumilon	*St.-Pierre-de-Mons*	wh	2	5	4
Château Tourteau-Cholet	*Arbanats*	wh	13	32·5	30
Clos de la Tuilerie	*Portets*	wh	3	7·5	10
		r	2	5	10
Cru La Tuilerie	*Landiras*	wh	2	5	7
Château de Tuileries	*Virelade*	wh	3	7·5	14
		r	7	17·5	19
Château Tuquet	*Beautiran*	wh } r	26	65	76 / 6
Château Tustoc	*Toulenne*	wh	8	20	26
Clos d'Uza (*see* Château Queyrats)					
Domaine des Vergnes	*Portets*	wh	2	5	4
		r	1	2·5	4
Clos Viaut	*St.-Pardon-de-Conques*	wh	2	5	4
Clos Viaut	*St.-Pierre-de-Mons*	wh	9	22·5	25
Cru Videau	*Pujols*	wh	6	15	25

	COMMUNE		*Hectares*	*Acres*	*Tonneaux*
Château La Vieille-France	*Portets*	wh / r	8	20	16 / 7
Château de Virelade	*Arbanats*	r	20	50	65

VIII *Sauternes and Barsac*

As in the Médoc, the Sauternes vineyards were officially classified in 1855. This classification is known as the Official Classification of the Great Growths of the Gironde.

The total production from these vineyards represents approximately 25 per cent of the total Sauternes production, amounting roughly to 350,000 cases per year.

The following figures of production are approximate, and indicate average annual output, as given by the communes and taken from their Déclarations de Récoltes records.

First Great Growth

	Tonneaux	*Cases*
Château d'Yquem	110	9,000

First Growths

	Tonneaux	*Cases*
Château Guiraud	125	10,250
Château La Tour-Blanche	50	4,000
Château Lafaurie-Peyraguey	35	3,000
Château de Rayne-Vigneau	95	7,700
Château Rabaud-Sigalas	30	2,100
Château Rabaud-Promis	105	8,700
Clos Haut-Peyraguey	20	1,900
Château Coutet	75	6,000
Château Climens	55	4,500
Château de Suduiraut	115	9,600
Château Rieussec	85	7,000

Second Growths

	Tonneaux	*Cases*
Château d'Arche	10	950
Château Filhot	50	4,000
Château Lamothe	10	750
Château Myrat	35	3,100
Château Doisy-Védrines	35	3,100
Château Doisy-Daëne	30	2,400
Château Suau	15	1,200
Château Broustet	30	2,300
Château Caillou	40	3,200
Château Nairac	30	2,300
Château de Malle	40	3,200
Château Romer	15	1,200

Minor Growths

	COMMUNE	*Hectares*	*Acres*	*Tonneaux*
Château d'Arche-Lafaurie	*Sauternes*	19	47·5	48
Cru d'Arche-Pugnau, Château Peyraguey-le-Rousset	*Preignac*	15	37·5	32
Château d'Arches, Château Lamothe	*Sauternes*	15	37·5	40

	COMMUNE	*Hectares*	*Acres*	*Tonneaux*
Château d'Arche-Vimeney	*Sauternes*	5	12·5	11
Château d'Armajan-des-Ormes	*Preignac*	7	17·5	18
Cru d'Arrançon	*Preignac*	5	12·5	10
Cru Arrançon-Boutoc	*Preignac*	3	7·5	9
Château Augey	*Bommes*	10	25	26
Cru Baboye	*Fargues*	2	5	5
Château Barbier	*Fargues*	6	15	16
Cru de Barboye	*Bommes*	2	5	4
Cru Barjumeau	*Sauternes*	3	7·5	6
Château Barjumeau-Chauvin	*Sauternes*	3	7·5	9
Clos Barreau	*Fargues*	1	2·5	4
Château Barrette	*Sauternes*	5	12·5	14
Cru Barrette	*Fargues*	1	2·5	2
Cru Bas-Peyraguey	*Preignac*	2	5	4
Château Bastor-Lamontagne	*Preignac*	38	95	90
Château Batsalle	*Fargues*	4	10	9
Cru Batsalle	*Fargues*	1	2·5	3
Château Baulac-Dodigeos	*Barsac*	5	12·5	12
Cru Baylieu	*Fargues*	7	17·5	13
Château Béchereau	*Bommes*	12	30	22
Cru Bel-Air	*Preignac*	2	5	4
Château Bergeron	*Bommes*	5	12·5	15
Cru Bergeron	*Preignac*	4	10	11
Château Bernisse	*Barsac*	3	7·5	8
Cru Bernisse	*Barsac*	1	2·5	4
Cru Bignon	*Bommes*	1	2·5	3
Cru Bordesoulles	*Preignac*	3	7·5	7
Château Bousclas	*Barsac*	3	7·5	8
Cru Bousclas	*Barsac*	4	10	12
Cru Boutoc	*Preignac*	5	12·5	10
Cru Boutoc	*Sauternes*	2	5	5
Château Bouyot	*Barsac*	6	15	15
Cru Bouyreou	*Preignac*	1	2·5	2
Château Brassens-Guitteronde	*Barsac*	5	12·5	14
Cru Camelong	*Bommes*	1	2·5	2
Château Cameron et Raymond-Louis	*Bommes*	9	22·5	35
Château Camperos, Château Montalivet, Château Mayne-Bert	*Barsac*	12	30	27
Château Cantegril	*Barsac*	14	35	38
Cru Caplane	*Bommes*	2	5	5
Cru Caplane	*Sauternes*	5	12·5	16
Domaine de Caplane	*Sauternes*	5	12·5	25
Cru Carbonnieu	*Bommes*	6	15	23
Château de Carles	*Barsac*	6	15	16
Cru du Carrefour	*Sauternes*	1	2·5	2
Cru de la Cave	*Preignac*	2	5	5
Cru du Chalet	*Barsac*	2	5	5
Cru du Chalet	*Preignac*	1	2·5	3
Domaine de la Chapelle	*Preignac*	2	5	4
Château de la Chartreuse	*Preignac*	5	12·5	10
Cru Chauvin	*Sauternes*	2	5	4
Cru Claverie	*Fargues*	2	5	6
Château Closiot	*Barsac*	5	12·5	11

	COMMUNE	*Hectares*	*Acres*	*Tonneaux*
Clos Cloziot	*Barsac*	1	2·5	2
Cru Cluziot	*Barsac*	1	2·5	2
Cru Commarque	*Bommes*	1	2·5	3
Château Commarque	*Sauternes*	4	10	10
Cru Commarque	*Sauternes*	6	15	11
Cru Commet-Magey	*Preignac*	4	10	8
Cru Commet-Magey-Briatte	*Preignac*	4	10	11
Domaine Cosse	*Fargues*	6	15	12
Domaine de Couite	*Preignac*	3	7·5	8
Cru Coussères	*Fargues*	1	2·5	2
Château Coustet	*Barsac*	6	15	21
Cru Coustet	*Barsac*	1	2·5	2
Domaine du Coy	*Sauternes*	3	7·5	8
Château de Coye	*Sauternes*	1	2·5	3
Cru Druenn	*Bommes*	2	5	4
Château Ducasse	*Barsac*	5	12·5	12
Cru Ducasse	*Fargues*	2	5	5
Château Dudon	*Barsac*	8	20	20
Domaine Duperneau	*Bommes*	3	7·5	9
Cru Duzan	*Barsac*	1	2·5	3
Clos d'Espagnet (*see* Château Esterlin)				
Château Esterlin, Clos d'Espagnet	*Sauternes*	3	7·5	7
Château de Fargues	*Fargues*	7	17·5	16
Château Farluret	*Barsac*	4	10	11
Cru Fillau	*Fargues*	4	10	10
Château Fleury, Château Terre-Noble	*Barsac*	2	5	4
Clos Fontaine	*Fargues*	2	5	6
Château Fontebride	*Preignac*	2	5	7
Domaine de la Forêt	*Preignac*	21	52·5	61
Cru Gavach	*Fargues*	3	7·5	7
Château Gilette, Domaine des Justices, Château Les Rochers, Château Les Remparts, Château Lamothe	*Preignac*	14	35	30
Clos Girautin	*Barsac*	1	2·5	3
Château Grand-Carretey	*Barsac*	1	2·5	2
Cru Grand-Carretey	*Barsac*	6	15	16
Cru Grand-Jauga	*Barsac*	2	5	6
Château Grand-Mayne-Qui-Né-Marc	*Barsac*	1	2·5	3
Cru Gravailles	*Preignac*	2	5	4
Château Gravas	*Barsac*	8	20	20
Château Grillon	*Barsac*	6	15	18
Cru Guillen-du-Rey	*Preignac*	7	17·5	22
Château Guimbalet	*Preignac*	1	2·5	4
Cru Guitteronde	*Barsac*	1	2·5	3
Château Guitteronde-Sarraute	*Barsac*	4	10	10
Château Guitteronde-Bert	*Barsac*	9	22·5	22
Château du Haire	*Preignac*	4	10	9
Cru du Haire	*Preignac*	6	15	18
Château Hallet	*Barsac*	10	25	24
Château Haut-Bergeron	*Preignac*	4	10	13
Château Haut-Bommes	*Bommes*	7	17·5	14
Château Haut-Claverie	*Fargues*	4	10	8
Cru Haut-Laguerítte	*Bommes*	2	5	4

	COMMUNE	*Hectares*	*Acres*	*Tonneaux*
Château Haut-Mayne	*Fargues*	2	5	5
Cru Haut-Piquan	*Sauternes*	1	2·5	3
Cru du Hère	*Preignac*	2	5	2
Château Hourmalas (*see* Château St.-Marc)				
Cru Hourmalas	*Barsac*	2	5	6
Château Jany	*Barsac*	2	5	6
Clos Jauguet	*Barsac*	1	2·5	3
Cru Jauguet	*Barsac*	5	12·5	14
Château Jean-Galant	*Bommes*	2	5	7
Château Jean-Laive	*Barsac*	4	10	11
Clos de Jeanlaive	*Barsac*	5	12·5	11
Cru Jeannonier	*Bommes*	3	7·5	4
Domaine Jean-Robert	*Preignac*	1	2·5	3
Château du Juge	*Preignac*	4	10	10
Cru Junka	*Preignac*	3	7·5	4
Château Les Justices	*Preignac*	3	7·5	6
Domaine des Justices (*see* Château Gilette)				
Cru La Bernisse	*Barsac*	3	7·5	7
Château La Bouade	*Barsac*	12	30	31
Clos La Bouade	*Barsac*	3	7·5	8
Domaine de Labouade-Rambaud	*Barsac*	1	2·5	3
Cru La Bouchette	*Bommes*	1	2·5	2
Cru Labouchette	*Preignac*	2	5	5
Château La Brouillère	*Bommes*	4	10	9
Cru Labrousse	*Barsac*	2	5	5
Château La Chapelle-St.-Aubin	*Bommes*	3	7·5	6
Château La Clotte	*Barsac*	5	12·5	12
Cru Lacoste	*Barsac*	2	5	4
Cru La Côte	*Fargues*	5	12·5	9
Château Lafon, Château Le Mayne	*Sauternes*	6	15	19
Château Lafon-Laroze	*Sauternes*	3	7·5	5
Cru Lagardan	*Bommes*	3	7·5	10
Cru l'Agnet	*Bommes*	2	5	3
Château Lagravette	*Bommes*	2	5	5
Cru La Gravière	*Preignac*	2	5	5
Cru Lahonade-Peyraguey	*Bommes*	2	5	6
Château Lahouilley	*Barsac*	3	7·5	9
Château La Hourcade	*Preignac*	4	10	13
Cru Lalot	*Preignac*	6	15	16
Cru La Maringue	*Bommes*	4	10	8
Château Lamothe (*see* Château d'Arches)				
Château Lamothe (*see* Château Gilette)				
Cru Lamothe	*Sauternes*	6	15	14
Château La Mourette	*Bommes*	3	7·5	8
Cru Lanère	*Sauternes*	11	27·5	21
Château Lange	*Bommes*	5	12·5	12
Cru Lanusquet	*Fargues*	2	5	5
Clos Lapachère	*Barsac*	4	10	10
Château Lapelou	*Barsac*	6	15	16
Château Lapinesse	*Barsac*	16	40	44
Cru Lapinesse	*Barsac*	7	17·5	19
Cru La Pinesse	*Barsac*	2	5	5

	COMMUNE	*Hectares*	*Acres*	*Tonneaux*
Domaine de Laraude	*Sauternes*	2	5	5
Château Laribotte	*Preignac*	5	12·5	9
Domaine de l'Arieste	*Preignac*	8	20	21
Clos l'Arieste	*Preignac*	3	7·5	8
Cru Larode	*Sauternes*	1	2·5	2
Château La Tour	*Barsac*	2	5	4
Château Latrezotte	*Barsac*	7	17·5	20
Cru l'Aubépin	*Bommes*	10	25	26
Cru l'Aubépine	*Bommes*	2	5	4
Cru l'Aubépins	*Sauternes*	3	7·5	6
Château Lauvignac	*Preignac*	3	7·5	6
Château Laville	*Preignac*	11	27·5	22
Château Le Coustet	*Barsac*	5	12·5	10
Cru Le Haut Bommes	*Bommes*	0·5	1·2	2
Château Le Hère	*Bommes*	6	15	10
Château Le Mayne (*see* Château Lafon)				
Château Le Mayne	*Preignac*	13	32·5	34
Château Le Mouret	*Fargues*	6	15	6
Cru Le Pageot	*Bommes*	2	5	4
Château l'Ermitage	*Preignac*	7	17·5	13
Cru Le Roc	*Preignac*	1	2·5	3
Château Le Rose-et-Monteil	*Preignac*	5	12·5	14
Cru Le Rousseau	*Bommes*	2	5	3
Château Les Arrieux	*Preignac*	5	12·5	15
Château Le Sauhuc	*Preignac*	3	7·5	9
Cru Les Cailloux	*Bommes*	2	5	4
Cru Les Gravilles	*Barsac*	1	2·5	2
Château Les Plantes	*Barsac*	5	12·5	14
Cru Les Quints	*Barsac*	1	2·5	2
Château Les Remparts (*see* Château Gilette)				
Château Les Rochers	*Preignac*	7	17·5	18
Château Les Rochers (*see* Château Gilette)				
Cru Les Rochers	*Preignac*	2	5	4
Cru Les Tuileries	*Fargues*	1	2·5	3
Château Liot	*Barsac*	11	27·5	29
Château de Luzies	*Barsac*	3	7·5	9
Cru Mahon	*Bommes*	1	2·5	4
Cru Mahon	*Preignac*	2	5	6
Cru de Mahon	*Preignac*	2	5	3
Clos des Maraings	*Preignac*	3	7·5	6
Château Masereau	*Barsac*	7	17·5	15
Château Mathalin	*Barsac*	11	27·5	35
Domaine de Mathalin	*Barsac*	1	2·5	3
Château Mauras	*Bommes*	10	25	24
Cru Mauras	*Bommes*	3	7·5	5
Cru Mauvin	*Preignac*	6	15	16
Château du Mayne	*Barsac*	7	17·5	17
Château du Mayne	*Preignac*	2	5	5
Château Mayne-Bert (*see* Château Camperos)				
Clos Mayne-Lamouroux	*Barsac*	2	5	5
Cru Menate	*Barsac*	1	2·5	2
Château Menota, Château Menota-Labat	*Barsac*	17	42·5	54

	COMMUNE	*Hectares*	*Acres*	*Tonneaux*
Château Menota-Labat (*see* Château Menota)				
Château Mercier	*Barsac*	2	5	4
Clos Mercier	*Barsac*	3	7·5	8
Cru Mercier	*Barsac*	1	2·5	4
Clos de Miaille	*Barsac*	1	2·5	2
Cru Miaille	*Barsac*	1	2·5	3
Cru Miselle	*Preignac*	3	7·5	7
Château du Mont	*Preignac*	4	10	11
Château Montalivet (*see* Château Camperos)				
Château Monteau	*Preignac*	9	22·5	21
Cru Monteil	*Bommes*	3	7·5	7
Cru Monteils	*Preignac*	1	2·5	2
Domaine de Monteils	*Preignac*	7	17·5	19
Cru Montjoie	*Preignac*	2	5	4
Château Montjou (*see* Château Terre Noble)				
Cru Mothes	*Fargues*	8	20	13
Cru du Moulin Neuf	*Preignac*	1	2·5	2
Château Mounic	*Fargues*	1	2·5	2
Domaine de Mounic	*Fargues*	1	2·5	2
Château Moura	*Barsac*	1	2·5	4
Cru Mouret	*Fargues*	3	7·5	7
Cru Mussotte	*Fargues*	1	2·5	3
Clos de Nauton	*Fargues*	4	10	7
Château Padonen-Terre-Noble	*Barsac*	7	17·5	10
Château Pageot	*Sauternes*	5	12·5	12
Cru du Pajeot	*Bommes*	4	10	7
Château Paloumat	*Fargues*	2	5	2
Château du Pape	*Preignac*	3	7·5	12
Clos du Pape	*Fargues*	5	12·5	11
Château Partarrieu	*Fargues*	8	20	9
Cru Passérieux	*Barsac*	3	7·5	7
Château Pébayle	*Barsac*	5	12·5	15
Château Peillon-Claverie	*Fargues*	9	22·5	26
Château Pechon-Terre-Noble	*Barsac*	3	7·5	9
Château Pernaud	*Barsac*	17	42·5	35
Cru du Perret	*Bommes*	2	5	6
Château Perroy-Jean-Blanc	*Bommes*	7	17·5	17
Cru Petit-Grillon	*Barsac*	2	5	5
Cru Peyraguey	*Preignac*	8	20	22
Château Peyraguey-le-Rousset (*see* Cru d'Arche-Pugnau)				
Château de Peyre	*Fargues*	1	2·5	3
Cru de Peyre	*Fargues*	1	2·5	3
Clos Peyret	*Preignac*	1	2·5	3
Château Peyron	*Fargues*	4	10	17
Château Piada, Clos du Roy	*Barsac*	11	27·5	29
Cru Pian	*Barsac*	2	5	7
Château Piaut	*Barsac*	9	22·5	22
Château du Pick	*Preignac*	23	57·5	59
Clos de Pierrefeu	*Preignac*	4	10	10
Cru Pilote	*Fargues*	3	7·5	8
Cru Piquey	*Bommes*	1	2·5	2
Cru de Pistoulet-Peyraguey	*Bommes*	2	5	4
Cru du Placey	*Barsac*	1	2·5	3

	COMMUNE	*Hectares*	*Acres*	*Tonneaux*
Cru Planton	*Barsac*	1	2·5	3
Château Pleytegeat	*Preignac*	12	30	51
Cru Pouteau	*Fargues*	2	5	4
Cru Pouton	*Preignac*	2	5	6
Clos des Princes	*Barsac*	2	5	6
Château Prost	*Barsac*	8	20	21
Château Pugnau	*Preignac*	3	7·5	8
Cru Puydomine	*Bommes*	2	5	4
Château Raspide	*Barsac*	5	12·5	16
Château Raymond-Lafon	*Sauternes*	3	7·5	4
Château des Remparts	*Preignac*	1	2·5	4
Cru Richard Barbe	*Bommes*	2	5	5
Cru Ripaille	*Preignac*	1	2·5	2
Château du Roc	*Barsac*	2	5	5
Château des Rocs	*Preignac*	1	2·5	3
Château de Rolland	*Barsac*	14	35	39
Domaine de la Roudette	*Sauternes*	2	5	6
Château Roumieu	*Barsac*	18	45	46
Château Roumieu-Lacoste	*Barsac*	5	12·5	14
Clos Rouquette	*Preignac*	6	15	17
Clos du Roy (*see* Château Piada)				
Château St.-Amand	*Preignac*	7	17·5	20
Château St.-Marc, Château Hourmalas	*Barsac*	6	15	14
Château St.-Michel	*Barsac*	1	2·5	3
Cru St.-Michel	*Barsac*	1	2·5	3
Clos St.-Robert	*Barsac*	1	2·5	3
Cru. St.-Sardeau	*Fargues*	2	5	6
Château Sahuc	*Preignac*	2	5	5
Château Sahuc-Latour	*Preignac*	4	10	8
Cru Saubade-Terrefort	*Sauternes*	2	5	3
Château Simon	*Barsac*	4	10	12
Château Simon-Carretey	*Barsac*	4	10	7
Château Solon	*Preignac*	4	10	13
Cru Soula	*Fargues*	4	10	9
Château Suau	*Barsac*	5	12·5	14
Domaine Tchit	*Fargues*	1	2·5	3
Cru Terrefort	*Bommes*	4	10	11
Domaine de Terrefort	*Sauternes*	3	7·5	6
Château Terre Noble, Château Montjou	*Barsac*	9	22·5	24
Château Terre-Noble (*see* Château Fleury)				
Cru des Terres Rouges	*Barsac*	2	5	4
Château Thibaut	*Fargues*	2	5	4
Cru Thibaut	*Fargues*	7	17·5	15
Château de Touilla	*Fargues*	3	7·5	4
Château Trillon	*Sauternes*	8	20	20
Cru Tucan	*Barsac*	2	5	3
Château Tucau	*Barsac*	3	7·5	9
Cru Tucou	*Preignac*	1	2·5	2
Château Valmont-Mayne	*Barsac*	2	5	4
Château Veyres	*Preignac*	10	25	30
Cru Vigne-Vieille	*Barsac*	3	7·5	8
Château Villefranche	*Barsac*	6	15	13
Château du Violet	*Preignac*	7	17·5	24

	COMMUNE	*Hectares*	*Acres*	*Tonneaux*
Cru du Violet	*Preignac*	1	2·5	5
Cru du Violet-et-Lamothe	*Preignac*	5	12·5	12
Château Voigny	*Preignac*	6	15	18

IX *Cérons*

The following figures of production are approximate, and indicate average annual output, as given by the communes and taken from their Déclarations de Récoltes records.

Principal Growths

	COMMUNE	*Hectares*	*Acres*	*Tonneaux*
Château Archambeau	*Illats*	4	10	34
Clos Avocat	*Cérons*	4	10	8
Clos de la Avocat	*Cérons*	3	7·5	9
Château Balestey	*Cérons*	10	25	20
Clos de Barial	*Illats*	9	22·5	22
Clos du Barrail	*Cérons*	8	20	19
Château Beaulac	*Illats*	3	7·5	7
Cru Bel-Air	*Illats*	3	7·5	12
Clos de Bos-Lancon	*Illats*	4	10	12
Cru de Bouley	*Illats*	4	10	8
Domaine de Bourdac	*Illats*	7	17·5	40
Clos Bourgelet	*Cérons*	7	17·5	15
Cru de Boutec	*Illats*	5	12·5	20
Cru de Braze	*Illats*	7	17·5	18
Cru Brouillaou	*Podensac*	11	27·5	28
Cru de Cabiro	*Illats*	3	7·5	11
Château Cages	*Illats*	5	12·5	17
Domaine du Caillou	*Cérons*	5	12·5	10
Domaine Caillou Rouley	*Podensac*	8	20	15
Château Cantau	*Illats*	4	10	9
Clos Cantemerle	*Cérons*	3	7·5	7
Château de Cérons	*Cérons*	15	37·5	28
Domaine de la Citadelle	*Illats*	4	10	14
Cru Cleyrac	*Cérons*	5	12·5	15
Cru des Deux Moulins	*Illats*	4	10	8
Cru Ducas	*Illats*	2	5	6
Domaine du Freyron	*Cérons*	3	7·5	5
Domaine de Gardennes	*Illats*	3	7·5	6
Château Grand Chemin	*Cérons*	4	10	8
Cru du Grand-Chênes	*Cérons*	3	7·5	6
Grand Enclos du Château de Cérons	*Cérons*	11	27·5	30
Château Hauret	*Illats*	4	10	9
Cru Haut-Buhan	*Illats*	7	17·5	18
Château du Haut-Gravier	*Illats*	11	27·5	22
Cru Haut La Hountasse (P. Banos)	*Illats*	3	7·5	6
Cru Haut La Hountasse (R. Banos, J. Banos)	*Illats*	5	12·5	15
Château Haut-Mayne	*Cérons*	5	12·5	10
Cru Haut-Mayne	*Cérons*	2	5	5
Cru de Haut-Mayne	*Cérons*	3	7·5	6
Château Haut-Rat	*Illats*	16	40	40
Château Huradin, Domaine du Salut	*Cérons*	8	20	30
Clos du Jaugua	*Illats*	4	10	8

	COMMUNE	*Hectares*	*Acres*	*Tonneaux*
Domaine de Jaussans	*Illats*	8	20	20
Château LaLanette Ferbos	*Cérons*	5	12·5	22
Château Lamouroux	*Cérons*	10	25	22
Château Lanette	*Cérons*	5	12·5	12
Cru Larrouquey	*Cérons*	7	17·5	18
Domaine Larrouquey	*Cérons*	5	12·5	12
Château La Salette	*Cérons*	5	12·5	12
Domaine Le Cossu	*Podensac*	5	12·5	11
Château Le Huzet	*Illats*	7	17·5	18
Château de L'Émigré	*Cérons*	2	5	5
Cru Le Tinan	*Illats*	3	7·5	6
Cru de Lionne	*Illats*	7	17·5	18
Château Madère	*Podensac*	12	30	28
Cru Madérot (Étienne Sterlin)	*Podensac*	2	5	6
Cru Majans	*Cérons*	3	7·5	6
Cru Marc	*Illats*	5	12·5	16
Château des Mauves	*Podensac*	10	25	40
Château Mayne d'Anice	*Podensac*	4	10	9
Cru Maynine	*Illats*	3	7·5	10
Domaine de Menaut Larrouquey	*Cérons*	12	30	32
Cru de Menjon	*Illats*	3	7·5	9
Cru Moulin de La Glorie	*Illats*	2	5	7
Château Moulin-à-Vent	*Cérons*	4	10	12
Cru du Moulin-à-Vent (Baron)	*Illats*	2	5	6
Cru Moulin-à-Vent (Biarnes)	*Illats*	16	40	51
Clos des Moulins-à-Vent	*Cérons*	5	12·5	14
Cru des Moulins-à-Vent (Lafond)	*Cérons*	3	7·5	6
Cru des Moulins-à-Vent (Lapujade, Despujols)	*Cérons*	9	22·5	14
Domaine des Moulins-à-Vent	*Illats*	9	22·5	21
Cru du Noulin	*Cérons*	3	7·5	6
Cru des Parrajots	*Illats*	3	7·5	8
Cru du Perliques	*Illats*	3	7·5	8
Château du Peyrat	*Cérons*	8	20	21
Cru Peyroutene	*Cérons*	4	10	9
Cru Pinaud	*Cérons*	4	10	10
Domaine de Prouzet	*Illats*	7	17·5	13
Château du Roc	*Cérons*	5	12·5	8
Clos des Roches	*Illats*	2	5	6
Cru St.-Roch	*Illats*	2	5	5
Domaine du Salut (*see* Château Huradin)				
Château du Seuil	*Cérons*	3	7·5	13
Château Sylvain	*Cérons*	11	27·5	28
Château Thomé-Brousterot	*Illats*	8	20	18
Château Uferic	*Cérons*	6	15	14
Cru Voltaire	*Cérons*	4	10	7

X *Loupiac*

The following figures of production are approximate, and indicate average annual output, as given by the communes and taken from their Déclarations de Récoltes records.

Principal Growths

	Hectares	*Acres*	*Tonneaux*
Château Barbe Morin	5	12·5	16
Cru Barberousse	4	10	15
Château Bel-Air	5	12·5	16
Château Bertranon	2	5	5
Château Bouchoc	2	5	4
Château Caudiet	10	25	36
Domaine du Chay	12	30	29
Château Chichoye	2	5	7
Clos de Ciron	4	10	9
Château Clos Jean	12	30	40
Château Couloumet	5	12·5	12
Château du Cros	21	52·5	56
Château Dauphine Rondillon	15	37·5	55
Château de l'Ermitage	2	5	7
Château La Nère	9	22·5	40
Château Le Tarey	5	12·5	13
Château Le Pavillon	4	10	14
Château Loupiac-Gaudiet	10	25	45
Château de Malendure	3	7·5	6
Cru Marges Dusseau	4	10	17
Château Mazarin	16	40	42
Côtes de Mossac	2	5	7
Château Moulin Neuf	10	25	40
Cru du Moulin Vieux	5	12·5	18
Château du Noble	7	17·5	15
Château Peyruchet	12	30	34
Cru du Plainier	5	12·5	14
Château Pontac	10	25	36
Château Ricaud	36	90	78
Domaine de Roby	5	12·5	20
Château Rondillon	12	30	40
Cru de Rouquette	8	20	18
Cru du la Sablière	4	10	13
Cru St.-Romain	4	10	11
Château Terrefort	8	20	34
Cru de Terrefort	4	10	16
Clos de Terrefort	3	7·5	6
Cru de Terrefort Pierre Noire	3	7·5	11
Château Turon La Nère (Dalas)	3	7·5	10
Château Turon La Nère (David)	5	12·5	18
Château du Vieux-Moulin	9	22·5	40

XI *Sainte-Croix-du-Mont*

The following figures of production are approximate, and indicate average annual output, as given by the communes and taken from their Déclarations de Récoltes records.

Principal Growths

	Hectares	*Acres*	*Tonneaux*
Cru Abraham	4	10	15
Cru Baret-les-Arrivaux	3	7·5	12
Château Bel-Air	12	30	46
Clos Belle-Vue	4	10	17
Château de Bertranon	2	5	9
Château Bouchoc	3	7·5	13
Domaine du Bougan	3	7·5	6
Domaine du Bugat	3	7·5	14
Cru du Canet	3	7·5	6
Château des Coulinats	3	7·5	13
Château Coullac	5	12·5	26
Domaine de Coullander	1	2·5	5
Clos du Crabitan	5	12·5	21
Domaine Damanieu	3	7·5	12
Domaine de d'Escaley	2	5	9
Domaine du Gaël	2	5	10
Cru de Gaillardet	1	2·5	4
Château Gensonne	2	5	5
Cru de Guerisson	3	7·5	7
Château Haut de Baritault	5	12·5	15
Cru Haut-Larrivat	3	7·5	12
Cru Haut-Medouc	3	7·5	15
Domaine de l'If	3	7·5	15
Château Jean-Lamat	4	10	16
Château Laborie	6	15	24
Château La Caussade	5	12·5	20
Domaine de Lacoste	2	5	9
Cru de La Côte Doré	2	5	8
Château Lafuë	10	25	35
Cru La Grave	2	5	6
Château La Grave	6	15	17
Château La Gravière	11	27·5	51
Château La Graville	4	10	19
Château Lamarque	15	37·5	60
Château La Mouleyre	4	10	8
Clos La Mouleyre	4	10	16
Cru La Mouleyre	3	7·5	12
Chateâu Lapeyrère	5	12·5	26
Clos L'Arabey	2	5	7
Château La Rame	5	12·5	20
Cru La Rame	6	15	27
Clos Larrivat	3	7·5	13
Château Laurette	15	37·5	66
Château Le Grand Peyrot	5	12·5	11
Clos Le Haut-Crabitan	2	5	8
Château Le Pin	3	7·5	13
Château L'Escaley	5	12·5	23

	Hectares	*Acres*	*Tonneaux*
Clos Les Arrivaux	3	7·5	11
Cru Les Arroucats	2	5	7
Domaine Les Marcottes	4	10	20
Cru Le Tarey	5	12·5	23
Château Loubens	10	25	34
Domaine de Louqsor	1	2·5	5
Château Lousteau Vieil	7	17·5	33
Château des Mailles	6	15	24
Cru Medouc	4	10	8
Clos du Medouc	2	5	7
Cru Medouc La Grave	2	5	8
Château Megnien	3	7·5	13
Château du Mont	7	17·5	30
Cru de Montagne	5	12·5	19
Domaine des Noyers	7	17·5	25
Clos du Palmiers	3	7·5	12
Domaine de Pampelune	3	7·5	15
Domaine de Parenteau	4	10	19
Château du Pavillon	4	10	17
Cru Peillot	2	5	9
Cru du Pin	2	5	6
Château de la Princesse	2	5	9
Château Roustit	9	22·5	40
Château de Tastes	6	15	18
Château Terfort	3	7·5	11
Cru du Terrefort	2	5	9
Château Vertheuil	10	25	25
Domaine du Vignots	2	5	7

NOTE. In addition to all the châteaux listed in this Appendix there are approximately 1,500 others in the communes of Bordeaux which do not have separate listings.

Appendix B Containers and Measures

I. *Bottle Sizes*

WINE	*Bottles*	*Metric capacity*	*British ounces*	*U.S. ounces*	*British equivalent*				*U.S. equivalent*			
					Gal.	*Qt.*	*Pt.*	*Oz.*	*Gal.*	*Qt.*	*Pt.*	*Oz.*
ALSACE	Half-Bottle	36·00 cl.	12·67	12·17				13				12
	Bottle	72·00 cl.	25·34	24·34			1	5			1	8
ANJOU	Half-Bottle	37·50 cl.	13·20	12·68				13				13
	Bottle	75·00 cl.	26·40	25·36			1	6			1	9
BEAUJOLAIS	Half-Bottle	37·50 cl.	13·20	12·68				13				13
'Pot'	¾ Bottle	50·00 cl.	17·60	16·90				18			1	1
	Bottle	75·00 cl.	26·40	25·36			1	6			1	9
BORDEAUX												
Fillette	Half-Bottle	37·50 cl.	13·20	12·68				13				13
	Bottle	75·00 cl.	26·40	25·36			1	6			1	9
Magnum	Two Bottles	1·50 l.	52·79	50·71		1	–	13		1	1	3
Marie-Jeanne	Three Bottles (approx.)	2·50 l.	88·00	84·53		2	1	8		2	1	4
Double Magnum	Four Bottles	3·00 l.	105·59	101·42		2	1	6		3	–	5
Jeroboam	Six Bottles	4·50 l	158·40	152·16		3	1	18	1	–	1	8
Imperial	Eight Bottles	6·00 l.	211·18	202·85	1	1	–	11	1	2	–	11
BURGUNDY	Half-Bottle	37·50 cl.	13·20	12·68				13				13
	Bottle	75·00 cl.	26·40	25·36			1	6			1	9
Magnum	Two Bottles	1·50 l.	52·79	50·71		1	–	13		1	1	3
CHAMPAGNE												
Split	¼ Bottle	20·00 cl.	7·04	6·76				7				7
Pint	Half-Bottle	40·00 cl.	14·08	13·52				14				14
Quart	Bottle	80·00 cl.	28·16	27·05			1	8			1	11
Magnum	Two Bottles	1·60 l.	56·31	54·09		1	–	16			1	6
Jeroboam	Four Bottles	3·20 l.	112·63	108·19		2	1	13		3	–	12
Rehoboam	Six Bottles	4·80 l.	168·94	162·28	1	–	–	9	1	1	–	2
Methuselah	Eight Bottles	6·40 l.	225·25	216·37	1	1	1	5	1	2	1	8
Salmanazar	Twelve Bottles	9·60 l.	337·88	324·46	2	–	–	18	2	2	–	4
Balthazar	Sixteen Bottles	12·80 l.	450·51	432·74	2	3	–	10	3	1	1	1
Nebuchadnezzar	Twenty Bottles	16.00 l.	563·14	540·93	3	2	–	3	4	–	1	13
MOSELLE	Half-Bottle	35·00 cl.	12·32	11·83				12				12
	Bottle	70·00 cl.	24·63	23·67			1	5			1	8
PORT												
Quart	Bottle	75·75 cl.	26·66	25·61			1	7			1	10
Magnum	Two Bottles	1·51 l.	53·15	51·20		1	–	13		1	1	3
Tappit Hen	Three Bottles	2·27 l.	79·89	76·84		2	–	–		2	–	13
Jeroboam	Four Bottles	3·03 l.	106·64	102·45		2	1	7		3	–	6
RHINE	Half-Bottle	35·00 cl.	12·32	11·83				12				12
	Bottle	70·00 cl.	24·63	23·67			1	5			1	8
SHERRY												
Pint	Half-Bottle	37·86 cl.	13·32	12·80				13				13
Quart	Bottle	75·75 cl.	26·66	25·61			1	7			1	10

TABLE I—(*continued*)

WINE	*Bottles*	*Metric capacity*	*British ounces*	*U.S. ounces*	*British equivalent*				*U.S. equivalent*			
					Gal.	*Qt.*	*Pt.*	*Oz.*	*Gal.*	*Qt.*	*Pt.*	*Oz.*
U.S.												
Tenth	Half-Bottle	37·86 cl.	13·32	12·80				13				13
Fifth	Bottle	75·72 cl.	26·65	25·60			1	7			1	10
Magnum	Two Bottles	1·51 l.	53·15	51·20			1	13		1	1	3

NOTE: Basic metric capacities, and in some cases ounces, upon which most figures in this table are based, are those fixed by law. Actual contents will almost always vary because of differences in corking space.

II. *Cooperage*

	Cask or barrel	*Description*	*Metric capacity litres*	*British equivalent imp. gallons*	*U.S. equivalent U.S. gallons*
FRANCE					
Alsace	*Foudre*	As in Germany, a huge barrel for sales and storage purposes	1,000 litres or any other size. No standard size is adhered to	220.0	264·2
	Aume	Used principally for shipping. Same size as Burgundy *feuillette*	114	25·1	30·1
Beaujolais	*Pièce*		216	47·5	57·1
	Feuillette	One half *pièce*	108	23·7	28·5
	Quartaut	One-quarter *pièce*	54	11·9	14·3
Bordeaux	*Barrique*	*Hogshead*—so-called. Most common Bordeaux cask. Yields 24 cases of 12 bottles each	225	49·5	59·4
	Tonneau	A measure comprised of 4 *barriques*. No actual barrel this size. Château production and price quotations stated in *tonneaux*. Yields 96 cases of 12 bottles each	900	197·9	237·8
	Demi-Barrique or Feuillette	One-half *barrique*	112	24·6	29·6
	Quartaut	One-quarter *barrique*	56	12·3	14·8
Burgundy	*Pièce*	Regular Burgundy barrel. When bottled, yields 24–25 cases of 12 bottles each	228	50·1	60·2
	Queue	Old French measure consisting of 2 *pièces*. No actual cask this size. Sales by Hospices de Beaune made in terms of *queue*	456	100·3	120·5
	Feuillette	One-half *pièce*	114	25·1	30·1
	Quartaut	One-quarter *pièce*	57	12·6	15·1

Table II—(*continued*)

	Cask or barrel	*Description*	*Metric capacity litres*	*British equivalent imp. gallons*	*U.S. equivalent U.S. gallons*
FRANCE—(*continued*)					
Chablis	*Feuillette*	Standard Chablis barrel. Larger than *feuillette* of Côte d'Or	132	29·0	34·9
Champagne	*Queue*	Regular Champagne cask. Also called a *pièce*	216	47·5	57·0
	Demi-Queue	One-half *queue*	108	23·7	28·5
Loire Valley					
Anjou, Layon, Saumur	*Pièce*	Capacity variable	220	48·4	58·1
Vouvray	*Pièce*	Capacity same as Bordeaux *hogshead*	225	49·5	59·4
Mâconnais	*Pièce*	Nearly the same size as the Beaujolais *pièce*	215	47·3	56·8
The Midi and Algeria	*Demi-Muid*	Storage barrel	600–700 (approx.)	143·0 (approx.)	171·7 (approx.)
Rhône Valley	*Pièce*	Standard barrel in the area of Châteauneuf-du-Pape. Slightly smaller than *pièce* of Côte d'Or	225	49·5	59·4
GERMANY					
Rhine and Moselle	*Ohm**	An old Hock or Rhine measure which is now obsolete	150	33·0	39·6
	Doppelohm	Double *ohm* equal to a quarter-*stück*	300	66·0	79·2
	Fuder (Moselle)	Large storage cask	1,000	219·9	264·2
	Stück (Rhine)	Huge storage cask	1,200	264·0	317·0
	Doppelstück (Rhine)	Double *stück*	2,400	527·8	634·0
	Halbstück (Rhine)	One-half *stück*	600	132·0	158·4
	Viertelstück (Rhine)	One-quarter *stück*	300	66·0	79·2
AUSTRALIA AND SOUTH AFRICA	*Hogshead*		295·3	64·9	78·0
LISBON	*Pipe*		531·4	117·0	140·4
MADEIRA	*Pipe*	Standard Madeira shipping cask. Yields on average 44½ cases of 12 bottles each	418·0	92·0	110·4
	Hogshead	One-half Madeira *pipe*	209·0	46·0	55·2
MARSALA	*Pipe*	Slightly larger than Madeira *pipe*. Yields 45 cases of 12 bottles each	422·6	93·0	111·6
	Hogshead	Same size as Madeira *hogshead*	209·0	46·0	55·2
PORT	*Pipe*	Standard Port cask. Average yield is 56 dozen reputed quarts	522·5	115·0	138·0

* No longer used.

TABLE II—(*continued*)

	Cask or barrel	*Description*	*Metric capacity litres*	*British equivalent imp. gallons*	*U.S. equivalent U.S. gallons*
PORT (*continued*)	*Hogshead*		259·0	57·0	68·4
	Quarter Cask	One-quarter standard	127·2	28.0	33·6
SHERRY	*Butt*	Standard Sherry cask. Yields, when bottled, 52 cases of 12 bottles each	490·7	108·0	129·6
	Hogshead	One-half *butt*, yields 26 cases of 12 bottles each	245·4	54·0	64·8
	Quarter Cask	One-quarter standard, or one-half *hogshead*	122·7	27·0	32·4
	Octave	One-eighth standard	61·4	13·5	16·2
TARRAGONA	*Pipe*	Same capacity as *pipe* of Port	522·5	114·9	138·0
	Hogshead		263·5	57·9	69·6
BRANDY	*Puncheon*	Most commonly used brandy cask	545·2	120·0	144·0
	Hogshead	One-half *puncheon*	272·6	60·0	72·0
	Quarter Cask	One-quarter *puncheon* or one-half *hogshead*	136·3	30·0	36·0
RUM	*Puncheon*	Size varies considerably	422·6–518·0	92·9–113·9	111·6–136·8
	Hogshead	Equally variable in size	245·4–272·6	54·0–59·9	64·8–72·0
WHISKY—SCOTCH	*Butt*	Standard distillery cask. Sometimes a rum *puncheon*, made from oak, cut down to the *butt* length of stave and gallonage	491·0 (approx.)	108·0 (approx.)	129·7 (approx.)
	Puncheon	Capacity varies between 95 and 120 imp. gallons	431·9–545·5	95·0–120·0	114·1–144·1
WHISKEY—U.S.	*Barrel*	Standard new barrel for either Rye or Bourbon whiskey as required by law	181·7	40·0	48·0
WHISKY—CANADIAN	*Barrel*	Capacity variable. Usually exceeds slightly the standard U.S. 48-gallon barrel	181·7 (approx.)	40·0 (approx.)	48·0 (approx.)
SPIRITS (*Aged*) U.S.	*Barrel*	Used cooperage: same U.S. barrel and size as for whiskey	181·7	40·0	48·0
	Hogshead	Cask holding between 45 and 80 imp. gals.		45·0–80.0	54·0–96·0
	Barrel	Cask holding between 35 and 45 imp. gals.		35·0–45·0	42·0–54·0
	Quarter	Cask holding between 15 and 30 imp. gals.		15·0–30·0	18·0–36·0
	Octave	Cask holding between 9 and 15 imp. gals.		9·0–15·0	10·8–18·0

CASE			
Bordeaux and Burgundy	8.52	1·87	2·25
Champagne	9·23	2·0304	2·4375

Appendix C **Comparative Table of Spirit Strength**

Sikes (British)	*American*	*Gay-Lussac and Tralles*
U.P. (Under proof)		
60·0°	45·7°	22·9°
59·8	46·0	23·0
59·0	46·9	23·4
58·9	47.0	23·5
58·0	48.0	24·0
57·1	49·0	24·5
57·0	49·1	24·6
56·3	50·0	25·0
56·0	50·3	25·1
55·4	51·0	25·5
55·0	51·4	25.7
54·5	52·0	26·0
54·0	52·6	26·3
53·6	53·0	26·5
53·0	53·7	26·9
52·8	54·0	27·0
52·0	54·9	27·4
51·9	55·0	27·5
51·0	56·0	28·0
50·1	57·0	28·5
50·0	57·1	28·6
49·3	58·0	29·0
49·0	58·3	29·1
48·4	59·0	29·5
48·0	59·4	29·7
47·5	60.0	30·0
47·0	60·6	30·3
46·6	61·0	30·5
46·0	61·7	30·9
45·8	62·0	31·0
45·0	62·9	31·4
44·9	63·0	31·5
44·0	64·0	32·0
43·1	65·0	32·5
43·0	65·1	32·6
42·3	66·0	33·0
42·0	66·3	33·1
41·4	67·0	33·5
41·0	67·4	33.7
40·5	68·0	34·0
40·0	68·6	34·3
39·6	69·0	34·5
39·0	69·7	34·9
38·8	70·0	35·0
38·0	70·9	35·4
37·9	71·0	35·5
37·0	72·0	36·0
36·1	73·0	36·5
36·0	73·1	36·6
35·3	74·0	37·0
35·0°	74·3°	37·1°
34·4	75·0	37·5
34·0	75·4	37·7
33·5	76·0	38·0
33·0	76·6	38·3
32·6	77·0	38·5
32·0	77·7	38·9
31·8	78·0	39·0
31·0	78·9	39·4
30·9	79·0	39·5
30·0	80·0	40·0
29·1	81·0	40·5
29·0	81·1	40·6
28·3	82·0	41·0
28·0	82·3	41·1
27·4	83·0	41·5
27·0	83·4	41·7
26·5	84·0	42·0
26·0	84·6	42·3
25·6	85·0	42·5
25·0	85·7	42·9
24·8	86·0	43·0
24·0	86·9	43·4
23·9	87·0	43·5
23·0	88·0	44·0
22·1	89·0	44·5
22·0	89·1	44·6
21·3	90·0	45·0
21·0	90·3	45·1
20·4	91·0	45·5
20·0	91·4	45·7
19·5	92·0	46·0
19·0	92·6	46·3
18·6	93·0	46·5
18·0	93·7	46·9
17·8	94·0	47·0
17·0	94·9	47·4
16·9	95·0	47·5
16·0	96·0	48·0
15·1	97·0	48·5
15·0	97·1	48·6
14·3	98·0	49·0
14·0	98·3	49·1
13·4	99·0	49·5
13·0	99·4	49·7
12·50	Proof	50·00
12·0	100·6	50·3
11·6	101·0	50·5
11·0	101·7	50·9
10·8	102·0	51·0
10·0	102·9	51·4
9·9	103·0	51·5

Appendix C—*(continued)*

Sikes (British)	*American*	*Gay-Lussac and Tralles*
9·0°	104·0°	52·0°
8·1	105·0	52·5
8·0	105·1	52·6
7·3	106·0	53·0
7·0	106·3	53·1
6·4	107·0	53·5
6·c	107·4	53·7
5·5	108·0	54·0
5·c	108·6	54·3
4·6	109·0	54·5
4·0	109·7	54·9
3·8	110·0	55·0
3·0	110·9	55·4
2·9	111·0	55·5
2·0	112·0	56·0
1·1	113·0	56·5
1·0	113·1	56·6
0·3	114·0	57·0
Proof	114·29	57·14
O.P. (Over proof)		
0·6	115·0	57·5
1·0	115·4	57·7
1·5	116·0	58·0
2·0	116·6	58·3
2·4	117·0	58·5
3·0	117·7	58·9
3·3	118·0	59·0
4·0	118·9	59·4
4·1	119·0	59·5
5·0	120·0	60·0
5·9	121·0	60·5
6·0°	121·1	60·6°
6·8	122·0	61·0
7·0	122·3	61·1
7·6	123·0	61·5
8·0	123·4	61·7
8·5	124·0	62·0
9·0	124·6	62·3
9·4	125·0	62·5
10·0	125·7	62·9
10·3	126·0	63·0
11.0	126·9	63·4
11·1	127·0	63·5
12·0	128·0	64·0
12·9	129·0	64·5
13·0	129·1	64·6
13·8	130·0	65·0
14·0	130·3	65·1
14·6	131·0	65·5
15.0	131·4	65·7

Sikes (British)	*American*	*Gay-Lussac and Tralles*
15·5°	132·0°	66·0°
16·0	132·6	66·3
16·4	133·0	66·5
17·0	133·7	66·9
17·3	134·0	67·0
18·0	134·9	67·4
18·1	135·0	67·5
19·0	136·0	68·0
19·9	137·0	68·5
20·0	137·1	68·6
20·8	138·0	69·0
21·0	138·3	69·1
21·6	139·0	69·5
22·0	139·4	69·7
22·5	140·0	70·0
23·0	140·6	70·3
23·4	141·0	70·5
24·0	141·7	70·9
24·3	142·0	71·0
25·0	142·9	71·4
25·1	143·0	71·5
26·0	144·0	72·0
26·9	145·0	72·5
27·0	145·1	72·6
27·8	146·0	73·0
28·0	146·3	73·1
28·6	147·0	73·5
29·0	147·4	73·7
29·5	148·0	74·0
30·0	148·6	74·3
30·4	149·0	74·5
31·0	149·7	74·9
31·3	150·0	75·0
32·0	150·9	75·4
32·1	151·0	75·5
33·0	152·0	76·0
33·9	153·0	76·5
34·0	153·1	76·6
34·8	154·0	77·0
35·0	154·3	77·1
35·6	155·0	77·5
36·0	155·4	77·7
36·5	156·0	78·0
37·0	156·6	78·3
37·4	157·0	78·5
38·0	157·7	78·9
38·3	158·0	79·0
39·0	158·9	79·4
39·1	159·0	79·5
40·0	160·0	80·0
40·9	161·0	80·5
41·0	161·1	80·6

Appendix C—*(continued)*

Sikes (British)	American	Gay-Lussac and Tralles	Sikes (British)	American	Gay-Lussac and Tralles
41·8°	162·0°	81·0°	58·4°	181·0°	90·5°
42·0	162·3	81·1	50·9	181·7	90·9
42·6	163·0	81·5	59·3	182·0	91·0
43·0	163·4	81·7	60·0	182·9	91·4
43·5	164·0	82·0	60·1	183·0	91·5
44·0	164·6	82·3	61·0	184·0	92·0
44·4	165·0	82·5	61·9	185·0	92·5
45·0	165·7	82·9	62·0	185·1	92·6
45·3	166·0	83·0	62·8	186·0	93·0
46·0	166·9	83·4	63·0	186·3	93·1
46·1	167·0	83·5	63·6	187·0	93·5
47·0	168·0	84·0	64·0	187·4	93·7
47·9	169·0	84·5	64·5	188·0	94·0
48·0	169·1	84·6	65·0	188·6	94·3
48·8	170·0	85·0	65·4	189·0	94·5
49·0	170·3	85·1	66·0	189·7	94·9
49·6	171·0	85·5	66·3	190·0	95·0
50·0	171·4	85·7	67·0	190·9	95·4
50·5	172·0	86·0	67·1	191·0	95·5
51·0	172·6	86·3	68·0	192·0	96·0
51·4	173·0	86·5	68·9	193·0	96·5
52·0	173·7	86·9	69·0	193·1	96·6
52·3	174·0	87·0	69·8	194·0	97·0
53·0	174·9	87·4	70·0	194·3	97·1
53·1	175·0	87·5	70·6	195·0	97·5
54·0	176·0	88·0	71·0	195·4	97·7
54·9	177·0	88·5	71·5	196·0	98·0
55·0	177·1	88·6	72·0	196·6	98·3
55·8	178·0	89·0	72·4	197·0	98·5
56·0	178·3	89·1	73·0	197·7	98·9
56·6	179·0	89·5	73·3	198·0	99·0
57·0	179·4	89·7	74·0	198·9	99·4
57·5	180·0	90·0	74·1	199·0	99·5
58·0	180·6	90·3	75·0	200.0	100·0

Appendix D **Conversion Tables**

I. MEASUREMENT OF LENGTH

Centimetres	*Inches*	*Ft.*	*Ins.*	*Metres*	*Ft.*	*Yds.*	*Ft.*	*Ins.*	*Yds.*	*Kilometres*	*Miles*
1	0·394		$\frac{2}{5}$	1	3·281	1		$3\frac{2}{5}$	1·094	1	0·621
2	0·787		$\frac{4}{5}$	2	6·562	2		$6\frac{7}{10}$	2·187	2	1·243
3	1·181		$1\frac{1}{5}$	3	9·843	3		$10\frac{1}{10}$	3·281	3	1·864
4	1·575		$1\frac{3}{5}$	4	13·123	4	1	$1\frac{1}{2}$	4·374	4	2·486
5	1·969		2	5	16·404	5	1	$4\frac{4}{5}$	5·468	5	3·107
6	2·362		$2\frac{2}{5}$	6	19·685	6	1	$8\frac{1}{5}$	6·562	6	3·728
7	2·756		$2\frac{4}{5}$	7	22·966	7	1	$11\frac{3}{5}$	7·655	7	4·350
8	3·150		$3\frac{1}{5}$	8	26·247	8	2	3	8·749	8	4·971
9	3·543		$3\frac{1}{2}$	9	29·528	9	2	$6\frac{3}{10}$	9·843	9	5·592
10	3·937		$3\frac{9}{10}$	10	32·808	10	2	$9\frac{7}{10}$	10·936	10	6·214
20	7·874		$7\frac{9}{10}$	20	65·617	21	2	$7\frac{2}{5}$	21·872	20	12·427
30	11·811		$11\frac{4}{5}$	30	98·425	32	2	$5\frac{1}{10}$	32·808	30	18·641
40	15·748	1	$3\frac{7}{10}$	40	131·234	43	2	$2\frac{4}{5}$	43·745	40	24·855
50	19·685	1	$7\frac{7}{10}$	50	164·042	54	2	$\frac{1}{2}$	54·681	50	31·069
60	23·622	1	$11\frac{3}{5}$	60	196·850	65	1	$10\frac{1}{5}$	65·617	60	37·282
70	27·559	2	$3\frac{3}{5}$	70	229·659	76	1	$7\frac{9}{10}$	76·553	70	43·496
80	31·496	2	$7\frac{1}{2}$	80	262·467	87	1	$5\frac{3}{5}$	87·489	80	49·710
90	35·433	2	$11\frac{2}{5}$	90	295·276	98	1	$3\frac{3}{10}$	98·425	90	55·923
100 = 1 metre	39·370	3	$3\frac{2}{5}$	100	328·084	109	1	1	109·361	100	62·137

10 millimetres = 1 centimetre
10 centimetres = 1 decimetre
10 decimetres = 1 metre

10 metres = 1 dekametre
10 dekametres = 1 hectometre
10 hectometres = 1 kilometre

I. Measurement of Length (*continued*)

Inches	*Centimetres*
1	2·540
2	5·080
3	7·620
4	10·160
5	12·700
6	15·240
7	17·780
8	20·320
9	22·860
10	25·400
11	27·940
12 = 1 foot	30·480
20	50·800
30	76·200
40	101·600
50	127·000
60	152·400
70	177·800
80	203·200
90	228·600
100	254·000

Feet	*Metres*	*Yards*	*Metres*	*Miles*	*Kilometres*
1	0·305	1	0·914	1	1·609
2	0·610	2	1·829	2	3·219
3 = 1 yard	0·914	3	2·743	3	4·828
4	1·219	4	3·658	4	6·437
5	1·524	5	4·572	5	8·047
6	1·829	6	5·486	6	9·656
7	2·134	7	6·401	7	11·265
8	2·438	8	7·315	8	12·875
9	2·743	9	8·230	9	14·484
10	3·048	10	9·144	10	16·093
20	6·096	20	18·288	20	32·187
30	9·144	30	27·432	30	40·280
40	12·192	40	36·576	40	64·374
50	15·240	50	45·720	50	80·467
60	18·288	60	54·864	60	96·561
70	21·336	70	64·008	70	112·654
80	24·384	80	73·152	80	128·748
90	27·432	90	82·296	90	144·841
100	30·480	100	91·440	100	160·934

12 inches (in.) = 1 foot (ft.)
3 feet = 1 yard (yd.)
1,760 yards = 1 mile

II. SQUARE MEASURE

Square centimetres	*Square inches*	*Square metres*	*Square feet*	*Hectares*	*Acres*	*Square kilometres*	*Square miles*
1	0·155	1	10·764	1	2·471	1	0·368
2	0·310	2	21·528	2	4·942	2	0·722
3	0·465	3	32·292	3	7·413	3	1·158
4	0·620	4	43·056	4	9·884	4	1·544
5	0·775	5	53·820	5	12·355	5	1·931
6	0·930	6	64·583	6	14·826	6	2·317
7	1·085	7	75·347	7	17·297	7	2·703
8	1·240	8	86·111	8	19·768	8	3·089
9	1·395	9	96·875	9	22·239	9	3·475
10	1·550	10	107·639	10	24·711	10	3·861
20	3·100	20	215·278	20	49·421	20	7·722
30	4·650	30	322·917	30	74·132	30	11·583
40	6·200	40	430·556	40	98·842	40	15·444
50	7·750	50	538·196	50	123·553	50	19·305
60	9·300	60	645·835	60	148·263	60	23·166
70	10·850	70	753·474	70	172·974	70	27·027
80	12·400	80	861·113	80	197·684	80	30·888
90	13·950	90	968·752	90	222·395	90	34·749
100	15·500	100	1,076·391	100 = 1 square kilometre	247·105	100	38·610

10,000 square centimetres = 1 square metre
10,000 square metres = 1 hectare
100 hectares = 1 square kilometre

II. Square Measure—(*continued*)

Square inches	*Square centimetres*	*Square feet*	*Square metres*	*Acres*	*Hectares*	*Square miles*	*Square kilometres*
1	6·452	1	0·093	1	0·405	1	2·590
2	12·903	2	0·186	2	0·809	2	5·180
3	19·355	3	0·279	3	1·214	3	7·770
4	25·806	4	0·372	4	1·619	4	10·360
5	32·258	5	0·465	5	2·023	5	12·950
6	38·710	6	0·557	6	2·428	6	15·540
7	45·161	7	0·650	7	2·833	7	18·130
8	51·613	8	0·743	8	3·238	8	20·720
9	58·064	9 = 1 sq. yd.	0·836	9	3·642	9	23·310
10	64·516	10	0·929	10	4·047	10	25·900
20	129·032	20	1·858	20	8·094	20	51·800
30	193·548	30	2·787	30	12·141	30	77·700
40	258·064	40	3·716	40	16·187	40	103·600
50	322·580	50	4·645	50	20·234	50	129·499
60	387·096	60	5·574	60	24·281	60	155·399
70	451·612	70	6·503	70	28·328	70	181·299
80	516·128	80	7·432	80	32·375	80	207·199
90	580·644	90	8·361	90	36·422	90	233·099
100	645·160	100	9·290	100	40·469	100	258·999

144 square inches = 1 square foot
9 square feet = 1 square yard
4,840 square yards = 1 acre
640 acres = 1 square mile

III. CUBIC MEASURE

Cubic centimetres	*Cubic inches*	*Cubic decimetres*	*Cubic feet*	*Cubic metres*	*Cubic yards*
1	0·061	1	0·035	1	1·308
2	0·122	2	0·071	2	2·616
3	0·183	3	0·106	3	3·924
4	0·244	4	0·141	4	5·232
5	0·305	5	0·177	5	6·540
6	0·366	6	0·212	6	7·848
7	0·427	7	0·247	7	9·156
8	0·488	8	0·283	8	10·464
9	0·549	9	0·318	9	11·772
10	0·610	10	0·353	10	13·080
20	1·220	20	0·706	20	26·159
30	1·831	30	1·059	30	39·239
40	2·441	40	1·413	40	52·318
50	3·051	50	1·766	50	65·398
60	3·661	60	2·119	60	78·477
70	4·272	70	2·472	70	91·557
80	4·882	80	2·825	80	104·636
90	5·492	90	3·178	90	117·716
100	6·102	100	3·531	100	130·795

1,000 cubic centimetres = 1 cubic decimetre
1,000 cubic decimetres = 1 cubic metre = 1 stere

III. Cubic Measure (*continued*)

Cubic inches	*Cubic centimetres*	*Cubic feet*	*Cubic decimetres*	*Cubic yards*	*Cubic metres*
1	16·387	1	28·317	1	0·765
2	32·774	2	56·633	2	1.529
3	49·161	3	84·951	3	2·294
4	65·548	4	113·267	4	3·058
5	81·935	5	141·584	5	3·823
6	98·322	6	169·901	6	4·587
7	114·709	7	198·218	7	5·352
8	131·097	8	226·535	8	6·116
9	147·484	9	254·852	9	6·881
10	163·871	10	283·168	10	7·646
20	327·741	20	566·337	20	15·291
30	491·612	30	849·505	30	22·937
40	655·483	40	1,132·674	40	30·582
50	819·353	50	1,415·842	50	38·228
60	983·224	60	1,699·011	60	45·873
70	1,147·094	70	1,982·179	70	53·519
80	1,310·965	80	2,265·348	80	61·164
90	1,474·836	90	2,548·516	90	68·810
100	1,638·706	100	2,831·685	100	76·455

1,728 cubic inches = 1 cubic foot
27 cubic feet = 1 cubic yard

IV. WEIGHTS

Grams	*Avoirdupois ounces*	*Lb.*	*Oz.*	*Kilograms*	*Avoirdupois pounds*	*Cwts.*	*Qtrs.*	*Sts.*	*Lb.*	*Oz.*
1	0·035		—	1	2·205				2	3
2	0·071		—	2	4·409				4	7
3	0·106		—	3	6·614				6	10
4	0·141		—	4	8·818				8	13
5	0·176		—	5	11·023				11	—
6	0·212		—	6	13·228				13	4
7	0·247		—	7	15·432			1	1	7
8	0·282		—	8	17·637			1	3	10
9	0·317		—	9	19·842			1	5	13
10	0·353		—	10	22·046			1	8	1
20	0·705		—	20	44·092		1	1	2	1
30	1·058		1	30	66·139		2	—	10	2
40	1·411		1½	40	88·185		3	—	4	3
50	1·764		1¾	50	110·231		3	1	12	4
60	2·116		2	60	132·277	1	—	1	6	4
70	2·469		2½	70	154·324	1	1	1	—	5
80	2·822		2¾	80	176·370	1	2	—	8	6
90	3·175		3¼	90	198·416	1	3	—	2	7
100	3·527		3½	100	220·463	1	3	1	10	7
150	5·291		5¼	150	330·69	2	3	1	8	11
200	7·055		7	200	440·92	3	3	1	6	15
250	8·818		8¾	250	551·16	4	3	1	5	3
300	10·592		10½	300	661·39	5	3	1	3	6
350	12·346		12½	350	771·62	6	3	1	1	10
400	14·110		14	400	881·85	7	3	—	13	14
450	15·873		15¾	450	992·08	8	3	—	12	1
500	17·637	1	1¾	500	1,102·31	9	3	—	10	5
550	19·401	1	3½	550	1,212·54	10	3	—	8	9
600	21·164	1	5¼	600	1,322·77	11	3	—	6	12
650	22·928	1	7	650	1,433·00	12	3	—	4	—
700	24·691	1	8¾	700	1,543·24	13	3	—	3	4
750	26·455	1	10½	750	1,653·47	14	3	—	1	7
800	28·219	1	12¼	800	1,763·70	15	2	1	13	11
850	29·983	1	14	850	1,873·93	16	2	1	11	15
900	31·746	1	15¾	900	1,984·16	17	2	1	10	2
950	33·510	2	1½	950	2,094·39	18	2	1	8	6
1,000 = 1 kilogram	35·274	2	3¼	1,000 = 1 ton (metric)	2,204·63	19	2	1	6	10

IV. Weights (*continued*)

Metric tons	*Long or gross tons*	*Tons*	*Cwts.*	*Qtrs.*	*Sts.*	*Lb.*	*Oz.*	*Metric tons*	*Long or gross tons*	*Tons*	*Cwts.*	*Qtrs.*	*Sts.*	*Lb.*	*Oz.*
1	0·984		19	2	1	6	9¾	20	19·684	19	13	2	1	6	6¼
2	1·968	1	19	1	–	13	3½	30	29·526	29	10	2	–	2	11
3	2·953	2	19	–	–	5	13¼	40	39·368	39	7	1	–	12	15¾
4	3·937	3	18	2	1	12	7	50	49·210	49	4	–	1	9	1¼
5	4·921	4	18	1	1	5	¾	60	59·052	59	1	–	–	5	6
6	5·905	5	18	–	–	11	10¼	70	68·895	68	17	3	1	1	11
7	6·889	6	17	3	–	4	4	80	78·737	78	14	2	1	11	12¼
8	7·874	7	17	1	1	11	1½	90	88·579	88	11	2	–	8	1
9	8·858	8	17	–	1	3	11¼	100	98·421	98	8	1	1	4	6
10	9·842	9	16	3	–	10	4¾								

IV. Weights (*continued*)

Avoirdupois ounces	*Grams*	*Avoirdupois pounds*	*Kilograms*	*Long or gross tons*	*Metric tons*
1	28·350	1	0·454	1	1·016
2	56·699	2	0·907	2	2·032
3	85·049	3	1·361	3	3·048
4	113·398	4	1·814	4	4·064
5	141·748	5	2·268	5	5·080
6	170·097	6	2·722	6	6·096
7	198·447	7	3·175	7	7·112
8	226·796	8	3·629	8	8·128
9	255·146	9	4·082	9	9·144
10	283·495	10	4·536	10	10.161
16 = 1 pound	453·592	14 = 1 stone	6·350	20	20·321
20	566·990	20	9·072	30	30·481
30	850·486	28 = 1 quarter	12·701	40	40·642
40	1,133·981	30	13·608	50	50·802
50	1,417·476	40	18·144	60	60·963
60	1,700·971	50	22·680	70	71·123
70	1,984·467	60	27·216	80	81·284
80	2,267·962	70	31·751	90	91·444
90	2,551·457	80	36·287	100	101·605
100	2,834·952	90	40·823		
		100	45·359		
		112 = 1 hundred-weight	50·802		

16 ounces (oz.) = 1 pound (lb.)
14 pounds = 1 stone (st.)
28 pounds = 1 quarter (qtr.)
112 pounds = 1 hundredweight (cwt.)
20 hundredweight = 2,240 lb. = 1 ton (long)
2,000 lb. = 1 ton (short)

V. CAPACITY

Centilitres	*Ounces (British)*	*British equivalent*		*Ounces (U.S.)*	*U.S. equivalent*		
		Pts.	*Oz.*		*Qts.*	*Pts.*	*Oz.*
20	7·039		7	6·763			6¾
25	8·799		8¾	8·454			6½
30	10·599		10½	10·144			10¼
35	12·319		12¼	11·835			11¾
36	12·671		12¾	12·173			12¼
37·5	13·199		13¼	12·681			12¾
40	14·078		14	13·526			13½
45	15·838		15¾	15·217			15¼
50	17·598		17½	16·907		1	1
55	19·358		19¼	18·598		1	2½
60	21·118	1	1	20·289		1	4¼
65	22·877	1	2¾	21·980		1	6
70	24·637	1	4¾	23·670		1	7¾
75	26·397	1	6½	25·361		1	9¼
80	28·175	1	8¼	27·052		1	11
85	29·917	1	10	28·742		1	12¾
90	31·676	1	11¾	30·433		1	14½
95	33·436	1	13½	32·124	1	—	—
100 = 1 litre	35·196	1	15¼	33·814	1	—	1¾

100 centilitres = 1 litre

V. Capacity (*continued*)

Litres	*Pints (British)*	*Gallons (British)*	*British equivalent* Gals.	Qts.	Pts.	Oz.	*Pints (U.S.)*	*Gallons (U.S.)*	*U.S. equivalent* Gals.	Qts.	Pts.	Oz.
1	1·760	0·220			1	15¼	2·113	0·264		1	–	1¾
2	3·520	0·440		1	1	10½	4·227	0·528		2	–	3½
3	5·279	0·660		2	1	5½	6·340	0·793		3	–	5½
4	7·039	0·880		3	1	¾	8·454	1·057	1	–	–	7¼
5	8·799	1·100	1	–	–	16	10·567	1·321	1	1	–	9
6	10·559	1·320	1	1	–	11¼	12·681	1·585	1	2	–	11
7	12·319	1·540	1	2	–	6½	14·794	1·849	1	3	–	12¾
8	14·078	1·760	1	3	–	1½	16·908	2·113	2	–	–	14½
9	15·838	1·980	1	3	1	16¾	19·021	2·378	2	1	1	¼
10	17·598	2·200	2	–	1	12	21·134	2·642	2	2	1	2¼
11	19·358	2·420	2	1	1	7¼	23·248	2·906	2	3	1	4
12	21·118	2·640	2	2	1	2½	25·361	3·170	3	–	1	5¾
13	22·877	2·860	2	3	–	17½	27·475	3·434	3	1	1	7½
14	24·637	3·080	3	–	–	12¾	29·588	3·699	3	2	1	9½
15	26·397	3·300	3	1	–	8	31·702	3·963	3	3	1	11¼
16	28·157	3·520	3	2	–	3¼	33·815	4·227	4	–	1	13
17	29·917	3·740	3	2	1	18½	35·928	4·491	4	1	1	14¾
18	31·676	3·960	3	3	1	13½	38·042	4·755	4	3	–	¾
19	33·436	4·180	4	–	1	8¾	40·155	5·019	5	–	–	2½
20	35·196	4·400	4	1	1	3¾	42·269	5·284	5	1	–	4¼
30	52·794	6·599	6	2	–	15¾	63·403	7·925	7	3	1	6½
40	70·392	8·799	8	3	–	7¾	84·538	10·567	10	2	–	8½
50	87·990	10·999	10	3	1	19¾	105·672	13·209	13	–	1	10¾
60	105·588	13·199	13	–	1	11¾	126·806	15·851	15	3	–	13
70	123·186	15·398	15	1	1	3¾	147·941	18·493	18	1	1	15
80	140·784	17·598	17	2	–	15¾	169·075	21·134	21	–	1	1¼
90	158·382	19·798	19	3	–	7¾	190·210	23·776	23	3	–	3¼
100= 1 hectolitre	175·980	21·998	21	3	1	19¾	211·344	26·418	26	1	1	5½

V. Capacity (*continued*)

Fluid ounces (British)	*Centilitres*	*Fluid ounces (U.S.)*	*U.S. equivalent* Qts.	Pts.	Oz.	*Pints (British)*	*Litres*	*Pints (U.S.)*	*U.S. equivalent* Gals.	Qts.	Pts.	Oz.
6	17·047	5·765			5¾	1	0·568	1·201			1	3¼
7	19·889	6·725			6¾	2= 1 qt.	1·136	2·402		1	–	6½
8	22·730	7·686			7¾	3	1·705	3·603		1	1	9¾
9	25·571	8·647			8¾	4= 2 qts.	2·273	4·804		2	–	12¾
10	28·412	9·608			9½	5	2·841	6·005		3	–	—
11	31·253	10·568			10½	6= 3 qts.	3·409	7·206		3	1	3¼
12	34·095	11·529			11½	7	3·978	8·407	1	–	–	6½
13	36·936	12·490			12½	8= 1 gal.	4·546	9·608	1	–	1	9¾
14	39·777	13·451			13½	9	5·114	10·809	1	1	–	13
15	42·618	14·411			14½	10	5·682	12·010	1	2	–	¼
16	45·460	15·372			15¼	11	6·251	13·210	1	2	1	3¼
17	48·301	16·333		1	¼	12	6·819	14·411	1	3	–	6½
18	51·142	17·294		1	1¼	13	7·387	15·612	1	3	1	9¾
19	53·983	18·254		1	2¼	14	7·955	16·813	2	–	–	13

V. Capacity (*continued*)

Fluid ounces (British)	*Centilitres*	*Fluid ounces (U.S.)*	*U.S. equivalent Qts.*	*Pts.*	*Oz.*	*Pints (British)*	*Litres*	*Pints (U.S.)*	*U.S. equivalent Gals.*	*Qts.*	*Pts.*	*Oz.*
20=1 pt.	56·824	19·215		1	3¼	15	8·524	18·014	2	1	–	¼
30	85·237	28·823		1	12¾	16=2 gals.	9·092	19·215	2	1	1	3½
40= 1 qt.	113·649	38·430	1	–	6½	17	9·660	20·416	2	2	–	6¾
50	142·061	48·038	1	1	–	18	10·228	21·617	2	2	1	9¾
60	170·473	57·646	1	1	9¾	19	10·797	22·818	2	3	–	13
70	198·885	67·253	2	–	3¼	20	11·365	24·019	3	–	–	¼
80=2 qts.	227·298	76·861	2	–	12¾	30	17·047	36·029	4	2	–	½
90	255·710	86·469	2	1	6½	40	22·730	48·038	6	–	–	½
100	284·122	96·076	3	–	–	50	28·412	60·048	7	2	–	¾
						60	34·095	72·057	9	–	–	1
						70	39·777	84·067	10	2	–	1
						80=10 gals.	45·460	96·076	12	–	–	1¼
						90	51·142	108·086	13	2	–	1½
						100	56·825	120·095	15	–	–	1½

20 fluid oz. (British) = 1 pint
2 pints = 1 quart

V. Capacity (*continued*)

Fluid ounces (U.S.)	*Centilitres*	*Fluid ounces (British)*	*British equivalent Qts.*	*Pts.*	*Oz.*	*Pints (U.S.)*	*Litres*	*Pints (British)*	*British equivalent Gals.*	*Qts.*	*Pts.*	*Oz.*
6	17·744	6·245			6¼	1	0·473	0·833				16¾
7	20·701	7·286			7¼	2=1 qt.	0·946	1·665			1	13¼
8	23·658	8·327			8¼	3	1·419	2·498		1	–	10
9	26·615	9·368			9¼	4=2 qts.	1·893	3·331		1	1	6½
10	29·573	10·408			10½	5	2·366	4·163		2	–	3¼
11	32·530	11·449			11½	6=3 qts.	2·839	4·996		2	1	—
12	35·487	12·490			12½	7	3·312	5·829		2	1	16½
13	38·445	13·531			13½	8=1 gal.	3·785	6·661		3	–	13¼
14	41·402	14·572			14½	9	4·258	7·494		3	1	10
15	44·359	15·613			15½	10	4·732	8·327	1	–	–	6½
16=1 pt.	47·316	16·653			16¾	11	5·205	9·159	1	–	1	3¼
17	50·274	17·694			17¾	12	5·678	9·992	1	–	1	19¾
18	53·231	18·735			18¾	13	6·151	10·825	1	1	–	16½
19	56·188	19·776			19¾	14	6·624	11·657	1	1	1	13¼
20	59·145	20·817		1	¾	15	7·097	12·490	1	2	–	9¾
30	88·718	31·225		1	11¼	16=2 gals.	7·571	13·323	1	2	1	6½
40	118·291	41·634	1	–	1¾	17	8·044	14·155	1	3	–	3
50	147·864	52·042	1	–	12	18	8·517	14·988	1	3	–	19¾
60	177·436	62·450	1	1	2½	19	8·990	15·821	1	3	1	16½
70	207·009	72·859	1	1	12¾	20	9·463	16·653	2	–	–	13
80	236·582	83·267	2	–	3¼	30	14·195	24·980	3	–	–	19½
90	266·154	93·676	2	–	13¾	40	18·927	33·307	4	–	1	6¼
100	295·727	104·084	2	1	4	50	23·658	41·634	5	–	1	12¾
						60	28·390	49·960	6	–	1	19¼
						70	33·121	58·287	7	1	–	5¾
						80=10 gals.	37·853	66·614	8	1	–	12¼
						90	42·585	74·940	9	1	–	18¾
						100	47·316	83·267	10	1	1	5¼

16 fluid oz. (U.S.) = 1 pint
2 pints = 1 quart
4 quarts = 1 gallon

V. Capacity (*continued*)

Gallons (British Imperial)	*Litres*	*Gallons (U.S.)*	*American equivalent* *Gals.*	*Qts.*	*Pts.*	*Oz.*
1	4·546	1·201	1	–	1	9¾
2	9·092	2·402	2	1	1	3½
3	13·638	3·603	3	2	–	13¼
4	18·184	4·804	4	3	–	7
5	22·730	6·005	6	–	–	¾
6	27·276	7·206	7	–	1	10¼
7	31·822	8·407	8	1	1	4
8	36·368	9·608	9	2	–	13¾
9	40·914	10·809	10	3	–	7½
10	45·460	12·010	12	–	–	1¼
11	50·006	13·210	13	–	1	11
12	54·552	14·411	14	1	1	4½
13	59·097	15·612	15	2	–	14¼
14	63·643	16·813	16	3	–	8
15	68·189	18·014	18	–	–	1¾
16	72·735	19·215	19	–	1	11½
17	77·281	20·416	20	1	1	5¼
18	81·827	21·617	21	2	–	15
19	86·373	22·818	22	3	–	8¾
20	90·919	24·019	24	–	–	2½
30	136·379	36·029	36	–	–	3¾
40	181·838	48·038	48	–	–	4¾
50	227·298	60·048	60	–	–	6¼
60	272·758	72·057	72	–	–	7¼
70	318·217	84·067	84	–	–	8½
80	363·677	96·076	96	–	–	9¾
90	409·136	108·086	108	–	–	11
100	454·596	120·095	120	–	–	12¼

V. Capacity (*continued*)

Gallons (U.S.)	*Litres*	*Gallons (Imperial)*	*British equivalent* *Gals.*	*Qts.*	*Pts.*	*Oz.*
1	3·785	0·833		3	–	13¼
2	7·571	1·665	1	2	1	6½
3	11·356	2·498	2	3	–	19¾
4	15·141	3·331	3	1	–	13
5	18·927	4·163	4	–	1	6
6	22·712	4·996	4	3	1	19¼
7	26·497	5·829	5	3	–	12¾
8	30·282	6·661	6	2	1	5¾
9	34·068	7·494	7	1	1	19
10	37·853	8·327	8	1	–	12¼
11	41·638	9·159	9	–	1	5½
12	45·424	9·992	9	3	1	18¾
13	49·209	10·825	10	3	–	12
14	52·994	11·657	11	2	1	5
15	56·780	12·490	12	1	1	18½
16	60·565	13·323	13	1	–	11¾

V. Capacity (*continued*)

Gallons (U.S.)	*Litres*	*Gallons (Imperial)*	*British equivalent* Gals.	Qts.	Pts.	Oz.
17	64·350	14·155	14	–	1	4¾
18	68·136	14·988	14	3	1	18
19	71·921	15·821	15	3	–	11¼
20	75·706	16·653	16	2	1	4½
30	113·559	24·980	24	3	1	16¾
40	151·412	33·307	33	1	–	9
50	189·265	41·634	41	2	1	1½
60	227·118	49·960	49	3	1	13½
70	264·971	58·287	58	1	–	6
80	302·824	66·614	66	2	–	18¼
90	340·678	74·940	74	3	1	10½
100	378·531	83·267	83	1	–	2¾

VI. TEMPERATURE

Centigrade degrees	*Fahrenheit degrees*	*Centigrade degrees*	*Fahrenheit degrees*
100·0	212·0	40·0	104·0
97·2	207·0	38·9	102·0
95·0	203·0	36·1	97·0
94·4	202·0	35·0	95·0
91·7	197·0	33·3	92·0
90·0	194·0	30·5	87·0
88·9	192·0	30·0	86·0
86·1	187·0	27·8	82·0
85·0	185·0	25·0	77·0
83·3	182·0	22·2	72·0
80·5	177·0	20·0	68·0
80·0	176·0	19·4	67·0
77·8	172·0	16·7	62·0
75·0	167·0	15·0	59·0
72·2	162·0	13·9	57·0
70·0	158·0	11·1	52·0
69·4	157·0	10·0	50·0
66·7	152·0	8·3	47·0
65·0	149·0	5·5	42·0
63·9	147·0	5·0	41·0
61·1	142·0	2·8	37·0
60·0	140·0	0·0	32·0
58·3	137·0	– 2·8	27·0
55·5	132·0	– 5·0	23·0
55·0	131·0	– 5·5	22·0
52·8	127·0	– 8·3	17·0
50·0	122·0	– 10·0	14·0
47·2	117·0	– 11·1	12·0
45·0	113·0	– 13·9	7·0
44·4	112·0	– 15·0	5·0
41·7	107·0		

Appendix E **Vintage Chart**

No vintage chart is a sure guide to the wines rated, for great wines cannot be standardized. Wines are a product of inconstant nature and fallible man. There will be enough enjoyable bottles in any one district in any off year to make exceptions invalidating anything so dogmatic as a vintage chart. Often overlooked, nevertheless a major factor in the purchase of wines, is the proper selection of wines that are sufficiently mature for present-day consumption. Very great years are often slow in maturing, hence your consideration of whether the wines will be consumed immediately or laid away for future consumption should be a determining factor in your selections.

EXPLANATION OF RATINGS

20, 19—exceptionally great	14, 13, 12—very good	7, 6—low average
18, 17—very great	11, 10—good	5, 4—poor
16, 15—great	9, 8—fair	3, 2, 1—very poor

N.B.: Many dry white wines may be too old for present-day consumption. All such wines are indicated by *italic figures*. All white Bordeaux older than 1961 which are not Sauternes, Barsac or Ste. Croix-du-Mont should be considered as possibly being maderized.

Vintage	*Red Bordeaux*	*White Bordeaux*	*Red Burgundy (Côte d'Or)*	*White Burgundy*	*Red Burgundy (Beaujolais)*	*Rhône*	*Loire*	*Alsace*	*Champagne*
1926	13	*14*	12	*12*	*11*	12	*11*	12	*12*
1927	*2*	*6*	*2*	*2*	*3*	7	*5*	*3*	*3*
1928	19	18	18	*15*	*17*	16	*15*	*15*	*20*
1929	19	19	19	*19*	*19*	19	*16*	*17*	*17*
1930	0	*0*	*4*	*4*	*4*	9	*6*	*4*	*4*
1931	3	*2*	*4*	*4*	*3*	10	*7*	*5*	*6*
1932	*1*	*1*	3	*4*	*5*	11	*7*	*5*	*6*
1933	10	*6*	17	*16*	*17*	14	*14*	*12*	*15*
1934	17	16	17	*17*	*17*	16	*13*	*14*	15
1935	5	*6*	*12*	*13*	*12*	9	*12*	*14*	*11*
1936	8	*8*	8	*6*	*9*	14	*9*	*10*	*10*
1937	15	18	17	*16*	*13*	16	*14*	*15*	*16*
1938	9	*8*	14	13	*10*	13	*9*	*10*	*12*
1939	5	*6*	3	*3*	*8*	10	*8*	*4*	*8*
1940	8	*9*	9	*9*	*8*	9	*8*	*11*	*8*
1941	2	*1*	4	*4*	*5*	9	*7*	*8*	*12*
1942	12	15	12	*15*	*14*	15	*11*	*13*	*15*
1943	15	15	14	15	*15*	15	*14*	*15*	*18*
1944	11	9	4	*5*	*7*	9	*7*	*5*	*9*
1945	19	19	19	*16*	*20*	19	*18*	*17*	*16*
1946	8	7	*12*	*9*	*10*	15	*10*	*10*	*11*
1947	19	19	19	*20*	*19*	19	*19*	*19*	*19*
1948	13	13	14	*15*	*9*	*9*	*10*	*12*	*11*
1949	18	18	19	*17*	*19*	16	*13*	*16*	*17*
1950	14	15	*12*	*18*	*12*	15	*10*	*8*	*11*
1951	9	6	8	*8*	*7*	9	*7*	*9*	*7*
1952	16	16	16	*16*	*16*	18	*14*	*14*	18
1953	17	17	19	*17*	*19*	13	*17*	*17*	17
1954	12	9	*10*	*11*	*10*	16	*10*	*11*	*10*
1955	18–19	17	17	*18*	*17*	18	*18*	15	19
1956	12	10	10	*14–17*	*9*	14	*12*	*13*	*10*
1957	15	16	17	*18*	18	18	*18*	*17*	11

Vintage	*Red Bordeaux*	*White Bordeaux*	*Red Burgundy (Côte d'Or)*	*White Burgundy*	*Red Burgundy (Beaujolais)*	*Rhône*	*Loire*	*Alsace*	*Champagne*
1958	11	13	9	*17*	13	16	*15*	*16*	*12*
1959	18	18	19	*18*	17	17	*19*	*19*	19
1960	12	12	7	*13*	9	19	*11*	*11*	15
1961	19	18	19	19	18	14	17	17	18
1962	16	12	15	16	16	12	16	16	16
1963	8	6	9	11	9	11	9	11	7
1964	17	*	15	15	17	13	15	15	17
1965	12	11	6	11	11	15	10	10	6
1966	17	†	15	16	16	15	15	14	18

* 16 dry 10 sweet † 16 dry 11 sweet

NOTE Figures for subsequent years will be obtainable on application to the publishers.

Appendix F Pronouncing Glossary

Abbreviations used in the glossary: *Fr.*—French; *Ger.*—German; *Sp.*—Spanish; *Port.*—Portuguese; *It.*—Italian; *Gk.*—Greek; *Bulg.*—Bulgarian; *Czech.*—Czechoslovak; *Du.*—Dutch; *Russ.*—Russian; *Scand.*—Scandinavian; *Serb.-Cro.*—Serbo-Croatian; *pl.*—plural

General Pronunciation Guide

The symbol (′), as in **moth·er** (muth′ər), **blue′ dev′ils,** is used to mark primary stress; the syllable preceding it is pronounced with greater prominence than the other syllables in the word or phrase. The symbol (ʹ), as in **grand·moth·er** (grandʹmuth′ər), **buzz′ bomb**ʹ, is used to mark secondary stress; a syllable marked for secondary stress is pronounced with less prominence than one marked (′) but with more prominence than those bearing no stress mark at all.

a act, bat, marry
ā aid, cape, way
â(r) air, dare, Mary
ä alms, art, calm

b back, cabin, cab

ch chief, butcher, beach

d do, rudder, bed

e ebb, set, merry
ē equal, seat, bee, mighty
ēr ear, mere

f fit, differ, puff

g give, trigger, beg

h hit, behave, hear
hw white, nowhere

i if, big, mirror, furniture
ī ice, bite, pirate, deny

j just, badger, fudge

k kept, token, make

l low, mellow, all

m my, simmer, him

n now, sinner, on
ng sing, Washington

o ox, box, wasp
ō over, boat, no
ô ought, ball, raw
oi oil, joint, joy
o͝o book, poor
o͞o ooze, fool, too
ou out, loud, prow

p pot, supper, stop

r read, hurry, near

s see, passing, miss
sh shoe, fashion, push

t ten, butter, bit
th thin, ether, path
th that, either, smooth

u up, love
û(r) urge, burn, cur

v voice, river, live

w west, away

y yes, lawyer

z zeal, lazy, those
zh vision, mirage

ə occurs only in unaccented syllables and indicates the sound of
a *in* alone
e *in* system
i *in* easily
o *in* gallop
u *in* circus

ə occurs in unaccented syllables before *l* preceded by *t*, *d*, or *n*, or before *n* preceded by *t* or *d* to show syllabic quality, as in
cra·dle (krād′əl)
red·den (red′ən)
met·al (met′əl)
men·tal (men′təl)
and in accented syllables between *i* and *r* to show diphthongal quality, as in
fire (fīər), *hire* (hīər)

Foreign Sounds

A as in French *a·mi* (A mē′) [a vowel intermediate in quality between the *a* of *cat* and the *a* of *calm*, but closer to the former]

KH as in German *ach* (äKH) or *ich* (iKH); Scottish *loch* (lôKH) [a consonant made by bringing the tongue into the position for *k* as in *key*, *coo*, while pronouncing a strong, rasping *h*]

N as in French *bon* (bôN) [used to indicate that the preceding vowel is nasalized. Four such vowels are found in French: *un bon vin blanc* (œN bôN vaN blän)]

Œ as in French *feu* (fœ); German *schön* (shœn) [a vowel made with the lips rounded in the position for *o* as in *over*, while trying to say *a* as in *able*]

R as in French *rouge* (Ro͞ozh), German *rot* (Rōt), Italian *ma·re* (mä′Re), Spanish *pe·ro* (pe′Rô) [a symbol for any non-English *r*, including a trill or flap in Italian and Spanish and a sound in French and German similar to KH but pronounced with voice]

Y as in French *tu* (tY); German *über* (Y′bəR) [a vowel made with the lips rounded in position for *oo* as in *ooze*, while trying to say *e* as in *east*]

ə as in French *Bas·togne* (bAstôn′yə) [a faint prolongation of the preceding voiced consonant or glide]

[1] Reprinted from *The Random House Dictionary of the English Language*, Copyright © 1966 by Random House, Inc., by permission.

French Pronunciation Guide

FRENCH LETTER	DESCRIPTION OF PRONUNCIATION
a, à	Between *a* in *calm* and *a* in *hat.*
â	Like *a* in *calm.*
ai	Like *e* in *bed.*
au	Like *oa* in *coat.*
b	As in English. At end of words, usually silent.
c	Before *e, i, y,* like *s.* Elsewhere, like *k.* When *c* occurs at the end of a word and is preceded by a consonant, it is usually silent.
ç	Like *s.*
cc	Before *e, i,* like *x.* Elsewhere like *k.*
ch	Usually like *sh* in *short.* *ch* is pronounced like *k* in words of Greek origin; before *a, o,* and *u;* and before consonants.
d	At beginning and in middle of words, as in English. At end of words, usually silent.
e	At end of words, normally silent; indicates that preceding consonant letter is pronounced. Between two single consonant sounds, usually silent. Elsewhere, like English *a* in *sofa.*
é	Approximately like *a* in *hate.*
è, ê, ei	Like *e* in *bed.*
eau	Like *au.*
ent	Silent when it is the third person plural ending.
er (end of words)	At end of words of more than one syllable, usually like *a* in *hate,* the *r* being silent; otherwise like *air* in *chair.*
es	Silent at end of words.
eu	A vowel sound not found in English; pronounced with the lips rounded for *o* as in *over,* while trying to say *a* as in *able.*
ez	At end of words, almost always like English *a* in *hate,* the *z* being silent.
f	As in English; silent at the end of a few words.
g	Before *e, i, y,* like *z* in *azure.* Elsewhere, like *g* in *get.* At end of words, usually silent.
gn	Like *ni* in *onion.*
gu	Before *e, i, y,* like *g* in *get.* Elsewhere, like *g* in *get* plus French *u* (see below).
h	In some words, represents a slight tightening of the throat muscles (in French, called "aspiration"). In most words, silent.
i, î	Like *i* in *machine.*
ill	(-il at end of words) like *y* in *yes,* in many but not all words.
j	Like *z* in *azure.*
k	As in English.
l	As in English, but always pronounced "bright," with tongue in front of mouth.
m, n	When double, and when single between two vowel letters or at beginning of word, like English *m* and *n* respectively. When single at end of syllable (at end of word or before another consonant), indicates nasalization of preceding vowel.
o	Usually like *u* in English *mud,* but rounder. When final sound in word, and often before *s* and *z,* like *o.*
ô	Approximately like *oa* in *coat.*
oe, oeu	Like *eu.*
oi	Approximately like a combination of the consonant *w* and the *a* of *calm.*
ou, oû, où	Like *ou* in *tour.*
p	At end of words, usually silent. Between *m* and *t, m* and *s, r* and *s,* usually silent. Elsewhere, as in English.
pn, ps	Unlike English, when *pn* and *ps* occur at the beginning of words the *p* is usually sounded.
ph	Like *f.*
qu	Usually like *k.*
r	A vibration either of the uvula, or of the tip of the tongue against the upper front teeth. See above under *er.*
s	Generally, like *s* in *sea.* Single *s* between vowels, like *z* in *zone.* At end of words, normally silent.
sc	Before *e* or *i,* like *s.* Elsewhere, like *sk.*
t	Approximately like English *t,* but pronounced with tongue tip against teeth. At end of words, normally silent. When followed by *ie, ion, ium, ius,* and other diphthongs beginning with a vowel, *t* generally is like English *s* in *sea* (unless the *t* itself is preceded by an *s* or an *x*).
th	Like *t.*
u, û	A vowel sound not found in English; pronounced with the lips rounded for *oo* as in *ooze,* while trying to say *e* as in *east.*
ue	After *c* or *g* and before *il,* like *eu.*
v	As in English.
w	Usually like *v;* in some people's pronunciation, like English *w.*
x	Generally sounds like *ks;* but when the syllable *ex* begins a word and is followed by a vowel, *x* sounds like *gz.* At end of words, usually silent.
y	Generally like *i* in *machine;* but when between two vowels, like *y* in *yes.*
z	Like *z* in *zone.* At end of words, often silent (see above under *ez*).

German Pronunciation Guide

CONSONANTS

b Usually like English *b:* **Bett, graben.** But when final or before *s* or *t,* like English *p:* **das Grab, des Grabs, er gräbt.**

c In foreign words only. Before *a, o, u,* like English *k:* **Café′.** Before *ä, e, i* in words borrowed from Latin, like English *ts:* **Cicero;** otherwise usually with the foreign pronunciation.

ch After *a, o, u, au,* a scraping sound like Scottish *ch* in *loch,* made between the back of the tongue and the roof of the mouth: **Dach, Loch, Buch, auch.** In other positions, much like English *h* in *hue:* **Dächer, Löcher, Bücher, ich, manch, welch, durch.** In words borrowed from Greek or Latin, initial *ch* before *a, o, u, l, r* is like English *k:* **Charak′ter, Chor, Christ.** In words borrowed from French it is like German *sch:* **Chance.**

chs As a fixed combination, like English *ks:* **der Dachs,** *the badger.* But when the *s* is an ending, like German *ch* plus *s:* **des Dachs,** genitive of **das Dach,** *the roof.*

ck As in English: **backen, Stock.**

d Usually like English *d:* **Ding, Rede.** But when final or before *s,* like English *t:* **das Band, des Bands.**

dt Like English *tt:* **Stadt** just like **statt.**

f As in English: **Feuer, Ofen, Schaf.**

g Usually like English *g* in *get:* **Geld, schlagen, Könige, reinigen.** But when final or before *s* or *t,* like English *k:* **der Schlag, des Schlags, er schlägt.** However, *ig* when final or before *s* or *t* is like German *ich:* **der König, des Königs, er reinigt.** In words borrowed from French, *g* before *e* is like English *z* in *azure:* **Loge.**

h As in English: **hier.** But after vowels it is only a sign of vowel length, and is not pronounced: **gehen, Bahn, Kuh.**

j Like English *y:* **Jahr.** In a few words borrowed from French, like English *z* in *azure:* **Journal′.**

CONSONANTS

- **k** As in English: **kennen, Haken, buk.**
- **l** Not the "dark *l*" of English *mill, bill*, but the "bright *l*" of English *million, billion:* **lang, fallen, hell.**
- **m** As in English: **mehr, kommen, dumm.**
- **n** As in English: **neu, kennen, kann.**
- **ng** Always like English *ng* in *singer*, never like English *ng* + *g* in *finger*. German **Finger, Hunger.**
- **p** As in English: **Post, Rippe, Tip.**
- **pf** Like English *pf* in *cupful:* **Kopf, Apfel, Pfund.**
- **ph** As in English: **Philosophie′.**
- **qu** Like English *kv:* **Quelle, Aqua′rium.**
- **r** When followed by a vowel, either a gargled sound made between the back of the tongue and the roof of the mouth, or (less commonly) a quick flip of the tongue tip against the gum ridge: **Ring, Haare, bessere.** When not followed by a vowel, a sound much like the *ah* of English *yeah*, or the *a* of *sofa:* **Haar, besser.**
- **s** Usually like English *z* in *zebra*, or *s* in *rose:* **sie, Rose.** But when final or before a consonant, like English *s* in *this:* **das, Wespe, Liste, Maske.**
- **sch** Like English *sh* in *ship*, but with the lips rounded: **Schiff, waschen, Tisch.**
- **sp, st** At the beginning of a word, like *sch* + *p*, *sch* + *t:* **Spiel, Stahl.**
- **ss, ß** Like English *ss* in *miss*. *ss* is written only after a short vowel when another vowel follows: **müssen.** Otherwise ß is written: finally **muß,** before a consonant **mußte,** or after a long vowel **Muße.**
- **t** As in English: **tun, bitter, Blatt.**
- **th** Always like *t:* **Thea′ter;** never like English *th.*
- **tion** Pronounced *tsyohn:* **Nation′, Aktion′.**
- **tsch** Like *t* + *sch:* **deutsch.**
- **tz** Like English *ts:* **sitzen, Platz.**
- **v** In German words, like English *f:* **Vater, Frevel.** In foreign words, like English *v:* **Novem′ber, Moti′ve;** but finally and before *s*, like *f* again: **das Motiv′, des Motivs′.**
- **w** Like English *v:* **Wagen, Löwe.**
- **x** As in English: **Hexe.**
- **z** Always like English *ts:* **zehn, Kreuz, Salz.**

SHORT VOWELS

a Satz	Between English *o* in *hot* and *u* in *hut.*
ä Sätze, **e** setze	Like English *e* in *set.*
i sitze	Like English *i* in *sit.*
o Stock	Like English *o* in *gonna*, or the "New England short *o*" in *coat, road;* shorter than English *o* in *cost.*
ö Stöcke	Tongue position as for short *e*, lips rounded as for short *o.*
u Busch	Like English *u* in *bush.*
ü Büsche, **y** mystisch	Tongue position as for short *i*, lips rounded as for short *u.*

UNACCENTED SHORT E

e beginne	Like English *e* in *begin, pocket.*

LONG VOWELS

a Tal, **ah** Zahl, **aa** Saal	Like English *a* in *father.*
ä Täler, **äh** zählen	In elevated speech, like English *ai* in *fair;* otherwise just like German long *e.*
e wer, **eh** mehr, **ee** Meer	Like English *ey* in *they*, but with no glide toward a *y* sound.
i mir, **ih** ihr, **ie** Bier	Like English *i* in *machine*, but with no glide toward a *y* sound.
o Ton, **oh** Sohn, **oo** Boot	Like English *ow* in *slow*, but with no glide toward a *w* sound.
ö Töne, **öh** Söhne	Tongue position as for *a* in *able*, lips rounded as for *o* in *over.*
u Hut, **uh** Kuh	Like English *u* in *rule*, but with no glide toward a *w* sound.
ü Hüte, **üh** Kühe, **y** Typ	Tongue position as for *e* in *east*, lips rounded as for *oo* in *ooze.*

DIPHTHONGS

ei Seite, **ai** Saite	Like English *i* in *side.* Also spelled *ey, ay* in names: *Meyer, Bayern.*
au Haut	Like English *ou* in *out.*
eu heute, **äu** Häute	Like English *oi* in *oil.*

THE SPELLING OF VOWEL LENGTH

	SHORT	LONG
An accented vowel is always short when followed by a doubled consonant letter, but nearly always long when followed by a single consonant letter.	schla**ff**	Schla**f**
	we**nn**	we**n**
	sti**ll**	Sti**l**
	o**ff**en	**O**fen
	ö**ff**nen	**Ö**fen
	Bu**tt**er	Pu**t**er
	dü**nn**e	Dü**n**e
Note that **ck** counts as the doubled form of **k:**	hacken	Haken
tz counts as the doubled form of **z:**	putzen	duzen

THE SPELLING OF VOWEL LENGTH

	SHORT	LONG
ss counts as the doubled form of ß:	Masse	Maße
Vowels are always long when followed by (unpronounced) **h:**	wann	Wa**h**n
	stelle	ste**h**le
	irre	i**h**re
	Wonne	wo**h**ne
	gönne	Sö**h**ne
	Rum	Ru**h**m
	dünn	kü**h**n
Vowels are always long when they are written double:	Stadt	St**aa**t
	Bett	B**ee**t
	Gott	B**oo**t
In this respect, **ie** counts as the doubled form of **i:**	bitte	b**ie**te

Italian Pronunciation Guide

ITALIAN LETTER — PRONUNCIATION

- **a** Like English *a* in *father.*
- **b** As in English.
- **c** Before *e* or *i*, and sometimes at the end of words, like English *ch.*
  Elsewhere, like English *k.*
- **ch** Before *e* or *i*, like English *k.*
- **ci** Before *a, o,* or *u*, like English *ch.*
- **d** As in English.
- **é** ("close *e*") Like English *ay* in *day*, but with no final *y*-like glide.
- **è** ("open *e*") Like English *e* in *bet.*
- **e** Like English *e* in *bet.*
- **f** As in English.
- **g** Before *e* or *i*, like English *g* in *gem.*
  Elsewhere, like English *g* in *go.*
- **gh** Before *e* or *i*, like English *g* in *go.*
- **gi** Before *a, o,* or *u*, like English *g* in *gem.*
- **gl** Before *i*, normally like English *lli* in *million.*
- **gli** Before *a, e, o,* or *u*, like English *lli* in *million.*
- **gn** Like English *ny* in *canyon.*
- **h** After *c* and *g*, indicates "hard" pronunciation of preceding consonant letter.
  Elsewhere, silent.
- **i** After *c, g,* and (normally) *sc*, before *a, o,* or *u*, indicates "soft" pronunciation of preceding consonant letter or letters.
  Elsewhere:
  - When unstressed and before or after another vowel, like English *y.*
  - Otherwise, like English *i* in *machine*, but with no final *y*-like glide.
- **j** At the end of words, when replacing *ii* in some noun

ITALIAN LETTER — PRONUNCIATION

plurals, like Italian *i*.
Otherwise, like English *y*.

k As in English.

Like English *l* in *like*, but with the tongue behind the upper front teeth.

m As in English.

n As in English.

ó ("close *o*") Like English *o* in *go*, but with no final *w*-like glide.

ò ("open *o*") Like English *o* in *bought*.

o Like English *o* in *bought*.

p As in English.

qu Like English *qu* in *quick*.

n Not at all like American English *r*; a quick flap of the tip of the tongue on the gumridge.

s Between vowels, like English *s* in *lease* (in southern Italy); like *s* in *please* (in northern Italy); sometimes like *s* in *lease* and sometimes like *s* in *please* (in central Italy).
Before *b, d, g, l, m, n, r, v*, like English *z*.
Elsewhere, like English *s* in *same, stick*.

ITALIAN LETTERS — PRONUNCIATION

sc Before *e* or *i*, and occasionally at the end of words, like English *sh*.
Elsewhere, like English *sk*.

sch Before *e* or *i*, like English *sk*.

sci Before *a, o*, or *u*, like English *sh*.

t As in English.

u When unstressed and before or after another vowel, like English *w*.
Otherwise, like English *oo* in *boot*, but without final *w*-like glide.

v As in English.

w Rare; like English *v*.

x Rare; like English *x*.

z Like English *ts* in *cats* or like English *dz* in *adze*.

CONSONANT LENGTH

All Italian consonants occur both single (short) and double (long); in the latter instance, the time of their pronunciation lasts from one-and-a-half to two times that of the single consonants.

Spanish Pronunciation Guide

SPANISH LETTER — PRONUNCIATION

a Like English *a* in *father*.

b, v At beginning of word group and after *m* or *n*, like English *b*.
Elsewhere, like English *v*, but pronounced with both lips instead of upper teeth and lower lip.

c Before *e* or *i*, like English *th* in *thin* (in Northern Spain); like Spanish *s* (in Southern Spain and the Americas).

d At beginning of word group and after *n* or *l*, like English *d*.
Elsewhere, like English *th* in *either*.

e Like English *e* in *bet*.

f As in English.

g Before *e* or *i*, the same as Spanish *j*.
Elsewhere, like English *g* in *get*.

gu Before *e* or *i*, like English *g* in *get*.
Elsewhere, like English *gw* in *Gwynn*.

gü Like English *gw* in *Gwynn*.

h Silent.

i Like English *i* in *machine*, but more clipped.
Before or after another vowel, like English *y* (except when accented.)

j Like English *h*, but more rasping.

k Like English *k*.

l Like English *l* in *like*, but with the tongue behind the upper front teeth.

ll Like English *lli*, in *million* (in Northern Spain); like Spanish *y* (in Southern Spain and the Americas).

m As in English.

n As in English.

ñ Like English *ny* in *canyon*.

o Approximately like English *o* in *vote*, but more clipped.

p As in English.

qu Like English *k*.

r Not at all like American English *r*; a quick flap of the tongue-tip on the roof of the mouth.

rr A strongly "rolled" or trilled version of Spanish *r*.

s Like English *s* in *lease*.

t As in English.

u Like English *oo* in *boot*, but more clipped.
Before *e* or after another vowel, like English *w* (except when accented.)

v See *b* above.

x Like English *x*; although before consonants many speakers pronounce it like Spanish *s*.

y Approximately like English *y* in *yes*.

z Like English *th* in *thin* (in Northern Spain); like English *s* in *lease* (in Southern Spain and the Americas).

Glossary

abboccato (äb′bôk kä′tô)
Abfullung (äp′fo͞ol o͞ong)
abocado (ä′bô kä′ᵺô)
Abran (ä bRän′)
Abricotine (A bRē kô tēn′)
Abruzzi (ä bRo͞od′dzē)
acescence (A se säNS′)
Aconcagua (ä′kông kä′gwä)
acquit (A kē′)
acquit-à-caution (A kē tA kō-syôN′)
acquit jaune d'or (A kē′ zhōn-dôR′)
adega (ə de′ gə)
Adom Atic (ä dôm′ ä tēk′)
Advocaat (äd′vô kät′)
agave (ä gä′ve)
Aglianico del Vulture (ä lyä′nē-kô del vo͞ol to͞o′Re)
agrafe, agraffe (A gRAf′)
Aguardiente (ä′gwäR dyen′te)
Ahr (äR)
Ahrweiler (äR′ vīl əR)
Aigle (e′glə)
Aiguebelle (eg bel′)
Aïn-Bessem-Bouïra (ä ēn′be-sem′ bo͞o ē Rä′)
Aïn-el-Hadjar (ä ēn′ el hA jär′)
Airén (ī Ren′)
Aisne (en)
Aix-en-Provence (eks äN pRô-väNS′)
Ajaccio (ä yät′chô)
Akvavit (ä′kvä vēt′)
Alavesa (ä′lä ve′sä)
Alba Flora (äl′bä flô′Rä)
Albana (äl bä′nä)
Albana di Romagna (äl bä′nä dē Rô mä′nyä)
Albanello (äl′bä nel′lô)
albariza (äl′bä Rē′thä)
Albillo (äl bē′lyô)
alcools blancs (Al kôl bläN′)
Aldegund (äl′də go͞ont′)
Aleatico di Portoferraio (ä′le-ä′tē kô dē pōR′tô feR Rä′yô)
Aleatico di Puglia (ä′le ä′tē kô dē po͞o′lyä)
À l'Écu (A lā KY′)
Aleksandrovac (ä′lek sän′dRô-väts)
Alella (ä le′lyä)
Aleyor (ä le yôR′)
Alf (älf)
Alger (Al zhā′)
Alicante (al′ə kan′tē; *Sp.* ä′lē-kän′te)
Alicante-Bouschet (al′ə kan′tē bo͞o shā′; *Fr.* A lē käNt′ bo͞o-she′)
Alicantina (ä′lē kän tē′nä)
Aligoté (A lē gô tā′)
alises (A lēz′)
Alkermes (al kûr′mēz)
Allasch, Alasch (ä läsh′)
Almadén (al′mə den′; *Sp.* al′-mä ᵺen′)
Aloxe-Corton (A lôs kôR tôN′)
Alsace (al sās′, al′sas; *Fr.* Al-zAs′)
Alsheim (äls′ hīm′)
Altenbamberg (äl′tən bäm′-beRk)
Altenberg (äl′tən beRk′)

Altenburg (äl′tᵊn bo͞oRk′)
Alupka (ä lo͞op′kä)
Alvarelhão (ôl′və Re′lyouN)
Amara (ä mä′Rä)
Amargo (ä mäR′gô)
Ambonnay (äN bô ne′)
Ambrato (äm bRä′tô)
Amer Picon (A meR pē kôN′)
Amertume (A meR tYm′)
Ammerschwihr (A meR shvēR′)
Amontillado (ə mon′tᵊlä′dō; *Sp.* ä môn′tē lyä′thô)
Amoureuses, Les (lā zA mo͞o-Rœz′)
Ampuis (äN pwē′)
Anberg (än′beRk′)
Angers (äN zhā′)
Angles, Les (lā zäN′glᵊ)
Angostura (äng′gô sto͞o′Rä)
anis (an′is; *Sp.* ä′nēs; *Fr.* A nē′)
Anisado (ä′nē sä′thô)
anisette (A nē zet′)
Anjou (äN zho͞o′)
Appellation Complète (A pel lA-syôN′ kôN plet′)
Appellation d'Origine Contrôlée (A pel lA syôN′ dô Rē zhēn′ kôN tRô lā′)
Appellation Simple (A pel lA-syôN′ saN′plᵊ)
Apry (A pRē′)
Aquavit (ak′wə vēt′; *Scand.* a′kvä vēt′)
Arak (a Rak′)
Aramon (A KA môN′)
Arbia (äR′byä)
Arbois (AR bwA′)
Arbuissonnas (AR bwē sô nA′)
Ardine (AR dēn′)
arena (ä Re′nä)
Armagnac (AR mä nyAk′)
armazem (äR mə zäN′)
Arroba (äR Rô′bä)
Arrondissement de Châlons (A RôN dēs mäN′ də shä lôN′)
Arrondissement d'Épernay (A RôN dēs mäN′ dā peR ne′)
Arrondissement de Reims (A RôN dēs mäN′ RaNs)
Arsac-Margaux (AR sAk′ mAR-gō′)
Arvelets, Les (lā zARvᵊle′)
asciutto (ä sho͞ot′tô)
assemblage (A säN blAzh′)
Assmannshausen (äs′mäns-hou′zən)
Asti Spumante (äs′tē spo͞o-män′te)
Asztalibor (os′to li bôR′)
Athol Brose (ath′əl brōz)
Aubaine (ō ben′)
Aude (ōd)
Auerbach (ou′əR bäkh′)
Auflangen (ouf′läng ən)
Aurum (ou′rəm; *It.* ou′Ro͞om)
Auslese (ous′lā zə)
Äussere Leiste (ois′ə Rə lis′tə)
Auvernier (ō veR nyā′)
Aux Argillats (ō zAR zhē lA′)
Aux Boudots (ō bo͞o dō′)
Aux Combottes (ō kôN bôt′)
Aux Cras (ō kRA′)
Aux Murgers (ō mYR zhā′)
Aux Perdrix (ō peR dRē′)
Aux Petits-Monts (ō pə tē môN′)
Aux Reignots (ō Re nyō′)
Aux Thorey (ō tô Re′)
Auxerrois (ôk se RwA′)
Auxey-Duresses (ôk se′ dY Res′)
Avaux, Les (lā zA vō′)
Avelsbach (ä′vəls bäkh′)
Avenay (Avᵊ ne′)
Avensan (A vaN säN′)
Avize (A vēz′)
Ay (ä ē′)
Ay-Champagne (ä ē′ shäN-pan′yᵊ)
Ayl (īl)
Ayler Kupp (ī′ləR ko͞op′)
Ayler Scheiderberg (ī′ləR shī′-dəR beRk′)

Bacardi (bə kär′dē; *Sp.* bä-käR′dē)
Bacharach (bäkh′ä Räkh′)
Bächel (bekh′əl)
Bad Dürkheim (bät dYRk′hīm′)
Bad Kreuznach (bät kRoits′-näkh′)
Bad Münster am Stein (bät mYn′stəR äm shtīn′)
Bad Neuenahr (bät noi′ən äR′)
Badacsony (bo′do chôn′yᵊ)
Badacsonyi Furmint (bo′do-chô′nyi fo͞oR′mint)
Badacsonyi Kéknyelü (bo′do-chô′nyi kâk′nye lY)
Badacsonyi Rizling (bo′do-chô′nyi Riz′ling)
Badacsonyi Szürkebarát (bo′do-cho′nyi sYR′ke bo Rät′)
Baden (bäd′ᵊn)
Badstube (bät′shto͞o′bə)
Bagaceira (bägə sā′Rə)
Bagrina (bä′gRi nä)
Baiken (bī′kən)
Baladí (bä lä thē′)
Balatonfüredi Rizling (bo′lo-tôn fY′Re di Riz′ling)
Balnana (bäl nä′nä)
Balzner (bälts′nəR)
Banadry (bA nA dRē′)
Bandol (bäN dôl′)
Banyuls (bA nyYls′)
Barack Pálinka (bo′Rok pä′-ling ko)
Barbacarlo (bäR′bä käR′lô)
Barbaresco (bäR′bä Res′kô)
Barbera (bäR be′Rä)
Barbera Amabile (bäR be′Rä ä mä′bē le)
Bardolino (bäR′dô lē′nô)
Bärentrank (be′Rən tRängk′)
Barolo (bä Rô′lô)
Barr (bAR)
Barre (bAR)
barricas (bäR Rē′käs)
barricas bordelesas (bäR Rē′-käs bôR′de le′säs)
barriquant (bA Rē käN′)
barrique (bA Rēk′)
barro (bäR′Rô)
Barsac (bAR sAk′)
Bas-des-Duresses (bä dā dY-Res′)
Bas des Teurons (bä dā tœ-RôN′)
Basi (bä′sē)
Basilicata (bä sē′lē kä′tä)
Basler Kirschwasser (bäz′ləR kiRsh′väs′əR)
basquaise (bAs kez′)
Bastia (bäs′tyä)
Bâtard-Montrachet (bä tAR′ môN RA she′)
Batzi (bä′tsē)
Baudes (bōd)
Baudes Bas (bōd bä′)
Baudes Saint-Martin (bōd saN mAR taN′)
Béarn (bā ARn′)
Beaujeu (bō zhœ′)
Beaujolais (bō′zhə lā′; *Fr.* bō-zhô le′)
Beaulieu-sur-Layon (bō lyœ′-sYR le yôN′)
Beaumes-de-Venise (bōm də və-nēz′)
Beaumont-sur-Vesle (bō môN′-sYR vel′)
Beaune (bōn)
Beaunois (bō nwA′)
Beauroy (bō RwA′)
Beaux-Monts (bō môN′)
Bechtheim (bekht′hīm′)
Beerenauslese (bā′Rən ous′-lā zə)
Beilstein (bīl′shtīn′)
Beines (ben)
Bel-Air (bel eR′)
Bellegarde (bel gARd′)
Bellet (be le′)
Benejama (be′ne hä′mä)
Benicarlo (be′nē käR′lô)
Bensheim (bens′hīm′)
Béquignol (bā kē nyôl′)
Berg (beRk)
Berg Bronnen (beRk bRôn′ən)
Berg Lay (beRk lī)
Berg Paares (beRk pä′Rəs)
Berg Roseneck (beRk Rō′zə-nek′)
Berg Rottland (beRk Rôt′länt′)
Berg Stumpfenort (beRk shto͞ompf′ən ôRt′)
Berg Zollhaus (beRk tsôl′hous′)
Bergerac (beR zhə RAk′)
Bergheim (*Ger.* beRk′hīm′; *Fr.* beRg hīm′)
Bergstrasse (beRk′shtRäs′ə)
Bergweiler (beRk′vīl′əR)
Bernkastel-Kues (beRn′käs′tᵊl ko͞o′əs)
Bernkasteler Doctor (or **Doktor**) (beRn′käs′tᵊl əR dôk′tôR)
Bernkasteler Graben (beRn′-käs′tᵊl əR gRä′bən)
Bessards (be sAR′)
Beugnon (bœ nyôN′)
bianco (byäng′kô)
Bianco dell'Elba (byäng′kô del-lel′bä)
Biancolella (byäng′kô lel′lä)
Biancone (byäng kô′ne)
Biar (byäR)
Bienengarten (bēn′ən gäR′tᵊn)
Bienvenue-Bâtard-Montrachet (byaN və nY′ bä tAR′ môN RA-she′)
Bildstock (bilt′shtôk′)
Bingen (bing′ən)
Bingen-Büdesheim (bing′ən bY′-dəs hīm′)
Bingen-Kempten (bing′ən kemp′tən)
Binger Rochusberg (bing′ər Rôkh′o͞os beRk′)
Bischöfliches Konvikt (bish′-œf likh′əs kôn′vikt)
Bischöfliches Priesterseminar (bish′œf likh′əs pRēst′əR ze-mi näR′)
Bischofsberg (bish′ôfs beRk′)
Blacé (blA sā′)
Blagny (blA nyē′)
Blagny-Blanc (blA nyē bläN′)
blanc (bläN)
Blanc d'Anjou (bläN däN zho͞o′)
Blanc de Blancs (bläN də bläN′)
Blanc de Noirs (bläN də nwAR′)
Blanc Fumé de Pouilly (bläN fY mā′ də po͞o yē′)
Blanchots (bläN shō′)
blanco (bläng′kô)
Blanquette de Limoux (bläN-ket′ də lē mo͞o′)
Blauer Portugieser (blou′əR pôR to͞o gē′zəR)
Blaurock (blou′Rôk)
Blayais (blA ye′)
Blaye (blA′yᵊ)
Bleichert (blīkh′əRt)

Boal (bo͞o äl′)
Bõa Vista (bouɴ′ä vis′tä)
Bobal (bô bäl′)
Boca Chica (bô′kä c͟hē′kä)
Bock (bôk)
Bocksberg (bôks′bеʀk′)
Bocksbeutel (bôks′boit′ᵊl)
Bockstein (bôk′s͟htīn′)
bodega (bō dā′gə; *Sp.* bô the′gä)
Bodenheim (bōd′ᵊn hīm′)
Bodensee (bōd′ᵊn zā′)
Bogdanuša (bôg′dä no͞o′s͟hä)
Bois Ordinaires (bwᴀ zôʀ dē-neʀ′)
Bombino (bôm bē′nô)
Bombom Crema (bôm′bôm kʀe′mä)
Bonarda (bô näʀ′dä)
Bonarda di Gattinara (bô näʀ′-dä dē gät′tē nä′ʀä)
bonde (bôɴd)
Bondola (bôn dô′lä)
Bonifacio (bô′nē fä′c͟hô)
Bonne Mares (bôn mᴀʀ′)
Bonnezeaux (bôn zō′)
Bons Bois (bôɴ bwᴀ′)
Boppard Hamm (bôp′äʀt häm′)
bor (bôʀ)
Bordeaux (bôʀ dō′)
Bordeaux clairet (bôʀ dō kle-ʀe′)
Bordeaux mousseux (bôʀ dō mo͞o sœ′)
Bordeaux rosé (bôʀ dō ʀō zā′)
Bordeaux supérieur (bôʀ dō sʏ pā ʀyœʀ′)
Borderies (bôʀ də ʀē′)
Bosa (bô′zä)
Bosenheim (bō′zən hīm′)
bota (bô′tä)
Botrys (bôt′ʀēs)
bouché (bo͞o s͟hā′)
Bouchet (bo͞o s͟he′)
bouchon (bo͞o s͟hôɴ′)
bouchonné (bo͞o s͟hô nā′)
Boudriottes (bo͞o dʀē ôt′)
Bougros (bo͞o gʀō′)
Bougy (bo͞o z͟hē′)
Bourg (bo͞oʀ)
Bourgas (bo͞oʀ′gäs)
Bourgeais (bo͞oʀ z͟he′)
Bourgeuil (bo͞oʀ gœ′yᵊ)
Bourgogne (bo͞oʀ gôn′yᵊ)
Bourgogne-Passe-Tout-Grains (bo͞oʀ gôn′yᵊ pᴀs to͞o gʀᴀɴ′)
Boutière (bo͞o tyeʀ′)
Boutières (bo͞o tyeʀ′)
Bouzy (bo͞o zē′)
Boxbeutel (bôks′boit′ᵊl)
Boyer (bwᴀ ye′)
Brachetto (bʀä ket′tô)
Brandewijn (bʀän′de wīn′)
Branntwein (bʀänt′vīn′)
Brännvin (bʀen′vēn′)
Braune Kupp (bʀou′nə ko͝op′)
Brauneberg (bʀou′nə beʀk′)
Brauneberger Falkenberg (bʀou′nə beʀ′gəʀ fälk′ən-beʀk′)
Brauneberger Juffer (bʀou′nə-beʀ′gəʀ yo͝of′əʀ)
Braunes (bʀou′nəs)
Braunfels (bʀoun′fels)
Braunloch (bʀoun′lôᴋʜ′)
Brède (bʀed)
brenner (bʀen′əʀ)
Bressandes (bʀə säɴd′)
Bresse-sur-Grosne (bʀes′ sʏʀ gʀōn′)
Breton (bʀə tôɴ′)
Briedern (bʀē′dəʀn)
Brizard (bʀē zᴀʀ′)
Brno (bʀ′nô)
Brolio (bʀô′lyô)
brouillis (bʀo͞o yē′)
Brouilly (bʀo͞o yē′)
Brückes (bʀʏk′əs)
Brûlets (bʀʏ le′)
Brunello di Montalcino (bʀo͞o-nel′lô dē môn′tälc͟hē′nô)
brunissure (bʀʏ nē sʏʀ′)
Brünnchen (bʀʏn′ᴋʜən)
brut (bro͞ot; *Fr.* bʀʏt)
Bruttig (bʀo͞ot′iᴋʜ)
Bual (bʏ ᴀl′)
Bucelas (bo͞o se′ ləs͟h)
Burdin (bʏʀ dᴀɴ′)
Burgenland (bo͞oʀ′gən länt′)
Burggraben (bo͞oʀk′gʀä′bən)
Burgunder (bo͞oʀ′go͞on dəʀ)
Burgweg (bo͞oʀk′vāk′)
Bursins (bʏʀ sᴀɴ′)
Bussley (bo͞os′lī)
Buttafuoco (bo͞ot′tä fwô′kô)
Byrrh (bēʀ)

Cabernet (kab′ər nā′; *Fr.* kᴀ-beʀ ne′)
Cabernet Franc (kᴀ beʀ ne′ fʀäɴ′)
Cabernet Sauvignon (kᴀ beʀ ne′ sō vē nyôɴ′)
Cabrières (kᴀ bʀē yeʀ′)
Cachiri (kä c͟hē′ʀē)
Cadaujac (kᴀ dō z͟hᴀk′)
Cahors (kᴀ ôʀ′)
Caillerets (kᴀ ye ʀe′)
Cailles (kᴀ′yᵊ)
Cairanne (ke ʀᴀn′)
Calabrese (kä′lä bʀe′ze)
Calabria (kä lä′bʀyä)
Calagraño (kä′lä gʀä′nyô)
Caldaro (käl dä′ʀô)
Calisaya (kä′lē sä′yä)
Caluso (kä lo͞o′sô)
Calvados (kal′və dōs′, -dos′, kal′və dōs′, -dos′; *Fr.* kᴀl vᴀ-dôs′)
Camaralet (kᴀ mᴀ ʀᴀ le′)
Campania (käm pä′nyä)
Campari (käm pä′ʀē)
Caña (kä′nyä)
Canaiolo (kä′nä yô′lô)
Candia (kan′dē ə)
Cannelle (kᴀ nel′)
Cañocazo (kä′nyô kä′t͟hô)
Canteiro (kan târ′ō; *Port.* känntā′ʀo͞o)
Cantenac (käɴtᵊ nᴀk′)
Cantenac-Margaux (käɴtᵊ nᴀk′ mᴀʀ gō′)
Canton d'Avize (käɴ tôɴ′ dᴀ-vēz′)
Canton d'Ay (käɴ tôɴ′ dᴀ ē′)
Canton d'Épernay (käɴ tôɴ dā-peʀ ne′)
Canton de Beine (käɴ tôɴ′ də ben′)
Canton de Bourgogne (käɴ tôɴ′ də bo͞oʀ gôn′yᵊ)
Canton de Condé-en-Brie (käɴ-tôɴ′ də kôn dā′ äɴ bʀē′)
Canton de l'Aube (käɴ tôɴ′ də lōb′)
Canton de Reims (käɴ tôɴ′ də ʀᴀɴs)
Canton de Verzy (käɴ tôɴ′ də veʀ zē′)
Cap Corse (kᴀp kôʀs′)
Capri (kə prē′; *It.* kä′pʀē)
caque (kᴀk)
carafe (kᴀ ʀᴀf′)
carafon (kᴀ ʀᴀ fôɴ′)
Carcavelos (käʀ′kə ve′lo͞os͟h)
Carema (kä ʀe′mä)
Carignan (kᴀ ʀē nyäɴ′)
Carignane Rousse (kᴀ ʀē nyᴀn ʀo͞os′)
Cariñena (kä′ʀē nye′nä)
Carioca (kä ʀyô′kä)
Carrascal (käʀ′ʀäs käl′)
Carricante (käʀ′ʀē kän′te)
Carta Blanca (käʀ′tä bläɴg′kä)
Carta Oro (käʀ′tä ô′ʀô)
casse (käs)
Cassis (kᴀ sēs′)
Castalla (käs tä′lyä)
Castelli Romani (käs tel′lē ʀô-mä′nē)
Cataratto (kä′tä ʀät′tô)
Cauché Gris (kō s͟hā gʀē′)
Cauro (kou′ʀô)
cave (kᴀv)
caviste (kᴀ vēst′)
Cazeau (kᴀ zō′)
Cazetiers (k zə tyā′)
Cencibel (t͟hen t͟hē bel′)
Cent Vignes (säɴ vēn′yᵊ)
Cepa (t͟he′pä)
cépage (sā pᴀz͟h′)
Cerasella (c͟he′ʀä sel′lä)
Cerasuolo di Abruzzo (c͟he′ʀä-swô′lô dē ä bʀo͞od′dzô)
Cercié (seʀ syā′)
Cerise d'Alsace (sə ʀēz′ dᴀl-zᴀs′)
Cérons (sā ʀôɴ′)
Certosa (c͟heʀ tô′zä)
Cesanese (c͟he′zä ne′ze)
Cesanese di Piglio (c͟he′zä-ne′ze dē pē′lyô)
César (sā zᴀʀ′)
Chablis (s͟hab′lē, s͟häblē′; *Fr.* s͟hᴀ blē′)
chai (s͟he)
Chai Fan (c͟hī′ fän′)
Chailloux (s͟hᴀ yo͞o′)
Chalonnais (s͟hᴀ lô ne′)
Chalumeaux (s͟hᴀ lʏ mō′)
Chambertin (s͟häɴ beʀ tᴀɴ′)
Chambertin-Clos de Bèze (s͟häɴ-beʀ tᴀɴ′ klō də bez′)
Chambéry (s͟häɴ bā ʀē′)
Chambolle (s͟häɴ bôl′)
Chambolle-Musigny (s͟häɴ bôl′ mʏ sē nyē′)
Chambord (s͟häɴ bôʀ′)
chambre (s͟häɴ bʀä′)
chambrer (s͟häɴ bʀā′)
Champagne (s͟ham pān′; *Fr.* s͟häɴ pᴀn′yᵊ)
Champans (s͟häɴ pᴀɴ′)
Champ-Canet (s͟häɴ kᴀ ne′)
Champillon (s͟häɴ pē yôɴ′)
Champimonts (s͟häɴ pē môɴ′)
Champlieu (s͟häɴ lyœ′)
Champlot (s͟häɴ plō′)
Chânes (s͟hän)
Chanière (s͟hᴀ nyeʀ′)
Chanlins-Bas (s͟häɴ lᴀɴ bä′)
Chanrue (s͟hän ʀʏ′)
Chante-Alouette (s͟häɴ tᴀl wet′)
chanteau (s͟häɴ tō)
chantepleure (s͟häɴt plœʀ′)
chapeau (s͟hᴀ pō′)
Chapelle-Chambertin (s͟hᴀ pel′ s͟häɴ beʀ tᴀɴ′)
Chapelle-de-Guinchay (s͟hᴀ pel′ də gᴀɴ s͟he′)
Chapelle-Vaupelteigne (s͟hᴀ pel′ vō pel ten′yᵊ)
Chapelot (s͟hᴀpᵊ lō′)
Chardonnay (s͟hᴀʀ dô ne′)
Charentay (s͟hᴀ ʀäɴ te′)
Charente (s͟hᴀ ʀäɴt′)
Charlemagne (s͟hᴀʀ lə mᴀn′yᵊ)
Charmat (s͟hᴀʀ mᴀ′)
Charmes (s͟hᴀʀm)
Charmes-Chambertin (s͟hᴀʀm′ s͟häɴ beʀ tᴀɴ′)
charnu (s͟hᴀʀ nʏ′)
Chartreuse (s͟här tro͞oz′; *Fr.* s͟hᴀʀ tʀœz′)

Chassagne-Montrachet (shA-sAN′yə môN RA she′)
Chasselas (shASə LA′)
Chasselas Doré (shASə LA′ dô-RĀ′)
Château Angludet (shä tō′ äN gly de′)
Château Ansone (shä tō′ ō zôn′)
Château Baleau (shä tō′ BA lō′)
Château Balestard-La-Tonnelle (shä tō′ BA les TAR′ LA tô nel′)
Château Batailley (shä tō′ BA-TA ye′)
Château Baulac (shä tō′ bō LAK′)
Château Beauregard (shä tō′ bō Rə GAR′)
Château Beauséjour-Duffau-Lagarrosse (shä tō′ bō sā-zho͞oR′ DY fō′ LA GA RÔS′)
Château Beauséjour-Fagouet (shä tō′ bō sā zho͞oR′ FA gwe′)
Château Belair (shä tō′ bel ER′)
Château Bel-Air-Marquis-d'Aligre (shä tō′ bel ER′ MAR kē′ DA lē′GRə)
Château Belgrave (shä tō′ bel-GRAV′)
Château Beychevelle (shä tō′ beshə vel′)
Château Bouscaut (shä tō′ bo͞os-kō′)
Château Boyd-Cantenac (shä tō′ boid käNtə NAK′)
Château Branaire-Ducru (shä-tō′ brA NER′ DY KRY′)
Château Brane-Cantenac (shä-tō′ BRAn käNtə NAK′)
Château Broustet (shä tō′ BRo͞os te′)
Château Caillou (shä tō′ KA-yo͞o′)
Château Calon Ségur (shä tō′ KA lôN sā GYR′)
Château Calvé-Croizet-Bages (shä tō′ KAl vā′ KRWA ze BAzh′)
Château Camensac (shä tō′ KA-mäN SAK′)
Château Canon (shä tō′ KA nôN′)
Château Canon-la-Gaffelière (shä tō′ KA nôN′ LA GAfə lyer′)
Château Cantemerle (shä tō′ käntə meRl′)
Château Cantenac-Brown (shä-tō′ käntə NAK′ broun′)
Château Cap-de-Mourlin (shä-tō′ KAP′də mo͞oR lan′)
Château Capbern (shä tō′ KAP-beRn′)
Château Carbonnieux (shä tō′ KAR bô nyœ′)
Château Certan de May (shä-tō′ seR täN′ də me′)
Château Certan-Giraud (shä-tō′ seR täN′ zhē RŌ′)
Château-Chalon (shä tō′ shA-lôN′)
Château Chasse-Spleen (shä tō′ shAS splēn′)
Château Cheval-Blanc (shä tō′ shə VAl bläN′)
Château Clerc-Milon-Mondon (shä tō′ kleR mē lôN′ môN-dôN′)
Château Climens (shä tō′ klē-mäNS′)
Château Corbin (shä tō′ kôR-baN′)
Château Corbin-Michotte (shä-tō′ kôR baN′ mē shôt′)
Château Cos d'Estournel (shä-tō′ kôs des to͞oR nel′)
Château Cos-Labory (shä tō′ kôs LA bô RĒ′)
Château Couhins (shä tō′ ko͞o-ANS′)
Château Coutet (shä tō′ ko͞o tē′)
Château Croizet-Bages (shä tō′ KRWA ze BAzh′)
Château Croque-Michotte (shä-tō′ KRôk mē shôt′)
Château Curé-Bon-la Madeleine (shä tō′ KY RĀ bôN LA MADə-len′)
Château Dauzac (shä tō′ dō-ZAK′)
Château de Bourg (shä tō′ də bo͞oR′)
Château de la Brède (shä tō′ də LA bRed′)
Château de Pez (shä tō′ də pez′)
Château de Rayne-Vigneau (shä tō′ də Ren vē nyō′)
Château de Sales (shä tō′ də SAl′)
Château de Suduiraut (shä tō′ də SY dwē RŌ′)
Château de Vaudieu (shä tō′ də vō dyœ′)
Château Desmirail (shä tō′ dā-mē RA′yə, dez-)
Château d'Issan (shä tō′ dē säN′)
Château Doisy-Daëne (shä tō′ dWA zē′ DA en′)
Château Doisy-Dubroca (shä-tō′ dWA zē′ DY bRÔ KA′)
Château Doisy-Védrines (shä-tō′ dWA zē′ vā dRēn′)
Château du Tertre (shä tō′ DY teR′tRə)
Château Ducru-Beaucaillou (shä tō′ DY KRY′ bō KA yo͞o′)
Château Duhart-Milon (shä tō′ DY AR′ mē lôN′)
Château Durfort (shä tō′ DYR-fôR′)
Château Durfort-Vivens (shä-tō′ DYR fôR′ vē väNS′, -väN′)
Château d'Yquem (shä tō′ dē-kem′)
Château Ferrière (shä tō′ fe-RyeR′)
Château Feytit-Clinet (shä tō′ fe tē′ klē ne′)
Château Fieuzal (shä tō′ fyœ-ZAl′)
Château Figeac (shä tō′ fē-zhAk′)
Château Filhot (shä tō′ fē lō′)
Château Fonroque (shä tō′ fôN-RÔk′)
Château Fourcas-Dupré (shä-tō′ fo͞oR KA′ DY PRĀ′)
Château Fourcas-Hostein (shä-tō′ fo͞oR KA′ ôs TAN′; hô stīn)
Château Fourtet (shä tō′ fo͞oR-te′)
Château Fortia (shä tō′ fôR-sya′)
Château Fuiosé (shä tō′ fwē sā′)
Château Gaffelière-Naudes (shä tō′ GAfə lyeR nōd′)
Château Gazin (shä tō′ GA ZAN′)
Château Giscours (shä tō′ zhēs ko͞oR′)
Château Gloria (shä tō′ glô-RYA′)
Chateau Gombaude-Guillot (shä tō′ gôN bōd′ gē yō′)
Château Grand-Barrail-Lamarzelle-Figeac (shä tō′ GRäN BA RA′yə LA MAR zel′ fē-zhAk′)
Château Grand-Corbin (shä tō′ GRäN kôR baN′)
Château Grand-Corbin-Despagne (shä tō′ GRäN kôR-baN′ des PAN′yə)
Château Grand-La Lagune (shä tō′ GRäN LA LA GYN′)
Château Grand-Puy-Ducasse (shä tō′ GRäN pwē′ DY KAS′)
Château Grand-Puy-Lacoste (shä tō′ GRäN pwē′ LA kôst′)
Château Grandes-Murailles (shä tō′ GRäNd MY RA′yə)
Château Grillet (shä tō′ GRē ye′)
Château Gruaud-Larose (shä-tō′ GRY ō′ LA RŌz′)
Château Guiraud (shä tō′ gē RŌ′)
Château Haut-Bages-Libéral (shä tō′ ō BAzh′ lē bā RAl′)
Château Haut-Bailly (shä tō′ ō BA yē′)
Château Haut-Batailley (shä-tō′ ō BA TA ye′)
Château Haut-Brion (shä tō′ ō bRē ôN′)
Château Kirwan (shä tō′ kēR-wäN′)
Château La Clotte (shä tō′ LA klôt′)
Château La Conseillante (shä-tō′ LA kôN se yäNt′)
Château La Couronne (shä tō′ LA ko͞o RÔn′)
Château La Croix (shä tō′ LA KRWä)
Château La Croix de Gay (shä tō′ LA KRWä də ge′)
Château La Dominique (shä tō′ LA dô mē nēk′)
Château La Fleur-Pourret (shä tō′ LA flœR′ po͞oRe′)
Château La Lagune (shä tō′ LA LA GYN′)
Château La Mission-Haut-Brion (shä tō′ LA mē syôn′ ō bRē ôN′)
Château La Pointe (shä tō′ LA pwANt′)
Château La Rose-Capbern (shä tō′ LA RŌz KAP beRN′)
Château La Tour-Blanche (shä tō′ LA to͞oR bläNsh′)
Château La Tour-Carnet (shä-tō′ LA to͞oR KAR ne′)
Château La Tour-de-Mons (shä tō′ LA to͞oR də môNS′)
Château La Tour du Pin Figeac (shä tō′ LA to͞oR′ DY PAN fē-zhAk′)
Château La Tour-Haut-Brion (shä tō′ LA to͞oR′ ō bRē ôN′)
Château La Tour-Martillac (shä tō′ la to͞oR MAR tē YAK′)
Château Lafaurie-Peyraguey (shä tō′ LA fōRē′ pe RA ge′)
Château Lafite (shä tō′ LAfēt′)
Château Lafite-Rothschild (shä tō′ LA fēt′ RÔt shēld′; rôth′chīld)
Château Lafleur (shä tō′ LA-flœR′)
Chateau Lafleur-Pétrus (shä-tō′ LA flœR′ pā TRYS′)
Château Lafon-Rochet (shätō′ LA fôN′ RÔ she′)
Château Lagrange (shä tō′ LA-GRäNzh′)
Château Lanessan (shä tō′ LA-ne säN′)
Château l'Angélus (shä tō′ läN zhā LYS′)
Château Langoa-Barton (shä-tō′ läNGWA′ BAR tôN′)
Château Lapointe (shä tō′ LA-pwANt′)
Château Lascombes (*preferred* (shä tō′ LAs kôNb′; *sometimes* (shä tō′ LA kôNb′)
Château Latour (shä tō′ LA-to͞oR′)
Château Latour-Haut-Brion (shä tō′ LA to͞oR′ ō bRē ôN′)

Château Latour-Lichine (shä tō′ lA tōōR′ lē shēn′)
Château Latour-Pomerol (shä-tō′ lA tōōR′ pômə RôL′)
Châteaux Laville-Haut-Brion (shä tō′ lA vēl′ ō bRē ôN′)
Château Le Chatelet (shä tō′ lə shAtə le′)
Château Léoville-Barton (shä-tō′ lā ô vēl′ bAR tôN′)
Château Léoville-Las-Cases (shä tō′ lā ô vēl′ lAs kAz′)
Château Léoville-Poyferré (shä tō′ lā ô vēl′ pwA fe Rā′)
Château Les Ormes de Pez (shä tō′ lā zôRm də pez′)
Château L'Évangile (shä tō′ lā väN zhēl′)
Château Lynch-Bages (shä tō′ lANsh bAzh′; *Eng.* shä tō′ linch′ bäzh′)
Château Lynch-Moussas (shä-tō′ lANsh mōō sä′; *Eng.* (shä-tō′ linch mōō sä′)
Château Magdelaine (shä tō′ mAg də len′)
Château Malartic-Lagravière (shä tō′ mA lAR tēk′ lA gRA-vyeR′)
Château Malescot-Saint-Exupéry (shä tō′ mA les kō′ sAN teg zY pā Rē′)
Château Margaux (shä tō′ mAR gō′)
Château Marquis d'Alesme-Becker (shä tō′ mAR kē′ dA lem be keR′)
Château Marquis-de-Terme (shä tō′ mAR kē′ də teRm′)
Château Mazeyres (shä tō′ mA zeR′)
Château Montrose (shä tō′ môN Rōz′)
Château Moulin-Riche (shä tō′ mōō lAN Rēsh′)
Château Mouton-d'Armailhacq (shä tō′ mōō tôN′ dAR mA-yAk′)
Château Mouton du Baron Philippe (shä tō′ mōō tôN′ dY bA RôN fē lēp′)
Château Mouton-Rothschild (shä tō′ mōō tôN′ Rôt shēld′, rôth chīld)
Château Myrat (shä tō′ mē RA′)
Château Nairac (shä tō′ ne-RAk′)
Château Olivier (shä tō′ ô lē-vyā′)
Château Palmer (shä tō′ pä′-mər; *Fr.* (shä tō′ pAl meR′)
Château Pape-Clément (shä tō′ pAp klā mäN′)
Château Paveil (shä tō′ pA-ve′yə)
Château Pavie (shä tō′ pA vē′)
Château Pédesclaux (shä tō′ pā des klō′)
Château Petit-Mayne (shä tō′ pə tē men′)
Château Petit-Village (shä tō′ pə tē vē lAzh′)
Château Pétrus (shä tō′ pā-tRYs′)
Château Phélan-Ségur (shä tō′ fā läN′ sā gYR′)
Château Pichon-Longueville (shä tō′ pē shôN′ lông vēl′)
Château Pontet-Canet (shä tō′ pôN te kA ne′)
Château Pouget (shä tō′ pōō-zhe′)
Château Poujeaux-Theil (shä-tō′ pōō zhō′ te′yə)
Château Prieuré-Lichine (shä-tō′ pRē œ Rā′ lē shēn′)
Château Rabaud-Promis (shä-tō′ RA bō′ pRô mē′)
Château Rauzan-Gassies (shä-tō′ Rō zäN′ gA sē′, -sēs′)
Château Rausan-Ségla (shä tō′ Rō zäN′ sā glA′)
Château Rieussec (shä tō′ RYœ-sek′)
Château Ripeau (shä tō′ Rē pō′)
Château Rouget (shä tō′ Rōō-zhe′)
Château Saint-Georges-Côte Pavie (shä tō′ sAN zhôRzh′ kōt pA vē′)
Château Saint-Pierre (shä tō′ sAN pyeR′)
Château Sigalas-Rabaud (shä-tō′ sē gA lA′ RA bō′)
Château Siran (shä tō′ sē RäN′)
Château Smith-Haut-Lafitte (shä tō′ smēt ō lA fēt′, smith-)
Château Soutard (shä tō′ sōō-tAR′)
Château Suau (shä tō′ sYō′)
Château Talbot (shä tō′ tAl bō′)
Château Troplong-Mondot (shä-tō′ tRō lôN′ môN dō′)
Château Trotanoy (shä tō′ tRō-tA nwA′)
Château Trottevieille (shä tō′ tRôt vye′yə)
Château Valoux (shä tō′ vA-lōō′)
Château Vieux-Château Certan (shä tō′ vyœ shä tō ser täN′)
Château Villegeorge (shä tō′ vēl zhôRzh′)
Château Villemaurine (shä tō′ vēl mō Rēn′)
Châteauneuf-du-Pape (shä tō-nœf′ dY pAp′)
Châtenet (shätə ne′)
Chatenière (shA tə nyeR′)
Châtillon-en-Diois (shä tē yôn′ äN dē wA′)
Chauché Gris (shō shā gRē′)
Chaume (shōm)
Chaumées (shō mā′)
Chaumes (shōm)
Chautagne (shō tAN′yə)
Cheilly-les-Maranges (she yē′ lā mA räNzh′)
Chekiang (ju′ gyäng′)
Chénas (shā nA′)
Chenin Blanc (shə nAN bläN′)
Cherry Rocher (cher′ē rō shā′; *Fr.* she Re′ Rô she′)
Cheste (ches′te)
Chevalier-Montrachet (shə vA-lyā′ môN RA she′)
Chianti (kē än′tē, -an′-; *It.* kyän′tē)
Chianti Colli Arentini (kyän′tē kôl′lē ä′Ren tē′nē)
Chianti Colli Fiorentini (kyän′-tē kôl′lē fyô′Rentē′nē)
Chianti Colli Pizane (kyän′tē kôl′lē pē dzä′ne)
Chianti Colli Senesi (kyän′tē kôl′lē se ne′zē)
Chianti Rufino (kyän′tē Rōō fē′-nô)
Chiaretto (kyä Ret′tô)
Chiaretto del Garda (kyä Ret′-tô del gär′dä)
Chica (chē′kä)
chicha (chē′chä)
Chichée (shē shā′)
Chiclana de la Frontera (che-klä′nä the lä fRôn te′Rä)
Chinon (shē nôN′)
Chipiona (chē pyô′nä)
Chiroubles (shē Rōō′blə)
chopine (shô pēn′)
Chorey-les-Beaune (shô Re′ lā bōn′)
Cinque Terre (chēng′kwe teR′Re)
Cinquièmes Crus (sAN kyem kRY′)
Cinsault, Cinsaut (sAN sō′)
Cinzano (chēn dzä′nô)
Cirial (thē Ryäl′)
Ciro de Calabria (chē′Rô de kä-lä′bRyä)
Clairet (kle Re′)
Clairette de Bellegarde (kle-Ret′ də bel gARd′)
Clairette de Die (kle Ret′ də dē′)
Clairette du Languedoc (kle-Ret′ dY läNg dôk′)
Clairin (kle RAN′)
Clape (klAp)
clarete (klä Re′te)
Clavelins (klAv lAN′)
Climat (klē mA′)
Clos (klō)
Clos Arlots (klō zAR lō′)
Clos Blanc de Vongeot (klō bläN də vōō zhō′)
Clos Bussière (klō bY syeR′)
Clos de Bèze (klō də bez)
Clos de Corton (klō də kôR tôN′)
Clos de la Boudriotte (klō də lA bōō dRē ôt′)
Clos de la Chapelle (klō də lA shA pel′)
Clos de la Commaraine (klō də lA kô mA Ren′)
Clos de la Maréchale (klō də lA mA Rā shAl′)
Clos de la Mousse (klō də lA mōōs)
Clos de la Perrière (klō də lA pe RyeR′)
Clos de la Roche (klō də lA Rôsh)
Clos de l'Église-Clinet (klō də lā glēz klē ne′)
Clos de Tart (klō də tAR)
Clos de Vougeot (klō də vōō zhō′)
Clos des Argillières (klō dā zAR zhē lyeR′)
Clos des Corvées (klō dā kôR-vā′)
Clos des Forêts (klō dā fô Re′)
Clos des Jacobins (klō dā zhA-kô bAN′)
Clos des Lambrays (klō dā läN bRe′)
Clos des Moines (klō dā mwAn)
Clos des Mouches (klō dā mōōsh)
Clos des Papes (klō dā pAp)
Clos des Porrets-Saint-Georges (klō dā pô Re′ sAN zhôRzh′)
Clos des Réas (klō dā RA ä′)
Clos du Chapitre (klō dY shA-pē′tRə)
Clos du Roi (klō dY RwA′)
Clos Fourtet (klō fōōR te′)
Clos Haut-Peyraguey (klō ō pe RA ge′)
Clos Napoléon (klō nA pô lā ôN′)
Clos Saint-Denis (klō sAN də-nē′)
Clos Saint-Jacques (klō sAN zhAk′)
Clos Saint-Jean (klō sAN zhäN′)
Clos Sorbet (klō sôR be′)
Cocuy (kô kwē′)
Cognac (kōn′yak, kon′-; *Fr.* kô nyAk′)
Cointreau (kwAN tRō′)
Colares, Collares (kōō lä′Rəsh)
collage (kô lAzh′)
collerette (kô lə Ret′)
Colli Trevigiani (kôl′lē tRe′vē-jä′nē)

Colline di Caldaro (kôl lē′ne dē käl dä′RÔ)
Colmar (kôl MAR′)
Colombard (kô lôN BAR′)
Colombaud (kô lôN bō′)
Combe-au-Moine (kôNb ō mWAN′)
Combe d'Orveau (kôNb dôR vō′)
Combes-Dessus (kôNb də SY′)
Combettes (kôN bet′)
Comète, Vin de la (VAN də LA kô met′)
Commandaria (kô′män dä RĒ′ä)
Commanderie du Bontemps de Médoc (kô mänDəRĒ′ DY bôN täN′ də mā dôk′)
commune (kô MYN′)
Coñac (kô nyäk′)
Conca (kông′kä)
Conca de Barbará (kông′kä the bär bä RÄ′)
Concise (kôn sēz′)
Condrieu (kôN DRĒ YŒ′)
Confrérie (kôN FRĀ RĒ′)
congé (kôN zhā′)
connétable (kô nā TA′blə)
Connétablie de Guyenne (kô-nā TA blē′ də GY yen′)
Consorzio (kôn sôR′dzyô)
Constantinovka (kôn′stän tyi-nôf′kä)
consumo (kôn so͞o′mo͞o)
Corbières (kôR byeR′)
Corbières du Roussillon (kôR-byeR′ DY RO͞O sē yôN′)
Corbières Supérieur (kōR-byeR′ SY pā RYŒR′)
Cordial Médoc (kôR dyAl′ mā-dôk′)
cordon (kôR′dən; *Fr.* kôR dôN′)
Cormondrèche (kôR môN-dResh′)
Cornas (kôR NA′)
Coronata (kô′Rô nä′tä)
corriente (kôR Ryen′te)
corsé (kôR sā′)
Cortaillod (kôR TA yō′)
Corte (kôR′te)
Cortese (kôR te′ze)
Corton (kôR tôN′)
Corton-Charlemagne (kôR tôN′-shAR lə MAN′yə)
Corvino (kôR vē′nô)
Corvo di Casteldaccia (kōR′vô dē käs′tel dät′chä)
cosecha (kô se′chä)
Costières du Gard (kôs tyeR′ DY gAR′)
Côt (kō)
côte (kōt)
Côte Blonde (kōt blôND′)
Côte Brune (kōt BRYN)
Côte Chalonnaise (kōt shA lô-nez′)
Côte de Beaune (kōt də bōn′)
Côte de Brouilly (kōt də BRo͞o-yē′)
Côte de Fontenay (kōt də fôN-tə ne′)
Côte de Nuits (kōt də nwē)
Côte des Blancs (kōt dā bläN′)
Côte d'Or (kōt dôR′)
Côte Roannaise (kōt RÔ A nez′)
Côte Rôtie (kōt RŌ tē′)
Coteaux d'Aix (kô tō deks′)
Coteaux d'Aix et des Baux (kô tō deks ā dā bō′)
Coteaux d'Ancenis (kô tō däN-sə nē′)
Coteaux de la Loire (kô tō də lä LWAR′)
Coteaux de l'Aubance (kô tō də lō bäNS′)
Coteaux de Mascara (kô tō də MAS KA RÄ′)
Coteaux de Saint-Christol (kô-tō də SAN KRĒ stôl′)
Coteaux de Saumur (kô tō də sō MYR′)
Coteaux de Tlemcen (kô tō də tlem sen′)
Coteaux de Touraine (kô tō də to͞o Ren′)
Coteaux de Touraine-Monsseux (kô tō də to͞o Ren mo͞o sō′)
Coteaux de Vérargues (kô tō də vā RARg′)
Coteaux des Baux (kô tō dā bō)
Coteaux du Giennois (kô tō DY zhyAN NWA′)
Coteaux du Layon (kô tō DY le-yôN′)
Coteaux du Loir (kô tō DY lWAR′)
Côtes Canon Fronsac (kōt KA-nôN′ FRôN SAK′)
Côtes d'Agly (kōt DA glē′)
Côtes d' Auvergne (kōt dō-veRN′yə)
Côtes de Bergerac (kōt də beR-zhə RAK′)
Côtes de Blaye (kōt də blA′yə)
Côtes de Bordeaux (kōt də bôR dō′)
Côtes de Bordeaux Saint-Macaire (kōt də bôR dō′ SAN MA keR′)
Côtes de Bourg (kōt də bo͞oR)
Côtes de Castillon (kōt də KAS-tē yôN′)
Côtes de Duras (kōt də DY RA′)
Côtes de Fronsac (kōt də FRôN-SAK′)
Côtes de Gien (kōt də zhyAN)
Côtes de Haut-Roussillon (kōt də ō Ro͞o sē yôn′)
Côtes de Jura (kōt də zhY RA′)
Côtes de Jura-Mousseux (kōt də zhY RA mo͞o SŒ′)
Côtes de Montravel (kōt də môN RA vel′)
Côtes de Provence (kōt də PRÔ väNS′)
Côtes de Toul (kōt də to͞ol)
Côtes de Ventoux (kōt də väN-to͞o′)
Côtes de Vérargues (kōt də vā-RARg′)
Côtes du Buzet (kōt DY BY ze′)
Côtes du Forez (kōt DY fô Re′)
Côtes du Jura (kōt DY zhY RA′)
Côtes du Lubéron (kōt DY lY-bā Rôn′)
Côtes du Marmandais (kōt DY MAR män de′)
Côtes du Rhône (kōt DY Rōn)
Côtes du Zaccar (kōt DY ZA-KAR′)
Couderc (ko͞o deR′)
coulure (ko͞o LYR′)
coupage (ko͞o PAzh′)
Courbu (ko͞oR BY′)
court noué (ko͞oR no͞o ā′)
courtier (ko͞oR tyā′)
Cramant (KRA mäN′)
Cras (KRA)
crémant (KRā mäN′)
Crème (*Fr.* kRem; *Eng.* krem, krēm, krām)
Crème d'Ananas (kRem DA NA nä′)
Crème de Banane (kRem də BA-NAN′)
Crème de Cacao (*Fr.* kRem də KA KA ô′; *Eng.* krem, krēm, krām də kō′kō)
Crème de Café (kRem də KA fā′)
Crème de Cassis (kRem də KA sēs′)
Crème de Chocolat (kRem də shô kô lA′)
Crème de Cumin (kRem də KY MAN′)
Crème de Fraise (kRem də fRez)
Crème de Framboise (kRem də fRäN bWAZ′)
Crème de Mandarine (kRem də män DA Rēn′)
Crème de Menthe (*Fr.* kRem də mäNT; *Eng.* krem, krēm, krām də menth, mint)
Crème de Moka (kRem də mô KA′)
Crème de Noyau (kRem də NWA yō′)
Crème de Prunelle (kRem də PRY nel′)
Crème de Roses (kRem də Rōz)
Crème de Thé (kRem də tā)
Crème de Vanille (kRem də VA nē′yə)
Crème de Violette (*Fr.* kRem də vyô let′; *Eng.* krem, krēm, krām də vī′ə lit)
Crème Yvette (kRem ē vet′)
crémeux (KRā MŒ′)
Crépy (KRā pē′)
Cressier (KRe syā′)
Criollas (KRē ô′yäs)
Criots-Bâtard-Montrachet (KRē ō bä TAR′ môN RA she′)
Croattina (KRô′ät tē′nä)
Croix des Bouquets (krwä dā bo͞o ke′)
Cröv (KRŒf)
Crozes-Hermitage (KRôz eR mē-TAzh′)
cru (KRY) *pl.* **crus** (KRY)
Cru Classé (KRY klA sā′)
Cru Gressier-Grand Poujeaux (KRY gRe syā′ gRäN po͞o zhō′)
Crujidera (KRo͞o′hē the′Rä)
crus artisans (KRY zär tē zäN′)
crus bourgeois (KRY bo͞oR-zhWA′)
crus exceptionnels (KRY zek-sep syô nel′)
Cruzan Rum (KRo͞o′zhən rum)
Csopaki Rizling (chō′po ki Riz′ling)
Cully (KY lē′)
Curaçao (kyo͝or′ə sō′, -sō′ə)
cuve (KYV)
cuvée (KY vā′)
Cuvée Dr. Peste (KY vā′ dôk-tôR pest′)
Cuvée Nicolas Rollin (KY vā′ nē kô LA RÔ lAN′)
cuverie (KYVə Rē′)
Cviček (tsvē′chek)

Dackenheim (däk′ən hīm′)
Dalheim (däl′hīm′)
Dalsheim (däls′hīm′)
Dame-Jeanne (DAM zhAN′)
Damien (DA myAN′)
Dampierre (däN pyeR′)
Danziger Goldwasser (dän′tsi-gəR gôlt′väs′əR)
Dão (douN)
Daubhaus (doup′hous′)
débourrement (dā bo͞o Rə mäN′)
Debrö (deb′RŒ)
Debröi Hárslevelü (deb′RŒ i härsh′le ve lY)
Decker (dek′əR)
dégorgement (dā gôRzh mäN′)
Deidesheim (dī′dəs hīm′)
Deidesheimer Grainhübel (dī′dəs hīm′əR gRīn′hY bəl)
Deidesheimer Herrgottsacker (dī′dəs hīm′əR heR′gôt zäk′-əR)

Deidesheimer Leinhöhle (dī′dəs-hīm′əR līn′hœ′lə)
délicat (dā lē KA′)
delikat (de li kät′)
Demerara (dem′ə râr′ə)
demie-queue (də mē kœ′)
demi-sec (də mē sek′)
Demir Kapija (de′mēR kä′pē-yä)
Denominación de Origen (de-nô mē nä thyôn′ de ô Rē′hen)
Denominazione di Origine Controllata (de nô′mē nä-tsyô′ne dē ō Rē′jē ne kôn′tRôl-lä′tä)
Denominazione di Origine Controllata e Garantita (de nô′mē nä tsyô′ne dē ô Rē′jē ne kôn tRôl lä′tä e gä′Rän tē′tä)
Denominazione di Origine Semplice (de nô′mē nä-tsyô′ne dē ô Rē′jē ne sem′plē-che)
Detzem (de′tsəm)
Deutelsberg (doit′əls beRk′)
deuxième taille (dœ zyem tA′yə)
Dexheim (deks′hīm′)
Dézaley (dā zA le′)
Dezize-les-Maranges (də zēz′-lā mA RäNzh′)
Dhron (dRōn)
Dhroner Hofberg (dRō′nəR hôf′beRk′)
Dicampidano (dē käm′pē dä′nô)
Didiers (dē dyā′)
Die (dē)
Dienheim (dēn′hīm′)
Dimyat (dim′yät)
Dingač (ding′gäch)
Dix Journaux (dē zho͞oR nō′)
Dizy (dē zē′)
Dniepropetrovsk (dnye′pRo-pe tRôfsk′)
Dolceacqua (dôl′che äk′wä)
Dolcetto (dôl chet′tô)
Dôle (dōl)
Dôle de Sion (dōl də sē ôN′)
Dom Avelsbach (dôm ä′vəls-bäkh′)
Dom Herrenberg (dôm heR′ən-beRk′)
Dom Pérignon (dôN pā Rē nyôN′)
domaine (dô men′)
Domaine de Chevalier (dô-men′ də shə vA lyā′)
Domaine de la Nerte (dô men′ də lA neRt′)
Domaine de Nalys (dô men′ də nA lē′, -lēs′)
Domaine de Saint-Préfert (dô-men′ də saN pRā feR′)
Domaine des Fine Roches (dô-men′ dā fēn Rôsh′)
Domaine des Sénéchaux (dô-men′ dā sā nā shō′)
Domäne (dô me′nə)
Domdechaney (dôm′də kä′nī)
Dominikanerberg (dô′mi ni-kä′nəR beRk′)
Dominode (dô mē nôd′)
Domtal (dôm′täl)
Donski (dôn′skē)
Dorsheim (dôRs′hīm′)
dosage (dô zAzh′)
doux (do͞o)
Drain (dRaN)
Dreimännerwein (dRī′men′əR-vīn′)
Dromersheim (dRō′məRs hīm′)
Dubonnet (dY bô ne′)
dulce (do͞ol′the)
dur (dYR)
Duras (dY RA′)
Duresses (dY Res′)
Durette (dY Ret′)
Dürkheim (dYRk′hīm′)
Dürnsteiner (dYRn′shtīn′əR)

Eau-de-Vie (ō də vē′)
Eau-de-Vie d'Andaye (ō də vē′ däN dA′yə)
Eau-de-Vie de Cidre (ō də vē′ sē′dRə)
Eau-de-Vie de Dantzig (ō də vē′ də dan′sig; *Fr.* däN tsēg′; *Ger.* dän′tsikh)
Eau-de-Vie de Lie (ō də vē′ də lē)
Eau-de-Vie de Marc (ō də vē′ də mAR)
Eau-de-Vie de Marc de Cidre (ō də vē′ də mAR də sē′dRə)
Eau-de-Vie de Poire (ō də vē′ də pwAR)
Eau-de-Vie de Vin (ō də vē′ də vaN)
Ebernburg (ā′bəRn bo͝oRk′)
Ebersberg (ā′bəRs beRk′)
Échezeaux (ā shə zō′)
echt (ekht)
Edelbeerenauslese (äd′əl bā′-Rən ous′lā zə)
Edelfäule (äd′əl foi′lə)
Edelgewächs (äd′əl gə veks′)
Edelweiss (äd′əl vīs′)
Edelzwicker (äd′əl tsvik′əR)
Edenkobener (äd′ən kō′bə nəR)
Édes (â′desh)
Ediger (ā′di gəR)
Eger (e′geR)
égrappage (ā gRA pAzh′)
égrappoir (ā gRA pwAR′)
Egri Bikavér (eg′Ri bi′ko vâR′)
Ehr (āR)
Eigengewächs (ī′gən gə veks′)
Eisel (ī′zəl)
Eisenstadt (ī′zən shtät′)
Eiserberg (ī′zəR beRk′)
Eisweg (īs′vāk′)
Eitelsbach (īt′əls bäkh′)
Eitelsbacher Karthäuserhof-berg (īt′əls bäkh′əR kärt′-hoi zəR hôf′beRk)
Elbling (el′bling)
Elefantenwein (e lə fän′tən-vīn′)
Élixir d'Anvers (ā lēk sēR′-däN veR′)
Ellenz-Poltersdorf (el′ənts pôl′təRs dôRf′)
Eller (el′əR)
Eloro (e lô′Rô)
Elsheim (els′hīm′)
Eltville (elt′vilə)
Eltviller Langenstück (elt′vil-əR läng′ən shtYk′)
Eltviller Sonnenberg (elt′vil əR zôn′ən beRk′)
Eltzerberg (el′tsəR beRk′)
Emeringes (œ me RaNzh′)
Emilia-Romagna (e mē′lya Rō-mä′nyä)
en dentelle (äN däN tel′)
En Remilly (äN Rə mē yē′)
en vrac (äN vRAk′)
Engehöll (eng′ə hœl′)
Engelmannsberg (eng′əl mäns-beRk′)
Engerweg (eng′əR vāk′)
Enkirch (en′kiRkh′)
Entre-Deux-Mers (äN tRə dœ meR′)
Entre-Fino (en′tRe fē′nô)
enveloppe (äN və lôp′)
Enzian (äN zyäN′)
Epenottes (e pə nôt′)
Épernay (ā peR ne′)
Épesses (ā pes′)
Erbach (eR′bäkh′)
Erbacher Markobrunn (eR′-bäkh′əR mäR′kô bRo͞on′)
Erden (eR′dən)
Erdener Treppchen (eR′dən-əR tRep′khən)
Ermitage (eR mē tAzh′)
Erntebringer (eRn′tə bRing′ər)
Escherndorf (esh′əRn dôRf′)
espalier (es pA lyā′)
espumoso (es′po͞o mô′sô)
Est! Est!! Est!!! (est′ est′ est′)
Estremadura (es′tRe mä tho͞o′-Rä)
estufa (ish to͞o′fə)
estufagem (ish′to͞o fä′gəm)
étampé (ā täN pā′)
etiquette (e tē ket′)
Étoile (ā twAl′)
Étoile, L' (lā twAl′)
Etrigny (e tRē nyē′)
extra sec (ek stRA sek′)
Ezerjó (e′zeR yō′)

faible (fe′blə)
Falerno (fä leR′nô)
Falkenberg (fälk′ən beRk′)
Falkenstein (fälk′ən shtīn′)
Fargues (fARg)
Faro (fä′Rô)
Fass (fäs)
Fassle (fäs′lə)
Faugères (fō zheR′)
Faye d'Anjou (fA′yə däN zho͞o′)
Fecciarossa (fet′chä Rôs′sä)
Féchy (fā shē′)
Federberg (fā′dəR beRk′)
Federweisser (fā′dəR vīs′əR)
Feherbór (fe′hâR bôR)
Felsenberg (fel′zən beRk′)
Felsenleiste (fel′zən līs′tə)
Fendant (fäN däN′)
ferme (feRm)
Fèves (fev)
Fiano (fyä′nô)
Fiano di Avellino (fyä′nô de ä′vel lē′nô)
fiasco (fē as′kō; *It.* fyäs′kô)
fillette (fē yet′)
Filzen (fil′tsən)
Fine Champagne (fēn shäN-pAN′yə)
Fine Maison (fēn me zôN′)
finesse (fē nes′)
Fino (fē′nô)
Finos de mesa (fē′nôs de me′sä)
Fins Bois (faN bwA′)
Fior d'Alpe (fyôR′ däl′pe)
Fitou (fē to͞o′)
Fixin (fē saN′)
Flagey-Échezeaux (flA zhe′ ā shə zō′)
fleur (flœR)
Fleurie (flœ Rē′)
Flohpeter (flō′pā təR)
flor (flôR)
floraison (flô Re zôn′)
Flur (flo͞oR)
Fockenberg (fôk′ən beRk′)
Folatières (fô lA tyeR′)
Folle Blanche (fôl bläNsh′)
Foochien (fo͞o′chyen′)
Forêts (fôRe′)
Forst (fôRst)
Forster Jesuitengarten (fôR′-stəR yā zo͞o ēt′ən gäR′tən)
Forster Kirchenstück (fôR′-stəR kiRkh′ən shtYk′)
forzato (fôR tsä′tô)
foudre (fo͞o′dRə)
Fourchaume (fo͞oR shōm′)
Fourtet (fo͞oR te′)
Fraise (fRez)

Framboise (fRäN bwAz′)
franc-de-goût (fRäN də go͞o′)
Frappato (fRäp pä′tô)
Frappato di Vittoria (fRäp-pä′tô dē vēt tô′ryä)
Franken (fRäng′kən)
frappé (fRA pā′)
Frascati (fRäs kä′tē)
Freihand (fRī′hänt′)
Freinsheim (fRīns′hīm′)
Freisa (fRā′zä)
Freisa d'Asti (fRā′zä däs′tē)
Freisa di Chieri (fRā′zä dē kye′Rē)
Fremiets (fRe myā′)
Friesenheim (fRē′zən hīm′)
Frionnes (fRē ôn′)
frizzante (fRēt tsän′te)
Fronsac (fRôN sAk′)
Frontignan (fRôn tē nyän′)
Frontignan-Muscat (fRôN tē nyäN′ mYs kA′)
Fronton (fRôN tôN′)
Frühburgunder (fRY′bo͞oR′-go͞on dəR)
Fruška Gora (fRo͞osh′kä gô′Rä)
Fuder (fo͞o′dəR)
Fumé de Pouilly (fY mā′ də po͞o yē′)
Furmint (fo͞oR′mint)
fût (fY)
fütyülös (fY′tyY lœsh′)
Fyé (fyā)

Gaillac (gA yAk′)
Gaillac Mousseux (gA yAk′ mo͞o sœ′)
Galgenwein (gäl′gən vīn′)
Gallais (gA le′)
Gamay (gA me′)
Gamay à Jus Coloré (gA me′ A zhY kô lô Rā′)
Gamay Beaujolais (gA me′ bō zhô le′)
Gamay-Teinturier (gA me′ taN tY Ryā′)
Gamza (gäm′zä)
Gancia (gän′chä)
Gänsberg (gens′beRk′)
Gard (gAR)
Garda (gäR′dä)
Gardine (gAR dēn′)
Garenne (gA Ren′)
Garganega di Gambellara (gäR′gä ne′gä dē gäm′bel-lä′Rä)
Garnacha (gäR nä′chä)
Garnacha Blanca (gäR nä′chä bläng′kä)
garrafeira (gäR′Rä fā′Rə)
Gattinara (gät′tē nä′Rä)
Gau-Algesheim (gou′äl′gəs-hīm′)
Gau-Bischofheim (gou′bish′ôf-hīm′)
Gaudichots (gō dē shō′)
gazéifié (gA zā fyā′)
Gegend (gā′gənt)
Gehrn (gāRn)
Geierstein (gī′əR shtīn′)
Geisberg (gīs′beRk′)
Geisenheim (gī′zən hīm′)
Gemarkung (gā mäR′ko͞ong)
Genevrières (zhənə vRyeR′)
Genièvre (zhə nye′vRə)
Genovesella (je′nô ve zel′lä)
Gentiane (zhäN tyAn′)
gentil (zhäN tē′)
Geropiga (zhi′Ro͞o pē′gə)
Gerümpel (ge RYm′pəl)
Geschwister Berres (ge-shvist′əR beR′əs)
Gevrey-Chambertin (zhə vRe′ shäN beR taN′)
Gewächs (gə veks′)
Gewürztraminer (gə vYRts′-tRä′mi nəR)
Gigondas (zhē gôN dA′)
Gimmeldingen (gim′əl ding′ən)
Giro di Sardegna (jē′Rô dē säR de′nyä)
Gironde (zhē RôNd′)
Gitelsbach (git′əls bäkh′)
Givry (zhē vRē′)
gobelet (gôbə le′)
Goldatzel (gôlt′äts′əl)
Goldberg (gôlt′beRk′)
Goldwasser (gôlt′väs′əR)
Goltbeerenauslese (gôlt′bā′-Rən ous′lā zə)
Gorges (gôRzh)
Gottesfuss (gôt′əs fo͞os′)
gourmet (go͞oR me′)
goût américain (go͞o A mā Rē kAN′)
goût anglais (go͞o äN gle′)
goût de capsule (go͞o də kAp-sYl′)
goût de pierre à fusil (go͞o də pyeR A fY zē′)
goût de terroir (go͞o də te-RWAR′)
Goutte d'Or (go͞ot dôR′)
Graach (gRäkh)
Graacher Himmelreich (gRä′-khəR him′əl Rīkh′)
Graben (gRä′bən)
Gräfenberg (gRef′ən beRk′)
Graciano (gRä thyä′nô)
Gragnano (gRä nyä′nô)
graisse (gRes)
Grand Arôme (gRän tA Rōm′)
Grand Cru (gRäN kRY′)
Grand Cru Classé (gRäN kRY klA sā′)
Grand Marnier (gRäN mAR-nyā′)
Grand Roussillon (gRäN Ro͞o sē-yôN′)
Grand Saint-Bernard (gRäN saN beR nAR′)
Grand Vin (gRäN vaN′)
Grande (Fine) Champagne (gRäNd fēn shäN pAN′yə)
Grande Rue (gRäNd RY′)
Grandes Ruchottes (gRäNd RY-shôt′)
Grands Échezeaux (gRäN zā-shə zō′)
Granja União (gRäNn′zhə o͞o-nyouN′)
Granjo (gRäNn′zho͞o)
Grappa (gRäp′pä)
Grappe Blanche (gRAp bläNsh′)
grasse (gRäs)
Grauerburgunder (gRou′əR-bo͞oR′go͞on dəR)
Graves (gRAv)
Graves de Vayres (gRAv də veR′)
Graves Supérieures (gRAv′ sY-pā Ryœr′)
Greco (gRe′kô)
Greco di Gerace (gRe′kô dē je Rä′che)
Greco di Tufo (gRe′kô dē to͞o′fô)
Greffieux (gRe fyœ′)
Grenache (gRə nAsh′)
Grenouilles (gRə no͞o′yə)
Grèves (gRev)
Grignolino (gRē′nyô lē′nô)
Grignolino d'Asti (gRē′nyô-lē′nô däs′tē)
Grillet (gRē ye′)
Grillo (gRēl′lô)
Grinzing (gRin′tsing)
Griotte (gRē ôt′)
Griotte-Chambertin (gRē ôt′ shäN beR taN′)
Grk (gûrk; *Serb.-Cro.* gRk)
Grolleau (gRô lō′)
Gros Mansenc (gRō mäN säN′)
Gros Plant de Pays Nantais (gRō pläN də pe ē′ näN te′)
Groslot (gRō lō′)
Grossenstück (gRôs′ən shtYk′)
Grumello (gRo͞o mel′lô)
Grünberg (gRYn′beRk′)
Grüner Veltliner (gRY′nəR felt′li nəR)
Guarapo (gwä Rä′pô)
Guebwiller (gYb vē leR′)
Guignolet (gē nyō le′)
Guindado (gēn dä′thô)
Gumpoldskirchner (go͞om′pôlts-kiRkh′nəR)
Guntersblum (go͞on′təRs blo͞om′)
Gutsname (go͞ots′nä′mə)
Guyenne, Connétablie de (kô-nā tA blē′ də gY yen′)
guyot (gY yō′)
Gyöngyös (dyœn′dyœsh)
Gyöngyösi Kadarka (dyœn′-dyœ shi ko′doR ko)

Haardt (häRt)
Hahnheim (hän′hīm′)
Halbrot (Al bRō′)
Halbstück (hälp′shtYk′)
Hallau (häl′ou)
Hallgarten (häl′gäR′tən)
Hallgartner Schönhell (häl′-gäRt′nəR shœn′hel′)
Hameau de Blagny (A mō də blA nyē′)
Hansenberg (hän′sən beRk′)
Harfe (häR′fə)
Hárslevelü (häRsh′le ve lY′)
Hartenberg (häR′tən beRk′)
Harxheim (häRks′hīm′)
Hasensprung (hä′zən-shpRo͞ong′)
Hassel (häs′əl)
Hattenheim (hät′ən hīm′)
Hattenheimer Nussbrunnen (hät′ən hīm′əR no͞os′ bRo͞on′-ən)
Hattenheimer Wisselbrunnen (hät′ən hīm′əR vis′əl bRo͞on′-ən)
haut (ō)
Haut-Combat (ō kôN bA′)
Haut-Dahra (ō dA Rä′)
Haut-Médoc (ō mā dôk′)
Haut-Montravel (ō môN RA vel′)
Haut-Peyraguey (ō pe RA ge′)
Haut-Pruliers (ō pRY lyā′)
haute (ōt)
Haute-Savoie (ōt sA vwA′)
Hautvillers (ō vē leR′)
Heddesheim (hed′əs hīm′)
Hegyaljai (he′dyol yo′i)
Heidelberg Tun (hīd′əl beRk′ to͞on′)
Heiligenbaum (hī′li gən boum′)
Heiligenberg (hī′li gən beRk′)
Hendelberg (hen′dəl beRk′)
Heppenheim (hep′ən hīm′)
Heppenstein (hep′ən shtīn′)
Hérault (ā Rō′)
Herberg (hāR′beRk′)
Hermannshöhle (heR′mäns-hœ′lə)
Hermitage (eR mē tAzh′)
Hermitage, L' (leR mē tAzh′)
Herrenberg (heR′ən beRk′)
Herrenweiher (heR′ən vī′əR)
Herrliberg (heR′li beRk′)
Hervelets (eRvə le′)

Herxheim am Berg (heRks′-hīm′ äm beRk′)
Herzley (heRts′lī)
Heurige (hoi′Ri gə)
Hilbitz (hil′bits)
Hinkelstein (hing′kəl shtīn′)
Hinter Eisel (hin′təR ī′zəl)
Hinterhaus (hin′təR hous′)
Hinterhäuser (hin′təR hoi′zəR)
Hipping (hip′ing)
Hitzlay (hits′lī)
Hoch (hōKH)
Hochgewächs (hōKH′gə veks′)
Hochheim (hōKH′hīm′)
Hochheimer-Domdechaney (hōKH′hīm′əR dōm′də kä′nī)
Hohe Domkirche (hō′ə dōm′-kiRKH ə)
Hohenrain (hō′ən Rīn′)
Hölle (hœl′ə)
Höllenberg (hœl′ən beRk′)
Homburg (hōm′bo͞oRk′)
Honigsäckel (hō′niKH zek′əl)
Horgazuela (ôR′gä thwe′lä)
Hörstein (hœR′shtīn′)
Hospices de Beaune (ôs pēs′ də bōn′)
hotte (ôt)
Houx (o͞o)
Huelva (wel′vä)
Hühnerberg (hY′nəR beRk′)
Hustopeče (ho͞os′tô pe′che)
Hütte (hYt′ə)

Île des Vergelesses (ēl dā veR-zhə les′)
impériale (aN pā RYAl′)
Inferno (ēn feR′nô)
Ingelheim (ing′əl hīm′)
Ingelheimer (ing′əl hīm′əR)
Innere Leiste (in′əR ə līs′tə)
Insolia (ēn sô′lyä)
Institut National des Appellations d'Origine (aN stē tY nA syô nAl′dā zA pel lA syôN′ dô Rē zhēn′)
Irancy (ē RäN sē′)
Ischia (ēs′kyä)
Istituzione del Comitato Nazionale per la Tutela della Denominazioni di Origine (ēs′tē to͞o tsyô′ne del kô′mē tä′tô nä′tsyô nä′le peR lä to͞o te′lä del′lä de nô′-mē nä tsyô′nē dē ô Rē′jē ne)
Izarra (ē zA Rä′)

Jaén Blanco (hä en′ bläng′kô)
Jaén Doradillo (dô Rä thē′lyô)
Jaén Tinto (tēn′tô)
Jarollières (zhA Rô lyeR′)
Jarzębiak (yäR zhan′byäk)
Jasnières (zhA nyeR′)
Jerez (he Reth′, -Res′)
Jerez de la Frontera (he Reth′ de lä fRôn te′Rä)
Jeriñac (he Rē nyäk′)
jeroboam (jer′ə bō′əm; *Fr.* zhā-Rô bô Am′)
jeropiga (zhi′Ro͞o pē′gə)
Jesuitengarten (ye zo͞o ēt′ən-gäR′tən)
Johannisberg (yō hän′is beRk′)
Johanniswein (yō hän′is vīn′)
Josephshof (yō′zefs hōf′)
Juffer (yo͞of′əR)
Juliénas (zhY lyā nA′)
Jullié (zhY lyā′)
Junkerberg (yo͞ong′kəR beRk′)
Jura (zhY RA′)
Jurançon (zhY RäN sôN′)

Kabinett (kä′bi net′)
Kabinettwein (kä′bi net′vīn′)
Kadarka (ko′doR ko)
Kaefferkopf (kef′əR kôpf′)
Kaffia (käf′ē ä)
Kahlenberg (kä′lən beRk′)
Kaiserstuhl (kī′zəR shto͞ol′)
Kallstadt (käl′shtät′)
Kambas (käm bäs′)
Kammer (käm′əR)
Kammerhof (käm′əR hōf′)
Kamptal (kämp′täl)
Kanzem (kän′tsəm)
Karlovo (käR′lô vô)
Karlsberg (käRls′beRk′)
Karthäuserhofberg (käRt′hoi′-zəR hōf′beRk′)
Kasel (kä′zəl)
Kaštel (käsh′tel)
Katharinenberg (kä tä Rē′nən-beRk′)
Katzenloch (käts′ən lôKH′)
Kaufmannsberg (kouf′mäns-beRk′)
Käulgen (koil′gən)
Kaysersberg (kī′zəRs beRk′)
Kecskemét (kech′ke māt′)
Kefersteiner (kā′fəR shtīn′əR)
Kehrnagel (kāR′nä′gəl)
Kéknyelü (kâk′nye lY′)
Kellerabfüllung (kel′əR äp′fY-lo͞ong)
Kellerabzug (kel′əR äp′tso͞ok)
Kelterberg (kel′təR beRk′)
Kerz (keRts)
Kerzenstück (keRts′ən shtYk′)
Kesselberg (kes′əl beRk′)
Kesselring (kes′əl Ring′)
Kesten (kes′tən)
Kette (ket′ə)
Kichelberg (kiKH′əl beRk′)
Kiedrich (kēt′RiKH)
Kieselberg (kē′zəl beRk′)
Kinheim (kin′hīm′)
Kipperlé (kē peR lā′)
Kirchberg (kiRKH′beRk′)
Kirchenstück (kiR′KHən shtYk′)
Kirchgrube (kiRKH′gRo͞o′bə)
Kirsch (*Ger.* kiRsh; *Fr.* kēRsh)
Kirschplatt (kiRsh′plät′)
Kirschwasser (kiRsh′väs′əR)
Klaus (klous)
Kleiner Rauschling (klīn′əR Roush′ling)
Kleinergelber (klīn′əR gel′bəR)
Klettgau (klet′gou)
Klevner (klef′nəR)
Klöch (klœKH)
Kloster Eberbach (klôs′təR ā′bəR bäKH′)
Klosterberg (klôs′təR beRk′)
Klostergarten (klôs′təR gäR-tən)
Klosterkiesel (klôs′təR kē′zəl)
Klosterlay (klôs′təR lī′)
Klotten (klôt′ən)
Klüsserath (klYs′ə Rät′)
Knipperlé (knē peR lā′)
Kobern (kō′beRn)
Kohlenberg (kō′lən beRk′)
Königsbach (kœ′niKHs bäKH′)
Königsbacher (kœ′niKHs-bäKH′əR)
Königsberg (kœ′niKHs beRk′)
Königsstuhl (kœ′niKHs shto͞ol′)
Konsumwein (kôn zo͞om′vīn′)
Kontuszówka (kôn′to͞o sho͞of′-kä)
Konz-Karthaus (kônts′ käRt′-hous′)
Korkbrand (kôRk′bRänt′)
Kornbranntwein (kôRn′bRänt-vīn′)
Kornschnapps (kôRn′shnäps′)
Kraichgau (kRīKH′gou)
Krajina (kRä′yi nä)

Krampen (kRäm′pən)
Kranklay (kRängk′lī)
Kremser (kRem′zəR)
Kreszenz (kRes′tsents)
Krettnach (kRet′näKH)
Kreuz (kRoits)
Krone (kRō′nə)
Kronenberg (kRō′nən beRk′)
Krötenbrunnen (kRœt′ən-bRo͞on′ən)
Krötenpfuhl (kRœt′ən pfo͞ol′)
Kröv (kRœf)
Krück (kRYk)
Küchelberger (kYKH′əl beR′-gəR)
Kues (ko͞o′əs)
Kugel (ko͞o′gəl)
Kümmel (kYm′əl)
Kupfergrube (ko͞op′fəR gRo͞o′bə)
Kutjevo (ko͞ot′ye vô)
Kvass (kväs)

Lacrima Christi (lak′rə mə kris′tē; *It.* lä′kRē mä kRēs′tē)
Ladoix-Serrigny (lA dwA′ se Rē-nyē′)
lagares (lä gä′Rəsh)
Lagarino Rosato (lä′gä Rē′nô Rô zä′tô)
lager (lä′gəR)
Lago di Caldaro (lä′gô dē käl-dä′Rô)
Lagrima (lä′gRē mä)
Lairén (lī Ren′)
Lalande de Pomerol (lA länd′ də pôm[ə] Rôl′)
Lambrusco (läm bRo͞os′kô)
Lambrusco di Sorbara (läm-bRo͞os′kô dē sôR bä′Rä)
Lancié (läN syā′)
Landkreis Bingen (länt′kRīs′ bing′ən)
Landkreis Mainz (mīnts)
Landkreis Worms (vôRms)
Landot (läN dō′)
Landwein (länt′vīn′)
Langenlohnsheim (läng′ən lōns′-hīm)
Langenstück (läng′ən shtYk′)
Languedoc (läng dôk′)
Lantigné (läN tē nyā′)
Latricières (lA tRē syeR′)
Latricières-Chambertin (lA-tRē syeR′ shäN beR taN′)
Laubenheim (lou′bən hīm′)
Laudun (lō dœN′)
Lauerbaum (lou′əR boum′)
Lauzet (lō ze′)
Lavaux (lA vō′)
Layon (le ôN′)
Lazio (lä′tsyô)
Lebuja (le bo͞o′hä)
Leidhecke (līt′hek′ə)
Leimen (lī′mən)
Leistadt (lī′shtät′)
Leisten (līs′tən)
Leistenberg (līs′tən beRk′)
Leiwen (lī′vən)
Lenchen (len′KHən)
Léognan (lā ô nyäN′)
lesen (lā′zən)
Leutschach-Ehrenhausen (loit′-shäKH′ ā′Rən hou′zən)
levure (lə vYR′)
Leyenkaul (lī′ən koul′)
Leynes (len)
Lhomme (lôm)
Lickerstein (lik′əR shtīn′)
Liebfrauenstift (lēp′fRou′ən-shtift′)
Liebfraumilch (lēp′fRou milKH′)
Lies (lēs)
Lieser (lē′zəR)

Liguria (lē go͞o′Ryä)
Likier Ziałowy (li′kyeR zhyä-lô′vi)
Likörwein (li kŒR′vīn′)
Lillet (lē le′)
Limoux (lē mo͞o′)
Lindos (lēn′dôs)
Lípovina (lē′pô vi′nä)
liqueur d'expédition (lē kŒR′ dek spā dē syôN′)
liqueur de tirage (lē kŒR′ də tē RAzh′)
Liqueur d'Or (lē kŒR dôR′)
Liqueur Jaune (lē kŒR zhōn′)
Liqueur Verte (lē kŒR veRt′)
liquoreux (lē kô RŒ′)
Lirac (lē RAk′)
Liré (lē Rā′)
Listán (lēs tän′)
Listrac (lēs tRAk′)
Litoměřice (li′tô mye Rzhi tse)
Lizas (lē′zäs)
Ljutomer (lyo͞o′tô meR)
locaux (lô kō′)
Logroño (lô gRô′nyô)
Loir (lwAR)
Loire (lwAR)
loja (lô′zhə)
Lorch (lôRKH)
Lorenzberg (lō′Rents beRk′)
Lorraine (lô Ren′)
Lösnich (lŒs′niKH)
Loupiac (lo͞o pyAk′)
Louvois (lo͞o vwA′)
loyaux (lwA yō′)
Ludon (lY dôN′)
Ludwigshöhe (lo͞ot′viKHs hŒ′ə)
Lugana (lo͞o gä′nä)
Luginsland (lo͞o′gins länt′)
Lussac-Saint-Émilion (lY sAk′ saN tā mē lyôN′)
Lutry (lY tRē′)
Luttenberger (lo͞ot′ən beR′gəR)
Lys (lē)

Maasborn (mäs′bôRn)
Macadam (mA kA dAm′)
Macau (mA kō′)
Macharnudo (mä′chäR no͞o′thô)
mâché (mä shā′)
Mâcon (mä kôN′)
Mâcon Supérieur (mA kôN sY-pā RyŒR′)
Mâconnais (mä kô ne′)
Mâconnais blanc (mä kô ne bläN′)
Madiran (mA dē RäN′)
Magyar Állami Export Pince-gazdaság (mo′dyoR äl′lo-mi ek′spôRt pin′tse goz do-shäg′)
Mai Lao (mī′ lou′)
Maikammerer (mī′käm′əR əR)
Mailly (mA yē′)
Maipo (mī′pô)
maître de chai (me′tRə də she′)
Málaga (mal′ə gə; *Sp.* mä′lä gä)
Malbec (mAl bek′)
Malconsorts, Les (mAl kôN sôR′)
Mali Plavac (mä′lē plä′väts)
Maltroie, La (mAl tRwA′)
Malvagia (mäl vä′hyä)
Malvasia (mäl vä′zyä)
Malvasia di Bosa (mäl vä′zyä dē bô′zä)
Malvasia di Lipari (mäl vä′zyä dē lē pä′Rē)
Malvasía de Sitges (mäl′vä-sē′ä the sēt′hes)
Malvoisie (mAl vwA zē′)
Mamertino (mä′meR tē′nô)
Mancha (män′chä)
Manchego (män che′gô)
Mandarine (mäN dA Rēn′)
Manègue (mA neg′)
Mannberg (män′beRk′)
Mantúo (män to͞o′ô)
Manzanares (män′thä nä′Res)
Manzanilla (man′zə nēl′yə; *Sp.* män′thä nē′lyä)
Maraca (mä Rä′kä)
Maranges (mA RäNzh′)
Maraština (mä′Räsh ti′nä)
marc (mAR)
Marconnets (mAR kô ne′)
marcottage (mAR kô tAzh′)
Maréchaude (mA Rā shōd′)
Mareuil-sur-Ay (mA RŒ′yə sYR A ē′)
Margaux (mAR gō′)
Marie-Jeanne (mA Rē zhAn′)
Marienholz (mä Rē′ən hôlts′)
Maring (mä′Ring)
Markgräflerland (mäRk′gRef′-ləR länt′)
Markobrunn, Marcobrunn (mäR′kô bRo͞on′)
Marne (mARn)
Marsala (mäR sä′lä)
Marsaluova (mäR′sä lwô′vô)
Marsanne (mAR sAn′)
Martinsthal (mäR′tins täl)
Marzenino (mäR′dze nē′nô)
mas (mä)
Mascara (mAs kA Rä′)
Mastika (mä stē′kä)
Mattersburg (mät′əRs bo͞oRk′)
Mauerchen (mou′əR KHən)
Maury (mō Rē′)
Mavrodaphne (mä′vRô däf′nē)
Mavroud (mäv Ro͞od′)
Maximin Grünhäuser Herrenberg (mäk′si min gRYN′hoi′-zəR heR′ən beRk′)
Mazis (mA zē′)
Mazis-Chambertin (mA zē′ shäN beR tAN′)
Mazoyères-Chambertin (mA-zô yeR′ shän beR tAN′)
Mazuelo (mä thwe′lô)
Mazys (mA zē′)
Méal (mā Al′)
Médéa (mā dā ä′)
Médoc (mā dôk′)
Mehring (mā′Ring)
Meilen (mī′lən)
Meisenberg (mī′zən beRk′)
Meleto (me le′tô)
Melnik (*Bul.* mel′nik)
Melněk (*Czech.* myel′nyek)
Melon d'Arbois (mə lôN dAR-bwA′)
Melon de Bourgogne (mə lôN də bo͞oR gôn′yə)
Mendoza (men dô′sä)
Mentuccia (men to͞ot′chä)
Meranese di Collina (me′Rä-ne′ze dē kôl lē′nä)
Mercurey (meR kY Re′)
Merito (me Rē′tô)
Merlot (meR lō′)
Mersault-Blagny (meR sō′ blA-nyē′)
Mertesdorf (meR′təs dôRf′)
mescal (me skal′; *Sp.* mes käl′)
Mesnil (mā nēl′)
Mesnil-sur-Oger (mā nēl sYR ō zhā′)
Messeguera (mes′se ge′Rä)
Metaxa (me täk′sä)
Mettenheim (met′ən hīm′)
Meursault (mûr sō′; *Fr.* mŒR-sō′)
Mezcal (mes käl′)
Midi (mē dē′)
Miguel del Arco (mē gel′ del äR′kô)
Millefiori (mēl′le fyô′Rē)
millerandage (mēl RäN dAzh′)
Mikulov (mi′ko͞o lôf)
Millandes (mē läNd′)
millésime (mē lā zēm′)
Milly (mē yē′)
Minas Gerais (mē′näz zhe-Rīsh′)
Minervois (mē neR vwA′)
Minnella (mēn nel′lä)
Mirabelle (mē RA bel′)
Mirabelle de Lorraine (mē RA-bel′ də lô Ren′)
Mirabelle Fine du Val de Metz (mē RA bel fēn′ dY vAl də mets′)
Miraflores (mē′Rä flô′Res)
Mirande (mē RäNd′)
Mis au Domaine (mē zō dô-men′)
Mis en Bouteille à la Propriété (mē zäN bo͞o te′yə A lA pRô-pRē ā tā′)
Mis en Bouteille au Château (mē zäN bo͞o te′yə ō shä tō′)
Mis en Bouteille au Domaine (mē zäN bo͞o te′yə ō dô men′)
mise sur pointe (mēz sYR pwANt′)
mistelle (mē stel′)
Mittelhaardt (mit′əl häRt′)
Mittelheim (mit′əl hīm′)
moelleux (mwA lŒ′)
Molinara (mô′lē nä′Rä)
Monastrel (mô näs tRel′)
Monbazillac (môN bA zē yAk′)
Mönchberg (mŒNKH′beRk′)
Monica di Sardegna (mô′nē kä dē säR de′nyä)
Monières (mô nyeR′)
Moniga-del-Garda (mô′nē gä del gäR′dä)
Monopole (mô nô pôl′)
Monóvar (mô nô′väR)
monpeyroux (môN pe Ro͞o′)
Mont de Milieu (môN də mē-lyŒ′)
Mont Près (môN pRe′)
Mont-sur-Rolle (môN sYR Rôl′)
Montagne-Saint-Émilion (môN-tAN′yə sAN tā mē lyôN′)
Montagny (môN tA nyē′)
Montalbano (môn′täl bä′nô)
Montaña (môn tä′nyä)
Montecarlo (môn′te käR′lô)
Monte Massico (môn′te mäs′-sē kô)
Montée de Tonnerre (môN tā də tô neR′)
Montefiascone (môn′te fyäs-kô′ne)
Montepulciano (môn′te po͞ol-chä′nô)
Montepulciano di Abruzzo (môn′te po͞ol chä′nô dē ä bRo͞od′dzô)
Monthélie (môN tā lē′)
Montilla (môn tē′lyä)
Montilla Moriles (môn tē′lyä mô Rē′les)
Montilla Sierra (môn tē′lya syeR′Rä)
Montiottes Hautes (môN tyôt ōt′)
Montlouis (môN lwē′)
Montmain (môN mAN′)
Montmélas-Saint-Sorlin (môN-mā lA′ sAN sôR lAN′)
Montrachet (môn RA she′)
Montravel (môN RA vel′)
Monts du Tessalah (môN dY te sA lä′)
Monts Luisants (môN lwē säN′)
Mór (mōR)
Mörbisch (mŒR′bish)
Morey-Saint-Denis (mô Re′ sAN də nē′)
Morgeot (môR zhō′)
Morgon (môR gôN′)

Móri Ezerjó (mō′ri e′zer yō′)
Moriles (mô rē′les)
Morschberg (môrsh′berk′)
Moscata (môs kä′tä)
Moscata di Noto (môs kä′tä dē nô′tô)
Moscatel (môs kä tel′)
Moscatel de Setúbal (môs kä-tel′ de si tōō′bôl)
Moscatello di Montalcino môs′kä tel′lô dē môn′täl-chē′nô)
Moscatel Morisca (môs kä-tel′ mô rēs′kä)
Moscato Atesino (môs kä′tô ä′te sē′nô)
Moscato d'Asti (môs kä′tô däs′tē)
Moscato del Salento (môs kä′tô del sä len′tô)
Moscato di Campidano (môs-kä′tô dē käm′pē dä′nô)
Moscato di Casteggio (môs-kä′tô dē käs ted′jô)
Moscato di Pantelleria (môs-kä′tô dē pän′tel le′ryä)
Moscato di Siracusa (môs-kä′tô dē sē′rä kōō′zä)
Moscato di Tempio (môs kä′tô dē tem′pyô)
Mosel (mō zel′; *Ger.* mō′zəl)
Moselblümchen (mō′zəl blym′-khən)
Moselkern (mō′zəl kern′)
Moselle (mō zel′; *Fr.* mô zel′)
Mostaganem-Kenenda (môs ta-ga nem′ ke nen dä′)
mosto (môsh′tōō)
mou (mōō)
mouillage (mōō yazh′)
Moulin-à-Vent (mōō lan na vän′)
Moulis (mōō lē′)
Mourvèdre (mōōr ve′drᵊ)
mousseux (mōō sœ′)
mout (mōō)
Mou-Tai (mō′ dī′)
Moutonne (mōō tôn′)
Mouzillon (mōō zē yôn′)
Mühlberg (myl′berk′)
Mülheim (myl′hīm′)
Müller-Thurgau (myl′ər tōōr′-gou)
Münster-bei-Bingerbruck (myn′stər bī bing′ər brōōk′)
Münster-Sarmsheim (myn′-stər zärms′hīm′)
Murcia (mōōr′thyä)
mûres (myr)
Murgers des Dents de Chien (myr zhā′ dā dän də shyan′)
Muscadelle (mys ka del′)
Muscadet (mys ka de′)
Muscat (mus′kət, -kat; *Fr.* mys ka′)
Muscat d'Alsace (mys ka′ dal-zas′)
Muscat de Lunel (mys ka′ də lynel′)
Muscat-Ottonel (mys ka′-ôtô nel′)
muselage (my sə lazh′)
Musigny (*Fr.* my zē nyē′; *Eng.* mōō zēn yē′)
Musigny de Clos de Vougeot (my zē nyē′ də klō də vōō zhō′)
Mussbach (mōōs′bäkh′)
mutage (my tazh′)
myrtilles (mēr tēl′)
Myshako (mi′shä kô)

Nackenheim (näk′ən hīm′)
Nackenheimer Rothenberg (näk′ən hīm′er rôt′ᵊn berk′)
Nahe (nä′ə)
Nanton (nän tôn′)
Nareuil sur Ay (na rœ′yᵊ syr a ē)
Narrenkappe (När′ən käp′ə)
nartjie (när′tyē)
Natur (nä tōōr′)
Naturrein (nä tōōr′rīn′)
Naturwein (nä tōōr′vīn′)
Navarra (nä vär′rä)
Néac (nā ak′)
Nebbiolo (neb byô′lô)
Nebbiolo Piemontese (neb-byô′lô pye′môn te′ze)
Nerello (ne rel′lô)
nerveux (ner vœ′)
Neuberg (noi′berk′)
Neuberger (noi′ber′gər)
Neuchâtel (nœ shä tel′)
Neudorf (noi′dôrf′)
Neumagen (noi′mä′gən)
Neustadt (noi′shtät′)
Niederhausen (nē′dər hou′zən)
Niederhäuser Hermannshöhle (nē′dər hoi′zər her′mäns-hœ′lə)
Niedermennig (nē′dər men′-ikh)
Nierstein (nēr′shtīn′)
Niersteiner (nēr′shtīn′ər)
Nies'chen (nēs′khən)
Nittel (nit′ᵊl)
noble (nô′blᵊ)
Noblejas (nô ble′häs)
Noilly-Prat (noi′lē prat′; *Fr.* nwa yē pra′)
Nonnenberg (nôn′ən berk′)
Norheim (nōr′hīm′)
Nostrano (nôs trä′nô)
Noyau (nwa yō′)
nu (ny)
Nuits-Saint-Georges (nwē san zhôrzh′)
Nuragus (nōō rä′gōōs)
Nussbrunnen (nōōs′brōōn′ən)

Obere Wolfshöhle (ō′bə rə vôlfs′hœ lə)
Oberemmeler (ō′bə rem′ə lər)
Obersberg (ō′bərs berk′)
Oberwesel (ō′bər vā′zəl)
Obol (ô′bôl)
Ocaña (ô kä′nyä)
Ockenheim (ôk′ən hīm′)
Ockfen (ôk′fən)
Ockfener Bockstein (ôk′fen ər bôk′shtīn′)
Odenas (ô dᵊna′)
oeil de perdrix (œ′yᵊ də per drē′)
Oger (ō zhā′)
Oggau (ôg′ou)
Ohligberg (ō′likh berk′)
ojo de gallo (ô′hô ŧħe gä′lyô)
Ojo de Liebre (ô′hô ŧħe lye′-bre)
Ölberg (œl′berk′)
Oliena (ô lye′nä)
Ollon (ô lôn′)
Oloroso (ō′lə rō′sō; *Sp.* ô′lô-rô′sô)
Oporto (ōō pôr′tōō)
Oppenheim (ôp′ən hīm′)
Oppenheimer (ôp′ən hīm′ər)
Oran (ô ran′; *Fr.* ô rän′)
Orbe (ôrb)
Orbel (ôr′bel)
ordinaire (ôr dē ner′)
orgeat (ôr′zhat; *Fr.* ôr zha′)
Originalabfüllung (ô ri gi näl′-äp′fyl′ōōng)
Originalabzug (ô ri gi näl′-ap′tsōōk′)
Originalwein (ô ri gi näl′vīn′)
Ormeau, L' (lôr mō′)
Ormož (ôr′môzh)
Ortenau (ôr′tᵊn ou)
Orvieto (ôr′vē ā′tō; *It.* ôr vye′-tô)
Osann (ō′zän)
Osterberg (ôst′ər berk′)
Osthofen (ôst′hō′fən)
Östrich (œst′rikh)
Oudon (ōō dôn′)
Oued-Imbert (wed an ber′)
ouillage (ōō yazh′)
Ouzo (ōō′zō)

Paarl (pärl)
Paceta (pä the′tä)
pagos (pä′gôs)
País (pä ēs′)
Pajarete (pä′hä re′te)
Palette (pa let′)
Pallet (pa le′)
Pallini (pä lē′nē)
Palma (päl′mä)
Palo Cortado (pä′lô kôr tä′ŧħô)
Palo Viejo (pä′lô bye′hô)
Palomino (pä′lô mē′nô)
palus (pa ly′)
Panadés (pä nä ŧħes′)
Panay (pä nī′)
paradise (pa ra dēz′)
Pardillo (pär dē′lyô)
Pares (pä′rəs)
Parfait Amour (par fe ta mōōr′)
Parras (pär′räs)
Parsac-Saint-Émilion (par-sak′ san tā mē lyôn′)
pasado (pä sä′ŧħô)
Passe-Tout-Grains (pas tōō gran′)
passerillage (pas rē yazh′)
passes (pas)
passito (päs sē′tô)
Pastis (pa stēs′)
Paterberg (pä′tər berk′)
Patrimonio Rosé (pä′trē mô′-nyô rô zā′)
Pauillac (pō yak′)
Paulinsberg (pou′lins berk′)
pays, vin de (van də pe ē′)
Pécharmant (pā shar män′)
Pécs (pâch)
pecsenyebór (pe′che nye bôr′)
Pécsi Furmint (pâ′chi fōōr′-mint)
Pedro Ximénez (pā′drō hē mā′-nās, -men′is; *Sp.* pe′ŧħrô hē me′neth)
Peissy (pe sē′)
Peloux (pe lōō′)
pelure d'oignon (pə lyr dwa-nyôn′)
perlant (per län′)
perlé (per lā′)
Perlwein (perl′vīn′)
Pernand-Vergelesses (per nän′ ver zhə les′)
Pernod (pâr nō′; *Fr.* per nō′)
Perpignan (per pē nyän′)
Perréon (pe rā ôn′)
Perrière (pe ryer′)
Perrières (pe ryer′)
Perroy (pe rwa′)
Pessac (pe sak′)
pétillant (pā tē yän′)
Petit-Chablis (pə tē sha blē′)
Petit Mansenc (pə tē män sän′)
Petit Verdot (pə tē ver dō′)
Petite Champagne (pə tēt shän-pan′yᵊ)
Petits-Vougeots (pə tē vōō zhō′)
Pézerolles (pāzᵊ rôl′)
Pfaffenberg (pfäf′ən berk′)
Pfaffenberger (pfäf′ən ber′gər)
Pfalz (pfälts)

Pfalzgraben Schlossberg (pfälts′grä′bən shlôs′beRK′)
Pfarrgarten (pfäR′gäR′tᵊn)
phylloxera (fil′ək sēr′ə, fi lok′-sər ə; *Fr.* fē lôk se RA′)
pichet (pe she′)
Picpoule (pēk po͞ol′)
Picpoule de Pinet (pēk po͞ol′ də pē ne′)
Pic-Saint-Loup (pēk saN lo͞o′)
pièce (pyes)
Pierelle (pye Rel′)
piments (pē mäN′)
Pineau d'Aunis (pē nō′ dō nē′)
Pineau de la Loire (pē nō′ də lA lwAR′)
Pineau des Charentes (pē nō′ dā shA RäNt′)
Pinot (pē nō′)
Pinot Blanc (pē nō bläN′)
Pinot Chardonnay (pē nō′ shAR dô ne′)
Pinot Gris (pē nō gRe′)
Pinot Liebault (pē nō′ lye bō′)
Pinot Meunier (pē nō′ mœ-nyā′)
Pinot Noir (pē nō nwAR′)
pipette (pē pet′)
piquant (pē käN′)
piqué (pē kā′)
piquette (pē ket′)
piqûre (pē kYR′)
Pisco brandy (pēs′kô)
Plante Abbé (pläNt A bā′)
Plante Chamel (pläNt shA mel′)
Plantes (pläNt)
Plantes-de-Maranges (pläNt′ də mA RäNzh′)
Platière (plA tyeR′)
Plavac (plä′väts)
Plješivica (plye′shi vi′tsä)
Plovdina (plôv′di nä)
Pohorje (pô′hôR ye)
Poinchy (pwaN shē′)
pointe de douceur (pwaNt də do͞o sœR′)
Pointes d'Angles (pwaNt däN′glᵊ)
poire (pwAR)
poiré (pwA Rā′)
Polcevera (pôl′che ve′Rä)
Polja (pô′lyä)
Pomerol (pômᵊ Rôl′)
Pommard (pô mAR′)
Pommern (pôm′əRn)
Pomoriye (pô mô′Ri ye)
Ponsigue (pôn sē′ge)
Porrets, Les (pô Re′)
porrón (pôR Rôn′)
Port-au-Prince (pôrt′ō prins′; *Fr.* pôR tō pRaNs′)
Pošip (pô′ship)
pot (pō)
Pougets, Les (po͞o zhā′)
Pouilly-Fuissé (po͞o yē fwē sā′)
Pouilly-Fumé (po͞o yē fY mā′)
Pouilly-Loché (po͞o yē lō shā′)
Pouilly-sur-Loire (po͞o yē SYR lwAR′)
Pouilly-Vinzelles (po͞o yē vaN-zel′)
pourridié (po͞o Rē dyā′)
pourriture grise (po͞o Rē tYR gRēz′)
pourriture noble (po͞o Rē tYR nô′blᵊ)
Pousse d'Or (po͞os dôR′)
Požega (pô′zhe gä)
Prälat (pRe′lät)
Preignac (pRe nyAk′)
Prémeaux (pRā mō′)
première taille (pRə myeR tA′yᵊ)
Premières Côtes de Blaye (pRə myeR kōt də blA′yᵊ)
Premières Côtes de Bordeaux (pRə myeR kōt də bôR dō′)
Premières Côtes de Gaillac (pRə myeR kōt də gA yAk′)
Premiers Crus (pRə myā kRY′)
Premiers Grand Crus Classés (pRə myā gRäN kRY klA sā′)
Preuses (pRœz)
preuve (pRœv)
Prévot (pRā vō′)
Priorato (pRyô Rä′tô)
prise (pRēz)
Prokupac (pRô′ko͞o päts)
Prolongeau (pRô lôN zhō′)
Provence (pRô väNs′)
Prosecco (pRô sek′kô)
Prošek (pRô′shek)
provignage (pRô vē nyAzh′)
Pruliers (pRY lyā′)
Prüm (pRYm)
Prunelle (pRY nel′)
Prunellia (pRY nel yä′)
Pruzilly (pRY zē′yᵊ)
Pucelles (pY sel′)
Puerto de Santa María (pweR′-tô the sän′tä mä Rē′ä)
Puerto Real (pweR′tô Re äl′)
Puglia (po͞o′lyä)
Puisseguin-Saint-Émilion (pwēs gaN′ saN tā mē lyôN′)
Pukhliakovski (po͞okh′lyä kôf′-skē)
Pulchen (po͞ol′khən)
Puligny-Montrachet (pY lē nye′-môN RA she′)
pulque (po͞ol′ke)
Punch Martiniquais (pœNsh mAR tē nē ke′)
pupitre (pY pē′tRᵊ)
puttonyos (po͞ot′tô nyôsh)

Quart de Chaume (kAR də shōm′)
Quartier de Marci Haut (kAR tyā də mAR sē ō′)
Quatourze (kA to͞oRz′)
Quatrièmes Crus (kA tRyem kRY′)
Quetsch (*Ger.* kvech; *Fr.* kwech)
Quincié (kaN syā′)
Quincy (kaN sē′)
Quinquina (kaN kē nA′)
Quinta (kēn′tə)

Rabigato (Rä′bē gä′tô)
Rablay-sur-Layon (RA ble′ SYR le yôN′)
race (RAs)
raki (rä kē′, rak′ē)
rakija (Rä′kē yä)
rancio (*Fr.* RäN syō′; *Sp.* Rän′-thyô)
Randersacker (Ränt′əR zäk′əR)
Raspail (RAs pA′yᵊ)
Rasteau (RAs tō′)
Ratafia (rat′ə fē′ə; *Fr.* RA tA-fyA′)
Rauschling (Roush′ling)
Rauchloch (Roukh′lôkh′)
Rauenthal (Rou′ən täl)
Rauenthaler (Rou′ən tä′ləR)
Rauschbier (Roush′bēR′)
Ravat (RA vA′)
Ravello (Rä vel′lô)
Raya (Rä′yä)
rebêche (Rə besh′)
Rechbächel (Rekh′bekh′əl)
Recioto Veronese (Re chô′tô ve′Rô ne′ze)
récolte (Rā kôlt′)
Refène (Rə fen′)
Refert (Rə feR′)
Régnié (Rā nyā′)
Rehbach (Rā′bäkh′)
rehoboam (rē′ə bō′əm; *Fr.* Rā-ô bô Am′)
Reil (Rīl)
Reims (RaNs)
Reims (lot Brisset) (RaNs lō bRē se′)
Rein (Rīn)
Reine-Claude (Ren klōd′)
Reiskahr (Rīs′käR)
remuage (Rə mY Azh′)
remueur (Rə mY œR′)
Renardes, Les (Rə nARd′)
Rennacker (Ren′äk əR)
Reserva (Re seR′vä)
retsina (ret′sə nə; *Gk.* Re tsē′nä)
Rettberg (Ret′beRk′)
Reuilly (Rœ yē′)
Réunion (rē yo͞on′yən; *Fr.* Rā Y-nyôN′)
Rhein (Rīn)
Rheinberg (Rīn′beRk′)
Rheingau (Rīn′gou)
Rheinhell (Rīn′hel′)
Rheinhessen (Rīn′hes′ən)
Rheinpfalz (Rīn′pfälts′)
Rheinriesling (Rīn′Rēs′ling)
Rhône (Rōn)
Rhum (rum; *Fr.* Rôm)
Rhum Barbancourt (bAR bäN-ko͞oR′)
Rhum Champion (shäN pyôN′)
Rhum Clément (klā mäN′)
Rhum Duquesne (do͞o kān′, dyo͞o-; *Fr.* dY ken′)
Rhum Marie Colas (mA Rē kô lA′)
Rhum Nazon (nA zôN′)
Rhum Tesserot (tesᵊ Rō′)
Rhum Tropical (trop′i kəl; *Fr.* tRô pē kAl′)
Ribeauvillé (Rē bō vē lyā′)
Ribero (Rē be′Rô)
Ricard (Rē kAR′)
Ricasoli (Rē′kä zô′lē)
Riceys (Rē se′)
Richebourg, Les (Rēsh bo͞oR′)
Richemone (Rēsh môn′)
Riesling (rēz′ling, rēs′-; *Ger.* Rēs′ling; *Fr.* Rēz lēng′)
Rilly-la-Montagne (Rē yē lA môN tAn′yᵊ)
Rio Grande do Sul (Rē′o͞o gRäNn′de do͞o so͞ol′)
Río Negro (rē′ō nā′grō; *Sp.* Rē′ô ne′gRô)
Rioja (Ryô′hä)
Rioja Alta (Ryô′hä äl′tä)
Rioja Baja (bä′hä)
Riquewihr (Rēk vēR′)
Rishon-le-Zion (Ri shôn′ le tsē ôn′)
Rivesaltes (Rēv zAlt′)
Riviera del Garda (Rē vye′Rä del gäR′dä)
Rivolet (Rē vô le′)
Roche (Rôsh)
Rochefort-sur-Loire (Rôsh fôR SYR lwAR′)
Rochusberg (Rôkh′o͞os beRk′)
Rochusweg (Rôkh′o͞os vāk′)
Rödelsee (Rœd′ᵊl zā′)
Rognet-Corton (Rô nye kôR tôN′)
Rohrgasse (RōR′gäs′ə)
Romana (Rô mä′nä)
Romanèche-Thorins (Rô mA-nesh tô RaN′)
Romanée (Rô mA nā′)
Romanée-Conti (Rô mA nā kôN-tē′)
Romanée-Saint-Vivant (Rô mA-nā′ saN vē väN′)
Ron Llave (Rôn yä′ve)
Ronrico (Rôn Rē′kô)
rosado (Rô sä′thô)

rosato (RÔ zä′tô)
rosé (RŌ zā′)
Rosé d'Arbois (RŌ zā DAR BWA′)
Rosé de Béarn (bā ARN′)
Rosé de Riceys (RĒ se′)
Rosenberg (RŌ′zən beRk′)
Rosengarten (RŌ′zən gäR′tən)
Rosenheck (RŌ′zən hek′)
Rosette (RÔ zet′)
Rosolio (rō zō′lē ō′, rə-; *It.* RÔ zô′lyô)
Rossese (RÔs se′ze)
Rossignola (RÔs′sē nyô′lä)
Rossolis (RÔ sô lē′)
Rosso Piceno (RÔs′sô pē che′nô)
Rosso Vallaggarina (RÔs′sô väl′läg gä RĒ′nä)
Rota (RÔ′tä)
rot blanc (RÔt bläN′)
Rotes Haus (RŌ′təs hous′)
Rotgipfler (RÔt′gipf′ləR)
Rothenberg (RÔt′ən beRk′)
rouge (ROOzh)
rougeau (ROO zhō′)
Roudnice (Rōd′nyi tse)
Rousselet de Béarn (ROOsə le′ də bā ARN′)
Roussette (ROO set′)
Roussillon (ROO sē yôN′)
Roussillon des Aspres (ROO sē-yôN′ dā ZAS′pRə)
Roxheim (RÔks′hīm′)
Ruchottes (RY shôt′)
Ruchottes-Chambertin (RY-shôt′ shäN beR taN′)
Rüdesheim (RY′dəs hīm′)
Rüdesheimer Berg, Rüdes-heimerberg (RY′dəs hīm′əR-beRk′)
Rüdesheim-Nahe (RY′dəs hīm′-nä′ə)
Rugiens (RY zhyaN′)
Ruillé-sur-Loir (RWĒ yā SYR LWAR′)
Ruländer (ROO′len dəR)
Rully (RY yē′)
Rueda (RWe′thä)
Ruppertsberg (ROOp′əRts beRk′)
Ruppertsberger (ROOp′əRts-beR′gəR)
Russin (RY saN′)
Rust (ROOst)
Ruster Ausbruch (ROOs′təR ous′bROOKH′)
Ruwer (ROO′väR)

Saar (zär, sär)
Saarburg (zäR′bOORk′)
Sables-Saint-Émilion (SA′blə saN tā mē lyôN′)
Sackträger (zäk′tRe′gəR)
Sacy (SA sē′)
Saint-Amour (saN tA mOOR′)
Saint-Aubin (saN tō baN′)
Saint-Aubin-de-Luigné (də lwē-nyā′)
St.-Blaise (saN blez′)
Saint-Chinian (saN shē nyäN′)
Saint-Denis (saN də nē′)
Saint-Drézéry (saN dRā zā RĒ′)
Saint-Émilion (saN tā mē lyôN′)
Saint-Estèphe (saN te stef′)
Saint-Étienne-des-Ouillières (saN tā tyen dāz wē lyeR′, dā zOO lyeR′)
Saint-Étienne-La-Varenne (lA vA Ren′)
Saint-Fiacre (saN fē A′kRə)
Saint-Foy-Bordeaux (saN fWA bôR dō′)
Saint Gall (gAl)
Saint-Georges (saN zhôRzh′)
Saint-Georges-d'Orgues (dôRg)
Saint-Géréon (saN zhā Rā ôN′)
Saint-Jean-de-Minervois (saN zhäN də mē neR VWA′)
Saint-Joseph (saN zhô zef′)
Saint-Julien (saN zhY lyaN′)
Saint-Julien-en-Montmélas (äN môN mā lA′)
Saint-Lager (saN lA zhā′)
Saint-Lambert-du-Lattay (saN läN beR dY lA te′)
St.-Laurent (saN lōRäN′)
Saint-Nicholas-de-Bourgeuil (saN nē kô lA də bOOR gœ′yə)
Saint-Péray (saN pā Re′)
Saint-Raphaël (saN RA fA el′)
Saint-Romain (saN RÔ maN′)
Saint-Saphorin (saN SA fô RaN′)
Saint Saturnin (saN SA tYR-naN′)
Saint-Symphorien-d'Ancelles (saN saN fô RyaN däN sel′)
Saint-Vérand (saN vā RäN′)
Sainte-Croix-du-Mont (saNt kRwä dY môN′)
saké (sä′kē)
Salles (SAl)
Salta (säl′tä)
Saltillo (säl tē′yō)
Samogon (sä mo gôn′)
Samos (sä′môs)
Sampigny-les-Maranges (säN-pē nyē′ lā mA RäNzh′)
Samshu (sam′shOO, -syOO)
San Juan (sän hwän)
Sancerre (säN seR′)
Sandgrub (zänt′gROOp′)
Sandgrube (zänt′gROO′bə)
Sandweine (zänt′vī′nə)
Sangiovese (sän′jô ve′ze)
Sanlúcar de Barrameda (sän-lOO′käR de bäR′Rä me′thä)
Sansevero (sän′se ve′RÔ)
Santa Catarina (sän′tə kä′tə-RĒ′nə)
Santa Giustina (sän′tä jOOs tē′-nä)
Santa-Lucia-di-Tallano (sän′tä lOO chē′ä dē täl lä′nô)
Santa Maddalena (sän′tä mäd′-dä le′nä)
Santenay (säNtə ne′)
Santenots (säNtə nō′)
Santenots-Blancs, Les (säNtə-nō bläN′)
Santiago (san′tē ā′gō; *Sp.* sän′-tē ä′gô)
Santo Stefano (sän′tô ste′fä nô)
São Paulo (souN pou′lOO)
Saperavi (sä′pe Rä′vē)
Sartène (SAR ten′)
Sassella (säs sel′lä)
Satigny (SA tē nyē′)
Saumagen (zou′mä′gən)
Saumur (sō mYR′)
Sausal-Leibnitz (zou′zəl līb′nits)
Saussignac (sō sē nyAk′)
saute bouchon (sōt bOO shôN′)
Sauternes (sō tûrn′, sô-; *Fr.* sô teRn′)
Sauvignon Blanc (sō vē nyôN bläN′)
Sauvignon Vert (sō vē nyôN veR′)
Savagnin (SA VA nyaN′)
Savennières (SA ve nyeR′)
Savigny-les-Beaune (SA vē nyē lā bōn′)
Savoy, Savoie (SA VWA′)
Schaaner (shä′nəR)
Schaffhausen (shäf′hou′zən)
Schalksberg (shälks′beRk′)
Scharlachberg (shäR′läKH-beRk′)
Scharzberg (shäRts′beRk′)
Schaumwein (shoum′vīn′)
Schiave (skyä′ve)
Schiedam (sKHē däm′)
Schilcher (shil′KHəR)
Schiller (shil′əR)
Schlangengraben (shläng′ən-gRä′bən)
Schloss Böckelheim (shlôs′ bœk′əl hīm′)
Schloss Böckelheimer Kupfer-grube (bœk′əl hīm′əR kOOp′-fəR gROO′bə)
Schloss Johannisberg (yō hä′-nis beRk′)
Schloss Marienlay (mä RĒ′-ən lī′)
Schloss Vollrads (fôl′räts)
Schlossabzug (shlôs′ap′tsOOk)
Schlossberg (shlôs′beRk′)
Schnack (shnäk)
Schnapps (shnäps)
Schönhell (shœn′hel′)
Schützenhaus (shYts′ən hous′)
Schwabsburg (shväps′bOORk′)
Schwanen (shvä′nən)
Schwarzlay (shväRts′lī′)
Schwarzwalder (shväRts′-väl′dəR)
Schwätzerchen (shvets′əR-KHən)
Sciaccarello (shäk′kä Rel′lô)
sec (sek)
secco (sek′kô)
séché (sā shā′)
Séchet (sā she′)
seco (se′kô)
Seconds Crus (sə gôN kRY′)
Seeweine (zā′vī′nə)
Seewinkel (zā′ving′kəl)
Sekt (zekt)
Sémillon (sā mē yôN′)
Senancole, La (se näN kôl′)
Senheim (zen′hīm′)
Sercial (sûr′shəl)
serre (seR)
Serrig (zeR′iKH)
sève (sev)
Sèvre-et-Maine (se′vRə ā men′)
Seyssel (se sel′)
Shekar (she KHäR′)
Šibenik (shi′be nik)
Siebenmorgen (zē′bən môR′-gən)
Siegelsberg (zē′gəls beRk′)
Silberberg (zil′bəR beRk′)
Sillery (sē lə RĒ′)
Silverwasser (zil′vəR väs′əR)
Silvestro (sēl ves′tRô)
Šipon (shi′pôn)
Sirah (sē Rä′)
Slavianka (slä vyäng′kä)
Slivovica (sli′vô vi′tsä)
Slivowica (shli′vô vi′tsä)
Šljiva (shlyi′vä)
Šljivovica (shlyi′vô vi′tsä)
Smederovo (sme′de RÔ′vô)
Soave (swä′ve)
solera (sô le′Rä)
Soleras (sô le′Räs)
Solopaca (sô′lô pä′kä)
Somlói Furmint (shôm′lō i fOOR′mint)
sommelier (sômə lyā′)
Sonnenberg (zôn′ən beRk′)
Sonnenglanz (zôn′ən glänts′)
Soplica (sô plē′tsä)
Soproni Kékfrankos (shôp′RÔ-ni kâk′fRong kôsh)
Sorbet, Les (sôR be′)
Sorni (sôR′nē)
Soussans (sOO säN′)
Spätburgunder (shpet′bOOR′-gOOn dəR)
Spätlese (shpet′lā′zə)
Spätrot (shpet′RÔt′)
Spiegelberg (shpē′gəl beRk′)
Spielberg (shpēl′beRk′)

Spitzengewächs (shpits′ən gə-veks′)
Spitzenweine (shpits′ən vī′nə)
Spitzle (shpits′lə)
Spritzer (shpRits′əR)
Spritzig (shpRits′iKH)
spumante (spo͞o män′te)
Stabel (shtä′bəl)
Ständerbühl (shten′dəR bYl′)
Starka (stäR′kä)
Steig (shtīk)
Stein (shtīn)
Steinberg (shtīn′beRk′)
Steinberger (shtīn′beR′gəR)
Steinhaeger (shtīn′he′gəR)
Steinhaufen (shtīn′hou′fən)
Steininger (shtīn′ing əR)
Steinkautweg (shtīn′kout wāk′)
Steinkopf (shtīn′kôpf′)
Steinmächer (shtīn′mäKH′əR)
Steinmantel (shtīn′män′t^{ə}l)
Steinweine (shtīn′vī′nə)
Steinwingert (shtīn′ving′əRt)
stravecchio (stRä vek′kyô)
Strega (stRe′gä)
Streichling (shtRīKH′ling)
Stück (shtYk)
Stumpfenort (shto͝ompf′ən ôRt)
Subotica (so͞o′bô ti′tsä)
Suchot (sY shō′)
Šumadiya (sho͞o′mä dē′yä)
Sur-le-Sentier-du-Clou (sYR lə sän tyā′ dY klo͞o′)
Sur-les-Grèves (sYR lā gRev′)
Sur Pile (sYR pēl′)
Süssdruck (zYs′dRo͝ok′)
Suze (sYz)
Sveta Nedjelja (sve′tä ne′dye-lyä)
Sylvaner (sil van′ər; *Ger.* zil-vä′nəR; *Fr.* sēl vA neR′)
Syrah (sē Rä′)
Száraz (sä′Roz)
Szatmár (sot′mäR)
Szekszárd (sek′säRd)
Szekszárdi Kadarka (sek′-säR di ko′doR ko)
szemelt (se′melt)

Tâche (täsh)
taglio (tä′lyô)
Tanduay (tan′dwā; *Sp.* tän-dwī′)
Tannat (tA nA′)
Tarniówka (täR nyo͝of′kä)
Tarragona (täR′Rä gô′nä)
Tart (tAR)
tastevin (tät^{ə} vAN′, täst^{ə})
Taubenberg (tou′bən beRk′)
taupette (tō pet′)
Taurasi (tou Rä′zē)
Tavel (tA vel′)
Temprana (tem pRä′nä)
Tempranillo (tem′pRä nē′lyô)
tequila (tə kē′lə; *Sp.* te kē′lä)
Terlaner (teR lä′nəR)
Terlano (teR lä′nô)
Termeno d'Avio (teR me′nô dä′vyô)
Teroldego (te′Rôl de′gô)
Teurons (tŒ RôN′)
Thörnich (tŒR′niKH)
Tibi (tē′bē)
Ticino (tē chē′nô)
Tielslay (tēls′lī′)
tierçon (tyeR sôN′)
Tikveš (tik′vesh)
Tinta Cão (tēn′tə kouN′)
Tinta Madeira (tēn′tə mä dā′rə)
tinto (tēn′tô)
tirage (tē RAzh′)
Tischwein (tish′vīn′)
Tokaier (tō′kī əR)
Tokaj (tô′kī)
Tokaj Hegyaljai Szamorodni (tô′kī he′dyol yo′i so′mô-Rod′ni)
Tokaji Aszy (tô′ko yi ä′so͞o)
Tokaji Forditás (tô′ko yi fôR′di täsh′)
Tokaji Máslás (tô′ko yi mäsh′-läsh′)
Tokaji Pecsenyebor (tô′ko yi pe′che nye bôR)
Tokaji Szamorodni (tô′ko yi so′mô Rôd′ni)
Tokay d'Alsace (tô ke dAl zAs′)
Tondonia (tôn dô′nyä)
tonneau (tô nō′), *pl.* **tonneaux** tô nō′)
Toro (tô′Rô)
Torre Giulia (tôR′Re jo͞o′lyä)
Torricelli (tôR′Rē chel′lē)
Toulon-la-Montagne (to͞o lôN′ lA mON tAN′y^{ə})
Touraine (to͞o Ren′)
Touraine-Amboise (to͞o Ren äN bwAz′)
Touraine-Azay-le Rideau (to͞o Ren A ze′ lə Rē dō′)
Touraine-Mesland (to͞o Ren mā läN′)
tourne (to͞oRn)
Tours-sur-Marne-blancs (to͞oR sYR mARn bläN)
Tours-sur-Marne-noir (to͞oR sYR mARn nwAR′)
Traben-Trarbach (tRä′bən tRäR′bäKH′)
Traminer (*Ger.* tRä′mi nəR; *Fr.* tRA mē neR′)
Trappistine (tRA pē stēn′)
Trebbiano di Abruzzo (tReb-byä′nô dē ä bRo͞od′dzô)
Trebujena (tRe′bo͞o he′nä)
Treis (tRīs)
Trentino-Alto Adige (tRen tē′nô äl′tô ä′dē je)
Treppchen (tRep′KHən)
Tressot (tRə sō′)
Trier (tRēR)
Triesner (tRēs′nəR)
Triple Sec (tRē′pl^{ə} sek′)
Trittenheim (tRit′^{ə}n hīm′)
Trockenbeerenauslese (tRôk′ən-bā′Rən ous′lā′zə)
Troisièmes Crus (tRwA zyem kRY′)
Trois-Puits (tRwA pwē′)
Trollinger (tRôl′ing əR)
Turruntés (to͞oR′Ro͞on tes′)

Ugni Blanc (Y nyē bläN′)
Ülversheim (Yl′vəRs hīm′)
Ungezuckert (o͞ong′ge tso͝ok′-əRt)
Ungstein (o͞ong′shtīn′)
Unterberg (o͞on′təR beRk′)
Untere Wolfshöhle (o͞on′tə Rə vôlfs′hŒ′lə)
Urbelt (o͞oR′belt)
Ürzig (YR′tsiKH)
Ürziger Würzgarten (YR′tsi gəR vYRts′gäR′t^{ə}n)
Usquebaugh (us′kwi bô′, -bä′)
Utiel-Requena (o͞o tyel′ Re-ke′nä)

Vacqueyras (vA ke RAs′)
Vaduzer (vä′do͞o tsəR)
Vaillon (ve yôN′)
Val d'Adige, Valdadige (väl′-dä′dē je)
Valais (vA le′)
Valdeorras (bäl′de ôR′Räs)
Valdepeñas (bäl′de pe′nyäs)
Valencia (və len′shē ə, -shə; *Sp.* bä len′thyä)
Valgella (väl jel′lä)
Vallet (vA le′)
Valmur (vAl mYR′)
Valozières (vA lô zyeR′)
Valpantena (väl′pän te′nä)
Valpolicella (väl′pô lē chel′lä)
Valtanesi (väl′tä ne′zē)
Valtellina (väl′tel lē′nä)
Valwig (väl′viKH)
Van der Hum (van′ dər ho͞om′; *Du.* vän′ dəR hYm′)
Varaždin (vä Räzh′din)
Varogne (vA Rôn′y^{ə})
Varoilles (vA Rô′y^{ə}, -RwAl′)
Vaucluse (vō klYz′)
Vaucoupin (vō ko͞o pAN′)
Vaucrains (vō kRAN′)
Vaud (vō)
Vaudésir (vō dā zēR′)
Vaudois Chablais (vō dwA shA-ble′)
Vaulorent (vō lô RäN′)
Vaupulent (vō pY läN′)
Vaux-en-Beaujolais (vō zäN bō zhô le′)
Veldenz (vel′dents)
Veltliner (felt′li nəR)
Venčac-Oplenac (ven′chäts ôp′le näts)
vendange (väN dAN zh′)
vendangeoir (väN däN zhwAR′)
venencia (be nen′thyä)
Veneto (ve′ne tô)
vente sur souches (väNt sYR so͞osh′)
véraison (vā Re zôN′)
Verband Deutscher Naturwein-Versteigerer (feR bänt′ doi′chəR nä to͞oR′vīn′ feR-shtī′gə RəR)
Verbessert (fəR bes′əRt)
Verbesserung (fəR bes′ə Ro͞ong)
Verde (veR′di)
Verdelho (veR de′lyo͞o)
Verdello (veR del′lô)
Verdicchio dei Castelli di Jesi (veR dēk′kyô dā käs tel′lē dē ye′zē)
Verdiso (veR dē′zô)
Verdot (veR dō′)
Vergelesses (veR zhə les′)
Vergennes-Corton (veR gen′ kôR tôN′)
verjus (veR zhY′)
Vermentino (veR′men tē′nô)
Vermentino Ligure (veR′men-tē′nô lē′go͞o Re)
Vernaccia (veR nät′chä)
Vernaccia di San Gimignano (veR nät′chä dē sän jē′mē-nyä′nô)
Verroilles (ve RwA′y^{ə}, -RwAl′)
Versarmières (veR sAR myeR′)
Verseuil (veR sŒ′y^{ə})
Vertou (veR to͞o′)
Vertus (veR tY′)
Verveine du Vélay (veR ven′ dY vā le′)
Verzenay (veR zə ne′)
Verzy (veR zē′)
Vesuvio (ve so͞o′vyô)
Vidiella (bē thye′yä)
Vieille Cure (vye′y^{ə} kYR′)
Viertälerwein (fēR′tel əR vīn′)
Viertelstück (fēR′t^{ə}l shtYk′)
Vieux-Château-Certan (vyŒ chä tō seR täN′)
vigneron (vē nyə RôN′)
Vignes-Blanches, Les (vēn′y^{ə} bläNsh′)
vignoble (vē nyôbl^{ə})
Vila Nova de Gaia (vē′lə nô′və dē gä′yə)

Villafranca del Panadés bē′lyä fRäñg′kä thel pä nä-thes′)
Villány (vil′län′y[ə])
Villányi Burgundi (vil′lä nyi bo͞oR′go͞on di)
Villányi Kadarka (vil′lä nyi ko′doR ko)
Villány-Péçs (vil′län′y[ə] pâch′)
Villaudric (vē lō dRēk′
Villeneuve (vēl nœv′)
Villette (vē let′)
Villié-Morgon (vē yā′ môR gôN′)
vin (vaN), *pl.* **vins** (vaN)
vin blanc (vaN bläN′)
vin bourru (vaN bo͞o RY′)
Vin de Blanquette (vaN də bläN ket′)
Vin de Bourgeoisie (vaN də bo͞oR zhWA zē′)
Vin de Coucher (vaN də ko͞o-shā′)
Vin de coule (vaN də ko͞ol′)
vin de cru (vaN də kRY′)
vin de cuvée (vaN də kY vā′)
vin de goutte (vaN də go͞ot′)
Vin de l'Étrier (vaN də lā tRyā′)
vin de liqueur (vaN də lē kœR′)
Vin de Macadam (vaN də mA-kA dAm′)
Vin de marc (vaN də mAR′)
Vin de paille (vaN də pA′y[ə])
vin de pays (vaN də pā ē′)
vin de presse (vaN də pRes′)
vin de primeur (vaN də pRē-mœR′)
vin de queue (vaN də kœ′)
vin de tête (vaN də tet′)
Vin de Veille (vaN də ve′y[ə])
vin d'honneur (vaN dô nœR′)
vin diable (vaN dyA′bl[ə])
vin doux naturel (vaN do͞o nA tY Rel′)
Vin de Garde (vaN də gARd′)
Vin du Clerc (vaN dY kleR′)
Vin du Curé (vaN dY kY Rā′)
Vin du Glacier (vaN dY glA syā′)
vin du pays (vaN dY pāē′)
vin fin (vaN faN′)
vin gris (vaN gRē′)
vin jaune (vaN zhōn′)
vin mousseux (vaN mo͞o sœ′)
vin nature (vaN nA tYR′)
vin ordinaire (vaN ôR dē neR′)
vin rosé (vaN Rō zā′)
vin rouge (vaN Ro͞ozh′)
Vin Santo (vēn′ sän′tô)
vinage (vē nAzh′)
vinasse (vē nAs′)
vinello (vē nel′lô)
vinettino (vē′net tē′nô)
vinho claro (vē′nyo͝o klä′Ro͞o)
vinho do rodo (vē′nyo͝o do͞o Rô′do͞o)
vinho liquoroso (vē′nyo͝o li′kwô Rô′zo͞o)
vihno trasfugado (vē′nyo͝o tRäs′fo͞o gä′do͞o)
Vinhos Verdes (vē′nyo͝osh veR′desh)
Vinica (vi′ni tsä)
vino aromatizado (bē′nô ä′Rô-mä′tē sä′thô)
vino bianco (vē′nô byäñg′kô)
vino blanco (bē′nô bläñg′kô)
vino corriente (bē′nô kôR-Ryen′te)
vino da arrosto (vē′nô dä äR Rôs′tô)
vino de color (bē′nô the kô lôR′)
Vino de Fruta (bē′nô the fRo͞o′tä)
vino de la tierra (bē′nô the lä tyeR′Rä)
Vino de Pasto (bē′nô the päs′tô)
vino dulce (bē′nô do͞ol′the -se)
vino espumoso (bē′nô es′po͞o-mô′sô)
Vino Nobile di Montepulciano (vē′nō nô′bē le dē môn′te-po͞ol chä′nô)
Vino Quinado (bē′nô kē nä′thô)
Vino Santo (vē′nô sän′tô)
vino seco (bē′nô se′kô)
vino tierno (bē′nô tyeR′nô)
vino tinto (bē′nô tēn′tô)
Vino Veronese (vē′nô ve′Rô-ne′ze)
Vins d'Auvergne (vaN dō-veRn′y[ə])
Vins de la Moselle (vaN də lA mô zel′)
Vins de Lavilledieu (lA vēl-dyœ′)
Vins de l'Orléanais (lôR lā A-ne′)
Vins de Renaison (Rə ne zôN′)
Vins de Saint-Pourçain-sur-Sioule (saN po͞oR saN′ sYR sē o͞ol′)
Vins de Savoie-Roussette (sA vWA′ Ro͞o set′)
Vins Délimités de Qualité Supérieure (vaN dā lē mē tā′ də kA lē tā′ sY pā RYœR′)
Vins d'Irouléguy (dē Ro͞o lā gē′)
Vins du Lyonnais (dY lē ô ne′)
Vins Fins de la Côte de Nuits (vaN faN′ də lA kōt də nwē′)
Vins Natures de la Champagne (vaN nA tYR′ də lA shän-pAn′y[ə])
Vinzel (vaN zel′)
Visonta (vi′shôn to)
Viti (vē′tē)
Viura (vyo͞o′Rä)
Vlasotinci (vlä′sô tin′tsi)
vodka (vod′kə; *Russ.* vôt′kä)
Vogelsang (fōgəl zäñg′)
Volnay (vôl ne′)
Vöslau (vœs′lou)
Vosne-Romanée (vōn Rô mA nā′)
Vougeot (vo͞o zhō′)
Vouvray (vo͞o vRe′)
vrac (vRAk)
Vranac (vRä′näts)
Vršac (vR′shäts)
Vully (vY lē′)
Vyborova (vi′bô Rô′vä)

Wachau (väkh′ou)
Wachenheim (väkh′ən hīm′)
Wachstum (väks′to͞om)
Wagenkehr (vä′gən kāR′)
Waldböckelheim (vält′bœk əl-hīm′)
Waldmeister (vält′mīs′təR)
Waldrach (vält′Räkh)
Walporzheim (väl′pôRts hīm′)
Walporzheimer (väl′pôRts-hī′məR)
Wandkaut (vänt′kout)
Wasserros (väs′əR Rōs′)
Wasserrose (väs′əR Rō′zə)
Wawern (vä′vəRn)
Wehlen (vā′lən)
Wehlener Sonnenuhr (vā′lə nəR zôn′ən o͞oR′)
Weid (vīt)
Wein (vīn)
Weinbauer (vīn′bou′əR)
Weinberg (vīn′beRk′)
Weingut (vīn′go͞ot′)
Weinviertel (vīn′fēR′t[ə]l)
Weissbier (vīs′bēR′)
Weissburgunder (vīs′bo͞oR′-go͞on dəR)
Weissenstein (vīs′ən shtīn′)
Weisserd (vīs′əRt)
Weissherbst (vīs′heRpst′)
Wellen (vel′ən)
Welschriesling (velsh′Rēs′liñg)
Wermut (vāR′mo͞ot)
Westhofen (vest′hō′fən)
Westrum (vest′Ro͞om)
Wienerwald-Steinfeld (vē′nəR-vält′ shtīn′felt′)
Wiesberg (vēs′beRk′)
Wieshell (vēs′hel′)
Wilgert (vil′gəRt)
Willborn (vil′bôRn)
Wiltingen Scharzhofberg (vil′tiñg ən shäRts′hōf beRk′)
Wincheringen (vin′khəR iñg ən)
Winiak Luksusowy (vi′nyäk lo͞ok′so͞o sô′vi)
Winkel (viñgk′əl)
Winningen (vin′iñg ən)
Wintrich (vin′tRikh)
Winzenheim (vin′tsən hīm′)
Winzer (vin′tsəR)
Wiśniówka (vish nyo͞of′kä)
Wisselbrunnen (vis′əl bRo͞on′ən)
Wolfsdarm (vôlfs′däRm)
Worms (vôRms)
Wülfen (vYl′fən)
Wurstmarkt (vo͞oRst′mäRkt′)
Württemberg (vYRt′əm beRk′)
Würzburg (vYRts′bo͞oRk′)
Wüst (vYst)
Wyborowa (vi′bô Rô′vä)

Xérès (kā Res′)

Yepes (ye′pes)
yeso (ye′sô)
Yvonne (ē vôn′)

Začinak (zä′chi näk)
Zaco (thä′kô)
Zadar (zä′däR)
Zamora (thä mô′Rä)
Zell (tsel)
Zeller Schwarze Katz (tsel′əR shväR′tsə käts′)
Zeltinger (tsel′tiñg əR)
Zeltinger Sonnuhr (tsel′tiñg əR zôn′o͞oR′)
Zierfandler (tsēR′fänt′ləR)
Žilavka (zhi′läf kä)
Zinfandel (zin′fən del′)
Złota Woda (zlô′tä vô′dä)
Znojmo (znoi′mô)
Żubrówka (zho͞o bRo͞of′kä)
Zuckerberg (tso͝ok′əR beRk′)
Župa (zho͞o′pä)
Zürich (zo͞or′ik; *Ger.* tsY′Rikh)
Zurück (tso͞o RYk′)
Zwicker (*Ger.* tsvik′əR; *Fr.* tsvē keR′)
Żytnia (zhit′nyä)

Select Bibliography

Allen, H. Warner. *Claret.* (LONDON: 1924)
A Contemplation of Wine. (LONDON: 1951)
A History of Wine. (LONDON: 1961)
Natural Red Wines. (LONDON: 1951)
Rum. (LONDON: 1931)
Sherry and Port. (LONDON: 1954)
White Wines and Cognac. (LONDON: 1952)
The Wines of Portugal. (LONDON: 1963; NEW YORK: 1964)

Amerine, Maynard A. and Joslyn, Maynard A. *Commercial Production of Table Wines.* (A pamphlet). (BERKELEY: 1940)
Dessert Appetizer & Related Flavored Wines. (BERKELEY: 1964)
Table Wines: The Technology of their Production in California. (BERKELEY AND LOS ANGELES; LONDON: 1951)

Amerine, Maynard A., Berg, Harold W. and Cruess, William V. *The Technology of Wine Making.* (Second Edition; WESTPORT, CONNECTICUT: 1967)

Amerine, Maynard A. and Singleton, Vernon L. *Wine: An Introduction for Americans.* (BERKELEY and LOS ANGELES: 1966)

Balzer, Robert Lawrence. *The Pleasures of Wine.* (NEW YORK: 1964)

Barbadillo, Manuel. *El Vino de la Alegría.* (JEREZ DE LA FRONTERA: 1951)

Barry, (Sir) Edward. *Wines of the Ancients.* (LONDON: 1775)

Benvegnin, Lucien, Capt. Émile and Piguet, Gustave. *Traité de Vinification.* (Second Edition; LAUSANNE: 1951)

Berry, Charles W. *In Search of Wine.* (LONDON: 1935)

Bertall, —. *La Vigne: Voyage autour des Vins de France.* (PARIS: 1878)

Bijur, George. *Wines with Long Noses.* (LONDON: 1951)

Bode, Charles G. *Wines of Italy.* (LONDON; NEW YORK: 1956)

Bourke, Arthur. *Winecraft: The Encyclopaedia of Wines and Spirits.* (LONDON: 1935)

Bréjoux, Pierre. *Les Vins de Loire.* (Paris: 1956)

Brunet, R. *Dictionnaire d'Œnologie et de Viticulture.* (PARIS: 1946)

Burklin, Albert; Schultz, F. R.; von Bassermann-Jordan; von Diersburg, Rœder; Weingarth, Otto. (Eds.) *Verband Deutscher Naturwein Versteigerer.* (1953)

Butler, Frank Hedges. *Wine and the Wine Lands of the World.* (LONDON: 1926)

Capus, Joseph. *L'Evolution de la Législation sur les Appellations d'Origine et la Genèse des Appellations Contrôlées.* (PARIS: 1947)

Carling, T. E. *The Complete Book of Drink.* (LONDON: 1951)

Carosso, Vincent P. *The California Wine Industry, 1830–1895.* (BERKELEY AND LOS ANGELES: 1951)

Carter, Youngman. *Drinking Bordeaux.* (NEW YORK; LONDON: 1966)

Casabianca, A. *Guida Storica del Chianti.* (FLORENCE: 1957)

Cassagnac, Paul de. *French Wines.* (Trs. by Guy Knowles) (LONDON: 1930)

Chappaz, Georges. *Le Vignoble et le Vin de Champagne.* (PARIS: 1951)

Churchill, Creighton. *The World of Wines.* (NEW YORK: 1964)

Ciais, Adrien; Quittanson, Charles; Vanhoutte, René. *La Protection des Appellations d'Origine des Vins et Eaux-de-vie et le Commerce des Vins.* (MONTPELLIER: 1949)

Cocks, Charles and Féret, Eduard. *Bordeaux et ses Vins, Classés par Ordre de Mérite.* (Eleventh Edition; BORDEAUX: 1949)

Cornelssen, F. A. (Ed.) *Das Buch vom Deutschen Wein.* (MAINZ: 1954)

Croft-Cooke, Rupert. *Madeira.* (LONDON: 1961)
Port. (LONDON: 1957)
Sherry. (LONDON: 1955; NEW YORK: 1956)

De Bosdari, C. *Wines of the Cape.* (Third Edition; CAPE TOWN; AMSTERDAM: 1967)

Delamain, Robert. *Histoire de Cognac.* (PARIS: 1935)

Desgraves, Louis. *Bordeaux au Cours des Siècles.* (BORDEAUX: 1954)

Dettori, Renato G. *Italian Wines and Liqueurs.* (ROME: 1953)

Dion, Roger. *Histoire de la Vigne et du Vin de France.* (PARIS: 1959)

Engel, Ferdinand. *Wirtschaftssicherung des österreichischen Weinbaus.* (VIENNA: 1946)

Faes, H. (Ed.) *Lexique viti-vinicole international: français, italien, espagnol, allemand.* (PARIS: 1940)

Ferré, Louis. *Traité d'Oenologie Bourguignonne.* (PARIS: 1958)

Fisher, M. I. *Liqueurs: Dictionary and Survey.* (LONDON: 1959)

Francisque, Michel. *Histoire du Commerce et de la Navigation à Bordeaux.* (BORDEAUX: 1867–70)

Frolov-Bagreev, Anton M. *Ampelografia S.S.S.R.* 7 volumes. (MOSCOW: 1946–1962)

Galet, P. *Cépages et Vignobles de France.* 4 volumes. (MONTPELLIER: 1956; 1958; 1962; 1964)

Goldschmidt, Eduard (Ed.) *Deutschlands Weinbauorte und Weinbergslagen.* (Sixth Edition; MAINZ: 1951)

González Gordon, Manuel M. *Jerez—Xerez—Scheris.* (JEREZ DE LA FRONTERA: 1948)

Grossman, Harold J. *Grossman's Guide to Wines, Spirits and Beers.* (Revised Edition; NEW YORK: 1964)

Halász, Zoltán. *Hungarian Wines Through the Ages.* (BUDAPEST: 1962).

Hallgarten, S. F. *Rhineland, Wineland.* (LONDON: 1951)
Alsace and Its Wine Gardens. (Revised Edition; LONDON: 1965)

Harrison, Godfrey. *Bristol Cream.* (LONDON: 1955)

Healy, Maurice. *Stay Me with Flagons.* (LONDON: 1963)

Hedrick, Ulysses P. *The Grapes of New York.* (ALBANY: 1908)
Grapes and Wines from Home Vineyards. (NEW YORK: 1945)

Henderson, Alexander L. *The History of Ancient and Modern Wines.* (LONDON: 1824)

Hyams, Edward, *Dionysos, A Social History of the Wine Vine.* (LONDON: 1965)

Isnard, Hildebert. *La Vigne en Algérie.* 2 volumes (GAP: 1951–1954)

Jacquelin, Louis and Poulain, René. *The Wines and Vineyards of France.* Trs. T. A. Layton. (LONDON; NEW YORK: 1962)

Jacques-Petit, F. *Les Appellations des Vins et Eaux-de-Vie de France.* (ANGERS: 1957)

James, Walter. *Wine in Australia.* (Revised Edition; MELBOURNE: 1963)

A Word Book of Wine. (LONDON: 1959; NEW YORK: 1960)

Jeffs, Julian. *Sherry.* (LONDON: 1961)

Johnson, Hugh. *Wine.* (LONDON: 1966)

Jones, Idwal. *Vines in the Sun.* (NEW YORK: 1949)

Keller, D. Josef (Ed.). *Pfalzwein Almanach.* (NEUSTADT: 1953)

Kittel, J. B. and Breider, Hans. *Das Buch vom Frankenweine.* (WÜRZBURG: 1958)

Kraemer, Ado. *Im Lande des Bocksbeutels.* (Third Edition; WÜRZBURG: 1961)

Laffer, H. E. *The Wine Industry of Australia.* (ADELAIDE: 1949)

Lafforgue, Germain. *Le Vignoble Girondin.* (PARIS: 1947)

Lafon, René; Lafon, Jean; Couillaud, Pierre. *Le Cognac: sa Distillation.* (Fourth Edition; PARIS: 1964)

Langenbach, Alfred. *German Wines and Vines.* (LONDON: 1962)

The Wines of Germany. (LONDON: 1951)

Larmat, Louis, (Ed.). *Atlas de la France Vinicole; Les Vins de Bourgogne.* (PARIS: 1953); *Les Vins des Côtes du Rhône.* (PARIS: 1943)

Layton, T. A. *Wines of Italy.* (LONDON: 1961)

Lebensfreude aus Rheinhessen. (A collection of articles). (MAINZ: 1954)

Léon-Gauthier, Pierre. *Les Clos de Bourgogne.* (BEAUNE: 1931)

Leonhardt, George. *Das Weinbuch; Werden des Weines von der Reb bis zum Glase.* (Second Edition; LEIPZIG: 1963)

Lichine, Alexis. *Wines of France.* (Revised Edition; NEW YORK: 1963; LONDON: 1964)

Lucia, Salvatore P. *Wine as Food and Medicine.* (NEW YORK; TORONTO: 1954)

A History of Wine as Therapy. (PHILADELPHIA AND MONTREAL: 1963)

Lutz, H. F. *Viticulture and Brewing in the Ancient Orient.* (LEIPZIG; NEW YORK: 1922)

Magistocchi, Gaudencio. *Tratado de Enología adaptado a la República Argentina.* (BUENOS AIRES: 1955)

Malvezin, F. *Histoire de la Vigne et du Vin en Aquitaine.* (BORDEAUX: 1919)

Marchou, Gaston. *Bordeaux sur la Règne de la Vigne.* (BORDEAUX: 1947)

Marrison, L. W. *Wines and Spirits.* (LONDON: 1957)

Melville, John. *Guide to California Wines.* (Second Edition; SAN CARLOS; CALIFORNIA: 1960)

Mendelsohn, Oscar A. *The Earnest Drinker.* (LONDON: 1950)

Morris, Dennis. *The French Vineyards.* (LONDON: 1958)

Mouillefert, P. *Les Vignobles et les Vins de France et de l'Étranger.* (PARIS: 1891)

Muir, Augustus (Ed.). *How to Choose and Enjoy Wine.* (LONDON: 1953)

Müller, Karl. *Weinbau-Lexikon für Winzer, Weinhändler, Küfer und Gastwirte.* (BERLIN: 1930)

Office International de la Vigne et du Vin. *Lexique de la Vigne et du Vin: Français, Italiano, Español, Deutsch, Portugues, English, Russk.* (PARIS: 1963)

Pacottet, Paul and Guittonneau, L. *Vins de Champagne et Vins Mousseux.* (PARIS: 1930)

Perold, A. I. *A Treatise on Viticulture.* (LONDON: 1927)

Pestel, H. *Les Vins et Eaux-de-vie à Appellations d'Origine Contrôlées en France.* (MÂCON: 1959)

Ponsot, Maurice (Ed.). *Vins, Alcools et Spiritueux de France.* (Third Edition; PARIS: 1949)

Postgate, Raymond. *An Alphabet of Choosing and Serving Wine.* (LONDON: 1955)

The Plain Man's Guide to Wine. (LONDON: 1951)

Poupon, Pierre and Forgeot, Pierre. *Les Vins de Bourgogne.* (Revised Edition; PARIS: 1964)

Quelques Aspects du Problème viti-vinicole luxembourgeois. (A pamphlet). (LUXEMBOURG: 1956)

Rainbird, George. *Sherry and the Wines of Spain.* (LONDON: 1966)

Ray, Cyril. *The Wines of Italy.* (LONDON; NEW YORK: 1966)

Reboux, Paul. *L'Algérie et ses Vins.* (ALGIERS: 1945)

Redding, Cyrus. *A History and Description of Modern Wines.* (LONDON: 1833)

French Wines and Vineyards. (LONDON: 1860)

Rendu, Victor. *Ampélographie française.* (PARIS: 1857)

Renouil, Yves. *Dictionnaire du Vin.* (BORDEAUX: 1962)

Ribéreau-Gayon, Jean and Peynaud, Emile. *Traité d'Œnologie.* 2 volumes. (PARIS: 1960)

Robb, J. Marshall. *Scotch Whisky.* (LONDON; EDINBURGH; NEW YORK: 1950)

Rodier, Camille. *Le Vin de Bourgogne.* (Third Edition; DIJON: 1948)

Roger, J. R. *The Wines of Bordeaux.* (NEW YORK: 1960)

Roupnel, Gaston. *La Bourgogne.* (PARIS: 1946)

Rozet, Georges. *La Bourgogne Tastevin au Main.* (PARIS: 1949)

Rudd, Hugh R. *Hocks and Moselles.* (Constable's Wine Library; LONDON: 1935)

Saintsbury, George. *Notes on a Cellar-Book.* (LONDON: 1920, 1963; NEW YORK: 1933)

Sandeman, Sons & Company, Ltd., George G. *Port and Sherry.* (LONDON: 1955)

Schoonmaker, Frank. *Encyclopedia of Wine.* (NEW YORK: 1964)

Schoonmaker, Frank. *The Wines of Germany.* (Revised Edition; NEW YORK: 1966)

Schoonmaker, and Marvel, Tom. *American Wines.* (NEW YORK: 1941)
The Complete Wine Book. (NEW YORK: 1934; LONDON: 1935)
Scott, J. M. *Vineyards of France.* (LONDON: 1950)
Seltman, Charles. *Wine in the Ancient World.* (LONDON: 1957)
Shand, P. Morton. *A Book of French Wines.* (LONDON: 1960)
A Book of Other Wines than French. (LONDON: 1929)
Simon, André L. *Champagne.* (LONDON; NEW YORK: 1962)
Concise Encyclopaedia of Gastronomy, Section VIII. (LONDON: 1946)
A Dictionary of Wines, Spirits and Liqueurs. (LONDON: 1958)
Know your Wines. (LONDON: 1956)
A Wine Primer. (LONDON: 1946)
The Wines of the World. (LONDON: 1949)
Simon, André L. and Hallgarten, S. E. *The Great Wines of Germany.* (LONDON; NEW YORK: 1963)
Stein, Gottfried: *Reise durch die Deutschen Weingärten.* (MUNICH: 1957)
Street, Julian L. *Wines.* (Third Edition; NEW YORK: 1961)
Thudichum, John L. W. and Dupré, August. *A Treatise on the Origin, Nature and Varieties of Wine.* (LONDON; NEW YORK: 1872)
Todd, W. J. *Port.* (LONDON: 1926)
Tovey, Charles. *Wine and Wine Countries.* (LONDON: 1862)
Tucker, T. G. *Life in Ancient Athens.* (LONDON: 1912)
Union Générale de Syndicats pour la Défense des Grands Vins de Bourgogne. *Décrets définissant les Vins à Appellation d'Origine Contrôlée de la Région de Bourgogne.* (NUITS-SAINT-GEORGES: 1944)
Valente-Perfeito, J. C. *Let's Talk about Port.* (OPORTO: 1948)
Viala, Pierre and Vermorel, Victor. *Traité Général de Viticulture.* 7 volumes. (PARIS: 1901–1910)
Wagner, Philip M. *American Wines and Wine-Making.* (NEW YORK: 1956)
A Wine-Grower's Guide. (Revised Edition; NEW YORK: 1965)
Waugh, Alec. *In Praise of Wine.* (LONDON: 1959)
Weeks, C. C. *Modern Science and Alcoholic Beverages.* (MANCHESTER: 1921)
Weiss, Harry B. *The History of Applejack or Apple Brandy in New Jersey from Colonial Times to the Present.* (TRENTON: 1954)
Wilkinson, P. W. *First Steps in Ampelography.* (1900)
Nomenclature of Australian Wines. (1919)
Wilson, Rev. A. M. *Wines of the Bible.* (LONDON: 1877)
A Brief Discourse on Wines. (LONDON: 1861)
Wine and Spirit Trade Record. *Clarets and Sauternes.* (LONDON: 1920)
Winkler, Albert J. *General Viticulture.* (BERKELEY and LOS ANGELES: 1962)
Xandri Tagüeña, J. M. *Elaboración de Aguardientes Simples, Compuestos y Licores.* (BARCELONA; MADRID: 1958)

Acknowledgements

A work of this scope could not have become a reality without the knowledgeable and willing assistance of persons, institutions, and associations identified in many ways with the wines and spirits of the world.

First, I want to thank my assistants and other members of Alexis Lichine & Co. and those who worked for it for their continued helpfulness: in particular, the Hon. Julian Grenfell, Peter C. Handler, Philip I. Togni, Pierre Gauthier, Anthony Wood, Harold Jurgenson, Paul Zuckerman and Parker R. Reis.

To those listed below and to all the other unnamed people who furnished indispensable data and information through pamphlets and brochures I am deeply grateful.

INTRODUCTORY CHAPTERS

Dr. Maynard A. Amerine, Department of Viticulture and Enology, University of California, Davis, California.

James A. Beard, of New York, author of *The Fireside Cookbook* and *Fish Cookery*.

Doctor Charles A. Fox, of New York.

Dr. Herbert L. Gould, New York.

Dr. Charles P. Mathé, of San Francisco, Chairman of Board of Governors, The Society of Medical Friends of Wine.

Dr. E. Peynaud, of the Station Œnologique de Bordeaux.

GENERAL

Sam Aaron, of Sherry-Lehman, New York.

Luis Hurtado de Amezage, of Rioja.

E. C. Anagurstopoulos, Royal Greek Embassy, London.

José Ramón García de Angulo, President of the Consejo Regulador, Jerez.

Luigi Artusio, of the Stabilimento Fontanafredda.

Australian Wine Board.

Raul Azparren, President, Camara de Comercio del Estado Lara, Barquisimeto.

John Baker, Managing Director, Walter Symons and Hedges & Butler, London.

André Balaresque, Wine Broker, of Bordeaux.

Fernando Augusto Bandeira, of the Casa do Douro, Regua.

Dr. Lajos Bánlaki, Legation of the Hungarian People's Republic, Washington, D.C.

Manuel Barbadillo, of Sanlúcar de Barrameda.

Dr. Friedrich von Bassermann-Jordan, of Deidesheim.

Joe Baum, of New York.

Joseph Bavard, of Puligny-Montrachet.

Jean Beliard, of Paris and New York.

Comte Hubert de Beaumont, of Château Latour, Pauillac.

Dr. Amos Becciolini, of the Consorzio of Chianti, Florence.

The Right Honourable Joseph Bech, former Prime Minister, Grand Duchy of Luxembourg.

The late E. Besserat de Bellefon, of Ay.

V. Besserat de Bellefon, of Ay.

Louis Benoist, owner of Almadén Vineyards, San Francisco.

M. V. Benzi, of Provence.

Lennart Berenmark, of the Company Aktiebolaget Vin-Spritcentralen, Stockholm.

Paul Bergweiler, of Bernkastel-Kues.

Cavalier Guglielmo Bertani, of Verona.

G. Biehler, of Málaga.

R. Bigot, of Noyers-sur-Cher.

Max Bilan, Union of Chambers of Commerce and Industry, Ankara.

Henri Binaud, former President, Syndicat des Négociants en Vins, Bordeaux.

Alain Blanchy, of Bordeaux.

H. Blechner, Austrian Embassy, London.

R. E. Boillot, of Volnay.

D. I. Bonarjee, High Commission of India, London.

E. Bonvin, Swiss Growers' Association, London.

Sr. Bosch, President, Compañía Ron Bacardi, S.A., Santiago de Cuba.

The late J. Bouteiller, of Château Pichon-Longueville (Baron), Pauillac.

Julian Boyd, of Princeton, New Jersey.

Lloyd H. Brandon, Managing Director, H. M. Brandon and Company, Ltd., Jamaica, B.W.I.

Marc Bredif, of Vouvray.

Giovanni Bressano, of the Stabilimento Fontanafredda.

Toni Bromser, Diplom Weinbauinspektor, Staatsweinkellerei, of Kloster-Eberbach.

Dr. Á. Burklin-Wolf, of Wachenheim, President of the German Natural Wine Association.

W. D. Burnet, Distillers' Co. Ltd., Edinburgh.

Joseph Burrier, of Beauregard and Moulin-à-Vent, President of the Cave Coopérative, Chénas.

Eng. Vieira de Campos, of Colares.

Inspector Canal, of the Institut National des Appellations d'Origine des Vins et Eaux-de-Vie, Armagnac.

Daniel F. Canning, Press Officer, Mexican National Tourist Council, New York.

R. E. Dejean de Castillo, Argentine Embassy, London.

Dr. J. Cavadias, of the Royal Greek Embassy, Paris, Delegate to the Office International du Vin.

Mademoiselle Chabert, President of the Cave Coopérative, Fleurie.

Georges S. Chappaz, of the Institut National des Appellations d'Origine des Vins et Eaux-de-Vie, Paris.

Pierre Chauveau, of Cognac.

Pierre Chauvot, of Bordeaux.

Miss M. Clark, F. & E. May, London.

John A. Clarke, of David Sandeman and Son, Ltd., London.

Ralph H. Cobbold, Director, Justerini and Brooks, Ltd., London.

H. K. H. Cook, Australian Government Trade Commission, New York.

Henri Coquillaud, Director, Bureau National Interprofessionnel du Cognac.

Pierre Couillaud, of the Viticultural Station, Cognac.

Emmanuel Cruse, of Château d'Issan, Margaux.

F. Jiménez Cuende, of Madrid.

Prof. Dalmasso, of the University of Turin, and Vice-President of the International Wine Office.

Paul Damiens, Technical Adviser of the I.N.A.O.

Pierre Damoy, of Gevrey-Chambertin.

Virgilio Augusto Dantas, of Lisbon.

J. Dargent, of the Comité Interprofessionnel du Vin de Champagne, Épernay.

C. V. Dayns, New Zealand House, London.

Kenneth Dean, of New York.

Jean Delamain, of Jarnac.

Leonard A. T. Dennis, Director, Grants of St. James's, London.

Stanley Dennis, Director, Grants of St. James's, London.

A. Devlétian, of the Institut National des Appellations d'Origine des Vins et Eaux-de-Vie, Paris.

Mauriceo González Diez, of Jerez.

J. Diris, Director, Bureau National Interprofessionnel de l'Armagnac, Eauze.

J. Dolezal, Pilsner Urquell Co. Ltd., London.

Beltráu Domecq, of Williams & Humbert, Jerez de la Frontera.

José Ignacio Domecq, of Pedro Domecq, Jerez de la Frontera.

Matthew W. Downer, Public and Trade Relations Department, Brown-Forman Distillers Corporation, Louisville, Kentucky.

Georges Dubœuf, of Romanèche-Thorins.

Jean Dubois-Challon, of Château Ausone, Saint-Émilion.

The late Pierre J. Dubos, of Château Cantemerle, Macau-Médoc.

Jean Ducamin, Secretary General, Union des Coopératives de Bas-Armagnac, Réans.

S. Dumer, Turkish Embassy, Washington, D.C.

Albert J. Durante, Bourbon Institute, New York.

José M. Elizalde, of José M. Elizalde and Company, San Francisco.

Jakob Graf zu Eltz, of Eltville.

F. O. Emery, of London.

René Engel, of Vosne-Romanée.

H. B. Estrada, President, Bacardi Imports, Inc., New York.

R. L. Exshaw, of John Jameson and Son, Ltd. Dublin.

Aldo J. Fabrini, Beaulieu Vineyard Company, San Francisco.

Julio Faesler, Mexican Embassy, London.

Federal Press Service, Vienna.

Frederic L. Felton. President, Felton and Son, Distillers, South Boston, Massachusetts.

R. W. Finlayson, President, Toronto Wine and Food Society.

Don A. Fisher, Distilled Spirits Institute, New York.

Sir Guy Fison, of Courage & Barclay, London.

Armand Achille Fould, owner of Château Beychevelle, Saint-Julien.

Georges Fouquier, of Bordeaux.

J. Fourcaud-Laussac, of Château Cheval Blanc, Saint-Émilion.

M. Franchini-Netto, Brazilian Embassy, London.

Lord Fraser of Lonsdale, Chairman of the Board of Charrington Vintners, London.

H. A. S. Fraser, Association of Canadian Distillers, Montreal.

M. Friedas, Office International de la Vigne et du Vin, Paris.

Edoardo Gancia, Director of Gancia and Company, Canelli.

Rudolf Gareis, retired Weinbaudirektor, of Eltville.

Prof. Pier G. Garoglio, of the Istituto di Industrie Agrarie, University of Florence.

Dr. E. Ercole Garrone, Director of the Consorzio, Asti.

The late Edouard Gasqueton, proprietor, Château Calon-Ségur, Saint-Estèphe.

Philippe Gasqueton, manager, Château Calon-Ségur, Saint-Estèphe.

The late Claude Geoffray, of Château Thivin, Côtes de Brouilly.

Gerald de Geoffre, of Cognac.

Whitney Gerard, of Boston and New York.

Bernard Ginestet, of Château Margaux.

Pierre Ginestet, of Château Margaux, Margaux.

Pierre Giovetti, Wine Broker, of Bordeaux.

Jean Godet, of La Rochelle.
Pierre Goffre-Viaud, Controller of the I.N.A.O.
Mrs. Goldschmidt, Israeli Embassy, London.
Manuel González Gordon, of Jerez.
Henri Gouges, President of the Burgundy Growers Association, Nuits-Saint-Georges.
M. Graffé, Luxembourg Embassy, London.
G. Maxwell A. Graham, of Oporto.
John A. Grant, Dumbarton, Scotland.
A. O. Grass, Canadian Wine Institute, Ontario.
Count Matuschka V. Greiffenclau, of Schloss Vollrads, former President of the German Wine Growers' Association.
The late Franz Greis, of Bernkastel-Kues.
Lord Grenfell, of London.
Louis Gros and Sons, of Vosne-Romanée.
Lester Gruber, Detroit.
Sydney Gruson, of Paris.
M. de la Guignaraye, Dusquene Rhums, Bordeaux.
Herman Guntrum, of Weingut Louis Guntrum, Nierstein.
Francis G. Guth, of Mexico City and Vienna.

Fritzi Haskell, of Minneapolis, Minnesota.
A. J. Hasslacher, M.C., Madeira Association, London.
J. Hastings-Trew, formerly of the Cyprus Viticultural Board, London.
Maurice Hennessy, of Cognac.
E. Hiitonen, O.Y. Alkoholilike, Helsinki.
François Hine, of Jarnac.
Robert Hine, of Jarnac.
H. Hjorth-Nielsen, Royal Danish Consulate General, London.
P. M. P. Hodsoll, formerly Chairman, Grierson, Oldham and Company, Ltd., London.
P. Höhl, of the Section de la Viticulture et de l'Économie vinicole, Division de l'Agriculture, Berne.
J. H. Hopkins, John Jameson & Son, Ltd., Dublin.
G. Horumba, Rumanian Legation, London.
Jean Hugel, of Riquewihr, Alsace.
Anthony Hughes, Cyprus Viticultural Board, London.

Dot. Augusto Ippoliti, of Florence.
Dr. Lorenzetto B. R. Luigi Ispettore, of the Consorzio of Chianti, Florence.

Michel Jaboulet-Vercherre, of Pommard.
Pierre Janneau, of Condom.
Guy Jarach, of Bordeaux.
Douglas Jooste, Deputy Chairman, J. Sedgwick & Co. Ltd., Cape Town, S. Africa.
Peter Jurgens, Vice-President, Almadén Vineyards, San Francisco.

Gabriel Kallay, of New York.
Gaetano Kano, of Montevideo, Uruguay.
R. H. King, Board of Trade, London.
Alfred A. Knopf, of New York.
Professor Kosinsky, Professor of Viticulture, University of Agriculture, Budapest.
Henrik Kraft, Public Relations Officer, Tuborg Breweries, Ltd., Copenhagen.
Edouard Kressmann, of Bordeaux.
René Kuehn, of Ammerschwihr.

Comte Durieu de Lacarelle, Château Filhot, Sauternes.
Henry Lacoste, President, Syndicat Régional des Courtiers des Vins et Spiritueux de Bordeaux, de la Gironde et du Sud-Ouest.
Jean Lafon, Director of the Viticultural Station, Cognac.
M. Lahlon, Moroccan Office for Control and Export.
Don Antonio Larrea, Chief of the Viticultural Station at Haro, Rioja.
Paul Lasserre and Mme. Lasserre, of the Domaine de Micquer.
L. Lavadoux, of the Centre de Recherches Agronomiques, Bordeaux.
Daniel Lawton, of Bordeaux.
Daniel-Georges Lawton, of Bordeaux.
Jerome J. Lehrer, Swiss Wine Bureau, New York.
Baron LeRoy de Boiseaumarié, of Châteauneuf-du-Pape, President of the Institut National des Appellations d'Origine des Vins et Eaux-de-Vie.
Henri Levèque, Wine broker, Podensac, Gironde.
José Joaquim da Costa Lima, Director of the Port Wine Institute, Oporto.
O. Lindo, J. Wray & Nephew, Ltd., Kingston, Jamaica.
The late Madame Edmond Loubat, of Château Pétrus, Pomerol.
Marquis de Lur-Saluces, of Château d'Yquem, Sauternes.

Alexander McNally, of New York and Connecticut.
Miss Eleanor C. Maloney, Washington, D.C.
Karel Masek, North American Director, Cedok Czechoslovak Travel Bureau, New York.
Cavaliere Capurso Marino, of the Consorzio of Verona.
Ed. Marjary, manager, Château Mouton-Rothschild, Pauillac.
Michel Firino Martell, of Cognac.
Henri Martin, President, Comité Interprofessionnel des Vins de Bordeaux, and Mayor of Saint-Julien.
John G. Martin, of Heublein, Inc., Hartford, Connecticut.

Egon Mauer, manager of the Langwerth von Simmern Estate, Eltville.
Abel Médard, Director, Comité Interprofessionnel du Vin de Champagne, Épernay.
D. Homen de Mello, of Lisbon.
Pierre F. Mendes, Casa de Portugal, London.
A. B. Meslier, régisseur of Château d'Yquem, Sauternes.
Prince P. von Metternich, of Schloss Johannisberg.
S. H. Miller, London Manager, John Jameson and Son, Ltd.
Robert Mondavi, of C. Mondavi and Sons, Charles Krug Winery, St. Helena, California.
Monimpex, Budapest.
Duc Pierre de Montesquiou-Fezensac, Château de Marsan, Auch.
Miss Marcia Moore, Swiss Wine Bureau, New York.
Jean-Pierre Moueix, of Libourne.

Dr. Antonio Niederbacher, of the Unione Italiana Vini, Milan.
Milos Nikolic, Yugoslav Information Center, New York.
Tom J. Noonan, Director, Grierson, Oldham and Company, Ltd., Dublin.

Dr. Giorgio Odero, proprietor, Frecciarosso Vineyards, Casteggio.
President de Oliveira, of the Junta Nacional do Vinho, Lisbon.

Frank W. Packard, of New York.
Raymond-Julien Pagès, President, Fédération d'Auvergne des Vins et Spiritueux, Clermont-Ferrand.
H. F. M. Palmer, Secretary, Australian Wine Board, Adelaide.
Peter Palmer, London.
M. Paran, Israeli Embassy, London.
Andrés de Blas Pardilla, of Madrid.
John Parkinson, of New York.
Sp. Phylaktis, Cyprus High Commission, London.
Karel Pichl, Embassy of the Czechoslovak Socialist Republic, Washington, D.C.
Claudio R. Porrero, Spanish Embassy, London.
R. Protin, Director, Office International du Vin, Paris.
Sebastian Prüm, of the Johann Josef Prüm Estate, Wehlen.

Charles Quittanson, Inspector of Fraud, Institut National des Appellations d'Origine des Vins et Eaux-de-Vie, Dijon.

Claude Ramonet, of Chassagne-Montrachet.
Jean de Premio Real, of Mexico City.
Theodor Rettinger, and son, of Wachenheim.
Dr. Guglielmo Ricaldone, Director General, Stabilimento Cinzano, S. Vittoria d'Alba.
Bettino Ricasoli, of Florence.
Pedro Rivero, of Jerez.
J. Bernard Robb, of the Virginia Alcoholic Beverage Control Board, Richmond, Virginia.
Gaspar Roca, Puerto Rico.
Comte E. de Rohan-Chabot, Château de Saint-Martin, Taradeau, President of the Syndicat de Défense des Côtes de Provence.
Ed. Rolland, of the Académie des Vins de Bordeaux, and Château Coutet, Barsac.
Baron Philippe de Rothschild.
Jean-Pierre Rouff.
I. M. Roushdy, United Arab Republic.
Armand Rousseau, of Gevrey-Chambertin.
E. J. Rozier, President, Fédération Méridionale du Commerce en Gros des Vins et Spiritueux, Béziers.

Francisco Salamero, of Rioja.
Joseph Salzmann, of Kaysersberg.
Jean Samalens, of Laujuzan.
Étienne Sauzet, of Puligny-Montrachet.
Noël Sauzet, of Jarnac.
Miss Elliseva Sayers, Portuguese Information Trade Office, New York.
D. V. Schiazzano, Italian Chamber of Commerce, London.
Guy Schyler, of Château Lafite, Pauillac.
M. D. L. Scott, Vice-President, Public Relations Division, Heublein, Inc., Hartford, Connecticut.
R. I. C. Scott-Hayward, Johannesburg.
Tom Seabrook, W. & J. Seabrook, Melbourne.
Fernand Sentou, of Eauze.
Marcel Servin, of Chablis.
Pierre Sevez, President, Société du Vermouth Dolin, Chambéry.
The late Allan H. Sichel, Director, Sichel and Company, Bordeaux and London.
Freiherr Langwerth von Simmern, of Eltville.
Werner Sitzmann, of Málaga.
S. Sklar, London.
Luis Solari, Peruvian Embassy, London.
Prof. Dr. Steinberg, Director, Viticultural School and Research Station, Geisenheim.
John Symms, Director, Charrington Vintners, Procurement.
George Szczeniowski, of San Antonio, Texas.
Claude Taittinger, of Rheims.
Dr. Clemente Tarantola, of the University of Turin.
Thomás López Tello, of Valdepeñas.
Richard & William Teltscher, London.
H. Gregory Thomas, Grand Master, Commanderie de Bordeaux, New York.
Carmel J. Tintle, Public Relations Department, Schenley Industries, Inc., New York.

Nicolas Trambitsky, of Paris.

Louis Trapet, of Gevrey-Chambertin.

Brigadier C. E. Tryon-Wilson, former Chairman, Associated Wine and Spirit Traders, London.

Mario Carlo Tucci, of Florence and New York.

The Ulster Magazine, Belfast.

Ramiro Valadão, Director, Portuguese Information Trade Office, New York.

Jean Vermorel, of Vaux-en-Beaujolais.

André-Jacques Vernaison, President, Fédération du Sud-Est, Lyon.

Maître Jacques Vivez, of Bordeaux.

Philip Wagner, Proprietor, Boordy Vineyard, Riderwood, Maryland.

D. D. Ward, Managing Director, Mount Gay Distilleries Ltd., Barbados, B.W.I.

Harry H. Waugh, Director, John Harvey and Sons, Ltd., Bristol and London.

H. Seymour Weller, Château Haut-Brion, Pessac.

William Widmer, Widmer's Wine Cellars, Naples, New York.

Stanley Williams, Managing Director of Charrington Vintners Ltd.

Prof. Albert J. Winkler, of the College of Agriculture, University of California, Davis, California.

Basil J. Winston, of New York.

Georges Yard, of Beaune.

V. Zanko, of the Poduzeće Industrijskih Vinarija, Zagreb.

Carlos J. Zitta, Centro de Vitacultores del Uruguay.

Index

Where an item has its own entry in the alphabetical text the reference to it precedes all other page references. Vineyard names which start with the word Château will be found under the next part of the name.

Abbreviations:
Fr. = French
Germ. = German
Gk = Greek
Hung. = Hungarian
Ital. = Italian
Portug. = Portuguese
Sp. = Spanish
Ch., Chx = Château, Châteaux
co. = county
comm. = commune
dept. = department
dist. = district
prov. = province
vd = vineyard

A NOTE ABOUT THE AUTHOR

ALEXIS LICHINE—winegrower, wine merchant, author, and lecturer—is one of the leading figures on the international wine scene today. He produces wines at Château Prieuré-Lichine and Château Lascombes, in Bordeaux, and at three vineyards in Burgundy. His shipping organization, Alexis Lichine and Co., in Bordeaux, is a leading exporter of fine French wines. He has written wine lists and created cellars for leading hotels, restaurants, and shipping lines and for individuals. His innovations in the wine field are numerous, ranging from an annual art exhibition on "Wine and the Vine" at Château Lascombes to a reclassification of Bordeaux wines. He gives an award, the Tasse d'Or, each year for the best Burgundies at a competition among the winegrowers. He belongs to the Académie des Vins de Bordeaux, the only American among the forty members. Mr. Lichine has been awarded the Légion d'Honneur.

Born in Moscow in 1913, Lichine was taken to France at the time of the Revolution and in 1919 to the United States, of which he is a naturalized citizen. During the Second World War, he served in Europe and North Africa as a major in the United States Army Military Intelligence. Although his base of operations is now New York, he undoubtedly spends more time in the vineyards of France than any other man writing in English.

A NOTE ON THE TYPE

❧ The text of this was set on the Monotype in a type face named Garamond. Based on Garamond's original models, this face is much lighter and more open than Garamond's original form. Jean Jannon has been identified as its designer. The italic is taken from a font of Granjon, which appeared in the repertory of the Imprimerie Royale and was probably cut in the middle of the sixteenth century.

Printed by Halliday Lithograph Corporation, West Hanover, Mass., and bound by The Haddon Craftsmen, Inc., Scranton, Penn.